PSYCHOLOGY

Diane E. Papalia
University of Wisconsin-Madison

Sally Wendkos Olds

McGraw-Hill Book Company
*New York   St. Louis   San Francisco   Auckland   Bogotá   Hamburg
Johannesburg   London   Madrid   Mexico   Montreal   New Delhi
Panama   Paris   São Paulo   Singapore   Sydney   Tokyo   Toronto*

As an additional learning tool, McGraw-Hill also publishes a study guide to supplement your understanding of this textbook. Here is the information your bookstore manager will need to order it for you: 48403-1 STUDY GUIDE TO ACCOMPANY PSYCHOLOGY

PSYCHOLOGY

3 4 5 6 7 8 9 0 V N H V N H 8 9 8 7 6 5

ISBN 0-07-048401-5

See Acknowledgments on pages A1 to A4.
Copyrights included on this page by reference.

Library of Congress Cataloging in Publication Data

Papalia, Diane E.
Psychology.

Bibliography: p.
Includes indexes.
1. Psychology.   I. Olds, Sally Wendkos.   II. Title.
BF111.P25   1985   150   84-19403
ISBN 0-07-048401-5

This book was set in Palatino by York Graphic Services, Inc.
The editors were David V. Serbun, Rhona Robbin, and James R. Belser;
the designer was Joan E. O'Connor;
the production supervisor was Phil Galea.
The drawings were done by Fine Line Illustrations, Inc.
The photo editor was Inge King.
Von Hoffmann Press, Inc., was printer and binder.

Cover credit
Rene Magritte, *The Ready-Made
Bouquet* by permission of Umeda
Art Boeki, Osaka.

TO OUR FAMILIES

Jonathan L. Finlay
Madeline and Edward Papalia
Edward, Jr., Daphne, Marie, and Edward Papalia, III

David Mark Olds
Nancy and Dorri Olds
Jennifer, Manfred, and Stefan Moebus

whose interest, inspiration,
confidence, and love
make it all possible.

CONTENTS IN BRIEF

CONTENTS

PREFACE

Aside from fulfilling a social science course requirement, what is the point of taking a course in introductory psychology? We, the authors of this book, believe that psychology underlies the most important learning we are capable of—finding out more about ourselves and the people whose lives intersect with ours. Not until we have some basic knowledge about ourselves and others can we put any of our other learning to work in an effective way. We feel that every literate person should take at least one course in psychology. And so, in this firm conviction, we tried to think about the most effective ways to present psychological concepts, both to those students for whom this will be the only course in the subject that they will take and for those who will go on to make psychology the basis for their life's work. With this in mind, let's look at what we consider the most important elements of this book.

OUR AIMS FOR THIS BOOK

It's hard to imagine anyone's being bored by the study of who we are. And yet basic facts and theories *can* be presented in a dry way, remote from the excitement of new discoveries about the way we live, the way we learn, the way we love. It's hard to imagine anyone not stretching his or her horizons through the study of psychology. On the other hand, the temptations are great to present these topics in a "pop-psychology" way that sugarcoats information and fails to anchor it in a meaningful context. In this book we sought to avoid both these traps, in an effort to make it easier for the student to learn and for the instructor to teach.

First and foremost, we recognize psychology as a science, and throughout this book we treat it as such. We scrutinize research reports to evaluate their findings, and we show respect to those theories that pass the rigorous requirements established by scientific seekers after truth.

Our aims are to present the basic matter of psychology—its areas of study, its methods, its findings, and their implications—as clearly as possible, with as much attention as possible to their practical value, and with a constant focus on encouraging students to think for themselves as they read. We don't want them to accept our words blindly but to learn how to evaluate our biases, as well as those they'll encounter elsewhere in life.

What are our biases? First, we're unquestionably prejudiced toward people: While we present information about animal studies when appropriate, we do so primarily to emphasize their implications for teaching us something about our own species. (What animal biology can teach us about human memory.) Second, we're oriented toward the here-and-now: While we report the findings of basic research, we always keep our eyes closely focused on the practical applications of the research we cite. (How students can apply what they've learned about memory to help them do better in school.) And third, in recognition of the enormous amount of research going on today, we're closely tuned into the present moment: Again, while we report the classic research and theories that have built the foundations of psychology, we have made special efforts to be up to date with "cutting edge" studies going on even as the book was being set in type. (How the newest technology can diagnose problems deep within the brain or the womb, that were not detectable as recently as a year ago.)

In our respect for the individual and in our humble awareness of human fallibility (including our own), we don't pretend to know all the answers. While we highlight our own views on ethics and on numerous controversial issues, we leave room for students to search their own consciences to determine the morality of various research projects and to weigh opposing arguments in controversial issues to come up with their own conclusions. In fact, we encourage this kind of critical thinking in the belief that it will serve students well when they see or hear stories in the media about "breakthrough" discoveries in psychology or are engaged in conversations with people announcing their own pet theories as "scientific facts."

ORGANIZATION

The book has seven principal parts. In Part 1, "Psychology as a Science," we introduce the student to the goals, the history, and the methods of psychology. Part 2, "Biological Foundations of Behavior," comprises three chapters: Chapter 2 on the biological structure of the brain and the nervous system, Chapter 3 on the mechanisms of sensation and perception, and Chapter 4 on states of consciousness. In Part 3, "Learning, Memory, and Cognitive Processes," we include four chapters: Chapter 5 deals with learning, Chapter 6 with memory, Chapter 7 with intelligence, and Chapter 8 with language and thought. Part 4, "Motivation, Emotion, and Stress," consists of Chapter 9 on motivation and emotion and of Chapter 10, which discusses the way stress affects motivation, emotion, and behavior, and how people cope with stress. The three chapters in Part 5 cover development through the life cycle, from conception through old age. Chapter 11 discusses the influences of heredity and environment, the process of conception, prenatal development, and various issues around childbirth. Chapter 12 explores physical, intellectual, and social-emotional development in childhood, and Chapter 13 deals with these aspects of development from adolescence through old age. Part 6, "Personality and Abnormality," consists of three chapters: Chapter 14 examines theories of personality and ways to measure it, Chapter 15 looks at abnormal psychology, and Chapter 16 describes many ways to treat people with psychological problems. In the final two chapters of the book, in Part 7, "Social Psychology," we look at the ways we influence and are influenced by other people, both in group situations and in intimate relationships.

Through the way the book is structured, we offer various options for those teaching the course. As the preceding listing shows, this book has all the chapters "standard" to almost all psychology texts, such as biology and behavior, sensation and perception, learning, memory, motivation and emotion, child development, personality, abnormal psychology, therapy, and social influences. You'll note that we've also given full-chapter treatment to other high-interest and important topics that are often treated very briefly if at all, such as stress and coping, intelligence, language and thought, the beginnings of life, adolescent and adult development, and intimate relationships.

While we cover these topics in a way that seems logical to us, we recognize that some instructors may want to organize their courses differently, either because of personal preference or scheduling requirements. All chapters are self-contained and can, therefore, be presented in a variety of different sequences. A professor choosing to emphasize the developmental-social-personality approach might, then, teach Chapters 1, 5, 6, 7 (optional), 8, and 10 through 18. One with more of an experimental-physiological approach could teach Chapters 1 through 9, 12, 13 (optional), 14, 15, and 17. Either of these arrangements would provide a course of 13 or 14 chapters, rather than the 18 as written.

REVIEWERS' COMMENTS ON THE BOOK'S SPECIAL FEATURES

One of this book's major strengths, according to academic reviewers who saw the manuscript before publication, is its effective integration of theory, research, and application as described earlier in the section on "Our Aims for This Book." In fact, the consensus of our reviewers was that we integrate these aspects more consistently than many other books. Other elements specially remarked on by reviewers include our attention to high-interest and timely topics, our reference to "cutting edge" studies as well as classic ones, and our approach to ethical issues. And over and over again, we were gratified to hear praise of the book's writing style, which was commended for its clarity, its ability to hold the reader's interest, and its engaging qualities—all elements that we've worked hard on, to make both the teaching and the learning of psychology easier and more rewarding.

LEARNING AIDS

You'll find in this book a number of basic teaching aids whose value has been demonstrated through experience, as well as research. These include:

- *Part overviews:* At the beginning of each part, an overview provides the rationale for the chapters that follow.
- *Spotlights on:* At the beginning of each chapter several key themes are spotlighted.
- *Chapter overviews:* At the beginning of each chapter an outline clearly previews the major topics included in the chapter.
- *Chapter summaries:* At the end of each chapter there's a clearly restated summary of the most important points.
- *Extensive illustrations:* Since one picture is often "worth a thousand words," many of the points in the text are underscored pictorially through carefully selected drawings, graphs, and photographs (many in full color to illustrate important points better and to enhance the reader's esthetic enjoyment of the book).
- *Pedagogically sound captions:* The captions for these illustrations also serve a teaching purpose, either by emphasizing important points made in the text, posing questions calling for student thought, or bringing in interesting new information.
- *Highlighting of key terms:* Whenever a new, important term is introduced in the text, it is highlighted in blue and defined. These terms also appear in the glossary.
- *Glossary:* The extensive glossary at the back of the book clearly defines key terms. These terms are highlighted in blue in the index next to the page numbers indicating where in the book they first appear.
- *Bibliography:* A complete listing of references enables students to evaluate the sources for major statements of fact or theory.
- *Recommended Readings:* Annotated lists of suggested readings (classic works or lively contemporary treatments) at the end of each chapter serve those who want to explore issues in greater depth than is possible within these covers.
- *Boxes:* Every chapter has self-contained, boxed discussions of especially high-interest topics.

SUPPLEMENTARY MATERIALS

An extensive package of supplementary materials add to the value of this book as a teaching and learning tool.

The Study Guide, by Virginia Nichols Quinn of Northern Virginia Community College and Jolyne S. Daughtry of the University of Richmond, includes readings from journals and pop-

cludes such standard elements as outlines, objectives, key terms and concepts, and 800 questions with answers. Questions from the study guide are also available on *Study Disk*™, interactive microcomputer software designed for students' use.

The Test Bank, also developed by Quinn and Daughtry (and by George J. Downing of Gloucester County College) to ensure consistency with the Study Guide in the level and types of questions, contains 2000 questions keyed to the learning objectives in the Study Guide and the Instructor's Manual. The Test Bank can be used with the Computer-Generated Testing System (Examiner and Microexaminer). Correct answers and text page references are included for all questions. An alternate test bank by James J. Johnson of Illinois State University will also be available in 1985.

The Instructor's Manual, also by James J. Johnson of Illinois State University, includes chapter outlines, learning objectives, key terms and concepts, mini-lectures, demonstrations, short-answer and essay questions, and a media guide. It also has a distinctive "Teaching the Chapter" section for each chapter, which integrates all these elements to assist the instructor.

Psychworld, by John C. Hay of the University of Wisconsin in Milwaukee, is an elaborate, colorful, and intriguing generic software package that contains 15 simulations of classic psychology experiments. Professors can use it in the classroom, and students can use it in a lab. It enables the user to perform such activities as identifying different sections of the brain and varying reinforcement patterns for a pigeon pecking at food.

Slides and Transparencies, a new package from McGraw-Hill, includes 100 generic slides, 100 generic transparencies, and 50 transparencies keyed specifically to this book, with instructor booklets describing each slide and transparency.

McGraw-Hill/CRM Films will also be available to adopters.

We hope that we have been able to communicate the excitement we feel about the study of psychology. We want to share this with you, our readers, as much as we want to share any of the facts, figures, and philosophies contained within these pages. For if we succeed in this, we know we will have enriched your lives as the study of psychology has enriched ours.

ACKNOWLEDGMENTS

We are indebted to many colleagues and friends whose help was invaluable in the gestation and birth of this book. For contributing their deeply informed expertise in specific psychological subfields, we're grateful to Jason Brandt and Howard Egeth, both at Johns Hopkins University; to Robert Franken, University of Calgary; and to Howard Hughes, Dartmouth College. We also appreciate the contribution of Virginia Nichols Quinn, Northern Virginia Community College, who wrote the Statistics Appendix.

For their help in reviewing sections of the manuscript within their areas of specialty, we would like to thank John Altrocchi, University of Nevada; Allen E. Bergin, Brigham Young University; Ellen S. Berscheid, University of Minnesota; Philip Costanzo, Duke University; Helen Joan Crawford, University of Wyoming; James T. Lamiell, Georgetown University; John M. Neale, State University of New York at Stony Brook; Neil J. Salkind, University of Kansas; and Robert Sternberg, Yale University.

And for their readings of all or part of the manuscript in various stages of development and the helpful comments they offered, we thank Mary Bayless, Brevard Community College; David Berg, Community College of Philadelphia; Stephen F. Davis, Emporia State University; David C. Edwards, Iowa State University; Jim Eison, Roane State Community College; George Goedel, Northern Kentucky University; Lyllian B. Hix, Houston Community College; Thomas Jackson, Fort Hays State University; James J. Johnson, Illinois State University; Stanley Kary, St. Louis Community College; John M. Knight, Central State University; Linda Lamwers, St. Cloud State University; Robert M. Levy, Indiana State University; Walter A. Pieper, Georgia State University; Daniel W. Richards, III, Houston Community College System; Barbara Robinson, Portland Community College; Rebecca M. Warner, University of New Hampshire; and Stephen Weissman, Plymouth State College.

We deeply appreciate the strong support we have received from our publisher. Rhona Robbin, our editor, became a friend not only to both the authors but also to the readers of this book, who will benefit from her careful attention to detail, her dedication to clarity, and her perceptive questions that continually forced us to reevaluate our presentation. James R. Belser gave this project the same painstakingly careful attention through the production process that he has given all five editions of our previous books. Inge King found beautiful and pedagogically perfect photographs. Elsa Peterson pursued and obtained needed permissions. Others at McGraw-Hill helped in ways large and small.

We would also like to express special thanks to Betsey Eidinoff, who tracked down elusive reports, typed up recalcitrant tables, and assisted in ways too numerous to list; to Louise M. Frye, researcher *extraordinaire* at the University of Wisconsin; to Stanford University student Ann Marie Boss for her help with research; to Thomas Rabak of the University of Wisconsin for his help with the bibliography; and to Jane A. Weier, who typed *all* those definitions in the glossary.

And, of course, this list would not be complete if we didn't acknowledge the constant encouragement of our husbands, Jonathan Finlay and David Mark Olds. In deference to our deadlines, they postponed things they wanted to do and did things that needed to be done. In support of our aims, they asked the right questions and made us come up with answers. They knew when to hold our hands and when to make us laugh. Throughout, they were there for us when we needed them, and this book is better for that.

Thank you, one and all. We could not have done it without you!

Diane E. Papalia   Sally Wendkos Olds

ABOUT THE AUTHORS

DIANE E. PAPALIA is a professor who has taught thousands of undergraduates at the University of Wisconsin. She received her bachelor's degree, majoring in psychology, from Vassar College, and both her master's degree in child development and family relations, and her Ph.D. in life-span developmental psychology from West Virginia University. She has published numerous articles in professional journals, most of which have reported on her major research focus, cognitive development across the life span from childhood through old age. She is especially interested in intelligence in old age and the factors that contribute to the maintenance of intellectual functioning in late adulthood. She is a Fellow in the Gerontological Society of America.

SALLY WENDKOS OLDS is an award-winning professional writer who has written more than 200 articles in leading magazines and is the author or coauthor of six books addressed to general readers, in addition to the three textbooks she has coauthored with Dr. Papalia. She received her bachelor's degree from the University of Pennsylvania, where she majored in English literature and minored in psychology. She was elected to Phi Beta Kappa in her junior year and was graduated *summa cum laude*. Her book, *The Complete Book of Breastfeeding,* has become a classic since its 1972 publication, and her most recent book, published in 1983, is *The Working Parents Survival Guide.*

DIANE E. PAPALIA and SALLY WENDKOS OLDS are the coauthors of the extremely successful textbooks *A Child's World* (now in its third edition) and *Human Development* (third edition scheduled for 1986 publication).

PART
1
PSYCHOLOGY AS A SCIENCE

The study of why people do what they do has long been a favorite topic of philosophers and poets, historians and novelists, and everyone else, including neighborhood gossips. Psychology, however, focuses on these same issues, all within a scientific framework.

Psychology is the scientific study of behavior and of mental processes. Although a large body of psychological research uses animals (like rats, dogs, and monkeys) as subjects, in this book we emphasize what psychology can tell us about what most of us consider the highest order of animals, human beings.

In Chapter 1, "Introduction to Psychology," which will present some of the issues and findings to be reported and discussed in the rest of the book, we'll look at the roots of this relatively young science, the offspring, as it were, of the two ancient disciplines of philosophy and physiology.

We'll look at different schools of thought within psychology and at the ways different viewpoints influence the nature of research projects. We'll examine the different techniques employed by psychological researchers. And we'll give a contemporary overview of the field, showing the many different settings in which psychologists work and the many different facets of the work that they do.

CHAPTER 1

INTRODUCTION TO PSYCHOLOGY

SPOTLIGHT ON

How psychology broke away from philosophy and physiology and became an independent science just over 100 years ago.

How the controversies surrounding the early schools of psychology shaped the discipline.

What psychologists do today.

Prospects for a career in psychology.

How psychologists study behavior.

The ethical principles that guide psychological research.

If you're like most people, your life is going as well as you would like in some ways and not so well as you would like in others. The chances are good that some of the problems that worry you are among the topics that interest psychologists.

For example, you may weigh more than you would like to. In their studies of motivation, psychologists have found certain differences between overweight and normal-weight people that have led to programs that have helped people to shed pounds. Or maybe you have a sleep problem: You may sleep nine or ten hours a night and worry that this is an abnormal pattern (It isn't) or have trouble falling asleep and wonder whether there are ways to solve your insomnia (There are). You may be overwhelmed because you have so much schoolwork to remember. In their studies of memory, psychologists have come up with a number of findings that can help you to remember better. Or the major problem in your life right now may revolve around a love affair. Even in this mysterious realm, psychologists have delved and have come up with insights that can help us understand our personal relationships better.

In this book you'll read about psychological study on all these issues and about the practical implications of both research and theories. And you'll read about much more that's relevant to your own life. For the very essence of this field is the study of you. When psychologists study the human brain, they learn about *your* brain. When they study the way people learn, they find out how *you* learn. When they study influences on human intelligence, they discover what has affected the development of *your* intelligence. No field of study has more personal relevance for your life than has psychology.

In this chapter we'll talk about the way the field of psychology developed and how it functions today. We'll talk about the methods of study that psychologists use—and the criteria you can use yourself to determine how scientific these methods are and how valid are the reports you read in newspapers, magazines, and professional journals. We'll also consider the very important ethical questions pertaining to psychological research—and the standards you might use to judge the ethicality of any particular study. And finally, we'll talk about the various subspecialties in psychology and the kind of work in the field that you yourself might do if you decide upon psychology as a vocation.

WHAT IS PSYCHOLOGY?

Psychology is the scientific study of behavior and mental processes. Let's look at this definition, word by word. The term "psychology" comes from the Greek words "psyche" (the soul) and "logos" (study) and reveals the original definition as the study of the soul (later, of the mind). *Scientific study* implies using such tools as observation, description, and experimental investigation to gather information and then organizing this information. *Behavior* is defined broadly to include actions that can be readily observed, such as physical activity and speaking, as well as other "mental processes" that occur even though they cannot be observed directly, such as perceiving, thinking, remembering, and feeling.

Psychologists are not content to stop at describing behavior. They go beyond this to try to explain, predict, and ultimately modify it to enhance the lives of individuals and of society in general.

In presenting an overview of the field of psychology, we, the authors, do so in line with our own biases. One of these biases is a celebration of the human being. While many of the most important experiments in psychology have been performed on nonhuman animals—most notably rats, pigeons, and monkeys—our emphasis in these pages will be upon what psychological research and theory has to tell us about human beings. When we do discuss important animal studies, we'll do so in order to shed light on human behavior.

Another bias you'll find throughout this book is an emphasis on the way research findings can be applied (used) to solve practical problems. While we *will* report on basic research, which is performed in the spirit of intellectual curiosity, and on the kinds of questions psychologists ask as they explore the universe of the mind, whenever possible we'll translate the results of such studies into knowledge that can be applied to better the human condition.

The scope of this book is broad. For convenience we've divided it into seven major parts. In the first part we'll look at the scientific and historical aspects of the field; then we'll consider how human beings are wired biologically and how this influences behavior; we'll look at our intellectual processes—how we learn, remember, think, and use language—and also at what intelligence is; we'll see how we are motivated, what role our emotions play in our lives, and how we are affected by and cope with stress; we'll look at our physical, cognitive, and personality development throughout life; we'll explore issues of personality and of psychological disorders and their treatment; and finally we'll examine the way we get along with other people, both in close relationships and in groups.

To simplify our discussion of physical, cognitive, and personality development, we will be examining these aspects separately—in effect "cutting" human beings into interlocking parts.

This description sounds as if we are cutting up human beings into arbitrary little jigsaw-puzzle-like pieces. We are, just for the purposes of simplicity. But according to the Gestalt philosophy, which you'll read about soon, the whole is greater than the sum of its parts, a viewpoint that applies well to our study of the psychology of human beings. By the time you've finished reading this book, we hope that your picture of the human being will be a cohesive whole, made up of your understanding of these various parts of our natures.

THE HISTORY OF PSYCHOLOGY

In a sense the history of psychology reaches back to ancient times when philosophers and religious leaders were asking questions about human nature and trying to explain human behavior. Psychology as a science is a much younger discipline, however, little more than 100 years old, as seen by some of its milestones shown in Table 1-1. What turned psychology from a philosophical search into a science? Principally the use of the tools and techniques that had been used successfully in the natural sciences. When those looking for answers turned from relying on their own intuition and their own experiences to carefully collecting information through systematic observation and controlled experiments, they transformed themselves from philosophers into scientists.

Psychology is, in effect, the child of two parents: philosophy (the pursuit of wisdom through logical reasoning) and physiology (the study of the vital life processes of an organism, such as respiration, digestion, and reproduction). During the eighteenth and nineteenth centuries, physiological researchers used the newly invented microscope to examine animal and human cadavers (dead bodies), making important discoveries about the functions of the spinal cord, the electrical nature of nerve im-

G. Stanley Hall. (National Library of Medicine)

William James. (Library of Congress)

TABLE 1-1 Famous Firsts in Psychology

1875–1876	First course in experimental psychology was offered at Harvard University by William James. The first psychology lecture James attended was his own.
1878	First Ph.D. in psychology in America was awarded to G. Stanley Hall.
1879	First laboratory for psychological research was founded in Leipzig, Germany, by Wilhelm Wundt.
1879	First American student to work with Wundt in Leipzig was G. Stanley Hall.
1881	First professional journal of psychology in the world was established in Germany by Wilhelm Wundt.
1883	First psychology laboratory in America was established at Johns Hopkins University by G. Stanley Hall.
1886	The first American textbook in psychology, *Psychology* by John Dewey, was published.
1887	First professional journal of psychology in the United States was established by G. Stanley Hall (*American Journal of Psychology*).
1888	First professorship of psychology in the world was established at the University of Pennsylvania, naming James McKeen Cattell.
1890	William James's classic textbook, *The Principles of Psychology*, was published (which took him twelve years to write, compared to the two he had originally estimated).
1892	American Psychological Association was founded, largely through the efforts of G. Stanley Hall, who served as its first president. (It grew to 400 members in 1920 and now has more than 50,000 members.)

pulses, and other biological mechanisms. Almost all the early experimental psychologists in Germany had been educated in medicine or physiology. Psychology's search to understand how people think, feel, and act continues to rest on a knowledge of human biology. Let's see how this science has evolved to its present state.

SCHOOLS OF PSYCHOLOGY

Controversy swirls around many psychological issues, mostly because of basic differences in the way different psychologists see the very nature of human beings. Within the field, bitter and violent disputes have erupted—as happens in any enterprise filled with brilliant, creative, strong-minded innovators. While some of these controversies are eventually resolved with the prevalence of one generally accepted viewpoint, others have continued for years and show no signs of any universal agreement. Many of these controversies were born in the very early days of psychology, with the emergence in the late nineteenth and early twentieth centuries of a number of different schools, or groups of psychologists who shared a theoretical outlook and approached psychological issues with a common orientation. As these schools flourished—and then often declined—the history of psychology was written.

Structuralism

Wilhelm Wundt, M.D. (1832–1920), is usually called the "father of psychology." He called himself a "psychologist," he formally established psychology as an independent and organized discipline, he set up the first laboratory for psychological experimentation in Leipzig, Germany, and he attracted many of the early leaders in the field as his pupils there (Hearst, 1979).

Wundt's book *Principles of Physiological Psychology* (published in two parts in 1873 and 1874) established psychology as a laboratory science that used methods derived from physiology. Wundt wanted to study the basic structure of the human mind, or what it *is*, rather than its functions or purposes, or what it *does*. To do this, he developed the method of *analytic introspection*. He made the centuries-old technique of introspection, or self-observation, new by adding precise experimental controls. He then proceeded to analyze, or break down, the mind into its component elements (such as a basic experience of seeing a color). Wundt emphasized physiological experiments, much of them involving fairly simple measures like those of reaction time (the amount of time it takes to react to a new stimulus, like the number of seconds between the flashing of a bright light and the blink of the subject's eyelid). His work ran into considerable resistance, however, partly because some of his fellow professors thought that too much examination of the mind could cause insanity and others felt that such experiments would "insult religion by putting the human soul on a pair of scales" (Hearst, 1979, p. 7).

One of Wundt's students, Edward Bradford Titchener (1867–1927), named Wundt's work "structuralism" and brought it to America. Titchener felt that the new science of psychology should analyze consciousness by reducing it to its elemental units. According to him, the structure of the human mind was made up of more than 30,000 separate sensations, feelings, and images, and nothing else.

It's not hard to see why structuralism died when Titchener did, in 1927.

Wilhelm Wundt, the father of psychology. (Bettmann Archive)

Aside from the fact that it left out such important topics as motivation, individual differences, and psychological disorders (among others), isolating the individual elements of the human mind seemed unnatural and silly to many people. For example, a structuralist could not say "I see a penny" because such a statement fails to break the penny down into its various elements—that it is small, round, flat, copper-colored, and made of metal, and because referring to the object as a "penny," rather than in terms of the elements that an observer would see, would be interpreting the object, not describing it. Similarly, a structuralist could not say that two people standing at different distances are the same size because the visual image of the distant person is smaller than that of the closer person. Furthermore, the method was not truly scientific because each introspectionist (who had to be rigorously trained in the method) described his own sensations uniquely and there was little reliability from one observer to another.

Functionalism

Considered the first truly American system of psychology, functionalism was both more scientific and more practical than structuralism, which early functionalists like William James (1842–1910) and John Dewey (1859–1952) objected to as irrelevant. They and the other functionalist thinkers wanted to amass knowledge that they could apply in everyday life. In their concern with the way the organism adapts to the environment, they wanted to know how the mind functions—what it *does*. The functionalists broadened the scope of psychology. They developed many research methods beyond introspection, including questionnaires, mental tests, and objective descriptions of behavior. In addition, using children, animals, and the mentally retarded, they broadened their subject base beyond trained introspectionists.

John Dewey's 1896 paper attacked as meaningless the structuralist view of breaking down behavior into its elements and is widely credited with launching functionalism and turning this pragmatic philosophy toward education. He felt that the emphasis of education should not be on the subject matter but on the needs of students, a radical view at the time. Dewey went on to found school psychology and to leave a lasting impression on this country's entire system of public education. American psychology is still functionalist in its outlook, with its emphasis on scientific methods of data collection and on the practical application of the knowledge gleaned from these methods.

Gestalt Psychology

The German psychologists who founded the Gestalt school early in the twentieth century advanced the idea that it's not the individual elements in the mind that are important (as the structuralists maintained) but the "gestalt," the form or pattern that these elements form. For example, they emphasized the importance of the new entity formed by the different elements such as a melody formed by the combination of individual notes or the sight of a leafy tree, in its grandeur much more than a mere combination of patches of light, shade, and separate forms. Unlike the behaviorists, the gestaltists acknowledged consciousness; they just refused to look at it in little pieces. They held that the whole is greater than the sum of its parts, a viewpoint that had particular impact on the study of perception.

Psychoanalysis

When Sigmund Freud (1856–1939) developed psychoanalysis, he complemented Wundt's "psychology of consciousness" with his "psychology of the unconscious." Unlike the preceding laboratory-centered approaches, psychoanalysis didn't try to be a pure science. Its emphasis was not the amassing of knowledge about the normal mind but the immediate application of a new way to treat individuals who showed abnormal behavior. It drew much of its data from clinical observation rather than controlled laboratory experimentation. Freud believed that powerful biological urges, most often sexual in nature, influenced human behavior. He felt that these drives were unconscious and that they created conflict between the individual and the mores of society.

The Freudian approach generated storms of controversy, some of which are still raging today, as we'll see in a number of places in this book. Some of Freud's disciples (like Erik Erikson) modified his basic approach, while others (like Carl Jung, Alfred Adler, and Karen Horney) broke away from him. While the psychoanalytic view of human behavior (described later in this book) has had an enormous influence on psychological thought, it has never become part of mainstream experimental psychology.

Behaviorism

With the publication of the article by John B. Watson (1878–1958) in 1913, "Psychology as the Behaviorist Views It," the new school of behaviorism, which grew out of studies of animal behavior, was born. The behaviorists felt there was no point in trying to figure out what people were seeing or feeling (as the structuralists did) or how they were thinking and why (as the functionalists did). Instead, they focused on what they could actually see people doing. In other words, they studied *observable* behaviors and events. They replaced introspection as a research method with laboratory studies of conditioning, a type of learning. If they could determine what kind of response a person or animal would make to a particular kind of stimulus, they felt they could learn what was most important about the mind. With this orientation, the nature of the research shifted to research with animals and work on learning. The behaviorists emphasized the role of the environment in shaping human nature and played down hereditary characteristics.

B. F. Skinner (b. 1904) is not only the leading behaviorist today; he is also one of the most important influences in all of psychology. The major thrust of his work has been in the area of operant conditioning (which we'll discuss in Chapter 5). While he used rats and pigeons to determine the effects of different patterns of reinforcement (rewards), he also did a great deal of work directly applicable to people. One of his inventions, the "aircrib," a roomy, temperature-controlled box in which he kept his own baby for the first two years of her life, never became commercially successful, although it was much talked about. Far more influential were the teaching machines that he popularized and the behavior modification programs that he developed, using the principles of rewards that he developed with rats and pigeons.

Behaviorism's major contribution was its use of the scientific method to study behavior; this method emphasized observable behaviors and events as opposed to earlier introspective measures. Behaviorism also expanded the scope of psychology to include the study of animals as a

Programming praise and encouragement into computer teaching programs like this one is a natural extension of the behaviorist stance that positive reinforcement for correct responses helps people to learn. (Mark Antman/The Image Works)

way to learn more about people. This school helped psychology become a truly scientific discipline and shaped the field for years to come, despite the deliberate simplicity that prevented it from dealing satisfactorily with any psychological factors that could not be seen, which included almost all emotion and thought. Today, a major area of discontent with behaviorism is its denial of cognitive processes; this concern has given rise to what has become known as the "cognitive revolution," which we'll discuss shortly. Still, behaviorism had a major impact and is still an important presence on the American psychological landscape.

Humanistic Psychology

This branch of psychology, often called the "third force"—after behaviorism and psychoanalysis—began in the early 1950s and has become increasingly influential since then. Humanistic psychologists, like Abraham Maslow (1908–1970) and Carl Rogers (b. 1902), protest what they consider the narrowness of the first two forces. They maintain that behaviorism tells us much about behavior but little about people and that psychoanalysis tells us much about the emotionally disturbed but little about the healthy. Humanism has sought to expand the content of psychology to include such uniquely human experiences as love, hate, fear, hope, happiness, humor, affection, responsibility, and the meaning of life, all of which are aspects of our lives that are usually not studied or written about in scientific ways because they resist being defined, manipulated, and measured (Schultz, 1981).

Cognitive Psychology

The most recent psychological school is an outgrowth of mainstream experimental psychology that seeks to find out what kinds of thought processes go on in the mind. Cognitive psychologists are not content with analyzing behavior in terms of simple stimulus-response connections but seek instead to understand the ways by which the mind processes the information it perceives—that is, organizes, remembers, and uses. This rapidly growing field is influencing the study of psychology in many ways, as you'll see throughout this book.

AREAS OF SPECIALIZATION IN PSYCHOLOGY

As the preceding brief rundown shows, psychology is a complex science with many different ways of looking at the human mind and human behavior and of applying the knowledge acquired. The field is so varied that it offers a rich selection of professional opportunities for individuals of widely differing interests, personalities, and abilities. See Box 1-1 for information on how you would prepare for a career in psychology and Figure 1-1 for graphic presentations of the settings in which psychologists with doctoral and master's degrees, respectively, work. The following thumbnail descriptions of the various psychological specialties can give you some idea of the kinds of work that psychologists do.

Clinical Psychology

Upon hearing that you're studying psychology, your friends and family may tease you by asking you for advice or accusing you of "analyzing" everything they say. They are showing the common belief that the clinical psychologist represents the entire field, which is understandable since this specialty is the largest in psychology. Clinical psychologists diagnose and treat emotional and behavioral disorders that range from mild to very severe. Abnormal psychology, a related specialty, is devoted to the study of such disorders. Clinicians differ among themselves about the causes of many of these disorders and about the best ways of treating them. In

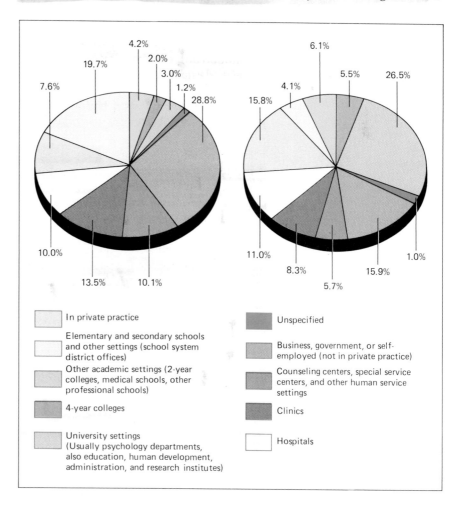

FIGURE 1-1 *The chart on the left indicates where psychologists with doctorates work while the chart on the right shows where psychologists with master's degrees work. (From Stapp and Fulcher, 1983)*

Counseling psychologists work in schools and colleges, where they help students with problems in such areas as academic work, career goals, and personal relationships. (Erika Stone/Photo Researchers, Inc.)

practice, they operate similarly to psychiatrists, who also treat disturbed individuals but who have a medical degree. Psychiatrists are able to prescribe medication, while psychologists cannot.

Counseling Psychology

Your college probably operates a counseling service, where you could go for help with problems revolving around your academic work, your career goals, the way you get along with your fellow students, or other aspects of your adjustment. Counseling psychologists give and interpret psychological tests, interview and observe those who come for help, and offer practical suggestions for resolving the problem that brought the counselee in in the first place. Many counseling psychologists work in schools.

Educational and School Psychology

Do children learn better with classmates of about the same level of ability? How can we help both gifted and mentally retarded children to develop to their fullest potential? What can the schools do to overcome social, physical, and cultural handicaps? Educational psychologists look to psychological principles and techniques for help in answering questions like these. School psychologists work directly with schoolchildren and their parents and teachers to help the children get the most from their school years. They operate similarly to counseling psychologists, focusing on the children's school achievement, mental health, and social adjustment.

Experimental Psychology

Are you interested in the phenomenon of color blindness? How we are motivated by our sex drives? Why somebody's name may be "on the tip of your tongue" but you can't bring it to the surface? All these topics are investigated by psychologists in this specialty with a name that's misleading since psychologists in *all* the subfields conduct experiments and since experimental psychologists use other research techniques, as well. Exper-

BOX 1-1

PREPARING FOR A CAREER IN PSYCHOLOGY

By taking this course, you will have fulfilled your first requirement for a major in psychology. If you decide that this field is for you, you'll be taking more courses in the psychology department of this or another college. Some junior and community colleges grant associate's degrees that prepare you to work in various psychological settings, as, for example, an aide in an institution or school. If you're enrolled in a four-year college, you'll be getting your bachelor's degree with a major in psychology, which may prepare you for employment as a welfare caseworker, a worker in a rehabilitation program or a community health center, or in some other psychological facility. Or you may find that your psychology background is

especially helpful for a career in any of a number of fields such as advertising or labor-management relations.

If you decide to pursue more education in the field, you can go on for a master's degree (usually one to two years of graduate school), which may help you find employment as a school psychologist, as a counselor in a mental health facility, or as a teacher in a community or junior college.

The next higher step is a doctorate. Most psychologists in the traditional areas of research and clinical work prepare for their careers by earning a Ph.D. (doctor of philosophy) degree, which entails three to six years of postgraduate study. All Ph.D. candidates design and carry out

an independent research project, which they describe in a detailed report called a *doctoral dissertation*. In addition, candidates take courses that give them a broad background in the different subfields and provide intensive training in their specialty.

If you want a doctorate with a more applied focus, you might instead pursue the Psy.D. (doctor of psychology) degree. Instead of a research dissertation, Psy.D. candidates usually conduct a doctoral project related to their future goal, which might be in psychotherapy, school psychology, or one of the other subfields. Preparation generally takes about the same time as that for the Ph.D.

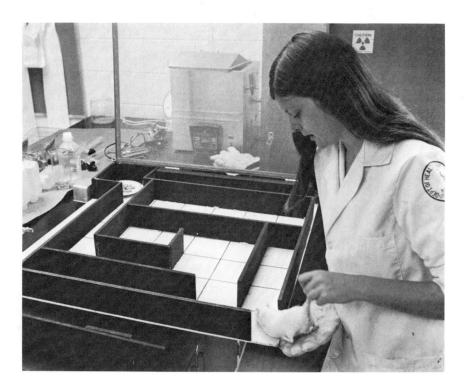

Experimental psychologists, who study basic psychological processes, work mostly in the laboratory, using both people and animals as subjects. Much psychological knowledge has been gleaned from studying the way rats learn how to run a maze, as this researcher is doing. (© Ken Robert Buck/The Picture Cube)

imental psychologists study such basic psychological processes as sensation and perception, learning, memory, cognition, motivation, and emotion. They work mostly in the laboratory and may use animals as well as human beings in their research.

Physiological Psychology

Why is it that someone with a spinal cord injury can show the familiar knee-jerk reflex even though he can't move his legs voluntarily? Why do injuries to certain regions of the brain cause memory loss, while others cause speech disorders? How does a baby's cry activate his mother's mammary glands to produce milk? These questions are among those studied by physiological psychologists, who study the biological bases for behavior, especially the nervous system and the endocrine system. While they sometimes study human beings who have suffered injury to some part of the brain or spinal cord, they more often conduct research with animals such as rats, cats, and monkeys. Recent work on the physiological underpinnings of memory highlights the close association between experimental and physiological psychologists.

Developmental Psychology

When does a baby learn that an object that she can't see still exists, an understanding that's vital for recognizing that even though her father walks out of the room he will very likely return? How do the hormonal changes of adolescence affect young people's emotional development? Do old people really suffer a decline in their intellectual abilities? Developmental psychologists study change over the life span, with some concentrating on particular times of life (such as infancy or old age) and others concentrating on relatively specific issues that persist throughout life (like the development of moral reasoning from childhood through adulthood). They describe, explain, predict, and try to modify behavior from birth through old age.

Personality Psychology

What makes one person trusting and another suspicious? One honest and another devious? One optimistic and another pessimistic? Are our personalities formed by our early experiences, or are we born the way we are? Are we likely to show the same personality characteristics in most situations, or do most of us show different faces in different settings? All these questions are investigated by personality psychologists, who measure and describe personality through interviews and specially designed tests and who formulate theories about its development.

Social Psychology

What makes people go along with a group even when they disagree with what the group is saying or doing? Why do people sometimes rush to the aid of accident victims and at other times ignore their plight? What attracts individuals to one another? These are some of the questions raised by social psychology, the branch that studies the way we affect and are influenced by other people, both in groups and in intimate relationships. Applied social psychologists use such knowledge to solve practical problems that arise in public relations and advertising, in communities composed of members of different ethnic backgrounds, in the workplace, and in just about every kind of situation in which people are together.

Developmental psychologists observe people of many different ages to determine how behaviors change across the life span. (Mimi Forsyth/Monkmeyer)

Psychometrics

You've undoubtedly taken various kinds of "intelligence" tests throughout your school years, some of which may have yielded an IQ (intelligence quotient). In applying for certain jobs or seeking vocational or emotional counseling, you may have taken personality tests that aimed to assess your social and emotional characteristics. Psychometric psychologists design such tests by identifying the characteristics they want to measure, developing the test items, and then developing statistical methods to interpret the scores.

Industrial and Organizational Psychology

People and their work are the province of industrial psychologists, who focus on making the workplace more fulfilling and more productive for both workers and their employers. These personnel specialists develop procedures for matching the job to the worker; for training workers; for evaluating internal organization; and for examining issues related to effective supervision, communication, and employee morale.

Engineering Psychology

This book was composed on a computer with word processing capabilities. Each person using this system can modify it to meet his or her individual comfort—can adjust the brightness of the letters on the screen, tilt the screen to the most comfortable angle, and move the keyboard to the best height and location. The kind of thought that goes into such design considerations—to make machines meet human needs—is the work of engineering psychologists. These applied experimental psychologists design, evaluate, and adapt equipment so that it can be used efficiently and effectively.

HOW PSYCHOLOGISTS STUDY BEHAVIOR

Since you've already seen how differently various psychological specialists conceptualize human behavior and how diverse the uses are to which

"To my data, right or wrong."

Happily for our state of scientific knowledge, most psychologists take a far less casual attitude toward their findings than does this "researcher." (Drawing by Levin; © 1984 The New Yorker Magazine, Inc.)

There is no uniform scientific method which, if scrupulously followed, will produce scientific knowledge. Scientific discoveries have been made in many ways, some of which are highly subjective, such as dreams. Scientific theories have been built both on flashes of insight and on plodding fact-gathering. Creativity in science cannot be put into a methodological straightjacket. Science progresses as it can. (Leahey, 1980, p. 4)

they apply psychological knowledge, it shouldn't come as any surprise to learn that the methods by which psychologists gather their information are just as varied. We'll look at the most important research techniques used by contemporary psychologists, examine their strengths and weaknesses, and see how they contribute to our understanding of human beings. We'll look at the participants in such research. And we'll probe into the ethical issues that arise in carrying out studies.

Before a researcher launches a particular project, she or he may develop a tentative theory to explain a particular behavior. Based on such a theory, the researcher will generate one or more hypotheses. A hypothesis is an "educated guess," a prediction of the results of the study. The researcher tests these hypotheses by conducting research, the systematic and objective collection of data. Data (a plural noun) represent the information collected, a body of facts (such as the scores on tests). The researcher then makes sense of the data by analyzing them using various statistical techniques, the most important of which are described in the appendix. Often researchers modify their original theories considerably as the research disproves their original hypotheses. The theorizing is an important part of this process since theories provide a framework for organizing the findings from research studies and for fitting them into our general state of knowledge.

As you become familiar with the ways these techniques are used, you'll be able to develop the kind of healthy skepticism that careful scientists develop in analyzing the results of their own and others' studies. You'll be able, for example, to read a newspaper report about "an exciting new discovery" and ask yourself, "Was this experiment carefully set up? Were there enough subjects to warrant drawing a general conclusion? Are the findings clear-cut or ambiguous? Are there other possible explanations for the results besides the ones given by the researchers?" A major element in any research project is the makeup of the people or animals being studied.

Who Takes Part in Psychological Research

COLLEGE STUDENTS   Modern psychology has sometimes been referred to as "the science of the behavior of the college sophomore" (Rubenstein, 1982, p. 83), reflecting the fact that some 80 percent of contemporary psychological research uses college students (who make up only 26 percent of 18- to 24-year-olds) as subjects (Rubenstein, 1982; Schultz, 1969). Why are students so popular with researchers? First of all, they're *there*, on the campuses where so much research is done. Furthermore, they require little outlay of scarce research funds: They can be motivated by rewards of course credits for participating in research studies; in some colleges students taking psychology courses are *required* to take part in studies.

For some kinds of studies, such as those involving basic sensory responses (like vision, hearing, and taste) or psychological processes (like concept formation, perception, and memory), students are eminently suitable subjects. For other kinds of studies, the heavy reliance on these young adults from a fairly narrow social range (usually white and middle-class) may be highly misleading. For example, most of what we "know" about normal sleep is based on the sleep of college students, while other research has shown that patterns of sleep vary greatly over the life cycle, making it impossible to generalize these findings either to children or to older adults. It's probably just as dangerous to generalize to the general public research findings about forming friendships, falling in love, conforming to group standards, and so forth, based only on studies of this

College students are the most popular subjects for psychological research because they're convenient, inexpensive, and well motivated. Overreliance on this subject pool may, however, lead to misleading conclusions. (© Van Bucher/Photo Researchers, Inc.)

one group. While psychologists are aware of the dangers in overstudying college students, no one seems to be coming up with a way around the dilemma.

ANIMALS Psychology has also been called "the science of the white rat," in recognition of the role this animal has played in so many research studies. Why do so many psychologists, whose field is, after all, the study of human behavior, aim their research microscope at animals like dogs, pigeons, monkeys, chimpanzees, and even such primitive organisms as snails? Partly for convenience: Since animals are less complex than people, we can often isolate a particular kind of behavior and get clearer, faster results. And partly for ethical reasons: We do many things with animals that we would not dream of doing with human beings such as performing surgery that removes sections of the animal's brain to see how the animal is affected, and observing the development of baby monkeys who have been removed from their mothers.

We have learned a great deal from such animal studies about learning, thought, memory, attachment, the biology of the brain, and so forth, but again, we have to be careful when we generalize findings from animals to human beings. Pigeons are not people, and we need to allow for differences between animals and human beings.

SAMPLING Since it's usually impossible to test all the members of a group (called a population) that a psychologist wants to study, such as all children from disadvantaged homes or all 1989 college graduates, researchers select subgroups, or samples, of these populations. They aim for a sample large enough to be representative of the population, while small enough to be manageable in a study. Careful thought goes into the selection of a sample. For example, if you wanted a sample of all the people over 70 years old in the United States, you wouldn't draw all your subjects from Florida but would choose people from various places around the country. You'd probably try for a mix of urban and rural residents of various racial and ethnic origins and a balance of both sexes and of married and single people.

You'd probably want a random sample, one in which each member of the population has an equal chance of being chosen. This selection is sometimes done by choosing every tenth name in a telephone directory (in which case you would be narrowing your population to those people who live in private residences and have telephones), in a list of couples who have just applied for marriage licenses, or in a list of first-year students enrolled in a particular college. Another way to get a random sample would be to put all the names of people in the desired population on individual pieces of paper, put all the papers in a drum, shake it up, and withdraw, say, one-fifth of the slips.

Samples are most reliable when they are stratified, that is, when they show a proportional representation of various important characteristics found in the larger population. For example, in a survey of the sexual attitudes and behaviors of the elderly, you would probably want your sample to reflect the same proportion of males and females, urban and rural dwellers, and married and single people as are in the entire population. (The technique of stratification is discussed in more detail in the appendix.)

Basic and Applied Research

One psychologist may ask, "How do people learn?" while another may inquire, "How can we help retarded children learn how to care for themselves?" One may wonder, "What causes aggression?" while another asks, "How can we reduce gang wars on our city streets?" In both these cases the first questioner's queries inspire basic, or "pure," research, while the second's questions are related to applied, or practical, research. The two orientations complement each other. Psychologists doing basic research look for answers that increase the total fund of human knowledge; while they're not addressing an immediate practical problem, the results of their work are often used in very down-to-earth ways. While a basic researcher, for example, may tell us what infants seem to like to look at, an applied researcher will use those findings to develop colorful mobiles to be hung over babies' beds.

Research Methods

The systematic and objective techniques that psychologists use all have their own strengths and weaknesses. Each of the following methods has made a major contribution to our understanding of human behavior. As we survey them briefly, we'll see the place each has earned in the science of psychology.

CASE HISTORY In Chapter 8 you'll read about Genie (not her real name), who at the age of 13 could not speak because from the age of 20 months she had been confined in a tiny room where no one spoke to her. One of the psychologists who worked with Genie over the nine years after her discovery kept close records of her progress in learning to speak, in forming relationships with hospital personnel, and in other aspects of her development (Curtiss, 1977). The book about Genie that resulted has shed light on the way people learn to speak. This is an example of the case history, or case study, method, in which intensive information is collected about one person or just a few people. The method is especially useful in a clinical setting when we need information to decide what kind of therapy to offer a particular individual.

SURVEYS When psychologists need information about a large group of people, they cannot use the case study method because it isn't valid to generalize from the experiences of one person. So they turn to survey methods such as questionnaires and interviews.

Questionnaires Researchers may design a written questionnaire which they send to a random sample of the population they want to reach. Sending a questionnaire to a sample of female college seniors at the University of Wisconsin-Madison could give us information about the students' religious preferences, political leanings, premarital sexual experiences, and so forth, which we could then generalize to female university students as a whole.

We might also find important relationships between two or more questions. We might, for example, find a relationship between political attitudes and sexual experience if students with liberal attitudes were more active sexually. We would say, then, that there was a correlation between, say, liberal politics and sexual permissiveness.

A correlation refers to the strength and direction of a relationship between two variables. The direction is positive when both variables increase; it's negative when one variable increases while the other one decreases. In the preceding example, then, the correlation would be positive for political liberalism and sexual permissiveness and negative for political conservatism and sexual permissiveness. The strength of the relationship is represented by a score between $+1.0$ (a perfect positive correlation) and -1.0 (a perfect negative correlation). (The uses of correlation as a statistical technique are described in greater detail in the appendix.)

While correlational analysis shows a relationship between two measures, it tells us nothing about cause and effect. We don't know whether one of these variables caused the other or whether the two variables are related because both stem from a third factor. We'll say more about cause-and-effect relationships when we talk about experiments.

While questionnaires can provide a lot of information about a lot of people in a short time, they have drawbacks. Answers are sometimes suspect because of faulty memory or because of subjects' giving answers they think they "should" give. Furthermore, there's no way to follow up a response to explore its meaning or delve deeper.

Interviews Psychologists or trained interviewers often ask questions in person. Usually the interviews are standardized so that everyone is asked the same questions, but sometimes respondents are asked to clarify or elaborate upon their answers. In Jean Piaget's interviews with children, he was more interested in the reasoning underlying the youngsters' answers than in the answers themselves, so he customized each interview to the individual child. In this way, he got a window into children's minds and attained many insights into children's thought processes.

Interviews are subject to faulty memory and the distortion of answers, either consciously or unconsciously. People answering questions on a sensitive topic like sex may, for example, exaggerate either their naiveté or their experience. Furthermore, interviews are expensive and time-consuming.

Sometimes questionnaires and interviews are used in the same study. In a survey of adolescent sexuality, 411 boys and girls filled out questionnaires, and an additional 200 were interviewed at length (Sorensen, 1973). Combining these two approaches provides depth as well as breadth.

NATURALISTIC OBSERVATION Just like biologists who observe the feeding habits of raccoons in their natural habitats, psychologists often observe human behavior in nursery schools, subway trains, singles' bars, or whatever natural environment is appropriate for the population and the behavior being studied. Researchers often keep meticulous records of their observations, such as tape-recording the interactions between parents and babies, recording the number of instances of aggression by preschoolers, or carefully describing the responses of fellow passengers in an elevator in response to some staged incident. Such records can provide valuable information about what people actually do in real-life situations.

Like every other study method, however, this one has its drawbacks. Sometimes the very presence of an observer can affect the subjects' behavior: If they know they're being watched, they behave differently. Researchers address this problem in several ways—by staying in a situation long enough so that the subjects get used to them, by blending into a crowd, or by remaining behind a one-way mirror through which they can observe others but cannot be seen themselves. Observation can be time-consuming and tedious, especially if the observer has to wait for a given behavior to occur to observe it. And it's hard for an independent investigator to verify observations since events are unlikely to recur in exactly the same way.

Probably the biggest disadvantage of naturalistic observation is that the observer cannot manipulate the variables and therefore cannot make cause-and-effect statements. If, for example, we note that children who watch a lot of violent television shows act aggressively, we can't say that the TV shows make them more aggressive; maybe aggressive children are more likely to view that kind of show. What naturalistic observation does help us do is generate a hypothesis that we can then test in an experiment.

EXPERIMENTS Psychologists design experiments to test hypotheses about causes and effects. They manipulate, or change, one aspect of a situation, called the independent variable, and observe its effect upon one aspect of behavior, called the dependent variable. The dependent variable thus *depends* upon the independent variable. For example, if a psychologist studied the effect of listening to music during an examination on test anxiety, the music would be the independent variable and test anxiety would be the dependent variable.

A well-designed experiment usually needs two groups of subjects, an experimental group and a control group. These groups would be similar in every way except for their exposure to the independent variable. The experimental group is exposed to the independent variable while the control group is not. The researcher then compares the two groups. (Statistical methods for determining the significance of the difference between the experimental and the control group are explained in the appendix.)

If the experimental group, which has been exposed to a treatment, behaves differently from the control group, which has not been exposed, we can assume that the treatment is responsible for the difference. If we didn't have a control group, we wouldn't know whether some other factor, like the simple passage of time, was responsible for the changed behavior. Some more complex experiments use more than one experimental group and more than one control group. Let's see how these principles work in both a laboratory and a field experiment.

A Laboratory Experiment In this kind of experiment, researchers bring subjects into a psychological laboratory. One classic experiment was on children's imitation of aggressive models (Bandura, Ross, & Ross, 1961). The researchers hypothesized that children who saw adults acting aggressively would copy their behaviors while children who did not see these models would not behave aggressively. To test this hypothesis, 72 preschool boys and girls were divided into three groups. One *experimental* group of 24 children saw an adult hitting and punching a rubber doll; the second *experimental* group of 24 saw an adult playing quietly with Tinker-toys; and the third group, the *controls*, didn't see any adults. (Seeing an aggressive or nonaggressive adult, then, was the *independent* variable; the children's aggressive or nonaggressive behavior was the *dependent* variable.)

The results supported the hypothesis. When children were observed in a free-play situation, those who saw the aggressive adults behaved aggressively. The children who saw the nonaggressive adults and those in the control group showed very little aggressive behavior. So this experiment seems to bear out the researchers' theory that children learn to be aggressive by seeing aggressive models, whom they then imitate. The big question, however, is whether the cause-and-effect relationships discovered in this carefully set up laboratory situation would generalize to settings outside the psychological laboratory.

A Field Experiment In this type of study, researchers introduce a change in a real-life setting, as in one study that took place in a nursing home (Langer & Rodin, 1976). The researchers wanted to see whether the decline in health, alertness, and activity that usually occurs among people in nursing homes could be slowed or reversed by giving these people the chance to make decisions and exert some control over their lives.

A total of 91 people were tested and rated on various measures of happiness and activity and then divided into two groups that were about the same on these measures. The 47 people in the *experimental group* were told that they were responsible for seeing that they got good care, for making decisions about how they spent their time, and for changing things they didn't like. They were also asked to choose and care for a plant. The 44 people in the *control group* were told that the staff was responsible for caring for them and making them happy. They were handed a plant and were told that the nurses would water and care for it.

Three weeks after the experiment began, 93 percent of the experimental subjects were more active, more alert, and happier, and were involved in many different kinds of activities. In the control group, however, 71 percent were weaker and more disabled. A follow-up evaluation eighteen months later showed that the benefits held up: Only 15 percent of the experimental subjects had died in this period, compared to 30 percent of the control subjects (Rodin & Langer, 1977). While the results of this study are more generalizable to the "real world" since it took place outside of the lab, the researchers did acknowledge one difficulty common to field experiments: Because of ethical and practical problems, they were not able to control all the important factors (in this case, random assignment of subjects and certain aspects of the nurses' involvements).

Strengths and Weaknesses of the Experimental Method Because experimental procedures can be tightly controlled, we can assume cause-and-effect relationships as with no other method. Furthermore, because these procedures can be standardized, other investigators can repeat them (can replicate the experiment) to see whether they get the same results.

We've already pointed out two difficulties: that of generalizing from laboratory findings to the real world and that of maintaining sufficient control over a field situation. Another problem may stem from experimenter bias. An experimenter who expects (and wants) a certain result to occur may unwittingly communicate these expectations to the subjects and thus influence the results. There are two ways to prevent such bias. In the single-blind technique, the experimenter who gives the posttest (the test given *after* the experiment to compare with the pretest, the one given *before* the experiment) doesn't know which subjects are in which group. In the double-blind technique, neither subjects nor experimenter know which group the subjects are in. In testing a drug that's supposed to alleviate depression, for example, the control group may be given a placebo (a sugar pill), but none of the subjects know which pill they're getting and none of the experimenters know which subjects received which pill.

ETHICS IN PSYCHOLOGICAL RESEARCH

> Absolute rules do not offer useful solutions to conflicts in values. What is needed is wisdom and restraint, compromise and tolerance, and as wholesome a respect for the dignity of the individual as the respect accorded the dignity of science.
> (Ruebhausen & Brim, 1966)

When Steve Kaufman, an 18-year-old college student, agreed to take part in an experiment on the effect of hypnotism on problem-solving ability, he didn't realize that during the course of the experiment he would become partially deaf through hypnosis, he would be placed in a room with two other students whom he thought were fellow subjects but who were actually confederates of the experimenter, and he would become convinced that these two were deliberately excluding him from their conversation and laughing at him (Hunt, 1982). By the time he learned what was going on, his experience had confirmed the experimenter's hypothesis—that deafness makes people paranoid, a highly significant conclusion for people with hearing problems (Zimbardo, Andersen, & Kabat, 1981). During the course of the experiment, Steve had some anxious, upsetting moments, but afterwards, when he was *debriefed* (told the actual purpose of the procedures), he expressed a feeling of pride that he had played an important role in this research.

This experiment demonstrates a major ethical issue in psychological research today—the use of deception. While this study and a number of others have been denounced by some critics for deceiving subjects into taking part in an experiment they weren't prepared for, defenders point to the obvious fact that this and other experiments in social psychology would be impossible to do without deception and that, in fact, a great deal of psychological knowledge has come to us precisely through such techniques. Recent emphasis on downplaying deception has resulted in a change in the nature of social psychology experiments, a change that many psychologists feel has seriously restricted the pursuit of psychological knowledge. This—along with certain other ethical dilemmas—is still not completely resolved.

During the 1970s, the U.S. Department of Health, Education, and Welfare (now the Department of Health and Human Services) mandated the establishment of institutional review boards to review psychological research from an ethical standpoint. As a result, colleges and other research facilities usually have committees that pass on the proposed research plans of investigators before they're allowed to go on. In 1982, the American Psychological Association (APA) developed a set of guidelines on ethical issues to protect subjects while permitting important research to continue. Essentially, these are the most important principles:

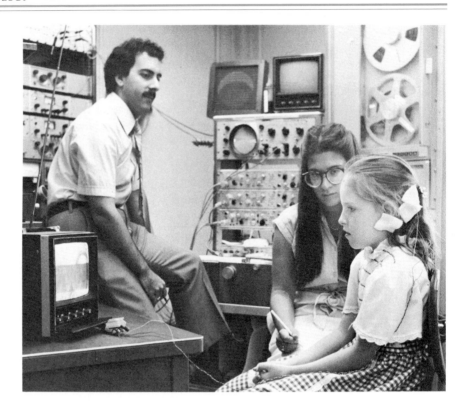

In designing their studies, psychologists must be keenly sensitive to ethical issues. For example, they need to be especially careful to avoid upsetting or frightening the children taking part in research even for the sake of benefits to future generations. (© 1982 Jim Holland/Black Star)

- *Subjects should be protected* from both physical and mental harm. As experimenters design their research studies, they are obliged to consider the best interest of the subjects. They must treat participants with respect and with concern for their dignity. They need to evaluate their designs to determine whether the subjects will be at risk of harm or will be at "minimal" risk.
- All subjects should give their *informed consent* to participate in research studies. In order to do this, they need to know what their participation will involve, what the study is about, what any risks might be, and anything else that might influence their decision about participating. The only time this obligation can be relaxed, according to the APA, is when a study is considered to hold minimal risk for the subject.
- Before an experimenter designs a study involving *deception*, she or he should try to come up with alternate procedures that would be equally effective. If this is impossible, the investigator then has to ask himself whether this study is really necessary. Will its results be sufficiently important to justify its use? If so, the investigator must then be sure that whatever deception is used will not harm the subject and that the subject be debriefed as soon as possible afterward.
- *Subjects must be able to decline to participate in a study or to withdraw* from it at any time, even if they are students, clients, or employees of the investigator.
- *The chief investigator in a research project is responsible* not only for his or her own ethical conduct but also for that of collaborators, assistants,

students, and employees on the project. All these people are also responsible for their own behavior.

- If a subject does suffer any harm from participation, *the investigator is
obliged to detect and to remove or correct any undesirable consequences,* including any long-term effects.
- All information obtained from participants is to be kept confidential,
unless subjects agree in advance that it may be divulged. Investigators
are obliged to guarantee the *right of privacy* to participants.

At various points throughout this book, we'll be turning our attention
to ethical issues when discussing specific research projects. Meanwhile
you might want to keep ethical considerations in mind when evaluating
the studies you'll read about here and elsewhere. You'll want to read with
a critical eye, looking not only at the ethical issues involved but also at the
value of the information that's presented, both for the field in general and
for your own life in particular. We have presented data that we feel are
important and have met the tests of scientific validity. We've found the
collection and presentation of these findings to be an exciting and chal-
lenging task, especially since the field of psychology is continuing to
grow, to expand, to enrich our lives with what it can tell us about ourselves. We wish you bon voyage as you journey along that most exciting
route of all, the one that leads into the very nature of your own being.

SUMMARY

1 *Psychology* is the scientific study of behavior and
mental processes. Psychologists want to *describe,
explain, predict,* and *modify* behavior.

2 Psychology as a science is just over 100 years old.
Its two main historical roots are *philosophy* and
physiology.

3 During the late nineteenth and twentieth centuries, a number of different *schools* of psychology
emerged. These schools represented different theoretical outlooks concerning psychological issues.

4 *Wilhelm Wundt,* the "father of psychology," set up
the first laboratory for psychological experimentation in Liepzig, Germany, in 1879. He developed
the technique of *analytic introspection* in an attempt
to study the basic structure of the mind.

5 *E. B. Titchener* named Wundt's work *structuralism*
and brought it to America. Titchener wanted to
analyze consciousness by reducing it to its elemental units.

6 The first truly American psychological school was
functionalism. Functionalists were concerned with
applying knowledge in practical situations, particularly educational settings.

7 *Gestalt* psychologists believed that the whole was
greater than its individual parts. They felt that
experiences could not be broken down into elements.

8 With the development of *psychoanalysis, Sigmund
Freud* started a revolution of the unconscious. This
approach focused on the unconscious drives
which motivate behavior.

9 *Behaviorists* focus on *observable* behaviors and
events. They are not concerned with unobservable
events or the impact of unconscious forces on behavior. They emphasize the role of the environment in shaping behavior. Behaviorism was
launched in 1913 with *John B. Watson's* article on
psychology as the behaviorist views it. Today, the
most prominent behaviorist is *B. F. Skinner,* who
has uncovered the basic principles of *operant conditioning* and has applied these principles to the solution of practical problems.

10 Humanistic psychologists such as *Maslow* and
Rogers have primarily been interested in healthy
human behavior. They believe that psychoanalytic
and behaviorist approaches are too narrow.

11   The most recent psychological school is *cognitive psychology* which is concerned with the way the mind processes information.

12   There are a number of different subfields in psychology. These include *clinical* and *abnormal; counseling; educational* and *school; experimental; physiological; developmental; personality; social; psychometrics; industrial* and *organizational;* and *engineering* psychology. There are career opportunities in psychology for individuals with different interests, abilities, and academic credentials.

13   Psychologists use a variety of *research techniques* in collecting psychological data. In designing research, an experimenter begins with a *theory,* or explanation about the cause of behavior. Based on this theory, the researcher generates *hypotheses,* or predictions, about the results of the study. A research project is then designed to test the hypotheses. The data collected are analyzed using appropriate statistical techniques, and the original theory is supported or modified based on these findings.

14   Since psychologists usually cannot test all members of a target *population,* they select subgroups, or *samples,* of these populations. There are two major sampling techniques. In a *random sample,* each member of a population has an equal chance of being selected. *Stratified samples* show various characteristics in the same proportion as they are found in the population.

15   College students and white rats have been somewhat overrepresented as subjects in psychological research.

16   Data collection techniques include *case histories, surveys* (including *questionnaires* and *interviews*), *naturalistic observations,* and *experiments.*

17   In a case study intensive information is gathered about one or a few subjects.

18   Using survey methods, psychologists can gather information about large groups of subjects. They may use questionnaires or they may conduct interviews. Sometimes questionnaires and interviews are used in the same study.

19   In naturalistic observation, subjects are observed in some "natural" setting rather than the experimental laboratory.

20   When psychologists want to make statements about *cause-and-effect* relationships, they design experiments. These are highly controlled procedures which can be readily replicated by the same or other experimenters. In an experiment, the psychologist manipulates the *independent variable* and observes the effect of this manipulation on the *dependent variable.* The two groups of subjects in an experiment are the *experimental group* (the group which experiences the experimental condition or *treatment*) and the *control* group (which does not receive the experimental treatment). By comparing the experimental and control groups, researchers can determine the effects of their treatment. Psychological experiments are usually done in the *laboratory* although they may also be carried out in the *field.*

21   In designing psychological research, psychologists must consider ethical guidelines developed to protect subjects.

SUGGESTED READINGS

American Psychological Association. (1982). *Ethical principles in the conduct of research with human participants.* Washington, D.C.: American Psychological Association. A guidebook by the APA to the ethics of psychological experimentation.

Diener, E., & Crandall, R. (1978). *Ethics in social and behavioral research.* Chicago: University of Chicago Press. Contains an interesting discussion of the ethical dilemmas faced by psychologists in designing and carrying out research.

Hearst, E. (Ed.). (1979). *The first century of experimental psychology.* Hillsdale, N.J.: Lawrence Erlbaum Associates. A collection of articles tracing the development of the subfields of experimental psychology during its first 100 years.

Nordby, V. J., & Hall, C. S. (1974). *A guide to psychologists and their concepts.* San Francisco: W. H. Freeman. A highly readable presentation containing information about the lives and major concepts of twenty-eight important psychologists from the past and present.

Schultz, D. (1975). *A history of modern psychology* (2d ed.). New York: Academic Press. A fascinating account of the most important schools of psychology and the people associated with them.

Super, C., & Super, D. (1982). *Opportunities in psychology.* Skokie, Ill.: VGM Career Horizons. An account of the many opportunities for careers in psychology.

Woods, P. J. (1976). *Career opportunities for psychologists.* Washington, D.C.: American Psychological Association. A collection of articles on careers in psychology emphasizing emerging and expanding areas.

PART

2

BIOLOGICAL FOUNDATIONS OF BEHAVIOR

Underlying everything we feel and do is the complex mechanism of our physical selves. To understand human behavior, then, we need to understand the basic biological structures and processes that bring us information about our world and enable us to respond to it.

In Chapter 2, "Biology and Behavior," we'll explore the intricate workings of the brain and the nervous system to see how they affect every mental and physical process we are capable of. Some of our knowledge about biological influences on behavior is as fresh as today's newspaper, since brain research continues to come up with ever more sophisticated tools for studying the nervous system and for treating disorders.

In Chapter 3, "Sensation and Perception," we'll describe the ways we receive information through our various senses, including the five "special" senses (vision, hearing, touch, taste, and smell). We'll also investigate the ways our brains interpret and organize such information to create meaningful patterns of perception.

Then, in Chapter 4, "States of Consciousness," we'll see how our abilities to sense, to perceive, and to act depend on our state of consciousness. We experience the world differently and behave differently, depending on whether we are awake and alert, asleep, or in an alternate state induced by meditation, drugs, or hypnosis.

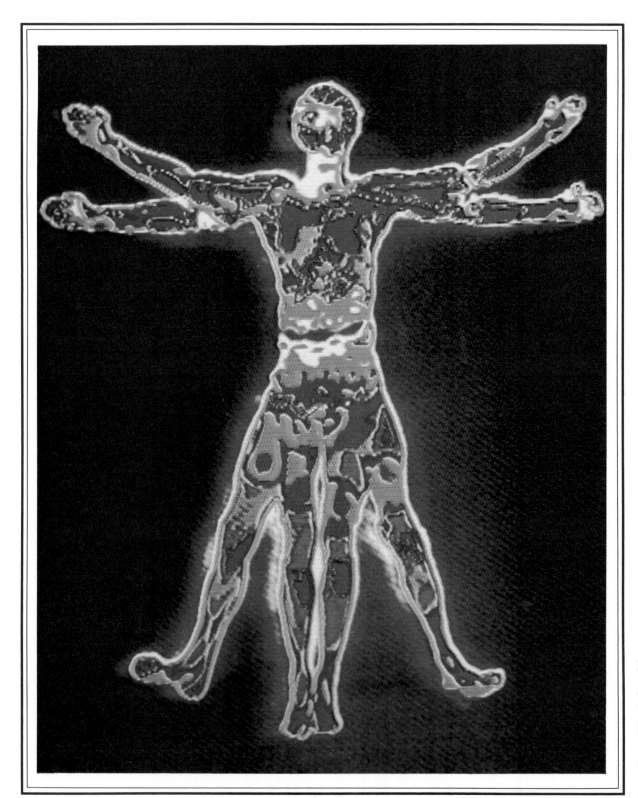

CHAPTER 2

BIOLOGY AND BEHAVIOR

SPOTLIGHT ON

How the nervous system works.

New ways to study the brain.

How the brain affects behavior, and the effects of brain injury.

The role of the endocrine system.

A popular theme in science fiction stories involves implanting one person's brain into another person's body. The reason this plot device is so intriguing is in the question it asks: "Who is the person? The body or the brain?" The almost invariable conclusion: The brain rules the body.

We can see this in our daily lives. It is, for example, this one wrinkled little organ that told your body to wake up this morning, that allowed you to recognize where you were, that directed you to get up out of bed, move your arms and legs, remember that you had a class to attend, remember how to get there, understand the words you've been hearing and reading, and formulate your own original thoughts and express them in speech. This same organ tells you when you're happy, sad, fearful, enraged, or in the grip of some other emotion.

The brain and the spinal cord comprise the central nervous system (CNS). The central nervous system, together with the peripheral nervous system (PNS) (the network of nerves that control the muscles and glands of the body), control every activity of our bodies and our minds.

The brain can be considered the chief engineer of both these nervous systems. While physical shortcomings or defects can interfere with the brain's work, no other part of the body can replace it or surpass it. For all practical purposes, then, we *are* our brains. Virtually all the subject matter included in the study of psychology is traceable to processes within our brains or to interactions between our brain and other organ systems in our bodies, such as the endocrine system. Programmed in our biology— in our brain and other parts of the nervous system—are the crucial elements that separate human beings from all other beasts of field, sea, and sky. These elements are the nerve cells, which permit us to think in abstract terms, to speak, to write, to study ourselves. All these activities are beyond the reach of all other animals.

As long as people have studied the brain, they have been in awe of its complexity. Through the centuries, theorists have tried to explain the mysteries of the way the brain works in terms of the most advanced technology of the day. During the seventeenth century, the French mathematician and philosopher René Descartes compared it to the science of hydraulics (the study of fluids), suggesting that information gets transmitted in the form of fluids through a system of pipes and tubes (See Figure 2-1). Later, others compared brain activity to the gears and wheels of clockworks, to electrical cables, and to telephone switchboards. Today's favorite analogy is with an electronic computer since the brain, like the computer, is a processor of information. None of these comparisons are totally accurate because the brain is still vastly more complicated than anything people have been able to invent. (See Table 2-1 for a comparison between the brain and the computer.) Still, the electrical analogy is apt since minute electrical currents in brain cells direct our every activity.

In this chapter we'll look at the biological basis for human behavior, at the way the brain receives and transmits information and communicates with other parts of the body. First, we'll describe the various components of the nervous system. Then we'll look closely at the basic building blocks of the system, the *neurons*, or *nerve cells*, and the *glial cells*, and the basic means of communication among these cells.

Until artificial intelligence can duplicate human mental development from birth onward; until it can absorb the intricacies and subtleties of cultural values; until it can acquire consciousness of self; until it becomes capable of playfulness and curiosity; until it can create new goals for itself, unplanned and uninstigated by any human programmer; until it is motivated not by goals alone but by some restless compulsion to be doing and exploring; until it can care about, and be pleased or annoyed by, its own thoughts; until it can make wise moral judgments—until all these conditions exist, the computer, it seems to me, will not match or even palely imitate the most valuable aspects of human thinking.
(Hunt, 1982, p. 360)

FIGURE 2-1 *This illustration of Descartes' comparison of the brain to the science of hydraulics shows the fire (A) pulling the tiny thread (CC), which opens a pore (d) in the ventricle (F) of the brain, allowing "animal spirit" to flow out through hollow tubes in the centers of the nerves connected to the leg muscles, making the foot (B) pull away from the fire. (Blakemore, 1977)*

TABLE 2-1 The Brain and the Computer

Computer	Brain
Processes information quickly.	Processes information quickly—but slower than computer.
Processes information serially, one item at a time.	Handles information simultaneously; millions of cells are active at the same time.
Removing one or two parts can upset an entire computation.	Injury or illness causing several neurons to cease functioning often makes no appreciable difference in some brain operations. Sometimes other parts of the brain substitute for the damaged ones.
Can execute only those programs and process only those data already in the system.	Can make intuitive leaps (called "insight"—see Chapter 8). Can understand, organize experiences into new concepts; can create new hypotheses and test them; can adapt to new situations and new information.
Can match incoming information with that stored in memory only if it is an exact copy.	Can abstract the meaning of a symbol and generalize to similar symbols (such as the letter A or a similar command in somewhat different language, etc.). Hunt (1982) tells of a computer that could understand spoken commands—but only when they were issued by one of the two designers who programmed the computer, both of whom had foreign accents!
Is only as good as its human input (how it is programmed, what requests are made of it).	
Can do long and intricate mathematical calculations much faster and more reliably than humans can do.	Maximum memory: 1 hundred trillion to 280 quintillion (280,000,000,000,000,000,000) bits* (Hunt, 1982; von Neumann, 1958) or several billion times more information than a large modern computer.

*A bit is the smallest unit of information.
Source: Adapted from Crick, 1979.

WHAT THE NERVOUS SYSTEM IS

The brain may be the most obvious component of the human nervous system, but it isn't the only one. The nervous system comprises two main divisions—the central nervous system (CNS) and the peripheral nervous system (PNS). These systems are shown in Figure 2-2.

The central nervous system consists of the spinal cord and the brain. The *spinal cord* is a long bundle of nerves, located in the hollow spaces between the *vertebrae*, the little bones that make up the backbone. The human *brain* is a spongy organ that weighs in at a tiny fraction of total body weight, only about 3 pounds in an adult. It contains several specialized structures: the brain stem, which is made up of the *pons,* the *medulla oblongata,* and the *midbrain;* the cerebellum (which means "little brain"); and the cerebrum (or *forebrain*), which is made up of the *thalamus,* the *hypothalamus,* the *limbic system,* and the *cerebral cortex.* We'll see in a little while what each of these structures does.

The peripheral nervous system is made up of two kinds of nerves: the sensory nerves transmit information from your body organs (such as skin or muscles) to your brain. The motor nerves transmit information from your brain to the muscles and glands of your body. Motor nerves can be part of the somatic or the autonomic nervous systems. Before we go into

FIGURE 2-2 *The central and peripheral nervous systems.*

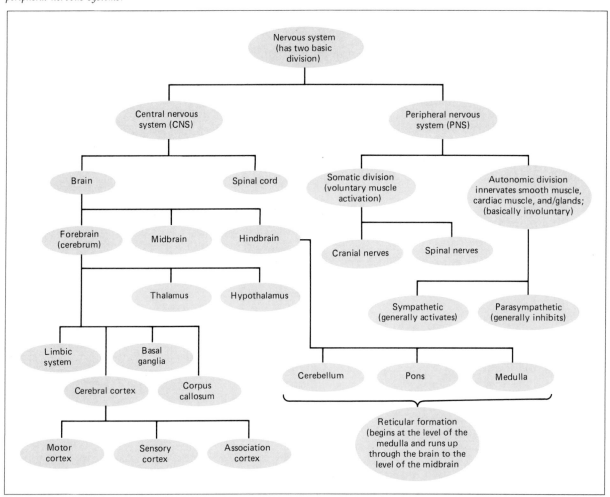

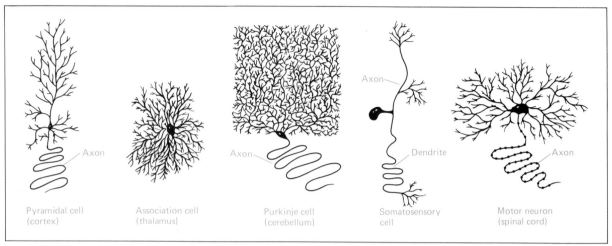

Pyramidal cell (cortex)   Association cell (thalamus)   Purkinje cell (cerebellum)   Somatosensory cell   Motor neuron (spinal cord)

FIGURE 2-3 *Each neuron, or nerve cell, is specialized for function. The drawings above show the different shapes and sizes of neurons in various parts of the nervous system.*

HOW THE NERVOUS SYSTEM WORKS

The Cells

detail about the specific functions of these various elements of the nervous system, however, let's look at the basic mechanisms underlying the way the system works.

The human nervous system is made up of billions of cells, of which there are two basic kinds. The neurons, or nerve cells, do the vital job of receiving and sending information to other parts of the body. The neurons are supported and protected in various ways by the glial cells (or glia). One type of glial cell covers parts of the neuron with a sheath, or covering, composed of a fatty tissue called myelin. Other types help remove dead nerve cells, while still others support the neurons in other ways. At least 12 billion neurons and at least the same number of glia are present in the human nervous system. Neurons, which were seen for the first time in 1950 under an electron microscope, vary widely in size and in shape, depending largely on the different functions they perform. Some examples of different kinds of neurons are shown in Figure 2-3.

Despite their differences, all neurons have certain characteristics in common. They all have a *cell body*, with a *nucleus* that contains the cell's genetic information (that is, the programming that determines what each cell can do) in deoxyribonucleic acid (DNA). They all have dendrites, narrow, branching extensions of the cell body, which receive incoming signals. The longer and more complex a neuron's dendrites, the more connections can be made. Most neurons have a tail-like extension called an axon, which may be as short as a tiny fraction of an inch for a brain neuron or as long as 2 or 3 feet for an axon on a neuron in the spinal cord. A neuron receives information from other neurons through its dendrites and cell body, while it transmits information down its axon (see Figure 2-4).

The Activity

Our brains are incredibly busy centers of electrical activity for as long as we live, even when we're asleep. Each neuron, like a battery, has potential energy stored within it because the inside of the neuron has more negative than positive ions (charged particles), while it is surrounded on the outside by positive ions. This potential energy is known as the resting potential (see Figure 2-4).

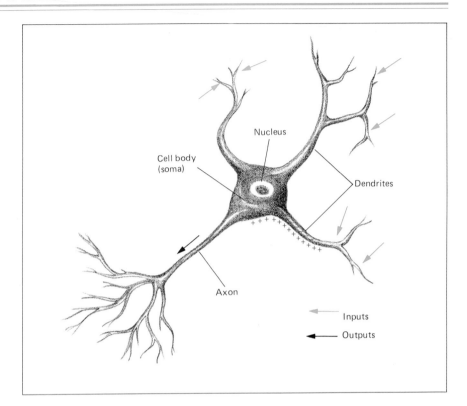

FIGURE 2-4 *Schematic diagram of a "typical" neuron, showing the cell body, nucleus, dendrites, and the axon. Also shown is the distribution of positive and negative ions that generates the resting potential.*

If you were in a very large city library with a million volumes, and every volume were five hundred pages long, and every page reproduced the neuron diagram [in Figure 2-4], there still wouldn't be as many neurons pictured as you have in your cortex alone.
(Hunt, 1982, p. 38)

The "firing" of a neuron, or sending a nerve impulse down its axon, from one end of the neuron to the other, is known as an action potential (see Figure 2-5). The action potential begins at a specialized part of the axon near the cell body (the *axon hillock*), and the impulse travels all the way along the axon to the axon terminal. Impulses travel faster along axons that are covered with myelin. Since myelin acts as an electrical insulator, the action potential cannot occur beneath the myelin sheath but instead jumps rapidly between the *nodes,* or gaps, in the myelin (see Figure 2-6).

The process of myelinization (the formation of myelin on axons) extends through at least the first ten years of life in human beings, and dendrites continue to grow and become more elaborate. In old age, however, there is a shriveling of dendrites and, thus, less communication among cells. The enormous growth in human abilities that takes place during the first ten years of life parallels the process of myelinization and the growth of dendrites during this period, pointing to a close relationship between brain development and human abilities.

When you touch a hot stove and instantly pull your hand away, you are acting upon information received by sensory neurons (that an intense stimulus is present) and sent by motor neurons (ordering your muscles to move your hand). Since these are different neurons, they must communicate with each other in some way. How do the neurons receive and pass along such information? They communicate with each other at specialized junctions called synapses. These synapses are spaces between the axon of one neuron and the dendrites or cell body of a second. When the action potential reaches the end of an axon, it causes release of a chemical called

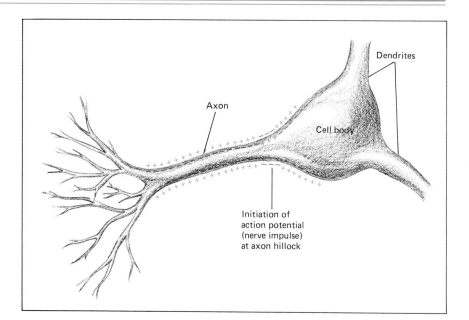

FIGURE 2-5 *Schematic diagram of reversal of resting potential that occurs during an action potential.*

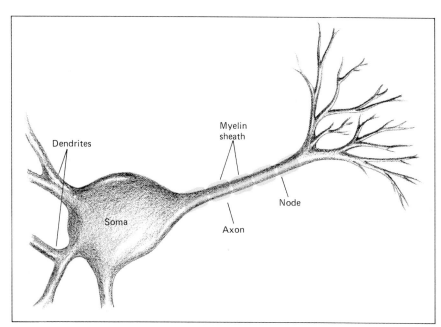

FIGURE 2-6 A Myelineated Axon *Myelin sheaths are specialized glial cells.*

a *transmitter substance*, or a neurotransmitter, into the synapse. Synaptic vesicles, specialized organs at the axon terminal of the sending neuron, squirt the chemical into the synapse. Receptor sites, specialized molecules on the receiving neuron, "catch," or bind with, the chemical (see Figure 2-7 for a diagram of a typical synapse).

There are many different transmitter substances, but each neuron typically sends only one chemical from all of its synapses. However, any receiving cell has many different receptor sites, which are specialized for the different types of neurotransmitters that can be sent by different neurons. Neurotransmitters in the synapse can either *excite* the receiving neu-

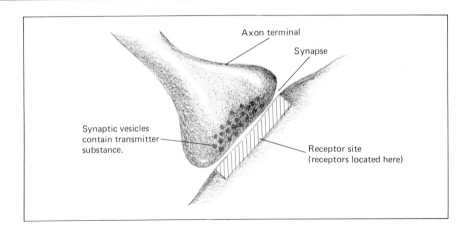

FIGURE 2-7 *Diagram of a typical synapse.*

ron, making it fire its own impulses, or they can *inhibit* it from firing. In the "hot stove" example, sensory neurons in your fingers that are specially designed to feel pain send impulses that excite the motor neurons that control the biceps muscle of your arm, making it contract so you can flex your arm and pull it away from the heat. At the same time, a "copy" of the message goes to the motor neurons that control your triceps muscle (the one that is used to extend your arm straight out in front of you), inhibiting those neurons from firing, to provide the necessary triceps relaxation that will allow your biceps to contract.

Neurons can receive many synaptic inputs at about the same time from different sources, and it's the sum total of the excitatory and inhibitory synaptic currents that decide whether a given cell will fire. So each neuron acts like a tiny calculator, adding up information (in the form of excitatory and inhibitory synaptic currents) from many sources and making "decisions" about whether to pass that information on to other cells.

Since each nerve cell can receive messages from about 1000 other nerve cells, the number of synaptic connections in the human brain probably exceed a trillion (1,000,000,000,000). This astronomically high number of communicative possibilities underlies everything we think, feel, and do. No wonder this small, squishy organ is still the most complicated mechanism in the known universe.

The Neurotransmitters

It's difficult to prove that any specific chemical acts as a neurotransmitter, although researchers have identified a number of substances that appear to be likely candidates. They meet these criteria: They are released by neurons, they can generate excitatory or inhibitory electrical currents, and the enzymes that break them down occur naturally in the brain.

We often learn what these substances are supposed to do when something goes wrong. For example, there is strong evidence that faulty transmission of one such chemical, dopamine, can lead to at least two disorders. Too much dopamine may cause the psychological disorder of schizophrenia (discussed in detail in Chapter 15), and too little may lead to the nervous disorder of Parkinson's disease, an ailment characterized by involuntary shaking and by depression. Researchers have come to these conclusions by observing the effects of certain chemicals on people affected with these disorders. Schizophrenics are often helped by a class of drugs known as the phenothiazines, which are known to block transmission in synapses that use dopamine, suggesting that overactive dopamine synapses are present in schizophrenia. And Parkinson's sufferers are helped by a drug called L-DOPA, a substance that the brain can convert to dopamine (Kolb & Whishaw, 1980).

Another neurotransmitter, acetylcholine, may be implicated in Alzheimer's disease. This is a degenerative disorder of the brain resulting in extreme forgetfulness and other intellectual losses. It is usually seen in the elderly (and often called "senility") but sometimes occurs in the middle-aged. (This is discussed in detail in Chapter 13.) Postmortem examinations of Alzheimer's patients have shown that their brains are deficient in acetylcholine and that they lose a group of neurons that are known to provide this neurotransmitter to the rest of the brain. Researchers hope that a chemical therapy will therefore help such patients, for whom no other treatment has yet been found (Coyle, Price, & DeLong, 1983).

Drugs that alter behavior seem to affect specific brain processes by introducing into the body chemicals whose action is similar to specific transmitters. Chemically, these drugs either speed up or reverse the effects of neurotransmitters and affect our sensations, our perceptions, our thinking processes, or our motor behavior accordingly. These effects may be short-lived, long-lasting, or even permanent. Table 2-2 provides a brief rundown of a number of psychoactive drugs (drugs that affect psychological processes), the neurotransmitters they affect, and the way they affect them: either by facilitating their release at the synapses, preventing their destruction by enzymes, or by blocking their attachment to receptor sites.

THE CENTRAL NERVOUS SYSTEM (CNS)

We'll now look at the activities within the two major structures of the central nervous system, the brain and the spinal cord. First we'll examine the simpler structure, the spinal cord.

The Spinal Cord

The spinal cord is a long, stemlike structure that consists of nerve cell bodies and axons. It operates as a pathway, taking sensory information to the brain and transmitting motor impulses from the brain to the muscles. It controls all the body's activities from the neck down and is also involved in simple sensorimotor reflexes.

When you kick your lower leg out in response to a tap just under the kneecap or pull your hand away from a hot stove, you are demonstrating a reflex, an involuntary response to a stimulus. This is one of the simplest forms of behavior, a connection between sensory input and motor output that we share with the lower animals. Human beings have many reflexes, all of which are supported by connections between sensory and motor neurons that appear to be built into our systems through our genetic structure.

There are two basic types of reflexes, the monosynaptic and the polysynaptic. The simpler kind, the monosynaptic, occurs as a result of a direct connection between a sensory neuron and a motor neuron, with no intervening *interneurons*. It has only one synapse between sensory input (what you feel) and motor output (what you do). The familiar *patellar*, or "knee-jerk," reflex is in this category (see Figure 2-8). Both kinds of neurons involved in this reflex—sensory and motor—are located in the spi-

TABLE 2-2 Common Psychoactive Drugs and Effects on Neurotransmitter Systems

Drug Class	Examples	Medical Use	Mechanism of Action
Barbiturates	Secobarbital (Seconal®) Pentobarbital (Nembutal®)	Sleep, sedation	Decrease levels of many neuro-transmitters
Benzodiazepines	Diazepam (Valium®) Chlordiazepoxide (Librium®)	Reduce anxiety	Act at benzodiazepine receptor
Alcohol	Distilled spirits, wine, beer	Relaxation	Decreased norepinephrine
Stimulants			
Amphetamines	Benzedrine® Dexedrine® Methylphenidate (Ritalin®)	Appetite suppressant Increased arousal Hyperkinesis	Increase release of norepineph-rine and dopamine
Cocaine		Surgical local anes-thetic, diagnostic	
Antidepressants			
MAO inhibitors	Nardil® Marplan®	Reduce depression	Prevent breakdown of norepi-nephrines and serotonin
Tricyclics	Imipramine (Tofranil®) Amitryptamine (Elavil®) Desipramine (Norpramin®)	Reduce depression	Decrease norepinephrine and serotonin reuptake
Major Tranquilizers			
Rauwolfia alkaloids	Reserpine (Serpasil®)	Treatment of psychoses Antihypertensive	Block dopamine, norepineph-rine, and serotonin storage
Phenothiazines	Chlorpromazine (Thorazine®) Trifluoperazine (Stelazine®) Thioridazine (Mellaril®)	Treatment of schizo-phrenia	Block dopamine receptors
Butyrophenones	Haloperidol (Haldol®)		
Analgesics			
Narcotics	Morphine Heroin Meperidine (Demerol®)	Reduces pain None Reduces pain	Mimic endorphins and bind with same receptors
Psychedelics			
	Atropine	Preoperative sedation	Blocks acetylcholine
	Muscarine	None	Increases acetylcholine
	Mescaline	None	Interacts with serotonin
	Cannabis (marijuana, hashish)	Antiglaucoma, antinausea	Interacts with serotonin*
	LSD Psilocybin	None	Interact with serotonin

*Mechanism uncertain

nal cord, so the brain itself does not directly participate. This is a dramatic demonstration of the fact that you can make some responses to sensory stimulation without being consciously aware of the stimulus.

Paraplegics are people whose lower limbs are paralyzed because an injury to the spinal cord has cut off communication between the brain and the spinal cord. Because of the injury, their brains don't receive sensory

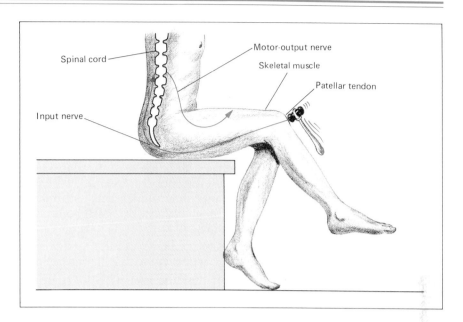

FIGURE 2-8 *The patellar, or knee-jerk, reflex is a simple, monosynaptic reflex that has only one synapse between sensory input (what you feel) and motor output (what you do).*

Within the figure: Spinal cord, Input nerve, Motor-output nerve, Skeletal muscle, Patellar tendon

information from the spinal cord. As a result, they don't feel pain even if something ordinarily painful is occurring to an affected part of the body. The lack of a pathway from the brain to the spinal cord also prevents information from traveling along a pathway from the brain to the rest of the body, thus preventing *voluntary* control over affected muscles. However, people with spinal cord injuries do exercise some *involuntary* control because of synaptic connections that are completely within the spinal cord. Thus, a paraplegic will still move his leg away after a pinprick, even though he isn't conscious of the sensation of pain.

When you blink to a loud noise, withdraw your hand from pain, or contract the pupils of your eyes in bright light, you are showing one of the more complex polysynaptic reflexes, which involve many synapses in an unknown number of interneurons. We have many different reflexes, all of which follow the same basic patterns of coupling between the sensory and motor systems.

The spinal cord of human beings is very similar to the structure in the lower animals. The organ that sets us apart is our brain, especially the part of the brain known as the "cortex."

The Brain

The brain has three major parts: the brain stem (medulla, pons, and midbrain); the cerebellum ("little brain"); and the cerebrum (hypothalamus, thalamus, basal ganglia, limbic system, and cortex). The positions of these structures are shown in Figure 2-9.

The brain stem is responsible for many basic functions. It takes in information from several senses through sensory regions for vision, hearing, taste, balance, and touch in the facial area. It controls involuntary activity of the tongue, the larynx, the eyes, and the facial muscles through specific motor neurons for these areas. It controls levels of sleep and arousal through the reticular formation, nestled within its central core, and it coordinates the motor neurons in the spinal cord that control such activities as walking, breathing, and the beating of our hearts.

The cerebellum, which is connected to the back of the brain stem, is involved primarily in the coordination of motor activity, especially the fine-tuning of voluntary movements. It is the functioning of this organ that enables a pianist to play a difficult and rapid arpeggio. The cerebellum also helps to maintain posture and balance. Damage to the cerebellum will not affect a person's movements at rest but will result in tremors when an affected individual attempts any kind of intricate activity.

The cerebrum, the most highly developed section of the human brain, is also multifunctional. It contains the hypothalamus, which, as we'll see, keeps many body systems in balance, largely through its close involvement with the endocrine system, which releases hormones into our bodies; the thalamus, which acts as a relay center to the cortex; the basal ganglia, large collections of cell bodies that are involved in bodily movements; the limbic system, which mediates emotional responses and is also involved in memory; and the cerebral cortex, the gray outer covering of the brain, which is involved in most higher-level functions such as thinking, remembering, and solving problems.

HOW WE STUDY THE BRAIN

As we said, the human brain has been of enormous interest to the human species. What makes us tick? What brings about the countless activities we are engaged in all the time, asleep or awake, sick or well? To find out, researchers have developed a variety of ways to study the brain.

One way that was popular in the nineteenth century involved feeling the bumps on people's heads. According to the pseudoscience of *phrenology*, your psychological attributes correspond to the swellings and hollows in your skull, which demonstrate the development of particular areas of your brain. In other words, areas of the brain exist for such traits as secretiveness, calculation, and a tendency toward amorous behavior, and if those areas are well developed, you have the personality characteristic in question. Most of the tenets underlying phrenology, however,

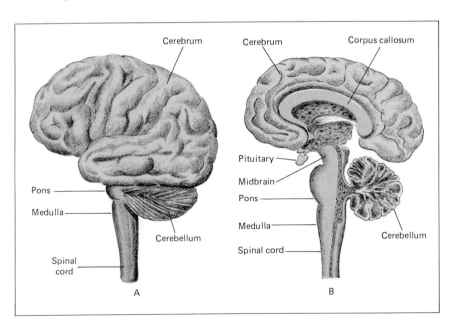

FIGURE 2-9(a) *A view of the left side of the human brain* (b) *Here, the brain has been split in half. We are looking at the medial (inside) surface of the right hemisphere.* (From Thompson, 1967)

The waterfront hi-jinks of this quartet are made possible by the normal functioning of the cerebellum. This brain structure helps to coordinate motor activity and maintain posture and balance. (©Michael Philip Manheim/Photo Researchers, Inc.)

were clearly unscientific and have been completely discredited. For example, the theory was based on faulty anatomy. Some of the areas of the skull shown in Figure 2-10 don't even lie over the brain. Furthermore, the way these areas are charted does not correspond in any way to functionally significant divisions of the cortex.

This theory is historically important, however, because it stimulated thinking and research aimed at finding out which regions of the brain control which functions of body and mind, a major focus of contemporary brain research. Fortunately, however, we now have far more scientific and effective ways to unlock the mysteries of the brain.

The oldest study technique is still in use: *surgery* in which researchers create *lesions*, or areas of brain damage in the brains of experimental animals. They then observe the impact such damage has on the animals' behavior. For obvious reasons, this technique is not used on human beings, but researchers have obtained similar kinds of knowledge from studying people who have suffered brain damage because of strokes or head injury or who have had surgery performed to correct some physiological condition (such as a tumor or epilepsy). Such individuals often show severe deficits that teach us a great deal about the relationship between specific areas of the brain and particular psychological functions.

Another method that researchers have used to locate a number of specific functions in the brain is *electrical stimulation* of various brain regions. This involves implanting wire electrodes (electrical probes) in the brain of an anesthetized, but conscious, animal or person and then sending small electric currents into the brain. The human subject can report on what she or he is feeling or shows the effects of the stimulation through his or her behavior. Electrical stimulation of the brain is painless in most brain areas since there are no pain receptors in the brain itself. The only time the subject feels pain is when the pain pathways of the brain are the regions stimulated.

Modern technology has made possible a variety of study techniques that are *noninvasive,* that is, they do not require surgery. They yield information that can prove invaluable in diagnosing injuries and disorders and in expanding our knowledge of the way the brain works. These techniques include the following.

Electroencephalography (EEG) records the electrical signals of the brain, which are generated in the form of waves. The very small electrical potentials of the brain cells are amplified thousands of times and are recorded on paper. Abnormal wave patterns on the EEG are very helpful in the diagnosis of epilepsy, brain tumors, and other neurological disorders.

A new EEG technique uses high-speed computers to construct brain-wave patterns that appear in response to specific stimuli such as a word, a tone, or electric shock. These "evoked potentials" make use of the computer to eliminate the background EEG and to magnify the brain's specific responses to stimuli.

The *computerized axial tomography (CAT)* scan takes x-rays from many

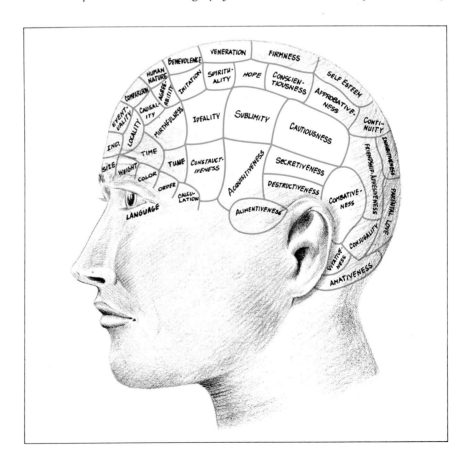

FIGURE 2-10 *This nineteenth-century phrenology chart shows different regions of the brain that were supposedly devoted to the development of different personality characteristics. Its anatomical inaccuracies are most obvious in its depiction of language as existing under the eye, an area where no brain tissue exists. (From Kolb & Whishaw, 1980.)*

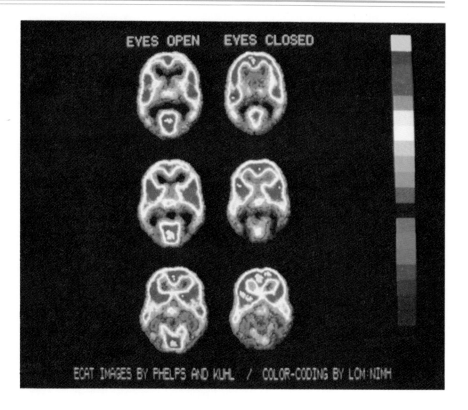

EYES OPEN   EYES CLOSED

ECAT IMAGES BY PHELPS AND KUHL / COLOR-CODING BY LOM·NIMH

These computerized images produced by the PETT scanner show that what we see influences the way our cerebral cortex utilizes glucose. Here we see three horizontal sections of the brain of a normal conscious man. Those in the left-hand column were made when his eyes were open; those in the right, with his eyes closed. When the eyes are closed, there is less glucose utilization in the occipital cortex and more metabolic activity in the frontal cortex. (NIH, ECAT images by Dr. Phelps and Dr. Kuhl; color coding by Dr. Sokoloff, NIMH; photo courtesy of National Institutes of Health)

points around the head. A computer analyzes these multiple images and arranges them into an image that resembles a slice of the brain. The newest CAT scanners produce very clear pictures of brain anatomy and can be used to diagnose a variety of neurologic disorders, including strokes and tumors.

To measure *cerebral blood flow,* or the rate at which the blood travels to different regions of the brain, investigators inject a radioactive sugar substance into the bloodstream. With special detectors, scientists can tell how fast this sugar reaches the brain. Since blood flow and sugar utilization are related to neuronal activity, these techniques allow us to see which brain areas are active during various types of tasks and mental operations.

The *positron emission transaxial tomography (PETT)* scanner uses radiation-sensitive detectors to record the location of molecules inside the brain that have been labeled with a radioactive sugar injected into the subject 30 minutes before the scan is performed. Unlike the cerebral blood flow technique, however, the PETT scan uses a computer to construct intricate and detailed color pictures of the brain. Since the most active parts of the brain use the most sugar for energy, these areas will have the largest amount of radioactive substance in them. The newest version of the PETT scan can examine seven "slices" of the brain in 1 minute and put these images together in a way that gives dynamic information about cerebral metabolism. Thus, the PETT scan is like a "movie" version of the CAT scan.

Nuclear Magnetic Resonance (NMR) is a very new technology currently in development. NMR uses radio waves and magnetic fields to produce

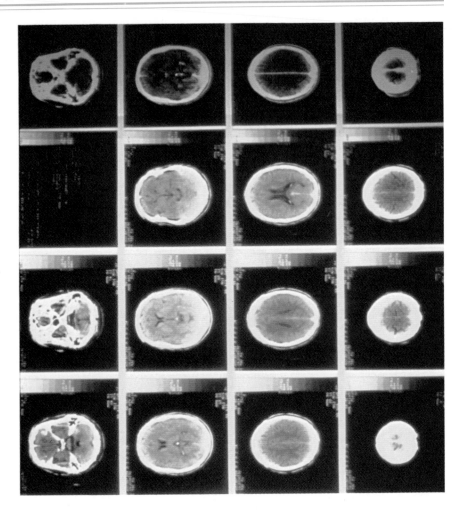

These computerized images produced by the CAT scanner show "slices" of a normal brain. (National Institutes of Health, National Cancer Institute)

three-dimensional images of the ridges, folds, and crevices of the brain. Like the CAT scan, NMR also shows a static picture, but one that is much sharper and more detailed. In addition to revealing anatomical detail, it may also be able to show physiological and biochemical information about organs and tissues. It is particularly helpful in diagnosing problems involving soft tissue, such as tumors of the brain stem and cerebellum, minute lesions of the brain, and abnormalities of the spinal cord.

THE SENSORY AND MOTOR SYSTEMS OF THE BRAIN

Hierarchical Organization of These Systems

The simplest motor activities are controlled by the spinal cord; somewhat more complicated ones by the brain stem; and the most complicated of all are controlled by the cerebrum. The complicated operations depend upon the control of simpler operations. We can see how this enables us to walk.

The spinal cord contains a number of simple reflex circuits, many of which provide elementary components of normal walking, which are the same in all animals. Paraplegics can execute the stepping motions basic to walking if their body weight is supported and if they are positioned above a treadmill. This tells us that these motions are controlled by the spinal cord. The spinal cord cannot by itself support walking, however, since it contains no mechanisms for balance and cannot support standing. So we need the motor centers in the brain stem. The spinal cord and the brain stem working together can control normal walking.

But walking depends on other systems, too. It's useful to be able to see where you're going so you don't bump into trees or fall over cliffs. These considerations make it easy to understand why what you see (visual input) eventually finds its way to the reticular formation in the brain stem. Finally, if you want to use walking to accomplish a goal, to procure food, for example, you need to know when you're hungry (a function accomplished by the *hypothalamus*), you need to know how to search for food (through hypothalamic activation of brain stem locomotor centers), and you may need to sniff out the food (through sensory control over the locomotor centers). Thus, we carry out increasingly complex behaviors by building on systems that are basically controlled by the brain stem but that can be modified by processes in the brain.

How Sensory and Motor Systems Work Together

We're all familiar with the five so-called special senses—sight, hearing, touch, taste, and smell—all of which receive information that comes from stimuli *outside* the body (and which will be fully explained in the next chapter). We also receive a great deal of sensory information that originates *inside* the body. For example, thanks to sensory receptors in our

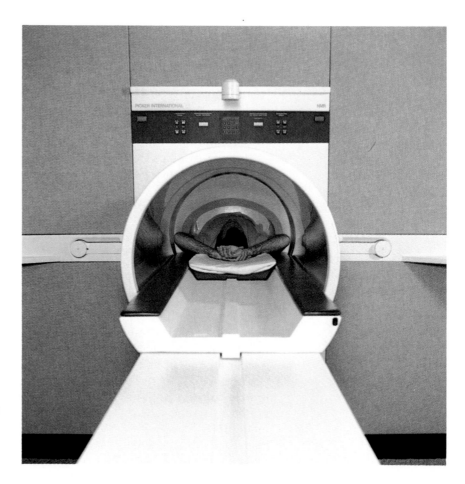

The patient in this nuclear magnetic resonance unit does not feel anything for the 5 to 30 minutes he remains inside. He hears loud noises caused by magnetic fields grating on metal, and he may become claustrophobic. Some hospitals supply patients with a little bell to signal technicians that they want something. (©1983 Will McIntyre/Photo Researchers, Inc.)

muscles, tendons, and joints, we know the positions of our limbs in space (a phenomenon known as proprioception, which allows us, for example, to touch our noses with our hands with our eyes closed) and the kinds of movements our muscles are making, which our brain needs to know but which we are usually not consciously aware of (kinesthesis).

We also receive a wide variety of sensory inputs from our internal organs. Blood pressure and oxygen levels in the blood, for example, are monitored by specialized receptors located at strategic points in the body. And the level of glucose in the blood is monitored by receptors inside the brain itself. Such sensory information is transmitted from the receptors to the motor neurons via bundles of nerve fibers called "sensory nerves."

Any neuron that terminates on a muscle cell is a motor neuron and is part of the motor system. The major structures of the central nervous system that comprise the motor system are the motor cortex, the basal ganglia, the cerebellum, parts of the reticular formation, and parts of the spinal cord. All these structures interact with each other in the way they control motor neuron activity, which then controls muscle activity, which then controls body movement. Every movement we make—from the tops of our heads to the bottoms of our feet, from blinking an eye to running a race—is controlled by the motor system.

We know that there's a connection between what our senses tell us (through our sensory neurons) and what we do (through our motor neurons). At the simplest level we have the spinal reflexes, discussed earlier in this chapter. Any more complicated behavior, which involves the integration of sensory and motor information, requires the brain. Suppose, for example, you hear a loud roar (auditory sensory input). You move your eyes (motor response). You see a lion that has escaped from the zoo (visual sensory input). Your sympathetic system becomes activated immediately, setting up a host of motor reactions, not the least of which is quick movement away from the basic stimulus (the maned stranger). So we see how the systems are integrated.

We human beings are endowed with a remarkable flexibility in the way we use sensory information. A big-game hunter equipped with a powerful gun would have reacted quite differently to that lion: Instead of running, he would have put himself in position to shoot. You and I may see very different things in an abstract painting. And at a concert, you may absorb the overall effect of the music, while I attend only to the sounds of the guitars. Such flexibility is certainly one ability that sets us apart from the lower animals.

Indeed, the major difference in our brains compared to those of other animals is the number of neurons that comprise the central integrating system. For such complicated processes, we need many millions of nerve cells. As you can see in Figure 2-11, the cerebral cortex in human beings is proportionately larger than the cerebral cortex in all other animals. The greater number of nerve cells in the cortex make possible the many complicated operations the human brain is able to perform. Furthermore, the human cortex is not only larger overall—it also has more area that does not have specific sensory or motor function assigned to it but is free for higher intellectual activities (see Figure 2-12). In the case of human beings, these other activities comprise the high levels of thought that we— and only we in all the animal kingdom—are capable of.

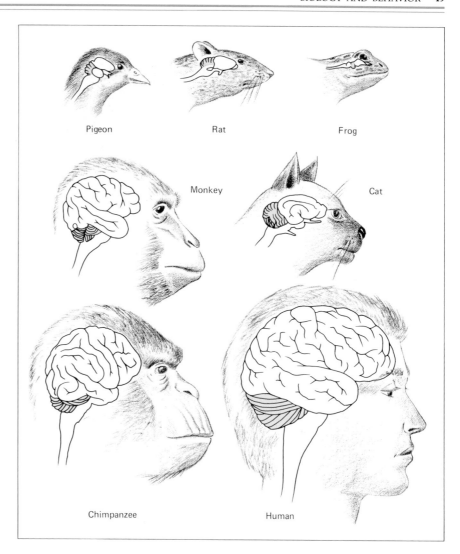

Pigeon

Rat

Frog

Monkey

Cat

Chimpanzee

Human

FIGURE 2-11 *As we go up the evolutionary scale, the brain becomes proportionately larger, as we can see in this comparison of the sizes and shapes of the brains in different vertebrate animals, all shown about four-tenths life size. Within these brains, the cortex (C) also becomes progressively larger. (From Rosenzweig & Leiman, 1982.)*

A great deal of the brain is given over to the sensory and motor systems, although it's very difficult to draw distinctions among these two systems and the *central integrating systems,* which enable the sensory and motor systems to interact with each other, because of the close interconnections among all three (see Figure 2-13). The thalamus, for example, receives sensory information, which it sends to appropriate sensory areas of the cerebral cortex; the thalamus also sends motor information to the motor area of the cortex.

The Central Integrating Systems

These structures are the links between the sensory and motor systems. They consist of the reticular formation, parts of the thalamus, the hypothalamus, the limbic system, and the association cortex. Every kind of sensory input involves one of these integrating systems. It can be a baby's cry that's sent to the limbic system, where it activates the hypothalamus to create an emotional response from you (especially if it's your baby). It can be the sight of a sharp drop at the edge of a cliff that sends informa-

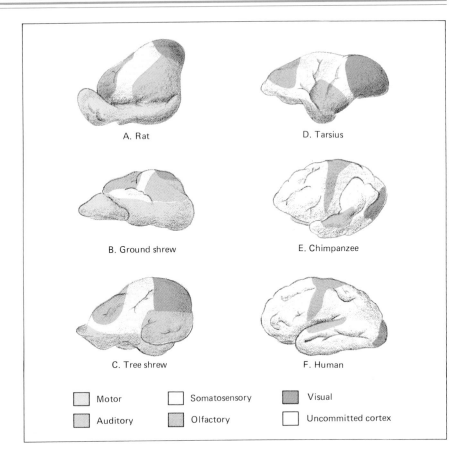

A. Rat

D. Tarsius

B. Ground shrew

E. Chimpanzee

C. Tree shrew

F. Human

☐ Motor   ☐ Somatosensory   ☐ Visual

☐ Auditory   ☐ Olfactory   ☐ Uncommitted cortex

FIGURE 2-12 *The human cortex is not only larger than the cerebral cortex in all other animals; it also has more area that does not have specific sensory or motor functions assigned to it and is thus free for higher intellectual activities. (From Hunt, 1982.)*

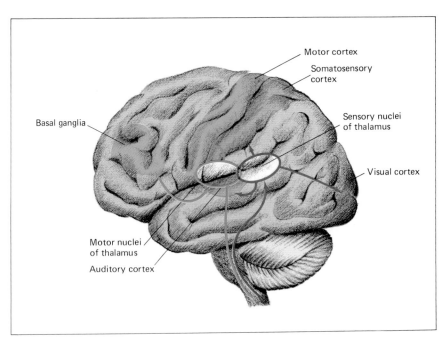

Motor cortex

Somatosensory cortex

Basal ganglia

Sensory nuclei of thalamus

Visual cortex

Motor nuclei of thalamus

Auditory cortex

FIGURE 2-13 *Sensory (orange) and motor (blue) systems of the brain.*

tion into the reticular formation, which tells the spinal cord to stop making walking movements, thus saving you from going over the edge. It can be a chilly feeling in the middle of the night, which sends information to the reticular formation, which wakes you up so you can pull up the blanket. Let's see what happens in these several integrative areas, each of which has its own functions.

THE RETICULAR FORMATION   A principal function of the reticular formation (which is, as we noted earlier, inside the central core of the brain stem), is to wake us up and put us to sleep. The part of this nerve network that wakes us up is called the ascending reticular activation system: It activates the cerebral cortex, thus awakening us. A part of the activating system goes through the thalamus which, as we have indicated, sends information to the cortex. Damage to its arousal areas can result in coma, while damage to other areas can cause long-lasting insomnia. An anesthetized animal will wake up if its arousal areas are electrically stimulated.

   The reticular formation also exerts control over motor activity such as the balance and coordination we need for walking. It also directs the more complicated reflexive movements. The *auditory startle reflex,* for example, the involuntary jump we make when we hear an unexpected loud sound, occurs at the end of a chain that begins with input to the auditory sensory nerve and ends with motor orders from the reticular formation to the spinal cord.

THE HYPOTHALAMUS   As its name indicates ("hypo" means "below"), this walnut-sized organ lies below the thalamus, in the cerebrum, as shown in Figure 2-14. It serves as a mediator between the brain and the endocrine system. It is responsible for the regulation of hormone release. The hypothalamus is often referred to as the "seat of emotion." It is a

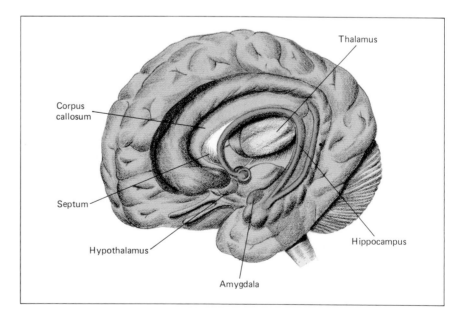

FIGURE 2-14 *Diagram of the limbic system. (From Rosenzweig & Leiman, 1982.)*

source of an individual's feelings and sends its orders to the glands in the endocrine system, translating emotions into physiological reactions. Its control of the pituitary gland allows the brain to control the endocrine system, and its receptors for hormones allow the endocrine system to exert control over the brain. We'll have more to say later about the endocrine system.

In its sensitive position, the hypothalamus is the principal controller and organizer of the body's vital functions. It maintains homeostasis, or equilibrium, of many body systems. Behaviors connected with eating, drinking, temperature regulation, sexuality, anger, and fear are intimately involved with the endocrine system. Since all are also involved with motivation, the hypothalamus' role in regulating motivation is very important. This has been shown experimentally by inducing such motivated states as fear, anger, hunger, and sexual interest through electrical stimulation of specific hypothalamic sites.

THE LIMBIC SYSTEM   When you're furiously angry or curiously calm, you're showing effects mediated through your limbic system. This set of structures includes the septal area, the hippocampus, the amygdala, and parts of the thalamus (see Figure 2-14). People or animals that have suffered injury to specific areas of the limbic system (like the amygdala) do not show some basic emotions (like rage), which, however, do appear when these limbic structures are electrically stimulated. *Amygdalectomy*, the surgical destruction of the amygdala, has been performed to alleviate uncontrollable rage in some psychiatric patients. This operation has never been widely performed.

The different limbic structures seem to maintain a balance between opposite emotional states. Thus, while stimulation of the amygdala causes rage and damage causes tameness, the opposite holds true for the septum. Memory is also an important function of the limbic system, as shown by the degeneration of a section of the thalamus in people with the memory disorder Korsakoff's syndrome. Also, you'll meet a man in Chapter 6 whose hippocampus was surgically removed from both sides of his brain, resulting in a dense amnesia, an inability to create new memories.

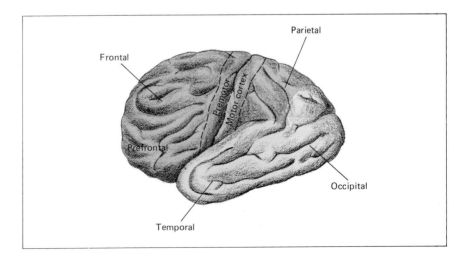

FIGURE 2-15 *The brain is divided into four lobes: the frontal, the temporal, the parietal, and the occipital.*

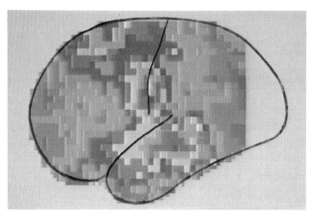 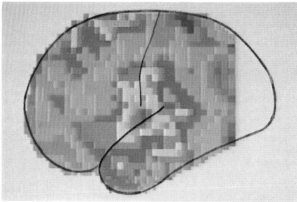

FIGURE 2-16 Inferring Localization of Function from Patterns of Blood Flow   *In these pictures, showing CAT-scan images averaged from the brain activity of nine different subjects, the colors indicate the average level of blood flow during speech: The green areas show average flow; yellow and red areas show higher-than-average flow; and the blue areas show lower-than-average flow. (The squared shapes are due to the recording and averaging procedure and don't accurately reflect the shapes of areas in the brain.) The areas in the cortex that control the activities of the mouth, tongue, and larynx are active, as is the area that directs auditory activity. (We hear ourselves speaking.) The mouth and auditory areas are more active in the left hemisphere than in the right. (From Lassen, Ingvar & Skinhoj, 1978)*

THE CEREBRAL CORTEX   If we compare the brains of a variety of mammals at different levels of evolutionary development, we see that the major differences in those brains is that the cortex, the gray matter that surrounds most of the brain, gets proportionately bigger in more highly developed animals (see Figure 2-11). In human beings, this wrinkled covering makes up most of the brain. The many functions carried out by cells in the cortex require a large area; the wrinkling allows more surface area to fit into the small area bounded by the human skull. The cortex is the part of the brain that makes us human, the place where we take in and then sift and make sense of what we see, hear, and perceive in other ways. It's the site where we think, plan, speak, write, remember, evaluate.

For convenience in studying and talking about the brain, neuroanatomists have divided each of the hemispheres (left and right halves) of the brain into four separate areas, called *lobes*. They are the *frontal* (which contains the prefrontal, the premotor, and the motor cortices), the *temporal*, the *parietal*, and the *occipital* lobes (see Figure 2-15). The most forward part of the cerebral cortex, that portion just behind the eyes and forehead, is the *prefrontal cortex*, a region involved in planning, forethought, and judgment. Just behind this is the *premotor cortex*, which programs complex movement. Behind the premotor cortex is the *motor cortex*, which controls movements of the various body parts. The *temporal lobes* play a major role in auditory perception and in some learning and memory functions. The *parietal lobes* play a major role in spatial perception, tactile perception, and body image. At the very back of the brain is the *occipital lobe*, an area primarily concerned with vision. While recent research points to some specialization within these lobes, each one is involved with a variety of different functions.

A dramatic—and colorful—demonstration of the localization of various brain functions can be seen in Figure 2-16. With the cerebral blood flow technique described earlier, we can infer the importance of different areas in different operations. This illustration shows images averaged from the brain activity of nine different subjects who engaged in a variety of activities, including speaking, following a moving object with the eyes, and listening to spoken words. Blood flow measurements showed increased activity in certain areas of the brain, depending on what the subjects were doing at the time.

The sensorimotor pathways between the hemispheres and the body

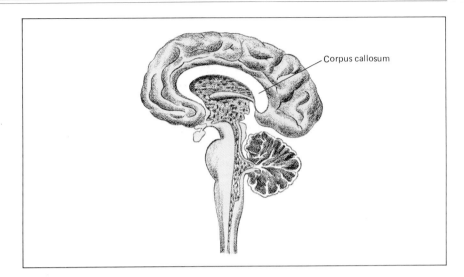

Corpus callosum

FIGURE 2-17 *The corpus callosum.*

FIGURE 2-18 *Self-portrait of stroke victim Anton Raderscheidt after damage to right association cortex of the parietal lobe. In portraits executed after his stroke, the artist failed to depict the left side of his face; here, he also ignores the left side of the canvas. (Courtesy of Dr. Richard Jung.)*

parts they control are crossed, so the right hemisphere controls the left side of the body and vice versa. Each eye projects to each hemisphere, with the left visual field of each eye going to the right side of the brain and the right visual field going to the left side of the brain. Motor signals cross sides, too, so that when you move your right arm, it is the result of a direction sent by your left hemisphere.

While the hemispheres look alike on the surface, they are different anatomically. The region that seems to control language in the left hemisphere is larger than the comparable region in the right hemisphere, for example. Furthermore, the two sides of the brain perform different functions. For most people, the left hemisphere controls the ability to use language, handle numbers, and think analytically. The right side generally directs complex spatial abilities, like pattern perception, and aspects of artistic and musical performance.

The two hemispheres communicate with each other by means of a massive bundle of axons called the corpus callosum (see Figure 2-17). If this body has been severed, as it sometimes is during operations performed to restrict epileptic seizures to one hemisphere, the two sides of the brain cannot communicate. Roger Sperry, a 1982 Nobel Prize winner, and his colleagues at the California Institute of Technology (Sperry, 1982) have done a great deal of research with such "split-brain" patients and in the process have learned much about the way the brain works. If such a patient sees a word on his right side, for example, he can say the word since the information is being processed by his left hemisphere, where the speech areas are located. If he sees the word on his left side, however, he cannot say it. If a patient touches a familiar object that is hidden from her sight, she can report what it is if she feels it with her right hand, but not if she feels it with her left. Such patients are suffering from *disconnection syndromes*. Their experiences demonstrate the seat of language abilities in the left hemisphere and of spatial abilities in the right.

Damage to different parts of the cortex results in many different kinds of disturbances. For example, damage to the association areas of the parietal lobes impairs the way people see spatial relations as well as the way they perceive their own bodies. In severe cases, affected people deny the existence of body parts opposite the side where the brain lesion is. They will not shave half their face, will not dress half their body, and, when questioned, will deny that an arm or leg is their own. Figure 2-18 illustrates the way one artist, after suffering a right-hemisphere stroke, ignored the left half of his face in two self-portraits and the left side of his canvas in others. A *stroke* is sustained when a blood vessel in the brain suddenly bursts or is blocked, preventing oxygen from reaching parts of the brain and thus causing damage to a specific area. A variety of symptoms, including paralysis of one entire side of the body, personality changes, and difficulties in speaking and writing, often result.

HOW DAMAGE TO THE LEFT HEMISPHERE AFFECTS LANGUAGE   The most dramatic examples of hemispheric asymmetries are in the domain of language. In the late 1800s, the French neurologist Paul Broca and others discovered that language disturbances, called *aphasias,* often occurred following damage to the left hemisphere due to a stroke or injury. When the right hemisphere was injured, however, language was rarely affected. Such findings have demonstrated that the left hemisphere controls language abilities. The kind of language deficit depends on where in the left hemisphere the damage has occurred. If the damage is in the left frontal lobe, in the region called *Broca's area* (see Figure 2-19), it produces *motor aphasia,* which affects production of speech and writing. People have trouble finding the right words and often cannot name everyday objects, but what they do say has meaning. They write or speak very simple noun-verb sentences and rarely use adjectives, adverbs, and other parts of speech. They usually understand what they hear and what they read, know what they want to say, and are painfully aware that they are not saying it.

Sensory aphasia occurs when damage is in the left posterior temporal area, in the region known as Wernicke's area (see Figure 2-19), after its discoverer. When this area is damaged, people have trouble understand-

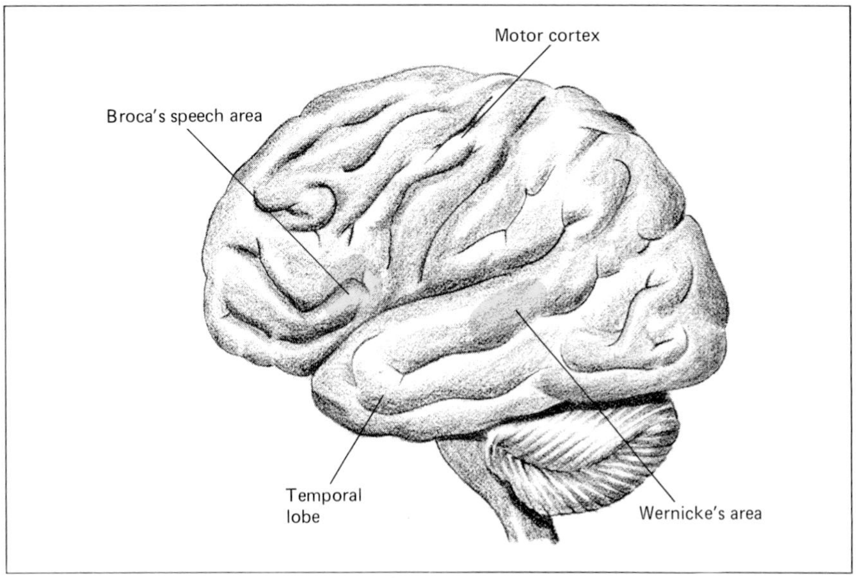

When shown a fork, a person with motor aphasia may say, "I know, it's a . . . , wait . . . , you eat with it." Another patient, asked about a dental appointment, said: "Yes . . . Monday . . . Dad and Dick . . . Wednesday nine o'clock . . . 10 o'clock . . . doctors . . . and . . . teeth."
(Geschwind, 1979, p. 186)

FIGURE 2-19 *Wernicke's area and Broca's area are two of the specialized language regions found in the left hemisphere.*

Motor cortex

Broca's speech area

Temporal lobe

Wernicke's area

BOX 2-1

BRAIN TRANSPLANTS HELP INJURED RATS

Brain injury is one of the most devastating things that can happen to a person, possibly transforming personality or diminishing capabilities and sometimes resulting in a completely incompetent existence. So while we always need to be very cautious in extrapolating the results from animal studies to apply them to human beings, it's encouraging to note findings from recent experiments with rats which may hold out the promise of helping brain-injured people (Labbe, Firl, Mufson, & Stein, 1983).

The subjects in this study were rats whose frontal cortex had been damaged. This part of the brain, as we've seen, controls the higher mental processes involved in planning, learning, and memory. The researchers implanted in these brain-injured rats tissues from the brains of rat fetuses—either from the frontal cortex or from the cerebellum, the area that controls movement. The rats that received the frontal cortex tissues did much better on tests of learning (solving mazes) than did the rats that received cerebellar implants or the ones that didn't receive any transplant at all.

The researchers determined that the transplants had "taken," that is, they became attached to the rats' brains. It's possible that another factor was also at work. The fetal tissue that the grafts consisted of may have released chemicals that foster neuron growth in the adult brain-damaged rats. If this is the answer, then it might be possible to identify the chemicals responsible and to administer them directly to brain-injured individuals, without resorting to the surgery of brain transplant.

ing the speech of others, and while they speak fluently, the sentences they utter make no sense. See the example in the margin of page 55.

Damage to other parts of the brain produces other disorders—one in which patients can understand speech and speak fluently but cannot repeat words spoken to them and another in which people cannot read despite normal vision. Damage to the left visual cortex and the corpus callosum may produce *alexia*, an inability to read, without *agraphia*, an inability to write. Affected people (usually stroke victims) can write a long passage from dictation or even generate their own writing—but then cannot read what they have just written.

LANGUAGE IS NOT ALWAYS CONTROLLED BY THE LEFT HEMISPHERE In some people the right hemisphere controls language, and in some both hemispheres do. Localization of language is related to some degree to hand preference. For 96 percent of right-handed people, language control is in the left side, while this is true for only 70 percent of left-handers. Of the remaining 30 percent of lefties, half have their language centers in the

FIGURE 2-20 *When split-brain patients were shown pictures of faces that had been split down the center and recombined, the patients didn't notice the gross discrepancies between the two sides of the pictures. When asked to describe the face they saw, they reported the half-face on the right side, which registers in the left hemisphere. But when asked to choose the face they saw from a set of unified faces, they picked the one that had been shown on the left side, which registered in the right hemisphere. So it seems that the right hemisphere is the one that recognizes faces. (From Levy, Trevarthen & Sperry, 1972; Photo by Jack Deutsch.)*

right side of the brain and the other half are bilateral (Milner, 1974). While some researchers have theorized about the significance of these differences in lateral specialization, we still don't know the implications of these findings for left- and right-handed people.

How can we tell which side controls language in a given individual? One way is to inject a short-lived anesthetic into the cerebral blood supply of one hemisphere. If speech is disrupted, this is the language hemisphere. If not, language is controlled either by the other hemisphere or by both. Another way to tell is by stimulating the cortex electrically. When the speech area is stimulated, the person may produce long vowel sounds ("ahhhh") or slurred speech, or may stop in the middle of speaking. Stimulation of Broca's area may produce an inability to name items similar to that seen in aphasics, apparently as a result of the unnatural activity patterns caused by the electrical stimulation.

FUNCTIONS OF THE RIGHT HEMISPHERE Is the "right brain" the dreamer, while the left one is the thinker? Popular interpretations of the different functions of the two hemispheres suggest this since the right hemisphere is more involved in artistic, musical, and whole-pattern perception. The right hemisphere is the one that lets us recognize faces and read people's facial expressions, as indicated in the experiments described in Figures 2-20 and 2-21. However, the "dual personalities" of the two hemispheres are not so clear-cut since there is a great deal of cooperation between them and since one hemisphere can often take over for the other, especially when damage occurs early in life. When children suffer an injury to the left hemisphere before the age of 5, the right hemisphere apparently takes over the speech functions. If the injury occurs later in childhood, recovery is better than it would be for an adult, but the recovery apparently takes place within the left hemisphere, not by a shift to the right hemisphere. If such an injury occurs later in life, recovery is much more limited (Kolb & Whishaw, 1980).

THE PERIPHERAL NERVOUS SYSTEM

Your ability both to see this book and to pick it up relies on the bundles of nerve fibers known as "peripheral nerves." One kind of peripheral nerve, the sensory nerves, transmit information from your body (your eyes, for example) to your brain. Once you have that information, the other kind,

FIGURE 2-21 *Which of the two faces shown here would you say is happier? If you're typical, you'll choose the one on the left. The two are mirror images, but because more of the left side of the picture goes directly to your right hemisphere, that's likely to be the side you'll focus on. (From Jaynes, 1976)*

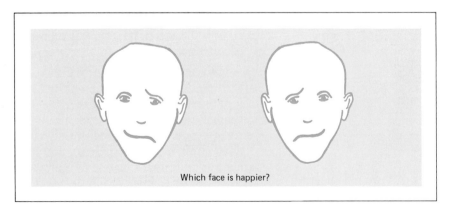

Which face is happier?

The popularity of fitness equipment like this Nautilus machine may be due to the fact that it exercises synergistic muscle groups, resulting in a more efficient workout for the body. (©1981 Will McIntyre/Photo Researchers, Inc.)

your motor nerves, transmit information from your brain to your muscles (telling your arms to reach out and your hands to close around the book). Motor nerves can be part of either the somatic or the autonomic nervous system, the two subdivisions of the peripheral motor system.

The Somatic Nervous System

The kind of nerves that directed your arms and hands to pick up this book are part of the somatic nervous system, which controls reflex actions as well as those actions you voluntarily choose to perform. These nerves control the *striated* muscles of the body, so-called because they appear striped, or striated, when seen under a microscope. Let's look at the way this system works.

The movements you make are accomplished through the way your muscles are attached to your bones, your skin, and your other muscles. This applies to all movements—large ones like running and jumping and small ones like subtle changes in facial expression. Muscles work together, sometimes in *antagonistic,* or opposing, pairs. When you raise your forearm, for example, you contract your biceps muscle (as described earlier in the hot stove example). The muscle antagonistic to that one, the triceps, relaxes. In certain movements other muscles work together in *synergistic,* or cooperative, ways. When you lift a bar bell, the biceps work together with finger muscles that allow you to hold onto the bell, with back muscles that maintain posture, and with leg muscles that either straighten or bend your knees. Some muscles that work as synergists in one movement will act as antagonists in another. Different patterns of muscular contractions produce different movements. And all these patterns are coordinated in the nervous system.

What controls your facial expression and the way you hold your head while you're lifting a heavy weight? What about those arm, finger, leg, and back muscles involved in the exercise itself? All these movements are controlled by somatic motor neurons located in the spinal cord and in the brain stem. The motor neurons in the brain stem (the so-called cranial nerves) control muscles in the face, the neck, and the head, while those in the spinal cord control muscles in the rest of the body. Each motor neuron contacts only one muscle, but each muscle receives contacts from many different motor neurons. The strength of a contraction depends on two factors: the number of active motor neurons and the frequency of the impulses they send. These impulses are sent by synaptic transmission as described earlier, and the neurotransmitter involved in such muscle movements is acetylcholine (Ach).

The motor neurons release Ach, which crosses over the synaptic bridge and conveys the command to the appropriate muscle. Meanwhile, circuits within the spinal cord and brain stem simultaneously inhibit antagonistic muscles. By modifying the number of neurons involved and the frequency of their impulses, the brain can produce an amazing variety of complex movement patterns. Thus a pianist produces an arpeggio or a chord, a tennis player slams a ball or lobs it lightly, a driver maneuvers along a winding mountain road or drives straight ahead on a wide open highway.

The Autonomic Nervous System

While you are lifting that heavy barbell, your body is functioning in other ways, too. Your heart is beating, your breathing goes on, and your digestive system is active. All these activities are being conducted by two other kinds of muscles—the *cardiac*, or heart, muscles, and the *smooth* muscles that control the throat, the viscera (internal organs such as stomach and intestines), the diaphragm (which controls breathing), and other organs. Both cardiac and smooth muscles are controlled by the nervous system and the endocrine system. We'll discuss the endocrine system later in this chapter, but for now let's see how the autonomic nervous system controls these life-support functions that are usually considered as *involuntary*, or beyond conscious control. In some cases, as we'll see in our discussion of biofeedback in Chapter 5, we *can* exert control over these functions, but usually they work more or less automatically.

The autonomic nervous system itself consists of two parts—the sympathetic and the parasympathetic divisions—which operate quite differently and often have opposing effects in many body parts, as shown in Figure 2-22. While the striated muscles of the somatic system contract only when they receive neuronal messages, the autonomic system's smooth muscles of viscera (body organs) and heart never relax totally but always generate some contractions. This is why heart muscle can continue to pulsate even after it has been removed from the body. To relax heart and visceral muscles, then, the muscles themselves (not just the motor neurons) must be inhibited. The sympathetic and parasympathetic divisions work in concert in the autonomic system: One division stimulates a muscle and the other inhibits it. The roles of the two systems change, depending on the target organ, so that each division is capable of triggering contraction or relaxation.

SYMPATHETIC FUNCTIONS   The sympathetic division works as a unit ("in sympathy") to mobilize the body's resources so it can *expend* energy. It creates the "fight or flight" response to stress (discussed in Chapter 10) and the physiological signs of such emotional states as fear, anger, and

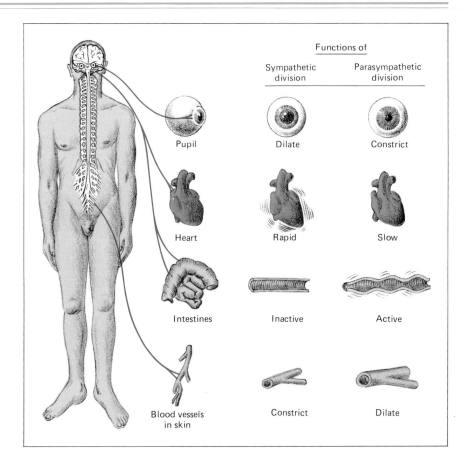

FIGURE 2-22 *The sympathetic and parasympathetic divisions of the autonomic nervous system often have opposing effects in many body parts. (From Rosenzweig & Leiman, 1982.)*

rage. Sympathetic activation makes your heart beat faster, makes you breathe more rapidly, and makes you sweat. To give you the oxygen and glucose (an energy-providing sugar) you need for vigorous activity, it directs blood from your skin and your stomach to your skeletal muscles, and makes your adrenal gland release epinephrine (adrenalin).

PARASYMPATHETIC FUNCTIONS   The parasympathetic system restores the body by increasing its supply of stored energy. How many times in your life have you been told not to go swimming right after eating? The reason for this warning lies in a dual action by the parasympathetic system, which directs blood to the stomach to help digestion and slows the heart. When so much blood has been diverted to the stomach that not enough reaches the muscles to enable them to engage in strenuous exercise, cramping takes place.

HOW BOTH SYSTEMS WORK TOGETHER   Most of the time, both sympathetic and parasympathetic divisions are active, creating a balance between them. After you eat lunch on a hot day, for example, you both perspire (sympathetic activity) and digest your food (parasympathetic). For any given organ, however, the two systems are antagonistic. This antagonism is especially evident in sexual behavior. Penile erection, for example, is a parasympathetic activity, which explains why men sometimes have difficulty achieving erection when they are anxious, angry, or afraid (emotions that indicate sympathetic activation), or after they have taken amphetamines or other drugs that mimic sympathetic activity.

HOW THE BRAIN ACTIVATES THE AUTONOMIC MOTOR SYSTEM   This system can be activated in different ways. What happens, for example, when you receive information through your senses—when you receive a painful injury, see a menacing figure, hear a baby's cry? All these stimuli can produce an emotional reaction in your limbic system, which—as we saw— is the brain's center of emotion. It sends messages to the hypothalamus, which in turn activates such autonomic responses as a racing heart or quickened breathing. Effects of learning can bring about autonomic responses, as in Ivan Pavlov's famous experiments in which dogs learned to salivate in response to a tone (discussed in detail in Chapter 5). Reflex pathways in the spinal cord and brain stem also activate autonomic responses. Filling the stomach with food, for example, activates "stretch" receptors, which send impulses to the brain stem, which activates interneurons (intermediary neurons that send messages from one kind of neuron to another), which then activate neurons that increase the secretion of gastric juices.

A fundamental principle of the control of many body systems, including these, is homeostasis, the maintenance of vital functions within their optimum range by coordinated automatic adjustments. Thus, when blood pressure rises, neurons in the brain stem are activated that reduce the heart rate, leading to lower blood pressure. The autonomic system is also controlled by the endocrine system and by areas of the brain that include the limbic system, the frontal cortex, and the hypothalamus.

THE ENDOCRINE SYSTEM

The nervous system is not the only biological system governing behavior. Both the central and peripheral nervous systems work closely with the endocrine system, the webbing of glands that secrete chemicals, called hormones, directly into the bloodstream.

Hormones are active in the process of homeostasis, which maintains the proper balance in the body's internal state. Thus, both the autonomic nervous system and the endocrine system work together to achieve bodily equilibrium. The crucial coordinator of both systems is the hypothalamus, which provides the mechanism by which the brain exerts control over the endocrine system and by which the endocrine system exerts control over the brain.

If we think of endocrine glands as members of a musical group, playing together to orchestrate the body's workings, the conductor of that orchestra is the so-called master gland, the pituitary. This gland has two subdivisions: the *anterior pituitary*, which is made of the same embryological tissue as the throat and is a true endocrine organ, and the *posterior pituitary*, which is made up of nerve tissue and is, therefore, part of the nervous system. The pituitary gland controls the activity of all the other glands from its position at the base of the brain, directly below the hypothalamus.

The anterior pituitary secretes a large number of hormones, each one of which affects the secretions of a different gland. Glands such as the adre-

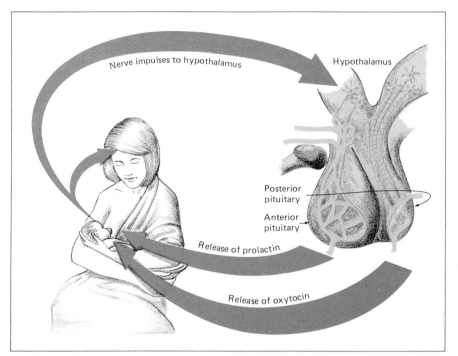

FIGURE 2-23 *The let-down response experienced by breastfeeding mothers shows how the brain and the endocrine system work together to make the milk and to get it to the baby. The baby's suckling produces nerve impulses that direct the endocrine system to produce the hormone prolactin, which makes the milk, and another hormone, oxytocin, which causes contractions that send the milk into the area just behind the nipples where the baby can get to it. (From Rosenzweig & Leiman, 1982.)*

nal, the thyroid, the testes, and the ovaries change the body in various ways. They build up glucose to prepare the body for strenuous activity, launch surges of adrenalin to enable it to respond to an emergency, send out sex hormones such as estrogen and testosterone to differentiate sexual organs and control sexual behavior, and regulate the body's balance of salt.

The posterior pituitary releases two hormones, *vasopressin,* which decreases the volume of urine, and *oxytocin,* which stimulates contraction of the uterus during childbirth and then sends rushes of milk into the mammary glands in a new mother's breasts. Both these hormones are actually manufactured by neurons in the hypothalamus, transported down their axons, and released into the bloodstream.

The "let-down" response experienced by breastfeeding mothers (which enables the mother to let down her milk to the baby) provides a classic example of neural-endocrine interactions (see Figure 2-23). The baby's suckling at the breast activates skin receptors in the mother's nipple, which transmit messages to the brain stem. Interneurons carry the message along to the hypothalamus, which signals the anterior pituitary to produce the hormone prolactin and the posterior pituitary to produce oxytocin. The *prolactin* produces the milk in the mammary glands, and the *oxytocin* causes the contractions that squeeze the milk through the ducts and into the milk pools behind the nipples where the baby can get to it. So while prolactin stimulates the mammary glands to make the milk, oxytocin makes it available to the baby.

The emotions play a powerful role in this reflex. Simply hearing her baby cry or just thinking about the baby at feeding time will often send a tingling rush of milk into the mother's breasts. On the other hand, anxiety or discomfort can inhibit the let-down reflex and is the source of most breastfeeding failures (Olds & Eiger, 1972). So we can see the intricate interconnections between mind and body, between neurons and hormones.

The let-down reflex demonstrates the powerful control the nervous system has over the endocrine system. But the reverse also holds true. Endocrine hormones get into the brain and bind with neurons in the limbic system and the hypothalamus, influencing the brain cells and the activities they direct.

One of the most dramatic examples of endocrine effects on the brain lies in the area of sexual behavior. The presence or absence of male and female sex hormones exerts potent effects on sexuality. Two sex-related behaviors include the aggressive play of male rats and *lordosis*, the "presenting" behavior of female rats (a position they assume for mating, similar to that of most four-legged animals). Depriving young rats of the appropriate sex hormones, by removing the ovaries of females or the testes of males, changes certain aspects of their behavior. For females, these changes can be reversed by giving them female hormones, even in adulthood. This shows that normal female behavior depends on the presence of female hormones but that these hormones don't need to be present early in the animal's development. Male behaviors do depend, however, on the presence of male sex hormones very early in life.

Recent anatomical studies of the hypothalamus of the rat have shown an area called the *medial preoptic nucleus (MPON)*. The MPON is ten times larger in males than in females, and there are certain differences in the patterns of the synapses in male and female MPONs. To produce a male-patterned MPON, male hormones have to be in the body of the male rat at about the time of birth. Otherwise, the MPON will develop in the female form. These differences parallel differences in sex-typed behavior as a result of hormonal activity, apparently showing the effects of circulating hormones on the development of the MPON. Furthermore, when the MPON is stimulated electrically, both males and females that have received male sex hormones engage in *mounting* (male sexual behavior). Thus we see the close relationship between the endocrine system and the brain. This research also suggests that some of the differences in the behaviors of males and females are due to physiological differences in the nervous system.

While this chapter has peered through some windows into the brain, it seems that every time we answer one question about its workings, we realize that we have dozens of other questions, which spur new research. It seems fairly safe to predict that psychobiology will never completely unravel the mysteries of the ways our brains function. Among some of the current frontiers of brain research are explorations into such topics as the factors that make one nerve cell different from another, the reasons why cell bodies don't always die even after their axons have been damaged, and the ways by which some cells can take over the functions of other cells in some circumstances. When we can answer questions like these, we'll not only have more knowledge about the most mysterious realm in the universe—what one writer (Hunt, 1982) has called "the universe within"—but we'll also have clues that will help us help those people whose brains are not functioning normally because of injury or illness.

SUMMARY

1 The *central nervous system* (CNS) consists of the brain and the spinal cord. The CNS and the *peripheral nervous system*, the network of nerves that control muscles and glands, control all human activity.

2 The brain contains several specialized structures: the *brain stem*, made up of the *pons*, the *medulla oblongata*, and the *midbrain*; the *cerebellum*; and the *cerebrum (forebrain)*, made up of the *thalamus*, the *hypothalamus*, the *limbic system*, and the *cerebral cortex*.

3 The *peripheral nervous system* is made up of two kinds of nerves. *Sensory* nerves transmit information from the body organs to the brain. *Motor* nerves send information from the brain to the muscles and glands.

4 There are two basic kinds of cells in the nervous system. *Neurons* (nerve cells) receive and send information to and from other neurons. *Glia* (glial cells) support and protect the neurons. One type of glia covers parts of the neuron with *myelin*, a fatty tissue.

5 All neurons have a *cell body*, with a nucleus that contains DNA, the cell's genetic information. All neurons have *dendrites*, branching extensions of the cell body. Most neurons have tail-like extensions called *axons*. A neuron receives information on its dendrites and cell body, and transmits information down its axon.

6 An *action potential* is the "firing" of a neuron. It is the transmission of a nerve impulse down the axon, from one end of the neuron to the other.

7 Neurons communicate with each other at *synapses*, spaces between the axon of one neuron and the dendrites or cell body of a second.

8 *Neurotransmitters* are chemical substances released by neurons. They bind on *receptor sites* on the receiving neuron. Neurotransmitters either *excite* the receiving neuron, making it fire, or they *inhibit* it from firing.

9 *Psychoactive* drugs change behavior by introducing chemicals into the body. Some mimic specific transmitters, others speed up the action of neurotransmitters, and others reverse the effects of neurotransmitters.

10 A *reflex* is an involuntary response to a stimulus. The simplest kind, like the knee-jerk reflex, is *monosynaptic*. More complex reflexes, like blinking to a loud noise, are *polysynaptic*.

11 The *brain stem* controls many basic functions, like breathing, heartbeat, digestion, and other bodily activities. The *reticular formation*, inside the brain stem, controls sleep, arousal, and attention.

12 The *cerebellum*, connected to the back of the brain stem, coordinates motor activity, especially the fine-tuning of voluntary movements.

13 The *cerebrum* is the most highly developed section of the human brain. It contains the *hypothalamus*, the *thalamus*, the *limbic system*, and the *cerebral cortex*.

14 Research techniques used to study the brain include *surgery*, *electrical stimulation*, and several noninvasive techniques such as *electroencephalography (EEG)*, *computerized axial tomography* (CAT) scan, *cerebral blood flow*, *positron emission transaxial tomography* (PETT) scan, and *nuclear magnetic resonance* (NMR).

15 The *sensory system* of the CNS includes brain mechanisms responsible for the five *special senses* (sight, hearing, touch, taste, and smell), plus the senses of *proprioception* and *kinesthesis*.

16 The *motor system* of the CNS includes the *motor cortex*, the *basal ganglia*, the *cerebellum*, parts of the *reticular formation*, and parts of the *spinal cord*.

17 The *central integrating systems* enable the sensory and motor systems to interact. They include the reticular formation, parts of the thalamus, the hypothalamus, the limbic system, and the association cortex.

18 The *hypothalamus* mediates between the brain and the *endocrine system*. It is often called the "seat of emotion" because it produces the physiological reactions associated with emotional states.

19 The *limbic system* consists of the *septal area*, the *hippocampus*, the *amygdala*, and parts of the *thalamus*. It maintains an individual's emotional balance, and memory.

20 The *cerebral cortex*, the gray matter that surrounds most of the brain, is proportionately larger in more highly developed animals. In human beings it makes up most of the brain.

21 The brain is divided into four *lobes*. Each is specialized to some degree. The *frontal* lobe contains areas that are involved in planning and judgment; the *temporal* lobes play a major role in auditory perception, learning, and memory; the *parietal* lobes, in spatial and tactile perception and in body image; the *occipital* lobe is primarily concerned with vision.

22 The two sides of the brain, the *left* and the *right hemispheres*, perform different functions. The left usually controls language, numeric, and analytic thought; the right usually directs artistic, musical, and complex spatial abilities.

23 The two hemispheres communicate through the *corpus callosum*, a large bundle of axons. If this

body is severed by injury or surgery, the two sides of the brain cannot communicate. By studying "split-brain" patients, researchers have learned much about the workings of the brain.

24 Damage to the left hemisphere affects language abilities. When *Broca's area* in the left frontal lobe is injured, *motor aphasia* results, and the person has trouble expressing thoughts in speech and writing. When *Wernicke's area* in the left posterial temporal lobe is injured, *sensory aphasia* results, in which the person has trouble speaking meaningfully and understanding other people's speech. Sometimes the right hemisphere can take over for the left, in case of early brain damage.

25 Motor nerves of the peripheral nervous system can be part of the *somatic* or the *autonomic* nervous system.

26 The somatic nervous system controls both reflex and voluntary actions. Motor neurons in the brain stem control muscles in the face, neck, and head; neurons in the spinal cord control muscles in the rest of the body. Motor neurons release the transmitter *acetylcholine* (Ach), which conveys a command to the appropriate muscle.

27 The *autonomic nervous system* consists of the *sympathetic* and *parasympathetic* divisions, which often have opposing effects in specific body parts. The sympathetic division mobilizes resources to *expend* energy (as in the "fight or flight" response); the parasympathetic division *restores* the body by increasing its supply of stored energy.

28 The *endocrine system* consists of a webbing of glands that secrete *hormones* into the bloodstream. Hormones maintain *homeostasis*, a balance in the body's internal state. The hypothalamus coordinates the endocrine system and the autonomic nervous system.

29 The *pituitary gland* controls the activity of all other glands, such as the adrenal, thyroid, testes, and ovaries. All these glands secrete hormones, which affect the body in various ways. The mechanisms involved in breastfeeding demonstrate neural-endocrine interactions.

SUGGESTED READINGS

Calvin, W. H. (1983). *The throwing madonna.* New York: McGraw-Hill. A series of clear, well-written essays on the brain written by a neurobiologist who draws on his own research, on psychology journals, and on poetry, biography, and art. The title essay asks whether the reason most of us throw with our right arm is related to the possibility that mothers more often hold their babies with the left arm.

Editors of *Scientific American.* (1980). *The brain.* San Francisco: W. H. Freeman. Originally published in September 1979 as a special issue of *Scientific American* magazine. It includes articles by some of the preeminent brain scientists of the day. The brain mechanisms of vision and movement are also discussed, as are the specializations of the human brain and its disorders.

Hunt, M. (1982). *The universe within: A new science explores the human mind.* New York: Simon and Schuster. A fascinating book, for the layperson, that presents a wide range of information on every aspect of the mind, including the evolution and physiology of the brain; the way we think, remember, and solve problems; and the differences between human and artificial intelligence.

Springer, S. P., & Deutsch, G. (1981). *Left brain, right brain.* San Francisco: W. H. Freeman. Discusses the exciting work that has been done in the study of the differences between the cerebral hemispheres. It includes studies of split-brain subjects as well as normal individuals.

CHAPTER 3

SENSATION AND PERCEPTION

SPOTLIGHT ON

How our senses work.

Some common sensory problems and what we can do about them.

Perception: How the brain organizes sensory information.

Visual illusions.

When you first woke up this morning, as in every single moment of your life, you were actively taking in an enormous amount of information through your senses. If it was still dark when you first opened your eyes, you may have walked to the bathroom in pitch darkness, making your way easily even though you couldn't see a thing, simply from knowing how your body was moving through familiar space. Or, turning on the light, you may have looked over at your clock. Quite possibly, you might have been able to tell what time it was by the music from your radio alarm or by the sounds of activity outside your bedroom door. When your bare feet hit the floor, you may have felt the comfortable plush of thick carpeting—or the icy cold shock of stone tile. You may have awakened to the seductive aroma of freshly brewed coffee or sizzling bacon. Before going down to breakfast, you probably brushed your teeth with your favorite flavor of toothpaste.

The preceding familiar morning experiences barely begin to scratch the richly textured surface of the vital role our senses play in our lives. From birth to death our senses are constantly bombarded by one stimulus after another, bringing us information and presenting us with decisions, first on how we'll perceive these stimuli and then on how we'll behave in response. In this chapter we'll look at the way we take in sensory information, from the basic operation of the sensory organs to the complex ways in which experience shapes our perceptions.

Before we go on, let's define some terms. A stimulus is any form of energy to which we can respond (such as light waves, sound waves, and pressure on the skin), a sense is a particular physiological pathway for responding to a specific kind of energy, sensation is the feeling we have in response to information that comes in through our sensory organs, and perception is the way our brain organizes these feelings to make sense out of them, that is, the recognition of objects that comes from a combination of sensations and the memory of previous sensory experiences.

In this chapter we are concerned, then, with two meanings of the word "sense" as the dictionary defines it. First, with the sense that brings us information—the functions of vision, hearing, touch, taste, smell, balance, and body orientation, which give rise to sensations. And then with the sense that gives this information meaning, which we define as perception.

HOW OUR SENSES WORK: PSYCHOPHYSICS

Psychophysics is the study of the relationship between the physical aspects of stimuli and our psychological perceptions of them, which aims to form a bridge between the physical and psychological worlds. It examines our sensitivity to stimuli and the ways in which variation in stimuli affect the way we perceive them. Let's look at some of the findings from this branch of study.

Sensory Thresholds

Do you remember the last time you looked up at a night sky and saw no stars at all, looked away, and then looked back to see one faint glimmer? How bright did that star have to be before you could see it? When the second star of the evening appeared to you, how much brighter did it have to be before you could say that it was brighter than the first star?

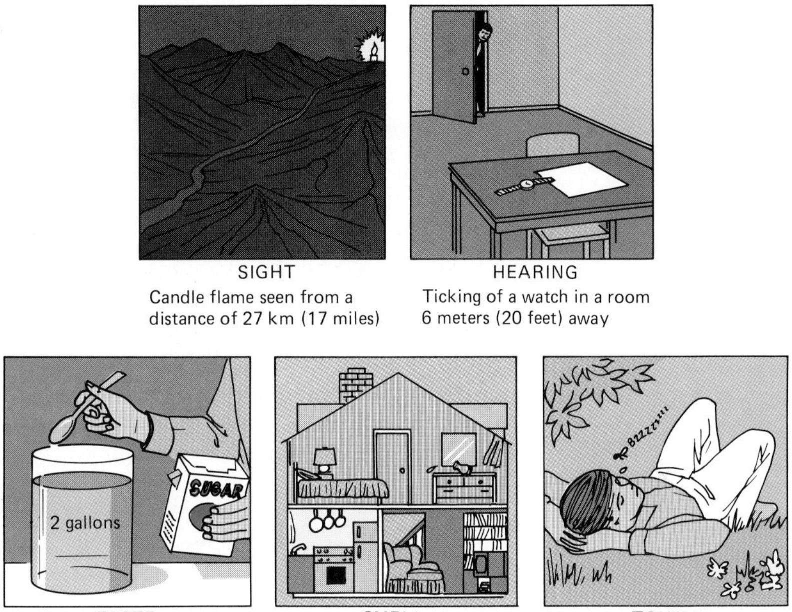

SIGHT
Candle flame seen from a distance of 27 km (17 miles)

HEARING
Ticking of a watch in a room 6 meters (20 feet) away

TASTE
One teaspoon sugar dissolved in 2 gallons of distilled water (1 part in 2000)

SMELL
One drop of perfume in a three-room house (1 part in 500,000,000)

TOUCH
The wing of a bee falling on your cheek from a distance of 1 centimeter (0.39 inch)

FIGURE 3-1 *Absolute sensory thresholds established by laboratory experiments, as shown by equivalent real-life approximations of stimuli presented in the laboratory.*

Both of these are "threshold" questions. The first question asked about an *absolute* threshold, while the second asked about a *difference* threshold.

THE ABSOLUTE THRESHOLD The absolute threshold is the smallest intensity of a stimulus that can be perceived. The ordinary hearing test that we get in school or in a doctor's office produces an *audiogram,* a graph of *sensitivity* (which in this case is essentially an absolute threshold) versus *frequency* (which will be discussed later in this chapter). As you can see in Figure 3-1, our senses are incredibly sensitive. Laboratory tests have demonstrated that under ideal conditions the human senses are capable of perceiving stimuli as subtle as the estimated real-life equivalents shown in this illustration (Hecht, Schlaer, & Pirenne, 1942; Cornsweet, 1970). Of course, that phrase "under ideal conditions" is significant since the sensitivity of our senses depends on the background level of stimulation. For example, you can see the stars best on a dark night when the moon isn't out; even though they're there in the daytime, you can't see them at all because of the brightness of the sun. You could hear a coin drop on a quiet street but not during a fireworks display.

THE DIFFERENCE THRESHOLD The difference threshold, also known as the *jnd* (just noticeable difference), is the smallest difference in intensity that you can tell between two stimuli. This threshold is variable depending not only on the background level but also on the intensity of the original stimulus. If you have a 53-pound pack on your back and someone adds a 1-ounce letter to it, you won't feel the difference, but you will feel the addition of a 1-pound package. If the pack weighs 106 pounds, you won't feel the addition of 1 pound, but you will feel a 2-pound change. This ratio between the original stimulus and any addition or subtraction is called Weber's law after the nineteenth-century German psychologist who first noticed that the larger the stimulus, the larger a change has to be before it is perceived. Weber worked out a set of ratios for different kinds of stimuli, ratios that hold true in the middle ranges of stimulation but not for very weak or very strong levels of intensity. These ratios are shown in Table 3-1.

Adaptation

Can you feel your watchband encircling your wrist? Are you conscious of the temperature in the room? Of the intensity of the light you're reading by? If none of these stimuli are so intense as to interfere with the primary focus of your attention (reading this book), chances are that you are not aware of any of them. In psychological terms, you have adapted to them. You have adjusted to a certain level of stimulation and are not consciously responding to it. Adaptation, then, is the decrease in the response of sensory receptors, with continued stimulations.

This mechanism protects you from being distracted by the many stimuli that impinge upon your senses at any given moment. You aren't likely to notice such constant levels of stimulation unless they change—unless the watchband is so tight that it begins to hurt, unless the heat goes off and you feel your feet getting cold, unless the lights flicker or dim, unless a trailer truck rumbles by, or unless someone brings your attention to one of these sensations. Our receptors for smell are the quickest to adapt, a fact that becomes apparent if you walk into a chemical plant spewing noxious fumes that the workers are not even aware of. We can get used to many extremes of temperature, noise, brightness, odor, and other stimuli so that they fade from conscious awareness. The phenomenon of adaptation explains why a 40-degree day in early spring after a cold winter seems warm, while you feel chilly on a 55-degree day in early fall after a hot summer.

The degree to which we've adapted affects our sensitivity to stimula-

---

TABLE 3-1 Weber's Law: Ratios of the Difference Threshold (the Proportional Increase in Intensity Required to Create a Just Noticeable Difference)

Weight	1:53
Sound	1:11
Skin pressure	1:7
Saltiness	1:5
Light	1:1.016
Smell	1:10
Brightness	1:62

Source: Woodworth & Schlosberg, 1955.

In this table, the initial figure (1) represents the proportion of the original stimulus, compared to the second figure, required to create a jnd. Thus, to detect a difference in weight, a change equivalent to one-fifty-third of the original stimulus is necessary; to detect a difference in sound, you have to make a proportionately larger change, equivalent to one-eleventh of the original stimulus; and so forth.

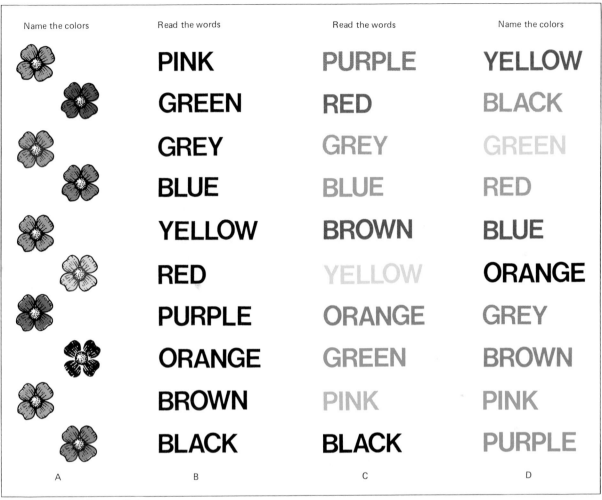

Name the colors	Read the words	Read the words	Name the colors
	PINK	PURPLE	YELLOW
	GREEN	RED	BLACK
	GREY	GREY	GREEN
	BLUE	BLUE	RED
	YELLOW	BROWN	BLUE
	RED	YELLOW	ORANGE
	PURPLE	ORANGE	GREY
	ORANGE	GREEN	BROWN
	BROWN	PINK	PINK
	BLACK	BLACK	PURPLE
A	B	C	D

FIGURE 3-2 *The Stroop effect demonstrates how hard it is to ignore certain stimuli. You may be able to demonstrate this to yourself by looking at the different columns. First, name the colors of the flowers in column A; you should be able to answer quickly. Then read the color names in columns B and C. This should be easy, too. Finally, name the colors in column D. You may find yourself responding more slowly to this last task. When laboratory subjects are asked to name the colors of words like those in column D, written in a color different from the ones the words describe, they respond much more slowly, showing how hard it is to ignore the meanings of the words (Stroop, 1935).*

tion. You can see this for yourself in a simple test: Put your left hand in ice-cold water and your right hand in water as hot as you can stand. After a minute or so, put both hands in warm water. This water will feel hot to your left hand and cold to the right, showing the effect of adaptation.

Attention

Now that you've just read about adaptation, you're probably aware of some of the stimuli just mentioned. That's because you turned your attention to them. Because we live constantly surrounded by stimuli, we can't be aware of all of them at once. But when we tune into certain ones, because of our own interest in concentrating on them, they leap to the fore of our consciousness. You've probably noticed this if you've ever been at a big party when you've been part of one conversation but have suddenly been drawn to another when you heard something of special interest—perhaps your own name or maybe a subject of special interest to you. One demonstration of the near impossibility of ignoring some kinds of stimuli, such as the meanings of words, can be seen in the Stroop effect, as shown in Figure 3-2 (Stroop, 1935).

All the preceding phenomena—thresholds, adaptation, and attention—affect the way we perceive information that comes through our senses. We'll talk more about perception throughout this chapter, but first let's look at the actual physiological mechanisms that permit basic sensations to take place.

THE SENSORY SYSTEMS

Most of us have heard from early childhood about the five senses—vision, hearing, touch, taste, and smell. These don't tell the whole story, however. For one thing, the sense of touch is complex, involving the separate sensations of heat, cold, pressure, and pain. For another, we have additional senses, such as the vestibular, which tells us whether we are right side up, going up or down, forward or backward, and so forth; the proprioceptive, which tells us the positions of our limbs in space (letting us know, for example, whether our arms are reaching forward or sideways, even when our eyes are closed); the kinesthetic, which relates information about our muscle tension, and the internal, which transmit such information from our internal organs as a full bladder, a painful kidney stone, or a quickly beating heart. Let's look at some basic information about our sensory systems.

VISION

For most people, the sense of vision assumes more importance than any of the other sensory systems. More of the brain is devoted to mechanisms for vision than to any other sense, and what we see gives us some 80 percent of our information about the world.

Vision dominates information from the other senses. If you've ever seen a skillful ventriloquist in action, you probably wondered how he could make those sounds come from that little dummy. If you close your eyes while the ventriloquist is talking, you'll be aware that both voices come from the same place, but when your eyes are open and you see the dummy's mouth moving, what you see becomes more important than what you hear. This phenomenon, by which visual information assumes more importance in our minds than information from the other senses, is called visual capture and is one example of the many reasons why we can't always trust the evidence of our own senses.

What We See

The human eye sees electromagnetic energy in the form of light waves. We don't see all the electromagnetic waves in the universe, however, such as x-rays, ultraviolet rays, or infrared rays, as you can see in Figure 3-3. The energy that we can see comes to us in photons, or *quanta*, the smallest units of light that can be measured. A single photon can activate a receptor in the eye, and, under the right conditions, as few as 10 photons produce an absolute threshold. This is an astonishingly small amount of energy. As Figure 3-1 shows, the human eye can see a source of light that is as faint as an ordinary candle from a distance of 27 kilometers through a nonabsorbing atmosphere. So a powerful searchlight directed from a new moon should be visible on earth with the naked eye (Pirenne, 1948).

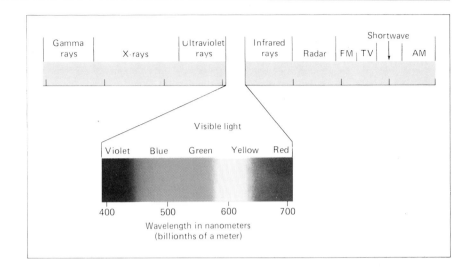

FIGURE 3-3 The Electromagnetic Energy Spectrum *The portion of the spectrum perceived as visible light is enlarged in the lower portion of the figure.*

How We See: The Anatomy of the Eye

As you can see in Figure 3-4, the miraculous organ that we know as the human eye is a sphere that contains a variety of structures. We can look at these structures in turn as we trace the path that light takes when it enters our eyes.

Light passes first through the cornea, the transparent tissue in front of the eye. The cornea is made of the same material as the sclera, the white outer part of the eyeball, but is transparent because of the way the corneal molecules are arranged. The sclera, the "skin" of the eye, contains receptors for pressure, temperature, and pain.

The light then enters the anterior (front) chamber of the eye, located just behind the cornea, in front of the lens. This chamber is filled with a watery fluid called aqueous humor, which helps to "feed" the cornea and which is continually secreted, released, and replaced.

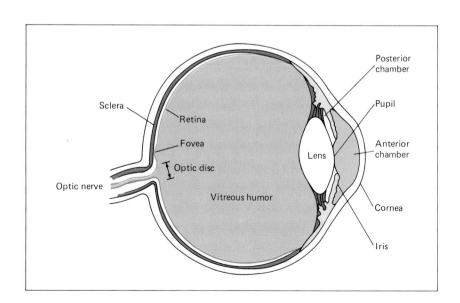

FIGURE 3-4 *Cross-section of the human eye.*

BOX 3-1

COMMON VISION PROBLEMS

- Damage to the cornea can make it lose its transparency and become opaque like the sclera, which prevents light from coming through. This kind of vision loss can be corrected through the transplant of a cornea from the healthy eye of a person who has just died.
- If the canal between the sclera and the iris becomes blocked, the buildup of vitreous humor in the anterior chamber can create an increase in pressure inside the eye, causing

glaucoma. Persons with this disease have a smaller field of vision, see a colored halo around artificial lights, and can eventually become completely blind through damage to the optic nerve in the back of the eye. An individual usually cannot feel the increase of pressure, but an opthalmologist can generally detect it at a fairly early stage and can control it with drops of medicine.

- If the eyeball is too long, the

lens cannot focus far images on the retina, causing nearsightedness (myopia), a difficulty in seeing objects that are far away. Since the shape of the eye can change over time, periodic checkups by an eye doctor can keep a lens prescription up to date.

- If the eyeball is too short, the lens cannot focus near images on the retina, causing farsightedness (presbyopia), a difficulty in seeing objects that are closeup. Another reason for

FIGURE 3-5(a) *Nearsightedness and farsightedness are caused by abnormalities in eye shape. In the normal eye (top), light is focused on the retina; when the eye is elongated (bottom left), nearsightedness results because the light focuses in front of the retina; when the eye is too short (bottom right), light focuses behind the retina, causing farsightedness.*

FIGURE 3-5(b) *A person with normal vision will see a "clockface" figure (a), while someone with astigmatism will have difficulty seeing some or all of the vertical lines (b) or the horizontal lines (c). (From Mitchell, Freeman, Millodot, & Haegerstrom, 1973)*

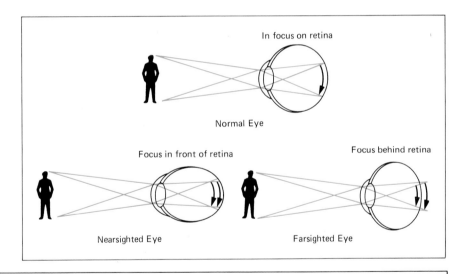

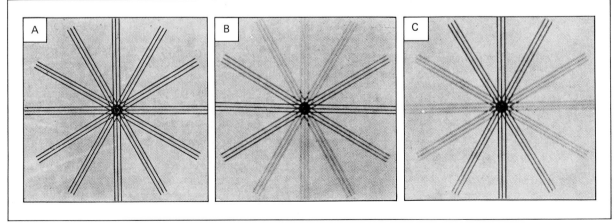

farsightedness, which affects most people past middle age, is a loss of elasticity in the lens, making it lose its ability to focus on near objects. People with normal-distance vision can wear half-glasses ("granny" glasses) that allow them to look through the glasses at nearby objects and to look over the tops of the glasses at far-away objects. People who are both nearsighted and farsighted wear bifocals, which correct the myopia in most of the lens and the presbyopia just at the bottom. (See Figure 3-5(a) for a graphic comparison of normal vision, nearsightedness, and farsightedness.)

- If the eyeball is not perfectly round, a condition called astigmatism results. People who are astigmatic cannot see equally well along horizontal and vertical axes; they have trouble seeing either sideways or up and down, as shown in Figure 3-5(b). If children's astigmatism is not corrected with eyeglasses at an early age, they are likely to have a permanent loss in the ability to see clearly either vertical or horizontal lines, apparently because the appropriate neural connections do not develop in the visual cortex (Mitchell et al.,

1973). Glasses prescribed in adulthood will not be able to totally make up for this visual defect.

- In the condition known as amblyopia ("lazy" or "weak eye"), there seems to be a problem in the processing of visual messages to the brain. Both eyes are normal, as are the optic nerve fibers, but for some reason the brain does not receive the visual information from one eye. As a result, the affected person has a fuzzy, distorted view of the world. Amblyopia, which occurs in 2 percent of the population, is the most common visual defect in children and the most common cause of legal blindness in children and young adults.

- Sometimes amblyopia is associated with an inborn defect of the eye muscles which keeps the two eyes from focusing together, resulting in strabismus (often called "crossed eyes," "wall-eyes," or "wandering eye"). People with this condition use their eyes one at a time, quickly alternating between them, but if one eye has poorer vision than the other, they will stop using that eye altogether. As a result, the vision in that eye will get even worse, until good vision

remains in only one eye. If amblyopia and strabismus are not corrected early (before age 5), either with exercises or with surgery, a permanent visual impairment will occur (Banks, Aslin, & Letson, 1975; Srebo, in press).

- Sometimes the lens loses its transparency, causing an opaque condition known as a cataract, which results in a progressive, painless loss of vision. It can be caused by trauma, x-ray treatment, exposure to microwaves (for example, in cases of leakage from microwave ovens), a disease such as diabetes, dietary deficiencies, or the degeneration of aging. Recent advances make the surgical removal of the lens a very quick and usually effective treatment. With new glasses, the patient often achieves excellent vision.

- A reduction of the ability to see in dim light, known as night blindness, often results from a deficiency of Vitamin A or from retinal disease. When a vitamin deficiency is at fault, the administration of vitamins will sometimes reverse the difficulty.

After passing through the anterior chamber, light enters the chamber just behind it through a small hole called the pupil, which looks like a little black circle. The pupil *dilates* (opens wide) to let more light in under conditions of darkness, and it *constricts* (becomes smaller) in bright light. The size of the pupil is controlled by the iris, the colored part of the eye, a pigmented set of muscles surrounding the pupil. Eyes with a great deal of pigment appear brown; those with little or none are blue; and other colors are caused by varying amounts of pigmentation.

Light then passes through the lens, a round elastic structure that focuses the light into a clear image that is projected through the vitreous humor to the photosensitive part of the eye, the retina. The vitreous humor is a clear fluid that is not recycled like the aqueous humor but stays in our eyes all our lives. The lens changes its shape to focus near or far images onto the retina, a process known as accommodation. Problems with accommodation cause either nearsightedness or farsightedness as shown in Figure 3-5(a). These and other vision problems are described in Box 3-1.

The most important and most complicated part of the eye is the retina, which consists of neurons, glial cells, and photoreceptor cells called rods and cones. Each retina contains approximately 120 million rods and 6 million cones. As shown in the diagram in Figure 3-6, light passes through all the neurons before it reaches the photoreceptors (the rods and cones), where the visual responses originate. These responses are then transmitted through a complicated network of nerves to the ganglion cells. Each eye has about 1 million ganglion cells, which carry all of our visual information to the brain. The axons of these cells converge to one spot on the retina known as the optic disk and then send impulses to the brain, where the messages brought by the ganglion cells are decoded, so that we know what we see. (More about this later in the chapter, when we discuss the way the brain organizes sensory information.)

As you can see in Figure 3-6, the retina contains two different kinds of receptor neurons, long, narrow rods and thicker cones. The rods and the cones both contain light-sensitive chemicals, but each kind of receptor has specialized functions and appears in different concentrations in different regions of the retina. The cones function best in bright light, where they are responsible for color vision and for seeing small details. They are located mostly in and near the fovea, a region of the retina specialized for detail vision, which contains no rods at all. As we move away from the fovea, we see fewer cones.

Rods begin to appear in the peripheral retina, the region responsible for *peripheral vision*, what we see from the corners of our eyes. Since the rods are more sensitive to light, they allow us to see in dim light. With the rods we see mostly outlines and shapes, all in black and white. This explains why we see little or no color or sharp details in dim light or out of the corner of the eye. Rod-controlled peripheral vision does have an important role, however, which you can test by trying to see something dim,

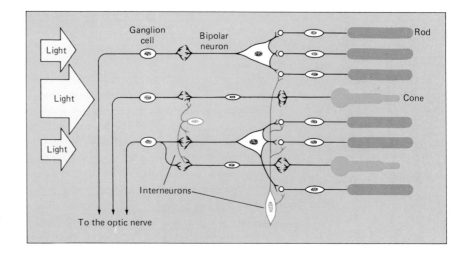

FIGURE 3-6 The Layers of the Retina *Light passes through the ganglion cells and the bipolar neurons to the photoreceptors, the rods and cones. Sensory messages go back from these receptor cells through the bipolar neurons to the ganglion cells. The axons of the ganglion cells form the optic nerve, which conveys visual messages to the brain. (From Hubel, 1963)*

FIGURE 3-7 Finding the Blind Spot *Close your right eye and line up the lamp with your left eye. Then move the book slowly back and forth and see the genie disappear when it is about a foot from your eye. Why? Because its image falls on your optic disk, which has no photoreceptors.*

like a faint star. If you look slightly away from your target, you'll see it better than if you gaze right at it. The phenomenon becomes especially dramatic when you move your head back and forth and find that the star becomes clear when seen from the side, while it may disappear when you look straight at it.

The optic disk has no photoreceptors at all, and therefore when an image is projected on the disk it hits a *blind spot* in either eye. We usually don't notice this blind spot for the following reasons: (1) because an image that hits it in one eye is hitting another place in the other eye so the other eye compensates, (2) because we move our eyes so fast that we quickly pick up the image, and (3) because the visual system has a tendency to "fill in" missing information. You can find your own blind spots, however, by following the instructions given with Figure 3-7.

How We See: What Happens in the Brain

RETINAL GANGLION CELLS AND RECEPTIVE FIELDS   What kinds of messages do 2 million ganglion cell axons send to our brains? The first recordings of the activity of individual ganglion cells (Kuffler, 1953) showed that each individual ganglion cell receives inputs from specific receptor cells and therefore "looks at" a particular part of the world. The message it sends to the brain apparently lets the brain know which ganglion cells are active, since there is a relationship between the retinal location of an image and its position in space. The area of the retina to which a given cell responds is called the cell's receptive field. Ganglion cells signal differences in the intensity of light falling on the central and surrounding portions of their receptive fields and thus give us better information in detecting changing levels of brightness than in perceiving areas of constant brightness.

One common visual illusion may well be due to the organization of receptive fields of ganglion cells. If you look at Figure 3-8(a), you'll probably see dark spots at all the intersections of the squares other than the one you're focusing on. What makes this illusion occur?

At the bottom right of the pattern you can see two ganglion cell receptive fields. Now look at Figure 3-8(b), which shows diagrams of two different kinds of ganglion cells. Those like the one shown in *a* are excited (that is, caused to fire more frequently) by light falling on their central areas and *inhibited* by light that falls on the area that surrounds the center. For cells like the one shown in 3-8b, the opposite reactions occur. For a 3-8a type of cell, then, a small spot of light that just covers the central area would appear brighter than a somewhat larger spot that covers the surrounding area as well. This is because the larger spot of light stimulates

FIGURE 3-8(a) *The dark spots you probably see at the intersections of the squares other than the one you're focusing on appear because of the different patterns of excitation and inhibition of the ganglion cells that are responsible for our sense of light and darkness.*

FIGURE 3-8(b) *Cells like those shown in a are excited by light falling on their central areas (+) and inhibited by light that falls on the surrounding areas (− − − −); cells like b are excited by light falling on the surrounding areas (+ + + +) and inhibited by light that falls in the center (−).*

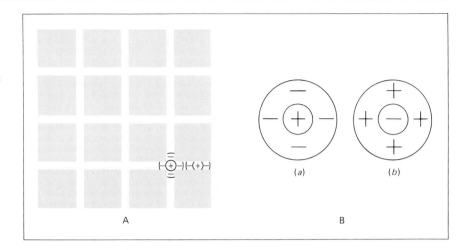

the inhibitory region (shown in the diagram as minus signs), in addition to the excitatory region (shown as plus signs).

The explanation for the phenomenon shown in Figure 3-8 is that the cell that is focused on an intersection has more of its surrounding area stimulated than the cell that is focused on a line. Since the former cell receives less excitatory stimulation, the intersection appears darker.

CENTRAL PROJECTIONS OF THE RETINA   The ganglion cells, then, *encode* retinal images, that is, they put information about what we see into sequences of action potential (explained in Chapter 2). These images are *decoded* in the brain, mainly in the visual cortex, so that we understand what we see. The central projections of the retina are the brain areas that receive synaptic inputs from the ganglion cells. The receptive fields of the cells in the visual cortex are not circular like the ganglion cells but are elongated. The discovery of receptive field organization (which won its discoverers, David H. Hubel and Torsten W. Wiesel, the Nobel Prize for medicine in 1981) has given us valuable information about the way we see. These cortical cells respond well to lines and contours in particular orientations—a different orientation for each cell. It seems, then, that the visual cortex changes images into "line drawings" in the brain. Later in the chapter we'll see what happens when young animals see lines only in one orientation, either vertical or horizontal.

Adaptation to Light and Dark

When you go to the movies on a sunny afternoon, two things happen. First you have to adapt to the dark, and then when you come out of the theater you have to adapt to the light. When you first walk into the dark auditorium, it takes a while before you can see clearly enough to walk down the aisle without bumping into things (or people). Gradually, your eyes adapt and you can see more clearly. Your *detection threshold*, the level at which you begin to see, drops as a function of the time you spend in dim light.

Both rods and cones begin to become more sensitive to light as soon as you step into a dark place. For the cones, the adaptation process is over within the first 10 minutes, whereas the rods continue adapting for another 20 minutes. By the end of half an hour, you are seeing as well as you are going to see in the dim light. Figure 3-9 shows the time course of dark adaptation and the different effects on rods and cones. Light adaptation is faster than dark adaptation, so it will take you less time to readapt to the daylight after you come out of the theater.

Color Vision

The human sense of color is not, of course, limited to the *primary* colors, which physicists consider as red, green, and blue because different mixtures of *lights* of these hues produce all the other colors, and which art teachers consider as red, yellow, and blue because different mixtures of their *pigments* (coloring agents) produce all the others. If you have normal color vision, you can tell apart hundreds of thousands of combinations of six basic hues—red, yellow, green, and blue, and of two hueless colors, black and white (Hurvich, 1982).

Exactly how do our eyes see colors produced by the mixing of lights? There are two major theories to explain how we see colors, the *trichromatic theory* and the *opponent-process theory*. We'll look at both of them (in color, of course). First, let's define color vision. When we see light waves, our sensations depend on three different qualities—their wavelength, their intensity, and their purity. Color vision is the ability to discriminate by wavelength independent of intensity. If your color vision is normal, you'll be able to tell colors apart regardless of the intensity of each wavelength. Let's see what these terms mean.

The *wavelength*, that is, the distance between the tops of the waves, is what chiefly determines what we think of as color and what scientists call *hue*. As you can see by looking again at Figure 3-3, the shortest wavelengths in the rainbow create the color we call violet, and the longest produce red. The rainbow itself is created by the breaking down of sunlight into different wavelengths as it passes through drops of moisture in the air.

The intensity of light is the amount of energy in the waves. The greater

FIGURE 3-9 Dark Adaptation *This graph shows what happens when a test flash affects the rods and cones. There is a decrease in visual threshold as a function of time in the dark. The upper curve shows cone sensitivity; the lower curve shows rod sensitivity. (From Cornsweet, 1970)*

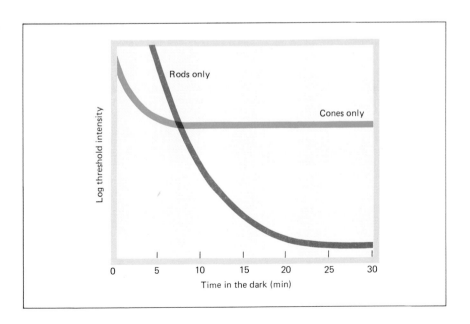

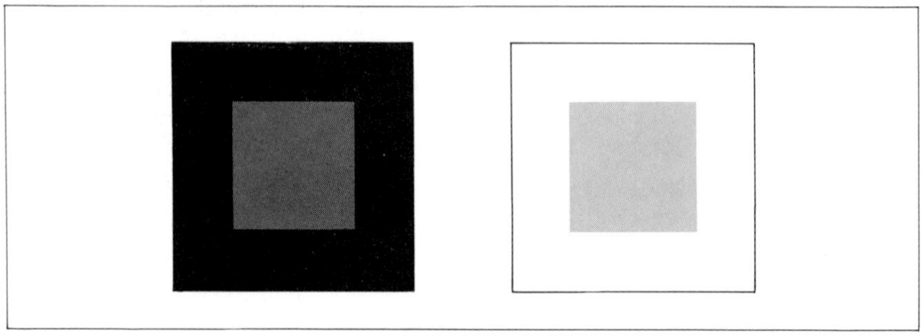

FIGURE 3-10 Simultaneous Brightness Contrast *Gray on black looks brighter than gray on white.*

the intensity of the light wave, the brighter it appears—in most cases. There are some exceptions, however, one of which can be seen in Figure 3-10. The center square in each larger square reflects the same amount of light to the eyes. However, the one on the left looks brighter by contrast with its dark background than does the one on the right, against a white background.

The *purity* of a light wave depends on whether what we see is composed primarily of waves of the same length (in which case we'll see a bright, "pure" color) or of mixtures of different wavelengths (in which case a color will be duller). The purest hues are said to be "highly saturated." You can see the effects of intensity and saturation in Figure 3-11.

The beginning of modern knowledge of color vision came with Sir Isaac Newton's discovery in 1730 that white light contains all wavelengths. Newton developed a prism that showed that different wavelengths are *refracted* (turned aside) by different amounts when they pass through the prism, so the different wavelengths are spread out, revealing the familiar rainbow pattern. The next major development came in 1802, when Thomas Young showed that you don't need all the colors of the spectrum

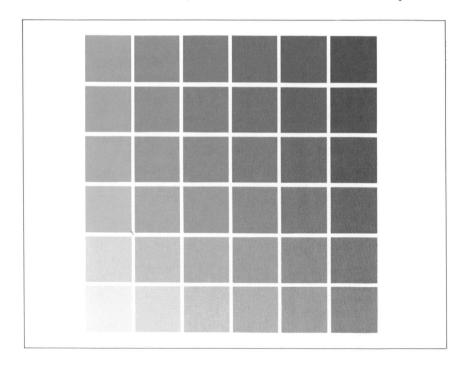

FIGURE 3-11 *Variations of intensity and saturation make these squares of the same color look different. In the far left column the squares are saturated (pure) blue. Moving to the right, the pure blue is increasingly diluted with gray of equal intensity (brightness), so that the squares on the far right are the least saturated blues that can be told apart from pure gray. The intensity of the squares decreases from top to bottom, so that the bottom ones appear less bright.*

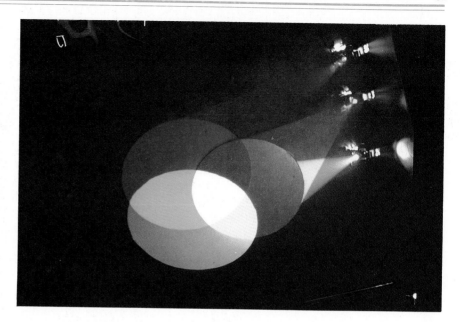

FIGURE 3-12(a) Additive Color Mixture *Different mixtures of lights produce different colors. Here we see what happens when green and red lights are combined and when green, red, and violet lights are combined. (Fritz Goro,* Life Magazine, © *Time, Inc.)*

to make white light but only two *complementary*, or opposite, colors, as shown in Figure 3-12(a). Complementary colors are pairs of hues that, combined with each other, create gray or white. They're opposite each other on a standard color wheel [see Figure 3-12(b)].

THE TRICHROMATIC THEORY OF COLOR VISION Young showed that combinations of the three colors red, green, and blue can produce every other

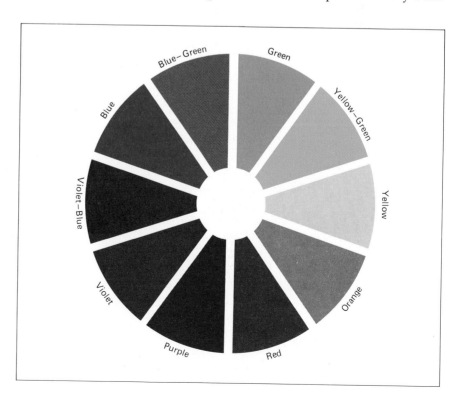

FIGURE 3-12(b) The Color Wheel *Any two colors that are opposite each other are complementary colors; that is, combining them produces gray.*

color. These observations led to the trichromatic theory (also known as the *Young-Helmholtz theory*)—that the visual system contains three color mechanisms (one for red, one for green, and one for blue), and that combinations of the responses of these three mechanisms produce all colored lights. Although this theory was developed in the 1800s by Young, and then by Hermann von Helmholtz (1911), it was not proved until the 1960s (Marks, Dobelle, & MacNichol, 1964; Brown & Wald, 1964). At this time experiments showed the existence of three types of cones, each of which has its own kind of *visual pigment*, made up of molecules that absorb the light and activate the visual process. Each kind of cone absorbs light at its own wavelength (peaking at either red, green, or blue) very effectively but is less effective at other wavelengths. The combined outputs of each of the three cone systems can signal the presence of any wavelength and enable us to see any color in the world.

THE OPPONENT-PROCESS THEORY OF COLOR VISION   While the trichromatic theory explains the effects of mixing colors of different wavelengths, it cannot explain some other aspects of color vision. One is the phenomenon of the *afterimage*, which *can* be explained by the opponent-process theory, first proposed by Hering (1920) and then developed by Hurvich and Jameson (1957). After you see a very brief flash of a very intense light (like the flashbulb of a camera or the high beams of an oncoming car at night), you'll see a series of both positive and negative afterimages. In a *positive afterimage,* you'll see an image in the same color as the original sight, while a *negative afterimage* will show the complements of the original colors. Negative afterimages also occur after you've been staring at colored objects for a long period of time. You can see how this works by following the instructions for Figure 3-13.

The opponent-process theory proposes the existence of opposite processes that occur in the cells of three systems—a blue-yellow system and a red-green system (each of which is made up of complementary colors), along with an *achromatic* (no hue) system of black and white. We see reds, for example, because red wavelengths excite some cells in that system, while inhibiting "opposite" cells (the ones that are excited by green wavelengths). The blue-yellow system works similarly, while the black-white system essentially responds to different levels of brightness. Let's see how this system explains colored afterimages.

When you stare at the yellow field of the flag, you are fatiguing the yellow system, while the blue system is unaffected since the cells in that system don't respond to yellow wavelengths. The same thing happens with the green stripes, and the black stripes and stars. As a result, after you look away from this image at plain white paper, the complementary systems will take over for the various fatigued systems, and you'll see the colors that are opposite those you originally stared at.

The trichromatic and opponent-process theories are not incompatible. In fact, combining the two theories suggests that the three cone mechanisms of trichromatic theory are the basis for the action of the opponent processes. The combination of both theories helps to explain color blindness.

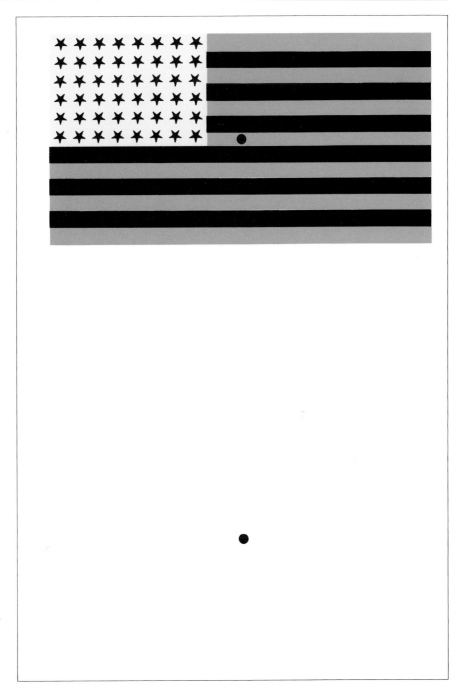

FIGURE 3-13 Afterimage   *To see a "normal" American flag, stare at the dot in the middle of the flag for 30 to 45 seconds. Then look at the dot in the white space below to see an afterimage in the familiar red, white, and blue pattern.*

COLOR BLINDNESS   Some people cannot see all the differences in color: Most of those who have a problem in distinguishing colors don't see reds and greens, some don't see blues and yellows, and a very few see all of life in shades of grays, blacks, and whites (See Figure 3-14). More males than females are color-blind, the deficiency is more common among some racial groups than others (see Table 3-2), and it is hereditary, usually

FIGURE 3-14 A Test of Color Blindness *What numbers, if any, do you see in these circles? People with normal color vision see the number 48 in red. If you don't see the number, you have red-green color blindness. (From The Psychological Corporation)*

passed on by a recessive gene carried by the mother. (For a description of this mechanism, see Chapter 11.)

It's possible that color-blind people are missing one or more cone systems. The missing cone system leaves the opponent-process system without an input, and the person is, therefore, unable to distinguish between the two opposing colors. Thus, someone missing the red cones can't tell the difference between red or green and sees them in shades of gray. People who don't see any colors at all may be missing all the visual pigments in the cones or possibly all the cones, so that they see only with their rods.

HEARING

A great deal of what we know about the world comes to us through our ears. Probably the commonest use to which we put our sense of hearing is in communicating with other people. In today's world, most of our con-

TABLE 3-2 Incidence of Color Blindness (in Percentage of Population)

Racial Group	Males	Females
Caucasians (Northern Europeans, Americans, and Australians)	8.08	0.74
Asiatics (Japanese, Chinese, and others)	4.90	0.64
American Blacks, Native Americans, Mexicans, and Eskimos	3.12	0.69

Adapted from Hurvich, 1981, p. 267.

tact with those we are close to, either personally or professionally, is either face to face or over the phone. It seems to be no accident that our keenest hearing is in those frequency ranges that include the human voice.

What We Hear

Do you remember the last western movie you saw that showed an Indian putting his ear to the ground to listen for the wagon train or to the track to listen for the "iron horse"? The Indian was showing his awareness of the fact that sound can travel in any medium—through air, water, metal, or the ground. The sound that we hear comes to us, like light, in the form of waves.

How do sound waves travel? Sound waves are actually movements of the molecules in the medium. The motion of the sound source alternately pushes molecules together (*compressing* the air, making it denser) and pulls them apart (*rarefying* the air, making it thinner), causing vibrations in the form of sound waves. When sound is generated by a loudspeaker, the air pressure goes up during compression and drops during rarefaction. Thus sound waves are actually changes in air pressure that move at about 340 meters per second. As you can see in Figure 3-15, the pattern of sound waves closely resembles the pattern of the ripples that spread out after you've tossed a pebble into a creek. Basically, a similar process is taking place in both situations: Waves of energy are passing through a medium, temporarily displacing molecules. Sound needs a medium: In a vacuum, a ringing bell would be as silent as a scream in a nightmare.

We differentiate among sounds on two basic measures—their loudness (a function of the height of sound waves) and their pitch (a function of frequency). The intensity, or loudness, of sound is measured in *decibels (db)*, which describe the amplitude or height of sound waves. The higher the decibel level, the louder the sound. Figure 3-16 shows the decibel levels of a number of common sounds. Regular exposure to 80 decibels or more and even a single exposure to much higher levels can cause permanent hearing loss.

Sound waves, then, are repetitive changes in air pressure. The number of cycles that occur in the wave each second are measured in *hertz (Hz)*, and human beings normally hear sound waves in the range between 20 and 20,000 Hz. The higher the frequency, the higher the *pitch* of a sound and the shriller it will sound. Most human speech is in a range between 100 and 3500 Hz, the frequency range to which human ears are most sensitive, thus showing an elegance in the way we have evolved. Dogs, however, can hear up to about 80,000 Hz, a fact that explains why you can buy a special dog whistle to call your pet without disturbing your neighbors. Bats and dolphins can hear at even more impressive ranges—beyond 100,000 Hz. Now that we're humbled by these comparisons, let's look at the way the human ear hears and discriminates so many different frequencies.

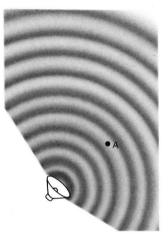

FIGURE 3-15 *Sound from a loudspeaker creates cyclic movement of molecules in the air as they are pushed together (compressed) and then pulled apart (rarefied).*

How We Hear: The Anatomy of the Ear

What we think of as the ear—that flap on the side of the head that serves variously as a hat rack or a jewelry stand—is only one small part of a complex structure, as you can see in Figure 3-17.

Let's follow a sound wave through the center of that skin-covered cartilage known as the *outer ear* (technically known as the pinna) and see

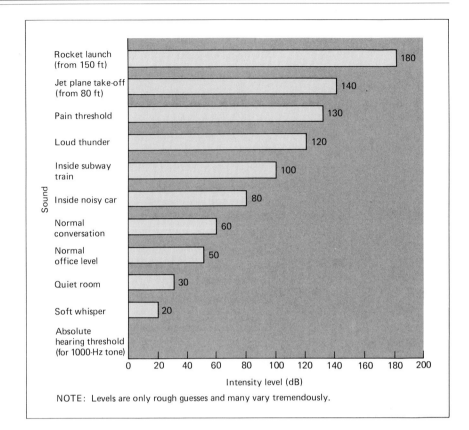

FIGURE 3-16 *Sound levels in decibels for a number of common sounds. (From Levine & Shefner, 1981)*

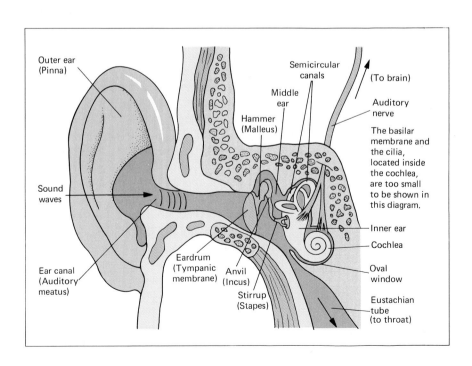

FIGURE 3-17 *Cross-section of the ear.*

where it takes us. The outer ear funnels sound waves into the *middle ear* through the tubelike *ear canal* (auditory meatus). This is lubricated by wax glands and protected by its lining of tiny hairs that keep out dirt and bugs. At the end of the ear canal is the *eardrum* (tympanic membrane), which moves back and forth as sound waves enter the ear. As the eardrum moves, it nudges the tiny bone, the *hammer* (malleus), which moves the *anvil* (incus), which moves the *stirrup* (stapes). (These three bones in the ear, named for their shapes, are the three smallest bones in the body.) The stirrup then presses against a small membrane called the *oval window,* which leads to the *inner ear.*

The inner ear consists of a coiled, snail-like structure called the cochlea, which is filled with fluid. When the stirrup presses against the oval window, it transmits sound energy to this fluid, creating pressure waves in it that cause the basilar membrane inside the cochlea to move at the same rate as the vibrations of the sound wave itself. Lying above the basilar membrane are rows of *hair cells,* with little hairs (*cilia*) protruding from them. When the basilar membrane moves up and down, the cilia move, making currents flow through the hair cells. These currents cause the release of neurotransmitters onto the dendrites of auditory nerve fibers, which then send impulses to the brain. These impulses represent the sound, and the brain processes this information to let us know what we hear.

Thus, the hair cells are the receptors for hearing, corresponding to the rods and cones for vision, and the auditory nerve fibers correspond to the ganglion cells in their function of transmitting sensory information to the brain.

HOW WE HEAR SOUNDS OF DIFFERENT FREQUENCIES: PLACE VERSUS FREQUENCY THEORY   How do we hear the different notes in a bar of music? How do our ears tell the difference between the high-pitched piping of a flute and the deeper tones of an oboe? Two alternate explanations for this ability are the place theory and the frequency theory.

According to the place theory, we hear a certain sound depending upon the particular spot on the basilar membrane that it stimulates. According to the frequency theory, it's the rate with which the basilar membrane is stimulated that determines what we hear. A variation of frequency theory is the *volley principle,* which suggests that groups of nerve fibers form "squads," and that individual neurons take turns firing in volleys.

Scientists generally agree that place theory seems to explain how we hear high-pitched sounds (above 3000 Hz, as in the warning tone of a civil defense alert) and that frequency theory explains our hearing of very low-pitched sounds, below 50 Hz, like the hum in a bad stereo system. Controversy still goes on, however, about which theory better explains our hearing of sounds between 50 and 3000 Hz, which includes most speech—or whether we need to look for a different theory altogether. Determining this may aid us in helping the hearing-impaired hear people talking to them.

HOW WE CAN TELL WHERE SOUND COMES FROM   Right from birth infants will turn their heads to hear a sound coming from one side, showing that

In some circles, President Ronald Reagan may become remembered more for his adoption of a tiny, almost invisible device than for his global policies. The 72-year-old former actor acknowledged the disorder he shares with some 16 million other Americans—a hearing impairment—by beginning to wear a new hearing aid specially designed for his kind of hearing loss (Clark & Witherspoon, 1983). The President suffers from sensorineural hearing loss, the most common type of impairment, supposedly brought on by a movie scene he played when someone fired a gun too close to his ear. The combination of that early experience and the normal tendency of hair cells to die off in later life culminated in increasing hearing problems, most noticeable in high frequencies and in situations where there's a lot of background noise. (Wide World Photos)

they can locate sounds in space (Castillo & Butterworth, 1981). This ability obviously has important survival value. How can we tell where a sound is coming from? The two major ways both rest on the fact that our ears are on different sides of our head.

If an elephant trumpets right in front of you, for example, the sound waves will travel the same length to reach each ear. But if the elephant is off to your left, the roar will have to travel a shorter distance to your left ear than to your right, and so it will be heard in that ear a fraction of a second sooner. Another clue to sound is the difference in intensity between the two ears. As this elephant bellows off to your left, your right ear is in a "sound shadow" created by your head, so the sound is louder in your left ear. Time of arrival is more important in locating low-frequency sounds, while intensity differences are more important for high-frequency sounds.

Suppose you have no hearing in one ear. Does this mean you can't locate sounds in space? Not completely. There are also monaural cues. Since covering the nooks and crannies of the outer ear with putty impairs localization, we know that they help us locate sounds. These cues, however, work well only for complex acoustic signals like human speech, again showing how well adapted we are for getting along with others of our species.

Hearing Loss

When the Swedish Navy wanted to track a suspected submarine in local waters, it had trouble finding sailors whose hearing was keen enough to use the sensitive listening devices. One navy captain ascribed the problem to permanent damage to the ears of young people caused by years of listening to loud rock music. Similar hearing loss has been seen among high school and college students who listen to a lot of loud music, among students who are "addicted" to headphones, and among people who work in noisy environments (Brody, 1982). People with this kind of hearing loss are often afflicted with tinnitus, a continuous ringing or hissing sound. In this kind of loss, called sensorineural hearing loss, the hair cells of the cochlea or the auditory nerve have been damaged. This is similar to the hearing loss that commonly comes with advancing age, caused by the normal tendency of hair cells to die off in later life. This kind of loss, called presbycusis (from the Greek words for "old age" and "hearing"), is particularly marked for high-frequency sounds and in situations with a lot of background noise (see Figure 3-18).

Until the recent development of a new hearing aid, consisting of a microphone, amplifier, and speaker in a tiny plastic case that nestles inside the ear canal, this kind of deafness could not be treated effectively. It could sometimes be prevented by avoiding excessive noise. Under federal

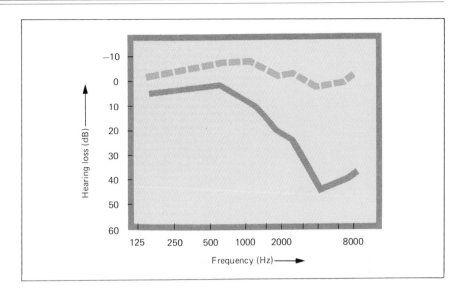

FIGURE 3-18 Hearing Loss as a Function of Frequency *The dashed curve shows losses for men between the ages of 18 and 30; the solid curve shows losses for men over the age of 65. (From Weiss, 1963)*

law, employers whose workers are regularly exposed to noise levels of 85 decibels or more are required to provide some kind of hearing conservation program (Brody, 1982). You can help yourself by keeping the volume in your head sets low and by not sitting right in front of the speakers when you attend rock concerts.

The other major type of hearing loss is conductive deafness, caused by a ruptured eardrum or a defect in the bones of the middle ear, which blocks sound waves from reaching the cochlea. This kind of impairment is easier to treat, either by surgery or a hearing aid that picks up sound from a bone behind the ear and transmits it to the cochlea, bypassing the middle ear.

THE SKIN SENSES

What's generally known as the "sense of touch" is in reality several different senses, which yield sensations of heat and cold, pressure, and pain. As long ago as the early 1800s, scientists knew that the skin has a variety of receptors to feel different sensations, and different kinds of receptors respond to different types of the preceding skin stimuli. These receptors, made up of nerve fibers, are so specific that when the individual fibers are stimulated, they will produce the sensation they are programmed for, no matter what the stimulus. The experiments of von Frey, for example, suggested that when a "cold" spot is stimulated, you will feel cold, even if the stimulus itself is hot. Similarly, a cold stimulus applied to a "warm" spot will produce a sensation of warmth. However, researchers have not been able to find a consistent relationship between the type of receptor and the kind of spot on the skin directly over that receptor.

Pressure

We are much more sensitive to touch in some parts of our bodies than in others, as shown in Figure 3-19. According to laboratory tests, our most sensitive parts are our face (especially our lips) and our hands (especially our fingers). The relative sensitivity of most body regions has been demonstrated scientifically by the *two-point discrimination threshold*, or the ability of a person to tell whether a single probe or two probes very close

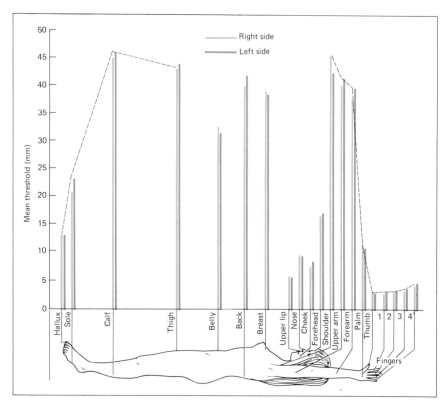

FIGURE 3-19 Two-Point Discrimination Thresholds *The mean threshold values represent the minimum distance between two points that is required for a person to sense two probes rather than one. The closer this distance is, the more sensitive the body is. The shortest lines in the figure show that the most sensitive parts of our bodies are the thumb and fingers, the lips, the cheeks, the big toe, and the forehead. (From Weinstein & Kenshalo, 1968)*

together are being applied to the skin. There is a close relationship between the ability to tell whether one or two probes are being applied to a particular body region and the size of the area in the cortex that represents this part of the body. There is also a close relationship between this threshold and the numbers of nerve fibers for each body region. The most sensitive areas have a larger number of skin receptors than the less sensitive areas.

Pain

The sense of pain serves a valuable evolutionary function by signaling danger—for letting us know, for example, when tissue is being destroyed by fire, injury, or illness, so that we can avoid harm. Once we are injured, however, that pain can be physically and emotionally draining, and so a great deal of research has explored the mechanisms that give rise to physical pain with the aim of finding ways to reduce or eliminate it.

So far, we're not sure whether a specific pathway for pain exists in the brain, but it does seem likely. Certain sensory nerve fibers respond only to pain, while others seem to signal pain along with other sensations as well. The assumption that there is a "pain pathway" comes from our knowledge of a condition known as the *Brown-Sequard syndrome*, which arises when half of the spinal cord is severed. In such a case, sensory information does not go from the legs to the brain in a normal way.

If the spinal cord is cut on the right side, for example, the right leg loses the sense of fine touch (as in the two-point threshold), but the leg feels pain. The left leg, on the other hand, becomes insensitive to pain but retains the sense of fine touch. (The same thing happens in reverse if it's the left side of the spinal cord that is severed.)

This phenomenon occurs because of the different sites where the two different kinds of sensory fibers cross from one side of the nervous system to the other. The pain fibers cross in the spinal cord, causing the pain fibers from the right leg to ascend on the left side of the spinal cord and thus reach the brain, while the touch fibers cross in the brain, so the touch fibers from the left leg ascend directly up the left side of the spinal cord to the brain.

If such specific pain pathways do exist, how does the brain control them? Some dramatic light on this question has been shed by research over the past ten years, which has demonstrated that the brain itself produces opiatelike substances that reduce or eliminate pain (Bolles & Fanselow, 1980; Snyder & Childers, 1979; Wall, 1978). These substances, called beta-endorphins, or sometimes just "endorphins," are not neurotransmitters, but *neuromodulators*, which adapt synaptic connections in certain ways. The endorphins seem to fill in the body's pain receptors in such a way that pain signals cannot get from the spinal cord to the brain (Fields & Basbaum, 1978). The smallest endorphin, enkephalin, is a very powerful painkiller when injected into animals or human beings.

Various situations seem to activate the brain's own antipain mechanism. One is physical exertion: marathon runners, for example, often don't feel the excruciating pain caused by pounding the pavements for more than 26 miles until after they have completed the race (Zaslow, 1984). Fear and stress are also common inhibitors of pain. A common casualty of war is the injured soldier who doesn't feel the pain from a bullet wound until after the battle is over, and a similar phenomenon is seen in other stressful situations, like the often reported instances of relatively slight women exposing themselves to what would ordinarily be painful ordeals to save their children from danger (Bolles & Fanselow, 1980).

Acupuncture, hypnosis, and placebos are all commonly known to block pain, and the big question is how they do it. Since a drug called *naloxone* reverses the action of enkephalin, apparently by blocking the receptors in the brain for opiates, one way that researchers test to see whether pain is being inhibited by the brain's own opiate system is to administer naloxone. If the naloxone reverses the effect, then the opiate system in the brain is probably what's relieving pain in a given situation. Using this approach, researchers have determined that acupuncture and placebos seem to activate the brain's own opiates but that hypnosis does not. Obviously, research along these lines has valuable implications for the well-being of the human race.

THE CHEMICAL SENSES

Our *gustatory sense* (taste) and our *olfactory sense* (smell) are considered chemical senses because they both respond to the chemical substances in various stimuli. They are also closely related.

Taste

No matter what makes your mouth water—a hot fudge sundae, a double cheeseburger, the finest imported caviar, or a juicy red slice of watermelon—it's obvious that your sense of taste adds a great deal to your enjoyment of life. Your sense of taste also has survival value—at least in the wild—since most foods in nature that are poisonous have a bitter or

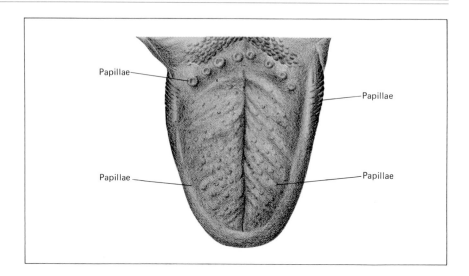

Papillae

Papillae

Papillae

Papillae

FIGURE 3-20 *The tongue showing different types of papillae.*

otherwise unpleasant taste. In any case, with the vast smorgasbord of different flavors that we can tell apart, it's surprising that our receptors for taste distinguish among only four different sensations—sweet, salty, sour, and bitter. Human beings describe virtually all tastes in terms of combinations of these four qualities (McBurney, 1969).

Our receptors for taste, the *taste buds,* are located on the tongue, inside the little bumps on it, called papillae. These taste buds are distributed in different places on the tongue, as shown in Figure 3-20. The tip of the tongue is most sensitive to sweet, salty, and bitter tastes, and the sides to sour (McBurney & Collings, 1977). These regional differences are applicable only to the zones of greatest sensitivity. All areas of the tongue that have papillae (that is, all areas except the middle of the tongue) can sense all taste qualities.

As you can see from Figure 3-21, nerve fibers convey information from the cells within the taste bud to the brain. These individual nerve fibers are also differentially sensitive to the four basic tastes. While they respond to a wide range of taste stimuli, they respond best to only one (Frank, 1973).

Have you ever wondered why some people have a ''sweet tooth,'' while others never eat dessert? Why some people love hot spicy foods, while others prefer bland foods? Why some people salt their food even before they taste it, while others prefer a minimum of salt? While some of these food preferences are undoubtedly the result of learning, others may well be due to hereditary differences in our taste buds. This is the conclusion of some interesting studies done with a bitter-tasting substance called *phenylthiocarbamide (PTC).* Laboratory experiments have shown that about one person in three cannot taste this chemical, apparently due to the absence of a particular ''bitter'' taste bud. The same people who can't taste PTC usually don't object to the bitter taste of caffeine and are likely to use less sugar in their coffee (Bartoshuk, 1974).

Taste cells die and are replaced by new cells about every ten days, but as we age, fewer new cells are generated; thus, the older we are, the fewer taste buds we have. This is why many elderly people complain that food doesn't taste so good to them anymore.

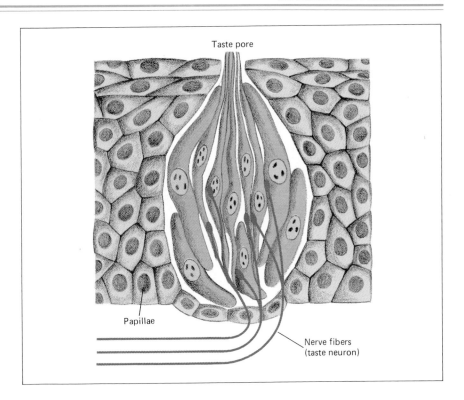

Taste pore

Papillae

Nerve fibers
(taste neuron)

FIGURE 3-21 *A taste bud is made up of taste cells and supporting cells.*

Smell

While we don't depend on our sense of smell for survival, as do so many of the lower animals—whose sense of smell is much more highly developed than our own—it does have value in detecting some poisonous gases and foods. It also enhances our enjoyment of life, especially in connection with the foods we eat. Do you remember the last time you had a cold and couldn't smell anything? Even though the taste buds in your tongue were not affected, you couldn't taste foods well, either. Your taste sensations themselves were not really impaired, but what most of us call "taste" is actually a global sensation that also includes the sense of smell. The olfactory sense (smell) and the gustatory one (taste) are indeed closely related. Figure 3-22 graphically shows this close relationship by demonstrating the olfactory pathways, through which the molecules of whatever we eat or drink make their way from the mouth up into the nasal passages to the olfactory receptors.

Odors come into the body as molecules in the air, either through the nostrils or from the back of the mouth, into the smell receptors in the nasal cavity. The nasal cavity is lined with the olfactory mucosa, a mucous membrane that contains the smell receptors, which have hairlike projections (cilia) that catch the molecules and send an electrical signal through nerve fibers to the *olfactory bulb*. The olfactory bulb is like the retina in that it is here that the signals sent by the receptors are processed and then sent to the brain.

It's harder to study the sense of smell than that of taste for several reasons. For one thing, it's harder to control odors: It's hard to say when and in what degree of concentration an odor reaches a receptor cell. The most difficult thing is to identify the fundamental physical variables that produce a given smell, as we can do for visual and auditory wavelengths

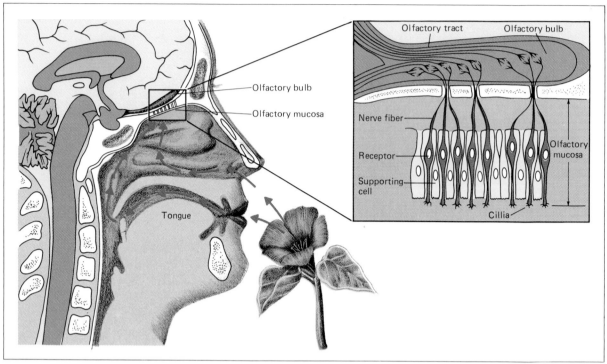

FIGURE 3-22 *Molecules of substances that we smell and also those that we eat or drink travel from the mouth into the nasal passages to the olfactory receptors in the brain. (Adapted from Amoore et al., 1964)*

or for the chemical properties that produce the four taste qualities. Researchers who have tried to determine the mechanisms for smell have come up with several different theories.

One branch of "smell" research has sought to determine how many different odors people can identify. Although the average person can name only a few, recent research shows that this seems due to an inability to think of the names of smells rather than an inability to tell the difference among them. When people are given the right names for odors, they can name correctly most of eighty different ones (Cain, 1981). This shows the importance of cognition in sensation. In fact, some researchers have suggested that older people have trouble identifying the flavors of foods because they cannot identify the smells connected to the tastes and that their difficulty is more closely tied to difficulties in remembering the names of tastes and smells rather than in perceiving them (Schiffman & Murphy, cited in Cain, 1981, p. 55).

According to the stereochemical theory, there are seven basic smells: ethereal (as in dry-cleaning fluid); floral (as in a rose); minty (as in spearmint); pungent (as in vinegar), camphoraceous (as in some kinds of mothballs); musky (as in certain perfumes); and putrid (as in a rotten egg) (Amoore, 1970; Geldard, 1972). Of course, even though there may be a limited number of basic smells, we can discriminate among hundreds of different variations and combinations, just as we can discriminate among thousands of colors based on just the three primary hues. The stereochemical theory suggests that smell receptors have particular shapes and that the molecular combinations of the various odor types fit into these shapes (see Figure 3-23). While no firm evidence has been found for this shape relationship between odor and receptor site, it does seem fairly

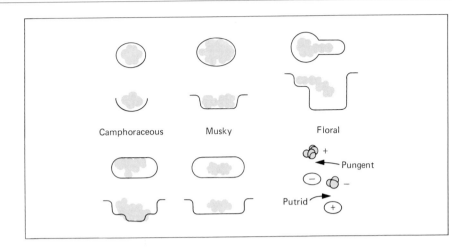

FIGURE 3-23 *Molecular models and the receptor sites into which these molecules fit according to Amoore's (1964; 1970) stereochemical theory of odor.*

clear that there is a relationship between the shape of a molecule and its odor (Matthews, 1972).

The chromatographic theory suggests that we perceive various smells because different odors travel different distances inside the nasal cavity, and the place they land in the mucous lining of the nose determines the way they smell to us (Mozell & Jagodowiez, 1973). This theory is similar to the place theory for the way we hear different pitches of sound. Experiments with salamanders show that neurons in the front of the olfactory bulb respond best to some chemicals, whereas other chemicals stimulate neurons in the middle or the rear of the bulb (Kauer & Moulton, 1974).

OTHER SENSES

Proprioception

The sense of proprioception provides information to us about the movement of our body parts and their position in space. The sensory receptors are located in the joints and muscles. This is the sense that lets us close our eyes and know whether our arms are stretched out in front of us or by our sides. People can have problems with this sense, too. If you've ever had to wear a cast for a long time, for example, you might have had the sensation sometimes that the encased limb was in a different posture from the one it actually was in. Another case of proprioceptive "hallucination" is the *phantom limb* phenomenon often experienced by amputees, who feel pain and other sensations in a leg or arm that is not there.

Balance: The Vestibular System

Have you ever felt the misery of seasickness, when first you were afraid you were going to die—and then you were afraid you weren't going to? This, as well as other forms of motion sickness, seems to be at least partially related to a discrepancy between two senses—the visual and the vestibular. The vestibular labyrinth is a complex arrangement of canals within the inner ear that help us to maintain our sense of balance. Within this labyrinth are receptor cells that can sense movement of the head in any direction. The receptors themselves are *hair cells*, which feel movements of a fluid inside the labyrinth. When your head moves, the fluid stays behind (in the same way water in a glass stays still when you roll the glass around in your hand), and the hair cells are displaced, sending neural impulses to the brain that signal the change in head position. The reason a person walks unsteadily after having drunk too much is that liquor changes the density of the fluid in the vestibular labyrinth (Barlow & Mollon, 1982).

The connection between our visual and our vestibular systems is apparent in the fact that many people feel the effects of car sickness less if they ride in the front seat of the car, where they can see—and thus anticipate—the movements of the car, and that people are less likely to be seasick if they can fixate their eyes above deck on the stable horizon rather than riding in a cabin below deck where they cannot compensate for the rolling sensation.

PERCEPTION: HOW THE BRAIN ORGANIZES SENSORY INFORMATION

There's an old story about two strollers in a little town that boasts a church known the world over for its tower bells. One turns to the other to say, "Aren't those bells magnificent?" and the other answers, "I can't hear you because of all that noise." The same sort of exchange goes on in any household that contains a lover of symphonies and a devotee of rock music. The same sounds may be perceived very differently by different people.

Perception is more than what we see or hear or feel or taste or smell. It's also the meaning that we ascribe to these sensations. We arrive at this meaning by the way our brain organizes all the information we take in through our senses. Reading this book, for example, you see more than an assortment of little black marks on a white page. You see letters that make up words. Because you have learned how to read, your brain organizes these little marks as symbols that represent meaning. The same process takes place in many other areas of life as we interpret sensory information.

Gestalt Laws of Perceptual Organization

While psychologists have established the individual elements, or basic units, of visual and auditory patterns, what we see and hear is much more than the sum of those units, as you can see in the portrait of Abraham Lincoln shown in Figure 3-24, in which meaningless shapes produce an instantly recognizable picture. We routinely organize lines and shadings into scenes and individual sounds into speech and music. Thus, these bits of information become meaningful patterns.

As we noted in Chapter 1, the Gestalt psychologists emphasized the significance of overall patterns. (The German word *gestalt* means "whole" or "pattern.") This approach is particularly applicable in perception. Look at the picture in Figure 3-25, for example. We see more than a random selection of lines. We even see more than the front half of a lion, a tree, and the back half of a lion. We immediately know that the front and back of the lion are parts of the same animal, even though we don't see this continuity in the picture itself. We know because we impose our own structure on what we see.

This picture illustrates one of the rules, or laws, which govern the ways in which we organize sensory information according to various characteristics. The lion demonstrates the *rule of continuity*, by which our minds continue in the direction suggested by the stimulus. Other basic rules

FIGURE 3-24 *If you look at this computer-processed portrait, your sense of vision will tell you that you're looking at an arrangement of geometric forms of varying shapes, sizes, and intensities. If you squint or move away from the picture, you'll see something else: The face of the sixteenth president of the United States will emerge from this pattern. Squinting, moving away, or defocusing lets us perceive an overall pattern that is not visible when we concentrate too closely on the geometric forms. Comic-book illustrations, made up of many tiny dots, illustrate the same concept.*

FIGURE 3-25 *We see more than a random selection of lines, more than a front half of a lion, a tree, and the back half of a lion. By the rule of continuity we impose our own structure on this drawing to see a lion behind a tree.*

described by Gestalt psychologists include the *rule of proximity* (we group elements that are near each other); the *rule of similarity* (we group elements that are like each other); and the *rule of closure* (we complete unfinished patterns). All these are illustrated in Figure 3-26.

The Gestaltists also pointed out another common way of organizing sensation—dividing it into a *figure* (the object we focus our attention on) and a *ground* (the background for the focal object). When figure-ground relations are ambiguous, our perceptions of figure and ground shift back and forth. You can see this in Figure 3-27. When you look at it one way, you see a white vase on a dark background; another way, it becomes two dark profiles facing each other over a white background. This figure dramatically demonstrates the active nature of our perceptual system since you can choose to see two different perceptions from the same stimulus. You can't, however, see them both at the same time.

These rules apply to other sensations, too, involving touch, taste, smell, and hearing. In a bar of music we may hear the melody as the figure, with the chords as the ground, until a change in volume or rhythm brings the chord to the center of our consciousness. Or, sitting in a classroom, we can attend either to the lecture or a conversation behind us. While extremely quick reversals of figure and ground can occur, we can-

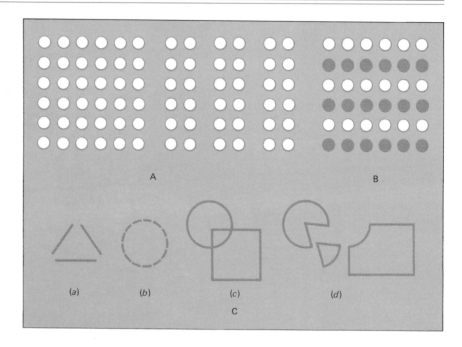

FIGURE 3-26(a) The Rule of Proximity   *The pattern on the left can be seen as either rows (across) or columns (down) because the circles are spaced equally in both directions. The pattern on the right appears as pairs of columns because the horizontal spacing has been altered.*

FIGURE 3-26(b) The Rule of Similarity   *We now see the circles in rows because we group together elements that look alike (the colored circles and the plain ones).*

FIGURE 3-26(c) The Rule of Closure   *We fill in the gaps. Thus we see figures A and B as a triangle and a circle. And we see figure C as a circle and a square, not as the assortment of incomplete figures shown in D.*

not simultaneously attend to both. So when we're studying, listening to music, and watching television, we may think we're paying attention to all three at once, but what's actually happening is that we're rapidly bringing each stimulus into our consciousness in turn.

Perceptual Set

The power we have over our own perceptions is great. We often see (or hear, taste, smell, etc.) what we expect to see or what fits our preconceptions of what makes sense, a phenomenon known as perceptual set. Overhearing a snatch of conversation, you may think you heard something far different from what was actually said; when told you are about to see pictures, you may see them even when none are actually shown. As we'll see in Chapter 6, this common tendency affects the reliability of eyewitness testimony. For example, when researchers showed people a drawing of a white man holding a razor, standing on a bus next to a black man, a surprisingly large number of people "remembered" having seen the razor in the black man's hand (Allport & Postman, 1958). You can demonstrate the power of perceptual set to yourself by doing the experiment shown in Figure 3-28.

This principle of the way our expectations shape our perceptions is an important one for our judgments of people. Two people, for example, may say exactly the same few words in the same gruff tone of voice. If you have the picture of one as good-natured and one as cranky, you'll assume the first one is joking and the second is hostile, and your own emotional reaction will be quite different toward the two speakers.

FIGURE 3-27 *A pattern in which figure and ground may exchange roles. The pattern may be seen either as two silhouetted faces or as a white vase.*

Perceptual Constancy

When you say good-bye to a friend and watch her walk down the street, her image on your retina gets smaller and smaller. You don't see her as the "incredible shrinking woman," however. You know that she's staying the same size and that the reason she looks smaller is the growing distance between you. This perception that objects and events in our envi-

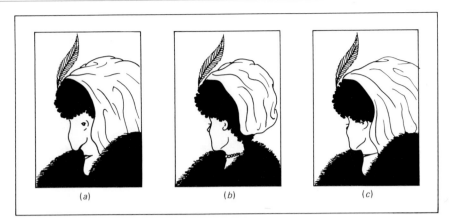

FIGURE 3-28 *The figure c is ambiguous. If you cover up b, both a and c will look like an old woman in profile, but if you cover up a, b and c will both look like a young woman whose face is turned away. Try showing c to a friend while covering up both other drawings. Ask, "What do you see?" And then: "Do you see anything else?" Then show each of the other drawings.*

ronment remain the same even though they may look different because of varying conditions in the environment is known as perceptual constancy. Because we can make allowances for varying environmental cues, we can maintain a stable view of the world and the people and objects in it. We also can make a variety of judgments about distance, lighting, and other aspects of our environment.

- *Size constancy:* If we know the size of an object (such as the friend in the preceding example), we know by its (her) relative size in our field of vision whether it (she) is close or far away (see Figure 3-29).
- *Texture constancy:* If we know that a particular surface is heavily tex-

FIGURE 3-29 *One way we judge distance is through size constancy. When we see this photo of hikers in the Italian Alps, we know that even though the last person in line seems much larger than the leader of the group, there cannot be that much difference in their sizes. Therefore, we rightly assume that the leader appears smaller because he is so far away, and we have some basis for estimating just how far away he is. (©Werner H. Müller/Peter Arnold, Inc.)*

FIGURE 3-30 *Another clue to distance is texture constancy. Note how clearly you can see the shapes, colors, and markings of the stones that are up close, and how little detail is observable on the stones in the distance. (©Bohdan Hrynewych/Stock, Boston, Inc.)*

FIGURE 3-31 *This photo illustrates shape constancy. We know that the oil drums shown here are round, so when they appear oval to our eyes, we know that that means we are seeing them from a distance. (©Sepp Seitz/ Woodfin Camp & Assoc.)*

tured up close, we'll know that when the surface seems to "smooth out" and we can see fewer details that it's farther away (see Figure 3-30).

* *Shape constancy:* If we know that oil drums remain round, then when they appear oval to us, we'll know that they're at a certain distance and angle of sight (see Figure 3-31).
* *Brightness constancy:* We see an object's brightness as constant even under different lighting conditions, so whether you read this page in bright sunlight or semidarkness, you'll still know that the paper is white and the printing is black. When the paper looks duller, you can judge the level of illumination.
* *Color constancy:* If we know the color of an object, we'll know that when it looks lighter, darker, or of a different hue, it's the lighting that makes it appear different.

Perceptual constancy also occurs with regard to the other senses, such as hearing. If we hear the very faint sound of a fire engine, we'll recognize the siren, know that it's ordinarily loud, and assume that it's far away. We'll then be able to relax, free from worry that our own house is on fire.

There are two basic explanations of perceptual constancies. One, the unconscious inference theory, rests on what we know from experience. If we know certain basic information—like the true size or shape of an object—we make unconscious inferences when that object *seems* different. According to this theory, we unconsciously know that nearby objects look bigger because they cast a larger image on the retina, so if we know the distance between our eyes and an object, we can derive the size of the object (Rock, 1977).

An alternative explanation, the ecological theory, says that the relationships between different objects in a scene give us information about their sizes (Gibson, 1979). Thus, when our friend walks away, the relationship between her size and the size of the trees and cars remains the same, so we see all the sizes as remaining constant, despite the change in retinal image. Or when we look at this book in the dark, the ratio between the white of the page and the black of the letters remains constant even though the actual amount of light reflected differs.

The Ames room [shown in Figure 3-32(a)] draws on the ecological theory to mislead the viewer into a distortion of the sizes of the people in the room. In this photo of an observer's view of the room, the boy looks much larger than the woman, even though she is, in fact, taller. This is because the room was designed to look like a normal rectangular room when viewed from one particular observation point, but as you can see from the drawing Figure 3-32(b), the room is shaped so that the woman is almost twice as far away from the viewer as the boy. The relationships between the sizes of the windows and walls have been altered, changing the relationships between the people and their environment and fooling the viewer. Constancy, then, needs a context.

Perceptual constancies are important because they free us from depending on the characteristics of the retinal image when we try to perceive the nature of an object. They make our perceptions object oriented

FIGURE 3-32(a) *The woman in this picture taken in the Ames room is actually taller than the boy, although he looks like a giant next to her. A drawing of the top view of the room explains the illusion. (©Baron Wolman 1981/ Woodfin Camp & Assoc.)*

Depth Perception

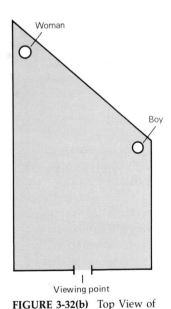

FIGURE 3-32(b) Top View of the Ames Room *The woman on the left is almost twice as far away as the boy on the right, although when the room is seen from the viewing point, this difference in distance is not apparent. (From Gregory, 1973)*

rather than retina oriented. They help us maintain a realistic sense of the world we live in.

Wesley Walker, a professional football player with the New York Jets, has to make fine judgments of speed and motion every time he makes a play. As a wide receiver, he has to estimate where the ball will land while both he and it are still in motion, and he has to keep modifying his estimate as he runs after the ball. Obviously, he needs a keen sense of depth perception. Judging from his success in the stadium, he has one—despite the fact that he is practically blind in his left eye (*New York Times*, 1983).

Depth perception is not, of course, important only to football players. It's vital for anyone who drives a car, walks in the street, performs the most elementary motor activities. How, then, do we judge the distance of objects? In two major ways: those that depend on the vision of both eyes working together (*binocular cues*) and those can be used with only one eye (*monocular cues*).

The binocular cue, which is more accurate, depends on the fact that the two eyes are several centimeters apart. Each eye has a slightly different view of the world, and the way the brain fuses these two images creates the impression of depth. When you "see double," you are seeing the separate views of both your eyes; for some reason (possibly fatigue, intoxication, or a weakness of the eye muscles), they are not fusing.

You can easily demonstrate this difference in what your eyes see, called *retinal disparity*. Close your right eye and hold one finger upright about eight inches in front of your left eye. Then position a finger from your other hand behind the first finger until the second finger is completely hidden. If you now close your left eye and open your right eye, you'll be able to see the previously hidden finger. This slightly different view of your fingers seen by each eye demonstrates the principle of *stereopsis*,

FIGURE 3-33 *Stereoscopic photos of football player "Mean" Joe Greene, former defensive lineman for the Pittsburgh Steelers. The left eye sees the view as shown on the left, and the right eye sees the view on the right. In the photo on the right, Player "23" seems closer to Greene, showing that our two eyes perceive the world just a little differently. (Stereogram by Mike Chikiris, 1977)*

which is the basis for 3-D movies and slide viewers, which project a slightly different image to each eye and thus create the illusion of depth. The stereoscopic photographs of the football players in Figure 3-33 show a scene the way it would be seen by each eye. The brain determines the speed of an object (say, a ball being thrown to you) through *stereomotion*, by processing the change in the disparity between the two images of the ball as it moves closer or farther away.

Wesley Walker and other people with sight in only one eye can still play tennis or football, drive a car, or even fly an airplane by depending on monocular cues, which do not depend on the vision from both eyes.

The monocular cues include size, motion parallax, partial overlap, texture gradients, linear and atmospheric perspective, and shading.

Size is a prime clue: Nearby objects look bigger because they cast a larger image on the retina. As a thrown ball comes closer it gets bigger, and, based on the rapidly changing retinal image, the brain can quickly calculate speed and direction. When the body is moving too, the brain also takes this into account, and the monocular cue of *motion parallax* becomes important. In this phenomenon, which is especially noticeable when we're riding in a car or train, nearby objects move past our field of vision at a faster rate than distant ones do: Bushes seen outside a bus window seem to fly by, compared to distant mountains which "move" at a more measured pace. The speed of the apparent movement is directly related to distance (see Figure 3-34). Other important monocular cues include:

FIGURE 3-34 *These successive views of a row of fence posts show motion parallax. As you move at right angles to the posts, the direction of the line seems to change because of the change in your position and your line of sight.*

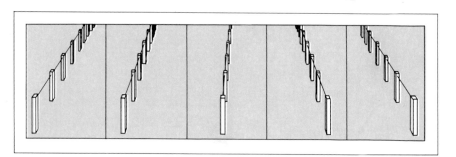

FIGURE 3-35 *This magnificent photograph of Dumont Dunes in California demonstrates the important monocular cue to depth perception known as "texture gradients." The fact that the sand grooves closer to us seem more widely spaced than do those in the distance allows us to draw inferences about the distances involved. (©C. Max Dunham/ Photo Researchers, Inc.)*

Partial overlap: When one object is in front of and partially blocks our view of another object, it's clear that the one in front is closer.

Texture gradients: When we look at a textured surface—either one with natural texture, like a grooved sand dune, or one composed of many objects stored close to each other, like a roomful of barrels—the elements closest to us seem to be spaced farther apart than the ones that are farthest away (see Figure 3-35).

FIGURE 3-36 An Example of Linear Perspective *When we see the parallel lines of the squares in the street and the fronts of the buildings converging to a vanishing point in the distance, we get an illusion of depth. (Museum of Art, Carnegie Institute, Pittsburgh; Director's Discretionary Fund, 1974)*

FIGURE 3-37 *Shading gives us a cue to the size and distance of an object. (Minneapolis Institute of Art)*

- *Linear perspective (convergence of parallel lines):* When two lines that we know are parallel appear to be converging to a point, we infer that that point is some distance away from us (see Figure 3-36).
- *Atmospheric perspective:* We see objects that are far away from us less clearly than nearby objects. The farther ones look fuzzier because of haze, smog, and dust in the air, and they also look bluer than closer objects. (Remember the lyrics, "purple mountains' majesty"?)
- *Shading:* By noting where the shadows fall, we often get a sense of the size and distance of an object. Artists who specialize in *trompe l'oeil* painting, which "fools the eye," use shading skilfully to make a viewer think that a flat painting actually has three-dimensional elements in it (see Figure 3-37).

The ability to calculate speed and motion on the basis of the changing size of retinal images is harder for people who lose sight in one eye after

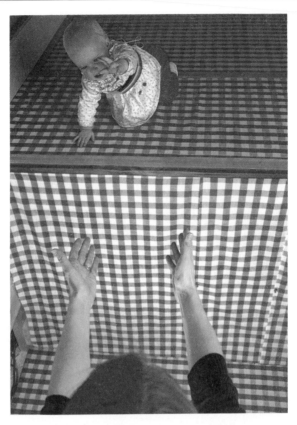

FIGURE 3-38 *Babies perceive the illusion of depth from a very early age. Even a mother cannot induce this baby to crawl across what looks like a cliff. (Enrico Ferorelli/DOT)*

the age of 7, indicating that the cortical cells especially developed for binocular depth perception are probably formed during the first few years of life (Regan, 1983). In fact, depth perception is either an innate ability or something learned extremely early. When babies as young as 6 months are placed on a "visual cliff" that consists of a flat, glass-covered board that creates an illusion of a chasm, they won't crawl on the side that looks deep, even to reach their mothers (Walk & Gibson, 1961). Two- to three-month-olds show slower heart rates on the "deep" than "shallow" side, suggesting that they're responding to the illusion of depth (Campos, Langer, & Krowitz, 1970) (see Figure 3-38).

Visual Illusions

While perceptual constancies help us perceive the world accurately, our perceptual systems are not infallible. We're subject to many false perceptions, called illusions. Some illusions are caused by misleading context, as in the size illusion produced by the Ames room and in the *Muller-Lyer* and *Ponzo illusions*.

Look at the lines in Figure 3-39(a). Ignoring the angled lines on the end of each vertical line, decide which vertical line is longer. If you measure them, you'll see that they're both the same, but it's hard to believe, because the one on the right looks longer to virtually everyone. The Muller-Lyer illusion, as this is called, is caused by those angled lines. Perhaps the effect is caused by the tendency of our eyes to be drawn back into the center of the line on the left-hand one and for them to move out into space on the right-hand one. Or the effect may be related to a false impression of depth, as indicated in Figure 3-39(b).

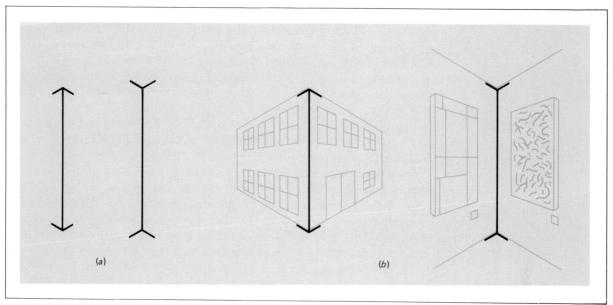

(a)   (b)

FIGURE 3-39(a) The Muller-Lyer Illusion *The two vertical lines are equal.*

FIGURE 3-39(b) *Drawing indicating how the Muller-Lyer figures could be perceived as indicating depth. (Van Bucher/ Photo Researchers, Inc.)*

The Ponzo illusion, shown in Figure 3-40, confuses us because of the illusion of depth caused by the converging railway tracks, which makes us expect the rectangle in the distance to appear smaller. When it does not, we assume it's larger than the one in the foreground of the photo.

Since at least the second century A.D., scientists have been trying to explain the *moon illusion,* which makes the moon look much larger when

FIGURE 3-40 *The Ponzo illusion.*

it's low in the sky, on the horizon, than when it's high overhead, at its zenith (see Figure 3-41). According to the *apparent-distance theory,* an object on the horizon seen across the filled distance of the landscape (that is, filled by hills, trees, buildings, etc.) seems farther away than an object seen across the empty space of the sky. This is partly because we can use visual cues given by the landscape (like texture gradients, perspective, and size) to figure out that the moon is indeed very far away. We don't have any cues at all in the vastness of the sky, however, and the moon is so far away that it's hard for the human mind to imagine the distance, and so we underestimate it.

Since the moon on the horizon seems farther away than the moon at its zenith, and since the moon is actually the same size at both points and projects the same size retinal image, and since we know that the farther away objects are the smaller they become, the moon that seems farther away appears larger. Eighteen centuries after Ptolemy, the early astronomer who gave us a sun-centered theory of the universe (that the earth revolves around the sun and not vice versa) put forth the apparent-distance theory, scientific experiments have confirmed it (Kaufman & Rock, 1962; Rock & Kaufman, 1962).

The Role of Experience

While some of the concepts we've been talking about seem obvious, they're far from universal. The use of perspective to show depth in painting (as in Figure 3-36) is a fairly recent artistic convention, for example. Roman paintings of the first century B.C. showed only an elementary perspective, "without any convergence of parallel lines toward a single vanishing point" (Robb, 1951, p. 54). It was not until the time of the Renaissance that artists discovered that by using the principles of perspective, they could add a convincingly realistic feeling of depth to their paintings. Even now, however, there are some cultures that apparently do not recognize the role of linear perspective in showing depth.

Cultural differences are also obvious in other ways. While you would look at the drawing in Figure 3-42 and know immediately that the hunter was trying to spear the antelope, some people from other cultures would ignore the size cues and assume the hunter was aiming for the elephant (Deregowski, 1972).

We also see differences in the way people from different cultures react to various tastes, smells, and physical sensations, based on their earlier

FIGURE 3-41 *An artist's conception of the moon illusion showing the moon on the horizon* (a) *and high in the sky* (b).

(a) (b)

FIGURE 3-42 *Members of remote tribes who are unfamiliar with pictorial cues for depth think that this picture shows a hunter trying to spear the elephant in the distance, not the antelope up close. (From Deregowski, 1972)*

experiences. So much of the way we organize our sensations is based on what we've learned.

Recent research has shown an actual physical change that occurs in response to early experience. When young cats have been fitted with goggles (like the ones shown in Figure 3-43) that allow them to see only vertical lines, when they mature, they won't be able to see horizontal lines and will bump into sideways boards right in front of them (Hirsch & Spinelli, 1971). If the goggles let them see only horizontal lines, they'll be effectively blind to up-and-down columns. This seems to be due to modifications in the cortex. Apparently, most of the neurons in the visual cortex become programmed to respond to the lines only in the direction (vertical or horizontal) that the cats have been permitted to see.

This does not happen when the same procedure is carried out with adult cats, suggesting that crucial cells in the visual cortex develop early in life. This points to a critical period in the development of vision. A *critical period* is a specific time during development when an animal or person needs to have appropriate experiences to bring about normal adult functioning.

The relevance of these findings for human beings lies in some recent findings about *astigmatism*, a visual defect in which a person has difficulty seeing lines in a particular orientation, either vertical or horizontal, as was shown in Figure 3-5(b). If children's astigmatism is not corrected with eyeglasses at an early age, they are likely to have a permanent loss of visual acuity for either vertical or horizontal dimensions (Mitchell et al., 1973). Similarly, children with *strabismus* who use only one eye at a time will have poor depth perception all their lives unless they receive treatment before age 5 (Banks, Aslin, & Letson, 1975).

As you'll see elsewhere in this book, there is a basis for the belief that there may be critical periods for various other kinds of development, such as learning language skills or sexual behaviors. Apparently brain development is preprogrammed to conform to certain sequential patterns. In this chapter we've seen how our brain helps us organize and give meaning to the information that comes to us through our sensory organs. In the next chapter, we'll see how the *state of consciousness* we are in at any particular moment influences the way we sense and perceive the world around us.

FIGURE 3-43 *This kitten is wearing training goggles. One lens contains horizontal stripes and the other vertical stripes. The eye that sees only horizontal stripes will be blind to vertical lines when the animal matures, and vice versa.*

SUMMARY

1 *Sensation* is the feeling we have in response to information that comes in through the sensory organs. *Perception* is the way the brain organizes these feelings to give them meaning. A *stimulus* is any form of energy to which we can respond. *Psychophysics* is the study of the relationship between the physical aspects of stimuli and our psychological perceptions of them.

2 The *absolute threshold* is the smallest intensity of a stimulus that can be perceived. This threshold depends on the background level of stimulation. The *difference threshold* is the smallest difference in intensity that you can tell between two stimuli. This threshold is variable, depending on the intensity of the original stimulus.

3 *Adaptation* is the decrease in the response of sensory receptors, with continued stimulations. *Attention* is the concentration upon certain stimuli, which makes them come to consciousness. Thresholds, adaptation, and attention all affect the way we perceive sensory information.

4 In addition to the familiar five senses—vision, hearing, touch, taste, and smell—we have other senses, which are the vestibular, the proprioceptive, the kinesthetic, and the internal.

5 *Vision:* The human eye sees electromagnetic energy in the form of light waves. This energy comes to us in *photons,* the smallest units of light that can be measured. The most important and most complicated part of the eye is the *retina,* which consists of neurons, glial cells, and photoreceptor cells called rods and cones. The rods and cones are sensitive to light and dark.

6 *Color vision:* According to the *trichromatic theory,* we see the primary colors of red, green, and blue, and all the different colors produced by combinations of these colors, by three color mechanisms in the eye—one for red, one for green, and one for blue. The *opponent-process theory* explains the phenomenon of the afterimage.

7 Common vision problems include glaucoma, nearsightedness, farsightedness, astigmatism, amblyopia, cataracts, night blindness, and color blindness.

8 *Hearing:* We differentiate among sounds on two basic measures—their *loudness* and their *pitch.* Loudness is measured in *decibels (db),* which describe the height of sound waves. Pitch depends on the frequency of the waves, which is measured in *hertz (Hz).* Hair cells in the ear are the receptors for hearing, and auditory nerve fibers transmit auditory information to the brain.

9 According to the *place theory,* we hear a certain sound depending upon the particular spot on the basilar membrane that it stimulates. The *frequency theory* says that the rate with which this membrane is stimulated determines what we hear. Place theory seems to explain hearing of high-pitched sounds, while frequency theory explains low-pitched sounds.

10 The two major kinds of hearing loss are *sensorineural,* in which the hair cells have been damaged (sometimes by loud noises, including listening to loud music and wearing headphones), and *conductive deafness,* caused by a ruptured eardrum or bone defect.

11 The sense of touch is really several different senses, which yield sensations of heat and cold, pressure, and pain. Some parts of the body are much more sensitive to touch than others, as measured by the *two-point discrimination threshold.* Pain serves an important function by signaling danger; it may occur through a "pain pathway." Certain sensory fibers respond only to pain, while others seem to signal pain along with other sensations. The brain produces *endorphins,* substances that reduce or eliminate pain. Fear, stress, and physical exertion often inhibit pain.

12 *The chemical senses:* Our taste receptors distinguish among four different sensations—sweet, salty, sour, and bitter. All tastes are described in terms of combinations of these qualities. Some taste preferences are learned, while others seem to be hereditary. What most people call "taste" is a global sensation that also includes the sense of smell. Odors come into the body as molecules in the air, either through the nostrils or from the back of the mouth, into smell receptors in the nasal cavity.

13 The sense of *proprioception* gives us information about the movement of our body parts and their position in space. The *vestibular system* is responsible for our sense of balance.

14 *Gestalt laws* emphasize the significance of overall patterns. These include the rules of continuity, proximity, similarity, and closure. Another Gestalt concept is the figure-ground relationship.

15 *Perceptual set* is the phenomenon by which we often see, hear, taste, smell, or touch what we expect to see.

16 *Perceptual constancy* is the awareness that objects and events in our environment remain the same even though they may look different because of varying conditions in the environment. Because we can make allowances for cues based on size,

texture, shape, brightness, and color constancy, we can maintain a stable view of the world.

17 We judge distance in two ways. *Binocular* cues, which depend on the vision of both eyes working together, are more accurate. These are based on the slightly different view of the world held by each eye. *Monocular* cues, which can be used with only one eye, include size, motion parallax, partial overlap, texture gradients, linear and atmospheric perspective, and shading.

18 *Illusions* are false perceptions, often caused by misleading context, as in the Ames, Muller-Lyer, and Ponzo illusions. We organize our sensations largely on what we've learned.

19 There appears to be a *critical period* in the development of vision. If certain kinds of vision do not occur at specific stages of development, normal adult functioning will not take place. This is so with regard to the ability to see in horizontal and vertical planes.

SUGGESTED READINGS

Coren, S., & Girgus, J. S. (1978). *Seeing is deceiving: The psychology of visual illusions*. Hillsdale, N.J.: Lawrence Erlbaum Associates. An extended treatment of visual illusions.

Cornsweet, T. N. (1970). *Visual perception*. New York: Academic Press. Sophisticated, clearly written description of vision.

Goldstein, E. B. (1980). *Sensation and perception*. Belmont, Calif.: Wadsworth. Well-written broad coverage on visual processes in general, especially perception.

Green, D. M. (1976). *An introduction to hearing*. Hillsdale, N.J.: Lawrence Erlbaum Associates. Well-written, thorough, and sophisticated coverage.

Spoehr, K. T., & Lehmkuhle, S. W. (1982). *Visual information processing*. San Francisco: W. H. Freeman. A good introduction to cognitive psychology, considering perception as a cognitive process, with coverage of topics such as pattern recognition, letter identification, reading, and other high-level processes.

CHAPTER 4

STATES OF CONSCIOUSNESS

SPOTLIGHT ON

How the ability to measure brain waves led to the discovery of different "stages" of sleep.

How meditation is being used to treat stress, hypertension, and other medical conditions.

The effectiveness of hypnosis in treating several medical conditions, despite the controversy over whether it is a unique state of consciousness.

The effects of a wide range of psychoactive drugs.

How aware are you right now? Chances are that you are not reading this book in your sleep, in a hypnotic spell, under the influence of drugs, or in a meditative trance but are, instead, in your normal waking state. What do we call this state? In psychological terms, you are in a *normal* state of consciousness as opposed to an *altered,* or *alternate,* state of consciousness, as you would be if you were in any of the other circumstances just mentioned.

In this chapter we'll discuss the normal state of consciousness, as well as such alternate states as sleep, meditation, hypnosis, and drug-induced states.

Consciousness is one of those concepts that seem straightforward but are surprisingly hard to define. Its very familiarity makes laypersons take it for granted and challenges psychologists to come up with precise descriptions. We need such descriptions to pin down the state well enough so that when you and I say "consciousness," we know we are both talking about the same state.

WHAT IS CONSCIOUSNESS?

The word itself (Latin: "knowing things together") was first used in the seventeenth century by Francis Bacon. Later in the century, John Locke defined it as "the perception of what passes in a man's own mind" (1690, p. 138). In the early nineteenth century, the new science of psychology was often referred to as the "science of consciousness."

The study of consciousness received a major setback in psychological circles when the behaviorists exerted their influence. In 1913, the year before he was elected president of the American Psychological Association, John B. Watson issued his behaviorist manifesto, in which he proclaimed, "The time has come when psychology must discard all reference to consciousness." Agreeing with Watson's proposition that psychology could be scientific only if it studied observable, measurable behaviors, most psychologists dropped the study of what goes on inside the human brain. Those who persisted in delving into thoughts and feelings tended to study them within a neurological and physiological framework rather than a psychological one. Not until the middle of the twentieth century did the study of consciousness again become respectable in psychological circles.

Today the emphasis on the study of this commonplace, yet elusive, phenomenon lies in defining it and describing its various levels, called either "alternate states" or "altered states." While there is no universally agreed-upon definition of "consciousness," we can adopt as a working definition: "our awareness of ourselves and of the world around us."

THE NORMAL STATE VERSUS ALTERED STATES OF CONSCIOUSNESS

Just as news reports do not point out the circumstances in daily life that proceed more or less normally but only those that disrupt the usual course of events, the study of consciousness has concentrated on altered states rather than the usual state. Before we go on to discuss these other levels, let's see how they differ from the normal condition.

Your normal state of consciousness is generally considered to be the one in which you spend most of your waking hours. Any qualitative change from your usual state is considered an alternative, or altered,

As part of their ritual, Turkish whirling dervishes spin furiously until they are in a euphoric trance state. (© Ira Friedlander/Woodfin Camp & Assoc.)

state. "Qualitative" is the key word since the difference has to be one of *kind*, not just of *degree*. It's not a question, for example, of your being more or less alert. You have to feel as if your mental processes are working in a different way from the way they usually function. You may be aware of mental functions that don't operate at all in your usual state, you may see or hear or feel things that normally you don't perceive, you may be more preoccupied than usual with your internal sensations or the way you think, you may actually think differently, and you may be out of touch with reality (Tart, 1969; Ludwig, 1966). Often you may be in a borderline state, as when you are in a semidoze, lying out in the hot sun, and you realize that you don't know whether you have been awake or asleep.

The concept of normality varies from one person to another. A musician may often hear melodies as she goes through her daily activities, while another person may hear a musical theme only under the influence of drugs. One person may be only dimly aware of time, another conscious of it almost to the minute. Individuals' senses about bodily sensations, visual images, and their surroundings vary considerably. Your normal state of consciousness is likely to differ from mine in countless ways.

Normality also differs among time frames, physical settings, and cultures. A normal state of consciousness to a cowboy in the American West of the nineteenth century was undoubtedly quite different from the normal state for a fourteenth-century Oriental priest. As Tart (1969) points out, "Many 'primitive' peoples believe that almost every normal adult has the ability to go into a trance state and be possessed by a god; the adult who cannot do this is a psychological cripple. How deficient Americans would seem to a person from such a culture" (p. 3).

Characteristics of Alternate and Altered States of Consciousness (ASCs)

We have all experienced changed states of consciousness when we have been asleep, dreaming, or sick with high fever. Some of us have also experienced the ASCs that come from meditation, hypnosis, and drugs. The first group comprises *alternate* states, while the second is made up of

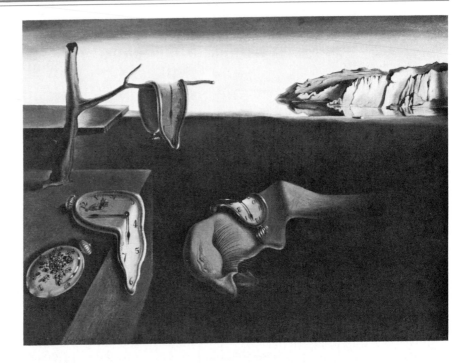

In his famous painting, The Persistence of Memory, *surrealist artist Salvador Dali projects a mood of an altered state of consciousness. He blends the actual (recognizable objects) with the imaginary (we have never seen watches like these!), creating images like those in dreams. The watches imply a sense of distorted time, commonly felt by people in an alternate state of consciousness. (Collection, The Museum of Modern Art, New York. Given anonymously.)*

what we consider *altered* states. These latter states do not occur spontaneously; they must be deliberately evoked. We'll look at both kinds of ASCs, all of which differ from each other, while some have characteristics in common, such as the following (Ludwig, 1966).

- *Alterations in thinking:* You experience varying degrees of change in concentrating, paying attention, remembering, and exercising judgment. You're not sure what is real and what isn't, and you get mixed up between cause and effect. Things that ordinarily seem inconsistent suddenly go unquestioned, as in a dream when one minute you are on a beach under a summer sun and the next minute are faced by mountainous snowdrifts.
- *Disturbed time sense:* You may feel that time is either standing still or moving very fast. Totally immersed in a creative activity, you may not realize that you have worked all day, until the darkening shadows let you know how many hours have elapsed.
- *Loss of control:* You may resist loss of control as you fight the onset of sleep. Or you may eagerly give up self-control as you try to go into a mystical state or onto a trip induced by a hallucinogenic drug. Sex therapists have found that one factor preventing some people from experiencing orgasm is their fear of losing control.
- *Change in emotional expression:* You may show your emotions much more freely, like the man who weeps copiously, laughs uproariously, or violently beats his wife only when he is drunk. Or you may become withdrawn, not showing any emotion at all, in a meditative state.
- *Body image change:* You may have a sense of being out of your body, feeling very heavy or very light, or feeling that certain body parts have shrunk or grown or become rubbery or rigid.

Ludwig (1966) has related his own experience, after having taken the drug LSD for experimental purposes:

Sometime during the height of the reaction, I remember experiencing an intense desire to urinate. Standing by the urinal, I noticed a sign above it which read "Please Flush After Using!" As I weighted (sic) these words in my mind, I suddenly realized their profound meaning. Thrilled by this startling revelation, I rushed back to my colleague to share this universal truth with him. Unfortunately, being a mere mortal, he could not appreciate the world-shaking import of my communication and responded by laughing!
(in Tart, 1969, p. 15)

Bringing on Altered States

- *Perceptual distortions:* You may see visions, hear voices or strange music, or feel you are perceiving things in a heightened way. Paintings done by people under the influence of drugs or in schizophrenic episodes generally show such distortions.
- *Change in meaning or significance:* You may have an "ah-ha!" experience in which you feel you have attained some exciting new insight. The dreamer, the meditator, the drunkard—all may feel as if they have finally hit upon the meaning of life. In all too many cases, however, once the state has passed, the insight has either withered away or become humdrum.
- *Sense of being indescribable:* "I can't explain it," you may say. While part of your problem may be a deficient vocabulary to describe experiences so far outside your ordinary realm, another may be an element of amnesia and another may be that your thinking processes were so dulled or different during the experience that you were not sufficiently aware of what was happening to you to be able to describe it.
- *Feelings of rejuvenation:* You may experience a sense of rebirth after emerging from certain kinds of ASCs such as very deep sleep, primitive puberty rites, and religious conversion.
- *Hypersuggestibility:* The hypnotic trance is, of course, the prime example of the degree to which a person in an altered state is apt to express beliefs and perform actions suggested by another person. However, you might be subjected to this in other circumstances, as well. Ludwig explains this suggestibility in terms of various attributes of the altered state including the loss of contact with reality, the diminished critical faculties, and the acceptance of contradictions.

The way you induce a particular altered state has a lot to do with the kind of state you want to induce, the kind of person you are yourself, and the circumstances around you. Methods of induction vary from overstimulation to the complete withdrawal of stimulation, as listed here (adapted from Ludwig, 1966):

- *Repetition, monotony, restricted movement:* Solitary confinement, trudging across unmarked snow-covered Arctic slopes, driving along miles of high-speed highway, immobilization after surgery
- *Barrage of stimulation, extensive activity:* "Third-degree" grilling, brainwashing, crowd influence as in a revivalist meeting or tribal ceremony, frenzied dancing, prolonged masturbation, long-distance running, emotional conflict
- *Mental concentration:* Praying, sentry duty, reading, writing, problem solving, listening to a charismatic speaker
- *Passivity:* Daydreaming, drowsiness, meditation, autohypnotism, soothing music, free association during psychoanalysis, muscular relaxation as in sunbathing
- *Physiological factors:* Changes in body chemistry brought about by drugs, dehydration, sleep deprivation, fasting, hyperventilation, fever, illness, withdrawal from addicting drugs

Now let's take a look at some of these alternate states, beginning with one that we all experience practically every day of our lives—sleep.

SLEEP

We can see the impact of technology on psychology when we look at what has happened in the growing field of sleep research. Until some thirty to fifty years ago, scientists had focused almost entirely on the waking state. This changed in 1929 with the invention of the electroencephalograph (EEG), the instrument that measures brain-wave activity, and then with the 1937 discovery by Loomis and his associates that certain stages of sleep were related to EEG states.

It was not, however, until the 1950s, in a series of studies conducted at the University of Chicago, that sleep research really took off. Eugene Aserinsky, a graduate student working with Nathaniel Kleitman, was studying the eye movements of sleeping infants. He noted times when the eyes moved very quickly in sleep, in patterns very similar to waking eye movements, and that these times were followed by periods of little or no eye movement. This discovery led to the distinction between REM (rapid eye movement) sleep and NREM (non-rapid eye movement) sleep, which show different brain-wave patterns, levels of breathing and heart rates, and dream patterns (Aserinsky & Kleitman, 1953). It also led to differentiation among four stages of NREM sleep. The two types of sleep (REM and NREM) and the stages within them show unique kinds of activity in many body processes, not just simple reduction of activity in all systems (Williams, Holloway, & Griffiths, 1973).

For most of what we have learned about sleep, we are indebted to volunteers who agree to spend varying numbers of nights in sleep laboratories, hooked up to such measuring devices as the electroencephalograph, which measures brain waves; the electromyograph, which measures muscle movements; and the electrooculograph, which measures eye movements.

Stages and Kinds of Sleep

An EEG tracing shows the *amplitude* of brain waves, the height of each wave when its voltage level is shown in pen movements on the page, and

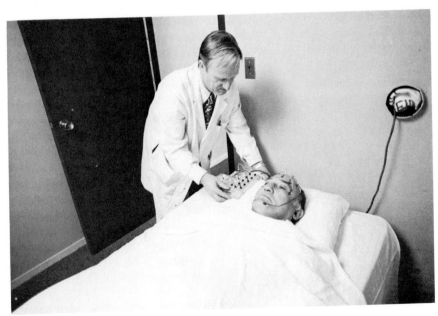

Many people have contributed to psychological research simply by going to sleep. Here at the Sleep-Wake Disorders Center at Montefiore Medical Center in New York, a researcher checks a machine that records a volunteer's breathing, brain waves, heart rate, and eye movements. (Courtesy of the Sleep-Wake Disorders Center, Montefiore Medical Center, The Bronx, New York.)

their *frequency*, the rate of up-and-down pen movements. When you are fully awake, an electroencephalogram (EEG) of your brain waves would show small, fast *beta* waves. Just before you fall asleep, when you are relaxed but still awake, your brain waves would show an *alpha* rhythm of larger, slower waves (8 to 12 cycles per second). Your eyes begin to close, your breathing and heart rates slow down, and your body temperature drops. (See Figure 4-1 for graphic depictions of these processes.)

STAGE 1   For just a few minutes after you fall asleep, you are in the stage of light sleep, when you can be awakened fairly easily. Your eyes move more slowly, beginning to roll from side to side. Your brain waves are 3 to 7 cycles per second, just a little slower than they were just before you fell asleep. Your breathing becomes irregular and your muscles relax.

STAGE 2   As you drift into a deeper sleep, either one of two brain-wave patterns that occur only in this stage will show up on your EEG. One, demonstrating short bursts of brain activity, is the *sleep spindle* (12 to 14 cycles per second, so-called because they look like thread wrapped around an old-fashioned sewing spindle, or spool). The other is a *K complex*, a low-frequency, high-amplitude wave that occurs in response to some stimulus—external like the ring of the telephone or internal like the pain of indigestion.

STAGE 3   As you sleep more deeply, your brain slows down even more as a *delta* rhythm, of 0.5 to 2 cycles per second, appears.

STAGE 4   When delta waves become more prominent, they signal your descent into the deepest sleep of all when you are very hard to arouse. If suddenly awakened, you may bolt upright, disoriented and confused. It will usually take you about half an hour to reach this point, and you will remain in this deep sleep for 30 to 40 minutes. You will then rise up through levels 3, 2, and 1 in a pattern that occurs in regular cycles of about 90 minutes throughout the night. At some point, you will emerge into a very different stage—REM sleep.

If you are a woman, your nipples may harden and your vagina is apt to swell during REM sleep. If you are a man, your penis is likely to become erect. This discovery has made it possible for sex therapists to determine whether a particular man's impotence has a physiological or emotional cause. If a man does not have erections during sleep, doctors look for a physical reason, but if his sleeping erections are normal, they look for psychological causes.

REM SLEEP   Here you are, about 40 to 80 minutes after you fell asleep: Your eyes, which had been quite still, suddenly dart around as if you are watching something. The breathing and heart rate that had been slow and regular speed up irregularly as your blood pressure rises. Your brain-wave tracings move back into a pattern very similar to the stage 1 EEG. In this stage, known as "emergent" stage 1, it is very hard to wake you up, as opposed to the initial stage 1 when it is very easy.

REM sleep is also known as "active" or "paradoxical" sleep because all the signs are so similar to the waking state even though you are clearly asleep. Another paradox is that even though there are so many signs of activity, the muscles are so relaxed that any movement is impossible. This is why sleepwalking never occurs during REM. Your first episode of REM sleep may last for only 2 to 5 minutes, while later episodes may last for as long as an hour. This is the time when you are most likely to dream.

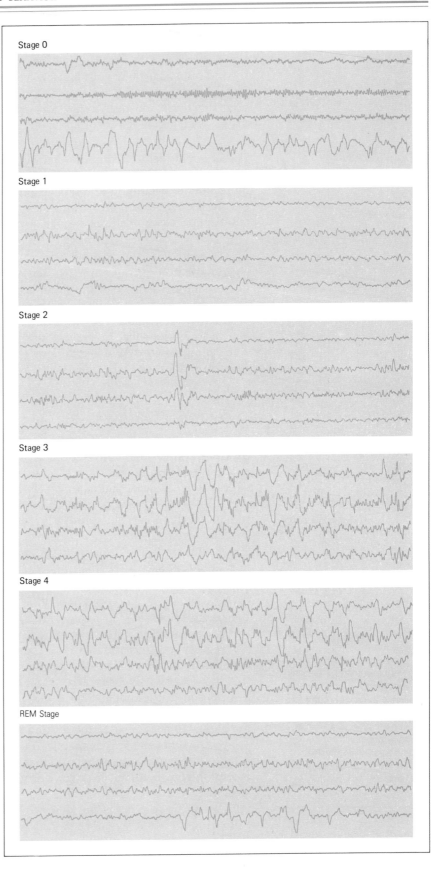

Stage 0

Stage 1

Stage 2

Stage 3

Stage 4

REM Stage

FIGURE 4-1 EEG Tracings of the Stages of Wakefulness and Sleep *Stage 0 is the awake stage. In Stages 1 through 4, sleep becomes progressively deeper. REM sleep, which is represented in the final tracing, is associated with dreaming. (From Webb, 1984)*

Characteristics of Sleep

Sleep is universal throughout the animal kingdom. Whether an animal sleeps a lot (like the bat, which sleeps about twenty hours a day) or a little (like the elephant, which sleeps from two to four hours a day), no animal can go without sleep. The lower animals seem to go through periods of REM and NREM sleep, just as human beings do.

The awareness of the brain's functioning during sleep has tantalized researchers and busy students with the possibility of learning during sleep. Wouldn't it be wonderful if you could turn on a cassette by your bed at night and wake up in the morning with a brain full of new knowledge! Unfortunately, however, "no study has been able to convincingly show an ability to learn complex verbal material during sleep" (Webb & Cartwright, 1978, p. 227). It looks as if we'll have to keep studying the old-fashioned way, awake.

CIRCADIAN RHYTHMS Plants, animals, and human beings operate by inner daily time clocks. These circadian (Latin for "about a day") rhythms govern the amount of sleep we need during a typical day. What if people didn't have to eat or sleep or be awake at any special time? An experiment in the early 1960s placed subjects in a windowless basement apartment with no clocks, no radio or TV, and nothing else to indicate the time of day or night (Aschoff & Wever, cited by Moore-Ede, 1982). The participants ate and slept whenever they wanted to. Through this study and others, we have learned that most human beings drift into a twenty-five-hour day.

Our body temperature also follows a twenty-five-hour pattern, fluctuating in a rhythm that correlates with our sleeping patterns. Most of us go to bed when our body temperature is falling and sleep for seven or eight hours. If our schedule changed so we went to bed when body temperature was at its peak, we would sleep much longer—for fifteen or sixteen hours. So the *time* we go to sleep, not how long we have been awake, seems to be more important in determining how long we will stay asleep.

This information has some very practical applications. One can be applied to diminishing jet lag on trips into other time zones. It's easier, for example, to adjust to new time zones on east-to-west trips, when we lengthen our day, than on west-to-east trips, when we shorten it.

Another important way to use this information is in planning work schedules for shift workers. Since it takes several days for an individual to adjust his or her circadian rhythms to a new schedule, it would make the most sense from the point of physiological functioning for people who work the night shift to continue on those shifts and not have to alternate between day (8 a.m. to 4 p.m.), swing (4 p.m. to midnight), and night (midnight to 8 a.m.) shifts, on a regular basis.

How to get around this constant need to change sleep-wake patterns? One way is to plan schedules so that workers go from earlier to later shifts. When workers who did this ("phase delay" system) were compared with those who went from a later shift to the preceding one ("phase advancing"), the phase delay workers were more productive and more satisfied, felt better, and were less likely to quit (Czeisler, Moore-Ede, & Coleman, 1982).

WHY WE SLEEP If we rest quietly in bed, eyes closed and muscles relaxed, will such rest do the same for our bodies that sleep does? Research says

The tendency for the human sleep-wake cycle to drift later each day by about an hour is a matter of common experience. During weekends, freed from the tyranny of alarm clocks or school or work schedules, most of us stay up later and sleep later. The result is that by Monday morning, our internal circadian systems have shifted two or three hours out of sync with solar time. Hence, when we get up on Monday morning at 7:00 and feel terrible, our body time may actually be 4:00 a.m.— thus accounting for the Monday morning blues.
(Moore-Ede, 1982, p. 32)

no. Rest alone cannot replace sleep loss (Webb & Cartwright, 1978). No one knows for sure why we sleep, even though sleep students have thought about and researched this puzzle. Most of the research has deprived people of sleep and then looked at the consequences. The results: People are surprisingly adaptable with regard to amount of sleep, but they cannot do without it totally for an unlimited period of time.

WHAT CAUSES SLEEP? Researchers have not yet learned exactly what cues our body into the awareness that sleep is necessary, but one recent discovery may provide some clues. When a "sleep-promoting substance" isolated from human urine was injected into the brains of rabbits, the rabbits showed a 50 percent increase in slow-wave sleep, a sleep that showed up under testing as normal. This sleep was similar to the deep, nondreaming state that occurs after animals who have been deprived of sleep are then allowed to sleep when they want (Krueger, Pappenheimer, & Karnovsky, 1982). Identification of a sleep-promoting factor could possibly help researchers to develop a safe, natural sleeping pill.

THE FUNCTION OF SLEEP What, then, does sleep do for us? Traditional wisdom has long believed in its ability to restore bodies and brains from the fatigue of daily activity. A recent study, which found an increase in slow-wave sleep and in total sleep time after running a 92-kilometer (57-mile) road race, seems to support this theory (Shapiro, Bortz, Mitchell, Bartel, & Jooste, 1981). Since sleep research has shown continual activity of one kind or another during sleep, however, this is probably not the whole story.

Another possibility is that we sleep not to *restore* our bodies after we get exhausted but to *prevent* exhaustion. If we're sleeping, we can't be doing all the other things that would tire us out.

Still another explanation is the evolutionary one advanced by Webb (1971) which proposes that we sleep because of ancient adaptive patterns that once ensured our survival. By curling up at night inside cozy caves, early humans were safe against predatory animals and other perils of the dark; those who slept at night survived and passed down their nocturnal sleeping patterns to their descendants. This theory explains the different schedule of sleep for different animals (those whose predators are up and about during the day sleep at night), but it doesn't, of course, answer the big question: Why do any of us sleep at all? So far, there is no answer.

THE FUNCTION OF REM SLEEP To find out whether REM sleep has special value, psychiatrist William Dement (1960) conducted experiments in which he awakened subjects each time they entered REM sleep and then let them go back to sleep. Over a period of three to seven nights, this procedure reduced REM sleep by about 75 percent. After this time, the same procedure was followed for NREM sleep. Those sleepers who had been awakened during REM became more anxious and irritable and had trouble concentrating. They caught up on their lost REM periods by showing more REM sleep on the "recovery night," the first night when they could sleep without being interrupted.

After reviewing some eighty studies of human beings and animals, however, Webb (1975) concluded that while REM is hard to suppress and insists on making up for its absence, it cannot be linked to any particular psychological function.

SLEEP DEPRIVATION   What happens when animals and people are not allowed to sleep at all for various periods of time? Relatively little of a physiological nature. Human beings often develop hand tremors, double vision, droopy eyelids, and a lower pain threshold after five to ten sleepless days, and animals often lose a lot of weight, possibly because of the stress the animal is under to stay awake and the total disruption of the body's biorhythms (Webb, 1975).

What about the ability to function? Here, too, while there are symptoms, they are not so severe as we might have supposed. People who have gone without sleep for as long as three nights can still carry out most tasks fairly well. They will have the most trouble with tasks that take a long time to do; that are difficult or complex, requiring several different operations; that must be finished in a short period of time; that use recently acquired skills; that require new short-term learning; and those for which they don't receive any feedback as to how well they are doing (Webb & Bonnet, 1979).

Sleep loss shows up in several other ways, too. After being deprived of sleep, you can't pay attention to the task at hand, you can't follow simple routine, you're less vigilant, and you don't bother to do things you know you *should* do. Soldiers who don't get enough sleep can still hit a target as well as ever, but they don't do the extras: Israeli soldiers on war games fail to keep their water canteens filled, a necessity for desert warfare, and English soldiers don't change their wet socks, running the risk of frostbite. If you're hospitalized, you can be fairly confident that a tired night nurse will give you the right drugs, but she may not walk down the hall to check on you (Webb, in Coleman, 1982).

People totally deprived of sleep do get confused and disoriented and become irritable, but their personality is likely to remain intact. They do show an overwhelming need to sleep and struggle hard to fight this need. Few human beings, however, can match the ingenuity of one experimental rat, kept from sleep by a cage floor made up of a slowly rotating wheel surrounded by water:

> He managed to climb to the top of his chamber, up smooth steel walls, and hook his teeth into a meshed wire covering the chamber. There he was found sleeping while suspended by his teeth! (Webb, 1975, p. 121)

This research seems to contradict the common feelings most of us have when we have slept too little the night before. The reason we don't feel well after not sleeping well or enough may have more to do with factors other than the actual loss of sleep itself—the stress we are under that prevented our sleeping in the first place or the energy we are expending by doing whatever we are doing when we are not sleeping, whether it's working, playing, or worrying (Webb, 1975).

So does all of this mean that sleep isn't that important after all? Not at all. Even though little or no physical or psychological damage seems to result from loss of sleep itself, such deprivation does, of course, have other effects. Real damage can occur when the driver of a car or the

As Lord Chesterfield wrote to his son, "A light supper, a good night's sleep, and a fine morning have sometimes made a hero of the same man who, by an indigestion, a restless night, and a rainy morning would have proved a coward." (1748)

BOX 4-1

SLEEP THROUGHOUT THE LIFE CYCLE

The next time you say, "I slept like a baby," remember that new babies usually wake up every two to three hours around the clock. Fortunately for all concerned (especially their parents), this pattern soon changes. Sleep is a dynamic system, whose patterns keep changing throughout life.

INFANCY

Newborn babies sleep an average of 16.3 hours every day, with one healthy baby sleeping as little as 11 hours and another as much as $21\frac{1}{2}$ (Parmalee, Wenner, & Schulz, 1964). They start to sleep through the night at varying times, and by 6 months, more than half their sleep takes place at night (Moore & Ucko, 1957). Newborns have about six to eight sleep periods, which alternate between quiet and active sleep. Active sleep, probably the equivalent of the REM sleep of maturity, appears rhythmically in cycles of about one hour, and accounts for 50 to 80 percent of the newborn's total sleep. Over the first six months REM sleep diminishes in both total time and percentage of sleep time (now accounting for only 30 percent), and cycle lengths become more consistent (Coons & Guilleminault, 1982).

CHILDHOOD

In early childhood the average amount of sleep declines, with wide individual differences. Preschoolers tend to sleep through the night with one daytime nap, and between the ages of 6 to 16 sleep drops from eleven to eight hours. By age 5, REM sleep accounts for only a little over two hours (Webb & Bonnet, 1979). Stage 4 sleep is at its highest in early childhood, with 100-plus minutes seen in the 2-year-old.

ADOLESCENCE

Teenagers are less likely to wake up spontaneously in the morning and are apt to sleep later and take afternoon naps, possibly due to a chronic lack of sleep associated with contemporary lifestyles (Anders, Carskadon, & Dement, 1980).

ADULTHOOD

We know the most about the sleep habits of 18- to 22-year-old college students, the group that provides the largest pool of research volunteers. On average, they take from 5 to 15 minutes to fall asleep, awaken only once every other night, and stay awake for less than 5 minutes. No sex differences show up, and both sexes average between seven and eight hours at night (ranging from about six to ten hours), with great variability from day to day. While they go to bed at varying times, they tend to have more regular times for awakening. They spend the most time—about half the night—in stage 2 and about one-fourth the night in REM sleep. The first REM period (5 to 10 minutes) is the shortest, with later ones getting progressively longer, up to an hour in length. Almost all stage 4 sleep occurs in the first four hours after falling asleep.

Sleep patterns undergo major changes for most people between early adulthood and late middle age. By age 60, people who used to wake up once during the night are now waking up six times, and their sleep is much lighter than it used to be. Women's sleep patterns do not change as dramatically as do those of men and resemble the sleep of men ten years younger (Webb, 1975, 1982).

operator of heavy machinery succumbs to a need for sleep and either goes off the road or gets a limb caught in the machine.

Sleep patterns vary among individuals along a number of dimensions. While little of the research is conclusive, it raises interesting questions.

What Is Your Sleep Personality Profile?

HOW LONG DO YOU SLEEP?   Do you regularly sleep less than six hours a night, not because you have insomnia but because this is all the sleep you need? Or do you usually sleep more than nine hours? Does either pattern say anything about your personality? It depends on which study you read.

When Webb and Friel (1971) compared fifty-four 17- and 18-year-old first-year college students, they found no significant differences between short and long sleepers in scores on personality or aptitude tests or in physical examinations. However, when Hartmann, Baekeland, and Zwilling (1972) conducted the same kind of study with twenty-nine men over age 20, they came up with two different personalities: *Short sleepers* tend to be energetic, efficient, outgoing people who are satisfied with themselves and their lives, rarely complain, and are somewhat conforming, socially and politically. They handle stress by keeping busy and denying it. *Long sleepers* are depressed, anxious worriers—nonconformist, critical, and unsure of themselves. They dream more than short sleepers and are more likely to be artistic and creative.

Although clinical observations suggest that short sleepers are "high-drive" people and long sleepers are "down" and "depressed," Webb (1979) maintains that the research to date has not demonstrated this difference. It's possible that more sophisticated kinds of tests would identify differences more consistently, but at the moment we just don't know.

DO YOU NEED MORE SLEEP AT CERTAIN TIMES IN YOUR LIFE?   About one out of three people are *variable sleepers* whose sleep needs change for weeks at a time at different periods of their lives (Hartmann & Brewer, 1976). If you need less sleep when things in your life are going well and more when you change jobs or schools, when depressed or under stress (especially after the death of a family member or the end of a love affair), or when you have to expend more mental activity, you are a variable sleeper. Physical factors also play a part since both pregnancy and illness require extra sleep. Since these findings mirror, within individuals, the differences between long and short sleepers and since it's the need for REM sleep that seems to change, these findings seem to show that REM sleep may help to restore psychic equilibrium at times of stress and upheaval.

HOW WELL DO YOU SLEEP?   Are you a "good" sleeper who falls asleep in 10 minutes, doesn't wake up during the night, and doesn't feel troubled about either falling asleep or staying asleep? Or a "poor" sleeper who takes an hour or more to fall asleep and wakes up at least once each night? Sleepers who described themselves in these two ways went into a sleep lab for two nights. Scientific measures confirmed the self-ratings, and personality tests found more emotional problems among the poor sleepers. The more disturbed the sleepers, the higher their REM time, possibly indicating that REM does help to alleviate emotional stress (Monroe, 1967).

HOW SOUNDLY DO YOU SLEEP?   Are you the kind of heavy sleeper who sleeps through thunderstorms, slammed doors, and the sudden flooding of a room with light? Or a light sleeper who is awakened by a whisper or a light seeping into the room through a closed door? Most people stay in the same classification from one night to another (Zimmerman, 1970). Both light and heavy sleepers awakened during REM sleep report about the same number of dreams, but when sleepers have been awakened from NREM sleep, light sleepers are much more likely to report having been dreaming and heavy sleepers more likely to report drifting kinds of thoughts such as those in daydreams.

Even if you are ordinarily a heavy sleeper, a stimulus with special meaning for you—someone's whispering your name in your ear or the sound of an expected friend tapping lightly on your door—may rouse you, confirming the continuing activity of your brain even during the deepest stages of sleep.

DREAMING

Dreams assumed an important, if mysterious, place in people's lives long before the Bible reported Joseph's prophetic interpretation of the pharaoh's dreams of lean and fat cattle. Some 4000 years later, Sigmund Freud, recognizing that dreams came not from divine forces but from the dreamer's own mind, drew from them clues to the workings of the unconscious. But not until the middle of this century have dreams become accessible to scientific research. Technology again: Until outside observers could tell when someone was dreaming, the only person who could discuss a dream was the dreamer himself. Once scientists had made the connection between REM sleep and dreaming and had the tools to tell when a dream was occurring, they could begin to solve some of the puzzles locked in our dreams.

What *is* a dream? A dream is a mental experience that occurs during sleep, consisting of a series of vivid, usually visual and often hallucinatory images. In our dreams we jump bizarrely from one time and place to another, among people who may be dead, fictional, or unknown. The strangest part is that, when we are dreaming, we accept such bizarre happenings without question.

How do researchers know when someone is dreaming? Four criteria have evolved:

- *An increase in pulse and breathing rates.*
- *The typical brain-wave EEG of an emergent stage 1 pattern:* This sign during REM sleep is most reliably associated with dreaming. Although some sleepers awakened during NREM sleep report having been dreaming, their dreams are usually much shorter, less distinct, and more like waking thoughts than like typical dream images.
- *The lack of body movement:* That terrifying sensation of being frozen to the spot while someone is chasing you or of opening your mouth to scream but being unable to utter a sound may have a basis in the reality that in fact we are unable to move our muscles while we are dreaming. This "dreamer's paralysis" may be due to a brain chemical that inhibits the motoneurons that ordinarily cause our muscles to contract (Chase, 1981). If such inhibition did not occur, we might act out our dreams and wouldn't get the rest that sleep provides. Furthermore, since our sense of judgment is suspended when we dream, we might get ourselves into dangerous situations.
- *The appearance of rapid eye movements:* Earlier dream researchers thought that the movements that can be seen under the closed eyelids of a sleeper were related to the action in the dream. The typical side-to-side

movements indicated that you were looking at the scene in your dream; vertical movements were thought to occur in those dreams where the action was up and down. Newer evidence, however, indicates that eye movements are probably unrelated to dream content. Cats raised in the dark, which have never seen anything, still show eye movement during sleep, as do adults who have been blind for as long as fifty-five years and who "hear" their dreams rather than "see" them (Webb & Bonnet, 1979).

Patterns of Dreaming

After monitoring the sleep of thousands of volunteers, dream researchers have come up with answers to some of the most common questions about dreaming.

- *What is a typical night of dreaming like?* Your first dream, occurring after about an hour of sleep, will last from less than 1 minute to up to about 10 minutes. You'll have a total of five or six periods of dreaming throughout the night, lasting from about 10 to 35 minutes, for a total of one to two hours of dream time.
- *Is is possible that I never dream?* All subjects in dream laboratories have "reported dreaming upon being awakened at appropriate times" (Kleitman, 1960, p. 241). Everyone seems to dream every night, but some people remember dreams more clearly.
- *Why don't I remember my dreams?* Most people don't remember most of their dreams. Freud (1900) attributed this forgetting to the repression of anxiety-laden thoughts. Hobson and McCarley (1977) refer, instead, to a "state-dependent amnesia." In other words, when we're awake and alert we don't remember experiences that occurred in another state, like sleep—unless we're barely out of the state, as when we're awakened immediately after dreaming. When this does happen, we do remember our dreams, even the very emotional ones, indicating that forgetting may have a physiological, state-related basis.

A new explanation for the forgetting of dreams has just been proposed—that dreams are *meant* to be forgotten. The very purpose of REM dreaming, say Crick and Mitchison (1983), is to clear our brains of unnecessary information so we won't be troubled by obsessions and hallucinations during our waking hours. They maintain that the brain has a "reverse learning mechanism," triggered by the intense electrical activity in the cortex that occurs during REM sleep, which erases various random memory associations that have formed during the day. This helps the cortex to work better and helps prevent the recurrence of dreams. (Those dreams that do recur are, they say, the ones that have tended to awaken us, possibly because they are anxiety-producing.)

Probably the full explanation for why we forget most of our dreams is a combination of psychology and physiology. Some people seem to forget emotional dreams because they repress anxious thoughts in waking life, also, and others forget unemotional dreams because they're not memorable (Koulack & Goodenough, 1976). It *is* harder to remember a dream if you were under stress before falling asleep (Goodenough, 1967; Koulack, 1970). The dream we do remember tends to be the one dreamed most recently, just before awakening; this dream also tends to be the longest, most vivid, and most emotional one of the night. When we remember an earlier dream, it may be because we awakened at that point either because of the dream itself or for some other reason, or it may be because we've had this same dream before. The dreams we remember are probably not typical of most of our dreams (Cartwright, 1977).

- *How much time do my dreams really take?* The notion that a long and complicated dream actually takes place in the space of a moment may owe its origin to the report given by the French writer André Maury, who ascribed a long and complicated dream about being guillotined during the French Revolution to the fact that the top of his bed had fallen upon the back of his neck, just where the guillotine blade would have struck (1861). Laboratory research, however, has determined that dreams take varying amounts of time and that sleepers awakened either 5 to 15 minutes after REM onset correctly estimate the length of their dreams as either 5 to 15 minutes long. People seem to tell dream time fairly accurately (Webb & Bonnet, 1979).
- *Do objective aspects of my environment during sleep affect the content of my dreams?* Very rarely, despite André Maury's experience. When a bell rang in the sleep lab, a ringing bell showed up in only 20 out of 204 dreams and only 5 out of 15 dreams told by sleepers who had gone without fluids for twenty-four hours contained any content related to thirst (Kleitman, 1960). There is, however, some carryover from the waking environment into dreams. Studies of subjects who during their waking hours wore goggles that gave everything they saw a reddish tint had more dreams with the color red or with colors near red on the spectrum than they did when they didn't wear the red goggles (Roffwarg, Herman, Bowe-Anders, & Tauber, 1976).

Content of Dreams

Where do the "stories" of our dreams come from? Most of them appear as a montage of the day's events in somewhat altered form. Based on some 10,000 dreams reported by normal people, Calvin Hall (1966) found that most dreams are commonplace. They are most often played out in familiar settings, such as a house, although the house is usually not the dreamer's own home. The most popular room is the living room, followed by—in order—bedroom, kitchen, stairway, basement, bathroom, dining room, and hall. The room is often a composite of several rooms the dreamer has known. Women's dreams more commonly take place indoors, men's out-of-doors.

Only 15 out of 100 dreams show the dreamer alone. We dream most often about the people we're emotionally involved with—our parents, spouses, and children. Men dream more often about male friends and acquaintances, while women dream of both sexes equally. About 4 out of 10 dream characters are strangers. What do we do? Mostly, ordinary everyday activities, more often related to leisure than to work. We walk, run, or ride, rather than float or fly. Most dreams have negative tones, with apprehension the most common emotion and hostile acts more than twice as common as friendly ones.

Why We Dream

An activity all of us engage in every night must be serving an important function. For clues to the purpose of dreaming, let's look at some of the possible explanations.

TO FULFILL WISHES AND GUARD SLEEP   Freud placed great importance on the function of dreams, calling them "the royal road to the unconscious." He felt that their *psychological* purpose was to let us express the wishes we repress during our waking lives. At the same time, they serve the *biological* function of acting as the "guardians" of sleep. When we move into REM sleep, we seem to be trying to wake up, perhaps because our emotional conflicts are insisting on surfacing. If we can deal with these conflicts in dreams, we can sleep.

Freud called the part of our dreams that we remember the *manifest content*. These events express through symbolism what is really behind the dream, the *latent content*, or *dream-thoughts*, the desires and conflicts we have repressed, most of which are sexual. The individual dreamer transforms latent content into manifest content by *dream-work* that uses symbols and other kinds of psychological shorthand to make his or her deepest desires more acceptable. Freudians might interpret a young man's dream of walking up the steps to his mother's house, carrying his open umbrella, as a dream of making love to his mother because of such symbols as a long object for the penis (with the opening of the umbrella a symbol for an erection), an enclosed place (the house) for the vagina; and the activity of walking up stairs for the act of sexual intercourse.

Modern-day interpreters of dreams recognize their symbolism but are more likely to interpret symbols in a variety of ways depending on an

In this scene from the movie, Who Is Harry Kellerman and Why Is He Saying Those Terrible Things About Me?, *Dustin Hoffman dreams he is running in an endless tunnel. A psychoanalyst would interpret the meaning of this dream differently from a cognitive psychologist. (Museum of Modern Art/Film Stills Archive)*

individual's unique situation rather than limiting them to sexual meaning. "For different persons, boarding a train may either represent a flight from a problem, engaging in a new adventure, worry about car repairs, or, simply, a concern about making a plane reservation for an upcoming trip" (Webb, 1975, p. 149). The manifest content may not be standing for something else in the dreamer's past but may, in fact, show a straightforward picture of present concerns (Foulkes, 1964).

TO RESOLVE PERSONAL ISSUES AND SOLVE EVERYDAY PROBLEMS   Alfred Adler (1936) called dreams "the factory of the emotions." Their job in this factory is to awaken the dreamer's emotions so that she or he will be pushed into solving real-life problems in a realistic way. The dreamer's problems are not repressed in the Freudian sense but are issues the dreamer is well aware of and wants to resolve. Thus, there is a continuity of thought during waking and sleep.

C. G. Jung (1933) felt that dreams help us learn about ignored or suppressed aspects of ourselves. The unconscious is an instrument of self-discovery, not a repository of uncomfortable forces. Dreams provide the images that compensate for any psychic imbalance in our waking lives and help us plan our future. Jung feels it's not necessary to look for a hidden meaning in a dream—that the manifest content will give us its personal significance.

We seem to use dreams to dispel the anxiety around experiences, often by "rehearsing" things we will have to do. People commonly dream about going away to college, taking a trip, working at a new job, getting married, and having a baby just before all these events. "Dreams are often safe experiments to prepare the way for coping with a future which may be anxiety provoking" (Cartwright, 1978, p. 28).

TO MAINTAIN SLEEP IN THE FACE OF PHYSIOLOGICAL ACTIVATION OF THE BRAIN   Hobson and McCarley (1977) explain the purpose of dreaming by describing its origins in basic physiological processes. The bizarre shifts and symbols of dreams may not be the product of disguised unconscious thoughts but the logical results of the way the brain functions during sleep. The brain creates its own electrical energy, and the forebrain becomes especially active during REM sleep. Rapid bursts of electrical activity in different parts of the brain determine what we dream about and how we put dream images together. The largely random or reflex process by which the various parts of the brain are stimulated accounts for illogical shifts in time, place, and other dream elements. Since such stimulation brings forth incomplete information, the brain tries to fill in with other material culled from memory, becoming like "a computer searching its addresses for key words" (p. 1347). This explanation looks to dreaming as a cognitive process that may give us clues to the learning process and virtually ignores the psychological ramifications of dreams, lending no particular significance to the events and people we dream about and to our emotions about them.

Finally, then, we don't have conclusive research evidence to explain why we dream. The quest for this evidence continues.

SLEEP DISORDERS

Whether it's sleeping too little, sleeping too much, or doing things during sleep that we'd rather not do, a variety of sleep disorders affect people throughout the life cycle.

Narcolepsy

Narcolepsy, an uncontrollable need to sleep for brief periods, usually during the day, accompanied by loss of muscle tone and sometimes hallucinations, generally shows up for the first time between ages 10 and 25, affects between 2 and 10 people in 10,000—some 250,000 people in the United States—and may last throughout life (Fenton, 1975; Dement & Baird, 1977). Some three to four hours after waking up, the narcoleptic feels overpoweringly sleepy and often does fall asleep while talking, standing, or even moving about. He may go into many episodes of microsleep lasting 5 to 15 seconds and eventually has to take a nap. Narcolepsy is not associated with any kind of emotional disorder, yields normal EEGs, runs in families, and may be a genetic disturbance of the mechanism that regulates REM sleep. Treatment so far is inadequate, relying on frequent napping and sometimes stimulant or antidepressant drugs.

Insomnia

Some 20 to 25 million Americans, 14 percent of the population, spend countless anxious hours tossing and turning in bed, trying to go to sleep, at bedtime (the biggest problem for eight out of ten insomniacs) or after awakening during the night or very early morning (U.S. Department of Health and Human Services, 1980). What causes an inability to sleep? Virtually everything, ranging through poor health, high stress, an irregular lifestyle, inadequate nutrition, drug ingestion, and emotional prob-

As this narcoleptic dog shows, nonhuman animals, too, sometimes experience an uncontrollable need to sleep. (Courtesy of Dr. William Dement, Sleep Disorders Center, Stanford University)

lems. Most people go through occasional periods of insomnia, but for the majority normal sleeping patterns soon return.

What about the minority? Will sleeping pills help? By and large, only under restricted, medically supervised conditions. Over-the-counter drugs do no more good than sugar pills and are only as effective as people's faith that they will help (Webb & Bonnet, 1979). Overdoses, taken in a vain effort to strengthen their effect, can be harmful. Medically prescribed barbiturates do help people fall asleep, sleep soundly, and stay asleep, but the problem with them is that people usually develop tolerance and require larger and larger doses. When dosage goes up, the person is likely to be groggy in the morning. At this point he will often take amphetamines, and the combined dependence on two kinds of drugs creates a problem far worse than the original sleep problem (Webb & Bonnet, 1979).

There is no simple cure for a complicated complaint with so many causes, but sleep researchers have come up with common-sense measures that have helped many. For suggestions on sleeping better, see Box 4-2.

Sleep Apnea

Earlier called the Pickwickian syndrome (after the fat messenger boy, Joe, in Charles Dickens' *The Pickwick Papers,* who fell asleep while knocking on a door), this disorder is characterized by loud snoring, poor sleep at night, extreme daytime sleepiness, and brief periods when breathing stops during sleep (Brouillette, Fernbach, & Hunt, 1982; Anders et al., 1980). The syndrome may affect intellectual functioning, possibly because the flow of oxygen to the brain is continually interrupted, accounting for a report that some 35 percent of affected children were diagnosed as borderline mentally retarded (Guilleminault, Eldridge, & Simmons, 1976). Many patients are obese men over age 40 whose airways may be obstructed by thick necks, previous surgery, or a jaw deformity. Treatment may include a *tracheostomy* (a surgical opening of the windpipe) that functions during the night and is closed off during the day; major weight loss; and drugs (Orr, Martin, & Patterson, 1979; Anders et al., 1980; Parkes, 1977; Cherniack, 1981).

Night Terrors (Pavor Nocturnus)

Night terrors and nightmares, which are very different, both begin to appear in early childhood, with about one in four children between ages 3 and 8 suffering from one or the other (Hartmann, 1981). In a night terror the sleeper awakens abruptly in a state of panic, usually within an hour of falling asleep. He may scream and sit up in bed, while breathing quickly and staring unseeingly ahead. He isn't aware of any scary dreams or thoughts, he goes back to sleep quickly, and in the morning he won't remember awakening. These episodes usually go away by themselves, don't signal underlying emotional problems, and probably occur as an effect of sudden awakening from very deep sleep. They may be a mild neurological disorder, which sets off an electrical discharge like a minor epileptic seizure.

Nightmares

Unlike night terrors, nightmares come toward the morning and are often vividly recalled. Persistent nightmares, especially those that make a child

BOX 4-2

SUGGESTIONS FOR POOR SLEEPERS

The following dos and don'ts offered by sleep experts may help you get to sleep and stay asleep.

- Follow a regular schedule: Go to sleep and get up at about the same times every day, even on weekends.
- Do some exercise every day, fairly early in the day.
- Do not eat or drink anything containing caffeine after midday. This includes coffee, tea, cola drinks, and chocolate.
- Develop a relaxing before-bed routine. Avoid stimulating work or play, family arguments, high-stress activities. Do whatever relaxes you—take a hot bath, read, watch TV, listen to music.
- Eat or drink something before bedtime. Grandma's old remedy of hot milk has now

achieved scientific validity. An ingredient found in certain foods, including milk and such carbohydrates as sweets, bread, pasta, and rice, has been found to induce sleep. The substance *tryptophan* is an amino acid that turns into the neurotransmitter *serotonin*.

- Do not drink a large quantity of beer, wine, or whiskey before you go to bed. They may help you *fall* asleep but will interfere with your *staying* asleep. When the sedative effects of the alcohol wear off, you're likely to wake up.
- Get into bed only when you plan to go to sleep. Using your bed as a center for working, studying, paying bills, talking on the telephone, and watching TV detracts from the association between getting

into bed and falling asleep.
- Sleep in the dark. Get room-darkening window shades or blinds or wear sleep goggles.
- Sleep in quiet. If you can't (or don't want to) kick out your snoring roommate, get earplugs. Get an electrical "white noise" machine to block out outside noises.
- Don't worry about *not* sleeping. The more you worry about how tired you'll be the next day, the harder it will be for you to go to sleep. Remember that human beings are flexible and can function quite well on little sleep, and then get up and do something relaxing (like reading a dull book, unlike this one) until you start to feel sleepy.

fearful and anxious during waking hours, may be a signal that a child is under too much stress. Repetitive themes often indicate a specific problem that a person cannot solve when awake and that, consequently, comes to the fore during sleep. (Hartmann, 1981).

Sleepwalking and Sleep Talking

Some 15 percent of all children between ages 5 and 12 sleepwalk at least once, and some 1 to 6 percent do it regularly (Anders et al., 1980). As in a night terror, the sleepwalking child will typically sit up abruptly, with her eyes wide open. She'll get out of bed and move about so clumsily that she needs to be protected from hurting herself. Her surroundings should be "sleepwalk-proofed," with gates at the top of stairs and in front of windows, but nothing else needs to be done since she will probably outgrow this tendency. Talking during sleep is also purposeless (and not in need of any corrective action.) It's usually difficult, if not impossible, to understand what the child is saying, and, contrary to popular belief, next to impossible to engage him in conversation.

In the rest of this chapter, we'll consider some of the less common states of consciousness—the altered states, which do not typically occur spontaneously but must be deliberately evoked.

MEDITATION

In our battery of survival mechanisms, the "fight-or-flight" reaction is one of the most powerful. This arsenal of responses (described in detail in Chapter 10), which equips us to react to perceived danger, includes increases in heart and breathing rates, blood pressure, blood flow to the muscles, and oxygen consumption. When we were beset by wild animals and hostile tribes on all sides, we needed the hyperalertness such responses brought. In most situations in contemporary life, however, our health and survival might be better served by a state in which we take in less oxygen, release less carbon dioxide, breathe more slowly, and have a slower pulse rate. This is the state induced by meditation (Wallace & Benson, 1972).

There is not, however, a single, unique, easily described meditative state. Despite considerable research on meditation over the past twenty years, this phenomenon retains an aura of mysticism. Some researchers describe it as a state of relaxed wakefulness in which bodily processes are slowed down (Wallace & Benson, 1972), while others note that the body processes of *experienced* meditators show a great deal of activity, possibly reflecting the intensity of their concentration (Corby, Roth, Zarcone, & Kopell, 1978), and still others have found that the EEGs of meditators show much time spent in actual sleep in stages 2, 3, and 4 (Pagano, Rose, Stivers, & Warrenburg, 1976). At present, then, the meditative state defies precise definition.

We do know that people can often do things in this state that they are ordinarily not capable of, such as controlling such autonomic systems as skin resistance to electricity, heart and breathing rates, and reflex reactions to heat, cold, and pain. Tibetan monks are said to be able to raise the

While meditating, we take in less oxygen, release less carbon dioxide, and our breathing and pulse rates are slower. Such a state may have benefits in our hypertense contemporary world. (Peter Vandermark/Stock, Boston)

temperature in their fingers and toes by almost 150 degrees Fahrenheit and increase body heat enough to dry wet sheets wrapped around them (*San Francisco Chronicle*, 1982).

People get into the meditative state in a variety of ways. They may whirl or dance, or sit still and concentrate on a nonsensical question, look at or imagine looking at an object, or repeat a prayer, a word, or a chant. The technique best known in the West is the easily learned transcendental meditation (TM) developed by Maharishi Mahesh Yogi. TM consists of two daily sessions of 15 to 30 minutes each and is practiced by some one-half to 2 million people worldwide (Benson, 1975). The meditator sits in any comfortable position, closes his or her eyes, and thinks of his mantra, a specific word or thought that has been given especially to him and is not publicly revealed. The purpose of repeating the mantra is to prevent distracting thoughts.

Regular periods of meditation help many people to deal with stress. It has been used in various therapeutic programs to reduce insomnia, to cut back the use of alcohol, tobacco, and other drugs, and to reduce the pain of angina pectoris, a frequent complication of heart disease (Kanellakos, 1978). It has also been helpful in reducing blood pressure in hypertensive patients *as long as the patients meditate regularly.* The initial high blood pressure returns within four weeks if they stop meditating (Benson, 1975). Meditation is also used to create a new positive condition, in addition to overcoming negative ones. After taking, through meditation, a "vacation" from ordinary awareness, meditators return to full, conscious awareness even more alive to the sights and sounds around them that had faded into the backgrounds of awareness simply from being taken for granted. This freshness of perception gives many meditators the sense of being reborn.

HYPNOSIS

A woman bites into a lemon and raves about the sweetness of the "peach." An old man talks in the babyish lilt of a 3-year-old as he expresses his feelings upon his father's death. A witness to a fire describes a suspicious-looking man on the scene whose features are dim in her conscious memory but seem clear to her now. All these people are demonstrating the power and lure of the little understood phenomenon of hypnosis. Let's explore its mysteries.

Being hypnotized means you will fall asleep, lose touch with your surroundings, be able to remember details buried from conscious memory, do whatever the hypnotist tells you to do, and forget whatever you did under the hypnotic spell when you wake up. Right? Wrong.

What Is Hypnosis?

The hypnotic state is very different from the sleeping state, and there is much disagreement about whether the hypnotic state can accurately be called a "trance." It has been difficult to identify physiological differences between hypnotized and unhypnotized people in terms of brain-wave patterns, eye movements, pulse or breathing rates, or galvanic skin response. But recent research does show that highly hypnotizable subjects change from left-hemisphere to right-hemisphere dominance as they go into hypnosis (MacLeod-Morgan, 1982).

The definition of hypnosis is controversial, often depending on such

The hypnotized person is in a state of heightened suggestibility, leading this woman to follow the commands of the hypnotist. Someday her ability to be hypnotized may help her manage pain or kick a habit. (© Ken Robert Buck 1981/The Picture Cube)

elusive reports as what the hypnotist or the hypnotized person does or on the subject's own report of how she or he feels, criteria that are unsatisfactory by scientific standards. Hypnotized people see this state as different from their normal state. They feel more susceptible to outside influence and less able to tell what is real and what isn't; they fantasize more and experience changes in body image (Crawford, 1982). Such self-reports are, of course, highly subjective, with no way of being confirmed. This problem of definition is so thorny that some scientists say the hypnotic state doesn't exist at all.

We believe that there is such a thing as the hypnotic state, that it is different from the normal state of consciousness, and that some day we may have the tools to define it—as we now have the criterion of rapid eye movements to define, more or less, the state of dreaming. We define "hypnosis" as a procedure practiced by a person with special skills who is able to induce in a subject a condition of heightened suggestibility in which the subject's perceptions have changed along lines suggested by the practitioner. Some common behaviors observed among hypnotized people are rigidity of the arm, loss of voluntary control, hallucinations, failure to feel pain, amnesia, and responsiveness to posthypnotic suggestion (performing an action *after* coming out of the hypnotic state in response to a suggestion made *during* hypnosis) (Hilgard, 1977).

Who Gets Hypnotized?

As much as you might like to become hypnotized, you may never be able to. You may be among that 5 or 10 percent of the population who cannot "go under," no matter how hard you try. On the other hand, you may be in that 15 percent who go into a deep trance so easily that you seem to be hypnotizing yourself. Or you may be like the great majority, responsive to some degree or another (Orne, 1977). Whatever your tendency, it is likely to remain with you throughout life. College students who had been tested for hypnotizability and then retested some eight to twelve years later showed remarkably stable scores (Hilgard, 1977). There are some changes over the life cycle: Susceptibility is lowest among young children, highest among preadolescents, and in slow decline from that point on (Hilgard, 1977).

What makes a person hypnotizable? There are some physiological differences between people who readily go into the hypnotic state and those who don't. Those who are easily susceptible show, in their normal waking state, strong theta-wave production, which seems to be related to attention and imagery ability (Sabourin, 1982).

Psychological differences show up, too. Easily hypnotized adults tend to have been very imaginative children who often lost themselves in flights of fantasy. Furthermore, they're also likely to have been severely disciplined in childhood and may be responsive to hypnosis perhaps because they learned to ''escape'' punishment through fantasy (J. Hilgard, 1979). Perhaps ready acceptance of an authority figure (the parent and then the hypnotist), along with the ability to escape into another state of consciousness, is a key element. The ability to be hypnotized may be at least partly hereditary since identical twins are more alike in hypnotizability than fraternal twins (Morgan, 1973).

How Can We Explain Hypnosis?

Is hypnosis a unique state, that is, a trance? There are a number of different viewpoints on this issue, ranging from the notion that the hypnotized person is indeed in a trance to the view that she or he is role-playing. Let's take a look at four current views.

TRANCE-STATE THEORY Is the hypnotized person in a trance state qualitatively different from normal consciousness? Research says yes. When six hypnotized college students were compared with six who were pretending to be hypnotized, enough of a difference showed up between the groups to warrant a conclusion that the hypnotized subjects were, indeed, in a different state of consciousness (Evans & Orne, 1971).

A ''blind'' experimenter (one who did not know which subjects had been hypnotized and which were pretending) made suggestions to all of them with a tape-recorded message, getting the subjects to tap their feet in time to imaginary music. During the procedure a switch was thrown in another room, stopping the tape recorder and turning out the lights. Five out of the six subjects simulating hypnosis immediately stopped pretending as soon as the experimenter left the room. When the power went on again they resumed faking. On the other hand, five out of the six hypnotized subjects showed no immediate signs of being aware of the power failure or the experimenter's departure. It took more than 10 minutes for them to stop tapping their feet and more than 16 minutes to open their eyes. They didn't try to pretend they were still hypnotized when the experimenter walked back in, confirming the hypothesis that hypnotized subjects will come out of a trance spontaneously and that they are not playing a role of being in a trance.

SPLIT-CONSCIOUSNESS (NEODISSOCIATION) A young woman was told she would awaken from hypnosis to find she had no hands but that this would not trouble her (Hilgard, 1970). When she was given a strong electric shock in those hands, she didn't feel anything—even though she hadn't been told she would feel no pain.

In the late eighteenth century an Austrian physician named Franz Mesmer believed that electrical magnetism in people's bodies controlled their health. Here, a ''mesmerizer'' is putting a patient into a trance and issuing suggestions. Although such patients often seemed cured of their ailments, a royal commission discredited Mesmer and his methods. (National Library of Medicine)

Her experience demonstrates Hilgard's neodissociation theory, which holds that the hypnotized person is functioning on more than one level of awareness. This is similar to the common sensation of knowing, while you are asleep and dreaming, that what seems real is only a dream and that there is another real world beyond your present perceptions.

Hilgard (1977) coined the term "hidden observer" to explain a phenomenon he discovered during experiments in which people kept their hands in ice water for 45 seconds, which usually produces intense pain. Hypnotized subjects reported little or no pain, but when they were asked to give reports from a "hidden observer," either by a kind of automatic writing or by pressing a key with one hand while the other was in the ice water, about half of the particularly "good" subjects showed that they did feel the pain at some level of awareness. Apparently, through hypnosis, they were blocking this pain from full consciousness.

ROLE-PLAYING   A "theatrical" explanation maintains that both hypnotist and subject are actors, enmeshed in a drama complete with plot and roles (Coe & Sarbin, 1977). The susceptible subject picks up cues from the hypnotist and starts to act out his or her part, throwing himself into the role and believing in it totally.

A dramatic illustration that gives backing to this point of view is in a follow-up to Reiff and Scheerer's 1959 study in which hypnotized adults regressed to the age of 4 had mud all over their hands. The experimenter held out lollipops in such a way that it was awkward to take them by the stick. Hypnotized subjects took the eating end of the lollipop into their muddy hands and put it into their mouths. When other researchers decided to see what real 4-year-olds would do in the same situation, they found, "To our surprise, none of the four-year-olds was willing to take the lollipop by its eating end—all sensibly insisting on taking it by the stick!" (Orne, 1977, p. 25). Apparently the hypnotized subjects were not trying to fool anyone but neither were they the 4-year-olds they had been. They were adults acting as they thought they had acted at age 4.

COGNITIVE-BEHAVIORAL THEORY   In this view the hypnotic state does not depend on any trance-induction techniques and can occur even in their total absence (Barber, 1970). It depends on the subject's readiness to think along with and imagine the themes suggested by the hypnotist. If the hypnotist says the subject won't feel pain, won't be able to lift an arm, or will become a 4-year-old again, the subject in the right frame of mind will go along with these themes and behave accordingly. Subjects with passive, negative, or cynical attitudes will not think along with these themes.

Three groups totaling sixty-six student nurses were compared (Barber & Wilson, 1977). The twenty-two in the first group were hypnotized in traditional ways, the twenty-two in the second were given "think-with" instructions designed to encourage them to focus their imaginative powers and to discourage negative and passive attitudes, and the others were a control group. The think-with group was told: "Let me give you an example of the kind of tests I might give you. I might ask you . . . to feel as if you're looking at a TV program." The experimenter then gave the subjects three ways they could respond: They could say negative things to themselves, such as "This is ridiculous, there is no TV there," and nothing at all would happen; they could wait for a TV screen to appear and again nothing would happen; or they could recall a program they liked and let themselves "see" it again in their mind's eye.

All three groups were then tested on a scale of creative imagination, which measured subjects' reports of arm heaviness, hand levitation, finger numbness, drinking imaginary water, smelling and tasting an imaginary orange, hearing nonexistent music, feeling imagined sunshine, sensing a slowdown of time, regressing to childhood, and feeling relaxed. The students in the think-with group achieved higher scores than those in either of the other groups, lending support to the viewpoint that hypnosis comes about because of the subject's ability to think along the lines suggested by the hypnotist.

At this point we cannot say which of these four theories is the right one. If we ever do arrive at a definitive explanation, that will affect the practical uses for which hypnosis is put. Right now it's being used in a number of ways in everyday life, including aiding therapy and solving crimes, as shown in Box 4-3.

Is Hypnosis Safe?

The U.S. Department of Health, Education, and Welfare (1971) listed hypnosis among several procedures that it considered potentially stressful. However, one study that looked at the aftereffects of five different kinds of activities participated in by 209 introductory psychology students, found being hypnotized no more troubling than taking part in a verbal learning experiment, attending a class, taking an exam, or college life in general (Coe & Ryken, 1979). In fact, exams, college classes, and college life in general seemed to make students more anxious, fearful, depressed, or unhappy than hypnosis did, and the 70 students who had been hypnotized often found hypnosis a pleasant experience that left them refreshed and rested.

Can hypnosis make you do something you ordinarily wouldn't do—such as kill a person or take off your clothes in front of strangers? One school maintains that you would resist such suggestions, while the other claims that a hypnotist could get you to do such things by couching his suggestions along lines you could accept such as telling you that someone was threatening your life and killing him would be a matter of self-defense or that you're in a doctor's office where getting undressed would be appropriate.

If you have a problem that you think hypnosis might help, you should consult an experienced, reputable practitioner to see whether you'd be a good candidate. To find or check the credentials of one, you could contact the American Psychological Association (1200 17th Street, NW, Washington, D.C. 20036); the psychiatry department of the closest university-affiliated hospital; your local medical society; the American Society of Clinical Hypnosis, 2250 East Devon Avenue, Suite 336, Des Plaines, Ill. 60018; or The Society for Clinical and Experimental Hypnosis, 129-A Kings Park Drive, Liverpool, N.Y. 13088.

DRUGS

If you're a typical adult, you regularly take some kind of chemical that alters your state of consciousness. Maybe it's the cup of coffee that helps

BOX 4-3

PRACTICAL APPLICATIONS OF HYPNOSIS

THERAPY

The list of ailments treated with hypnosis is a varied one, including:

- Pain from childbirth, angina pectoris, burns, back problems, dentistry, headaches, cancer, arthritis, and major surgery
- Other conditions including nausea from chemicals used to treat cancer; obesity; insomnia; abuse of alcohol, nicotine, and other drugs; warts; asthma; nail-biting; phobias; fecal incontinence; the apprehension felt by a patient about to undergo surgery; and various psychosomatic illnesses

The effectiveness of hypnosis varies enormously depending on the individual, the practitioner, and the ailment. It seems most successful in treating pain, warts, and asthma but is of little or no value in treating obesity, alcoholism, and cigarette smoking (Wadden & Anderton, 1982). By and large, the conditions best treated by hypnosis seem to be unlearned, ones the individual seems to have no control over. The self-initiated addictive disorders present a complex problem of ingrained habits and of having to give up some immediate gratification like the pleasure of eating, smoking, or drinking (unlike pain or the inability to breathe, which are not rewarding in themselves).

Hypnosis is particularly effective in alleviating pain. It is nonaddictive, inexpensive, and safe and can be used alone or along with medical treatments. One 33-year-old aviator had had surgery and been on medication for years to relieve disabling leg and back pain. After receiving a hypnotic strategy based on his flying in his airplane, along with psychotherapy and a small dose of medication, this flyer was able to return to active duty (Wain, 1980).

Hypnosis distracts attention by giving a person something besides the pain to focus on. It relaxes the individual, diminishing the anxiety that often makes pain feel worse. It may enable a person to block painful perceptions from full consciousness. And it makes him or her forget the pain upon awakening from the hypnotic state.

SOLVING CRIMES

An executive who escaped from a hotel fire that killed twenty-six fellow executives testified at the trial of the accused arsonist (Feron, 1982). Earlier the witness had undergone hypnosis to try to bring to consciousness details he might have forgotten. During his conscious testimony he described having seen a man "dressed in the uniform of those who serve coffee"; under hypnosis, he saw this man wearing a short-sleeved blouse and described him as

"chunky, with perhaps a mustache," a description that might have helped the suspect, who was slightly built and clean-shaven. The jury, however, did not hear the testimony given under hypnosis—and it did convict the defendant (Press, 1982). Would the hypnosis testimony have changed the verdict? Should it have?

The use of hypnosis in criminal trials is highly controversial. While police departments are using it more often these days, there is real doubt that it is as accurate a memory prodder as supporters maintain. Critics charge: "Far from enhancing memory of a past event so that it can be recalled, hypnosis makes it more likely that memory will be altered" (Neisser, in Colen, 1982). Martin Orne (in Colen, 1982) tells of a case in which a hypnotized child described the murder of his mother by his father, only to have the mother turn up alive after the father's conviction. Several such incidents, bolstered by research on the faulty memories of eyewitnesses (Loftus, 1979), have led at least one professor of law and medicine to conclude: "The possibility of contamination of remembered fact by fantasy and suggestion is so great that no witness who has undergone hypnosis should be allowed to testify in court" (Diamond, in Colen, 1982).

you wake up in the morning, the after-dinner cigarette that helps you relax, the glass of wine, beer, or liquor that puts you into a lighter mood, the marijuana joint that heightens your enjoyment of music, the tranquilizer that calms you during a crisis, or one of many other commonly used substances. From the beginnings of recorded time, people in every cul-

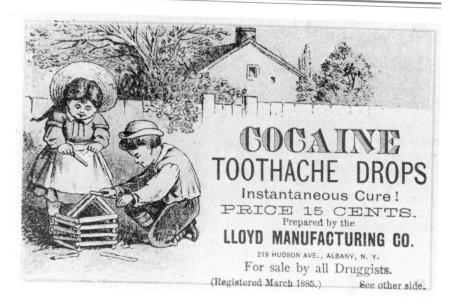

Before the sale of narcotics was regulated by the Food and Drug Administration, substances like alcohol, cocaine, and heroin were dispensed freely in over-the-counter patent medicines. (National Library of Medicine)

ture around the world have taken various substances that changed their states of consciousness. Sometimes these elements have helped people cope better, and sometimes they've created problems far worse than those that led to their use in the first place.

The U.S. Department of Health and Human Services (1980) defines a drug as "any chemical substance that produces physical, mental, emotional, or behavioral change in the user" (p. 3). Those we are talking about here are the psychoactive, or mind-altering, drugs. They range from those common substances just described through the coca leaves chewed by natives of the Peruvian Andes, the cocaine sniffed by members of underworld and Hollywood circles, the heroin injected by the junkie who steals to keep alive an expensive habit, and the amphetamines swallowed by the fashion model trying to lose weight.

Why do people take these foreign elements? Sometimes just to enhance slightly their enjoyment of everyday life, sometimes to solve—or escape from—a problem that seems insoluble by any other means, sometimes to reach a state of mind that promises new experiences of a spiritual or an esthetic nature, sometimes just because it's "the thing to do." Often the reason a person *continues* to use drugs—a psychological or physiological dependence on it—has little to do with the original purpose in trying it. Anyone taking a drug because she or he is afraid of or unable to give it up is a *drug abuser*. Drug abuse has varying stages, involving any kind of physical, mental, emotional, or social impairment of the drug taker's life. To test your own knowledge of drug abuse, you might want to answer the quiz in Box 4-4.

Let's take a look at some of the most common psychoactive drugs, how they change states of consciousness, and what they do to overall functioning on both short- and long-term bases.

Caffeine

That cup of coffee or tea, can of cola, or bar of chocolate that you sometimes take for a "pick-me-up" all contain the stimulant *caffeine*, which raises your heart and breathing rates and your blood pressure. It can

BOX 4-4

DRUG ABUSE: SOME QUESTIONS AND ANSWERS

DRUG QUIZ

The following quiz is designed to probe your knowledge about drug abuse. By drug abuse, we mean the use of any chemical substance for nonmedicinal purposes which results in the impaired physical, mental, emotional or social health of the user.

Some questions have more than one answer. It's not so important that you get the right answers—this quiz won't be graded. What *is* important is that you start thinking about the impact drug abuse has on all our lives.

Circle the correct answer(s) to each of the questions. Answers are on page 143.

1 During which period(s) was drug abuse a problem in the United States?
(a) during the Civil War
(b) in the 1950s
(c) in the 1960s
(d) all of the above

2 Which age group has the highest percentage of drug abusers?
(a) 10-17
(b) 18-25
(c) 26-35
(d) 36-60
(e) 61 and over

3 How do most drug users make their first contact with illicit drugs?
(a) through "pushers"
(b) through their friends
(c) accidently
(d) through the media

4 Which of the following is the most commonly abused drug in the United States?
(a) marijuana
(b) alcohol
(c) cocaine

(d) heroin

5 Which of the following poses the greatest health hazard to the most people in the United States?
(a) cigarettes
(b) heroin
(c) codeine
(d) LSD
(e) caffeine

6 Which of the following is not a narcotic?
(a) heroin
(b) marijuana
(c) morphine
(d) methadone

7 Which of the following is not a stimulant?
(a) amphetamine
(b) caffeine
(c) methaqualone
(d) methamphetamine

8 Which of the following drugs does not cause physical dependence?
(a) alcohol
(b) morphine
(c) peyote
(d) secobarbital
(e) codeine

9 Which of the following poses the highest *immediate* risk to experimenters?
(a) inhalants
(b) marijuana
(c) nicotine
(d) LSD

10 Overall, why is intravenous injection the most dangerous method of using illicit drugs?
(a) because the drug enters the system so rapidly
(b) because nonsterile equipment and solutions can cause serious complications
(c) because users usually get a larger amount of the drug by this method

(d) (a) and (c) only
(e) (a), (b), and (c)

11 When does a person who uses heroin become physically dependent?
(a) immediately (first time)
(b) after four or five times
(c) after prolonged use (20 times or more)
(d) different for each person

12 When people become dependent on heroin, what is the primary reason they continue to take it?
(a) experience pleasure
(b) avoid withdrawal
(c) escape reality
(d) gain acceptance among friends

13 Which of the following has (have) been used effectively to treat drug abusers?
(a) methadone maintenance
(b) detoxification (medically supervised drug withdrawal)
(c) drug-free therapy
(d) psychotherapy
(e) all of the above

14 Which of the following are social costs of drug abuse?
(a) loss of employee productivity
(b) increased possibility of auto accidents
(c) depletion of already scarce drug abuse services
(d) (b) and (c) only
(e) (a), (b), and (c)

15 What is the most unpredictable drug of abuse on the street today?
(a) PCP
(b) heroin
(c) LSD
(d) alcohol

ANSWERS TO DRUG QUIZ

1 (d) All of the above. Drug use is as old as history, and certain periods of U.S. history are associated with special drug abuse problems. During the Civil War, for example, morphine was used as a pain killer. Morphine's addictive properties were not well understood, and many soldiers became dependent on it. Throughout the century, there were periodic "drug scares" created by the use of cocaine at the turn of the century, heroin in the 1920s, marijuana in the 1930s, and heroin again in the 1950s. The 1960s saw a social explosion of drug use of all kinds from LSD to heroin and marijuana.
Since the 1970s, phencyclidine (PCP), a psychedelic of the 1960s, has reappeared on the street and is causing concern because of its bizarre effects. And new compounds, marketed as "room odorizers" are being inhaled for a "high."

2 (b) 18-25

3 (b) Through their friends.

4 (b) Alcohol. Many people in the United States have trouble with alcohol, and estimates show that about 10 million are dependent on the drug.

5 (a) Cigarettes. Approximately 300,000 deaths annually from coronary disease, other heart disease, lung cancer, respiratory disease, and other types of cancer have been linked to cigarette smoking.

6 (b) Marijuana. In the past, marijuana was legally classified as a narcotic, but it isn't now. Marijuana's psychopharmacological effects (the way a drug works on a person's mental and physical system) differ from the effects of narcotics.

7 (c) Methaqualone. Methaqualone is a nonbarbiturate sedative-hypnotic called a "lude" or "soaper" on the street. But it, like the stimulant drugs, is also a drug of abuse.

8 (c) Peyote. Physical dependence on mescaline (the active ingredient of the peyote cactus) or other hallucinogens not verified.

9 (a) Inhalants. Sniffing aerosols or other volatile substances can result in immediate death.

10 (e) The danger of contracting hepatitis or other infection is often overlooked by drug users who inject with nonsterile equipment.

11 (d) Different for each person. Although the time it takes for a person to become physically dependent on heroin varies, we do know that repeated use ultimately causes physical dependence. Some people become physically dependent after using heroin as few as three or four times.

12 (b) Avoid withdrawal. When people stop taking heroin after they have become physically dependent, they develop withdrawal symptoms: vomiting, muscle spasms, profuse sweating, insomnia, and other physical conditions. If they once again begin to take the drug, withdrawal symptoms disappear.

13 (e) All of the above. All have been used successfully, both individually and in combination, to treat drug abusers.

14 (e) Hours lost from productive work, increased traffic accidents caused by driving under the influence of drugs, and dollars spent on treatment and law enforcement programs—these are the social costs we all pay, one way or another, for drug abuse.

15 (a) Phencyclidine (PCP, "angel dust"). Phencyclidine is an unpredictable and highly dangerous drug. Its use has been associated with bizarre and violent behavior, with accidents, and with psychotic episodes.

Source: Department of Health and Human Services   Public Health Service Alcohol, Drug Abuse, and Mental Health Administration

stimulate you mentally and physically for brief periods of time, giving you short bursts of energy. In large doses (the amount in seven to ten cups of coffee), caffeine can make you restless, jittery, and irritable, give you headaches or diarrhea, keep you from falling asleep or make you wake up in the middle of the night, interfere with your ability to concentrate, produce ringing in your ears, and, at times, even produce mild delirium. Coffee can irritate the stomach lining, especially when taken on an empty stomach.

Americans ingest a lot of caffeine, mostly through coffee, with one out of four people over age 17 drinking six or more cups a day (Dusek & Girdano, 1980). Most adults seem to suffer no extreme side-effects, but children who take in the amount of caffeine present in 6 to 8 ounces of coffee (or the equivalent in cola or chocolate) often become anxious and have learning difficulties (Dusek & Girdano, 1980). While questions have been raised as to the danger of caffeine to the developing fetus, recent research shows no association between the pregnant mother's coffee drinking and any ill effects for the baby (Linn, Schoenbaum, Monson, Rosner, Stubblefield, & Ryan, 1982).

Nicotine

The second most widely used stimulant, nicotine is present in the tobacco in cigarettes, cigars, and pipes. Smoking may help you feel more relaxed, but it is actually stimulating your heart and nervous system, raising your blood pressure, and making your heart beat faster. If you have ever stopped smoking or tried to, you are familiar with nicotine's addictive properties. Giving it up causes such withdrawal symptoms as irritability, cramps, headache, anxiety, nervousness, and depression. Continuing to smoke produces even worse effects. Cigarette smoking is the major cause of death from cancer of the lung, esophagus, larynx, and mouth, and contribute to death from cancer of the pancreas, kidney, and bladder; it also contributes to heart disease (U.S. Public Health Service, 1982). Smoking during pregnancy affects the baby as well as the mother: It increases the chances of producing a small baby or one who is dead at birth or dies soon afterwards (U.S. Department of Health and Human Services, 1980).

Fortunately, cigarette smoking is on the decline among Americans, with only 20 percent of high school seniors smoking in 1981, compared to 29 percent in 1977, and with 32 percent of adults smoking, compared to 42 percent in 1965 (U.S. Public Health Service, 1982). People who want to stop smoking often look for help from counseling, behavior modification, hypnosis, or certain medications. While none of the official programs report impressive success rates, many people break the habit on their own. Of a sample of seventy-five smokers who never sought help in stopping, more than sixty-five percent stopped by themselves (Schachter, 1982).

Alcohol

Seeing the exuberance at a beer party or the violence of a drunken wife-beater, you might think that alcohol is a stimulant. It is not. It is a central nervous system depressant that causes blood pressure to drop while heart rate increases. The effects of alcohol vary. While small amounts tranquilize most people, others become stimulated, probably because the alcohol suppresses the mechanisms that ordinarily control active behaviors, so they lose their inhibitions and act exuberant, sociable, silly, or aggressive. Large amounts of alcohol tranquilize most people, dulling sensation, impairing judgment, memory, and muscular coordination, and eventually causing unconsciousness. Shakespeare recognized the effect of alcohol on sexuality, noting, "Drink . . . provokes the desire, but it takes away the performance" (*Macbeth,* Act II, scene iii).

Alcohol is this country's number 1 drug problem. Ten million Americans can't handle it and are either "problem drinkers" or full-fledged alcoholics. When does alcohol become a problem? When it interferes with a person's ability to function on the job or in personal relationships and

Alcohol is the leading drug abuse problem in the United States today. Most people who drink do so in moderation, but 10 million Americans are either problem drinkers or full-fledged alcoholics. This young man is at the Mardi Gras in New Orleans. Is he using the occasion as an excuse to overindulge? (Charles Gatewood/ The Image Works)

when the drinker cannot control the desire for or use of alcohol. People dependent on alcohol experience a variety of withdrawal symptoms. Drinkers can die from a large amount of alcohol at one time—or from liver or heart disease brought on by drinking over a period of years.

The mixture of alcohol and other drugs, especially tranquilizers, anticoagulants, barbiturates, and other sedatives, can cause depression, coma, or death. Drinking during pregnancy—especially heavy drinking and binge drinking—can produce the fetal alcohol syndrome, which causes retarded growth, low intelligence, and poor motor development in the baby (Jones, Smith, Ulleland, & Streissguth, 1973). Because alcohol impairs judgment, reaction time, and motor ability, one of its most lethal effects is in the high number of traffic accidents caused by drivers who have been drinking.

With all these dangers, why would anyone ever drink? Partly because most people can handle alcohol in moderation and find that it enhances their enjoyment of life. Wine is a part of the rituals of many religions, a small amount of brandy is often recommended by doctors as a painkiller, and the relaxing qualities of alcohol contribute to social celebrations. With alcohol such a pervasive presence in modern society, individuals need to monitor themselves to determine whether they are among those people who either cannot drink at all or who need to exercise special care. At the same time societal institutions need to continue to develop ways to help those people who already have drinking problems regain their ability to become fully functioning. The most effective approaches so far have been group-oriented programs like Alcoholics Anonymous, which focus on individuals' recognition of their problems, total abstinence, and the emotional support of fellow alcoholics (Zimberg, 1982).

A major controversy over the past ten years has swirled around claims that alcoholics taught "controlled-drinking" techniques do better than those given conventional therapy aimed at staying away from alcohol totally (Sobell & Sobell, 1975; Sobell, Sobell, & Ward, 1980). Critics have contested these conclusions, claiming that patients taught controlled drinking were often sick and rehospitalized within a year and that over a ten-year period four died of alcohol-related causes (Pendery, Maltzman, & West, 1982). A Canadian review panel supported the controlled-drinking approach (Boffey, 1982), but the controversy will undoubtedly persist for some time.

Marijuana

This derivative of the common plant *cannabis sativa* contains more than 400 chemicals, of which the mind-altering component is delta-9-tetrahydrocannabinol (THC). Marijuana increases heart rate and sometimes blood pressure, reddens the eyes, produces a dry mouth and throat. It alters the sense of time, making minutes seem like hours or vice versa. It impairs the ability to perform tasks requiring concentration, coordination, and quick reaction time. Mood often changes, possibly into euphoria, melancholy, or almost emotionless detachment. Powers of perception may seem heightened so that colors are seen more vividly, music heard more acutely, or physical sensations felt more intensely. Short-term memory is affected. Depending on the amount and strength of the marijuana and the underlying psychological condition of the smoker, confusion, anxiety, or delirium can result (Relman, 1982).

Marijuana has several therapeutic uses, such as in treating the eye disorder glaucoma, alleviating nausea and vomiting caused by chemotherapy in the treatment of cancer, and treating such ailments as asthma, seizures, and spastic conditions (Relman, 1982).

The long-term effects of smoking marijuana are still unknown. There is no evidence of any permanent change in the human nervous system or on brain function. Neither addiction nor physical dependence seem to take place, although mild withdrawal symptoms do appear and psychological dependence sometimes occurs. Some research indicates that marijuana may affect both male and female reproductive systems, but there's no proof that it affects either sex's fertility (Relman, 1982). It may have the same kinds of effects on the lungs that tobacco does, but this has not been firmly established (U.S. Department of Health and Human Services, 1980).

In recent years young people have been smoking less as shown in Table 4-1.

TABLE 4-1 Marijuana Use Reported in 1979 and 1982 (Percentages)

	12–17 YEARS OLD		18–25 YEARS OLD	
	1979	1982	1979	1982
Ever used	30.9	26.7	68.2	64.1
Used in previous month	16.7	11.5	35.4	27.4
Used in past year	24.1	20.6	46.9	40.4

Source: U.S. Department of Health and Human Services, 1983.

Stimulants: Amphetamines and Cocaine

Stimulants stronger than caffeine and nicotine, such as amphetamines and cocaine, increase energy levels and wakefulness to a greater degree, elevate mood, and have other effects.

AMPHETAMINES People who take these drugs known collectively as "uppers" or "speed" do so for various reasons. Some find them helpful in focusing concentration on a demanding task like writing a paper. Others take them to stay awake to study, do a boring job, or drive long distances. Athletes take them to marshal energy for a big game. Dieters take them to suppress the appetite (which they do, but only on a short-term basis). Doctors often prescribe them for hyperactive children to lengthen attention span and control restlessness, to narcoleptics to keep them awake, to sufferers of short-term depression. People who buy them on the street take them just to feel good—to gain self-confidence and feel they can meet any challenge life has to offer.

Amphetamines used to be readily available without a prescription, and then freely obtainable from a friendly physician, but since they've led to so much abuse, they are now much harder to obtain legally. Doctors are now required by law to justify any prescriptions for them.

Amphetamines make the heart beat faster, harder, and sometimes irregularly; constrict blood vessels; cause a rise in blood pressure and blood sugar level; stimulate adrenal glands; and increase muscle tension. The person taking them is apt to be very talkative, energetic, alert, in a good mood, uninterested in sleep but very interested in sexual activity. These effects seem to occur because of the drugs' action on the brain chemicals dopamine and norepinephrine.

Abuse can lead to weight loss and malnutrition, pain in muscles and joints, unconsciousness, and a feeling of paralysis. It can also lead to *amphetamine psychosis*, in which paranoia, hallucinations, and an inability to recognize familiar faces are often present. Violence and aggression are common in the heavy user, especially in the depression that often follows a high.

COCAINE Among the most expensive and fashionable illicit drugs on the market today is cocaine, the stimulant made from the leaves of the South American shrub *erythroxylon coca*. Cocaine has a colorful history dating from ancient times, when it was first used to induce meditative trances in religious ceremonies. Freud was an enthusiastic user and proselytizer for cocaine, which he originally thought would be a cure for morphine addiction, depression, and fatigue. Coca Cola™ got its name from the coca leaves that, along with cola nuts, are used as flavoring for the drink. Since just after 1900, the company has closely overseen production to make sure every trace of cocaine is removed from the manufacture of its product. It sells the refined cocaine, under government supervision, to pharmaceutical companies.

How does cocaine alter consciousness? Either sniffed in the form of powder or injected as a liquid, it acts on the central nervous system to produce feelings of euphoria and excitement. Temperature and blood pressure rise, the pupils of the eyes dilate, blood vessels constrict, and appetite diminishes. The user generally feels strong, energetic, and optimistic. Judgment is impaired, inhibitions are unblocked, and perception may be altered. Large doses often create hallucinations and may lead to

Marijuana, here being prepared in tablets by a hospital pharmacist, is used therapeutically to alleviate the nausea caused by cancer chemotherapy, as well as to treat such other ailments as asthma, seizures, and glaucoma. The drug's long-term effects are still unknown. (Wide World Photos)

Cocaine, which has gone in and out of fashion for years, is not physically addictive, but its harmful side-effects include paranoia, impotence, destruction of nasal tissues, panic attacks, and depression. (Yvonne Hemsey/ Liaison Agency)

paranoia, panic attacks, anxiety, depression, impotence, or insomnia. Cocaine may make a person dangerous to others or result in death to the user. People don't become physically addicted, but they may become psychologically hooked since "coke" users often feel depressed and tired after its effects have worn off. Another side-effect caused by sniffing cocaine is injury to the nose.

Barbiturates and Other Sedatives

Sedatives, which have a calming effect and bring on sleep, comprise three kinds of drugs: *barbiturates,* or *sedative hypnotics* (Nembutal, Seconal, Amytal); *nonbarbiturates* (Miltown and Quaalude); and the *major and minor tranquilizers* (Thorazine, Compazine, Valium, Librium, and others, whose psychotherapeutic uses are discussed more fully in Chapter 16). These "downers" are often used by people who have gone too far "up" on amphetamines. Unable to sleep or calm down, the "speed freak" turns to the drugs in this class to counteract the uppers, thus boarding a chemical roller coaster. Sedatives are also taken by anxious people, those dealing with a life crisis such as the death of a family member, and insomniacs. Physicians often prescribe them to relieve the anxiety of patients with heart, respiratory, gastrointestinal, or other physical illnesses.

Barbiturates are easily abused. They have profound effects, impairing memory and judgment, and sometimes leading to coma or even death. They are particularly dangerous when taken with alcohol since the combination magnifies the effects of both these central nervous system depressants. Nearly one-third of accidental drug-related deaths are related to barbiturate overdose (U.S. Department of Health and Human Services, 1980). Barbiturate users develop a tolerance, need greater and greater amounts, and eventually become addicted. Withdrawal can be a grueling experience, with the addict's suffering from tremors, nausea, abdominal cramps, vomiting, hallucinations, and a disoriented sense of time and space. Withdrawal can even lead to death.

LSD and Other Hallucinogens

Hallucinogens, or psychedelics, affect consciousness in many ways. They influence perceptions, thoughts, and emotions, making them all different from the normal waking state. Time and space expand and contract, delusions appear, logical judgment is suspended, and the imaginary visual, auditory, and tactile sensations that characterize hallucinations show up.

Users may feel chills, nausea, tremors, and palpitations of the heart. Memory plays strange tricks, bringing long-buried images to vivid consciousness in unexpected ways. The combination of unfamiliar feelings may lead to euphoria or panic. A frightening aftermath of LSD use is the flashback that often occurs long after taking the drug. A bad trip may recur as long as eighteen months later, with troubling and dangerous emotions.

LSD (d-lysergic acid diethylamide) was synthesized in the laboratory in 1938, but its psychoactive properties were not discovered until 1943. During the 1950s it was used in psychotherapy, in treating drug and alcohol addiction and mental disorders, and to relieve pain in terminal cancer patients. By the 1960s it had attracted a following among people seeking creative and spiritual visions, and Congress restricted its use as an experimental drug. The black market stepped in, making LSD easily available on the street.

LSD seems to work by affecting the production of the chemical brain transmitter *serotonin*. It is rapidly absorbed into the bloodstream and disseminated throughout the body. Experiments on monkeys have shown that only 1 percent concentrates in the brain, mostly in the pituitary and pineal glands, but also in the hypothalamus, the limbic system, and the auditory and visual reflex regions (Snyder & Reivich, 1966). It can impair memory, attention span, and the ability to think abstractly and may bring about organic brain damage in some heavy users. Does it damage chromosomes? The research on this is inconclusive, with findings indicating that pure LSD does not seem to do so but that street LSD, mixed with other substances, may have far-reaching genetic implications.

Will LSD make you more creative? Many defenders of this drug, like historical supporters of cocaine and nitrous oxide, claim that it will. If you have a good trip, you'll probably agree. You may see and hear all sorts of things that may never have appeared in your normal waking life. Under the drug's influence, you may feel you have new insights and answers to all sorts of questions. Chances are, however, that you won't be able to demonstrate this new creativity to anyone else.

The relationship between psychedelic drugs and creativity is complex, and one of the problems with relying on a drug for creative production is that the drug does not provide "the checks and balances between intuition and analytic reason required for genuine creation" (Grinspoon & Bakalar, 1979, p. 267). During the drug experience, you can't transmit your new insights, partly because of the drug's effects on motor abilities. After taking LSD, users don't show any more creativity than they did beforehand (Dusek & Girdano, 1980). So while some creative artists—like the poet Samuel Coleridge and the novelist Robert Louis Stevenson, as well as contemporary poet Allen Ginsberg and novelist Ken Kesey— credit drug-induced states for some achievements, there's no proof that these artists produced more creative work drugged than undrugged.

PCP (phencyclidine hydrochloride) is a frequently abused street drug

A person tripping on LSD might feel all sorts of distorted sensations:

His foot may seem to be five yards away from his eye or right under his chin, his hand shriveled with age or shrunken to a baby's, his body large enough to cover the landscape from horizon to horizon. The body may feel hollow, boneless, transparent; its substance may seem to change to wood, metal or glass; it may feel heavy and light at once, or hot and cold at once.
(Grinspoon & Bakalar, 1979, p. 95)

People in every culture around the world have often turned to mind-altering drugs, with varying consequences. Opium was widely used in China to heal, relieve pain, and give courage, as shown in this wood-cut of an opium den that appeared in Harper's Weekly *in 1880. (National Library of Medicine)*

that is a stimulant, a depressant, and a painkiller, as well as a hallucinogen. Originally developed as an anesthetic, it is no longer used legally on human beings because of the agitation and thought disturbance it produces. Users take it for its few favorable effects—mood elevation, relaxation, stimulation, and heightened sensitivity—even though they seem greatly outweighed by its negative ones. These include memory and speech problems, depression, anxiety, paranoia, violence, hallucinations, convulsions, depersonalization, poor coordination, numbness, and possibly psychosis or even death from convulsions or interference with breathing. The most dangerous aspect of PCP is its utter unpredictability.

Other common hallucinogens are mescaline, peyote, psilocybin, STP, DMT, and nitrous oxide.

Heroin and Other Narcotics

In today's climate it's hard to believe the way the use of narcotics, a class of depressant drugs that relieve pain and induce sleep, flourished openly in this country during the nineteenth and early twentieth centuries. Opium was used in China and India to heal, relieve pain, and give warriors courage. It appeared in this country in patent medicines for coughs, diarrhea, and just about every other human ailment. Morphine, an opium derivative, was freely given to injured Civil War and World War I soldiers. Then a promising new drug that seemed to have the advantages of both of these, without their addicting properties, burst on the scene. Unfortunately, heroin did not live up to the expectations held for it but instead became more of a problem than the other narcotics, today accounting for 90 percent of narcotic abuse in the United States (Shorter & McDarby, 1979).

Heroin users, who typically shoot a solution of the drug directly into the bloodstream with a hypodermic syringe, feel its effects quickly. They soon feel euphoric, peaceful, content, and safe, detached from any dangers or challenges. Breathing becomes slower and more shallow, pupils constrict, sex drive diminishes, and intense itching, nausea, and vomiting may occur. Despite these effects, they can hold a job and lead a relatively normal life—as long as they take the drug. Physical addiction occurs, with severe withdrawal symptoms when the drug wears off, and tolerance develops with prolonged use, so heroin addicts need progressively greater amounts.

Within four to six hours after an addict stops taking the drug, she or he begins to experience withdrawal discomforts, which turn into agonies by twelve to sixteen hours after the last dose. Sweating, shaking, vomiting, running nose and eyes, chills, aching muscles, abdominal pain, and diarrhea are common (U.S. Department of Health and Human Services, 1980). Withdrawal doesn't cause death, but an overdose can. Heroin users often contract serum hepatitis from using dirty needles and syringes and nonsterile solutions. They also develop vein inflammations, skin abscesses, and lung congestion.

One common way of countering addiction is to give the addict a daily dose of methadone, an addictive narcotic that lasts longer and is less likely to cause harmful side-effects. Another approach tries to free the addict from physical or psychological dependence on *any* drug through group therapy and peer support, often at a residential treatment center. As users break the physical addiction, they progress to a halfway house and then to life in the community, perhaps with regular supportive help.

The major problem in curing heroin addicts is not releasing them from the physiological hold of the drug—but meeting the underlying psychological needs that drove them to take it in the first place. The typical addict has low self-esteem and self-confidence, is afraid of life, has a generally negative and pessimistic outlook, feels that whatever she or he does is futile, and looks to heroin as a means of escaping reality (Dusek & Girdano, 1980). Such deep-seated psychological problems often defy resolution and send the "cured" addict back into the arms of the comforting drug.

Many people who originally sought altered states of consciousness through drugs have since discovered they can obtain some of the same benefits without the same risks from meditation, hypnosis, and other mind-altering techniques. Part of the appeal of long-distance running seems to lie in the "high" that many runners experience. Since moving into other states of consciousness seems to be a basic human tendency, it's likely that people will continue to develop still more ways to expand or limit consciousness.

SUMMARY

1   *Consciousness* refers to our awareness of ourselves and the world around us. The *normal state of consciousness* is one's normal waking state. Any qualitative change from the normal state is an *alternate* or *altered state of consciousness.* Such states include *sleep* and states induced by *meditation, hypnosis,* and *drugs.*

2   The characteristics of altered and alternate states

of consciousness (ASCs) include the following: *alterations in thinking, disturbed time sense, loss of control, change in emotional expression, body image change, perceptual distortion, change in meaning or significance, sense of being indescribable, feelings of rejuvenation,* and *hypersuggestibility.*

3 Altered states may be induced in a number of different ways ranging from overstimulation to complete withdrawal of stimulation.

4 While sleeping, we pass through *four sleep stages* that exhibit different brain-wave patterns. Sleep gets progressively deeper as we progress from stage 1 through stage 4. These four stages are called *non-REM (non-rapid eye movement)* sleep.

5 After progressing through the four stages, our sleep gets lighter again, and, about 40 to 80 minutes after we fall asleep, we enter *REM (rapid eye movement)* sleep. This is the time when we are most likely to dream.

6 Sleep is universal throughout the animal kingdom although there is wide difference in the average amount of sleep different species need. Recently a "sleep-promoting substance" has been isolated from human urine, which, when injected into rabbits, brings on a 50 percent increase in deep, nondreaming sleep.

7 There are a number of different theories about the function of sleep. People deprived of sleep show some relatively minor physiological symptoms including hand tremors, double vision, and lowered pain threshold. Sleep loss especially affects the ability to do complex or difficult tasks. People totally deprived of sleep are apt to become confused and irritable although their personality is likely to remain intact. People awakened during REM sleep become anxious and irritable and have trouble concentrating. They "catch up" on REM sleep when they are allowed to sleep uninterrupted.

8 The average amount of sleep varies depending on the age of the person. Infants sleep the most and elderly people sleep the least.

9 Research on personality differences between long and short sleepers is contradictory. People may need different amounts of sleep depending on how their lives are going.

10 The presence of *dreaming* is associated with: the typical brain wave of an emergent stage 1 sleep pattern; an increase in pulse and breathing rate; lack of body movement; appearance of rapid eye movements. People dream for about one to two hours a night. A number of theories exist to explain why we forget dreams. *Freud* maintained that this was due to *repression* of anxiety-laden thoughts; *Hobson and McCarley* point to *state-dependent amnesia; Crick and Mitchison* believe dreams *clear our brains* of unnecessary material.

11 There are a number of very different theories about the reasons for dreaming. Sigmund Freud felt we dream to fulfill the wishes we repress while awake. He believed that dreams have both *manifest content* (the actual description of our dreams) and *latent content* (their underlying meaning). According to Freud, much of what we dream is symbolic of repressed desires and conflicts, most of which are sexual.

12 *Alfred Adler* believed our dreams assist us in solving problems. *Carl Jung* felt dreams help us learn about ignored or suppressed aspects of ourselves.

13 *Hobson and McCarley* proposed the *activation-synthesis model* of dreaming. They feel that the bizarre shifts and symbols of dreams are not disguised unconscious thoughts but are the result of how the brain functions during sleep. During dreaming, parts of the brain are stimulated; which part is stimulated determines what we dream about and how dream images are put together.

14 Sleep disorders include *narcolepsy* (an uncontrollable urge to sleep); *insomnia* (difficulty getting to sleep and/or staying asleep); *sleep apnea* (periods of sleep when breathing stops briefly); *night terrors* (panic attacks); *nightmares; sleepwalking* and *sleeptalking.*

15 There does not seem to be a single, unique *meditative state.* While Wallace and Benson describe it as a state of relaxed wakefulness, others have noted that *experienced* meditators show a great deal of activity in their body processes.

16 The best-known meditative technique in the West is *transcendental meditation (TM),* developed by Maharishi Mahesh Yogi.

17 Regular periods of meditation seem to help many people deal with stress and have been useful in the treatment of insomnia, angina pectoris, and hypertension. Meditation has been used in programs to cut back the use of alcohol, tobacco, and other drugs.

18 *Hypnosis* is a state of heightened suggestibility or susceptibility to outside influence. Some common behaviors among hypnotized people include rigidity of the arm, loss of voluntary control, hallucinations, failure to feel pain, amnesia, and responsiveness to posthypnotic suggestion. Not all people can be hypnotized.

19 Opinions differ on what *hypnosis* is. According to *trance-state theory,* the hypnotized person is in a state of consciousness different from the normal one. Experiments comparing the behaviors of sub-

jects who were hypnotized with those who were told to simulate hypnosis suggest that the hypnotized state *is* qualitatively different from normal consciousness.

20 *Hilgard* believes that hypnotized people experience little or no pain because they block pain from full consciousness through hypnosis. He maintains that during hypnosis there is a *dissociation* or *split-in consciousness,* that is, that the hypnotized person is functioning on more than one level of awareness.

21 The *role-playing approach* holds that "hypnosis," rather than being a special state of consciousness, is a case of role-playing. *Cognitive-behavioral theory* maintains that the hypnotic state doesn't depend on any trance-induction technique but, rather, depends on the subject's readiness to think along with and imagine the themes suggested by the hypnotist.

22 Hypnosis is being used in a number of practical settings. It has been used to treat a number of *medical conditions* and has been particularly effective in alleviating *pain.* Hypnosis is becoming a highly controversial element in *criminal trials.*

23 A *drug* is any chemical substance that produces physical, mental, emotional, and/or behavioral changes in the user. *Psychoactive drugs* are mind altering. Anyone using a drug because he or she is unable or afraid to give it up is a *drug abuser.*

24 Commonly ingested substances such as *caffeine* (in coffee, cola, and chocolate), *nicotine* (in cigarettes, cigars, and pipe tobacco), and *alcohol* are drugs. Caffeine and nicotine are *stimulants* while alcohol is a central nervous system *depressant.* Alcohol abuse is the number 1 drug problem in America today.

25 *Marijuana* is a commonly used drug derived from the *cannabis sativa* plant. When it is smoked, it often conveys upon the smoker a sense of well-being. However, depending on the amount and strength, it can also cause anxiety, confusion, or delirium. Its long-term effects are as yet unknown. It seems to be of use in several types of medical treatments.

26 *Stimulants* such as *amphetamines* and *cocaine* lead to increased energy levels, wakefulness, and mood elevation although they have considerable negative side-effects.

27 *Sedatives* have a calming effect and bring on sleep. There are three types: *barbiturates, nonbarbiturates,* and *major and minor tranquilizers.* Although they have appropriate medicinal uses, they are easily abused. They can impair memory and judgment, sometimes leading to coma and death. They are particularly dangerous when taken with alcohol since both are central nervous system *depressants* whose effects are magnified when taken together.

28 *LSD* and other *hallucinogens,* such as *PCP,* are *psychedelics,* which influence perceptions, thoughts, and emotions by making them different from the normal waking state.

29 *Heroin* and other *narcotics* are depressants that relieve pain and induce sleep. Today heroin accounts for 90 percent of narcotic abuse in the United States. Addiction is sometimes treated by giving *methadone,* an addictive narcotic that lasts longer and is less likely to cause negative side-effects.

SUGGESTED READINGS

Dusek, D., & Girdano, D. A. (1980). *Drugs: A factual account* (3d ed.). Reading, Mass. Addison-Wesley. A comprehensive account of drug use and abuse. Contains information on how drugs affect the nervous system and on drugs and the law.

Edmonston, W. E. (1981). *Hypnosis and relaxation.* New York: Wiley: Examines the relationship between hypnosis and relaxation. Contains interesting historical information about hypnosis.

Naranjo, C., & Ornstein, R. E. (1976). *On the psychology of meditation.* New York: Penguin. In the first part of this book Naranjo discusses the spirit and techniques of meditation. In Part II, Ornstein describes the implications of meditation techniques for modern psychology.

Pattison, E. M., & Kaufman, E. (Eds.) (1982). *Encyclopedic handbook of alcoholism.* New York: Gardner Press. A monumental book that includes sections on the definition and diagnosis of alcoholism as well as discussions of medical, biological, social, and psychological aspects of alcoholism.

U.S. Department of Health and Human Services. (1980). *The health consequences of smoking for women.* Washington, D.C.: USDHHS. A 400-page analysis of the scientific documents related to women and smoking. It includes information on the effects of smoking on prenatal development and childbirth and on women's increasing rates of lung cancer.

Webb, W. (1975) *Sleep: The Gentle Tyrant.* Englewood Cliffs, N.J.: Prentice-Hall. A brief and easy-to-read discussion of experimental findings about sleep by a prominent researcher. The book has a practical orientation.

PART
3

LEARNING, MEMORY, AND COGNITIVE PROCESSES

You could not be taking this course and reading this book if you were not capable of the abilities described in the next four chapters—learning, remembering, and thinking. These abilities are not exclusively reserved for human beings; in fact, considerable controversy rages in psychological circles over the extent to which certain nonhuman animals can think and can learn a language. There is no controversy, however, about the indisputable fact that all normal human beings can perform all these mental processes.

In Chapter 5, "Learning," we'll look at some of the principles of learning and at the practical implications of psychological findings, which have been applied to such everyday concerns as overcoming writer's block, doing well on final exams, and teaching tricks to pets.

How do we remember? Why do we forget? These questions are posed and answered (to the best of current knowledge) in Chapter 6, "Memory." While much of the memory research that has taken place so far aims to sort out the basic processes of remembering and forgetting, here, too, we can turn to the research for practical clues for improving our memories.

Chapter 7 takes up the controversial topic of intelligence, asking what it is, how we measure it, and what factors affect it. All these issues have been—and continue to be—hotly debated by educators, politicians, laypeople, and, of course, psychologists. We'll look at some exciting new directions in intelligence testing and talk about what's right and what's wrong with the tests in common use today. The chapter ends with discussions of people at the two extremes of intelligence—the intellectually gifted and the mentally retarded.

Chapter 8, "Language and Thought," focuses on the cognitive abilities examined in the previous three chapters, as we consider the ways in which both people and animals apply their intelligence to learn and remember, in the service of thought and language. We'll examine the various theories that try to explain how we learn to speak and understand language, describe several apes who are said to know a language, and consider the important role of "motherese" in children's linguistic development. The kind of thinking that solves problems will be discussed, along with suggestions for more creative problem solving.

CHAPTER 5

LEARNING

SPOTLIGHT ON

Two simple types of associative learning, classical and operant conditioning, and cognitive aspects of learning.

How Pavlov's experiments with dogs, Thorndike's experiments with cats, and Skinner's experiments with rats and pigeons led to basic laws of learning.

How psychologists have used learning principles to deal with practical problems such as how and when to use punishment with children, how to overcome writer's block, how to teach a pet a trick, and how to control certain bodily responses.

The importance of a sense of control in the lives of people of all ages and how the feeling that we cannot control events in our lives (learned helplessness) can undermine our ability to learn.

As you watch a spider spin a graceful gossamer web, or see a mother bird drop worms into the wide open mouths of her nestlings, or peer at a column of ants carrying crumbs to the anthill they call home, you are not watching any learned activity. All these behaviors are carried out by an inborn sort of species-specific program that each of these creatures is born with, known as "instinct." Instincts are relatively complex patterns of behavior that are biologically determined and usually important for species survival. All members of a particular species show this instinctive behavior. One swallow, for example, does not stay "home" while all the others migrate to Capistrano every year at some genetically programmed signal.

Today, most psychologists and other observers of human behavior agree that human beings have no abilities that could properly be called "instincts." Prevailing professional opinions hold that we come into this world with a functioning body, a handful of reflexes, a maturational time-table, and a capacity for infinite learning.

Reflexes, the closest thing human beings have to instinct, are inborn, unlearned, involuntary reactions to stimulation. These simple behaviors arise not through our planning or even our will but involuntarily in response to certain aspects of our environment. We blink at a bright light or a puff of air, kick out when we are tapped at a certain spot just below the kneecap, and, as infants, respond to a stroke on the cheek by turning our head, opening our mouth, and beginning to suck. (The primitive reflexes, such as the sucking reflex just described, that infants are born with, drop out in the first year of life as they are no longer needed. We will discuss these further in Chapter 12.) Why don't we consider these reflexes learned behavior? To answer this question we need to define learning.

Learning is a relatively permanent change in behavior, which reflects a gain of knowledge, understanding, or skill achieved through experience, which may include study, instruction, observation, or practice. Changes in behavior are reasonably objective and, therefore, can be measured.

This definition specifically excludes any ability or skill that is attained by maturation, the process by which biologically predetermined patterns of behavior unfold, more or less on schedule. Development is often described as the result of maturation *and* learning. An unfriendly environment can delay maturation, but a supportive one can rarely hurry it up. Before certain kinds of learning can take place, a person has to have achieved a certain level of maturation. A 6-month-old baby cannot learn how to control his bowel movements because neither his brain nor his body is mature enough. When we hear parents proudly talk of their very young "toilet-trained" infants, we know that it is the parent who is trained—to know when the baby is about to move his bowels and to rush him to the "potty seat."

This concept of learning also excludes reflexes because they are innate, involuntary responses to stimulation rather than the relatively permanent changes of behavior brought about by experience. Nor does learning include temporarily induced states brought about by physiological factors like illness, medication, or fatigue. If, for example, you perform much better on a test this week than you did last week, it may not be because you have learned so much in the meantime. Your first performance may not have been as good as it could have been because you were tired or not feeling well. Similarly, if your second performance is much worse, the explanation may again be laid to the door of fatigue or poor health rather than to the likelihood that you have forgotten what you have already learned.

The presence of learning can often be deduced by a change in behavior. But not always. There is a difference between learning and performance. Even though you have learned something, you may not demonstrate that learning by your behavior if you are not motivated and paying attention. A college student's score on a psychology exam, for example, may not adequately reflect what she has learned if she had an argument with her roommate just before the test, if she is suffering from a bout of hay fever, if she slept poorly or not at all the night before, or if she gets extremely anxious in a testing situation. (See Chapter 10 for a discussion of test anxiety.) Latent learning, to be discussed later, is another example of disparity between learning and performance.

Despite the fact that performance is not necessarily a perfect indicator of learning, however, psychologists generally assess what a person or animal has learned based on what she or he does because behavior is the only criterion they can observe and measure.

Because so much of what human beings do, both in and out of society, depends on learning, psychologists have devoted considerable attention to finding out how people learn. They have found that we learn in a number of different ways. The simplest kind of learning, habituation, is the phenomenon by which we "get used to" something, thus showing that we know what it is. The next level of learning, in which we form new associations between a stimulus and a response, is called associative learning. In the two simple types of associative learning, classical and operant conditioning, new responses seem to be "stamped" into an animal or person. These two types of learning have received a lot of attention over the years, but today, many psychologists are looking at learning as a more cognitive, less automatic acquisition of knowledge about the environment.

Cognitive psychologists focus on the thought processes that go on in the mind of an animal or person. While behaviorists say that an organism making a particular response is showing an automatic stimulus-response connection, cognitive psychologists maintain that there is a step between the stimulus and the response. This step is mental activity, or thought, whose nature will be described in detail later in this chapter. Cognitive psychologists also feel that there are other types of learning besides associative learning or conditioning. They define learning to include learning by observation and latent learning.

CLASSICAL CONDITIONING

You meet your friend at noon, in front of the Science Building, and head toward the student union. As you walk together, she tells you about the restaurant where she had dinner the night before. As she describes, in delicious detail, the pungent aromas and the subtle flavors of the food she ate, you realize that your mouth is watering. "Hey!" you say. "I'm like those dogs I just learned about."

Pavlov and His Salivating Dogs

"Those dogs" are the subjects in what is probably the most famous scientific experiment in the field of learning. Ivan Pavlov, a Russian physiologist who won the Nobel Prize in 1904 for his work on the digestive system, also had a great interest in studying the brain and the nervous system. His research into the workings of these two systems demonstrated the presence of the learning phenomenon that has come to be known as classical conditioning. Classical, or Pavlovian, conditioning involves some kind of reflex behavior. As we noted earlier, reflexes are involuntary responses to stimulation. We see in classical conditioning that the organism learns to make a reflex response (that is, becomes classically conditioned) to some stimulus that was previously *neutral* (that is, it did not automatically bring forth this response). Let's see how this works in our discussion of Pavlov's dogs.

Pavlov knew that when he placed meat powder in a dog's mouth, saliva would flow as the first step in the process of digestion. Salivation is an unlearned, or reflex, response to the food. After noting that his dogs would salivate when they first *saw* the meat, he designed the experiment that has become famous. First, a minor operation was performed on the laboratory dogs so that their saliva could be collected and measured. As a dog stood quietly on a table, loosely harnessed, an experimenter sounded a tone on a tuning fork, and then, seven to eight seconds later, moved a plate of powdered meat within reach of the dog. At first, the animal did not salivate upon hearing the tone, although it did salivate copiously while it was eating (see Figure 5-1).

The experimenter then presented different combinations of the tone and food, varying the intervals between them. Eventually the dog salivated when it heard the tone, even before the meat appeared. Apparently, it had learned that the tone would soon be followed by dinner, and its salivary reflexes had been conditioned to respond to the tone as they did to food. Its salivary juices had begun to flow in the expectation of receiving food, just as yours might as you smell dinner cooking or as you listen to your friend describe that delectable meal.

How do we talk about this phenomenon in psychological terms? In this experiment the *tone* is a neutral stimulus, a stimulus that does not automatically elicit a response. The food is an unconditioned stimulus (UCS), a stimulus that automatically elicits a response. This response, known as the unconditioned response or unconditioned reflex (UCR), does not have to be learned. Salivation is the UCR to food.

During classical conditioning, the organism learns a new association between two events. In this experiment, an association is learned between the tone and the food. How does this occur? By repeatedly pairing the neutral stimulus (the tone) with the unconditioned stimulus (the food). Once the organism has learned to associate the food and the tone and to respond essentially the same way to both (salivation), we say conditioning has occurred. At this point the tone is called the conditioned stimulus (CS) and salivation is the conditioned response (CR). A conditioned stimulus, then, is an initially neutral stimulus that, after repeated pairings with a UCS, comes to elicit a conditioned (or learned) response. A diagram showing the phenomenon graphically appears in Figure 5-2.

Pavlov (1927) and those who came after him felt that conditioning is strongly influenced by the timing of the interstimulus interval, the period

Ivan Pavlov and one of his famous salivating dogs, subjects in an experiment that demonstrated that dogs can learn to salivate in response to a tone they have learned to associate with food. (National Library of Medicine)

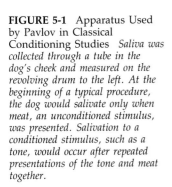

FIGURE 5-1 Apparatus Used by Pavlov in Classical Conditioning Studies *Saliva was collected through a tube in the dog's cheek and measured on the revolving drum to the left. At the beginning of a typical procedure, the dog would salivate only when meat, an unconditioned stimulus, was presented. Salivation to a conditioned stimulus, such as a tone, would occur after repeated presentations of the tone and meat together.*

of time between the presentation of the neutral stimulus and the UCS. Generally, it's most effective to present the neutral stimulus (the tone) just before and overlapping with the UCS (the meat). This is called a *delayed relationship*. A *trace relationship* occurs when the CS (the tone—after conditioning has taken place) is presented and then withdrawn before the UCS (the meat) appears. If the tone sounds too far before the meat appears, the dog would have trouble learning the association between the two. If the tone sounded at the same time the dog saw the meat (*simultaneous conditioning*) or afterwards (*backward conditioning*), he might not notice the tone and might not learn to associate the tone with the meat (see Figure 5-3).

What happens when the experimenter changes the ground rules and begins to sound the tone without following it with the meat? The dog eventually learns that food is not forthcoming, after all, and no longer salivates. This is the process of extinction, the removal of reinforcement for a behavior that has been reinforced in the past.

After the conditioned response has been extinguished, spontaneous recovery often takes place. How does this work? Several days after the dog has stopped salivating in response to the tone, taking her back to the lab where the original conditioning took place and again sounding the tone will make her start salivating again. This response shows that she has not forgotten the original learning but has inhibited the learned response. We say that this recovery is "spontaneous" because it occurs without any new conditioning trials (see Figure 5-4).

Another Pavlovian concept is stimulus generalization, the tendency to make the conditioned response to a stimulus that is similar but not identical to the one that was originally paired with the unconditioned stimulus. For example, a dog that has learned to salivate to one tone may also salivate to another tone, to a bell, or to some other sound. *Discrimination* is the opposite of generalization; the animal learns to respond only to the tone and not to something similar like a bell.

Pavlov used the concept of discrimination to create an *experimental neurosis* in some dogs (1927). First the dogs learned how to discriminate be-

FIGURE 5-2 Classical conditioning *Classical conditioning occurs in three stages. The neutral stimulus eventually produces a conditioned response.*

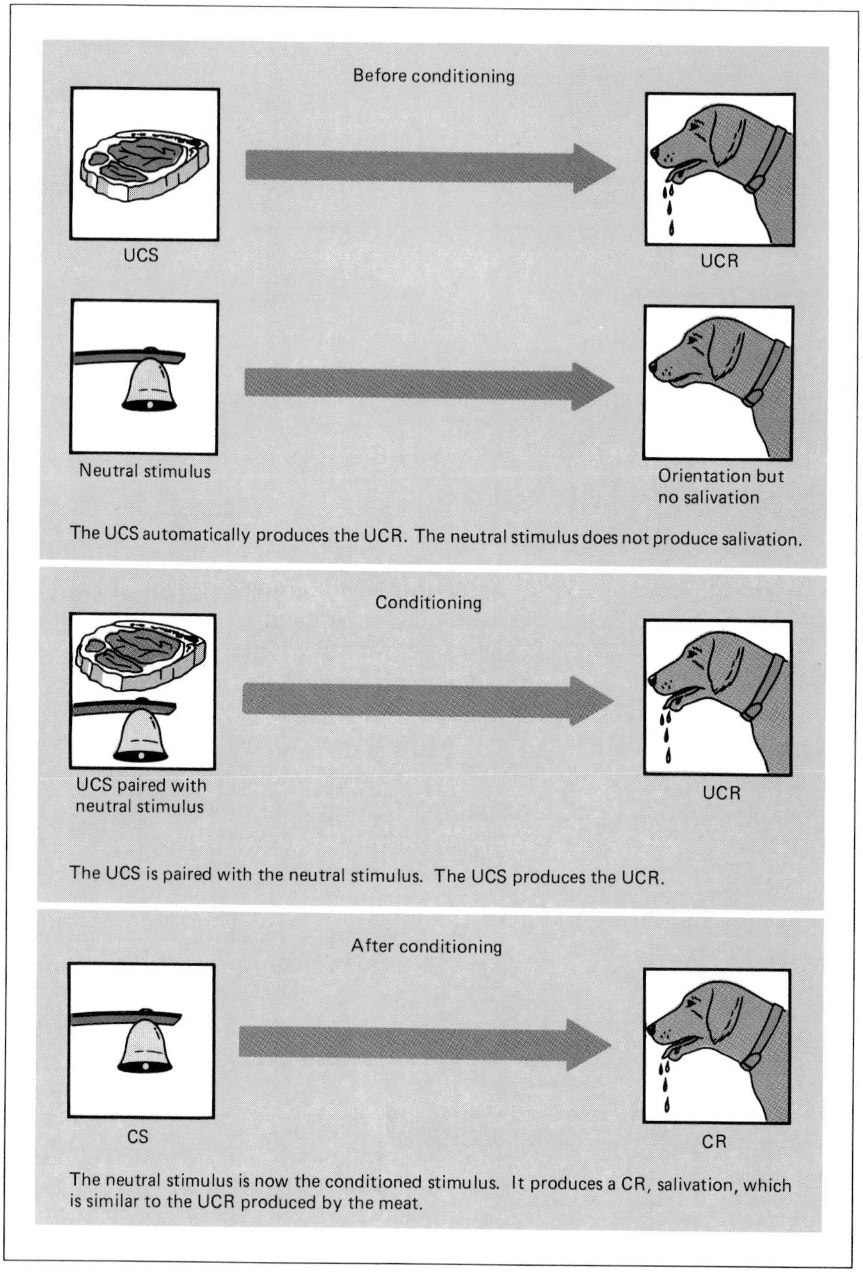

Before conditioning

UCS → UCR

Neutral stimulus → Orientation but no salivation

The UCS automatically produces the UCR. The neutral stimulus does not produce salivation.

Conditioning

UCS paired with neutral stimulus → UCR

The UCS is paired with the neutral stimulus. The UCS produces the UCR.

After conditioning

CS → CR

The neutral stimulus is now the conditioned stimulus. It produces a CR, salivation, which is similar to the UCR produced by the meat.

FIGURE 5-3 Pairing of CS with UCS in four temporal relations *Acquisition of conditioning is quickest using the "delayed" sequence. (From Hulse, Egeth, & Deese, 1980)*

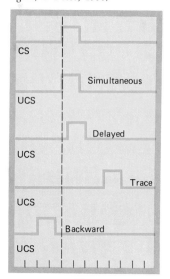

tween a circle, which was a signal for food, and an ellipse (an elongated circle, or an oval shape), which meant that no food would be forthcoming. When the circle and the ellipse were quite different from each other, the dogs quickly learned to salivate to the circle but not to the ellipse. But when the experimenter gradually changed the shapes so that the two figures came to look more and more alike, the dogs could no longer tell the difference between the shape that signaled food and the one that didn't.

Once the dogs could no longer discriminate between the two shapes,

FIGURE 5-4 Acquisition, extinction, and spontaneous recovery of a conditioned response *During acquisition, the CS and UCS are paired, and learning increases. During extinction, the CS is presented without the UCS; responding weakens and eventually stops. After a rest period, spontaneous recovery occurs. In other words, the learned response reappears without further conditioning trials.*

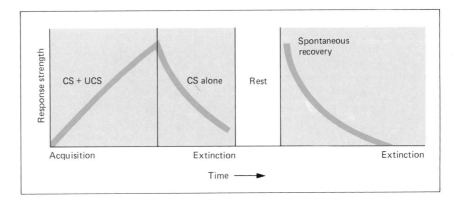

they began to act strangely. They barked, acted fearful, and tried to destroy the conditioning apparatus.

Since these behaviors are similar to those that we often see among neurotic people, this experiment may help us understand human neuroses. For one thing, it suggests that neuroses are learned. For another, the situation the dogs were put in, in which they essentially lost control of their environments, resembles the situations many people often feel they are in, in which they are unable to pick up cues from their environment and, therefore, feel they have no control over their lives. Later in this chapter we will talk about the emotionally debilitating condition known as "learned helplessness," which resembles the plight of these dogs.

Can People Be Conditioned?

A salesperson takes a potential client out to dinner. After associating the salesperson's proposal with the good feelings engendered by a pleasant dinner in a lovely restaurant, the prospect will be more likely to become a client than if the salesperson had approached him in less appealing surroundings. At least, this is the basis for much of the expense-account wining and dining that supports many overpriced restaurants across the country.

A soldier sees a man in the uniform of an opposing nation. Having seen that uniform only in conjunction with stories of atrocities committed by people wearing it, rage bubbles up in the soldier's heart as soon as he sees the man who has been designated his enemy.

These are only two examples of the many ways in which we are conditioned, throughout our lives, to associate pairs of stimuli and to react accordingly.

Give me a dozen healthy infants, well formed, and my own special world to bring them up in, and I'll guarantee to take any one at random and train him to become any type of specialist I might select—doctor, lawyer, artist, merchant, chief, and yes, even beggar and thief, regardless of his talents, penchants, tendencies, abilities, vocations and race of his ancestors.
(Watson, 1958, p. 104)

LITTLE ALBERT John B. Watson, the "father of behaviorism," and the student who became his wife, Rosalie Rayner (1920) maintained that infants are born with three basic emotions: fear, rage, and love. They felt that children's early home lives are the laboratories in which they are conditioned to show these emotions and the more complex feelings that grow out of them. To test these beliefs, they brought Albert, the healthy, good-natured, emotionally stable 9-month-old son of a hospital wet nurse, into the lab. The baby showed no fear to any stimulus—until they made a loud sound by striking a steel bar with a hammer just behind Albert's head. Finally, Albert trembled and wept.

When children have positive experiences with animals, they're not likely to fear them. By deliberately associating furry white animals with a loud noise, behaviorist John B. Watson created fear in a small child who had formerly embraced such animals eagerly. (© 1981 Dean Abramson/Stock, Boston)

Two months later, they brought Albert back. Just as he was starting to touch a white rat (which he had shown no fear of at first), an experimenter sounded a loud noise. Albert jumped, fell forward, and cried. A week later, Albert again saw the rat at the same time he heard the loud noise. Again, frightened tears. This happened again and again.

Eventually, as soon as the baby saw the rat, he whimpered in fear. His fear generalized to a rabbit, a dog, a seal coat, cotton wool, a Santa Claus mask, and Watson's hair. One month later, Albert was found to be afraid of the Santa Claus mask, the fur coat, and to various degrees, the rat, the rabbit, and the dog. Watson and Rayner concluded that "directly conditioned emotional responses as well as those conditioned by transfer persist . . . for a longer period than one month. Our view is that they persist and modify personality throughout life" (p. 12).

Since these psychologists believed so strongly in the power of early experience to bring about lifelong fears, their willingness to subject a healthy baby to these procedures seems especially irresponsible. They did pay lip service to the project's questionability and talked about the counterconditioning they "would" have done if Albert had not been removed from the hospital before they could carry it out. They indicated, however, that they had known from the start that they would have access to Albert for only a short time. Experiments like this have given rise to the Code of Ethics of the American Psychological Association, which today would not allow such an intrusion into a child's psyche.

While psychologists have long faulted Watson and Rayner's ethics, serious criticism of their conclusions surfaced only recently. Let's look at some of the reservations voiced by Harris (1979). First, the results did not prove stimulus generalization since separate conditioning trials were held for both the rabbit and the dog. Second, Albert did not have as strong a fear reaction as indicated. In fact, he was ambivalent toward the animals after the experiment, sometimes letting them approach, sometimes reaching out to them, sometimes avoiding them but not crying. Furthermore, a number of researchers tried to replicate the work, but were unable to induce fears in infants by conditioning them to a loud noise (Jones, 1930; Valentine, 1930; Bregman, 1934). While this study is usually called a pure example of classical conditioning, the punishing aspect of the frighteningly loud noise interposes elements of operant conditioning, which will be discussed later. We have discussed this experiment in detail because of its status as a classic study.

COUNTERCONDITIONING   Suppose that Watson and Rayner had gone ahead with their expressed intention to free Albert of the fears they had instilled in him. How might they have gone about it? They spoke of pairing the feared objects with stroking of the child's erogenous zones (sensitive body areas that produce pleasurable sexual sensations when stroked, like the genitals and breasts) or feeding him candy or other food, or encouraging him to imitate a model (p. 12). It's probably just as well they never went through with this first approach since they well might have produced sexual pathology on top of Albert's other problems. Their other two suggestions, however, were used successfully by another student of Watson's, Mary Cover Jones (1924).

Peter was a healthy, normal, interesting almost-3-year-old, except for his exaggerated fears, which resembled Albert's laboratory-induced fears so closely that Jones said he "seemed almost to be Albert grown a bit older" (p. 153). No one knew what had made Peter so afraid of such objects as a white rat, a rabbit, a fur coat, a feather, and cotton wool. (Like Albert, Peter had no fear of blocks.) Jones wanted to "uncondition" Peter's fear to an animal and then see whether this unconditioning would generalize, without further training, to the other feared items.

First, she set up a modeling procedure, bringing Peter to the lab together with three other children who were not afraid of the rabbit. (Modeling, which we'll discuss in detail later, is the process by which individuals observe and imitate the behavior of others, who are termed "models.") Peter watched the other children playing near or with the rabbit and gradually lost his own fear. He went from the point of being afraid if the rabbit was caged up anywhere in the room, to letting the rabbit nibble his fingers and exulting over the fact that "I touched him on the end."

After this advance, Peter was in the hospital for two months with scarlet fever. When he came back to the lab he was showing his old fears again, partly, no doubt, because both he and his nurse had been frightened by a large dog who jumped at them as they were leaving the hospital. At this point, Jones started a new phase of treatment, in which Peter got food he liked when the rabbit was present so he would associate the rabbit with a pleasant experience. This method was also effective in helping Peter overcome his fear not only of the rabbit but also of the other objects and of strange animals like a mouse and a tangled mass of angleworms. Therapeutic approaches based on these principles will be discussed in Chapter 16.

PRACTICAL ASPECTS OF CLASSICAL CONDITIONING   We are all conditioned to many aspects of the world about us. It helps to be aware of the mecha-

BOX 5-1

THE MEDICAL POTENTIAL OF CLASSICAL CONDITIONING

Gloria, a 28-year-old former dancer, suffers periodically from rashes, pain, fever, and debilitating weakness. Her dancing career, like her general health, has fallen victim to the disease, *systemic lupus erythematosis*. "Lupus" is a disorder of the immune system in which the body turns against itself. Gloria regularly takes a drug called cyclophosphamide, which suppresses the immune response and keeps many of her lupus symptoms under control. On the drug, however, she often doubles over from the painful stomach cramps that are one of its side-effects. If the dosage could be lowered to a level that would still be effective in controlling the symptoms of lupus but that would not produce the undesirable side-effects, Gloria and other fellow-sufferers would benefit greatly.

Recent research indicates that this may be possible. A psychologist and an immunologist have been able to classically condition rats and mice to suppress their bodies' immune response as a result of drinking saccharin-flavored water, after saccharin had been paired repeatedly with cyclophosphamide (Ader & Cohen, 1982). The researchers injected cyclophosphamide into the animals immediately after they received water sweetened with saccharin. The immune systems of the rodents that had received sweetened water along with the drug then reacted to the sweetened water alone as if it had the immunosuppressive qualities of the drug.

If such classically conditioned mice received only half the usual dosage of cyclophosphamide, bolstered with the sweetened water the animals had been conditioned to, their bodies' immune systems were suppressed as completely as if they had been given full dosages of the drug. These mice lived as long as did other mice that received full dosages.

The implications of these findings for the human condition are exciting since the usefulness of many drugs is limited by the severity of their side-effects. If classical conditioning could fool human bodies into responding to greatly lowered dosages of powerful drugs, many people would have access to treatments that are now out of the question because of their side-effects. This kind of research demonstrates the powerful influence of the mind over such autonomic body systems as the immune response, which we don't ordinarily think of as under our control. It also demonstrates the promise that psychology holds for advancing medical progress.

nism that prepares us to feel spiritual as soon as we step into a church, patriotic when the flag passes by, emotional upon reading or hearing certain phrases of a poem or a bar of music. As the psychologist B. F. Skinner has pointed out, society uses the process of classical conditioning "to arrange for the control of behavior" (1953, p. 56). Classical conditioning procedures are also used to help people overcome phobias (irrational fears) as well as undesirable habits like excessive drinking or smoking. One practical potential of classical conditioning is described in Box 5-1.

OPERANT CONDITIONING

In a large gambling casino on the boardwalk in Atlantic City, a middle-aged woman stands for hours in front of a metal box with pictures. Over and over again, she puts a coin into a slot and pulls down a lever to make the pictures come up in a certain pattern. Why does she engage in this monotonous, arm-tiring behavior? Because from time to time a pattern she is trying for does appear and coins cascade out of the machine, for her to scoop up and reinsert, in hopes of bigger and bigger returns. Here we see a prime example of operant conditioning.

How does operant conditioning differ from classical conditioning?

Classical conditioning applies to behaviors that automatically follow a stimulus, like salivation to the presence of food. The food *elicits* the behavior, and through conditioning, a new stimulus like a tone eventually elicits the same behavior. Operant conditioning applies to behavior that the organism *emits* because it has learned that doing so (*operating* on the environment) will bring about a reward or will avoid or escape a punishment. The reward is *contingent* on a particular behavior. This kind of learning is also called *instrumental conditioning* because the person or animal is instrumental in changing its environment in some way. The starring role that Pavlov's dogs played in demonstrating the principles of classical conditioning is assumed for operant conditioning by Thorndike's cats and Skinner's pigeons and rats.

Thorndike: His Cats and His Law of Effect

An American psychologist, Edward Lee Thorndike, was discovering the basic laws of operant conditioning at about the same time Pavlov was discovering the basic principles of classical conditioning in Russia. Thorndike put hungry cats inside locked "puzzle boxes." The cat could see and smell food that was placed outside the box but couldn't get at it. Unless it could learn some way to get outside the box. Which it gradually did. The animals learned to pull on a piece of rope that would open the box, let them get out, and allow them to get at the food. This feline learning achievement was the basis of Thorndike's doctoral dissertation, a research project required for the Ph.D. degree, which he received in 1898.

The cats learned by trial and error. They engaged in a number of different behaviors while they were in the box and only by accident happened upon the right one. Once they learned the trick of opening the box, however, they were able to escape rapidly. On subsequent stays in the box, they did not engage in any of the other unproductive behaviors they had initially tried but instead zeroed in on pulling the rope.

Thorndike explained the cats' learning by referring to the reward they got (the food) and the association the cats made between pulling the rope and eating. He put it into words as the *law of effect* (1911), which states, basically, that when an animal's actions in any given situation are accompanied or closely followed by a satisfying experience, the animal will connect the actions with the satisfaction and will be likely to perform the same actions if a similar situation comes up again. When the animal's actions become linked with discomfort, the animal won't repeat those actions. In other words, if it feels good, the cat will do it again. If not, it won't. This association, said Thorndike, is automatic.

Skinner: Principles Derived from the "Skinner Box"

Burrhus Frederic Skinner is the foremost proponent of operant conditioning today. He is concerned chiefly with the way behavior affects the environment to produce consequences and with the way a favorable consequence, or reinforcement, works to increase the probability of a behavior's occurring again. Skinner maintains that reinforcement is the basic means of controlling behavior. The kind of behavior that is influenced by reinforcement is called an operant. In Skinner's work with animals, operants were often pecking or bar-pressing.

In his laboratory work with rats, and then with pigeons, Skinner designed an apparatus that has since become one of the most common tools

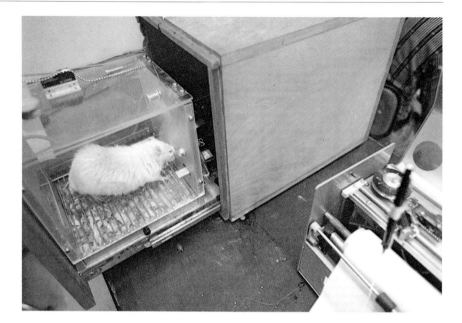

The principles of operant conditioning, first demonstrated by B. F. Skinner, explain how rats learn to press a lever to get food. This rat is part of a pharmaceutical company's efforts to discover new drugs. It feeds trained rats a variety of drugs and then runs tests to compare the actions of the different drugs on the rats' behavior. (© Sepp Seitz, 1978. Woodfin Camp & Assoc.)

of psychological research. This was a cage, or box, equipped with a simple mechanism that the animal itself could activate to get its reward. This was usually a bar or lever that the animal could press. He also designed a moving paper tape that would automatically record the animal's behavior.

Skinner developed a standard procedure for studying operant conditioning, which can be applied to people as well as to animals. Briefly, this is how the procedure works:

1 Identify the response to be studied (that is, the *operant*). The easiest kind to study is a simple response like pressing a bar.
2 Determine the *base-line rate* of that response. That is, how often does the animal normally take this action?
3 Choose something that you think the animal will consider a reward and that will, therefore, serve to *reinforce* the behavior you want the animal to emit. Food is most often chosen, but other reinforcers are also used from time to time such as the opportunity for a mother to reach her offspring or for an adult to reach a sexual partner.
4 Apply the reinforcer according to some set schedule until the animal has increased the response you want.
5 Stop awarding the reinforcer to see whether the animal's rate of response will drop back to the base-line rate. If so, *extinction* has occurred, and you can safely assume that the reinforcer was responsible for the animal's changed behavior.

Reinforcement

There are two basic kinds of reinforcers: *positive* and *negative.* Positive reinforcers are stimuli that increase the probability of a response when they are *added* to a situation. Examples are such desirables as food, water, or sexual contact. Negative reinforcers are unpleasant stimuli whose re-

moval from a situation increases the probability of a response. Common examples are a loud noise, a very bright light, or electric shock. In either case, the effect of the reinforcer is the same: It increases the response. Negative reinforcement is *not* the same as punishment. While both kinds of reinforcement—positive and negative—result in the probability that a given behavior will occur more often, punishment is administered to make a behavior occur less often. We'll see how this works when we discuss punishment in more detail later in this chapter.

Reinforcers can be primary or secondary. Primary reinforcers are biologically important: They include food, water, sex, and escape from harmful conditions. Secondary reinforcers are learned; they become reinforcing only because of their association with primary reinforcers. In this category we would put money, school grades, gold stars on a chart, and praise. Tokens, which can be exchanged for desired merchandise or for other kinds of rewards, can be effective secondary reinforcers to change the behavior of people in different situations.

How do you know what will serve as a reinforcement? Only, according to Skinner (1953), by making a direct test. An event is reinforcing if it brings about an increase in the frequency of a specific response. No matter how good something might seem to you, it is not a reinforcer if it either doesn't change the animal's or person's rate of response or if it lowers it. Conversely, something that on the face of it does not seem like a reinforcer may actually be one.

In many homes, for example, parents tend to ignore small children when they are quietly behaving themselves. But when Melissa starts to tease the cat, poke a finger in the baby's eye, or get into the cookie jar, her parents don't ignore her any longer. They may scold, scream, or spank. None of these behaviors seem like reinforcers, but if what Melissa wants is attention, that is what she is getting. And so the attention itself is the reinforcer for the child's obstreperous behavior.

In an experiment that has since become a classic, two psychologists decided to test the reinforcing power of attention to eliminate aggressive behavior among nursery school children (Brown & Elliott, 1965). Over an eight-week period, nursery school teachers focused on eliminating aggressive behavior among 3- and 4-year-old boys. They paid special attention to the children when they were being cooperative, saying things like "That's good, Mike," and "Look what Eric made." They tried to ignore aggression unless it seemed dangerous.

The average number of physically aggressive acts dropped from forty-one during the pretreatment week to twenty-one by the end of the treatment period, and the number of instances of verbal aggression plummeted from twenty-three to five. Why did verbal aggression drop so much more? Probably because it's harder to ignore fighting than threats and insults. In any case, both kinds of aggression did drop, and the two most troublesome boys in the class became friendly and cooperative to a degree none of the teachers had thought possible.

TIMING OF REINFORCEMENT   For reinforcement to be effective, it must be prompt. If it follows too long after the action, no learning will take place. The other events that take place during the period of delay will make the

The allure of slot machines lies in the gambler's knowledge that he has a chance to win a lot of money. He may not be familiar with the terms, intermittent reinforcement *and* variable ratio schedule, *but these are principles that govern the slot machine's payoff—and its popularity. (© Michael S. Yamashita 1981/ Woodfin Camp & Assoc.)*

person or animal miss the connection between what he or she did and the fact that he is now experiencing something unpleasant.

The major exception to this general rule is in regard to food preferences and aversions, which we'll discuss in the section on punishment.

SCHEDULES OF REINFORCEMENT   Schedules of reinforcement refer to the patterns by which reinforcement is given. There are two broad categories of patterns—continuous and partial. Partial reinforcement is also known as *intermittent* reinforcement. If a pigeon gets food every time it pecks a particular spot, it is receiving continuous reinforcement. If the pigeon receives food only every tenth time it pecks the spot, it is receiving intermittent, or partial, reinforcement, which is more common.

Animals learn more quickly when they receive continuous reinforcement, but they will perform the behavior longer under intermittent reinforcement. Why is partial reinforcement more resistant to extinction? Because the animal receiving continuous reinforcement quickly learns when no further reinforcement is forthcoming and quickly stops making the response, while the animal being reinforced only part of the time takes longer to recognize that reinforcement has stopped. As a result, it keeps making the response for a longer time.

The power of intermittent reinforcement can be seen in practically any supermarket any day of the week. Here is a typical scenario: Three-year-old Michael, sitting in a cart, asks his mother for a box of cookies. The mother says, "No, we have some at home." Michael asks again. Again, the mother refuses. Michael starts to scream and flail about, trying to get out of the seat. His mother refuses one more time. Other shoppers look at the child, who is getting noisier and more out of control by the minute. Finally, the embarrassed mother grabs a box of cookies from the shelf and hurls them into Michael's lap. The child has learned something that he will use to his advantage in the future. He has learned that he has a tool for getting what he wants. He has learned that sometimes it will work and sometimes it won't, so he might as well keep trying it.

Partial reinforcement can be given according to a number of different schedules. The most basic of these are fixed and variable interval schedules, and fixed and variable ratio schedules (see Figure 5-5).

Interval schedules require a certain amount of time to pass between the presentation of reinforcement. According to this kind of schedule, a pigeon might get food every 5 minutes, regardless of the number of pecks it makes during that period, as long as it pecks after each 5-minute waiting period. Animals on a fixed-interval schedule will show a drop in responding immediately after reinforcement since they have learned they will not be reinforced again for quite some time.

On a variable interval basis, the time period that must pass before a response will be reinforced is varied, so that the animal might get food every 5 minutes, *on the average*. Sometimes, however, the organism may be reinforced after only, say, 30 seconds, and another time it might have to wait longer than 10 minutes. Skinner (1953) points out that pigeons reinforced under this type of schedule give a "remarkably stable and uniform" performance (p. 102) that is very resistant to extinction. Skinner (1953) observed that pigeons will peck for as long as fifteen hours straight, pecking two to three times per second, without pausing longer than 15 or 20 seconds during the entire time span.

In *ratio reinforcement*, the time interval doesn't matter. It's the number of responses that count. A pigeon will be reinforced, say, every tenth time it presses the bar, and a writer will receive a check for every three completed chapters of a book. In a fixed ratio schedule, like these, reinforcement is contingent upon the organism's making a fixed number of responses. Ratio reinforcement is the basis for sales commissions, most professional pay, and certain kinds of industrial work.

FIGURE 5-5 Typical curves for different reinforcement schedules *The different reinforcement schedules produce typical response curves. Note that both ratio schedules are associated with high levels of responding, as demonstrated by the steepness of the curve. The interval schedules are associated with intermediate rates of responding. Note the drop in responding immediately after reinforcement in the fixed-interval schedule; this produces the typical "scalloped" curve. The presentation of reinforcement is indicated by the small lines perpendicular to each curve. (Adapted from "Teaching Machines" by B. F. Skinner, © 1961 by Scientific American, Inc. All rights reserved.)*

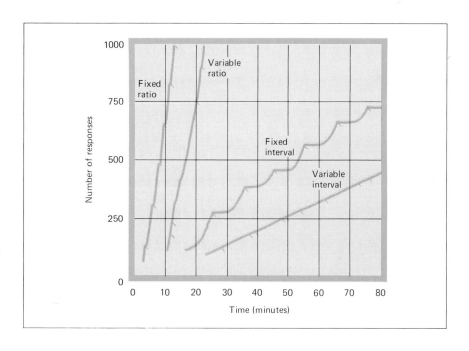

BOX 5-2

OVERCOMING "WRITER'S BLOCK" THROUGH OPERANT CONDITIONING

While we usually think of "writer's block" as a tragic condition afflicting a once-successful novelist or playwright who suddenly cannot put words on paper, the inability to write afflicts people in all fields who have to do a certain amount of professional writing. Certain kinds of writing, for example, are essential for academic success: Undergraduate students have to write term papers, graduate students have to write dissertations, professors have to write for scholarly journals, and administrators have to write reports. Since the inability to write can doom a career to failure, it's encouraging to learn that writing problems can respond to operant learning principles.

Robert Boice (1982) developed a program custom tailored to help several academicians with writing complaints. Let's see how this four-step program could help you overcome a difficulty in writing:

STEP 1: GETTING BASE-LINE INFORMATION

First, you would need to find out how much writing you're producing over a two- to three-week period. You would need to keep a record of the amount of writing you're doing (in written or typed pages) and the conditions under which you write (such as time of day, amount of time you devote to writing, and location). Don't count note taking or thinking about writing—just the actual putting down of words on paper.

STEP 2: FIRST CONTINGENCY PERIOD

For six weeks you would give yourself rewards on the basis of a certain amount of writing, perhaps five pages a day. It's important to set realistic goals since expecting too much of yourself will doom your whole program to failure. Boice's investigations of the work habits of professional writers indicate that regularly scheduled, relatively brief writing periods will, in the long run, be more productive than the kind of writing binges and dry spells that break momentum.

Your rewards could be as simple as taking your daily shower, reading the newspaper, watching TV, or phoning a friend. You couldn't do any of these activities until you had produced the set number of pages. (One of Boice's subjects went without a shower for nearly three weeks. Let's hope he lived alone.)

If you found that rewards like these didn't work, you would switch to something else. Another subject of Boice's, whose first reinforcer was not effective, switched to a "productive-avoidance" technique: She placed $250 in the hands of a colleague; if she failed to meet her agreed-upon production of written work in any given week, the colleague would send the $250 to an agency that held a policy on abortion completely opposite to the subject's own attitude and whose aims, therefore, she violently opposed. The subject made sure

to meet her writing quota.

You might follow Boice's suggestions for maintaining your schedule during this period: Begin each writing day by rewriting the last page from the previous session's work; stop writing once you produced the agreed-upon output; and take a break after every half hour of writing.

STEP 3: REMOVAL OF EXTERNAL CONTINGENCIES

For about four weeks, you would keep to your writing schedule, without rewarding yourself on the basis of your literary output. (Whether or not you took a shower, for example, would depend on personal need or inclination—or strong hints from a close friend—instead of whether or not you had produced your daily page quota.)

STEP 4: REESTABLISHMENT OF EXTERNAL CONTINGENCIES

You would go back to your earlier reward system or switch to a more effective one. If you reached the point where you had worked for twenty days without going below your criterion level three times, you would consider yourself successful. Boice's subjects found that by this time they had established a momentum for writing, which would carry them ahead even without their external contingencies. The writing itself became a reinforcer.

An animal being reinforced by a high fixed ratio will show a drop in responding just after reinforcement, just as it does in the case of fixed-interval reinforcement. Skinner (1953) points out that the same principle applies to people: "Wherever a piecework schedule is used—in industry, education, salesmanship, or the professions—low morale or low interest is most often observed just after a unit of work has been completed" (p. 103). (*Piecework* is the term used in industry to denote payment to workers on the basis of the number of units of work they complete. A tailor who gets paid for every finished garment he turns in provides an example of ratio reinforcement.)

In a variable ratio schedule, the organism is reinforced for variable numbers of responses, around some average number. Since the probability of reinforcement at any moment remains essentially the same, the animal continues responding on a constant basis. This kind of schedule is much more powerful than a fixed-ratio schedule with the same average number of responses, showing much more resistance to extinction. The gambler stationed at the "one-arm bandit" is operating on a variable ratio schedule. She knows that the casino management has set the slot machine to pay off according to some kind of average that will, in the long run, make money for the house. She also knows, however, that occasionally there will be big payoffs, and she keeps playing in the hope that she will be lucky enough to be around for one of those payoffs. This is the lure for all gamblers.

It is also possible to combine interval and ratio schedules, to reward a certain number of responses made during a particular time period. A psychology student, for example, might get an A in a sixteen-week course if he gets a grade of 90 percent in each of four exams taken during that time span.

Superstitious Behavior

Things looked bad to Tony LaRussa, manager of the Chicago White Sox. His team had lost twelve games out of fifteen, his job was in danger, and he had just received a telephone death threat. Maybe that's why he pulled his warm-up jacket around him, even though it was a hot, muggy night. That night his team won. From that time on, Tony put on his jacket every time the team played, no matter how blistering the weather. The White Sox won the next nine games out of eleven, and LaRussa said, "I don't put much faith in it, but you never know" (*New York Times*, 1982, p. B8).

Athletes, actors, and gamblers are all famous for wearing their "lucky" clothes, carrying "lucky" charms, performing "lucky" behaviors. Why do they do it? Because on one or more occasions they associated great success with one of these other events. Superstitious behavior is behavior that has been strengthened or weakened because it was accidentally reinforced or punished.

Pigeons can learn to be superstitious, too. In one series of experiments, Skinner (1953) gave pigeons a small amount of food every 15 seconds, no matter what the bird was doing. The first time the pigeon got the food, it was doing something—if only standing still. The pigeon apparently made some connection between the activity and the food, and the second time

Animal trainers teach tricks to their pupils by the use of operant conditioning techniques like shaping, in which they reward any effort in the right direction, no matter how small. The results often make circus audiences gasp and marvel. (© Jeff Albertson/The Picture Cube)

it got the food, it was more prone to be doing what it was doing previously than some other activity. The more it did this, the more the act was reinforced, since the food kept coming. Pigeons that have been conditioned in this way have started hopping from one foot to the other, turning sharply to one side, bowing and scraping, turning around, strutting, and raising their heads.

Such accidental connections have been the basis for the success of innumerable nonscientific medical "cures." Many medical conditions run their course over a certain time period, and any measure that is taken to cure them will meet with success if it is adopted at the right time. Thus are true "believers" created.

Shaping

A favorite saying among behavior modifiers is that the trick to encouraging a child to do what you want him to do is to "catch him being good" and then to reward his goodness. Suppose, though, that you never do catch the child doing exactly what you want him to do. What, then, can you reward?

You reward any effort, no matter how small, that is going in the right direction. This is called shaping, and this approach can be very effective in bringing about all sorts of new behavior—getting a child to make the bed, getting an animal to do a trick, getting a college teacher to stand in a certain corner of a room. To see how shaping works, see Box 5-3, "How to Teach an Animal." We'll talk more about the use of operant conditioning principles in Chapter 16, when we discuss its applications in therapy.

Biological Influences on Learning:

Long before "Miss Piggy" pranced into the public consciousness, a real porker named "Priscilla the Fastidious Pig" was performing on TV, as well as at fairs and conventions, turning on the radio, eating breakfast at a table, picking up dirty clothes and putting them in a hamper, running a vacuum cleaner, and answering yes or no to audience-posed questions by lighting up the proper signs.

Priscilla was the apt pupil of Keller and Marian Breland (1951), a husband-and-wife team of psychologists who applied the principles of operant conditioning to teach chickens, a calf, a turkey, rats, hamsters, guinea pigs, ducks, pigeons, rabbits, cats, dogs, and crows. While their work was almost exclusively in the field of entertainment, they envisioned the use of their techniques for making farm animals more useful and for training dogs to work with the blind, hunt, do detective work, and guard children and property.

In 1961, ten years after publishing a first enthusiastic paper about the promise of this new field of what they called "applied animal psychology," the Brelands published a report about what they called their "failures." These failures teach us a vital lesson about the biological parameters of learning.

Can Any Animal Learn to Do Any Trick?

In one experiment, the Brelands wanted to teach chickens to stand on a platform for 12 to 15 seconds. More than half the chickens would not stand still but instead began to scratch vigorously, round and round at the rate of about two scratches per second. The trainers changed the act and billed it as the "dancing chickens."

In another experiment, they wanted to teach a raccoon to pick up coins and put them in a piggy bank. The raccoon quickly learned to pick up the coin but was very reluctant to let go. He would rub it against the inside of the container, pull it back out, and hold it firmly for several seconds before finally dropping it in the bank. Even though the rubbing behavior was not reinforced, the raccoon did so much of it that the act never worked out.

Because higher-level animals are capable of extremely complex learning, Crystal, a capuchin monkey, has changed the life of Bill, a man left completely dependent on others by a motorcycle accident that made him a quadriplegic. Taught by a professional animal trainer, Crystal picks up books, turns the TV on and off, opens the door, and even does Bill's grocery shopping. (Ira Wyman/Sygma)

BOX 5-3

HOW TO TEACH AN ANIMAL

You can use shaping yourself to train a pet:

1 Choose your subject. You could pick any household pet, including a mouse, a parrot, or a gerbil. (Skinner suggests saving any available children until you have had practice with less valuable material.) Let's say you want to teach your Samoyed dog, Sami, a new trick.
2 Choose a reinforcer. Food is usually the easiest to use. For food to be reinforcing, Sami has to be hungry. So don't try to teach her right after she has eaten.
3 Since reinforcement is most effective when given almost simultaneously with the desired behavior, and since it's hard to hand out food as quickly as you would like to, develop a conditioned reinforcer by pairing the food with something else. That something might be one of those little metal toys

that make a "cricket" sound when you click them.

Condition the cricket by getting together thirty or forty small scraps of food or tiny dog biscuits. Toss a few to Sami, one at a time, no oftener than once or twice a minute. As soon as Sami is eating all the scraps eagerly, sound the cricket—and then toss a piece of food. Wait about 30 seconds and repeat. When you sound the cricket, make no other movement. Sound the cricket and give food only when Sami is not facing you and is at the spot where she receives food.
4 When Sami goes to the food place whenever you sound the cricket, you are ready to begin teaching.
5 Choose the behavior you want to teach. One relatively simple trick, good as a starter, is getting Sami to touch the handle on a low cupboard door with her nose.
6 Shape Sami's behavior by reinforcing anything that

remotely resembles the behavior you want. First, reinforce any turn toward the cupboard. Then reinforce any move toward the cupboard. When Sami is standing close to the cupboard, reinforce any movement of her head that brings her nose close to the cupboard handle. Every time you reinforce, sound the cricket as nearly simultaneously with Sami's movement as possible, and then give her a piece of food. During the teaching, do not touch Sami, talk to her, coax her, or in any other way divert her attention from the task at hand. As a normal dog, Sami should, according to Skinner, learn the desired behavior within 5 minutes.
7 Before you teach Sami another trick, extinguish this one by no longer reinforcing it. Eventually Sami will stop touching her nose to the cupboard handle and will be ready to learn something new.

(Based on Skinner, 1951)

These failures of conditioning theory can be seen as triumphs of biology. What was happening was that these animals were persisting in carrying out the behavior that came to them instinctively and were resisting the most sophisticated use of operant conditioning techniques. They were drifting toward their own instinctive behaviors, even when these behaviors delayed or eliminated reinforcement. The Brelands termed this inner agenda *instinctive drift*, the phenomenon by which "learned behavior drifts toward instinctive behavior."

The existence of instinctive drift seemed to have been confirmed by another study in which pigeons learned to peck at a light even though the pecking actually *prevented* them from getting food (Williams & Williams, 1969). Reinforcement, then, is not all-powerful. It works best when teaching animals to perform behaviors that are compatible with their natural responses (Wickelgren, 1977).

GENERALIZATION AND DISCRIMINATION   As in classical conditioning, stimulus generalization describes the phenomenon whereby an animal or person has learned a response to one stimulus and then applies it to other similar stimuli. So a pigeon who learns to peck at a card colored red will also peck at a green card. If you want to teach the pigeon to discriminate between the two cards, you continue to reinforce the pecks at the red card and stop reinforcing the pecks at the green card. The red card is then said to be the *discriminative stimulus* because that's the one that rewards, and thus controls, behavior. We say that the red card has acquired *stimulus control* over the pigeon's behavior. Since it signals potential reinforcement, the pigeon is likely to respond in a certain way when it is present (in this case, peck).

If we were not able to generalize learning from one stimulus to another, getting along in the world would be very difficult. We would, for example, have to learn how to drive all over again every time we borrowed a friend's car, drove on a new road, or were in some other driving situation. Similarly, it's just as important to learn how to discriminate among different although somewhat similar stimuli. If we could not learn that when we see a green light at a traffic crossing we are supposed to keep on going and when we see a red light we are supposed to stop, chaos would reign on modern thoroughfares.

EXTINCTION   How do you get an animal or person to stop responding in a certain way? One way is to stop reinforcing the response. As we have pointed out, the rapidity with which you can extinguish a response depends on the kind of reinforcement schedule you have been using. You can extinguish continuously reinforced behaviors faster than intermittently reinforced behaviors. Of the intermittently reinforced responses, you can extinguish the ones that were reinforced on a fixed schedule faster than those on a variable schedule. You can also get an organism to stop responding by using punishment, which we'll discuss in the next section.

SPONTANEOUS RECOVERY   Just as in classical conditioning, animals and people whose operant behaviors have been extinguished may recover them. If you take a pigeon whose pecking behavior has been extinguished and put it back in the Skinner box at a later date, the pigeon may well start to peck again. Or a "cured" habitual gambler may start to play blackjack again when he goes back into a casino.

Punishment

A rat receives a shock when he runs up the wrong alley in a maze. A child gets a spanking when she runs into the street. A pigeon has her food taken away from her when she pecks at a bar the experimenter wants her to avoid. A motorist has to pay a fine when he runs a red light. The first two types of punishment described here represent the presenting of a stimulus the subject does not like, and the second two represent the withdrawal of a stimulus the subject does like. Punishment is defined as an event that, when administered following a response, decreases the probability of that response occurring again. Clearly, punishment can and does take many forms. Its popularity throughout society seems to show that for most people the idea of punishing undesirable behavior seems more natural than rewarding desirable behavior—in child rearing, in family relations, at work, and in the community. Is this belief justified?

As we pointed out earlier, punishment is different from negative reinforcement. Punishment is administered for the express purpose of reducing the tendency to behave in a certain way, and it often does. Administering electric shock to an animal every time it presses a bar will make it stop pressing the bar. A child who is bitten by a dog she or he tries to pet will probably stop approaching strange animals.

In other cases, however, punishment does not seem very effective. Thieves who have been imprisoned for their crimes routinely go out to steal again as soon as they are released from jail. A dog that has been whipped for eating food off the table will often continue to gobble up any meat it can find, as long as its master is not around. A teenage girl who is "grounded" because she sneaked out to meet a boyfriend will devise ever more ingenious ways of getting out of the house without being caught.

Why does punishment work some of the time but not all of the time? And when it does work, why does it still have so many drawbacks that most behavioral scientists, animal trainers, and child-rearing authorities recommend that it take a backseat to reinforcement?

HOW PUNISHMENT WORKS   Punishment often works dramatically right away, in the immediate situation. Its long-term effects are much more questionable. We can see this with rats that had been trained to press the bar in a Skinner box and were then slapped on the paw every time they pressed it. On the first day of the punishment trial, these rats pressed the bar less often than a control group of rats that were not punished for pressing but were not reinforced for it, either. By the second day, however, there was no difference between the two groups of rats. The response was extinguished just as quickly in the nonpunished rats as in the punished ones (Skinner, 1938) (see Figure 5-4).

When does punishment work best? A number of factors determine its effectiveness. Ross D. Parke has identified timing and consistency as among the most important (1977). Other research has shown severity and the availability of an alternative, reinforced response as significant elements.

TIMING   Earlier is better than later. The closer the time interval between a given behavior and its punishment, the more effective the punishment will be. When children are punished as they *begin* to engage in a forbidden act (such as approach an object they have been told to stay away from), they will go to it less often than if they are not punished until *after* they have actually touched it. The same principle applies with animals. Telling a child to "wait until your father gets home!" or coming home to find a table leg chewed up and then hitting the dog (which is at the moment happily napping) are both tactics of limited value. In practical terms, of course, it's not always possible to punish a child, a pet, or a criminal as they are misbehaving or immediately afterwards. So timing often works against the effectiveness of punishment.

As we pointed out earlier, an exception to this with animals can be seen with learned food aversions. A rat that eats a food that makes him ill as much as twelve hours later quickly learns to avoid that food. This is obviously a survival mechanism. Apparently, the kind of learning that helps an animal to survive in its basic environment will persist (Garcia & Koelling, 1966). Thus, rats, which depend for their daily rations on whatever they can scavenge, need to learn quickly which foods to stay away from. Such learning is relatively easy for rats partly because they are conservative gourmets who tend to eat only one new food at a time. If they then become nauseated soon after eating that new substance, they will be able to identify it as the culprit and will thereafter avoid it (Wickelgren, 1977). Interestingly, rats do learn to avoid tastes associated with nausea but not those associated with pain. This may be because their biological systems are programmed to recognize the nausea as something associated with eating, whereas they don't make the same connection to pain.

CONSISTENCY   The more consistently a person or animal is punished, the more effective the punishment will be. Erratic punishment prolongs undesirable behavior more than if it had not been punished at all. The father who punishes 4-year-old Kimberly on one occasion for using four-letter words, rewards her with his amused smile on another, and ignores her on a third is helping to cement these words in his daughter's vocabulary. Again, looking at the situation practically, parents, pet owners, and police officers are not always on the scene. So people and animals often get away with behavior on one occasion that they will be punished for on another. Inconsistency sabotages punishment, and in the real world inconsistency is unavoidable.

AVAILABILITY OF ALTERNATIVE, REINFORCED RESPONSE   A rat will quickly learn to take an alternative route in a maze if he is not only shocked for taking the wrong route but is rewarded with food for taking the right one. A 3-year-old will learn not to poke his finger in his baby sister's eye if he is not only scolded for eye-poking behavior but is also shown how to tickle her gently and is then commended for being "such a big boy who knows how to treat a baby." Skinner (1953) stresses the importance of specifying the kind of behavior that will avoid punishment—whether it is a different act or simply doing nothing (p. 189). Very often punishment doesn't work because the animal or person being punished realizes what he should *not* be doing but keeps on doing it because he doesn't know what he *should* be doing. This is only one of the problems with punishment. Let's see what some of the others are.

THE PROBLEMS WITH PUNISHMENT   Even if all these conditions that maximize the effectiveness of punishment could be met, we'd still have to say that it's still less desirable than reinforcement.

People don't learn any new acceptable responses from punishment. Reinforcement helps a person or animal make new associations to perform some new action. Punishment, though, doesn't teach people what *to* do—it tells them what they should *not* do. It leads them to suppress a behavior that they already know and that they are already doing.

If the impulse to carry out this suppressed behavior is strong enough and if the rewards for doing it are great enough, the behavior will bubble to the surface. That teenage girl wants so desperately to be with her boyfriend that she is willing to risk whatever punishments her parents can dream up. That dog just can't resist the tempting smell of meat left to defrost on a reachable kitchen counter, no matter how many times he gets whipped for eating it. The rewards of the behavior more than make up for the punishment that might follow.

This principle is seen throughout society. Many people regularly break the law, knowing that they will eventually have to pay the piper. It's worth it to them since they get more from committing the transgression than they suffer from the punishment. The president of a company that looses poisonous chemicals into the environment may, for example, make a business decision that it's cheaper for the company to continue to do business as usual and to pay fines from time to time than it is to overhaul the operations of the plant.

Another problem with the use of punishment is that what may be a punishment for one person is a reinforcement for another. As we pointed out earlier, the spanking that Melissa gets when she acts up may be a reinforcer since it's more attention than she got when she was being good. If punishment is a reward, it encourages the very behavior it seeks to extinguish.

Even when punishment is effective in eliminating behavior that parents or teachers or other agents of society consider undesirable, it may have other unwanted side-effects. The person who is punished for sexual behavior in childhood or adolescence may encounter difficulties in forming a healthy sexual relationship in adulthood. The child who is punished for being curious and exploratory may withdraw into herself and not ask the questions that could stretch her mind and abilities. The feelings of guilt or rage or fear that come from the suppression of natural impulses often cause emotional problems later in life. Children who are punished with physical abuse often grow up to abuse their own children.

"In the long run," says Skinner (1953, p. 190), "punishment does not actually eliminate behavior from a repertoire, and its temporary achievement is obtained at tremendous cost in reducing the over-all efficiency and happiness of the group."

COGNITIVE PERSPECTIVES ON LEARNING

So far we have been talking about learning as a simple formation of associations. A dog learns to associate a tone with the taste and smell of food. A child becomes afraid of objects associated with a loud noise. A pigeon learns that, if she pecks, she'll get fed. A teenager learns that, if he does his schoolwork, he'll get to shoot pool. We have interpreted these events in an environmental way. That is, it doesn't matter who or what the subject is. Whether it's a person or a pigeon, behaviorists feel that by knowing the reinforcement contingencies, we can explain and predict the behaviors.

Cognitive psychologists believe that there's more to the story. While they agree that classical and operant conditioning are important ways of learning, they maintain that they are not the only ways. Furthermore, they maintain that even in associative learning, more than a simple mechanistic explanation is called for to account for the important thought processes that intervene between the stimulus and the response.

At the core of cognitive interpretations of learning is the conviction that human beings—and even lower-order animals—are not just creatures of our environment but that we bring to it our own capacities for understanding the nature of the world and for demonstrating that understanding when we are motivated to do so. Although the environment certainly affects behavior, the person or animal also has an important impact on his own learning. Learning is not only the result of external forces like conditioning. It is also internal. A process that we cannot see is taking place.

For example, the dog that comes running to the kitchen as soon as he hears the rustle of dry dog food being shaken from the bag or the soft thump of the feeding dish being placed on the floor has learned more than a simple mechanical response. Like Pavlov's laboratory animals, our pet has developed an *expectation* that these previously neutral sounds will be followed by an unconditioned stimulus, like dinner. Cognitive psychologists maintain that such learned expectations are at the root of all learning, including classical and operant conditioning.

Higher-level animals are capable of extremely complex learning. They learn concepts like sameness and difference, large and small, up and down, and the alternation of left and right. They learn by imitating other animals, both those like themselves and those that are different. They learn how to use tools. They learn to cooperate with others like themselves. Furthermore, they put this learning to work in totally new ways to solve new problems. We cannot explain much of the elaborate learning shown by primates and by human beings simply by referring to classical and operant conditioning principles. How, then, do cognitive psychologists explain learning?

One way psychologists have shown the cognitive aspects of learning is through the phenomenon of *blocking,* which demonstrates the importance of the animal's ability to pay attention before conditioning can take place. If we wanted to show how blocking works, we would first establish standard Pavlovian conditioning. We could pair a bell (the CS) with meat (the UCS) until we got a dog to salivate to the bell alone. At this point, we might add a second neutral stimulus, say, the sound of chimes, to the bell, to form a compound CS. At this point we would pair the compound— bell plus chimes—with the meat for several trials. Then we would sound only the chimes, to see whether the dog would salivate to this sound. In all probability, he would *not.* Why? Because previous conditioning to the first stimulus, the bell, *blocked* any conditioning from occurring to the chimes.

Why does blocking occur? There are two theoretical explanations. According to Mackintosh (1975), adding the second stimulus (the chimes) to the bell *after* conditioning has taken place gives the organism (in this case, the dog) no new information. The sound of the bell is such a strong signal to the dog that the meat will appear that the animal does not pay attention to anything else that accompanies the bell such as the chimes.

Rescorla and Wagner (1972; Wagner & Rescorla, 1972) offer another explanation—that there is a limit to the amount of conditioning the UCS (the meat, in this example) can support. If an organism is conditioned to one stimulus (the bell), there's not enough conditioning "strength" left to permit another stimulus (such as the chimes) to take effect as a CS.

Which of these explanations is the true one? According to Hulse, Egeth, & Deese (1980), both are useful in that they are able to predict accurately

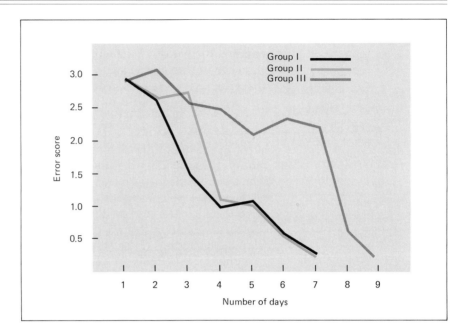

FIGURE 5-6 Error scores for three groups of rats in Blodgett's (1929) study. (*Adapted from Blodgett, 1929*)

that if we increase the intensity of the UCS at the time we add the second stimulus (by, for example, offering more meat or a new and tastier kind of meat when the chimes are first sounded), the second stimulus can become a CS. Is this because the dog is paying more attention because the UCS has changed or because increasing its intensity gives it enough additional strength to support a second CS? It's hard to know.

Latent Learning

Latent learning is a type of learning that occurs but is not displayed until the organism is motivated to do so. Blodgett (1929) ran three groups of rats through a maze over a nine-day period. The rats in the first group were rewarded with food after every successful run, from the first day forward. Those in the second group found no food in the maze for the first two days (they were fed in their home cages during this time) but were rewarded for successful maze runs from the third day on. And those in the third group were treated similarly except that they didn't find any food in the maze until the seventh day. The graph in Figure 5-6 shows the error scores for these three groups of rats, that is, the number of wrong turns they continued to make on each day.

It's clear from looking at the sharp drops in the error curves of the two groups of rats who received food later that they had been learning the maze route even when they were not being rewarded for doing so. In the absence of reward they had apparently meandered their way through, not showing what they knew, but when they had a *purpose* for using that learning, they showed how much they had learned.

Edward C. Tolman conducted a number of experiments that confirmed these findings and that also confirmed his strong belief in the importance of purpose in learning, a belief he expressed in his 1932 book, *Purposive Behavior in Animals and Men*. He also maintained that understanding, rather than conditioning, is the essence of learning and that animals and people learn innumerable things through life for which they are reinforced by no other reward than the satisfaction of the learning itself. Often, of course, they don't show this learning until they have some reason, or purpose, for doing so—as the rats did when they knew they could get food by traversing the maze.

Tolman and His "Map-making" Rats

Tolman, a behaviorist who took issue with the stimulus-response analysis of learning, likened that view of learning to a telephone switchboard in which there is a very simple, straightforward connection between stimuli and responses, "the incoming calls from sense-organs" and the "outgoing messages to muscles" (1948, reprinted in Gazzaniga & Lovejoy, 1971, p. 225). He agreed that stimulus leads to response but felt that complicated, patterned brain processes were taking place between the two, and that an animal even as lowly as the rat is "surprisingly selective as to which of these stimuli it will let in at any given time" (p. 227). Tolman compared the "telephone exchange" view of learning to his own concept, which saw learning taking place in something that more closely resembled a map control room:

> The stimuli, which are allowed in, are not connected by just simple one-to-one switches to the outgoing responses. Rather, the incoming impulses are usually worked over and elaborated in the central control room into a tentative, *cognitive-like* map of the environment. And it is this tentative map, indicating routes and paths and environmental relationships, which finally determines what responses, if any, the animal will finally release (p. 227).

Tolman developed his concept of *cognitive maps* through a series of experiments in which rats who had learned how to negotiate a maze to get food then found their initial routes blocked. The fact that they were still able to reach their goal quickly indicated that they had not learned only to make such simple responses as "turn left" or "turn right" but that they had constructed a mental map of their environment. To construct this map, they had undoubtedly used information gained from their senses (like the smell of the food), as well as kinetic clues about direction and distance. They processed this information in their brains and ended up knowing something they had not known before. The rats showed that they were *goal-oriented* rather than *response-oriented*, demonstrating that they could use any of "many paths to Rome."

This map-making ability is crucial to the way we manage our everyday life. We see it in those cases when our favorite route to school is blocked by construction, and we take for granted the need to figure out another route. We also see it when we break an arm and learn to do things with our left hand that we have always done with our right. It is the goal that counts, and cognitive creatures are not kept from reaching it by a limited repertoire of responses.

Learning by Observing

Can you imagine learning how to knit, square dance, play tennis, or drive a car without having seen someone else go through the motions? We learn specific skills like these, which we deliberately set out to learn, by watching other people carry them out. We also learn a great deal more simply by seeing and listening to other people.

Parents who try to raise their children according to the principle of "Do

Both children and adults learn by watching other people. Here we see an adult model acting aggressively toward a "Bobo" doll, and then we see children who saw this particular adult. They're behaving aggressively themselves, more so than children who saw a quiet model. (Albert Bandura, Stanford University)

as I say, not as I do" soon find that this won't work. Children *will* do what their parents do. If their parents hit them in anger, the children learn that this is an acceptable way to express their own anger. An experience familiar to virtually every parent of small children is the sudden awareness that the youngsters are copying in their play not only the parent's actions but also his or her exact vocabulary and tone of voice. (Sometimes this recognition brings the parent up short. "Do I really act like that?" a mother may wonder, using her own learning to change her behavior!)

The power of observational learning has been confirmed in experiments in which children who see an adult model punching, throwing, and kicking a 5-foot inflated doll are more likely to act aggressively themselves when they have the chance to do the same thing than are children who see a quiet model (Bandura, Ross, & Ross, 1961).

The cognitive psychologists who emphasize the role of learning by observation are adherents of social learning theory, which will be discussed in detail in our discussions of personality theory, psychotherapy, and developmental psychology. Albert Bandura, the most prominent social learning theorist in the United States, has conducted many experiments that confirm the importance of this kind of learning, also called *vicarious learning* or modeling. The people whose behavior we observe, and often imitate, are called *models*.

If all learning resulted from rewards and punishments actually received by the individual, our capacity for learning would be severely restricted. We would have to go through every experience ourselves and would not be able to learn from the examples of others. Mistakes made through trial and error would be costly and often tragic. Society as we know it could not exist.

One does not teach children to swim, adolescents to drive automobiles, and novice medical students to perform surgery by having them discover the appropriate behavior through the consequences of their successes or failures. The more costly and hazardous the possible mistakes, the heavier is the reliance on observational learning from competent examples.
(Bandura, 1977, p. 12)

HOW OBSERVATIONAL LEARNING OCCURS   Bandura (1977) has identified the following four steps in the process of learning by observation:

1 Paying attention and perceiving the relevant aspects of the behavior
2 Remembering the behavior, either through words or mental images

3 Converting the remembered observation into action
4 Being motivated to adopt the behavior

Let's see how this process might work. Suppose 6-year-old Jessica is riding in the car with her father, who has taken a wrong turn. He stops next to a traffic officer, asks for the name of the street he's looking for, thanks the officer, and continues on his way. Jessica may never mention this incident. If she herself becomes lost someday, however, the mental image of the incident may swim back into her consciousness. She may even remember the exact words her father spoke to the police officer. Since she knew those words were effective in getting help, she is motivated to act similarly.

Modeling can in certain instances be more effective than shaping in encouraging socially withdrawn children to become more sociable (O'Connor, 1972). Teachers from four different Illinois nursery schools identified eighty children as "social isolates" who avoided playing with other children. The researchers put these youngsters in one of four categories: Those in the Modeling group saw a film showing sociable children; those in the Shaping group received a total of five hours of praise and attention, during a two-week period, as they showed signs of going toward other children—they also saw a film about fish; those in the Modeling-and-Shaping group saw the film about children and also received praise and attention; and those in the Control group saw the film about fish.

In this study, modeling was a faster agent of change than shaping, and the changes held up better: All sixteen of the children who saw the film about children played more with other children afterward. While the youngsters in the two Shaping groups also played more with others right after the program ended, after three more weeks all the other children in these two groups were as isolated as they had been before the program began.

Modeling has been demonstrated to be such a powerful influence on the behavior of both children and adults that it has become the basis for a popular psychotherapeutic approach in the treatment of phobias. With the help of specially planned programs, people who are afraid of dogs, snakes, the dark or other things manage to overcome these fears, partly by seeing other people behave fearlessly. This approach will be described in detail in Chapter 16.

SELF-REINFORCEMENT The concept of *self-reinforcement* is important in the cognitive view of learning. In this view of humankind, individuals are seen to have a major impact on their own environment. They are not only dependent on the rewards and punishments that may waft their way from outside forces but are also capable of rewarding and punishing themselves in a way that helps them develop new ways of behaving. Bandura (1977) uses the term *self-regulation* to encompass both reinforcing and punishing influences that people impose upon themselves.

How do people regulate their behavior? Mostly, by developing standards and making efforts to live up to them. Very often they develop these standards in relation to what they have observed in other people. For example, a middle-aged woman who takes up running as a sport may

The process of self-regulation actively affects the act of writing: Authors do not need someone sitting at their sides selectively reinforcing each written statement until a satisfactory manuscript is produced. Rather, they possess a standard of what constitutes an acceptable piece of work. Ideas are generated and phrased in thought several times before anything is committed to paper. Initial constructions are successively revised until authors are satisfied with what they have written. The more exacting the personal standards, the more extensive are the corrective improvements. Self-editing often exceeds external requirements of what would be acceptable to others. Indeed, some people are such critical self-editors that they essentially paralyze their own writing efforts. Others who lack suitable standards exercise little self-correction.
(Bandura, 1977, p. 129)

gauge her performance by comparing herself to other women of her own age and general level of physical fitness. If she runs faster than other 40- to 50-year-old casual athletes, she may feel highly reinforced even if she knows that she will never outdistance younger, more athletic women—or men. People who set unrealistically high standards for themselves are unlikely to obtain reinforcement for their efforts, a phenomenon we'll look at in Chapter 9 when we talk about motivation.

If we can learn how people learn, we can help them learn in more self-fulfilling, socially productive ways. Having such knowledge about learning imposes a special responsibility, of course, on those society leaders and child rearers who are in a position to decide what they want others to learn.

PRACTICAL INSIGHTS INTO LEARNING: BIOFEEDBACK AND LEARNED HELPLESSNESS

Psychological researchers are constantly exploring topics that have great relevance for people's day-to-day lives. We will talk about two issues, one that tells us how some people are learning to control something that was once thought beyond our reach and another that explains a mechanism through which some people have learned to feel helpless about controlling the aspects of their lives that most of us take for granted.

Biofeedback appears to hold great promise for sufferers of many physical conditions that have up to now been resistant to treatment. The exciting premise of this technique is that people can now learn about their bodies in new ways. Through the use of electronic monitoring, people learn how their internal body processes are functioning, and they then learn how to control this functioning to improve their health.

The other kind of learning, which has motivational, cognitive, and emotional elements, is learned helplessness, a state that exists when a person or animal feels that she or he cannot control important events in the environment. This condition has important ramifications for the care of children, the ill, and the elderly.

Biofeedback

The apparatus looks intimidating at first sight—rather like those pictures we have seen of people hooked up to the electric chair. Three electronic sensors are attached to the man's forehead with adhesive disks. Wires connect the man in the reclining chair to a complex instrument panel where lights flash and dials flicker. It seems as if being plugged in would be a painful experience. But then, why is the "victim" smiling so peacefully? Because this man is getting relief from the excruciating pain of recurrent tension headaches with the help of the machine he is hooked up to.

The machine is an electromyograph, which measures and records tension in the muscles, as evidenced by their electrical potential. As the electrical charges reach the machine, it emits a series of clicks. The faster the clicks, the tighter the muscles. By listening to the clicks, this man "learns to recognize which feelings and thoughts make the machine click faster. His job is to discover what it feels like to relax his muscles, to notice how he feels when he makes the clicks slow down. Then he tries to maintain that state. If the training sessions work, he gradually learns to reproduce the state of relaxation without need of the clicking machine" (Runk, 1980, p. 4).

Many who, through biofeedback, are now receiving relief for the first time in their lives from a variety of troubling conditions consider it a miracle.

But why are we talking about this kind of psychophysiological therapy in a chapter on learning? Because biofeedback involves a very special kind of learning—learning about the internal physiological processes most people are not aware of. Biofeedback is the detection of the processes that go on inside an individual's body (usually through monitoring performed by electrical machines especially designed for this purpose) and the transmittal of information about these processes to that person. What are people using biofeedback actually learning?

> The skills learned in a biofeedback clinic involve functions and responses that are usually outside the patient's ability to control—blood pressure and circulation, for example, or a tight, spastic, or paralyzed muscle. These normally inconspicuous responses become detectable because they are monitored, amplified, recorded, and fed back to the patient by a mechanical or electronic device. Biofeedback patients can, in effect, "watch" or "hear" fluctuations in their blood pressure or heartbeat or in the activity of a single muscle cell. Then, using a variety of maneuvers that are already voluntary, the patient may learn to control the formerly involuntary response (Runk, 1980, p. 2).

What Biofeedback Does   There have undoubtedly been times in your life when you have been conscious of your heart beating faster. Generally, however, an increase has to be enormous before you notice it. If you suffered from a cardiac disorder in which it was dangerous for your heart to beat too quickly, it would be important for you to know when it was *starting* to speed up. Biofeedback can give you this information. It's not enough, of course, just to know what's happening. The ultimate aim of biofeedback is to enable you to do something about the condition, to control the process you're getting data about. So an important part of the therapeutic process involves giving you the tools to prevent your heart from reaching that dangerously high rate.

Physicians and psychologists alike used to believe that people had no control over the autonomic systems of the body—heart and breathing rates, blood pressure, skin temperature, salivation, and the galvanic skin response (the electrical reactions of the skin to a stimulus). During the 1960s, however, researchers in the United States became impressed by the reports of practitioners of various Eastern disciplines who demonstrated that they could stop the heart rate, remain buried for long periods of time without suffocating, and seemingly experience no pain from actions that seemed excruciating (like piercing the skin with a bicycle spoke, walking on red-hot coals, and swallowing broken glass). At about the same time, some psychologists were proposing that people and animals did not learn in two different ways—one way for autonomic responses and one for voluntary responses—but that one kind of learning controlled both kinds of functions (Miller, 1969).

As a result of a great deal of research over the past twenty years, we now know that both people and animals can indeed control many aspects of the autonomic system and that such control can help people handle a wide range of physical conditions. Biofeedback is particularly effective in controlling irregular heartbeat and tension headaches. It holds promise in

Have you ever wanted to wiggle your ears? Ever tried and not been able to figure out how to make those appendages move? Many years ago, several young men learned this socially dubious skill in the course of studies on developing voluntary control over muscle movement (Bair, 1901). The men gave themselves a mild electric shock through electrodes wired to their ears. The shock made their ears contract and wiggle. Then the men tried to move their ears on their own by clenching their jaws and knitting their brows. Because they remembered what a wiggling ear felt like, they could detect an extremely faint movement from their strenuous efforts, which spurred them to enthusiastic practice, eventually perfecting this ability. This principle—that to control a response, you must first be able to feel it—is the basis for biofeedback (Runk, 1980).

Through biofeedback, people learn to detect irregularities in their internal physiological processes and can often control such mechanisms as heart and breathing rates, blood pressure, and skin temperature. Such control enables people to treat their own tension headaches and holds promise for many other medical conditions. (© Ray Ellis/ Photo Researchers, Inc.)

controlling such other conditions as high blood pressure, epilepsy, asthma, stuttering, migraine headaches, ulcers, nervous stomach, teeth grinding, and pain.

Electroencephalograms (EEGs) have been used to measure the electrical activity of the brain (Kamiya, 1969). In this kind of measure, electrodes attached to the scalp record and communicate the amount of electricity the brain gives off. Kamiya differentiated three different kinds of brain waves—the fairly slow *alpha* waves that appear when a person is quietly relaxed, the fast *beta* waves that show up when a person is thinking, and the very slow *theta* waves that are seen when a person is about to fall asleep. He found that people can learn to tell whether they are in the alpha or beta state and that they can, in fact, control brain-wave activity to get into the alpha state.

We can also measure the amount of electrical activity given off by muscle contractions with the use of an electromyogram (EMG). This graphic representation is given on a screen from two electrodes placed over the muscle, which are connected to an amplifier and then a recorder. A dramatic early use of EMGs emerged during the 1950s before anyone even called it "biofeedback." Hospital personnel were trying to get children whose muscles had atrophied because of polio to exercise, to strengthen those muscles. The children would not exercise, mostly because their muscles were so weak that, when they tried to flex them, they couldn't see or feel anything happening. A psychologist had an inspiration. Why not record each child's EMG for the particular muscle needing to be exercised and using the electrical signal to light up a clown's face? The children were so happy about seeing the results of their efforts in this way that they gladly did their exercises (Stern & Ray, 1977).

Evaluating Biofeedback   The great strength of biofeedback is the way it puts the individual in charge of his or her own body. He learns how to listen to his body signals and to recognize when something might lead to trouble. For example, the man who suffers from tension headaches can learn to sense tension in his neck before the headache comes on. Then, using special relaxation techniques, he can dispel the tension and prevent the headache. No one else is doing this for him. He is responsible for himself.

We do have to be a little cautious, however, in assessing the value of biofeedback. First, because it is so new, there is no long-term follow-up data to let us know how its successes hold up. (Are many cases of apparent improvement that seem to be due to biofeedback simply reflections of natural, possibly temporary improvements in the condition itself, or due to placebo effects?)

Secondly, the machinery is expensive and the practitioner needs specialized training, so the technique is limited to those who can afford the fees and the time. Usually treatment is given in weekly sessions of 30 to 60 minutes over a period of six to twenty weeks, and in 1981 fees in the New York metropolitan area ranged from $40 to $75 per session (Wineburg, 1981).

Another problem is weaning the individual off the biofeedback machines. Many people are helped as long as they can continue to use the machine in the practitioner's office, but once they stop going, they often lose whatever gains they made. It's risky to assume a cure prematurely. Taking a patient off hypertensive medication because he has shown he can lower his blood pressure in the laboratory might, for example, be dangerous if he cannot continue to do this in everyday life.

Finally, biofeedback sometimes produces its own side-effects: Some people feel out of control experiencing alpha brain waves, some have frightening thoughts during the procedures, and some substitute other symptoms for the ones being treated (Runk, 1980).

Still, biofeedback seems like a worthwhile way to go since it "is bringing about improvement in the condition of numerous patients with a variety of problems, some of whom have not been helped by any other type of therapy" (Stern & Ray, 1977, p. 152).

Learned Helplessness

During the 1960s a team of psychologists studying the relationship between fear and learning noticed that the dogs they were working with were behaving in bizarre ways. As part of one experiment, they gave moderately painful but not physically harmful electric shocks to the dogs. No matter how much the dogs struggled to get out of the hammock, barked, or wagged their tails, they could not escape the shocks. There was nothing the dogs could do to avoid being shocked. The next part of the experiment involved putting the dogs in a two-sided chamber with a barrier. By jumping over the barrier after the shock began, the dogs could turn it off; by jumping over beforehand, the shock would be completely avoided.

Most dogs put into an apparatus like this without ever having experienced shock before will run about the chamber until they accidentally scale the barrier, and they then learn very quickly how to avoid the shock. This was what the experimenters expected their unescapable-shock dogs to do once they had the chance to stop the shocks. What happened was eerily different. At first, the unescapable-shock dogs ran around frantically for about 30 seconds. But then they stopped moving, lay down, and whined. After 1 minute the shock was turned off. On all trials after that, the dogs gave up. They never did learn how to escape the shock (Seligman, 1975, p. 22).

This, then, is what Seligman termed learned helplessness, the conviction by an animal or person that she or he is out of control—that nothing she or he can do would make any difference in changing an important feature of his or her life. This demoralizing condition has also been seen in cats, rats, fish and nonhuman primates, as well as in human beings. What does learned helplessness do to both people and animals? Since they believe they can't do anything to change a situation, they don't have any motivation even to try. They are rendered incapable of learning a response that would in fact control the outcome. If the outcome is likely to be traumatic, they will be afraid and will then lapse into depression.

Fortunately, the experimenters who had caused learned helplessness in their laboratory dogs were able to figure out a way to reverse it. They *forced* the dogs to learn what would turn off the shock by leashing and dragging them from one side of the box to the other, with the barrier removed. As the dog's body scudded over the center of the chamber, the shock stopped, and eventually the dog learned to initiate the move itself. A complete and lasting recovery from helplessness has been effected for both dogs and rats.

PREVENTING LEARNED HELPLESSNESS   Seligman and his colleagues asked themselves questions, which they answered through lab experiments:

- "Suppose dogs *first* learned how to escape shock before being presented with the unescapable shock?" Their findings: Dogs who had ten escape trials first did not thereafter lapse into the helpless state.
- "What effects does a dog's early history have on its later tendency to become helpless?" Findings: Dogs raised in cages in which they controlled practically nothing in their lives turned out to be much more susceptible to helplessness than other dogs.

These results confirmed earlier reports showing that wild rats that had been squeezed in the hands of an experimenter drowned within 30 minutes of being put in a water tank, compared to unsqueezed rats, who swam for sixty hours before drowning (Richter, 1957). Apparently, the squeezing took away from these rats the sense that they could save themselves.

HOW HUMAN BEINGS CAN LEARN THEY DO HAVE POWER   These findings seem to hold great significance for the lives of human beings. If early experiences of mastery over one's environment immunize animals against the paralysis of helplessness and if early experiences of lack of control predispose animals to give up under adversity, it seems apparent that if we want to raise human beings who will exert the maximum effort toward improving their situation in life, we must imbue them early on with the sense that they have the power to do so. This implies a sensitivity on the part of parents and those who work with small children to

BOX 5-4

HOW A SENSE OF CONTROL HELPS CHILDREN TO PROTECT THEMSELVES

Sexual assaults against children are alarmingly frequent today, with many of them coming from people whom the children know and believe they have to obey because the assaulters are adults. A New York City organization called the Safety and Fitness Exchange (SAFE) advises that one way of preventing child molestation is to allow children to take control of their own bodies from a very early age. In a pamphlet for adults, SAFE recommends:

One of the ways to help children prevent sexual assault is to encourage them to develop a sense of physical integrity. Just as we allow them to close the door when they use the bathroom, we must also allow them to say no to any unwanted physical affection and touch. Such a situation might take place after a visit with Grandma:

Grandma wants a kiss good-bye
Child: I don't want to.
Grandma: Just one kiss. Don't you love me?
Mother to Grandma: She's not in the mood to kiss you right now.
Mother to child: Would you like to throw Grandma a kiss or shake her hand? (Colao & Hosansky, 1982)

respond to their needs on the basis of the cues the children themselves give. What are some ways this can be done?

A baby's first signal showing that she or he needs something is the cry. Parents who take a baby's crying seriously and respond by feeding, changing, or just holding an infant show that baby that she or he can make the world a more comfortable place. Parents don't have to worry about "spoiling" infants; a more serious error is ignoring the calls of these dependent little creatures for help in doing the things they cannot do for themselves.

Learned helplessness is a danger not only in childhood but throughout life. Adults who feel powerless to escape from traumatic situations often give up and simply die. "Hex deaths," in which people die following a kind of "voodoo" curse or pronouncements are common in societies around the world, a phenomenon clearly related to the victim's sense of helplessness in preventing the death that has been prophesied. People who feel helpless because they have lost a loved one on whom they depended often respond by dying themselves. The ill and the elderly who are institutionalized and deprived of control over the everyday details of their lives often respond by weakening, sickening, and even dying. Learned helplessness is also discussed in Chapter 10 as it relates to stress and in Chapter 15 as it relates to depression.

People learn through every experience in life. When this learning shows them they have little control over their lives, the result may be as devastating as death or as wasteful as the failure to try to achieve. When they learn that what they do does make a difference, they are inspired to make the most of their time here on earth. The vital importance of learning for the way we live our lives justifies the great interest and involvement the topic of learning has received and continues to get from psychological researchers.

SUMMARY

1   *Learning* is a relatively permanent change in behavior, which reflects a gain of knowledge, understanding, or skill, achieved through experience, which may include study, instruction, observation, or practice. Learning does not include changes brought about by factors such as maturation, fatigue, illness, or medication. Psychologists infer that learning has taken place through changes in performance.

2   There are several different types of learning. The simplest type is *habituation,* in which an organism stops responding because it has grown used to something. The next level of learning is called *associative learning,* in which an organism forms an association between two events. Two types of associative learning are *classical conditioning* and *operant conditioning.* Another type of learning is *cognitive,* which focuses on the thought processes that are involved in learning.

3   Classical conditioning involves *reflex* (or involuntary) behavior. In classical conditioning, the animal or person learns to make a response to some previously *neutral stimulus* (that is, a stimulus which originally did not bring forth a particular response) which has been paired repeatedly with an *unconditioned stimulus.* An unconditioned stimulus is one that automatically brings forth an *unconditioned response.* At the point where the neutral stimulus alone brings forth the response, the neutral stimulus becomes known as the *conditioned stimulus* and the response becomes known as the *conditioned response.*

4   Conditioning is influenced by the period of time between the presentation of the conditioned stimulus and the unconditioned stimulus. When the conditioned stimulus is presented alone, without being paired at least once in a while with the unconditioned stimulus, the conditioned response will be *extinguished* (that is, will weaken and eventually stop). When the extinguished response appears spontaneously, with no additional pairings of the unconditioned stimulus and the conditioned stimulus, the organism is exhibiting *spontaneous recovery.* Classical conditioning is the basis for a number of psychotherapeutic techniques.

5   In operant conditioning, an organism emits a response known as an *operant.* When a response is rewarded, it is likely to be repeated. Responses that are not rewarded or are punished are likely to be suppressed. There are two basic kinds of *reinforcers: positive* and *negative.* Positive reinforcers are rewards that increase the probability of a response when they are added to a situation. Negative reinforcers are unpleasant stimuli that increase the probability of a response when they are removed from a situation. Positive or negative reinforcers increase the probability of a response recurring. Reinforcers can also be primary or secondary. *Primary reinforcers* are biologically important—that is, they satisfy needs such as those for food, water, or sex. *Secondary reinforcers* are learned—they become reinforcing through their association with primary reinforcers.

6   Reinforcements are administered according to patterns or *schedules.* The type of reinforcement schedule chosen influences the rate of response and resistance of the response to extinction. In *continuous reinforcement,* reinforcement is given after every response. In *partial* (or *intermittent*) reinforcement responses are reinforced after a certain number of responses have been emitted (this is called a *ratio schedule* of reinforcement) or after a certain time period has passed (this is called an *interval schedule*).

7   *Superstitious behavior* occurs when an organism is reinforced accidentally. In *shaping,* rewards are given for behaviors that come progressively closer to the desired behavior until the desired behavior is reached. *Generalization* refers to responding similarly to similar stimuli, and *discrimination* refers to responding to a particular stimulus while not responding to another similar (but not identical) one. As in classical conditioning, responses learned through operant conditioning are subject to extinction and spontaneous recovery.

8   In *punishment* a behavior is followed by an unpleasant event. The purpose of punishment is to reduce responding. The effectiveness of punishment is associated with a number of factors including its *timing, consistency,* and the *availability of alternative responses.* Problems with punishment include the failure to provide new, acceptable responses to replace the punished ones, the fact that what may be punishment for one may be reinforcement for another, and the unwarranted side-effects that may accompany punishment.

9   Recently psychologists have been concerned with cognitive aspects of learning. Two types of cognitive learning are *latent learning* and *learning by observation.* In latent learning, we learn but do not demonstrate the learning until we are motivated to do so. In learning by observation, we learn by observing and imitating the behavior of a model.

10 Through *biofeedback* we learn to control involun-

tary responses, and this learning holds promise for the treatment of medical conditions such as irregular heartbeat and tension headaches.

11 *Learned helplessness* refers to the conviction that one cannot control events in one's life. This lack of control undermines the ability of both animals and humans to learn.

SUGGESTED READINGS

Bandura, A. (1977). *Social learning theory.* Englewood Cliffs, N.J.: Prentice-Hall. A brief overview of the social learning theory perspective, written by the leading spokesperson for this approach.

Hulse, S. H., Egeth, H., & Deese, J. (1980). *The psychology of learning* (5th ed.). New York: McGraw-Hill. A clearly written textbook which presents the basic principles of learning and memory.

Pavlov, I. P. (1927). *Conditioned reflexes.* London: Oxford University Press. Pavlov's own discussion of the experiments which revealed the basic laws of classical conditioning.

Seligman, M. E. P. (1975). *Helplessness: On depression, development, and death.* San Francisco: W. H. Freeman. Drawing on experimental evidence, the author discusses the importance of a sense of control at all stages in the life course.

Skinner, B. F. (1974). *About behaviorism.* New York: Knopf. An interesting and clearly written discussion of how the environment controls human behavior, as described by America's most influential behaviorist.

Stern, R. M., & Ray, W. J. (1977). *Biofeedback.* Lincoln: University of Nebraska Press. The authors of this award-winning book provide information about the potential and limitations of biofeedback in an easy-to-read style.

CHAPTER 6

MEMORY

SPOTLIGHT ON

A model of memory that proposes that there is not one but three types of memory: sensory, short-term, and long-term.

An alternative view of memory proposing that how well we remember depends on how deeply we process information.

What the tip-of-the-tongue phenomenon tells us about how we remember.

Some factors that influence what we remember and some ideas about why we forget.

How mnemonics can help us remember better.

The unreliability of childhood memories is dramatically apparent in this statement by the cognitive development theorist Jean Piaget (1951):

I can still see, most clearly, the following scene, in which I believed until I was about fifteen. [At the age of 2 years] I was sitting in my pram, which my nurse was pushing in the Champs Élysées, when a man tried to kidnap me. I was held in by the strap fastened round me while my nurse bravely tried to stand between me and the thief. She received various scratches, and I can still see vaguely those on her face. Then a crowd gathered, a policeman with a short cloak and a white baton came up, and the man took to his heels. I can still see the whole scene, and can even place it near the tube station. When I was about fifteen, my parents received a letter from my former nurse saying that she had been converted to the Salvation Army. She wanted to confess her past faults, and in particular to return the watch she had been given as a reward on this occasion. She had made up the whole story, faking the scratches. I therefore must have heard, as a child, the account of this story, which my parents believed, and projected it into the past in the form of a visual memory, which was a memory of a memory, but false. Many real memories are doubtless of the same order.
(pp. 187–188)

The next time you're with a couple of friends and the conversation is flagging, ask everyone to describe the very earliest memory they can think of. You'll learn something about memory and something about your friends at the same time.

Think about your own earliest memory. Unless you're very unusual, it will not be about anything that took place before the age of 3 or 4, and it may well not have taken place before you were 6 or 7 (Kihlstrom & Harackiewicz, 1982). For most of us, the memories of early childhood are frustratingly fragmentary and elusive. Even the great writer Leo Tolstoy could remember only four memories before the age of 5 (Salaman, 1970).

What can we learn about memory—and people—by focusing on the memories of early childhood? First, we may gain clues to our personalities—to the events that either shaped us or that, reaching back into our distant past, we consider important. Personality theorist Alfred Adler wrote, "The first memory will show the individual's fundamental view of life, his first satisfactory crystallization of his attitude. . . . I would never investigate a personality without asking for the first memory" (quoted in Nelson, 1982, p. C1).

A dramatic illustration of this is the first memory of a sophomore woman in a demanding premedical program who remembers sitting in her frilly pink bedroom at the age of 3, listening to the record of *The Little Engine That Could*. John Kihlstrom, senior author of a study on the early memories of 314 high school and college students (Kihlstrom & Harackiewicz, 1982), pinpoints this memory as capturing "what she was all about—trying to combine a feminine role with high achievement" (quoted in Nelson, 1982, p. C7).

The search for childhood memories can also raise questions that may lead to fruitful answers to the enigma of memory in general. For example, how important is the use of language in incorporating and preserving memories? It is possible that the reason we have so few memories from our earliest years is because we didn't have the tools—that is, the words—to organize them in a way they could be stored. Or perhaps we have repressed them: Freud maintained that we forgot so many of our childhood feelings and experiences because they were too troubling to us.

Another clue from childhood memories relates to the utter unreliability of so many of the things we remember with absolute certainty, and to the way actual events become entangled with the stories we've heard and photos we've seen. In your earliest memory, for example, do you see yourself as a small child as if you were observing yourself from the outside? This may be because your memory was shaped not so much by what you actually remember but by photographs you have seen or family stories you have heard.

Research into childhood memories represents a new focus in the study of memory—directing our attention to the way memory actually operates in everyday life rather than to the way we can make it operate in a psychological laboratory. Research on memory has been going on for about a hundred years, most of it based in the laboratory. Such work has provided a great deal of basic information about how memory works. Today, however, while the study of memory continues in the lab, there is a growing interest in the way memory operates "in real life." In this chapter we will discuss what we know about memory as a basic psychological process. In addition, we'll take up some of the practical implications of memory research, such as what it tells us about the reliability of eyewitness testimony and what it suggests for improving our memories.

HOW DO WE REMEMBER?

Your memory works through four basic steps: First you have to perceive something—to see it, hear it, or become aware of it through some other sense. Second, you have to get it into your memory. Third, you put it away. And finally, you have to be able to find it so you can take it out.

Perception, the first step in this process, may be involuntary. You see or hear something, and it makes an impression on you. Or it may involve a deliberate effort to pay close attention to information so that your perception will be keener.

The second step requires you to encode whatever you want to remember. Encoding is the process of classifying information. You need to get information ready for storage by organizing it in some meaningful way. One way is by coding letters of the alphabet into words, coding words into sentences, and coding sentences into ideas. We also encode material by sound and meaning. Only encoded information can be remembered.

Third, you store the material so that it stays in memory.

The final, crucial step in this sequence is retrieval, or getting the remembered information out of storage. The thoroughness with which we prepare information for memory and store it determines the efficiency with which we retrieve it.

The two most popular explanations of the way these processes occur are the storage and transfer model of memory proposed by Richard Atkinson and Richard Shiffrin (1968, 1971) and the levels of processing model of Fergus I. M. Craik and Robert S. Lockhart (1972).

Atkinson and Shiffrin's Storage and Transfer Model

According to this explanation for the way memory works, all of us have three different types of memory. First, material comes through our senses—our eyes, our ears, our nose, and so forth—into sensory memory (SM). In less than a second, this information either disappears or is transferred from sensory memory into short-term memory (STM), where it may stay for up to 20 seconds. If it does not disappear at this stage, it moves into long-term memory (LTM), where it may remain for the rest of our life. Let's take an in-depth view at each of these types of memory (see Figure 6-1).

SENSORY MEMORY (SM) Here you are a camera. You take an instantaneous "photo" of whatever you see, hear, smell, taste, or touch. For a fraction of a second, your brain absorbs the overall appearance of the room you step into, with its colors, shapes, and arrangements, or the buzz and rumble of sounds around you on a busy city street, or the bouquet of fragrances in a summer garden. This information is the raw data of life, which you can either act upon by taking it into your memory or ignore and forget it. The way this kind of memory works has been demonstrated by a series of experiments performed by George Sperling.

HOW SPERLING'S EXPERIMENTS DEMONSTRATE THE SHORT-LIVED BUT BROAD-BASED CAPACITY OF SENSORY MEMORY Before Sperling did his

You probably have a lot of questions about memory. Why do the most trivial facts fly unbidden into your mind while you forget vital information? Why can a classmate who doesn't seem especially bright remember more than you? Can you improve your memory? If you witnessed an accident, would you be a reliable eyewitness?

You'll be able to answer some of these questions from the information in this chapter. Others, however, will remain unanswered until researchers—maybe you, someday—explore hitherto ignored aspects of memory.

*"The matters about which I'm being questioned, Your Honor, are all
things I should have included in my long-term memory but which
I mistakenly inserted in my short-term memory."*

experiments in 1960, psychologists had performed many studies showing
people visual arrays of letters like the grid in Figure 6-1. No matter how
many items were shown—from as few as eight to as many as twenty—
most people could only remember four or five. The natural assumption,
then, was that this was the maximum number of items people could take
in in a single glimpse.

Yet Sperling knew that many people insisted they had seen more items
but that they forgot the others during the time it took them to report the
first four or five. So he devised his "partial report" experiment as part of
the work for his doctoral dissertation.

If you were a subject in this study, you would see a grid like the one in
Figure 6-2. After you could no longer see the grid, you would hear a tone
telling you to report all the letters you remember from one of the rows. A
high-pitched tone would mean the top row, a medium tone the middle
row, and a low tone the bottom row. No matter which tone you heard,

FIGURE 6-1 Atkinson and
Shiffrin's storage and transfer
model of memory *According to
this model, there are three memory
systems. Information comes
through our senses and enters
sensory memory. In less than a
second it is either forgotten or
transferred into short-term
memory. Information remains in
short-term memory for about 20
seconds unless it is held there
longer by rehearsal. Information
that is not forgotten enters long-
term memory, where it is organized
and stored. Information is retrieved
from long-term memory and is
transferred back to short-term
memory when it is recalled.
Although the capacity of short-term
memory is limited, the capacity of
long-term memory is virtually
limitless.*

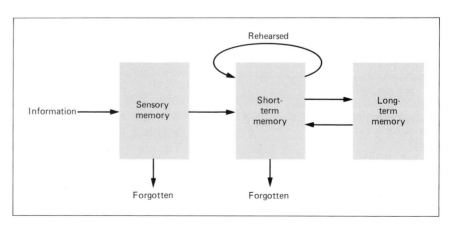

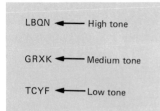

FIGURE 6-2 Sperling's partial report technique to assess sensory memory *Subjects in Sperling's experiments were shown a letter grid for a brief period. They then heard one of three tones and were instructed to report the letters from either the first, second, or third row of the grid depending on whether they heard a high, medium, or low tone. For an array of letters of the size in the example, subjects typically were able to report three out of four letters in a row. (From Sperling, 1960)*

you would probably report three out of the four letters in a row. Since you didn't know in advance which row you'd be asked about, you must have known about three letters from each row, or nine letters, about twice the earlier estimate of what people can absorb into sensory memory.

Sperling also established the fleeting nature of sensory memory. He found that if he sounded the tone after a delay of only 1 second, his subjects would remember very little (see Figure 6-3).

KINDS OF SENSORY MEMORY   The kind of memory we have just been talking about, which comes in through our vision, is known as iconic memory. Apparently iconic images fade more quickly than those that come in through our ears, known as echoic memory. Echoic images last a bit longer, as you might have noticed if you have ever seemed to hear the radio continue playing *after* you had turned it off. We do, of course, have sensory memories for our other senses, too. One of the authors (D. E. P.) sometimes comes across a soap with a strong floral scent. When she smells this fragrance, childhood memories of her grandmother, her grandmother's apartment, and the long-ago times the author had spent with her waft into her mind. Another psychologist, James Johnson (1983), recently noted an experience that might demonstrate either smell or kinesthetic memory. As he opened a can of cat food, he asked his son if he wanted anything. The father later recalled that the night before, as he had been opening a can of cat food, the boy had asked him to get him a light bulb. Thus, the father associated the child's wanting something with the activity of opening the can. While other sensory memories are familiar to all of us, little research has been done on any besides the iconic and the echoic.

SHORT-TERM MEMORY (STM)   Short-term memory is our working memory, our active memory that contains the information we are currently using. What happened the last time you had to look up a telephone number to make a call at a public booth, when you didn't have anything to write the number down? You probably repeated the number in your head

FIGURE 6-3 The fleeting nature of sensory memory *The longer the time between seeing the letter grid and being asked to report, the fewer letters subjects remember. (From Sperling, 1960)*

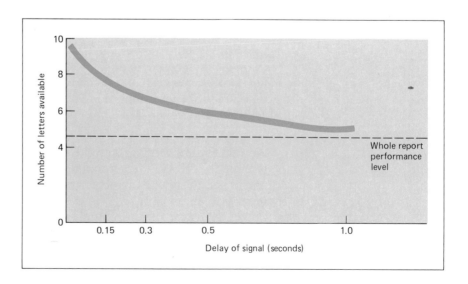

The concept of short-term memory has been with us since William James poetically described it in 1890, calling it *primary memory* to distinguish it from long-term, or *secondary memory:*

The stream of thought flows on; but most of its segments fall into the bottomless abyss of oblivion. Of some, no memory survives the instant of their passage. Of others, it is confined to a few moments, hours, or days. Others, again, leave vestiges which are indestructible, and by means of which they may be recalled as long as life endures. (p. 643)

two or three times before dialing it. If a friend came up to speak to you before you reached the phone, you most likely forgot the number and had to look it up all over again. What does this common situation tell us about STM?

Short-Term Memory Fades Rapidly If you had not repeated the telephone number to yourself (i.e., rehearsed the material), you would have forgotten the number within 15 to 18 seconds (Peterson & Peterson, 1959).

Rehearsal Helps to Retain Material in STM With rehearsal, you will be able to hold onto material for a longer time. As long as you keep repeating it, you'll remember it, but unless you take your rehearsing a step further into elaborative rehearsal (discussed in the section on long-term memory), you will probably forget the item after you have used it.

Short-Term Memory Is like Your Attention Span If you're distracted, you'll forget whatever is in short-term memory. This can be a nuisance sometimes but a sanity-saver at others. Suppose you remembered every trivial transaction you were involved in all day long? Such information would interfere with your ability to go on with other activities and to take in the new material you would need. If you were waiting on tables and could not put out of your mind the previous ten customers' orders after they had left your restaurant, you would have a hard time remembering the orders of your current customers.

The experience of a famous memory prodigy, known as S, bears this out (Luria, 1968). S remembered *everything* and forgot nothing. As a result, he could not read, for the image from one passage would intrude upon his reading of the next one, and he would be ensnared in a thicket of overlapping images. He could not dismiss an image when it was no longer needed.

The Capacity of Short-Term Memory Is Small What George Miller (1956) called "the magical number . . . plus or minus two" usually defines the limits of STM. The magic number is 7, and as an average, this is the largest number of items we can keep in short-term memory. An item is a meaningful unit, such as a letter, digit, word, or phrase. It is true, however, that some people at some times can remember no more than five items, and others can often remember up to nine. (Is it just a coincidence that American telephone numbers—without area codes—comprise exactly seven numbers?)

We Can Expand the Capacity of Short-Term Memory One way to do this is through chunking, or grouping items into meaningful units. You can remember telephone numbers more easily, for example, if you break them into three chunks—the exchange, plus two groups of two-digit numbers, instead of seven numbers in a row. Chunking does not expand short-term memory indefinitely, however. Once you reach the limit of the amount of information you can store there, adding new information will cause the old information to be displaced, unless it has been stored in long-term memory.

Retrieval from Short-Term Memory Is Rapid and Exhaustive If we have stored information in STM, we can get at it quickly. This has been demonstrated in the experiments performed by Saul Sternberg (1966, 1967, 1969). If you were a subject in these studies, you would see a *memory set* consisting of letters or numbers, say, the digits 5 8 4 2. Next, you would press a button that would flash a single digit, known as a *test item*, or a *probe*, and you would say whether or not this had been in the memory set. If the probe was 4, you would say yes, but if it were 6, you would say no. You would be asked to answer as quickly as possible but to avoid errors. Errors are very rare in this experiment, so researchers can concentrate on response time.

By focusing on response time, the researchers explored two basic questions about the way we retrieve information from short-term memory. Do people examine items in STM one at a time (*serial processing*) or globally, all at once (*parallel processing*)? One way to answer this is by varying the size of the memory set. If people examine everything in STM at one time, the size of the set shouldn't affect response time; if we examine items one at a time, the more items we have to look through, the longer our search will take. Sternberg found that searches for longer memory sets take longer, leading to the conclusion that we probably look for things one at a time.

HOW SHORT-TERM AND LONG-TERM MEMORY WORK TOGETHER Imagine yourself as a carpenter in your workroom, with all your materials neatly organized on wall-hung shelves. As you prepare to build a cabinet, you take the wood, a saw, and a hammer from the shelves and put them on your workbench, saving some room for you to work on. Soon you realize you need some nails and clamps, so you lay them down on the bench, too. Before long your bench is such a jumble of tools and materials that there's no room to work. You stack some boards in a neat pile, but still things keep falling off onto the floor. So you put some of the materials and tools you're finished with back onto the shelves to leave some room to work on, and you go ahead to finish the job.

In this analogy, created by Klatzky (1980)—and expanded by us—the workbench represents short-term memory, known as our "working memory," while the shelves represent long-term memory, the repository of much information we don't need at the moment but have stored. Short-term memory contains a limited amount of *activated* material in current use, while long-term memory contains a great deal of encoded, currently *inactive* material.

If we stretch this analogy and assume that the shelves have the magical quality of refilling themselves when we take materials to the workbench, we can appreciate the way short-term and long-term memory overlap. Something can be in both STM and LTM at the same time. You may have known the road over the meadow and through the woods to Grandmother's house ever since you were a child, so it is in your long-term memory. The next time you go there, though, you will be activating it into your short-term memory so that you can put your knowledge of the route to work for you.

Another way to look at the difference and the relatedness of these two types of memory is to realize that, according to the model we've presented, everything we learn has to go through STM before it reaches

LTM. Once it does, it is (at least theoretically) capable of being activated so we can work with it. Whatever we want to retrieve from LTM has to go through STM before we can use it. Not all information, though, gets into LTM: Some of it falls off the workbench onto the floor, where it gets swept up and thrown out rather than put on the shelves.

It's easy and more or less automatic to pick up materials from the workbench (and memories from STM) while you have to search for what you want on the shelves (or in LTM). However, once you have stored something on the shelf (in LTM), it's not as likely to fall off and disappear—even if you get distracted. What does happen, though, is that material stored on the shelves for a long time sometimes gets warped, bent out of shape, distorted. So do memories, as we'll see when we discuss forgetting later in this chapter.

THE IMPORTANCE OF TRANSFER FROM STM TO LTM   Suppose you never transferred anything from short-term to long-term memory. If you met someone today, you would have to learn his or her name again tomorrow, and the next day, and the day after that. If you moved to a new place, you would not be able to remember your way home from one day to the next. You would have to keep relearning the same information over and over again because of the limited capacity of short-term memory. As we will see later in this chapter, there *are* people who are in this limbo of perpetual short-term memory, due to injury, surgery, or other interferences with brain function.

LONG-TERM MEMORY   Back to your carpenter's workroom. Those wall shelves that represent long-term memory seem to have the magical quality of unlimited capacity. However, the way you place your tools on the shelves is crucial for their later retrieval. If you throw everything on haphazardly, you may never be able to find them when you want them. If you organize them according to a system, they will be easier to find. Long-term memory is often described as being similar to a card catalog in a library, a complicated filing system, or a book index.

CROSS-INDEXING IN LONG-TERM MEMORY   How would you get to your memory of your birthday in 1984? Suppose you had celebrated it with a picnic in Fairmount Park in Philadelphia: You might get to it by thinking of picnics or parks in general, of Fairmount Park, of Philadelphia, of the people you were with that day, of the foods you ate, of the mosquitoes that ate you, of birthday celebrations, of the aroma of new-mown grass, of the feel of the wind or the color of the sky that were like the conditions on the day of the picnic, or by any of a number of other indexes.

The more associations you have with a piece of information, the easier it will be for you to remember it. You won't, however, store every single detail of an experience. You won't remember every word spoken during the three hours you were at the park, nor every person seen, nor every mouthful eaten. As memory researcher Elizabeth F. Loftus writes, you'll just remember the highlights:

> The brain condenses experiences for us. It seems to edit the boring parts in order to highlight the interesting parts and cross-reference them for storage.

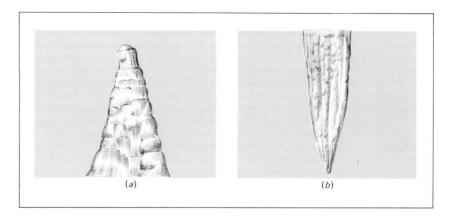

(a)   (b)

FIGURE 6-4(a) *A stalagmite.*
(b) *A stalactite.*

While there are many similarities in the ways in which different people's memories are organized, each memory is also unique. This is because memory is a result of a collection of life experiences, and everybody's life experiences are different (1980, pp. 27–28).

ENCODING BY ASSOCIATION   While rehearsing something—going over it several times, either silently or out loud—will fix it for short-term memory, a different kind of process is needed to embed something in long-term memory. You need to make associations between what you now want to remember and something else that you already know, that is, to make the new material personally meaningful in some way. This kind of meaningful organization is one type of encoding. Simple rehearsal actually works better for immediate recall, but this kind of encoding, *associational rehearsal*, is better for remembering something in the long run.

If you can find a meaning in material that you want to remember, you'll have an easier time holding on to it. Suppose, for example, you want to remember the difference between stalagmites and stalactites, those mineral deposits that form in caverns. With these words, it's easy to find something in the words that will be associated to their meaning. The g in "stalagmite" is the initial letter of the word "*g*round," reminding you that stalagmites form from the ground of a cave. The t in "stalac*t*ite" begins the word "*t*op"; ergo, it's easy to remember that stalactites form from the *top* of a cave (Figure 6-4).

ENCODING BY ORGANIZATION   Associational rehearsal is one kind of organization. Remember the shelves in the workroom? The better you can organize the material to stack on those shelves, the easier it will be to find it. When material is presented in an organized way, such as by categories, it is easier to remember than when it is presented in random fashion (Bousfield, 1953). When it is presented randomly, most people tend to organize it themselves through the technique of clustering, that is, grouping items into categories, rearranging in the mind the order in which the items were presented. This is a common way to convert material from short-term to long-term memory.

Endel Tulving (1962) presented sixteen unrelated words in sixteen different sequences to sixteen college women for sixteen different trials. The words are listed in Figure 6-5.

ACCENT	LAGOON
BARRACK	MAXIM
DRUMLIN	OFFICE
FINDING	POMADE
GARDEN	QUILLET
HOYDEN	TREASON
ISSUE	VALLEY
JUNGLE	WALKER

FIGURE 6-5 *The sixteen unrelated words used in Tulving's study of memory.*

When the students were then asked to recall the words in any order that came to mind (free recall), they tended to recall them in the same order on different trials, no matter how they were presented, indicating that the women had organized them in their own minds. They organized the words in many different ways—meaning, sound, familiarity, and so forth. There were a number of common patterns, indicating either that the subjects discovered sources of organization in the material itself rather than imposing it arbitrarily or that the women's similar life experiences may have led them to similar styles of clustering.

WHAT WE'VE LEARNED FROM "THE TIP OF THE TONGUE" You run into someone whose name you're sure you know, but no matter how hard you try, you can't come up with it. Is it Nadine? Natalie? Nadia? No, you know none of those are right—but you have the feeling you're on the right track. You try to remember where you met her. You keep probing until you visualize the party in the loft apartment, and you see the mystery lady wearing a red dress. Suddenly you remember. Natasha! Of course!

Sequences like this go on in our heads all the time. They're called tip-of-the-tongue (TOT) states and describe situations in which a person cannot recall a word, image, or other memory immediately but does have knowledge of it. Sometimes we solve the riddle quickly, sometimes after several hours, sometimes never. After fifty-six college students heard definitions of forty-nine fairly uncommon words (such as *apse, nepotism, cloaca, ambergris,* and *sampan*) and were asked to supply the word, they came up with a total of 360 (TOT) states. One of the definitions was "a navigational instrument used in measuring angular distances, especially the altitude of sun, moon, and stars at sea." Before you read the next paragraph, take a couple of minutes to write down the word or words that you think would fit this definition.

If you don't know the proper word, chances are that you'll search your memory for it, meanwhile coming up with words like *astrolabe, compass, dividers,* and *protractor,* all of which are similar in meaning to the target word. Or you would go off in a different direction, coming up with words like *secant, sextet,* and *sexton,* all of which resemble the sound of the word you're looking for. Most people encode material into memory according to two basic signals—how a word sounds and what the word means (Brown & McNeill, 1966).

In all cases of positive TOTs (those in which the target word was known and eventually recalled or recognized), 48 percent of the subjects came up with a word that had the same number of syllables as the target word, 57 percent guessed the initial letter, and substantial numbers of subjects came up with the correct prefix or suffix.

While 95 words similar in meaning were called forth, 224 words similar in sound were given. The researchers called this second kind of recall *generic* recall, or recall of the general type of the word, if not the actual word itself. Such generic recall can be *partial,* when only a letter or two, or a prefix or suffix is remembered, or *abstract,* such as "a two-syllable word with the stress on the first syllable."

In a follow-up study, fifty-three students saw photos of fifty personalities from the fields of entertainment, politics, the arts, and so forth. When

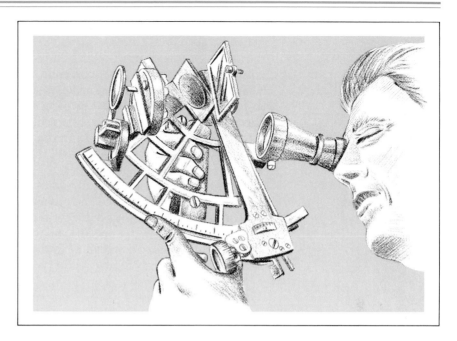

FIGURE 6-6 *A sextant*

subjects didn't recognize the face immediately, they tried first to locate the person's profession ("movie star") and then to remember when they last saw him or her ("latest film was *Bob, Carol, Ted and Alice*"). Then they guessed the first letter of the last name, the number of syllables, and, finally, a similar sounding name, and were quite accurate in these approaches (Yarmey, 1973).

Both these experiments show that items in long-term memory are encoded in ways other than meaning alone and that we retrieve a word or name from our long-term memory by the way it looks or the way it sounds, in addition to whatever it means to us. (By the way, did you ever come up with *sextant?*) (See Figure 6-6.)

Other research has shown that we store, organize, and retrieve material in memory through two basic systems—one using words and one using images—and that these two ways seem to be processed differently. According to this *dual-coding hypothesis* (Paivio, 1975), we use imagery for information about concrete objects and events, and we use words for ideas and language. Both systems are independent but interconnected: Either one can be approached individually, but they transfer information back and forth to each other. Some material seems to be stored in each of these systems, although the amount and type in each is controversial.

Craik and Lockhart's Levels of Processing Model

There is another way of looking at the way memory works. Craik and Lockhart (1972) disagree with the concept of memory as a division into three completely separate memory structures—sensory, short-term, and long-term memory. They identify only one kind of memory and maintain that the ability to remember is dependent on how deeply we process information. We process material along a continuum of ever-increasing depth, running it through on levels that range from quite shallow to very deep. The deeper we process it, the longer it lasts.

This concept of memory sees it as more of an active than a reactive process, with memory performance a direct result of the learner's mental activity.

How does this concept work? The shallowest level of processing, according to this model, involves your awareness of a sensory feature—what a word or number looks like or sounds like, what a food smells or tastes like, and so forth. As you recognize some kind of pattern in your sensory impression, you'll process it more deeply. And when you make an association, that is, give a meaning, to your impression, you will be at the deepest level of processing of all, the kind that will form the strongest and most enduring memory trace.

If you were a subject in a study that Craik and Tulving (1975) ran to test this thesis, you would have been asked to look at a number of different words. You would be asked whether the word is in capital letters, whether it rhymes with a specific sound, whether it would fit into a given category, or whether it would fit into a particular sentence with a blank spot. To get a picture of the levels of processing for these words, see Table 6-1.

After these questions, you would have received a surprise quiz on the words, in which you would be asked to *recall* or *recognize* them. Recall and recognition are two different measures of memory. (See Box 6-1.)

In these experiments, Craik and Tulving found that deeper levels of processing generally took longer to accomplish and produced stronger memories of the words. Follow-up tests suggested that it was not the time itself but the depth of processing that was important. When a complex but shallow task was assigned (such as classifying vowel-and-consonant patterns according to a complicated formula), it took longer to carry out than an easy but deeper task (deciding whether a word would fit into a sentence).

The levels of processing explanation has some gaps in it. For one thing, the type of test used to measure memory may well influence the conclusions drawn. In other experiments, questions like "Was there something [in the words you saw] that rhymed with pain?" gave better results than the sentence task (Morris, Bransford, & Franks, 1977). Apparently, then, there are cases where a shallower depth of processing (at the phonemic level in this case, as described in Table 6-1) gives better retention than a deeper processing level. Furthermore, another contradictory finding has appeared: When subjects are presented with the same item and the same

TABLE 6-1 Typical Questions and Answers in Levels of Processing Experiment

Level of Processing	Depth of Processing	Question	Answer YES	NO
Structural	Shallow	Is the word in capital letters?	TABLE	Table
Phonemic (sound)	Intermediate	Does the word rhyme with *weight*?	Crate	Market
Category	Deep	Is the word a type of fish?	Shark	Heaven
Sentence	Deep	Would the word fit this sentence: "He met a _____ in the street"?	Friend	Cloud

Source: Based on Craik & Tulving (1975).

BOX 6-1

TESTING MEMORY: RECOGNITION, RECALL, AND RELEARNING

Of the three basic ways used to test and study learning and memory, *recognition* and *recall* are most often used today. The most sensitive measure, *relearning,* is not commonly used today because it's so time-consuming, but it is historically important.

RECOGNITION

In this kind of test you're given an array of possible answers from which you're asked to choose the right one. These answers are cues that help you search your memory. Multiple-choice and true-false tests are tests of *recognition.* This task is usually easier than recall since you're given the answer (even if it's one among several) and you have to perform only *one* memory task—deciding whether what you see (or hear, etc.) is a copy of the information you have in your memory or not.

RECALL

In these tests you may be given clues, but you have to pull the information out of memory yourself. Essay tests are tests of *recall.* The reason why recall is usually harder than recognition is that you have to go through *two* steps—generating possible answers from your memory and then identifying them.

There are two kinds of recall tests: In free recall you can recall the material in any order. In serial recall you have to recall it in a particular sequence, usually the order in which it was originally presented. You might be shown twelve nonsense syllables and be asked to recall them by either free or serial recall. Or you might learn pairs of nonsense syllables and then be shown the first member of each pair and asked to recall the second.

RELEARNING

This technique attempts to measure the amount of time you save in learning material if you had already learned it at some earlier time. It's easier, for example, to prepare for a comprehensive final exam in a subject if you've already learned the material earlier in the semester than if you're learning it for the first time during your "cram" session.

As a research method, relearning takes so much time because it involves teaching information, allowing enough time to go by for the information to be forgotten, and then presenting the same information again. The savings is calculated in one of two ways: either comparing the ease with which a single person learns brand-new material compared with material that had been learned earlier, or comparing two groups of subjects, one of which had been exposed to material earlier while the other had not.

In the first systematic study of memory, in 1885, Hermann Ebbinghaus demonstrated this concept. Ebbinghaus decided to use the most convenient, economical research subject around—himself. (This, of course, raises the possibility of experimenter bias.) He invented the concept of the nonsense syllable—a set of three letters, arranged in consonant-vowel-consonant order—as the basis for his experiments. Why nonsense syllables such as SUJ, FUB, HIW, and the like? Because he felt that people would make various associations to meaningful items and would differ in their ability to learn and remember them. (Another problem with this work is that some nonsense syllables are not all equally meaningless and thus differ in the ease with which they can be learned.)

Ebbinghaus learned lists of nonsense syllables and determined how long it took him to learn them perfectly. He let enough time go by for him to forget the syllables and then he relearned them, calculating how long it took him to once again recite them perfectly. The difference between the number of trials it took him to learn the nonsense syllables the first time and the amount of time it took him to relearn them gave him a measure of savings.

encoding question more than once ("Does the word 'train' have an *n* sound?"), they remember it better (Nelson, 1977). The second presentation doesn't call for any deeper processing, only more of the same, so the explanation for better recall after two trials has to be sought outside the levels of processing model.

Furthermore, we don't yet have an objective way to measure depth of processing. We can't go by the time required, as we have seen. So all we're left with is the intuitive assumption that processing by meaning is "deeper" than processing by physical characteristics. It may well be, but where is the proof?

What we can do is use the best parts of both explanations. It's useful to think about memory in terms of short-term and long-term memory. At the same time, we recognize that they are related—not divided into two completely separate memory structures. Furthermore, we note that both models have some elements in common, like the emphasis in each one on the importance of meaningful associations.

WHAT DO WE REMEMBER?

We've already learned that we remember meaningful, well-organized information best. Well-remembered material also has some other characteristics. Here are a few of them.

We Remember Best What We Learn First and What We Learn Last: The Serial Position Curve

If you have ever gone through a receiving line at a wedding or other social affair, you may remember being introduced to eight or ten or so new people, one right after the other. By the time you had shaken the last hand, it's probable that you remembered the names of the two people you met first and the two you met last—and forgot the names of those in the middle.

This phenomenon incorporates the effects of primacy (the tendency to remember the items you learned first) and of recency (the tendency to remember those you learned last). You can get a graphic picture of it by looking at the serial position curve shown in Figure 6-7. One possible explanation for this common situation is that the first two names you learned entered your long-term memory while the others made it only into short-term memory. Because of the way material in short-term memory gets displaced by new information, the only names you could remem-

Remembering the names of the first and the last people you meet in a receiving line—and forgetting those of the people in the middle— illustrates the primacy and recency effects. (© Jim Kalett/Photo Researchers, Inc.)

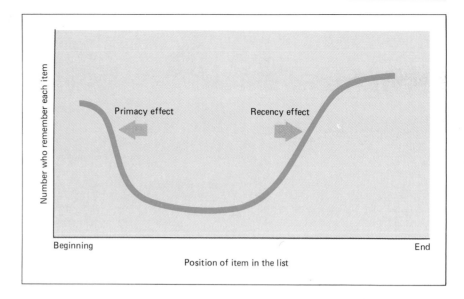

FIGURE 6-7 The serial position curve *This curve indicates that subjects are most likely to remember items at the end (recency effect) and beginning (primacy effect) of a list and are least likely to remember items in the middle. (From Loftus, 1980)*

ber at the end of the line were those that had not yet been replaced, the last two (Glanzer & Cunitz, 1966).

We Remember Best the Unusual: The von Restorff Effect

If one of the names in the middle of the line had been famous or distinctive, you probably would have remembered it—provided it was not so difficult for you to pronounce or spell that you were unable to get it into your memory in the first place. This tendency to remember an unusual item, regardless of its position in a list, is named after the psychologist who first presented it.

We Remember Best What We Learned in a Similar Mood: State-Dependent Memory

Let's go to the movies for a minute and see Charlie Chaplin in *City Lights:*

> In one very funny sequence, Charlie saves a drunk from leaping to his death. The drunk turns out to be a millionaire who befriends Charlie, and the two spend the evening together drinking and carousing. The next day, when sober, the millionaire does not recognize Charlie and even snubs him. Later the millionaire gets drunk again, and when he spots Charlie treats him as his long-lost companion (Bower, 1981, p. 129).

Gordon Bower (1981) cites the case of Sirhan Sirhan, Robert Kennedy's assassin, who had no memory of the murder until, under hypnosis, he reached the same frenzied state in which he shot Kennedy and then reenacted the crime. These examples illustrate a relationship between mood and memory that Bower has termed state-dependent memory. It also shows up in less extreme circumstances. When you're feeling sad, it's easier to remember memories formed during another sad time in your life and harder to remember what you learned in happier moods. Furthermore, when you're sad, you're more likely to remember unhappy experiences than happy ones.

Bower confirmed the existence of this phenomenon with lab experiments that showed that people who learned lists of words in a hypnotically induced state of happiness or sadness recalled the material much better when they were again in a similar emotional state. Apparently, we

This scene from Charlie Chaplin's movie, City Lights, *shows the relationship between mood and memory. Charlie saves the life of a drunken millionaire who then befriends his rescuer. The next day when the millionaire is sober, he doesn't recognize the little tramp. When the millionaire gets drunk again, however, he hails Charlie as his friend. Bower terms this phenomenon state-dependent memory. (Museum of Modern Art/Film Stills Archive)*

come to associate a particular emotion with a particular idea or event, and one helps to bring back the other.

Knowing this tendency can work for us in daily life. We can help to get ourselves out of low moods by deliberately focusing on a happy memory or thought and then letting the positive momentum carry us into a better frame of mind. Aaron Beck's cognitive therapy (discussed in Chapter 16) focuses on trying to get depressed people to change the way they think about the events in their lives, partly by concentrating on the positives in their lives.

We Remember Best Links to Emotionally Significant Events: Flashbulb Memories

During the last century a researcher asked 179 middle-aged and elderly people whether they remembered where they had been when they heard that President Abraham Lincoln had been shot (Colegrove, 1899). Thirty-three years after the assassination, 127 of those questioned were able to give a full description, including time of day, exact location, and the identity of the news bearer.

This kind of recollection has been termed a flashbulb memory (Brown & Kulik, 1977). It is "simply *there,* ready to appear in stunning detail at the merest hint. It's as if our nervous system took a multimedia snapshot of the sounds, sights, smells, weather, emotional climate, even the body postures we experience at certain moments" (Benderly, 1982, p. 71). The snapshot is not complete, however. While it usually includes certain basic elements like where you were, what you were doing before the shock, who gave you the news, what you did next, and how you and those about you felt about the event, it generally captures some trivial details while leaving out others. You may remember the expression on the face of the department store stockroom worker who said, wheeling his cart past

Millions of John Lennon's fans will always remember what they were doing when they heard the news of the singer's murder. Do you have such a "flashbulb memory" for this or any other event in your life? (Owen Franken/Sygma)

My father and I were on the road to A—in the State of Maine to purchase the "fixings" needed for my graduation. When we were driving down a steep hill into the city we felt that something was wrong. Everybody looked so sad, and there was such terrible excitement that my father stopped his horse and leaning from the carriage called: "What is it, my friends? What has happened?" "Haven't you heard?" was the reply—"Lincoln has been assassinated." The lines fell from my father's limp hands, and with tears streaming from his eyes he sat as one bereft of motion. We were far from home, and much must be done, so he rallied after a time, and we finished our work as well as our heavy hearts would allow.
(Colegrove, 1899, p. 247–248)

We Fill In the Gaps

you, "The president's been shot!" while not remembering what kind of merchandise was on display around you.

What kind of event captures such a memory? It can be a moment out of history or out of your personal life. You may remember that formaldehyde smell mingling with the scents of cut flowers as you sat in a hospital room listening to a red-bearded doctor tell you that an illness was even more serious than you had feared. The flashbulb memory occurs at a moment of surprise, or shock, and of great personal, biological significance say Brown and Kulik. In 1977 they asked eighty people aged 20 to 60 (forty blacks, forty whites) to recall the circumstances in which they had first heard the news of nine public events (including the killings or assassination attempts of seven Americans—four white, three black), as well as a personal, unexpected shock, such as death of a friend or relative, a serious accident, or the diagnosis of a deadly disease.

These subjects had flashbulb memories of a number of events—all but one for the murder of John F. Kennedy, and seventy-three out of the eighty for a personal shock. Some racial differences showed up, the most dramatic being the difference surrounding the news of the murder of the Rev. Martin Luther King, Jr. While 75 percent of the black subjects reported a flashbulb memory for this event, only 33 percent of the whites did. By and large, black people reacted more emotionally to Dr. King's death than did white people.

Why would people remember details from their own lives that had no significance other than coincidence with a historic event—what you were eating, what someone was wearing, the feel of a rubber tread underfoot? Brown and Kulik believe that printing such a record in our memories held survival value in premedia days. It would have been important to remember significant events. Suppose you saw a dangerous animal attack someone in front of you? Your life could be saved by remembering exactly what time of day it was, where you were, and what you were doing at the time of the attack so you could avoid such an encounter in the future.

Neisser (1982) puts forth another explanation for such memories. He offers evidence that such memories are often inaccurate and that, years later, we rarely have any way of checking an individual's memory of what she or he was doing at the time. While Brown and Kulik feel that the memory is set at the time the event occurs, Neisser refers to evidence showing that people often relate their accounts of these memories many times and maintains that the "photo" is taken retroactively because of the significance the event acquires in the person's mind *after* the event. Neisser feels that public flashbulb memories are "benchmarks," "places where we line up our own lives with the course of history and say 'I was there'" (p. 48). By holding onto a scrap of our personal history, we attach ourselves to the larger tapestry through which our civilization's tale is told. We become a part of something grander and more important than our own personal existence.

We can see how our retrieval mechanism works when we search our minds for a memory, using certain clues to lead us to our goal. Suppose someone asks you what you were doing at 12:00 noon exactly one year ago today. First you'll establish the date; then you're likely to place yourself geographically; then you may think in terms of your usual weekly schedule; then you'll narrow down your possibilities until you come up with what you want. In the following example you can see that recalling this kind of memory is like solving a logical problem:

> January 7, 1977. Let's see, that was during Christmas break so I suppose I was at home. No, wait a minute, that year Christmas break ended January 6, that was before we switched schedules. So let's see, I must have been back at school. In fact that was review week so I assume I was in class. Let's see, we came back on a Monday, so the 7th would have been a Tuesday. What classes was I taking that term—Renaissance poetry, physics—wait, I must have been in statistics because it met over the noon hour on Tuesdays and Thursdays. Now I remember the review session. Dr. Shaw was having trouble with all the nervous students demanding to know if they were responsible for this or that particular piece of information (Glass, Holyoak, & Santa, 1979, p. 119).

This process does help us come up with many elusive memories. It also, however, leads us to nonexistent ones. A number of different lines of research—with childhood memories, with the reconstruction of a story we have read or heard, with parents' memories of their children's development, with eyewitness testimony—all lead to the same conclusion. In the zeal to be logical and to fill in the gaps, people often invent material they're sure they actually remember as the truth.

The parents of forty-seven 3-year-olds were asked about various aspects of their children's development and their own child-rearing practices over the previous three years (Robbins, 1963). All these parents had been participating in a longitudinal study since their children's birth, so researchers had a way to evaluate their answers.

The parents turned out to be poor reporters. They made mistakes about such marker events as the age when a child was weaned from breast or bottle, age of bowel and bladder training, and the end of the 2 a.m. feeding. The mothers' memories tended to be distorted in the direction of currently popular professional recommendations. For example, they were more likely to report they had fed on demand when they had not. The fathers' errors varied more randomly, possibly showing lack of awareness of current trends in child rearing since the study covered a period of time when fathers were less involved in their children's day-to-day care than many men are today.

This report is especially significant when we realize how many research projects have been based on *retrospective* reports, that is, reports relying on individuals' memories. As this study shows, we cannot count on the accuracy of human memory.

Apparently, in the absence of memory for the events in question, these mothers filled in the gaps and created memories for the dates and experiences they had forgotten. Filling in the gaps can have life-or-death implications when we turn to the topic of eyewitness testimony, the kind of testimony that is believed in most strongly by jurors and a kind that has been shown, both experimentally and in real life, to be distressingly prone to error. This is largely because witnesses tend to use information from a number of different sources in reconstructing past events.

When 150 subjects were shown a film of a traffic accident and asked questions about it, those who were asked, "About how fast were the cars going when they smashed into one another?" gave higher estimates of speed than the ones asked how fast the cars were going when they "hit" one another. Furthermore, the ones who heard the verb "smashed" were more likely to say they had seen broken glass than were the ones who had heard the word "hit." In fact, there was no broken glass in the accident. Obviously, hearing the word "smashed" gave these "witnesses" new information. Associating the word with higher speeds and more severe accidents, they "filled in the gaps" and drew their own conclusions (Loftus & Palmer, 1974).

This study suggests that our memories respond to two kinds of information—that received during the perception of the original event and that received afterward, and that the material that comes later may act like paint on a wet watercolor picture, seeping into the earlier impression and changing it forever.

WHY DO WE FORGET?

How much do you remember of what you learned over the past academic year? How many of your high school classmates could you call by name right now? How many times a week do you forget appointments, chores, and other details of everyday life? Before you groan in self-disgust, take heart at how normal you are. We all forget all kinds of things all the time. Psychologists have even shown that people forget in an orderly fashion and according to a number of well-established principles.

Pioneer memory researcher Hermann Ebbinghaus (1885) gave us a picture of the *curve of forgetting* (see Figure 6-8), which shows that forgetting is very rapid at first and then slows down markedly. After Ebbinghaus had learned his nonsense syllables, he forgot them in an orderly—and quite rapid—way. Twenty minutes after having learned a list of thirteen syllables well enough to recite the list twice in order without a mistake, he forgot about 40 percent of what he had learned, and by the end of the first hour he remembered only about $33\frac{1}{3}$ percent. Over the next few days additional forgetting took place at a much slower pace, so that six days later he remembered 25 percent, and a month later, he still remembered

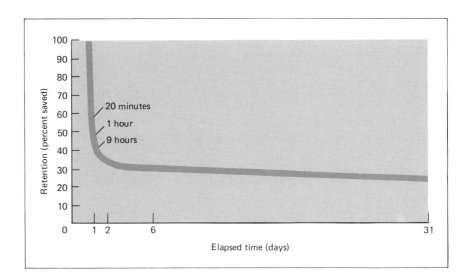

FIGURE 6-8 Ebbinghaus's forgetting curve *This curve demonstrates that forgetting is initially very rapid and then slows down markedly. (From Ebbinghaus, 1895)*

BOX 6-2

WE REMEMBER BEST WHAT WE NEED TO REMEMBER

Before you go on, take out pencil and paper and draw a picture of an ordinary American penny—both sides, putting in all the picture, number, and letter details you can think of. After you've done the best you can, look at the drawings in Figure 6-9. Which of these seems most accurate to you? Now take a penny out of your pocket and see how well you did in recalling what is on a penny, as shown by your own drawing, and in recognizing an accurate depiction of a penny. (This little exercise is fun to do with a couple of friends.)

If you're like most people, you gave an abysmal performance in trying to draw a penny. When twenty adults (all U.S. citizens) were asked to draw both sides of a penny from memory, only one (an avid penny collector) put in all eight features listed in Figure 6-10. Only four people got as many as half (Nickerson & Adams, 1979). Some examples of the drawings produced are shown in Figure 6-11. In another experiment the same researchers showed 127 adult citizens one of the drawings like the ones in Figure 6-9 and asked them to decide whether it was accurate and if not, why not. Again, performance was generally poor, both in recognizing the accurate drawing and in spotting errors on the inaccurate ones.

Five such experiments show that most people have very incomplete and imprecise memories of the details of an object that we have been handling constantly since childhood. Apparently, we don't store the details of a penny in our memory because we don't need to. We remember only what we need to remember. We can identify a penny by size and color, without looking at its features. We don't have to know which way Lincoln's head faces in order to recognize a penny as a penny. This report seems to show that recognition makes much smaller demands on memory than most of us have believed.

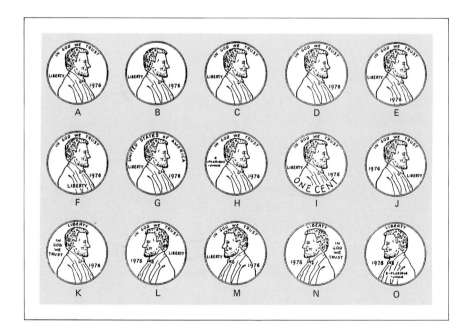

FIGURE 6-9 *Which is the "real" penny?*

FIGURE 6-10 *Examples of drawings of "pennies."*

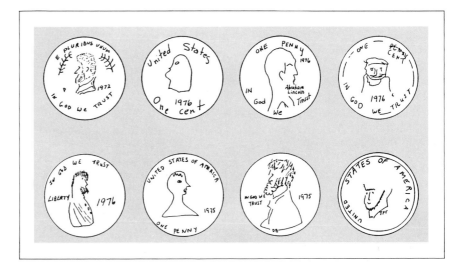

FIGURE 6-11 *Types of errors made in trying to draw a penny.*

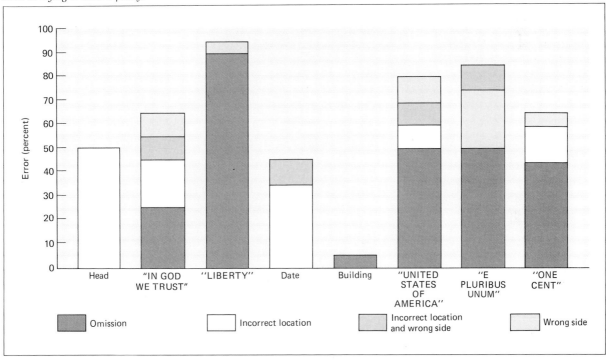

about 20 percent. Ebbinghaus felt that the slowness of this forgetting strongly suggested that it would have taken a very long time to forget the series entirely (Sahakian, 1976).

If Ebbinghaus rehearsed his list thirty additional times immediately after learning it, he remembered his syllables much better, showing that extra time spent *overlearning*, or studying, material that you want to remember can often pay off. Eventually, even the effects of overlearning decrease, so this, too, needs to be done within reason.

Forgetting is normal: We all do it, all the time. Memory researchers have shown that we forget in an orderly fashion and according to a number of well-established principles. Do you remember what these principles are? (Drawing by Ziegler; © 1977 The New Yorker Magazine, Inc.)

We seem to forget for a number of different reasons. Each of the following theories probably gives us at least part of the answer for why we forget. The complete answer to this question, however, is still unknown.

Motivated Forgetting: Repression

Sometimes we forget material in our long-term memories because there seems to be some personal benefit to *not* remembering. Thus, you forget the name of someone you don't like or the dentist's appointment you don't want to keep. You repress memories that are sad, embarrassing, or painful. (Freud felt that repression is a defense mechanism to combat anxiety.) Or you glorify your past, bringing your memories more in line with an ideal picture you would like to have of yourself (as in the case of the mothers in the child-rearing study referred to earlier who saw themselves as going along with currently recommended child-care practices more than they actually had [Robbins, 1963]).

Decay of the Memory Trace

The basic question about most other—unmotivated—forgetting is whether we forget because a memory just deteriorates or because even though the memory is there—possibly for as long as we live—we can't get at it to retrieve it. Some influential theorists, such as Shiffrin and Atkinson (1969) and Tulving (1974), maintain that we lose material from short-term memory because of decay of a memory trace, but that anything stored in long-term memory stays there forever, and any forgetting of that material is due to difficulty in retrieval. A *memory trace*, or engram, is a pathway left in the nervous system after learning has taken place. Other researchers (Loftus, 1979, 1980) take strong issue with this point of view, claiming that there is little basis for the widespread belief in the permanence of long-term memories. Theorists who maintain that there is a memory trace and that it is subject to decay believe it will persist when used but will disappear with time if it is not used. We'll examine these possibilities below and later in this chapter when we discuss the physiological basis for memory. First, let's consider the possible reasons for the decay of a memory.

POOR PERCEPTION   A memory may decay because your perception was too weak to make much of an impression in the first place. This may come about because of external conditions like noise, darkness, or some other circumstance that interferes with observation. If, for example, you saw a man in a moving car at least 60 feet away from you, who was visible only for the time it took the car to travel 50 or 60 feet, it would be hard to remember what the man looked like because you never got a good look at him. (Yet it was just this kind of eyewitness identification that helped to convict Nicolo Sacco, a shoemaker, an anarchist, and the codefendant in the famous Sacco and Vanzetti trial, of murder and to send him to his death in 1927 [Loftus, 1979].)

Poor perception may also be due to some quality of the observer. You might be distracted, under stress, or not paying attention because you don't think a particular item is terribly significant. This becomes a problem when a bystander who has not been paying close attention is suddenly called upon to testify about a crime, an accident, or some other event that caught him or her by surprise. In ordinary life, it's possible that most people can't remember names and faces because they've never learned them in the first place—they don't listen closely enough when they are first introduced to people.

INABILITY TO REHEARSE   At other times a memory decays because we don't have the opportunity to rehearse what we want to remember. If you look up a phone number and are prevented from going over it in your head, you may not be able to remember it long enough to make your call and will almost certainly lose it right afterwards. This applies only to short-term memory. Once something has been stored in long-term memory, we don't have to keep rehearsing it.

How well eyewitnesses remember an event like an accident depends on how accurate their initial perception was. If they weren't paying close attention or if it was dark out, the scene will not have made enough of an impression on their memory for them to recall the details. (© Miriam Reinhart, 1975/Photo Researchers, Inc.)

Interference

A different theory of forgetting holds that the reason we forget is because other information, learned earlier or later, *interferes* with our memory, either short- or long-term. When some kind of material similar to what we want to remember prevents us from rehearsing material in short-term memory (like someone's calling your name just after you've looked up a phone number), we forget it. Different processes are involved in interference with long-term memory.

Proactive interference (PI) describes a situation in which information that you learned first interferes with your ability to remember new material. An experimental group learns one list of words (material A), then a second list (material B), and then is asked to recall the second list. A control group is asked only to learn and then recall the words in the B list. The control group usually remembers the words better, indicating that the earlier-learned words are interfering with the experimental group's ability to remember the later ones.

In real life, this effect often shows up when you run into a woman you knew when she was single, who then took her husband's last name after marriage. Even though you have learned her married surname, you are apt to think of her by the name you first learned rather than the one you had to learn later, if you remember her name at all. The principle of proactive interference would suggest that you would remember a person's name more easily if you had to learn only one name, which might be a good argument for women's retaining their birth names!

In retroactive interference (RI), information that we learn later causes a kind of memory barrier that interferes with our remembering previously learned material. The new material takes over, obliterating the old, even if we learned it well. In studies of this phenomenon, the experimental group learns material A, then B, then recalls A, while the control group is not exposed to B at all. In these experiments, too, the control group remembers the material better, indicating that the experimental group's attention to new material is blocking the memory of the old material (Table 6-2).

Loftus's (1980) experiments with eyewitness testimony indicate that information received after the initial perception often replaces the original information in our memories, and we are prepared to swear that the

---

An example of proactive interference:

Dear Miss Manners:
What can you do after accidentally calling your present lover by your former lover's name?

Gentle Reader:
Seek a future lover. Such a mistake is easy to do and impossible to undo. Why do you think the term "darling" was invented?
From *Miss Manners' Guide to Excruciatingly Correct Behavior* (Martin, 1982, p. 292).

TABLE 6-2 Experimental Designs for the Study of Retroactive and Proactive Interference

Group	Step 1	Step 2	Step 3
Retroactive Interference			
Experimental	Learns A	Learns B	Retention test on A
Control	Learns A	Rest	Retention test on A
Proactive Interference			
Experimental	Learns A	Learns B	Retention test on B
Control	Rest	Learns B	Retention test on B

Adapted from Hulse, Egeth, & Deese, *Psychology of learning*, New York: McGraw-Hill, 5th ed., 1980, p. 308.

second impression is the only one. Many people who saw a film of a traffic accident and were then asked, "How fast was the car going when it ran the stop sign?" later believed that they had seen a stop sign even though they had actually seen a yield sign.

Retrieval Failure

Have you ever seen someone you usually see at the beach or the tennis court in a situation where you're both wearing more formal clothes and had a terrible time figuring out who that familiar-looking person could be? When one of you finally makes the connection, either is sure to say, "Oh, I didn't recognize you with your clothes on." This is cue-dependent forgetting.

In this kind of forgetting, the memory trace is there, but we just can't get at it, showing that normal people often have difficulty retrieving memories, just as amnesics do. Our environment is different, the cues we depend on for retrieval are no longer present, and the memory is, therefore, inaccessible. In the preceding example, you're away from the usual environment where you see this person, and the person is dressed differently; in other words, the cues for recognition are not there. Many contemporary psychologists feel that we often can't get at our long-term memories because we don't have appropriate cues to call them up rather than because of decay or interference.

Tulving (1974) has shown that when retrieval cues are given to subjects when they first learn something, these cues will help them remember it later on. Such cues may be words that rhyme with or are associated with a list of words a subject has learned, or the first letter or letters of the word. This work suggests that material will be easier to retrieve later if we encode it with some kind of cue when we first commit it to memory. The possibilities are fascinating: If we play a certain piece of music while we're learning material—and then play it again during the exam (a take-home exam or through earphones), will our memory be better?

ARE MEMORIES PERMANENT? Which of the following statements best reflects your own opinion?

1 Everything we learn is permanently stored in the mind, although sometimes particular details are not accessible. With hypnosis, or other special techniques, these inaccessible details could eventually be recovered.
2 Some details that we learn may be permanently lost from memory. Such details would never be able to be recovered by hypnosis, or any other special technique, because these details are simply no longer there.

The specific words used to ask questions of eyewitnesses influence what they "remember." Witnesses asked "How fast were the cars going when they smashed into one another?" gave higher estimates of speed than those asked how fast the cars were going when they hit one another. (© 1982 Charles Cocaine/Photo Researchers, Inc.)

When Elizabeth F. Loftus and Geoffrey R. Loftus (1980, p. 410) asked 169 people (75 psychologists and 94 in other occupations) to answer this question, they found that 84 percent of the psychologists and 69 percent of the nonpsychologists believed in the permanence of memories. Loftus and Loftus maintain that many memories cannot be recovered because the memories no longer exist. We are indebted to their discussion for much of the following evidence for and against this belief.

One of the authors (S.W.O.) remembers an association during a math course in college. She used to do home assignments while listening to dramatic radio shows. Then, when going over the math problems in class the next day, the entire drama she had heard while doing a particular assignment would come back to her. The principle of cue-dependent remembering seems clear here, but the practical way to use this principle would seem to involve playing the radio to bring back the memory of the work. The way it worked for her didn't seem to accomplish anything beyond extending her memory of some rather forgettable melodrama!

HYPNOSIS A woman who witnessed her boyfriend's murder could not remember the incident because of two factors—the shock and the state of intoxication she had been in. Under hypnosis she gave previously unreported information that helped police find the killer (Stump, 1975). Hypnosis has successfully unblocked suppressed memories in a number of similar cases. It has also in other cases apparently unleashed "memories" of events that never took place. An article in the *American Bar Association Journal* reported:

> People can flat-out lie under hypnosis, and the examiner is no better equipped to detect the hypnotic lie than any other kind. Even more serious, a willing hypnotic subject is more pliable than he normally would be, more anxious to please his questioner. Knowing even a few details of an event, often supplied in early contacts with police, may provide the subject with enough basis to create a highly detailed "memory" of what transpired, whether he was there or not (1978, p. 187).

EYEWITNESS TESTIMONY Although this kind of testimony is often relied upon in courts of law and often strongly believed in, it is highly inaccurate in many instances. In Elizabeth Loftus's many experiments in this area, she has shown that information provided after an event can erase an accurate memory, substituting an inaccurate one.

In one experiment (Loftus, Miller, & Burns, 1978), subjects saw a series of thirty color slides showing successive stages in an auto-pedestrian accident. Half the subjects saw the car going toward an intersection with a stop sign; the other half saw a yield sign. The subjects were then asked, "Did another car pass the red Datsun while it was stopped at the stop sign?" or the same question, substituting "yield" for "stop," with some subjects getting a question consistent with what they had seen, and others getting a misleading question.

Over 80 percent of subjects who heard the misleading question answered as if they had seen the slide that corresponded to what they had been *told* rather than the one they had actually *seen*. However, when no misleading information was given, over 90 percent of subjects correctly identified the sign they had seen. Apparently, what people learn after an event can replace the information they originally learned. When this happens, "in the process, the original information is forever banished from the subject's memory" (Loftus and Loftus, 1980, p. 416). If one memory can be completely displaced by another, the disappearance of the original memory seems to disprove the notion of the permanence of memory.

This and other similar findings have enormous practical implications in a society in which a person can be imprisoned for life or even executed on the basis of testimony from a witness convinced that she or he is telling the truth. What people *think* is the truth is often a hodgepodge of remembered events, statements by other people, and logical "filling in the gaps."

THE BIOLOGICAL BASIS OF MEMORY

For decades psychologists have tried to pinpoint the exact physiological mechanisms that underlie memory—principally, how and where memories are stored in the brain. Research has given us important clues to help us answer these questions, but since many of these findings are not definitive, the search for answers continues. Let's look at some of the most compelling theories and at the evidence for them.

How Memories Are Stored in the Brain

An influential model of the way the brain stores memories was proposed by one of the founders of physiological psychology, D. O. Hebb (1949). Hebb assumed that the physiological bases are different in short-term memory (STM) and long-term memory (LTM). In short-term memory a circuit of neurons, which Hebb called the "cell assembly," fires in repeated patterns, creating a memory trace. This trace is unstable and does not cause a change in the physical structure of the brain. For material to go from short-term to long-term memory, an actual physical change of the brain is required; this change takes the form of new connections between neurons.

The findings from several lines of research support the basic thrust of Hebb's theory. The evidence for the existence of an unstable short-term memory that has not been consolidated into long-term memory comes from experiments using electroconvulsive shock on animals, usually rats. The experimenter places electrodes on an animal's head and passes a strong electric current—strong enough to produce a seizure—through the animal's brain. If the animal is shocked immediately after having learned a task, such as running a pathway in a maze, it will lose all memory of the experience. But if the shock is delayed for some time after the learning experience, perhaps an hour or so after a rat has learned a maze, the animal doesn't forget what it has learned. Why should this difference exist? Presumably because when the shock comes immediately after learning, it disrupts the specific neural firing patterns that provide the *code*, or the system of symbols, for short-term memory. Once the code has been established, it's not so vulnerable to disruption. So, when the shock comes sometime afterward, it has no effect on material that has already been coded and consolidated into long-term memory (Duncan, 1949).

Other evidence supports the notion that long-term memory is based on changes in brain structure. As described in Chapter 2, dendritic spines are thornlike projections on dendrites, the parts of neurons that carry nerve impulses toward cell bodies. These spines form synapses, or connections, with axons, those parts of neurons that carry impulses away from the cells. The number of dendritic spines in the brain correlates roughly with intelligence, a finding that has emerged from postmortem examinations of the brains of mentally retarded persons, and the number of these spines increases as a result of learning experiences (Purpura, 1974; Crick, 1982). Other researchers have found that when electrical stimulation is given to the hippocampus, a brain structure thought to be important in memory, the dendritic spines physically swell (Van Harreveld & Fifkova, 1975). When we compare animals that have matured in enriched environments with those that have suffered sensory deprivation with few learning opportunities, and then do post mortum examinations on their brains, we find that the brains of the deprived animals have fewer dendritic spines and fewer synaptic connections (Sokolov, 1977).

Researchers have devoted considerable effort to try to learn precisely how these structural changes come about. Since protein molecules serve as the "building blocks" for all cells, including neurons, much research has sought to determine whether learning experiences produce changes in *protein synthesis*, that is, the body's building of protein molecules from amino acids. So far, the biochemical changes that seem to be most consistently correlated with memory are changes in *ribonucleic acid (RNA)*, a chemical found in plant and animal cells that appears to direct the life-sustaining functions of cells. The RNA molecule provides a framework on which proteins are built. Many research studies over the past couple of decades have shown both qualitative and quantitative changes in RNA in brain cells as a result of experience (Hyden & Lange, 1970). For example, the brain cells of rats that have been given enriched learning experiences have higher ratios of RNA to DNA (deoxyribonucleic acid, another basic compound). This suggests that these rats are synthesizing RNA at a higher rate and suggests that such synthesis may be the physiological mechanism underlying memory consolidation.

In an intriguing series of studies, McConnell (1962) tried to transfer memory from one organism to another on the basis of biochemical changes. Through classical conditioning, he taught *planaria* (a species of flatworm) to curl up in response to light. He chopped up the conditioned worms and fed them to untrained worms. He then taught the "cannibal" planaria the same conditioned response—and found that they learned to curl significantly faster than the original group of animals, suggesting that some kind of physiological change occurs in memory. In another study, extracting RNA molecules from conditioned planaria and injecting them into untrained worms also resulted in faster curling (Zelman, Kabot, Jacobsen, & McConnell, 1963). However, since other researchers have not been able to replicate these experiments because of a variety of methodological problems (Gaito, 1970), this explanation is still highly controversial.

Other researchers have turned to a different primitive animal to establish physiological bases for learning and memory—the invertebrate sea snail *Aplysia*, which has a simple, easy-to-study nervous system (Kandel, 1976; Carew, Hawkins, & Kandel, 1983) (see Figure 6-12). Aplysia nor-

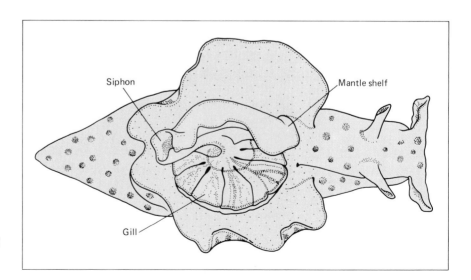

FIGURE 6-12 Aplysia *This invertebrate sea snail has a simple, easy-to-study nervous system. Scientists have recently studied aplysia to establish the physiological bases for learning and memory. (From Kandel, 1979)*

Siphon

Mantle shelf

Gill

mally retracts its gill in response to tactile stimuli, such as would occur in turbulent waters, probably as a protective mechanism. When researchers squirt water at a certain spot on the snail (mimicking a stormy ocean), a nerve impulse in sensory neurons releases a neurotransmitter onto motor neurons, which in turn activates the muscles that retract the gill. But if they squirt ten times or more, say, once every minute, less transmitter is released from the sensory neuron, apparently because repeated squirts cause chemical changes at the synapses. The snail has become habituated to the turbulence and has stopped releasing the transmitter; therefore the gill does not retract.

If, however, the snail receives an electric shock and then a squirt of water, it becomes *sensitized,* and the gill-withdrawal reflex is more vigorous than ever. This seems to be due to the fact that other synapses become active and release the neurotransmitter *serotonin,* which facilitates transmission in the reflex pathway. Now more transmitter is released from the sensory neurons. These simple animals can even respond to differential conditioning; that is, they can acquire two different conditioned responses to stimulation of different sites on the animal's body. The mechanism of the conditioning appears to be an extension of the same mechanism that underlies the simpler form of learning known as "sensitization."

This basic research may help us find answers to some of the questions we ask about human learning and memory, including the relationship between classical and operant conditioning, the one between habituation and extinction, and the nature of the differences between short-term and long-term memory.

Where Memories Are Stored in the Brain

For most of his professional life, physiological psychologist Karl Lashley was occupied by one consuming activity, the search for the engram, a memory trace that is "engraved" upon the nervous system. He tried to find specific locations in the brain where memory traces existed. In his search rats learned various tasks, including running mazes and discriminating between stimuli; then *lesions* (injuries) were surgically produced in various parts of the rats' cortices; and finally, the rats' memories were tested for the tasks they had learned. After decades of this research, Lashley was unable to find a specific region of the cortex which, when lesioned, invariably produced impairments in memory.

While it's probably true that memories do not settle into isolated chunks of brain tissue, more recent studies indicate that certain brain structures play more important roles in memory than others do. In particular, parts of the limbic system that lie under the *temporal lobes* seem to be essential in the establishment of new permanent memories. (See Chapter 2 for a review of these sections of the brain.)

This became dramatically apparent in 1953 through the traumatic experience of a man who has come to be known as "HM." He suffered from such severe epileptic seizures that his life was constant misery. None of the remedies that had been tried were at all effective. So in a desperate attempt to control these seizures, surgeons removed both temporal lobes of his brain, as well as the deeper structures, including the hippocampus. The seizures went away—but so did much of HM's ability to remember new information.

In summarizing his work, Lashley (1950, p. 477) jokingly reported, "I sometimes feel, in reviewing the evidence on the localization of the memory trace, that the necessary conclusion is that learning is just not possible."

Although HM had no apparent memory problems before his operation, neuropsychologist Brenda Milner (1966) has described his life afterward. While he remembered whatever he had learned before the operation, he couldn't learn the most basic facts afterward. After his operation he couldn't recognize hospital staff, even though he saw them every day; he couldn't learn the way to the bathroom; and when his family moved to a new house, he couldn't learn the way to get there and would keep returning to his old house. While HM is able to hold a conversation and is able to keep information as long as it stays in consciousness, even a moment's distraction will wipe out the memory. His short-term memory, then, seems relatively intact. His essential disorder seems to be in the transfer of information from the fragile short-term store to the more permanent long-term storage.

HM has shown a few interesting exceptions to his otherwise severe amnesia, or pathological loss of memory, in his ability to learn a variety of perceptual and motor tasks. For example, he learned how to play tennis after his surgery. Milner (1966) raises the possibility that memory for motor skills may be different from other memories. After all, once we've learned how to swim or ride a bicycle, we never forget how to do either one. HM has also shown the ability to solve puzzles and perform maze tasks and to improve on these tasks with practice. Most strikingly, however, he has no recollection of ever having done them.

In other studies, Milner (1970) has shown that the hippocampus and the amygdala, both parts of the limbic system, are the crucial brain structures responsible for memory loss after temporal lobe removal in humans. Patients whose temporal lobe removals had been restricted to the cerebral cortex, without the destruction of the hippocampus and the amygdala, do not show the profound amnesia suffered by HM. Animal research supports this conclusion: Surgical lesions of both of these structures affect the ability to learn new information (Horel, 1979; Mishkin, 1982). Rats with lesions of the hippocampus have problems with spatial memory tasks (Olton, 1979), and monkeys with bilateral lesions of hippocampus and amygdala develop memory deficits similar to HM's (Mishkin, 1982).

Another line of evidence suggesting the importance of temporal lobe structures in memory comes from the cortical stimulation studies of neurosurgeon Wilder Penfield. During the 1940s, while operating on conscious patients, he touched certain portions of their brains with a stimulating electrode. Some of the patients responded to the stimulation of specific locations of their brains with a flashback of previous experiences. One man "heard" a song, saying, ". . . it was not as though I were imagining the tune to myself. I actually heard it." A woman said, "I think I heard a mother calling her little boy somewhere. It seemed to be something that happened years ago . . . in the neighborhood where I live." These experiences led Penfield (1969) to conclude that the brain contains a complete, deeply detailed record of past experience in which all of an individual's memories are stored for as long as that person lives.

However, only 40 out of the 520 patients whose temporal lobes were stimulated gave such responses, and some of these seemed more like the description of a dream than an actual memory. For example, the woman just quoted also heard a mother calling her child "at the lumberyard," even though the patient said she had never been around a lumberyard.

Loftus and Loftus (1980) conclude, "These so-called memories, then, appear to consist merely of the thoughts and ideas that happened to exist just prior to and during the stimulation" (p. 414).

EXCEPTIONAL MEMORIES

Memorists

Russian psychologist Alexander Luria (1968) was stymied by the man he called "S." Luria wanted to measure the limits of human memory, as exemplified by this famous case of a memorist (a person with an exceptional memory), but he was thwarted in his goal because he could never establish a point at which S forgot anything. No matter what task Luria posed nor how long a period of time passed afterward, S never forgot.

S produced a veritable explosion of visual images with virtually everything he learned, an ability that fixed information in his mind but that also produced difficulties for him, as we pointed out earlier. He had trouble reading or being read to because images would form so quickly they would collide with one another in his mind, become contorted, and create mental chaos. Much of the time he was, however, able to distribute these images along a road or street he "saw" in his mind, along the lines of the method of loci memory-aid system described later in this chapter.

There have been other people whose feats of memory dazzle us. There is, for example, VP (Hunt & Love, 1972), who could play seven blindfold games of chess at the same time and constantly carried on correspondence chess games, for which he kept no written record. There is "Nancy" (Gummerman & Gray, 1971), who could provide a 9-minute, 25-second, greatly detailed description of a picture she had seen for only 30 seconds. Ulric Neisser (1982) feels that such abilities may be more common than we realize and that studying such individuals may shed light on the potential of human memory.

Eidetikers

Then, there are people—mostly children—who have the power of eidetic imagery. After looking at a picture for 10 to 30 seconds, such children can still see it for from 2 to 5 minutes after it has been removed from view. Parts of the image fade before others, and usually the first part to fade is the first part of the image looked at by the child. In describing the smile of the Cheshire cat in *Alice in Wonderland*, which remained after every other part of the cat had faded from view, Lewis Carroll seems to have been describing an eidetic image.

About 5 percent of 6- to 12-year-olds have the ability to "see" a picture even when it is no longer in front of them, although practically no adults can do so (Haber, 1980). Eidetic children do not seem significantly different from noneidetic children in IQ, reading ability, vision, personality, neurological status, or any other characteristic that has been tested. They are different principally in their remarkable visual memory. The images they see, says Ralph Haber (1980), are not hallucinations or a form of photographic memory or afterimages (like the spot we see after a flashbulb has popped in front of us). They are manifestations of a distinct kind of visual memory, which is still little understood.

Memory Disorders

Amnesia is the general term for a variety of memory disorders that arise from different causes and affect the memory in different ways. A number of neurologic conditions that cause damage to the brain produce memory deficits of one kind or another. They're probably the most frequent com-

PIG AND PEPPER.   91

"Well then," the Cat
went on, "you see a dog
growls when it's angry,
and wags its tail when it's
pleased. Now *I* growl when
I'm pleased, and wag my
tail when I'm angry. Therefore I'm mad."

"*I* call it purring, not
growling," said Alice.

"Call it what you like,"
said the Cat. "Do you
play croquet with the Queen to-day?"

The smile of the Cheshire cat in
Alice in Wonderland, *described
by Lewis Carroll as remaining after
every other part of the cat had
disappeared, seems to be an eidetic
image. (Culver Pictures, Inc.)*

plaint of patients who have suffered strokes, infectious diseases of the brain, and traumatic injuries. In addition, memory disorders are often the earliest signs of a number of neurologic illnesses, including Alzheimer's disease, a progressive degenerative disease of the brain that usually occurs in old age and that will be discussed in Chapter 13.

There are two basic kinds of memory loss. In anterograde amnesia, the inability to create new permanent memories, patients typically cannot learn the names of their doctors, the hospitals they're in, or any other new information they're exposed to after the traumatic event or illness that caused the amnesia. In retrograde amnesia, the inability to recall information that had been learned before the onset of the amnesia, patients may not remember experiences in their earlier life or the name of the president of the United States. HM, of course, suffers from a profound anterograde amnesia but only very limited retrograde amnesia. (Can you invent a mnemonic to help you remember these two types of amnesia?)

For obvious reasons, bilateral temporal lobectomy (the operation that caused HM's amnesia) is no longer used as a treatment for epilepsy, but similar symptoms sometimes arise from diseases that attack the temporal lobes (Drachman & Arbit, 1966). We referred earlier to the effects of electroconvulsive shock in animals. In Chapter 16 we'll discuss electroconvulsive therapy (ECT), which is sometimes used to treat severe depression in humans. Shock therapy produces both anterograde and retrograde amnesia (Squire, Slater, & Chance, 1975). This memory loss is probably the most notable side-effect of the therapy, and it may even be the key to its effectiveness. That is, one reason why shock treatment may lift a severe depression is that it disrupts the depressed person's pattern of brooding over (remembering) the elements causing unhappiness.

Damage to regions of the brain other than temporal and limbic structures can also produce severe memory disorders. Korsakoff's syndrome is a neuropsychiatric disorder caused by prolonged, excessive alcohol abuse, coupled with a deficiency in the vitamin *thiamine.* Affected people suffer both kinds of amnesia discussed above and try to fill in their gaps in memory with incorrect details. They can use language normally but have trouble carrying on a conversation because they can't think of anything to say (Talland, 1969). Postmortem examinations have shown that the lesions most typical of this syndrome are not in the hippocampus but in the thalamus and the hypothalamus (Victor, Adams, & Collins, 1971; Butters & Cermak, 1980).

Another instance of memory loss arising from injury to the thalamus can be seen in the case of a young man, NA, who suffered a lesion in his left dorsal medial thalamus (Teuber, Milner, & Vaughan, 1968). A friend who had been fooling around with a miniature fencing foil accidentally stabbed NA. The foil entered the nostril and went to the base of his brain, causing a severe anterograde amnesia. NA's memory loss is largely restricted to verbal activities, probably because his lesion occurred in a portion of the left thalamus. His retrograde amnesia is limited to only one year before his accident (Squire & Slater, 1978).

The kind of amnesia most people hear more about is actually much rarer than the kind caused by organic brain damage. This is psychogenic amnesia, a memory disorder caused by emotionally disturbing events. It differs from organic amnesia in several ways. Patients with this kind usually display much worse retrograde than anterograde amnesia, the opposite of the usual situation in an organic amnesia. Furthermore, psychogenic amnesics often lose their personal identities, which organic amnesics almost never do. The characteristics of this kind of memory loss are poorly understood and have only recently begun to be explored through research (Kihlstrom & Evans, 1979).

THEORIES OF AMNESIA   Debate and controversy swirl around the issue of precisely where memory breaks down. Some of the cognitive processes that have been implicated follow, but the most likely conclusion is that there is no one single cause; in any individual patient one or more information processing mechanisms may be faulty (Brandt, 1983).

ENCODING   A substantial amount of research evidence in recent years has supported the possibility that amnesics, especially those with Korsakoff's syndrome, analyze incoming information too superficially, failing to engage in the deep-level encoding that, according to depth of processing theory, makes for stable memory traces (Butters & Cermak, 1980).

CONSOLIDATION   Since electroconvulsive shock experiments have shown that information is most susceptible to forgetting during a finite period of time after learning, it's possible that amnesia is caused by the failure to consolidate information into more permanent memory traces.

RETRIEVAL   The tendency of some amnesics to make an unusual number of "intrusion errors" (the reporting of previously acquired information when trying to retrieve task-relevant material) suggests the possibility of faulty retrieval based on proactive interference or excessive interference from previously learned information (Warrington & Weiskrantz, 1970).

We have seen how complex memory is and how it is inextricably tied into the entire learning process. Both learning and memory have major implications for the development and the measurement of intelligence, as we'll see in the following chapter.

BOX 6-3
HOW CAN YOU IMPROVE YOUR MEMORY?

You can improve your memory at every step in the processes described earlier. You can improve at the first stage, *perception*, or *sensory memory*, by paying close attention. You cannot remember something you never saw or heard, so if you want to remember it, you have to first get it into your consciousness.

You can improve your *short-term memory* by *rote rehearsal*, just going over and over something in your head for the short time you need to hold onto it. You can also hold things better in short-term memory by *chunking*—organizing long lists or numbers so that you can remember them in seven or fewer chunks.

The major improvement you can make, however, is in your *long-term memory*. The way you *encode* and *store* material will help you when you go to *retrieve* it. The all-embracing concept that will help you remember what you want to remember is *organization for meaningful association*. The more meaning you can give to something and the more associations you can make between the new information you are now learning and other information you already know, the better you'll remember.

If you ever took piano lessons, you must have learned the sentence, "*Every Good Boy Does Fine*," because the first letter of every word represents the lines in the treble clef, and the acronym "FACE," whose letters represent the spaces in the treble clef. In grammar school you probably learned the spelling rhyme, "i before e except after c, or when sounded like A as in neighbor or weigh." A device that helps you remember information is known as a mnemonic, and an entire system to improve or develop your memory is called *mnemonics*.

These systems really work. When Gordon H. Bower (1973) gave five different lists of twenty words to two different groups of college students, those who had used mnemonics remembered an average of 72 out of the 100 items, while those using either simple or rote learning remembered only an average of 28. Some of the most popular of these systems are given on the next page. They all require time and attention until you get used to using them. People who have learned them, however, often swear by them, and some professional memorists base their performances on them.

Most of us rely less on the kind of internal memory aids represented by these mnemonic systems than we do on a variety of external aids, such as the ones that follow. Writing something down usually requires less thought, but tying it to a mnemonic system frees you from reliance on paper and pencil. You might want to try one or two of the mnemonic systems described in the following pages and see how

they work, compared to whatever system you have been using up until now.

HOW CAN MEMORY RESEARCH HELP YOU TO STUDY BETTER?

1   Probably the best way to remember material is to make it yours by making it personally meaningful (Craik & Lockhart, 1972). Make associations with your own life and your own beliefs as much as possible. It's especially easy to do this in a course like psychology, which has so many applications to your own life, so make those connections. For example, think of a time you personally have experienced the tip-of-the-tongue phenomenon or a flashbulb memory, and so forth. Do the memory and other exercises presented in the text. Answer the quizzes.

In other course material you may have to stretch to make connections with your own life, but you *can* do it, using your imagination. For example, in studying a foreign language, fantasize yourself falling in love using that language. Or to make history come alive, go into a time machine and put yourself in the time and place you're learning about. In biology, imagine yourself living the life of a frog.

2   Concentrate on concentrating. Much forgetting is caused by not paying enough attention in the first place.

3   The first time you study, absorb the material in as large a chunk as possible. You'll remember it better than by just doing it a little at a time. (When you go over it before an exam, spread out your study periods, since

relearning over several days works better than doing it all in one day.)

4   Take notes, putting what you learn in your own words. This kind of recoding helps to imprint the material and aids retention.

5   Rehearse what you learn as you go along. Every now and then look up and ask yourself questions. (Helpful ones are in the study guide that accompanies this and many other textbooks.) Recite key points silently or out loud. It may be helpful to speak into a tape recorder, which you can then play back while you're getting dressed, driving, or doing some other activity.

6   Give yourself cues for retrieval. Use headings in your notes, and make up personally meaningful catch phrases and/or visual images that you associate with various blocks of material. Some doctor with a sense of humor, for example, taught medical students the sentence: "Never Lower Tilley's Pants—Mamma Might Come Home," to help them remember the bones of the wrist, whose names start with the first letters of the words of this sentence [Navicular, Lunate, Triquetrum, Pisiform, greater Multangular, lesser Multangular, Capitate, and Hamate (Rubenstein, 1983)].

7   Combine verbal and visual images whenever possible.

8   Eliminate as much interference as possible. Don't study for two tests on the same day. It will be more productive for you to plan your studying so that you can study one subject, go to sleep, and wake up early to study the other. The material from the first will have been

integrated sufficiently, so that the two topics won't inhibit retention of each other, and neither retroactive nor proactive inhibition will take place.

9   Study the most important or most difficult topics first or last, since the primacy and recency effects will tend to make you most likely to forget whatever you study in the middle.

10   Pick out the most important points. Don't try to remember every little detail.

11   Allot extra time to studying difficult subjects. Ebbinghaus found that the more time he devoted to learning his words, the better he remembered them. The same applies to other material.

MNEMONICS

The following memory systems all use visual imagery to help you make the associations that can help you to remember. Such systems seem to come naturally to some people with exceptional memories, like the memory whiz S. Other people, however, can also learn them and can often achieve remarkable results.

Method of Loci

This mnemonic has a long history, having originated in ancient Greece and been related to us by the Roman writer Cicero (which explains the use of the word "loci," which means "locations" or "places" in Latin). It works through the use of imagery, based on keying what you want to remember to the stops along a route that you take in your mind:

- *Develop your route:* Think of an orderly progression of places that you are already familiar with—possibly your street, the

sidewalk in front of your building, the outer door, the vestibule, the inner lobby, the stairway, the first landing, the landing in front of your door, the door into your apartment, your living room, your kitchen, your bathroom, and your bedroom. The same kind of progression could be set up for a private house, a rural setting, a walk along campus, or any other familiar route. Whichever one you choose, it's important to stick to the same route, so you don't have to keep learning a new one.

- *Make up an image associating each item you want to remember with each stop on your route:* Suppose you want to remember to buy the following items—milk, eggs, tomatoes, bananas, sunflower seeds, tea, toilet paper, peanut butter, soap, and window cleaner. You might imagine your street covered with puddles of milk, your outer door splattered with eggs, the vestibule piled so high with tomatoes that you can't get in, the inner lobby sporting a big banana tree where the Christmas tree usually stands, the stairway slippery with sunflower seeds, a giant teapot on the first landing, the landing in front of your door piled high with rolls of toilet paper, the door into your apartment smeared thick with peanut butter, your living room awash with soap bubbles, and a little gremlin busily cleaning your kitchen window. The more vivid your images, the better you'll remember them.

- *When you want to remember your list, take a mental walk:* Ask yourself, "What did I put in the street? On the outer door? In the vestibule?" And so forth. Remembering the scene at each stop will give you a cue

to help you remember what's in it. You can also use this system for remembering people, errands, chores, and so forth.

The Peg-Word Method

- *Learn a series of words that correspond to the numbers 1 through 20:* The ones most often used for 1 through 10 are these:

One is a bun	Six is sticks
Two is a shoe	Seven is Heaven
Three is a tree	Eight is a gate
Four is a door	Nine is wine
Five is a hive	Ten is a hen

- *Make up a series of images that let you "hang" the items you want to remember on the pegs:* Each item interacts with one peg-word. For the previous shopping list, you might imagine milk sloshing over a bun (or a quart of milk inside it—a milk sandwich), a broken egg in your shoe, a tree laden down with tomatoes, a bunch of bananas hanging on a door, bees carrying sunflower seeds into their hive, tea bags attached like flags to sticks, rolls of toilet paper decorating the gates of Heaven, jars of peanut butter impaled on a gate, a wine bottle whose label declares the brand of soap you want, and a hen cleaning your window.

- *When you want to remember the list, go through your peg-words in numerical order:* The peg-words serve as your cues, and the numbers will help you keep track of how many items you want to remember.

Narrative-Chaining Method

If you have to remember only a single list of items, either of the preceding methods is as good as this one. But if you need to remember more than one list or a variety of different kinds of items, this method is more effective: *Make up a story built around whatever you want to remember.* Back to our shopping list. Imagine that you're a tourist visiting a farm, and the farmer asks you whether you want to milk the cow. You sit down on the milking stool to do it, but you didn't realize that there were a bunch of eggs on the stool, and when you sit down, you smash them and come up covered with egg yolk. The farmer says, "I know what will remove the egg stains!" and rubs at your pants with a cut-open tomato, making the stain worse, of course. You get so mad you throw a banana at her. She ducks, and the banana flies past her into a bag of sunflower seeds, puncturing the bag and sending seeds all over the barn floor. The farmer's husband runs in and says, "You two look pretty upset. Why don't you calm down with a nice cup of tea." The three of you mop up the mess with gobs of toilet paper . . . and, well, you see how this works.

HOW TO REMEMBER NAMES AND FACES BETTER

1   Pay attention when you first hear someone's name. Many cases of "forgetting" a name are caused by never having absorbed it in the first place.
2   Use the name immediately. Say something like "Hello, Mary. Smith is an unusual name, isn't it?" Speaking the name out loud provides a valuable form of rehearsal. Use it once or twice more during your conversation or focus on it silently.
3   Make an emotional association with the person's face. Would you buy a used car from this person? Would you trust them with money or a confidence? Does she or he remind you of anyone you know?
4   Notice an outstanding physical feature and conjure up some kind of mental image that will hook the feature to the person's name. [For example, if Mr. Bell has large ears, imagine them as ringing bells (Lorayne, 1975).]

POPULAR EXTERNAL MEMORY AIDS THAT HELP IN EVERYDAY LIFE

- Write a note to yourself and put it where you are sure to see it. (Tape it to the bathroom mirror before you go to sleep at night or to the inside of the door you'll use to leave home in the morning.)
- Put an object you have to do something with (book to library or shoes to shoemaker) in a place where you can't miss it (such as in front of door).
- Write appointments, obligations, and activities in a daily diary or calendar, which you check automatically every morning.
- Ask someone reliable to remind you of something.
- Make lists of items you have to buy, activities you have to do, people you have to phone, assignments you have to fulfill, etc.
- Set an alarm or a kitchen timer to remind you to turn off the stove, leave your room for an appointment, make a phone call, or end one activity and begin another.
- Change a ring you ordinarily wear on one finger to a different finger, transfer your watch to your other wrist or turn it to the underside of the customary arm; or make some other change you'll be conscious of.
- Write a note to yourself on your hand.
- Integrate an activity into your everyday routine such as taking a daily pill with your morning juice instead of at haphazard times during the day. Keep your pillbox in a prominent spot.

Most of the preceding suggestions were used by thirty college students surveyed by John E. Harris [1978, in Gruneberg, M. M.; Morris, P. E.; & Sykes, R. N. (eds.), *Practical Aspects of Memory,* London: Academic Press, 1978.], as well as by the authors of this book. Such aids are recommended for older people, who often find that they are more forgetful than they used to be.

SUMMARY

1   Memory works through four basic steps: *perception, encoding, storage,* and *retrieval.*

2   According to *Atkinson and Shiffrin's storage and transfer model,* there are three different types of memory: *sensory memory, short-term memory,* and *long-term memory.*

3   Sensory memory involves stimuli that come to us through the senses. These impressions either disappear in about a second or are transferred into short-term memory.

4   Short-term memory is *working memory.* It has a limited capacity of about seven meaningful units. Information in short-term memory disappears in about 20 seconds unless it is held there through rehearsal. The amount of information in short-term memory can be expanded by chunking. Material that is not forgotten enters long-term memory.

5   Long-term memory appears to have an unlimited capacity and the capability of storing information permanently. Retrieval from long-term memory depends upon how efficiently the material was stored there in the first place. The more *associations* you make between what you now want to remember and what you already know, the more likely you will be to remember something in the long run. In other words, we are more likely to remember material that is meaningful. *Clustering* is an organizational technique in which we encode material to be remembered by grouping items into categories.

6   The *"tip-of-the-tongue" phenomenon* refers to a retrieval problem in which a person cannot recall information although he or she has knowledge of it. Research on this phenomenon indicates that information is coded in ways other than meaning alone, such as by sound.

7   Not all psychologists see memory as consisting of separate storage systems as Shiffrin and Atkinson propose. *Craik and Lockhart,* for example, feel that the ability to remember depends on how deeply we process information. The deeper we process the information, the longer it lasts. This is known as the *levels of processing model.*

8   *Recognition, recall,* and *relearning* are three ways to measure retention. In *recognition* one must pick out (or recognize) previously learned information. In *recall* one has to reproduce previously learned material. In *free recall* the material may be reproduced in any order while in *serial recall* it must be reproduced in the order in which it was originally presented. The *relearning* technique measures the amount of time saved learning material which had been learned originally at some prior time.

9   Research on the *serial position curve* indicates that we tend to remember materials we learned first *(the primacy effect)* and last *(the recency effect).* However, if there is an unusual item in the middle of the material to be remembered, we also tend to remember this. This is called the *von Restorff effect.*

10 The relationship between mood and memory is called *state-dependent memory.*

11 *Flashbulb memories* are vivid recollections of what one was doing when one heard about certain significant events, such as the assassination of President Kennedy. The ability to have these may at one time have had survival value.

12 Research has shown that at least some of what we "remember" is the result of mental *reconstruction.* In other words, we fill in the gaps of our memories.

13 *Ebbinghaus's curve of forgetting* indicates that forgetting is initially quite rapid, and the rate of loss slows down markedly over time.

14 A number of theories for why we forget have been suggested. According to the theory of *motivated forgetting,* we forget material we need to forget; in other words, we *repress* certain uncomfortable memories. *Decay theory* holds that certain memories decay or fade with the passage of time if we do not use the information. *Interference theory* holds that we forget information because other information interferes with or confounds our memory. *Proactive interference* describes a situation where the material we learned first interferes with the ability to remember new material. *Retroactive interference* refers to a situation where information learned later interferes with our remembering previously learned material.

15 Psychologists disagree about the permanence of memory. Some hold that forgetting is a case of retrieval failure. That is, we sometimes cannot get at information because we lack the appropriate cues needed for retrieval. Other psychologists maintain that at least some memories are permanently lost or altered in some way.

16 A number of researchers have been concerned with the way memories are stored in the brain although they have relatively little knowledge of this process. Different processes are believed to take place for short-term memory and long-term memory. According to Hebb, in short-term memory a circuit of neurons, the "cell assembly," fires in repeated patterns, creating a memory trace. This trace is unstable, not causing any actual change in the physical structure of the brain. For material to go from short-term memory to long-term memory, an actual physical change is re-

quired, taking the form of new connections between neurons. A number of lines of research have supported this distinction.

17 Recent studies indicate that certain brain structures play important roles in memory. The parts of the limbic system that lie under the temporal lobes seem to be essential for the establishment of new permanent memories.

18 A *memorist* has an exceptional memory. Russian psychologist Alexander Luria studied S who seemed never to forget. An *eidetiker* is a person, typically a child, who can see an image from 2 to 5 minutes after it has been removed from view.

19 There are a number of different memory disorders. *Amnesia* is a general term for a variety of memory disorders. A person with *anterograde amnesia* cannot create new memories. *Retrograde amnesia* is a condition in which a person cannot recall information learned before the onset of the amnesia. *Shock therapy*, which is used to treat severe depression, produces both types of amnesia. *Korsakoff's syndrome*, a neuropsychiatric disorder caused by prolonged, excessive alcohol use, entails both anterograde and retrograde amnesia. *Psychogenic amnesia* is a memory disorder caused by emotionally disturbing events. Theories of amnesia have considered difficulties in encoding, consolidation, and retrieval. Most likely there is no one single cause of all amnesias. In any individual patient, one or more information processing mechanisms may be faulty.

20 A *mnemonic* is a device to aid memory. Useful mnemonics include the *method of loci* (where items to be remembered are imagined as placed along a familiar route); the *peg-word method* (where words to be remembered are associated with certain peg-words or cues); and the *narrative-chaining method* (where a story is made up containing the information to be remembered). *External aids* such as writing notes, making lists, and keeping an appointment calendar are also useful.

21 Memory research can help students study better. Material should be made as meaningful as possible. Other effective study techniques include: concentrating; studying the material initially in large chunks; taking notes; rehearsing the material; developing meaningful retrieval cues; combining verbal and visual images; picking out the main points; allotting extra time to difficult subjects.

SUGGESTED READINGS

Baddeley, A. (1982). *Memory: A user's guide.* New York: Macmillan. A beautifully illustrated, fascinating compendium of up-to-date information about memory, complete with tests and exercises to improve your memory.

Loftus, E. (1979). *Eyewitness testimony.* Cambridge, Mass.: Harvard University Press. A powerful and absorbing book presenting a massive array of evidence on the unreliability of eyewitness testimony.

Loftus, E. (1980). *Memory.* Reading, Mass.: Addison-Wesley. A comprehensive account by a memory expert of recent research findings on such topics as memory in old age, the use of computers as memory substitutes, the effects of drugs on memory, along with suggestions for improving one's memory.

Neisser, U. (1982). *Memory observed: Remembering in natural contexts.* San Francisco: W. H. Freeman. A fascinating look at a generally neglected area of psychological research on memory and forgetting—their manifestations in everyday life.

CHAPTER 7

INTELLIGENCE

SPOTLIGHT ON

How psychologists through the years have disagreed about what intelligence is and how to measure it.

The strengths and weaknesses of intelligence tests in use today.

Some new directions in intelligence testing.

How hereditary and environmental factors influence intelligence.

The extremes of intelligence: the intellectually gifted and the mentally retarded.

You probably have strong opinions about the intelligence of your friends, people you know at school or work, your family members, and yourself. How, though, do you decide whether or not a person is "smart"? If you're like most of the people canvassed in a recent study (Sternberg, Conway, Ketron, & Bernstein, 1981), you base your opinions on the way other people act, and your ability to judge intelligence in others is fairly accurate.

Psychologist Robert J. Sternberg and his colleagues interviewed or mailed questionnaires to 476 men and women—students, working people, supermarket shoppers, and people located by newspaper ads or the phone book. They also questioned 140 research psychologists who specialize in studying intelligence. Both experts and laypeople listed various kinds of behavior that they thought characterized "intelligence," "academic intelligence," "everyday intelligence," and "unintelligence." Some 250 different behaviors emerged: 170 indicators of different aspects of intelligence and 80 signs of a lack of intelligence.

Most of the intelligent behaviors can be grouped in three categories: *practical problem-solving ability* ("identifies connections among ideas"), *verbal ability* ("reads with high comprehension"), and *social competence* ("thinks before speaking and doing"). Academic intelligence was composed of the same three basic categories, with a greater emphasis on academic skills such as studying hard, and everyday intelligence consisted of practical problem-solving ability, social competence, character, and interest in learning and culture.

The ideas advanced by laypeople turn out to be very close to the most widely accepted scientific theories of intelligence—with one major difference. The ordinary person goes further in his or her definition, adding social and cultural dimensions (such as sensitivity to other people's needs and desires, honesty, and getting along well with others) to the cognitive dimensions (like logical reasoning, display of curiosity, and rapid learning).

While people aren't very good at judging their own intelligence, they are good at describing the way they act, so that an outside observer can get a pretty accurate idea of their intelligence. When the subjects in this study rated themselves on the 250 behaviors, the researchers were able to predict quite well their overall scores on standard intelligence tests, as well as the subjects' scores on the parts of the tests that measure verbal ability, social competence, and the ability to solve problems.

This finding points to a brand-new possibility in intelligence testing—a checklist that could supplement, or in some cases, replace the elaborate intelligence tests that follow most of us throughout our school and work years. A checklist would have several advantages: its simplicity, its focus on typical performance rather than with the best performance a person is capable of, its nonstressful nature; its emphasis on behaviors that matter in the real world, and its ability to be tailored to different cultural groups, including behaviors important within that culture or subculture.

While there were some differences between the experts (who emphasized motivation more) and the laypeople (who were more tuned in to competence in getting along with other people), one of the most interesting conclusions from this study is the close connection between what the average person on the street means by "intelligence" and what psychologists say it is (Sternberg, 1982).

The chapter that follows this one on language, thought, and problem solving, deals with issues that are closely related to intelligence. In this chapter we'll look at the global concept of this capacity. Psychologists have shown increased interest recently in doing research on issues related to intelligence, a number of which have had major political and social impact. One such issue is the definition of intelligence through the years to the present day. Another is the whole area of intelligence testing—how psychologists have measured, or tried to measure, it—some of the uses and abuses of testing, and some promising new directions for assessing intelligence. We'll explore the relationships—or their absence—between intelligence and such factors as heredity, race, sex, and environment. Finally, we'll consider the extremes of intelligence among the intellectually gifted and the mentally retarded.

DEFINING INTELLIGENCE

Despite agreement among both scholars and laypeople about various elements that contribute to intelligence, there is no universally agreed-upon definition of this attribute. Lewis Terman (1921), an early researcher who developed the Stanford-Binet Intelligence Scale, the most influential test in this country, and who launched a major longitudinal study of gifted children that is still going on today more than sixty years later, defined intelligence as *the ability to think abstractly.* Jean Piaget (1952), the Swiss psychologist who applied his broad knowledge of biology, philosophy, and logic to meticulous observations of children and constructed complex theories about the ways children acquire knowledge, defined intelligence as *the ability to adapt to one's surroundings.* And David Wechsler (1944), the developer of widely used intelligence tests for different ages, came up with a practical definition—*the ability to "act purposefully, to think rationally, and to deal effectively with the environment"* (p. 3). More cynical psychologists define it as "whatever intelligence tests measure."

When we use the term *intelligence* in this book, we are referring to *a constantly active interaction between inherited ability and environmental experience, which results in an individual's being able to acquire, remember, and use knowledge; to understand both concrete and (eventually) abstract concepts; to understand relationships among objects, events, and ideas; and to apply and use all the above in a purposeful way to solve problems in everyday life.*

This definition is—deliberately—extremely broad. While we consider intelligence to result from the interplay between heredity and environment, we feel that venturing a guess on the proportions involved is so inaccurate as to be foolhardy. In such an interaction, the two influences cannot be separated as if we were adding one scoop of nature and one scoop of nurture. Our definition also blends the practical and adaptive with the abstract. We recognize, for example, that the verbal abilities you need to get along in mainstream American society are different from the abilities you would need if you lived in a culture where you had to hunt and fish to survive.

THEORIES OF INTELLIGENCE

There are almost as many theories of intelligence as there are definitions. We will present two basically different approaches. The first, as exemplified in the theories of Spearman, Thurstone, Guilford, and Cattell and Horn, employs the statistical technique of factor analysis* as a tool to discover the nature of intelligence. These theories' emphasis on individual differences in intelligence has had great impact on the development of the intelligence tests in use today. In fact, the approach is often called the psychometric approach because it emphasizes the measurement of intelligence.

The second major approach is seen in Sternberg's work. Instead of identifying the particular *factors* that define intelligence, Sternberg looks at the *processes* by which a person uses information to solve problems.

Spearman's Two-Factor Theory

One of the earliest theorists, Charles Spearman (1904), proposed a *g* and several *s* factors in intelligence. The *g* factor (general intelligence), was thought to be an inherited intellectual capacity that influences all-around performance, and the *s* factors (specific abilities) were said to account for the differences between scores on different tasks, say, verbal and mathematical. Spearman justified this division by pointing to the common phenomenon that people who score high on one kind of test usually do well on others but that their scores on various abilities do differ somewhat.

Thurstone's Primary Mental Abilities

Using factor analysis on intelligence test scores of a large number of children, L. L. Thurstone (1938) identified seven relatively distinct factors: *word fluency* (the ability to think of words rapidly); *verbal comprehension* (the ability to define words); *space* (the ability to recognize a figure whose position in space has been changed); *perceptual speed* (the ability to detect similarities and differences between designs); *reasoning* (logical thought); *number*; and *memory*.

Guilford's Structure of Intellect Theory

J. P. Guilford (1959, 1982) took factor analysis several steps further into a three-dimensional, cube-shaped model of intelligence made up of some 120 separate factors, with *no* overall general intelligence factor. Guilford recently expanded his model to include 150 factors. These separate factors result from the interaction of *operations* (the ways we think); *contents* (what we think about); and *products* (the results of the application of a certain operation to a certain content, or our thinking a certain way about a certain subject). (See Figure 7-1.)

Cattell and Horn's Concepts of Fluid and Crystallized Intelligence

R. B. Cattell (1965) and J. L. Horn (1967, 1968) propose a distinction between two types of intelligence, which they term "fluid" and "crystallized." Suppose you are asked to group letters and numbers according to some criterion, to pair related words, or to remember a series of digits. The kind of intelligence you use for these tasks—to figure out relations between two different items or concepts, to form concepts in the first place, to reason, or to abstract—is fluid intelligence. These problems are novel for everyone or else call into play an element just about everyone in

*Factor analysis is used to identify a factor common to a variety of items. A factor is composed of a group of measures that correlate highly with each other. People who score highly on reading tests, for example, would usually also score highly on vocabulary tests. A common factor to both tests would be what Thurstone called "verbal comprehension."

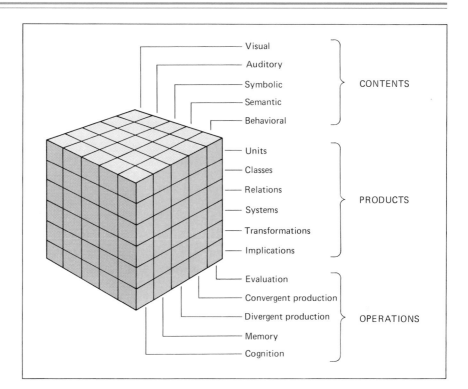

Visual
Auditory
Symbolic
Semantic
Behavioral

CONTENTS

Units
Classes
Relations
Systems
Transformations
Implications

PRODUCTS

Evaluation
Convergent production
Divergent production
Memory
Cognition

OPERATIONS

FIGURE 7-1 Guilford's Structure of Intellect Model *Guilford has proposed that there are 150 intelligence factors. These result from an interaction of operations, contents, and products. (From Guilford, 1977)*

a culture would know. This kind of intelligence is considered dependent on neurological development and relatively free from the influences of education and culture. It reaches full development in the late teens and begins a slow, steady decline in the twenties. The decline usually doesn't have much practical significance until very late in life—well into the eighties—because most people learn to compensate, often simply by allowing a little more time to learn this kind of information.

The other kind of intelligence in this theory—crystallized intelligence—involves the ability to use an accumulated body of general information to make judgments and solve problems. This kind of information has to be specially learned and is, therefore, dependent on education and culture. It includes knowledge like the meanings of words, the customs of Peruvian Indians, and which fork to use at a formal dinner. This is the kind of knowledge we depend on for solving problems where there's no one "right" answer but a range of possible solutions. This kind of intelligence increases throughout the life span, until near the end of life. In fact, recent research that measured age differences in "world knowledge" (like the names of world leaders, signs of danger in the street, and so forth) found that people in their seventies remembered such information better than young and middle-aged adults (Lachman & Lachman, cited in Goleman, 1984) (see Figure 7-2).

Sternberg's Information Processing Approach

Instead of asking how *well* people solve different kinds of problems, some researchers, like Robert Sternberg (1979), ask *how* we approach problems, seeing problem solving as an aspect of intelligence. What do you *do* with information from the time you perceive it until the time you have finished using it to solve your problem? This theory identifies a series of steps in

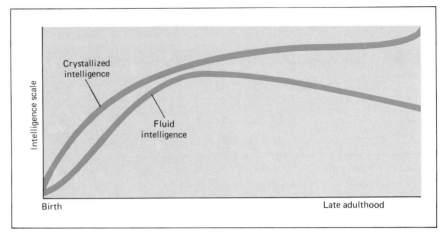

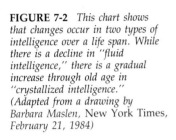

FIGURE 7-2 *This chart shows that changes occur in two types of intelligence over a life span. While there is a decline in "fluid intelligence," there is a gradual increase through old age in "crystallized intelligence." (Adapted from a drawing by Barbara Maslen,* New York Times, *February 21, 1984)*

the way we process information. We can see these steps by analyzing the way you might solve an analogy typical of the ones in many intelligence tests: WASHINGTON is to ONE as LINCOLN is to: (a) FIVE; (b) TEN; (c) FIFTEEN; (d) FIFTY.

1 *Encoding:* You have to identify the terms in the analogy and retrieve from your long-term memory whatever information you have that might be relevant. What do you know about Washington and Lincoln? What would be pertinent to this particular question?

2 *Inferring:* What relationship can you draw between the first two terms in your information—that is, between WASHINGTON and ONE? The one most people think of immediately is that Washington was the first president of the United States. Can you think of another relationship between WASHINGTON and ONE?

3 *Mapping:* What is the relationship between a previous situation and a present one? To *map,* or establish the higher-order relationship that links the two halves, we need to know that in this example, the previous situation is the first half of the analogy (WASHINGTON is to ONE) and the present situation is the second half (LINCOLN is to ?).

4 *Application:* How can you apply the relationship between WASHINGTON and ONE to LINCOLN and one of the numbers given in the multiple-choice section? Was Lincoln, for example, the fifth, tenth, fifteenth, or fiftieth president?

5 *Justification:* How can you justify your answer? If you remember that Lincoln was the sixteenth president, you may say that he was FIFTEEN presidents after Washington. This may not seem quite right to you, and so you conclude that the question is not well worded but that your answer is the best of all the choices given.

6 *Response:* You give the answer you think is best. The final correct answer depends on correct thinking at each stage. For example, if in step 1, you remembered that Washington's picture is on a one-dollar bill and that Lincoln's is on a five, you would have helpful information, which you could use at each succeeding step to come up eventually with the correct answer of FIVE.

By adding the prefix "meta" to a word, we change the root word to one that reaches a higher level than the original meaning. In Sternberg's theory we have components of intelligence (the preceding steps in solving a problem), and we have metacomponents, the steps you go through when you decide *how* to solve a problem. These higher-order processes help you decide which of the preceding steps you need to use for any particular problem, how you'll combine the steps, what order you'll use them in, how much time you'll spend on any one step, and how well you're doing on your solution.

Why do some people perform poorly on intelligence tests? They may not have the components they need—the information or the strategies. (Someone might not know that Lincoln's picture is on a five-dollar bill or might not know how to look for relationships between Washington and Lincoln.) Or they may not know how to use what they do have in the best way possible. They may spend too much time on one step and not enough on another. (Good problem solvers usually invest more of their time in the encoding stage, which gives them a good basis for working quickly on later steps.) By looking at the way people use the different steps, we can see where they get bogged down and can then teach specific strategies at each step. We can point out to an impulsive problem solver the importance of taking time to lay out a variety of options rather than just guessing at the first answer that sounds at all possible.

A more basic reason for poor performance is at the metacomponential level. Some people don't know how to go about solving a problem; they can't decide what the problem is and what components they need to use to solve it. So it may be more helpful to teach people how to construct their own problem-solving strategies rather than to teach any particular strategy. Sternberg recommends training people to think about how they are approaching a problem, to ask themselves how well they're doing, and to learn how and when to change strategies. Since problem solving is a major element in intelligence and an ability measured by virtually all intelligence tests, learning how to solve problems better should have the effect of increasing demonstrated intelligence.

AN HISTORICAL VIEW OF INTELLIGENCE TESTING

Intelligence testing has become such a controversial political issue in recent years that it's hard to remember it was born in the mid-nineteenth century out of an interest in the humane treatment of institutionalized retarded and disturbed people in the United States and Europe. The first intelligence tests were devised by a couple of French physicians, one of whom emphasized verbal ability and another of whom stressed such performance tasks as inserting different-shaped blocks into a formboard (Esquirol, 1838; Seguin, 1866). Later in the century, Sir Francis Galton (1883), an English biologist who believed strongly that intelligence was inherited, translated his conviction that keen sensory discrimination held the key to intelligence into various measures based on the Galton bar (to visually estimate length), the Galton whistle (to judge the highest audible pitch), and a series of weights to measure kinesthetic discrimination.

Another important early contributor was the American psychologist

Alfred Binet, pioneer in the study of intelligence. (National Library of Medicine)

James McKeen Cattell, who in 1890 coined the term "mental test." He developed easy-to-give tests that focused on such simple tasks as reaction time, word association, keenness of vision, and weight discrimination. Since scores on the tests did not predict college grades, as Cattell had hoped, the tests were forgotten. Their failure apparently lay in the fact that the tasks were not complex enough to measure intelligence.

Not until 1905 was intelligence testing as we know it launched upon the educational scene. At the time, school administrators in Paris wanted to relieve overcrowding by removing from class those children who didn't have the mental capacity to benefit from an academic education. They called in psychologist Alfred Binet and asked him to devise a test to identify such children so they could get special help that would improve their ability to get along in school. A variation of this test devised by Binet and his colleague, Theophile Simon, is still widely used.

Binet invented the term *mental level* to express a child's test score. This level, later widely called *mental age*, corresponded to the age of the normal children who had received a similar score on these items during the preparation of the test. Binet and Simon had given the tests they had devised to large numbers of normal children between the ages of 3 and 13. A child who passed all the test items passed by 80 to 90 percent of the normal 3-year-olds in the standardization groups (as described later in this chapter) would be considered to have a mental age of 3. Binet did not regard intelligence as fixed and urged that students who did poorly on his test be given "mental orthopedics" to increase their intelligence (Kamin, 1981).

The term IQ (for intelligence quotient) was devised later to translate mental age into a number that could be used for all age groups. IQ is the ratio of a person's mental age (MA) to chronological (CA) age multiplied by 100. The equation looks like this:

$$IQ = \frac{MA}{CA} \times 100$$

When mental age is the same as chronological age, the test taker has an IQ of 100, which is average; when mental age is greater than chronological age, the IQ is over 100; and when mental age is less than chronological age, the IQ is under 100. Thus:

- A 10-year-old child (CA = 10) whose test score yields a mental age of 10 years (MA = 10) has an IQ of 100.
- A 10-year-old (CA = 10) who scores a mental age of 8 (MA = 8) has an IQ of 80.
- A 10-year-old (CA = 10) who scores a mental age of 12 (MA = 12) has an IQ of 120.

The distribution of IQ scores in the general population takes the form of a bell-shaped curve. That is, the great majority of scores will cluster around the middle, with fewer and fewer at either end (see Figure 7-3).

One problem with this traditional calculation was that the same IQ did not mean the same thing at different ages because the variability in scores (the average deviation around the mean, or standard deviation) was not

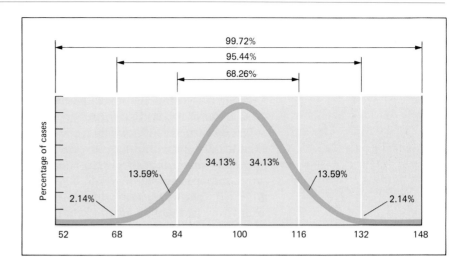

FIGURE 7-3 Percentage Distribution of Cases in a Normal Curve   *IQ scores are distributed in a normal curve. Most of the population fall in the middle range of scores; extremely high and extremely low scores are relatively rare. The curve indicates that on an IQ test with a standard deviation of 16 points, 68.26 percent of the population have IQs between 84 and 116; 95.44 percent have IQ's in the 68–132 range; and 99.72 percent have IQs between 52 and 148. (From Anastasi, 1982)*

the same at all age levels. The standard deviation might be 10 at one age, and so someone with an IQ of 110 would be superior to 84 percent of the sample. At another age, at which the standard deviation was 16, the test taker would need to attain an IQ of 116 to keep the same level of superiority. Since 1960, IQ scores at all ages have been reported as a *deviation IQ,* a standard score considered to have an average of 100 and a standard deviation of 16. (See the statistical appendix for explanation of these terms.)

The Binet-Simon tests set the stage for all the intelligence tests that were to follow, even though subsequent tests differ in a number of ways. For one thing, all the Binet-Simon tests were administered only to individuals, and the major growth in IQ testing came with the development of group tests at the time of World War I. The terms "mental age" and "IQ" captured the fancy of the public, as well as the psychological profession, and the heavily verbal content of these tests influenced the nature of most other tests, even though nonverbal tasks have been used increasingly in recent years.

Binet's tests leaped the English Channel and the Atlantic Ocean and became widely used in Great Britain and the United States. Lewis Terman, a psychologist at Stanford University, revised the test, which became known as the Stanford-Binet and was standardized on American children. Since 1916 it has been revised and updated several times, most recently in 1973, but after nearly three-quarters of a century some of the original items are still included.

INTELLIGENCE TESTING TODAY

Before we take up some of the political and philosophical issues swirling around intelligence testing, we'll focus on its more technical aspects—the kinds of tests in most common use, the strengths and weaknesses of each kind, and the criteria for developing both intelligence and personality tests. (We will talk specifically about personality tests in Chapter 14.)

Test Construction and Standardization

The constructors of a test must first decide what they want it to evaluate and predict. They then develop a large pool of items that seem to fit their purpose, either inventing new ones or adapting some that have been used in other tests. Construction and standardization go hand-in-hand in these early stages, as constructors standardize a test, that is, develop uniform procedures both for *giving* and *scoring* it. To make the testing situation as identical as possible for all subjects, test givers give the same directions, the same materials, and the same demonstrations, impose the same time limits, and so forth.

Test constructors try out their prospective items on a group of subjects like the ones for whom they are devising the test. (If the test is supposed to predict the ability of ghetto children to benefit from an educational program, for example, it would be given to a sample of children from an inner city, not to a group from a wealthy suburb.) They analyze the answers from the sample group, keeping the items that differentiate among people of different abilities and discarding the ones that don't. The final step involves giving the refined test to a different group, a large, representative group of people known as the standardization sample.

At this point the test designers establish norms, so they can standardize scoring. A *norm* is a normal or average performance. The average performance in the standardization sample is determined to get a basic norm, and then the frequency of deviations around this average is calculated to assess the superiority or inferiority of other scores. Norms, then, are standards of performance.

Reliability

A test is reliable when it is consistent in measuring the performance of an individual or a group. How do we calculate reliability? The most common way is to give the same person or group the same test more than once (test-retest reliability). The consistency between scores can be undermined by a number of different factors, including the effects of practice in taking the test and differences in the testing condition or in the physical circumstances of the individual. If you're in a quiet room one time and a noisy one the next, or if you're tired on one occasion and alert on another, your scores are likely to be fairly different from time to time. One problem with calculating reliability in this way is that people are likely to do better on the test the second time they take it because they have become familiar with the general aims of the test, the principles underlying the items, or the actual items themselves, or simply because they feel more comfortable in the testing situation.

So testers often use other ways to establish reliability. One way is to develop *alternate*, or parallel forms of a test, which are very similar, but not identical, in format, content, and level of difficulty. Instructions must also be comparable. This eliminates the possibility of the subject's familiarity with specific items but does not get around the effects of practice in taking this kind of a test. Split-half reliability can be calculated after a single administration of the test by seeing how a test taker did on half the test items compared to the other half. Usually the test is split according to odd- and even-numbered items. This procedure gives a measure of the test's internal consistency.

Validity

A test is valid if it measures what it is supposed to measure, as judged by how well scores correlate with other measures. One kind of validity is content validity, which refers to a test's ability to show a broad picture of whatever you want to measure. For example, a final exam in psychology has content validity if it covers all major aspects of what the course covers rather than only one or two topics. It's much easier to determine content validity for achievement tests, like final exams, than for intelligence tests, which cannot draw on a particular course of instruction or basic content.

Criterion-related validity measures the relationship between test performance and some criterion. The criterion is an outcome that is completely independent of the test; one does not affect the other. Criteria vary, depending on individual tests and what they measure. The two types of criterion validity are concurrent and predictive. Concurrent validity is related to test performance and a situation in the present (e.g., a child's IQ and his present classroom grades), while predictive validity looks at the relationship between test performance and some future situation (like Scholastic Aptitude Tests taken in high school and grades during the first year of college).

Do Intelligence Tests Measure Aptitude or Achievement?

If you were to encounter the WASHINGTON-LINCOLN analogy in an intelligence test, what would it measure? Reasoning ability? Yes. Your ability to determine relevant information? Yes. Your ability to see relationships among different items? Yes. All these are elements of aptitude, or general intelligence. Would it also measure what you had learned? Of course. If you had never seen a one-dollar and a five-dollar bill, you would not be able to solve the analogy. Sternberg (1979) refers to "a bit of conventional wisdom among those in the field" that achievement tests measure what you have learned recently, while IQ tests measure what you learned in the more distant past (p. 47).

The items on most traditional intelligence tests reflect to a great extent what we have learned, with that "we" generally taken to mean members of the dominant culture in the United States—middle- and upper-middle-class whites. Many efforts have been made to assess "pure" unlearned intelligence, but so far it hasn't been possible to separate what you might be capable of learning from what you have already learned. Later in this chapter, we'll talk about some of the new ways psychologists are tackling this challenge.

TESTS IN USE TODAY

You might have had your intelligence measured on a test specially designed for infants, for children, or for adults. You can be tested as an individual or in a group. (Individual tests are used primarily in clinical settings, for help in counseling or therapy, while group tests are used for mass screening, primarily in educational, military, and business settings.) You can have your motor ability or your verbal ability tested—or both. We'll take a look at some of the traditional measures of intelligence and then at some new kinds of tests whose designers are responding to some of the criticisms of current testing practices.

Infant Intelligence Tests

Why would anyone want to measure a baby's intelligence? Usually to see whether a particular child is developing normally. Sometimes to evaluate a particular environment. At other times for research purposes, to see, for example, whether babies in day care respond differently from babies raised at home. The aims are worthwhile, but the tests are of limited value. They have a little value in assessing a baby's current level of development even though they're low on reliability, but they're almost useless in foretelling future development. It's virtually impossible to predict intelligence scores in adulthood or even childhood based on scores of normal children obtained before the age of 2.

Even though early scores are better at predicting later IQ for retarded or neurologically impaired infants, we need to be cautious in interpreting findings about these children, too. Some of the research affirming predictability, for example, involved adopted children. A baby who tested low may have been placed in a home that didn't offer intellectual stimulation, and therefore his low initial score may have served as a *self-fulfilling prophecy* (Brooks & Weinraub, 1976). That is, because he tested low, those in charge of placement did not expect much from him, and they put him in a home that didn't help him to develop his potential mental abilities.

Infants are intelligent right from birth, but assessing that intelligence is another matter altogether. They can't speak or read. You can't ask them a question and get an answer. They can't give you any clues as to how they reason. The only thing you can do is watch what they do. But very young babies don't do all that much. Furthermore, even though all the infant tests are administered individually, you can't always capture a baby's attention or motivate her to do what you want her to do. If a 16-month-old doesn't pick up a block (a typical item on infant intelligence tests), you don't know whether it's because she doesn't know how to do it, she doesn't know you want her to do it, or she just doesn't feel like doing it.

Why are early scores so unrelated to those in later life? Quite possibly because early intelligence tests, which focus on motor activity, are so different from the heavily verbal tests for older children. The tests may be measuring two different things. Let's look at the most popular scales for assessing infant intelligence, all of which are individual tests.

THE GESELL DEVELOPMENTAL SCHEDULES   Covering ages between 4 weeks and 6 years, these four schedules (i.e., batteries of tests and observations) measure a wide range of activities appropriate for children of the ages covered: *motor behavior* (holding the head erect, sitting, and creeping); *adaptive behavior* (eye-hand coordination in reaching for things, exploring new surroundings); *language behavior* (understanding people, reacting through facial expressions and babbling); *personal social behavior* (toileting, smiling, feeding self) (Gesell & Amatruda, 1947). (See Figure 7-4.)

THE CATTELL INFANT INTELLIGENCE SCALE (1940)   An adaptation of the Stanford-Binet designed for younger children, this scale covers ages from 2 to 30 months. It tests *perception* (paying attention to a voice or a bell, or following movement with the eyes) and *motor abilities* (lifting the head or using the fingers).

The Stanford-Binet Intelligence Scale

Still given as an individual test to one person at a time, the Stanford-Binet is used primarily for children, although it may also be given to adults. It takes about 30 to 45 minutes to test a child and up to an hour and a half for an adult. Test takers at different age levels have to answer six items at each level (except for the "average adult," who is given eight items), but

GESELL AND AMATRUDA

(Key age, 28 weeks)

Lifts head.

Sits erect momentarily.

Radial palmar grasp of cube.

Whole hand rakes pellet.

Holds two cubes more than momentarily.

Retains bell.

Vocalizes m-m-m and polysyllabic vowel sounds.

Takes solid food well.

Brings feet to mouth.

Pats mirror image.

(Key age, 52 weeks)

Walks with one hand held.

Tries to build tower of cubes, fairly.

Dangles ring by string.

Tries to insert pellet in bottle.

Two words besides "mama" and "dada."

Gives toy on request.

Cooperates in dressing.

FIGURE 7-4 Sample Items from the Gesell Developmental Schedules, an Infant Assessment Test *The items on the top are suitable for 28-week-old infants, and those on the bottom for 52-week-old infants. (Gesell & Amatruda, 1947)*

Language, essentially, is the shorthand of the higher thought processes, and the level at which this shorthand functions is one of the most important determinants of the level of the processes themselves. (Terman & Merrill, 1937, p. 5)

no one is expected to answer all the items. The test is heavily verbal at all age levels beyond infancy, with items involving vocabulary, analogies, proverb interpretation, and so forth. This verbal emphasis is deliberate. (Later in this chapter we'll talk about the implications of this emphasis.)

The examiner begins by presenting items on a level slightly below the expected mental ability of the person taking the test. If the examiner misjudged and the subject has trouble passing any of these initial items, the examiner drops back and gives the subject easier items, so that a "floor," or *basal age*, can be established at which the person passes all items. The examiner then goes through higher levels until a level is reached at which the person fails all items; once this *ceiling age* is reached, testing stops. The IQ is the subject's basal age plus months of credit for items passed above this.

Generally, a person's IQ is considered to be roughly equal to those in a range of 10 points higher or lower since one person's score may vary that much from test to test. While some guidelines have been developed to interpret IQ scores, there are no hard-and-fast rules. Many people with IQs at the average level make outstanding contributions during their lifetime, while some at the extreme upper levels do not distinguish themselves. At the low end of the scale, retardation is defined by the way a person acts as well as by IQ.

It's important to remember that IQ can be modified. Changes in environment often produce changes in IQ scores, as we'll see when we discuss the influence of environment on intelligence.

The Stanford-Binet is very reliable, especially for older test takers and for those at the lower end of the IQ scale. It's impressively valid in predicting the ability to do well in school: IQ scores correlate highly with high school and college grades, especially on highly verbal courses like English and history, more moderately on courses like biology and geometry. These meaningful correlations (ranging from .40 to .60) are not surprising since this test was originally developed to predict success in school.

A correlation does not, of course, need to be a perfect 1.0 in order to have meaning. When correlations are, however, less than that, as these are, it appears that performance in school is also influenced by other factors such as nutrition, child-rearing practices, motivation, teachers' expectations, and educational opportunities.

A major criticism of the Stanford-Binet is its heavy verbal emphasis, which serves to discriminate against people for whom English is a second language, for those in a subculture with its own way of speaking (like low-income blacks), and for individuals whose special strengths are in nonverbal areas such as mechanical aptitude.

Compelling evidence that even this well-standardized, popular test does not measure "pure" intelligence can be seen in the changes in test takers' scores over the many years it has been administered. Test takers of all ages have been doing better on the test in recent years, with improvements especially notable among preschoolers and those aged 15 and older (Anastasi, 1976). The person who scores 100 now has passed more items than the one who got 100 in 1937. Higher scores for older test takers probably reflect increased years of education for this age group, while young children's higher scores may be related to the increasing literacy and higher educational level of their parents, as well as the impact of radio and television on the children themselves.

The Wechsler Scales

David Wechsler originally developed his own test because he felt the Stanford-Binet was too oriented toward children, even with the addition of more difficult items geared to adults. As he put it, "Asking . . . an ex-army sergeant to give you a sentence with the words, 'boy,' 'river,' 'ball,' is not particularly apt to evoke either interest or respect" (1939, p. 17). So he developed a test for adults (1939; 1955; 1981); then one for schoolchildren (1958; 1974); and finally one for preschoolers (1967). All three contain two separate scales—verbal and performance—which yield separate scores as well as a full-scale IQ. This approach allows us to analyze test scores to see precisely where someone may excel or be behind most other people. It also overcomes some of the objections to the heavily verbal content of tests like the Stanford-Binet.

WECHSLER ADULT INTELLIGENCE SCALE (WAIS) The WAIS contains six verbal subtests (information, comprehension, arithmetic, similarities, digit span, and vocabulary) and five performance subtests (digit symbol, picture completion, block design, picture arrangement, and object assembly). (See Figure 7-5.)

The WAIS, which was revised most recently in 1981, includes specially developed norms for adults and the elderly and is very reliable. It's valid on several measures, including relationship to job category (white-collar workers do better in verbal IQ, while skilled workers do better in performance IQ) and prediction of work adjustment for mental retardates released from institutions (Anastasi, 1976).

WECHSLER INTELLIGENCE SCALE FOR CHILDREN (WISC-R) Tailored for children aged 6 to 16, the separate verbal and performance scales of the WISC-R (revised in 1974) let us pick up problems with language development (when verbal score is much lower than performance score) or with perceptual and/or motor development (when performance score is much lower). Reliability is good. The verbal items are very similar to the Stanford-Binet, and so WISC IQ correlates highly with Stanford-Binet IQ and gives rise to the same charges of cultural bias against test takers from low socioeconomic groups.

WECHSLER PRESCHOOL AND PRIMARY SCALE OF INTELLIGENCE (WPPSI) This test is used with children from 4 to 6½ years old, takes about an hour, and is sometimes given in two separate sessions since young children are distracted easily and tire out soon. Reliability is good on this test, too, which has not been revised since 1967. There is some relationship with socioeconomic status since children of professional fathers score higher than children of unskilled workers (Anastasi, 1976).

Group Tests

As the United States entered World War I in 1914, the American Psychological Association pressured the government to administer group intelligence tests to all recruits (Gould, 1981). The immediate rationale was to help place soldiers in appropriate jobs, but the major incentive for the

FIGURE 7-5 *A psychologist administers the Block Design Test, a subtest of the Wechsler Adult Intelligence Scale (WAIS). This is one of five performance and six verbal subtests, which yield separate verbal performance scores, as well as a full-scale IQ. (© Sepp Seitz 1982/Woodfin Camp & Assoc.)*

APA, which developed the tests, was to generate data on large numbers of people and to advance the "science" of intelligence testing. The written Alpha test was given to men who could read and write, and the performance Beta test was administered to illiterates and the foreign-speaking. The tests didn't help in job placement (except for screening men out of officer training), but they did generate a mass of data on some 3 million people (leading to abuses we'll discuss later) and served as models for the group tests that most of us have encountered throughout our lives in school, in applying for jobs, and in the military.

The best part about group tests is their speed and ease of administration. Generally, good norms are provided for their scores, and they don't need the same kind of clinical interpretation that individual tests do. They have several drawbacks, though. That same clinical interpretation that takes time on an individual test offers the chance for the examiner to establish rapport and to use clinical insight in assessing the test taker's ability. This is not available under group testing. Preschoolers, who seem to need rapport with the examiner, cannot be tested in a group.

Furthermore, the multiple-choice nature of most group tests penalizes the creative thinker who offers a different slant on a question and provides an unusual answer. Recently Daniel Lowen, a high school student in Cocoa Beach, Florida, correctly solved a geometry problem on the Preliminary Scholastic Aptitude Test (PSAT) but had his answer marked wrong. He appealed the decision and won, which forced the Educational Testing Service to raise the scores of 240,000 other students as well (Fiske, 1981) (see Figure 7-6). This story had a happy ending, but there are undoubtedly many more cases when an answer is ambiguous, a student with an unusual answer is not given credit, and no one questions the decision.

WHAT'S RIGHT—OR WRONG—WITH INTELLIGENCE TESTING

The controversies that swirl around intelligence testing sound like a meeting between advocates of gun control and the National Rifle Association. Are the tests themselves okay for certain specified purposes but dangerous when used in the wrong way by the wrong people? Or is the whole concept of intelligence testing as we know it a mistake bound to have unfavorable consequences for society? Let's take a look at the basis for some of the arguments for and against testing.

The Value of Testing Intelligence

There are many situations when it's useful to have some method of predicting academic performance, which intelligence tests do quite well. Test scores can alert parents and teachers to the fact that a child will need special help, the extent of that help, and possibly the kind of help that will be most useful. A high school student's performance on an intelligence test can help him decide which college to go to—and can help the college decide whether he will be able to keep up with the level of work it requires. IQ tests provide one way to judge whether a special educational program, like Head Start, which was designed for children from economically disadvantaged families, improves children's performance enough to justify the expenditures of effort and money. Sometimes such tests are used to provide opportunities by identifying and offering scholarships to

The Question:

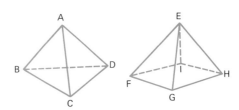

44. In pyramids ABCD and EFGHI shown above, all faces except base FGHI are equilateral triangles of equal size. If face ABC were placed on face EFG so that the vertices of the triangles coincide, how many exposed faces would the resulting solid have?

(A) Five   (B) Six   (C) Seven
(D) Eight   (E) Nine

Discussion of Solution:

Depending on whether the faces considered are those of the original two solids or those of the combined solid, both choices (A) Five and (C) Seven have merit as correct answers. When the question was originally scored, only choice C was considered correct. Although seven of the original faces remain exposed, the solid that results if face ABC is placed on face EFG contains but five distinguishable faces. Some of the faces of the original figures (for example, faces ABD and EGH in the diagram below) lie in the same plane and form a parallelogram when the solids are placed together. The diagram provides an illustration.

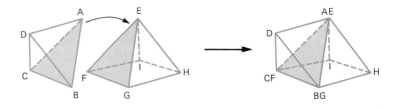

FIGURE 7-6 *Preliminary Scholastic Aptitude Test problem and Daniel Lowen's solution. (Educational Testing Service)*

gifted youths whose families cannot afford to send them to college or are not educationally oriented and might not even consider the possibility.

The IQ tests have a number of strengths that help them accomplish the foregoing aims. They are well-standardized instruments whose norms, validity, and reliability are well established. They are readily available and often easy to give. Since many researchers have used them, results can be compared to those in other studies. At the moment they are the best available predictor of school performance and the best available measure of mental retardation.

While the tests do have many valid and socially beneficial uses, then, it's dismaying to note that they have often been misused, with far-reaching ramifications for society.

Current Misuse of Intelligence Tests

JUSTIFYING RACIAL DISCRIMINATION   Ever since the second decade of this century, when Terman found that Spanish-Indian, Mexican, and black test takers tended to score in the 70 to 80 IQ range, one expert after another has used this information to maintain that intelligence levels are inborn and unchangeable and that test scores demonstrate the superiority of whites over everyone else. Such convictions have been used to justify providing a poorer education to minority-group children and to keep adults out of jobs.

There *are* differences in IQ scores between racial groups, but they don't always favor white Anglo-Saxons. Later in this chapter we discuss the current superiority of Japanese intelligence scores over those of Americans. The increases in Japanese IQ scores over the past generation are very relevant to the ongoing discussion over the disparity in this country between black and white scores.

On the average, black children tend to test some 15 points lower than whites on IQ tests, attaining an average IQ of about 85. There is, of course, some overlap: Some blacks score higher than almost all whites, and many blacks score higher than most whites. Furthermore, urban northern blacks score higher than rural southern blacks. The range of scores within any ethnic or racial group goes from very low to very high, indicating that the differences among individuals of the same group are much greater than the differences in average scores between groups (Brody & Brody, 1976).

In 1969 Arthur Jensen, a California professor of education, inflamed many readers (and excited others) with an article published in the *Harvard Educational Review* titled, "How Much Can We Boost IQ and Scholastic Achievement?" Referring to a large body of evidence suggesting that genetic factors seem to determine much of the differences in measured intelligence among members of the same ethnic groups (i.e., white Europeans and Americans), Jensen proclaimed that the difference in IQ scores between different groups (i.e., blacks and whites in the United States) must also be hereditary. While the vast majority of psychologists do not agree with this position—and even Jensen has backed off from it considerably, this dubious and unproven argument has been used to suggest that compensatory education is a waste of teachers' time and efforts and of taxpayers' money. If intelligence is determined almost entirely by our genes, an enriched environment can do nothing.

Later in this chapter we'll discuss the relative influences of heredity and environment. For now, let's just say that the unproven assumption that blacks are genetically and unalterably less intelligent than whites creates a host of self-fulfilling prophecies. Parents, teachers, and others who think a child is dumb lower their expectations, do not devote to the child the kind of attention that would encourage him or her to do better, undermine the child's self-confidence, discourage ambitious educational and career goals, and end up producing an adult who lives down to everyone's expectations. Furthermore, when intelligence tests that discriminate against a major portion of the population are used to screen admission to schools or entry into employment, those people who do not do well on the test will be deprived of future opportunities to do well in life.

OVERRELIANCE ON TESTING   After a four-year study, a panel named by the National Academy of Sciences (1982) concluded that standardized tests *are* reliable predictors of narrowly defined areas of performance (such as first-year college grades) but that they do reflect the inequities in the educational and home backgrounds of many minority-group youngsters. How to get around this dilemma? The authors of the report warn against rigid overreliance on such tests for placing children in special classes, for admitting students to college, and for hiring job applicants. They recommend the use of flexible criteria that take into account motivation and other factors. They also suggest that one test you the reader probably took, the Scholastic Aptitude Test (SAT) or another college entrance examination, is usually an unnecessary expense and inconvenience since most applicants (other than those applying to a very few highly selective schools) are accepted to the college of their choice.

UNDERESTIMATION OF IQ IN THE ELDERLY Older people may not do as well on intelligence tests as younger adults, particularly when the test asks them to solve problems they have never seen before. Even when elderly test takers do know the answers, they cannot always show it. Impairment in vision, hearing, coordination, and agility often make it hard to perceive instructions or carry them out. Speed of response is especially affected: When elderly test takers are allowed as much time as they need to finish a task, they do better than when they are timed (Bromley, 1974). Such physical conditions as fatigue, high blood pressure, and various other ailments seem to interfere with performance (Schaie & Gribbin, 1975). Test anxiety is another factor, especially for an old person who has never seen a machine-scored answer sheet and may be embarrassed to ask questions. Finally, the test items may have so little relevance to the life of an older test taker that she or he is not motivated to make much effort to answer them.

Such tests, then, may limit the ability of older people to get a job or to go back to college. Instead of closing off opportunities to the elderly, the psychological community needs to devise new kinds of tests that will more realistically assess intellectual ability in late life. (For a continuation of this discussion of intellectual activity in old age, see Chapter 13.)

UNDERESTIMATING THE INTELLECTUAL ABILITIES OF HANDICAPPED CHILDREN Traditional intelligence tests often underestimate the intelligence of children with various motor and speech handicaps. Considered mentally deficient, they are then consigned to classes for the retarded and prevented from realizing their intellectual potential. Tests like those discussed in the next section can be administered to handicapped children for a truer picture of their ability.

New Directions in Intelligence Testing

Ever since the concept of intelligence testing was born, one psychologist after another has tinkered with the tests already in use, trying to improve them to overcome the shortcomings every one has had. Wechsler's addition of performance tasks to lessen the heavy verbal emphasis of IQ tests was one such innovation. In recent years, a number of other approaches have been tried.

MEASURING COGNITIVE DEVELOPMENT Jean Piaget, whom you will be reading more about in Chapter 12, devised an elaborate theory of cognitive development—how children acquire knowledge about the world and learn to solve logical problems. Piaget stressed the fact that children who

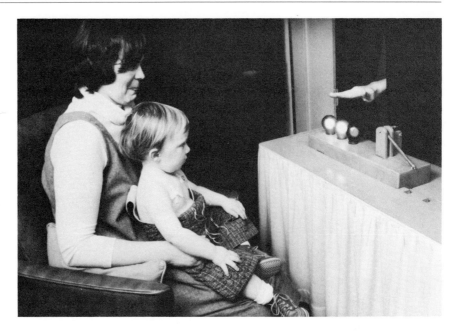

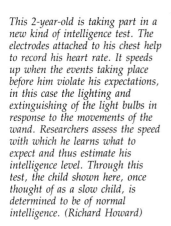

This 2-year-old is taking part in a new kind of intelligence test. The electrodes attached to his chest help to record his heart rate. It speeds up when the events taking place before him violate his expectations, in this case the lighting and extinguishing of the light bulbs in response to the movements of the wand. Researchers assess the speed with which he learns what to expect and thus estimate his intelligence level. Through this test, the child shown here, once thought of as a slow child, is determined to be of normal intelligence. (Richard Howard)

have not yet learned how to understand language show that they are intelligent by their *adaptive behavior,* that is, the way they get along in their environment. One adaptive concept developed between 12 and 18 months of age is object permanence, the realization that an object (or person) continues to exist even when out of sight. A number of standardized scales have been developed to measure the acquisition of such concepts, and one of these, the Uzgiris and Hunt Infant Psychological Development Scale, seems to predict intelligence later in childhood fairly well.

ZELAZO AND KEARSLEY'S INFORMATION PROCESSING APPROACH Troubled by the frequent underestimation of the intelligence of physically handicapped children because of the large motor component of infant tests, Zelazo and Kearsley (1981) developed a completely new testing approach. Drawing on research that shows that even infants only a few days old can become habituated to sounds, sights, and smells, thus demonstrating the presence of infant memory, Zelazo and Kearsley test children from the ages of 3 months to 3 years.

The baby sits, usually on his mother's lap, in a room set up like a puppet theatre. Through wires attached to his chest, the child is hooked up to an instrument that records changes in his heartbeat, while hidden observers watch and record his facial and physical changes. Over a 45-minute period, the child sees or hears five episodes that are designed to set up expectations and then to surprise the child by changing the expected pattern. In one of the little dramas, a toy car rolls down a ramp and knocks over a doll. A hand stands the doll back up and rolls the car back up the ramp. The same action occurs six times. The seventh time, the doll does not fall down when it is hit by the car. This happens twice more, and then there are a few more trials of the original sequence.

The child reacts to these events in a number of ways: He may stare at the stage, point or clap, wave, twist, or turn to his mother. At two points—

the first time the doll does not fall down and the first time it falls down again—his heart is likely to speed up; he may frown the first time the doll doesn't fall and smile the next time it does. The researchers have charted the ways children typically react and have developed standards for different age levels, paying special attention to the speed with which a child reacts to the episodes. In this way, they have been able to assess intellectual development quite apart from motor development. Thus they can test children with major physical handicaps whose intelligence would be vastly underestimated by traditional tests.

This approach has advantages for testing normal children, as well, since we don't have to worry about whether the child understands, likes, or is willing to cooperate with the examiner. The test itself is so interesting that the child pays attention to what is going on.

CONSIDERING THE ENVIRONMENT One recent attempt to take into account environmental factors and the way a child functions in daily life is embodied in *SOMPA*, the *System of Multicultural Pluralistic Assessment* developed by sociologist Jane Mercer and now being used in some states to place students in special-education programs. This battery of measures for 5- to 11-year-olds includes a medical exam, a Wechsler IQ test, and an interview with the parents. The interview yields information about the environment (how many people live in the home, their levels of education, etc.) and the child's level of social competence (how many classmates he knows by name, whether he prepares his own lunch, etc.).

Thus, a 9-year-old who scored only 68 on the Wechsler IQ test might be eligible for placement in a class for the mentally retarded. But when we take into account her impoverished cultural background in a family living on welfare in an urban ghetto and compare her with other children from similar backgrounds, we realize that her IQ score of 68 is only 9 points below the mean for that group. Her adaptive-behavior scores show that she is unusually capable of taking care of herself and getting along in her community. Her estimated learning potential, or "adjusted IQ," of 89 means she belongs in a regular class that takes her background into account (Rice, 1979).

CULTURE-FREE AND CULTURE-FAIR INTELLIGENCE TESTS When a group of Oriental immigrant children in Israel were asked to provide the missing detail for a picture of a face with no mouth, they said that the *body* was missing. They were not used to considering a drawing of a head as a complete picture and "regarded the absence of the body as more important than the omission of a mere detail like the mouth" (Anastasi, 1976, p. 347). This experience illustrates the difficulties in designing a test that can measure innate intelligence without introducing cultural bias.

It's possible to design a test that doesn't require language. Examiners use gestures, pantomime, and demonstrations for tasks such as tracing mazes, finding absurdities in pictures, putting the right shapes in the right holes, and completing pictures. But our way of thinking and of behaving is affected much more broadly by our culture than most of us realize. As in the case of the Israeli children, we need to be familiar with commonly accepted artistic conventions. We also need to be familiar with objects pictured, as biology professor Stephen Jay Gould (1981) confirmed when he gave the army Beta test to his present-day Harvard University students and found that many of them were stumped by the challenge to supply the missing part of a Victrola that their "innate intelligence" should have told them was the horn.

Furthermore, our standards of behavior exert a powerful influence. A person living in a culture that emphasizes the importance of doing something thoroughly even if that means doing it slowly, will do poorly in tests that value speed and the number of items answered. On the other hand, children from poor families tend to rush through a test, marking their answers almost at random and finishing ahead of time (Anastasi, 1976). Whether this is because they're not interested in the test, don't care about the results, don't expect to do well at it, or just want to get it over with as quickly as possible, the end result is that their score underestimates their ability.

Recognizing the impossibility of designing a *culture-free* test, test makers have tried to produce *culture-fair* tests that deal with experiences common to various cultures. But they've found that it's almost impossible to screen for culturally determined values and attitudes and that the tests almost always favor people from the same culture as the test constructor. Some conditions differ among cultures: "intrinsic interest of the test content, rapport with the examiner, drive to do well on a test, desire to excel others, and past habits of solving problems individually or cooperatively" (Anastasi, 1976, p. 345). Ironically, some of these "culture-fair" tests have yielded larger discrepancies between the scores of black and white children than verbal tests do (Anastasi, 1976). Obviously, these nonlanguage tests must be heavily loaded with cultural baggage that we can't even allow for because it's largely invisible.

Even as efforts continue to devise tests that minimize cultural influences, the ultimate question remains: Suppose we could devise a test that had no relevance to culture—what would we be measuring? Doesn't intelligence have something to do with how well people perceive and adapt to their culture? Isn't culture so pervasive that it's bound to affect every aspect of our intelligent functioning?

RECOGNIZING CULTURAL DIFFERENCES   It may be impossible to eliminate cultural bias from intelligence tests that try to compare one regional, ethnic, or social group with another. One way to get around this might be to test each group in its own cultural idiom, choosing test elements, vocabulary, conventions of time, and so forth separately from the background of each group (Garcia, 1981). If testers paid less attention to identifying those people who will do well in the future and focused more on opening up opportunities for minority-group and economically disadvantaged people (as Gordon & Terrell, 1981, suggest), we will have come full circle. Alfred Binet, who devised the earliest intelligence tests, felt that the tests could provide a valuable service by identifying children who needed special help, which could then be given to improve their functioning in school. The early translators of Binet's tests, including Terman and God-

Dr. Robert K. Jarvik, brilliant inventor of an artificial heart, whose college grades were too low for admission to an American Medical school is shown here with his invention. What does this say about our traditional methods of measuring intellectual ability? (Enrico Ferrorelli/Dot)

dard, took the opposite view, setting the stage for years of using intelligence tests to screen out the less qualified rather than to make them more qualified.

TESTING FOR COMPETENCE   David C. McClelland (1973) couldn't believe the research findings showing that career success in life is virtually unrelated to college grades—or, by extension, to intelligence tests (whose only reliable correlations are with grades in school). So he conducted his own survey of some of his own former Wesleyan College students, some fifteen to eighteen years after college graduation. There was no difference between a group of straight A students and a group of C- or below students. Lawyers, doctors, research scientists, and teachers were in both groups. Recognizing the fact that under today's stricter admission testing standards for graduate and professional schools, the C- students probably couldn't get into even second-rate law and medical schools, McClelland points out how our society might be depriving itself of some excellent practitioners who do not do well on traditional tests. [Proof of such occurrence can be seen in the case of Dr. Robert Jarvik, inventor of an artificial heart, who had to attend an Italian medical school because his college grades were too low for acceptance to an American medical school (Webster, 1982). If that foreign medical school had been as strict, Dr. Jarvik's creative genius might well have been lost to medicine.]

McClelland proposes some nontraditional methods of testing. One is criterion sampling, in which tests are developed that sample what the test taker is actually expected to do in real life. The best example of this is the road test you take to get your driver's license. You are thrust into the situation you'll be in when you'll be driving on the public roads.

This principle can be applied in many other areas. Instead of giving police academy applicants paper-and-pencil tests that ask them to define words like "quell" and "lexicon," which they don't need to know to do their job, testers should find out what a good police officer does and what she or he needs to know. McClelland suggests following a good officer on his or her rounds, making a list of the activities performed, and then sampling from that list in screening applicants. It's probably more important for an officer to know street language than "dictionary" words.

Developing such tests will not be easy, concedes McClelland. "It will require new psychological skills not ordinarily in the repertoire of the traditional tester. What is called for is nothing less than a revision of the role itself—moving it away from word games and statistics toward behavioral analysis" (p. 8). His other suggestions include:

- *Follow-up tests:* Such tests should assess what someone has learned through experience instead of trying to measure intelligence as an inborn, unchangeable trait.
- *Testing realistic behavior:* Most tests ask the subject to choose among several clearly defined choices, but life doesn't usually work in this tightly structured way. So McClelland recommends the development of test items to which there are many correct answers, with one that's best. A test taker could be faced with a checkbook-balancing problem

BOX 7-1

CRITERION SAMPLING IN NEW YORK'S PARKS

The principle of criterion sampling was recently confirmed in New York City. After 800 in a group of 1000 parks service workers who took a civil service test scored so low that they would have had to be fired, the city's personnel department decided to throw out the test. The sixty-question written test, given to people who were already working at such jobs as picking up trash, cutting grass, and feeding zoo animals, included definitions of such words as "inflammable" and "ingest." Recognizing that the test would have thrown the city parks and recreation department into turmoil because of the necessity of having to dismiss four out of five employees and would have resulted in the dismissal of effective workers, officials decided to discard the test.

As one union leader said, "We're glad the city did the right thing. There's something unreal in a test that would eliminate people already performing the job well" (Gotbaum, quoted in Carroll, 1982). New York City's personnel director held out the possibility of devising a new job-related test or else just determining qualifications for the job and hiring any eligible applicant, without requiring a formal test.

(City of New York, Department of Recreation)

or an airlines scheduling problem in which basic information would be given to enable him or her to come up with the best solution.

Should we, then, get rid of all the tests now in use until better instruments can be developed? Not yet. While they're not perfect, they're all we have, and if used properly, they're better than nothing at all. As long as we're aware of the dangers in overreliance on tests, we can use what we have and carefully weigh the results.

INFLUENCES ON INTELLIGENCE

If I had any desire to lead a life of indolent ease, I would wish to be an identical twin, separated at birth from my brother and raised in a different social class. We could hire ourselves out to a host of social scientists and practically name our fee (Gould, 1981, p. 234).

Why do Professor Gould's fantasies run to separated twinship? Because such a situation would make him and his brother extremely rare specimens—people whose genes are identical and whose environments are different. Psychologists have been trying to track down people like these for more than half a century and are still looking, to try to resolve the old nature versus nurture question: How much of our intelligence is determined by our genes and how much by our means?

It's difficult to determine with any certainty the relative roles of heredity and environment in determining intelligence. The only way we could prove this would be to compare children with different heredity growing up in identical environments or children with identical genes growing up in different environments. The first alternative is impossible since no two children—not even identical twins—grow up in identical environments, and each person's experience is unique. If this is true for two children in the same family, it is infinitely more true for children from different racial groups, different socioeconomic levels, different neighborhoods. In America, black children are more likely to come from poor families, and so any comparison of white with black is likely to confound the effects of poverty, cultural differences, and race. Even controlling for financial circumstances does not eliminate the problem since the cultural heritage of black and white children differs in innumerable subtle ways.

The second alternative—comparing the IQs of identical twins who grew up in different environments—has been attempted but has met with difficulty because such twins are hard to find. Some other ways of trying to measure the relative inputs of heredity and environment are studies of adopted children and their biological and adoptive families; comparisons among relatives of various degrees of closeness and unrelated persons; and measures of intelligence before and after a known change in environment.

Heredity

The belief that intelligence comes to us as a hereditary legacy is an old one. Sir Francis Galton (1869) based his studies of eminent men largely on his beliefs that heredity, race, and class (this last attribute attained by virtue of the first two) were the basic determinants of achievement; he estimated the chances for relatives of the most eminent men to achieve eminence themselves. (This tack may have been influenced by the fact that Galton himself was Charles Darwin's cousin.) Given the point of view Galton started out with, it's not surprising that he concluded: The closer the blood tie, the better the chance for fame.

While Binet, the framer of the first intelligence test, felt that intelligence scores were often the result of past experience and education and that they could be improved with special help, the translators of his tests in this country—such as Terman and Goddard—took a strong hereditarian point of view that has influenced psychological thought throughout the twentieth century, culminating in Jensen's (1969) adamant arguments that heredity accounts for 80 percent of the differences in IQ and that environment accounts for only 20 percent. What evidence have these and other hereditarians cited to bolster their belief in the heritability of IQ?

Back to Professor Gould's dream of fame and fortune. From early in this century, various social scientists have tried to fix the proportions of he-

The belief that intelligence is largely hereditary stems from evidence showing high correlations in intelligence between identical twins, even when they have been reared separately. Such twins, like the "Jim" twins shown here, are hard to find. These twins, both named James by their adoptive parents, have other striking similarities: Before they were reunited, each had married a woman named "Linda," each drank the same brand of beer, each had a carpentry workshop in his basement, and in these pictures we see the benches that each one built around a tree in his yard, the only person on his block to do so. (Enrico Ferorelli/DOT)

redity and environment by comparing identical twins raised together and apart and fraternal twins raised together and apart. Separated twins have been hard to find, and even when located, are often found to have been reared in very similar environments, by relatives, friends, or like-minded adoptive parents (Kamin, 1981).

For years hereditarians pointed to the research of the British psychologist Cyril Burt, which appeared to be the most complete study of fifty-three pairs of separated identical twins. Burt's findings showed that separated twins were remarkably similar in IQ, despite differences in their upbringing. This remarkable similarity, showing unheard-of high correlations over time and under different research conditions, was the "fatal flaw" in Burt's work that made Kamin (1974) suspicious of Burt's findings and that led to the exposure of Burt's massive hoax. Compelling evidence has surfaced, showing without a doubt that he invented much of his data—the twins themselves, two colleagues who never existed, and the statistics that were supposed to prove his theory (Hearnshaw, 1979).

The major implication of Burt's fakery has been to eliminate the most persuasive bit of evidence for the heritability of intelligence. It has not eliminated *all* the evidence, of course. There is still a body of research in comparisons of forty pairs of separated identical twins, which found high correlations in intelligence between them (Shields, 1962). These twins, however, turned out to have been reared similarly and often to have been in touch with each other over the years. Furthermore, the more the two twins' family environments differed, the less alike their IQ scores were.

The IQs of twins raised by relatives (one by the mother, the other by an aunt or a grandmother) had a correlation of .83; those by unrelated families had a correlation of only .51. (Check the meaning of correlations like these in the statistical appendix.) Since the twins' genes were, of course, identical, such differences offer clear evidence of a strong environmental component to intelligence (Kamin, 1974).

Efforts to locate and study twins reared apart continue. An ongoing study has so far reported preliminary findings on fifteen pairs of identical twins and four pairs of fraternal twins who have been reared apart. High degrees of similarity have been found in the identical twins in mental abilities, emotional disturbances, temperament, and such disorders as phobias and speech impediments (Bouchard, Heston, Eckert, Keyes, & Resnick, 1981; Bouchard, 1981; 1982; Eckert, Heston, & Bouchard, 1981). The study still lends support to the importance of environment, however. When twins grew up in vastly different environments, as did two brothers, one of whom was raised by a poorly educated fisherman and the other by a much more cosmopolitan family, IQ differences were greater—in this case, by 20 points in favor of the twin with the more sophisticated background.

The evidence from twin studies, from adoption studies, and from other research does seem to indicate that heredity does play a significant part in determining intelligence. Most behavior geneticists conclude that about half the difference in IQ between American and European whites is the result of genetic differences; Jensen claims an 80:20 ratio; Loehlin (1979), a director of an adoption study in Texas, cites a heritability of only about 38 percent; and Kamin (1981) points to recent estimates by behavior geneticists that the heritability of intelligence may even be zero. As we pointed out earlier, it is difficult to pinpoint the exact proportion of responsibility to be borne by heredity and environment since the way these two influences interact prevents our being able to look at them as separate ingredients.

Environment

What has happened to Japan since World War II? Besides its high position in the world's marketplace as manufacturer of all sorts of items from transistors to cars, it has undergone vast changes in the way its people live. Psychologists are particularly interested in those societal shifts because the average IQ among Japanese children aged 6 to 16 is now the highest in the world, having risen by some 7 points over the past generation. Young Japanese now score a mean IQ of 111, compared to the American 100, with Japanese superiority showing up particularly on block design, mazes, picture arrangement, and object assembly (Lynn, 1982). More than three-quarters of Japanese children have higher IQs than the average American or European, and while only about 2 percent of Americans and Europeans score over 130, about 10 percent of Japanese now reach this level.

"It seems doubtful whether a rise of this magnitude could be accounted for by a change in the genetic structure of the population. Instead, the explanation probably lies largely in environmental improvements" (Lynn, 1982, p. 223). Among the changes in Japanese society that probably contribute to this rise in scores are the mixing of previously isolated

The average IQ among Japanese children aged 6 to 16 is now the highest in the world, a phenomenon which probably can be explained largely by environmental improvements. These Japanese students from a school outside Tokyo are learning algebra by using the computer. (Wide World Photos)

peasant communities as almost 40 percent of the population moved from the country to the cities and married people from other areas; the country's rapid economic growth that brought out improvements in welfare, health, and education; and the growing exposure to the Western culture that developed these tests (Anderson, 1982).

It isn't clear why the Japanese IQ has surpassed the American average, but one possibility might be differences in the two countries' educational systems. The Japanese system aims to produce not a brilliant elite but rather a high average level of capability in its graduates, thus "shaping a whole population, workers as well as managers, to a standard inconceivable in the United States" (Rohlen, quoted in Silk, 1982, p. D2).

Evidence of the impact of environment on intelligence scores has also shown up in a number of different situations in this country. In one classic study (Skeels, 1966; Skeels & Dye, 1939; Skodak & Skeels, 1949), thirteen apparently retarded 2-year-olds, who were taken from an orphanage to an institution where mentally retarded young women spent a great deal of time "mothering" them, grew up to be functioning adults. By contrast, a control group of twelve children who had stayed in the orphanage until later placement had a much lower IQ in adulthood, and four were still institutionalized.

Additional dramatic evidence comes from an important study of 130 black and interracial children who had been adopted by 101 white families in Minnesota (Scarr & Weinberg, 1976). These families were well above the average in education, occupation, income, and IQ—in short, the kinds that usually rear children who do well on IQ tests and in school. The children's biological mothers were at a slightly lower social echelon, with an educational level averaging four to five years less than the adoptive mothers. When these adopted children were tested, they averaged 106—higher than the average IQ of 90 usually achieved by black children reared in their own homes in the area. Furthermore, the adopted black children were performing above the national norms on the standard scholastic achievement tests.

These researchers conclude that if all black children had environments like the ones provided by the adoptive families in this study, their IQ scores might well be 10 to 20 points higher. It's not the interracial aspect of the adoption that seems important but the presence of elements that encourage intellectual skills. Here again, it seems obvious that IQ is not a fixed trait, present from birth, but a changeable one that is highly responsive to changes in the environment.

The intertwining of genetic and environmental issues comes through in this study in several ways. First of all, the IQs of the adopted children were not quite as high as the IQs of the adoptive parents' biologic children, and secondly, there was a slightly higher correlation between the IQs of the mothers and their biological children (.34) than with their adopted children (.29). Back to environment and the importance of the caretaking parent: While the correlation in IQ between the father and his biological child was the same as that of the mother (.34), his correlation with his adopted child was considerably lower (.07), which might reflect the typical situation in which the father is less involved than the mother in the child's day-to-day care.

In another adoption study, in Texas (Horn, Loehlin, & Willerman, 1979), the correlation between parents' and adopted children's IQ scores was considerably higher, possibly because these children were placed in their adoptive homes as newborns, directly from the hospital, while the Scarr and Weinberg study included children adopted as late as 1 year of age.

What goes on in homes that produce children who do well on intelligence tests, in school, and in life in general? A number of studies (Clarke-Stewart, 1977; White, 1971) have shown that certain parental characteristics are associated with intellectual growth. Parents of achieving children tend to be sensitive, warm, and loving. They are accepting of their children's behavior, letting them explore and express themselves. When they do want to change certain aspects of the child's behavior, they use reasoning or appeals to feelings rather than rigid rules. They use fairly sophisticated language and teaching strategies, and they encourage their children's independence, creativity, and growth by reading, teaching, and playing. They give their children a sense of control over the environment: The children know that what they do counts. The children respond by expressing curiosity, being creative, exploring new situations, and doing well in school. Such a climate for excellence need not be created exclusively by a child's biological parents. Other relatives and caregivers outside the family (such as day-care providers) can all contribute to a child's intellectual growth.

Another factor that influences intellectual development is nutrition. Severe early malnutrition seems to retard intellectual development by affecting brain development, the *orienting response* (which shows that a baby is paying attention to some sight or sound), and the ability to pay attention (Winick, Brasel, & Ross, 1969; Lester, 1975). Giving a pregnant mother, a new baby, or a preschooler extra food often has positive effects on the child's intelligence (Harrell, Woodyard, & Gates, 1955; Lloyd-Still, Hurwitz, Wolff, & Schwachmar, 1974).

So it seems clear that *both* heredity and environment exert some influence on the intellectual heights any of us can reach. Since we can't do anything about the former and we can do a great deal about the latter, it makes sense for us to continue to ask which environmental factors seem most important in encouraging intellectual development and, as individuals and members of society, to do as much as we can to introduce those factors into the lives of all children.

Sex

Your sex is not likely to affect your overall IQ. This isn't surprising since both the Wechsler and the Stanford-Binet tests were designed to eliminate any sex bias. A persistent thread running through these and other intelligence tests, however, has been a sex difference in some specific abilities. If you're a woman, you are more likely to excel in verbal ability, and if you're a man, in spatial ability. Of course, you may not fit this general pattern. While group differences between the sexes do exist in these abilities, there is considerable overlap between male and female scores.

VERBAL ABILITY   From the age of 1 month up to about 6 years, and then again from adolescence throughout adulthood, females outperform males in reading, speaking, spelling, and grammar. They start to talk earlier and do better on vocabulary and similarities tests in old age (Oetzel, 1966; Maccoby & Jacklin, 1974; Shipman, 1971; Stanford Research Institute, 1972; Eichhorn, 1973; Blum, Garvik, & Clark, 1970; Blum, Fosshage, & Jarvik, 1972).

SPATIAL ABILITY   From the age of about 6 or 8, males start to excel at spatial relations, and they continue to do better than females throughout life. They are better able to grasp the position and form of objects in space and to imagine the parts they can't see. This seems to be why males generally do better at mazes, formboards, block designs, and the like (Oetzel, 1966; Maccoby & Jacklin, 1974; Hall, 1978; Cohen, Schaie, & Gribbin, 1977).

WHY "LA DIFFERENCE"?   Researchers trying to figure out why these differences exist have generally looked at two major areas—biological and cultural. Do our hormones organize male and female brains differently? Since the left hemisphere, which typically controls verbal abilities, matures earlier in girls, and the right hemisphere, which seems to control spatial abilities, matures earlier in boys, this *may* account for the differences (Burstein et al., 1980).

Another possibility is that girls and boys are socialized differently. Ten-year-olds whose verbal abilities are much higher than their spatial abilities tend to have mothers who encourage them to be dependent, and mothers of children with better spatial ability give their children more freedom (Bing, 1963). This sounds like a stereotypical difference in the ways parents raise their sons and daughters, but research in sex-related child-rearing practices has not picked up any such clear-cut differences along these lines (Burstein et al., 1980). So the search for answers goes on.

THE INTELLECTUALLY GIFTED

When Robert R. Sears was a little boy in California, his teacher gave his name to Lewis Terman (1922), who was looking for exceptionally bright children, with a view to following them through life to see which ones would achieve success. Robert was tested for intelligence (scoring over 140, the requirement for inclusion in the study), school achievement, character, personality, and interests. He was examined medically, his physical measurements were taken, and his parents and teachers were interviewed for case-history material and a rating of Robert's personality.

The data that emerged for the 1500 children studied demolished the popular stereotype of the bright child as a puny, pasty-faced bookworm. On the contrary, these children were superior all around: healthier, taller, better coordinated, better adjusted, and more popular than the average child.

Over the years the Stanford University researchers kept in touch with as many of the original subjects as possible. Their intellectual, scholastic, and vocational superiority continued. They were ten times more likely than an unselected group to have graduated from college and three times more likely than other students to have been elected to honorary societies like Phi Beta Kappa. By midlife, they were highly represented in listings such as *American Men of Science* (which includes women) and *Who's Who*. Almost 90 percent of the men* were in the two highest occupational categories: the professions and the semiprofessions and higher echelons of business (Terman & Oden, 1959).

Surprisingly, this unusually bright group turned out not to be especially creative, never producing a great musician, an exceptional painter, or a Nobel Prize winner (Goleman, 1980). It's possible that the tests and other methods of selection tended to screen out the highly creative in favor of the highly competent. Or, as Goleman (1980) says, "Perhaps it is unfair to expect that among this particular pool of intelligence there would happen to be a Beethoven or an Einstein" (p. 34). While these people scored in the top 1 percent of intelligence in the nation, two or three million other Americans were in the same category.

Robert Sears did his fair share to advance the reputation of "Terman's children," becoming a prominent psychologist who directed a major study of child-rearing practices (Sears, Maccoby, & Levin, 1957), head of the psychology department at Stanford University (a post held earlier by Terman himself), and then dean of the university. Now, more than sixty years after the study began, Dr. Sears and his wife, Pauline, also a psychologist, are examining the trends that have emerged over the years from this longitudinal study of the intellectually gifted (Sears, 1977; Sears & Barbee, 1978).

While most of these adults were more successful than the average person in our society, there was a range of achievement in the group itself. When the 100 most successful (A) and the 100 least successful (C) men were compared in relation to their life histories and personalities, a number of differences emerged. The A's made more money, had higher-level occupations, came from more advantaged families and more stable homes, were better adjusted as children, were encouraged to be inde-

---

*Because of different societal attitudes toward careers for men and women, the sexes were evaluated separately. Both sexes made a good showing.

pendent, felt more parental pressure to excel in school and go to college, were healthier, better educated, more active physically, and happier in family life. They were more ambitious even as children—more goal-oriented, self-confident, persevering, and eager for acknowledgment for their achievements. Obviously, factors other than intelligence affect success since the average intelligence level in both groups was about the same.

In 1972, at an average age of 62, the subjects reported on their sources of life satisfaction (P. Sears, 1977; R. Sears, 1977). Overall, the men and the employed women rated work highly, the women at home rated family life highly, and both men and women gave their highest satisfaction scores for family life. Both men and women needed to feel competent. Sixty-nine percent of the women said they would choose their work lifestyle again. The happiest women had been working outside the home for years, had been single for a long time, and had no children.

What does this study tell us? That people who score high on intelligence tests do well in life? Possibly. McClelland suggests somewhat cynically that it "may show only that the rich and powerful have more opportunities, and therefore do better in life" (1973, p. 5). The sample in the study was not representative of the U.S. population: All were Californians, most came from relatively advantaged homes, Jewish children were overrepresented and black and Asian children underrepresented. The most interesting findings to emerge from the study may well be those *within* the sample, such as the ones that set off the super-successful A's from the less successful C's. Given so much in common, what differences mattered? With answers to a question like this, we may be able to improve the lives of people at all levels of intelligence—and society.

THE MENTALLY RETARDED

At the other extreme of the IQ spectrum are those people whose intelligence is *below* the average. The most widely accepted definition of mental retardation includes below-average general intellectual functioning, deficiency in the level of adaptive behavior appropriate to current age, and the appearance of such retardation before age 18 (American Psychiatric Association, 1980). It's important to note that while low-level intellectual functioning (as detected by IQ tests) is one component, behavioral performance is also important.

There are several levels of retardation, as shown in Box 7-2. People in the borderline and mild categories, who account for about 80 percent of all retarded people and may constitute about 15 percent of the American population (Zigler & Seitz, 1982; APA, 1980), can hold jobs and function fairly well in society, while those at the very lowest levels have to be cared for constantly, usually in institutions.

We also categorize retardation another way—in terms of whether it is organic, with a known physical cause, or familial, in which we can't identify a specific reason.

Organic retardation may be due to a number of different physical reasons. It may stem from a chromosomal disorder like Down's syndrome, which also produces certain distinct physical characteristics. (Down's syndrome is discussed in Chapter 11.) It may come from a disorder of metabolism, like phenylketonuria (PKU). Or it may result from problems

Given a supportive environment, Down's syndrome children like the one on the right can learn important skills. (Peter Vandermark/Stock, Boston)

during the prenatal period such as maternal illness, infection, or drug ingestion. Sometimes it accompanies a major physical birth defect like hydrocephaly, in which a baby is born with an abnormally large head. In this and other instances, the cause is unknown although it is clearly physical in origin. This type of defect can usually be detected before or shortly after birth. About one in four mentally retarded persons—some 2 million people—are in this class. Their IQs are usually below 50, and they are equally likely to come from the highest social classes as from the lowest (Zigler & Seitz, 1982).

In familial retardation, the cause is more elusive, probably involving a complex interaction between genetic factors and such environmental influences as poor nutrition, mild lead poisoning, and deprivation of social and intellectual stimulation. It is usually less severe than the organic kind, is most common among the lower socioeconomic classes, and often appears in several members of the same family. Often it isn't diagnosed until the child goes to school, and even then the diagnosis may be controversial.

The way a mentally retarded person gets along in our world today depends on society's attitudes and willingness to take action to prevent retardation in the first place, to provide supports for the retarded and their families, to make it easier for people to live in the community, and to offer humane institutional care for the most severely affected. Prevention of retardation seems most feasible when we talk about organic retardation. In fact, Zigler and Seitz (1982) maintain that if techniques like genetic counseling, amniocentesis, routine screening and health care for newborns, prenatal health care, and nutritional services for pregnant women and infants had been in full use for the past generation, the number of organic retarded people in our society could have been reduced from about 2 million to 1 million.

A number of intervention programs have been successful in enhancing the levels of functioning of many mild to moderately retarded people. As a result, many are able to be more independent and to live in the community. Such additional supports as day-care centers and hotels for retarded

BOX 7-2

LEVELS OF MENTAL RETARDATION

Type of Retardation	IQ Range*	Level of Functioning
Borderline retardation	70–85	May be able to function adequately in society
Mild retardation	50–55— +70	"Educable": Can learn academic skills up to sixth grade level and can support self minimally, with special help at times of unusual stress
Moderate retardation	35–40— 50–55	"Trainable": Can learn up to second grade level, care for self, do skilled work in sheltered workshop with supervision and guidance
Severe retardation	20–25— 35–40	Does not learn to talk or practice basic hygiene until school years, cannot learn vocational skills, may be able to perform simple work tasks under close supervision
Profound retardation	Below 20– 25	Requires constant care and supervision

*Scores are not rigid since level of adaptive behavior is also important.
Source: The material in the box is based on DSM III and Grossman, H. J. *Classification in Mental Retardation.* Washington, DC: American Association on Mental Deficiency, 1983.

adults, and homemaking services for families caring for retarded children are enormously valuable, and from a societal point of view are financially sound when compared to the high costs of institutional care. Finally, the schools can play an important role in providing special educational services for that great proportion of people in the upper ranges of retardation, to enable them to become contributing members of society to the best of their ability.

SUMMARY

1 There are a number of different theories and definitions of intelligence. In this book we define intelligence as a constantly active interaction between inherited ability and environmental experience, which results in an individual's being able to acquire, remember, and use knowledge; to understand both concrete and (eventually) abstract concepts; to understand relationships among objects, events, and ideas; and to apply and use all the above in a powerful way to solve problems in everyday life.

2 *Spearman's two-factor theory* of intelligence proposed that there is a general (or g) factor and several specific (or s factors) in intelligence. *Thurstone* identified seven relatively distinct factors. *Guilford's structure of intellect model* has included 150 factors which result from an interaction of opera-

tions, contents, and products. *Horn and Cattell* propose that there are two types of intelligence: *fluid and crystallized.*

3 *Sternberg's information processing* approach considers the steps people use to process information needed to solve intelligence test problems.

4 It was not until 1905 that intelligence testing as we know it was developed in the laboratory of Alfred Binet in Paris. The test he developed there to measure intelligence was the forerunner of the American test called the *Stanford-Binet.*

5 In order to develop an intelligence test a number of factors must be considered. These include *test standardization, reliability,* and *validity.*

6 A wide range of intelligence tests are in use today. Some of these are administered individually and others to groups. Intelligence tests have been de-

veloped for infants (e.g., *The Cattell Infant Intelligence Scale* and the *Gesell Developmental Schedule*), but it is difficult to predict adult or even childhood intelligence on the basis of infant scores. Other tests have been developed primarily for children (*The Stanford-Binet. WISC-R, WPPSI*) and others for adults (*WAIS*).

7   Intelligence tests are particularly useful in predicting academic performance. However, they have also been used in ways that have resulted in underestimating the intelligence of such groups as ethnic minorities and the elderly.

8   In recent years a number of novel approaches at assessing intelligence have been developed. These include scales based on *Piagetian concepts,* an *information-processing approach,* tests which consider the *atmosphere* in which the child lives, *culture-free and culture-fair tests,* and tests assessing job-related *competence.*

9   Psychologists today believe that both heredity and environment influence intelligence although there is considerable disagreement about the relative contribution of each factor.

10 There is no sex difference in overall IQ. However, females tend to excel in verbal ability and males in spatial ability. Possible reasons for these sex differences include differences in male and female brains and socialization experiences between the sexes.

11 The Terman longitudinal study of *gifted children,* with measured IQs of over 140, indicated that these children were healthier, taller, better coordinated, better adjusted, and more popular than the average child. They maintained their intellectual, scholastic, and vocational superiority in adulthood, although a range of success levels was noted in this sample during adulthood.

12 *Mental retardation* includes below-average general intellectual functioning, deficiency in the level of adaptive behavior appropriate to current age, and the appearance of such retardation before age 18. *Organic retardation* has a physical basis and applies to about 25 percent of mentally retarded people, and *familial retardation* probably involves an interaction of environmental and genetic factors. A number of intervention programs have helped people with mild to moderate retardation to be more independent and better able to live in the community.

SUGGESTED READINGS

Feldman, R. D. (1982). *Whatever happened to the quiz kids? Perils and profits of growing up gifted.* Chicago: Chicago Review Press. A highly readable series of minibiographies of precocious children who became premature celebrities. The last chapter, "Reflections on Growing Up Gifted," treats questions such as the relationship between intelligence and adult success, the difference between academic ability and creativity, and the effect of societal pressures and expectations on the psychological development of gifted children.

Gardner, H: (1983). *Frames of mind: The theory of multiple intelligence.* New York: Basic Books. A view of intelligence that draws upon research in cognitive psychology and neuropsychology to argue that people are all born with the potential to develop several different intelligences. Besides the logical-mathematical and linguistic skills that are tested by standard intelligence tests, other intellectual competences include the potential for musical accomplishment, bodily mastery, spatial reasoning, and the capacity to understand ourselves and others. The author suggests ways to mobilize these intelligences for maximum benefits to society and individuals.

Gould, Stephen Jay. (1981). *The mismeasure of man.* New York: Norton. A dramatic account of the history of intelligence testing in this country that reads like a scientific detective story. Harvard biology professor Gould uncovers a vast amount of evidence that many proponents of intelligence as a single hereditary ability fudged statistics, altered photos, and made up entire research projects to bolster their preconceived notions.

Hearnshaw, L. S. (1979). *Cyril Burt, psychologist.* Ithaca, N.Y.: Cornell University Press. An authoritative biography of a major figure in British psychology which was written by a fellow psychologist who came to the project with a vast admiration for Burt. Faced with the clear evidence that Burt had made up his studies on identical twins reared separately to put forth his own conviction that intelligence is inherited, the admirer became a historian, revealing the extent of Burt's massive scientific fraud.

Eysenck, H. J., & Kamin, Leon. (1981). *The intelligence controversy.* New York: Wiley. A lively debate on whether intelligence is the result of heredity or environment by two prominent advocates of each point of view, complete with attacks, counterattacks, and rebuttals.

CHAPTER 8

LANGUAGE AND THOUGHT

SPOTLIGHT ON

The development of language in childhood and the role of "motherese" in language learning.

The controversy over whether apes can learn language.

The question of whether the years before puberty are a critical period for learning language.

How the ability to organize different people, places, and events into categories imposes order on our world.

Routine and creative problem solving and some ideas about how to be more creative.

You would automatically expect the science of psychology, which we can define as the scientific study of mental processes and behavior, to include the study of the way people think. But for many years, the study of thought was "out of fashion" among American psychologists. For much of the first half of the twentieth century, experimental psychology was *behaviorist* in its orientation. Trying to get away from the ponderings of philosophers and to make this new study more rigorously scientific, it focused only on behavior, on what could be seen and measured.

The behaviorists felt that psychologists could not properly study "thinking" because they could not observe it directly and could not, therefore, measure it objectively. They coined the term *mentalism* and generally used it somewhat contemptuously to describe the interpretation of behavior in terms of mental processes as opposed to observable behavior. While the twists and turns that our brains take when we think are rapid and basic and not readily available to scientific measure, we are making enormous strides in this area, and most psychologists today seem to feel that the study of mental activities is not only important but is also possible. Today, with the rise of cognitive psychology, that branch of the science that strives to understand human thought, the cognitive revolution has done much to foster our understanding of mental processes.

In *thinking*, we're able to use symbols to stand for things, events, and ideas, which allows us to manipulate concepts and images so that we can acquire knowledge, remember it, and use it to solve problems. The subjects we'll talk about in this chapter—language, problem solving, and creativity—are all topics that psychologists consider to be aspects of thinking. The impact of cognitive psychology goes beyond these topics, however, as you'll note throughout this book. The influence of the "cognitive revolution" can now be seen in the study of virtually every issue discussed in these chapters.

Even though human thought is still complex, still resistant in many ways to the kind of study that yields positive answers about its nature, thanks to the ways intelligent and creative researchers have solved some of the problems of studying it, we now have access to some of its secrets. One of the most absorbing topics studied by cognitive psychologists is the development of language, a basic tool for most human thought.

LANGUAGE

"Does the bus stop here?" "I've come up with some possible solutions—here's my report." "I love you." "What time will you be back?" "Ladies and gentlemen of the jury. . . ." "Please stop at the store and pick up milk, bread, and apples." "To be or not to be, that is the question. . . ." "If you agree to limit your nuclear weapons, we'll limit ours."

When we consider the role that language plays in our day-by-day functioning, in our relationships with other people, in our ability to do our work, in our enjoyment of leisure-time activities, in the governance of the nations of the world, we realize how indispensable it is for normal human interaction. If you've ever been in a country whose language you didn't know, you know how much of a handicap you suffered. The occasional stories that surface of individuals without language—like the young Helen Keller or like the abused and neglected "Genie," whom we'll meet in this chapter—are among the saddest we hear. Without language we wouldn't be able to build a society, establish and enforce laws, pass on knowledge, do most of the things that we take for granted as part of human life. No wonder cognitive psychology devotes so much emphasis to the study of language!

Studying Language

To even begin to understand linguistics, the study of language, we need to learn a few terms and their meanings (presented graphically in Figure 8-1). Language is a means of communicating through spoken sounds (or, in the case of American Sign Language, used by the deaf, through gestures) that express specific meanings and are arranged according to rules. Every language has a grammar, a set of rules that specify its three basic components—*sound, meaning,* and *structure.* The phoneme is the minimal unit of sound. English has about forty-six basic speech sounds, while other languages have from fifteen to eighty-five phonemes. The morpheme is the smallest element of speech that has meaning. Made up of phonemes, it consists of a word stem, a prefix, or a suffix. The word "date" is composed of three phonemes (d, a, and t sounds). It consists of one morpheme. Words like "dates," "dating," or "predate," which consist of the word stem plus a prefix or suffix, have two morphemes each (as in "pre" and "date"). "Predates" (prefix, word stem, and suffix) has three morphemes. Semantics is the study of meaning in a language. Syntax is the set of rules for structuring a language, that is, for ordering words into sentences. Grammar, then, is the general term that includes the rules of sound, the rules of meaning, and the rules of syntax.

Psychologists investigate language abilities in many different ways. To learn about the production of speech, they observe the way people speak and then analyze their speech; to learn about understanding, they observe the way people respond to the speech of others. An important way to learn about human linguistic abilities is to study the way they first appear among young children.

In recent years, researchers have devised ingenious ways of studying the language abilities of young children. Infants who are sucking on a pacifier while listening to a sound decrease their sucking rate when they habituate, or get used to, the sound; they will step up their rate when a new sound is presented, thus showing the experimenter that they can tell the difference between one sound and another. Another measure of habituation is a slowing of the heart rate, which also increases in response to a new sound. The rate at which babies turn their heads to a new sound is another behavioral measure. Another recent way to measure the discrimi-

FIGURE 8-1 Grammar *Every language has a grammar which includes rules of sound, meaning, and structure.*

Phonology: The study of speech sounds	*Semantics:* The study of meaning	*Syntax:* The study of linguistic structure
Phonemes: s, k, a, t	*Morphemes:*	(*Example:* "The girl skates." instead of "Skates girl the." or "Girl the skates" or "The skates girl.")
Single morphemes { "skate" (noun) "skate" (verb) ". . . s" ". . . ed"		
"skates" "skated" } These words each consist of two morphemes.		

nation of different sounds is through *auditory evoked responses (AER)*. In this procedure, electrodes fastened to a baby's scalp measure the brain responses elicited by sounds, and differences in these responses are interpreted as evidence that the baby is discriminating between the sounds (Molfese, Molfese, & Carrell, 1982).

It's easier, of course, to study the language abilities of older children. Researchers tape-record samples of their speech, perhaps for an hour or two a week, and then analyze what they say. Since it's often important to know what a child is doing as she's speaking, videotaping has become popular. To test the ability to hear or reproduce speech sounds, children are asked to imitate a word or a sentence. To find out what they know about linguistic rules, they may be asked to say something. For example, a child may be shown a funny-looking creature and told, "This is a wug. There's another one. There are two . . .?" If he says "wugs," he has shown that he knows how to make plurals in English since he could not have heard this made-up word anywhere else. To measure comprehension, researchers ask children to choose among pictures or objects or to act out something ["Make the (toy) horse kick the (toy) cow"].

How Children Learn a Language

Long before a child says his first word, generally some time between 12 and 18 months of age, an enormous amount of language learning has taken place. Some of this learning occurs so early that it seems as if the basic form and structure of a language system are programmed into our genes, so that we are born with built-in mechanisms for the acquisition of language. A 1-day-old baby will move her body, for example, in the same rhythm as the adult speech sounds she hears around her (Condon & Sander, 1974). A 3-day-old baby can tell his mother's voice from a stranger's (DeCasper & Fifer, 1980). And a 1-month-old can tell the difference

Language gives us tools for learning about the world. As we get more sophisticated, we learn that a cloud can be a nimbus, a cumulus, a stratus, or a cirrus, but at the beginning all we need to know is that "they're all clouds." (Drawing by Gahan Wilson; © 1984 The New Yorker Magazine, Inc.)

"That's a cloud, too. They're all clouds."

This little girl seems to be remembering what it felt like to touch the cactus. She's probably using a single word to describe it— maybe a modifier like "sharp" or "hurt." Such modifiers are often among children's first spoken words, along with names of things ("flower"), words that express feelings ("ouch"), and action words ("touch"). (© Michal Heron/ Woodfin Camp & Assoc.)

between sounds as alike as "pah" and "bah" (Eimas, Siqueland, Jusczyk, & Vigorito, 1971).

PRELINGUISTIC SPEECH   Before babies say that first real word, they utter a variety of sounds in a sequence tied fairly closely to chronological age. First they *cry*, with the crying taking on different patterns, intensities, and pitches to indicate hunger, sleepiness, anger, or pain. At about six weeks they *coo* when they're happy, and at 4 to 6 months they *babble*, repeating a variety of simple consonant and vowel sounds ("ma-ma-ma-ma"). During the second half of the first year, they listen to sounds around them, *accidentally imitate* these sounds, then imitate themselves. At about nine or ten months they *consciously imitate* other people's sounds even though they don't understand them. During these last three stages babies acquire their basic repertoire of sounds, and during the second year they string these sounds together in ways that mimic the patterns and rhythms of sentences, even though they make no sense—at least to anyone besides the baby (Lenneberg, 1967; Eisenson, Auer, & Irwin, 1963).

LINGUISTIC SPEECH
The First Words   Baby says her first word! Usually this happens at about one year. This word can be any simple syllable and can have a variety of meanings, the one at any given time having to be interpreted by those close to her by the context in which she says it. She points to a cracker or toy and says "da." (Meaning: "I want that.") She crawls to the door and says "da." (Meaning: "I want to go out.") She smiles at her father and says "da." (Meaning: "I'm glad you're home, Daddy.") These first words are called *holophrases* because they express a complete thought in a single word.

Children differ considerably in the kinds of words they use first (Nelson, 1973; 1981). Among the first fifty words spoken by one group of eighteen 1- and 2-year-olds, the most common were *names* of things, either in the general sense ("da" for "dog") or the specific sense (the name of one particular dog). Others were *action* words ("bye-bye"); *modifiers* ("hot"); words that express *feelings or relationships* ("no"); and a very few words that fulfill a solely *grammatical function* ("for") (Nelson, 1973).

After children acquire a few words at about one year, there seems to be a plateau of several months when they add very few additional words (Nelson, 1979). This may be a period of growing language understanding, when children use words to structure their own thinking more than for communication.

The First Sentences: Brown's First and Second Stages At twenty-six months, Nancy said her first four-word sentence. She looked up from the stroller in which she was riding and told her father, "I dropped my shoe." Clearly a practical thing to be able to say. Some children speak in sentences earlier than this, some later. While prelinguistic speech is fairly closely tied to chronological age, linguistic speech is not. In fact, Roger Brown (1973a; 1973b) of Harvard University, who has done a great deal of work on this phase of language acquisition, maintains that knowing a child's age tells us very little about his or her language development.

Brown prefers to discuss syntactic skill in terms of mean length of utterance (MLU), the average length of utterances in morphemes (units of meaning). A child is in stage 1 when he first begins to combine morphemes and words, making his MLU over 1.0 and in stage 2 when it is 2.0 (and when he can actually utter as many as seven morphemes, even though the mean, or average, is only two). The child advances with each increase of 0.5 MLU, up to stage 5.

Stage 1 is primitive speech, when tense and case endings, articles, and prepositions are missing (as in "That ball," "More ball," "All gone ball," "Hit ball," "Big ball," "Book table," "Go store," "Mommy sock"). When the MLU is 1.5, the child may string two basic relations together ("Adam hit" and "Hit ball") to get a more complicated relation ("Adam hit ball").

In *stage 2*, children acquire fourteen functional morphemes, including articles ("a," "the"), prepositions ("in," "on"), plurals, verb endings, and forms of the verb "to be" ("am," "are," "is"). Children start to use these forms gradually, sometimes over several years. In his intensive study of three children, Adam, Eve, and Sarah, Brown (1973a) noted that the variation in rate of development even among such a small sample is great, but that the order in which the children acquired the different constructions was almost constant.

Stages 3, 4, and 5 Children leave stage 2 at a variety of ages, and their speech becomes longer and more complex. Speech in *stage 3* has been called *telegraphic* because it contains many utterances like "Put dolly table," but this term is misleading because it implies that children edit their sentences as adults do with telegrams. Stage 4 grammar is close to that of adults, even though children are still learning some syntactical niceties. They can string together two sentences but still make a lot of grammatical mistakes and often can't use the subjunctive ("I wish we were going swimming today"); can't make up tag questions ("You are coming, aren't you?"); and can't deal with the meaning in such sentences as "John promised Mary to shovel the driveway" (they think Mary's

---

First words of several children:

Nancy: "da-da"—11 months
Jennifer: "da-da"—10 months
Dorri: "bye-bye"—9 months
Stefan: "dis"—11 months
Eddie: "da-dee"—10 months
Marie (Eddie's twin sister): "da-dee" and "bird"—10 months
Elizabeth: "mom-mom" and "bagel"—11 months

going to do the shoveling) (N. Chomsky, 1969). While *stage 5*, embodying full competence, occurs by late childhood, and no change in handling syntax occurs beyond puberty, vocabulary and style continue to improve into adulthood. Very little research has been done on these last two stages.

Some Characteristics of Early Speech (Stages 1, 2, and 3) Just as children are not miniature adults, neither is their speech a simplified version of adult language. It has a character all its own, with its own rules—even though these rules change over time. Children speaking German, Russian, Finnish, Samoan, or even English, show similar patterns (Slobin, 1971). How, then, do young children form their speech?

- *They simplify:* Children utter just enough to get their meaning across, omitting many parts of speech that adults consider essential (as in "Nancy go store" for "I want to go to the store" or "No drink milk" for "I don't want to drink any more milk").
- *They overregularize rules:* At the beginning of stage 3 many children who had used the correct words for "mice" and "went" and other exceptions to grammatical rules begin to say things like "mouses" and "goed." Why? They haven't regressed to a lower stage; instead, they've learned the rules of their grammar for forming past tense and plural nouns and are now using these rules consistently. Now they need to learn the exceptions to the rules.
- *They overgeneralize:* Sometimes children apply concepts too broadly. Young children's tendency to call all men "Daddy" and all furry creatures "kitty" is exemplified by one child who called both her older sisters "Mom," in addition to her mother (Nelson, 1973). Apparently this child had overgeneralized the caretaking role.
- *They understand grammatical relations that they cannot yet express:* A child early in stage 1 may understand that a dog is chasing a cat but cannot explain the complete action. He may say "puppy chase," "chase kitty," or "puppy kitty," but not until the end of this stage will he be able to string together "puppy chase kitty."

Theories about the Way We Acquire Language

The major theories about why and how children learn language range along a continuum on the relative influences of environment and heredity. Those who believe most strongly in the power of the environment are the learning theorists, while those most convinced of an inborn capacity for learning language are the nativists. We'll look at these views at either extreme and then examine one based on interaction between the two.

LEARNING THEORIES   According to the behaviorist B. F. Skinner (1957), we learn language the way we learn everything else—through reinforcement, discrimination, and generalization. Parents shape their children's production of speech by reinforcing those sounds that are like adult speech. Children learn to generalize and abstract from the sounds they're reinforced for and eventually produce an effective language. Evidence favoring this view is the greater amount of babbling by babies reared at

All over the world the first sentences of small children are being as painstakingly taped, transcribed, and analyzed as if they were the last sayings of great sages. Which is a surprising fate for the likes of "That doggie," "No more milk," and "Hit ball."
(Brown, 1973a, p. 97)

home, who presumably are noticed and reinforced more often than those reared in an institution, who vocalize less (Brodbeck & Irwin, 1946). Evidence against it is the fact that parents generally do not correct the grammar of their young children (Brown, Cazden, & Bellugi, 1969).

Social learning theory stresses the importance of observation and imitation (Bandura, 1977; Mowrer, 1960). In other words, children hear their parents speak, copy them, are reinforced for this behavior, and thus learn the language. Certainly this theory explains some aspects of language acquisition since children in English-speaking nations speak English rather than French or Swahili. But imitation does not explain many aspects of language development. For one thing, many of the things children say are novel. The little girl who didn't know the word for "knee" and called it an "elbow of the leg" had not heard this description before and so could not have imitated a model. Furthermore, it's highly unlikely that children come up with words like "mouses" and "goed" through observation and imitation.

NATIVISM   According to this view, human beings have an inborn capacity for acquiring language and learn to talk as naturally as they learn to walk. Noam Chomsky (1965; 1968) of the Massachusetts Institute of Technology proposes that the human brain is specifically constructed to give us this innate ability. He calls this inborn ability to learn language the language acquisition device (LAD). LAD enables children to analyze the language they hear and extract grammatical rules, with which they are able to create new sentences that no one has ever spoken before. Our brains are programmed to extract these rules; all we need are the basic experiences that will activate our innate language capacity.

Evidence for this viewpoint rests partly in the fact that all normal children learn their native language, no matter how complex, mastering the basics in the same age-related sequence. It also draws credibility from certain biological characteristics of human beings. We are, for example, the only species whose brain is larger on one side than on the other. This size difference between the hemispheres is consistent with the speculation that there is an innate mechanism for language in the left hemisphere. Our language skills may be impaired by lesions in the brain that do not affect other mental and motor skills, pointing to a localized structure specifically designed to provide language capacity (Lenneberg, 1969). Furthermore, the "ongoing dance of the neonate with human speech" that Condon and Sanders (1974) found in the tendency of newborns to move at the same tempo as the speech sounds they heard suggests that even before birth something in our brains may lay down the form and structure of language.

The extreme nativist approach has its own shortcomings in explaining the development of speech. Some learning has to take place, of course, if children are to learn the rules of English rather than the rules of German or Japanese. Also, this theory does not take into account the considerable individual differences among children which do exist. And finally, Chomsky has not addressed issues related to the meaning of the words children use nor to the social context in which they use it.

The distinction between what Skinner and Chomsky are saying is made easier for me by imagining moving to a new city, say Washington, D.C., and finding my way around. Suppose I knew nothing about the layout of streets. Gradually through many forays, mistakes, instructions from others, I would get my bearings. If I lived in the city long enough, I might even get to a point at which I had a kind of cognitive map. But this cognitive model of Washington's structure would be induced from my experience. In the second case I imagine going to Washington with a street map in my possession and constantly in use. I would check all my experiences against the map, filling in details with time. I would not have to discover, for example, that streets are laid out like spokes and wheels, that being given by the street map. I would have to discover the physical appearance of the various streets, that not being evident from the map. If I imagine that the map is given innately in the second case instead of by Exxon, I have a grasp of the essentially philosophical difference between Chomsky and Skinner. (Whitehurst, 1982, in Wolman, 1982, pp. 368–369)

Even young children intuitively simplify their vocabulary and syntax when they talk to infants and toddlers. (Susan Johns/Photo Researchers, Inc.)

Today, most psychologists believe that language develops through the active interaction between children and those who care for them. Infants enter the world with some inborn language capacity, as seen in their ability to discriminate fine variations in sounds, to distinguish and respond to their mothers' voices as compared to the voices of other women, and to move in rhythm with adult speech. This basic capacity lets them benefit from the specialized environmental input called "motherese."

Here we see a classic example of the failure to imitate:

She said, "My teacher holded the baby rabbits and we patted them."
I asked, "Did you say the teacher held the baby rabbits?"
She answered: "Yes."
I then asked: "What did you say she did?"
She answered again: "She holded the baby rabbits and we patted them."
"Did you say she held them tightly?" I asked.
"No," she answered. "She holded them loosely."
(Gleason, 1967, cited in Cazden, 1971)

MOTHERESE   When you're with a baby or toddler, do you find yourself talking "baby talk" and using a higher voice pitch than usual? If so, you're speaking "motherese," something most adults do intuitively and something that's important in helping children learn a language. While the word "motherese" reflects the fact that most research in this area has studied language between children and their mothers, the term is, in fact, more general. It refers to language addressed to children by mothers, fathers, other adults, and even older children, who generally talk to small children differently from the way they speak to their age-mates. Studies of the social context of language learning have led to explorations of the way adults talk to children and have led to the conclusion that such modifications in speech are essential in teaching children their native language.

How do adults change their speech in talking to small children? Catherine E. Snow (1972) examined the speech of middle-class mothers and of women who had no children themselves and were rarely with children. Mothers and nonmothers alike made similar adjustments, speaking quite

Fathers, too, speak "motherese," a simplified form of speech in which word endings are omitted, pronouns are avoided, sentences are short, and a great deal of repetition occurs. These modifications of usual adult speech help children learn the language. (© Harold W. Hoffman 1976/Photo Researchers, Inc.)

differently to 2-year-olds than to 10-year-olds. They simplified what they said, repeated it either exactly or by rephrasing the same idea, and used fewer pronouns and verbs.

When the child was not actually present, however, as in experiments in which the adults were asked to make tapes addressed to children of these ages, the adult did not modify her speech as much. Other studies have found that motherese does not begin to function fully early in infancy—only when babies respond with a glimmer of understanding to what the adult is saying (Molfese, Molfese, & Carrell, 1982). Mothers tend to overestimate the conversational abilities of infants, but as they attribute such skills to them and talk to them as if they had them, the children develop them. Children, then, are active partners in these conversations, showing by their expressions, their actions, and their own speech how closely they're following the adults' speech.

Other studies have shown that adults speaking to small children modify what they talk about, as well as the way they talk about it. They tend to talk about down-to-earth, everyday topics—what the child can see or hear, what he has just seen or done or is about to see or do, what the child himself might want to know. As Snow (1977, p. 41) points out, "Mothers make very predictable comments about very predictable topics," a tendency that helps children learn language because they can add their own knowledge to what they hear to help them work out the meaning.

What is the function of motherese? Emotionally, it provides a framework for social interaction between adult and child, helping to develop the relationship between them. Socially, it teaches the child how to carry on a conversation—how to introduce a topic, comment and expand on an idea, and take turns talking. Linguistically, it teaches a child how to use new words, how to structure phrases, how to put ideas into language. It appears vital to the learning of speech.

We see this in the language retardation of children with normal hearing who grow up in homes with deaf parents who communicate with them through sign language. No matter how fluent the children are in "signing" (showing their ability to learn a language) and no matter how much television they watch, they don't develop fluency in spoken language unless adults speak to them, which may not happen until they go to school (Moskowitz, 1978). Other research has shown that young Dutch children who watched German TV every day didn't learn German (Snow, Arlman-Rupp, Hassing, Jobse, Joosten, & Vorster, 1976). To learn how to speak, children need practice.

It seems, then, that language development is based on an innate mechanism that depends both on maturation and on certain kinds of language experience for its full flowering.

Two Controversies in Linguistics

IS THERE A CRITICAL PERIOD FOR ACQUIRING LANGUAGE?   You may know an older person who came to this country twenty, thirty, or more years ago—and yet still speaks with a pronounced foreign accent. On the other hand, if you know someone who came to this country as a small child, she or he probably speaks English in tones as unaccented as those spoken by a native. This common phenomenon is one of the bases for thinking that there is a *critical period* for learning a language, that the brain of a child who has not yet reached puberty is organized to encourage the acquisition of language, while something happens in the brain during the early teens that changes this linguistic ability.

Eric Lenneberg (1969), one of the strongest proponents of the critical period for acquiring language, offers other evidence for this viewpoint. He points to the fact that language correlates better with motor development, an important index of maturation, than it does with chronological age (see Table 8-1). Furthermore, he notes that children who suffer injury to the left hemisphere of the brain before their early teens may temporarily lose some speech ability but quickly regain it if the right hemisphere is intact. If such lesions occur during adolescence or adulthood, however, any loss of language skills is likely to be irreversible. Apparently, says Lenneberg, left-right specialization does not take place until puberty. Until then, the right hemisphere can take over if injury occurs to the left. He maintains that the critical period "coincides with the time at which the human brain attains its final state of maturity in terms of structure, function, and biochemistry" (p. 639).

A poignant test of this hypothesis occurred in the case of "Genie," a girl discovered in 1970 (Fromkin, Krashen, Curtiss, Rigler, & Rigler, 1974; Curtiss, 1977; Pines, 1981). From the age of 20 months until her discovery at age 13½, Genie (not her real name) had been kept confined in a small room where no one spoke to her. When Genie was brought to a California

Ten linguists working full time for ten years to analyze the structure of the English language could not program a computer with the ability for language acquired by an average child in the first ten or even five years of life. (Moskowitz, 1978, p. 92)

TABLE 8-1   Correlation of Motor and Language Development

Age (Years)	Motor Milestones	Language Milestones
0.5	Sits using hands for support; unilateral reaching	Cooing sounds change to babbling by introduction of consonantal sounds
1	Stands; walks when held by one hand	Syllabic reduplication; signs of understanding some words; applies some sounds regularly to signify persons or objects, that is, the first words
1.5	Prehension and release fully developed; gait propulsive; creeps downstairs backward	Repertoire of 3 to 50 words not joined in phrases; trains of sounds and intonation patterns resembling discourse; good progress in understanding
2	Runs (with falls); walks stairs with one foot forward only	More than 50 words; two-word phrases most common; more interest in verbal communication; no more babbling
2.5	Jumps with both feet; stands on one foot for 1 second; builds tower of six cubes	Every day new words; utterances of three and more words; seems to understand almost everything said to him; still many grammatical deviations
3	Tiptoes 3 yards (2.7 meters); walks stairs with alternating feet; jumps 0.9 meter	Vocabulary of some 1000 words; about 80 percent intelligibility; grammar of utterances close approximation to colloquial adult; syntactic mistakes fewer in variety, systematic, predictable
4.5	Jumps over rope; hops on one foot; walks on line.	Language well established; grammatical anomalies restricted either to unusual constructions or to the more literate aspects of discourse

Lenneberg, *Science*, Vol. 164, May 9, 1969, p. 636.

hospital, she weighed only 59 pounds, could not straighten her arms or legs, could not chew, had no control over bladder and bowel functions, and did not speak. She recognized only her own name and the word "sorry."

Genie's linguistic progress during the following nine years (until her mother regained custody and cut her off from the professionals who had been caring for her and teaching her) both disconfirms and supports the critical period hypothesis. The fact that she learned any language at all at this age may be a refutation of the existence of a critical period. Then again, it may not. She did acquire quite a bit of language ability, learning many words and stringing them together in primitive though rule-governed sentences. Yet even after nine years of progress and intensive work with psycholinguists, she never used language normally. She never asked questions, and, four years after putting words together, "her speech remained, for the most part, like a somewhat garbled telegram" (Pines, 1981, p. 29).

The fact that she was just beginning to show signs of puberty may indicate that she was still in the critical period, although near its endpoint. The fact that she had apparently said a few words before being locked up at the age of 20 months may mean that her language learning mechanisms had been triggered early in the critical period, thus allowing later learning to occur. And the fact that she was so abused and neglected may have retarded her so much emotionally, socially, and intellectually that she cannot be considered a true test of the critical period. A number of tests suggested that Genie was using her right hemisphere to learn language, possibly because development of the left hemisphere is limited to a critical period following the acquisition of language at the proper time (Curtiss, 1977).

DOES THOUGHT STRUCTURE LANGUAGE OR DOES LANGUAGE STRUCTURE THOUGHT? While we have only one word for snow, Eskimos have separate words for "snow packed hard like ice," "falling snow," and "snow on the ground." The question is: Do they think differently about snow because they have the vocabulary to do so? Or have they made up those words because they think differently? Can Eskimos make discriminations among types of snow that we, with our meager vocabulary of snow words, cannot?

This concept, that the language we use affects the way we perceive and think, is known as the linguistic relativity hypothesis, or the Whorfian hypothesis, after its most vigorous modern proponent, Benjamin Lee Whorf (1956). Whorf maintains that language does not simply provide a neutral means for giving voice to ideas but instead plays an active part in shaping those ideas. Thus people who speak different languages perceive the world differently and think differently.

As fascinating as Whorf's observations are, they are not decisive. People from Florida can distinguish the preceding types of snow and can describe them with phrases. Furthermore, if these Floridians go to Colorado to ski, they are likely to add new words to their vocabulary like "powder," "corn," and "ice" to describe kinds of snow. They can learn to make distinctions, or *discriminations,* among the different kinds of snow. Brown and Lenneberg (1954) maintain that the major distinctions in such vocabulary differences arise from differences in the frequency of referring to a particular phenomenon. The more you talk about something, the more likely you are to have developed a short word for it.

Recent efforts to make the English language less sexist (gender-biased) have built on this view that language structure shapes a person's view of reality and, therefore, carries serious psychological implications. Thus, a language that uses masculine words to apply to both sexes ("mankind") and that defines occupational titles by sex ("mailman," "laundress") puts forth a stereotyped view of people and suggests that the male is the more important sex.

Another instance of the interrelationship between grammatical structure and thought can be seen in the lack of a structure in the Chinese language for the kind of abstract thinking known as a *counterfactual hypothesis,* such as: "If John F. Kennedy had not been assassinated, Lyndon Johnson might never have become President of the United States." As a speaker of English, you probably had no trouble following the meaning of this sentence. If your native language were Chinese, however, you probably would (Bloom, 1981).

The Chinese language has no structure to express this kind of thinking, and would have to cast the sentence differently: "Since John F. Kennedy was assassinated, Lyndon Johnson was able to become President." As you can see, the meaning is changed. How does this difference in language structure affect thought? It seems to cause difficulty in certain labo-

The languages of the world, like the professional vocabularies within one language, are so many different windows on reality. We should no more wish away the differences among languages than we should wish away the differences among ourselves.
(Brown and Lenneberg, 1958, p. 18)

ratory reasoning tasks and in some areas of science and math. However, the proficiency of many native-born Chinese in these last two fields seems to indicate that speakers of Chinese are able to overcome the obstacles.

TESTS OF THE LINGUISTIC RELATIVITY HYPOTHESIS   To test this hypothesis, Brown and Lenneberg (1954) developed the concept of *codability* of words. Highly codable words are those that speakers of the same language respond quickly to and agree on, both with one another and from one occasion to another for the same person. Applying codability to colors, "red" would be highly codable, while "mauve" would not be. Brown and Lenneberg found that the most codable colors were the best remembered. For many years this finding was considered a demonstration of the effect of language on perception and memory.

More recently, the same concept was applied in color naming and memory tests given to English-speaking Americans and to New Guinea Dani, a stone-age tribe who have just two names for color, emphasizing brightness rather than hue (Heider & Olivier, 1972). The Americans, with their large color vocabulary, named many more colors. However, when subjects were shown a single color chip for 5 seconds and then, 30 seconds later, were asked to pick it out from an array of 40 chips, both groups performed similarly. Not having names for colors did not seriously handicap the Dani from perceiving and remembering them. Colors that were highly codable in English were remembered best by both groups, suggesting that certain colors are remembered best by everyone, no matter what their language. These findings have led many psychologists to discard the Whorfian hypothesis, while others think that color naming is the wrong place to look for an effect of language on thought.

The development of language gives us a symbol system that lets us label the people, places, events, and things in our lives. Through these

"What we have here is a failure to communicate," a common problem in everyday life when we forget to take the viewpoint of our listener. To the police officer in this cartoon, the route to (X) *is clear; as a result, he may be talking too fast or he may be omitting crucial information. (Drawing by Stevenson;* ©1976 *The New Yorker Magazine, Inc.)*

BOX 8-1

CAN ANIMALS LEARN LANGUAGE?

During the 1970s, a stir was created in linguistic circles by the likes of Washoe, Sarah, Lana, and Nim Chimpsky (Fouts, 1974; Premack & Premack, 1972; Rumbaugh & Gill, 1977; Terrace, 1979). All these celebrities are chimpanzees who had been taught to communicate to varying degrees through such mediums as American Sign Language (ASL), the set of hand gestures used by deaf persons (Washoe and Nim); Yerkish, an artificial visual language (Lana); and an artificial language of different colored and shaped plastic chips (Sarah). Earlier studies had recognized the impossibility of teaching apes actually to speak because of their inadequate vocal apparatus (Hayes, 1951; Kellogg & Kellogg, 1933), but these new researchers seemed to be getting around this problem by using nonvocal languages. (ASL is considered a language even though it doesn't

include one defined feature of language, spoken sounds, since it does embody the other crucial elements, especially the rules that allow signers to create new sentences.)

Enthusiasm greeted such news as Washoe's definition of a duck as a "waterbird," Sarah's ability to follow such directions as "Sarah, insert apple pail banana dish," Lana's ability to "say" "Please machine give juice," and Nim's sixteen-sign utterance, "Give orange me give eat orange me eat orange give me eat orange give me you." The trainer of Koko, a gorilla, even said, "Language is no longer the exclusive domain of man" (Patterson, quoted in Terrace, 1979).

However, recent critics of these and other projects that purported to teach apes various kinds of language state that the apes' performances do not demonstrate an ability for learning a language

as we define it (Limber, 1977; Terrace, 1979; Terrace, Petitto, Sanders, & Bever, 1979). It all seems to come down to the fact that while apes can learn to use meaningful symbols, can generalize them correctly to new situations, and can communicate after a fashion with human beings, they don't learn the creative aspect of language, which involves knowing how to use rules to create an infinite number of new expressions and complex sentences.

One psychologist had initially felt that "his" chimp, Nim Chimpsky, was indeed using a grammar—until he analyzed videotapes of Nim's "conversations" with his teacher. At that point, Terrace (1979) discovered that the word sequences that had seemed like sentences were, in fact, subtle imitations of the teacher's own sequences. Furthermore, even

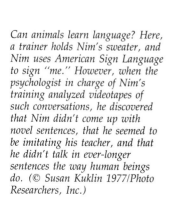

Can animals learn language? Here, a trainer holds Nim's sweater, and Nim uses American Sign Language to sign "me." However, when the psychologist in charge of Nim's training analyzed videotapes of such conversations, he discovered that Nim didn't come up with novel sentences, that he seemed to be imitating his teacher, and that he didn't talk in ever-longer sentences the way human beings do. (© Susan Kuklin 1977/Photo Researchers, Inc.)

though Nim learned more and more words, he didn't show the kind of increase in mean length of utterance that accompanies normal human speech development. Nim was not as grammatically competent as he had first seemed, and, according to Terrace, neither were any of the other "talking" apes.

At this point none of the apes have shown the kind of creative, complex production of meaningful phrases that are part of a full-fledged language. However, we do have to remember that none of the apes have had the many years or the intensity of language training that children receive automatically before they're able to understand and speak a language. If it were possible to provide such training (so far unworkable because chimpanzees become unmanageable and dangerous as they grow older), we might be able to draw a different conclusion.

labels we can communicate with others in our culture who attach similar meanings to these labels. In the next section, we'll see how individuals learn to apply similar labels to stimuli that they categorize into concepts.

FORMING CONCEPTS

If you were to be asked what you have in your closet, you might answer, "clothing." Or you might say "jackets, jeans, shirts, and shoes." In either case, you would not feel you had to describe every individual object in the closet. Both these answers demonstrate a vital aspect of human thought, the ability to organize a variety of different objects or events into concepts, which are categories of objects, events, or people. In forming categories, we group together items that have defining features in common. These concepts range from fairly narrow ones like *pullover sweaters*, to broader ones like *tops* (including sweaters, blouses, T-shirts), *sportswear*, *outerwear*, and so forth, to the broad category of *clothing*.

This ability to classify nonidentical things enables us to impose order on a world full of unique objects and happenings. It lets us generalize from previous experience and formulate general rules for thought and action. Early in life, for example, we learn to stay out of the way of fast-moving cars, trucks, and buses because we have formed the concept that speed and a large vehicle can be a dangerous combination. On the more abstract level, systems of morality, justice, and government rest on a foundation of concepts.

Well-Defined Concepts

A well-defined concept is one that can be specified by a set of clear, unambiguous *features*—such aspects as color, size, shape, or function, connected by a *rule*, or a relationship among them. Thus a baseball is a spherical object of a certain composition, size, weight, *and* texture, used for the purpose of playing a particular game. An eligible candidate for president of the United States is someone who was born in this country *and* is over 35 years old. A promising applicant for college is a high school student who has achieved good grades, *or* has scored high on aptitude and/or achievement tests, *or* has an interesting extracurricular background. The rules or relations in these examples are the words "and" and "or." In the first two examples, *all* the features have to be present for category membership ("and"), while in the last example, *only one* of the three features has to be present ("or").

In studying the way people form concepts, researchers often use a series of symbolic forms that differ in such features as size, shape, and

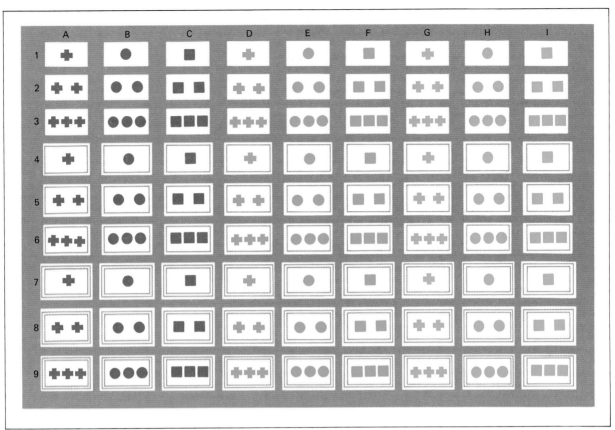

FIGURE 8-2 Stimuli from a
Concept-Learning Task *Stimuli
such as these are often used to
investigate the way people arrive at
the rules that define concepts.
(From Bruner, Goodnow, &
Austin, 1956, p. 42)*

color, and then ask subjects to tell which items are examples of an *unde-
fined* concept. The experimenter does not define the concept in question
for the subject but requires him or her to determine what the concept is
("all green circles") by figuring out which stimuli are and are not positive
examples of the concept in question (see Figure 8-2). In this way it's possible to see the kind of reasoning used in forming concepts. People usually
use systematic strategies rather than trial-and-error guessing. This shows
that concept formation is a thinking process. As such, it goes far beyond
the mindless strengthening or weakening of stimulus-response associations, as behaviorists had maintained. In fact, people do better in solving
concept formation problems if they have had training in formal logic
(Dodd, Kinsman, Klipp, & Bourne, 1971) or a great deal of practice in
learning concepts in the laboratory (Bourne, 1967, 1970).

People usually focus on one feature at a time. If the first positive example was "three red circles in two borders," a subject may choose "three
green circles in two borders." If he is told the second item is *not* an instance of the concept, what does he know? He knows color is crucial
because it's the only feature that has changed between the two examples.
If he's told the second item *is* an instance, he knows that color is not
relevant, but that number of circles or borders and/or shapes might be.

If the subject feels like gambling, after he has been told that the first
positive instance is three red circles in two borders, he might choose "*two
green* circles in two borders." If this *is* an instance, he has learned two

facts—that both number and color are irrelevant. If this is *not* an instance, he doesn't know which was crucial—changing the color or the number. This "focus gambling" is like the kind sometimes used in the game Botticelli, in which players try to guess which famous person another person is thinking of, by using questions that can only be answered yes or no. If I ask, "Is this a living, American male?" and you say "yes," I have three pieces of information; but if you say "no," I don't know whether any of these attributes apply. If I had asked, "Is this person living?" I would have one definite, specific place of information, no matter what your answer was.

Ill-Defined Concepts

The concepts we just described are considered well-defined because there's no likelihood of confusion between red and green, between circles and squares, between one border and two. All these distinctions are very clear. In real life, however, where we cannot control conditions the way we can in a laboratory, most concepts are ill-defined. That is, the features of one category often overlap with those in another, making it difficult to distinguish between them.

What, for example, is the difference between a magazine and a book? Is it the fact that a book is bound and a magazine is stapled? That a book is issued once and a magazine periodically? That a book is sold in bookstores and a magazine at newsstands? Suppose a publisher issues a yearly publication in a binding typical of that used for books. Is it a magazine, even though most magazines are published weekly or monthly? Or is it a book? If the publisher calls it a book, does that make it a book? If bookstores refuse to sell it, does that make it a magazine? Who decides?

In ill-defined concepts, then, the features and the rules that connect members of a category are not obvious. Ill-defined concepts tend to be learned by experience over time with members of the category rather than by learning a specific definition. The concept of clothing, for instance, is usually taught by example, not by definition. Young children learn to distinguish coats from hats not by being given lists of the features of each one but by being told, "This is a coat. That is a hat." In other words, we learn what comprises a concept by being given a series of examples and abstracting the rules for concept membership from these examples.

For example, you know what a game is. Come up with a definition for "game" before reading on.

Now check your definition. Does it include checkers but exclude dancing? Does it distinguish between amateur and professional sports? Should it? What are its features? What rules connect them?

TYPICALITY Even though many different items may fit into a particular concept category, some things have a firmer place in it than others. Some items seem to be more typical (that is, better examples) of a concept than others. To see how this works, let's say you were asked to respond yes or no as quickly as possible to such questions as "Is a robin a bird?" and "Is a penguin a bird?" Most people correctly answer yes to both questions, but are faster in replying to the question about robins than the one about penguins (Rips, Shohen, & Smith, 1973). A robin is more typical of bird than is penguin, probably because it has more of the defining features of

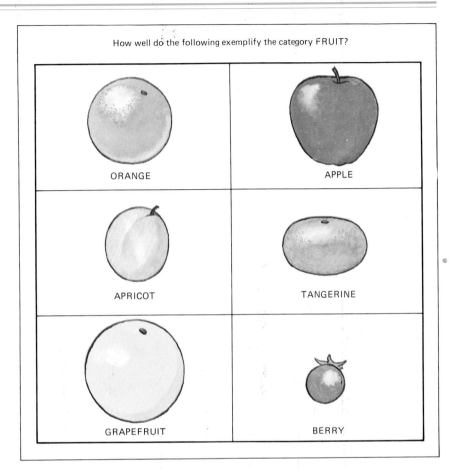

How well do the following exemplify the category FRUIT?

ORANGE

APPLE

APRICOT

TANGERINE

GRAPEFRUIT

BERRY

FIGURE 8-3 Typicality in Concept Formation *How well do each of the following exemplify the category "fruit"? (From Rosch, 1975)*

the category bird: A robin lays eggs and has feathers and wings, and it also flies, which a penguin does not do. When asked to rate different kinds of fruits on typicality (pictured in Figure 8-3), subjects rated orange and apple as good examples, apricot and tangerine as intermediate, and grapefruit and berry the lowest. These ratings correlated with reaction times, with answers affirming the more typical examples being faster (Rosch, 1975).

FAMILY RESEMBLANCE   One way of explaining the phenomenon of typicality is through the theory of family resemblance. You may, for example, look like your father, especially around the eyes. Your sister's nose may look like his. But you and your sister may not look much like each other. In a family, members resemble each other in various ways, and the essence of this family resemblance is a successive overlap of similarities. Members of a natural language category may be linked by the same type of "family resemblance" in which all the members have at least one feature in common with another member and some members share many of the same features (Wittgenstein, 1953).

To test the theory that typicality is related to the degree of feature overlap, college students were asked to rate the typicality of twenty objects from each of six categories (furniture, vehicle, fruit, etc.) (Rosch & Mervis,

FIGURE 8-4   *A Basic-Level Category: Chair*

1975). Another group of students were asked to list the attributes possessed by each item (for *bicycle*, features might include "two wheels," "pedals," and "you ride on them"). When scores between the two groups were compared, typicality and family resemblance ratings correlated very highly. The more features an item has in common with other members of a category, the more it will be considered a good and representative member.

BASIC-LEVEL CATEGORIES   In the real world, concepts are not arbitrary combinations of features and rules. Nor do they necessarily look, sound, or feel alike. Yet there is a basic level of abstraction at which we naturally divide things into categories (Rosch & Mervis, 1975). For example, what would you call the object pictured in Figure 8-4? You would probably say, "A chair," the answer most likely to be given by both children and adults. Yet this object also belongs to a higher-order category ("furniture") and a lower-order category ("kitchen chair"). People *can* classify an object (like a chair) in any of several ways. They could correctly indicate that it is a chair, a kitchen chair, a piece of furniture, or a manufactured object. Reaction time tasks show that people classify fastest at the basic level (chair). This suggests that basic-level categories are the ones we use in our daily dealings with objects. These basic-level categories are probably the ones that children learn to use earliest in naming and classifying objects (Rosch, Mervis, Gray, Johnson, & Boyer-Braem, 1976).

PROBLEM SOLVING

The world would be a totally chaotic place if we could not use language and form concepts. Concepts, as we've seen, allow us to generalize and thus to give order to our world. With this order, we know how to act when we meet new members of a category so we don't have to relearn how to behave at each encounter. Thus, by having a concept of "car," we know that this is a four-wheeled vehicle with the potential for taking us someplace—and also for damage. Since we have this concept, we can apply it to new cars (such as foreign ones, racers, and so forth) that we have never seen before.

With this ability, then, to form concepts, we can make generalizations about the world that let us impose our own order on its complexity, we can communicate with other people, and we can go on and solve at least some of the many problems we encounter as we go through life.

Consider this: It's Saturday night. Sara is getting married the following day. The shoes that go with her wedding dress are in the store where she bought them, being repaired. She forgot to pick them up, and now the store is closed, not to reopen till Monday. Sara has a problem. Finally, Sara's mother remembers that a friend of hers is a friend of the sister of the man who owns the shoe store. She calls her friend, who calls her friend, who calls her brother, who takes pity on the distraught bride and arranges to meet her at the store early the next morning to give her the shoes. Sara gets married in full wedding garb and everyone is happy. The problem has been solved.

The ability to find an answer to a question or a predicament, that is, to solve a problem, is a cognitive activity aimed at a goal. In this case, the goal was obtaining the shoes before Sunday afternoon. Problem solving can be either *routine* (using existing procedures) or *creative* (developing new procedures). Sara's mother's use of a familiar tool (the telephone) and a familiar activity (contacting people) puts her solution in the category of the routine. What creative procedures might Sara have devised for this problem?

Unlike language, problem solving seems to be a common activity among animals of lower orders. To explain how both people and animals solve problems, psychologists turn to one of several theories.

Theories on Problem Solving

LEARNING THEORY The learning theory, or associationist, approach to problem solving is exemplified in the work of Ivan Pavlov, John B. Watson, and Edward Lee Thorndike, whose philosophies and research were all introduced in Chapter 5. According to Thorndike, cats placed in "puzzle boxes" learned to pull the string that got them out by a trial-and-error process, rather than by a sudden flash of insight. He felt the cat was only learning a new habit because of the reward, or reinforcement, of getting out of the box and did not understand why tugging on the string led to escape.

GESTALT Sultan, a chimpanzee, is the star of the most famous experiments exemplifying the *Gestalt* approach (explained in Chapter 1), which were conducted by Wolfgang Kohler (1927). If bananas were placed outside Sultan's cage, out of reach, and he was given a stick, he would use the stick to pull the bananas to him. Sultan's problem occurred when neither of the two sticks he had was long enough to reach the bananas. He tried both to no avail and then walked away. Suddenly, however, he went back and figured out a way to put one stick inside the other, making the combination long enough to reach the bananas. According to Kohler, Sultan used *insight,* or what is often known as an "aha!" experience. He came up with a completely new, creative solution to his problem, which he continued to use in similar situations. (Repeat uses fell into the category of routine problem solving.)

Similar flashes of insight may have occurred to the black bears in the Great Smoky Mountains National Park, which have become expert at stealing food from human beings. One creative bear nicknamed the "Deep Creek Leaper" climbs a tree from which a camper has suspended a pack containing food until the bear is above the pack; the bear then leaps from the tree, grabbing the pack on her way down. Another was spotted stretching to her full length up a pole so that a cub clinging to her shoulders could reach the pack at the top (*New York Times,* 1983).

Gestalt psychologist Karl Duncker considers a major barrier to effective problem solving to be functional fixedness, or an overreliance on old ways of seeing and doing things that keeps the individual from thinking of novel possibilities.

INFORMATION PROCESSING According to this approach (discussed in Chapters 5, 6, and 7), problem solving is a complex activity comprising several processes. These processes include: registering information, retrieving material from memory that's related to this information, and using both kinds of knowledge in a purposeful way. Study of information processing has grown along with use of computers, starting in the 1950s. Scientists have tried to figure out how people solve problems so they could program computers to use similar processes, producing *artificial intelligence*. This area of research is called *computer simulation*.

Stages of Problem Solving

Generally, say psychologists, we go through three or four stages in solving problems. According to one theory (Bourne, Dominowski, & Loftus, 1979), we *prepare*, we *produce*, and we *evaluate*.

1. PREPARATION   First, we need to understand what the problem is. Our interpretation can be affected by the way the problem is presented, as seen in Figure 8-5. Duncker (1945) gave one group of subjects three cardboard boxes, one holding matches, one holding thumbtacks, and one holding candles. He then asked them to mount a candle upright on a nearby screen. These subjects had a great deal of trouble solving the problem, whereas other subjects given the same materials solved it much more easily. The difference lay in the way the materials were presented. The second group received the boxes empty, thus allowing them to visualize one of the boxes as a base to mount the candle. Those in the first group suffered from functional fixedness in their inability to overcome the notion that the boxes were containers and thus not candle holders.

2. PRODUCTION   Then we need to generate possible solutions. Simple problems may require nothing more than getting the correct information from long-term memory, while more complicated problems require more complex strategies. The two basic kinds of solution strategies are algorithms and heuristics.

An algorithm is a strategy that exhausts every possible answer till it comes up with the correct solution; used diligently, it guarantees a correct solution. For example, given the anagram UHB, an algorithm would put the three letters in every possible combination (BUH, BHU, HBU, UBH) until the correct order (HUB) is found. Algorithms are rarely used partly because they don't exist for many problems and partly because when they do they can be too time-consuming.

A heuristic is a "rule of thumb" that can lead to a very quick solution or to no solution at all. Heuristics may involve *planning* that ignores some of the problem information while focusing on other information (solving a three-letter anagram quickly by realizing that the vowel probably goes between the two consonants and not even trying out words that don't fit this pattern). Or it may involve a *means-end analysis* that tests for a difference between the state that currently exists (your king in check in a chess game, meaning that you'll lose if you don't get him out of check) and one that is desired (winning the game) and doing something to reduce the difference (planning moves that will first get the king out of check and will then, one by one, put you in a stronger position). Heuristics may also involve *working backward*, figuring out what the ideal situation would be (Sara's possession of the shoes) and then determining what step will lead to the ideal and what has to be done before that step (contacting the owner of the store, who can be reached by his sister, who can be called by her friend, etc.).

The study of information processing—the way human beings register it, retrieve it from memory, and use it in a purposeful way—has grown along with the use of computers, as researchers try to program computers to "think" like humans. (© 1983 Robin Moyer/Black Star)

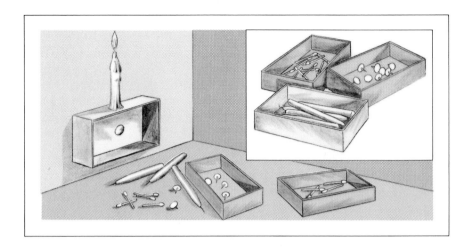

FIGURE 8-5 The Candle Problem *Given the tacks, matches, and candles, mount the candle upright on a screen.*

3. EVALUATION We have to decide how good our solution is. This is easy for some problems. If we unscramble an anagram and come up with a word, we know we're right. If we get the shoes in time for the wedding, we've solved the problem as well as we need to. Many problems, however, have less precise goals and are harder to judge. There may be more than one possible solution, and we then have to determine which one is best. (This is often the case in a multiple-choice exam in which two answers may be correct but one is better than the other.)

When a problem is solved in a moment of *insight*, evaluation is so quick that the person or animal is not aware of it, simply knowing that he has come up with the solution. Before we say more about insight, we want to emphasize that the three stages we've just presented are not necessarily gone through 1–2–3. Often there's a great deal of moving back and forth as we produce a possible solution (stage 2), evaluate it (stage 3), then go back to reinterpret the problem (stage 1).

"Aha" Solutions: Flashes of Insight and Leaps of Logic

How can two men play five games of checkers and each win the same number of games without any ties? How can you plant a total of ten trees in five rows of four trees each? If you have black and brown socks in your drawer in a ratio of 4:5, how many socks will you have to take out to make sure of having a pair the same color? How did the museum director know that the "old Roman coin" stamped with the date 350 B.C. was a fake?

SOLVING INSIGHT PROBLEMS Problems like the foregoing are generally solved through insight rather than from prior knowledge or laborious computation. From study of the way people reach their conclusions, Sternberg and Davidson (1982) identified three necessary intellectual processes—*selective encoding*, the ability to *encode* information (to see what's relevant, even if it isn't obvious, and to sort it out from the irrelevant); *selective combination*, the ability to *combine* different and seemingly unrelated bits of information; and *selective comparison*, the ability to discover a nonobvious relationship between new and old information. The role of selection is important in all three types of information processing.

If you assumed the checkers players were playing each other, faulty

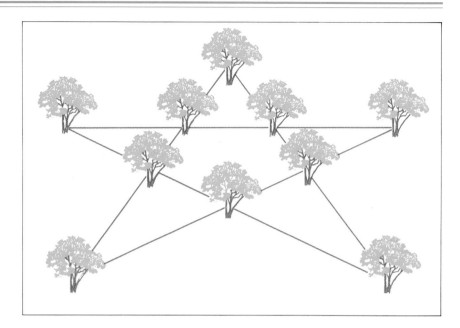

FIGURE 8-6 *Ten trees can be planted in five rows of four each if they are arranged in this nonparallel pattern.*

encoding got in the way of your solution. Since there were no ties and each player won the same number of games, they could not have been playing each other. If you did not think of planting the trees in a nonparallel pattern (see Figure 8-6), you were not combining the facts productively. If you didn't realize you need to draw out three socks to be sure of a pair, you were misled by the irrelevant 4:5 ratio and neglected to use prior knowledge. (Of any three items of two different kinds, two are bound to be the same.)

The final problem demonstrates that insight is not enough. Prior knowledge is also important (the meaning of "B.C." and the fact that coins are stamped with the date when they are first made, a combination that leads to the conclusion that the coin could not have been stamped "B.C." 350 years before the birth of Christ). Other elements important for solving problems are the basic processes of planning, production, and evaluation; motivation (leading the solver to exert necessary effort); and style (being impulsive at some times, reflective at others).

INSIGHT AND INTELLIGENCE   The insight required to solve problems like these correlates with IQ but is not the same, discovered Sternberg and Davidson (1982) when they gave a battery of tests to thirty urban residents. They included tests of intelligence; insight; *deductive* reasoning (drawing a conclusion that is certain if the information given is true, as in "If all robins are birds and all birds lay eggs, then all robins lay eggs"); and *inductive* reasoning [drawing a probable conclusion, as in "Mary and John live in the same house and have the same name and Mary has a picture of John on her desk; therefore Mary and John are married." While Mary and John could be siblings or lovers with the same name, the conclusion is probably correct (Anderson, 1980, p. 329)].

High correlations showed up for insight and IQ, insight and inductive reasoning, with much more modest correlations between insight and deductive reasoning. The best indicators of IQ were insight problems that required the subject to sort out relevant from irrelevant information,

Water lilies double in area every 24 hours. At the beginning of the summer there is one water lily on a lake. It takes 60 days for the lake to become covered with water lilies. On what day is the lake half covered?

FIGURE 8-7 *Sternberg and Davidson (1982) found this problem to be a good predictor of IQ. To solve it, people had to realize that the key fact is that the number of lilies double every twenty-four hours.* Answer: day 59. *(From Sternberg & Davidson, 1982)*

while the poorest were "trick" questions that the subjects misread (see Figures 8-7 and 8-8). So performance on insight problems does, then, provide a good measure of intelligence. It would be interesting to see a similar testing program of the relationship between insight and creativity.

A farmer has 17 cows. All but nine break through a hole in the fence and wander away. How many are left?

FIGURE 8-8 *Sternberg and Davidson (1982) found this problem to be a poor predictor of IQ since answering it depends only on a careful reading of the second sentence.* Answer: 9. *(From Sternberg & Davidson, 1982)*

CREATIVITY

If Sir Isaac Newton had not had the creative ability to see things in a new and unusual light, he could have watched a million apples fall and never have come up with the law of gravity. (Culver Pictures, Inc.)

Einstein's discovery of the theory of relativity. Newton's of the law of gravity. Shakespeare's playwriting. Picasso's painting. Henry Ford's establishment of assembly-line production. The U.S. government's creation of the Social Security system. All of these are examples of creativity, the ability to see things in a new and unusual light, to see problems that no one else may even realize exist, and then to come up with new, unusual, and effective solutions. While creativity may seem a "more exalted topic" than problem solving (Hayes, 1978), it is, in fact, reasonable to think of creativity in terms of solutions to problems. The poet writing a sonnet is solving a problem, as is the scientist seeking a new alloy, the musician composing a symphony, the sculptor chiseling form from a block of marble, the social planner who'll be able to bail out the Social Security system from its present financial problems.

We can see the relationship between creativity and problem solving in the famous 9-dot problem. Look at Figure 8-9 and see whether you can come up with a solution. After a reasonable amount of time, look at Figure 8-10 and see some of the solutions others have come up with.

Measuring Creativity

Standard intelligence tests measure what Guilford (1967) calls *convergent thinking*, the ability to come up with a single correct or best answer. It's hard to measure *divergent thinking*, the ability to come up with new and unusual answers to a problem, but creative researchers have devised several tests to do just this. They ask questions like: "List all the uses you can think of for a brick," "Name all the words you can think of that start with A and end with D," and "Suppose that all humans had eyes in back of their heads as well as in front. List all the consequences and implications you can think of." Then these items are scored for *quantity* (how many different answers you came up with); *originality* (how different your answers are from those given by others); and *usefulness* (how important your answers are).

So far these tests are more important for research than for educational or vocational counseling. One problem is that they depend heavily on speed for their scoring, and creative people do not always give quick responses. Another is that while the tests are reliable (consistent), there's little or no evidence of their validity (their ability to predict creativity in real life). Results are mixed as to whether they really measure creativity in nontest situations (Anastasi, 1976). In one study, for example, advertising copywriters judged to be high on creativity did better on several tests of divergent thinking than did those judged low (Elliott, 1964). In another, little correlation showed between creativity and divergent thinking in a group of research scientists (Taylor, Smith, & Ghiselin, 1963). This kind of discrepancy isn't surprising. There may be many specific kinds of divergent thinking abilities—Guilford (1967) claims at least twenty-four. It's difficult to know just which ones are required for any given real-life problem. In addition, creativity seems to involve more than just divergent thinking. Motivation, prior knowledge, training, independence of spirit, and purposefulness all seem to play a part in producing creative work (Perkins, 1981),

FIGURE 8-9 The Nine-Dot Problem *Without lifting your pencil from the paper, draw no more than four lines that will cross through all nine dots.*

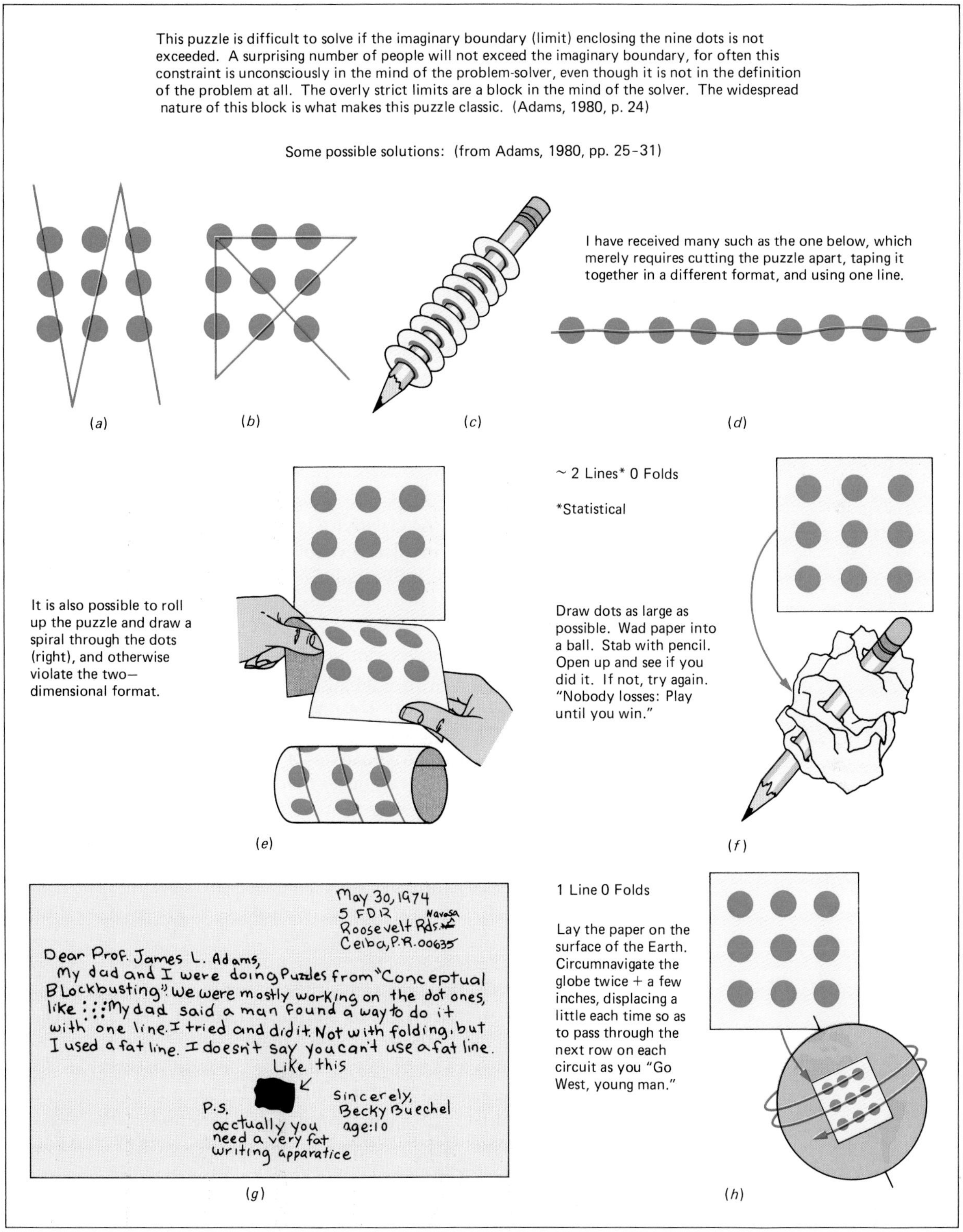

This puzzle is difficult to solve if the imaginary boundary (limit) enclosing the nine dots is not exceeded. A surprising number of people will not exceed the imaginary boundary, for often this constraint is unconsciously in the mind of the problem-solver, even though it is not in the definition of the problem at all. The overly strict limits are a block in the mind of the solver. The widespread nature of this block is what makes this puzzle classic. (Adams, 1980, p. 24)

Some possible solutions: (from Adams, 1980, pp. 25-31)

(a)   (b)   (c)

I have received many such as the one below, which merely requires cutting the puzzle apart, taping it together in a different format, and using one line.

(d)

It is also possible to roll up the puzzle and draw a spiral through the dots (right), and otherwise violate the two—dimensional format.

(e)

~ 2 Lines* 0 Folds

*Statistical

Draw dots as large as possible. Wad paper into a ball. Stab with pencil. Open up and see if you did it. If not, try again. "Nobody losses: Play until you win."

(f)

1 Line 0 Folds

Lay the paper on the surface of the Earth. Circumnavigate the globe twice + a few inches, displacing a little each time so as to pass through the next row on each circuit as you "Go West, young man."

(h)

May 30, 1974
5 FDR
Roosevelt Rds. Navasa
Ceiba, P.R. 00635

Dear Prof. James L. Adams,
My dad and I were doing Puzzles from "Conceptual Blockbusting" We were mostly working on the dot ones, like ⋮⋮⋮ My dad found a way to do it with one line. I tried and did it. Not with folding, but I used a fat line. I doesn't say you can't use a fat line. Like this

P.S. acctually you need a very fat writing apparatice

Sincerely,
Becky Buechel
age: 10

(g)

FIGURE 8-10 Some Possible Solutions for the Nine-Dot Problem *(From Adams, 1980, pp. 25–30)*

Creativity and Intelligence

We all know bright people who do well in school or on the job but who exhibit "little evidence of the quality that advances rather than enhances the status quo" (Goertzel & Goertzel, 1962, p. 280). These people are intelligent but not creative. We also know people who test poorly and muddle their way through school but who constantly come up with original ideas. These people score high in creativity, low in intelligence. The two traits often do not go hand-in-hand. When investigators have tested schoolchildren, they have found only modest correlations between creativity and intelligence (Anastasi & Schaefer, 1971; Getzels & Jackson, 1963).

We come up with similar findings when we look at adults. Creative people tend to be relatively intelligent, but beyond a certain level, higher IQs do not predict creativity. When groups of architects, mathematicians, and research scientists (all of whom were well above average in intelligence, with IQs ranging from 120 to 140) were divided into groups that *had* made distinguished contributions to their fields and other competent practitioners who had *not,* no differences in IQ showed up between the two groups (McKinnon, 1968). Nor were school grades related to later creativity.

Enhancing Creativity

A major reason for exploring creativity is the desire to encourage individuals to be more inventive in all aspects of life, both for the good of society and the fulfillment of the individual. To this end, many programs have been devised over the past fifty years, but the results have been generally disappointing. High hopes had been held for such tactics as brainstorming (group problem-solving techniques in which participants are encouraged to produce as many new and original ideas as possible, without evaluating any until the end of the session); so-called productive thinking, and specific problem-solving strategies. Most studies, however, show that specific strategies that can be used on problems similar to those presented during instruction can be learned, especially in highly technical fields such as mathematics, engineering, and product design, but that creative problem solving that applies to many different skills does not appear to be teachable (Mayer, 1983).

A number of specific strategies have emerged from these studies, however, which have helped some people. Some of these are presented in Box 8-2.

One way to become more creative is to rid ourselves of conceptual blocks, "mental walls that block the problem-solver from correctly perceiving a problem or conceiving its solution" (Adams, 1980, p. 11). The difficulty in solving the nine-dot problem results from a perceptual block, an inability to perceive the problem itself or the information needed to solve it. Most people have trouble with this because they impose their own constraints on the problem, limiting it too closely. Even though nothing in the problem specifies that the line must stay within the bounds of the square, most people automatically assume this limitation.

Other blocks are *emotional,* such as the fear of looking foolish from saying or suggesting an unusual idea; *cultural,* such as the taboo that keeps most people from thinking of urinating in a pipe to free a Ping-Pong ball stuck in it; and *intellectual or expressive,* such as the use of an inappropriate problem-solving language (trying to solve a problem mathematically when visualizing it or using words would be more effective).

BOX 8-2

HOW TO BE MORE CREATIVE

Based on the research and thinking on creativity, some of the following suggestions may help you be more creative in your work, your hobbies, your daily life.

- Take time to understand the problem before you begin trying to solve it.
- Get all the facts clearly in mind.
- Identify the facts that seem to be the most important.
- Work out a plan for attacking the problem.
- Consciously try to be original, to come up with new ideas.
- Don't worry about looking foolish if you say or suggest something unusual or if you come up with the wrong answer.
- Eliminate cultural taboos in your thinking that might interfere with your ability to come up with a novel solution.
- Draw a diagram to help you visualize the problem.
- Write out your thoughts to capture important points, and let you look for patterns, and come back to them later.
- Imagine yourself acting out the problem. (With the sock problem you might imagine yourself going to the drawer and beginning to fish out socks.)
- Actually act out the problem.
- Establish subgoals: Solve part of the problem and go on from there.
- Use analogies whenever possible: Think of a similar situation and see whether you can generalize from that one to your current problem.
- Think of a similar problem you've solved in the past and build on the strategy you used then.
- Keep an open mind. If your initial approach doesn't work, ask what assumptions you made that may not be true.
- Use several different problem-solving strategies—verbal, visual, mathematical, acting out the situation.
- If you get stuck with one approach, try to get to the solution by another route.
- Be alert to odd or puzzling facts. If you can explain them, your solution may be at hand.
- Look for relationships among various facts.
- Trust your intuition. Take a guess and see whether you can back it up.
- Try to be right the first time, but if you're not, explore as many alternatives as you need to.
- Think of unconventional ways to use objects and the environment.
- Consider taking a detour that delays your goal but eventually leads to it.
- Discard habitual ways of doing things and force yourself to figure out new ways.
- Strive for objectivity: Evaluate your own ideas as you would those of a stranger.

SUMMARY

1. In *thinking*, people use symbols to stand for things, events, and ideas so they are able to manipulate concepts and ideas. A major concern of *cognitive psychology* is the study of human thought processes that include *language, concept formation, problem solving*, and *creativity*.

2. Language is a means of communicating, generally through spoken sounds that express specific meaning and are arranged according to rules. Every language has a *grammar*, a set of rules for ordering words into sentences.

3. The *phoneme* is the minimal unit of sound. The *morpheme* is the smallest element of meaningful speech. *Semantics* is the study of meaning in a language. *Syntax* is the set of rules for ordering words into sentences.

4. *Prelinguistic speech* occurs in a sequence that is tied fairly closely to chronological age. Prelinguistic speech includes *crying, cooing, babbling*, and *imitation of sounds*.

5. *Holophrases* are single words that express a complete thought. They are the earliest form of linguistic speech, generally occurring at about age 1. The second year of life is an important time for *understanding* language.

6. *Mean length of utterance (MLU)* is the average length of utterances in morphemes (units of meaning). A child in stage 1 has an MLU over 1.0 and in stage 2 has an MLU of 2.0. The child advances with each increase of 0.5 MLU, up to stage 5.

7. Speech in early childhood is different from adult language. Young children simplify, overregularize

rules, overgeneralize concepts, and understand some grammatical relationships they cannot yet express.

8 *Learning theories* emphasize the role of the environment in language acquisition. According to Skinner, language is learned through reinforcement, discrimination, and generalization. *Social learning theorists* stress the roles of observation, imitation, and reinforcement. Although learning theories do account for why children learn to speak a particular language, they do not account for novel speech.

9 *Nativists* believe that human beings have an inborn capacity for language. Chomsky calls the inborn ability to learn language the *language acquisition device (LAD)*. While this approach accounts for novel speech and the rapidity with which children acquire language, it fails to consider individual differences and the learned aspects of language.

10 Today psychologists believe that language develops through an active interaction between caregiver and child. The infant has some innate capacity to learn language as demonstrated in his or her ability to discriminate fine variations in sound, respond differentially to the mother's voice, and move in synchrony with adult speech. This capacity probably allows the child to benefit from the specialized kind of speech known as *"motherese."*

11 Motherese is language addressed to small children by people who interact with them. Its characteristics include high pitch, simplification, and repetition. These modifications appear to be essential in language learning.

12 Lenneberg proposed that the years *before puberty* are a *critical period* for language acquisition. Although several types of evidence support this assertion, no clear-cut conclusion can as yet be made.

13 The *linguistic relativity hypothesis* (the *Whorfian hypothesis*) holds that language affects perception and thinking. Research has not conclusively supported this hypothesis.

14 Psychologists disagree about whether animals can learn language. Although apes can learn to use meaningful symbols, can generalize them correctly to new situations, and can communicate with humans to some extent, they seem unable to learn the creative aspects of language, which involve using linguistic rules to create novel and complex sentences.

15 An important aspect of human thought is the ability to organize different stimuli into *concepts*, which are *categories* of objects, events, or people.

This ability enables us to impose order on a world full of unique objects and events.

16 A *well-defined concept* is the one that can be specified by a set of clear, unambiguous *features*, such as color, size, shape, or function, connected by a *rule* or relationship among them.

17 Most concepts are *ill-defined*. That is, the features of one category often overlap with those in another, making it difficult to distinguish between them. In ill-defined categories, the features and the rules that connect the members of a category are not obvious.

18 Some examples of a category are more typical (i.e., better examples) than are others. The theory of *family resemblance* can be used to explain the phenomenon of *typicality*. *Basic-level categories* are the ones we use in our daily dealing with objects.

19 *Problem-solving* is a cognitive activity aimed at a goal. It can be either *routine* (using existing procedures) or *creative* (developing new procedures).

20 There are several theories of problem solving. *Learning theory* is concerned with the *trial-and-error process* of problem solution. *Gestalt theorists* consider the role of *insight* in solving problems. *Functional fixedness* is an overreliance on old methods of dealing with problems that hinder novel approaches. *Information processing* approaches consider problem solving to be a complex activity consisting of several processes.

21 Stages of problem solving include *preparation, production*, and *evaluation*. In the preparation stage we must determine exactly what the problem is. In the production stage we generate possible solutions. Two basic kinds of solution strategies are *algorithms* (which *exhaust* every possible solution until the correct one is discovered) and *heuristics* (which are rules of thumb which lead to either rapid problem solution or no solution). In the evaluation stage we must consider the adequacy of the solution.

22 There appear to be three intellectual processes involved in solving "insight" problems: *selective encoding, selective combination,* and *selective comparison*. The ability to solve insight problems is related to IQ but is not the same.

23 *Creativity* is the ability to see things in a new and unusual light, to see problems that no one else may even realize exist, and then to come up with new, unusual, and effective solutions. It is, then, a type of problem solving. While standard intelligence tests measure *convergent thinking* (the ability to produce the one best answer), creativity is concerned with *divergent thinking* (the ability to produce new and unusual answers). Programs geared

toward "teaching" creative problem solving indicate that specific strategies that can be used on problems similar to those presented during instruction can be learned but that creative problem solving that applies to many different skills does not appear to be teachable.

Suggested Readings

Anderson, J. R. (1980). *Cognitive psychology and its implications.* San Francisco: W. H. Freeman. A basic college textbook that contains discussions of all the major topics in cognitive psychology in a readable style.

Brown, R. (1973). *A first language: The early stages.* Cambridge, Mass.: Harvard University Press. A classic book that describes the language development of three young children, Adam, Eve, and Sarah.

Curtiss, S. (1977). *Genie: A psycholinguistic study of a modern-day "wild child."* New York: Academic Press. The absorbing story of the discovery and treatment of Genie, a child who suffered severe neglect during most of her childhood.

deVilliers, P. A., & deVilliers, J. (1979). *Early language.* Cambridge, Mass.: Harvard University Press. An engaging discussion of early linguistic development containing many examples of child language.

Ferguson, C. A., & Snow, C. E. (Eds.) (1977). *Talking to children: Language input and acquisition.* Cambridge, England: Cambridge University Press. A collection of articles by language scholars that highlight the effects of mother's speech on child's language.

Goertzel, V., & Goertzel, M. G. (1962). *Cradles of eminence.* Boston: Little, Brown. An absorbing study of the childhoods of some 400 prominent people that seeks to relate early-life factors to eventual success in life.

Kohler, W. (1927). *The mentality of apes.* New York: Harcourt, Brace, and World. Kohler's own discussions of his classic studies of insight in apes.

PART

4

MOTIVATION, EMOTION, AND STRESS

The links between body and mind are especially clear when we talk about the forces that motivate us toward certain behaviors. A major element of motivation lies in the way we feel emotionally in any given situation. And specific emotional and motivational factors often occur in response to a stressful experience.

In Chapter 9, "Motivation and Emotion," we'll delve into the complexities of motivation, especially in the areas of eating, sex, achievement, aggression, curiosity, and arousal. We'll look at some of the theories proposed to explain why some people behave one way and others another, or why the same person acts differently in different situations.

Chapter 10, "Stress and Coping," focuses on a topic that has become increasingly important in this modern world—stress and how to handle it. Not all stress is bad; some of it provides a stimulating challenge. Each of us needs to find our own optimal stress level. We'll examine ways by which stress affects the entire family as well as the individual. Finally, we'll offer a look at some of the ways individuals and families can cope with stress.

CHAPTER 9

MOTIVATION AND EMOTION

SPOTLIGHT ON

Why we get hungry and how motivational principles can help us lose weight.

How our sexual responses are affected by our bodies and our minds.

Why we are aggressive.

The importance of moderate levels of arousal.

The need to achieve.

Biological, learned, and cognitive aspects of emotions.

Almost as soon as we learn to put a sentence together, we begin to ask ''Why?'' Aside from wondering why the world is as it is—an element of curiosity that spurs scientists, artists, explorers, and others to do their finest work—most of us spend a great deal of time wondering why we and those around us behave in certain ways. Why, for example, you ate that second doughnut this morning after you had resolved to lose 10 pounds. Why your roommate spent so many hours on her last homework assignment, even though it was only a one-credit course. Why you're sexually attracted to someone who doesn't seem to know you're alive, and why you can't work up any enthusiasm at all for someone who's obviously crazy about you. Why a mugger not only stole your friend's wallet but cruelly beat him for no apparent purpose.

When you ask questions like these, you're asking about motivation, that force that energizes behavior, that gives direction to behavior, and that underlies the tendency to persist. This definition of motivation recognizes that in order to achieve goals, people must be sufficiently aroused and energetic, they must have a clear focus, and they must be able and willing to commit their energy for a period of time long enough to fulfill their aim.

Motivation researchers assess the roles of three kinds of factors. *Biological, learned,* and *cognitive* components join together in the motivation of most behaviors. The way we eat, for example, is determined by a combination of the bodily sensations of hunger caused by our need for food (biological), our preferences for steak over fried ants (learned), and our knowledge about the nutrients in various kinds of food, which leads us to choose milk over a soda (cognitive). In asking why people behave as they do, we need to look at each of these components.

A major element in motivation is the way we feel, our emotions, those subjective reactions to our environment that are accompanied by neural and hormonal responses, generally experienced as pleasant or unpleasant and considered adaptive reactions that affect the way we think. You act quite differently toward someone you love than toward someone you hate, and you respond to incidents differently when you're feeling cheerful than when you're feeling sad or angry. Where, then, do our emotions fit into the three-component theory of motivation? As we'll see when we discuss research on emotions, these, too, have biological, learned, and cognitive components.

Emotional states like fear, anger, and excitement are characterized by such physiological signals as a rapid heartbeat and breathing rate, high blood pressure, and a flushing of the skin. Such changes are apparently caused by the activation of certain parts of the brain and the production of various hormones in the body. Emotions also have their learned and cognitive aspects, which contribute to the differences in the ways different people react to the same experiences. So, while you experience euphoria while parachuting out of an airplane, I am terrified by the experience. We respond to our feelings sometimes unthinkingly (screaming, crying, laughing, or running away) and sometimes in ways that we've learned are appropriate (climbing a tree to get away from a bear or counting to ten to prevent an angry outburst). Sometimes we label ambiguous feelings with the names of emotions that we think are pertinent to the situation. In the end, the combination of our biological, learned, and cognitive reactions affect both the way we think about the world around us and the way we act (Kleinginna & Kleinginna, 1981).

It's often hard to distinguish between motivation and emotion because the two are so closely linked. In general, motivation theorists believe that there's a close link between feelings and action. We often do things because they make us feel good, and we avoid doing things that make us feel bad. Sometimes, however, we do things even though we know they'll make us unhappy and we don't do things even though we think they'd make us happy. Researchers are beginning to be able to explain such paradoxes, especially when they focus on people's reactions to stress (see Chapter 10) and on the emotional disturbance of depression (see Chapter 15).

If you've ever wondered why people endanger their own lives to save strangers, eat themselves into obesity or starve themselves to death, fly into a jealous rage, torture people who've done them no harm, become addicted to drugs, become workaholics, fall in love, climb forbidding mountains, set out for unexplored territory—you've asked some of the same questions posed by motivation and emotion researchers. Some of the major issues that confront human beings have aroused so much interest that entire fields of study have grown up around them, and many of them are treated in other sections of this book.

In this chapter we'll concentrate on only a few of these topics—hunger and eating, sex, aggression, achievement, and arousal. We'll look at the way researchers study the motivational and emotional factors associated with them, the way the various components of motivation and emotion contribute to our behavior around these issues, the theories that have been developed to explain motivation and emotion, and the questions that still exist. While there will be some overlap in our discussion of these two important phenomena in our lives, we'll treat them separately, first taking up the issues of why we do what we do and then of how we feel about it.

MOTIVATION

In their studies of the reasons why we behave the way we do, psychologists have drawn up a number of different kinds of theories and have followed different approaches to try to confirm or refute these theories. In this section we'll discuss the theories of motivation, the ways we study it, and the specific insights into our behavior in six major areas of our lives—eating, sex, aggression, achievement, curiosity, and arousal.

Theories of Motivation

Theories of motivation generally fall into three categories. Some stress the *biological* basis of motivation, some emphasize the importance of *learning*, and some focus on the role of *cognitive* factors.

BIOLOGICAL THEORIES   One of the oldest theories in this group is the one that attributed human behavior to the inheritance of instincts, which we now define as relatively complex patterns of behavior that don't have to be learned, like nest building in birds or food gathering in ants. These early theorists, however, termed as "instincts" traits like curiosity, gregariousness, and acquisition but still couldn't find a limited number of instincts to account for all human behavior. Furthermore, instinct theory

Human beings do seem biologically predisposed to do such things as care for our children. We don't call this an instinct, however, since the way we carry out these activities varies so widely across cultures and among individuals within a culture. (Ira Kirschenbaum/Stock, Boston)

couldn't account for individual differences. These reasons, as well as psychologists' growing realization of the important roles that learning and thinking play in human behavior, made them abandon instinct theory.

Drive theory, as developed by Hull (1943) tried to overcome these shortcomings. Hull stressed the importance of *biological drives,* internal tension states that propel animals or persons to act. Unlike instincts, which are assumed to give both direction and energy to behavior, drives provide only the energy that propels the action. They do this by producing an undesirable state that the person or animal wants to change. The reduction of this drive is enough of a reinforcement to make learning occur. Thus, if a dog is driven by hunger and happens to find food in a garbage can, it would learn to seek out garbage cans whenever it was hungry. While drive theory has fallen out of favor, partly because it failed to take into account new information about the cognitive processes underlying human behavior, there's still a widespread belief in the existence of both learned and unlearned human drives.

Other psychologists added psychological to biological *needs* as explanations for human behavior. Since 1938, when Henry A. Murray first suggested that satisfying a variety of needs energizes and directs behavior, some psychologists have tried to identify and measure such needs. While Hull had focused mainly on physiological needs like hunger, thirst, and sex, a growing emphasis on psychological needs and on the difference in these needs from one person to another led eventually to the humanistic approach exemplified by Abraham Maslow (1970).

Maslow organized human needs in the form of a pyramid, with the most elemental physiological needs at the bottom (see Figure 9-1). These are the needs basic to survival that have to be met before we can even think about anything else. A starving man, for example, will take great risks to obtain food; once he knows he'll live, he has the luxury of worrying about his personal safety. Then his needs for security must be met, at least in part, before he can even think about meeting his needs for love. As each succeeding layer of needs is addressed, we are motivated to look to the needs at the next higher step until we attain the summit of self-actualization, the full realization of our true potential. While there seems to be a strong basis for accepting this progression, it's not invariant. History is full of the accounts of incidents of self-sacrifice, in which individuals have sacrificed what they need for survival so that another (a loved one or even a complete stranger) may live.

LEARNING THEORIES   As we noted in Chapter 5, proponents of these theories argue that while biological needs may play a role in behavior, learning plays a much more important role in directing animal and human behaviors. (Here we see the great importance of emphasis, especially when we realize that some need theorists, including Hull, acknowledged that some needs are learned but emphasized the common unlearned needs that they felt were characteristic of human beings.) The main proponent of learning theory was B. F. Skinner (1953), who showed that a great number of behaviors can be taught by rewarding an animal or person immediately after the desired behavior occurs.

Social learning theorists like Albert Bandura (1977) expanded on Skinner's ideas to argue that some of the most powerful rewards for human beings are social rewards like praise. Thus, a child who is praised for doing well in school will develop the "habit" of achieving academically.

FIGURE 9-1 Maslow's Hierarchy of Needs *According to Maslow (1954), human needs have different orders of priorities. First comes survival, represented by the needs described at the base of this pyramid. A starving man will take great risks to obtain food; once he knows he'll live, he has the luxury of worrying about his personal safety. Then his needs for security must be met, at least in part, before he can even think about meeting his needs for love. As each succeeding layer of needs is addressed, says Maslow, the individual is motivated to look to the needs at the next higher step. While there seems to be a strong basis for accepting this progression, it's not invariant, however. History is full of the accounts of incidents of self-sacrifice, in which individuals have sacrificed what they need for survival so that another (a loved one or even a complete stranger) may live.*

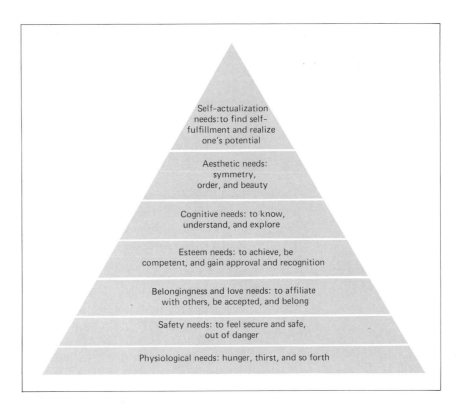

Because of the human ability to process symbolic information, we can also learn by observation. A child who sees someone else getting what he wants by throwing a tantrum is likely to imitate that behavior. We choose as models those people who seem to get the most rewards; to children, such people are often their parents. While learning theories account for many important behaviors, they ignore physical factors like the effects of chemicals in the blood and cognitive ones like different thinking styles.

COGNITIVE THEORIES These theories draw on the human thought processes to explain why we do what we do. Cognitive psychologists point out that the way we respond to events depends on how we interpret them. If a strange woman steps on my toe, for example, I can interpret the action in several different ways: She did it on purpose, she's drunk, she's clumsy, or she's disabled. The interpretation I choose affects the way I'll act. Attribution theorists, who look for the causes of behavior, represent this approach. Cognitive-consistency theorists point out the way we selectively process information and the way we change our thinking to match our behavior, and vice versa. (We reject or forget information that's inconsistent with our beliefs and actions, for example.) Both attribution and cognitive consistency are explained in more detail in Chapters 17 and 18.

Goal-directed behavior depends on how I evaluate a number of factors. Goals have incentive values, or *valence.* When one goal has a greater valence for me than another, I'm more likely to select it. (If I have a choice of running in two different races on the same day, I'll choose the one that has the more scenic course or the one I have a better chance of winning.) *Expectancies* are also important—such as my expectancy about whether a goal is realistic, whether I have the ability to achieve it, and how long it will take. (I'll run in 5-mile races, but not marathons, because I feel this is a goal I'm capable of accomplishing, without the sacrifice of too much time and energy.)

Each of the preceding approaches has something to offer. While at one time psychologists were quick to dismiss the instinct theorists, for example, we now realize that human beings *are* biologically predisposed to do certain things (like care for our children), even though we don't do them in a predetermined way. Similarly, the other motivation theories explain some behaviors in some situations.

How Psychologists Study Motivation

Because the field of motivation is so broad, most researchers concentrate their efforts fairly narrowly on one specific topic such as hunger, sex, aggression, or achievement. Within these topics the research focus may narrow in on biological, learned, or cognitive factors, and/or the way the different kinds of factors interact with each other.

Motivation researchers use virtually all the psychological techniques described throughout this book. They may explore hereditary mechanisms and prenatal influences (described in Chapter 11). They may perform surgery to alter brain structures and observe the effects. They may track the concentrations of hormones and other chemicals in the body. They may design laboratory experiments to study the effects of learning. They may develop tests to investigate the way people think. They then interpret their findings to develop an explanation for certain kinds of behavior.

When Motives Conflict

Life—as you may have learned by now—is rarely simple. We're often torn between two or more choices of action, all of which are motivating to some degree. Suppose, for example, you're about to kiss your "steady" when your stomach starts to growl, reminding you that you haven't eaten since the day before. Do you draw back immediately and suggest going for a pizza? Or do you follow through with the kiss, ignoring both the embarrassment of your stomach rumblings and the discomfort of your growing hunger? Motivation researchers have classified just such competing motives into the following four categories (Lewin, 1938; 1948).

- Approach-approach conflicts occur when you're simultaneously attracted to two desirable outcomes or activities, as in the preceding example, when the kiss and the pizza both have their (somewhat different) appeals. You're also in this situation when you're trying to decide which of two good movies to see on a given night.
- Avoidance-avoidance conflicts arise when you're repelled by two or more undesirable outcomes or activities. Suppose there's a required course you have to take that meets either at 8:00 A.M. or on Saturdays, neither of which time appeals to you. Still, you know that if you want to graduate, you have to choose one of these unwanted alternatives.
- Approach-avoidance conflicts come up when a *single* option has both positive and negative elements. Suppose you're asked to speak to a group that can be influential in helping you to get a good job, but you're terrified of speaking in public. In this kind of conflict, individuals sometimes turn to an outside prop like a drug (to give them courage or allay their anxiety).
- Multiple approach-avoidance conflicts are the ones we most often face in life. These involve situations in which several options exist, with each one containing both positive and negative elements. Not surprisingly, these are the hardest to resolve, and the most stressful. For example, you want to do well in school (for your own self-esteem, to make your family happy, to get a good job), and you want to pursue the relationship you have with the person you're in love with (for your self-esteem, to fulfill your sexual desires, to build a family). The night before your most important final exam, your loved one is giving a musical performance in another city. Do you stay home and study, or do you go to the concert? However you resolve this dilemma, your choice will involve some fairly sophisticated decision making.

Now let's turn to six important areas of behavior that are often characterized by conflict—hunger and eating, sex, aggression, achievement, curiosity, and arousal.

WHAT MAKES US HUNGRY AND WHY WE EAT

While most of us take for granted the daily activity of eating, food means more than fuel for the body. Virtually every society around the world has developed rituals revolving around food. Food may symbolize love, social bonding, the display of affluence. The way we eat may reflect our attitudes toward ourselves, our families, and our society. Let's look at the various components driving us to the dinner table, the snack bar, or the four-star restaurant.

Body Signals for Hunger

How does our body tell us we want or need food? Most of us, fortunately, are more likely to feel the stirrings of appetite rather than the pangs of a body depleted by hunger. In either case, however, the underlying mechanism is probably the same. A basic signal for hunger is the presence of stomach contractions, a finding from classic experiments early in this century in which subjects swallowed a balloon that recorded the contractions of their stomach (Cannon & Washburn, 1912). A close relationship existed between the presence of these contractions and the subjects' sensations of hunger pangs. The question then arises: What causes the stomach contractions?

One cause seems to be a low level of *glucose* (sugar) in the blood. More than fifty years ago, studies with dogs manipulated blood glucose levels by transfusing blood from a starved dog to one that had just eaten and vice versa (Templeton & Quigley, 1930). When the blood from the hungry dog was given to the recently fed dog, it developed stomach contractions even though its stomach was full, and when blood from the dog that had just eaten was given to a hungry dog, the stomach contractions of the hungry dog stopped, even though it received no food.

These findings have been complemented by research with people who have *diabetes*, a disorder caused by a disturbance of the body's mechanism for producing *insulin*, a necessary hormone that converts blood glucose and carbohydrates into energy. Since diabetics don't produce enough of their own insulin, they either inject it or take it in pill form. After injecting insulin, they experience stomach contractions and feelings of hunger (Goodner & Russell, 1965). Since insulin tends to be secreted whenever glucose levels increase, it has been difficult to conclude whether hunger is caused by changes in levels of glucose or insulin. Recently, research that manipulated the two independently found that hunger follows changes in insulin rather than glucose (Rodin, 1983).

One implication of this finding is that eating can prime us to become hungry! When we begin to eat, our insulin levels rise, explaining why we may be more hungry *after* snacking on a candy bar than we had been *before* we ate it. Sugar, which leads to increased glucose in the blood, raises our insulin levels more than many other foods; furthermore, it keeps insulin levels higher for longer periods of time. Therefore, eating sweets often makes us hungry again after a short period of time. On the other hand, fruits, which contain the "fruit sugar" *fructose*, increase insulin levels for only short periods of time. Thus, fruits can satisfy hunger without making us want to eat again soon (Rodin, 1983).

Why We Eat the Way We Do

One of the major health problems in the United States today is overweight. People who are 10 percent heavier than the "ideal" weight for their height and body build are considered *overweight*, while the term *obese* is reserved for people who are at least 20 percent over desirable weight. Current estimates indicate that about 70 million American adults are overweight, 7.5 million are obese, and some 7 million are severely obese [30 percent above desirable weight for men; 50 percent above for women (Kreutler, 1980)]. While simple overweight is most often a cosmetic problem in a society that worships at the altar of slenderness, obesity can lead to a variety of health problems, including high blood pressure, heart disease, allergies, and sinus attacks. Obesity can also become a psychological problem since it so drastically violates our society's aesthetic standards for beauty. The combination of its high incidence in the population and its unpopularity has spawned a major industry based on dieting and has spurred a great deal of research into the mechanisms of weight. Let's look at some of the theories that seek to explain eating patterns, especially *overeating* patterns.

PREPARATION FOR FAMINE   Some theorists look to our early evolutionary history to explain the inability of many people to control their food intake, saying that our tendency toward retaining fat was once adaptive. At one time, human beings didn't have a dependable food supply and would go for long periods of time on a subsistence level before having the chance to eat their fill. To deal with periodic food shortages, they developed the capacity to store energy in the form of fat. When a large animal, say, was killed, they would gorge themselves on it and put on extra weight, which would sustain them over a time of scarcity.

A chemical linked to the conservation and expenditure of energy may be responsible for this kind of fat storage, claim researchers who have shown that genetically obese mice have high beta-endorphin levels (Margules, Moisset, Lewis, Shibuya, & Part, 1978). Since recent work with humans has failed to find a direct link between beta-endorphin levels and obesity (O'Brien, Stunkard, & Ternes, 1982), however, the evidence for this theory is far from conclusive.

SET-POINT THEORY   Most of us do not become obese. We tend to reach a certain body weight and to stay at about that weight with minor fluctuations. This may be because we're equipped with a *set-point*, a mechanism that signals us to stop eating, once our own individual ideal weight has been reached. The set-point, then, controls body fat the way a thermostat keeps room temperature at a certain level. It varies from person to person so that two people of the same height may be "programmed" at different body weights.

Research with rats suggests that such a mechanism may be located in the hypothalamus. When surgical lesions are made in one site in the hypothalamus (the ventromedial nuclei), rats tend to become obese. They don't eat until they burst but put on weight until they reach some maximum level and then reduce their food intake and maintain their weight. When rats are lesioned at another site (the lateral hypothalamus), they tend to stop eating. Again, they don't starve themselves to death; after reaching some abnormally low body weight, they begin to eat again and maintain that low weight. These two hypothalamic sites may work together to determine an individual's set-point (Keesey & Powley, 1975). The way these sites affect appetite is shown graphically in Figure 9-2.

According to set-point theory, some people have higher set-points than others, therefore eat more, and therefore weigh more. When these set-points are disrupted, as by dieting, the dieters feel deprived, and their set-point rises still more, and so they eat more. This explains why some people gain more after going off a diet that was temporarily successful (Bennett & Gurin, 1982). What accounts for individual differences in set-points? Some researchers suggest that we inherit our set-points, others that we learn them. At this point, no one really knows.

There is some evidence that we may be able to raise or lower our set-points. Such external influences as the taste and smell of rich foods seem to raise set-point, leading us to eat more. Other influences seem to make us eat less, most notably drugs like amphetamines and nicotine, which depress appetite *only* so long as they are being taken. A healthier appetite depressant is regular physical exercise: People who exercise daily often eat less than people who are less active. It's possible that physical activity alters the *basal metabolism rate (BMR)*, which controls the amount of energy the body expends in digesting food (Thompson, Jarvis, Lahey, & Cureton, 1982). The more energy we expend, the more calories we use up.

ENJOYMENT OF SENSORY QUALITIES OF FOOD   One reason for eating is the sensuous pleasure it gives us. We like biting into and chewing a tender steak, we like the crispness of a fresh salad, we like the rich flavor of a chocolate mousse. Both humans and animals seem to be born with a preference for sweet foods. Rats will learn to press a bar to get the sweet taste of a nonnutritive food additive like saccharin, and human beings often select sweet foods over others that have more nutritive values (Nisbett, 1968).

We receive pleasant sensations of taste and texture via the *trigeminal nerve pathway*, which links receptors in the mouth to the lateral hypothalamus. When this nerve was cut in a group of rats, they stopped eating (Zeigler, 1973; 1975) probably because they got no more pleasure from

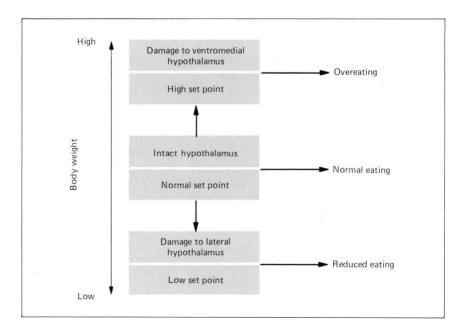

FIGURE 9-2 *Damage (or lesions) to the ventromedial hypothalamus raises the set-point, while damage (or lesions) to the lateral hypothalamus lowers the set-point.*

Regular physical exercise is a healthy appetite depressant: People who exercise daily often eat less than people who are less active. (© Russ Kinne 1977/Photo Researchers, Inc.)

their food than you would if your meals consisted of a tasteless semiliquid. One reason for the success of commercial liquid-diet preparations is their uninteresting blandness. In one experiment, when obese people were told they could eat all they wanted of such a substance, their calorie intake dropped from about 3000 calories a day down to 500, while the intake of normal subjects continued at about 2400 calories a day (Hashim & Van Itallie, 1965) (see Figure 9-3). While this isn't a practical solution for obesity since we can't control the environment of most obese people, this does demonstrate the seductive qualities of appealing food. It also raises the question of the different reactions to food by normal and overweight people.

LEARNED CUES FOR EATING   Do you ever look at your watch and, after finding out what time it is, decide that you're hungry? Do you eat more popcorn when the bowl is on your desk than when it's in the other room? Do you eat more when you're the guest of an unusually good cook than you do at home? If your answer to any of these questions is yes, you're responding to external rather than internal cues for eating. *Internal cues* are those that originate within our bodies—stomach contractions, low blood glucose or insulin levels, or any other indication that we require nourishment. *External cues* are outside our bodies, such as time of day, ads and commercials, sensory qualities of food, or simply its availability; they are factors in the environment that we have learned to associate with eating. After conducting a series of ingenious experiments in which overweight people ate more food than normal-weights did in response to various external cues, Schachter (1971; Schachter & Gross, 1968; Goldman, Jaffa, & Schachter, 1968) concluded that obese people are more in-

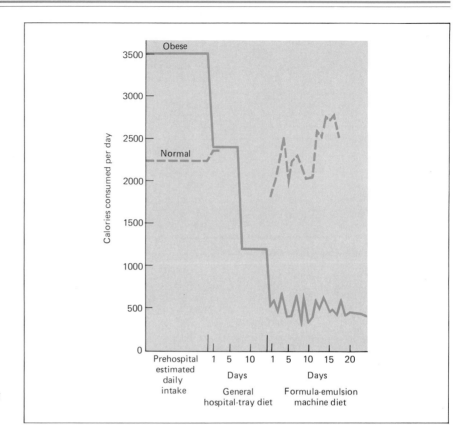

FIGURE 9-3 *The effect of a formula emulsion diet on the eating behavior of a normal and an obese subject. (From Schachter, 1971)*

fluenced by external cues (what time they think it is, how much trouble it is to eat something, qualities of taste and texture), and that normal-weight people are more influenced by internal cues.

Following up this research, Rodin (1981) found that "externals" (people who eat more in response to external cues) show a large insulin reaction when presented with a sizzling steak, while "internals" do not. There may, then, be a physiological difference between these two types of eaters. The difference, however, is not always reflected in different weight levels. Rodin has also found that many people of normal weight are also affected by external cues but that they manage to control their tendency to overeat. The management of external cues is the basis for many *behavior modification* approaches to dieting. That is, if you can change your environment so that it presents you with fewer cues for eating, you'll be likely to eat less. Some basic guidelines for putting into practice this and other research findings about eating and weight are given in Box 9-1.

Eating Disorders

Robert Earl Hughes of Monticello, Missouri, died in 1958 at the age of 32, weighing 1041 pounds. According to the *Guinness Book of World Records*, he was the heaviest man ever weighed (Bennett & Gurin, 1982). Overeating to such obesity, which prevents a normal life and is a menace to health is, of course, a major problem. Two other kinds of eating disorders, which seem to have become more common in recent years, especially among young women, are anorexia nervosa, a form of self-starvation that

BOX 9-1

LOSING WEIGHT BY APPLYING MOTIVATIONAL PRINCIPLES

- *Eat in only one place at regular times:* This will help you cut down on snacking, by limiting the number of places and times that have associations with eating and thus suggest, "It's time to eat."
- *Eat slowly:* This helps you get the most pleasure from the least amount of food, helps you fool yourself into thinking you're eating more than you actually are, and gives your body time to give you feedback on when you've had enough.
- *Don't do anything else while you're eating such as reading or watching television:* This helps you make eating the "main event," so you can concentrate on your food and be more responsive to your body's internal cues. It also avoids establishing habits ("If I'm at the movies, it's time to eat popcorn").
- *Reduce the availability of fattening foods:* If you can't resist chocolate chip cookies, peanuts, or some other high-calorie food, don't bring them home. Throw out or freeze leftovers immediately so you won't be tempted to eat them. If you buy nuts, buy them with

their shells on so you'll have to expend more effort to eat them; you'll eat less.
- *Allow for some variety in your diet—but not too much:* If you deprive yourself of all the foods you love, you'll binge when you get the chance so it's better to incorporate a small serving of cake or ice cream or some other high-calorie treat into your menu plan instead of avoiding it completely. However, since people (and animals) eat more food when faced with a large variety, limit your meals to a few basic dishes instead of a wide choice.
- *Avoid fatty and rich-tasting foods, even when they're "dietetic":* Foods that look, smell, and taste rich or fatty—even when they're not—seem to stimulate the appetite.
- *Eat in the company of other people who are moderate eaters themselves:* You'll be inclined to eat more moderately when other people are witnesses to what you eat. Also, you'll be able to guide your intake by theirs.
- *Use small serving plates and glasses:* Food heaped on a small plate looks like more than

the same amount on a large plate. Take advantage of this visual illusion to fool yourself into eating less.
- *Incorporate exercise into your daily schedule:* Aside from the direct expenditure of energy in the activity itself, exercise seems to reduce appetite. Programs that combine dieting, changes in behavior, and exercise result in more weight loss than any one of these changes alone. The most effective exercise schedules include sessions of at least 20 minutes each, three times a week, of activities that are strenuous enough to expend 300 calories per session or to raise the heart rate to 60 to 70 percent of its maximum (Thompson et al., 1982). This generally means swimming, running, bicycling, dancing, or some other kind of *aerobic* activity (requiring high consumption of oxygen for a sustained period of time) rather than a more static exercise like weight lifting or sit-ups.

can actually lead to death, and bulimia, in which an individual regularly eats vast quantities of food and then purges the body of them either by induced vomiting or laxative use. While we don't have the answers to why people would mistreat their bodies in these ways, the latter two disorders seem closely linked to the great emphasis in our society on slenderness as an ideal of beauty. There are also some indications that both may be linked to depression and that anorexia may also have a physiological basis (Sugarman, Quinlan, & Devenis, in press; Herzog, 1982; Walsh, Katz, Levin, Kream, Fukushima, Hellman, Weiner, & Zumoff, 1978; Gwirtsman & Germer, 1981).

Popular singer Karen Carpenter died in 1983 at the age of 32, a victim of complications of anorexia nervosa, a form of self-starvation that afflicts increasing numbers of young women in our intensely weight-conscious society. (Johnny Horne/Picture Group)

ANOREXIA NERVOSA This perplexing syndrome is a prolonged and severe refusal to eat, which causes a person to lose at least 25 percent of original body weight and can lead to death. While the disorder affects both sexes of varying ages (beginning as early as 9 years of age or during the decade of the 30s or even later), the typical patient is a bright, well-behaved, appealing female somewhere between puberty and the early 20s, from an apparently stable, well-educated, well-off family.

She is preoccupied with food—with cooking it, talking about it, and urging others to eat—but she either doesn't eat herself or gorges herself and then purges by vomiting or using laxatives (a variant known as bulimia, described below). She has a distorted sense of body image and sees herself as beautiful when she is at her most pathetically and grotesquely skeletal. Once the starvation begins, other symptoms appear: Menstruation usually stops, thick soft hair may grow over the body, and intense overactivity may occur.

We don't know what causes anorexia. Differing suggestions include a physical disorder caused by a hypothalamic disturbance, a deficiency of a crucial neurotransmitter, a psychological disturbance related to depression, a fear of growing up, an extreme symptom of family malfunctioning, and societal pressures for slenderness upon a vulnerable individual (Walsh, Katz, Levin, Kream, Fukushima, Hellman, Winer, & Zumoff, 1978; Gwirtsman & Germer, 1981; Sugarman, Quinlan, & Devenis, in press; Barker, 1979; Bruch, 1977). So far, research evidence has not conclusively borne out any of the hypotheses, and further study is needed (Yager, 1982).

BULIMIA A related disorder also most common in teenage and young adult women is characterized by episodes of binge eating of huge quantities of food (of up to 5000 calories in a single sitting), followed by vomiting or laxative use to empty the body. Bulimics are often depressed and commonly suffer such physical complications as hair loss, extensive tooth decay, and gastric irritation. While some bulimics are also anorexic, others maintain normal weight, and the syndrome is far from rare. Conservative estimates indicate that it affects 5 percent of the general population (Nagelberg, Hale, & Ware, 1983). In several recent surveys, half the college women queried said they binge and purge sometimes (Herzog, 1982). While bulimics have traditionally been secretive about their bizarre eating habits, recent reports indicate that more young women openly admit this unhealthy method of weight control (Squire, 1983).

SEXUALITY

While we don't need to be sexually active to survive in the way we need to eat to live, the sexual drive is one of the most powerful for all animals. It is, of course, needed for species survival. The very basis of our physiology equips us for sexual behavior, provides a mechanism that makes it enjoyable, and readies us for a variety of reinforcing stimuli from the environment.

The Physiology of Human Sexual Response

While research on eating, on aggression, on achievement, and on many other human endeavors has gone on since early in this century, it wasn't until the 1950s that the pioneering work of William H. Masters, M.D., and

Virginia E. Johnson began to discover exactly what happens inside the human body during sexual activity. With the help of more than 600 men and women who volunteered to come to their laboratory in St. Louis, Masters and Johnson used an array of technological instruments to measure physiological responses (1966).

On the basis of their research, Masters and Johnson identified four stages of sexual response, based on two basic physiological processes, *vasocongestion* (the flow of blood into a region's blood vessels as a result of the dilation of the vessels) and *myotonia* (the contraction of muscles in the genitals and throughout the body). Let's look at the four stages:

* *Excitement:* In this beginning stage, the female experiences lubrication of the vagina, enlargement of the breasts, erection of the nipples, swelling of the glans (tip) of the clitoris, and an expansion of the upper two-thirds of the vagina. The male achieves an erection, tension of the scrotal sac, and elevation of the testes. Both sexes may experience a sex flush (a transitory rash) and an increase in pulse rate and blood pressure.
* *Plateau:* With vasocongestion at its peak, the woman's vaginal walls thicken, the opening becomes smaller, enabling the vagina to grip the penis snugly, the clitoris draws up into the body, the uterus enlarges, and the color of the inner labia deepens. The man's penis is completely erect, the testes are enlarged, and a few drops of fluid (which may contain active sperm) appear at the tip of the penis. Breathing, pulse rate, and blood pressure continue to mount for both sexes.
* *Orgasm:* In both sexes orgasm consists of a series of rhythmic muscular contractions of the pelvic organs at about 0.8-second intervals. The male orgasm has two stages, the first one of "ejaculatory inevitability," that is, the sense that ejaculation is about to occur and cannot be stopped, and the second of the ejaculation itself, during which semen is forcefully expelled from the penis. In the female orgasm, the uterus also contracts.
* *Resolution:* In this final phase the body returns to the unaroused state. This reversal of the preceding processes usually takes 15 to 30 minutes but may take up to an hour for women who have been aroused but have not experienced orgasm. Men enter a *refractory period,* a time during which they are incapable of having an erection or an orgasm. This period may last only a few minutes for some men, for twenty-four hours in others. It is longer for older men. Women do not experience a refractory period, making multiple orgasms possible for them.

The many pleasurable sensations associated with sexual contact go far beyond intercourse alone. We have many sexually sensitive areas in our bodies. These places are known as the erogenous zones, and people can experience arousal or orgasm from being touched in some of these spots. The most common means of reaching orgasm, besides intercourse, are manual and oral stimulation of the genitals. Besides the genital region (clitoris and vagina, penis and testes), the erogenous zones usually include the breasts, thighs, lips, and buttocks—and may also include such other sites as the ears or armpits, depending on the individual. Different people are sensitive in different parts of their bodies; what one person may ignore, another may find highly erotic.

Arousal of Sexual Desire

What makes a person want sex at all? Research points to the interaction of physiology and learning. The key physiological factor underlying sexual desire in both males and females can be found in the role of hormones, and learning shows up in the way people respond to various stimuli.

HORMONES Of the androgens (the male sex hormones), testosterone is the most studied. When testosterone levels are high, the male is more inclined to engage in sexual behavior. During adolescence testosterone levels rise; it is during these years that many boys begin to masturbate to orgasm. Women have testosterone in their bodies, too, and there is evidence that women with high levels of testosterone engage in sex more frequently and enjoy it more (Persky, Lief, Strauss, Miller, & O'Brien, 1978).

Of the two major female sex hormones, estrogen and progesterone, estrogen has been linked specifically to female sexual arousal. Estrogen is released about once every twenty-eight days, when the ovum breaks through the wall of the follicle cell. In virtually all animals except the human, females will permit sexual intercourse only during those times in the reproductive cycle when estrogen levels are high (which is also the time when they are fertile). While the human female may tend to be more interested in sex when estrogen levels are high (Adams, Gold, & Burt, 1978), she is just as likely to engage in it when estrogen levels are low (Morris, 1969).

The relationship between sex and physiology is dramatically underscored by the large number of commonly used drugs that can impair sexual functioning in both men and women. Among 188 men in a recent study who suffered from impotence, medications were the single largest cause of their dysfunction. Drugs may also interfere with sexual desire in both sexes, with the ability to ejaculate in men, and with the ability to reach orgasm in women. They may do this by altering the production or action of sex hormones; by interfering with the autonomic nervous system, blocking the stimuli needed for a normal sexual response; or by altering emotional mood or level of arousal (Slag et al., 1983; Kaplan, 1979). Fortunately, nearly all drug-related effects on sexuality disappear when the individual stops taking the drug.

STIMULATION What makes us start thinking about sex at any particular time? Ethologist Desmond Morris (1977) suggests that sexuality is triggered by "gender signals," clues that enable us to recognize another person as male or female and that, in fact, emphasize maleness or femaleness. So anything that differentiates the sexes attracts our attention: the genitals; the breasts and rounded buttocks of the woman; the broad shoulders and flat buttocks of the man; and the culturally imposed gender signals like clothing and hairstyles.

We don't know exactly why certain physical characteristics of another person appeal to us. It may be because they remind us of someone else (like a parent), because they represent a societal ideal of beauty, or because we've learned in some other way to associate a certain mix of physical features with sexual arousal. When we do find we are "sexually attracted" to someone, our first response is to maintain visual contact, our next is to get physically close, and if the other is receptive, we'll move to touch him or her and then to escalate this touch into sexual contact.

Because human beings are capable of symbolic thinking, we can be aroused not only by the sight of a flesh-and-blood person in front of us but also by pictures, films, and descriptions of nudity and sexual behavior. Both males and females show such arousal (Mosher & Abramson, 1977). Exposure to erotic materials has been shown to increase the output of sex hormones, which we know are important for sexual arousal (LaFerla, Anderson, & Schalch, 1978).

LEARNING   While we don't have any scientific data on the role of learning with regard to our preference for sexual partners, there's a great deal of evidence that learning plays an important role in the mature sexual response. Most of this evidence comes from research with animals, and the assumption is that if learning plays an important role in the sexual behavior of animals, it's apt to play an even greater role in humans. Monkeys who don't have a chance to play with other monkeys their own age when they're young seem motivated to be sexually active when they mature, but they don't know what to do—how to engage in appropriate sexual behavior (Harlow, 1962; 1969). Apparently the presence of peers somehow stimulates young monkeys to practice certain behaviors in play (such as components of the mature sexual response) that are important for mature sexual behavior.

The importance of early sexual learning is undoubtedly crucial in human beings, also. While we don't have the same kind of data (since for obvious ethical and practical reasons we cannot bring up children for the

Learning is a major factor in our choice of sexual partner. We learn the standards of sexual attractiveness that are prevalent in the particular time and place that we happen to live. During the 19th century, the buxom, bosomy soprano, Lillian Russell, was the ideal of womanly beauty; today she seems quaintly soft and overblown next to the lean, athletic spareness of Jane Fonda. (a. Lillian Russell, Culver Pictures, Inc. b. Jane Fonda, Steve Schapiro/Gamma Liaison)

sake of a scientific experiment), sex therapists often comment on the preponderance of repressive upbringing among people with sexual dysfunctions (O'Connor, 1982).

Learning is clearly a factor in people's choice of sexual partners, as shown by the widely varying standards of attractiveness from one culture to another or even at different times within the same culture.

COGNITIVE FACTORS Since human beings are thinking creatures, it's not surprising that the way we think affects the way we act, sexually as well as other ways. For example, two different personality types—*extroverts* and *introverts*—seem to think differently in many ways. Extroverts like change and variety, like to be with other people, and tend to act impulsively, while introverts prefer the familiar, enjoy solitude, and are more reflective. In a study of English students, Eysenck (1976) found that extroverts petted more, engaged in intercourse more, and tried more different sexual positions than introverts; they were also more satisfied with their sexual experiences. Eysenck suggested that introverts may be more inhibited by feelings of guilt. Other research has shown that people often associate sexual arousal with feelings of guilt and therefore are inclined to label sexually arousing situations as disgusting or nauseating (Mosher, 1965; Mosher & Abramson, 1977).

Homosexuality

What makes people become sexually attracted to persons of the other sex or to persons of the same sex? While a great deal of research has been carried out to answer this question, we have many theories but no definitive answers. Both *heterosexuals* (people who are sexually attracted to persons of the other sex) and *homosexuals* (those sexually attracted to same-sex persons) show similar physiological responses during sexual arousal and are aroused by the same forms of tactile stimulation. Large-scale studies have indicated that homosexual men act in most ways like heterosexual men and homosexual women are very similar to heterosexual women (Blumstein & Schwartz, 1983; Bell & Weinberg, 1978). The major difference is in the preferred sex of the partner.

A number of hypotheses have been advanced to account for the existence of homosexuality. The oldest is that it represents a kind of *mental illness*. In a classic study, Hooker (1957) could find no evidence to support this contention, a result that eventually led the American Psychiatric Association (APA) to stop classifying homosexuality as a "mental disorder." The APA (1980) now considers homosexuality a disorder only for those people who want to become heterosexual.

Other theories include the possibility of a *genetic factor*, a *hormonal imbalance*, a *family constellation* with a dominating mother and a weak father, and a *chance-learning* situation, in which a young person who had been seduced by someone of the same sex would then develop a preference for that sex. So far, no scientific support has been found for the latter two of these theories, and only tentative evidence for the first two. The fifth hypothesis is that there are probably several different reasons why an individual may become homosexual and that it's the interaction among various hormonal and environmental events that's crucial. This hypothesis seems to have garnered the most support (Masters & Johnson, 1979; Bell, Weinberg, & Hammersmith, 1981; Durden-Smith & DeSimone, 1982).

What makes people become sexually attracted to others of the same sex? We have many theories but no conclusive answers. (Bettye Lane/ Photo Researchers, Inc.)

AGGRESSION

On January 18, 1984, Malcolm H. Kerr, the president of the American University of Beirut, was shot to death by unidentified gunmen as he was walking to his office. A caller who identified himself as a member of a supposedly pro-Iranian underground group, Islamic Holy War, said the group had assassinated Dr. Kerr in protest against the American military presence in Lebanon. The group had also assumed responsibility for the bombing of the American Embassy in Beirut on April 18, 1983, and the attack against the marine compound on October 23, 1983 (Friedman, 1984). While there is no hard evidence that the organization actually exists, the tragic truth is that more than 250 people are now dead as the result of these three incidents and that more are likely to die in the strife-torn Middle East.

The tiny town of Old Snake River, Texas, seems like an unlikely spot for an epidemic of violence. Yet within one year, one wife killed the husband who used to beat her, another killed hers while he was talking on the phone to his girlfriend, a mother killed her teenage son, and a 23-year-old woman was raped and murdered. In response, almost the entire population (which is about 200 people) of Old Snake River has armed itself against "undesirable outsiders," with, of course, the danger of more violent attacks among neighbors and relatives (Strasser, 1984).

Aggression—any behavior intended to hurt someone or something—is all around us. In most places around the world, not least in the United States, this aggression often explodes into violence, destructive action against people or property. At other times the aggressive impulse is confined to competition, verbal attack, or some other expression of hostility short of physical injury. When we talk about aggression, then, we are talking about behavior that the doer engages in with the intention of doing harm.

Scientists have offered a variety of explanations for aggressive behavior—inherited tendencies, the results of experience and learning, and an interaction between these two major forces. By and large, it looks as if we are born with a predisposition toward aggressiveness and then we learn when we should express this tendency and when we should inhibit it.

Do We Inherit the Aggressive Tendency?

In view of the widespread appearance of aggression among nonhuman animals, sociobiologists like David P. Barash (1977) suggest that it's adaptive behavior that has developed over the course of evolution. Animals threaten or attack other animals whenever they compete for any commodity that is in short supply, such as food, space, or a mate; when they're in pain or discomfort; when they're frustrated in reaching some goal; when they're up against a competitor against whom they have a chance of winning; and when strangers appear. Human beings often become aggressive under similar circumstances.

Konrad Lorenz (1963), an ethologist (a scientist who studies animal behavior in its natural environment), has proposed that an aggressive instinct exists in all animals, including humans, as a genetically determined, inevitable trait. Anthropologist J. Robin Fox (1983) suggests that human beings are "wired for" aggression—that the drive is an essential and functional part of the organism, which is always available. It can be easily turned on, and it can also be turned off when the expression of aggression would interfere with some other goal. However, the fact that some cultures and some individuals in every culture show practically no aggression while others show a great deal suggest that although we may inherit the tendency to act aggressively, other factors determine to what extent we will express aggressive behavior.

The biological basis for aggression, or at least a predisposition toward it, is indicated by a considerable body of research. Certain brain structures, for example, are implicated in the regulation of aggression. Electrical stimulation of certain areas of cats' brains cause normally nonaggressive cats to attack rats, even if the cats were busy eating at the time (Roberts & Kiess, 1964). Different brain structures are involved in the expression of different types of aggression, such as rage, attack, predatory behavior, and defensive behavior (Moyer, 1976). In some instances, as in the case of Charles Whitman, who went on a shooting spree in Texas in 1966, a brain tumor of the temporal lobes was implicated as a probable cause of his sudden, unexplained violent actions.

Various hormones and brain chemicals have also been linked to aggression. One is the male hormone testosterone. Among humans as among most other animal species, males are generally more aggressive than females (Maccoby, & Jacklin, 1974). In nearly all societies around the world, the men do the hunting and the fighting; in the United States they commit more violent crime; and lab experiments have often found men to be more aggressive than women and very rarely found women more aggressive than men (Myers, 1983). In one study of young criminals, those with a history of violent and aggressive crimes had higher testosterone levels than those with a nonviolent history (Kreuz & Rose, 1976). It also looks as if aggressiveness sometimes causes testosterone levels to rise rather than the other way around. Behavior does affect biology in some situations, as seen by studies of monkeys that show that the levels of whole-blood

On the night of July 31, 1966, Charles Whitman, an introspective 25-year-old, killed his wife and mother. The following morning he went to the administration building of the University of Texas where he shot the receptionist and then barricaded himself in the tower. Using a high-powered rifle with a telescopic lens, he then proceeded to shoot anyone in range. Over the next 90 minutes he killed fourteen people and wounded another twenty-four. His shooting spree ended only when he himself was shot and killed by the police. In a note he wrote before any of the killings, he described the agonizing headaches he had been suffering over the previous months and the unusual and irrational thoughts, including violent impulses, that had been tormenting him. The autopsy that he had requested showed a brain tumor of the temporal lobes (Johnson, 1972). (Wide World Photos)

serotonin in the system of a dominant male in a group rise *after* he becomes dominant (Raleigh et al., 1981).

Some researchers have pointed to an increase in irritability and hostility just before the menses of some women and have suggested that this is caused by changes in female hormones—a marked drop in progesterone and a rise in estrogen (Dalton, 1977). In recent years, the name premenstrual syndrome (PMS) has been given to this condition, with medication frequently prescribed, even though the existence of the syndrome is still controversial.

In an experiment that measured blood-pressure rates of persons taking part in a competitive, aggression-inducing task, Frodi (1978) found the kind of rates that are present when high levels of the neurotransmitter norepinephrine are released in the brain. Low blood glucose level, which marks the state of hypoglycemia, has also been implicated in aggression. In one group of people, under normal conditions only 7.7 percent were aggressive, but when they were moderately hypoglycemic, 84.6 percent were aggressive (Bolton, 1973). And the link between alcohol and aggression has been well established, in research as well as in everyday observation of people who become violent only when they're drunk (Pihl, Zeichner, Niaura, Nagy, & Zacchia, 1981). Alcohol's effects are probably largely due to the way it reduces inhibitions but may also come from its ability to produce a hypoglycemic state. A promising line of research is currently investigating the role of various substances in the brain that cause fear, which reduces aggression and which is notably absent among violence-prone sociopathic individuals (Redmond, 1983). It seems clear, then, that various hormones and chemicals can increase the likelihood of aggression.

What Triggers Aggression?

Hormones and chemicals don't produce aggressive behavior itself. What they do is lower our threshold for expressing aggression. In other words, if I encounter a situation that would call forth an aggressive response, I'm more likely to make that response if I have a higher level of these substances coursing through my body. Among the kinds of events that bring out aggressive responses are *frustration* (the thwarting of some goal-directed behavior), *insults*, and *negative evaluations*.

WE GET FRUSTRATED How do you feel when someone cuts in front of you in traffic or in a check out line when you're in a hurry? Chances are that you want to "get back" at the intruder.

Frustration doesn't *always* bring about aggression, however; it's likely to lead to aggression only when it's intense and unexpected or arbitrary

(Baron, 1977). You're less likely to become angry when you're refused a job if you hadn't counted on getting it and if you think the interview was fair. Furthermore, frustrated individuals aren't likely to become aggressive, no matter how angry they get, unless the stage is set for aggression. This stage setting may consist of "cues for aggression" such as an atmosphere that promotes violence (seeing a violent movie), the presence of weapons that remind you how they can be used to hurt someone, or a previous dislike for the person who frustrated you (Berkowitz, 1979).

WE ARE INSULTED OR WE RECEIVE A NEGATIVE EVALUATION Children learn from an early age that calling people names is almost sure to make them angry, and laboratory researchers have confirmed the aggression-eliciting power of insults by acting rudely toward subjects, sometimes questioning their intelligence (Baron & Bell, 1973). Similarly, most of us have felt angry at teachers who gave us a lower grade than we felt we deserved or supervisors who rated our work below the level we thought was fair. Here, too, intent is important. We're much less likely to become angry if an evaluation—no matter how negative—seems fair than if it seems arbitrary and undeserved (Greenwell & Dengerink, 1973; Donnerstein & Wilson, 1976).

How Do We Learn to Be Aggressive?

How, then, do we *learn* when to discharge frustration and anger through aggression? How do we learn that it's okay to hurt other people in certain circumstances? What in our environment teaches us? Social learning theorists consider aggression to be behavior that's learned as a result of rewards and punishments, as well as through imitating models.

WE LEARN FROM THE PEOPLE AROUND US Parents usually teach their children not to hit other children first, not to hit smaller children, and not to hit the parents. But when parents tell their children not to hit but then hit them themselves, they're sending mixed messages and providing a double incentive toward violence. Aside from suffering pain and humiliation, which is likely to elicit an aggressive reaction, the children see an example of an adult with whom they identify acting aggressively. Such parents provide a "living example of the use of aggression at the very moment they are trying to teach the child not to be aggressive" (Sears, Maccoby, & Levin, 1957, p. 266).

Parents exert a great deal of influence over children's aggressiveness. One major study found that the parents of children who were aggressive in school were less nurturant and accepting, punished their children for aggression at home, and, in general, gave them little support (Eron, 1980).

WE LEARN FROM SOCIETAL ATTITUDES When social scientists compare violent societies (like our own) with those in which very little violence occurs, they find a number of differences. In the valley of Oaxaca, Mexico, for example, there are several antiviolent communities, surrounded by others showing a more typical level of violence (Paddock, 1975). What are the differences? The antiviolent communities have very different attitudes toward sex differences, rearing boys and girls very similarly and showing practically no signs of *machismo*, or the necessity for male domi-

We can tell a great deal about a society's way of looking at things by knowing what activities it encourages. What do American sanctions for a "sport" that consists of efforts to injure other human beings say about our cultural attitudes toward violence? (© 1982 Frank Fournier/Contact)

nance in employment, income, and within the family. They discipline their children quite differently, correcting them verbally most of the time and rarely spanking. Adults ignore children's misbehavior when possible and teach children to ignore mistreatment by other children. Children are also kept much closer to the home.

In our society, even today, after many changes in the roles of men and women, prevailing attitudes are more like those of the more violent Mexican ones—men are expected to be the head of the household, children and adults alike are expected to get even with anyone who does them an injury, and corporal punishment is taken so much for granted as a way of disciplining children that even nonfamily members (like teachers) are often expected to spank youngsters.

Our attitudes about the relationship between men and women are closely linked to male behavior toward women. In recent years, there's been a disturbing upsurge in *aggressive pornography*, which shows men raping, mutilating, or otherwise hurting women. Young men who see these films in the laboratory tend to become more aggressive to women they actually encounter, probably because these films strengthen their belief in the myth that women like force and dominance and influence their behavior toward women in general (Donnerstein & Malamuth, in press; Malamuth & Donnerstein, 1982). Furthermore, men who see films showing a woman becoming aroused by rape (a common theme in hard-core pornography) see the victim as more responsible for her own rape than they do when the woman seems to suffer, giving rise to another myth—that rape is a sexually arousing act instead of the terror-producing one that actual rape victims report. Such pornography teaches that this kind of aggression is acceptable, a worrisome lesson.

WE LEARN FROM TELEVISION   One of the best message bearers of our society's values is television. What are children to conclude about aggression and violence when they sit before the TV set and watch grisly killings, beatings, and mayhem day after brutal day? Between the six violent acts per prime-time hour of network television and the twenty-seven violent acts per hour of Saturday morning cartoons, the average child has witnessed the violent destruction of more than 13,400 people during the ten years between his or her fifth and fifteenth birthdays (Sabin, 1972; Prial, 1983).

While some people argue that viewing aggression or even acting it out to a limited degree helps to "drain off" aggressive energy, there's a limited basis for this belief. Acting aggressively is just as likely in some situations to make someone *more*, rather than *less*, aggressive (Geen & Quanty, 1977). And the bulk of the research on viewing aggression indicates that children who watch a lot of television learn that we live in a society that condones aggression in many situations, and they learn what to do when they feel aggressive themselves (Bandura, 1973). But when parents let their children know that violence is not an acceptable means of settling disputes, watching TV does *not* lead to more aggression (Dominick & Greenberg, 1971; Huesmann, Eron, Klein, Brice, & Fisher, in press).

The influence of TV is hard to counter, though. Research on its effects has gone on since the 1950s, and the great majority of reports from then up until the present suggest that seeing violence on the screen makes children more aggressive in real life (NIMH, 1982). This effect is true across all geographic and socioeconomic levels, for both sexes, and for normal children as well as those with emotional problems. The report issued in 1982 by the National Institute of Mental Health concludes that television encourages aggressive behavior in two ways: Children imitate what they see on television, and they also absorb the values transmitted and come to accept aggression as appropriate behavior.

Let's take a look at the conclusions drawn by one researcher who's been concentrating on this issue since the early 1960s. After following up 427 young adults whose televiewing habits had been studied when they were in third grade as part of a larger study of parental practices, Eron (1980) found that the single best predictor of a young man's aggressiveness at age 19 is the violence of the television programs that he liked to watch at the age of 8. A similar relationship has since been found for girls and women (Eron, 1982). Third-graders may be at a critical period of development, making them unusually susceptible to the effects of television. Aggressive children watch more television in general, identifying more strongly with aggressive TV characters, and are more likely to believe that on-screen aggression reflects real life (Eron, 1982).

Child-care professionals suggest that parents who want to counteract the effects of violent TV place limits on the amount of TV viewing, monitor the programs their children watch, and engage their children in discussions that encourage them to think about what they're seeing and to question the acceptability of violence as a way to settle disputes (Kaye, 1974).

It seems, then, that while we may well inherit the tendency to act aggressively, the way we express or inhibit this kind of behavior is shaped by the world around us.

AROUSAL AND CURIOSITY

Anyone who has ever spent much time in the company of a 3-year-old knows that human beings are very curious creatures from a very early

Human beings take new paths, climb forbidding mountains, and even go to the moon to satisfy our curiosity. Wanting to know what the universe is like is a powerful motivator for many different kinds of activities. (NASA Photo)

age. We want to know about everything in our lives—why people act as they do, why events occur, how things work, what's on the other side of a hill, a mountain, an ocean. To satisfy our boundless curiosity, we begin as infants to touch, to put new objects in our mouths, to take our first faltering steps away from home. As we grow older, we continue to process the information that comes in through all our senses, we explore our surroundings, we ask questions, we study, we puzzle, we think. We seem to do many things for no intrinsic reward other than satisfying our curiosity. Most psychologists believe that a basic motivational system underlies this behavior and that curiosity and arousal are related in important ways.

How We Become Aroused

The more alert we are, the better we can analyze what we see, hear, and feel. If we're drowsy, we don't process information well. (How many times have you read the same paragraph six times before realizing you were just too sleepy to concentrate?) To satisfy our curiosity, then, we need to be at a relatively high level of arousal. *Arousal* is a physiological state, which we experience as an ability to process information, to react to an emergency, and to experience a wide range of emotions.

What's happening in our bodies when we are at such a high level? A number of things. Let's start in the cortex. As we learned earlier, brain-wave patterns can be measured by the use of the electroencephalogram. When we are in a state of moderate arousal, in which we're alert and attentive, our EEG patterns show regular, fast, short spikes. In this state there's also an increase in other physiological responses: Heart rate and blood pressure go up, along with the release of blood glucose and other

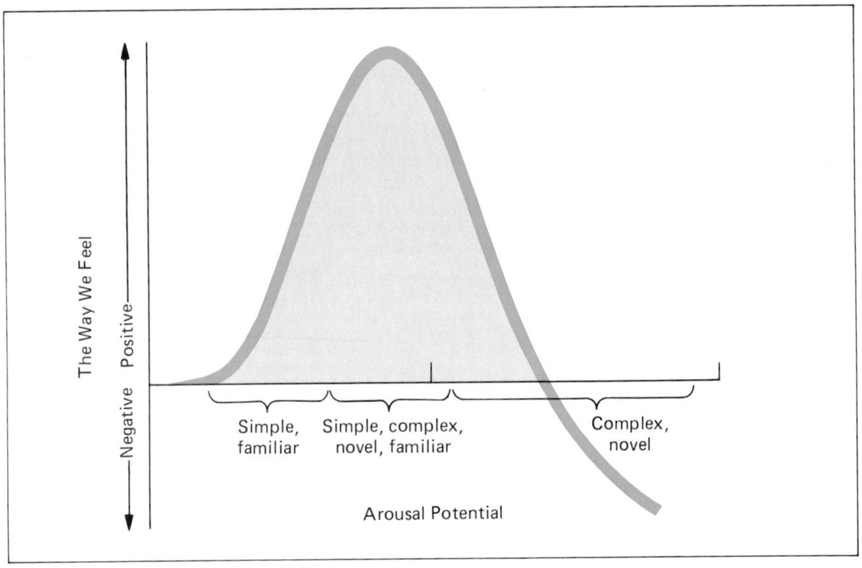

FIGURE 9-4 The Hypothesized Relation between the Way We Feel and the Arousal Potential of a Stimulus *Note that people are in the best frame of mind when faced with a stimulus that is moderately complex or moderately novel. A stimulus that is too simple and familiar or too complex and strange produces less pleasant feelings. (From Berlyne, 1970)*

reactions that prepare the body for expending energy. These increases are referred to as autonomic arousal since these reactions are mediated by the autonomic nervous system.

What produces these signs of cortical and autonomic arousal? There seems to be some biological mechanism, probably located in the reticular formation in the brain stem. This system, as we saw in Chapter 2, controls our levels of alertness and also plays a primary role in putting us to sleep. Incoming sensory stimulation activates sensory neurons, which stimulate the reticular formation. This in turn activates the cortex and other brain centers (such as the hypothalamus) that control autonomic arousal. Because the reticular formation activates these various brain centers, it has come to be called the reticular activating system.

How We Feel about Arousal

Human beings tend to prefer a moderate level of arousal—not so high that we're excited and disorganized and not so low that we're drowsy (Berlyne, 1971; Eysenck, 1967). This relationship between arousal and feeling state is shown in Figure 9-4, which demonstrates people's differing reactions to a variety of stimuli, ranging from the very simple and very familiar to the very complex and strange. Most people apparently like a stimulus that's moderately complex or moderately new.

Most people try to maintain a moderate level of arousal. Usually we do this by controlling our level of external stimulation: When we feel overstimulated, we're likely to retreat to a quiet spot where we can be alone, and when we feel understimulated, we're apt to seek out a noisy place full of people.

There are, however, large individual differences in the degree of arousal people feel comfortable with. You may be a very active person who likes or would like to engage in activities that carry risk and adventure, a very sociable individual who likes meeting and being with unconventional people. If so, you're what one psychologist has termed a "sensation-seeker" (Zuckerman, 1979). If, on the other hand, you prefer familiarity, stability, and a sense of peace, you're low on the sensation-seeking scale. To see where you fit on this characteristic, you may want to take the quiz in Table 9-1.

TABLE 9-1 Are You a High or a Low Sensation Seeker?

To test your own sensation-seeking tendencies, try this shortened version of one of Marvin Zuckerman's earlier scales. For each of the 13 items, circle the choice, A or B, that best describes your likes or dislikes or the way you feel. Instructions for scoring appear at the end of the test.

1 A I would like a job that requires a lot of traveling.
 B I would prefer a job in one location.
2 A I am invigorated by a brisk, cold day.
 B I can't wait to get indoors on a cold day.
3 A I get bored seeing the same old faces.
 B I like the comfortable familiarity of everyday friends.
4 A I would prefer living in an ideal society in which everyone is safe, secure, and happy.
 B I would have preferred living in the unsettled days of our history.
5 A I sometimes like to do things that are a little frightening.
 B A sensible person avoids activities that are dangerous.
6 A I would not like to be hypnotized.
 B I would like to have the experience of being hypnotized.
7 A The most important goal of life is to live it to the fullest and experience as much as possible.
 B The most important goal of life is to find peace and happiness.
8 A I would like to try parachute-jumping.
 B I would never want to try jumping out of a plane, with or without a parachute.
9 A I enter cold water gradually, giving myself time to get used to it.
 B I like to dive or jump right into the ocean or a cold pool.
10 A When I go on a vacation, I prefer the comfort of a good room and bed.
 B When I go on a vacation, I prefer the change of camping out.
11 A I prefer people who are emotionally expressive even if they are a bit unstable.
 B I prefer people who are calm and even-tempered.
12 A A good painting should shock or jolt the senses.
 B A good painting should give one a feeling of peace and security.
13 A People who ride motorcycles must have some kind of unconscious need to hurt themselves.
 B I would like to drive or ride a motorcycle.

Scoring

Count one point for each of the following items that you have circled: 1A, 2A, 3A, 4B, 5A, 6B, 7A, 8A, 9B, 10B, 11A, 12A, 13B. Add up your total and compare it with the norms below.

0-3 Very low on sensation seeking
4-5 Low
6-9 Average
10-11 High
12-13 Very High

Although the test gives some indication of a person's rating, it is not a highly reliable measure. One reason is, of course, that the test has been abbreviated. Another is that the norms are based largely on the scores of college students who have taken the test. As people get older, their scores on sensation seeking tend to go down.

From "The Search for High Sensation," by M. Zuckerman. In *Psychology Today*, February, 1978, *11*(9), 38–46. Copyright © 1978 by Ziff-Davis Publishing Company. Reprinted by permission.

Such differences in preferred arousal levels may be inherited, according to research evidence that one of the chemicals that regulate this tendency is, at least in part, genetically determined (Zuckerman, Buchsbaum, & Murphy, 1980). Since diversity is often important for the survival of a species, it's possible that such differences in sensation seeking may contribute to the vigor of the human race. In any case, the existence of people with such widely differing tendencies certainly helps keep life interesting.

How Arousal Affects Performance

Not only do most people like to feel moderately aroused but most of us are most efficient in this state. You've probably noticed yourself that you can't do your best work when you're excited and jumpy nor when you're really "laid back." You write your best papers, do your best studying, put forth your finest efforts at anything when you're in a state of moderate arousal. Figure 9-5 graphically shows this relationship between arousal and your best efforts.

According to the *Yerkes-Dodson law,* stated in 1908 by two psychologists, the optimal level of stimulation varies depending on what you're doing. If you're doing something very easy, you'll do best if the stimulus is very strong, while you'll do better at a more complicated or difficult task if the stimulus strength is somewhat lower. Since the discovery in 1949 of the reticular activating system, D. O. Hebb (1954) provided a new way of looking at how stimulation affects performance. Hebb said that the crucial determinant was not the stimulus itself but the state of arousal that it produced. A very strong stimulus produces high arousal, while a weaker stimulus produces low arousal.

Hebb pointed out that arousal narrows our attention. Thus, a narrowed focus, brought about by a strong stimulus and high arousal, helps us to concentrate on only one task. But when we need to solve problems in which we have to consider a number of factors and possible solutions, we have a broader approach. This has survival value. An animal who sees an enemy (a strong stimulus that causes high arousal) focuses his attention on one task—getting away. At such a time, he'll tend to use a familiar escape route. He needs to be at a lower level of arousal, when there is no immediate threat, to process information about the environment effectively enough to learn new routes.

According to Hebb, performance increases as arousal increases—up to a point. After the optimal level is reached, further increases in arousal don't *help* performance—they actually *interfere* with it. Hebb's model not only predicts performance, but predicts the kinds of tasks that human beings and animals are inclined to select. According to Hebb, we select tasks that provide us with optimal levels of arousal, and we often shift from one level of arousal to another—choosing to be quiet after being overstimulated or doing something new when we're bored. Individuals differ according to the level of arousal each of us finds comfortable. If you prefer to work in a state of high arousal, for example, in a room where people are constantly coming and going, where the walls are covered with attractive posters, and where loud music is playing, while your roommate likes to work alone in a quiet, sparsely furnished room, you'll have to do some careful negotiating—or else switch roommates.

Our bodies have the mechanisms for reacting to and dealing with new objects and events. In laboratory experiments, subjects faced with novel experiences have responded with autonomic arousal, increased galvanic skin response (the skin's reaction to a weak electric current), dilation of the pupils, and other signs of arousal (Lynn, 1966). There seems to be a clear evolutionary reason for this kind of reaction: It can save your life. For example, if you were suddenly to encounter a bear on the path, you'd need good cortical arousal to analyze how best to deal with this novel

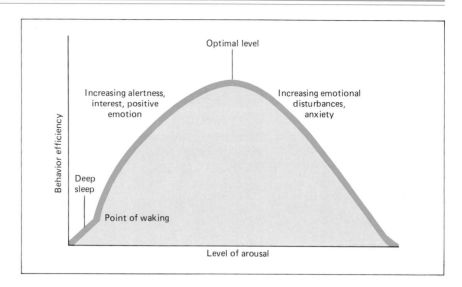

FIGURE 9-5 *The hypothetical relation between behavioral efficiency and level of arousal. (From Hebb, 1955)*

event, and you'd need autonomic arousal to provide the necessary energy backup to do whatever you'd decided was the appropriate action—climbing a tree, shooting, shouting for help, whatever.

Effects of Sensory Deprivation

Most of us today are beset on every side by a bewildering variety of sounds, sights, smells, movements, and other stimuli. Modern life—especially modern urban life—is a hubbub of stimulation, which some people (like "sensation seekers"?) thrive on and others long to escape. Some do escape, not by leaving the city but by regularly isolating themselves from stimulation. One way to do this is by immersion in a sensory deprivation chamber or tank, a facility that has become commercially available in some large cities. What does this do to people? Apparently, the effect depends partly on the individual and partly on the length of time one remains isolated from stimulation.

Some years ago a group of psychologists at McGill University built a sensory isolation chamber designed to keep stimulation to a minimum. They offered students who agreed to participate $20 a day (equivalent to $40 or $50 a day in today's economy) and asked them to be prepared to stay as long as possible. To the students, it sounded like an easy way to earn money by doing nothing. For nothing was exactly what they did. They were to lie motionless in this chamber whenever they weren't eating or drinking the adequate amounts of food and water available to them. They couldn't see anything but constant light because they wore translucent goggles, they couldn't touch things because they wore cardboard cuffs over their hands and lower arm, and they couldn't hear anything because the monotonous hum of an exhaust fan drowned out all other sounds. It turned out, however, that doing nothing was hard to do: Nearly all the subjects said the experience was unpleasant, and more than half asked to leave within forty-eight hours (Heron, 1961). Sensory deprivation for such an extended time turned out to be intolerable.

Other researchers have found some benefits in sensory deprivation, including its ability to improve performance in certain sensory abilities, such as the ability to respond quickly to a tone signal, the two-point touch discrimination threshold (described in Chapter 3), and sensitivity to

Clearly, reduced stimulation can be useful: while a student who wants to prepare an assigned paper should avoid environmental monotony, it could be an aid for one who needs to memorize a body of material.
(Suedfeld, 1975, p. 65)

The hallucinations often experienced by truck drivers who travel vast distances on flat, boring interstate highways seem to be caused by sensory deprivation. (Penelope Breese/Liaison Agency)

sweet and bitter tastes and to pain. Certain cognitive processes seem to be sharpened, also, such as rote learning of lists of words and recall or recognition of previously learned material; while such simple tasks often show improvement after deprivation, more complex tasks show impaired performance. Among the therapeutic benefits of sensory deprivation has been its use in a program that has helped people to stop smoking (Suedfeld, 1975).

Despite these individual findings, however, most people seem to need a great deal of sensory stimulation and find the kind of deprivation we're talking about here intolerable for any extended period of time.

ACHIEVEMENT

You may be trying to make the highest grade possible in this course, striving to make the dean's list, be graduated with honors, and go on to reach the top of your chosen profession. Or you may be content to pass the course, get through college somehow, and take a job that may give you a living but won't hold out the promise of high achievement. If the first sentence describes you, you probably have high achievement needs; if the second is more accurate, your achievement needs are lower. In 1938, Murray defined the need to achieve (often expressed as *n*Ach) as a desire or tendency "to overcome obstacles, to exercise power, to strive to do something difficult as well and as quickly as possible" (pp. 80–81). It wasn't until 1953, however, that psychologists tried to measure the strength of this need, using the Thematic Apperception Test (TAT) to do so (McClelland, Atkinson, Clark, & Lowell, 1953).

The TAT is made up of a set of pictures showing people in different kinds of situations. If you were taking this test, you would be asked to write a story indicating what led up to the event shown in the picture, what's happening now, and what will happen in the future. The assumption underlying the test is that people are inclined to write stories about themes that are important to them. (For this reason the TAT is often used as a general personality test, as explained in Chapter 14.) McClelland and his associates devised a system for scoring "achievement imagery." They analyzed the content of stories about the TAT pictures to see whether the writers had used achievement imagery or used words related to achievement. In other words, did people talk about setting difficult goals, persisting, overcoming obstacles, and so forth? Through answering these questions, they rated the test takers' needs for achievement.

Now that we have been studying achievement for more than twenty-five years, what do we know about it? We know that even 2-month-old babies seem to experience some sense of achievement since an experiment in which infants controlled the movement of an overhead mobile by turning their heads found that the babies who did this seemed to smile more when the mobile moved than did babies who saw the same kind of mobile but hadn't made it move themselves (Watson & Ramey, 1972). This finding seems to point to some kind of inborn human need to make things happen.

Several personality characteristics and behavioral styles of high-achievement-need people have also emerged. When given a choice of hard, easy, and in-between tasks, they usually pick the in-between, which seems to present enough of a challenge to be interesting but not so much to be discouraging (Mahone, 1960; Morris, 1966). They're usually optimistic about their chances of success, consider themselves capable of it, take personal responsibility for it, and are willing to delay gratification to achieve it (Feather, 1965; Kukla, 1972; Mischel, 1961).

It's possible that the need for achievement may be at least partly inherited; some people may be born with the drive to succeed. Whether or not this is so, we do know that there are ways to increase *n*Ach. We know, for example, that certain styles of child rearing seem to influence children to become high achievers (Feshbach & Weiner, 1982). In one classic study, Winterbottom (1958) found that mothers of children with strong achievement motivation tend to encourage independence and mastery before their children are 8 years old, expecting their youngsters to know their way around the city and to do well in competition.

Achievement performance can also be improved later in life. Men who took part in a three- to six-week training course (in which they learned about the importance of taking risks, the future-orientation of achievers, and how to set their own goals) achieved more afterward than men who had not taken the course (McClelland & Winter, 1969). Other approaches try to change people's explanations for success or failure, in the knowledge that low achievers tend to think they have little ability and won't succeed anyway, so they don't try hard. This results, of course, in a self-fulfilling prophecy since people who don't make the effort to achieve are more likely to fail. Some programs concentrate on simply instructing people about the role of effort in success (Ostrove, 1978).

Aside from personal, anecdotal guesses, we don't know whether *n*Ach cuts across different areas of people's lives, because researchers have not sought to find out whether someone with a high need for achievement will be just as competitive on the tennis court as in the law court or whether people have different achievement needs in different areas of their lives. Our knowledge about whether people's needs for achieve-

BOX 9-2

STUDENTS' STORIES ABOUT SUCCESS

When male and female undergraduates were asked to write stories based on clues that were alike in every detail except the sex of the protagonist, men writing about a male protagonist tended to describe success in glowing terms, while women emphasized the negative aspects of success. Here are some typical stories, based on the clue, "After first-term finals, John [Anne] finds himself [herself] at the top of his [her] medical-school class."

WRITTEN BY MALE UNDERGRADUATES

John is a conscientious young man who worked hard. He is pleased with himself. John has always wanted to go into medicine and is very dedicated. . . . John continues working hard and eventually graduates at the top of his class.

John has worked very hard and his long hours of study have paid off. . . . He is thinking about his girl, Cheri, whom he will marry at the end of med. school. He realizes he can give her all the things she desires after he becomes established. He will go on in med. school and be successful in the long run.

WRITTEN BY FEMALE UNDERGRADUATES

Anne starts proclaiming her surprise and joy. Her fellow classmates are so disgusted with her behavior that they jump on her in a body and beat her. She is maimed for life.

Although Anne is happy with her success she fears what will happen to her social life. The male med. students don't seem to think very highly of a female who has beaten them in their field. . . . She will be a proud and successful but alas a very *lonely* doctor.

From Horner, 1968.

ment remain fairly stable through life is fairly limited. We do know that college men who were high in *n*Ach in their early twenties tended to end up in entrepreneurial jobs (McClelland, 1965). And in studies of men in fifteen fields of creative endeavor and in ten fields of governmental, judicial, and military leadership, a strong relationship has shown up between achievement motivation and career success (Veroff, Atkinson, Feld, & Gurin, 1960). As in so many areas of psychological research, most of the study of achievement motivation has concentrated on its effect on men. In view of the different messages transmitted to girls and women in our society, we need to explore this phenomenon more intensively as it applies to women.

It seems that the need to achieve is modified in some people by their need to avoid failure (Atkinson, 1957). Those with a high need to avoid failure are reluctant to take the risks required to succeed. These people would choose easy tasks when they can; by not taking risks, they keep themselves from real achievement and end up hovering somewhere between success and failure. While this theory was reasonably good at predicting the way men would behave in a variety of laboratory situations, it was less accurate for women. Other evidence, too, indicated that women seemed to perceive achievement differently from men—and, in fact, achieved less. Students of achievement wondered why women were less likely to enter the higher professions and less likely to succeed when they did. Was this because they had less ability, less of a need to achieve, or were suffering discrimination?

Matina Horner, now president of Radcliffe College, was the first to tackle this question scientifically. She asked both male and female students to write stories based on themes of success and found that the stories women wrote about a woman's success emphasized the negative consequence success can bring, such as unpopularity, loneliness, and guilt, while both men and women wrote stories about male success that emphasized the positive advantages of doing well. Based on these responses, some of which are shown in Box 9-2, Horner (1968) suggested that women have a "fear of success" that keeps them from achieving.

Subsequent researchers have come to different conclusions, including the fact that males experience just as much fear of success as women (Tresemer, 1974). Today, then, many psychologists treat Horner's findings with some skepticism (Zuckerman & Wheeler, 1975). Nevertheless, several studies have confirmed the basic premise that women—at least in the 1960s, 1970s, and early 1980s—were having trouble reconciling their new-found freedom to achieve with traditional expectations about the role of women in society (Stephan, Rosenfield, & Stephan, 1976; Kruegar, 1983). Some women do feel ambivalent about achievement and may not compete because of what they see as the costs of achievement. There's also considerable evidence that women often don't compete against men when they think a task involves "masculine" skills (Deaux, White, & Farris, 1975).

Often, it seems that women refuse to compete not out of an irrational fear but from a realistic assessment of the negative side-effects that often accrue to successful women in our society. For many women, career success *has* resulted in conflicts in personal life. As cultural stereotypes diminish and attitudes change, such negative consequences may no longer follow a woman's achievement, and capable women will be able to seek and embrace success as enthusiastically as men can.

As we pointed out earlier, our feelings are an important element in motivating our behavior—and our own behavior and that of others are important elements in making us feel a wide range of emotions. Let's look at what psychology has determined to be significant about human emotions.

EMOTION

You're afraid. You're angry. You're happy. You're sad. What do these words mean? What are you experiencing when you're in an emotional state? Are you interpreting the physical sensations caused by the release of some chemical in your body or the activation of some region of your brain? Or is the strong feeling you're aware of a subjective thing that owes its existence to the thought processes in your brain that created it and labeled it? Much of the research into emotion has focused on answering these questions.

Theories of Emotion

The principal theories of emotion see this feeling state as physiological, as cognitive, or as a product of the interaction of physical and mental factors. For graphic depictions of the three major theories, see Figures 9-6, 9-7, and 9-8.

THE JAMES-LANGE THEORY (FEELINGS ARE PHYSICAL)   Two scientists working at the same time—the psychologist William James (1884) and the

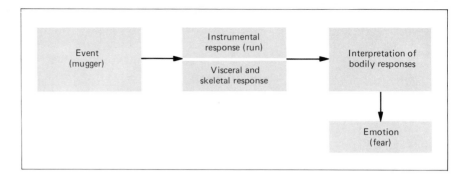

FIGURE 9-6 The James-Lange Theory of Emotion *Emotion occurs when the individual interprets his or her bodily responses: "I must be afraid because I am running and my heart is pounding."*

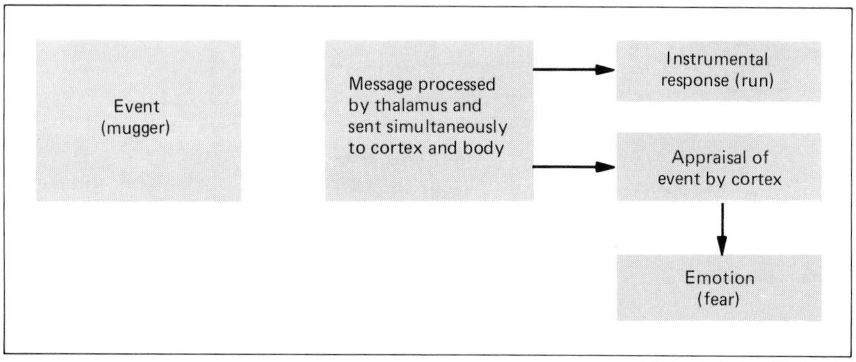

FIGURE 9-7 The Cannon-Bard Theory of Emotion *Emotion is solely a cognitive event: "I am afraid because I know muggers are dangerous."*

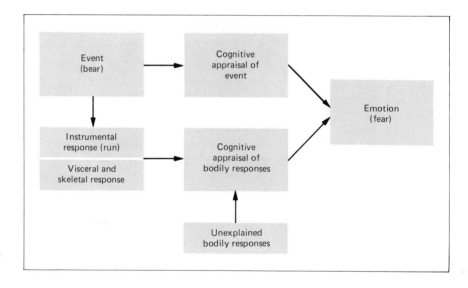

FIGURE 9-8 The Schachter-Singer Theory of Emotion *Emotion is due to two related but independent cognitive operations—appraisal of the event and appraisal of bodily reactions. The intensity of an emotion is due to how the individual appraises bodily responses. Unexplained bodily reactions can contribute to increases in perceived intensity.*

physiologist Carl Lange (1885)—came up with such similar points of view that we can treat their contributions jointly. Essentially, both questioned the traditional assumption that we experience some event (like being accosted by a mugger), feel an emotion (fear), and then experience the physiological sensations connected to that emotion (pounding heart, quickened breathing, sweaty palms, weakness in the knees, etc.) and behave in a way that seems appropriate to the situation (fight, shout, faint, or run away). Both James and Lange argued instead for a reversal of this sequence—that the basis for emotions arises from our perception of

Common sense says that we lose our fortune, are sorry, and weep; . . . [My] hypothesis . . . is that we feel sorry because we cry, angry because we strike, afraid because we tremble. . . . (James, 1890)

such physiological sensations as changes in heart rate and blood pressure and contractions of visceral and skeletal muscles.

According to this theory, when you're insulted, you don't feel angry and then experience the physiological symptoms of rage. Your heart and breathing speed up and your muscles tense and you then interpret these body changes to yourself as "I'm angry." This theory assumes that our physiological responses are different for each emotion, which is not *always* the case. So while the theory has a certain measure of validity, it does not provide a complete explanation for the experience of emotion.

The feedback from physiological responses is not *necessary* to experience an emotion, but it can be important. As discussed below, Schachter and Singer (1962) showed how it can help to make an emotional response more intense.

THE CANNON-BARD THEORY (FEELINGS ARE COGNITIVE) In 1927 Walter Cannon argued against the James-Lange position, an argument later extended by Philip Bard (1938). They pointed to laboratory research that showed that the physiological reactions that accompany different emotions are the same from emotion to emotion. In other words, that heart and breathing rates increase and muscles tense whether people are nervous, angry, afraid, or in love. So if we depended only on our physiological responses, we wouldn't be able to distinguish one emotion from another. Furthermore, they claimed that people are not normally aware of most of the internal changes (like contractions of visceral organs such as the kidney or the liver) and that even animals who were surgically prevented from experiencing such physiological sensations showed typical emotional reactions. They proposed instead that the emotional experience and the physiological arousal occur at the same time, rather than one after the other.

How does this happen? According to Cannon and Bard, for example, when you encounter a mugger, nerve impulses carry this information to two important places in your brain. Your *cortex*, the site of the higher thought processes, tells you that the mugger is a threat to your personal safety, and this realization, this thought, is enough to produce fear. At the same time, your *thalamus* produces a variety of nonspecific physiological changes (that is, they are not specific to any particular emotion but arise in response to any emotion). These changes are referred to as the "stress" reaction, or the "fight-or-flight" reaction (described more fully in the following chapter). This reaction prepares you to expend energy and deal with potential injury. If you then discovered that this threatening-looking person was not a mugger but just someone coming up to ask you directions, both sites would shut down: The cortex would turn off your feelings of fear and the thalamus would cancel the physiological reaction.

This theory integrated the research on the role of the thalamus in emotion. Its major shortcoming was its failure to recognize the complexity of emotional experiences and the way they can be influenced by an individual's interpretation of physiological feedback.

THE SCHACHTER-SINGER THEORY (EMOTIONS DEPEND ON DOUBLE COGNITIVE LABELING: HOW WE APPRAISE THE EVENT AND HOW WE EVALUATE WHAT'S GOING ON IN OUR BODIES) The view of emotion as a purely cognitive event became the accepted explanation until the 1960s, when two

One reason why roller coasters are so popular with lovers may be the possible association in people's minds between the physiological sensations brought on by being in a scary situation—and those of sexual arousal. In a recent study, men who met an attractive young woman on a high, rickety bridge were more likely to phone her later than those who met the same woman on a sturdier, lower, safer bridge. (© 1983 Michael Murphy/ Photo Researchers, Inc.)

innovative psychologists, Stanley Schachter and Jerome Singer (1962) questioned the concept that physiological responses play no role whatsoever.

Schachter and Singer performed a number of interesting laboratory experiments. In some of them they administered to a group of subjects epinephrine, a drug produced by the adrenal cortex, which causes autonomic arousal such as increased heart rate and blood pressure. They then put the subjects in situations that would encourage them either to be happy or to be angry. Meanwhile, they had told half the subjects in each situation (happy/angry) that the injection would cause certain physiological effects; the other half were not informed of the effects of the injection.

By and large, the results of the experiment confirmed the researchers' hypothesis. The subjects who had *not* been told of the probable effects of the injection claimed to be especially happy or angry and acted accordingly, while the ones who *had* been informed did not have a particularly emotional reaction. Apparently, the informed subjects attributed their physiological arousal to the effects of the drug, while the uninformed subjects, not knowing about the drug effects, noticed their arousal, cast about for an explanation, and concluded that it must be due to an emotion. In looking for an emotion, they hit upon the most available explanation and fit their emotion to the situation at hand.

The same thing seemed to happen in another intriguing experiment that took place on a rickety footbridge more than 200 feet above a rocky canyon. When young men standing on this bridge were approached by an attractive young woman who asked them to take part in a study that involved writing thoughts inspired by a picture she showed, they seemed to be more sexually aroused (based on their writing) than did young men who were approached by the same woman on a sturdier, lower, safer bridge. Furthermore, the men on the high-fear bridge were more likely to phone the woman afterward (Dutton & Aron, 1974). Apparently the men in the high-fear situation tended to attribute whatever signs of arousal they felt—a swiftly beating heart, clammy hands, quickened breathing—to sexual arousal in the presence of a likely candidate. Could the implications of this study lead people in love to take the objects of their affection to someplace scary to intensify their feelings? Maybe that's why roller coasters and ferris wheels are so popular with lovers.

While follow-up research has not supported Schachter and Singer's theory completely, it has confirmed some elements. For example, it does seem as if increased arousal (which can come from the injection of a drug like epinephrine, from physical exercise, or from being in a frightening situation) can *intensify* an emotion we already feel (Reisenzein, 1983).

Considerable support has been found for Schachter and Singer's suggestion that people show more intense emotional reactions when they experience increases in arousal that they can't attribute to some other source. Research has not supported their suggestion that reducing arousal automatically leads to a reduction in emotional intensity (Reisenzein, 1983). In other words, arousal can enhance intensity but doesn't necessarily cause it.

FACIAL FEEDBACK THEORY (OUR FACIAL EXPRESSIONS LEAD TO EMOTIONS) Recent findings about the effects of our facial expressions show a definite connection to theories William James enunciated a century ago.

Professional actor Tom Harrison is shown in these frames from a videotape as he responds to such instructions as "Raise your brows and pull them together" (left), "Now raise your upper eyelids" (center), and "Now also stretch your lips horizontally, back toward your ears" (right). Researchers designed these instructions to portray the facial expressions that accompany the emotion of fear, and in fact the actors who followed the instructions showed more bodily signs of emotion than they did when they just thought of a frightening experience. (© 1983 Paul Ekman)

If we wish to conquer undesirable emotional tendencies in ourselves, we must assiduously, and in the first instance cold-bloodedly, go through the *outward motions* of those contrary dispositions we prefer to cultivate.
(James, 1884)

(According to contemporary reports, James followed his own advice to get over his grief over his parents' deaths.)

Cognitive-Chemical Interactions in Emotion

Professional actors were the subjects in a two-phase experiment on emotion (Ekman, Levenson, & Friesen, 1983). In one part, researchers instructed the actors to think of an emotional experience in their own lives that mirrored each of the six emotions being studied—surprise, disgust, sadness, anger, fear, and happiness (as in "method acting"). In the other phase, the senior researcher coached each subject, with the help of a mirror, to assume a certain expression. He didn't ask them to feel a certain way but just to contract specific facial muscles, by which they created smiles, frowns, and expressions common in the six emotional states. In both phases, the subjects' autonomic nervous system responses were recorded—their heart rate, temperature of left and right hands, resistance of the skin to the passage of a very weak electric current, and muscle tension in the forearm.

Two significant sets of findings emerged from this study. First, this research found that physiological responses differed according to the emotion being studied. Hearts, for example, beat faster in anger and fear than in happiness, hands were colder in fear than in anger, and certain other physical differences showed up. It seems, then, that different emotions do elicit different responses, at least to some degree. This indicates, then, that the James-Lange theory described earlier does seem to have some validity: We do get feedback from our bodies, and we often get different kinds of feedback for different emotions.

The other major finding was that when subjects just moved their facial muscles, they produced more pronounced physiological signs of emotion than they did when they thought of emotional experiences. So the advice in the popular song to "put on a happy face" when you're feeling low may be psychologically sound, after all. Acting happy may make you feel happy.

Most of us have accepted the idea that the chemicals in our body affect the way we feel, think, and act. This is, after all, the rationale for taking psychoactive drugs that simulate the action of natural neurotransmitters. More recently, however, we have been discovering that the way we feel, think, and act affects the chemicals our bodies secrete. Males in a position of dominance, for example, seem to secrete more of the neurotransmitter *serotonin*. When members of a college fraternity were measured for serotonin levels, the officers were found to have higher levels than other members. Evidence that the leadership led to the serotonin, and not vice

The seated woman is taking a polygraph, or lie detector, test. The devices attached to her body measure her breathing rate, blood pressure, and electrodermal response as she responds to a range of questions. The theory behind the test is that an individual is more likely to show changes in these measures when lying than when telling the truth, but many factors other than lying can affect an individual's score, making the test far from foolproof. (Bruce Roberts/ Photo Researchers, Inc.)

FIGURE 9-9 Measures in a Typical Polygraph Test *At the right we see tracings in a polygraph recording. The top tracing shows breathing rate; the middle tracing shows electrodermal response (EDR); and the bottom tracing shows blood-pressure rate. The subject, who claimed not to have seen a stolen envelope, was asked whether it was brown (1), red (2), blue (3), yellow (4), or gray (5). You can see the sharp rise in the EDR when question 3 was asked. The subject finally admitted taking the money and returned it in its blue envelope. The electrodermal response is the most accurate of the three measures. (From Reid & Inbau, 1977)*

versa, comes from research with monkeys (McGuire, Raleigh, Brammer, & Yuwiler, 1983).

Dominant males in colonies of vervet monkeys have been shown to have twice as much circulating serotonin in their blood as other males. When the leader is isolated from the group, his serotonin levels drop. When another male assumes the dominant role, his serotonin level rises to about twice its normal level. Then, when the original leader returns, his serotonin level rises again and the deposed monkey's drops again.

Other research with monkeys (Brady, 1967; 1975) has shown that monkeys who are in control of an event secrete more of the neurotransmitter *norepinephrine*. High levels of this chemical usually lead to feelings of optimism and enthusiasm, while low levels are associated with depression (Schildkraut & Kety, 1967). Before taking part in shock-avoidance studies, the monkeys' levels of norepinephrine and epinephrine were fairly low, but after the monkeys had learned how to avoid a painful electric shock, their norepinephrine levels soared. This adaptive mechanism helps to explain why people who feel they have control over their lives have a much more positive outlook, as we saw when we discussed the phenomenon of learned helplessness in Chapter 5. Often, people who feel they have control feel better even when they don't exercise such control, which is a powerful argument for seeing life as a series of challenges rather than a series of blows dealt by fate.

The well-established fact that a relationship exists between our emotions and our bodies is the basis for the development of the lie detector. Since most people tend to feel anxious when they lie and since there are a number of common physical signs of anxiety—such as a faster heartbeat and breathing rate and an increase in perspiration, the notion that judging whether someone's telling the truth by measuring some of these physical signs is a seductive one. The ancient Hindus tried to do it by requiring people suspected of crimes to chew a mouthful of rice; those who couldn't spit it out on a sacred leaf were judged guilty. Why? People who are afraid salivate less, making the rice stick in their dry mouths and making it impossible to spit. Our technically advanced modern *polygraph* is based on the same physiological relationship, but it isn't always reliable, as shown in Box 9-3.

In the next chapter we'll see how people react when they're faced with stress—how it affects their emotions, when it overwhelms them, when and how they marshal their forces to cope with it, and when it's an energizing, motivating force in their lives.

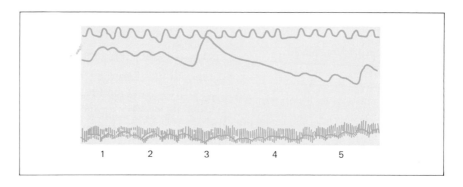

BOX 9-3

LIE DETECTORS: FOOLPROOF OR FRAUDULENT?

The owner of "Scooper Dupers," an ice cream parlor, finds a persistent shortage in the cash register, based on the amount of ice cream being sold. She questions her twelve employees and is unable to figure out who is either stealing money or giving away ice cream. So she administers "lie detector" tests to all twelve. Six "fail" the test and are fired. The question is: Have the real culprits been fired?

People selling such tests often tell prospective customers that psychologists have *proved* that they work. This is not true. What psychologists have found is that on a probability basis, they can detect more people who lie than don't lie. In any particular instance, however, they are not foolproof. (This is like the probability that when we toss a coin, we don't know on any given toss whether heads or tails will come up, but we do know that if we toss enough coins, we'll turn up half heads and half tails.)

So our Scooper Dupers owner is likely to be firing two honest people for every three liars. In other words, she's apt to continue to employ one out of four liars, while firing two out of four truth tellers. With the test, she can identify three out of four liars, but at the expense of labeling half of the truthful ones as liars (Waid & Orne, 1982). To see how this could be, let's see how these tests, called *polygraph tests,* work.

The examiner reminds the subject of his or her right not to take the test and has the person sign a consent form testifying that the test is being taken "voluntarily." (An ethical question is how voluntary such a step can be when the subject feels that refusing to take the test will make him or her the object of suspicion.) The examiner then discusses the questions that will be asked. Some are irrelevant ("Are you in the United States?"), some are designed to elicit an emotional response ("Besides what you told me about, have you ever stolen anything?"), and some are related to the specific purpose of the test ("What color was the envelope containing the stolen money?").

Before the examiner actually asks the questions—usually no more than twelve questions over a time period of 3 to 4 minutes—devices are attached to the subject's body. These measure breathing rate, blood pressure, and *electrodermal response,* or *EDR* (an index that detects changes in the resistance of the skin to the passage of a very weak electric current). This last measure is the most accurate (see Figure 9-9). The subject cannot see either the examiner or the machine's record of his or her responses.

The tests do show that certain physiological responses do reflect a high level of emotionality. But they don't necessarily prove that the emotions are linked to lying. The theory underlying these tests is that people who are guilty of whatever wrongdoing the test is being given to uncover will respond emotionally to the key questions and that these measures can correctly identify emotional responses. Often this is so: People show greater changes from their *base-line* scores (the scores they show when they're answering irrelevant questions) when they're lying than when they're telling the truth.

There are, however, many factors that affect an individual's score on a test. Some people react emotionally to certain words or phrases even when they're telling the truth. Those who believe that the lie detector is effective in detecting lies are more likely to receive accurate readings from it than people who don't (probably because they'll be more nervous about being found out when they lie than people who don't think that lie detectors work). It's also possible to reduce detectability in a number of ways. Laboratory studies have shown that it's harder to detect lying by subjects who have taken tranquilizers, people who are not paying close attention to the questions, habitual liars, those of the same ethnic group as the examiner, and those who were later-born children in large families (Waid & Orne, 1982).

Lie detectors are routinely used these days throughout society—by employers, by law enforcement agencies, and by such government agencies as the CIA and the National Security Agency. In view of the many factors that affect the accuracy of these tests and the 50:50 chance of labeling a truthful person a liar, and given the consequences of "flunking" a lie detector test—which may include being fired from a job (with a consequent reputation for lying and/or theft), being refused government security clearance (with this fact going on one's record), indictment on a criminal charge, trial, and perhaps a prison term—it is hard to justify pressuring people to take these tests.

SUMMARY

1   *Motivation* is the force that energizes and gives direction to behavior and that underlies the tendency to persist. Current research focuses mainly on the factors that arouse and energize behavior. *Emotions* are subjective reactions to our environment that are accompanied by neural and hormonal responses. They are generally experienced as pleasant or unpleasant and are considered adaptive reactions that affect the way we think.

2   Theories of motivation generally fall into three categories. Those that stress *biological* factors include theories based on *instincts* (inborn patterns of behavior); *drives* (internal tension states such as hunger that propel people or animals to act); or *needs* (which may be physiological or psychological and which operate in a hierarchical way, so we need to satisfy those most basic for survival first). The other two categories stress the importance of *learning* (our observations of the kinds of behavior that gets rewarded, either through our own or other people's actions) and of *cognitive* factors (our interpretations of events).

3   When two or more motives are aroused at the same time, four types of conflict may occur: *approach-approach, avoidance-avoidance, approach-avoidance,* and *multiple approach-avoidance.*

4   Six kinds of behavior often studied by motivational researchers are hunger and eating, sex, aggression, achievement, curiosity, and arousal.

5   *Hunger and Eating:* Subjective feelings of hunger are linked to insulin levels (a biological factor): Insulin is released when we eat and is important in the conversion of blood glucose and carbohydrates into energy; when insulin levels are high, we get hungry.

6   Four theories about why people become obese include: (a) the possibility that we are perpetuating an evolutionary mechanism by which we eat when we can and store energy in the form of fat against the possibility of famine; (b) in some people, the *set-point,* the mechanism controlled by the hypothalamus that signals us to stop eating when an ideal weight has been reached, is higher than average; (c) people who are addicted to the taste and texture of food eat too much of it; and (d) people who respond to *external* cues (like time of day, ads for food, or its availability) eat more than people who respond to *internal* cues (like stomach contractions or low blood glucose or insulin levels). Most current diet programs try to get overweight people to eat less and exercise more.

7   *Anorexia nervosa,* a form of self-starvation that can cause death, and *bulimia,* a harmful eating pattern characterized by binging and then vomiting or laxative-induced purging, have become more common in recent years, especially among young women, probably because of societal pressures to be thin.

8   *Sexuality:* The four stages of sexual response include *excitement, plateau, orgasm,* and *resolution.* Sexual desire is aroused by a combination of physiology and learning. *Testosterone,* one of the *androgens* (male sexual hormones), is an important source of sexual arousal in both men and women, and the female hormone *estrogen* is linked to female sexual arousal. Learning affects sexual arousal in many ways: We learn to act toward others by observing those around us, we choose sexual partners based on cultural standards of attractiveness, and we become aroused in situations we consider sexual ones.

9   We don't know what causes *heterosexuality* (sexual attraction to someone of the other sex) or *homosexuality* (attraction to someone of the same sex), although it's probable that an interaction among various hormonal and environmental events is crucial.

10 *Aggression:* A number of theories try to explain the cause of *aggression,* any behavior intended to harm someone or something. *Biological* theories point to the implication of several brain structures in the regulation of aggressive behavior and to hormones and other brain chemicals, such as *testosterone, estrogen,* and *norepinephrine. Learning theories* emphasize what we observe in the actions of other people and what messages we get from our culture. Violence depicted on television and in pornography seems to teach an acceptance of aggressive behavior to both adults and children. Events that trigger aggressive behavior include frustration, negative evaluation, and insults.

11 *Arousal and curiosity: Arousal* is a physiological state, which we experience as an ability to process information, react to an emergency, and experience a wide range of emotions. *Curiosity* is a desire to learn about new events or objects. Human beings are curious animals that seem to become aroused as we process information in the absence of any reward other than the satisfaction of our curiosity. While different people find different levels of arousal satisfying, most of us feel most comfortable and do our best work at a moderate level. Individual differences may be inherited.

12 *Achievement:* Human beings have different needs to attain goals by putting forth their best efforts. This need to achieve is often measured by the The-

matic Apperception Test (TAT). It may be partly inherited, but it can also be spurred by certain child-rearing techniques or incentives. Individual performance is affected by a person's fear of failure or fear of success.

13 The three major explanations for emotions are based on physiology, cognition, or the interaction of physical and mental factors. The *James-Lange theory* suggests that we base the way we feel on physical sensations like increased heart rate and muscle contractions. The *Cannon-Bard theory* suggests that feelings are purely cognitive since physical reactions are the same for different emotions and people can't tell one emotion from another on the basis of physiological signs. The *Schacter-Singer theory* maintains that emotions are due both to our cognitive appraisal of an event and our bodily reactions: People notice physiological changes, note what's going on around them, and label their emotions according to both kinds of observations.

14 When people experience an event as uncontrollable, they feel more negative about it than when they feel they can direct its outcome. Feelings of control are linked to the brain chemical *norepinephrine*.

15 Lie detectors *(polygraph tests)* are not very reliable in determining a subject's truthfulness by monitoring such physiological signs as breathing rate, blood pressure, and electrodermal response. This is because people sometimes react emotionally to questions that they answer truthfully and at other times are able to mask emotional responses when they are lying.

SUGGESTED READINGS

Geen, R. G., & Donnerstein, E. I. (Eds.). (1983). *Aggression: Theoretical and empirical reviews,* vol. 1: *Theoretical and methodological issues,* and vol. 2: *Issues and research.* New York: Academic Press. Provides a very comprehensive coverage of recent developments in the field of aggression that have taken place since the 1970s. Both theoretical and applied research is included.

Maslow, A. H. (1971). *The farther reaches of human nature.* New York: Viking Press. Discusses how humans can become self-actualized. Maslow's humanistic view is presented clearly and forcefully.

Spence, J. T. (Ed.). (1983). *Achievement and achievement motives.* New York: W. H. Freeman. Brings together the current research and thinking about achievement motivation.

Stuart, R. B. (1978). *Act thin, stay thin.* New York: Norton. The condensed version of a classic book on dieting. In this book Stuart explains why his behavioral approach to dieting works.

Tiger, L. (1979). *Optimism: The biology of hope.* New York: Simon and Schuster. Presents the case that humans are inclined to be optimistic. Tiger traces the origins of this tendency back through our evolutionary history, showing how and why this tendency evolved.

Zuckerman, M. (1979). *Sensation-seeking: Beyond the optimal level of arousal.* Hillsdale, N.J.: Lawrence Erlbaum Associates. Packed with information about the sensation seeker. For anyone interested in this topic, this book is a must.

CHAPTER 10

STRESS AND COPING

SPOTLIGHT ON

The positive value of stress.

How our reactions to a potentially stressful event are due not only to what the event is but to how we interpret it.

The "stress potential" of major life changes and life's little hassles.

How families cope with normal family transitions such as having a baby and the empty nest.

Stress-inoculation training as a stress-prevention technique.

Even before that first mysterious moment when something in our mother's body signaled our readiness to be cast out from the security of her womb, our prenatal existence was not free of stress. Despite the protection of the uterine environment, a fetus is likely to be assaulted by a barrage of such environmental insults as drugs, nicotine, maternal disease, x-rays, and environmental pollutants. From that point on, there is the trauma of birth, quickly followed by the discomfort of hunger, the fear of a crash of thunder, the anxiety of encountering a strange person, the frustration of not being able to make our wishes known, the difficulty of learning a new skill, the pain of a stomach cramp, and innumerable other reminders that no environment is all serenity and bliss.

On the other hand, some stress is positive, at every stage throughout life. Stress is not characterized only by experiences that cause pain. Stress is in the leap of excitement as a baby welcomes her mother's return at the end of the working day, in the bursts of giggling that follow a child's being tossed up in the air in exuberant play, in the heady excitement of a toddler's first shaky steps toward a wider world. Through coping, or dealing with both kinds of stress, we develop in many ways. There are effective and ineffective ways of responding to stress, as we'll see in our discussion of coping in this chapter.

What exactly is stress? Different researchers have looked at it on different levels and have, you'll not be surprised to find, defined it very differently according to their own orientations. As we'll soon discuss in more detail, Hans Selye, M.D., the pioneer in stress research, defined it in physiological terms as the body's response to any stressful demand. Richard S. Lazarus defined it in psychological terms as an individual's cognitive judgment that his or her personal resources will be taxed or incapable of dealing with the demands posed by a particular event. And Reuben Hill defines a stressor event as one that makes demands on the family system, rather than on the individual.

Infancy, of course, is only the beginning. For most of us, virtually every day in our lives contains some stress, some of which we welcome and some of which we weep at, and most of which most of us handle quite well. A great deal of stress is expected as part of the normal life cycle. Such stresses as assuming a new job, getting married, having a baby, and being widowed are, for example, not unexpected in the lives of most people. Such events are referred to as *normative stress,* as compared to *nonnormative stress,* which involves some totally unanticipated event like being caught up in an earthquake or a bank robbery. There is "good" stress, which Selye (1974) called *eustress,* and "bad" stress, which he termed *distress.*

Dr. Selye, former professor and director of the Institute of Experimental Medicine and Surgery at the University of Montreal, was a major figure in the history of stress research until his death in 1982. Since he began to investigate the body's physiological response to stress more than forty years ago, he formulated many key concepts about stress which have formed the basis for much of the research that has followed. One of Selye's most important contributions to our understanding of stress is his emphasis on the concept that some stress is essential for life. While too much stress can be damaging, too little is boring. Selye maintained that "complete freedom from stress is death" (1980, p. 128).

HOW WE REACT TO STRESS

Selye (1974; 1980; 1982) defined stress as "the nonspecific response of the body to any demand." The body responds similarly to any event it considers stressful. This reaction of the body is considered *nonspecific* because it is similar, regardless of the source or type of the stress. A *specific* response, on the other hand, is distinctive, in response to the kind of demand a particular stress makes on the individual.

Sweating is a specific response to heat, shivering to cold, tired leg muscles to bicycling up a steep hill. All of these demands—heat, cold, and muscular exertion, as well as others like joy, sorrow, drugs, hormones, and a host of other stimuli—require the body to *do* something to bring it back to a normal state. In other words, to adapt, or adjust. The overall process of adaptation is nonspecific in the sense that it overrides the specific individual response (i.e., sweating) to the specific individual demand for adjustment (i.e., heat). The work the body has to do to adapt to the demands of the stressing element is independent of the specific response.

This may seem clearer if we look at the body as being like a house powered by electricity. When the house is too cold, we turn on the furnace. When it is too hot, we turn on the air conditioner. When it is too dark, we turn on a light. Each kind of equipment performs a different function, thus making a specific response. Each one also draws on the house's overall supply of electricity. The increase in total electric power generated is the house's nonspecific response to the separate demands upon its ability to adapt. Similarly, the body's increased energy output is its nonspecific response to the demands created by stress.

The General Adaptation Syndrome (GAS)

Back in the 1930s, Hans Selye found that injecting rats with nonlethal doses of poison or exposing them to such noxious stimuli as cold, heat, infection, trauma, hemorrhage, and nervous irritation led to a predictable group of symptoms. Certain definite physiological changes showed up: The cortex, or outer layer, of the adrenal glands enlarged and became hyperactive; all the lymphatic structures (spleen, thymus, etc.) shrank; and bleeding ulcers developed in the stomach and upper intestines (Selye, 1982).

Selye called these physiological reactions the general adaptation syndrome, or GAS (1936). He then concluded that what happened to the rats was similar to what happened to people under stress. The GAS is a three-phase reaction to stress consisting of alarm, resistance, and exhaustion.

The workings of the GAS can be seen in a scenario like the following: Imagine that you are on vacation at a lush tropical island. Warm and relaxed from a stretch of sunbathing, you decide to cool off in the sparkling azure sea. As you slowly stroke through the calm waters, you suddenly spot the unmistakable fin of a shark headed right for you. What happens now?

1 *Alarm reaction:* This reaction is subdivided into two phases, *shock* and *countershock.*
   a. *Shock phase:* Your initial and immediate response to the sight of the telltale fins is a combination of several signs of injury: Your body temperature and your blood pressure both drop, your heartbeat quickens, and your muscles go slack. Then the next subphase takes over.

b. *Countershock phase:* Your body now rebounds to mobilize its defenses.

2 *Stage of resistance:* You have now adapted to the sight of the shark, and the symptoms you first showed either improve or go away entirely. At this stage you resist most other stimuli: You're concentrating so hard on swimming away from the shark as fast as possible that you don't notice that you're painfully sunburned, stiff from too much dancing the night before, and tired.

3 *Stage of exhaustion:* Let's hope you don't reach this stage totally because if the shark doesn't get you, the exhaustion will. When a stressful event is severe enough and prolonged enough, your symptoms will reappear and your body will eventually give in to the intolerable demands made upon it. A happier end to this tale will leave you exhausted to the point of collapse but not death, for you will be saved by vigilant fellow vacationers, one of whom manages to divert the shark from the chase, while another brings your fatigued body into shore. With sleep and rest you will be restored almost to your previous levels of functioning. This extreme effort by your body has, however, taken its toll, and this is the kind of experience that wears the body down over a period of time. (For a diagram showing the mechanism underlying the GAS, see Figure 10-1.)

Selye's concept of the GAS is not universally accepted. Some researchers contest his belief in the general, nonspecific response, claiming instead that some stressors produce their own unique profile of hormonal change (Lazarus, 1980). The work of Mason (1968) and his colleagues indicate, for example, that there are no general hormonal responses to all stimuli.

"Fight or Flight"

The first two phases of the GAS have prepared your body to respond to stress in one of two ways—either attacking the threatening force *(fight)* or escaping to safety *(flight)*. These physiological responses result from the action of the adrenal gland, which has been stimulated to increase the body's production of *adrenalin*. This hormone gives the body the energy it needs to adapt to the demands of the stressor.

As your heart begins to beat faster, it pumps more blood into your brain

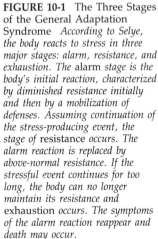

FIGURE 10-1 The Three Stages of the General Adaptation Syndrome *According to Selye, the body reacts to stress in three major stages: alarm, resistance, and exhaustion. The* alarm *stage is the body's initial reaction, characterized by diminished resistance initially and then by a mobilization of defenses. Assuming continuation of the stress-producing event, the stage of* resistance *occurs. The alarm reaction is replaced by above-normal resistance. If the stressful event continues for too long, the body can no longer maintain its resistance and* exhaustion *occurs. The symptoms of the alarm reaction reappear and death may occur.*

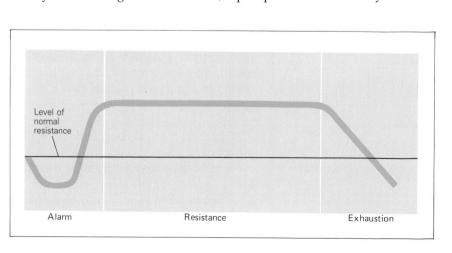

and muscles, sharpening the former to figure out what to do and strengthening the latter to carry out the brain's commands. The blood vessels close to your skin constrict, shortening clotting time, which helps to prevent severe bleeding from wounds. As you breathe faster and deeper, you take more oxygen into your body, which helps you to be more alert. The dry mouth commonly noted in a time of crisis signals the drying up of both saliva and mucus, which increases the size of the air passages to the lungs. The perspiration that suddenly breaks out at these times cools the body.

Your muscles are tensing and tightening to prepare your body for rapid, vigorous action. The pupils of your eyes dilate, making your eyes more sensitive and able to respond more quickly to a seen threat. Meanwhile, your body is rapidly mobilizing white corpuscles to help fight the infection that may ensue from wounds suffered in either the fight or the flight. While you may have been ravenous before the stressful event, thoughts of eating have totally left you. Even the digestion of any food already in your stomach is suspended to conserve your body's energy. Thus the various forces in your body automatically mobilize to aid you in your moment of need, whether that involves attacking the threatening force or escaping to safety.

Stress Is in the Mind of the Beholder

Remember that shark that galvanized you into action? What would your reaction to it have been if you were a marine biologist studying a rare species of the fish, encased in an underwater capsule that permitted you to be seen by this huge specimen while protected from any injury? Chances are that you would have been interested in the approach of the shark in question, excited if it turned out to be a member of the rare species you were seeking but activated in a much different way than had you been a lone, unprotected swimmer. If you were a passenger on the deck of an ocean liner and spotted the shark in the distance, it would probably not create any stress at all.

A stressor, "an event capable of causing change and stress but not necessarily doing so every time" (Boss, 1985, p. 10), is activated by the individual's reaction to it. The experience of failing a course will have a very different effect on a student's life, depending on whether she needs the credit from this course to be admitted to graduate school or whether she had wanted to drop out of college and has been trying to find a good excuse. The death of a father is apt to create different levels of stress for every one of four adult children affected, ranging from an extremely slight effect on the son who had never been close and was now living 3000 miles away to a major loss for the daughter who had been keeping house for him as a surrogate wife.

It is not the event itself that creates the stress; it is how the individual perceives it. Some situations, of course, are universally seen as stressful— like being in a hotel fire. Others, however, depend for their stressful impact more on the way the individual interprets them based on previous experience with similar circumstances and on present ability to cope.

Stress and Development

It is only by inviting things to go wrong, inviting them to go in unexpected and inappropriate directions, that we will find out where it is that they indeed intend to go.

The most painful loss in a person's life is likely to be the death of a spouse, according to psychiatrists Thomas Holmes and Richard Rahe, who rated this as the single most stressful event of many life changes that are associated with the onset of illness. (Abraham Menashe 1983/ Photo Researchers, Inc.)

People of high well-being are not insulated from difficult passages. On the contrary, they are the *most* likely to report having confronted at least one important passage or transition and having made a major change in their outlook, values, personal affiliations, or career. This contradicts the widespread assumption that a consistent life with no great changes or surprises is the most rewarding. Far from it.
(Sheehy, 1981, p. 13)

These words by poet William Dickey (1981) sum up a major reason why so many people continue to take risks, courting stress, throughout their lives. While the negative aspects of stress can be grave, the positive aspects can be uplifting. A good argument can be made that most of our development throughout life arises from the stressful situations we encounter or create, not from the rafts of tranquility we drift upon from time to time.

Many men and women achieve high peaks of life satisfaction by risking change and by successfully navigating the unpredictable accidents in life. It is precisely at those times when we reach out to try some new activity we're not at all sure we can bring off that we feel the familiar signs of stress. When we apply to a college we're not confident will accept us, when we take on a new job we don't have the experience to handle easily, when we make an overture to a man or woman whose interest in us we're in doubt about, we are actively—if not consciously—choosing a stress-inducing situation. If we didn't overreach ourselves to some degree, however, we would never advance beyond present levels of achievement and satisfaction. We would stop growing.

The key to achieving success seems to lie in the ability to cope with stress, both the kind we actively seek out and the kind thrust upon us by fate. Most of us do cope well most of the time. By analyzing the strategies effective copers use, it's possible to improve our ability to grow from stress instead of being overwhelmed by it. We'll talk about these strategies later.

There is no way we can escape stress throughout life. Even if we could, we would lose more than we would gain. As stress researchers continue to point out, we all *need* some degree of stress in our lives. What we have to do is find the level that's right for us, and then develop ways of coping that will enhance our lives, not constrict them.

Anxiety

From the time Rob had been a little boy, he had been determined to become a doctor. Now that he had applied to medical school, however, he was convinced that he wouldn't be accepted. No matter that his grades had been good, his character exemplary, his references sound. During the two months before the acceptances (and rejections) from medical schools were to go out, Rob was a walking wreck. His palms were constantly sweaty, his heart would startle him by beating so rapidly and so loudly that it seemed to fill his entire body, he picked at his food, woke up two or three times during every night, and trembled so much that he wouldn't trust himself to carry a cup of coffee across the room.

Rob was exhibiting a severe state of anxiety, a condition whose definition inspires just as much disagreement among researchers as does that of stress. We can come up with a working definition of it as a state characterized by feelings of apprehension, uncertainty, or tension arising from the anticipation of a threat, real or imagined. Individuals react with varying degrees of anxiety, depending on their own individual tendencies to be anxious and on the type of threat they're responding to. For a graphic illustration of the relationship between stress, personality variables, anxiety, and reactions, see Figure 10-2.

Anxiety is generally characterized as "normal" or "neurotic," depending on whether an individual's reaction seems appropriate to the situation that caused it. Psychoanalyst Sigmund Freud considered normal, or "objective," anxiety reactions to be reactions to real threats in the outside world, and neurotic anxiety reactions to be the result of unacceptable internal impulses that the individual is striving to control. (These neurotic reactions are discussed in detail in Chapter 15, "Abnormal Psychology.")

The symptoms of normal anxiety are danger signals that mobilize an individual for coping with harmful situations. Thus, normal anxiety is an adaptive mechanism that helps to preserve the human race. Anxiety is not considered neurotic unless it is experienced far out of proportion to the actual danger posed or unless it continues to be felt long after the real danger has passed.

A Cognitive Perspective on Stress and Anxiety

If our reactions to stress do not depend totally on what happens but rather on our reaction to it, then the way we *feel* depends to a great extent on the way we *think* about the events in our lives. Richard S. Lazarus (1980; Holroyd & Lazarus, 1982) sees stress as a result of a *transaction*

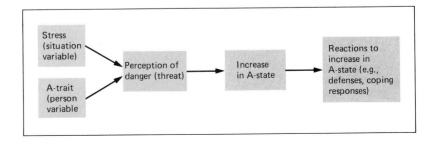

FIGURE 10-2 *Stress and the anxiety process.*

between person and environment. The way people appraise or construe their relationship with the environment is a function of *cognition*, or thought. These thoughts influence the way people feel. Contrariwise, people's emotions affect the way they make sense out of the world around them. Thus, emotion (feeling) follows cognition (thought), and vice versa.

The key, says Lazarus, rests in the transactions that take place between people and their environments. The way we all feel, think, and act is a product of the way we as individuals interact with events. All our experiences—the good and the bad—are filtered through our unique personalities, our personal histories, and our viewpoints on life. By and large, we determine which of these experiences will be uplifting and which will be degrading. We do this partly in the way we act to shape our own lives and partly in the way we react to the shapes our lives assume.

Stress-Induced Illness

"He died of fright." "She died of a broken heart." "Don't tell him that—you'll give him a coronary." These commonly heard sentences, often dismissed as superstitious folklore, now seem to have scientific validity as medical researchers discover more and more links between stress and illness.

Gastroenterologists, for example, have long told their ulcer patients, "It's not what you're eating that's making you sick—it's what's eating you." Emotional stress in the home aggravates the symptoms of diabetic children, sometimes sending them to the brink of death (Baker & Barcai, 1968). And a large body of research, which we'll discuss shortly, has identified the major predictor of heart attack as the stress-laden lifestyle of people driven by what is known as the "Type A" behavior pattern.

CORRELATES OF STRESS

What causes stress? A large and continually growing body of research keeps trying to find the answer to this question. It seems to point in certain directions. Since most of the data are correlational, we cannot come to definitive conclusions about causation, but we can certainly draw some fairly strong inferences. Let's take a look at these data.

Major Life Changes

Building on both the sensed and proven links between some stresses and some illnesses, two psychiatrists looked carefully at the life events that had preceded illness among 5000 hospital patients (Holmes & Rahe, 1976). They found strong evidence that the more changes that had taken place in a person's life, the greater the likelihood of illness within the next year or two. There were relationships between life changes and the occurrence or onset of heart attack, accidents, tuberculosis, leukemia, multiple sclerosis, diabetes, psychiatric disorders, and all sorts of minor medical complaints.

Surprisingly, some of the stressful events patients reported seemed positive in nature—such as marriage, a new baby, a new home, a promotion at work, or an outstanding personal achievement. Even happy events, though, require adjustments to change: change induces stress, and some people react to stress by getting sick.

Based on people's assessments of the amount of adjustment various life events required, the researchers assigned numerical values to the events

TABLE 10-1 Life Events and Weighted Values

Life Event	Value	Life Event	Value
Death of spouse	100	Son or daughter leaving home	29
Divorce	73	Trouble with in-laws	29
Marital separation	65	Outstanding personal	
Jail term	63	achievement	28
Death of close family	63	Wife beginning or stopping	
member		work	26
Personal injury or illness	53	Beginning or ending school	26
Marriage	50	Revision of habits	24
Fired at work	47	Trouble with boss	23
Marital reconciliation	45	Change in work hours	20
Retirement	45	Change in residence	20
Change in health of family	44	Change in schools	20
Pregnancy	40	Change in recreation	19
Sex difficulties	39	Change in social activity	18
Gain of new family member	39	Change in sleeping habits	16
Change in financial state	38	Change in number of family	
Death of close friend	37	get-togethers	15
Change of work	36	Change in eating habits	15
Change in number of		Vacation	13
arguments with spouse	35	Minor violations of law	11
Foreclosure of mortgage	30		
Change of responsibility			
at work	29		

SOURCE: Adapted from T. H. Holmes and R. H. Rahe, "The Social Readjustment Rating Scale, *Journal of Psychsomatic Research*, 11 (August 1967), 213. Reprinted with permission from the authors and Pergamon Press Ltd.

(see Table 10-1). About half the people who scored between 150 and 300 life change units (LCUs) in a single year became ill, and about 70 percent of those with 300 LCUs did.

While the concept of the relationship between life stress and illness seems to be firmly accepted, the Holmes and Rahe conclusions may be questioned on the following bases (Perkins, 1982; Kobasa, 1981; Lazarus, 1981; Lefcourt, Miller, Ware, & Sherk, 1981; Rabkin and Struening, 1976):

- The statistical correlation (indicating the strength and direction of the relationship) between life events and subsequent illness is fairly low.
- Some of their research depended on memory, which is often unreliable.
- In some cases, an illness in its early stages may trigger one or more life changes, but it may seem as if the life changes led to the illness rather than having been caused by it.
- Subsequent research has not supported the contention that *positive* life events contribute to poor health (Lefcourt et al., 1981).
- People are so complex that we can rarely analyze their lives only by numbers. Simply adding up LCUs doesn't tell us the context in which changes took place or how well a person dealt with them.
- The scale presents a view of human beings as passive creatures who react rather than act.
- It doesn't take into account individual differences in response to stress.
- It doesn't address the fact that much stress results from *lack* of change—

boredom, loneliness, inability to advance at work, stable but unrewarding personal relationships, and an absence of commitment in life.

To sum up, then, while the Holmes and Rahe research has earned an important place in the psychological literature by underscoring the relationship between stress and illness, we still need to look further for answers to the question, "Why do some people get sick from stress, while others are energized by it?"

The Hassles of Everyday Life

It's not the large things that send a man to the madhouse . . .
No, It's the continuing series of small tragedies
that send a man to the madhouse . . .
not the death of his love
but a shoelace that snaps
with no time left . . .

In his poem, "Shoelace," Charles Bukowski (1972) expresses lyrically what Richard C. Lazarus has established through research. Lazarus (1981) and his colleagues conducted a year-long study of the effects of the kinds of disagreements, disappointments, accidents, and unpleasant surprises that plague all of us daily. They gave both life event questionnaires and checklists, where people could record the "hassles," or irritating things that happened to them from day to day, as well as the "uplifts," or pleasant things, to 100 white middle-class, middle-aged Californians.

What did they find? That such mundane matters as losing a wallet, getting stuck in traffic, and fighting with a teenage child at home or a boss or subordinate at work were much better predictors of physical and psychological health than were the major events in people's lives. Furthermore, the effects that the major life events do have are basically outgrowths of the daily hassles they create.

Thus, a widow's grief at losing the man she loved is compounded by her need to learn how to balance a checkbook, how to handle household repairs, and how to manage on a smaller Social Security income. A man's distress over his divorce has as much to do with his problems in getting the stains out of his shirts as in getting his wife out of his mind.

Why should this be? One answer revolves around the issue of control. Most of us tend to feel as if we *should* be able to control the small things in our lives. We *should* pick the route that's free of traffic, we *should* safeguard our belongings so our wallet doesn't get stolen, we *should* get along with other people. When these "shoulds" don't operate, we feel at fault.

Lazarus (1981) emphasizes the importance of everyday life in a story about the man who has just learned that his brother, who lives far away, has died. While the man may grieve, his brother's death hardly affects his daily life. If the man's business partner were to die, however, he would not only miss him personally but would also have to cope with many business problems caused by the partner's death. Lazarus predicts that illness would be more of a likelihood upon the death of the partner than the death of the brother.

We cannot, however, conclude that hassles cause stress. As we pointed out earlier, the fact that two variables show a correlation (a mathematical relationship, as explained in the appendix) doesn't mean that one neces-

The same event may seem more stressful to one person than to another. (Sidney Harris)

sarily causes the other. It's possible, for example, that people in poorer physical and mental health take their hassles more seriously and are more gravely affected by them than are healthier people. It's also possible that the poor health itself *causes* some of the hassles—makes a person forgetful, clumsy, or argumentative. There does, however, seem to be a strong relationship between everyday hassles and poor health, and this is certainly an area to investigate further.

Unpredictability and Lack of Control

Some research efforts to assess the effects of the amount of control people have over their environments and the degree to which they can predict what will happen have yielded some fruit that bears out Lazarus's claim that feeling out of control and "in the dark" increases our vulnerability to stress. A wide range of stressors can affect the way people perform various tasks, and they affect people most negatively when the subjects can neither control the stressor nor predict its occurrence (Cohen, 1980). These stressors include such stimuli as noise, crowding, electric shock, arbitrary discrimination, bureaucratic stress, and increased task demands.

In one study, laboratory subjects did proofreading tasks while their ears were regularly assaulted by blasts of noise. When the subjects were told they could stop the noise by pushing a button, they performed better on the task than those who felt they could not do anything about the noise—even though the ones with control did not, in fact, push the button (Glass & Singer, 1972). In another study, subjects in crowded and in uncrowded rooms did a proofreading task. The ones in the crowded room who were told they could walk out and work in a larger room did not actually do so, but they did perform better as proofreaders than did those who didn't have the option of moving (Sherrod, 1974).

Other studies have found that uncontrollable, unpredictable stress also interferes with people's humanitarian tendencies. Laboratory subjects who have been exposed to stress that they can neither predict nor do anything about are less sensitive to other people. They are less likely to help a stranger look for a "lost" contact lens, more likely to administer an electric shock to another subject, and less likely to recognize individual differences among people. (The way people behave toward each other is discussed in more detail in Chapters 17 and 18, which deal with social psychology.)

Why does uncontrollable, unpredictable stress have such wide-ranging effects? One explanation is the learned helplessness theory (first introduced in Chapter 5, "Learning"). When a person feels that nothing he or she can do will change one aspect of his environment or help him to predict its future occurrence, he loses the will to try to change other aspects of the environment. Since he feels that nothing he does matters, the end result is a shrug of the shoulders and a "Why try?" This shows up in poor performances on both cognitive and emotional levels. It may lead to depression (as explained further in Chapter 15, "Abnormal Psychology") and, in severe cases, to death.

Support for the learned helplessness theory can be seen in the fact that people living under various conditions over which they have no control—college students in crowded dorms, poor residents in densely populated housing projects, and grade school pupils who go to schools located in

The shoelace might break, but a major part of the psychological stress created thereby is the implication that one cannot control one's life, that one is helpless in the face of the most stupid trivialities, or, even worse, that one's own inadequacies have made the obstacle occur in the first place. This is what brings the powerful, stressful, and pathogenic message that breaks one's morale. (Lazarus, 1980, p. 34)

the noisy air corridors of busy airports—show signs of helplessness (Cohen, 1980). Obviously, such findings have important implications for society at large. If people are to be more helpful and sensitive to one another and less aggressive, they have to learn ways by which they can better control and predict events in the world about them.

Type A Behavior Pattern

Here are two successful men, both in their early fifties. Paul, a brewery manager, is an impatient, harried man whose daily life is characterized by a sense of a race against time; an effort to do two or more things at once whenever possible; a low boiling point at such frustrations as delayed planes, queues at banks and theaters, and traffic jams; and a consuming involvement with his work. He has little time for his family, and none for hobbies, friends, or community activities.

Ralph, a bank president, is a relaxed, patient man who speaks slowly; takes delays in stride; takes time to exercise and to pursue his hobbies of book printing, listening to classical music, collecting fine books, and going to the theater; and invests time in a few close friendships as well as in his relationships with his wife and three children.

Paul's chances of developing heart trouble are about twice those of Ralph (Rosenman & Chesney, 1982). Why? Because Paul operates on a "Type A behavior pattern," while Ralph is "Type B."

Friedman and Rosenman (1974) maintain that coronary heart disease almost never occurs before 70 years of age in Type B people, even if they smoke, eat fatty foods, and don't exercise. But people with Type A behavior patterns are prone to coronary heart disease in their thirties or forties.

Since cardiac disease causes more than four out of ten deaths of men between 25 and 44 (Cooper, 1981), the effort to help Type A individuals modify their behavior has enormous health implications. This is not easy, however, since Type A behavior is associated in our society with occupational prestige, high income, and rapid career advancement as well as with competitiveness, impatience, and the potential for hostility (Rosenman & Chesney, 1982; Cooper, 1981). More than half the men in Friedman and Rosenman's samples were Type A, about 40 percent were B's, and 10 percent were a mixture of both. In general, more men than women show Type A behavior. Type A women are more vulnerable to heart disease if they are working at a paying job than if they are homemakers. With the steady influx of women into the labor force, the implications for the health of American women are grave.

These behavior patterns seem to have their origins in childhood (Matthews & Siegel, 1983) and appear to arise more from the environment than from the genes. Children seem to observe the way the adults around them act, learning either aggressive and competitive behavior or a more relaxed pattern (Rosenman & Chesney, 1982). Some evidence for environmental causes comes from the fact that Type A behavior is more common in industrial societies.

Type A people prefer to work alone in stressful situations (Dembroski & MacDougall, 1978), possibly because they feel more in control, they won't be distracted by other people, and they want to avoid the possibility of failing in front of other people. Yet this preference for working alone under stress may impose added stress. These authors recommend that Type A's learn to work with others in a way that "increases colleague

This harried, impatient man, an apparent Type A personality, is a prime candidate for an early heart attack unless he makes a deliberate effort to modify his behavior. (Robert V. Eckert, Jr./The Picture Cube)

support without at the same time producing interpersonal conflict or competitiveness" (p. 32).

People have to make their own decisions. Is the race for success worth dropping dead of an untimely heart attack? Some feel it is. Yet Friedman and Rosenman (1974) point out that many Type B's are also successful and that Type A's can modify their behavior with good results. They can combine *cognitive* efforts to change their way of thinking, *physiological* alterations to learn new ways to relax, and *behavioral* steps to reduce the number of appointments made or the amount of work taken home. They can, for example, allow themselves more time in their daily schedule by waking up a few minutes earlier, not answering the phone at certain times, and allotting more time to activities than they expect them to take. They can combat "hurry sickness" by forcing themselves, whenever they speed up to go through an amber light, to punish themselves by turning right at the next corner and going around the block. They can take many other ingenious and common-sensical steps to slow down.

Test Anxiety

Test anxiety, another stress-related factor that is a function of personality, is especially relevant for college students. Marcy, a successful executive, has been out of college for twenty-five years. Yet she has a recurring dream of being in a classroom about to take a test. As the "blue books" are being given out, she realizes that she is totally unprepared. Depending on which variation of the dream she is experiencing, she either forgot to study, studied for the wrong course, or has never even taken the course she is being tested in. The frequency of this "examination dream" among successful people attests to the anxiety-provoking aspect of academic tests.

Virtually all students experience some anxiety before a test. This was demonstrated as long ago as 1929 by Cannon's experiments, which showed the presence of sugar in the urine after a stressful examination when it had not been there previously (Spielberger, 1979). The sugar is a physiological marker of intense emotional reaction. While most students are more or less tense before exams, most come through with no more lasting effects than the kinds of dreams Marcy has. To some, however, test anxiety is more than a dream; it is a waking nightmare. These are the ones who "freeze up" when the time comes to show what they have learned.

Sometimes a moderate increase in anxiety helps a student to increase effort and focus attention on the test. A large increase, though, can wreak havoc with a student's performance. This is true mostly for students in the middle range of ability. No matter how nervous very bright students feel, they still tend to do well on tests. And no matter how relaxed students at the lowest levels are, they still do poorly. Florida psychologist Charles Spielberger (1979) has found that it is among the great majority of students in the middle that anxiety can make a big difference.

How does anxiety interfere with performance? Generally in the way it takes students' energies away from the actual work at hand and diverts them into self-defeating activities like worry and self-criticism. Overwhelmed by anxiety, they have trouble concentrating, often fail to follow directions, and either neglect or misinterpret obvious informational cues.

A major problem test-anxious students have is that they fill their minds with worrisome thoughts. Let's read the mind of one such student, Kevin:

> I'm probably going to fail this test. I'll bet everyone in this class is doing better than I am. Except maybe the real dummies. Look at them—everybody else looks as if they know the answers. What's wrong with me? What am I doing in this class, anyway? What am I doing in college? I can't do this work. I'm a dummy myself. When my grades come out, everyone's going to know it. My folks will kill me, my girlfriend will be disgusted, and I'll be embarrassed to face anyone. I'll have to drop out of school. Then what'll I do? Well, I can always drive a cab. Not everyone has to go to college. Uh-oh . . . I'm getting one of those sinus headaches again—that's a sure sign that I'm nervous. Now I'd better stop myself from feeling nervous or I'll never get through this exam. Now let me get back to the first question. I could answer it a hundred ways. I wonder which is the best one. I don't want to rush into a decision or I'll be sorry later.

This kind of thinking carries a triple whammy. Since Kevin's thoughts are focused on himself, he can't pay attention to the test itself. Since he is overwhelming himself with negative messages, he is eating away at his motivation to succeed. And the "automatic, stereotyped, 'run-on' character" of his thoughts raises his anxiety level rather than controlling it (Meichenbaum & Butler, 1978, p. 10).

Test-anxious students are their own worst enemies in other ways, too. There's some evidence that they have poor study habits, not covering the material well enough and not using their time effectively; they may not know how to get help and support before the test from faculty and fellow students; and they may not know the strategies of good test taking (going over problem-solving rules in their heads, giving themselves pep talks, handling multiple-choice questions, deciding on essay questions, and so forth) (Meichenbaum & Butler, 1978).

How, then, can test-anxious students be helped? A number of different approaches have evolved, with some counseling programs focusing

Virtually all students experience some anxiety before a test, but some become so overwhelmed that they cannot concentrate, don't follow directions, and neglect or misinterpret obvious clues, ending up failing the test, and often the course. Fortunately, test-anxious students can be helped in a variety of ways. (Alan Carey/The Image Works)

on teaching better study habits, some on teaching methods of relaxation, some on improving test-taking behavior, some on helping students change the messages they give themselves, and some on the entire sequence.

One comprehensive approach—stress-inoculation training—teaches the individual to understand the nature of stressful reactions, to tell when she or he is becoming anxious, and to learn various skills in overcoming anxiety. The client is then given the opportunity to practice these skills in the group setting and is then urged to put them into practice in a real-life situation (Meichenbaum, 1975). Stress-inoculation training will be discussed in more detail later in this chapter.

Burnout

We can see an example of another kind of stress when we look at what has happened to Dr. Lang, a young physician. She had changed. Everyone noticed the difference in her—the nurses at the hospital, the other doctors in her medical group, her husband, her children, her patients. She looked tired and sad most of the time and had lost the ready smile that had been so much a part of her personality. "That nice friendly Dr. Lang," who always had had time—or had *made* time—to listen to a patient's recital of aches and pains was now irritably asking people, "Yes, but what's your *major* complaint?" She was coming in late for clinic duty, and, when she realized that people had been waiting, would say to herself, "What difference does it make? How much good am I doing, anyway?"

Dr. Lang was suffering from a malady common among people in the "helping professions" such as medicine, social work, and police work—burnout. Burnout has been defined as "a syndrome of emotional exhaustion, depersonalization and reduced personal accomplishment" (Maslach & Jackson, in press, p. 2). A person suffering from this syndrome, like Dr. Lang, feels that she has used up all her emotional resources and has nothing left to give to others. She is likely to develop negative and callous

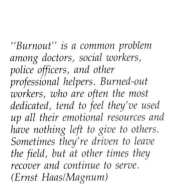

"Burnout" is a common problem among doctors, social workers, police officers, and other professional helpers. Burned-out workers, who are often the most dedicated, tend to feel they've used up all their emotional resources and have nothing left to give to others. Sometimes they're driven to leave the field, but at other times they recover and continue to serve. (Ernst Haas/Magnum)

attitudes about the people she is being paid to help. And she blames herself for not being able to solve all their problems.

At other times, the support of other people, especially coworkers, helps a person get some perspective on his or her work and herself. Such support can come from the kind of informal shoptalk that emerges over a shared cup of coffee as well as from formally organized meetings. Sometimes it can also come from a spouse or close friend with whom the practitioner can talk over his or her concerns.

It's usually hard to pinpoint the exact onset of burnout because it is generally a response to chronic rather than acute stress. Symptoms creep up, get worse, pile on top of each other—fatigue, insomnia, headaches, persistent colds, stomach troubles, alcohol and/or drug abuse, and troubles getting along with people. The burned-out practitioner gets fed up with the job and may quit suddenly, pulls away from family and friends, and sometimes even sinks into a suicidal depression (Maslach & Jackson, in press; Briley, 1980).

The factors of lack of control and unpredictability common to other stresses are major elements of burnout, too. It very often strikes those practitioners who had been the most dedicated, the most eager to help other people. When they see that no matter how hard they work, they cannot cure all illness, poverty, or despair, they often sink into despair themselves.

Fortunately, most people in high-burnout professions have evolved their own ways of coping with the syndrome—by withdrawing from people when they need to and by reaching out toward them when that seems helpful. Some of the most helpful "withdrawal" strategies include cutting down on working hours, taking frequent breaks from work, and changing the scene entirely by going away on vacation. Psychological withdrawal can be accomplished by focusing on thoughts and activities unconnected with the job. Many people in high-stress helping occupations rely on "decompression" routines at the end of the working day. They jog, listen to music, curl up with a novel, stretch out in a hot bath, or meditate. Once they have had time to withdraw into themselves for a little while, they are able to relate to other people, including their families.

COPING WITH STRESS

People who take on the physically and psychologically demanding job of air traffic controller generally have the kinds of personalities that flourish in stressful situations. Working on schedules that alternate long periods of boredom with short bursts of hectic activity, these workers know that as they guide airplanes into and out of airports, they hold the lives of hundreds of people in their hands. Most people in this occupation handle stress well since, as stress expert Charles D. Spielberger has said, "The demands of the job itself act as a screening device. Those individuals who would fall into the 'stress is the spice of life' category would be interested in this career opportunity because they feel challenged by the demands of a very difficult job and feel capable of handling the pressures" (quoted in *Behavioral Medicine*, 1981, p. 33).

Yet even these stress-hardy individuals have their tolerance levels—so much so that the union representing air traffic controllers cited the psychological strains inherent in their jobs as the major basis for their request for a shorter workweek. When their request was denied, in August of 1981, 13,000 union members went on strike. Ironically, the strike itself posed new stresses that energized some workers while it demoralized others.

Most of the striking controllers expected to be back at their jobs within a month. The President of the United States, however, declared the strike illegal and the controllers fired. By the end of the year, the former controllers were no longer measuring the strike in terms of days out or salaries lost. They talked about it, instead, in terms of the changes in their lives (Barron, 1981).

Some of these workers were suffering greatly. They were worried about money, feeling inadequate because their wives were now supporting the family (most air traffic controllers are men), they were having marital problems, and they were feeling generally anxious and upset.

After the initial shock, however, some of these displaced workers plucked victory from what to others was a crushing defeat. One 32-year-old, for example, went back to college, amassed a 3.3. grade-point average in prelaw political science courses, and was seriously considering becoming a lawyer. This man is obviously coping positively with a stressful situation in a way that promises ultimate reward.

What exactly *is* coping? According to Lazarus (1980), it is a response to stress that has two major functions. The first implies *solving the problem:* We either change the environment in some way or change our own actions or attitudes. For example, a striking air traffic controller can change the work environment by taking a different kind of job, or he might immerse himself in union-related activities to improve the working conditions of the present job. If he feels that, for one reason or another, he can't change the job itself, he might work on changing his own attitude—by seeking tension-releasing activities outside of work or by reminding himself that the gratifications of his job are partly due to its challenges and his ability to use his skills.

Secondly, coping allows us to *manage stress-related emotional and physical responses*, so that we keep up our morale and continue to function. We do this in a number of more or less successful ways—through defense mechanisms like denial, intellectualization, projection, and so forth (first enunciated by Sigmund Freud and described in Chapter 14); by taking drugs that range from medically prescribed sedatives and tranquilizers, through legally obtained over-the-counter nostrums and alcohol, into the subculture of illegal substances like marijuana, cocaine, and the entire lexicon of illicit street drugs; by changing state of consciousness through techniques like meditation (for a discussion on the way drugs and meditation affect us, see Chapter 4); and by forcing ourselves to think positive thoughts. While not all these techniques are effective, they all represent some attempt to cope.

Effective copers tend to use both kinds of techniques—those that help them solve the problem at hand and those that help them feel better. Less effective copers may solve the immediate problem but at a high cost in terms of emotional and physical well-being or may escape into a way of thinking that makes them feel better but doesn't do anything to change the basic source of their stress. Most of the time, of course, we use a combination of many acts and thoughts to cope with any specific situation.

Why do some people handle stressful situations better than others do? Why does one person build a new life after becoming permanently handicapped through illness or injury, or mourn a dead spouse but go on to form a close relationship with someone else, or rebound after losing a job under publicly embarrassing circumstances, to emerge apparently stronger for the ordeal, while another sinks into apathy, depression, or even suicide from the same stressor events? A number of factors play a role.

PERSONALITY   The personality style an individual develops affects the way she or he handles stress. According to Kobasa (1982), the first kind of person as just described shows "hardiness," a personality style that includes three characteristics—commitment, control, and challenge.

Commitment allows us to believe in the truth, importance, and interest value of who we are and what we are doing and thereby to feel an overall sense of purpose in life. *Control* is the belief that we are responsible for our own lives, that in some way we brought about these stressful events, and that, therefore, we can do something about them. And *challenge* is based on the belief that change, rather than stability, is the normal condition of life. When we hold this attitude, we can look at a stressful life event as an opportunity leading to personal growth rather than as a threat. We are likely to be open and flexible, and we may even seek out new and interesting experiences, in the full and open knowledge that when we do so, we invite a certain measure of stress into our lives.

EXPECTATION   "Executive stress" is a hot topic these days. As Kobasa (1982) has pointed out, the popular media are full of a new myth about the business executive, which shows him (and now her, with more women entering upper echelons of business) as "the classic stress victim." Stress is bad, often overwhelmingly so, and it should be avoided as

Some people thrive on stress. Lawyers seem to cope with it especially well and remain healthier after stressful life events than people in some other fields. It's possible that the kind of people who choose law as a profession do so because they like the kinds of pressures that come with this work. (Michelle Bogre/Black Star)

much as possible. On the other hand, the public has a different view of lawyers, a view that lawyers themselves share. According to this ideology, attorneys thrive under stress, perform best at times of great change and under a lot of pressure, never get sick, and live very long lives. In fact, lawyers do remain healthier after stressful life events than do executives and army officers (Kobasa, 1982). It's quite possible that much of life is a self-fulfilling prophecy, that is, when we *expect* something to happen, it does.

PERSONAL RESOURCES   The body we inherit, with whatever predispositions it may have, affects the way we respond to stress (Kobasa, 1982). According to Selye (1956), stress-provoked illness occurs in the weakest organ or system. Thus, while one person suffers asthmatic attacks from stress, another develops stomach ulcers, and a third is stricken by a heart attack. A fourth may have such reserves of physical strength that stress does not cause poor physical health.

FAMILY STRESS

Up to now we have been talking about stress as it is experienced by the individual. All of us who live in families, however, have also experienced the kind of stress that we share with others in our households. Family stress can take many forms. The kind experienced by the Urbancyk family of Detroit, Michigan, is one example.

When Bill Urbancyk was laid off from his job as an automotive worker, his initial reaction was panic. What would he do? Where would he go to get another job? What did this say about his manliness, when he couldn't support his family? After a while he lost his interest in making love to his wife, in playing ball with his daughters, and in going out with friends. The stress of Bill's unemployment was not limited to the one person now out of work but affected everyone in the family. Many stressors obviously affect the entire family—such events as childbirth or adoption, moving to another city, and the departure from the home of adult children.

In fact, stress is the biggest problem families face, according to a 1981

Stressful life events affect not only individuals but often their entire families. When this unemployed auto worker couldn't meet his mortgage payments and had to sell his home, his wife and child were affected, both by the husband's emotional distress and by the changes in their own day-to-day lives. (J. P. Laffont/Sygma)

report by the Family Service Association of America, whose biennial poll of twenty-four of its member social work agencies found stress topping the list of the problems families take to counselors. Family-stress researchers look at the family as a *system*, in which what happens to one part of the system (i.e., Bill) affects the other parts of the system (i.e., Bill's wife and children).

A formula that helps us look at the process of family stress is Reuben Hill's *ABC-X* model (1949), the outcome of his work on the effects of family separations and reunions during World War II. This model conceptualizes family stress in the following way:

- *A* represents the stressor event, which might be the husband and father's being in the service and away from home.
- *B* stands for the family's *resources* in coping with the stress, which could include the availability of relatives who could fill in for the husband and do some of the tasks he would ordinarily do, the family's access to money, and the emotional strength of the family. Other valuable family resources include the flexibility and willingness to shift traditional roles of husband/wife or mother/father; the acceptance of responsibility by all family members in performing family duties; the willingness to sacrifice personal interest to attain family objectives; a pride in family traditions; high family participation in joint activities; egalitarian patterns of decision making and family control; and strong affectional ties among family members.
- *C* refers to the family's *interpretation* of the event—positively, with pride in the father and in themselves for "giving" their man to the service of their country, or with a feeling of abandonment, thinking, "He could have gotten a deferment to stay with us if he had wanted one." This is similar to Lazarus's cognitive appraisal.
- *X* denotes the *outcome* following the stress. For a family with adequate resources and a positive interpretation, the outcome might be in-

creased family cohesiveness. For one with few resources and a negative interpretation, the result might be family disorganization and depression, which could well linger on even after the father had returned home.

A family in a state of such extreme disorganization that the system practically comes to a halt is, according to Boss (1985), not only under stress, but in a state of crisis. While stress is a state of disturbed equilibrium, or an upset in a steady state that can go on for long periods of time, a crisis is a state of acute disequilibrium so sharp and severe that the family can no longer perform its tasks and the individuals within it may not be functioning. Many families, like many individuals, live with high levels of stress and thrive on it, never reaching the crisis point.

The family that does go into crisis can be visualized like a "roller coaster" (Hill, 1949; Boss, 1985). First, the family plunges down into an initial period of *disorganization,* during which members find that the coping mechanisms they used in the past are not adequate to deal with this new event. Then the family pulls out of its well of disorganization and begins to pull itself together, by coming up with some new coping methods, or with some new combination of old ones, as it enters a period of *recovery.* Finally, the family reaches a new level of organization, which may be higher, lower, or at the same level as before the stressful event. Some families emerge stronger after a crisis, some are left in shambles, and others seem to show no effects at all.

Family Coping

As we pointed out earlier, an event that affects one human being—illness, a job promotion that requires a move out of town, the loss of a job, any major triumph or disappointment—is likely to affect everyone in that person's family. Not only does the affected individual have to cope with the stress; the entire family must deal with it.

Researchers who have studied family stress have found that families cope by the same basic means individuals do—by taking actions and changing their attitudes, both to solve the problems and to make themselves feel better. How, for example, do wives of corporate executives deal with their husbands' frequent absences from home? Some fit into the corporate lifestyle, becoming "company wives"; some make special efforts to develop their own personalities and interests; and some establish routines independent of their husbands', rather than seeking a "togetherness" their lifestyle will not permit (Boss, McCubbin, & Lester, 1979). Some do this so well that the families deny being stressed at all.

Normal Family Transitions

With a growing emphasis on the study of development throughout the life span, a great deal of research has focused on the various transitions that many families experience: having a new baby, moving to a different community, seeing children grow up and leave the family home until the "nest" is empty, and losing a parent or spouse to death. Most of the research has concluded that most people do cope well with these transitions, and that, while they may be stressful at the time, they usually do not lead to the state of disorganization typical of a family crisis.

It is, however, harder to cope with these events when several of them occur at once—such as the death of a parent coming right after the birth of a baby and the move to a new home (Boss, 1985). On the family level, this confirms the life change unit rating system for individuals, developed by Holmes and Rahe (1976), discussed earlier in this chapter.

A considerable amount of research on family stress concerns two aspects of parenting: becoming a parent and having one's grown children leave home. Let's look at some of these findings.

BECOMING A PARENT   The birth or adoption of a first baby marks a major transition point in its parents' lives. Moving from an intimate relationship involving two people to one involving a third—a helpless being totally dependent on these two people—changes people and changes marriages. While some of the early research on this event regards the birth of the first child as a troublesome crisis that creates a major upheaval for both parents and for their marital relationship (LeMasters, 1957; Dyer, 1963), more recent studies conclude that it is a somewhat stressful transition rather than a full-blown crisis (Hobbs & Cole, 1976; Hobbs & Wimbish, 1977; Russell, 1974).

The most stressful aspect of first-time parenthood seems to be the disruption in ongoing lifestyles that it causes. Thus, among women, those who find the experience most difficult are highly educated, career-oriented mothers who often resent the new demands on their time and energy as well as the interruption of their professional lives (Russell, 1974). For even in these "liberated" times, when the roles of men and women are undergoing great changes, in most homes most of the responsibility for raising the children still falls to the mother. It is not surprising, then, that both black and white women have more difficulty than their husbands in adjusting to their new roles as parents (Hobbs & Cole, 1976; Hobbs & Wimbish, 1977). New fathers are bothered by the necessity of changing plans because of the baby and by the additional work and money problems. Both parents are upset by fatigue, caused by interrupted sleep and rest, and by marital tension, caused partly by increased demands on time and reduced levels of sexual activity (Russell, 1974; Wandersman, 1980).

How do new parents cope with this transition? Researchers questioned more than 100 couples on their coping strategies, as well as on several measures of personal well-being and personal and marital stress at three successive time periods—midway during pregnancy, about six weeks after the baby's birth, and from six to eight months after birth (Miller & Sollie, 1980). When they analyzed the replies, they found that those couples who coped best reported that the following activities and attitudes were helpful:

- *Adaptability:* The ability to accept the unpredictability of a baby's day, to learn patience, and to be flexible.
- *Communication:* The ability of husband and wife to share their feelings with each other.
- *Seeing parenthood as a shared responsibility:* The ability to break away from stereotyped roles within the household and to negotiate new ones.
- *Pursuing adult interests:* Continuing to participate in activities that had been of interest before the birth of the baby.

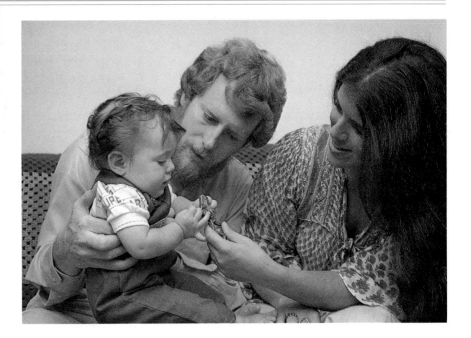

Becoming a parent brings stress along with joy. The most stressful aspect of first-time parenthood seems to be the disruption it causes in ongoing lifestyles. Fortunately, most new parents develop ways to cope with this transition. (Erika Stone/Peter Arnold, Inc.)

- *Spending some time away from the baby.*
- *Looking to the future:* Talking about career goals, planning to implement them, and recognizing that parenting responsibilities will ease as children mature.
- *Using friends, relatives, and neighbors as resources* for information, advice, and help with child care.

THE EMPTY NEST For years people talked about the crisis that afflicts parents whose children have grown up and left home to strike out on their own. Many observers of society have associated this time of life with depression, a sense of loss, and an inability to cope (Roberts & Lewis, 1981). In the past the syndrome was discussed almost entirely in terms of women, but recent studies have found that about the same percent of mothers and fathers—*less than one in four*—experience distress when their children leave home (Roberts & Lewis, 1981). For most parents, in fact, the experience is a positive one. The classic picture of the stressful "empty-nest syndrome" is not generally supported by research. On the contrary, parents now have more free time and energy, they can experience the satisfaction of having done their job of launching adult children, and they can invest more of themselves into their marriage and their own personal needs (Rubin, 1979; Bredehoft, 1981).

Those who come through this life passage most easily are usually those who have other interests in life, who have not been overinvolved in their children's lives, and who have anticipated the launching by thinking about it and planning for it. For those parents who do find this transition especially stressful, Roberts and Lewis (1981) suggest such coping strategies as:

- *Developing a new role:* A mother who had been a full-time homemaker's

finding a job or a father's becoming a scout leader.
* *Finding new sources for intimacy:* Friends, other family members, or colleagues at work or in volunteer commitments.
* *Joining a support group:* Either consciousness-raising or therapy, to share concerns with others and to learn from people who have weathered this transition.

PREVENTING STRESS: STRESS-INOCULATION TRAINING

Brian, a first-year college student, always breaks out in a cold sweat before taking an examination, is so tense and nervous that he forgets all the material he thought he had down pat, and goes on to get a low grade on the test. Since Brian wants to do well at the university, he knows he will have to do *something* to overcome this debilitating test anxiety.

One thing Brian might do is seek out a program of stress-inoculation training mentioned earlier in this chapter. This approach uses techniques of behavior modification to prevent stress in a variety of specific areas. These programs educate individuals about their stressful reactions through an active give-and-take between leader and participants, give them a chance to rehearse ways to cope with the specific stressor being discussed, and then have them practice these coping skills on a variety of stressors, from mild to severe.

In one program geared to test anxiety, students are encouraged to learn new, helpful statements that they can say to themselves to replace the former anxiety-producing ones. Some examples of coping self-statements are given in Box 10-1.

Stress-inoculation training has many other applications, too. It can help people overcome phobias, cope with pain, and control anger. All the applications we've talked about so far deal with the management of stress that is already present. One innovative way to use this same basic approach is to prevent stress before it occurs. With this aim in mind, Ray Novaco (1977) used stress-inoculation training to teach anger management techniques to police officers in training.

Much police work involves hostile confrontations, and anger can often cloud the officer's judgment and interfere with his or her management of the situation. Recognizing and controlling anger, therefore, helps the officers do their jobs in a way that's less upsetting to themselves and more effective for society.

In the first phase—education—the trainees as a group talk about the kinds of situations that could make them angry—a drunk's getting sick in the backseat of the police car, a citizen's refusal to help the officer, being called a name, being spat upon, and being suspended for something they felt they couldn't help. Then they set such incidents in a framework of the various other aspects that influence how the officer would respond—whether he'd had trouble with his car or she'd had a fight with the commander. The trainees come to realize how complex their reactions are and how they respond to a sequence of different events.

The second phase consists of skills training and rehearsal. The officers-in-training learn self-statements (such as those in Box 10-2) that have arisen from the group discussions and been shaped to some extent by the trainer. These statements help the officers feel a sense of control, with an accompanying feeling of confidence that they will be able to cope with whatever situations may come up.

BOX 10-1

SOME COPING SELF-STATEMENTS USED BY TEST-ANXIOUS STUDENTS IN A STRESS-INOCULATION PROGRAM*

PREPARING FOR A STRESSOR

What is it I have to do? I can develop a plan to deal with it. Just think about what I can do about it. That's better than getting anxious. No negative self-statements; just think rationally. Don't worry. Worry won't help anything. Maybe what I think is anxiety is eagerness to confront it.

CONFRONTING AND HANDLING A STRESSOR

Just "psych" myself up. I can meet this challenge. One step at a time; I can handle the situation. Don't think about fear, just about what I have to do. This anxiety is what the doctor said I would feel. It's a reminder to use my coping

exercises. This tenseness can be an ally, a cue to cope. Relax; I'm in control. Take a slow deep breath. Ah, good.

COPING WITH THE FEELING OF BEING OVERWHELMED

When fear comes, just pause. Keep focus on the present; what is it I have to do? Let me label my fear from 0 to 10 and watch it change. I was supposed to expect my fear to rise. Don't try to eliminate fear totally; just keep it manageable. I can convince myself to do it. I can reason my fear away. It will be over shortly. It's not the worst thing that can happen. Just think about something else. Do something that will prevent me from thinking

about fear. Just describe what is around me. That way I won't think about worrying.

REINFORCING SELF-STATEMENTS

It worked; I was able to do it. Wait until I tell my therapist about this. It wasn't as bad as I expected. I made more out of the fear than it was worth. My damn ideas, that's the problem. When I control them I control my fear. It's getting better each time I use the procedure. I'm really pleased with the progress I'm making. I did it!

*Adapted from Meichenbaum (1975, p. 250–251).

In the final phase of the training, the officers-to-be role-play provocative situations, using their new skills, and then get feedback from the other group members and by videotapes of the scenarios.

This kind of program offers a good illustration of the combination of two important psychological approaches: cognitive therapy, which makes people aware of their feelings and of what they themselves are doing and saying to themselves to bring about those feelings; and behavior modification, which shows them how to change their negative behaviors.

LIVING WITH STRESS

Do people who know how to handle stress live longer? The results of a recent study of 1200 people over the age of 100 seem to point in this direction: Centenarians who answered questions related to social, psychological, and biological factors seemed to exemplify the successful application of Selye's theory (Segerberg, 1982). They have positive outlooks on life and root out negative attitudes and emotions.

A major tenet in Selye's theory is the development of a "lofty long-range purpose" to live by (1974, p. 106). With such a purpose, people can make commitments, can express themselves fully, and can achieve a sense of security. "To accomplish this," says Selye (p. 110), "you must first find your optimal stress level, and then use your adaptation energy

BOX 10-2

SOME SELF-STATEMENTS USED BY POLICE TRAINEES IN A STRESS-INOCULATION PROGRAM*

PREPARING FOR A PROVOCATION

This could be a rough situation, but I know how to deal with it. I can work out a plan to handle this. Easy does it. Remember, stick to the issues and don't take it personally. There won't be any need for an argument. I know what to do.

IMPACT AND CONFRONTATION

As long as I keep my cool, *I'm* in control of the situation. You don't need to prove yourself. Don't make more out of this than you have to. There is no point in getting mad. Think of what you have to do. Look for the positive and don't jump to conclusions.

COPING WITH AROUSAL

Muscles are getting tight. Relax and slow things down. Time to take a deep breath. Let's take the issue point by point. My anger is a signal of what I need to do. Time for problem solving. He probably wants me to get angry, but I'm going to deal with it constructively.

SUBSEQUENT REFLECTION: CONFLICT UNRESOLVED

Forget about the aggravation. Thinking about it only makes you upset. Try to shake it off. Don't let it interfere with your job.

Remember relaxation. It's a lot better than anger. Don't take it personally. It's probably not so serious.

SUBSEQUENT REFLECTION— CONFLICT RESOLVED

I handled that one pretty well. That's doing a good job! I could have gotten more upset than it was worth. My pride can get me into trouble, but I'm doing better at this all the time. I actually got through that without getting angry.

*From Meichenbaum and Novaco (1978).

at a rate and in a direction adjusted to your innate qualifications and preferences.'' Selye does not suggest eliminating all stress from our lives. Nor would he. In some ways, life is like theater. Every good play is built around a basic conflict, the solving of which illuminates character, draws on the characters' reserves of strength, and maintains suspense by the uncertainty of the outcome. So it is with life.

Stress is not necessarily the villain in our lives. At times it may well be the hero in our life script. The role it plays depends largely on the way that we, the actors, read our lines and stage our actions. By responding creatively and effectively, we can often write our own happy endings.

SUMMARY

1. Different researchers have defined *stress* in different ways. *Selye* considers stress to be the nonspecific response of the body to any demand. He described a three-stage reaction to stress consisting of alarm, resistance, and exhaustion known as the *general adaptation syndrome* (GAS).

2. *Lazarus* sees stress as a result of a transaction between people and the environment. Whether or not an event is viewed as stressful depends on a person's interpretation of the particular event.

3. *Hill* considers stress in light of its effect on the family system rather than on the individual.

4. Some stress is normal throughout life. According to Selye, complete freedom from stress is death.

5. *Anxiety* is a state characterized by feelings of apprehension, uncertainty, or tension arising from

the anticipation of a threat, real or imagined. Anxiety can be considered either "normal" or "neurotic."

6 *Holmes and Rahe* found evidence for a relationship between *life changes* and illness. Although many of the life changes studied by Holmes and Rahe were basically negative (divorce, death of spouse, going to jail), others were happy events (marriage, having a baby). Holmes and Rahe's research has recently been criticized on methodological grounds.

7 Lazarus and his colleagues found that responses to *hassles* (irritating things that happened to people from day to day) were better predictors of physical and psychological health than the major events in people's lives.

8 Stressors such as noise, crowding, electric shock, arbitrary discrimination, bureaucratic stress, and increased task demands can affect the way people perform various tasks. They affect people most negatively when they can be neither predicted nor controlled.

9 *Type A behavior* has been associated with coronary heart disease. People displaying Type A behavior are impatient and competitive. It appears to be possible to modify Type A behavior patterns.

10 Although a moderate increase in anxiety before a test may help a student's performance, a large increase in anxiety can undermine it. *Test-anxious students'* test performance can suffer because their energy is diverted away from the work at hand and into self-defeating activities such as worry and self-criticism. A number of programs are available to help overcome test anxiety.

11 *Burnout* is a "syndrome of emotional exhaustion, depersonalization and reduced personal accomplishment," especially common among people in the helping professions. Techniques to help overcome burnout include cutting down on working hours, taking frequent breaks, and doing things unconnected with one's job.

12 According to Lazarus, *coping* is a response to stress that has two major functions. The first is *to solve the problem causing the stress* and the second is *to manage the stress-related emotional and physical responses.* We can solve the problem by changing the environment or our own actions and attitudes. We can manage stress-related responses in a number of more or less successful ways ranging from meditation to forcing ourselves to think positively to taking (and possibly abusing) legal and illegal drugs.

13 An individual's *personality, expectations,* and *personal resources* all contribute to how successfully he or she deals with stress.

14 *Family-stress* researchers look at the family as a *system,* in which what happens to one person in the system affects the others. Hill proposed the *ABC-X model of family stress* in which *A* represents the stressor event, *B* represents the family's resources for coping with stress, *C* refers to the family's interpretation of the event, and *X* denotes the outcome following the stress. A family's reaction to a stressor then depends on several factors including what the particular event is, how well a family is prepared to deal with it, and how the family regards the event.

15 A considerable amount of research has focused on the various transitions families typically experience such as having a baby and launching one's children. Studies have shown that these events are better viewed as transitions than as crises. In each case coping strategies ease the transition.

16 *Stress-inoculation training* is a behavior modification technique designed to prevent stress. Individuals are educated about their stressful reactions, given training in coping techniques, and allowed to role-play their new coping skills in various situations.

17 Selye recommends that people determine their optimal stress level. Selye feels that some stress is necessary for life.

SUGGESTED READINGS

Figley, C. R., & McCubbin, H. I. (Eds.) (1983). *Stress and the family: II: Coping with catastrophe.* New York: Brunner/Mazel. A collection of articles by leading stress researchers about coping with such catastrophic events as unemployment, rape, captivity, and chronic illness.

Goldberger, L., & Breznitz, S. (Eds.). (1982). *Handbook of stress: Theoretical and clinical aspects.* New York: Free Press. A series of articles on physiological and psychological aspects of stress as well as treatment and support strategies.

McCubbin, H. I., and Figley, C. R. (Eds.). (1983). *Stress and the family: I. Coping with normative transitions.* New York: Brunner/Mazel. The companion volume to Figley and McCubbin, discussed above. Chapters focus on the impact of family transitions such as marriage, parenthood, divorce, and dual-career situations.

Waldo Pierce: *Haircut by the Sea.* 1933. Metropolitan Museum of Art.

PART
5

LIFE-SPAN DEVELOPMENTAL PSYCHOLOGY

From that fateful moment of creation when each of us was conceived to that fatal final moment when we expel our last breath, our lives are governed by one overriding principle: change. As long as we live, we are in the process of becoming something other than what we were. Through every moment of every day of our lives, we change, we grow, we develop. This process of development throughout life is what the following three chapters are all about.

Our development is a continuous thread that marks conception; unravels through childhood, adolescence, and adulthood; and is snipped off only at the grave. The pattern made by this thread is formed by many influences: the biological ones that provide our genetic heritage and dictate the unfolding of new abilities as we mature—and the kaleidoscope of experiences we have through life.

This part presents the life span in three major segments. Chapter 11, "Origins," discusses the beginning of life, from conception through prenatal development and the experience of birth itself. We also consider the newest medical advances for helping infertile couples conceive, and we consider the psychological ramifications. And we discuss what it might mean to be an only, first-born, or later-born child in a family.

In Chapter 12, "Childhood," we are awed by the amazingly competent newborn, whose wide-ranging abilities have only begun to reveal themselves to us through innovative psychological measures. We examine the physical, the intellectual, and the socioemotional aspects of development for the first twelve years of life as we see the enormous strides that children make in controlling their bodies, in understanding and using intellectual concepts, and in expressing their unique personalities.

In Chapter 13, "From Adolescence On," we see the persistence of development throughout the adult years. The struggles still being waged with issues of identity foster growth, even through the final step in this struggle, dealing with our own death.

CHAPTER 11

ORIGINS: THE BEGINNINGS OF LIFE

SPOTLIGHT ON

How heredity and environment work together to affect the various aspects of our development.

How certain birth defects are transmitted and what techniques are available to diagnose and treat them prenatally.

Prenatal development and some hazards of the prenatal environment that can affect the developing fetus.

The recent progress in biological engineering.

Different ways of giving birth.

How your birth order may (or may not) influence your development.

Throughout this book we ask questions that have the most intimate relevance to our own lives. How do we function? What are the underlying causes for our behavior? How are the different threads of our lives interrelated? Developmental psychologists ask these questions with special emphasis on changes in behavior over the life span. They focus on the dramatic evolution of a human being from a tiny one-celled organism invisible to the naked eye into a fully formed infant, then a questioning child, and eventually an adult who continues to change throughout life.

Developmental psychologists are concerned with the ways people change throughout the life span. They look at the way the constantly changing individual acts upon and reacts to a constantly changing environment. As they concentrate on changes from conception through old age, they describe, explain, and predict behavior and make suggestions for modifying it, with the aim of helping people develop to their full potential (Baltes, Reese, & Lipsitt, 1980). When we study development, we concern ourselves not with the static situation at any given moment but with the process by which we ourselves change, by the influences on our own change, and by the way we change the world around us. We look at ourselves as active participants in our own development.

The three major paths of human development are closely interrelated, with each one affecting and being influenced by the other two. Developmental psychologists study physical development (changes in the body such as height, weight, brain development, and the acquisition and refinement of motor skills); cognitive development (changes in thought processes, which affect learning, language abilities, and memory); and psychosocial development (changes in the emotional and social aspects of personality).

We define development, then, as the ways by which people's physical, cognitive, and psychosocial characteristics change throughout the entire life span. This life span view contrasts with the view that most of the important developmental changes occur in childhood or, at the latest, by the end of adolescence. Development is seen as a lifelong process. There is potential for change throughout life. For example, even very old people continue to develop and often experience personality growth. Even at the very end of life, as people prepare for death, they often grasp this final opportunity to resolve their identity problems and come to terms with who they are.

Developmental change is of two main types: quantitative and qualitative. *Quantitative* changes are fairly easy to observe and measure. They include changes such as growth in height and weight and the expansion of vocabulary. *Qualitative* changes are more complex, involving "leaps" in functioning—those changes in kind that distinguish a talking child from a nonverbal baby, a mature adult from a self-absorbed adolescent. These changes trace the growth of intelligence, creativity, sociability, and morality. But even these leaps result from a series of small steps that we continue to take for as long as we live.

Developmental psychologists are concerned with a range of factors which influence developmental change. No one of us develops in a vacuum. We are all influenced by the interaction between maturation (the unfolding of biologically determined patterns of behavior—such as walking) and *past and present experience*. So developmental psychologists ask the kinds of questions that will assess the role these various influences play in our lives. First, they go back to the very beginnings of life to ask, "How are we made? What do we bring with us? How does our genetic heritage program the rest of our lives?" Then they explore how maturation affects the way we develop over time and how the decisions we make affect our physical status.

Psychologists consider other factors besides maturation. For instance, they study our first social network, the family. Although early theorists and researchers emphasized the impact the mother had on her developing child, those in the field today have broadened their awareness to consider the important influence of other relatives such as the father, brothers and sisters, and other caregivers. Furthermore, there is a growing recognition of the important changes over time in these relationships, as in the ties between adult children and their elderly parents and those among adult siblings. Today's spotlight has moved beyond the question of the ways in which older relatives affect children to illuminate the ways in which children—even as newborns—influence those around them. Through the constant interplay in relationships, people help to shape each other.

They consider the broader cultural context. The particular culture and subculture we live in influence our development. The child raised in a third world developing country and the one who grows up in a prosperous, highly industrialized nation have different cultural experiences, which leave their mark. The elderly person who lives in a society, like China, that reveres age accepts and appreciates this time of life much more than does an elderly person in the United States, where we tend to "shelve" the elderly as having outlived their usefulness.

And they explore the impact of the times we grow up in. The cohort, or generation we grow up in, exerts its effects. The history that occurs in our lifetimes—such as a major economic depression or a war—leaves indelible impressions. Furthermore, people who grow up in a time when medical advances in treating common illnesses keep alive both the young and the elderly, when we can pick up a telephone and call someone on the other side of the world, when we can get on an airplane and be on a distant continent on the same day are bound to be different in some ways from their ancestors whose historical context was very different.

And finally they consider the impact of nonnormative life events such as a chronic illness or the birth of a child with a defect. These events, although they do not occur to everyone, have considerable potential impact on those who do experience them.

The way we answer the questions raised by developmental psychologists helps to clarify the relationships among us and the people, places, and events in our lives. These relationships are almost never one-sided. Instead, *interaction* and *individuality* are the keys to understanding the process of development.

As we bring to life our own individual strengths, abilities, and predispositions, these are then affected by influences from the environment. These influences make us act in a certain way that will elicit new experiences. So the characteristics inside us constantly intermesh with factors outside us, and we find ourselves in a never-ending cycle of acting and reacting. As our bodies, for example, set boundaries on what we can do, the things we do affect our bodies. As our parents influence us, we influence them. As our culture constructs a place for us, we modify that place.

Through it all, we must bear in mind the individual differences among people. We all bring a unique genetic legacy into this world and then proceed to have a unique set of experiences. How, then, could we not be different from each other?

In this chapter we'll consider the roles that heredity and environment play in our development. First, we'll examine the mechanism for the transmission of the characteristics we inherit from our parents. Then we'll explore the very earliest effects of the environment—those that have their impact while we are still in the uterus. We'll look at the newest techniques for providing a "window on the womb" and for preventing or treating problems that develop prenatally. Then we'll look at the birth experience and at the impact of our place in the family—as first-born, later-born, or only child. In the following two chapters, we'll examine development during childhood, adolescence, and adulthood, into late life.

First, then, to understand where it all begins, let's go back to the very origins of life, to learn about the earliest influences we are likely to encounter, to ask what we are born with and what we acquire.

HEREDITY AND ENVIRONMENT

Throughout this book we have been talking about the many different abilities of human beings—how we perceive the world and how we act toward the people and situations in it. One question that has preoccupied students of humanity for centuries is how we develop these abilities. Do we inherit them or do we learn them? Through history, opinion on the answer to this question has varied, ranging between the extreme views that we are either the product of our nature (our inherited traits) or our nurture (our experiences).

While most contemporary thinkers recognize the difficulty of ever completely separating the two influences, which interact in various ways to make each of us a unique individual, the nature-nurture debate still goes on. Its findings are important since they determine the way we construct both our society and our personal lives.

In general, it seems that our heredity predisposes us toward and sets limits for certain behaviors, but our environment determines their expression. Your intelligence, for example, may be determined in large part by the genes you inherited from your parents, but the kind of home you grew up in, the degree to which you were encouraged to pursue intellectual interests, the kind of education you have received, and your own decisions in life have all had—and will continue to have—an effect on the way your intelligence will flower. Similarly, if you have inherited a family trait of shortness, you may never reach a height of 6 feet; but if you have been well cared for, you will grow taller than you would have if you were kept in cramped quarters and given too little food, too little exercise, and too little love.

Only in extreme cases does a specific genetic condition guarantee the expression of a particular disorder. No matter how supportive the prenatal or after-birth environment, all individuals who received an extra chromosome 21 at the moment of conception will develop Down's syndrome, which includes mental retardation and often heart defects, and other physical anomalies (see discussion later in this chapter). Even in an extreme case like this, however, a supportive environment can make the difference between total dependence in an institution and a measure of self-sufficiency, enabling the person to move about relatively freely in the community.

Through the science of behavior genetics, researchers have developed a number of methods to learn how people inherit various traits. They include:

- *Selective breeding in animals:* If animals can be bred for certain characteristics (such as the ability to run mazes or the tendency to become obese), we conclude that the trait is at least partly hereditary, and we generalize these findings to human beings, validly in some cases, less so in others.
- *The study of twins:* When identical twins (who have the exact same genetic legacy) are more alike (concordant) than fraternal twins (who are no more alike than any brother or sister), a hereditary basis for a trait seems indicated. Identical twins who have been raised in different homes are especially sought after to contrast their identical heredity with differing environments, but such individuals are hard to find. Even when we can locate them, their cultural environments usually turn out to be quite similar.
- *Adoption studies:* When adopted children are more like their biologic parents and siblings, we see the influence of heredity; when they resemble their adoptive families more, we see the influence of environment.
- *Consanguinity studies:* By examining as many blood relatives as possible in a particular family, we can discover the degree to which they share certain characteristics and whether the closeness of the relationship affects the degree of similarity.

Other lines of research concentrate on determining possible environmental causes for particular characteristics. These include:

- *Prenatal studies:* By investigating relationships between various conditions in individuals and their mothers' experiences during pregnancy, we can often pinpoint a specific cause for a specific condition. With this sort of detective work in the 1960s, researchers identified an innocent-seeming tranquilizer called *thalidomide* as the agent that caused thousands of children to be born without arms or legs.
- *Manipulating the environment:* Making changes in diet, exercise opportunities, intellectual enrichment, and sensory stimulation in one group of animals or people and then comparing this group with a control group enables us to draw conclusions about the effects of such environmental differences. A dramatic example of this kind of manipulation showed up in a classic study of enrichment, when thirteen apparently retarded 2-year-olds were moved from their orphanage to an institution for mentally retarded young adults who doted on the children and lavished care on them. As adults, all thirteen were functioning in the community, married, and raising their own normal children;

How We Study the Relative Effects of Heredity and Environment

Many people take away . . . the impression that the effect of genes is carved in granite, fixed and immutable from the moment of conception. The reality is that genes switch on and off, sometimes in response to developmental progression, sometimes as environment is filtered through physiologic processes.

What we need to study is that instability, which simply is another way of saying that we should examine the blueprint of development and how it is modified by genetic and environmental influences. . . . Once we begin to understand how genes and environment interact, . . . we may begin to understand something that is really worth knowing. (Farber, 1981, p. 80)

by comparison, twelve who had remained in the orphanage for a much longer time had a much lower average IQ, and four were still institutionalized (Skeels, 1966; Skeels & Dye, 1939).

Our ability to manipulate either the heredity or environment of human beings is, of course, limited by both ethical and practical considerations. We cannot, for example, mate human beings for selective characteristics, and we would not separate identical twins, make adoption placements, institutionalize children, or prescribe questionable drugs to pregnant women for experimental purposes. So we have to rely on animal studies or after-the-fact observations of events that have occurred naturally.

- *Comparisons of actual histories:* By interviewing parents about their child-rearing practices (remembering to discount the effects of faulty and distorted memories!) and by comparing other life-history factors, researchers can sometimes isolate specific environmental influences on specific characteristics.

Characteristics with Strong Hereditary Components

The results of many studies point to a strong hereditary basis for the characteristics listed in Table 11-1. These traits are also influenced by the environment.

HOW GENETIC TRAITS ARE TRANSMITTED

Creating a New Life

The moment of conception is a split-second event when a *sperm* from the father unites with an *ovum* (sometimes referred to as an "egg") from the mother to form a one-celled zygote, containing the new person's complete hereditary endowment. The question of which sperm joins which ovum has tremendous implications for the kind of person the new being will become.

Sperm and ovum each contain twenty-three rod-shaped particles called chromosomes, twenty-two of which are autosomes (nonsex chromosomes) and one of which is a sex chromosome (see Figure 11-1). The autosomes are the same for both sexes, but while the mother's sex chromosome is always an X, the father's may be either an X or a Y. If the new being inherits an X chromosome from each parent, it will be female; if it inherits a Y from the father, it will be male.

Each one of the zygote's forty-six chromosomes contains about 30,000

TABLE 11-1 Characteristics with Strong Hereditary Components

- *Physical:* Height and, to a lesser extent, weight (Newman, Freeman, & Holzinger, 1937); pulse and breathing rates, blood pressure, and perspiration (Jost & Sontag, 1944); patterns of tooth decay, voice tone and pitch, and posture (Farber, 1981); age of first menstruation (Petri, 1934); and age of death (Jarvik, Kallmann, & Klaber, 1957).
- *Intellectual:* Word fluency, memory, the timing of language and Piagetian stages of intellectual development (Wilson, 1980); maze-running abilities in rats (Tryon, 1940); and scores on various intelligence tests (DeFries & Plomin, 1978; Bouchard & McGue, 1981). For a discussion of environmental contributions to intelligence, see Chapter 7.
- *Personality:* Shyness and outgoingness, emotionality, and activity (Vandenberg, 1967); depression and psychopathic behaviors (Gottesman, 1963, 1965); anxiety and obsession (Gottesman, 1962; Inouye, 1965); and neuroticism (Eysenck & Prell, 1951; Slater, 1953; 1958); special aptitudes and interests, especially in the arts and athletics, and mannerisms such as a firm handshake (Farber, 1981).

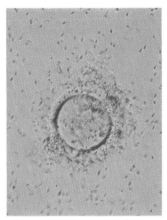

The moment of conception is a split-second event when a sperm unites with an ovum, as shown here. The question of which sperm joins which ovum has tremendous implications for the kind of person the new being will become. (© Alexander Tsiaras, Science Source/ Photo Researchers, Inc.)

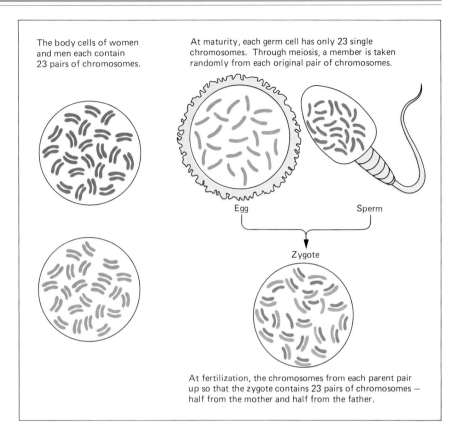

The body cells of women and men each contain 23 pairs of chromosomes.

At maturity, each germ cell has only 23 single chromosomes. Through meiosis, a member is taken randomly from each original pair of chromosomes.

Egg

Sperm

Zygote

At fertilization, the chromosomes from each parent pair up so that the zygote contains 23 pairs of chromosomes — half from the mother and half from the father.

FIGURE 11-1   Genetic Transmission   *(From Papalia & Olds, 1982)*

segments strung out on it lengthwise like beads. These segments are the genes, which are made up of DNA *(deoxyribonucleic acid)* and which determine all our hereditary characteristics. The assortment of genes we inherit constitutes our genotype, while the characteristics that can be seen make up our phenotype. These are not always the same, as seen in the case of people who have brown eyes (their phenotype) but carry genes for both brown and blue eyes (their genotype). The reason underlying this difference is the fact that genes come in alternate forms called alleles.

Patterns of Genetic Transmission

When you inherit identical alleles from both parents, you are homozygous for that trait; when you inherit different alleles, you are heterozygous. If you are homozygous for brown eyes, you will have brown eyes and will transmit only brown-eyed genes to your children. If you inherit one allele for brown eyes and one for blue eyes, you will have brown eyes yourself since brown-eyed genes are dominant over blue-eyed genes, which are recessive. However, you could pass on either allele to your children. If you and your spouse both pass on blue-eyed genes, your child will have blue eyes. While your pattern is that of autosomal dominant inheritance (since you showed the dominant characteristic of brown eyes), your child's will be autosomal recessive inheritance (showing the recessive trait of blue eyes).

Another major pattern is sex-linked inheritance, in which recessive genes for a specific (generally undesirable) trait are carried on the X chromosome, passed on by mothers to their sons. Females with these traits rarely express them since the recessive gene is usually countered by a dominant gene on the X chromosome received from the father. Males who have only the one X chromosome do not have the same protection: If they receive the X-linked gene, they express the trait.

The final form of inheriting characteristics is known as multifactorial inheritance, which is a more complicated combination of genes or an interaction between genetic predispositions and environmental factors that bring them out.

Some characteristics follow one of these patterns, others another. For example, hair type (curly or straight) is either autosomal dominant or recessive, baldness is sex-linked, and height and weight are probably multifactorial.

PROBLEMS IN GENETIC TRANSMISSION

Five years after their marriage, Joe and Ellen Gould decided they were ready to start their family. Ellen became pregnant right away. The couple turned their study into a nursery, and they eagerly looked forward to bringing the baby home. But when Joe and Ellen brought their baby home, they did so with a heavy heart. Their greatest fear—that their baby would be among the 100,000 to 150,000 infants born each year with a major genetic disorder or malformation—had come true. Their eagerly awaited child had been born with Tay-Sachs disease, an inherited condition that, they were told, would take her life before her fifth birthday.

The odds, of course, are overwhelmingly good that this will not happen. Still, babies with birth defects account for 3 to 5 percent of the total of 3 million births and for at least one in five infant deaths (Clinical Pediatrics, 1979). Some of these defects, while present at birth, do not become obvious until much later in life. Let's see how they are transmitted.

Genetic Defects

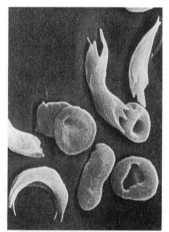

Sickle-cell anemia, a blood disorder most often seen in black people, results if both parents transmit a recessive gene for the sickle-cell trait. (Science Source/Photo Researchers, Inc.)

Inherited, or *congenital,* birth defects can follow any one of the preceding patterns. Those inherited by autosomal dominance include *achondroplasia* (a kind of dwarfism) and *Huntington's chorea* (a progressive degenerative disease of the nervous system that does not become apparent until middle age). When a person with a dominant gene for such a condition mates with a person with a normal gene, each child carries a 50 percent chance of inheriting the abnormal gene and developing the disorder [see Figure 11-2(a)].

Autosomal recessive conditions, which are often killers in infancy, include *Tay-Sachs disease* (a progressive degenerative central nervous system disease occurring mainly in Jews of Eastern European ancestry) and *sickle-cell anemia* (a blood disorder most often seen in black people). A person who inherits one recessive gene from each parent will develop the trait in question. The closer in genetic heritage two people are, the greater the chance of their both carrying the same recessive gene. This is why marriages between close relatives produce more abnormal offspring. Each child of two "carriers" of a recessive gene has a 25 percent chance of developing the trait [see Figure 11-2(b)].

The blood-clotting disorder of *hemophilia* is a sex-linked condition (see Figure 11-3). Examples of disorders believed to be transmitted multifactorially are *spina bifida* (a defect in the closure of the vertebral canal); *cleft palate* (incomplete fusion of the roof of the mouth or upper lip); and a tendency, or predisposition, toward the mental illness schizophrenia (discussed in Chapter 15).

Chromosomal Abnormalities

Some birth defects are caused not by transmission of a faulty gene but by an abnormality of the chromosome itself. While some chromosomal defects are passed on according to genetic patterns of inheritance, many result from accidents that occur during the development of an individual organism. Such accidental abnormalities are no more likely to recur in the same family than in any other.

There are a number of chromosomal disorders of varying degrees of severity caused by either a missing or an extra sex chromosome or by one or more recessive genes on one of these chromosomes. By and large, the long-term outlook for such children generally does not show serious mental retardation but does include reading and general learning disabilities (Lancet, 1982). Unfortunately, this is not the case for children born with Down's syndrome, the most common chromosomal disorder.

FIGURE 11-2(a) How Autosomal Dominant Inheritance Works *(From The March of Dimes, 1983)*

FIGURE 11-2(b) How Autosomal Recessive Inheritance Works *(From The March of Dimes, 1983)*

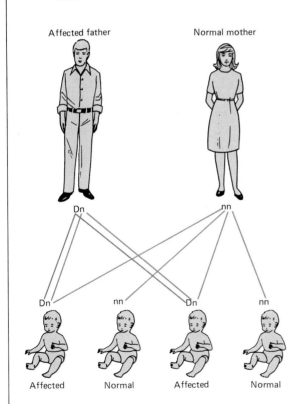

One affected parent has a single faulty gene (D) which *dominates* its normal counterpart (n).

Affected father — Normal mother

Dn — nn

Dn — nn — Dn — nn

Affected — Normal — Affected — Normal

Each child's chances of inheriting either the D or the n from the affected parent are 50 percent.

(a)

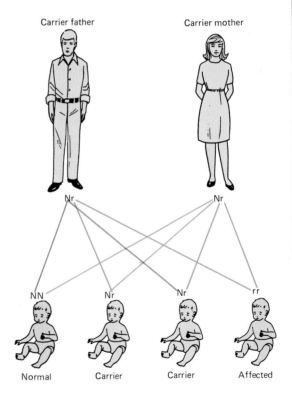

Both parents, usually unaffected, carry a normal gene (N) which takes precedence over its faulty recessive counterpart (*r*).

Carrier father — Carrier mother

Nr — Nr

NN — Nr — Nr — rr

Normal — Carrier — Carrier — Affected

The odds for each child are
1. A 25% risk of inheriting a "double dose" of r genes which may cause a serious birth defect
2. A 25% chance of inheriting two Ns, thus being unaffected
3. A 50% chance of being a carrier as both parents are

(b)

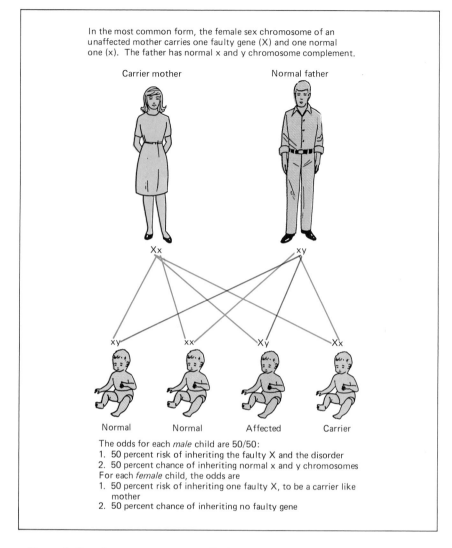

In the most common form, the female sex chromosome of an unaffected mother carries one faulty gene (X) and one normal one (x). The father has normal x and y chromosome complement.

Carrier mother   Normal father

Xx   xy

xy   xx   Xy   Xx

Normal   Normal   Affected   Carrier

The odds for each *male* child are 50/50:
1. 50 percent risk of inheriting the faulty X and the disorder
2. 50 percent chance of inheriting normal x and y chromosomes
For each *female* child, the odds are
1. 50 percent risk of inheriting one faulty X, to be a carrier like mother
2. 50 percent chance of inheriting no faulty gene

FIGURE 11-3 How Sex-Linked Inheritance Works *(From The March of Dimes, 1983)*

Down's Syndrome was once called "mongolism" because of the physical appearance of those afflicted, who have a downward-sloping skin fold at the inner corners of the eyes, a small head, flat nose, protruding tongue, defective heart, eyes, and ears, and mental and motor retardation. The syndrome is caused by an extra twenty-first chromosome (giving the child a total of forty-seven instead of the normal forty-six) or the attachment of part of chromosome 21 onto another chromosome. Down's syndrome occurs once in every 700 live births, and while older women are at greater risk for bearing Down's children, mothers under age 35 (who have more than 90 percent of all births) bear 65 to 80 percent of Down's babies (Holmes, 1978).

It is hereditary only about 3 percent of the time, usually among younger parents. Among older parents, chromosomal accidents are almost always to blame (Smith & Wilson, 1973) possibly because the mother's ova deteriorate over time or because of some problem with the father's sperm, which seems to be implicated in about one in four cases (Abroms & Bennett, 1981).

Since Down's children are usually cheerful and sociable, a growing number are being cared for by their biologic parents or in foster or adoptive homes rather than in institutions (Oelsner, 1979). Programs that offer supportive exercises and activities have been able to improve their limited intellectual abilities (Hyden & Haring, 1976). As a result, many learn simple skills and can, in time, help to support themselves.

Natural Selection

Without outside medical intervention, and sometimes even in spite of it, people afflicted with many handicapping conditions die before they can have children of their own. In this way, the transmission of many birth defects is prevented from afflicting a wide spectrum of the population.

One explanation for the fact that the great majority of the population (more than 95 percent) is born normal, with no handicap, lies in the evolutionary perspective presented by Charles Darwin (1859). In describing the great variety of species populating the earth and the diversity of characteristics within species, Darwin proposed that the reason some characteristics take hold and get passed on from generation to generation is that they have adaptive value and that the laws of nature dictate that animals possessing them will be selected to survive and reproduce.

For example, animals that can run swiftly to get away from predators will avoid being killed and will live to produce their own offspring, which will inherit genes for the same kind of body structure and/or motor abilities. Slow and clumsy animals will be killed early, will not reproduce, and will not pass on their physique. Those who are best adapted to their environments will survive. This is the meaning of the phrase, "survival of the fittest."

Today, with our sophisticated medical techniques, this basic natural law does not always apply. Down's syndrome children, for example, used to die in childhood but now the administration of antibiotics keeps many of them alive into middle age (Scully, 1973). The same technological progress that keeps many such individuals alive, however, is often able to detect their conditions before birth, giving the prospective parents the option to terminate the pregnancy, thus preventing their birth in the first place, or to prepare for the treatment of the child immediately after birth. This is the difficult decision often to be made by couples who go for genetic counseling.

Predicting Birth Defects

GENETIC COUNSELING In years past, a couple who had already borne one handicapped child, who had a family member with a major disorder, or who had a disabling condition themselves would often decide never to have children because they were afraid of what could happen. Today, such couples have a way to estimate their chances of conceiving and bearing a normal child.

They can consult a *genetic counselor*—a pediatrician, obstetrician, family doctor, or genetic specialist—who will try to determine the couple's odds for having children with certain conditions. Another type of couple helped by genetic counseling are those in which both partners come from a racial or ethnic group in which certain hereditary disorders are common (such as sickle-cell disease among blacks and Tay-Sachs disease among those of Eastern European Jewish ancestry). Counselors arrive at mathematical predictions by examining both spouses, taking their family histo-

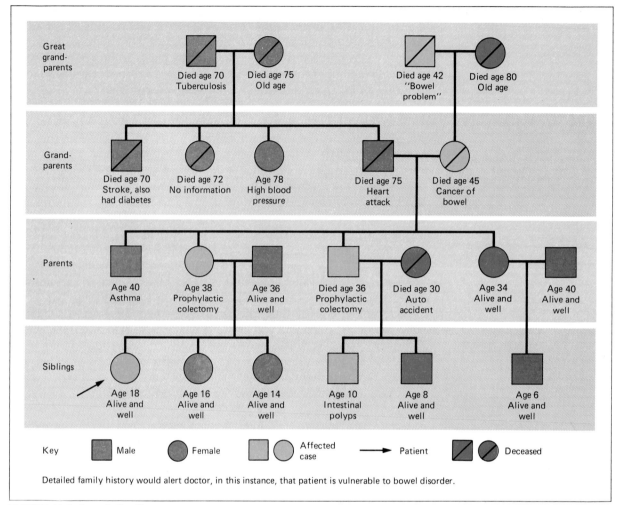

FIGURE 11-4 Sample Family History of an Inherited Disorder *This detailed history indicates that the patient is vulnerable to bowel disorders. Notice the high incidence of bowel disorders in his relatives. (From* The New York Times, *April 13, 1982, p. C-3)*

ries (as shown in Figure 11-4), and perhaps doing sophisticated laboratory examinations of their blood, skin, urine, or fingerprints, and/or making a chart called a karyotype, which shows the chromosomal pattern.

PRENATAL SCREENING   We now have an impressive array of revolutionary tools to assess fetal development. Coupled with the legalization of abortion, these new techniques have encouraged many couples with troubling medical histories to take a chance on conception. Many who would not have dared risk a pregnancy have been reassured by prenatal examinations that their babies would be normal, and other expectant parents have terminated problem pregnancies and gone on to embark on new, more fortunate conceptions. Those parents who have chosen to continue the pregnancy of a handicapped child have had more time to adjust to and plan for the child's special needs. The use of the following new techniques may have the happy result of decreasing the incidence of mental retardation and other congenital conditions.

Amniocentesis   At about the fifteenth week of pregnancy, a sample of the amniotic fluid (the fluid in which the fetus floats while in the uterus) can be withdrawn and analyzed to detect the presence of a variety of birth defects (see Figure 11-5 for a diagram showing this procedure). Through amniocentesis, we can also find out the baby's sex, which may be crucial in the case of a disorder much more likely to affect males, such as hemophilia. The procedure is indicated for women over 35 (at higher risk for Down's syndrome), of Eastern European Jewish ancestry (at risk for Tay-Sachs disease), or with a family history of other detectable diseases. Only 10 percent of women at risk now undergo it because of a combination of reasons: unavailability in their community, not knowing about it, the expense, and a very slightly increased risk of miscarriage (Fuchs, 1980; Clinical Pediatrics, 1979).

Chorionic Villus Biopsy   This new method for obtaining fetal cells, now being tested here and in Europe, has several advantages over amniocentesis (Kolata, 1983). It can be done during the first trimester when it's easier to terminate a problem pregnancy, and it yields results within days, or sometimes even hours. By inserting a thin catheter into a pregnant woman's cervix, a small section of tissue is suctioned from the end of one or more *villi* (hairlike projections of the membrane around the em-

FIGURE 11-5   Amniocentesis
Through amniocentesis a sample of the amniotic fluid can be withdrawn and analyzed for the presence of a variety of birth defects. A needle is inserted through the mother's abdominal wall to remove the fluid. Analysis of the sampled fluid generally takes two to four weeks. (From Fuchs, 1980)

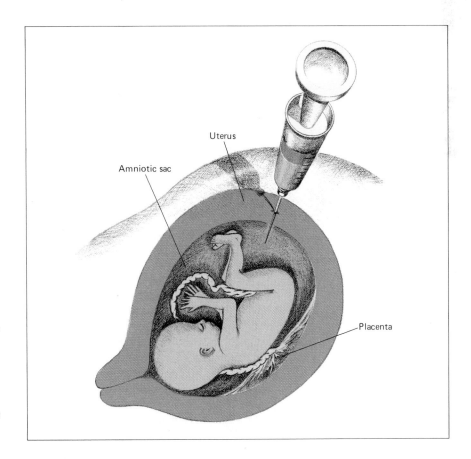

Uterus

Amniotic sac

Placenta

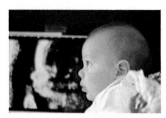

Here is a 6-month-old baby posing with his ultrasound picture taken during the fourth month of pregnancy. (J. Pavlovsky/Sygma)

bryo). This tissue, made up of rapidly dividing fetal cells, can be analyzed immediately for the presence of a variety of chromosomal and biochemical disorders. Since the procedure is still in the experimental stage, a number of questions remain, but it does appear highly promising as a replacement for amniocentesis in many cases.

Maternal Blood Testing Between the fourteenth and twentieth weeks of pregnancy, a woman's blood can be tested for its level of a substance called alpha fetoprotein (AFP). This is usually done only for women at risk of bearing a child with a neural tube defect (like spina bifida), the most common kind of birth defect in the United States. If a high level of AFP is found, amniocentesis and ultrasound can confirm or contradict the diagnosis (Fuchs, 1980; Kolata, 1980; Crandall, 1981).

Ultrasound High-frequency sound waves directed into the abdomen of the pregnant woman yield a picture of the fetus, placenta, and uterus that can detect multiple births, determine fetal age, locate the fetus before amniocentesis, and find out whether the fetus is still alive (Clinical Pediatrics, 1979). While studies have shown no ill effects from this "noninvasive" technique (Brent, 1981), it is still so new that it seems prudent to use it only when medically indicated.

Fetoscopy A tiny telescope, equipped with a light, can be inserted directly into the uterus to permit limited visual examination of the fetus and to permit the drawing of a fetal blood sample. This blood can be tested to determine the presence of such disorders as sickle-cell anemia and hemophilia. Because of a 5 percent risk of miscarriage when the procedure is used, it is still not ready for general use (Check, 1979).

Electronic Fetal Monitoring Machines that monitor the fetal heartbeat throughout labor and delivery came into general use in the 1960s and by 1978 were used in about seven out of ten births (Check, 1979). This technique is now recommended only for high-risk pregnancies where there seems to be a danger of prematurity or other complications of childbirth since it is costly, leads to more cesarean births (those in which the baby is delivered through an incision in the mother's abdomen rather than through the vagina), and occasionally injures the mother or child (Banta & Thacker, 1979).

**Therapy
inside the Womb**

One exciting development of recent years is the ability to use diagnostic techniques like those just described to correct a variety of inborn disabilities. While most disorders must still wait till after birth to be corrected, knowing of their existence ahead of time often permits better treatment. In some cases, for example, early delivery can be induced to prevent a defect from becoming worse or from interfering with childbirth. In other cases, advance warning of the advisability of a cesarean delivery can be given.

The most revolutionary treatments are those administered while the fetus is still inside the mother's body. A baby whose blood type is incompatible with the mother's, for example, might ordinarily be in danger of being attacked by the antibodies in her bloodstream, with possibly fatal

Identical twins result when one ovum divides in two after it has been fertilized by one sperm. Such twins have exactly the same hereditary traits. Fraternal twins, like the girls shown here, are no more alike genetically than any other pair of siblings and may be of the same or different sexes. (© Bruce Roberts/Rapho-Photo Researchers, Inc.)

results. Transfusions of compatible blood while the baby is still in the uterus sometimes save the lives of such babies (Zimmerman, 1973). Fetuses with certain other conditions are able to swallow and absorb medicines and nutrients that are injected into the amniotic fluid.

Experimental work with sheep and other animals shows promise for various forms of *in utero* surgery, and such surgery has already been performed on human fetuses: A catheter was recently implanted in the bladder of a fetus with a urinary tract obstruction (Harrison, Golbus, Filly, Nakayama, & DeLorimier, 1982). Even if these techniques can be improved to allow more widespread use, however, they will still carry some risk to both mother and fetus. Their dangers, then, will have to be weighed against the benefits of prenatal intervention.

MULTIPLE BIRTHS

Unlike most other animals, human babies usually come into this world alone. The exceptions—twins, triplets, quadruplets, and so forth—fascinate most of us. Let's see how they are conceived.

Two basic mechanisms account for all multiple births. In the case of fraternal (dizygotic, two-egg) twins, the woman's body releases two ova within a short time of each other. If both are fertilized by different sperm, two babies will be conceived. They are no more alike in their genetic makeup than any other siblings and may be of the same or different sexes. Identical (monozygotic, one-egg) twins result when one ovum divides in two after it has been fertilized by one sperm. These twins have exactly the same genetic heritage, and any differences they will later exhibit must be due to the influences of environment. They are, of course, always of the same sex. Multiple births of more than two babies result from one or a combination of these patterns and have become more common in recent years as the result of fertility drugs taken by women who have had trouble conceiving.

Twins are more common among black Americans, accounting for one birth in every seventy, compared to one in eighty-eight white births. Fraternal twins account for most twin births (from two-thirds to three-fourths) and seem to run in families, while identical twins do not. Older mothers, women who have borne two previous children, women who are fraternal twins themselves, and women who have taken fertility drugs have a higher proportion of fraternal twins (Vaughan, McKay, & Behrman, 1979).

Twin pregnancies have more problems, including higher rates of spontaneous abortion, hypertension of pregnancy, maternal anemia, hemorrhaging prematurity, low birthweight, congenital malformations, and more babies who are born dead or die soon after birth (University of Texas Health Science Center, 1980).

PRENATAL DEVELOPMENT

In recognition that what happens before birth is crucial to what happens afterward, scientists have devoted increasing attention to the approximately 266 days when the fetus develops inside the mother's body.

Three Stages of Prenatal Development

Each of the three stages of prenatal development has its own characteristics. Let's look at what happens in each stage.

During the germinal stage (fertilization to two weeks), the zygote enters a period of rapid cell division resulting in an increasingly complex organism that possesses rudimentary body organs, and such protective and nurturing organs as the *umbilical cord,* which connects the embryo to the placenta, the organ that brings oxygen and nourishment to the baby and absorbs its body wastes, and the amniotic sac, the membrane that encases the fetus.

In the embryonic stage (two to eight weeks), the embryo grows quickly, and its major body systems (respiratory, alimentary, and nervous) and organs develop. Because of this rapid growth and development, this is the most vulnerable time for prenatal environmental influence. Almost all developmental birth defects (such as cleft palate, incomplete limbs, and blindness) occur during the critical first trimester (three-month period) of pregnancy. This is the time when growth is most rapid and the organism is most vulnerable. Three out of four spontaneous abortions (miscarriages) also occur during this time, affecting an estimated 30 to 50 percent of all pregnancies. Chromosomal abnormalities are found in half of all spontaneous abortions (Ash, Vennart, & Carter, 1977).

The fetal stage (eight weeks to birth) begins with the appearance of the first bone cells and is characterized by rapid growth and changes in body form.

The milestones of prenatal development are presented in Table 11-2.

Hazards of the Prenatal Environment

If a pregnant woman is under stress, will her baby be affected? What if she has x-rays taken while she is pregnant? Or gets sick? Or smokes marijuana? How does her nutrition affect her unborn child? Questions like these have been—and continue to be—the subject of research in the relatively new field of prenatal psychology.

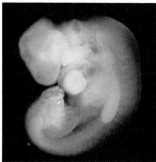

A 4-week-old embryo. Its body is about 0.3 inches long, with a head, a trunk, and a tail. Blood flows through its tiny arteries and veins, its heart beats 65 times a minute, and it has the beginnings of a brain, kidney, liver, and digestive tract. Its sex cannot yet be determined. Through a microscope you would be able to see the swellings on the head that will eventually become eyes, ears, mouth, and nose. In this photo you can see the beginnings of an arm and a leg on the side of the trunk. (© Lennart Nilsson: A Child Is Born. English translation © 1966, 1977 by Dell Publishing Company, Inc.)

A 3-month-old fetus. Over 3 inches long and weighing almost an ounce, this fetus has fully developed fingers and toes, and even fingernails and toenails. It also has eyelids (still closed), external ears, vocal cords, lips, and a prominent nose. Its organ systems are functioning, so it may breathe, swallow amniotic fluid, and urinate. It can move its legs, feet, thumbs, and head, and show such reflexes as sucking, fanning out its toes if the sole of its foot is touched, and making a fist if the palm of the hand is touched. Its head is about ⅓ its body length. Its sex can easily be determined. (© Lennart Nilsson: A Child Is Born. English translation © 1966, 1977 by Dell Publishing Company, Inc.)

TABLE 11-2   The Development of Embryo and Fetus

1 MONTH

During the first month, the new life has grown more quickly than it will at any other time during its lifetime, achieving a size 10,000 times greater than the zygote. It now measures from $\frac{1}{4}$ to $\frac{1}{2}$ inch in length.

Blood is flowing through its tiny veins and arteries. Its minuscule heart beats sixty-five times a minute. It already has the beginnings of a brain, kidney, liver, and digestive tract. The umbilical cord, its lifeline to its mother, is working. By looking very closely through a microscope, it is possible to see the swellings on the head that will eventually become its eyes, ears, mouth, and nose. Its sex cannot yet be distinguished.

2 MONTHS

The embryo now looks like a well-proportioned, small-scale baby. It is less than 1 inch long and weighs only $\frac{1}{3}$ ounce. Its head is one-half its total body length. Facial parts are clearly developed, with tongue and teeth buds. The arms have hands, fingers, and thumbs, and the legs have knees, ankles, and toes. It has a thin covering of skin and can even make hand and foot prints.

The embryo's brain impulses coordinate the function of its organ systems. Sex organs are developing; the heartbeat is steady. The stomach produces digestive juices; the liver, blood cells. The kidney removes uric acid from the blood. The skin is now sensitive enough to react to tactile stimulation. If an aborted 8-week-old embryo is stroked, it reacts by flexing its trunk, extending its head, and moving back its arms.

3 MONTHS

Now a fetus, the developing person weighs 1 ounce and measures about 3 inches in length. It has fingernails, toenails, eyelids (still closed), vocal cords, lips, and a prominent nose. Its head is still large—about one-third its total length—and its forehead is high. Its sex can easily be determined.

The organ systems are functioning, so that the fetus may now breathe, swallow amniotic fluid in and out of the lungs, and occasionally urinate. Its ribs and vertebrae have turned to cartilage, and its internal reproductive organs have primitive egg or sperm cells.

The fetus can now make a variety of specialized responses: It can move its legs, feet, thumbs, and head; its mouth can open and close and swallow. If its eyelids are touched, it squints; if its palm is touched, it makes a partial fist; if its lip is touched, it will suck; and if the sole of the foot is stroked, the toes will fan out. These reflex behaviors will be present at birth but will disappear during the first months of life.

4 MONTHS

The body is catching up to the head, which is now only one-fourth the total body length, the same proportion it will be at birth. The fetus now measures 8 to 10 inches and weighs about 6 ounces. The umbilical cord is as long as the fetus and will continue to grow with it. The placenta is now fully developed.

The mother may be able to feel the fetus kicking, a movement known as *quickening*, which some societies and religious groups consider the beginning of human life. The reflex activities that appeared in the third month are now brisker because of increased muscular development.

5 MONTHS

Now weighing about 12 ounces to 1 pound and measuring about 1 foot, the fetus begins to show signs of an individual personality. It has definite sleep-wake patterns, has a favorite position in the uterus (called its *lie*), and becomes more active—kicking, stretching, squirming, and even hiccuping. By putting an ear to the mother's abdomen, it is possible to hear the fetal heartbeat. The sweat and sebaceous glands are functioning. The respiratory system is not yet adequate to sustain life outside the womb; a baby born at this time has no hope of survival.

Coarse hair has begun to grow on the eyebrows and eyelashes, fine hair is on the head, and a woolly hair called lanugo covers the body.

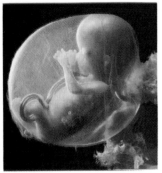

A 4-month-old fetus. This active boy, more than 6 inches long and weighing about 7 ounces, puts his feet against the amniotic sac, and his mother may feel him kicking. His head is now only ¼ of body length, the same proportion it will be at birth. All organs have been formed, and reflexes are brisker because of increased muscular development. (© Lennart Nilsson: Behold Man. English translation © 1974 by Albert Bonniers Förlag, Stockholm)

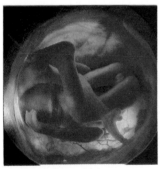

A 5-month-old fetus. This little girl is about 10 inches long and is beginning to show signs of her distinct personality. She has her own sleep-wake patterns and a favorite position in the uterus. She's more active—she kicks, stretches, squirms, and even hiccups; but because her respiratory system is not fully developed, she could not live outside the womb. This photo inside the amniotic sac was taken with a special super-wide-angle lens with an ultrashort focal length. (© Lennart Nilsson: A Child Is Born. English translation © 1966, 1977 by Dell Publishing Company, Inc.)

6 MONTHS

The rate of fetal growth has slowed down a little—the fetus is now about 14 inches long and 1¼ pounds. It is getting fat pads under the skin, and the eyes are complete, opening and closing and looking in all directions. It cries; and it can make a fist with a strong grip.

If the fetus were to be born now, it would have an extremely slim chance of survival because its breathing apparatus is still very immature. There have been instances, however, when a fetus of this age has survived outside the womb, and these are becoming more common with medical advances.

7 MONTHS

The 16-inch fetus, weighing 3 to 5 pounds, now has fully developed reflex patterns. It cries, breathes, and swallows and may suck its thumb. Head hair may continue to grow. Survival chances for a fetus weighing 3½ pounds are fairly good, provided it receives intensive medical attention. It will probably have to live in an incubator until a weight of 5 pounds is attained.

8 MONTHS

The 18- to 20-inch fetus now weighs between 5 and 7 pounds and is fast outgrowing its living quarters. Its movements are curtailed because of cramped conditions. During this month and the next, a layer of fat is developing over the fetus's entire body to enable it to adjust to varying temperatures outside the womb.

9 MONTHS

About a week before birth, the baby stops growing, having reached an average weight of 7 pounds and a length of about 20 inches, with boys tending to be a bit longer and heavier than girls. Fat pads continue to form, the organ system is operating more efficiently, the heart rate increases, and more wastes are expelled. The reddish color of the skin is fading. On its birthday, the fetus will have been in the womb for approximately 266 days, although gestation age is usually estimated at 280 days since doctors date the pregnancy from the mother's last menstrual period.

Most of our knowledge about prenatal hazards has been gleaned from animal research or from studies in which mothers reported after their babies had been born on such factors as what they ate while they were pregnant, what drugs they took, how much radiation they were exposed to, and what illnesses they had.

Particular influences in the prenatal environment affect different fetuses differently. Some environmental factors are teratogenic (birth-defect-producing) in some cases, while they have little or no effect in others. We still do not know why this should be so, but research seems to indicate that the timing of an environmental insult, its intensity, and its interaction with other factors are all important. For example, we have known for more than fifty years that radiation can cause gene mutations and that x-rays are most dangerous before the sixth week of conception, at the time of major organ development (Murphy, 1929). What, then, do we know about other prenatal influences?

MATERNAL NUTRITION   A woman's diet during pregnancy can have important ramifications for the future health of her child. Women who have been malnourished for long periods before and/or during pregnancy are more likely to have complications during pregnancy and childbirth and to bear low-birthweight babies or babies who are born dead or who die soon after birth (Burke, Beal, Kirkwood, & Stuart, 1943; Read, Habicht, Lechtig, & Klein, 1973). While supplementing the diets of pregnant women

BOX 11-1

BIOLOGICAL ENGINEERING

At one time we might have been able to make the simple statement that life begins in the same way for everyone. Now, this is no longer true. Techniques for achieving conception that were unheard of a century ago now make possible new means of creating human life. These possibilities are accompanied by innumerable biological, legal, and ethical questions.

INFERTILITY

The story begins with a couple who want to have a baby (often after years of preventing conception) and expect to conceive readily. Months, or even years, go by, however, with no conception taking place. Today, this disappointment is experienced by about 20 percent of American couples.

Medical tests often uncover the reasons for the infertility: The man may be releasing too few sperm, his sperm may not be able to exit because of a blocked passageway, or they may not be able to swim well enough to reach the cervix. The woman may be producing abnormal ova or none at all, her fallopian tubes may be obstructed, she may have endometriosis (a disease of the uterine lining), or for some poorly understood reason the mucus in her cervix may prevent sperm from penetrating it.

Sometimes medical intervention can solve the problem, possibly through surgery for either partner or the prescription of hormones to enhance ovulation or increase the sperm count. In more than one in ten cases, both man and woman seem perfectly normal according to all the medical tests but still for

95 percent of these couples conception never takes place (Boston Children's Medical Center, 1972).

Historically, childless couples have sought to adopt children whose own parents could not or did not want to take care of them. With recent advances in contraception and the legalization of abortion, however, fewer such children are being born. So an increasing number of couples are turning to alternative means of conception.

ARTIFICIAL INSEMINATION BY A DONOR (AID)

> As far as I'm concerned, this baby will be his, just like our daughter. From the minute she was born, we never mentioned it to each other. We won't tell her— or our friends and family— because there's no way she can find that father. It is our secret: It will go with us to the grave. (Fleming, 1980, p. 20)

This speaker is one of the 20,000 women every year who are inseminated with the sperm of an anonymous donor, a man whose name they will never know, because their own husbands are infertile. The man whose sperm is placed inside the woman's vagina has been matched for physical and ethnic characteristics with her husband, and in some cases the husband's sperm are mixed with the donor's, so that the possibility will always exist that the child may have been biologically fathered by the man who will raise him or her.

While AID has been performed since the beginning of the twentieth century, some of the

knotty questions about it still remain. Should the children know about their parentage? Should the agencies keep records so the children can find the identity of their fathers if there is ever a compelling reason to do so? Should chromosome tests be performed for all prospective donors, a procedure being done for only a few? How can we prevent the possibility that children fathered by the same donor (genetic half-siblings) might someday meet and marry, thus putting their own children at higher risk for birth defects?

IN VITRO FERTILIZATION

Another child conceived in an unorthodox way was born, not under a vow of secrecy, but to the trumpeting of headlines on the front pages of newspapers around the world. In 1978, in England, Louise Brown, the first "test-tube baby," was born. After twelve years of trying to conceive a baby, Louise's parents allowed Dr. Patrick C. Steptoe, a British gynecologist, to extract an ovum from Mrs. Brown's ovary, allow it to mature in an incubator, and fertilize it with a few drops of Mr. Brown's sperm. After the zygote had divided into eight cells, the doctor implanted the embryo in the mother's uterus, where it grew in a normal way.

This procedure is sometimes performed when a blockage in the woman's fallopian tubes prevents the fertilized ovum from reaching and implanting itself in the uterus. The first test-tube twins were born in 1981, followed by triplets in 1982 and quadruplets in 1984, and as of early 1984, some 350 test-tube babies had been born, about half in Australia (Renfrew, 1984). Several clinics have opened up around the world, and such transfers are expected to become more common and more reliable.

This kind of conception also raises questions. Does handling an embryo outside the human body injure it? What happens if a test-tube baby is born with a major defect—is the physician liable? If a donor's sperm or ovum is used, or if another woman carries the embryo to term, who would the legal parents be?

SURROGATE MOTHERHOOD

Another growing means of helping infertile couples have children that are at least half theirs biologically is resorted to when the man is fertile and the woman is not. In such cases, a different woman may be inseminated with the father's sperm, conceive his child, carry it to term, and then turn the

baby over to him and his wife. As in AID, the prospective surrogate is matched for characteristics with the adoptive mother. She is also certified not to be pregnant, is the mother of young children already (to prove her fertility and to be sure she understands what giving up a baby would mean), and wants no more children of her own. A number of such births have already taken place, and by early 1983 an estimated 100 women across the country were serving as surrogate expectant mothers (Peterson, 1983). The arrangement usually involves payment of from $5,000 to $15,000 in addition to the surrogate mother's medical expenses.

The psychological impact of this procedure is like the dilemma of a mother's giving up for adoption the baby she has nurtured for nine months in her own body. Its legal ramifications involve the payment of money, which is, at the time of this writing, forbidden for adoption purposes in about twenty-five

states. And what happens if the mother, having given birth, changes her mind and wants to keep the baby?

DONOR EGGS

Two baby boys, born within months of each other, one in Australia and one in California, are beautiful examples of two new methods by which a fertile woman can donate an ovum to an infertile woman who cannot produce normal ova. The Australian baby was a "test-tube" baby, the result of a procedure by which the donor's egg was taken from her body and then fertilized in a glass petri dish in the laboratory, after which the embryo was implanted in another woman's uterus (Lutjen, Trounson, Leeton, Findlay, Wood, & Renou, 1984). The California baby's birth was made possible after the donor's egg was fertilized through artificial insemination while it was still in the donor's body. Five days after the insemination, the donor's uterus was flushed out

Through in vitro *fertilization, an ovum is extracted from a woman's ovary, allowed to mature in an incubator, and fertilized in a glass dish with a few drops of sperm, as shown here. (© 1982 Dan McCoy/ Black Star)*

Twins can result from in vitro *fertilization as well as by the more usual route. These fraternal twins, Heather and Todd, were born at North Shore Hospital in Manhasset, New York, on March 24, 1983. (L. Gubb/Liaison Agency)*

and the healthy embryo inserted immediately into the uterus of the recipient (Bustillo, et al., 1984). In both cases, sperm from the recipient's husband was used to fertilize the ova.

Life was never simple, and it seems to become more complicated all the time. As if we didn't have enough questions dealing with human psychology when biology, at least, was relatively constant! No one really knows what the implications of these new means of conception will be for any of the principals— the children themselves, the parents who raise them, the people who contributed their genes to them, the physicians who worked with them. And yet the human hunger to bear and rear children is often so great that all involved (all except the babies themselves, who are not given a choice) are willing to take a chance on yet another revolutionary process of change.

reduces these problems (Jacobson, 1977; Prentice, Whitehead, Watkinson, Lamb, & Cole, 1983), good long-term nutrition for both mother and child is best.

Optimal weight gains during pregnancy seem to hover at about 20 to 25 pounds for the normal-weight woman, 16 for the overweight, and 30 for the underweight (Winick, 1981; Naeye, 1979). Recent large-scale studies found that when women gained much more or much less than these levels, they were more likely to lose their children either before or soon after birth. Other recent research has established the importance of eating breakfast during pregnancy since pregnant women who skip breakfast show changes in the levels of various bloodstream substances that are not shown by nonpregnant women (Metzger, Ravnikar, Vileisis, & Freinkel, 1982). (For a diagrammatic representation of where the weight goes, see Figure 11-6.)

SEXUAL INTERCOURSE   Most research over the years has not indicated any fetal harm from sexual intercourse, except just before delivery, when pregnant women have generally been advised to abstain (Pugh & Fernandez, 1953; Mills, Harlap, & Harley, 1981; Pekins, 1979; Rayburn & Wilson, 1980). Recent analyses of data from 26,886 pregnancies have, however,

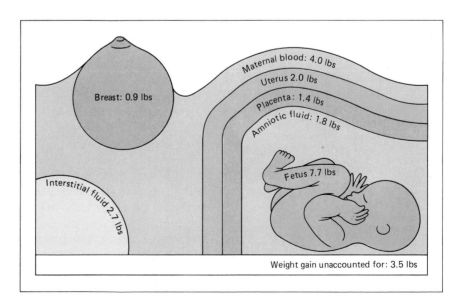

FIGURE 11-6 Distribution of Weight Gain in an Average Pregnancy *(From Newton & Modahl, 1978)*

pointed to the possibility that intercourse during the second and third trimesters can, in some cases, cause infection, premature birth, and, possibly, infant death (Naeye, 1979; 1983).

The data in this research program were gathered from 1959 to 1966, when neonatal mortality rates were higher than they are now, so these reports may overestimate the danger of prenatal intercourse. In any case, further research is warranted. Meanwhile, Naeye (1979) has suggested that since the problem may result from infections caused by sperm, it may be possible to avoid them by the use of condoms or precoital washing.

MATERNAL ILLNESS   A number of illnesses contracted during pregnancy can have serious effects on the developing fetus, depending partly on *when* the mother gets sick. While *rubella* (German measles) before the eleventh week of pregnancy is almost certain to cause deafness and heart defects in the baby, chances of such consequences are about one in three between thirteen and sixteen weeks of pregnancy, and almost nil after sixteen weeks (Miller, Cradock-Watson, & Pollock, 1982). Diabetes, tuberculosis, and syphilis have also been implicated in problems in fetal development, and both gonorrhea and genital herpes can have harmful effects on the baby at the time of delivery.

MATERNAL DRUG INTAKE   The discovery during the 1960s of the link between pregnant women's taking the tranquilizer *thalidomide* for the relief of morning sickness early in pregnancy and the subsequent birth of babies with no arms and legs and with other major abnormalities launched many investigations into the teratogenic effects of common drugs. The findings mean that any woman who thinks she might be pregnant should be very careful about taking any drug, whether prescribed or over the counter. She needs to weigh long-term potential effects on her unborn child against any discomfort she is feeling and should consult her obstetrician about the safety of any medication.

HORMONES   The hormone *diethylstilbestrol (DES)*, which for many years was prescribed (as it turned out, ineffectually) to prevent miscarriage, has apparently caused rare vaginal cancers in some teenage and adult women whose mothers took it (Herbst, Ulfelder, & Poskanzer, 1971). These "DES daughters" have experienced more problems bearing their own children (Barnes, Colton, Gundersen, Noller, Tilley, Strama, Townsend, Hatab, & O'Brien, 1980), and "DES sons" seem to show a higher rate of infertility and reproductive abnormalities (Stenchever, Williamson, Leonard, Karp, Ley, Shy, & Smith, 1981).

TOBACCO   The pregnant woman enjoying an after-dinner cigarette may not think that she is taking a potent drug. Research, however, shows that she is. Pregnant women who smoke are more likely to bear low-birthweight and premature babies; to have more spontaneous abortions; more stillbirths and more babies who die soon after birth (U.S. Department of Health and Human Services, 1981); more babies with cleft lip and palate (Ericson, Kallen, & Westerholm, 1979); and more children with learning disabilities (Landesman-Dwyer & Emanuel, 1979).

How will a baby be affected by a pregnant mother's diet, emotions, experiences, and general health? The relatively new field of prenatal psychology tries to answer these questions. (© Joseph Nettis/Photo Researchers, Inc.)

ALCOHOL   A small number of alcoholic women have given birth to babies who suffer from a rare ailment termed fetal alcohol syndrome and characterized by mental, motor, and growth retardation (Jones, Smith, Ulleland, & Streissguth, 1973; Golden, Sokol, Kuhnert, & Bottoms, 1982). Even when the children's intelligence is normal, they are apt to have problems with school work (Shaywitz, Cohen, & Shaywitz, 1980).

Studies of mice have indicated a critical exposure period equivalent to the third week in human pregnancy, a time when most women do not know they are pregnant (Sulik, Johnston, & Webb, 1981). Since many alcoholic women have alcoholic husbands, it is significant that sperm samples from alcoholic men are often highly abnormal (Lester & Van Thiel, 1977). While some researchers feel there is *no* safe level of prenatal alcohol exposure, recent reviews of the literature indicate that we have no clear-cut findings on the impact of occasional or social drinking (Abel, 1981; Rosett & Weiner, 1982). To be on the safe side, the National Foundation–March of Dimes recommends that women avoid alcoholic drinks completely for the duration of pregnancy.

MATERNAL LIFESTYLE   In a Boston study of 1690 mother-child pairs, researchers found that pregnant women who smoke marijuana are five times more likely than nonusers to deliver infants with features considered compatible with the fetal alcohol syndrome (Hingson et al., 1982). An important finding that emerged from this study was the significance of a mother's overall lifestyle. The authors point out the difficulty of isolating single variables and getting accurate information about drug use from mothers. Furthermore, they found that a general lifestyle combining smoking, drinking, marijuana use, poor nutrition, and so forth has a major impact on fetal and child development, even though the impact of each individual maternal behavior may be relatively minor.

MATERNAL STRESS   Unfortunately, the first question we asked in this section still cannot be answered. While a number of researchers have tried to pin down the effects of maternal emotions during pregnancy, there is still no consensus on the risk in prenatal emotional problems (Spezzano, 1981).

Although, as we have seen, many factors can affect the course of prenatal development, most babies are, fortunately, born healthy. The life force is powerful. We don't know, however, which fetuses will be harmed by the preceding factors, some of which are more dangerous than others and many of which seem to exert their influence most powerfully in combination with other crucial elements. It's difficult to control these influences since a woman may not always be aware enough to give an accurate report of her activities.

Furthermore, we need more research into the father's role in causing birth defects. As we have seen, advanced paternal age has been implicated in Down's syndrome and some rare genetic effects, and the father's drinking of alcoholic beverages has been suspected as a contaminant of sperm. More research is needed with regard to men's exposure to chemicals at work, to the drugs they take, to their health, and to other factors in their lives.

BIRTH

Struggling through a difficult passage, facing the demands of doing the most basic tasks that up till now have been done for you (like eating, breathing, eliminating), adapting to a changeable climate, getting along with hordes of strangers, learning how to recognize friends from foes, making your needs known and taken care of, doing the right thing at the right time and place. Sound familiar? It's what we've all done, beginning with that first launching from our mother's womb into an unknown world.

The Birth Process

While births differ greatly, all vaginal deliveries follow the same basic pattern of three stages. The initial one, when labor contractions begin and the neck of the uterus widens to let the baby begin to move down the birth canal, usually lasts from two to twenty-four hours, depending on such factors as the size of mother and baby and the baby's position in the womb. The second stage begins when the baby enters the birth canal (usually head first, occasionally feet or buttocks first) and ends with the birth, and the third stage is the delivery of the placenta.

In about 15 percent of all births, however, when labor is progressing too slowly, the mother's pelvis is too small to permit passage of the baby's head, the baby is in an awkward position for delivery or seems to be in trouble, the mother is bleeding vaginally, or there is some other problem, the doctor performs abdominal surgery and lifts the baby out of the uterus (NIH, 1981). Cesarean sections, as such deliveries are called, often save the lives of mothers and babies who could not have managed a traditional delivery. They pose somewhat more risk to mother and baby, however, since they always require some sort of anesthesia and do represent major surgery. Critics of current American childbirth practices claim that too many such births are being performed unnecessarily, pointing to their threefold increase during the 1970s.

Different Ways of Giving Birth

THE LEBOYER METHOD   Is it possible that many of the problems that we human beings experience throughout life—insecurity, unhappiness, anger, hostility—all stem from that initial traumatic way we enter the world, as we are ejected from the dim, warm, sheltering waters of our mother's body into the harsh, cold glare of the outside world? One French obstetrician, Frederick Leboyer (1975), thinks so, and has evolved a series of postdelivery procedures to make birth pleasant for the baby, rather than abrupt and painful.

Babies born by the Leboyer method are gently eased through the transition from womb to world by emerging into a softly lit room, a warm bath, and a gentle massage. Instead of being slapped to initiate breathing, a practice Leboyer considers unnecessary and inhumane, immediately after birth the babies are calmly placed face down on their mothers' abdomens, a position that keeps the baby's temperature up by contact with the mother's skin and that enables the infant to bring up any residual mucus.

So far the method is still controversial, with critics pointing out dangers of infection from the bath water or the mother's body and from other problems that the doctor may miss because of the dim lighting (Cohn, 1975). A 1980 study comparing a group of Leboyer-delivered babies and a group of conventionally delivered infants found no advantage in the Leboyer way over *gentle* conventional delivery, nor any greater risk of danger. There were no differences in maternal and infant health or in infant behavior at the first hour of life, at twenty-four and seventy-two hours, or at 8 months of age. Nor were there any differences in the mothers' perceptions of their babies and the experience of giving birth—except for the mothers' feelings, eight months later, that the event had influenced their children's behavior (Nelson et al., 1980).

It would be interesting to follow up these babies several years after birth to find out whether any differences in attitude and behavior do exist between these Leboyer-delivered individuals and others subjected to the more usual techniques. The problem in such research would, of course, lie in the near impossibility of controlling the children's later environments and thus isolating the difference in their births from all the other confounding differences in their lives. For example, would parents who choose a Leboyer birth be different in important ways from those who don't? Would they themselves be so influenced by the philosophy that they would treat their children more gently throughout life? Until we have well-designed studies that deal with these issues, the question of the psychological impact of the almost universal birth trauma, while intriguing, remains unanswered. On the other hand, we do have strong evidence for the effects of another aspect of childbirth—the medication the mother receives to lessen her discomfort.

MEDICATED DELIVERIES   Most western women take for granted the availability of some type of pain relief during labor and delivery. Women can receive *general anesthesia* which renders them unconscious, a *regional anesthetic* that blocks the awareness of pain from reaching the brain, or an *analgesic* for relaxation. In 1974, anesthesia was used in 95 percent of all deliveries performed in eighteen teaching hospitals (Brackbill & Broman, 1979). Yet all drugs pass through the placenta and enter the fetal blood supply and tissues, and the effects of childbirth medication on the baby are marked, well documented, and appear to last at least through the first year of life and perhaps longer.

Among 3500 healthy, full-term babies, progress bore a direct relationship to the amount of medication their mothers had received during delivery—none, regional, or general. The babies whose mothers had received no medication were the most advanced in sitting, standing, and moving around; those whose mothers had received regional blocks did less well; and the ones whose mothers had been anesthetized into unconsciousness did most poorly of all. This effect lasted at least through the first year of life (Brackbill & Broman, 1979).

CHILDBIRTH WITHOUT DRUGS   Do mothers have to suffer, then, to assure their babies a good start in life? Not according to a growing number of advocates of natural childbirth, a method of giving birth that provides alternate ways of making delivery more comfortable for the mother, safer for the baby, and more of a total family experience, involving the father. This philosophy is based on the fact that the uterine contractions that expel the baby from the mother's body are not always painful and that even when they are, women can learn how to minimize their discomfort.

In 1914 Dr. Grantly Dick-Read suggested that childbirth pain is often caused by a woman's expectation of pain, her ignorance about what is

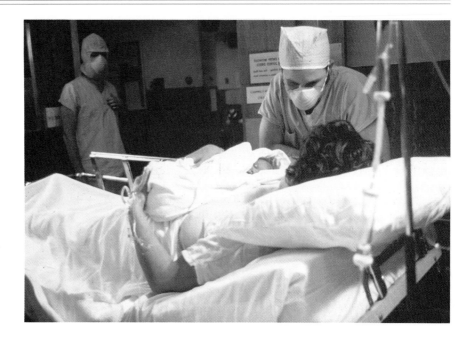

Today many fathers are assisting at the births of their children, making the delivery a total family experience. This gowned and masked father has just helped to deliver his child. (Sharon L. Fox/ The Picture Cube)

happening inside her body, and her fear of what is to come. He proceeded to educate women in the physiology of reproduction and delivery and to train them in breathing, relaxation, and physical fitness. Then, during the 1950s, Dr. Fernand Lamaze based his program of psychoprophylactic, or prepared childbirth, on the classical conditioning techniques of Ivan Pavlov (described in Chapter 5). Using this approach, a woman learns to substitute new breathing and muscular responses to the sensations of uterine contractions in place of the old responses of fear and pain. Both methods enlist the coaching help of the father or a friend who massages the mother's back and assists in other ways.

ALTERNATIVE WAYS OF GIVING BIRTH   Birth can take place in different kinds of settings, with different types of helpers. Recently, many couples have chosen to have their babies in the comfort and familiarity of home instead of in the hospital. Many of these, along with others who do go to the hospital, have elected to have the assistance of a *midwife* (a nurse or other nonphysician who has had special training in prenatal and childbirth care) rather than a doctor. In either case, the experience is often exhilarating when the birth goes smoothly. When complications arise, however, it is safer and happier for all involved to take advantage of the advanced medical techniques provided by a modern hospital, including, if necessary, the minimal amount of anesthesia that will make the mother comfortable with least risk to the baby. Most hospitals offer the option of natural childbirth, many have trained midwives on their staffs, and many have set up birthing rooms that have a comfortable, homelike atmosphere.

What are the psychological implications of the new birthing techniques? First, the techniques that steer clear of drugs seem to provide a healthier, more beneficial start in life to the babies. Secondly, the active participation of both parents seems to reinforce close family attachments among mother, father, and infant. Third, women's insistence on assuming a major role in the births of their children has helped to spur a major movement in family health, in which individuals have become more active in taking responsibility for their own health and less prone to sit back, passively relying on the doctor. Of course, there are many ways to have a baby, and many healthy, well-adjusted adults have been born in very traditional hospital settings. In view of what we have learned about the importance of people's feeling in control of their lives, the *availability* of alternative means of childbirth seems like a healthy trend, but choice is the crucial element. Children born through more conservative procedures can still grow up psychologically and physically healthy.

BIRTH COMPLICATIONS

Low Birthweight

All very small babies used to be considered premature, that is, born before the full term of a normal pregnancy. Today this term is used only for those babies born before the thirty-seventh week of gestation. Small-for-date babies, who are abnormally small for their gestational age, may or may not be premature. The 177,000 of these small babies who are born every year—about 6 percent of all newborns—are particularly vulnerable to infection and respiratory problems. In general, the smaller babies are at birth, the smaller their chances of survival, although in recent years we have made great progress. Today, babies born at or before twenty-seven weeks, weighing less than 2 pounds, often survive and often do well (U.S. Department of Health and Human Services, 1980; Bennett et al., 1983).

While three out of four prematures grow up without serious problems (U.S. Department of Health and Human Services, 1980), the consequences of low birthweight may be grave. One study of children who had weighed about 2 pounds at birth found that at the age of 2, they still tended to be shorter and lighter than other 2-year-olds and to have a higher than normal incidence of respiratory tract infections and severe developmental delays (Pape et al., 1978). Many premature children do, however, catch up in later years (Taub, Goldstein, & Caputo, 1977).

The very same medical progress that has saved the lives of these babies has often put them into an unfavorable psychological environment: They have been isolated in incubators, separated from their parents, and denied the sensory enrichment that human beings seem to need. In recent years, enrichment programs that include holding and handling these babies more often, singing to them, and stimulating them in other ways have helped these tiny babies to thrive (Leib, Benfield, & Guidubaldi, 1980; Stewart & Reynolds, 1974; Scarr-Salapatek & Williams, 1973).

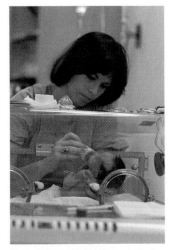

One of the most thrilling medical advances of recent years has been the progress in the technology to deliver and care for premature and low-birthweight babies. Today, babies born at or before a gestation of 27 weeks, weighing less than 2 pounds, often survive and grow up healthy. (© Allen Green/Photo Researchers, Inc.)

Birth Trauma

Fortunately, far fewer babies (less than 1 percent of those born at an excellent hospital, according to Rubin, 1977) suffer from birth-related brain injury caused by oxygen deprivation, mechanical injury, or disease. Those who suffer trauma at birth may be mentally retarded, have learning disabilities, or behavior problems, but the effects of minor or moderate trauma can often be overcome by favorable care afterward (Werner et al., 1968).

BIRTH ORDER

What do Margaret Mead, Pablo Picasso, Indira Gandhi, and Winston Churchill have in common? They have all graced the cover of *Time Magazine*. Furthermore, like a disproportionate number of other super-achievers featured on *Time* covers (Toman & Toman, 1970), they are all first-born children.

Up to this point we have been considering some factors that influence prenatal development and birth. Now we'll begin looking at influences that leave their mark *after* birth. A fair amount of research has centered on the implications of the order of birth. For example, a number of studies have found that first-born children, like those pictured here, are particularly likely to be high achievers. Other research has looked into the effect of having siblings (a relationship we'll be discussing in a little while) or of being an only child. The birth order effects that have been found are most probably due to the different experiences undergone by first-born, later-born, and only children.

Achievement

First-born and only children are more likely to make it into the pages of *Who's Who,* are more likely to earn Ph.D.s, and to become national merit scholars (Sutton-Smith, 1982; Helmreich, 1968). This pattern of achievement may be related to the fact that they're more likely to go to college and more likely to make it into an elite school, accomplishments that in turn are probably related to the fact that they do better in school at earlier ages and aim higher (Sutton-Smith, 1982).

Recent research on intelligence has confirmed this trend: Among 400,000 19-year-old Dutch men tested for intelligence, first-borns scored better on average than second-borns, who in turn scored better than third-borns, and so forth (Belmont & Marolla, 1973). Family size seemed to have an effect, too, since the men who grew up in small families had higher scores. Other research has found that middle-born children are underachievers (Bayer, 1967).

The effects of birth order on intellectual functioning may, however, be more complex than it seems at first. For one thing, some differences may be closely related to social class since better reading skills and higher educational goals held by first-born children seem to exist only for those coming from middle- and upper-middle-class families (Glass et al., 1974).

Robert Zajonc (1976) has developed a mathematical model, emphasizing the family configuration, as well as birth order alone. According to this theory, an individual's intelligence is affected by the average intellectual level in the family, uncorrected for age. The more children there are, the more they bring the average down. When there are large gaps between the children, however, they have more time to develop their intellects, thus raising the average. This model has been used to predict intelligence among large groups of children in the United States and several European countries, but it is limited in its applicability to individual families (Zajonc & Bargh, 1980).

How do we explain these findings? The most obvious explanation is that when parents spend more time with children and expect more from them, the children will achieve more. This is consistent with Zajonc's model and also with observations of mothers, who behave this way with their first children (Sutton-Smith, 1982). There are other possibilities, too. First-born children may be motivated to outperform those interlopers, their younger siblings, who have, in Alfred Adler's (1928) words, "dethroned" them from their initial position in the family. They may be more inspired by their adult models, their parents, than their younger brothers and sisters are by them.

In any case, Zajonc's research exemplifies two major trends in birth order research. First, it explores various relationships in the family instead of concentrating on the first-born as so many studies have done, and secondly, it explores the complex interactions children have with their siblings instead of focusing only on the parent-child relationship. We'll discuss the effects siblings have on each other in the next chapter.

Personality

While a relationship between birth order and intellectual and vocational achievement does seem to be fairly well established, only a few isolated personality differences have shown up between first- and later-born children. While one study found that first-born college women were more likely to want company when facing stress than were later-borns (Schachter, 1959), and others have found that middle-born teenage boys (Kidwell, 1981; 1982) had less self-esteem and considered their parents more punitive and less supportive than did their older and younger siblings, no persuasive profile has ever been drawn that conforms closely to birth order.

The middle-born child, in general, has been largely ignored in birth order research, which has focused on the first-born and lumped all other children in the single category, "later-borns." As one researcher has written, research that "focuses on comparing firstborns with a broad category of 'laterborns' is masking the apparently important and conceptually distinct birth-order category of middleborns" (Kidwell, 1982, p. 234).

The Only Child

About one in ten couples is now choosing to have only one child. The single, or only, child has generally had a bad press, usually considered to be spoiled, selfish, lonely and maladjusted. How valid is this picture? Not very, according to recent reviews of studies (Falbo, 1977; 1982; Hawke & Knox, 1978).

Only children tend to be bright and successful, self-confident, self-reliant, and resourceful; popular with other children; and just as likely as children with siblings to grow up to be successful in work, marriage, and parenting (Hawke & Knox, 1978).

Some differences that have shown up between single and other children are not necessarily negative and may have something to do with the kinds of personalities their parents have (Falbo, 1977; 1982). People who choose to have only one child show certain distinctive personality traits: Women who have voluntarily had only one child tend to be more highly educated and independent and to have fewer friends in general and fewer close friends in particular (Lewis, 1972; Falbo, 1978). So perhaps the fact that only children belong to fewer organizations, have fewer friends, and have a less intense social life is related to their (partly inherited) temperament and to a style of life they have absorbed from their parents. Since only children do have close friends, become leaders in the clubs they do join, and seem just as happy with their lives as others, their differences in sociability do not seem a handicap (Blake, 1981). From the little bit of research that we have, for example, their chances for success in marriage seem just as good as for those from two-child families (Groat, Wicks, & Neal, 1980; Claudy, Farrell, & Dayton, 1979; both cited in Falbo, 1982).

While single children do show up, right along with first-borns, in most lists of high achievers, they don't test as highly in intelligence (Belmont & Marolla, 1973). This can be explained through Zajonc's theory by recognizing the fact that they are more likely to come from single-parent families (which, by having only one adult in the home, have lower average intellectual levels). When family intactness is taken into consideration, only children turn out to be just as intelligent as others (Falbo, 1982).

It would be surprising if our position in the family did not have some effect on our development since this one fact reflects so many aspects of our relationships with our parents, our brothers and sisters, even other relatives like grandparents. The parents of a first child, for example, are less sure of themselves when that child is born; on the other hand, they are more delighted with the child's every new accomplishment. Everything is shiny and new. Later-born children benefit from their parents' experience and more relaxed manner but may lose out on that initial sense of wonder. Single children live in a predominantly adult world until they go to school and even then come home to a situation in which they play a unique role in their families. Does it all balance out in the end? We don't know yet.

The findings on the effect of birth order underscore the immense complexity of human beings and of the innumerable influences upon us, influences that, as we have seen, affect us well before birth. In the following two chapters we will consider the sweep of developmental change throughout the life span, emphasizing the three interrelated strands of physical, cognitive, and psychosocial development.

SUMMARY

1   *Developmental psychologists* are concerned with how people's physical, cognitive, and psychosocial characteristics change throughout the entire life span. They see development as a lifelong process with the potential for growth and change throughout life rather than one that ends in adolescence.

2   Development is influenced by a variety of factors including *maturation* (the unfolding of biologically determined patterns of behavior) and *past and present experience* (such as the family, culture, and cohort we grow up in and any nonnormative life events which may occur). These factors all contribute to the individual differences between people.

3   The *nature-nurture debate* concerns the relative influence of heredity and experience on development. The relative effects of heredity and environment are studied in a number of ways including *selective breeding in animals, studies of twins and adopted children, consanguinity studies, studies of prenatal and postnatal environmental influences,* and *studies that compare life-history factors.*

4   *Conception* occurs when the *sperm* from the father unites with an *ovum* from the mother to form a one-celled *zygote.* Sperm and ovum each contain twenty-three *chromosomes,* giving the zygote forty-six chromosomes. About 30,000 *genes* are located on each of the chromosomes. The genes we inherit constitute our *genotype;* the characteristics that can be seen make up our *phenotype.*

5   Genes come in alternate forms called *alleles.* If a person inherits identical alleles from each parent, he is *homozygous* for a trait; if he inherits different alleles, he is *heterozygous.* A *dominant gene* for a particular trait is one that is always expressed; a *recessive gene* for a trait is expressed only in cases where the dominant gene is not present. There are a number of patterns of genetic transmission including *autosomal dominant inheritance, autosomal recessive inheritance, sex-linked inheritance,* and *multifactorial inheritance.*

6   Each year from 100,000 to 150,000 infants are born with major *congenital* disorders or malformations. Genetic disorders can be passed on through any of the four patterns of genetic transmission. In a chromosomal abnormality the defect is caused not by the transmission of a faulty gene but by an abnormality of the chromosome. The most common chromosomal defect is *Down's syndrome,* which results from an extra twenty-first chromosome.

7   Today rapid advances are being made both in detecting birth defects and in treating them. *Genetic counselors* use a variety of techniques to determine the mathematical odds a couple has of giving birth to a child with particular birth defects. Prenatal screening techniques include *amniocentesis, chorionic villus biopsy, maternal blood testing, ultrasound, fetoscopy,* and *electronic fetal monitoring.* Newly developed *surgical techniques* to be used while the fetus is still *in utero* offer much promise for treating certain conditions prenatally.

8   When two ova are fertilized by different sperm, *fraternal* (also called *dizygotic,* or *two-egg*) twins result. *Identical twins* (also called *monozygotic,* or *one-egg*) are the result of one ovum's dividing in two shortly after it has been fertilized by one sperm. Fraternal twins account for most twin births.

9   There are *three stages of prenatal development.* During the *germinal stage* (fertilization to two weeks), the zygote enters a period of rapid cell division resulting in an increasingly complex organism. In the *embryonic stage* (two to eight weeks), the embryo grows quickly, and the major body systems and organs develop. The *fetal stage* (eight weeks to birth) begins with the appearance of the first bone cells. This period is characterized by rapid growth and changes in body form.

10 The organism is particularly vulnerable during the first three months (*trimester*) of pregnancy. The child can be affected by such prenatal factors as *maternal nutrition, sexual intercourse, maternal illness,* and *maternal drug use* including *hormones, tobacco, alcohol,* and *marijuana.* A *general lifestyle* combining smoking, drinking, marijuana use, and poor nutrition can have a major impact on fetal and child development, considerably greater than the impact of each factor alone.

11 Advances in *biological engineering* have provided couples who have experienced difficulties conceiving with a number of promising approaches for having a child. These include *artificial insemination, in vitro fertilization,* and *egg transfer.* Some couples have turned to surrogate mothers to bear a child who has the father's genes.

12 Although births differ greatly, all vaginal deliveries take place in three stages. In the first stage the labor contractions begin, and the neck of the uterus widens to let the baby begin to move down the birth canal. The second stage begins when the baby moves down the birth canal, and it ends at birth. About 15 percent of births are *cesarean sections* in which the doctor performs abdominal surgery and lifts the baby out of the uterus.

13 The pregnant woman has a number of choices about the way she will give birth. The *Leboyer method* is designed to minimize the baby's birth trauma. Women may choose *medicated* or *nonmedicated techniques.* In addition, they may be assisted by a *midwife* rather than a doctor and may give birth at home or in the hospital. *Low birthweight* and *birth trauma* are two complications that sometimes occur.

14 Psychologists have been interested in the effects of *birth order* on characteristics such as achievement and personality. When birth order effects do exist, they are particularly likely to be due to the different experiences undergone by first-borns, later-borns, and only children.

SUGGESTED READINGS

Baltes, P. B., & Brim, O. G. (Eds.). (1977–1984). *Life-span development and behavior.* Volumes 1–6. New York: Academic Press. A continuing series in which each volume contains about ten articles by leading life span researchers. The emphasis in each volume is on constancy and change in human development across the entire life span.

Corson, S. L. (1983). *Conquering infertility.* Norwalk, Conn.: Appleton-Century-Crofts. A practical guide about all aspects of infertility which stresses the infertile *couple;* written by a medical doctor specializing in the treatment of infertility.

Goldberg, S., & Divitto, B. A. (1983). *Born too soon: Preterm birth and early development.* San Francisco: W. H. Freeman. A sympathetic book focusing on the problems and unique experiences of the preterm infant, emphasizing the first three years of life.

Leboyer, F. (1975). *Birth without violence.* New York: Knopf. Presents Leboyer's controversial techniques to minimize the trauma of birth; includes beautiful photographs.

CHAPTER 12

CHILDHOOD

SPOTLIGHT ON

How the concept of childhood as a distinct period of the life span is a relatively new idea.

The enormous physical, cognitive, and social changes that occur from birth to about age 12, when adolescence begins.

How parents' child-rearing styles influence their children.

The bonds children form with their mothers, fathers, and others in their worlds.

Physical and psychological differences between the sexes and how these are affected by biological, parental, and cultural factors.

As we try to learn about the many factors that influence our development through life, we begin with the very early years. Many changes take place during these years, and, as we have said, the study of development is the study of change. As developmental psychologists learn about these changes, they describe, explain, predict, and make efforts to modify the kinds of changes that take place, with a view to helping people achieve the most they are capable of. Development continues throughout life in the three major realms we discuss—physical, cognitive, and psychosocial. While we separate these broad areas to make it easier to study them, we recognize that they are closely intertwined and that each affects the others.

In this chapter we'll examine physical, cognitive, and psychosocial development from birth to about age 12, when adolescence begins. The changes that occur in these years—especially in the first couple of years of life—are enormous. The distinctive nature of these first twelve years makes it even more surprising to realize that when we consider these years as distinct from the rest of life, we are drawing on a relatively new frame of reference—the idea that childhood is a special time of life.

CHILDHOOD IN HISTORY

From ancient times, philosophers have held various ideas about what children were like and how they should be raised to cause the least amount of trouble to their parents and to society. Not until the seventeenth century, however, were children considered as anything different from smaller, weaker, dumber versions of adults (Looft, 1971). Adults didn't think that children had a different nature or special needs. For centuries, even artists seemed unable to see that children *looked* different, with different proportions and different facial features. We can see this in many of the old portraits of children, who look out at us from the canvas with precocious expressions, as shrunken adults dressed in child-sized adult clothing.

In a classic study called *Centuries of Childhood*, Phillipe Aries (1962) states that a major reason for ignoring the appealing and unique aspects of childhood was the high infant mortality rate that prevailed until the eighteenth century: Since parents realized they were likely to lose their children in infancy or childhood, they did not dare become too attached to them too early. This argument is not totally persuasive, however, because of the biological and emotional demands that human infants make on their parents. As Hunt (1970) and others have pointed out, babies are totally dependent on the strength and experience of adults for their very survival. If parents had been so indifferent, their babies would have died in even greater numbers.

So, as in so many other aspects of the study of psychology and human development, we have to keep looking for an answer to the riddle of the historically invisible child. In any case, by the eighteenth century, the child as a child was more in evidence. With medical advances, children did, indeed, live longer. With the rise of Protestantism, parents were feeling more responsible for the way their children turned out, instead of just accepting misfortune or misbehavior as bestowed by fate. As children received more education, teachers were motivated to learn more about them. By the nineteenth century, these and other currents had come to-

Jean Piaget based his theories of cognitive development on careful observation of his own three infants and on skillful clinical interviews of children. (Yves de Braine/Black Star)

gether, and people of science were devising all manner of ways to put children under the psychological microscope.

WAYS TO STUDY DEVELOPMENT

In 1877, when the biologist Charles Darwin published his notes about his son's early development, he gave scientific respectability to a form of child-study report that had first appeared in 1601, the baby biography. The journals kept to record the progress of a single baby present detailed observations of day-to-day activities. Although baby biographies tend to suffer from the biases of proud-parent observers and only record behavior without explaining it, they do provide a great deal of descriptive information about the development of an individual child. The cognitive psychologist Jean Piaget (1952), for example, based his highly original theories about the way babies learn on his meticulous observations of his own three children.

Since the day of the baby biography, researchers have come up with many ingenious methods to get information about the capabilities of infants, who, unable to talk, cannot tell us what they know, think, or feel. Each of the methods described earlier in this book have contributed to our understanding of how people develop.

Collecting the Data

Today, two major avenues are used to collect information about development—the cross-sectional and the longitudinal methods. In the cross-sectional method, psychologists compare people of different ages at the same point in time, giving us information about age differences in behaviors, abilities, or growth patterns. In the longitudinal method, psychologists trace the development of one or more individuals at more than one point in time, giving us information about age changes. This design gives us information about individual developmental patterns rather than group averages.

The cross-sectional method: Sixty children—ten boys and ten girls of three age levels, 3 to 4 years, 7 to 8 years, and 11 to 12 years—were interviewed about their understanding of "how people get babies." (Bernstein and Cowan, 1977) The researchers also administered a number of cognitive tasks and found that children's thinking about the origin of babies proceeds in a definite developmental pattern, closely related to the child's level of cognitive functioning. So, a child at the first level of cognitive development might say, "You go to a baby store and buy one"; one at level 2 says, "You just make it. You put some eyes on it . . . and hair, all curls"; and so on up to cognitive level 6, which shows a sophisticated understanding of fertilization. (© Media Vision/Peter Arnold, Inc.)

Each of these methods has its own strengths and weaknesses. In the cross-sectional method, we sometimes confuse age differences with the effects of cohort (generational membership). Suppose the school we went into had changed its methods of teaching first-grade vocabulary during the past year: Since the older children would have had different experiences, we can't attribute the differences between them and the younger ones solely to the effect of age. Furthermore, cross-sectional data are usually presented as group averages, so it's difficult to pinpoint individual differences.

The longitudinal method is costlier and more time-consuming. Furthermore, we have to take into account people factors: By taking the same or similar tests more than once, subjects probably do better on the later ones because of practice; and by using people who volunteer for and stay with research projects, we are getting a self-selected sample that is probably brighter, of higher socioeconomic status, and different in other ways from those who don't take part or drop out.

Theories in Developmental Psychology

Developmental psychologists aren't content to describe the *how* of development; they want to explain the *why* of it as well. To do this, specialists in different areas have advanced theories about different aspects of development. There is no one theory that focuses on the development of the whole person, but some theories are broader than others, as they focus on how we develop our intellectual abilities, say, or on the way we develop emotionally or socially.

According to several of the broader theories, development occurs in a sequence of stages, through which we all go in the same order, if not at the same ages. Sigmund Freud's model of psychosexual development (discussed in Chapter 14) is just such a theory. Other stage theories are those of Erik Erikson, who built on Freud's structure but emphasized the

The longitudinal method: In 1922 Lewis M. Terman located more than 1300 exceptionally bright elementary children. Through a series of eleven questionnaires spanning sixty-three years, investigators at Stanford University have followed the progress of these subjects up to the present time, providing a large body of information on the school, vocational, and social careers of people of high intelligence. Psychologists Pauline and Robert Sears, shown here (he was a ''Termite'' in the original study) are now analyzing the data. (News & Publications Service/Stanford University)

role of society more heavily in the structure of personality, and of Jean Piaget, who proposed that cognitive development also proceeds in a series of ordered stages. Unlike these theories, which stress the importance of inner motivation and maturation as tempered by environmental forces, the behaviorist-oriented social learning theory emphasizes the overwhelming importance of the environment. We'll discuss each of these theories in connection with the phase of development they seek to explain.

Knowing a particular researcher or writer's theoretical leanings can be helpful in evaluating the conclusions she or he draws from a body of research. Often the very idea for a research project grows out of an individual's theoretical orientation, which influences the questions asked, the factors considered important influences on development, and the design and techniques the researcher draws on.

THE BODY: HOW WE DEVELOP PHYSICALLY

The way a baby grows in height and weight is obvious and enormous, as is his or her surge in motor abilities. Some infant capabilities are less apparent, a fact that led people to underestimate infants' abilities to perceive and respond to a great variety of events in their everyday world. Research in recent years, however, which has used a variety of ingenious study techniques, has shown that infants are very sophisticated little beings. Even though human babies are dependent in many ways, they are amazingly competent.

At the Beginning: Who Is the Neonate?

New arrivals do not look like the babies in magazine ads. They are usually wrinkled, with a misshapen head and a squashed nose resulting from the trip through the birth canal, and may be covered all over their bodies by a downy fuzz called lanugo. All of this changes during the neonatal period, the first two weeks for the normal, full-term infant (longer for the low-birthweight baby). During this time of transition from life in the uterus to an independent existence, all the newborn's body systems—circulatory, respiratory, gastrointestinal, and temperature regulation—adjust to functioning on their own, with no help from the mother's systems.

Even at this threshold of life, newborn babies can do much more than most people realize. From birth they blink at a bright light, follow a moving target, turn toward the light at the window, and see best at a distance of about 7½ inches—just about the distance a nursing baby is from the mother's face (Vaughan, McKay & Behrman, 1979; Haynes, White, & Held, 1965).

They turn their heads toward a sound, move in time to human speech, and respond to pain by trying to withdraw from a needle and being wakeful after being circumcised or being pricked for blood. Before one week of age, they prefer to look at a human face than at other patterns, recognize their mother's voice and smell, and are more alert when held at an angle or upright rather than lying down. By two weeks, they recognize their mother's face and can stick out their tongue to imitate someone (Mac-Farlane, 1978).

How do we know all of this? Thanks to techniques devised by ingenious researchers, which have let us discover that the infant's world is not what William James described it as in 1890: "one great blooming, buzzing confusion."

Some of the most interesting research on infant vision, which measures aspects of infant thought as well, is in the area of visual preference. If we see that a baby spends a longer time looking at one item rather than another, we conclude that she can tell the difference between the two and for some reason likes one of them better. Robert L. Fantz (1956) designed a special apparatus in which infants can lie and look at visual stimuli that differ in color, complexity of pattern, dimensionality, and familiarity. By measuring the length of time an item is reflected in the baby's cornea, an observer can tell what the baby likes to look at. Babies prefer curved lines over straight, color to black and white, complex patterns to simple, three-dimensional to flat, pictures of faces to nonfaces, and new sights to familiar ones (Fantz, 1963; 1964; 1965; Fantz & Nevis, 1967; Fantz, Fagan, & Miranda, 1975).

Another way to determine infant capabilities is by the phenomenon of habituation, in which babies stop responding to a stimulus they've gotten used to (see "How Babies Learn," in this chapter). In this way we've learned that newborns can distinguish among at least four distinct smells and prefer a sweet taste (MacFarlane, 1978). By one month, they can tell the difference between sounds as close as "pah" and "bah" (Eimas, Siqueland, Einar, Jusczyk, & Vigorito, 1971).

From research like the foregoing, we know that we enter this world as competent creatures who are ready to interact with the people and objects around us. So we see how competence in one domain (like the physical) affects our development in the cognitive and psychosocial realms.

How Nature and Nurture Affect Physical Development

Both physical growth and the development of motor skills like walking and running are strongly influenced by hereditary blueprints, or maturation. They tend to unfold in a biologically predetermined pattern within certain ranges. They can rarely be hurried, even through the most vigorous attempts to train a child in, say, walking stairs, before he is ready (Gesell, 1929). Furthermore, they persist despite deprivation. Even children who suffer from abuse and neglect learn to sit up, to crawl, to walk. Only when deprivation is unusually severe is development substantially affected.

One classic example of such severe deprivation and its effect on motor development was seen among institutionalized children in Iran who were hardly ever handled by their overworked attendants. As babies, they were in their cribs almost all the time, lying on their backs, never on their stomachs, never put in a sitting position. They drank from propped bottles, had no toys, and were not taken out of bed till they could sit unsupported.

They often didn't sit alone till 2 years of age, as compared with 9 months for the average American child—and for children in another Iranian institution who did get a more normal upbringing. When the children in the understaffed institutions did start to get about, they didn't crawl on their hands and knees but scooted on their behinds. Apparently, their lack of practice in using upper-body muscles had retarded their development. Even among these children, however, this retardation seemed only temporary. School-age children at one of the understaffed institutions, who presumably had also been retarded as toddlers, now worked and played normally (Dennis, 1960).

Growth during Childhood

During the first three years, children grow more quickly than they will at any other time throughout life. By the first birthday, they triple their birthweight (which averages 7 pounds for a normal full-term baby) and increase by one-half their height (average, 20 inches at birth). Between the first and third birthdays, they grow about another 8 inches and gain another 10 pounds. While the average boy is larger and heavier than the average girl, the difference is not significant.

Physical growth slows down somewhat after this but is more rapid during the next three years than it will be after age 6 till about age 12, when the pubertal growth spurt occurs and when girls will, for a period of a couple of years, tend to be larger than boys of the same age. Normal children show such a wide range in height "that if a child who was of exactly average height at his seventh birthday grew not at all for two years, he would still be just within the normal limits of height attained at age nine" (Tanner, 1973, p. 35).

Motor Development

Next time you're near a baby who's not yet walking, notice all the things that she (or he) can do with her hands. This exemplifies the cephalocaudal principle—that development proceeds in a head-to-toe direction, with the upper-body parts developing before the bottom ones. You'll also note that babies learn to use their arms and legs before they have fine control over their fingers and toes, in line with the proximodistal principle—that development proceeds from near to far, with the parts of the body near the center developing before the extremities.

You can see the great leaps in motor development undergone by all normal children, as shown in Figure 12-1. In interpreting *age norms*, or averages, for these motor milestones, we have to remember that many normal children achieve these abilities before the age listed, and many do so afterward. One child may walk at eight months, another not until seventeen months, and both are perfectly normal. The study of development is the study of the usual, but it is also the study of individual differences. In every aspect of development throughout life, there's a wide range of normality.

One fairly consistent set of differences does show up between the sexes, even in early childhood. Girls are better at hopping, catching a ball, and doing "jumping jacks," while boys are better at throwing a ball and using a ladder (Garai & Scheinfeld, 1968; McCaskill & Wellman, 1938; Cratty, 1979). Are these sex differences due to genetic programming? To body build and musculature? Or do they stem from society's tendency to

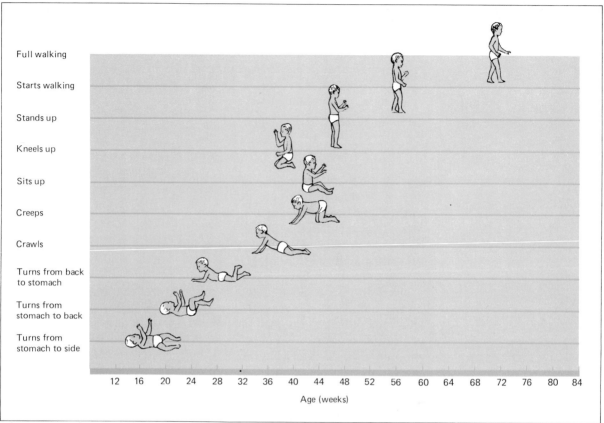

Full walking

Starts walking

Stands up

Kneels up

Sits up

Creeps

Crawls

Turns from back to stomach

Turns from stomach to back

Turns from stomach to side

Age (weeks)

12 16 20 24 28 32 36 40 44 48 52 56 60 64 68 72 76 80 84

FIGURE 12-1 The Development of Motor Abilities *The age norms given here are averages. Babies vary widely in the age when they acquire these abilities and still may be regarded as "normal." (From Pikler, 1971)*

Children cannot be hurried into learning how to walk. They have to have reached a certain level of maturation before they can take that first step. Children who are severely deprived can, however, be retarded in motor development so that they walk much later than the average. (©Michal Heron 1982/ Woodfin Camp & Assoc.)

The rooting reflex: Many mothers use their knowledge of the rooting reflex to help their newborns learn how to nurse. If they stroke the baby's cheek, she'll turn her head, open her mouth, and suck. (Suzanne Szasz/Photo Researchers, Inc.)

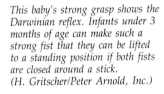

This baby's strong grasp shows the Darwinian reflex. Infants under 3 months of age can make such a strong fist that they can be lifted to a standing position if both fists are closed around a stick. (H. Gritscher/Peter Arnold, Inc.)

encourage different kinds of activities for boys and girls? With the current trend toward egalitarian physical education for the sexes, these differences may disappear—or at least diminish.

Reflex Behaviors   When we blink at a bright light or kick out a foot after being tapped lightly on the knee, we are not acting in a deliberate, planned, voluntary way. We are reacting through a reflex, an involuntary response to stimulation. Human beings have an arsenal of reflexes, some of which are clearly instrumental for survival and stay with us throughout life. The *primitive reflexes* are present at birth, drop out at various times throughout the first year, and provide an index for us to gauge a baby's neurological development. Two of these primitive reflexes are shown below.

- *Rooting reflex:* When the baby's cheek is stroked, she turns her head, opens her mouth, and sucks. This drops out by nine months.
- *Moro reflex:* When the baby hears a loud noise, is dropped, or is startled in some other way, he extends his legs, arms, and fingers, arches his back, and drops his head back. This drops out at about three months.
- *Swimming reflex:* When the baby is put in water face down, she makes well-coordinated swimming movements. This drops out at about six months.
- *Darwinian reflex:* When the baby's palm is stroked, he makes such a

strong fist that he can be lifted to a standing position if both fists are closed around a stick. This drops out at two or three months.

THE MIND: HOW WE DEVELOP INTELLECTUALLY

Even though infants do have some adaptive capacities at birth, the enormous leaps in intellectual functioning are still to come—learning about the world and the people in it, figuring out how to make their wants known, learning to speak and understand language (see Chapter 8), remembering what they have learned and how to use it. How do these vast developments come about?

Piaget's Theory of Cognitive Development

The most influential explanation of intellectual development of modern times was put forward by the Swiss biologist and psychologist Jean Piaget (1896–1980), who formulated a theory to explain the various levels of cognitive development, or the development of the acquisition of knowledge. Piaget presumes an ever-increasing ability to acquire knowledge that proceeds in an orderly sequence.

He is an *interactionist,* who considers the child to be an active constructor of his own cognitive world rather than a passive reactor to influences in the environment. Piaget's biological background led him to give maturation an important place in his scheme, but he went beyond this to emphasize the interaction between maturation and experience. In other words, a child has to be ready for new development to occur, but if she does not have certain types of experiences at crucial times, she will not achieve the level she is capable of. These experiences include direct contact with physical objects as well as education.

How did Piaget formulate this theory? Not through standardized experimental procedures but through his observations of his own children and through the clinical method, a flexible way of questioning children and basing additional questions on the children's earlier responses. He devised this technique early in his career when he worked with Alfred Binet in Paris, trying to standardize an intelligence test (as described in Chapter 7). Piaget became interested in the children's wrong answers, and in exploring the reasoning behind them, he found that this reasoning was age-related.

Piaget's theory has been criticized because of its stress on the average child and its ignoring of individual differences, because of its failure to give enough importance to the ways education and culture affect children's performance, and because it's based on a very personal and idiosyncratic point of view. Still, his analysis of intellectual growth has opened the door to a novel way of evaluating the development of logical thinking, has inspired more research than any other theorist in the last few decades, and has stimulated many practical changes in the way children are taught and cared for.

Let's take a look at three of Piaget's four major stages of cognitive development (see Table 12-1). We'll discuss the fourth stage in detail in the next chapter since, typically, it does not appear until adolescence.

SENSORIMOTOR (BIRTH TO 2 YEARS) Infants learn about their world through their senses and their motor behaviors rather than thinking

TABLE 12-1 Schema for Various Developmental Stages

Ages	Psychosexual Stages (Freud)*	Psychosocial Stages (Erikson)†	Cognitive Stages (Piaget)†
0–18 months	Oral	Basic trust vs. mistrust	Sensorimotor
18 months– 3 years	Anal	Autonomy vs. doubt, shame	Sensorimotor/ preoperational
3–5 years	Phallic	Initiative vs. guilt	Preoperational
6–11 years	Latency	Industry vs. inferiority	Concrete operational
12–17 years	Genital	Identity vs. role confusion	Formal operational (beginning to develop for some)
Young adult	‡	Intimacy vs. isolation	‡
Maturity	‡	Generativity vs. stagnation	‡
Old age	‡	Ego integrity vs. despair	‡

*Theory discussed in Chapter 14.
†Theories discussed in Chapters 12 and 13.
‡No additional stages described for these ages.

about it in the way that older children and adults are capable of. So this is a time of learning through action, as babies go from responding primarily through reflexes to organizing their activities in relation to the environment. They learn how to coordinate information from the different senses and to show goal-directed behavior. They learn the concept of object permanence.

The most important achievement of the sensorimotor period, object permanence is the realization that an object (or person) continues to exist even if it can no longer be seen. Up to about 4 months of age, babies do not look for an object they no longer see, but at about that time they'll look if they see any part of it. Between eight and twelve months, they'll look for it if they see it being hidden, but if it's moved several times—even right in front of their eyes—they'll look for it in the first place they saw it being hidden. Between twelve and eighteen months, they can follow moves that they see but cannot imagine movements they don't see. Not until after 18 months of age do children have a mature awareness of this concept. They can follow the movements of an object, look in the last place they saw it, and look for items they have not seen being hidden.

The concept of object permanence has many practical implications. For one thing, children who have achieved it are better able to handle separation from their parents because they know that these important people still exist and will return. They can also go to the closet to look for a favorite toy or item of clothing and take other actions that involve remembering where someone or something might be.

The popular game of "peekaboo" helps babies develop the concept of object permanence, the realization that an object (or person) continues to exist even if it can no longer be seen. According to Piaget, this is the most important cognitive acquisition of infancy. (© Elizabeth Crews)

PREOPERATIONAL STAGE (2 TO 7 YEARS)   Children make a qualitative leap forward, thanks to their new ability to use symbols such as words to represent people, places, and objects. They can now think about objects that are not right in front of them, imitate actions they don't see at the moment, learn how to do numbers, and to use language—the most remarkable of symbol systems—in a sophisticated way. They have the beginnings of the understanding that an object continues to be the same thing even if its form changes, and they can understand relationships between two events (like flipping a switch and a light going on).

There are, however, major limitations in thought. Children at this stage generally fail to take all the aspects of a situation into account and instead focus on only one aspect, ignoring other just as important ones. They also don't understand that actions can be reversed to restore an original state. Furthermore, they're still egocentric, that is, they have difficulty considering another person's point of view but often view life as if everyone were looking at it with their own eyes and perception and as if they're the cause of all significant events. For example, children of divorcing parents may feel that they caused the divorce ("If I hadn't been bad, Mommy and Daddy wouldn't have fought so much"). Sensitive adults will reassure children that they did not cause a divorce, a death, or another major event.

Some recent critics maintain that Piaget overstated children's egocentrism by posing problems that were too difficult for them. They point to recent studies showing that children in this stage *can* take another person's point of view and can communicate information effectively if they understand the task at hand (Dickson, 1979) and that even 4-year-olds change their way of speaking when they talk to 2-year-olds (Shatz & Gelman, 1973).

CONCRETE OPERATIONS (7 TO 11 YEARS)   Again, children make a qualitative leap as they shed their egocentrism and begin to understand and use new concepts. They can classify things into categories, deal with numbers, take all aspects of a situation into account, and understand reversibility. They are much better at putting themselves into another's place, which has implications for their understanding of other people and for making moral judgments.

The concept of conservation, which has probably intrigued more researchers than any other aspect of Piagetian theory, brings out the difference between preoperational and concrete operations. Conservation is the ability to recognize that two equal quantities of matter remain equal (in substance, weight, length, number, volume, or space), even if the matter is rearranged, as long as nothing is added or taken away.

In the conservation of substance task, a child agrees that two balls of clay are equal. He is said to "conserve substance" if he then recognizes that even after one of the balls is rolled into the shape of a worm (or a pancake or is divided into several smaller balls), both lumps still contain the same amount of clay. In weight conservation, he's asked whether the ball and the worm weigh the same. In conservation of volume, the question is whether the ball and the worm displace an equal amount of liquid when placed in glasses of water.

Children develop the ability to conserve the different dimensions at different times. At age 6 or 7, they can conserve mass, or substance; at 9 or 10, weight; and by 11 or 12, volume. This age difference is intriguing since each problem is based on exactly the same principle, but it does

When do children stop believing in Santa Claus? According to one theory (Fehr, 1976), disbelief occurs during the stage of concrete operations, when a child can think logically and is thus forced into disbelief by his or her answers to two questions: "Is one man able to deliver a virtually infinite number of presents in one night to children throughout the world?" and "How can Santa Claus be in so many different places (street corners, department stores, and so forth) at one time?" Younger children either do not ask these questions, or, if they do, are satisfied with an illogical answer. The concrete operations child has no choice but to stop believing. (Barbara Burnes/ Photo Researchers, Inc.)

When this child realizes that both these containers hold the same amount of liquid, even though the containers look different, he will have mastered the concept of conservation, an important acquisition of the concrete operations stage. (Mimi Forsyth/ Monkmeyer)

seem to hold true for most children—that even though the age of acquisition may vary, children first master mass, then weight, and then volume.

The reasons children give for their answers give us clues to their thinking. Concrete operations children show that they understand reversibility ("You can always turn the sausage back into a ball"); identity ("It's the same clay; you haven't added any or taken any away"); and compensation ("The ball is shorter and thicker, but the sausage is longer and narrower"). Preoperational children who say that the sausage has more clay or weighs more because it's longer show that they are fooled by what the clay looks like and that they are thus focusing on only one aspect of the situation. They also may have trouble understanding the precise meaning of the words "more," "less," and so forth. And since their memory is not so well developed, they may not remember that the two lumps were equal to begin with.

FORMAL OPERATIONS (12 YEARS AND OLDER)   This stage heralds the ability to think abstractly. People in this stage can approach a problem that isn't physically present, work out a hypothesis, and systematically go about testing it. While Piaget originally felt that this qualitative leap was made by all normal youngsters at about the age of 12, he later changed his stance, allowing for different kinds of experiences that might delay the arrival of this stage until later in the teens. Other researchers have discovered that some people may never attain formal operations (Papalia & Bielby, 1974; Tomlinson-Keasey, 1972).

How Infants Learn

Another aspect of early cognitive ability is the infant's ability to learn. In recent years, researchers have tried to determine how early babies can learn and what type of learning they are capable of. We've found out that from the first day of life children learn. They learn to make sucking movements with their mouths as soon as they see their mothers, and they learn to recognize sounds, patterns, and smells. Such early learning is possible because it builds upon powers that human beings are born with, such as reflexes and basic sensory capabilities. These inborn survival-promoting abilities can be thought of as "a gift of the species" (Lipsitt, 1982, p. 63).

There is no controversy about this infinite capacity for learning, which opens up a world of possibilities for the human infant, especially as the baby's brain matures and the cerebral cortex takes over many activities, allowing new learning to take place. Major questions still exist, however, about the *ways* babies learn.

CONDITIONING As we learned (in Chapter 5), human beings can be conditioned to associate pairs of stimuli, in other words, to learn. In classical conditioning, the learner forms a new association between a previously neutral stimulus and an unconditioned stimulus, and in operant conditioning, the organism learns that making a particular response will bring about either reward or punishment. Researchers have set up experiments in both classical and operant conditioning and have tried to determine how early human beings can be conditioned.

Some researchers (Spelt, 1948) have maintained that classical conditioning can take place even before birth, although such claims are controversial. The evidence for classical conditioning among newborn infants is also controversial. Some studies have seemed to show that it's possible to teach newborns to suck when they hear a buzzer or a tone (Marquis, 1931; Lipsitt & Kaye, 1964), but contemporary critics point to flaws in the way these experiments were conducted. At least one researcher (Sameroff, 1971) feels that no research has clearly established the possibility of teaching the newborn baby by means of classical conditioning techniques.

Classical conditioning seems harder to establish among newborns than operant conditioning. One reason may be that babies are just not tuned in enough to their environment to be able to identify a neutral stimulus. If a baby doesn't recognize a bell as something different from everything else around her, she won't be able to respond to it. Recent research coming out of the Soviet Union indicates that newborn infants cannot be conditioned to perform motor behaviors but that some autonomic (involuntary) responses, like heart rate, do show some promise of being classically conditioned.

Operant conditioning, or learning by a reinforcement system, seems easier to establish in infancy, especially when it's based on preexisting behavior patterns such as reflexes rather than on behaviors the infant would not ordinarily perform. For example, infants as young as 2 days old have learned to apply the sucking reflex to suck on a nipple that didn't produce any milk. Their reward was music, produced by their sucking. When sucking turned the music off (which was *not* a reward), the babies didn't learn to suck (Butterfield & Siperstein, 1972).

As we see, then, learning occurs in several ways (social learning will be discussed later in this chapter), and children—and adults—continue to learn along the lines we have discussed in Chapter 5. Other aspects of intellectual development in childhood—such as the growth of intelligence, its measurement, and learning the language—are covered elsewhere in this book.

BOX 12-1

HOW CONDITIONING MAY SAVE BABIES' LIVES

The conditionability of newborn babies may have a life-saving application. Sudden infant death syndrome (SIDS), the sudden death during sleep of an apparently healthy baby, is a condition that parents dread and health authorities are struggling to understand. Psychologist Lewis P. Lipsitt (1980) has suggested that these infants die because they don't make the normal transition from reflexive to voluntary control of body mechanisms, which usually occurs between 2 and 4 months of age, the most dangerous time for SIDS. As a result, they don't cry, move their heads, or take other steps to take in oxygen when air is blocked.

In the belief that it may be possible to teach such life-saving skills to very young babies, Lipsitt has launched a program at Brown University that uses the principles of operant conditioning. The experimenter plays a kind of peekaboo game with the baby, putting a gauze pad lightly over the baby's nose and mouth, threatening a brief reduction in the flow of air. If the baby moves her head or cries, she is rewarded by having a nipple placed in her mouth for a few seconds or by having a tape of a soothing human voice turned on. "These rewards reinforce the infant for taking proper action," says Lipsitt (p. 124), "making it more likely that it will respond similarly when it is alone and faced with a real-life respiratory problem."

This program has shown that such young babies can learn these skills, but Lipsitt himself points out that it will take years of follow-up studies to see whether babies who've received this kind of training have lower SIDS rates than similar high-risk infants who have not.

The Development of Memory

MEMORY IN INFANCY   What do babies know? What can they remember? When we see a baby beginning to make sucking motions with his mouth when he sees his mother come into sight, we deduce that he remembers that she's the one who feeds him. This doesn't happen at birth: Research has shown that a delay interval of only 1 second will interfere with the memory of a 1-month-old (Watson, 1967). As infants mature neurologically, their memories get better and better.

Because researchers have come up with creative methods of studying memory, we now know that early memory is much greater than we could have imagined. We now know that some degree of memory exists at 1 week of age. How do we know this? A major source has been the research establishing the existence of *visual recognition memory*, a baby's ability to remember something she or he has previously seen. We test this kind of memory using the apparatus developed by Fantz (1956) and described earlier in this chapter.

There are several ways to test infant memory, one of which makes use of the fairly primitive learning mechanism called habituation, in which an animal or a child becomes accustomed to a sound, a sight, or some other stimulus. Thus, a baby may be shown a particular design several times while sucking on a nipple. When he first saw the new sight, he probably stopped sucking so he could pay attention to looking at the design. After he had seen the same design several times, he tended to continue sucking, showing that he had become used to it. When a new design is shown, however, the baby stops sucking again. This shows that the baby has stored some information about the design he had seen before: He must remember enough about that to recognize that this new design is different.

During the first week of life, babies can discriminate stimuli that are considerably different from each other. If patterns differ along several dimensions (such as size, number, hue, and brightness), they can tell them apart. Not until the third or fourth month can they tell things apart that differ only in one dimension such as orientation, form, or patterning. By 5 months of age, they can make even more subtle distinctions such as those between black-and-white photos of two unfamiliar faces (Fagan, 1982).

One practical application of these findings on infant memory is the development of tests that may be able to predict later intelligence: A baby's visual recognition memory may be able to tell us about his or her later intellectual development. This is implied by the fact that tests of infant visual recognition memory are good predictors of verbal intelligence in 4- and 7-year-olds (Fagan, 1982; Fagan & McGrath, 1981).

MEMORY IN CHILDHOOD Between the ages of 2 and 5 memory improves considerably. Researchers have tested children through "memory games," asking them to *recognize* (point out familiar items) or *recall* (summon items from memory when they can't see them) a series of toys or pictures that they saw a short time before. As in adulthood, recognition is easier than recall. Four-year-olds recognize about 92 percent of items they've seen, but they can recall only about 35 percent (Myers & Perlmutter, 1978).

As children develop intellectually, their memory improves partly because they develop strategies that help them to remember. By the second grade, children *spontaneously* use *rehearsal* (that is, the silent or spoken repetition of something they want to remember like a phone number), and they can be *taught* to rehearse earlier, in first grade (Flavell, Beach, & Chinsky, 1966).

Later in childhood, at about the fifth-grade level, youngsters begin to use strategies like *clustering* (organizing materials in categories—like birds, foods, items of clothing) and *chunking* (organizing material in sections—remembering the area code, then the telephone exchange, and then the last four digits) (Forman & Sigel, 1979; Appel, Cooper, McCarrell, Sims-Knight, Yussen, & Flavell, 1972). Such strategies will help them remember the billions of items of information they'll be called upon to keep in their minds throughout their lives.

THE PSYCHE: HOW WE DEVELOP EMOTIONALLY

In the first days of life, babies are already manifesting their own unique temperaments; they are gaining a sense of the world—whether it is friendly and caring or cold and hostile; and they are responding to and evoking responses from the people around them. The way we develop emotionally depends on what we bring into this world and what we find in it. In turn, we affect others and contribute to our own future emotional development. And so it goes, throughout life.

Erikson's Theory of Psychosocial Development

The psychoanalyst Erik Erikson (b. 1902) developed the only major theory of normal human development that covers the entire life span. Erikson (1950) built on the Freudian concept of ego to consider society's influence on the developing personality. He outlined eight stages of development throughout life, each of which depends upon the successful resolution of

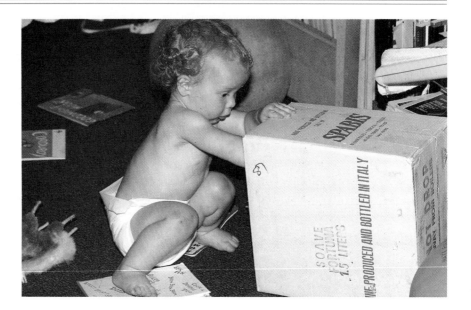

Autonomy versus shame and doubt, the second crisis in Erik Erikson's theory of psychosocial development: This toddler is becoming independent by exploring and testing limits. (© Stan Ries/ The Picture Cube)

a *crisis*, or turning point. Each crisis is an issue that needs to be resolved at a particular point in development, with the aim being a balance between the two alternatives (see Table 12-1). How such resolution does or does not occur has an impact on personality development.

While Erikson's theory has been criticized on several counts—most especially an antifemale bias that emerges from his acceptance of prevailing cultural standards (Gilligan, 1982) and the imprecise definition of his concepts that make it difficult to confirm them through research—its great strength is its broad-based viewpoint which considers the entire life span.

CRISIS 1: TRUST VERSUS MISTRUST (BIRTH TO 12–18 MONTHS)   Constant and reliable care is the basic determinant for the successful resolution of this crisis. Babies pick up their cues about such care primarily from the satisfaction of their feeding needs but also from the way they're handled, protected, and kept safe and comfortable. The child with trust in his mother (whom Erikson views as the primary caretaker) is able to let her out of his sight because he knows she's certain to return. At the same time, his trust in her becomes a barometer against which he can measure others and determine whom to trust, whom to mistrust.

CRISIS 2: AUTONOMY VERSUS SHAME AND DOUBT (18 MONTHS TO 3 YEARS) Building upon the sense of trust already established, children are now exploring their environments with their newly developed skills in moving around and in dealing with language. They are learning how independent (autonomous) they can be and what their limitations are. A healthy sense of doubt helps them set their own limits, and the development of shame marks the very beginnings of a sense of right and wrong. The parents' role at this stage is to provide the right amount of control—too much and they inhibit the child's autonomy, too little and the child may become compulsive about controlling herself.

CRISIS 3: INITIATIVE VERSUS GUILT (3 TO 6 YEARS)   The basic conflict now is between initiative in planning and carrying out activities and guilt over what the child wants to do. Children have to learn how to regulate these aspects of personality so they can develop a sense of responsibility and still be able to enjoy life. If too much guilt develops, for example, children overcontrol themselves, stifling their initiative and preventing the free expression of their personality.

CRISIS 4: INDUSTRY VERSUS INFERIORITY (6 TO 12 YEARS)   Children now must learn the skills of their cultures, either in school or at the feet of adults or older children. Productivity and a sense of competence are important, tempered by the child's awareness of how much he still has to learn. This stage coincides with the timing of the cognitive leap known as the *concrete operations stage*, whose abilities make possible many productive achievements. Children who feel inferior to their peers may retreat to the safety of the family, stifling cognitive and productive development; children consumed with the importance of industriousness may neglect the emotional sides of their personality.

We'll examine the last four Eriksonian crises in the next chapter since they occur in adolescence and adulthood.

Expressing Feelings

How can we tell what's happening in a baby's mind? We try to figure out what's going on based on what we can see—the crying and the smiling and the laughing and the way babies, and then older children, respond to those around them. But it's often hard to interpret these signs. The question about which emotions babies have at birth and soon after has given rise to considerable controversy. It's easy to tell when a baby is unhappy, but it's more difficult to know what other emotions an infant feels—and at what age these feelings develop. Early researchers felt that the young infant had only one emotion, undifferentiated excitement (Bridges, 1932), or perhaps three—love, rage, and fear (Watson, 1919).

More recently, researchers using sophisticated techniques have been able to plumb the mysteries of the world of the preverbal child. We have found that very young children are more complex and more adept than we had given them credit for. Babies do show a range of different feelings, and adults who don't know the babies can distinguish a variety of emotions. The facial expressions of thirty infants (ten each at the ages of 5, 7, and 9 months) in such circumstances as playing games with their mothers, being surprised by a jack-in-the-box, getting shots from a doctor, and being approached by a stranger were recorded on videotape. A panel of judges were trained with Izard's *Facial Expression Scoring Manual* (FESM—Izard, 1971; 1977), which gives verbal descriptions and photographs of brow, eye, and mouth regions of nine facial patterns that express fundamental emotions. These judges then classified the expressions.

Then untrained subjects—college students and female health service professionals (mostly public health and school nurses)—were asked to identify the babies' expressions. These volunteers were able to accurately identify such expressions as joy, sadness, interest, and fear, and to a lesser degree anger, surprise, and disgust (Izard, Huebner, Risser, McGinnes, & Dougherty, 1980). When the subjects were trained with the

Eriksonian crisis 4, industry versus inferiority: During the elementary school years children need to develop a sense of competence. While a child in some other culture might concentrate on learning domestic skills, this girl is learning the kind of intellectual knowledge that will be important to her in this society. (Betsy Cole/The Picture Cube)

Personality traits influence our lives in many ways. People who are shy as children tend to choose different kinds of careers and leisure activities in adulthood from the kinds chosen by those people who are more outgoing. (Suzanne Szasz)

FESM, they became even more accurate. While we can't be positive that these babies did have the emotions they were credited with, the fact that the judges and the untrained subjects agreed so closely in identifying the various expressions does seem to indicate that the babies were showing a variety of different feelings, and the fact that the babies' expressions resembled adult expressions in similar situations seems to provide some basis for attributing similar emotions to young infants.

CRYING Babies cry for many reasons, and both experienced parents and laboratory researchers are often able to tell whether they're hungry, angry, in pain, or frustrated (Wolff, 1969; Oswald & Peltzman, 1974). Babies whose cries of distress do bring relief are apparently able to gain a measure of self-confidence in the knowledge that they can affect their own lives: By the end of the first year, babies whose caregivers respond promptly and caringly to their crying cry less. The more the caregiver ignores, scolds, hits, commands, and restricts the baby, the more the baby cries, frets, and acts aggressively (Clarke-Stewart, 1977).

SMILING The smile of a baby is another powerfully irresistible means of communication. The probability of an infant's smile eliciting a smile from an adult ranges from 0.46 to 0.88 (Gewirtz & Gewirtz, 1968), and these reciprocal smiles go far to cement the bonds between babies and the important people in their lives. Babies smile fleetingly at the age of 1 week, more frequently at 1 month, and at $3\frac{1}{2}$ months they smile more to familiar faces than to unfamiliar ones (Kreutzer & Charlesworth, 1973).

LAUGHING At about the third month babies start to laugh out loud—when they're kissed on the stomach, when they hear certain sounds, and when they see their parents do unusual things. Laughter is a sign of cognitive development: By laughing at the unexpected, children show that they know what to expect (Sroufe & Wunsch, 1972). So we can see how an emotional expression signals cognitive development, demonstrating still another way in which different aspects of development are interrelated.

Individual Differences in Temperament

One baby seems to smile and laugh almost all the time, hardly ever crying, while another reverses the pattern. Such differences often show up right from birth, demonstrating distinct differences in temperament, or an individual's characteristic style of approaching people and situations. After following hundreds of babies from birth through middle childhood, researchers identified nine different aspects of temperament that appear inborn (Thomas, Chess, & Birch, 1968).

These include: activity level; regularity in biological functioning (sleeping, eating, eliminating); readiness to accept new people and situations; adaptability to change; sensitivity to noise, light, and other sensory stimuli; mood (cheerfulness or unhappiness); intensity of responses; distractibility; and persistence. Biological differences may be at the root of such temperamental diversity: Newborns with lower levels of the enzyme monoamine oxidase (MAO) are more active, more excitable, and crankier than those with higher MAO levels (Sostek & Wyatt, 1981). Previous research has established a probable genetic basis for such variations.

Jerome Kagan (1982), who has conducted a number of longitudinal

When my third daughter was an infant, I could place her against my shoulder and she would stick there like velvet. Only her eyes jumped from place to place. In a breeze, her bright-red hair might stir, but she would not. Even then, there was profundity in her repose.

When my fourth daughter was an infant, I wondered if her veins were full of ants. Placing her against a shoulder was a risk both to her and to the shoulder. Impulsively, constantly, everything about her moved. Her head seemed about to revolve as it followed the bestirring world."
(McPhee, 1983)

studies, has found that toddlers who were shy at 21 months of age continued to be bashful ten months later. Furthermore, men who had been shy little boys grew up to choose different kinds of careers and leisure activities than did those who had been more outgoing, leading Kagan to conclude that early temperamental style might influence later behavioral choices in subtle ways.

Certain combinations of the nine temperamental traits identified by Thomas, Chess, and Birch produce three distinctive personalities. About 40 percent of the children studied could be described as *easy* children: They're happy most of the time, adjust easily to new situations, and sleep, eat, and eliminate on a fairly predictable schedule. About 10 percent are *difficult:* They cry easily, are irregular in body functions, and take a long time to adjust to a new routine. And about 15 percent are *slow-to-warm-up:* mild in responses, with a need to take their time adjusting to new experiences and people (Thomas & Chess, 1977). Since not all children fit neatly into these categories, these percentages don't add up to 100 percent.

The significance of such characteristics lies in the degree to which children create their own worlds. One of the major trends in recent research has been the exploration of the degree to which children affect their parents, as well as the other way around. Some children are more likely, for example, to suffer abuse—premature and low-birthweight babies, hyperactive and retarded children, and youngsters who make other special demands on their parents (Reid, Loeber, & Patterson, 1982). Other research has shown that when experimenters encourage children to ask their parents for help, the children act more dependently and their parents become bossier and more restrictive; when the children are encouraged to be independent, parents are less likely to interfere (Segal & Yahraes, 1978).

A child's temperament, therefore, is an important element in the way other people, especially parents, will act toward him or her. It's easier to be warm and loving to a baby who's usually cheerful and whose wants you can anticipate and meet relatively easily than it is with a baby who cries constantly, resists being cuddled, and often seems impossible to please. Parents who get along best with difficult or slow-to-warm-up children are the ones who've learned how to adapt their child-rearing patterns to their children's individual needs (Thomas & Chess, 1977). Some children, in fact, seem to change their behavioral styles over the years, apparently reacting to the kind of parental handling they get.

ATTACHMENT

If you've ever seen a baby follow his mother's every move with his eyes, smile at her when she comes near, gurgle to her, cry when she leaves the room, then squeal with joy upon her return—you've seen a baby who has formed his first attachment to another person. Attachment is an active, affectionate, reciprocal relationship specifically between two individuals, as distinguished from all other persons. While babies do form attachments to their fathers, their brothers and sisters, their grandparents, and other consistent caregivers, most of the research on early attachment has focused on the bond between mother and child.

For attachment to take place, both parties have to reach out and respond to the other. Mothers (and other caregivers) do this by being sensitive to their babies' needs, picking up their signals, holding them closely. Babies do their share by smiling, crying, clinging, and looking into their caregivers' eyes. As early as the eighth week, babies initiate some of these behaviors more toward their mothers than toward anyone else and gain a sense of power and competence when their mothers respond warmly (Ainsworth, 1969).

Different levels of attachment exist, as measured by Mary D. Salter Ainsworth's *strange situation,* with its eight sequences: Mother and baby enter an unfamiliar room; mother sits down and baby is free to explore; an unfamiliar adult enters; mother leaves baby alone with stranger; mother returns and stranger leaves; mother leaves baby alone; stranger comes back; and finally, stranger leaves and mother returns (Ainsworth, Blehar, Waters, & Wall, 1978). One-year-olds observed through this sequence were either:

- *Securely attached,* using the mother as a safe base from which to explore, returning to her occasionally for comfort, acting distressed when she leaves, and going to her when she returns.
- *Avoidant,* rarely crying when the mother leaves but staying away from her when she returns, seeming to be very angry.
- *Ambivalent,* anxious before separation, becoming very upset when mother leaves, and on her return seeking close contact while resisting it by kicking or squirming.

What causes these different patterns, which seem to persist at least until age 5 (Matas, Arend, & Sroufe, 1978; Waters, Wippman, & Sroufe, 1979; Arend, Gove, & Sroufe, 1979)? Probably a combination of the infants' temperaments and the mothers' handling patterns. The mothers of the securely attached babies, for example, were most sensitive to them, while the mothers of the avoidant babies were the angriest; furthermore, the ambivalent babies were temperamentally "difficult" (Ainsworth, 1979).

The early development of a strong bond between parent and child seems to have far-reaching effects. For one thing, securely attached babies are more sociable with strangers, probably because they trust their mothers and generalize this trust to other people (Thompson & Lamb, 1983). This confirms Erikson's emphasis on the initial crisis in psychosocial development, "trust vs. mistrust."

Several long-lasting effects of attachment have been found. When securely attached 18-month-olds were followed up at the age of 2, they turned out to be more enthusiastic, persistent, cooperative, and, in general, more effective than children who had been insecurely attached babies (Matas, Arend, & Sroufe, 1978). At $3\frac{1}{2}$, securely attached children are described as "peer leaders, socially involved, attracting the attention of others, curious, and actively engaged in their surroundings" (Waters, Wippman, & Sroufe, 1979). At 4 or 5 years, they are more curious and more competent (Arend, Gove, & Sroufe, 1979).

How Attachment Occurs

How do babies and mothers become attached to each other? It's often not love at first sight: Only about half of one group of new mothers reported

In a series of classic experiments, Harry and Margaret Harlow showed that food is not the crucial path to a baby's heart. When baby rhesus monkeys could choose whether to go to a wire surrogate "mother" where they could feed from a bottle or to a terrycloth "mother" that offered warmth and softness but no food, the babies spent more time clinging to the cloth one. (Courtesy of Harry Harlow/University of Wisconsin Primate Laboratory)

that they had positive feelings when they first saw their babies, but by three weeks love was taking hold and by three months most were strongly attached (Robson & Moss, 1970).

Ainsworth (1979) feels that attachment depends on the mother's sensitivity, which lets the baby form expectations of her as generally accessible and responsive. The baby wakes up and cries; the mother comes into the room. He is hungry; she feeds him. He is wet; she changes his diaper. He smiles; she plays with him. He develops what Erikson calls a sense of trust. What happens, though, when babies' signals are not picked up? They become anxious, not knowing what to expect, and fail to form a strong attachment.

Even though Erikson felt that the feeding situation was paramount in developing the sense of trust, Harry and Margaret Harlow's classic experiments with monkeys have shown that food is not the crucial path to a baby's heart. In one famous study, monkeys were separated from their mothers six to twelve hours after birth and raised in the laboratory. The infants were put in cages with one of two surrogate "mothers"—one a plain cylindrical wire mesh form, the other covered with terrycloth. Some monkeys were fed from bottles connected to the wire mothers, others by the warm, cuddly cloth ones.

When the monkeys were allowed to spend time with either mother, all of them spent more time clinging to the cloth one, even if they were being fed by the wire one. Monkeys with cloth mothers also explored more than the wire-mothered babies (Harlow, 1958; Harlow & Zimmermann, 1959). Apparently body contact can be even more important than food.

Not surprisingly, even having a warm, cuddly cloth mother to cling to doesn't provide good enough mothering. The cloth-raised monkeys did not grow up normally, had difficulty mating, and were unable to mother their own infants (Harlow & Harlow, 1962; Suomi & Harlow, 1972). Obviously, mothers have to *do* something—not just stand there and allow themselves to be clung to—to let their children develop normally. An encouraging follow-up to the story of these motherless monkeys, however, can be seen in the success with which slightly younger normal monkeys were able to rehabilitate them (Suomi & Harlow, 1972; 1978). These "therapist" monkeys made normal social overtures, eventually eliciting normal playfulness in the unmothered monkeys.

The Role of Early Mother-Infant Contact

Harlow's success in rehabilitating monkeys deprived of normal mothering argues against the theory that primate animals, like some of the lower species, must receive mothering at a critical, early period. Among sheep and goats, certain standardized rituals occur right after birth to cement the mother-child relationship. If these rituals are prevented or interrupted, neither mother nor baby will recognize each other, no attachment will take place, and the baby is likely to die or develop abnormally. Klaus and Kennell (1976) proposed that the first hours after birth constitute a critical period for bonding between mother and child and that if the two are separated then, the attachment needed for the baby's healthy development may be harmed.

Their pioneering research, which promoted the beneficial effects of extended close contact right after birth between mother and baby, was widely accepted and quite influential in changing many restrictive hospital practices that kept mothers and babies apart. While these changes do seem more humane and natural, recent research indicates that they are not critical for the relationship between mother and child. As a result, Klaus and Kennell (1982) have modified their original position.

After analyzing more than twenty follow-up research projects, Michael E. Lamb (1982a; 1982b) concluded that early contact between a mother and her newborn has no lasting effect on either one, although it may sometimes have slight short-term effects on *some* mothers in *some* circumstances. Awareness that such early separation does not do permanent harm is particularly important for adoptive parents, for parents of sick and low-birthweight infants, and for parents in other circumstances of unavoidable separation after birth. Happily, the adaptability of the human infant is extraordinary.

Stranger Anxiety

If you've ever tried to pick up a baby over the age of 8 months with whom you have little or no acquaintance and been greeted by howls of fear and desperate attempts to go back to the safety of familiar arms, you don't have to worry that you did anything wrong. The baby is only showing a perfectly normal (although not universal) wariness of strangers, which usually appears sometime between 8 and 12 months of age.

Why do infants all over the world begin to become afraid of strangers at about this age, reach a peak of distress at about fifteen months, and accept their presence at about three years? This phenomenon occurs among blind babies, babies held almost constantly on their mothers' bodies, and babies raised in such disparate settings as nuclear families, communes, and day-care centers. According to Jerome Kagan (1982), the reason for this reaction, which appears at just about the same time as the concept of the permanent object, lies in the development of learning and memory. He suggests that it's the infant's new ability to learn and to remember the good feelings experienced in the presence of the familiar caretaker, combined with anxiety at not being able to predict what it will be like to be with a stranger, that gives rise to stranger anxiety.

It also seems related to temperament and to attachment. "Easy" children, for example, show little stranger anxiety, while difficult and slow-to-warm-up children exhibit it more (Thomas & Chess, 1977). Furthermore, babies who are securely attached to their mothers are particularly wary of strangers, while avoidant babies would often rather be picked up by a stranger than by their own mother (Harmon, Suwalsky, & Klein, 1979).

The Father-Child Bond

Most of the psychological literature about attachment has, as we said, focused on the mother-child tie, while the father has hovered in the shadows. In recent years, however, we have seen a surge of research interest in father-child bonds. This has, of course, paralleled changes in our society, in which many fathers (including research psychologists) are assuming a much larger role in the care of their children.

The soundness of this trend is confirmed by recent research showing that infants form attachments to their fathers in the first year of life, that fathers often become attached to their babies within the first three days after birth, and that the father-child bond throughout childhood has important implications for children's healthy development (Lamb, 1979; Greenberg & Morris, 1974; Lynn, 1974).

How do mothers' and fathers' relationships with their children differ? First, mothers spend more time with them. Then, they do different things. Mothers tend to hold their babies to take care of them—feeding, bathing, or changing; while fathers pick up their babies to play with them, usually more boisterously than play the mothers initiate (Lamb, 1979). On the other hand, fathers who take care of their babies seem to do just as good a job as mothers: They touch, look at, talk to, rock, and kiss their children as much as mothers do; respond equally well to the babies' signals; and are just as effective in feeding them (Parke, 1978). Still, when both parents are present, the mother usually gives basic care and the father plays with the baby.

IDENTIFICATION

How do children develop a sense of who they are? Partly by looking at the people around them and seeing who they want to be like. Through identification, children adopt certain characteristics, beliefs, attitudes, values and behaviors of another person or group. Identification is one of the most important personality developments in early childhood.

Psychoanalysts, who originated the concept of identification, see it as an outgrowth of the Oedipus and Electra complexes (discussed in Chapter 14). Unable to compete with the same-sex parent for the love of the opposite-sex parent, children resolve their conflicts by identifying with the same-sex parent. This is sometimes termed "identification with the aggressor" since the child sees the same-sex parent as a rival and potential aggressor.

Social learning theorists see identification as the result of copying a model who may be a parent but who might also be a sister or brother, a

Children imitate people they admire and want to be like, in the process of identification, one of the most important personality developments in early childhood. Children tend to adopt the model's beliefs, attitudes, and values, as well as his or her behavior. (© Larry Mulvehill/ Photo Researchers, Inc.)

neighbor, a teacher, a playmate, or a sports or television star. Furthermore, children often model themselves after several different people, picking up different characteristics from each. They choose their models largely on the basis of two main characteristics—power and nurturance (Bandura & Huston, 1961). The social-learning explanation theory for sex-role identification will be discussed later in this chapter.

According to Jerome Kagan (1958; 1971), four interrelated processes establish and strengthen identification:

1   *Children want to be like the model:* A little boy, for example, feels that if he's like his sports idol, he'll be able to do what the athlete can do.
2   *Children believe they are like the model:* They feel they look like the model, tell jokes like him, walk like him. This identification with a parent is often buttressed by the comments of other people ("You have your daddy's eyes").
3   *Children experience emotions like those the model is feeling:* When a little girl sees her mother cry after her own brother's death, the child feels sad and cries, too, not for an uncle she barely knew but because her mother's sadness makes her feel sad.
4   *Children act like the model:* In play and in everyday conversation, they often adopt mannerisms, voice inflections, and phrasing. Many a parent is startled to hear her own words and her own tone of voice come out of the mouth of a tot.

Through identification, then, children come to believe they have the same characteristics as a model. Thus, when they identify with a nurturant and competent model, the children are pleased and proud. When the model is inadequate, the children may feel unhappy and insecure.

THE SIBLING BOND

If you have brothers and sisters, your relationships with them are likely to be the longest-lasting you'll ever have with anyone. They began in infancy, long before you were to meet a future spouse, and are apt to end in old age, probably long after your parents will have died. The intensity and specialness in these relationships are rarely duplicated. These are the people who share your roots, who emerge from the same font of values, who deal with you more objectively than your parents and more candidly than practically everyone you'll ever know.

Sibling relationships are probably even more important today than they were in days gone by because of various changes in society (Cicirelli, 1980). With higher rates of divorce and remarriage, brothers and sisters tend to become closer to each other than to either their parents or their stepparents. Another change is the increased responsibility among middle-aged children for the care of aging parents, a burden that can either draw siblings closer together or inflame old rivalries. Not surprisingly, your siblings are a major influence in your life. What is surprising is the small amount of research on this unique relationship.

Until very recently, the only interest in sibling influence revolved around birth order and its effects on development. Over the past few years, however, researchers have become more interested in interaction among the siblings themselves rather than between parents and their

BOX 12-2

HOW PARENTS' CHILD-REARING STYLES AFFECT THEIR CHILDREN

What makes one child burst into tears of frustration when she can't finish a jigsaw puzzle, while another will shrug and walk away from it, and still another will sit with it for hours until he finishes? What makes one child independent and another a clinger? One ready to hit out at the slightest provocation and another loathe to fight? One answer, as we've seen, lies in the basic temperament children are born with. Another very important influence on behavioral styles is the early emotional environment, how they're treated by their parents.

Psychologist Diana Baumrind set out to discover relationships between different styles of child rearing and the social competence of children. She reviewed the research literature and conducted her own studies with ninety-five families of nursery school children. Using a combination of long interviews, standardized testing, and observations at school and

home, she identified three categories of parenting styles and linked them to children's behavior (Baumrind, 1967; 1970; Baumrind & Black, 1967).

Authoritative parents exert firm control when necessary, but they explain why they take their stands and encourage the children to express their opinions. They feel confident in their ability to guide their children, while respecting the children's interests, opinions, and unique personalities. They combine firm control with encouragement and love. Their children know they're expected to perform well, fulfill commitments, and carry out duties in the family. They know when they're meeting expectations and when it's worth risking parental displeasure to pursue some other goal. They seem to thrive on their parents' reasonable expectations and realistic standards, and are the most self-reliant, self-controlled, assertive, exploratory, and content.

Authoritarian parents value

unquestioning obedience and punish their children forcefully for not conforming to set and fairly absolute standards. They're fairly detached, controlling, and distant. Their children tend to be discontented, withdrawn, and distrustful.

Permissive parents make few demands on their children, set few rules, and hardly ever punish. As preschoolers, their children are immature, the least self-reliant, self-controlled, or exploratory.

Baumrind's work raises important issues about child-rearing practices, but before we conclude that parenting is all, we have to remember what children bring to the family. Through their own inborn temperaments, children influence their parents. It's possible, for example, that an easy child will elicit an authoritative attitude from his parents, while a difficult one may make tyrants out of his.

How can parents raise competent, socially responsible, independent children? Diana Baumrind (1970) suggests: teaching by example, that is, behaving the way you want your children to behave; rewarding the behaviors you want to encourage and punishing the ones you want to discourage and giving explanations in both cases; showing interest in children and bestowing your approval only when the child has earned it; demanding achievement and the meeting of standards, while being open to hearing the child's point of view; and encouraging original thinking. (© Michal Heron 1981/Woodfin Camp & Assoc.)

Even though relationships between siblings are the longest-lasting ones in most people's lives, psychologists have only recently begun to study this close bond to learn how siblings affect each other over the life span. (Jean-Claude Lejeune/ Stock, Boston)

different children, in the way siblings affect each other throughout life rather than just in childhood, and in process rather than effect (Lamb, 1982).

Most people grow up with at least one sibling, and the influence of one on the other begins even before the birth of the second child, as the anticipated birth affects both the parents and the first-born. The potential for rivalry is present in the coming "dethroning" of the first child, which was first pointed out by Alfred Adler (1928), a disciple of Freud's. Adler didn't invent the notion of sibling rivalry, which has been around since the days of Cain and Abel, but he emphasized the importance of its feelings of competition, jealousy, and hostility on personality development.

While some rivalry exists in all sibling relationships, it needn't be the dominant theme. Often the positive aspects of the sibling tie are uppermost—the ability siblings have to learn from each other and enjoy each other's company; the mutual support they give each other against pressures from outsiders and even parents; and the security formed by familiarity and shared experiences. Preadolescent siblings often become each other's primary confidantes and sources of emotional support (Lamb, 1982), and most siblings tend to stay close throughout adulthood, often becoming closer in old age (Cicirelli, 1982).

LEARNING TO GET ALONG WITH PEERS

Right from infancy, we human beings are social creatures who are intensely interested in other people, and especially other people about our own size. Even very young babies are fascinated by each other. From the age of 6 months, babies will smile, touch, and babble to another baby, and will tend to cry if another baby near them has been crying for a long time (Vandell, Wilson, & Buchanan, 1980; Hay, Pederson, & Nash, 1982). These responses become increasingly common toward the end of the first year and are more likely to occur when the babies are not distracted by the presence of either adults or toys.

Toddlers become even more social, and their sociability has more purpose. A 10-month-old may hold out a toy to another baby—but is just as likely to offer it when the other baby's back is turned as not. During the second year of life, children's social skills sharpen and they learn when such offers have the best chance of being accepted and how to respond to other children's overtures (Eckerman & Stein, 1982).

While even toddlers, then, are active in socializing with other children, real friendships usually don't emerge until sometime after 3 years of age. Even at this point, friendships are at a relatively primitive level compared to the form they'll take in later years. The distinctive ways children of different ages think about friendship emerge dramatically from a recent study about the ways people's ideas about this important relationship develop over the life span. Robert and Anne Selman (1979) interviewed more than 250 people between the ages of 3 and 45 to get a developmental perspective on friendship.

Up until about 9 years of age, children tend to define friendship in terms of themselves. The egocentric preschooler thinks about her own convenience ("She's my friend—she lives on my street"). Slightly older children consider a good friend as someone who does what *they* want him to do ("He's not my friend anymore because he wouldn't go with me when I wanted him to"). Not until the age of 9 or so, when children are well into the cognitive stage of concrete operations with the flexibility of thought such development allows, do friendships become more mutual. Still, children of this age may become possessive of each other and jealous of their friends' other friends. With the coming of adolescence, people respect their friends' needs for both mutual dependency and autonomy. Friends are especially important during these years of transition from childhood to adulthood, as teens break their early dependency on their parents, try out different roles in the process of achieving identity, and experiment with different ways of being (Selman & Selman, 1979; Coleman, 1980).

Even infants show special interest in other babies, and real friendships begin to emerge sometime after the age of 3, becoming more and more important in children's lives. Up till about 9 years of age, children tend to define friendship in terms of their own needs, and then, with their ability to put themselves in another's place, they develop more of a sense of mutuality. (Ira Berger 1981/Woodfin Camp & Assoc.)

MALE AND FEMALE:
SEX DIFFERENCES
AND SEX ROLES

If you were to spend a day visiting a typical nursery school, you'd see little girls and boys immersed in dozens of different activities. Somewhere you'd see the "housekeeping" corner, and the chances are better than even that little girls would be in that corner, playing with dolls, "cooking," cleaning up. Somewhere you'd see a couple of children fighting, and the chances are better than even that the fight would be between little boys. In our society, as in most societies around the world, girls and women are more nurturant, spending more time taking care of other people, and boys and men are more aggressive, putting more energy into physical encounters.

What accounts for these differences? How many other consistent differences are there between the sexes? And what are the implications of such differences for the healthy development of boys and girls?

How Different ARE
Males and Females?

PHYSICAL DIFFERENCES   Aside from their distinctive anatomies, other biological differences between the sexes begin to appear at the moment of conception. Males and females are born with different chromosomal patterns (XX sex chromosomes for females and XY for males), a difference that seems to give the female an immediate and lifelong advantage.

Males are more vulnerable in many ways from conception on. Although 120 to 170 males are conceived for every 100 females, only 106 males are actually born for every 100 females. Boys have a higher likelihood of being spontaneously aborted, born dead, or of dying in the first year of life (Rugh & Shettles, 1971; U.S. Department of Health and Human Services, 1983), and "until adulthood it is difficult to find a pathological condition in which the incidence among females is higher than among males" (Shepherd-Look, 1982, p. 408). At all ages, males die at higher rates than females (Lewis & Lewis, 1977).

Why are males more vulnerable? Explanations include the possibility of protective genes on the X chromosome, harmful genes on the Y, and a more efficient mechanism in females for forming antibodies to fight against infection (Purtilo & Sullivan, 1979). Whatever the basic cause of male vulnerability, poverty makes it worse, showing how biology and environment interact (Birns, 1976).

PSYCHOLOGICAL DIFFERENCES   In a major analysis of more than 2000 studies on this issue, Eleanor Maccoby and Carol Jacklin (1974) found only a few clear-cut dissimilarities between boys and girls. Only two cognitive differences showed up consistently, both of which usually develop in middle childhood. A very small difference appears after about the age of 10 or 11, when girls do better at a wide range of tasks involving word skills and boys do better at mathematics and spatial relations (the ability, for example, to visualize what an object would look like if it were seen from a different angle). From early childhood through adulthood, boys and men are more physically aggressive. More recent research indicates that girls and women show more empathy (Hoffman, 1977). The striking conclusion overall is that boys and girls are much more alike than they are different from each other.

What Makes the Sexes
Different from Each
Other?

HORMONES AND THEIR EFFECTS   One basic difference between the sexes is a different hormonal balance. All embryos begin life with female body structures, and not until about the sixth week, when androgens (male sex hormones, including testosterone) flood the bodies of those babies destined to be male do masculine body structures begin to form (Money & Ehrhardt, 1972; Hoyenga & Hoyenga, 1979). These hormones are responsible for the development of male internal and external sex organs. The basic structure is female. If nothing is added, the animal will develop as a female.

In recent years a number of researchers have explored the effects of the sex hormones on the development of brain structures. Evidence from research with animals indicates that hormones circulating before or at about the time of birth can cause sex differences in behavior, and even though it is often risky to make assumptions about human beings based on findings about rats, guinea pigs, dogs, sheep, or even our closer relatives, monkeys, some scientists believe there may be similarities (Hines, 1982).

Although different species of animals develop differently, in general, low levels of sex hormones before or at about the time of birth result in an animal's showing female characteristics, while higher levels result in typically male behaviors. Researchers have come to these conclusions after conducting many animal experiments in which they have manipulated hormone levels. Since for both ethical and practical reasons, this cannot be done with human beings, most human research has relied on two types of subjects—people who had unusual prenatal exposure to hormones and people born with certain disorders such as abnormal production of or sensitivity to sex hormones.

Some researchers have sought to explain behavioral differences along hormonal lines (Ehrhardt & Money, 1967). Nine girls whose mothers had received synthetic progestins during pregnancy were born with abnormal external sexual organs. After surgery, the girls looked normal and were capable of normal female reproduction. Though raised as girls from birth, they were called "tomboys," liked to play with trucks and guns, and competed with boys in active sports. There may be something in fetal masculinization that affects that part of the central nervous system that controls energy-expending behavior. However, these parents may have been influenced by their daughters' genital masculinity at birth, or the girls' own awareness of their endocrine problems may have led to their tomboyish behavior. Furthermore, tomboyishness is common, and since there was no control group, we don't even know how different from the norm these girls were, if at all.

"MALE" AND "FEMALE" BRAINS   Another line of research seeks to explain the cause of cognitive differences by pointing to different brain structures between males and females, which, in turn, may be caused by the effects of sex hormones. This line of reasoning points to studies that seem to show that men's brains are more specialized in terms of what the two hemispheres do, while women's are more flexible; that men are more right-brained, while women are more left-brained.

When two neurologists compared nineteen men in their twenties who suffered from *idiopathic hypogonatropic hypogonadism* (a disorder that causes low production of male hormones at puberty) with normal men, they found that those with low hormone levels did much worse on such spatial relations tasks as identifying geometric forms camouflaged by distracting lines and building geometric designs with blocks (Hier & Crowley, 1982).

They concluded, therefore, that androgens seem responsible for the development of spatial abilities.

While this line of research may eventually lead to clear-cut conclusions, we are not yet at that point. For one thing, sample sizes in these studies are often quite small, as in the ones previously mentioned, both of which have received a great deal of popular and scientific attention. For another, sex differences in right- and left-brain functioning are so small that only sophisticated statistical analysis can detect them. The variations among people of the same sex are always larger than the average differences between men and women, and they don't come near to explaining the great differences in behavior.

Furthermore, sex differences in spatial-relations tasks don't show up in all cultures. They seem to be especially large in cultures that expect them, like our own. People try harder when they expect to succeed: If women don't expect to do well on spatial tasks, they'll be more anxious, will expect to fail, and are apt to give up more easily; if men who see themselves as not fully masculine feel that spatial relations is a task for "real men," they'll react the same way (Kagan, 1982).

ENVIRONMENTAL INFLUENCES In some cases, small differences that exist between the sexes are encouraged and accentuated by societal forces. In other cases, the culture actually creates differences, apparently as part of a universal phenomenon that decrees that in every society some roles shall be appropriate for females and some for males. The flexibility of this rule is underscored by the fact that roles differ from culture to culture. How, though, are these beliefs handed down in any particular culture?

What Parents Do Even in these "liberated" times, parents treat their sons and daughters differently from infancy, often without realizing it. In one study, women who had small children of both sexes and who said they didn't see any differences between boys and girls in infancy were given the chance to play with a 6-month-old baby, variously labeled as a boy or a girl. When these women thought the baby was a girl, they were more likely to offer "her" a doll; when they thought it was a boy, they were more likely to offer a train (Will, Self, & Datan, 1976).

Furthermore, parents seem to be more actively involved with their male infants (Moss, 1967; Shepherd-Look, 1982) and to treat them more roughly (Yarrow, Rubenstein, & Pederson, 1971). Middle-class and better-educated mothers talk to their daughters more than to their sons (Maccoby & Jacklin, 1974).

In many ways, however, parents treat their sons and daughters about the same. They have similar expectations of their children in dressing and bathing themselves, similar limits on how far from home they may go, and similar limits on aggression; and mothers, at least, hold out similar expectations for competence. From their children's infancy on, fathers consistently show more sex-typing behavior. They tend to pay more attention to sons, emphasize competency for them but relationship issues for daughters, and tend to encourage dependency in their daughters while stressing achievement, career, and occupational success for their sons (Shepherd-Look, 1982).

Messages in the Media By the time the typical child has graduated from high school, she or he has watched more than 15,000 hours of television, including 360,000 commercials (Action for Children's Television, 1978). What messages are conveyed in this megaviewing?

Children will have seen about twice as many males as females on the little screen, and they will have observed that the sexes act quite differently—more differently, in fact, than real-life people. Males on TV are more apt to be aggressive and to build or plan something, while females are more submissive and inactive. Males are more likely to be rewarded for behavior in general and to escape punishment for acting aggressively, while females are more likely to receive no consequence for their actions, except when they give up the sedate female role and move quickly and actively, at which point they're punished in some way. In commercials, women are menial laborers within the house, waiting on their husbands and children, expecting nothing in return. Even in their housekeeping abilities they defer to male experts, and their only other major interest in life, aside from home and family, seems to be making themselves more beautiful (Sternglanz & Serbin, 1974; Mamay & Simpson, 1981). No wonder children who are heavy televiewers develop more traditional sex-role attitudes than those who watch little TV (Frueh & McGhee, 1975)! Similar content-analysis studies have found highly sex-stereotyped behaviors and attitudes in children's books (Weitzman, Eifler, Hokada, & Ross, 1972; Weitzman & Rizzo, 1974).

Cultural Attitudes In the 1930s anthropologist Margaret Mead (1935) dramatically demonstrated the influence of culture on male and female behaviors when she reported on three New Guinea tribes whose behavioral patterns didn't conform to typical stereotypes. Among the Arapesh, *both* men and women are "placid and contented, unaggressive and non-initiatory, non-competitive and responsive, warm, docile, and trusting" (p. 56) and nurturant toward children. Among the cannibalistic Mundugumor, "*both* men and women are expected to be violent, competitive, aggressively sexed, jealous and ready to see and avenge insult, delighting in display, in action, in fighting" (p. 213). The occasional mild or nurturant man or woman is a social misfit. The Tchambuli tribe has different expectations for males and females, but they are directly opposite to those in most societies. The woman is dominant, impersonal, and hardworking, while the man is less responsible, more concerned about personal appearance, and more emotionally dependent.

In most cultures around the world, men are more aggressive, have more authority than women, and usually do the dangerous, physically strenuous jobs, while the women do routine work closer to home. These patterns undoubtedly developed because the average man is taller, heavier, and more muscular than the average women, and the woman is the one who bears and nurses babies. Today, however, when most work can be performed as well by a 90-pound woman as a 200-pound man and when women are bearing fewer children and breastfeeding them more briefly, cultural attitudes about sex roles are changing—too slowly for some, too quickly for others.

Theories of Sex-Role Development

We've already looked at both biological and environmental explanations for differences between the sexes. In order to explain how these factors interact to produce people who think of themselves as male or female and who act accordingly, three major theories have evolved. According to psychoanalytic thinking, sex typing is the indirect result of anatomy and of the child's identification with the parent of the same sex, in many ways an outgrowth of the Oedipus and Electra complexes. The two other theories most often invoked today are *social learning theory* and *cognitive developmental theory*.

SOCIAL LEARNING THEORY Social learning theorists (whose point of view was introduced in Chapter 5) have proposed that children learn to act like boys or girls by imitating the parent of the same sex (especially when that parent is seen as nurturant, competent, and powerful) and that they're then rewarded for behavior their parents and other adults think is appropriate and punished for what's deemed inappropriate.

While this theory seems to make sense, it's been hard to prove. First of all, while children do imitate adults, research findings imply that they don't necessarily imitate the parent of the same sex nor even necessarily a parent at all. When children are tested on masculinity or femininity, they're no more like their own parents than like a random group of children's parents, and those who do test similarly to their own parents score no closer to the same-sex parent than to the one of the other sex (Hetherington, 1965; Mussen & Rutherford, 1963).

Furthermore, Maccoby and Jacklin (1974) cast doubt on the reinforcement aspect of this theory by their findings that parents do not treat their children very differently according to sex. In a critique of this conclusion, Block (1978) felt that the particular studies Maccoby and Jacklin reviewed might not have identified any differential treatment that existed because the great majority of them concentrated on the way mothers (not fathers) treated their children and because most dealt with children aged 5 and younger. Since fathers sex-type more than mothers and since sex differentiation increases with age, any analysis that does not take these factors into account is apt to be skewed. Another possibility is that the transmission of sex-role standards by parents may be so subtle that it can't be picked up by research instruments.

COGNITIVE-DEVELOPMENTAL THEORY According to this theory, proposed by Lawrence Kohlberg (1966), sex typing comes about as a natural corollary of cognitive development. Children don't depend on other people's serving as models to imitate or as dispensers of rewards and punishments as social learning theory proposes, but instead they actively categorize themselves as "male" or "female" and then organize their lives around their own category.

By the age of 2 or 3, a boy knows that he is a boy, decides he wants to do the things boys are supposed to do, does them, and is then rewarded by feeling secure in his gender identity. Sometime between the ages of 5 and 7, children achieve what Kohlberg calls "gender conservation," when they realize that they'll always be male or female. (At earlier ages, this awareness is not always present, as was clear in 3-year-old Eric's comment to his mother, "When I grow up I want to be a mommy just like you so I can play tennis and drive a car.")

Sex-role concepts, then, change as cognitive development advances. In fact, the brighter children are, the more quickly they adapt to the sex-role stereotypes of their cultures since they notice the physical differences between the sexes, learn the societal prescriptions for each sex's role, and try to live up to these roles themselves (Greenberg & Peck, 1974).

How Ideas about Sex Differences Affect Our Lives

Despite the demonstrated similarities between boys and girls, myths persist about important differences between them. These myths take shape as sex-role stereotypes, beliefs that males and females have—and should have—certain distinctive characteristics. Our culture, like other societies around the globe, defines some behaviors, emotions, and attitudes as acceptable for males, others for females. Boys are expected to be dominant, aggressive, active, independent, and competitive, while girls are expected to be nurturant, compliant, and dependent.

Very early in their lives children absorb these stereotypes. Even between the ages of 3 and 6 children see their adult lives quite differently depending on whether they are girls or boys, with the boys looking forward to a wide range of active, exciting, non-family-oriented careers and the girls seeing themselves mainly as mothers, nurses, or teachers (Papalia & Tennent, 1975).

The wholesale acceptance of sex-typed societal restrictions has many far-reaching implications. Individuals often deny their natural inclinations and abilities because they're "unmasculine" or "unfeminine," often forcing themselves into ill-fitting academic, vocational, and social molds. Sometimes not until adulthood do these stereotypes exert their fullest influence.

Convinced that sex-role stereotyping constricts both men and women, preventing either sex from achieving its potential, Sandra L. Bem (1974; 1976) developed a new concept of psychological well-being, which maintains that the healthiest individual is one whose personality includes a balanced combination of the most positive characteristics normally thought of as being appropriate for one sex or the other. In other words, such a person, whom Bem calls androgynous, might well be assertive, dominant, and self-reliant ("masculine" traits), as well as compassionate, sympathetic, and understanding ("feminine" traits).

Bem (1976) found that sex stereotyping restricts people in even the simplest, most everyday behaviors. Masculine men won't choose to prepare a baby bottle or wind yarn, and feminine women won't choose to nail boards together or attach artificial bait to a fishing hook, even if they could earn more money by doing these "cross-sex" activities than by doing sex-typed tasks. The major effect of femininity in women is not the inhibition of traditionally masculine behaviors but often the inhibition of any behavior at all in a situation where the woman isn't sure about the right thing to do. On the contrary, androgynous men and women show the most freedom to judge a particular situation on its own merits and to take action based on what seems most effective rather than what's most appropriate for their gender.

Many contemporary psychologists subscribe to Bem's (1976) goal of "freeing the human personality from the restricting prison of sex-role stereotyping" (p. 59) in the interest of healthy development throughout childhood and into adolescence and adulthood. In this very brief overview of childhood, we've seen how much progress children make in the three realms we've been discussing—the physical, the cognitive, and the psychosocial. We've also seen how many different factors influence this development. Now let's follow them as they move into adolescence and then into adulthood, where they'll grapple with the issues of defining their individual identity and giving purpose to their lives.

SUMMARY

1 The concept of *childhood* as a distinct time of life, with special characteristics different from those of adulthood, is a relatively new one. Until the seventeenth century children were considered smaller, weaker, dumber versions of adults.

2 Developmental psychologists use a variety of ways to study development. The two main data collection techniques are *cross-sectional* and *longitudinal.* In the cross-sectional method, psychologists compare people of different ages at the same point in time to determine *age differences* in behaviors, abilities, and growth patterns. In the longitudinal method, psychologists trace the development of one or more individuals at more than one point in time, obtaining information about *age changes.* Each method has its strengths and its weaknesses.

3 Developmental psychologists are concerned with describing, explaining, predicting, and modifying developmental change. Theories proposed by *Sigmund Freud, Erik Erikson,* and *Jean Piaget* see *psychosexual, psychosocial,* and *cognitive* development, respectively, as occurring in a series of stages.

4 The *neonatal period* is the first two weeks of life for the normal full-term baby. It is a transition period from prenatal to postnatal life. Neonates are amazingly competent; they can use all their senses and exhibit a variety of specialized responses.

5 Both physical growth and motor development are strongly influenced by maturation. During the first three years the child grows more quickly than at any other time postnatally. The growth rate slows down after this until the child reaches the prepubertal growth spurt at around age 12. The *cephalocaudal principle* indicates that development proceeds in a head-to-toe direction with the upper-body parts developing before the bottom ones. The *proximodistal principle* holds that development proceeds from near to far, with the parts of the body near the center developing before the extremities.

6 *Reflexes* are involuntary reactions to stimulation. The infant in the first few months of life shows a variety of primitive reflexes that will drop out as neurological development progresses.

7 According to Jean Piaget, children actively construct their own cognitive worlds. Piaget sees *cognitive development* as occurring in an invariant sequence of four stages which are roughly related to age: *sensorimotor* (birth to 2 years); *preoperational* (2 to 7 years); *concrete operations* (7 to 11 years); and *formal operations* (12 years and older, or perhaps never for some individuals). These stages represent qualitatively different ways children adapt to and think about their worlds. During the sensorimotor stage the infant acquires the concept of *object permanence,* the realization that people and objects do not cease to exist when they are out of sight. During the preoperational stage children become more proficient at using *symbols.* Their thought shows a high degree of *egocentrism,* or inability to consider another's point of view. Children in the concrete operations stage begin to think logically but are unable to think abstractly. They understand cognitive concepts such as *number, classification,* and *conservation.* During formal operations people are able to think abstractly, test hypotheses, and deal with problems that are not physically present. All people may not attain formal operations.

8 Recent research indicates that infants *learn* from the first day. Infants also show rapid gains in *memory.* At about the second grade children spontaneously use *rehearsal* as a memory strategy; at about fifth grade they use *clustering* and *chunking.*

9 Erik Erikson proposed a theory of *psychosocial development* which consists of eight stages throughout life. Each stage depends upon the successful resolution of a crisis or issue; how an individual resolves each crisis affects his or her personality development. The four stages of childhood are *trust versus mistrust* (birth to 12–18 months); *autonomy versus shame and doubt* (18 months to 3 years); *initiative versus guilt* (3 to 6 years); and *industry versus inferiority* (6 to 12 years).

10 Recent research suggests that even infants experience a variety of *emotions and emotional expressions.* There are individual differences in *temperament,* or a characteristic style of responding, which are

present from birth. According to the findings of a major longitudinal study, most children can be classified into one of three types: *easy, difficult,* and *slow-to-warm-up.* A child's temperament can influence the way others react to him or her.

11 *Attachment* is an active, affectionate reciprocal relationship between two individuals. Infants form attachments not only to their mothers but also to their fathers and others in their world. Infants show a variety of attachment patterns including *securely attached, avoidant,* and *ambivalent.* These attachment patterns seem to influence later development.

12 *Stranger anxiety* is a normal wariness of strangers that occurs between eight and twelve months. Not all children show stranger anxiety.

13 *Identification* is the process whereby a child takes on the values and behaviors of another person or group. Psychoanalysts say this is the result of identification with the aggressor (same-sex parent), which is an outgrowth of the Oedipus-Electra complex. Social learning theorists see identification as the result of observing and imitating models.

14 Diana Baumrind has identified three child-rearing techniques, *authoritative, authoritarian,* and *permissive.* The techniques used influence the child's development.

15 Right from infancy human beings express an interest in *peers.* The peer group becomes more important as children enter middle childhood.

16 There are certain physical and psychological differences between the sexes. Males seem to be more vulnerable to physical problems. Females excel in verbal abilities and males in spatial and mathematical abilities. A variety of theories have been proposed to account for these differences. They include hormonal effects, differences between "male" and "female" brains, and environmental influences such as parental child-rearing patterns, messages in the media, and cultural attitudes.

17 The three major theories of sex-role development are the *psychoanalytic, social learning,* and *cognitive developmental.* Psychoanalytic theory sees sex typing as the result of the Oedipus-Electra complex resolution. Social learning theorists propose that children learn to act like boys and girls by observing and imitating models (most frequently the same-sex parent) and by being reinforced for appropriate behaviors. Cognitive-developmental theorists feel that sex typing is related to a child's intellectual understanding that she or he is of a particular sex and is therefore expected to act in certain ways.

18 *Sex-role stereotypes* are beliefs that males and females *should* have certain (distinct) characteristics. For example, boys *should* be dominant and aggressive while girls *should* be dependent and compliant. Sandra Bem maintains that the healthiest personality is the one that integrates positive characteristics which are normally thought to be appropriate for one sex or the other. Such an individual is called *androgynous.*

SUGGESTED READINGS

Bringuier, J. (1980). *Conversations with Jean Piaget.* Chicago: University of Chicago Press. Fourteen conversations with Piaget which give insight into the man as well as his theory of cognitive development.

Kaplan, A. G., & Sedney, M. A. (1980). *Psychology and sex roles: An androgynous perspective.* Boston: Little, Brown. A thorough discussion of the nature and measurement of androgeny is followed by material on the impact of sex-role socialization in childhood and adulthood.

Lamb, M. E. (Ed.). (1981). *The role of the father in child development* (2d ed.). New York: Wiley. The most thorough collection of information currently available on the impact of the father on the developing child, written by leading researchers on paternal influences.

Lamb, M. E., & Sutton-Smith, B. (Eds.). (1982). *Sibling relationships.* Hillsdale, N.J.: Lawrence Erlbaum Associates. A collection of articles by leading researchers that focuses on the relationship between siblings throughout the entire life span.

Lewis, M., & Michalson, L. (1983). *Children's emotions and moods.* New York: Plenum. A discussion of the development of emotions and the complex issue of their measurement.

Papalia, D. E., & Olds, S. W. (1982). *A child's world: Infancy through adolescence* (3d ed.). New York: McGraw-Hill. A description of the development of two "typical" children, Vicky and Jason, through whom the authors describe normative physical, intellectual, personality, and social development during childhood and adolescence.

Parkes, C. M., and Stevenson-Hinde, J. (Eds.). (1982). *The place of attachment in human behavior.* New York: Basic Books. A collection of articles concerning the impact of attachment throughout the life span.

© Timothy Eagan 1981/Woodfin Camp & Assoc.

CHAPTER 13

FROM ADOLESCENCE ON

SPOTLIGHT ON

How the capacity for growth continues beyond age 12.

The importance of love and work in the years past childhood.

The search for identity that is prominent in adolescence and goes on throughout adulthood.

How the aging process affects us physically, intellectually, and emotionally.

How dying people and those close to them deal with death.

Adolescence is the point at which we teeter between the childhood we are leaving behind and the adulthood we are embarking upon. In broad terms, we tend to accept Sigmund Freud's definition of maturity: the capacity to love and to work. In many simpler cultures the adolescent is accepted as an adult, ready to assume full work responsibilities, ready to marry, ready to conceive and rear children. In more complex societies like our own, the adolescent is still, for the most part, considered a child.

Still, we now see glimmerings of the adult we will become as we develop new bodily proportions, and as we become more deeply invested in the concerns that will absorb us throughout the rest of life—getting a firm grasp on our sense of self, finding and concentrating on our life's work, and forming and handling the intimate relationships that have so much to do with our happiness and our well-being. The specific issues around these concerns vary over the life stages of adolescence, young adulthood, midlife, and old age, but there always *are* issues. We always have more questions than we have answers. And as we keep looking for answers, we keep developing.

ADOLESCENCE

With all its physical changes and its foreshadowing of adulthood, this stage marks the rebirth of the human being. The postpubertal adolescent looks almost as different from his or her childhood self as the butterfly emerging from its cocoon does from its former state as a caterpillar. There is nothing subtle or gradual about this transformation. After the bit-by-bit development of childhood, the changes of adolescence erupt like a sudden storm. A person's entire body form changes so that she or he now *looks* like an adult, even if emotions and intellectual ability are not at the same level of maturity. He sounds different; her life is affected by a new rhythm that will stay with her for the next several decades; they are both becoming absorbed with adult concerns.

The process begins with pubescence. In this stage of rapid growth the reproductive functions and sex organs mature, and the secondary sex characteristics (all other body changes not directly tied to reproduction such as breast development, body and facial hair, and voice changes)

Girls go through their adolescent growth spurt earlier than boys and reach puberty about two years ahead of them. During the years from 11 to 13, girls tend to be taller, heavier, and stronger than boys of the same age, a difference especially noticeable at early dances. (© Donald Dietz 1980/ Stock, Boston)

TABLE 13-1 Secondary Sex Characteristics

Girls	Boys
Breasts	Pubic hair
Pubic hair	Axillary hair
Axillary hair	Facial hair
Increased width and	Body hair
depth of pelvis	Voice change

appear (see Table 13-1). After about two years, this stage ends in puberty, when the individual is sexually mature and able to reproduce. While the average age of puberty is 12 for girls and 14 for boys, there is a tremendously wide normal age range. The end of adolescence is even harder to mark since it is defined by social, legal, and psychological measures such as being self-supporting, choosing a career, being eligible to vote or join the military, marrying—or, as one parent defines adulthood, "not calling home collect anymore."

Physiological Changes

Menarche, the first menstrual period, signals sexual maturity in girls, even though they are often not fertile for the first few cycles. Studies done over the past half-century reveal a variety of attitudes about menstruation. Although some girls express joy and excitement or accept the arrival of their menstrual periods matter-of-factly, many react with shame, embarrassment, and fear. Often this is because girls are poorly prepared or because adults overstress cleanliness and hygiene at the expense of the girls' psychological needs (Conklin, 1933; Shainess, 1961; Whisnant & Zegans, 1975; Rierdan & Koff, 1980).

The equivalent physiological marker for boys, the presence of sperm in the urine, found in about one in four 15-year-olds (Richardson & Short, 1979), is not readily observed and so has never achieved the same emotional or symbolic significance that menstruation does for girls. Both sexes appear to reach full adult height and sexual maturity earlier today than they did in previous centuries, probably because of improved nutrition, but this trend has leveled off in recent years (Wyshak & Frisch, 1982; Dreyer, 1982; Muuss, 1970; Schmeck, 1976). We see in this so-called secular trend the effects of the interrelationship between heredity (which has a large influence on the timing of maturation) and the environment.

Adolescents are acutely aware of their physical appearance. Boys want to be tall and broad-shouldered, while girls want to be slim though bosomy. The importance of good looks in adolescence looms large: Adults who considered themselves attractive as teenagers are more self-confident and happier than those who felt unattractive, and these differences don't disappear until the mid-forties (Berscheid, Walster, & Bohrnstedt, 1973).

Furthermore, both sexes want to be in step with their peers and are uncomfortable when they mature much earlier or later. Late maturing has especially pronounced effects for boys, as shown in classic studies (Mussen & Jones, 1957). Up until their early thirties, late-maturing boys continue to feel less self-assured, but then they turn out to be more flexible, assertive, and insightful (Jones, 1957). The effects of late or early maturation on girls is less clear, with research showing contradictory findings (Jones & Mussen, 1958).

Cognitive Development

A cognitive definition of maturity is the ability to think abstractly, an ability usually reached during adolescence—according to Piaget (1972), sometime between the ages of 11 and 20. Adolescents can now think in terms of what *might* be true, not just what they can see in a concrete situation. Since they can imagine an infinite variety of possibilities, they can think of hypothetical situations, they can consider all aspects of a situation, and they can approach an intellectual problem systematically.

We can see this development of thought by the different reactions to this story:

> Only brave pilots are allowed to fly over high mountains. A fighter pilot flying over the Alps collided with an aerial cable-way, and cut a main cable causing some cars to fall to the glacier below. Several people were killed (Peel, 1967).

A child still at the Piagetian level of concrete operations said, "I think that the pilot was not very good at flying. He would have been better off if he went on fighting." This child assumes only one possible reason for an event—in this case, the ineptness of the pilot. By contrast, a young person who had attained the level of thought Piaget called formal operations said, "He was either not informed of the mountain railway on his route or he way flying too low, also his flying compass may have been affected by something before or after take-off, this setting him off course causing collision with the cable" (Peel, 1967).

Formal operational thought, unlike the earlier Piagetian stages, does not always occur. It seems that a certain level of cultural support and education is essential for it to show up. In fact, many American adults—perhaps as many as half—never seem to reach it at all (Papalia, 1972; Clayton & Overton, 1973; Kohlberg & Gilligan, 1971).

Moral Development

According to the studies and theories of Jean Piaget (1932) and Lawrence Kohlberg (1964; 1968), the way children think about moral issues depends on their level of intellectual development as well as on their character and upbringing. Defining "moral development" as the development of an individual's sense of justice, Kohlberg has concentrated on how people think about morality rather than on what they actually do.

To test this thinking, he devised a set of moral dilemmas ("Should a man who cannot afford the medicine his dying wife needs steal it?" "Should a doctor 'mercy-kill' a fatally ill person suffering terrible pain?") and a system for scoring people's answers to these dilemmas. He then identified six stages in the development of moral judgment, as indicated in Table 13-2. While children begin to think about issues of right and wrong at a very early age, Kohlberg maintains that they cannot attain the highest stages of moral reasoning at least until adolescence and that some people never reach these levels.

Why does moral development depend on cognitive development? Largely because children cannot judge the morality of another person's actions until they can put themselves in the place of all the people who would be affected by those actions—the actor as well as all the people that his or her actions would affect. Until they have developed social

TABLE 13-2   Kohlberg's Six Stages of Moral Reasoning

LEVEL 1: PREMORAL (AGES 4 TO 10 YEARS)
Emphasis in this level is on external control. The standards are those of others, and they
are observed either to avoid punishment or to reap rewards.
  Type 1 Punishment and obedience orientation. "What will happen to me?" Children
    obey the rules of others to avoid punishment.
  Type 2 Instrumental purpose and exchange. "You scratch my back, I'll scratch yours."
    They conform to rules out of self-interest and consideration for what others can
    do for them in return.
LEVEL II: MORALITY OF CONVENTIONAL ROLE CONFORMITY (AGES 10 TO 13)
Children now want to please other people. They still observe the standards of others, but
  they have internalized these standards to some extent. Now they want to be considered
  "good" by those persons whose opinions count. They are now able to take the roles
  of authority figures well enough to decide whether some action is "good" by their
  standards.
  Type 3 Maintaining mutual relations, approval of others, the golden rule. "Am I a good
    girl [boy]?" Children want to please and help others, can judge the intentions of
    others, and develop their own ideas of what a good person is.
  Type 4 Social system and conscience. "What if everybody did it?" People are con-
    cerned with doing their duty, showing respect for higher authority, and main-
    taining the social order.
LEVEL III: MORALITY OF SELF-ACCEPTED MORAL PRINCIPLES (AGE 13, OR NOT
UNTIL YOUNG ADULTHOOD, OR NEVER)
This level marks the attainment of true morality. For the first time, the individual acknowl-
  edges the possibility of conflict between two socially accepted standards, and tries to
  decide between them. The control of conduct is now internal, both in the standards
  observed and in the reasoning about right and wrong. Types 5 and 6 may be alternate
  methods of the highest level of reasoning.
  Type 5 Morality of contract, of individual rights, and of democratically accepted law.
    People think in rational terms, valuing the will of the majority and the welfare of
    society. They generally see these values best supported by adherence to the
    law. While they recognize that there are times when there is a conflict between
    human need and the law, they believe that it is better for society in the long run
    if they obey the law.
  Type 6 Morality of universal ethical principles. People do what they as individuals think
    right, regardless of legal restrictions or the opinions of others. They act in ac-
    cordance with internalized standards, knowing that they would condemn them-
    selves if they did not.

Source: Adapted from Kohlberg (1976, in Lickona, 1976).

role-taking skills, they cannot weigh the effects of their own behavior, let
alone anyone else's.

Carol Gilligan (1982; 1977) has turned her attention to moral development in women, which seems to rest on an exquisite extension of role-
taking ability. Kohlberg's definition of morality as justice rather than compassion and his male-based research have led to women's generally scoring lower than men on tests of moral judgment, which are usually based
on Kohlberg's theory. Gilligan maintains that women define morality by
the ability to take another person's point of view and by a willingness to
sacrifice oneself to ensure the well-being of another. Her research shows
that women see morality not in terms of abstractions like justice and fairness but as a responsibility to look out for a specific other person or
persons. Her sequence of development can be seen in Table 13-3.

Gilligan contrasts Kohlberg's morality of rights with her own morality
of responsibility by recalling two stories from the Bible. The abstract mo-

TABLE 13-3 Gilligan's Levels of Moral Development in Women

LEVEL 1: ORIENTATION OF INDIVIDUAL SURVIVAL
First, a woman concentrates on what is practical and best for her. Then she makes the transition from selfishness to responsibility as she thinks about what would be best for other people.

LEVEL 2: GOODNESS AS SELF-SACRIFICE
This stage begins with her thinking that she has to sacrifice her own wishes to what other people want, being worried about what they will think of her, and feeling responsible for what they do. She tries to manipulate other people, sometimes through guilt. She then makes the transition from "goodness" to "truth," taking into account her own needs, *along with* those of others. Her own survival returns as a major concern.

LEVEL 3: THE MORALITY OF NONVIOLENCE
Finally, she has elevated the injunction against hurting anyone to include herself, thus establishing a "moral equality" between herself and others.

Source: Gilligan, 1982.

rality exemplified by Kohlberg's stage 6 led Abraham to be ready to sacrifice the life of his son when God demanded it as a proof of faith. Gilligan's person-centered morality can be seen in the story of the woman who proved to King Solomon that she was a baby's real mother when she agreed to give up the infant to another woman rather than see it harmed. To attain the highest levels of morality, Gilligan argues that justice and compassion must exist side by side.

Personality and Social Development

THE SEARCH FOR IDENTITY   The most important task of adolescence is the search for identity, the quest to find out "who I really am." This quest is not, of course, fully resolved in adolescence but is a theme we return to for the rest of our lives. Erik Erikson described this search as his fifth crisis: Identity versus role confusion (1950; 1963; 1965; 1968).

The sudden changes in their bodies bewilder young people and make them question who they have been and who they are becoming. "Am I the same person I used to be?" they wonder. "What will I be like from now on?" As teenagers continue to question and puzzle over their greatest preoccupation, their life's work, they are in danger of becoming confused. This confusion can show itself by the individual's taking an excessively long time to settle on a career. (Erikson himself wandered around Europe for seven years after leaving school before he even considered the possibility of becoming a psychoanalyst.) Confusion may also show up in childish impulsivity, in hero worship, or in intolerance of others.

Falling in love is seen by Erikson as an attempt to define identity. By becoming intimate with another and sharing thoughts and feelings, the adolescent offers up his or her own identity, sees it reflected in the loved one, and is better able to clarify the self.

Erikson's identity concept has received more research attention—and support—than any other aspects of his theory. Research with college students has found four different levels of identity related to intimacy, commitment, and sense of self (Marcia, 1967; Orlofsky, Marcia, & Lesser, 1973). Other research with undergraduates has confirmed Erikson's point that people who have resolved their own identity crises, especially with regard to their occupational goals, are better able to develop intimate relationships with other people (Kacerguis & Adams, 1980).

Identity versus role confusion
*Erikson placed this fifth crisis of
psychosocial development in
adolescence, when young people
eagerly embark on the search for
self. During these years, they
explore new interests, test
themselves in new competencies,
get in touch with the values they
believe in. (©Jim Anderson/
Woodfin Camp & Assoc.)*

THE ADOLESCENT REBELLION: FACT OR FANTASY?   The first psychologist to formulate a theory of adolescence, G. Stanley Hall (1916), contended that the physiological changes of adolescence necessarily would bring about psychological reactions and that the teenage years must be a time of storm and stress. The anthropologist Margaret Mead (1928) challenged this view after going to the South Seas and observing that teenage girls in Samoa were not stressed by the onset of adolescence but accepted it easily.

Mead's conclusions about the Samoans' smooth transition from childhood to adulthood have been questioned recently because of findings that delinquency shows up more often in adolescence than at any other time of life in Samoa, as well as in the United States, England, and Australia (Freeman, 1983). Still, a number of researchers have found that for most young people, adolescence is just one more of life's transitions, no stormier than any other (Bandura, 1964; Offer, 1969; Offer & Offer, 1974).

Most adolescents don't feel alienated from their parents. In fact, they are probably more inclined to accept their parents' values and opinions than those of their friends. Two separate studies, fifteen years apart, asked teenagers to choose solutions to various common problems, depending on whether they were suggested by parents or peers. Whether parent or peer carried more weight depended on the particular situation.

When deciding how to dress, how to resolve school-centered situations, and other day-to-day problems, the peers' opinions carried more influence. But when deciding about long-range issues like which job to take or how to resolve a deeper moral conflict, the girls in the first study leaned more toward their parents' opinions (Brittain, 1963). In the other study, which involved both sexes, the particular situation a student was considering also influenced whether he would pay more attention to parent or peer (Emmerick, 1978). When parents and peers hold similar values, as they often do, there is no real conflict between them.

Why does the myth of teenage turmoil persist? Partly because of our very belief in it, according to Albert Bandura (1964), who feels that a troubled adolescence is often a self-fulfilling prophecy: When society expects youth to be rebellious, they oblige. Also, researchers may pay more attention to certain troublesome segments of the adolescent population and surprisingly little to the bulk of normal teenagers (Adelson, 1979).

Erikson (1968) has offered another explanation for the tumult in some youths' coming of age. While young people who are gifted and well prepared for the future will eagerly embrace the responsibilities of adulthood, those who feel overwhelmed and ill-equipped to deal with new technology and new roles are, on the contrary, likely to "resist with the wild strength encountered in animals who are suddenly forced to defend their lives. For, indeed, in the social jungle of human existence there is no feeling of being alive without a sense of identity" (p. 130). This theory seems to shed some light on recent riots in English and American cities by young men who are so chronically out of work that they lose hope of being employable.

CAREER DEVELOPMENT   The role of work looms large in Erikson's concept of development in adolescence, even though he virtually ignores it in adulthood. At about age 17, teenagers are supposed to be entering a

Even though thinking about a future career looms large in the adolescent search for identity, many high school seniors don't know enough about occupations and the kinds of education and training they require to make good career choices. (Betsy Cole/The Picture Cube)

phase in which they realistically plan for their future careers (Ginzberg et al., 1951), but recent research indicates that many high school seniors are still not making realistic educational and career plans. More than 6000 high school seniors in Texas were found to have very limited knowledge about occupations and even less about the appropriate education for them. Moreover, relatively few seemed to be making good matches between career choice and their own interests (Grotevant & Durrett, 1980).

A greater proportion of teenage students are working today than at any other time over the past twenty-five years—about half of all high school juniors and seniors and some 30 percent of freshmen and sophomores (Cole, 1980). Some work because their families need the income, and others because they want the independence that comes from earning their own money.

Yet work doesn't seem to benefit teenagers' educational, social, or occupational development as much as you might think (Steinberg, 1982; Greenberger & Steinberg, 1985). Teenagers who work are no more independent in making financial or other decisions affecting their lives than their classmates who don't hold jobs (Greenberger et al., 1980). Most students who work part-time do not learn the kinds of skills that will be useful later in life (Hamilton & Crouter, 1980). And those who work during high school are not likely to earn any more money afterward than they would have had they not held jobs (Steinberg, 1982).

So work does not seem to aid development in adolescence. In fact, there seem to be a number of "hidden costs." Teenagers who work, especially those who put in more than fifteen or twenty hours per week, show declines in school grades, involvement, and attendance. Furthermore, there's a correlation between working and certain antisocial behaviors: Some teenage workers spend the money they earn on alcohol or drugs, develop cynical attitudes toward working, and cheat or steal from their employers by the time they've been on a job six or seven months. Working teenagers tend to spend less time with their families and feel less close to them. Furthermore, they have little contact with adults on the job, and they are usually exposed to sex-stereotyped occupational roles (Greenberger & Steinberg, 1985).

Some of these negative correlations may not be caused by working itself but by the factors that motivate some teenagers to take jobs. That is, they may already be uninterested in school, alienated from their families, and prone to drink or take drugs whenever they can afford to. In any case, working does not seem to help such young people manage their lives any better. Part of the reason is probably the fact that the kinds of jobs teens can get are usually of a menial, dead-end nature that are completely unrelated to their life goals. So while some adolescent workers do learn how to manage both money and time, how to find a job, and how to get along with a variety of people, work experience seems less important than a solid academic foundation.

ADOLESCENT SEXUALITY   Sexuality comes to the fore during adolescence, but it's still not most young people's primary interest, generally ranking lower among teenagers than future work, understanding other people, and even sports (Kermis, Monge, & Dusek, 1975). When sex *is* of prime interest, it's usually in the context of a relationship, apparently engaged in more because of the young person's search for identity through intimacy than for impulsive physical gratification. Aside from their interest in sex, adolescents also have other compelling concerns—friendships, school, sports, the struggle to be independent from their parents while still needing some guidance from them, and, of course, issues of identity and intimacy (Carrera, 1983).

How *do* modern teenagers feel and act with regard to sex? Since the pioneering work of Alfred C. Kinsey and his associates (Kinsey, Pomeroy, & Martin, 1948; Kinsey, Pomeroy, Martin, & Gebhard, 1953), some twenty-five major studies and many smaller studies of adolescent sexual behavior have, despite many methodological limitations, given us an overall picture.

Premarital Heterosexual Behavior   Things are very different now from what they were fifty years ago. Most young people approve of sex before marriage, especially within a loving and affectionate relationship. While the double standard that sanctioned more sexual activity for males than for females is not quite dead, it has almost disappeared in some segments of society (Dreyer, 1982). By 1979, 44 percent of high school girls, 56 percent of high school boys, and 74 percent of college students—both men and women—were no longer virgins (Dreyer, 1982). (These figures are for white students.) Furthermore, adolescents are sexually active at younger ages than they used to be, with 38 percent of boys and 24 percent of girls having had coitus by age 15 (Vener & Stewart, 1974).

What do these changes mean for today's adolescents? Older surveys often looked for special reasons to explain teenage sexual behavior, but contemporary observers seem to feel that "sexual activity is becoming part of the teenage experience and is being experienced by all types of young people, not just those who use sex as a way to express personal frustrations or to meet dependency and security needs" (Dreyer, 1982, p. 575).

In recent years there has been an enormous rise in teenage pregnancies, to more than 1 million a year. While most unmarried teenagers terminate their pregnancies by abortion, most who bear their children keep their babies rather than putting them up for adoption. Teenage parenthood has important implications for both the young mother and her baby. (Polly Brown/The Picture Cube)

The promiscuity that so many adults have feared is rare among adolescents, who, by and large, have strong moral feelings about sex, disapproving of exploitation and of casual sex outside a caring relationship (Zelnik, Kantner, & Ford, 1981). Yet most teenagers are still ambivalent and conflicted about sex, partly because they continue to get mixed messages from the society around them. Sexuality blares out from billboards, TV and movie screens, and newsstands. Their peers may be accepting and even encouraging of sexual activity, while their parents, teachers, and religious leaders discourage it. The more they venture out into the world beyond their own neighborhoods, the more conflicting value systems they are likely to encounter. As a result, they get very little consistent guidance (Dreyer, 1982). Furthermore, while they may be physically mature and able to reproduce, emotional development often lags behind, so that they are not ready or able to accept the mature responsibility that a sexual involvement demands.

Teenage Pregnancy This ambivalence can be seen in the enormous rise in teenage pregnancies in recent years—more than 1 million in 1979 (Alan Guttmacher Institute, 1981). Obviously, too many sexually active teens are not using effective birth control. Why not?

Even in today's generally accepting climate of premarital sex, the major cause of unwanted, unplanned pregnancies is still the refusal of many young people—especially young girls—to admit that they are sexually active (Oskamp & Mindick, 1981; Oskamp, Mindick, Berger, & Motta, 1978). They prefer to think of themselves as having been swept away in a moment of passion ("forgivable"), rather than having expected to engage in intercourse ("immoral"). They are not ready to think of themselves as sexually mature and responsible, and do not, therefore, plan ahead to prevent conception.

Other teens do not use birth control because they don't know about contraception, they don't know where to get it, they're afraid their parents will find out they're having sex, or they believe they cannot become pregnant (because they're too young, they're having intercourse for the first time, they're doing it standing up, or some other reason). When less experienced teens do try to prevent conception, they most often rely on male-controlled methods, the condom or withdrawal, rather than the more effective diaphragms, birth control pills, or intrauterine devices (IUDs), which are used more often by older, more sexually experienced girls (Dreyer, 1982; Alan Guttmacher Institute, 1981; Zelnik, Kantner, & Ford, 1981).

Most unmarried teenagers terminate their pregnancies by abortion, accounting for one-third of all abortions performed in this country, but many others keep their babies (Alan Guttmacher Institute, 1981; Chilman, 1982). With changing attitudes toward sexuality, the baby born out of wedlock presents less of a disgrace to the family. As a result, hardly any babies are given up for adoption; girls who choose to bear their babies usually keep them.

What, then, are the consequences of early childbearing and child rearing for both mother and child in these "two-child families"? Although problems exist, Chilman's 1982 review of the literature suggests that they're not so grave as had been believed, that, "in general, the direct social and psychological effects of early childbearing, per se, appear to be fairly minimal for young people in many aspects of their later lives" (p. 425).

Pregnant girls are more likely to drop out of school (but, then, some girls may become pregnant precisely because they're having school problems) and are more likely to get married early and to have larger families and to receive welfare assistance while their children are young. About half or more go back to school later on, earn about the same as comparable women who were not young mothers, and are generally as competent and caring as older mothers are. The babies' fathers seem to do just as well at work as comparable men who didn't father babies so young.

It's possible that earlier reports of negative health consequences for young mothers and their babies were due more to the girls' poverty and inability to get good medical care, both before and after the birth, than to their age. What about the psychological effects on the children, though? The children of teenage mothers, especially the sons, do seem to have more health, school, and behavior problems, an effect that may be due to the presence of only one parent in the home and to economic and social problems of the family.

The problems of adolescent parenthood are imbedded in the problems of society in general. "Teenage parenting is not a problem separate from other basic dysfunctions of contemporary society," writes Chilman (p. 429). On the contrary, it will respond to public policies that encourage full employment, adequate income, good family planning and other health services, all resting on a solid basis of racial equality.

EARLY AND MIDDLE ADULTHOOD

Hindu texts written in the second century described life as "a series of passages, in which former pleasures are outgrown and replaced by higher and more appropriate purposes" (Sheehy, 1976, p. 355). From that point, however, until the twentieth century, the concept of development throughout adult life was, for the most part, ignored by scientists even as artists recognized the ways in which adults keep developing. William Shakespeare, for example, immortalized the "seven ages of man" in *As You Like It.*

Now, developmental psychologists are looking closely at how we develop as grownups, dividing adult life into several stages. With fewer specific physical criteria to signal change from one period to another and with a bewildering array of social markers, the beginnings and endings from one stage to another are even more arbitrary than are the age divisions of childhood. For purposes of our discussion, we'll divide adulthood into three parts: young adulthood (20 to 40–45 years); middle adulthood (40–45 to about 65); and old age (from 65 or 70 on).

What does knowing a person's age really tell us in adulthood? Not very much since individual lives diverge so drastically, with all of us doing different things at different times. While biology shapes much of what we do in childhood, culture and individual personality play a much larger role in adult life. The older we get, the less our age tells about us. For example, two 40-year-old women may resemble each other physiologically, but the one who had three children in her twenties, stayed home with them, and is just starting to carve out a vocation has a very different outlook on life from that of her childless age-mate with a well-established career.

Traditionally, most adults have had strong feelings about the time in life when certain activities are considered acceptable (Neugarten, Moore, & Lowe, 1965). People are keenly aware of their own timing and describe themselves as "early," "late," or "on time" regarding the time they married, settled on a career, had children, or retired. This sense of timing seems to be shaped by environmental expectations, often affected by social class. The entire life cycle is speeded up for working-class people, who tend to finish school earlier than middle-class people, to take their first jobs sooner, to marry younger, have children earlier, and become grandparents earlier (Neugarten, 1968).

In recent years, however, as affluence has filtered down, as medical advances have kept people vigorous, and as the life span has lengthened, age-based expectations have become more flexible. We're more accepting of 40-year-old first-time parents and 40-year-old grandparents, 50-year-old retirees and 75-year-old workers, 60-year-olds in blue jeans and 30-year-olds in college presidencies. As Bernice Neugarten and Gunhild Hagestad (1976) point out, "We seem to be moving in the direction of what might be called an age-irrelevant society; and it can be argued that age, like race or sex, is diminishing in importance as a regulator of behavior" (p. 52).

We're much more flexible when it comes to dealing with the basic developmental tasks of adulthood. While most of us choose a career in young adulthood, many of us change careers again in middle age and sometimes even again in old age. We may become independent of our parents in our twenties, our forties, or our sixties. We may form our first intimate love relationship in our teens—or not until midlife. We may conceive our first child at 20 or at 40. Yet some tasks seem more age-related than others. It isn't until middle age, for example, that most people acknowledge the limitations of their bodies or accept the certainty of

While the word "grandparent" evokes images of white hair and rocking chairs, many middle-aged grandparents are leading such busy, active lives that it's often hard for them to find time to babysit. Age-based expectations are more flexible today than they used to be; a 40-year-old man holding a baby can be either the father or the grandfather. (David S. Strickler/ The Picture Cube)

their eventual deaths. Some ill or handicapped people do so early in life, of course, while some never think about these issues, denying them altogether.

These are years of good health and energy, especially in our twenties and thirties, with very slight, gradual changes not becoming noticeable till about age 50. We're at the peak of our muscular strength and our manual dexterity at about 25 or 30 (Bromley, 1974; Troll, 1975). We see and hear most sharply in our early twenties, gradually becoming farsighted and less able to hear high tones. Taste, smell, and sensitivity to pain, touch, and temperature remain stable until at least 45 or 50. We're at the peak of our reproductive capacities.

Most of the health changes from young adulthood to middle age are relatively minor. The organ systems are not as efficient as they had been, tending to lose some of their reserve capacity. Men's sexual capacity declines, and high blood pressure becomes a problem. Metabolism changes, and both sexes tend to put on weight.

How do individuals cope with physical changes, and, therefore, with the awareness of their aging? Past health history, family attitudes, and individual personalities play a large part. So does sex. Women tend to be more health conscious, both for themselves and their families. This may have something to do with the fact that pregnancy and childbirth have involved them more closely with medical care, as well as with their traditional role as guardian of the family's health. While men often turn to diets and exercise, they tend to ignore symptoms (Lewis & Lewis, 1977).

MIDLIFE CHANGES: THE MENOPAUSE AND THE MALE CLIMACTERIC   The ratio of the physical and the psychological in these midlife events vary, with the former affecting women universally and the latter becoming an increasingly recognized syndrome among men.

The Menopause   This biological event in every woman's life when she stops menstruating and can no longer bear children, may come any time between 38 and 60 years of age, with the average between 48 and 52 (Upjohn, 1983). The time span of some two to five years during which her body undergoes the various physiological changes that bring on the menopause is known technically as the climacteric. The only symptoms that seem directly related to the reduction of the body's production of the female hormone estrogen are hot flushes (sudden sensations of heat that flash through the body); thinning of the vaginal lining (which can make sexual intercourse very painful); and urinary dysfunction (caused by tissue shrinkage) (Ballinger, 1981).

The administration of artificial estrogen can resolve these problems dramatically. Estrogen therapy alone has been related to higher risks of cancer of the lining of the uterus, but recent research suggests when artificial progesterone is given along with the estrogen, the risk of developing this kind of cancer drops *below* the rate among women who received no hormone at all (Bush et al., 1983; Hammond et al., 1979).

At one time a number of psychological problems, especially depression, were blamed on the menopause, but recent research shows no rea-

FEIFFER

son to attribute psychiatric illness to the physical changes in a woman's body. Such problems are more likely caused by environmental pressures against aging, which remind a woman that menopause marks the end of her youth. In those cultures that value the older woman, few problems are associated with the menopause (Ballinger, 1981). A society's attitude toward aging seems to influence a menopausal woman's well-being far more than the level of hormones in her body.

The Male Climacteric   Despite the fact that men can continue to father children till quite late in life, there *are* some biological changes in middle-aged men. These include decreased fertility and frequency of orgasm, and an increase in impotency (Beard, 1975). Furthermore, men seem to have cyclic fluctuations in the production of hormones (Kimmel, 1974).

About 5 percent of middle-aged men are said to experience symptoms such as depression, fatigue, sexual inadequacy, and vaguely defined physical complaints (Henker, 1981). Since researchers have found no relationships between hormone levels and mood changes (Doering, Kraemer, Brodie, & Hamburg, 1975), it's probable that most men's complaints are just as subject to environmental pressures as women's are. Some of the problems may be related to disturbing life events, such as illness of the man or his wife, business or job problems, his children's leaving home, or the death of his parents.

Both sexes suffer from our society's premium on youth, even though women are especially oppressed by our double standard of aging. The gray hairs, coarsened skin, and crow's feet wrinkles that are attractive proofs of experience and mastery in men are telltale signs that women are "over the hill." The feminine look is "smooth, rounded, hairless, unlined, soft, unmuscled—the look of the very young; characteristics of the weak, of the vulnerable" (Sontag, 1972, p. 9). Once these signs of youth have faded, so has a woman's value as a sexual and romantic partner. Some homosexual men may also suffer from the loss of their appeal as they age (Berger, 1982). And even heterosexual men, who historically have had the most leeway in growing old naturally, are often at a disadvantage in the job and promotion market as they reach middle age.

These false values, added to the real losses people are apt to suffer as they get older, create undue burdens, often leading to what has been called the "midlife crisis," which we'll talk about a little later in this chapter. Not until attaining maturity is seen as a positive phenomenon for both sexes rather than as a relegation to the social wasteheap will human beings in our society be able to make the most of most of their lives.

Intellectual Development in Adulthood

For many years it was believed that general intellectual activity peaked at about age 20 and then declined. The good news is that this isn't so. We have strong evidence showing that certain types of intelligence continue to develop throughout life.

This conclusion rests on several bases. One of the most important comes from the results of two different kinds of tests. In Chapter 8 we talked about two types of intelligence, *fluid* and *crystallized*. Verbal abilities, a type of crystallized intelligence, appear to increase throughout adulthood and old age. Performance in solving new problems such as spatial-relations tasks, an aspect of fluid intelligence, peaks in the late teens and then begins a slow, steady decline. Furthermore, the accumulated wisdom that comes with adulthood may offset any decline in fluid abilities (Dittmann-Kohli & Baltes, in press). Wisdom, which can be defined as the "ability to exercise good judgment about important but uncertain matters of life" (Dittmann-Kohli & Baltes, in press, p. 34), also affects our relationships with other people, as we'll see in the next section.

Personality and Social Development during Adulthood

HOW WE CHANGE AND HOW WE STAY THE SAME   Few of us hold the same outlook on life at 40 that we did at 20, showing the growth and development that take place during adulthood. This growth comes about from many sources—the people we meet, the reading we do, the experiences we undergo, the challenges we face up to. Recent longitudinal studies of adults have dramatically illustrated the kinds of developmental tasks we deal with over the years. These tasks, as we'll see, are remarkably similar for large groups of people, even though the details vary widely in terms of circumstances and specific actions.

Yet despite the changes that occur in our lives and our thinking, we *are* still the same people. And we do tend to carry certain basic traits with us in all the twists and turns of life's pathways. If we had sunny dispositions as junior high schoolers, we're likely to be cheerful 40-year-olds; if we were complaining adolescents, we're apt to be querulous adults; if we were assertive at 20, we're likely to be outspoken ten years later (Block, 1981; Haan & Day, 1974; Livson, 1976).

Does this mean that our personalities are set in stone early in life? That change and growth and development are not possible, after all? Not at all, because other aspects of personality do show evidence of considerable change. For example, we're apt to show great leaps in self-esteem and in a sense of control over our lives, as the result of our own accomplishments (Brim & Kagan, 1980). Furthermore, the wisdom we accumulate over the years enhances our growth and changes us.

The two threads of stability and change are intertwined throughout all our lives, with some of us showing more change and others more continuity. Zick Rubin (1981) underscores this duality by referring to Richard Alpert, the competitive, ambitious, power-oriented Harvard University psychology professor of the 1960s who in the 1970s became Baba Ram Dass, a long-bearded mystical guru who taught people how to live in the present. Has this man changed? Of course, he has. Is he still charming, oriented to psychic concerns, and hard-driving? Yes, even despite his transformation.

One personality change common in midlife is the tendency to express aspects of our personalities that we had repressed during our younger years (Cytrynbaum, Blum, Patrick, Stein, Wadner, & Wilk, 1980). Sometimes these newly flowering personality traits are ones that are usually thought of as more appropriate for the other sex.

With the recognition at this stage of life that some of our basic goals have already been achieved—the children reared, the career established, the identity in large measure achieved—both men and women feel freer to veer from the stereotypical male or female they had modeled themselves after years earlier. They allow themselves to express long-buried aspects of their personalities, as many women become more assertive, competitive, and independent and many men allow themselves to be passive and dependent. The significant aspect of such change is not its "contrasexual" nature but the fact that any trait that has been repressed for the first half of life may now flower, with the increased self-confidence and relaxation that often accompany middle age.

One other common personality change, which may help uncover such buried characteristics, is a tendency for people to become more introspective as they grow older. While younger people invest more of their energies in action rather than in thought, people at midlife and beyond tend to think about themselves more, analyzing what they have done in their lives and why they have done it (Cytrynbaum et al., 1980).

ERIKSONIAN CRISES DURING EARLY AND MIDDLE ADULTHOOD   Erikson (1963) maintains that the search for individual identity begun in adolescence continues as adults focus on different issues, depending on their life stage. In a recent interview he expanded his emphasis on the necessary balance between the two extremes of each crisis (Hall, 1983).

Crisis 6: Intimacy versus Isolation   The young adult is now ready to make a commitment to a close relationship with another person, risking temporary ego loss in situations requiring self-abandon (like coitus and orgasm, marriage, or a very close friendship). While a certain degree of isolation is crucial to maintain one's individuality, too much may prevent the ability to merge with another in an intimate bond and may lead to loneliness and self-absorption. Erikson's original view of this crisis was limited, as he defined a "utopia of genitality" to include mutual orgasm in a loving heterosexual, child-producing relationship, thus eliminating from the realm of healthy development homosexuals, single people, and nonparents. Also, he omitted any discussion of career development, a major issue in the identity formation of the young adult.

Recently Erikson expanded on the implications of the decision not to have children. While he recognizes the rationale behind such an option, he calls upon child-free people to recognize that they are defying an instinctual urge: They need to acknowledge the sense of frustration and loss

Intimacy versus isolation: Erikson maintains that people are not ready to commit themselves to a close relationship with another person until they have a strong sense of self. Only then can they risk the temporary ego loss necessary in the merger demanded by love. (© Jim Anderson 1982/Woodfin Camp & Assoc.)

that may accompany this decision and to channel their procreative tendencies in other directions (Hall, 1983).

Stage 7: Generativity versus Stagnation   At about age 40, individuals face their need for generativity, a concern in establishing and guiding the next generation, which can be expressed through having and nurturing one's own children, by teaching, by taking on younger protégés, or by other productive and creative work that will live on. While the major emphasis is still on wanting to have and guide one's own children, thus demonstrating some "belief in the species," Erikson stresses the potential for generativity in any kind of work, from plumbing to artistic creation, and in a concern for the future shown in political and volunteer activities (Hall, 1983). Some degree of stagnation can serve as a counterbalance to allow creativity to lie fallow for a while, but too much can result in self-indulgence or even physical or psychological invalidism. Here again, Erikson seems to overemphasize the universal value of parenthood and to give insufficient recognition to the need for self-nurturance that often emerges at this time of life, after people have been focusing on others, either through work or family.

WORK AND ADULT DEVELOPMENT   It's surprising that Erikson should have ignored the role of work in adulthood, after having stressed the importance of competency in childhood and the urgency of career preparation in the adolescent search for identity. He isn't alone, however. Only recently has work been getting the attention it deserves, in view of its central importance in the lives of most people. "What do you do?" is usually the first question strangers ask about us. What we do—for pay—usually takes up at least half of our waking hours. And what we do and how we do it often play a major role in our own self-esteem.

Generativity versus stagnation
During middle age many people take an interest in establishing and guiding the next generation, often by passing on the fruits of their own experience to a young protégé. (Hugh Rogers/Monkmeyer)

Perhaps the recent increase in interest in work (as shown by some of the longitudinal research on adulthood, whose findings will be discussed later) parallels changes that have taken place in American society. One demonstration of these changes is presented in a 1981 report that presents findings from two national studies, of more than 2000 adults each, one in 1957 and the other almost twenty years later in 1976 (Veroff, Douvan, & Kulka, 1981).

What has happened in the work world over this generation? Women have moved into it in ever-increasing numbers, so that by 1969 more mothers of school-age children were out working than were staying at home. Meanwhile, men seemed to show more concern about their family roles, more young people had entered the work force, workers were thinking more about both leisure and retirement, and those born into the

Women have moved into the work world in increasing numbers. Are middle-aged working women physically and mentally healthier than homemakers (as found in one study) because of the benefits of the higher prestige our society grants to job-holders—or because healthier women are more likely to seek and hold jobs? (Drawings by Shirvanian; © 1983 The New Yorker Magazine, Inc.)

"Honey, I'm home!"

"Honey, I'm home!"

"baby boom" generation (born in the late 1940s) were pursuing higher educational goals. Some of these broad changes undoubtedly affected differences in the attitudes people in the 1970s displayed toward their work, compared to those in the 1950s.

About 12 or 13 percent of both sexes at both times (1957 and 1976) mention their jobs as a source of happiness, but in 1976 more people see their jobs as a source of worry and more women see them as a source of unhappiness. The women's answers probably reflect the greater importance their jobs hold for them; no longer just a source of pocket money or even needed income, they are now an important potential source of identity validation, as well. When a job doesn't live up to this promise, disappointment is keener.

Surprisingly, these researchers found that Americans don't mention their work prominently when they define themselves. Furthermore, married workers who have children rate their occupations below their roles as spouse and parent, confirming Erikson's emphasis on the importance of generativity in our lives. The way people hold their jobs often depends on their principal values and their stage in life. For example, older men who greatly value self-actualization consider work more of a source of self-actualization than marriage but still rate work lower than parenthood. Women seem to value the noneconomic benefits of their jobs (contact with people and interest) more than men do and more often say they would continue to work even if they didn't need the money. This may reflect the contrast between the social isolation and low prestige of home-making, which many women and few men have experienced.

Overall, while Americans today seem to value family roles over work roles, work is still a strong area of concern, stronger than ever for some people, especially young single women. The most sweeping changes with regard to work over these past twenty or thirty years have affected women, a fact confirmed by other researchers. An intensive study of about three hundred 35- to 55-year-old Boston-area women found a strong relationship between paid work and a woman's sense of pride and power, especially for women in high-prestige occupations (Baruch, Barnett, & Rivers, 1983). Work has a major impact on a woman's feeling of well-being.

HOW PARENTHOOD AFFECTS DEVELOPMENT Parenthood can be a creative self-growth experience as parents go through its several stages: anticipating ahead of time what parenthood will be like, adjusting to new demands and learning how to meet them at every stage of their children's growth, and then disengaging from the active parental role as children mature (Group for the Advancement of Psychiatry, 1973). As children grow, parents get a second chance to relive their own childhood experiences and to work out issues they had not resolved with their own parents. In addition, they're influenced by their children, who bring their own unique personalities and demands to this intimate, intensely emotional relationship.

Most women greet pregnancy with mixed emotions. At the same time that they feel special, potent, and creative, they may also feel a loss of individual identity and worry about the future. No matter how much a woman may want a baby, it can be depressing to see her familiar body

In the past a woman's love life, her age, and whether she was or was not a mother were considered more central to her life than her work. Our study shows that these aren't very useful in predicting a woman's sense of pride and power—her Mastery, in our terms. But the relationship between paid work and Mastery, particularly among women in high-prestige occupations, shows just how vital a role work plays. (Baruch, Barnett, & Rivers, 1983, p. 103)

looking and feeling so different. Furthermore, contemplating the unknown often arouses anxiety, and no one can ever imagine ahead of time the changes a baby will bring to her life. All these feelings—the positive, the negative, the ambivalent—are normal.

While we know less about the father's reaction to the impending birth, he also experiences a jumble of conflicting emotions. He is apt to feel virile and powerful, excited at the prospect of carrying on his genetic lineage, while at the same time feeling inadequate about his ability to be a good father, worried about the new responsibility a baby will bring, and estranged by the physical and emotional changes in his wife.

Parenthood is more of a freely chosen option today than at any time in history. As this choice has become more available, so has acceptance of those people who choose not to have children. Still, most people in their thirties still have children, most parents find this a significant experience, and most find parenting a major source of satisfaction (Veroff, Douvan, & Kulka, 1981).

Parenting does, of course, affect different people in different ways. By and large, the sexes hold different viewpoints, with women tending to think that the nicest thing about having children is the love and warmth in the relationship and men focusing on their role in influencing and forming the character of a child. When asked to describe the changes children bring to a person's life, women reflect the difficulties in meeting society's expectations of a good mother by focusing on restrictions on their freedom.

Those queried in 1976 felt more inadequate about their parenting than did the parents of 1957 (reported by Veroff et al. in the 1981 report referred to earlier) possibly because today's parents feel much more responsibility for their children's successful growth and development—emotional and intellectual as well as physical. Modern parents often feel it's their duty to see that their children are happy and successful. Since these outcomes aren't guaranteed for anyone, parental frustration and self-blame often result. (Some of the stresses of parenting are discussed in Chapter 10.) As children grow older, parenting gets easier, and older parents who see that their children have turned out all right are less anxious and more relaxed with their offspring.

STAGES IN ADULT DEVELOPMENT Not until very recently have researchers looked closely at the ways we develop as adults. Over the past ten years several reports of intensive longitudinal studies have yielded profiles of normal development from adolescence through middle age. We can't draw definitive conclusions from them since most of these studies have been limited largely to white, middle-class men, some are based on very small samples, and none have gone beyond the decade of the fifties. Further research is needed to determine whether the approximate sequence, if not the ages, of these developmental stages are appropriate for women, nonwhites, and those in lower social and economic echelons. But even the preliminary findings that we have confirm the premise that personality continues to evolve throughout life, that the end of adolescence does not mean the end of growth, and that each age period is significant.

Roger Gould (1972; 1978) conducted the only major study of adult development that includes women. He examined the attitudes and life histories of psychiatric outpatients in seven age groups ranging from 16 to over 60, and of 524 nonpatients of comparable ages. Another study followed up 268 men from the time they were freshmen at Harvard University in 1938 until they were in their fifties (Vaillant & McArthur, 1972).

The other major study of adult development is the one conducted by Daniel Levinson and his colleagues, who interviewed in depth forty men aged 35 to 45 (ten each from four different vocations: biologists, business executives, novelists, and hourly workers in industry), asking them about work, religion, politics, education, leisure, and personal relationships. While the sample was small and only men were studied, this work was important because it gave rise to a comprehensive theory of adult development, which was apparently confirmed by the research (Levinson, Darrow, Klein, Levinson, & McKee, 1978).

Levinson ties the findings from this work to his overall concept that the goal of adult development is the creation of a life structure. Such a structure has internal aspects made up of dreams, values, and emotions, and external aspects such as participation in work, family, and religious life. The significant developmental nature of this structure is that people continually go through periods of stability after they have built a part of it and then of transition as they keep reevaluating it.

These three separate studies show us a typical scenario of development through the adult years:

* *The early adult transition (17 to 22 years):* People feel halfway out of the family and sense a great need to get all the way out. They have a tenuous sense of their own autonomy and feel that real adult life is just around the corner.
* *Entering the adult world (22 to 28 years):* People now feel like adults. They're established in a chosen lifestyle, independent of their parents, and pursuing immediate goals without questioning themselves about whether they're following the right course.
* *The age-30 transition (28 to 34 years):* People ask themselves, "What is this life all about now that I am doing what I am supposed to?" and "Is what I am the only way for me to be?" They often reassess both work and family patterns. At this time, for example, career women think about having a baby, and homemakers begin to work outside the home.
* *Settling down (33 to 43 years):* People make deeper commitments to work, family, and other important aspects of their lives, setting specific goals with set timetables. Toward the end of this period is the stage Levinson calls "becoming one's own man," when men break away from the authorities in their lives and work at attaining senior status in their own right.
* *Midlife transition (40 to 45 years):* People question virtually every aspect of their lives and values with an increasing awareness that time is limited. They may lose their mooring for a time as they bridge the transition to the second half of life. They come to terms with the fact that the first part of adult life is over and they will not be able to do all that they had planned before they grow old and die. The transition

may be smoothly managed or it may assume crisis proportions, depending on their personalities and the specific situations they find themselves in.

For those who build a satisfying life structure, "middle adulthood is often the fullest and most creative season in the life cycle. They are less tyrannized by the ambitions, passions and illusions of youth. They can be more deeply attached to others and yet more separate, more centered in the self" (Levinson, Darrow, Klein, Levinson, & McKee, 1978, p. 62).

While Levinson and his colleagues tentatively proposed three later-life stages—"the age-50 transition" (50 to 55 years), "building a second middle adult structure" (55 to 60 years), and a "late adult transition" (60 to 65 years)—the research to flesh out the tasks of these years has yet to be done. In view of the evidence so far, it seems likely that the sequence of stable and transitional periods does indeed continue throughout life and that we are constantly facing new challenges and growing from them.

LATE ADULTHOOD

There is, of course, no arbitrary dividing line when old age begins. A vigorous-looking woman of 55 complains, "I hope I never get as old as I feel," while a frail 84-year-old talks about putting aside money for his "twilight years." There are tremendous differences among people in their later years, with some remaining intellectually and physically hale well into their nineties and others looking, feeling, and acting old in their fifties. Bernice Neugarten (1975) refers to the "young-old" aged 55 to 75, who have retired from full-time work and are still vigorous and active, as compared to the "old-old" of 75 and over.

Senescence, the period of the life span when one grows old, begins at different ages for different people, so we don't always know much about someone just by knowing when she or he was born. Official definitions used to peg old age at 65, when people could be forced to retire from a job and were eligible for Social Security payments. In recognition of the fact that people are staying vigorous longer, however, even the legal definition of old age is changing, so that mandatory retirement cannot be implemented for most jobs before age 70, and the age for full Social Security eligibility will soon be raised to 67.

Such regulations have far-reaching implications for social policies, political trends, fiscal stability, and family patterns in our society as the elderly become a larger segment of our population. Today some 11 percent of the U.S. population is 65 or older; by the year 2030, this will almost double, to 21 percent (Bureau of the Census, 1983).

Physical and Health Status of the Elderly

Despite widespread belief, being old does not mean being sick and disabled. Most elderly people are reasonably healthy, with 90 percent of people over 65 describing their health as fair, good, or excellent. Older people in the work force average only four or five absences a year, a rate similar to that among younger workers. A majority of the elderly (54 percent) report no limitations on their activities for health reasons, while about 40 percent report that they have had to curtail a major activity (compared to about 20 percent of people aged 45 to 64). Those most likely to suffer from handicapping health conditions are the rural elderly and those over 85, while those most apt to be in good health are those with high incomes (Bureau of the Census, 1983).

Chronic conditions are the most prevalent health problem for people over 65, with more than 80 percent reporting one or more. The most common are arthritis, rheumatism, heart problems, hypertension, and impairment of the lower extremities, the hips, the back, or the spine. On the other hand, acute conditions like colds and flu are less common in old age. The elderly visit the doctor an average of six times a year, compared with five times for the population in general, and are hospitalized twice as often as younger people. Still, only about 5 percent of the elderly live in nursing homes (about 1.3 million people in 1982), with institutionalization more prevalent among the very old. About 75 percent of elderly people in the United States die from heart disease, cancer, and stroke, although there has been a decrease in heart disease since 1968, especially for women (Bureau of the Census, 1983).

During the middle of the last century, Americans could expect to live to an average age of 40 years, and by 1900 life expectancy had risen only to 49. But children who were born in 1982 can now expect to live for 78.7 years if they are white females, 71.4 years if they are white males, 75.2 years if they are nonwhite females, and 66.5 years if they are nonwhite males (National Center for Health Statistics, 1983)—record highs for all groups, due largely to lower mortality rates in infancy and childbirth. What are these added years like?

SENSORY ABILITIES IN OLD AGE With age the acuity of the senses declines, but here, too, there are great individual differences. People over 65 are apt to have problems seeing in the dark, which often prevents them from driving at night. Half of the legally blind people in the country are over 65, but, fortunately, with the development of improved glasses and contact lenses and of new surgical techniques for the removal of cataracts, many vision losses are at least partly correctable.

Hearing problems are more common than visual ones, with older people having special difficulty following a conversation when there is competing noise from a radio or TV set, outside noises, or other people talking at the same time. Here again, we see a close relationship between physical and emotional development when we become sensitive to the way hearing loss can contribute to an elderly person's loneliness and sense of isolation. Another link between physical limitations and personality problems has been underscored by experiments that found that college students suffering from hypnotically induced partial deafness began to feel paranoid (Zimbardo, Andersen, & Kabat, 1981). People who may not admit their hearing problems to themselves may, therefore, develop personality quirks and become difficult to be with if they get the idea that others are whispering about them or are deliberately excluding them from conversations.

The elderly often complain that their food doesn't taste so good any more. This seems to be caused by a loss of sensitivity in taste and smell. The vestibular senses, which help to maintain posture and balance, often deteriorate in old age, which causes dizziness and falls.

PSYCHOMOTOR SKILLS Older people can do most of the same things they could when they were younger, but they do them more slowly. Their general slowing down affects the quality of their responses as well as the time since it takes them longer to assess the environment and make decisions. This slowdown has a number of implications. It depresses the elderly's scores on intelligence tests, for example, since many of these tests require completion within a certain time limit. On a more practical level, it affects their ability to drive and thus their ability to be independent.

Are you one of those people who lie down every time you feel the urge to exercise—until the urge passes? Reconsider: Physical exercise has benefits throughout life. Aside from its ability to make you feel virtuous, it helps tone your muscles, keep your weight down, and protect you from heart disease. In old age it proves its worth again. Older people who have exercised throughout adulthood show fewer losses in speed, stamina, and strength, and in various underlying functions such as circulation and breathing (Bromley, 1974). Many of the effects we associate with aging may well result more from lack of use of our bodies and their adaptation to nondemanding physical circumstances than from chronological age.

WHY DO OUR BODIES AGE? We still don't have the definitive answer to this question. We do know that aging is a complex process influenced by heredity, nutrition, disease, and various environmental influences. If you've chosen your ancestors well and observed various healthy practices, you'll stay vigorous longer and live longer. Still, that doesn't explain the process itself. What happens to the cells in our bodies? How are old cells different from young cells? What happens to make them different? Theories that try to answer these questions fall into two main categories, as follows.

The Programmed Theory Since each species has its own pattern of aging and its own life expectancy, aging must be built into every organism in some way. Leonard Hayflick (1974), who studied the cells of many different animals, found that normal cells will divide only a limited number of times, about fifty for human cells. He maintains that this limitation controls the life span, which, for humans, seems to be limited to 110 years. We may be born with genes that become harmful later in life, causing deterioration. One such deterioration may be in our bodies' immune system, which seems to become "confused" in old age, causing it to attack the body itself.

The Wear-and-Tear Theory Comparing our bodies to machines whose parts eventually wear out through continual usage, this theory proposes that internal and external stresses (which include the accumulation of harmful byproducts in our systems such as chemical byproducts of metabolism) aggravate the wearing-down process. As cells grow older, they are less able to repair or replace damaged components, and so they die. We know, for example, that the cells of the heart and brain can never replace themselves, even early in life. When they are damaged, they die. The same thing seems to happen to other cells later in life.

DEMENTIA The combination of physical and mental deterioration that we know as senility and that is known medically by the term dementia is not inevitable in old age. In fact, only about one in ten people over 65 show significant mental impairment (National Institute on Aging, 1980). When a person *is* disabled by such symptoms as forgetfulness, problems in paying attention, decline in general intellectual ability, and difficulties in responding to other people, there is usually some kind of physiological explanation (Butler, 1975).

The bulk of all cases of dementia are caused by Alzheimer's disease, whose early symptoms include signs of forgetfulness, followed by confusion, irritability, incontinence, and sometimes a complete inability to speak or care for oneself (National Institute on Aging, 1980). Some patients continue to function on some levels (playing tennis, gardening, maintaining personal relationships), while losing their capacities for other more complex tasks. About one in three cases seem to be hereditary, and these tend to show up earlier in life, sometimes as young as age 40, while the cases in families with no history of the disease don't appear till about age 70 (Kolata, 1981).

Alzheimer's seems to be caused by a disorder in the brain, possibly a defect in the manufacture or activity of the chemical neurotransmitter acetylcholine. Attempts to supply patients with more of this or similar substances have been ineffective so far, but research continues. As of now, there is no way to treat the illness itself. Antidepressant drugs, counseling, and the use of a variety of memory aids, however, can sometimes help to make life more pleasant for the patient and the family.

Many other cases of senile dementia are caused by a series of many small strokes. Since such strokes can often be prevented by treating the hypertension that leads to them, such cases may be rarer in the future. And some cases of what seem like dementia may be due to a number of causes that are treatable and reversible.

All too often, dementialike symptoms in the elderly are not accurately diagnosed and not treated because senility is *expected* in old age. However, many instances of confusion, memory loss, and similar symptoms do respond well to proper treatment. For example, when such states arise from *overmedication* (especially with a combination of drugs that interact poorly with each other), treatment is obvious—a reduction in dosage or a change of medicine. Other conditions that produce similar symptoms and are treatable include *depression* (possibly resulting from poor health, surgery, the death of a spouse, or some other actual event); *underlying disease* (alcoholism, malnutrition, or low thyroid function); and a *difficulty in adjusting to a social change* (like moving to a new apartment).

For most people, generalized intellectual deterioration is not an inevitable part of old age, as we'll see in the next section.

Intellectual Status

Two of psychology's most prominent intellectual giants recently made public statements about their own lessened intellectual abilities in old age. Behaviorist B. F. Skinner (1982) stated that at 78 he finds it harder to "think big thoughts" without losing the thread from one chapter to another, he sometimes forgets things that he said or wrote many years ago, and he's not as creative as he once was. And at 74, learning researcher Donald O. Hebb (1978) wrote that during his sixties he started to become forgetful, to lose some command of his vocabulary, and to be troubled by irrelevant thoughts he couldn't get out of his mind (like the words of an old nursery rhyme).

Both these men devised strategies to deal with what they perceived as

For most people, generalized intellectual deterioration is not an inevitable part of old age, and creativity often remains high. The foremost American artist Georgia O'Keeffe didn't begin making pottery until her mid-eighties. (© Dan Budnik/Woodfin Camp & Assoc.)

major losses. Skinner gave up intellectually demanding leisure activities like chess and made special efforts to continue meeting with fellow scholars, and Hebb began to be more discriminating in what he read and stopped working at night. Both began to rely more on external memory aids (like hanging an umbrella on the front doorknob so they'd remember to take it later).

As we pointed out earlier, crystallized intelligence holds up very well, even as fluid intelligence does show some decline. The elderly tend to be better at certain uses of intelligence than younger people. While they don't perform as well as younger people when facing a new problem whose solution requires geometric or spatial-relations abilities, they tend to be superior at remembering, combining, and drawing conclusions from information learned over the years. As Horn (quoted in Goleman, 1984, p. C5) says, "The ability to bring to mind and entertain many different facets of information improves in many people over their vital years. . . . Older people can say the same thing in five different ways. In our research, they're better in this sort of knowledge than the young people we see." Why are some abilities maintained while others seem to decline? Nancy Denney (1982) has proposed that people maintain *exercised* (or used) abilities and tend to show decline in *unexercised* abilities. In our society we often use many of the crystallized abilities—and call upon the fluid ones less often.

Many older people perform at a lower level than their true intellectual capacity because of nonintellectual reasons. Since they do things more slowly, anything that requires speed puts them at a disadvantage. They may have trouble seeing or hearing the test instructions or questions, may be anxious about their performance, and may just not be motivated highly enough to make the effort. [When elderly test takers were rewarded with S and H Green Stamps, they improved their speed on reaction time tasks, which is usually considered to be something that inevitably slows down in old age (Hoyer, Hoyer, Treat, & Baltes, 1978)]. What we are talking about here, then, is a distinction between competence and performance.

A number of studies have shown that the elderly can improve their intellectual performance (Crovitz, 1966; Meichenbaum, 1974). Elderly problem solvers can be trained to break down the processes of solving a problem into separate components and can get better at organizing information and coming up with alternative solutions through such simple techniques as talking to themselves, either silently or out loud. They can learn to get into the habit of asking themselves questions about how they're handling the task at hand. They can work out practical techniques to jog their memories. They can make special efforts to stay intellectually active and to be with stimulating people. They can set priorities, reserving their energies for the tasks they consider most important. Such simple techniques are applicable not only in the testing situation but in real life, as psychologists Hebb and Skinner point out.

Often, the decline in intellectual abilities that has been attributed to old age is, instead, a precursor of death. Shortly before death, people often experience terminal drop, a sudden drop in intellectual performance (Riegel & Riegel, 1972; Botwinick, West, & Storandt, 1978). While this affects all ages, the higher death rates among the elderly account for its association with old age.

Personality and Social Development

The years beyond age 65 constitute a normal stage of development during which people can experience growth as well as crisis. Yet our society seems to be devoted to preventing our elderly from experiencing their last years positively. We dismiss their ideas as outdated and irrelevant rather than valuing the wisdom gained through experience and the links with the past. We force them into retirement while many are still eager and able to work. We accept illness and depression as inevitable baggage of old age. And we stereotype the elderly in countless ways, treat them according to our mistaken ideas of what they are like, and thus create self-fulfilling prophecies. As a society, we fail, for the most part, to meet their needs for companionship, income, transportation, housing, health care, and safety. In the face of all this, it's amazing that so many of the elderly age so successfully. How do they do it?

SUCCESSFUL AGING   There's more than one way to age successfully, and the route any one of us takes depends on our personality, our past, and our present circumstances. Two major theories, which take diametrically opposite views and extreme views, have generated vast amounts of research. The research so far has shown that, not surprisingly, neither one seems to hold a complete explanation. With this in mind, let's look at the either-or theories.

Activity Theory   *The more active you remain, the more fulfilled you'll be in old age.* Ideally, according to this perspective, the elderly person has to stay as much like a middle-aged person as possible. You should keep up as many activities as you can and replace roles you've lost (such as spouse or worker) with other roles (like grandparent or volunteer). Research, however, has found that the degree of the elderlys' life satisfaction has little relationship to how busy they are (Lemon, Bengston, & Peterson, 1972).

According to the activity theory of aging, the more active you remain, the more fulfilled you'll be in old age. This works for many people, like the couple shown here, while other elderly people enjoy the tranquility of the rocking chair. (Michael Hayman/Stock, Boston)

Disengagement Theory *You'll be happiest if you gracefully withdraw from life.* According to this viewpoint, it's normal and healthy for the elderly to cut down activities and involvements, retreating into themselves and weakening emotional ties to others. Yet such disengagement has been found to be more closely tied to impending death than to age itself (Lieberman & Coplan, 1970).

Actual Patterns Other research has found that some people are happiest when they stay busy, while others enjoy the tranquility of the rocking chair. The approach a person takes usually reflects the kind of personality and the degree of activity that she or he engaged in long before middle age and shows that there is equal promise of a happy old age for the person who loves being frantically busy at work, volunteer activity, and in the social whirl, as well as for the retiree who enjoys indulging in the luxury of leisure time, possibly for the first time in his or her life (Reichard, Livson, & Peterson, 1962; Neugarten, Havighurst, & Tobin, 1965).

Retirement What impact does leaving the world of paid work have? As the preceding would indicate, it depends on whom you ask. The following statements by retirees who took part in a nationwide longitudinal study (Streib & Schneider, 1971) both express common points of view:

> I dislike retirement. Personally I think it is better to keep busy. When you are not occupied and not useful, you feel like a back number. The world gets along without you. Sometimes I think about suicide. There is nothing to do but read— it's hard keeping occupied. . . . Yesterday I answered an ad. Retirement is the bunk (p. 139).

> Retirement means everything to me! I'm so happy about the whole set-up. I'm having a good time. I don't have any trouble keeping busy. On Monday I gardened. On Tuesday I played 18 holes of golf. Sometimes I bowl. On Wednesday I did yard work all morning. On Saturday I went fishing. I read a lot. In the winter I go to my lodge, and play cards. I've had several job offers but I don't want to work (p. 142).

What makes the difference? By and large, it often comes down to money and health. Not surprisingly, those retirees who feel good and don't have money worries are more satisfied with retirement than are those who don't feel well enough to make full use of their leisure time and who miss the income. This conclusion emerged from Streib and Schneider's study and also from other cross-sectional studies of retirees (Barfield & Morgan, 1974; 1978).

Streib and Schneider began their study when all their respondents were gainfully employed, following them up as they continued working, as they retired, or as they returned to work after retiring. They began with questions derived from role theory: What does it mean when we drop, disrupt, or alter such a basic role as that of worker? How does this affect health, actual and perceived economic situation, self-image, and satisfaction with life?

Their findings were generally quite positive: Health doesn't decline after retirement, nor does satisfaction with life. Self-image doesn't change drastically, either; retirees do not feel suddenly old and useless. While income declines sharply, most retired people in this study felt prepared for this drop and didn't worry about money. This finding underscores the wisdom of preparing for retirement well ahead of time.

In general, the better educated workers are, the more prestigious their jobs, the more money they earn, and the longer they're likely to work.

Most research about the effects of retirement has concentrated on male workers, but with the increased role of work in the lives of women, this is changing. Streib and Schneider found that married and single women tended to retire earlier than widowed and divorced women. The earlier retirement of single women seems to belie the importance work has in their lives, but it may also reflect the fact that they have probably been working more continuously than women in the other groups and that retirement may give them their first chance to do the kinds of domestic and leisure activities that women in the other groups may have taken for granted and gotten tired of.

ERIKSON'S FINAL LIFE CRISIS: EGO INTEGRITY VERSUS DESPAIR   Ego integrity is the culmination of the successful resolution of the seven previous crises in development throughout life. It implies a love of the human ego, which is dependent on an acceptance of the life one has lived, without major regrets for what could have been or for what one should have done differently. The person who cannot accept the basic way she or he has lived may sink into despair at the knowledge that there's no time now to start another life, no time to do things right this time (Erikson, 1963). People who have not continually evaluated and modified their life structure (as recommended by Daniel Levinson and his colleagues) can become desperately afraid of death. On the other hand, those who have accepted their lives can more easily accept the inevitability of their deaths, at the end of a life lived as well as they knew how. (See the discussion on dealing with death in Box 13-1.)

Despair has its healthy side, too, however. As Erikson asks, "How could anybody have integrity and not also despair about certain things in his own life, in the human condition? Even if your own life was absolutely beautiful and wonderful, the fact that so many people were exploited or ignored must make you feel some despair" (Hall, 1983, p. 27). Again, it's the balance that's so important.

Elderly people often engage in what Robert Butler (1961) has called the life review, in which they go over the past and think about what to do with the future. In Ingmar Bergman's classic film *Wild Strawberries*, an elderly doctor realizes how cold he has been for most of his life and becomes warmer and more open in his last days. This film dramatically shows the fact often noted in real life that we are in control of our personalities and can make changes at any time in the life span, including old age.

As we have seen, all stages of the life cycle are important. Development winds continuously throughout the corridors of our lives as we take different directions to discover who we are and to give purpose to our quest. We never have all the answers to all of life's questions; all our days are illuminated by the search for them. This search persists right up to the end of life.

BOX 13-1

MOURNING AND DYING: HOW BOTH THE DYING AND THE SURVIVING DEAL WITH DEATH

Once death was very much a part of most people's daily lives. Children often died in infancy, and throughout life people succumbed to a frightening array of fatal illnesses. People feared death and yet accepted its presence as it hovered in the corners of their lives.

With advances in medicine, death has been receding farther away from the center of most people's daily existence and has become one of the few topics we hate to talk about. Recently, however, a healthier attitude toward death has arisen—an attitude that seeks to understand it, to explore the emotional, moral, and practical issues surrounding it, and to try to make this inevitable outcome of all our lives as positive as possible for both the dying and the surviving. Thanatology, the study of death and dying, is arousing much interest, with the recognition that dealing with death can teach us about life.

ATTITUDES ABOUT DEATH THROUGH THE LIFE SPAN

Young children consider death a temporary and reversible condition, often thinking the dead person will return. Their understanding gradually develops, until by early adolescence, virtually all youths realize that death comes to everyone and that its coming should not be seen as punishment but as part of the normal life cycle (Nagy, 1948). This gradual understanding is affected partly by normal cognitive development but also by the individual's own experiences. Chronically ill children and children who have lost a parent become precociously aware of the meaning of death (Bluebond-Langner, 1977).

Adolescents and young adults rarely think about it because it's usually not an imminent threat, either to themselves or those around them. Usually not until middle age do most people come to terms with the fact that they

themselves are going to die. This realization is often an impetus for a major life change. Knowing that time is limited, people take stock of their careers, marriages, friendships, parenting, and values—and often make major changes. Old people generally accept death more easily than do the middle-aged.

ACCEPTING ONE'S OWN DEATH

A pioneer in the study of the dying process, Elisabeth Kübler-Ross (1969) evolved a five-stage process in the acceptance of imminent death, based on her work with several hundred dying patients. She maintains that most people go through the stages of *denial* ("This can't be happening to *me!*"); *anger* ("*Why* me?"); *bargaining* ("God, if you let me live to see my daughter graduate, I won't ask for anything more"); *depression* ("I won't be able to do the things I had planned"); and

Friends are important throughout life. When people can share their worries and pain with someone who cares, they can deal better with such crises of old age as widowhood, ill health, and other losses. (© 1977 Warren D. Jorgensen/Photo Researchers, Inc.)

acceptance ("My time is close now, and it's okay").

Dr. Kübler-Ross has made a major contribution to our understanding of the dying and our ability to help the terminally ill, but her stages are not invariant for all people and should not be held up as the criterion for the "good death." Some people, for example, deal best with death by denying it; others find release in raging against it; and others skip one or more stages on the way to acceptance. We need to respect individual deathstyles just as we do lifestyles.

DEALING WITH THE DEATH OF A LOVED ONE

Bereaved people in America have no universal mourning rites to help them express their grief and provide a structure for building a new life. Mourners are expected to be brave, suppress their tears, and get on with the business of living. Yet the bereaved need to express and deal with their feelings of loss before they can reorganize their lives.

Normal grief often follows a fairly predictable three-stage pattern (Schulz, 1978). For the first few weeks after the death, survivors react with shock and disbelief. As their awareness of loss sinks in, initial numbness gives way to overwhelming sadness. Some cry almost constantly; many suffer physical symptoms like insomnia, shortness of breath, and loss of appetite; some fear an emotional breakdown; some drink too much or sedate themselves with tranquilizers.

About three weeks after the death, for about a year, the widow (or other bereaved person) relives the death in her mind in an obsessive search for its meaning. She may hallucinate the presence of the dead person, seeing his face, hearing his voice. At the start of the second year after the death, survivors become more active socially, getting out more, seeing people, resuming interests. At this point they feel an added strength, knowing they have survived a dreaded ordeal.

When people react to loss with an initial sense of well-being and then show personality changes like generalized hostility or irritability, when they sink into a long-lasting depression, or when they develop major physical symptoms like asthma or colitis, they can often benefit from some kind of help in managing their grief. This help can come from a lay organization like Widow to Widow or Compassionate Friends (for parents whose children have died) or from short-term psychotherapy.

WIDOWHOOD

Three out of four women can expect to suffer one of life's greatest traumas, the death of a spouse, an event that heads the list of Holmes and Rahe's (1976) stressful life events. About half of all women become widows before they turn 56, and about half afterward, setting middle age as the time women most often have to deal with this loss and old age as the time they integrate their widowed status into day-to-day life (Balkwell, 1981). In 1978 more than four out of ten women aged 65 to 74 and almost seven out of ten women over 75 were widows, compared to only one in ten men 65 to 74 and one in five men over 75 (Soldo, 1980). Why this disparity? Because women live longer than men, usually marry older men, and are less likely to remarry after their spouses' deaths than men are, partly because there are fewer men of their own age around and because they rarely marry younger men.

What does widowhood mean for day-to-day life? Men are more likely to die from a "broken heart." In one study of 4486 widowers over age 55, death rates during the six months following their wives' deaths were 40 percent above the expected rate, with the men tending to die mostly of heart ailments (Parkes, Benjamin, & Fitzgerald, 1969). Yet women are more apt to suffer from disabling chronic conditions (Verbrugge, 1979). Both sexes show a higher rate of mental illness than their married counterparts (Balkwell, 1981).

Helena Lopata (1977; 1979) of Loyola University has done extensive research with more than 1000 widows and widowers. One of the big problems faced by both sexes is economic hardship. When the husband was the principal breadwinner, his widow is now deprived of his income. The widowed man, on the other hand, now has to buy many of the services his wife had provided. Even when both spouses were employed, the loss of one income is often major. The biggest problem, though, is still the emotional blow. Even in a bad marriage the survivor feels the loss. The role of spouse has been lost, social life has changed from couple-oriented friendships to associations with other single people, and the widowed no longer have the day-in, day-out companionship that had become such a basic part of their lives.

People deal with these problems in various ways. Men usually remarry, and women usually become friendly with other widows. Few choose to live with their married children. Younger widows often feel more competent after they have made their basic adjustments to their husbands' death and carved out a more independent life for themselves (Lopata, 1973).

Like any other life crisis, widowhood affects people in different ways, depending on their personalities, the quality of the marital relationship, and the other elements in their lives (such as work, friendships, and financial assets). Married people can prepare themselves for the possibility of widowhood by gaining a strong sense of their own identity and a sturdy measure of self-sufficiency. A woman is less likely to be devastated by her husband's loss if, while he is still alive, she has pursued her own interests and assumed a large role in every aspect of family planning and management, including the financial. A man will cope better if he's used to handling day-to-day household tasks like cooking simple meals, doing laundry, and making social arrangements.

SUMMARY

1 *Adolescence* begins with *pubescence,* when the sex organs mature and the secondary sex characteristics develop. *Puberty* is the point when the individual is sexually mature and able to reproduce. *Menarche,* the first menstrual period, signals sexual maturity for girls. The closest physiological marker for boys is the presence of sperm in the urine.

2 According to Jean Piaget, adolescents are in the cognitive stage of *formal operations,* or abstract thought. Research indicates that not all adolescents (or adults) may reach this stage.

3 Kohlberg sees *moral development* as related to cognitive development. He considers moral development to be the development of a sense of justice, which progresses through six stages. Gilligan claims that women, who tend to score lower than men on Kohlberg's moral dilemmas, see morality not in terms of abstractions such as justice and fairness but in terms of responsibility to look out for another.

4 Erik Erikson describes the crisis of adolescence as *identity versus role confusion,* when a person tries to find out "who I really am."

5 Many adolescents have good relationships with their parents and do not feel alienated from them. The *adolescent rebellion* appears to be largely a myth.

6 Although many teenagers are working today, work does not seem to have any great benefit for their educational, social, or occupational development.

7 Many adolescents are sexually active today, although they tend not to be promiscuous. However, many are not using birth control, and over 1 million teenage pregnancies were reported in 1979. Most unmarried teenagers have abortions although many others keep their babies.

8 During young (20 to 40–45 years) and middle (40–45 to about 65 years) adulthood, health and energy are generally quite good. For women, the *menopause* (or *climacteric*) typically occurs between 48 and 52. Society's attitude toward the aging woman seems to have a more profound effect on her reaction to menopause than do the hormone levels in her body. Males also experience some biological changes during midlife, including decreased fertility, orgasm frequency, and potency.

9 Certain types of intelligence continue to develop throughout life. Although *fluid intelligence* begins a slow, steady decline in adulthood, *crystallized intelligence* stays the same or may improve.

10 There is the potential for personality growth in adulthood. According to Erikson the young adult must deal with the crisis of *intimacy versus isolation,* and the middle-age adult must deal with that of *generativity versus stagnation.* The young adult must make a commitment to another or risk isolation, according to Erikson. The adult in midlife must deal with issues concerning establishing and guiding the next generation.

11 Psychologists today are looking at the impact of work in adulthood. While Americans seem to value family roles over work roles, work is still a strong area of concern.

12 Many couples react to pregnancy with mixed emotions. Although effective birth control techniques make parenthood more of a "freely chosen option" than in the past, most people do have children. Most parents find this a major source of satisfaction.

13 Recent research has identified a number of "stages" of adult development, although much of this work has focused on narrow samples largely of white, middle-class men. According to Levinson the goal of adult development is the creation of a *life structure.* Individuals go through periods of stability after they have built part of the life structure and then transition as they reevaluate it.

14 Knowing an adult's chronological age does not tell us much about that person. While biology shapes much of what happens during childhood, culture and individual personality play a larger role in affecting development in adulthood. Individual difference is wide in adulthood, particularly in old

age. *Senescence,* the time when one grows old, begins at different ages for different people. Typically age 65 is often designated as the beginning of old age although there are wide individual differences among 65-year-olds.

15 Old age is not synonymous with sickness and disability. Sensory problems are fairly common in old age although many of these can be remedied. The elderly can do many of the same things they did when they were younger, although they tend to do them more slowly.

16 A number of theories have been advanced for physical aging, including the possibilities that aging is *programmed* into every organism in some way and that it is the result of the continual *wear-and-tear* on our bodies.

17 *Dementia,* the physical and mental deterioration experienced by one in ten people over 65, is not universal. Most cases of dementia are caused by *Alzheimer's disease,* which cannot yet be cured. Other causes of dementia, for example, a series of small *strokes* (which may be prevented by blood pressure monitoring and treatment of high blood pressure), and *overmedication, depression, underlying disease,* and *difficulty in adjusting to social change* can often be prevented or treated.

18 Generalized intellectual deterioration is not an inevitable part of old age. The elderly may perform less well than younger adults on intellectual tasks for a variety of nonintellectual reasons, including an inability to work on the tasks as quickly as younger adults, impaired sight or hearing, test anxiety, and poor motivation. A number of attempts to improve intellectual performance through "training" have been successful.

19 Two important theories of successful aging are *activity theory* and *disengagement theory.* Activity the-

ory holds that the more active you remain, the more fulfilled you will be. Disengagement theory maintains that successful aging involves the normal mutual withdrawal of an old person from society. Research indicates that there is no one pattern of "successful" aging. Different people adapt in different ways.

20 Research on *retirement* indicates that good health and an adequate income are important aids to good adjustment.

21 Erikson sees the life crisis of old age as the establishment of *ego integrity,* which is dependent on accepting the life one has lived. A person who cannot do this faces overwhelming *despair* since it is too late to start over.

22 Our society has long treated death as a "taboo" topic. Recently there has been an increased interest and healthier attitude toward death. People's attitudes and understanding of death change throughout the life span. Elisabeth Kübler-Ross suggests that people go through five stages in dealing with their own deaths: *denial, anger, bargaining, depression,* and *acceptance.*

23 Immediately following the death of a loved one, survivors often react with shock, disbelief, numbness, and sadness. This initial reaction may be followed by an attempt to give the death meaning and a feeling that the dead person is still there. After about a year or so, the survivor may become more active, feeling a sense of strength at having survived the loss. *Widowhood* will be experienced by 75 percent of women, with half becoming widows by age 56. Widowhood affects people differently depending on such factors as personality, life circumstances, and the quality of the marital relationship.

SUGGESTED READINGS

Gilligan, C. (1982). *In a different voice.* Cambridge, Mass.: Harvard University Press. A discussion of the misrepresentation of women by the major theorists in developmental psychology, with an emphasis on concepts of women's morality.

Heston, L. L., & White, J. A. (1983). *Dementia: A practical guide to Alzheimer's disease and related disorders.* San Francisco: W. H. Freeman. A very readable guidebook about all aspects of dementing illnesses. The authors provide information about current theories, treatment possibilities, and practical concerns.

Kübler-Ross, E. (1969). *On death and dying.* New York: Macmillan. A moving book that started the birth of a new interest in death; Kübler-Ross draws upon interviews with dying patients to conclude that there are five stages in the outlook of the dying person.

Levinson, D. J.; Darrow, C. N.; Klein, E. B.; Levinson, M. H.; & McKee, B., (1978). *The season's of a man's life.* New York: Ballantine. A detailed report of this research team's findings about male development from early adulthood through middle age. Highly readable, with interesting case histories, the authors spell out a number of theoretical concepts that guide adult development.

Papalia, D. E., & Olds, S. W. (1981). *Human development* (2d ed.). New York: McGraw-Hill. A college textbook which explores physical, intellectual, personality, and social development across the entire life span.

Pablo Picasso: *Girl Before a Mirror*, 1932. Collection The Museum of Modern Art, New York. Gift of Mrs. Simon Guggenheim.

PART
6

PERSONALITY AND ABNORMALITY

Individuality, for good and for ill, and the pursuit of mental health are the meat of this section of this book, and are also, for many people, the overwhelming reason for the existence of the science of psychology. The riddle of individual personality—What makes us the way we are?—is taken up, with some attempts to provide possible answers. Then we look at the difficulties that arise when the way some people are undermines their ability to function normally. We also examine the attempts through the years to treat those suffering from various kinds of psychological disturbances.

In Chapter 14, "Theories and Assessment of Personality," we ask what makes each of us unique and examine some of the explanations offered by various students of personality, including Sigmund Freud, who focused on the conflict between biological urges and the need to tame them; B. F. Skinner, the behaviorist, and Albert Bandura, the social learning theorist, who look to the role of the environment; and Abraham Maslow and other humanists, who consider the potential each of us has to fulfill ourselves. We then look at ways psychologists measure personality, through interviews, projective techniques like the interpretation of inkblots, and more objective pencil-and-paper tests.

Chapter 15, "Abnormal Psychology," discusses the ways we define emotional disturbance and abnormal behavior and the difficulties in arriving at such judgments. It describes and tries to shed some light on the causes of a range of emotional disorders, from the mild depression that affects almost all of us at some time to the break with reality that characterizes schizophrenia.

In Chapter 16, "Therapy," we point out the most widely used ways of treating psychological disorders. We also look at some of the innumerable differences within the three major approaches to therapy—*psychotherapy,* which relies most heavily on talking to help the individual change his or her attitudes and behavior; *medical treatment,* which uses physical techniques like drugs, electric shock, and surgery; and *social or environmental intervention,* which focuses on changing the individual's environment in some way.

CHAPTER 14

THEORIES AND ASSESSMENT OF PERSONALITY

THEORIES OF PERSONALITY
DEVELOPMENT
    Psychoanalytic Approaches
    Environmental (or Learning) Approaches
    Humanistic Approaches
    Type and Trait Theories

THE PERSON-SITUATION
CONTROVERSY

BOX 14-1: PRIMARY POINTS OF
CONTROVERSY IN MAJOR PERSONALITY
THEORIES

TESTING PERSONALITY
    Types of Personality Tests
    The Ethics of Personality Testing

SUMMARY

SUGGESTED READINGS

SPOTLIGHT ON

A theory of personality which views people as being in a constant struggle to tame their biological urges (Freud's psychoanalytic theory).

Several personality theorists who broke away from Freud because they felt he overemphasized the role of sex in motivating behavior (Carl Jung, Alfred Adler, Karen Horney, Erik Erikson).

Two theories of personality that focus on the role of the environment (Skinner's radical behaviorism and Bandura's social learning theory).

Two personality theories that emphasize each person's potential for self-fulfillment (Maslow's self-actualization theory and Rogers' person-centered theory).

Two theories that look to a person's physical or psychological attributes to explain personality (Sheldon's constitutional psychology and Allport's psychology of the individual).

Some ways to assess personality and some related ethical considerations.

Suppose we asked you to describe the personalities of your three closest friends:

- You might say that Jamie is fun to be with, enjoys trying new things, has an offbeat sense of humor that you enjoy even though you sometimes have to duck the sarcasm directed at you, has a quick temper, and is extremely generous.
- Bob, you'd tell us, is quiet and thoughtful, given to thinking and talking about serious things, tolerant of other people's foibles, easygoing even under stress, insightful in discussions of books and movies, and generally committed to traditional values.
- Sandy is intense, competitive, quick with praise, equally quick with criticism when friends don't measure up to her standards of behavior, honest often to the point of brutality, and frugal.

Even though we don't know any of these people, we could probably identify each of them after 5 minutes of conversation. The better we got to know them, the more facets of their personalities would show up. The more they revealed of themselves, the plainer it would be that each one is a unique human being, whose personality is like that of no one else on earth. And this is precisely the psychological definition of personality— that constellation of relatively consistent ways of dealing with people and situations that put the stamp of individuality on each of us. While our attitudes, our values, our opinions, and our emotions are the cornerstone of our individuality, the way we act upon these states of mind determine what others will see as our personalities.

No one, of course, is 100 percent consistent—always generous, always friendly, always tolerant, always callous, always honest. But as you know from your own experience and your reading of literature, certain characteristics do predominate in our psychological makeup so that we can be described by the traits that seem to govern our behavior much of the time.

The great puzzle in psychology, and the one that has spawned countless theories and research projects, is, What makes people develop these characteristics? What made Jamie so generous that she'd give away her last dollar to an almost total stranger, while Sandy finds it painful to spend even modest amounts? Why does Bob accept people pretty much as they are, while Sandy has room in her life only for those who think and act the way she does? Why is Jamie loud and Bob quiet? Why is one person "all wired up" and another "laid back"? One ready to question authority at every turn, while another finds comfort in established structures?

For insights into these questions, observers of human nature have evolved complex theories. We will look at the most important of these theories, which fall into four broad categories: *psychoanalytic, learning, humanist,* and *types and traits.* Learning theory sees personality as being determined by experiences outside oneself, in the environment, while the other three schools of thought see it as formed within ourselves, arising from basic inborn needs, drives, and characteristics.

THEORIES OF PERSONALITY DEVELOPMENT

As you read about the theories we'll be talking about in this chapter, you might ask yourself how each one would account for the personality characteristics we've described in the three friends, Jamie, Bob, and Sandy. You might also look at each theory with an eye to the way it differs along the dimensions brought out by the following questions. How do you think the answers to these questions affect the degree to which each theory has become accepted both by individuals and by broad segments of society?

1 Does it consider behavior to be motivated largely by conscious or unconscious factors?
2 Where did the theory originate—from looking at normal people, from observing troubled people who have sought out psychotherapy, or from observing animals in the laboratory and then generalizing to human beings?
3 How easily can researchers design programs to test the theory? Are terms defined precisely? How much research actually has been generated?
4 Does it emphasize biological or environmental causes of behavior?
5 Does it see people as basically good, basically bad, or neutrally reactive to experience?
6 Does it focus on behavior that can be seen or on internal traits?
7 Is its principal interest in universal laws of behavior or in individual uniqueness?

Psychoanalytic Approaches

THE CLASSICAL PSYCHOANALYTIC THEORY OF SIGMUND FREUD (1856–1939)   The most famous personality theorist the world has ever known, Freud revolutionized people's thinking about the development of personality. Many of the terms he coined have entered the common vocabulary so that most of us have heard the words *id, ego, superego, oral* and *anal personalities, libido, penis envy, Oedipus complex,* the *unconscious,* and many others. We'll take a look at what these and other terms mean in the context of Freudian theory.

The History of Freudian Theory   Freud's life spanned the second half of the nineteenth century and most of the first half of the twentieth, and left the world forever changed in the way people saw some basic concepts of human personality. In some ways he presented a totally new vision of the human mind, and in other ways he was a product of his own upbringing and of the Victorian era in which he lived. Freud began his career in Vienna, where he lived for almost eighty years. A physician in private practice, he became interested in the treatment of nervous disorders. First he tried hypnosis, but since he had little success with it, he dropped this technique. Continuing to search for a better way to help his patients, he finally felt he had found it in Dr. Joseph Breuer's "talking cure," through which patients were able to get rid of their symptoms by talking about their experiences and problems. Freud expanded and developed this technique into what we now know as psychoanalysis, which we'll discuss in greater detail in Chapter 16.

Sigmund Freud. (National Library of Medicine)

As Freud listened to his patients—mostly middle-aged, upper-middle-class Viennese women—talk about their concerns and recite many of their experiences, he began to see significant threads emerging—the life-long influence of early-childhood experiences, the existence and importance of infantile sexuality, the significance of the content of dreams, the way so much of our lives is ruled by deeply rooted elements of which we are not consciously aware. Based on these and other conclusions, he formulated his theories, sometimes illustrating his points by writing up individual case histories.

The Structure of Personality   The id, the ego, and the superego are the three different parts to the personality, each of which serves a different function and develops at a different time (Freud, 1932). These three components are not, of course, physically present in the brain but are forces that Freud assumed to exist, based on his observations of people's behaviors and expressed thoughts and feelings.

The id (Latin word for "it") is present at birth. It consists of such basic needs as hunger, thirst, and sex, which Freud called the *life instincts*, fueled by a form of energy called the libido. The life instinct is called "eros," which is also the name for the Greek god of love. The id also contains a *death instinct* (called "thanatos"), responsible for aggressiveness and destruction. The id cries out for satisfaction *now*. It operates on the pleasure principle, which demands immediate gratification no matter what. The hungry baby cries to be fed; he doesn't care if his mother is sound asleep or if his father is caring for his older sister; to the infant, his need is paramount, and he will stop his demands only when they are met.

To Freud, these life and death instincts are the bases for *all* human behavior throughout life. Each instinct consists of a bodily *need* (with hunger, the need is nutritional deficit) and a psychological *wish* (a desire for food). The need gives birth to the wish, and the wish leads to behavior.

People don't always gratify their instincts directly; sometimes they use substitute objects, a process known as displacement. This is what happens when you repress your desire to yell at your boss—and then go home and yell at the first family member unlucky enough to cross your path. When a displacement produces a socially valued achievement, it is called a sublimation. Thus, a hungry baby may suck on a pacifier when the breast is unavailable, a child discouraged from masturbation may play with blocks, and a Leonardo da Vinci may paint Madonnas when what he really wants is to feel close to his own mother, from whom he had been separated in childhood.

The ego (Latin for "I") develops soon after birth when the infant realizes that all that she wants will not automatically come to her and that she will have to figure out a way to get what she wants. It operates on the reality principle, by which a person works out a plan and then takes some kind of action to test the plan to see whether he is on the right track. This process is known as *reality testing*. So the infant ruled by its id lies screaming in its crib till it gets fed; the hungry toddler, under the guidance of his ego, makes his way to the cookie jar. The id (irrational and unconscious) feels and unthinkingly expresses emotion; the ego (rational and largely

This butcher may be sublimating his unacceptable aggressive impulses into the socially acceptable activity of butchering meat. (Ray Ellis © 1983/Photo Researchers, Inc.)

conscious) *thinks* and acts upon its analysis of the situation. The ego tries to find a way to gratify the id, while still considering reality.

The superego (Latin for "over-the-I"), the last part of the personality to develop, appears in early childhood. It operates on what we might call the *perfection principle*. It represents the values that parents and then other representatives of society communicate to the child as ideals. The superego lets the child internalize the concepts of right and wrong so that he can control his own behavior according to whether he himself considers a given action right or wrong. The superego consists of the *ego-ideal* (the "shoulds" for which we have been approved of, to which we aspire, and of which we feel proud) and the *conscience* (the "should-nots" for which we have been punished and now punish ourselves through guilt).

The superego is the moral taskmaster of the soul, the agent that tries to prevent the id from acting upon its impulses, especially the sexual and aggressive ones. It aims to divert the ego from its realistic approach to a moralistic orientation. Nonrational like the id, controlling like the ego, the superego is in opposition to both of them. It is the original killjoy: "Unlike the ego, the superego does not merely postpone instinctual gratification; it tries to block it permanently"(Hall & Lindzey, 1978, p. 40). If it succeeds too well, it produces a rigid, inhibited personality; when it fails, it looses an antisocial personality in our midst.

Defense Mechanisms of the Ego   Ideally, the three faces of the psyche—the id, the ego, and the superego—are in a state of equilibrium with each other. Their interplay is dynamic, and the energies called into play produce a happy balance that enables a person to retain the spontaneity of the id, the moral concern of the superego, and the reasonableness of the ego. When these forces are out of balance, however, people often become anxiety-ridden. To relieve the pressure, the ego often comes to the rescue with one or more defenses. All these defense mechanisms distort reality to make it easier for the individual to deal with it. Furthermore, they are unconscious so that the person is not even aware that any distortion has taken place and is completely convinced that his or her viewpoint is the only correct one. We all engage in these common defenses at some times; they become pathological only when they take a severe form. Displacement and sublimation, discussed earlier in this chapter, are two such mechanisms. What are some of the others?

- *Repression:* In an anxiety-producing situation, a person may block certain urges or experiences from consciousness. She or he may be unable to remember a painful experience, may be unable to see an object or person in plain sight, may be unaware of feelings that at one time she had freely expressed, or may be physically disabled without any organic reason (as in the case of a man who is sexually impotent with his wife because he considers the sexual impulse aggressive and is afraid of hurting her).
- *Regression:* In anxiety-producing situations, people often return to the behavior of an earlier time, to try to recapture remembered security. A child may react to the birth of a baby brother by wetting his bed and sucking his thumb, behaviors he engaged in when *he* was the baby.

Or, after the first marital quarrel, a newlywed may "go home to Mother." Once the crisis is past, the immature behavior will probably disappear, but if this is a person's pattern, it is likely to reappear at the next sign of trouble.

- *Projection:* One way of dealing with unacceptable thoughts and motives is to project them, or attribute them to someone else. Thus, Jimmy may talk about how much his sister hates him instead of how much he hates her. Or a man may accuse his wife of adultery not because she has given him any reason to doubt her fidelity but because he himself is attracted to other women.

- *Reaction formation:* When a person feels that some of her feelings are unacceptable (to her), she may replace them with their opposite. A woman who hates her mother because she always felt the mother favored her sister over her may loudly proclaim her love, complete with extravagant gifts and grand gestures. This kind of mechanism may have motivated a Tampa, Florida, marketing analyst, who led a drive against sex education books in public libraries because he claimed they would pervert the morals of children. While in the midst of this censorship attempt, the analyst was arrested for, and later pleaded no contest to, sexual misconduct involving an 8-year-old girl and a teenage boy (ASJA, 1982). This man may well have replaced his unacceptable sexual urges toward children with what he saw as the opposite, the wish to maintain the innocence of children by not exposing them to books about sex. How can we distinguish a reaction formation from the real thing? Usually by the compulsiveness and the going-to-extremes behavior that tend to mark the reaction formation. When "the lady doth protest too much," we are alerted to the fact that things may not be what they seem.

- *Rationalization:* Another way of dealing with a difficult situation is to justify our behavior by pretending that the difficulty doesn't exist. The fox tells himself that he doesn't want those grapes just out of reach because they must be sour. Or, biting into a particularly sour lemon, he praises himself for having chosen such a sweet fruit. The college we didn't get into wouldn't have been as much fun as the one we're at now, the job we didn't get would have been a dead end, the lover we lost would have kept us from meeting the far superior person we are now involved with.

  People rationalize for another purpose, too, to make themselves feel better about doing something they basically feel they shouldn't be doing. When a department store clerk makes a mistake in your favor, for example, do you pocket the money, telling yourself, "The store overcharges anyway, so this is really coming to me"? If so, you are rationalizing.

Psychosexual Development According to Freud (1905), personality develops in a sequence of five stages, beginning in infancy. Four of these stages are named for those parts of the body that are primary sources of gratification in each phase. These body parts are called the erogenous zones. A person whose needs are not met at any one stage or who is overindulged at that time may become *fixated* at a particular stage. While the order of the shifts of instinctual energy from one body zone to another is always the same, the level of a child's maturation determines when these shifts will take place. Freud felt that a person's lifelong personality is largely determined during the first three of the following stages. A major element of his theory is the concept of *infantile sexuality*—that the human sexual drive does not appear full-blown at puberty but that it has been present since birth, even though the sexual feelings of infants and young children are different in form from those of adolescents and adults.

The oral stage (birth to 12–18 months): The erogenous zone is the *mouth,* through which the baby gets pleasure from eating, sucking, and biting. Sucking, then, accomplishes more than getting nutrition into the body—it is a source of pleasure in itself. A person fixated in the oral stage may, as an adult, become so gullible that he will swallow anything, become dependent, or take the same kind of pleasure from absorbing knowledge and acquiring possessions as she once did from ingesting food.

The anal stage (12–18 months to 3 years): During the second year the erogenous zone shifts to the *anus* as the child learns to control elimination. Toddlers find the very act of withholding or expelling feces sensually gratifying. Toilet training is important: The child who is trained too strictly may become obsessively neat, cruel and destructive, or obstinate and stingy, while the one who is praised extravagantly for producing bowel movements may be inspired to be productive in other realms, as well.

The phallic stage (3 to 6 years): This stage, which gets its name from *phallus,* a term for the penis, begins when the child feels pleasure in the *genital* region. At this point the child may discover masturbation.

According to the scenario of the Oedipus complex, which arises during this stage, a little boy lavishes love and affection on his mother, thus competing with his father for the mother's love and affection. Unconsciously the boy wants to take his father's place, but, recognizing his father's power, he is afraid of him. Since he has learned that little girls don't have penises, he concludes that someone must have cut them off and fears that his father, angry at his attempted usurpation, will do the same to him. This is the *castration complex*. Fearful, the boy represses his sexual strivings toward his mother, stops trying to rival his father, and begins to identify with him.

The Electra complex is the female counterpart to the Oedipus. The little girl falls in love with her father and is ambivalent toward her mother. She even becomes afraid of her mother because she thinks that her mother has cut off the penis she thinks she (and other little girls) once had, and now she's afraid that her mother will do even worse things to her because of the child's rivalry for the father's affections. At the same time, she does love her mother and doesn't want to lose her mother's love. So she represses her ambivalent feelings, and eventually identifies with her mother.

All of this is said to come about because of the penis envy the little girl develops at this stage, which can be resolved somewhat only in adulthood when she gives birth to a son "who brings the longed-for penis with him" (Freud, 1905, quoted in Schaeffer, p. 19). (Apparently the woman who never has children or is blessed only with daughters is doomed to suffer penis envy all her life.) Freud felt that little girls never completely

According to Sigmund Freud's Electra complex, little girls fall in love with their fathers during the phallic stage of psychosexual development. (© Hazel Hankin/ Stock, Boston)

overcome penis envy (leaving females generally envious and suffering from low self-esteem) and that they don't resolve this stage as well as little boys do, leaving them with a less-well-developed superego than the male.

At about age 5 or 6, children resolve these complexes when they realize that the risks are too great. They identify with the parent of the same sex and internalize parental standards to develop a superego. Identification with the same-sex parent helps to relieve the anxiety brought about by the Oedipus and Electra complexes. This process is known as "identification with the aggressor." Freud felt, however, that identification with the same-sex parent is never total and that all people continue to possess some traits of the other sex. He also felt that boys develop a superego more readily than girls do. (For a discussion of identification, both in Freudian and in other terms, see Chapter 12.)

The latency stage (6 years to puberty) is a period of relative sexual calm. Boys and girls tend to avoid the opposite sex but are not totally asexual during this time since there is some interest in masturbation and in sex-oriented jokes.

The genital stage (from puberty on), which occurs because of the hormonal changes that accompany puberty, marks the entry into mature sexuality, when the person's major psychosexual task is to enter into heterosexual relationships with people outside the family.

We have barely touched on Freud's rich and complex theory, which he spelled out and elaborated upon in many volumes. We do discuss other aspects of his theoretical framework in other places in this book, for they permeate many of the individual topics in the study of psychology. For now, though, let's see how well it has held up over the years.

Evaluation of Freudian Theory Probably the single most important contribution Freud made to the study of human personality was his concept of the *unconscious*, that vast network of stored, often repressed passions and ideas that direct our conscious thoughts and behavior. Before his time, psychologists studied only conscious behavior and thoughts. Freud's likening the human mind to an iceberg, in which only the smallest part (the conscious, like the tip of the iceberg) is exposed, while the much larger part, the unconscious, is hidden beneath the surface, opened the way for deep exploration of the human psyche.

Another vastly important contribution was Freud's emphasis (even though it sometimes appears to be overemphasis) on the importance of early experience on later development.

The single most controversial element of his body of thought was his insistence on the sexual drive as the primary motivating force for behavior throughout life, even from infancy. Several of his followers, including Jung and Adler (discussed later in this chapter), broke with him over this issue. He is also criticized by contemporary critics for overemphasizing sex, but is generally respected for bringing out into the open the concept of infantile sexuality.

In more recent years, the focus of controversy has shifted to his perception of women as inferior creatures, anatomically (because they don't have a penis), psychologically (because, not having a penis, they do not experience either the Oedipus conflict or castration anxiety), morally (because, not undergoing these two conflicts, they do not develop as strong a superego as boys do), and culturally (because, not having such a strong superego, they are not capable of sublimating their more base desires into creative and productive work that will advance civilization). One of his early followers, Karen Horney, broke with Freud on his view of women.

Other voices have criticized Freud on other bases. The humanists, for example, take issue with his view of human beings as creatures at the mercy of base instincts that will cause trouble if they are not controlled. Because he based his theories on the lives of troubled people who had come to him for help, Freud did not appear to appreciate the strength of the healthy human psyche. Furthermore, it's questionable whether we can appropriately theorize about normal development based on the observations of people with emotional problems.

Because many of Freud's theories are vague and hard to define, it has been difficult to design research projects to confirm or refute them. Still, researchers have tried. And tried. Thousands of attempts to test Freud's theories have been made over the years, with varied results (Fisher & Greenberg, 1977). Research findings do show evidence for oral and anal personality types, for children's erotic feelings for the parent of the other sex and their hostility toward the same-sex parent, and for male fears of castration as related to erotic arousal. Other research, however, indicates that identification occurs for reasons having as much or more to do with parental characteristics of warmth and nurturance as with "fear of the aggressor," that women achieve sexual gratification as easily as men, and that, contrary to the notion of "penis envy," women are generally more accepting of their bodies than men are. As far as psychoanalysis as a treatment is concerned, the jury is still out: On the basis of available research, it cannot be either accepted or rejected. It did, however, serve to popularize "talk therapy," which in a number of forms is widely used today, as we'll see in Chapter 16.

A recent flood of criticism has focused on the way Freud's own defense mechanisms seem to have entered into the formulation of his theories.

Carl Jung. (National Library of Medicine)

For example, there is evidence that Freud may have ignored blatant evidence of parental maltreatment and sexual seduction of children, while claiming that children were naturally aggressive, masochistic, and sexually seductive toward their parents (Masson, 1984; Tribich & Klein, 1981). One reason advanced for this selective blindness is the possibility that Freud may have suspected—and not wanted to acknowledge—the likelihood of his own father's having been sexually seductive; another might be Freud's inability to own up to sexual fantasies about his own daughters (Tribich, 1982).

In general, Freud's followers differed from him in a number of ways. They did not place the same all-encompassing emphasis on sex and aggression as motivators of human behavior, and they were more concerned with the way social interaction affects development. Let's meet some of these neo-Freudians.

THE ANALYTIC PSYCHOLOGY OF CARL JUNG (1875–1961) At one time considered by Freud as his heir to the throne, Jung, a Swiss physician, split with Freud for both personal and intellectual reasons. Major theoretical differences included Jung's rejection of sexuality as the major determinant of behavior, his conviction that life is directed in large part by the positive and purposeful goals people set for themselves and not only by repressed intellectual factors, and his emphasis on growth and change throughout life, in contrast to Freud's belief that personality is unalterably set in childhood.

The most controversial aspect of Jung's theory is his mystical belief in the racial, or historical, origins of personality. He felt that the roots of personality go far back before the birth of the individual through past generations, way back to the dawn of humankind's origin on earth. From our distant ancestors we inherit common predispositions that mold the way we will look at and respond to life. Our personalities are thus racially determined. To learn more about the evolution of this racial, or collective, personality, Jung steeped himself in the study of mythology, religion, and primitive beliefs and rituals, as well as in dreams and the manifestations of neuroses and psychoses.

Jung saw the mind as consisting of the ego (the conscious mind); the personal unconscious (repressed or forgotten material); and the collective unconscious (that part of the mind derived from ancestral memories). The collective unconscious is made up of archetypes, emotionally charged ideas that link universal concepts to individual experience. Archetypes can best be thought of as symbols or common themes that are found through the generations and in all parts of the world. According to Jung, we have many archetypes that we are born with and that influence our behavior. For example, the *archetype of the mother* results when the baby perceives its mother not only according to the kind of woman she is and the experiences the baby has of her but also according to the preformed concept of a mother that the baby is born with. Other archetypes include the persona (the social mask one adopts); the anima (the feminine archetype in man); and the animus (the masculine archetype in woman). We also have archetypes for birth, death, God, the child, the wise old man, and others.

Much more widely accepted were Jung's constructs of the *introvert* (the

This painting by Magritte, "The Ready Made Bouquet," seems to illustrate Jung's concept that each of us carries within us an archetype of the other sex. Here we see the anima, *the feminine archetype, contained within a man.*

person oriented toward his or her inner, subjective world) and the *extrovert* (the person oriented toward the outer, objective world). A person may often be described in one of these terms till middle age, when the other attitude emerges from the personal unconscious. Jung considered the midlife transition important in other ways, too. This is the time of life, said Jung (1931), when a person wants to throw off the persona, or mask, that has characterized the way she or he has been dealing with other people, and to express the feelings and emotions that have been repressed up until now. This helps to explain the commonly noted phenomenon of men's becoming more nurturant and emotionally expressive in middle age, as women become more assertive and career oriented.

Like Freud's work, Jung's is hard to substantiate through research and experimentation. While he has not had nearly the impact of his "master," his influence reaches further than is generally recognized. It was Jung, for example, who first expressed the optimistic viewpoint that the humanists later expanded on, who first enunciated the concept of self-actualization through goal-directed behavior and the optimism that laid the foundation for humanistic theories. Furthermore, artistic expression of Jung's theories can be seen in many contemporary films, plays, and novels, and perhaps in the general move toward mysticism that has characterized many aspects of contemporary society.

THE INDIVIDUAL PSYCHOLOGY OF ALFRED ADLER (1870–1937) A Viennese physician like Freud, Adler also broke with him largely because of differences about sexuality and the role of the unconscious. Adler felt that people are primarily social, not sexual; that social motivations are more powerful than sexual; that the style of life a person chooses determines how he or she will satisfy sexual needs rather than vice versa; and that conscious, goal-directed behavior is more important to explore than unconscious motivation. While he felt that social nature is inborn, he also maintained that the kinds of social experiences one has early in life—

According to Alfred Adler, we overcome our inferiority complexes by striving for superiority over our own inadequacies. (Alan Oransky/ Stock, Boston)

Karen Horney. (Culver Pictures, Inc.)

Erik H. Erikson. (UPI/Bettmann Archive)

those with other people, especially one's parents and siblings, influence the way an individual will deal with relationships throughout life.

Adler coined the term inferiority complex. He felt that individuals try to compensate for their feelings of inferiority, sometimes by *overcompensating* and developing what he called a superiority complex. It's possible that he became interested in dealing with feelings of inferiority and with the importance of early experiences as an outgrowth of his own sickly childhood.

As the founder of "individual psychology," Adler emphasized the uniqueness of individuals. In this belief, he was the precursor of the humanists since he emphasized the concept of an individual style of life, or the way by which a person would strive to overcome his or her inferiority feelings and develop a sense of self-worth and, eventually, what the humanists were to call "self-actualization."

Adler was very influential through his analysis of the effect of birth order on personality, through his emphasis on the great influence of social, rather than sexual, factors, and through his stress on conscious, goal-directed behavior.

Like Jung, Adler also considered behavior to be goal-directed, instead of being motivated by unconscious factors. He believed in a *creative self*, a personal system that interprets the experiences one has and seeks out those that will be fulfilling. Instead of emphasizing basic universal drives, Adler focused on the *uniqueness* of personality, which prods each individual in a different direction to find those satisfactions in life that will be personally fulfilling.

A major impetus in life, according to Adler, is the urge toward superiority, not over other people but over one's own sense of inferiority, which stems initially from a child's feelings of inadequacy because of her small size and lack of power. The inferiority complex drives a person to achieve, to complete oneself, to overcome those early feelings of inferiority and achieve what later theorists, like Abraham Maslow, referred to as "self-actualization."

KAREN HORNEY (1885–1952) Another disciple of Freud who was strongly influenced by him and then went off in new directions, Horney was also a physician trained in psychoanalysis. She was convinced that Freud overestimated the importance of biological factors in determining personality while he neglected social and cultural ones. A particularly dramatic example of this was Horney's reaction to Freud's concept of penis envy. Horney maintained that when a woman does wish to be a man, it is not an anatomical feature that she would like to possess but "all those qualities or privileges which in our culture are regarded as masculine, such as strength, courage, independence, success, sexual freedom, right to choose a partner" (1939, p. 108).

Horney (1945) attributed neuroses to a child's difficulty in dealing with a potentially hostile world full of such adverse factors as domination, indifference, erratic behavior, lack of respect, too much or too little warmth, admiration, responsibility, and so forth. The anxious child, she theorized, goes on to deal with the world by "feeding" one or more of ten needs that she characterized as neurotic because she considered them irrational solutions. These needs are for affection and approval, for a part-

John B. Watson. (Culver Pictures, Inc.)

ner who will take over one's life, for power, for prestige, for personal achievement, for personal admiration, for self-sufficiency and independence, for perfection and unassailability, to exploit others, and to restrict one's life within narrow borders. She later grouped these needs into three basic ways of responding: moving *toward* people (becoming dependent upon them); moving *against* people (becoming hostile and rebellious); and moving *away* from people (withdrawing into the self).

The major difference between the healthy person and the neurotic one, she said, was that the healthy individual can integrate these three attitudes, sometimes giving in to others, sometimes fighting, and sometimes keeping to oneself, while the neurotic is inflexibly committed to one of these directions, regardless of the appropriateness in particular circumstances.

THE PSYCHOSOCIAL THEORY OF ERIK H. ERIKSON (1902–PRESENT)   A contemporary psychoanalytic theorist who was born in Germany but has spent most of his life in the United States, Erikson has carried on Freud's tradition of modifying original theories to keep up with changing times.

Erikson's major contribution to personality theory is his emphasis on the conflict between inborn instincts and societal demands. He maintains that the particular culture a person grows up in determines what these conflicts will be. This theory, which incorporates both psyche and society, describes a progression of eight stages throughout life. In each stage the individual is faced with a crisis, the resolution of which can have either a good or bad outcome, depending on the person's ability to strike a healthy balance. For example, beginning in infancy, the individual must develop the right ratio of *trust* (so that he can form intimate relationships) to *mistrust* (so that he can protect himself in a sometimes hostile world). While many of Erikson's writings (1950; 1963; 1968) focused on childhood and adolescence, he built upon both Jung and Adler's belief in adult development and extended his own life-cycle stages into old age. For a detailed discussion of Erikson's theory, see the chapters on development in Part 5.

Environmental (or Learning) Approaches

John B. Watson (1924), the American psychologist known as "the father of behaviorism," agreed with the *tabula rasa* (Latin for "blank slate") view of personality enunciated by the seventeenth-century British philosopher John Locke. According to this point of view, the newborn infant is an empty slate: The stylus of the environment will imprint both personality and destiny upon the child. The theories fitting this philosophy are quite different from the other three kinds of approaches we talk about in this chapter, which all place great emphasis on various inborn traits or drives. Environmental approaches view human beings as almost infinitely malleable, not only in childhood, but throughout life. Watson believed, for example, that most emotions are learned. In the "Little Albert" experiment described in Chapter 5, which has been regarded as a classic, he demonstrated how fear could be classically conditioned in a baby.

These theories have their roots in Ivan Pavlov's work on classical conditioning and in Edward Thorndike's work on operant conditioning (described in Chapter 5), as well as in Watson's experiments.

B. F. Skinner. (Harvard University News Office)

THE RADICAL BEHAVIORISM OF B. F. SKINNER (1904–PRESENT)   According to Skinner, whose research on the ways animals—and people—learn is also discussed in Chapter 5, we learn how to be the kind of person we are, just as we learn everything else. The entire concept that most people call "personality," with its unconscious motivation, its moral underpinnings, and its emotional overlay, does not exist. Human behavior, he says, can be divided into the different kinds of activity that we either do or don't do, depending on what we have been rewarded or punished for in the past and on the consequences we expect in the future. Rewards are much more powerful in shaping behavior than are punishments.

Human behavior, then, is *lawful*, in the sense that it follows certain basic laws, or principles, of learning. It is merely a result of the chaining together of a number of stimulus-response sequences. No matter how unproductive a behavior may seem to be, it would not persist unless there were some "payoff" for the individual. A child may throw frequent temper tantrums, for example, because they often bring results—either the object he wants or the attention of his parents. He will continue to pitch tantrums as long as he gets something from them.

As much as this theory has been criticized for seeing people as empty shells and for oversimplifying the significance of learning principles, it is optimistic in that it sees the possibility of change. An extreme view of the effect of change is demonstrated in *Walden Two*, the novel by B. F. Skinner. Here he describes a utopian community that would reward desirable behaviors, thus bringing about a perfect society. At least one Virginia commune tried to put these principles into effect, but it later dropped its emphasis on behavior principles (Samuel, 1981).

There are, however, many successful case histories of individuals who *have* seemed to change their behavior patterns as a direct result of these learning principles, structured in behavior modification treatment programs. We will be discussing these programs in Chapter 16.

THE SOCIAL LEARNING THEORY OF ALBERT BANDURA (1925–PRESENT)   Human beings are not pigeons confined to a cage whose only two stimuli are different-colored bars. Our infinitely varied behavior takes place in extremely complex surroundings. How do we learn to do things in the first place so that we can then be rewarded or punished for them? According to Bandura and other social learning theorists (whose social learning theory was first presented in Chapter 5), we see other people perform various behaviors, and we copy them, and then when we get rewarded, we continue to do them. When we don't get positive feedback, we eventually stop these behaviors. This point of view goes beyond basic learning principles to take into account the social context in which learning takes place.

The process of imitating others, called "modeling," apparently plays a part in the way children learn to be aggressive or altruistic. When children observe someone else—a real-life adult, an adult seen on film, or a cartoon character—hitting out, they'll be more likely to act that way than if they don't see any model at all or if they see a model acting in a kindly, gentle, helpful way. Furthermore, they'll be more likely to imitate behavior when they see the person responsible for it being rewarded than when

Give me a dozen infants well-formed, and my own specified world to bring them up in and I'll guarantee to take any one at random and train him to become any type of specialist I might select—doctor, lawyer, artist, merchant-chief, and yes, even into beggar-man and thief, regardless of his talents, penchants, tendencies, abilities, vocations, and race of his ancestors.
(Watson, 1924, p. 76)

they observe punishment or no consequence at all (Bandura, Ross, & Ross, 1961; 1963; Bandura & Walters, 1963; Bandura, 1965; 1977).

While social learning theory does not give a good picture of the whole person because of its strong emphasis on specific behaviors, it has made a strong contribution to personality theory. A major plus is the therapy derived from it that is used to help people rid themselves of phobias and other situation-related anxieties. (More about this in Chapter 16.)

Humanistic Approaches

The so-called "third force" in psychology, humanistic psychology, is more like psychoanalysis than behaviorism (the other two "forces") in its focus on internal motivators of behavior but differs from classical analytic thinking in its optimistic confidence in our positive natures. Philosophically, humanists are in the same camp as the eighteenth-century philosopher Jean-Jacques Rousseau, who believed that people are "noble savages," who will blossom into productive, fulfilled, happy, good human beings—unless unfavorable experiences interfere with their ability to express their finest natures. This contrasts sharply with the psychoanalysts' view of people as captives struggling to free themselves of dark and dangerous instinctual urges, or as the blank slates the behaviorists see us as.

Instead of the medical backgrounds held by the early psychoanalysts, the humanists tend to come from disciplines such as education and psychology. Their viewpoints, known as *phenomenological*, stress the importance of the subjective, unique experiences of the individual and emphasize the potential every one of us has for self-fulfillment through spontaneity, creativity, and personal growth.

THE SELF-ACTUALIZATION THEORY OF ABRAHAM H. MASLOW (1908–1970) The psychologist who named humanistic psychology the "third force," Maslow's greatest contribution to the field was probably his preoccupation with healthy people rather than sick ones. Focusing on joy, enthusiasm, love, and well-being rather than on conflict, shame, hostility, and unhappiness, Maslow studied creative people who were functioning at a high level in society. From these studies he drew conclusions about healthy personality development.

Maslow's theory of human motivation rests on what he saw as a *hierarchy of needs*. These needs are of two basic kinds: *D-needs* (to correct *deficiencies*) and *B-needs* (to achieve a higher level of *being*). He felt that we human beings have to meet certain basic needs of survival first, before we can even think about needs on the next higher level. Not until we are satisfied in our most basic needs can we strive to fulfill those higher-order needs that provide the most intense kinds of spiritual and psychic gratification.

Thus, a person gasping for air or suffering from starvation has one overriding motivation—basic survival. When that is assured, he can turn his attention to concerns of safety—freedom, say, from fear and pain. Feeling relatively safe, he then seeks intimacy in his relationships with family, friends, and lover. Once comfortably nurtured by affectionate ties with other people, he can then turn his attention to meeting his basic need for self-respect. Not, then, until an individual feels healthy, safe, loved, and competent can she or he seek the self-actualization that comes from the pursuit of knowledge, the appreciation of beauty, playfulness, self-sufficiency, insight into the truth, or any of the other fifteen principal B-values.

What kind of person does achieve this kind of self-actualization? Maslow (1950) identified thirty-eight persons who he thought had fully realized their potential. This select group included such historical giants as Albert Einstein, Ludwig von Beethoven, Abraham Lincoln, and Eleanor Roosevelt, along with lesser-known people whom Maslow knew personally. After closely studying these people's lives, Maslow identified sixteen characteristics that distinguished these self-actualizers from the average person: a realistic viewpoint toward life; acceptance of themselves, other people, and the world around them; spontaneity; a focus on solving problems rather than thinking about themselves; a need for privacy and a certain degree of detachment; independence and an ability to function on their own; an unstereotyped appreciation of people, things, and ideas; a history of peak experiences which are profoundly spiritual experiences that may be mystical or religious in nature and that often occur when a B-value is actualized, at the point at which a person gains insight into some truth; identification with the human race; deeply loving and intimate relationships with a few people; democratic values; the ability to separate means from ends; a sense of humor that is lively and not cruel; creativity; lack of conformity; and demonstrated ability to rise above the environment rather than merely adjust to it.

While Maslow's theory has been inspirational to many people and has introduced a welcome focus on the healthy personality capable of scaling the heights of self-fulfillment, he has been criticized for a lack of scientific rigorousness, especially in the subjectivity of his criteria for self-actualization. (This is not surprising since he protested an overreliance on science and described the detached, highly objective, proof-oriented scientist as an example of a closed-minded person who resists anything resembling a peak experience.)

THE PERSON-CENTERED THEORY OF CARL ROGERS (1902–PRESENT) One of the most influential contemporary theorists, Carl Rogers has a life-affirming view of human beings as powerful architects of themselves. From his background of studies in agriculture, theology, and clinical psychology, and from his experience as a therapist, Rogers has evolved a view of personality centered around the concept of the *self,* that element that is the core of personality. We all need to find out what our real self is, to become that person, and to accept and value ourselves for the person we are.

While Rogers came to his beliefs through his work with troubled people in therapy, he has an essentially optimistic view of the strength of the human psyche. He acknowledges an unconscious, which guides much of our behavior, but, unlike the psychoanalysts, he sees unconscious processes as *positive* motivators for behavior.

Self-knowledge and self-regard come about, says Rogers, through our early experiences in which we gain mastery over the environment; through the high regard of others shown by their expressions of affection, admiration, and acceptance; and through the *congruence,* or agreement, between the experiences we continue to have throughout life and the way

Carl Rogers. (Doug Land)

There is a natural tendency toward a more complex and complete development. The term that has most often been used for this is the "actualizing tendency," and it is present in all living organisms. Whether we are speaking of an earthworm or a beautiful bird, of an ape or a person, we will do well, I believe, to recognize that life is an active process, not a passive one. Whether the stimulus arises from within or without, whether the environment is favorable or unfavorable, the behaviors of an organism can be counted on to be in the direction of maintaining, enhancing, and reproducing itself. The actualizing tendency can be thwarted or warped, but it cannot be destroyed without destroying the organism. (Rogers, 1980, p. 118)

we view ourselves. Another aspect of congruence is the agreement between the person we would like to be and the person we see ourself as. The closer these two concepts are, the happier we are with the self.

The congruent person functions at the highest level. Open to experience and not defensive, such a person views people and things accurately, gets along well with others, and has a high level of self-esteem. The goal of this healthy personality is growth to self-actualization.

A person who has an *incongruent* view of the self becomes tense and anxious and may resort to defense mechanisms or even retreat into psychotic fantasy to preserve his or her view of the self. What causes such an incongruent view? Sometimes it comes about because a person is torn between what she thinks and what she believes other people think she should think or do. For example, a woman with a strong sex drive wants to think of herself as a good person. If she has been taught that sex is evil, she may repress her sexuality, even in marriage, so she will not think of herself as a bad woman. Rogers' person-centered approach aims to bring about congruence through a nurturing, nondirective method that will be discussed in Chapter 16.

Like Maslow, Rogers has done much to promote a positive view of humankind. He sees the brighter face of our personality rather than the darker side stressed by the Freudians, and he sees us as controlling ourselves rather than being buffeted by outside forces as the behaviorists do. His person-centered approach to therapy has been influential, and he has tried to stimulate research on his theories. Since many of his terms and concepts are vague and hard to define operationally, however, it has been difficult to design research projects to study them.

Type and Trait Theories

The fourth broad category of personality theories we'll talk about consists of several explanations for personality that resemble psychoanalytic and humanistic points of view in their focus on *internal* influences on personality, as opposed to the *external* factors emphasized by environmentalists. According to these viewpoints, personality is consistent from situation to situation not because of an emotional outlook colored by early experience, nor because of ancestral memories, nor because of universal needs. Rather, these explanations focus on specific attributes peculiar to the individual, in some cases physical and in others psychological.

Some of these approaches, like Sheldon's, which follows, are *type theories* that divide people into distinct categories and neatly classify them as being of one type or another. Jung's introverts and extroverts are types, as are Sheldon's endomorphs, mesomorphs, and ectomorphs. *Trait* theories look at people not so much in terms of extremes of one type or another but as blends of many different characteristics that people have to a greater or lesser extent.

THE CONSTITUTIONAL PSYCHOLOGY OF WILLIAM H. SHELDON (1898–1977)
Some 400 years ago, Shakespeare had Julius Caesar say,

> Let me have men about me that are fat;
> Sleek-headed men, and such as sleep o' nights
> Yond Cassius has a lean and hungry look;
> He thinks too much: such men are dangerous. (Act I, scene ii) (1959)

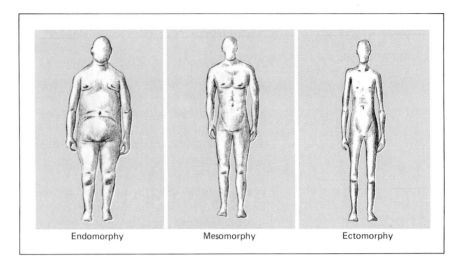

Endomorphy   Mesomorphy   Ectomorphy

FIGURE 14-1 *The three body types described by Sheldon.*

These comments fit into a long tradition of judging people's personalities based on the way they look. This tradition achieved scientific respectability in some quarters well into the twentieth century, with the theories of William H. Sheldon, a medical doctor and Ph.D. who believed that there was a strong relationship between people's body types, or somatotypes, and their personalities.

Sheldon described three types of physical physique: the *endomorph*, who is overweight, with poorly developed bones and muscles; the *mesomorph*, muscular, strong, and athletic; and the thin, fragile *ectomorph* (see Figure 14-1). He then came up with three clusters of personality traits: *viscerotonia* (comfort-loving, food-oriented, sociable, relaxed); *somatotonia* (aggressive, adventure-loving, risk-taking); and *cerebrotonia* (restrained, self-conscious, introverted). When Sheldon rated men according to where they stood with regard to both body types and personality traits, he found high correlations. Extremely endomorphic men were likely to be viscerotonic, mesomorphs tended to be somatotonic, and ectomorphs were cerebrotonic.

Since Sheldon did many of the ratings of both physique and personality himself, his results may well have been colored by his own bias. When other researchers have followed up on his findings, they have generally found lower correlations between physique and personality. There does seem to be somewhat of a relationship between physique and personality type, confirming popular beliefs, but this relationship is much slimmer than Sheldon's data show (Hall & Lindzey, 1978).

Furthermore, correlation does not mean causation. We cannot conclude that being muscular makes a person aggressive any more than we can say that being introverted makes a person thin. It seems a truism, of course, to conclude that loving food makes a person overweight, but even this may not always be true. In many cases, it's likely that people with particular traits learn to act a certain way because other people expect them to. Some overweight people, for example, think that they are supposed to be jolly, and so they live up to other people's expectations.

THE PSYCHOLOGY OF THE INDIVIDUAL OF GORDON W. ALLPORT (1897–1967) Concerned with the uniqueness of each individual rather than with the personality of the "average" person, Allport sought ways to identify those specific traits that would account for each person's characteristic ways of behavior.

Allport maintained that each of us has a personal disposition made up of cardinal, central, and secondary traits (1937; 1961). A cardinal trait is so dominant that it colors virtually every aspect of a person's behavior and attributes. One example might be the character played by Jack Lemmon in the film *Tribute*. The hero of this movie was *always* funny. He made jokes in every conceivable situation—when his marriage was breaking up, when his young son was trying to be intimate with him, when he was facing his own imminent death from cancer. For this man, humorousness was clearly a cardinal trait. Among historical figures, we think of the amorousness of Casanova and the power plotting of Prince Machiavelli. Few people have one overriding trait, such as these, which characterizes their whole personality.

Central traits are the handful of characteristic tendencies that we would ordinarily use to describe a person, such as those few phrases used at the beginning of this chapter which draw quick personality sketches of Jamie, Bob, and Sandy. According to Allport, we need to know only five to ten central traits to know a personality fairly well. Then there are secondary traits, which we display from time to time but which are not strong enough to be regarded as integral parts of our personality because they appear in only a relatively small range of situations. To Allport, personality is the dynamic organization of a person's traits, which determines how he or she will act. He distinguished personality from *character*, which he considered an ethical concept, a judgment of a person's personality, and from temperament, which he summed up as those biological aspects of functioning that show little change with development. (See the discussion of apparently inborn temperamental traits in Chapter 11.)

Allport was not interested in looking at large groups of people and identifying general principles of behavior (the *nomothetic,* or *dimensional,* approach to studying personality) but rather in determining what makes one individual "tick" (the *idiographic,* or *morphogenic,* approach). This very emphasis makes it difficult to study personality by his theory since every researcher would have to study every individual separately.

Allport was more interested in what people are like than in how they got that way. He was as uninterested in delving into their past for repressed unconscious motivation as in looking at the culture to come up with environmental influences on personality. He wanted to *describe* personality more than he wanted to *explain* it. In his effort to do this, Allport and a colleague, H. S. Odbert (1936), analyzed about 18,000 terms found in a dictionary to determine which ones represented true personality traits, which ones represented temporary states, and which ones were judgmental terms. They finally came up with a total of 4541 psychological traits.

Allport's influence led to a heightened interest in studying individual cases rather than large groups of people, in relating people's behavior to their underlying personality traits, and in the development of personality tests, which we'll discuss later in this chapter.

THE PERSON-SITUATION CONTROVERSY

Let's go back to our friends, Jamie, Bob, and Sandy, whom you met at the beginning of this chapter, in terms of a few of their personality traits. Now let's ask ourselves whether we can describe them in these ways consistently, or whether their behaviors vary across situations. Is Jamie almost always fun to be with, for example, or does she sink into long sieges of depression when her work isn't going well? Is Bob talkative and vivacious when he's with one or two people, while he keeps to himself at big parties? Is Sandy frugal when it comes to spending money on herself but a spendthrift when she buys presents for her family? In other words, how much of people's behavior retains an internal consistency, and how much responds to the particular situations they find themselves in (or maneuver themselves into)?

The person-situation controversy goes to the very heart of the distinction between theoretical viewpoints. Most people tend to think of personality as something that is fairly stable over time and across situations. This "common-sense" belief is in agreement with those psychoanalysts and type and trait theorists who see behavior as consistent because of certain characteristics within a person, while the other side is peopled by environmentalists, who maintain that situation-specific behavior is more typical. It's sometimes hard to judge consistency since we usually don't see people in a complete range of situations. If Jamie never calls her friends or makes excuses not to see them when she's feeling depressed, they'll have a limited view of her. Your point of view about Bob will vary depending on whether you usually see him in a small group or in a large crowd.

More than fifty years ago, Hugh Hartshorne and Mark May set out to study honesty in children. They set up a variety of circumstances giving children opportunities to lie, cheat, and steal. Contrary to common belief, they found that it was impossible to characterize some children as "honest," and others as "dishonest." Some would lie but not cheat, some would cheat but not steal, some would steal in one setting but not in another. Many factors seemed to influence the children's behavior, including the likelihood of their being caught. In any case, there was no way of predicting what any one child would do in any given situation.

Allport (1937) explained these findings by suggesting that the concept of an overall trait called "honesty," which includes lying, stealing, and cheating, may exist only in the head of the researcher and not in the mind of the child. Since the motivations for human behavior are so complex, it is almost impossible to lump different kinds of behavior to form one overall construct like this. This is also true, of course, for adults.

A person who cheats by letting someone else copy from his test paper is doing something of a different order from the one doing the copying. Yet both are participating in cheating. A woman who would never dream of lying to the Internal Revenue Service may lie to her husband about an extramarital affair. How could we give a single explanation for the desperate parent who steals a loaf of bread for a starving child, the kleptomaniac who feels compelled to steal items he cannot even use, the embezzler

BOX 14-1

PRIMARY POINTS OF CONTROVERSY IN MAJOR PERSONALITY THEORIES

- Is sex behind everything? Or are other drives—for power, achievement, recognition, and social standing—equally or at times more important?
- Are people controlled by "bad" primitive instincts that need to be repressed? Or are we "good" social creatures, the "noble savages" that the

French philosopher Rousseau described us as, unless harmful experiences interfere with our ability to express our noblest natures?

- Can the behaviorists' findings about the ways animals learn be applied to human beings to explain our personality development?

- Can we inherit the beliefs of our ancestors? Or are we born with no ancestral memory?
- Are we consistent in our behaviors? Or do we change according to the situation in which we find ourselves?
- Can we develop a theory of normal personality development by studying troubled people?

who finds she can amass money faster by stealing it than by earning it?

A recent questionnaire answered by readers of the magazine *Psychology Today* elicited similar findings, as shown in Table 14-1. You will be able to judge the significance of different situations if you ask yourself questions like the ones posed in this table.

While Stanford University psychologist Walter Mischel (1968; 1973) at one time took an extreme environmentalist position, feeling that the likelihood of reward or punishment in any given situation is more important in determining behavior than some internal trait within the individual, he has more recently (1977) modified this stance somewhat. For one thing, he has come to accept the point made by Kenneth Bowers (1973) that people often create the situations they find themselves in. Competitive people turn cooperative sessions into competitions, aggressive children create chaos as soon as they join a group, and certain people typically surround themselves with particular types of other people—such as the woman who always gets involved with a man who disappoints her or the employer who always hires incompetent workers. A man may justify his speeding, for example, by saying that his car rides so smoothly at high speeds that it's hard to keep it within the legal limit or that the highway he takes is so full of other fast-moving cars that he would feel foolish going any slower; yet this man *chose* both his car and his route. So what makes him a speeder—some risk-taking, aggressive, rebellious, or impatient characteristic within himself or the highly pressured situations he gets himself into?

Are person and situation so intertwined that trying to ascribe behavior to just one or the other is an exercise in futility? Daryl Bem and Andrea Allen (1974) think so, claiming that the more frequently used nomothetic research technique (which looks at large groups of people) cannot distinguish among individuals within the group. Some people in a group are likely to be quite consistent in a trait while others are not. When group

TABLE 14-1 Situational Ethics

The following responses indicate how 23,340 *Psychology Today* readers answered a variety of questions about moral behavior. The respondents tended to be female (69 percent); young (67 percent in twenties or thirties); well educated (only 12 percent had had no college experience); and relatively nonreligious (only 11 percent rated themselves as very religious). (From Hassett, 1981)

Would You:	Percent Who Said Yes or Probably	Percent Who Said It Is, or Probably Is, Unethical	Percent Who Would, or Probably Would, Be More Likely to Do It if Sure They Wouldn't Get Caught
Drive away after scratching a car without telling the owner?	44	89	52
Cover for a friend's secret affair?	41	66	33
Cheat on your spouse?	37	68	42
Keep $10 extra change at a local supermarket?	26	85	33
Knowingly buy a stolen color TV set?	22	87	31
Try to keep your neighborhood segregated?	13	81	8
Drive while drunk?	11	90	24
Accept praise for another's work?	4	96	8

norms are generated based on such a mixed group, the group average will make it seem as if the behavior is inconsistent. How, then, can we judge consistency?

One way is to ask people about themselves. Bem and Allen did this, with sixty-four male and female college students. The students filled out a questionnaire on friendliness and conscientiousness, indicating how consistent they considered themselves to be on these traits. The researchers bolstered these self-statements with their own observations and with statements from the students' parents and friends.

What did they find? That people who consider themselves consistently friendly or conscientious generally are seen as friendly or conscientious by other people, in a variety of situations. Those who saw themselves as variable on these traits did, in fact, show a low correlation between their self-reports on the questionnaire and the observations of other people. While these researchers were still looking at group correlations rather than consistency in individuals, the fact that they were studying small subgroups led them to discover greater consistency of behavior.

What, then, can we conclude about the person-situation controversy? That, as in so many other psychological issues, there does not seem to be one overriding, single explanation. In this case, it appears to be impossible to isolate the person from the situation. Behavior seems to arise from the interaction between a person's dominant personality characteristics and the particular dimensions of a specific situation.

TESTING PERSONALITY

As one Ph.D. candidate was thinking about a topic for her doctoral dissertation, a number of her friends were confiding in her about extramarital sexual relationships. She did a computer search of the social science literature and, although she found a number of articles pointing out the neuroticism and immaturity of people who engage in extramarital sex, she was not able to locate any studies that had used standard personality measures or standard measures of marital adjustment to compare women having affairs with monogamous women. Since she felt that this information would help marriage counselors to help couples dealing with this issue, she chose this topic and administered such tests to these two groups of women. Her findings: that the personalities of the two groups of women did not differ but that their marriages did (Oursler, 1980).

This, then, is one reason for developing personality tests—to come up with information that can help solve practical problems. Counselors use personality test information to advise people in making career decisions, in understanding their difficulties in getting along with other people, in making a wide range of decisions. The U.S. government has used personality tests to identify men who are too disturbed to serve in the armed forces. Employers sometimes require all job applicants to take personality tests to determine their emotional and temperamental suitability for the jobs they are applying for.

The other major purpose of personality testing is for basic research. By measuring different aspects of personality, researchers look for similarities and differences among individuals and among groups, they measure the effectiveness of various kinds of psychotherapy, they look for personality changes that occur throughout the life span, and they look for the relationship between personality and various kinds of behaviors.

How do we decide whether a particular personality test is a "good" measure? The same basic criteria of reliability and validity, which we discussed with regard to intelligence tests in Chapter 7, apply to personality tests. A test is reliable if it yields approximately the same results on retests, and it is valid if it measures what it is supposed to be measuring. We'll keep these criteria in mind as we look at some of the most common tests used to measure personality.

Types of Personality Tests

The type of personality test chosen in any particular situation usually reflects the test giver's own theory of personality, the purpose for which the test is being given, and the testing situation. Let's look at the differences in the most common objective and projective tests.

OBJECTIVE TESTS   Objective tests call for short replies, are usually answered in writing rather than through conversation, and consist of a standardized list of questions. While interpretation, being less subjective than for projective tests, does not call for the same level of skill and training from the examiner, it is still not cut-and-dried. These tests do come out better in terms of validity and reliability than do projective techniques.

The Minnesota Multiphasic Personality Inventory (MMPI)   During the 1930s, J. C. McKinley and Starke R. Hathaway, both from the University of Minnesota Medical School, wanted to find a way to bring some kind of standardization to psychiatric diagnosis. They collected more than 1000 potential questionnaire items, which they then posed to both mental patients and apparently healthy people. They then kept 550 items that clearly differentiated between the patients and the nonpatients. And the MMPI was born.

While the inventory is still used to look for evidence of emotional disturbance, it is also in wide usage as a general measure of personality traits. This test has generated so much research that by 1976, some 3500 references on the MMPI were in the literature (Anastasi). The test required considerable skill to interpret since the *patterns* of the answers are significant rather than the answer to any one question.

The answers are characterized in two ways—on four scales that check the overall validity of the test-taker's answers and on ten clinical scales that demonstrate specific traits. For sample items on some of these measures, see Table 14-2.

Despite its popularity, the MMPI is not without its critics. Some of the charges against it are: Since it was validated in the 1950s, it may not be valid for test takers of today; the original standardization sample was too small to begin with; and the test-retest reliability hovers around zero (Samuel, 1981). A major problem is that the test is often used outside of the clinical setting for which it was developed.

Cattell's Sixteen Personality Factor Questionnaire (16PF)   After rating several hundred adults on a large number of personality traits, Raymond Cattell (1965; 1973) came up with a basic list of sixteen *source traits*, using the statistical procedure known as *factor analysis*. Factor analysis provides a way to group highly correlated items together; a group of such items is then called a *factor*. Cattell feels that three of his basic sixteen factors are the most important in describing personality: how outgoing or reserved a person is, how stable or emotional, and how intelligent. Critics charge that Cattell was arbitrary in extracting and naming his source factors and that the scales are not valid predictors of behavior; however, Cattell is constantly refining the technique, and the test is well regarded in some quarters (Samuel, 1981).

PROJECTIVE TESTS   These relatively unstructured tests try to discover what and how a person is thinking, on both conscious and unconscious levels. They present ambiguous material in either words or pictures and ask questions that call for openended answers. The way the test taker interprets the material and then formulates his or her answer provides important clues to personality. The material in a projective test has been described as "a sort of screen" on which the test taker "'projects' his characteristic thought processes, needs, anxieties, and conflicts" (Anastasi, 1976, p. 559). These tests are used more often for people in therapy than for basic research or in nontherapeutic counseling situations such as academic or vocational counseling. The Rorschach and the TAT are the most frequently used projective tests.

TABLE 14-2 Some of the Validity and Clinical Scales of the MMPI and Paraphrases of Some Items from Each Kind of Scale. (Adapted from Samuel, 1981, p. 165)

Scale Name	Sample Item and Example of Response (These items are usually not answered in these ways by normal people.)	Characteristics of High Scores on This Scale
VALIDITY SCALES		
Lie	Once in a while I poke fun at others' mistakes. (False)	Denial of common personal faults; defensiveness.
Cannot say	Many blanks or "cannot say's"	Evasiveness or uncoop-erativeness.
Frequency	My nose often swells up so it is larger than normal size. (True)	Eccentricity or carelessness.
CLINICAL SCALES		
Hypochondriasis	I feel "butterflies" in my stomach several times a day or oftener. (True)	Overconcern about health; exaggeration of real or imagined physical ailments.
Depression	I have had several days in a row where I could not get over feeling "blue." (True)	Feelings of hopelessness and worthlessness.
Hysteria	I frequently notice trembling or shaking in various limbs of my body. (True)	Complaints of physical ailments when under stress; overenthusiasm suggestive of immaturity.
Paranoia	It is hard for me to think of anyone I could call an enemy. (False)	Defensiveness, suspiciousness, and jealousy.
Psychasthenia	I always wipe my feet two or three times before entering a building, even if there is no doormat. (True)	Obsessive-compulsiveness; excessive introspection that dwells on fears and self-doubts.

The Rorschach What do you see in the inkblot shown in Figure 14-2? This inkblot is similar to those used in the test developed in 1921 by the Swiss psychiatrist Hermann Rorschach. (The inkblot designs actually used in the test are never published anywhere else.) If you were actually taking this test, you would be shown some or all of ten standardized inkblot cards and asked to tell what you saw in each one. The examiner would keep a record of your answers, including any comments you might volunteer, any gestures you might make, and any emotional expressions you would show. You would then be questioned closely about your answers, to get you to clarify and elaborate upon them.

Your answers would then be analyzed and scored on several dimensions: *location* (What part of the blot did you talk about—the entire blot or part of it, and which parts?); *determinants* (Did you talk about color, form,

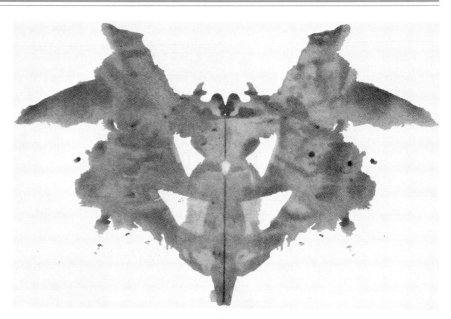

FIGURE 14-2 *This inkblot is similar to one used in The Rorschach, a projective personality test. (Hans Huber Publishers)*

or movement in the blot?); *content* (What did you see—animal or human forms or some other type of object?); and *popularity* (Is your response similar to those of many other people or is it novel?).

There are a number of questions about the reliability and validity of the Rorschach test. The number of responses a test taker makes is related to his or her age and levels of intellect and education, which should not, of course, be influencing a pure measure of personality (Anastasi, 1976). Then there are the effects of experience: You're more likely to see boots in the blots if you've just been hiking in the woods, whereas you're more apt to see an airplane if you live near an airport (Sundberg, 1977).

The Rorschach is widely used. Its most useful application may be as a direct measure of an individual's cognitive style or ways of organizing what she or he perceives or as a structured interview in the hands of a skilled clinician (Goldfried, Stricker, & Weiner, 1971).

Thematic Apperception Test (TAT)   Now, look at the picture in Figure 14-3 and make up a story describing what the people shown are thinking and doing, what went on beforehand, and what will happen next. If you were actually taking the TAT, this might be one of a series of cards you would be shown. Your stories would be analyzed according to which of the people you identify with, what personality characteristics and basic needs you ascribe to them, what environmental pressures you see as significant, the overall plot line of the story, and the story's eventual outcome.

The TAT has been modified for several special purposes—for children, vocational counselees, and participants in attitude surveys. One picture of four adults of different ages was specially drawn for a study looking at the way middle-aged adults perceived their age and sex roles in the family (Neugarten & Gutmann, 1958). The differences between the ways 40- to 54-year-olds saw the people in the cards and the ways people from 55 to 70 years old saw them enabled the researchers to draw some conclusions about personality changes in the years from 40 to 70. For example, the

FIGURE 14-3 *A sample item from Murray's Thematic Apperception Test (TAT). (Reprinted by permission of the publishers from Henry A. Murray,* Thematic Apperception Test, *Cambridge, Mass.: Harvard University Press. Copyright 1943 by the President and Fellows of Harvard College. © 1971 by Henry A. Murray.)*

younger group saw the older man in the picture as the authority figure, while the older group saw the older woman in that way. The researchers, Bernice L. Neugarten and David L. Gutmann, concluded that as women age, they become more tolerant of their own aggressive impulses, while men become more tolerant of their own nurturant impulses.

While considerable standardization has been done on this test, with published norms for all aspects of the ways people respond to each card, research has shown that responses are influenced by such states as fatigue, hunger, and emotional condition (Anastasi, 1976). Again, the impact of these temporary conditions interferes with the interpretation of more enduring personality characteristics. In order to put the stories in proper perspective, the examiner needs to know something about the test taker's life outside the testing situation. Age, for example, would be significant in terms of assessing the character a person identifies with. Other clues in the story might reflect events or circumstances of special significance to the test taker.

The Rorschach and the TAT share with other projective tests, such as sentence completion and word association tests, certain problems in interpretation. Because answers are so open-ended, interpretation relies to a great extent on the examiner's subjective assessment. It is, as a result, difficult to come up with good indexes of reliability among different scorers and between one test session and another. It is also difficult to assess validity.

On the positive side, these tests have several advantages. Because they are interesting, they often serve as a good way for an examiner or a therapist to establish good rapport with a client. Since the "right" answer is less obvious than in objective tests, they are harder to fake. And they seem to help therapists expand their knowledge of the client.

INTERVIEW TECHNIQUES Talking to people is, of course, a time-honored way of finding out about them. When we ask them questions, we not only get the basic reply but can also get clarification or expansion of their answers. Furthermore, we can see how a person behaves as he or she is talking to us. Does she seem comfortable and self-assured, answering our questions directly and easily, or does she avoid looking us in the eye, hesitate for a long time before answering, and change her answers frequently? What does he look like? Does he seem to pay reasonable attention to his grooming, is he dressed appropriately, is he clean?

Interviews vary along a number of dimensions, one of which is the degree of standardization. There is the highly *structured* interview, in which the interviewer has drawn up a particular set of questions, which she or he poses to every person interviewed. The *unstructured* interview, on the other hand, takes form as it progresses, differing in each case. With this procedure, the interviewer is not confined to a particular set of predetermined questions but can follow the interviewee along paths that she or he opens up, to explore any issues that arise, including some the interviewer may never have thought of. Virtually all therapists use some form of interview to find out about their clients, as we shall see in our discussion of therapeutic procedures in Chapter 16.

The Ethics of Personality Testing

"The Fourth Amendment was designed to protect our people from unreasonable search and seizure. Yet today our Government is engaged in a much more insidious form of search than going into someone's home or through personal papers. We are now searching their minds, trying to pry out the most hidden and intimate thoughts," said U.S. Congressman Cornelius E. Gallagher during the course of hearings on the use of personality tests by federal agencies (*American Psychologist*, 1965). The committee conducting the hearings maintained that it was none of the government's business how people feel about their parents, what their sex life is like, or what their religious beliefs are. Questions on all these topics appear in many personality tests.

When we realize how much confidential information about people can be learned through both projective and objective testing, we realize why this is such a sensitive area. Should these questions be asked at all in employment, academic, and other situations in daily life? Or does this constitute an invasion of privacy? When they are asked, who should ask them? And how should the results be handled? These are all difficult questions.

One danger in personality tests is the possibility of their falling into the wrong hands, being administered and interpreted by unqualified people, and thereby subjecting the test taker to biased treatment. Another is the possibility that the test *results* may fall into the wrong hands.

We also need to be aware of a different sort of ethical issue. Since different racial groups show different kinds of personality profiles on the MMPI, with blacks appearing to show more emotional disturbance than whites, we need to look closely at what the tests are really measuring. Since these tests were standardized and validated only with white populations, the differences in the scores of nonwhite test takers may have more to do with cultural differences than with emotional ones (Cross, Barclay, & Burger, 1978; Gynther, 1972). If so, black test takers might be unfairly denied entry into military service, employment, and other opportunities that depend on test results.

The entire issue of emotional health is, of course, extremely complex. How do we decide when a person crosses the line between health and illness? Who decides? How do we define various states and degrees of health or illness? And how can disturbed people best be helped? We will be grappling with these questions in the following two chapters.

SUMMARY

1 *Personality* is the constellation of relatively consistent ways of dealing with people and situations that makes each person unique.

2 According to the *psychoanalytic theory* of *Sigmund Freud*, people are in constant conflict between their biological urges and the need to tame them. In Freud's view there are three different parts to the personality: the *id*, the *ego*, and the *superego*. The id, which operates on the *pleasure principle*, wants immediate gratification of instinctual needs. The ego, which operates on the *reality principle*, tries to find acceptable ways to gratify the id. The superego represents parental and societal values.

3 According to Freud, individuals develop *defense mechanisms* to combat anxiety. These work unconsciously and distort reality. Among them are *displacement*, *sublimation*, *repression*, *regression*, *projection*, *reaction formation*, and *rationalization*.

4 *Psychosexual development* refers to a shift in areas of gratification, known as *erogenous zones*. According to Freud, there are five stages of psychosexual development. Failure to be appropriately gratified at a particular stage can result in *fixation* at that stage. This is reflected in a person's personality traits.

5 From birth to 12–18 months, the infant is in the *oral stage*, in which the erogenous zone is the area around the mouth. Feeding is particularly important in determining the successful (or unsuccessful) resolution of this stage. From 12 to 18 months until about 3 years, the toddler is in the *anal stage*, the erogenous zone is the anal region, and toilet training is important. During the *phallic stage* (from 3 to about 6), when the erogenous zone shifts to the phallic area, the young boy must resolve the Oedipus complex and the young girl the Electra complex. Identification with the same-sex parent is the upshot of this resolution. Between about 6 years and puberty the child is in a calm period called *latency*. From puberty on, the individual is in the *genital stage*.

6 Freud's theory is controversial. Probably his most important contribution is his emphasis on the role of the *unconscious* in motivating behavior. His emphasis on the *sexual drive* as being the primary motivating force for behavior throughout life, even in infancy, is the most controversial aspect of his theory.

7 *Carl Jung*, who broke away from Freud because of Freud's emphasis on sexuality, believed in the racial, or historical, aspects of personality. *Alfred Adler* also broke from Freud because of differences

with Freud over the role of sexuality in motivating behavior. According to Adler people struggle with the need to overcome inferiority. *Karen Horney* attributed neuroses to a child's difficulty in dealing with a potentially hostile world. *Erik Erikson* is particularly concerned with the effects of cultural and societal factors on personality development. He sees *psychosocial development* as a lifelong process that occurs in a series of eight stages. In each stage the individual has to resolve a particular crisis.

8   *Environmental approaches* include *Skinner's radical behaviorism* and *Bandura's social learning theory*. According to Skinner, we learn behaviors on the basis of reward and punishment. Bandura feels that we learn by observing and imitating *models*. If we get rewarded for imitating behaviors, we are likely to repeat them.

9   *Humanistic theories* of personality emphasize the subjective, unique experiences of the individual and the potential each person has for self-fulfillment.

10 Humanist theorist *Abraham Maslow* believed that individuals are motivated by a hierarchy of needs. Once an individual's basic needs are met, that individual can strive to fulfill the need for *self-actualization*.

11 Humanist theorist *Carl Rogers* believes that everyone needs to find out who his or her "real self" is, to become that person, and to find acceptance for the person he or she is. To function at the highest level, we need agreement (congruence) between the person we would like to be and the person we see ourselves as actually being.

12 *William H. Sheldon* believed that there is a strong relationship between *body type* and personality. He described three types of physique: *endomorphs, mesomorphs,* and *ectomorphs*. He found that extremely endomorphic men were likely to be *viscerotonic* (relaxed, lovers of food and comfort); mesomorphic men were likely to be *somatotonic* (aggressive and risk taking); and ectomorphs were likely to be *cerebrotonic* (introverted and restrained). His results, however, have been questioned on methodological grounds.

13 *Gordon Allport* believed that each person has a personal disposition made up of several types of *traits*. A *cardinal trait*, which few people have, is a dominant trait that colors virtually every aspect of a person's behavior and attributes. *Central traits* are the handful of characteristic tendencies that could be used to describe someone. *Secondary traits* are those displayed from time to time in a small number of situations.

14 The *person-situation controversy* revolves around the question of whether "personality" is consistent and stable over time and situations or whether people's behavior is more situation specific. Behavior seems to arise out of an interaction between a person's dominant personality characteristics and the particular situation he finds himself in.

15 Psychologists have devised different ways to assess personality. These include *objective tests* (such as the MMPI and the Cattell) and *projective tests* (such as the Rorschach and the TAT). In addition, *interviews*, which may be structured or unstructured, are often used. A number of important *ethical considerations* surround personality testing. These include using the tests inappropriately and having test results fall into the wrong hands.

SUGGESTED READINGS

Anastasi, A. (1982). *Psychological testing* (5th ed.). New York: Macmillan. A comprehensive textbook that covers the fundamental principles of psychological testing. It contains chapters on both personality and intelligence testing.

Bandura, A. (1977). *Social learning theory.* Englewood Cliffs, N.J.: Prentice-Hall. A brief statement of the principles of social learning, written by the leading spokesperson for this approach.

Freud, S. (1965). *The interpretation of dreams.* New York: Avon/Discus. First published in 1900, this book contains Freud's revolutionary and controversial analysis of the significance of dreams.

Hall, C. S., & Lindzey, G. (1978). *Theories of personality* (3d ed.). New York: Wiley. A comprehensive textbook that contains critical discussions of the major personality theorists as well as interesting information about their lives.

Rogers, C. R. (1980). *A way of being.* Boston: Houghton Mifflin. A recent statement by Rogers that describes his person-centered approach.

Skinner, B. F. (1972). *Beyond freedom and dignity.* New York: Bantam/Vintage. A controversial plan for a scientific program to alter man's behavior. This book is considered one of the most important in modern psychology.

Watson, J. B. (1970). *Behaviorism.* New York: Norton. Originally published in 1925, this is Watson's own statement of the principles and methods of behaviorism. He describes the behaviorists' view of emotions, instincts, and personality.

CHAPTER 15

ABNORMAL PSYCHOLOGY

SPOTLIGHT ON

How mental disorders have been explained variously as the result of a breach of morality, an illness, faulty learning, ineffective adaptation, or warped development.

The range of mental disorders suffered by some 55 million (or one in four) Americans.

The difficulty in diagnosing mental disorders and the controversy over the latest attempt: *The Diagnostic and Statistical Manual of Mental Disorders (DSM-III)*.

It is virtually impossible to pick up a newspaper without reading about people who are psychologically disturbed. A distraught father in Memphis, Tennessee, is shot by police after he himself has threatened to shoot four employees of a hospital where his son died of leukemia. An elderly "bag lady" in New York City froze to death because she insisted on living in a cardboard hut in subfreezing weather despite pleas from authorities to take the shelter they offered. We read of mass murderers, flamboyant suicides, child abusers, amoral criminals, drug addicts, power-mad dictators, the whole gamut of people whose disturbed behavior disturbs the public welfare.

Virtually all of us, moreover, have a more personal interest in abnormal psychology, the study of emotional disturbance and abnormal behavior. Who among us does not number among our own family members, our friends and neighbors, or our coworkers someone who displays eccentricities, who suffers from a depression that prevents him or her from working or studying, whose daily life is restricted by unrealistic fears, who drinks to such excess that his or her work or family life suffers, who cannot hold a job, or who shows some other sign of what is generally considered abnormal behavior? Who among us has not at some time behaved in a way that seemed odd even to ourselves?

Yet not every passing mood, unusual action, or quirk of personality assumes great significance. What, then, constitutes abnormal behavior? How do we explain it—as a breach of morality, an illness, faulty learning, ineffective adaptation, or warped development? What causes it? And what can be done about it? We will deal with these first two questions in this chapter and with the third one in the chapter to follow, which describes various types of therapies for psychological problems.

While this chapter is devoted to the study of psychological disorders, there is often no sharp break between what is "normal" and what "abnormal." So we'll be as explicit as we can in our definitions. All the disorders we'll discuss affect large numbers of people, even though they may represent only small percentages of the population at large. Like a pebble thrown into a pond, a troubled individual's problems ripple out to affect families and friends, the community that must arrange for care, and all of us who as taxpayers are called upon to support needed services. We become intensely aware of the truth in John Donne's poetic statement that "no man is an island entire of itself; every man is a piece of the Continent, a part of the main." Mental disorders affect us all.

WHAT IS ABNORMAL?

Shortly after midnight on Friday, June 16, 1978, Sylvia Frumkin decided to take a bath. Miss Frumkin, a heavy, ungainly young woman who lived in a two-story yellow brick building in Queens Village, New York, walked from her bedroom on the second floor to the bathroom next door and filled the tub with warm water. A few days earlier, she had had her hair cut and shaped in a bowl style, which she found especially becoming, and her spirits were high. She washed her brown hair with shampoo and also with red mouthwash. Some years earlier, she had tinted her hair red and had liked the way it looked. She had given up wearing her hair red only because she had found coloring it every six weeks too much of a bother. She imagined that the red mouthwash would somehow be absorbed into her scalp and make her hair red permanently. Miss Frumkin felt so cheerful about her new haircut that she suddenly thought she was Lori Lemaris, the mermaid whom Clark Kent had met in college and had fallen in love with in the old "Superman" comics. She blew bubbles into the water (Sheehan, 1982, p. 3).

It is immediately clear—not only to a psychiatrist but to any reasonably aware person—that the young woman here given the pseudonym of "Sylvia Frumkin" is acting and thinking in an extremely bizarre way, a way we would have no trouble at all designating as abnormal.

What is it in this woman's thinking and behavior, however, that is abnormal? Many normal, healthy people in our culture are heavy and ungainly, many wear their hair in unbecoming ways, many color their hair with ineffective products. Many daydream, fantasizing themselves as other persons. Sylvia Frumkin is not like these other people. She has been diagnosed as suffering from a *schizophrenic disorder*, which we'll define in this chapter.

For one thing, Sylvia Frumkin cannot distinguish reality from fantasy. She does not just imagine herself as "Lori Lemaris, the mermaid"; she is convinced that she *is* this fictional creature. For another thing, a person of Sylvia Frumkin's basic intelligence and position in society would be expected to know that mouthwash is not a hair dye and cannot be absorbed into the scalp. It is not ignorance or naiveté that makes her think this way but a disorder in the nature of her thinking.

This, then, is one element of abnormal behavior, the *inability to recognize reality*. People who "hear" voices, people who imagine that hordes of enemies are conspiring against them, people who fear injury at the hands of invaders from outer space are all out of touch with the real world. This lack of orientation to reality tends to make them act in strange ways, ways that may be destructive to themselves or to others.

Another element of abnormality in Sylvia Frumkin's behavior is its *statistical rarity*. Most people do not think the way she does, and most people do not act the way she does. During the thirteenth century, people who thought that the world was flat were mistaken, but they were not harboring an abnormal belief. Most people believed the earth was so constructed. Anyone thinking that now, however, would be in the distinct minority and would, therefore, be exhibiting an abnormal point of view, counter to the scientific facts that have been well established and widely taught in our society.

Being different from other people isn't always considered abnormal, of course. Albert Einstein, for example, exhibited thought processes that were unique, and yet he was honored for his difference, not institutionalized. So, to be considered abnormal, a person's unusual thoughts or behavior must also be considered *undesirable*. In this case they may be considered abnormal even if they are not rare, as, for example, in the case of clinical depression, a fairly common disorder.

Abnormality has other faces, too. Sylvia Frumkin does not perform productive work, does not have an intimate sexual relationship, has no friends, has great difficulty getting along with her parents and her sister, has trouble getting from one place to another, loses possessions constantly. She is *dysfunctional* in all these basic areas of life. Furthermore, Sylvia Frumkin is unhappy much of the time. While normal people are not always happy, of course, they are not subject to the severe bouts of depression, rage, fearfulness, or confusion that are often hallmarks of an abnormal condition. Since human beings are so variable, it is extremely difficult to come up with an all-encompassing definition of abnormality. The preceding points, however, cover the most important deviations from our society's model of a normal, psychologically healthy individual. This is someone who generally perceives reality fairly accurately, who behaves somewhat similarly to most other people in most situations, who does productive work either in the home or at a paid or volunteer job, who can handle the tasks of daily living, and whose moods remain on a fairly even keel as appropriate to life circumstances.

Not all people who deviate from this profile, of course, are severely disturbed. Some people may differ in just one respect. For example, a person may be unusually sad or fearful much of the time and yet still be able to hold a job, take care of a family, get along day by day. Or a person may have a temporary episode of strange behavior but then go back to leading a fairly normal life. Furthermore, the degree to which a person is affected at any one time may range from such a mild level that the person is on the borderline between normality and abnormality, to such severe impairment that the individual requires institutionalization and intensive treatment.

HOW COMMON IS ABNORMALITY?

The kind of behavior we talk about in this chapter is distressingly prevalent. According to a 1978 estimate by the President's Commission on Mental Health, one out of every four Americans, or more than 55 million people, suffer from some kind of psychological disturbance. About 7 million people a year receive treatment for mental health problems, but some 34 million are thought to need it.

Research has pointed to various societal factors as contributing to mental disturbance. These include poverty, discrimination based on race and sex, and stress (Ilfeld, 1978; Sroule, Langer, & Michael, 1962; Srole & Fischer, 1980; Schwab, Bell, Warheit, & Schwab, 1979). For example, a Chicago study (Ilfeld, 1978) found that women in upper- or upper-middle-class-status occupations are the only women whose psychological problems are not greater than those of men in comparable situations. And in their report of a Florida study, Schwab and his colleagues (1979) found that social factors (such as high rates of mobility and migration) and biological influences (such as a family history of mental illness and concurrent physical illness) seemed to contribute to the mental disorders of blacks more than their having had an unhappy or sickly childhood and concluded that this "points to the importance of [socioeconomic] and role factors for mental illness in the blacks" (p. 210).

MEASURING ABNORMALITY

In the studies just referred to, researchers used various measures to determine how "normal" people are. A major source of information came from interviews in which trained observers drew conclusions based on behavior and also asked subjects about the presence of various symptoms that are generally considered indicative of psychological difficulties (such as bouts of depression, certain physical ailments that have been linked to mental states—like stomach ulcers and migraine headaches—and drinking, eating, and sleeping habits). Sometimes during the course of the

[F]rom our findings comes a very practical implication for lowering women's symptomatology, namely, encouraging and enabling them to obtain jobs, especially of higher status. This implication in turn calls for new approaches to socializing girls and women for the job market, as well as for confronting the consequences of increased female employment on our child rearing practices. (Ilfeld, 1977, p. 3)

interview and sometimes by the administration of questionnaires, investigators asked questions designed to elicit attitudes (such as, ''Do you agree or disagree with this statement: 'I sometimes can't help wondering whether anything is worthwhile any more.'?''). The researchers then developed their indices of mental health based on the subjects' answers in the various categories and on their own observations.

Diagnosis of emotional disturbance is extremely difficult and a constant source of controversy among mental health professionals. In one well-known study, titled ''On Being Sane in Insane Places'' (1973), David Rosenhan got several colleagues to join him in faking a symptom, with the purpose of being admitted to mental hospitals. After saying they had been hearing voices over the past three weeks that said ''empty,'' ''hollow,'' and ''thud,'' the eight ''fakers'' were diagnosed as suffering from schizophrenia and admitted to twelve hospitals in five states. Immediately after admission the pseudopatients spoke no more about the voices and proceeded to act normally. Still, during the time they were in the hospital, anything they did—including taking notes—was considered to be a symptom of illness. While none of the hospital employees ever seemed to suspect that these people might not be disturbed after all, some of the *real* patients voiced their suspicions that the ''pseudos'' were journalists or investigators. After one to seven weeks of hospitalization, all the pseudopatients were discharged as ''schizophrenics in remission'' (temporarily symptom-free).

Rosenhan sees this study as evidence that psychiatrists cannot recognize mental health when they see it, since normal people were indeed admitted to mental hospitals and were then discharged not as healthy but as temporarily symptom-free ill people. Spitzer (1976), however, who has severely criticized the study's design, sees its findings as proof that diagnosis of mental illness is relatively accurate since the staff psychiatrists had no reason to think the pseudopatients were lying when they described their symptoms and because they were kept in the hospitals for a much shorter period than is usually the case. Spitzer also maintains that discharging them as ''in remission'' was correct inasmuch as it was a precaution warranted by the severity of their presenting symptoms.

What this study illuminates more than anything else is the great difficulty in deciding what is normal and who is not. What are the major dilemmas here? First, that it is difficult even for highly educated professionals to determine when someone is truly disturbed and when she or he is just pretending to be, a fact that is especially significant in our criminal justice system and in the military service. Secondly, that once someone has been labeled ''abnormal,'' other people (in this case, hospital staff) look at them in that way without stopping to question the diagnosis. And third, even though these ''patients'' were discharged more quickly than most real schizophrenics would have been and were recognized as being free of symptoms at discharge, they were still considered ill. Once having shown signs of abnormality, they were not considered to have recovered, even after they were seen to be behaving normally.

DSM-III

In an effort to make it easier to diagnose various mental disorders, the American Psychiatric Association drew up, in 1952, a guidebook called the *Diagnostic and Statistical Manual of Mental Disorders (DSM)*. The DSM has been revised twice. Its third edition, which appeared in 1980, is no less controversial than the first two. Even highly qualified mental health professionals disagree on the definitions of many disorders.

The goals of the framers of DSM seem clear enough—to help clinicians treat and manage patients, to make diagnostic categories as reliable as possible, to be relevant to clinicians of various theoretical persuasions, to reflect up-to-date research data, to bring some consistency to the use of diagnostic terms, and to eliminate terms that are no longer useful.

Normality and abnormality are not all-or-nothing propositions, of course. Most of us recognize that many people have idiosyncrasies that might be considered abnormal and yet they can still lead relatively normal lives, and even people who are so disturbed that they need to be institutionalized often have periods of acting quite normally. *DSM-III*'s position, therefore, that the state of having a mental disorder and the state of *not* having a disorder are not totally different conditions but, instead, are two different ends of a continuum, seems unassailable.

Then why has this document aroused such a storm of controversy in psychological and psychiatric circles? Partly because of the basic difficulty in diagnosing psychological problems. In the case of physical illness, we can often determine an abnormal condition by taking a temperature, measuring blood chemistry, seeing an obvious symptom like unusual bleeding. In the case of a criminal transgression, we can determine that a crime has been committed by such clear violations as stolen property or the inflicting of bodily harm. But with regard to psychological abnormality, personal opinions, attitudes, cultural norms, and moralistic standards enter in to muddy up the situation.

For example, one of the major controversial changes in *DSM-III* (from *DSM-II*, 1968) is the dropping of homosexuality as a mental disorder, unless the individual is unhappy about his or her sexual orientation and *wants* to become heterosexual. Some psychiatrists protest this definition, claiming that homosexuality is indeed a mental disorder, no matter how the individual feels. Another major controversy revolves around the elimination of the term "neuroses," because of *DSM-III*'s shift away from Freudian orientation, as well as its framers' conviction that there is no universally accepted definition of the term. (Since this word has become so widely used and is so familiar to many people, we will use "neuroses" in this book to describe those manifestations of abnormal behavior that are serious enough to interfere with daily life yet not so disabling as the psychoses described later in this chapter.)

Others criticize *DSM-III* for its medical explanations of abnormal behavior (see the discussion of the "medical model" in the next section). Many professionals reject the concept of considering *all* psychological disorders a form of mental illness, and some even reject the very concept of mental illness.

Despite all the objections to *DSM-III*, however, it is still the most comprehensive guide we have and the culmination (to date) of continuing efforts to define abnormal behavior as specifically as possible. The mental disorders classified therein are those that the American Psychiatric Association defines as a "clinically significant behavioral or psychological syndrome or pattern that occurs in an individual and that is typically associ-

TABLE 15-1   Major Categories of Disorders

Category	Examples
Disorders usually first evident in childhood or adolescence	Mental retardation, Tourette's syndrome, hyperactivity, anorexia nervosa
Organic mental disorders	Alzheimer's disease (senile dementia)
Substance-use disorders	Abuse of or dependence on such drugs as alcohol, barbiturates, amphetamines, PCP, LSD
Schizophrenic disorders	Disorganized, catatonic, paranoid, undifferentiated, and residual schizophrenia, all of which involve thought disturbances and/or hallucinations
Paranoid disorders	Differing severities of paranoia, which involves the delusion that one is being persecuted
Psychotic disorders not classified elsewhere	Brief reactive psychosis (psychotic symptoms lasting from a few hours to two weeks in response to a trauma)
Affective disorders	Disorders of mood such as depression and mania
Anxiety disorders	Phobias, panic disorders, obsessive-compulsive disorder, posttraumatic stress disorder
Somatoform disorders	Hypochondriasis, conversion disorder, psychogenic pain disorder, in all of which the person exhibits physical symptoms for which no physiological basis can be found
Dissociative disorders	Multiple personality, amnesia, fugue, all of which involve a sudden, temporary alteration in consciousness, identity, or motor behavior
Psychosexual disorders	Masochism, sadism, inhibited orgasm, premature ejaculation, gender identity disorders
Factitious disorders	Physical or psychological symptoms that are under the control of the individual, as determined by some outside observer (like the production of severe psychological symptoms that make the patient seem psychotic)
Disorders of impulse not classified elsewhere	Kleptomania (compulsive stealing), pyromania (fire setting), pathological gambling
Adjustment disorders	Impaired functioning in response to some stressful life event (divorce, illness, natural disaster) or a developmental stage (leaving the parental home, becoming a parent), which may include a depressed or anxious mood or inhibition with work
Psychological factors affecting physical condition	Tension headaches, asthma, ulcerative colitis, acne
Personality disorders	Paranoid, narcissistic, antisocial, passive-aggressive, schizoid
Conditions not attributable to a mental disorder that are a focus of attention or treatment	Malingering, problems in school or on the job, marital problems, parent-child problems

Source: From *DSM-III*, 1980.

ated with either a painful symptom (distress) or impairment in one or more important areas of functioning (disability)'' (p. 6). Implicit in this definition is the existence of some kind of behavioral, psychological, or biological dysfunction, as distinct from a social dysfunction, that is, a conflict between an individual and society (like juvenile delinquency). If a person's disturbance is only social, the APA considers it a social deviance rather than a mental disorder. For a listing of the major categories or disorders in *DSM-III*, see Table 15-1.

The manual organizes information along five different *axes*, or main organizational categories: three clusters summarizing ways to diagnose a specific disorder and two that provide additional information to be called upon to plan treatment and predict the outcome for a particular patient. For an illustration of the way therapists use these axes to help them in their diagnosis, see Box 15-1. The axes are organized as follows:

- Axis I   Clinical syndromes (such as organic mental disorders, affective disorders, schizophrenic disorders, etc.). Conditions that are a focus of attention or treatment but which are not attributable to a mental disorder (such as underachievement in school, isolated antisocial acts, and career uncertainty).
- Axis II   Personality disorders, in which specific personality traits interfere with social or occupational functioning or cause distress (such as dependent, paranoid, schizotypal, etc.).
- Axis III Specific developmental disorders (such as late speech or retarded arithmetical abilities). Physical disorders and conditions.
- Axis IV   Severity of psychosocial stressors (ranging from mild, like a change in work hours, to extreme, like a death in the family).
- Axis V   Highest level of adaptive functioning in the past year (with regard to social life, job, and use of leisure time).

WAYS OF LOOKING AT ABNORMAL BEHAVIOR

The woman dresses bizarrely, speaks incomprehensibly, behaves outlandishly, and frightens the neighbors who recognize her strangeness. She must be possessed by evil spirits, they believe. Thereby, to get rid of the evil, she must be put to death. At another time and another place, the same woman would be seen to be suffering from an unfathomable illness, which is best treated by one or more chemical substances whose manner of work is just as mysterious as the origins of her strange behavior. In still other circles, people believe that this woman learned to behave eccentrically as a response to her environment. Therefore, to help her adapt more normally, she must be taught the "right" responses.

The preceding interpretations of abnormal behavior see it as a moral lapse, a medical condition, or an example of learning the wrong things.

BOX 15-1

DIAGNOSIS OF PSYCHOLOGICAL DISTURBANCE USING THE DSM-III EVALUATION SCHEME

The director of psychological services at a major corporation has referred a long-term employee, a 62-year-old man who is slated for early retirement, to a psychiatrist because of the worker's depression, which has caused a high rate of absenteeism. While the psychologist knows that this worker used to be absent often because of a drinking problem, he thinks that the man is not drinking now and feels that there are other problems. The psychiatrist's diagnosis, based on the *DSM-III* axes, looks like this, as presented in *DSM-III* (1980), page 30:

- Axis I: Major depression, single episode, with melancholia Alcohol dependence, in remission
- Axis II: Dependent personality disorder (provisional, rule out borderline personality disorder)
- Axis III: Alcoholic cirrhosis of liver
- Axis IV: Psychosocial stressors: anticipated retirement and change in residence with loss of contact with friends Severity: Moderate
- Axis V: Highest level of adaptive functioning past year: Good

The view that mental illness was the result of sin and the devil set the stage for thousands of witchcraft trials, such as the 1692 trial of George Jacobs in Salem, Massachusetts, portrayed in this painting. (The Bettmann Archive, Inc.)

The way we explain abnormality influences the way we treat it and carries important ramifications for society at large, as well as the affected individuals. Therefore, it's important to understand the various *models*, or theories, that try to explain abnormal attitudes and behavior.

The Moral Model

During the Middle Ages, it was commonly thought that psychological disorders stem from a sinful rejection of divine wisdom. This point of view refuted much of the thinking of the previous two centuries and, in its tendencies to see abnormality in terms of sin and the devil, set the stage for the burning of thousands of people said to be witches and for the mistreatment of untold deranged persons in the name of a higher moral order.

While this thundering judgmentalism has largely disappeared, its traces remain in the words of mental patients themselves, who often speak of their conditions in moral terms, generally ascribing their problems to a lack of willpower or other personal inadequacies.

The Medical Model

By absolving the individual sufferer of blame for his or her condition, the explanation of abnormality as the result of some underlying illness represented a great stride forward in the treatment of mental patients.

The medical origins of some abnormal behavior are seen clearly in conditions in which a physical illness or event, such as a stroke or an accident, affects a person's personality and judgment as well as his or her physical functioning; in drug addiction; and in senile dementia, which presumes an organic deterioration of the brain. It is also assumed, as we'll see later in this chapter, as the result of findings of unusual chemical balances in the blood systems of people diagnosed with schizophrenic or depressive disorders.

When we speak of abnormal psychology in terms of "psychopathology" or "mental illness" as distinguished from "mental health," we are thinking in medical terms. An acceptance of this explanation leads to calling strange-acting people "sick," turning their care over to physicians, placing them in hospitals or treating them as "outpatients," and treating them with a wide variety of physical techniques (i.e., drugs, electric shock, sleep, vitamins, etc.). It tends to deemphasize both individual responsibility for behavior and social forces that may be contributing to the individual's problems.

A major criticism of *DSM-III* points to its reliance on the medical model to explain virtually all deviance. More than half of the more than 230 disorders listed in *DSM-III* are *not* attributable to organic causes, the origins of these problems are not necessarily under the person's skin, and looking at human behavior only in terms of illness limits our understanding and restricts our ability to help (Schacht & Nathan, 1977).

The Psychoanalytic Model

Lucy R., a young English governess, consulted Sigmund Freud because she had lost her sense of smell and yet was plagued by imaginary strong odors. She had also lost her appetite, her energy, and her ability to sleep normally. Freud diagnosed Lucy's problems as *hysteria*, a neurosis by which she had converted psychic energy into physical symptoms as a result of repression of some idea or feeling. During the course of treatment, Freud's initial diagnosis appeared to be confirmed by Lucy's admission that she was in love with her employer, a widower, but, embarrassed by those feelings, she was trying to put them out of her mind. As she expressed her repressed sexual longings, she became able to live with them, and her sense of smell returned to normal (Freeman & Strean, 1981).

According to Freud, whose theories explaining personality are presented in Chapter 14, abnormal behavior results from conflicts between the id and the superego, conflicts too great for the ego to handle. They can be aggravated by serious errors in child rearing committed by parents who either understimulate or overstimulate their children during the oral, anal, or phallic stages of early childhood. As a result of the child's own inborn needs and the parent's blunders, the child becomes fixated in one period or another and is unable to develop normally.

When psychoanalytic thought developed, at the beginning of the twentieth century, it, too, represented a major advance in thinking. "Unlike either the moral model or the organic-medical model, psychoanalysis did not place sole responsibility for abnormal behavior on either sin and weak will or diseased tissue; instead, it assigned the blame more broadly to family, friends, *and* physiology. The development was helpful because it forced behavioral scientists to broaden their search for the causes of psychopathology" (Nathan & Harris, 1980, p. 14).

On the other hand, by limiting its emphasis to the experiences of early childhood, psychoanalysts give short shrift to the possibility that some traumatic event in adulthood could trigger psychopathology. Furthermore, psychoanalysis's stress on early parenting may provide a ready target for blame, but this is not necessarily beneficial to the patient. "The advantage of a blame-free interpretation of behavior is that energy is not wasted on vendettas but can be spent on returning the mad person to normal" (Siegler & Osmond, 1974, p. 176).

The Behavioral Model

Psychologists who subscribe to the behavioral model do not draw upon unconscious id-superego conflict or physical illness to explain disorders. Instead, they believe that abnormal ways of thinking and acting are learned, largely through conditioning and modeling mechanisms. Thus, a little girl may have learned to protect herself against an abusive father, but when in adulthood she either avoids all men or seeks out abusive ones, her behavior is no longer *adaptive* (helping her to adapt to her environment) but is instead *maladaptive* (interfering with her adjustment). At this point, the learning theorists design a treatment that involves teaching new, adaptive ways of behaving.

While traditional learning theorists have been concerned with maladaptive *behaviors,* cognitive theorists have emphasized the way that maladaptive *thoughts* influence behavior. This orientation, spurred by the "cognitive revolution," suggests that how we think about events influences how we behave. A number of currently popular therapies emphasize changing these underlying thought patterns.

Other Models

With a subject as complex, as compelling, and as important for both individuals and society at large, it is not surprising that there should be so many different explanations for psychological disorder. Besides the models just described, a number of other viewpoints have their adherents.

SOCIAL CONSEQUENCE MODEL Thomas Szasz (1974), a psychiatrist (and thus medically trained), vigorously attacks the notion of considering psychological disorders as illnesses. Szasz is the most prominent proponent of the social consequence model, a viewpoint that holds that such disorders are problems of living, which arise out of difficulties in coping with society. Such difficulties—which include personal needs, opinions, social aspirations, and values that conflict with the needs of other individuals or of society—are not medical in origin. They stem instead from ethical conflicts, legal definitions, and cultural standards. Their consequences are social rather than medical. So instead of assuming the role of a patient, it's more appropriate for a person to take responsibility for his or her own actions, to do something about them, and to suffer the consequences when they are harmful to others. While Szasz's criticisms sometimes seem to oversimplify complicated situations and don't provide explanations for all abnormal behavior, they raise issues that are all too often ignored or taken for granted.

THE FAMILY, OR SYSTEMS, MODEL This viewpoint sees psychological difficulties as arising from an entire family setting rather than from an individual. The abnormal behavior that only one family member may show is not, by this way of thinking, confined to that person alone but is a symptom of psychopathology within the family. Practitioners of family therapy look at the family as a system, with its own patterns of functioning. The communications in a family that contains a disturbed individual are, according to this theory, specially constructed to create one disturbed person (called the "identified patient") so that the other family members can continue to function "normally." When the identified patient is helped,

As one of the most severe pressures people are subjected to, poverty can lead to or contribute to mental disturbance. Poor people suffer a disproportionately high degree of psychological disorders. (J. P. Laffont/Sygma)

the entire family may be thrown into turmoil and forced to develop new patterns of relating to each other (Bateson, Jackson, Haley, & Weakland, 1956; Herr & Weakland, 1979).

THE SOCIOCULTURAL MODEL   This way of thinking emphasizes society's role in causing disturbed behavior. As extreme examples, there are people who seem to flout every human tendency—a mother who roughly flings her baby to the ground and laughs when it is hurt, a husband who does not take his wife to the hospital but lets her die and buries her secretly so that he can make money by selling her medicine, an adult who'll snatch the food right out of a starving old man's mouth and then remorselessly leave him to die. Who are such people, whose behavior shouts out its abnormality? They're typical members of the Ik tribe, who live in the African mountains between Uganda, the Sudan, and Kenya (Turnbull, 1972). Their alienation from one another and from almost everything we have come to call "human" and "normal" demonstrates what living in a harsh environment, where food is murderously scarce and where survival depends on total selfishness, can do to an entire society.

Less severe pressures can also take their toll. Discrimination against women, blacks, the elderly, and homosexuals; poverty and its stresses; the strains of living in an overcrowded, high-pressured urban environment—all these factors are pointed to as causes of disturbed and disruptive behavior. This viewpoint gathers strength from surveys such as those cited earlier in this chapter which show that women, blacks, and the poor suffer more than their share of psychological disorders.

THE HUMANISTIC MODEL   According to the thinking of Carl Rogers (1970), Abraham Maslow (1970), and Rollo May (1969), abnormal behavior is the failure to achieve self-actualization. It is the result of a lack of growth, a fear of change, a culmination of poorly made choices in life. Like the behaviorists, the humanists pay little attention to what may have caused the abnormality, focusing instead on what can be done now. This perspective is optimistic since it assumes that the individual's own choices have done much to cause his troubles and that he can now make new choices that will change his life and resolve his psychological problems.

None of the models described here can, of course, serve as an umbrella explanation for all abnormality. In some instances, one basic approach may seem to hold the most reasonable explanation and implication for treatment, while in others a completely different perspective is more appropriate. The important things to realize are how little we actually do know about the causes of abnormal behavior, how much one disturbed person differs from another not only in the disturbance itself but in every other aspect of life capable of influencing the cause, the course and the treatment of the disturbance, and how vital it is to keep an open mind. With this understanding, it will be easier to consider some examples of the most common disorders affecting people in our society.

"NEUROTIC" DISORDERS

For months after the devastating automobile accident that left her two closest friends dead, 17-year-old Robin had nightmares about the crash, although during her waking hours she could not remember it. She could not concentrate on her schoolwork, she felt detached from her family and classmates, and she was plagued by guilt feelings because she had survived while her friends had not.

Laurie, a college senior, felt she was losing control of her life. She was overwhelmed with schoolwork and on academic probation for the first time ever. She had no friends, felt alienated from her family, and wanted a boyfriend desperately but was afraid to talk to men. She hated the way she looked, felt she never had any fun, had no energy or interest to pursue activities that might be enjoyable, and felt worthless and frightened. While this was the worst she ever felt, she couldn't remember a time since high school when she had been really happy.

Allan, a college sophomore, has to wake up two hours earlier than his roommate, even though both have the same schedule of morning classes. Allan's earlier wake-up time is required because of the elaborate rituals he goes through every single morning—brushing his teeth exactly 150 times, taking both a bath and a shower, changing his bedsheets, checking to be sure all his books are in alphabetical order, and so forth.

Many people experience mild degrees of the preceding conditions or others that are similar. Everyone who has experienced a trauma experiences some after-shock effects; most of us have been "in the doldrums" for some period of time; who among us has not double-checked something we were positive we had already done just a few minutes before (like turning on an alarm clock or engaging the emergency brake of a car)? Yet when feelings like these don't affect the way we function in day-to-day living over a period of time, we take them in our stride.

The people just described cannot do this because their functioning is severely impaired. They are suffering from conditions Sigmund Freud called neuroses, to describe mental disorders arising from anxiety, whose symptoms interfere with normal functioning but do not block it entirely. Conditions that used to be termed "neuroses" (until the 1980 publication of *DSM-III*) include phobias, obsessions and compulsions, some depressions, and amnesias. A neurosis does not represent a break from reality, and while it interferes with normal functioning, does not call for hospitalization.

Under the APA classification used in *DSM-III*, the term "neurosis" is no longer used. These disorders are now classified as *anxiety disorders, affective disorders, somatoform disorders,* and *dissociative disorders.* It's useful to look at some of these and other "neurotic" disorders before we go on to examine *psychoses,* those severe conditions that affect total functioning, involve a break from reality, and make it virtually impossible for the affected person to get along in the world without a major support like heavy medication or institutionalization.

Anxiety Disorders

In this group of disorders, anxiety is either the main symptom or it appears when people try to master their symptoms (confronting whatever they're phobic about or resisting a compulsion, for example). What do we mean by anxiety? It can be defined as a state of apprehension, fearful uncertainty, or dread caused by anticipated threat. It is often accompanied by such physical symptoms as shortness of breath, rapid heartbeat, sweating, and trembling. Anxiety disorders—phobic, obsessive-compulsive, panic, generalized anxiety, and posttraumatic stress disorders—are fairly common, affecting some 2 to 4 percent of the American population (*DSM-III,* 1980). Panic, phobic, and obsessive-compulsive disorders seem to run in families.

PHOBIC DISORDERS Agoraphobia, the most severe and most common phobia for which people seek treatment, generally shows up in an inability to go out of the house, be in large unfamiliar places (like theaters and department stores), drive, or travel by bus or train. The condition affects women about four times oftener than men and is experienced by about 0.5 percent of the population (*DSM-III,* 1980).

Two other phobias are social phobia, in which the individual is terrified of being in a situation where she or he can be scrutinized by others, and simple phobia, the most common phobia, in which a person has a persistent, irrational fear of some particular aspect of the environment. Such a person may be so afraid of animals that she won't visit a family that has a pet, so afraid of thunder and lightning that she goes down into the apartment house foyer during every thunderstorm (even in the middle of the night), so afraid of enclosed places that he won't ride in an elevator, or so afraid of heights that he won't go to his child's third-floor classroom on Open School Night.

OBSESSIVE-COMPULSIVE DISORDERS Allan, the fanatically fastidious college student, is plagued by obsessions (persistent ideas, thoughts, images, or impulses that seem senseless even to him and yet invade his consciousness against his will) and by compulsions (repetitive, irrational behaviors that he feels obliged to carry out even though he can't see any point to them himself).

The most common obsessions center around violence (fear of killing one's child); contamination (becoming infected by shaking hands or by eating from unclean utensils); and doubt (wondering over and over whether one has done something terrible, like hurting someone in a car accident). The most common compulsions drive someone to count (steps, actions, figures in wallpaper), to wash the hands or to touch (every piece of furniture in a room or every garment in a closet). Obsessive-compulsive adults almost always realize how senseless these thoughts and actions are, and they usually try to resist them. Resistance, however, causes so much anxiety that it's easier just to give into the symptoms, even when doing so may disrupt their lives to the point that they cannot go to school or hold a job (Spitzer, Skodol, Gibbin, & Williams, 1983).

So-called compulsive eating, sexual activity, gambling, or drinking are not true compulsions because the activities themselves can be pleasurable and the only reason a person drawn to them would want to resist them would be because of their consequences. So-called obsessive preoccupations with problems on the job, in an unrequited love affair, or in some other area are not true obsessions because no matter how much a person may brood about these things, the problems themselves are real and so the thoughts are meaningful, even if excessive.

POSTTRAUMATIC STRESS DISORDER   The kind of reaction Robin had to the car crash she had been in is neurotic only in its degree of severity. Virtually everyone who experiences a traumatic event feels some aftereffects. Only when these effects are more severe and long-lasting than usual is the individual considered to be suffering from posttraumatic stress disorder, a condition common among veterans of military combat and among survivors of rape, natural disasters, and such unnatural disasters as concentration camps and bombing attacks. When symptoms appear within six months of the trauma and last no longer than six months, the prognosis is more favorable than in cases when the symptoms emerge after a latency period of months or even years and when they last a longer time.

OTHER ANXIETY STATES   Panic disorders are characterized by recurrent attacks of terror of some nameless, formless doom. Sometimes these attacks occur unpredictably; at other times they develop a discernible pattern, coming up in connection with some particular activity (like driving a car or going into a dark room). The attacks are usually signaled by a rush of physical symptoms—dizziness, trouble breathing, choking, chest pain, sweating, faintness, and so forth. The person may suddenly be seized by a fear of dying, going crazy, or doing something uncontrolled. Women are more likely than men to experience these panic attacks, which usually last for several minutes but occasionally persist for hours.

Generalized anxiety disorder is a more diffuse kind of anxiety lasting at least a month, without the specific symptoms of any of the preceding anxiety disorders. Affected people usually cannot ascribe their discomfort to any particular situation or event. They just know they feel anxious, and they may exhibit such physical symptoms as shakiness, "the jitters," sweating, dry mouth, insomnia, distractibility, and a general state of uneasy anticipation.

Somatoform Disorders

You didn't hear it, you didn't see it,
You never heard it, not a word of it!
You won't say nothing to no one!
Never tell a soul
What you know is the truth.

After 10-year-old Tommy sees his mother's lover kill the boy's father, he is admonished by the preceding words. Going even further than his mother and eventual stepfather intended him to, Tommy dutifully becomes deaf, blind, and mute. The rest of the rock opera, *Tommy,* as sung by the group The Who, tells of the family's efforts to restore the boy's senses. The doctor who sees him reports,

The tests I gave him showed no sense at all.
His eyes react to light, the dials detect it.
He hears, but cannot answer to your call.

Neither gypsy (the "acid queen") nor faith healer can help the boy, who eventually regains his abilities only after his mother, in a violent outburst, smashes a mirror in front of him. (Townshend, 1969)

Tommy is a severe example of someone suffering from conversion hysteria, one of the somatoform disorders. These conditions, which derive their name from the Greek word "soma," meaning "body," are characterized by the display of physical symptoms for which no physical basis can be found. There is reason to believe that such symptoms, which are more common in wartime, arise from psychological needs.

Victims of conversion hysteria may become paralyzed, lose the senses of smell or pain, suffer seizures, or even experience false pregnancy. *DSM-III* offers two possible explanations for this condition. Tommy's case seems to fall into the first category, in which a person keeps an internal conflict or need out of awareness by losing the ability to perceive. An alternative reason for developing a severe symptom might be the "secondary gain" received through avoiding an activity. Thus, an opera singer who really hates to perform in public loses his voice and *cannot* go on. Or a woman whose husband wants a divorce becomes paralyzed and holds onto him through her need.

Dissociative Disorders

A shy, timid 22-year-old, who was given the pseudonym "Sybil" by the writer who told her story (Schreiber, 1975), first consulted a psychiatrist because there were periods in her life when she seemed to "black out" totally, forgetting what she had done for long stretches at a time. Soon after she entered into therapy, Sybil underwent a drastic personality change in the middle of a session, leading her psychiatrist to suspect that Sybil was a rare example of the dissociative disorder of multiple personality. In this condition, one person has more than one distinct personality, each of which comes to prominence at different times, totally submerging the other. The personalities are usually quite different from each other (as in the most famous multiple personality in literature, "Dr. Jekyll and Mr. Hyde") and may be unaware of the other self.

Sybil's case proved to be much more complicated even than her psychiatrist first suspected, however, as the course of therapy brought out a

After the hero of the rock opera Tommy *sees his mother's lover kill his father, the boy becomes deaf, blind, and mute. A mental health practitioner would probably diagnose him as suffering from conversion hysteria, one of the somatoform disorders. (© Columbia Pictures/Museum of Modern Art Film Stills Archive)*

total of sixteen separate personalities living at different times in Sybil's mind. These personalities were all very different from each other. They ranged in age from infancy to middle age; two were male; and they all had different talents, abilities, ways of speaking and moving, and different images of themselves.

Sybil's first additional personality had been born when as a 3-year-old she found this route to escape at least mentally from the horrendous tortures inflicted upon her by her cruel and disturbed mother. From that time on, Sybil would create new personalities whenever she had to deal with an unbearable situation in her life. Fortunately, Sybil's case had a happy ending. After more than eleven years of psychoanalysis, she was able to integrate all her personalities into one (the seventeenth) personality, which was, finally, a whole person capable of dealing with life.

Multiple personality, the disorder Sybil suffered from, is, fortunately, quite rare, as are the other dissociative disorders, psychogenic amnesia, psychogenic fugue, depersonalization disorder, and atypical dissociative disorder. In all these conditions, the individual experiences a sudden, temporary alteration in either consciousness, identity, or motor behavior.

A person with localized amnesia may forget events that occurred during a certain period of time, often for a few hours before or after a disturbing event, as Robin, the girl who had been in the automobile accident, forgot the events just before the crash. This kind of amnesia usually begins after an extremely stressful event and ends suddenly, without coming back. A more pervasive amnesia can cause a person to forget who she is, forcing her to assume a new identity. Or a person may feel that his reality is lost.

Causes of Neurotic Disorders

There are, of course, as many explanations for the causes of neurotic disorders as there are models, such as the ones described earlier in this chapter. The following specific theories that aim to explain the development of neuroses have grown out of the psychoanalytic, learning theory, and medical models.

Psychoanalysts consider neurosis as a four-element sequence along these lines:

1 An inner conflict between the drives of the id and the fears induced by the superego
2 The presence of sexual drives
3 The inability of the ego's logical, rational influence to help the person work through the conflict
4 The burrowing underground of powerful drives, which, not to be denied, seek expression through anxiety or other neurotic behaviors (Nathan & Harris, 1980)

Not all psychoanalysts, of course, subscribe to this four-stage explanation. As we pointed out in Chapter 14, several of Freud's followers broke with him over the key role he gave to sexual feelings. Alfred Adler, for example, maintained that neuroses ensue from feelings of inferiority (1929; 1930). These feelings have their roots in childhood when the child feels inadequate because of his small size and relative inability to help himself.

Learning theorists hold that neuroses come from learning the wrong behaviors (such as, for example, by a child's observing a phobic parent) and then from being reinforced for them (as in the case of a child who refuses to go to school who is rewarded for the stomach ache she gets every morning by being allowed to stay home from school with her mother). Some learning theorists take a fairly mechanistic view (Wolpe, 1969; 1978), feeling that thinking is just another kind of behavior governed by the same basic laws that direct our other behaviors. On the other hand, Bandura (1968; 1974) stresses the importance of the intervening influence of thought as essential in producing changes in human behavior.

Medical doctors often explain neuroses in terms of biochemistry. For example, new research has shown that barbiturates facilitate the transmission of an important inhibitor substance in the brain, which inhibits brain activity (Lancet, 1981). It's possible that antianxiety drugs stimulate the production or transmission of this substance, resulting in a reduction of arousal that lessens anxiety. If they do work this way, then it follows that anxiety may be due to the presence or absence of such brain chemicals.

AFFECTIVE DISORDERS: DEPRESSION AND MANIA

All of us have our good moods and our bad ones. Some of us are moodier than others, more prone to swings in that dominant emotional tone that colors our psychic lives. It's easy to understand the moods that seem related to the events in our lives—the euphoria when we fall in love or the depression when we are fired from a job. Most people also accept the notion of "waking up on the wrong side of the bed" or "waking up with a song in my heart" and think little about ordinary mood shifts. When these emotional states do not interfere with the way we lead our lives—or when such interference is confined to a brief period of time, most people can adapt quite well.

Sometimes, however, such moods are more severe. When they are either so good that a person seems to be flying, or so bad that his or her entire life looks bleak, and when moods like these persist over time to such a severe degree that they interfere with day-to-day functioning, that person is said to be suffering from one of the affective disorders, or disorders of mood.

John Custance was just such a person. He wrote that he had fallen in love "with the whole Universe" (1952). In a state of great well-being, his senses were keener than ever, allowing him to see, feel, and hear at high levels of intensity. He felt a mystic sense of communion with God, with all of humankind, with all people with whom he came in contact. Sexual activity had become a religious experience. He felt enormously powerful, as if all his wishes—even the most extravagant ones—were coming true and all his ambitions—even the most unrealistic ones—would be realized.

On the surface, this sounds like a state we would all like to be in. At the time John Custance was experiencing all these euphoric feelings, however, he was in an acute manic episode, which drove him into wild and irrational behavior. He insisted on giving away large sums of money that he could ill afford to prostitutes who accosted him on the street. He made a shambles of a church whose representatives had denied his request for money to help a particular young woman. Because of episodes like this, he landed in a psychiatric institution.

John Custance's illness had an even darker side—that of depression. From the heights of the grandiosity that characterized his manic periods, he would plunge into the depths of black moods in which he was overcome by an overpowering sense of a nameless dread, a sense of his own wickedness and worthlessness, and a terrifying succession of hallucinations that drove him to try to take his own life on three different occasions.

John Custance, whose accounts of his illness, written while he was in its throes, have made a major contribution to the psychiatric literature, was suffering from what is commonly known as *manic-depressive disorder*. It is categorized by *DSM-III* as bipolar disorder, one of the *major affective disorders*. Affective disorders take a number of different forms. They range in severity from a relatively mild mania (the elated phase of the disorder) or depression (the sad phase) to an extreme state of either mania or depression, or an alternating of the two extremes in mood swing. "Bipolar disorder" is the term given to the condition consisting of one or more manic episodes, which generally alternate with depressive episodes. Depression without mania, or unipolar disorder, may be classified as a chronic minor affective disorder, a chronic depressive disorder, or a major depressive disorder that is either psychotic or not, depending on the severity and other characteristics of the condition.

In some ways, depression and mania are but two faces of the same illness, with many characteristics in common. The course of either manifestation may be chronic, continuing over a span of years, with periods of normal functioning between episodes. Or a person may experience but a single episode. Episodes may occur singly, spaced years apart, or several may occur, one right after another and then not again for a long time. Either kind of affective episode often follows chronic physical illness, severe psychosocial stress, alcohol dependency, and less severe manic and depressive disorders. And both kinds tend to run in families, giving rise to the possibility that they may have a hereditary aspect to them. This possibility does, indeed, seem to be confirmed from recent research, which we'll look at in a little while.

In other ways, depression and mania do differ from each other, so that it makes sense to discuss them separately.

Depression

Cal, a successful advertising executive, has suddenly lost all interest in life. Nothing seems to matter anymore—not his job, his family, the tennis games he once enjoyed so much. Food no longer tastes good, and so Cal eats much less of it, losing 30 pounds over the course of a few weeks. He lies awake for hours and then falls asleep only to awaken abruptly after an hour or two, to lie awake again for hours before drifting off shortly before dawn.

Cal's difficulty in concentrating, his slower thinking, and his indecisiveness affect his work at the advertising agency, but even though his boss has expressed genuine concern, asking him what is wrong, Cal doesn't care about either his poor work performance, the opinion of his colleagues, or the danger of losing his job. Obsessed with thoughts of

Depression is the most common mental health problem in the United States today, with some 20 million Americans in need of treatment for this disabling condition. Unfortunately, only about one-quarter of all depressed people seek help. (© Arthur Tress 1981/Woodfin Camp & Assoc.)

suicide, his major preoccupation involves going over in his mind the various methods he might use to end his life. Cal is in the midst of a *major depressive episode.*

Laurie, however, the college senior whose plight was described earlier, is considered to be suffering from the fairly common chronic mild depression known as dysthmic disorder, and often referred to as *depressive personality.*

Depression is the most common mental health problem in the United States today, with some 20 million Americans in need of treatment for this disabling condition, although only 25 percent of these people seek help (U.S. Department of Health and Human Services, 1981a). The greatest danger of depression is suicide: About 15 percent of depressed people kill themselves, and the older they are, the more likely they are to take this drastic step. It's hard to know how many elderly people are depressed since symptoms of depression in the elderly are often misdiagnosed as organic brain syndrome. Women are twice as likely as men to become depressed, with some 18 to 23 percent of females and some 8 to 11 percent of males having had at least one major depressive episode. About 6 percent of women and 3 percent of men have been hospitalized for depression (*DSM-III*, 1980).

Major depressive episodes may begin at any age, even in infancy, and the symptoms of depression are somewhat different for people of different ages. Depressed children, for example, are likely to experience separation anxiety, to cling, refuse to go to school, and be afraid that their parents will die. Dysthmic depression usually begins early in adult life, although it may begin in childhood or adolescence, or in later adulthood, sometimes following a major depressive episode. The onset of a depressive episode is variable, developing sometimes over a period of days or weeks and at other times as a sudden reaction to severe stress.

WHAT IS DEPRESSION LIKE? Both Laurie's and Cal's symptoms are typical of their different levels of depression. They consist not only of the sad and despairing mood itself but of other kinds of behavior as well. Depressed people often experience some kind of change—sleeping or eating much more or less than usual, suddenly having trouble concentrating, suffering loss of energy or interest in previously enjoyed activities, losing all desire for sex or seeking it out constantly. In fact, sometimes these symptoms are present *without* the sadness, still leading to a diagnosis of depression. In major depressions with psychotic features, additional symptoms are often present. These may include delusions of persecution (in which the patient feels sinful, guilty, and deserving of punishment); somatic delusions (in which the person thinks that parts of his or her body are either missing or not functioning); auditory hallucinations (hearing voices); and disordered and confused thinking.

Depressions differ along several dimensions. As we have already noted, they can be unipolar or bipolar, and they can range in severity from a fairly mild interference with one's normal state to an extreme psychotic condition that calls for institutionalization. They can be *reactive*, or *exogenous*, by which we mean that they occur in response to some event in a person's life that would be upsetting to almost everyone—the death of a close relative, the loss of a job, or the end of a love affair. This kind of depression has a much better outlook for the future than does the *process*, or *endogenous*, type that descends upon someone for no apparent reason (Nathan & Harris, 1980). Not every bout of unhappiness, of course, should be termed "depression." Normal reactions to life stresses like the ones just mentioned usually include a period of sadness and grief. It is only when such a mood persists over a long time, interfering with ordinary functioning, that it is termed "depression."

CAUSES OF DEPRESSION In trying to locate the cause of depression, researchers have looked within the body, the psyche, the mind, and the environment. What have they discovered?

Genetic and Physiological Causes When psychiatrist Larry Pardue, who had suffered from depression as a college student and physician-in-training, began to suspect that an unusually large number of his relatives were depressed, he searched his family tree. After he came up with nineteen close relatives who showed signs of the condition, he published his findings, giving support to a theory that depression, or a tendency toward it, can be inherited (Pardue, 1975; Wingerson, 1982).

Other evidence for a hereditary basis comes from family studies. When identical twins, who have the same genetic inheritance, are more likely to be concordant for a trait (that is, to both show it) than are fraternal twins, who are no more alike than any two siblings, there seems to be a strong likelihood that the trait is at least partly hereditary. This is the case with affective disorders. Identical twins have a 70 percent rate of concordance, while the risk goes down to 15 percent for fraternal twins and other siblings, parents, and children, and only about 7 percent for grandchildren, nieces, and nephews (U.S. Department of Health and Human Services, 1981a). Since the concordance rate is not 100 percent, the disorder probably has an environmental component, as well.

Further support for the heritability of affective disorders comes from a recent report that one or more genes associated with depression have been located at a specific point on chromosome 6 (Weitkamp, Stancer, Persad, Flood, & Guttormsen, 1981). These genes are located near a cluster of genes that control the HLA system, a part of the body's immune system. Depression, then, may be related to a defect in the immune system of an affected individual.

A related physiological explanation for depression is a biochemical one, attributing the illness to a malfunction of neurotransmitters, certain chemicals in the brain that either stimulate or inhibit other cells. One group of neurotransmitters in particular, *serotonin, dopamine,* and *norepinephrine,* known as *biogenic amines,* have been implicated in the cause of both depression and mania. Too few of these amines sent through the brain may cause depression, while too many may produce a manic state (Wender & Klein, 1981). The research supporting this theory is in accord with findings that stimulating certain parts of the brains of animals and humans with electric current can cause a feeling of great pleasure, while removing the biogenic amines from the brain lessens the effect of this kind of stimulation.

Some other physiological changes associated with depression are increased muscle tension and heart and breathing rates, an imbalance in electric charges in the nervous system arising from an increase in salt retention, and increases in the production of the hormone cortisol (U.S. Department of Health and Human Services, 1981a). We still don't know which comes first: Do the biochemical changes cause depression? Or does the disorder cause the biochemical changes?

Psychoanalytic Explanations While "a unified, comprehensive, and precise psychoanalytic theory of depression has not fully emerged" (Isenberg & Schatzberg, 1978, p. 149), a number of different psychoanalytic explanations have been offered.

In the *libidinal* approach, Freud and his followers explain depression as the result of lowered self-esteem, which is the result of failure in adult love relationships, which in turn is the result of an oral fixation caused by problems in the mother-infant relationship. *Ego-psychological* theory sees depression as the result of a person's realization that she is unable to live up to the aspirations she held for herself. Feeling like a failure, she becomes depressed. According to *object-relations* theory (in which the word "object" is usually used with reference to a person), depression comes from a person's failure to reconcile his good and bad feelings toward his mother. The resultant ambivalence causes guilt and tension and can then bring about depression in later life at the loss of some important object (which may be, in addition to a person, a position in life or physical health or some other attribute). In apparent contrast to this approach, which sees depression as a reaction to loss, a recent review of the literature on the relationship between depression in adulthood and the loss of a parent in childhood found no evidence to show a cause-and-effect relationship (Crook & Eliot, 1980).

Distortions in Thinking   Both the *cognitive theory* of Aaron Beck and the *learned helplessness* theory of Martin E. P. Seligman rest on the way people interpret their life experiences.

Beck noted that depressed people think poorly of themselves, criticize themselves, feel deprived, exaggerate their problems, and dwell on thoughts of killing themselves. He feels that the depressive suffers from a basic distortion of thinking: She or he magnifies failures, misreads innocuous statements about the self to indicate that he or she is bad, puts a negative face on ordinary experiences, and is pessimistic about the future. Why do depressed people think this way? According to Beck, because they suffer from cognitive, as well as emotional, dysfunction.

Depressed people, for example, have trouble interpreting proverbs because they tend to think concretely rather than abstractly. They look at life in an all-or-nothing way, seeing things as either black or white. They misinterpret statements, focus on irrelevant details, draw global conclusions on the basis of a single incident, and evaluate experiences unrealistically, either making a mountain out of an unimportant event or a molehill of an important one.

As depressed people hold fast to their distortions in thinking, they become even more disturbed, and they develop a sense of purposelessness and hopelessness that makes them act in ways that make their depression worse. A depressed businessman, for example, stops seeing friends and colleagues, thinking, "What's the use? They'll be better off without me." By isolating himself, he loses the opportunity to get positive input that might raise his sense of self-esteem; by staying away from his business, he contributes to its decline; and so his disordered thinking feeds upon itself, creating a self-fulfilling prophecy (Beck & Burns, 1978).

Depressed people also show other cognitive deficits, as Seligman (1975) has pointed out. When they are hospitalized, their tested IQs drop and their ability to memorize definitions of new words deteriorates. This may be due to their belief that they can't do these tasks. Feeling this way, they don't try, and their beliefs become reality. Another self-fulfilling prophecy.

This lack of belief in one's effectiveness is the core of Seligman's learned helplessness theory. This can be seen most clearly in reactive depressions, which usually follow events like the death of a loved one, rejection by a loved one, physical illness or injury, money troubles, flunking out at school, being fired from a job, growing old, or being faced with any problem that seems insoluble. It is the apparent insolubility of the problem, the belief that nothing the person can do will overcome the terrible blow that has brought such suffering, which leads to depression. People who feel that they have put forth their best efforts—and that those best efforts have not been good enough—become depressed, feeling there is nothing further they can do.

Success, too, can bring about depression, when people feel they did not create their own successes but "fell into" them. What, for example, would make a Marilyn Monroe feel that life is not worth living? The depression of someone like this might result from her feelings that she gets attention, love, wealth, and other rewards not for who she is or what she does but only for what she looks like, a condition she had little or nothing to do with bringing about.

We'll talk about therapy for learned helplessness in the next chapter. What about prevention, though? This seems to lie in learning from an early age how to control important elements in one's life (Seligman, 1975).

Mania (Bipolar Disorder)

Normally, Ellen is a fairly reserved suburban real estate broker. In her manic phases, she is euphoric, talkative, and exuberant. Someone meeting her for the first time is likely to be fascinated by this flamboyant woman whose liveliness makes her the "life of the party." Only those who know her well realize how excessive her moods are at these times. When Ellen is in the middle of a manic episode, she goes off in all different directions at once, making extensive plans to take part in all sorts of activities—sexual, occupational, political, or religious (and sometimes all of these). She becomes very sociable and thinks nothing of picking up the phone to call old friends in the middle of the night. Since she seems to need practically no sleep, it doesn't occur to her that her friends do. As her powers of judgment fail, she spends money recklessly, takes risks in the car and on the ski slopes, and flirts outrageously with her friends' husbands, often ending up in bed with them. They are especially attracted to her at these times because she becomes flamboyantly dramatic, turning into a lively companion, full of jokes and amusing stories, as well as advice on a wide range of topics that she knows nothing about.

Manic episodes like this are equally common to both sexes and are much rarer than episodes of depression, affecting little more than 1 percent of the population (*DSM-III*, 1980). They differ from depressive episodes in other respects, too, notably in the nature of their onset. Manic episodes tend to come upon a person suddenly, rapidly escalate, and last from a period of a few days to a few months. They usually begin before age 30, and most people who have a manic episode will eventually experience a major depressive episode.

Less research has been conducted into the causes of the manic side of affective disorders than into the depressive face. From what has been done, however, it seems likely that some disturbance of brain chemistry underlies this condition. Strong evidence supporting this point of view is the effectiveness of the drug lithium in treating it, which we'll discuss in the following chapter.

PERSONALITY DISORDERS

In Chapter 14 we talked about the consistency over time of the characteristic ways of seeing, thinking about, and relating to the people and experiences in our lives that we know of as personality. When these traits do not contribute to a person's effective functioning, and when they are so rigid that even though they are maladaptive they continue to govern a person's life and to interfere with that individual's social or occupational functioning, we say that that person is suffering from a personality disorder.

Personality disorders encompass a wide range of behaviors. They are more vaguely defined than some of the other disorders discussed in this chapter, but they still present distinctive profiles. For a summary of the personality disorders described in *DSM-III*, see Table 15-2. Since there are

TABLE 15-2 Personality Disorders*

Cluster 1: Odd or Eccentric Behavior	Cluster 2: Dramatic, Emotional, or Erratic Behavior	Cluster 3: Anxious or Fearful Behavior
Paranoid: suspiciousness, mistrust, hypersensitivity, restricted expression of emotion, grandiosity.	*Antisocial:* chronic behavior that violates the rights of others, onset before age 15, consistent failure to perform on a job.	*Passive-aggressive:* Indirect resistance to demands for performance at work or in social life, through such maneuvers as dawdling, inefficiency, and forgetting.
Schizoid: inability to form social relationships, coldness, aloofness, lack of humor, indifference to praise or criticism, failure to show appropriate emotions, lack of humor.	*Narcissistic:* grandiose fantasies of unlimited success, craving for constant attention, feeling enraged, ashamed or haughtily indifferent in response to criticism or failure, expectation of special favors, disregard of others' rights, lack of empathy.	*Avoidant:* hypersensitivity to rejection or disapproval, preventing longed-for close ties.
Schizotypal: oddities of thought, perception, speech, and behavior not severe enough to be diagnosed as schizophrenic.	*Histrionic:* overly dramatic behavior, overreaction to minor events, tantrums, disturbed relationships due to self-indulgence and inconsiderateness, vanity, unreasonable demands, dependency, need for reassurance, or manipulativeness. *Borderline:* instability in several areas, including mood, self-image, and relationships, with no single feature invariably present; often associated with other personality disorders.	*Dependent:* lack of self-confidence that leads to giving up responsibility for one's life. While letting others make major decisions about one's life, the dependent person subordinates his or her own needs and desires to avoid jeopardizing the relationships depended upon. *Compulsive:* perfectionism, insistence that others do things his or her way, workaholism, restricted ability to express warmth and tenderness.

*Adapted from DSM-III, APA, 1980.

so many different personality disorders, we will describe in detail only one in each of the three clusters.

While these disorders vary considerably, they do have certain traits in common. Most, for example, show up at a very early age and become more deeply ingrained over the years. With most of them, the affected individual doesn't see anything wrong with the way he or she is functioning. He thinks it's the rest of the world that's out of step, that his own behavior is perfectly natural. It's easy to perpetuate this illusion since the behavior of someone with a personality disorder does not interfere with everyday life to the same extent as do the manifestations of some other disturbances. When it does, the individual usually does not recognize the degree to which he himself is creating his own difficulties.

The Paranoid Personality

Afflicted with this disorder, Ed peers at other people through a veil of suspicion. Instead of accepting responsibility for his own actions and his own mistakes, he finds it much easier to explain the loss of his job to the sabotage of his coworkers, who "wanted to make me look bad and so undermined me to my boss," or the loss of his wife to the perfidy of his best friend, who "told her all the worst things about me to make her lose her trust in me." No matter how much evidence Ed is shown to contradict his suspicions, he is unwilling to abandon his point of view.

Most people with this disorder tend to keep their thoughts to themselves, partly because they don't trust other people enough to confide in them. For this reason, impairment tends to be minimal. In fact, some people seem to ascend to great heights on the strength of their paranoia. Our history books seem to be full of individuals who bear out the American Psychiatric Association's observation in *DSM-III* (p. 308), that, "owing to a tendency of some [paranoid personalities] to be moralistic, grandiose, and extrapunitive, it seems likely that individuals with this disorder are over-represented among leaders of mystical or esoteric religions and of pseudoscientific and quasi-political groups."

The Antisocial Personality

Cult leader Charles Manson, an extreme example of a person with an antisocial personality disorder, showed antisocial behavior throughout his life, starting in childhood and culminating, at the age of 34, in the masterminding and execution of an especially brutal mass murder. (Wide World Photos)

Our prisons are full of them, and our hospitals and morgues are full of their victims. They frustrate law enforcement officers, social workers, the clergy, and their own parents, usually from a very early age. These people seem unreachable by most means. They commit acts that range from petty disobedience to the most unspeakable brutality and then seem to feel no remorse. As children they don't respond to the ordinary rewards and punishments that motivate other youngsters. As adults they're resistant to most societal structures.

Charles Manson, the cult leader who was convicted of the brutal murders of seven Californians, including the actress Sharon Tate, showed typical examples of antisocial behavior from a very early age. He lied, stole, and played hooky from school repeatedly. As a young teenager, he began to engage in petty theft, for which he wound up in a succession of eighteen state schools, reformatories, and other juvenile institutions. He graduated to car theft, the exploitation of naive young "hippies," and murder. Because of his charismatic personality, he was among those antisocial personalities who manage to attract many followers—and make it into our history books.

Charles Manson is typical of this kind of personality in other ways, too. The son of a teenage prostitute, he never knew his father and was abandoned by his stepfather when he was still a baby. At the age of 5, he lost his mother, too, since she was imprisoned for robbery. This pattern of growing up without both parents, removal from home (as Manson was when he was sent to live with an aunt and uncle, and then again when he was sent to one juvenile institution after another), and poverty is common.

About 3 percent of American men and less than 1 percent of American women are estimated to have antisocial personality disorder, a condition that seems to run in families, spurred by both genetic and environmental influences.

Passive-Aggressive Personality Disorder

People with this kind of disorder are less likely to make it into either newspapers or history books—but we are all familiar with them. With the roommate who is always full of promises to wash the dishes, make the bed, keep his or her side of the room up to the most minimal standards of sanitation and order but then never seems to get around to it. With the spouse who does such a poor job at raking leaves, scrubbing a floor, or whatever that we quickly decide it's easier to do it ourselves. With the coworker who forgets to deliver an important memo, thus impeding progress on a colleague's favorite project—and making the colleague look bad in the bargain.

These are the people who may be seething with rage on the inside but are unable to show it directly. So they express it in a variety of guises. Their passively expressed aggression tends to do more harm to a relationship than the most vehemently stated expressions of anger. Yet they often resort to this kind of veiled hostility because they have learned in the past that assertive behavior is likely to be punished.

SCHIZOPHRENIC DISORDERS

Some pages back we met Sylvia Frumkin, whose life has been sensitively and exhaustively detailed in a recent book (Sheehan, 1982). In many ways, Sylvia is typical of those suffering from schizophrenic disorders, the most severe and disabling of all the psychological disturbances. Her bizarre and handicapping symptoms, the early onset of her disorder, the great difficulty she has had receiving effective treatment, and the devastating impact her condition has had both on her own life and on that of her family are all typical. In other ways, no such patient is typical since no single feature is always present in this disorder and since, in fact, there may be a cluster of separate illnesses that comprise a schizophrenic syndrome.

When we look at Sylvia's symptoms next to an open copy of *DSM-III*, we are struck by the many ways in which she corresponds to the APA's definition. First of all, schizophrenia is clearly considered a *psychosis*, a psychological disorder characterized by a loss of contact with reality. Someone who is considered to be psychotic is suffering from delusions, hallucinations, or other disorders of thought that render him or her so out of touch with reality that it is extremely difficult for the person to function. How do schizophrenics show this split from the real world?

Symptoms of Schizophrenia

Schizophrenics show *disturbances in the content of their thought:* They may believe they are being persecuted, think that other people can hear their thoughts, be convinced that their thoughts have been removed from their head, or show other bizarre thought processes. They show *loosening of associations:* They shift ideas quickly from one topic to another completely unrelated one, without seeming to be aware of the disjointed quality of their thoughts. Their *speech is often vague,* and when they can't think of the word they want, they sometimes make one up. They experience *hallucinations,* in which they hear voices, see apparitions, or feel sensations (like snakes crawling around inside their bodies). Their *emotional responses* are unusual—*blunted* (showing a very low level of emotion), *flat* (showing virtually no emotion), or *inappropriate* (laughing when talking about a sad or frightening experience). Other features of schizophrenia are a disturbed sense of self, a withdrawal from the real world into a private world of fantasy, an inability to work toward a goal, and abnormalities of posture and motor movements (rigidity, jumping around, grimacing). While no single feature is always present, one of these three—delusions, hallucinations, or thought disturbances—always appears at some phase of the illness (*DSM-III,* 1980).

The Course of the Disorder

Schizophrenic disorders usually begin during adolescence or early adulthood. Here, too, Sylvia Frumkin is typical, having gone from a bright, achieving child to an adult who has been unable to function even marginally.

The disease generally goes through a preliminary phase, called *prodromal*, which marks a deterioration in functioning before the illness goes into its active phase. During the *active* phase, the psychotic symptoms appear. This is then followed by a *residual* phase, during which some of the psychotic symptoms may persist while others go into remission and disappear, at least for the time being. The symptoms must have lasted for at least six months to warrant a diagnosis of schizophrenic disorder.

The onset of schizophrenia may be acute or chronic. *Acute*, or sudden, occurrence of schizophrenic symptoms usually comes about in reaction to a specific situation and is more likely to appear relatively late in life in people who were previously functioning well. *Chronic schizophrenia* appears early—as we said, in adolescence or early adulthood, surfacing in individuals who were "different" in some way as children.

When a diagnosed schizophrenic shows no signs of the illness at all, she or he is considered to be "in remission." Most commonly, schizophrenics have increasingly more severe attacks of symptoms and become more and more impaired between episodes. Those who seem to have the best chance for a good prognosis are people who seemed quite healthy before they showed any schizophrenic symptoms, people whose illness seemed to have been precipitated by disturbing life events, people whose illness came on suddenly and in midlife as opposed to adolescence or early adulthood, and individuals whose relatives have suffered from depressive or manic disorders. In other words, those with the acute form have a better chance of recovery than those with the chronic form of the illness.

Men and women are equally likely to become schizophrenic, so sex is not a factor. Socioeconomic status is, however, since it is more common among the poor than among the middle and upper classes, with 6 percent of slum dwellers likely to be diagnosed as having a schizophrenic disorder at least once, compared to 1 to 2 percent in the general population (U.S. Department of Health and Human Services, 1981b).

Causes of Schizophrenic Disorders: Current Perspectives

While there are many theories of schizophrenia, most of the available research seems to point to a combination of an inherited biochemical predisposition to schizophrenia, which is then triggered by environmental stresses. Let's take a look at the evidence for this point of view.

PHYSIOLOGICAL EXPLANATIONS "Speed freaks," or people who overdose on the stimulants known as "uppers," often develop a disorder known as amphetamine psychosis. This condition is so much like paranoid schizophrenia that it can be diagnosed with certainty only after a urine test has been taken and analyzed to differentiate between the two disorders (Wender & Klein, 1981). This is just one of the many bits of evidence that scientists have been fitting together to come up with a picture of schizophrenia as a disorder involving a chemical imbalance in the brain.

Dopamine may be the critical factor. Dopamine is a neurochemical transmitter in the brain. Amphetamines, which as we just pointed out, can cause or worsen schizophrenic psychosis, release dopamine into the brain pathways. Neuroleptic drugs (like thorazine and chlorpromazine), on the other hand, which reduce agitation and are widely used to treat schizophrenics, work by blocking receptors and preventing the transmission of

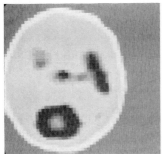

PETT scans are used to monitor the chemical activity in the brain. During a PETT scan a patient who has been injected with radioactive material is monitored by the scanner as the material passes through the brain. The first PETT scan in these photos is of a normal brain; the second is from a person diagnosed with schizophrenia. (© Dan McCoy 1983/Black Star)

dopamine. So just by knowing how these drugs work, we may be able to conclude that too much dopamine in the brain may cause schizophrenic symptoms. We still cannot come to a definitive conclusion, however, because even though an impressive amount of research points to dopamine as a causative factor, researchers have not been able to find any consistent changes in metabolites or enzymes related to the group of neurotransmitters that includes dopamine. It's possible, then, that dopamine may play a secondary rather than a primary role in causing schizophrenia (Nathan & Harris, 1980). On the other hand, recent research (Iversen, 1979) has uncovered another link to dopamine—nearly twice the usual number of dopamine receptors in the brains of schizophrenics. This may mean, then, that schizophrenics get double the effects from the same level of dopamine.

Research has established other physiological differences between persons with schizophrenia and normal people. By using the CAT scanner (described in Chapter 2), researchers have found that about one in five with schizophrenia have enlarged ventricles (small, pouchlike cavities) inside the brain (Wender & Klein, 1981). Enlarged ventricles are a typical sign of neurological disease. Furthermore, those whose CAT scans do show brain changes appear to be more severely affected than others with the disorder. They don't respond as well to treatment, and they are less likely to recover from the illness. It appears possible that permanent damage to the brain accounts for the incurability of some cases of schizophrenia. On the other hand, many people with schizophrenia do not have unusually large ventricles, and many normal people have ventricles that are as large or larger than those of many with the disorder. So it is clear that more research is needed in this area.

Another new technique has found physiological differences in the brain activities of people with schizophrenia and manic-depression. Through the PETT scanner (described in Chapter 2), scientists can actually monitor the chemical activity in the brain. Using this technique, they have seen differences in the metabolism of sugar glucose (which provides more than 80 percent of the brain's energy) in psychotic patients. Those with schizophrenia show a lower level of glucose metabolism in the frontal cortex, and those with manic-depression show a higher level of activity in the right temporal region during their manic phases. PETT scanning may thus aid in diagnosing a patient without clear-cut symptoms, as well as offer a clue to the origin of these psychoses.

Furthermore, there are other unexplained physical differences, such as the "peculiar-looking capillaries" found in schizophrenic brains, especially in chronic cases (Nicol & Heston, 1979). The fact that capillary peculiarities are also found in mentally retarded people, in elderly people with senile dementia, and in epileptics points to another possible avenue of research. Almost every line of research over the years has found some differences between normal people and at least some people with schizophrenia (Herbert, 1982). Since some of these differences—like higher rates of tuberculosis—were later explained as results of the disease rather than its cause (as outgrowths of poor care, for example), we need to be cautious about interpreting the meaning of any differences.

One question that researchers constantly have to ask themselves has to do with the difference between correlation and causation. Suppose faulty enzymes or differences in enzyme levels are, indeed, found between schizophrenic and healthy people. Is it possible that the schizophrenic behavior in some way changed the biochemical balance rather than having been caused by it? While this does not seem likely, it is possible and does have to be taken into account.

GENETIC TRANSMISSION   Can parents pass schizophrenia on to their children? Is there a schizophrenic gene that travels through the generations as one more hereditary condition? A large body of evidence points to the likelihood of a genetic predisposition for schizophrenic disorders. Where does this evidence come from? Mostly from studies of adopted children, of twins, and of families (Smith & Forrest, 1975). Let's consider each of these lines of research.

Adoption Studies   What happens to children born to schizophrenic women who are then removed from their mothers at an early age and adopted by families that have no schizophrenic members? Such children are more likely to develop schizophrenia themselves than are the adopted children of nonschizophrenic mothers (Heston, 1966). Another study found similar results but only for the offspring of mothers with *chronic*, rather than *acute*, schizophrenia (Kety, Rosenthal, Wender, & Schulsinger, 1968). These same researchers located a small number of children of normal biological mothers who were adopted into families in which the adoptive parent became schizophrenic and found that the rate of schizophrenia for these adoptees was no higher than would be expected in the normal population. So all these studies point to a hereditary factor in the condition.

Geneticist Irving I. Gottesman (1979, p. 57) has said, "If you are a betting person, the existence of an identical twin to a schizophrenic is still the best single predictor of future schizophrenia."

Twin Studies   A number of twin studies have found identical twins to be *more* concordant than fraternal twins, though even among identicals the concordance rate is not 100 percent. Even in the rare cases when identical twins have been reared apart, they are just as likely to be concordant for schizophrenic disorders as those brought up together (Gottesman & Shields, 1972).

Risk Studies   Another way of investigating the heritability of a trait is to look at a person's family tree and to ask, "What are the risk rates for this person's relatives' developing the disorder, as compared to the population at large?" When such consanguinity (blood relationship) studies have been done, researchers have found that relatives of people with schizophrenic disorders are more likely to develop the disease themselves than are unrelated people, and the closer the blood relationship, the higher the risk (Erlenmeyer-Kimling, Cornblatt, & Fleiss, 1979). In the general population, for example, the risk of developing schizophrenia is about 1 percent; the risk for a person with one schizophrenic parent is 11 to 12 percent, and the risk for a person with two schizophrenic parents is about 40 percent (Erlenmeyer-Kimling, Cornblatt, & Fleiss, 1979).

How Hereditary Are Schizophrenic Disorders?   In none of these lines of research—the adoption studies, the twin studies, and the consanguinity studies—is the risk rate 100 percent. Not all children of schizophrenic parents go on to develop schizophrenia, nor do all identical twins of affected people get the disease themselves. It is this imperfect correlation that leads to the assumption that some people inherit a predisposition to this disorder that may never be expressed unless something occurs to bring it out.

The predisposition may show up in other ways. For example, the relatives of schizophrenic patients sometimes show eccentricities that could be considered "muted forms" of schizophrenic symptoms—shyness, unsociability, coldness, sensitivity, fanaticism, or militancy—often leading them to be diagnosed as neurotics (Wender & Klein, 1981). It's possible that a "schizoid trait" can actually be desirable in some contexts (Claridge, 1972). This trait, when carried by a highly intelligent person who has grown up in a secure, nurturing environment, can lead to unusual creativity. This trait may lead a person to use language in unusual ways, to make up words, to put them together in new combinations, and to make other novel and creative connections among ideas. In less favorable circumstances, the trait may lead someone into the madness of schizophrenia.

We still do not know how a hereditary tendency toward schizophrenia interacts with the environment to produce the illness. Gottesman (1979) suggests that heredity accounts for about 80 percent of the cause of schizophrenia but that the 20 percent environmental factor is critical "in determining whether the person who is at high risk for genetic reasons does or does not break down" (p. 69). For example, a person with a very mild predisposition toward schizophrenia may function normally until late in life when major stresses—like, perhaps, the combination of the death of a spouse and the onset of deafness, both of which bring about social isolation—may trigger an acute schizophrenic reaction.

Furthermore, what one person experiences as highly stressful events, another may take in stride, not reacting strongly to them and, therefore, not experiencing ill effects. This may explain why two people with the same genetic predisposition (like identical twins) may not react identically to what appears to be the same environmental factors.

ENVIRONMENTAL THEORIES   In contrast to the physiological, genetic, and psychoanalytic explanations for schizophrenia, which look for answers *inside* the affected individual, an entirely different approach looks to the world the person lives in. Theodore Lidz, for example, looks to "family pathology" in families that are disorganized and unhealthy because of conflicts between the parents or because of mental illness in one or both parents as a possible cause (Lidz & Fleck, 1960).

Anthropologist Gregory Bateson looks to what he has termed the "schizophrenogenic" (schizophrenia-causing) mother, who makes her children crazy by saying one thing verbally but sending contradictory messages with body language, facial expressions, or actions. He called such mixed messages a "double-bind" because no matter how the receiver of them reacted, he would be "made wrong" by such a mother.

And the British psychiatrist R. D. Laing has made schizophrenia political by his viewpoint that schizophrenic behavior is the sanest response to living in an insane environment (1964; 1967). "What we call 'normal,'"

A young man who had fairly well recovered from an acute schizophrenic episode was visited in the hospital by his mother. He was glad to see her and impulsively put his arm around her shoulders whereupon she stiffened. He withdrew his arm and she asked, "Don't you love me anymore?" He then blushed and she said, "Dear, you must not be so easily embarrassed and afraid of your feelings." The patient was able to stay with her only a few minutes more and following her departure he assaulted an aide and was put in the tubs.
(Bateson, Jackson, Haley, & Weakland, 1956)

says Laing, "is a product of repression, denial, splitting, projection, introjection and other forms of destructive action on experience" (1967, p. 27). He sees the schizophrenic person as the one who *knows* that she or he has to explore the inner self to overcome the violation of the self that allows one to live in an impossible world.

The problem with all these explanations is that they don't explain well enough why some people growing up in chaotic families and in a topsy-turvy world do not become schizophrenic but instead are able to lead satisfying, fulfilling, normal lives. Nor why some people who grow up in homes that appear loving and orderly do go on to develop the disorder. In addition, we come back to the old problem of the difference between causation and correlation. It is eminently possible that parents become disturbed and that homes become disorganized because of the presence of a family member with schizophrenia—in other words, that the causation goes in the other direction. What, for example, does it do to parents never to know when they may have to be summoned by the police to pick up an adolescent or grown child who is undressing in public? How do parents feel when their attempts to be affectionate are rebuffed by an angry child? How do they react when their own children attack them violently?

How important is stress as a cause? Relatively weak, according to one review of the literature on the relationship between stressful life events and schizophrenia (Rabkin, 1980). People with this disorder do not report significantly more stressful events in their lives in the year or two before becoming sick than do other psychiatric patients. While they do seem to experience more stress before illness than normal people do, even this evidence is inconclusive. There is a relationship, however, between the number of stressful events and the probability of a relapse. By and large, then, stressful life events "seem to add the final straw" (p. 421). Stressful life events don't *cause* schizophrenia, but they may trigger an attack, influencing its timing rather than its occurrence at all.

It is a truism in science that the more theories we have about something, the less we know about it. This is certainly true of schizophrenia. Perhaps one of the problems we have is in trying to find one single cause for all the schizophrenias. We may have to look for many different causes. With this point of view, maybe we can come up with some partial answers here and some there, and eventually we'll be able to fit them all together to form a total picture. Till then, research continues.

Obviously, theories about the causes of psychological disturbances influence the ways these disturbances will be treated, as we'll see in the next chapter when we discuss various kinds of therapy now in use.

SUMMARY

1 *Abnormal psychology* is the study of emotional disturbance and abnormal behavior. It is difficult to come up with an all-encompassing definition of abnormality.

2 In our society the psychologically healthy person is considered to be someone who perceives reality fairly accurately, who behaves somewhat similarly to most other people in most situations, who does productive work, who can handle the tasks of daily living, and whose moods remain fairly even and appropriate to the situation. Of course, not all people who deviate from this profile are severely disturbed.

3 Over 55 million Americans suffer from some kind of psychological disturbance. About 7 million people receive treatment for a psychological disorder although some 34 million are thought to need it.

4 The societal factors that contribute to mental disorder include poverty, racial and sexual discrimination, and stress.

5 Diagnosis of mental disorders is difficult and controversial. The third edition of the *Diagnostic and Statistical Manual of Mental Disorders (DSM-III)* is a controversial document whose goal is to facilitate accurate diagnosis.

6 Throughout history people have offered different explanations about what causes abnormality and, therefore, how to treat it. During the Middle Ages mental disorders were thought to be the result of sin and devil possession, and the afflicted were treated as witches. This position is called the *moral model*.

7 The *medical model* considers mental disorder as the result of illness.

8 The *psychoanalytic model* holds that abnormal behavior is the result of conflict between the id and the superego.

9 The *behavioral model* maintains that abnormal ways of thinking and acting are learned, largely through the mechanisms of conditioning and modeling.

10 According to the *social consequence model,* many disorders that the medical model would view as illnesses are more appropriately considered as problems of living that arise out of difficulties in coping with society.

11 The *humanistic model* views abnormal behavior as a result of the failure to achieve self-actualization. None of the models presented here can account for all types of mental disorders.

12 The *DSM-III* has eliminated the term *neurosis*. Disorders that used to be called "neuroses" are now classified as *anxiety disorders*, certain *affective disorders*, *somatoform disorders*, and *dissociative disorders*. People with these disorders have difficulty coping with aspects of their lives but generally do not need hospitalization.

13 *Anxiety* is a state of apprehension, fearful uncertainty, or dread caused by some real or imagined anticipated threat. Anxiety disorders include *phobic disorders, obsessive-compulsive disorders, posttraumatic stress disorder, panic disorders,* and *generalized anxiety disorders*. These disorders affect 2 to 4 percent of the population.

14 A *phobia* is a persistent, intense, and unrealistic fear of an object or situation, such as snakes or open spaces. *Obsessions* are persistent unwanted ideas, thoughts, images, or impulses that cannot be eliminated logically; *compulsions* are urges to repeat certain unwanted acts. Obsessions and compulsions often occur together. *Posttraumatic stress disorder* may occur after experiencing a traumatic event such as military combat. It is characterized by reexperiencing the event and being overly responsive to stimuli that recall it. *Panic disorders* are attacks of terror that include physical symptoms such as dizziness, breathing difficulties, and sweating. In *generalized anxiety disorders*, people feel anxiety without being able to ascribe their discomfort to any particular situation or event.

15 *Somatoform disorders* are characterized by physical symptoms for which no physical basis can be found. They are thought to arise from psychological factors. *Conversion disorder* is an example of a somatoform disorder.

16 *Dissociative disorders* involve a sudden temporary alteration in either consciousness, identity, or motor behavior. Examples include *multiple personality, psychogenic amnesia, psychogenic fugue,* and *depersonalization disorder*.

17 *Psychoanalytic, learning,* and *medical* explanations of neuroses have been offered. According to the psychoanalytic approach, these conditions are the result of id-ego-superego conflict. Learning theorists hold that they are the result of inappropriate learning. The medical approach looks to biochemical explanations.

18 *Affective disorders* are disorders of mood. They take a number of different forms and levels of severity. *Depression* is the most common mental health problem in the United States, with some 20 million people in need of treatment. Depressed people

feel sad, have difficulty eating, sleeping, and concentrating. In depression with psychotic features they may also experience delusions, hallucinations, and disordered and confused thinking. Explanations of depression have looked to genetic and physiological causes, psychoanalytic interpretations, and distortions in thinking. During a *manic episode* people show extremely elated behavior. *Bipolar disorder* is the term given to the condition consisting of one or more manic episodes generally alternating with depressive episodes.

19   *Personality disorders* are maladaptive behavior patterns that appear at an early age, become more ingrained over time, and are not viewed as abnormal by the person exhibiting them. Three personality disorders are *paranoid* (characterized by suspiciousness); *antisocial* (characterized by behaviors which violate others' rights); and *passive-aggressive*

(characterized by indirect resistance to meeting demands through passively expressed aggression).

20   *Schizophrenia* is an example of a *psychosis*, a psychological disorder characterized by loss of contact with reality. The primary characteristics may include disturbances in the content of thought, loosening of associations, vague or made-up speech, hallucinations, delusions, and/or unusual emotional reactions. While no single feature is always present, *delusions, hallucinations,* or *thought disturbances* always appear at some phase of the illness. Schizophrenic disorders are found in 1 to 2 percent of the general population.

21   Current perspectives on the cause of schizophrenic disorders consider *physiological, genetic,* and *environmental* factors, such as the double-bind situation and stress.

SUGGESTED READINGS

American Psychiatric Association. (1980). *Diagnostic and statistical manual of mental disorders* (3d ed.). Washington, D.C.: American Psychiatric Association. The most recent edition of the *DSM*. A highly controversial document, it contains diagnostic criteria for mental disorders.

Nathan, P. E., & Harris, S. L. (1980). *Psychopathology and society* (2d ed.). New York: McGraw-Hill. A college textbook which reflects the viewpoint that psychopathology is both a response to and an influence on society.

Seidenberg, R., & DeCrow, K. (1983). *Women who marry houses*. New York: McGraw-Hill. A penetrating discussion of agoraphobia, the fear of leaving home, with an emphasis on the female case.

Sheehan, S. (1982). *Is there no place on earth for me?* Boston: Houghton Mifflin. A fascinating true account of Sylvia Frumkin, a paranoid schizophrenic who spent seventeen years of her life in and out of mental institutions.

Spitzer, R. L.; Skodol, A. E.; Gibbon, M.; & Williams, J. B. W. (1983). *Psychopathology: a case book*. New York: McGraw-Hill. A collection of fifty-four case histories which include information about diagnosis, the course of the disorder, treatment, and prognosis.

Wasow, M. (1982). *Coping with schizophrenia*. Palo Alto: Science and Behavioral Books. Written by a professor of social work whose 15-year-old son was diagnosed as having a schizophrenic disorder; contains information about resources and treatment options.

CHAPTER 16
THERAPY

SPOTLIGHT ON

Three major types of psychotherapy—dynamic, behavioral, and humanistic—and some current trends toward cognitive, interpersonal, and brief approaches.

The biochemical revolution: some pros and cons about the treatment of mental disorders with drugs.

Research on the effectiveness of psychotherapy which indicates that therapy is better than no therapy but that there is no one clearly superior method.

The importance of the "fit" between client and therapist.

The following dialogue marked the beginning of a psychoanalysis that was to change reporter Lucy Freeman's life, as she acknowledged in her book, *Fight Against Fears*.

"What are you thinking?" John [the therapist] asked softly.

I was worrying lest my shoes dirty the couch. It did not seem good manners to rest one's feet on furniture, even if that was accepted as high style for psychiatry.

"Nothing," I muttered. . . . "It doesn't seem right to talk about myself."

"Everyone should be interested in himself, first," John said. "The people who refuse to think about themselves realistically never understand themselves or anyone else."

He added, reflectively, "Perhaps you were never allowed to talk about yourself and now you feel nobody cares what you say."

Nobody cares? How often I felt nobody cared. Everyone but I seemed to have someone who cared.

"Maybe you don't care about yourself," he said.

"What difference does that make?" I asked sharply. I had never worried whether I liked myself or not.

"If you do not like yourself, you cannot like anyone else," he said.

I was too surprised to answer. The first tears in years flowed to my eyes (Freeman, 1951, pp. 35–37).

Psychoanalysis, of course, is not the only kind of treatment, or therapy, offered for emotional troubles. In this chapter we will look at many different kinds of therapy for psychological problems, some of which deal only with the mind (as in the "talking cure" of psychoanalysis); some of which treat the body (through drugs, surgery, or electric shock); and some of which combine physical and psychological approaches (such as administering drugs along with ongoing sessions of psychotherapy).

WHO GOES FOR THERAPY

Approximately 7 million people, or 3 percent of Americans, are presently under the care of a psychiatric facility, that is, private offices, outpatient clinics, community health centers, and hospitals (U.S. Department of Health and Human Services, 1981). More people are hospitalized for mental disorders than for any other kind of ailment.

Most recipients of help are either *psychotics* (who suffer from schizophrenic or depressive disorders—and are most likely to be receiving drugs and/or to be institutionalized); *neurotics* (whose functioning is impaired—most likely to be receiving psychotherapy); the *psychologically shaken* (who are temporarily overwhelmed by stressful events or experiences such as illness, job loss, childbirth, divorce, the death of someone close, and the like—and usually respond to a "first-aid" kind of therapy); the *unruly* (acting-out children or teenagers, self-indulgent spouses, antisocial personalities, alcoholics, compulsive gamblers—usually brought to therapy by others); the *discontented* (who seek more joy, happiness, and contentment—the bulk of the clients for the "human potential" programs that don't claim to cure any specific problem but promise life enhancement and self-fulfillment); and *professional therapists* (who undergo therapy themselves before offering it to other people) (Frank, 1979).

WHO PROVIDES THERAPY

Most of us receive help for psychological problems from many people. We talk to friends, relatives, teachers, family doctors. We often feel better after sharing our concerns with these people and often get good advice from them. We would not, however, refer to them as "therapists." A therapist is someone specially trained to offer a definite kind of treatment. In some societies this definition could apply to witch doctors and practitioners of voodoo. In our society a therapist is usually one of the following: a *clinical psychologist*, who holds a Ph.D. degree in psychology and generally has special clinical training; a *psychiatrist*, a medical doctor with advanced training in psychiatry (the only kind of therapist permitted to prescribe medication and the best qualified to identify physical conditions that may be causing psychological problems); a *social worker*, who has a master's degree and often advanced training in psychiatric theory and practice; a *psychoanalyst* (any of the foregoing, with advanced training in psychoanalysis, a technique based on Freudian theory, and who has undergone analysis as part of his or her training); a *psychiatric nurse*, who holds an R.N. degree and has advanced training in psychiatry; or a *counselor*, who may hold a doctoral or master's degree in education.

WHAT FORMS THERAPY TAKES

Therapy for psychological problems can take many forms. Problems are complex and people are complex. What helps one person will not necessarily work with another; the solution for a problem that stems from a physiological cause will necessarily be different from one for a problem arising from a troubled family environment.

The three major forms of therapy are *psychotherapy*, *somatic therapy* (medical treatment), and *environmental therapy* (social treatment). *Psychotherapy* focuses on thoughts, feelings, and behaviors. Psychotherapists use procedures that aim to make a person's personality, behavior, and/or attitudes more productive, more positive, and more life enhancing. Psychotherapy may focus on helping the recipient understand the reasons underlying his or her own problems, or it may ignore the reasons and concentrate only on changing undesirable behavior. It may explore the client's past history or focus almost entirely on the here and now. It may emphasize words or actions, thoughts or behavior.

The two other forms of treatment for psychological problems have different foci. The *medical* approach to treating emotional troubles focuses on the body and uses such tools as drugs, surgery, or electric shock. The third approach is *social*. It changes people's environment in some way, perhaps by placing them in an institution or in a foster home, changing the work situation, or structuring their life around a new set of activities.

PSYCHOTHERAPY

The nonmedical forms of treatment use words and behaviors as their tools rather than prescription pads and scalpels. Psychotherapists do not make any physiological changes in their clients' bodies. They do not prescribe drugs, perform surgery, or intervene physically in any other way—unless they are offering drugs and/or surgery in addition to the basic course of psychotherapy. By the conclusion of a successful course of psy-

BOX 16-1

HELP IS WHERE YOU FIND IT

A mother whose teenaged daughter wants to get married is distraught because they are constantly arguing. A young man who just lost his job is obsessed with the idea of taking an overdose of sleeping pills. An alcoholic is desperate about what is happening to her life. A man whose wife has left him cannot sleep or concentrate on his work.

All these troubled people are lucky to have knowledgeable helpers whom they can see regularly, to whom they can confide their problems, and who can give them some help in solving them. Their confidants are not professional counselors but a hairdresser, a bartender, a job supervisor, and a divorce lawyer, respectively.

Convinced that most people discuss their problems with people in their everyday lives rather than with mental health professionals for reasons that include lack of money, lack of availability, and a belief that "only crazy people go to psychiatrists," Cowen (1982) looked at the way people ask for and receive help from more informal helpers. When he interviewed representatives of the four occupations just mentioned, he found that four out of ten legal clients bring up personal problems, compared to one-third of hairdressers' clients, 16 percent of bar customers, and 7 percent of supervisors' staff. The problems raised varied, depending partly on the nature of the relationship between the individual and the

helper and partly on the context. Hairdressers most often heard about problems with children, health, and marriage, closely followed by depression and anxiety. Bartenders heard tales about marriage, job, money, and sex. Divorce lawyers, not surprisingly, were faced with problems related to spouses and depression, and supervisors heard mostly job-related worries, including problems with fellow workers. These problems, says Cowen, are *not* notably different from those brought to mental health professionals.

The kinds of help given varied, too. Hairdressers and bartenders tended to listen sympathetically, offer support, and try to be lighthearted. Lawyers also asked questions and pointed out the consequences of bad ideas, and supervisors also got people to come up with alternatives. Most of these people enjoyed giving help and felt it was an important part of their job. As one supervisor said, "Personal problems are part of everyone's life at one time or another, and if a supervisor doesn't deal with this fact he will pay the price with high reject rates, repairs, and absentee problems" (p. 390).

In recognition of the important role of such informal helpers, mental health workers in many communities have offered special courses for such "gatekeepers," people whose professions put them in places where they are accessible to people with

problems. Special courses have been given for hairdressers, lawyers, the clergy, and police officers to teach them skills for listening and responding and to inform them about community facilities (Cowen, 1982; Olds, 1972). Such programs do not try to turn untrained people into substitute psychotherapists but teach them how to make the most of their special places in people's lives. While preliminary attempts to evaluate such programs seem promising, it's still too early to tell whether teaching such skills actually make the troubled clients feel better.

Another kind of help for people with problems comes from *other* people with problems. Many people feel that they can get more help from others who have undergone similar experiences or have similar conditions than they can from any professional who has not lived through what they have. So they start self-help groups to share their feelings, perceptions and problems, and to get empathy and understanding, as well as practical solutions. By one estimate, some 15 million Americans are involved in 500,000 such groups. A clearinghouse of self-help groups in New York, one of twenty-one across the country, lists groups that help alcoholics, drug abusers, stutterers, schizophrenics, victims of crime, parents of murdered children, homosexuals, and those with many other health, psychological, and social concerns (Kerr, 1982).

Using a variety of different procedures, psychotherapists aim to make a person's personality, behavior, and/or attitudes more productive, more positive, and more life enhancing. (© Frank Siteman 1979/The Picture Cube)

chotherapy, the recipient should have learned something and should have gained greater control over his or her life.

The three major schools of psychotherapy are the dynamic, the humanistic, and the behavior therapies.

The dynamic school, which emphasizes the thoughts, feelings, and past life of the client and the need for insight into them in order to change personality, has grown out of the psychoanalytic theory of Sigmund Freud (see Chapter 14). While relatively few people today enter into classical analysis, Freudian philosophy is a basic element of most contemporary psychotherapy.

The humanistic therapies, which have their basic foundation in the view of personality espoused by Jung and Adler, and then enunciated by Maslow and Rogers (also described in Chapter 14), are much more diverse. They emphasize the unique qualities of each individual's vision of the self and attempt to change outlook.

The behavior therapies are based on learning theories that grew out of the work of such researchers as Pavlov, Watson, Skinner, and Bandura (as described in Chapter 5). These therapies do not delve into the client's thoughts and motives but focus instead on specific, observable actions. They concentrate on the behavior that the first two schools may regard only as *symptoms* of the deeper problem. Behavior therapists work primarily on changing behavior, using techniques developed from controlled research studies.

These orientations have arisen from different sources, draw on different techniques, and emphasize different aspects of development. They are all constantly evolving and giving birth to new outgrowths and approaches, some of which will be described later in this chapter. We'll discuss such important trends in therapy as the *cognitive, brief,* and *interpersonal* approaches.

In a recent survey of more than 400 counseling and clinical psychologists, about 11 percent identified their orientation as psychoanalytic, about 9 percent as person-centered (i.e., humanist), about 7 percent as behavioral, and about 10 percent as cognitive behavioral (see Table 16-1). Modern therapists tend to draw from more than one school. About 41 percent of these psychologists called themselves "eclectic," indicating that they integrate aspects of two or more schools into a treatment course for an individual client (Smith, 1982). This often works well since, as Strupp (1973; 1975) has pointed out, all kinds of psychotherapy contain certain common ingredients. They all include a helping relationship similar to the parent-child relationship, as well as a power base from which the therapist can influence the patient, and they all depend for their success on the client's ability and willingness to learn. Let's look more closely at each approach.

Dynamic Therapies

What do we mean when we say a therapy is "dynamic"? One of the meanings of "dynamic" is "characterized by or tending to produce continuous change" (*American Heritage Dictionary*, 1971). All therapy, of course, aims to bring about change—and is considered a dismal failure when it does not. Dynamic therapists, however, aim for a particularly far-reaching kind of change. They seek to restructure basic personality by changing the way a person looks at and reacts to life. How do they bring about change? By helping people develop *insight* into, or awareness of, the vast and powerful psychological forces buried deep within their unconscious.

The first type of therapy incorporating this goal and this approach was the psychoanalytic treatment invented by Sigmund Freud. Many of the therapists who followed him incorporated most of his ideas about the reasons for the psychological difficulties people encounter but have introduced a number of changes into the process. Today, therefore, a great

TABLE 16-1 Theoretical Orientations of Respondents

Orientation	N	Percent %
Psychoanalytic	45	10.84
Adlerian	12	2 .89
Behavioral	28	6.75
Reality	4	0.96
Cognitive behavioral	43	10.36
Person-centered	36	8.67
Gestalt	7	1.69
Existential	9	2.17
Rational-emotive	7	1.69
Transactional analysis	4	0.96
Family	11	2.65
Eclectic	171	41.20
Other	38	9.16
Total	415	99.99

Source: Smith, 1982.

many people receive therapy incorporating Freudian thought but with modifications in philosophy or technique.

PSYCHOANALYSIS If you were to embark upon a treatment of *classical psychoanalysis*, you'd be in an intense and long-lasting doctor-patient relationship. You'd be seeing your analyst from three to five times per week, 45 or 50 minutes each time, for several years. You might lie down on a couch as the analyst sat behind you, to free both of you from the distractions that might interfere with your free flow of thoughts and with your doctor's total concentration on what you were saying. The analyst would say very little, while you, as the *analysand,* would be encouraged to say whatever came into your mind, without censoring anything. This process is known as *free association.* You'd also be encouraged to talk about your dreams, whose content is considered very important in uncovering hidden thoughts. Your analyst would point out to you the symbolic nature of events and people in your dreams.

As you talked, you would give your analyst clues to the unconscious forces behind your anxiety. By asking questions, she or he would stimulate you to think about these influences on your personality and to gain insight into them. Freud felt that many of the causes that underlie the basic conflict between id and superego are sexual in nature and that repressed sexuality is the cause of most emotional problems.

When patients don't speak freely—have trouble free-associating or remembering dreams or discussing a particular topic—they're considered to be *resisting therapy* because talking about certain events causes them too much anxiety. (That's why they repressed them in the first place.) All analysands are expected to resist to some degree. Becoming aware of your resistance helps you identify especially significant elements.

Another important feature of analysis is *transference.* You'd often react to the therapist as if she or he were an important person in your life. You'd become angry or hurt by his reactions as if he were the mother who had neglected you or the lover who left you. The analyst will sometimes provoke a patient to bring about transference. As you recognized your emotions and reenacted conflicts based in an earlier relationship (usually parent-child), you'd get the opportunity to work through these strong feelings. *Countertransference* refers to the therapist's feelings for the patient, which arise from your awakening in her elements from her own emotional history.

Very few people go through strictly classical psychoanalysis today. For one thing, hardly anyone can afford it. At the going rate of $50 to $100 or more per analytic hour, the cost of several sessions per week for several years is completely out of the question for all but the very wealthy. For another, few people are able or willing to spend the time. Furthermore, not everyone can benefit from this type of help. The ideal analysand is bright, articulate, and not too sick. The person who does best in analysis is the one who does best in most treatment programs, the client therapists nickname the "YAVIS" (young, attractive, verbal, intelligent, and successful).

PSYCHOANALYTICALLY INSPIRED PSYCHOTHERAPY Another reason so few people receive classical psychoanalysis is that most therapists have

The 1982 movie Lovesick *dramatizes the psychoanalytic concept of "countertransference," through which a therapist becomes emotionally involved in some way with a patient. In this scene, we see Dudley Moore as a psychiatrist who falls in love with his patient, played by Elizabeth McGovern. (© 1982 The Ladd Company)*

moved toward a more directive, less frequent, short-term, goal-directed approach. The basic tenets of Freudian analysis are still alive and well but are most often offered in modified forms. Usually, therapy sessions take place only once or twice a week rather than three to five times. The therapist and patient generally sit in chairs facing each other. Contemporary therapists (like the one quoted in the opening paragraphs of this chapter) tend to be more directive than classical analysts, raising pertinent topics when they think it's appropriate rather than waiting until the patient brings them up.

Humanistic Therapies

As opposed to dynamic therapies, which aim to *rebuild* personalities, the goal of the humanistic therapies is to *free* them. The potentially actualized personalities are already there, buried under constricting attitudes. Humanistic therapists see their role as helping people to remove the constraints upon their self-fulfillment.

As we saw in Chapter 14, the humanists' explanations of personality are optimistic. They have an upbeat image of people and of our ability to live life to the fullest, even if that means changing long-held attitudes and behaviors. The person who receives therapy is not a "patient," a sick person under the care of a doctor. She or he is a "client," a partner in therapy. In fact, humanistic therapists respect the client as a sort of "senior partner" since it is the client, rather than the therapist, who is considered primarily responsible for the success of therapy. It is the client who has to want to change—and it is the client who is capable of the kind of improvement in living that will lead to self-actualization.

In keeping with the keenly individualistic flavor of humanism, this point of view has spawned many different therapeutic approaches. Each one emphasizes somewhat different goals and uses somewhat different techniques.

A PERSON-CENTERED APPROACH Developed by Carl Rogers (1951), this approach, formerly called *client-centered therapy*, views the client as an individual in search of self. It is based on the conviction that we all have within ourselves vast resources for self-understanding and for changing our self-concepts, basic attitudes, and behavior and that the therapist's role is to provide the climate for individuals to draw upon their own resources to *actualize*, that is, to reach complex, complete development (Rogers, 1980). Rogers was named most often as the most influential psychotherapist, living or dead, by the 400 practicing psychologists who answered Smith's (1982) survey.

In Rogerian philosophy, the client is a person in search of self. The therapist does not view himself or herself as an expert on whom the client can depend but as an accepting, understanding friend who will be the client's companion during the search. The therapist has no preconceived goal, does not seek to diagnose the client's problems, and does not try to lead the client. To the contrary, the therapist looks to the client—to see the world as the client sees it and to understand that world through the client's eyes. Progress toward the client's goal of *self-actualization* comes about through the relationship between client and therapist.

What conditions in this relationship create a growth-promoting climate? The three basic elements are not limited to the relationship between therapist and client but also apply to parent-child, teacher-student, and administrator-staff ties. They are:

1   *Acceptance*, or unconditional positive regard. If the therapist accepts the client totally and unconditionally as she actually is at that moment—even if she is expressing "negative" feelings—she will gain the strength from that acceptance to change and grow. Being accepted by someone else helps the client develop a more caring attitude toward herself.

2   *Empathic understanding*, a sensitive, active listening that allows the therapist to understand the client's feelings (even those the client may not be aware of), to clarify them, and to communicate this understanding to the client. Being heard in this way helps the client listen more accurately to himself. He can then feel emotions he had blocked.

3   *Congruence*, or genuineness or realness. A person who is congruent is not trying to appear other than who she is. She is herself. She isn't putting up a front (of, say, professionalism or authoritarianism), isn't trying to mask emotions, is letting the other person see what she's feeling and what she's thinking. As clients understand and prize themselves, they will accept their experiences as real and become more genuine. They perceive themselves differently, getting to know their own feelings and attitudes and not those that had been imposed upon them by other people.

By the end of therapy, clients have come to recognize their own responsibility for their emotions, opinions, and actions and are able to experience the new self in action. How do therapists help clients reach this point? They clarify the client's feelings and the topics under discussion often by doing nothing more than using different words to restate what the clients have just said; ask nonspecific questions to encourage clients to bring up those topics that are most important to them; and, throughout, show acceptance of clients and what they're saying.

GESTALT THERAPY The term "gestalt" refers to the arrangement of the parts of something into a whole that is meaningful in a way that the individual parts are not. Gestalt psychology explains personality through this concept of the whole being greater than the sum of its parts.

Gestalt psychologists believe that psychological problems often stem from a difficulty in not being able to integrate the various parts of the personality into a well-organized whole. Frederick S. Perls (1944) integrated the Gestalt viewpoint into a therapeutic approach that focuses on the patient's understanding the present rather than the past. Gestalt therapy helps clients make themselves aware of the whole self, mostly through direct appeals to the physical and the emotional selves rather than the intellectual self.

This kind of therapy incorporates a high level of activity and direction on the part of the therapist, who is much more in charge than in person-centered therapy. The therapist actively seeks to make the client aware of contradictions in his or her actions, often by pointing out the way the client's nonverbal behavior belies what he or she says. The therapist stresses the concept of each person's assuming responsibility for what she or he does, urging clients to speak in terms of "I did" rather than "it happened." Role-playing, games, and visual imagery are all important Gestalt techniques, which emphasize joining fragments of the self into a unified being.

Behavior Therapies

Behavior therapy, also known as "behavior modification," is markedly different from the other two major forces in psychotherapy. This therapy did not evolve entirely from the treatment of troubled individuals, as dynamic and humanistic therapies did, but in part from laboratory research on the way humans and animals learn. It is rooted, therefore, in the psychology of learning, which, as we saw in Chapter 14, explains human personality by basic learning principles. If maladaptive behavior has been learned, it can be unlearned. So we can define behavior therapy as the use of experimentally established principles of learning to overcome habits that are not adaptive for the individual.

Behaviorists maintain that negative habits and attitudes are learned responses and that the best way to get rid of them is to learn new, positive responses. They don't concern themselves with unconscious conflicts that underlie behavior. Instead, they're concerned with the behavior itself. Therefore, the therapist's job is to help the client unlearn the maladaptive behavior and learn some new replacement behavior. While dynamic therapists believe that eliminating any specific behavior will merely take away one symptom, which the individual will soon replace with another maladaptive behavior, behavior therapists disagree. They contend that the maladaptive behavior itself is usually the problem.

Since they believe that people learn *abnormal* behavior according to the same principles that govern the learning of *normal* behavior, they regard the abnormal not as an indication of mental illness but as the result of faulty learning. Behavior therapists refer to many of the conditions classified as "mental disorders" in DSM-III (such as sexual deviance, conduct disorders, and neuroses) as "behavior disorders" or "problems of living" (Rachman & Wilson, 1980).

Behaviorists delve into people's past experiences only as much as they have to, to find out how what happened *then* is maintaining undesirable behavior *now*. Their focus is on the present: What is the person doing now? And what should she or he be doing instead? They don't aim to reorganize people's personalities but confine their goal to eliminating the behavior that brought the client to therapy in the first place.

Behavior therapists apply scientific principles and show their ties to the laboratory by being as precise as possible in the criteria for using a particular technique for a particular problem, in the description of techniques, and in the measurement of results.

There have, however, been changes in the strict application of some of these standards. While behaviorists used to take a vehement "antimentalistic" approach that denied that thought, feelings, or social interaction had anything to do with controlling behavior, today these therapists, too, recognize that people *can* exercise self-control and self-direction to change the way they act. Not only in our environments are our behaviors shaped but in our hearts and minds, as well.

For example, if a client came to therapy with a drinking problem, a contemporary behavior therapist might decide not to focus directly on the problem behavior, the drinking. The therapist might consider it more productive to change the conditions that create the client's need or desire to drink. If the therapist felt that the drinking was related to problems at work, she or he might help the client become more assertive with his boss or learn techniques that would help him be more relaxed in the boss's presence. Or the therapist might use a cognitive approach to raise the client's level of self-esteem so he wouldn't feel so weak and helpless in relation to the boss.

While all these techniques would still be considered "behaviorist" because they are based on learning principles, are focused on the here and now, and are oriented toward changing current behavior, "focussing on the relationship rather than on the drinking per se clearly reflects a more mentalistic and complex approach to problem drinking than strict learning principles would admit" (Morse & Watson, 1977, p. 274).

Behavior therapists have developed a number of different techniques. The use of any particular procedure will depend on the specific problem being treated, the personality of the individual client, and the orientation of the therapist. What are some of these methods?

SYSTEMATIC DESENSITIZATION   Were you afraid of the ocean as a small child? If so, your father may have taken you to the water's edge and stood with you, holding your hand, till you were comfortable watching the waves. Next, he might have encouraged you to dip a foot in the water between waves, lifting you up when a wave approached. Then he may have stayed with you, still holding tight, while a wave washed over your ankles. In this way you would have conquered your fear, bit by bit, till you were able to splash merrily. If so, you experienced a form of system-

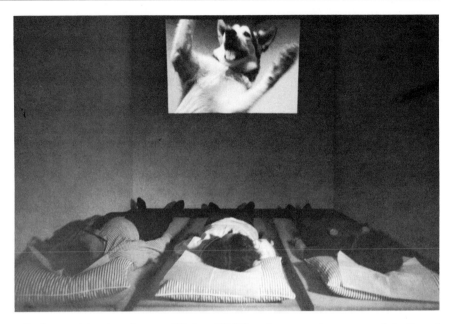

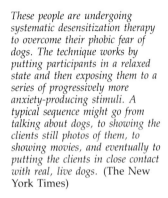

These people are undergoing systematic desensitization therapy to overcome their phobic fear of dogs. The technique works by putting participants in a relaxed state and then exposing them to a series of progressively more anxiety-producing stimuli. A typical sequence might go from talking about dogs, to showing the clients still photos of them, to showing movies, and eventually to putting the clients in close contact with real, live dogs. (The New York Times)

atic desensitization that, as Wolpe (1982) points out, is commonly offered not only to children but also to beginning mountain climbers, trapeze artists, and members of societies that require ceremonial ordeals.

This popular method, based on classical conditioning, aims to help a client replace undesirable responses with desirable ones in a piecemeal fashion. It works by inducing a relaxed (nonanxious) state and then exposing the client to a series of progressively stronger anxiety-producing stimuli, until she or he is ready to face them in real life. The treatment is often offered in two phases: *in imagination,* in which the client visualizes the anxiety-producing situations in his or her mind, and *in vivo,* in which the client actually confronts the anxiety-producing stimuli in real life. The first situation in either phase is a very weak anxiety producer, and the client does not go on to anything more threatening until she or he can respond without anxiety at each level. This approach has been effective in dealing with complex neuroses as well as phobias.

AVERSIVE COUNTERCONDITIONING   This technique combines an unpleasant situation with a behavior that a client wants to get rid of. It has been used successfully to help problem drinkers, smokers, and sexual offenders, among others. A person who has taken the drug *Antabus* (disulfiram), for example, will become violently ill if she or he drinks even the smallest amount of alcohol while the drug is in the drinker's system. Repeated experiences of drinking and feeling sick will often remove any desire to drink. Aversive conditioning is useful only when clients use the aversion as an aid to changing their behavior when they are not in the therapeutic situations (Bootzin, 1975).

MODELING THERAPY   Imitation is not only "the sincerest form of flattery"; is is often the most effective way to learn a new behavior. We learn how to swim, dance, play tennis, and do all sorts of other things by watching other people and then imitating what they do. We learn ways of getting along in the world by watching our parents. The people we copy, or *model* ourselves after, exert a major influence over us, say the learning theorists. If these models cope well with life, we're likely to learn and practice good coping mechanisms. If not, we copy their maladaptive ways. In any case, behavior therapists who maintain we can learn adaptive behavior by seeing and copying well-adjusted people consciously provide models of desirable behavior.

Modeling therapy can take several forms. *Live modeling* consists of observing actual people, while *symbolic modeling* involves watching people on film. Either one of these can be paired with *desensitization*, in which the client uses a relaxation technique along with seeing the models, and with *participation*, in which the client actually takes part in the anxiety-producing activity. This kind of therapy is used most often in the extinction of phobias as phobic people see others demonstrating a lack of anxiety. Modeling therapy is also used to help aggressive children learn more appropriate behavior patterns.

POSITIVE REINFORCEMENT (OPERANT THERAPY)   People learn to behave in ways they get rewarded for. With this knowledge in their pockets, behavior therapists have treated many psychological problems by rewarding clients for changing behavior. The secret to a successful reward program lies partly in the value of a specific reward to the specific individual. Such a program has to follow a sequence in which the therapist identifies the behavior to be changed, then establishes what the client would consider a motivating reward, and then gives the reward every time the client performs the target behavior.

Positive reinforcement works both with and without the client's awareness. In one case, a hospitalized woman in danger of starving to death because she had virtually stopped eating was rewarded by the therapist's speaking to her every time she lifted her fork to eat, and then as she lifted the food toward her mouth, chewed, and swallowed (Bachrach, Erwin, & Mohr, 1965). When she did not eat anything, the therapist left her alone until the next meal. After a while, weight gain, rather than the act of eating by itself, brought additional rewards. As her weight began to rise (from its low of 47 pounds), her rewards broadened to having another patient as company during mealtimes, going for walks around the hospital grounds, and being shampooed. Upon her discharge from the hospital, therapists instructed her family in ways to reward her behavior, and two and a half years after discharge she was maintaining an adequate weight.

Other Important Trends in Psychotherapy

COGNITIVE THERAPIES   The cognitive therapies stress the identification of distortions in thinking, show clients how such distortions contribute to their distress, and help them substitute more correct appraisals and interpretations. Cognitive therapists don't try to interpret unconscious factors. They use some behavioral techniques and also stress inner experience.

Rational-emotive therapy (RET), developed by Albert Ellis (1958), operates on a belief in the close intertwining of thought and emotion and a conviction that psychological problems are caused by faulty thought. This approach focuses on helping people solve their emotional troubles by examining their thinking, finding the flaws in it, and making it more logical and realistic.

TABLE 16-2 Summary of the Three Major Psychotherapeutic Schools

	Dynamic	Humanistic	Behaviorist
Roots of school	Psychoanalytic theory.	Humanism.	Learning theory.
Historical development	Treatment of troubled individuals.	Treatment of troubled individuals.	Laboratory research in learning.
Academic background of therapist	M.D., Ph.D., or Ed.D, often with special training in psychiatry and psychoanalysis. Analysts have undergone analysis themselves.	Ph.D. or Ed.D, usually with special training in clinical psychology.	Ph.D in psychology with either research or clinical background.
Theory about causes of abnormal behavior	Unconscious forces, especially sexual urges.	Inhibition of natural growth and motivation; distortion of self-perception.	Faulty learning.
Attitude toward recipient of therapy	"Patient" (sick person), to be healed by doctor/expert.	"Client," equal partner with therapist.	Student, to be taught by therapist.
Aim of therapy	Reorganize patient's total personality.	Help client move toward self-actualization.	Teach client new adaptive habits and attitudes to replace old maladaptive ones.
Approach	Patient may lie on couch and free-associate. Therapist does not raise issues but does interpret meaning of patient's information.	Client and therapist face each other as both raise issues.	Therapist devises specific program to focus on target behaviors.
Important time frame	The past.	The present and future.	The present and future.
Length of therapy	Three to five 45-minute sessions per week for several years.	Weekly 45-minute sessions for a variable time.	Variable.

RET uses an alphabet-soup approach to view personality. As explained by Ellis (1974), therapy usually starts at C, the client's upsetting emotional Consequence, the feeling of depression, anxiety, or worthlessness that has brought the client into therapy. The client usually attributes C to A, the Activating Experience, such as being rejected. It is up to the therapist to make the client see that there had to be some kind of intervening factor, B, the client's Belief System, to get him from A to C.

The therapist might point out to the client—let's call him "Joe"—that people get rejected all the time and that they don't all feel as depressed as Joe does. Some people get angry, some are inspired to write a song, and some just shrug their shoulders and find someone else. So it's obvious that A didn't *cause* C. What did? Joe's own irrational beliefs: his beliefs that Mary's rejecting him means that he's worthless, that something is terribly wrong with him, that he'll never find anyone else he'll love as much, and that he deserves to be punished for failing to get Mary to accept him.

The therapist then moves on to D—to Dispute with Joe his irrational beliefs, making Joe ask himself such questions as "Where is the evidence that no desirable woman will probably ever accept me?" and "By what law do I deserve to be punished for being so inept?" Joe can then rephrase his belief system to include such thoughts as "It is not awful, but merely very inconvenient and disadvantageous for Mary to reject me," "Although my life may be less enjoyable now and therefore worth less, I am never a worthless individual," and "It is highly likely that some day I'll find another desirable woman."

Joe can now move on to E—new and better functioning Effects. Such effects include his ability to stop indulging in irrational thought the next time he goes through a similar activating experience, whether it's being jilted by a woman, fired from a job, or refused for an apartment.

The cognitive therapist not only challenges and contradicts thoughts but she or he also tries to demonstrate through action how illogical they are. For example, a therapist will direct a woman who is afraid to speak to men to go out of her way to do so. Only by actually seeing that what she feared most does not come true will such a woman recognize the lack of logic in her thinking and will see how it has warped her life.

Psychiatrist Aaron T. Beck incorporates this active approach in a variety of short-term treatment programs in which the therapist helps the individual organize both thinking and behavior. Working with depressed suicidal outpatients in a psychiatric clinic, Beck and his colleagues used both behavioral and verbal techniques to change these people's thinking (Beck & Burns, 1978). In one case, the therapist asked a patient who spent most of his time in bed and protested that he was "too weak" to walk, how far he thought he could walk. When the man said, "Just a few feet," the therapist suggested they experiment to see whether the man might be able to walk farther than he had thought. This proved to be so, and after getting the patient to walk around the ward and get a soda as a reward, the therapist got his reward by seeing the patient playing Ping-Pong the next day.

BRIEF THERAPIES   Actor, writer, and film director Woody Allen has often spoken of his psychoanalysis, which has gone on for some twenty-five years. In something of an understatement, Allen has said, "You don't learn anything in a dramatic rush" (Gittelson, 1979). Classical Freudian analysis is the longest-lasting psychotherapy generally offered today, with five-year and longer spans of treatment fairly common. It's surprising, therefore, to realize that Freud started out offering analysis as a brief therapy, lasting from a few months to up to a year. In fact, he once used a single four-hour session to cure the composer Gustav Mahler's impotence with his wife.

In this session Freud pointed out to Mahler the way he was identifying his wife with his mother, saying, "I take it that your mother was called Marie. How come it is that you married someone with another name, Alma, since your mother evidently played a dominating part in your life?" Mahler, impressed, told Freud that his wife's full name was Alma Maria but that he always called her "Marie" (Goleman, 1981, p. 62). Thus the composer quickly arrived at the curative insight into his problem.

A contemporary therapist has reported a high success rate with single two-hour sessions, during which he identifies one major problem and offers at least one suggestion for beginning to solve it. While he doesn't claim that this kind of therapy will solve serious emotional problems, he sees it as an "impasse service," which helps overcome an emotional "roadblock" (Bloom, cited in Goleman, 1981).

For the most part, however, most conventional therapy is open-ended so that a client has no idea how long it will last. This often poses problems since therapy is expensive, time is precious, and there are not enough therapists to help all those who need help. As a result, over the past twenty years, a number of time-limited therapeutic approaches have developed, generally going up to no more than fifteen or twenty sessions (Goleman, 1981).

How do therapies operate within such strict limitations? Mainly, by focusing on one, or just a few, troubling symptoms, rather than trying to mount a global effort to reorganize a personality. Brief therapies come from all the schools we have discussed and have much in common. They tend to be supportive, emphasizing the client's strengths and offering a "safe," accepting atmosphere. The therapists are usually active, not hesitating to give practical advice rather than insisting that all insight develop from the client. They often use aids like hypnosis, drugs (prescribed by themselves if they are physicians or by doctors with whom they work closely), and various conditioning techniques.

The best candidates for brief therapy are intelligent people troubled by an easily identified, sharply focused problem and strongly motivated to change. The worst are impulsive, self-centered, self-destructive, masochistic, negativistic, rigid, and very dependent (Goleman, 1981). Again, the people who do best with brief therapy are the ones who do best with any therapy.

Group and Family Approaches

GROUP THERAPY   Like our closest animal relatives, the great apes, people are social creatures. We live in groups, we function in groups, and we malfunction in groups. A vast number of the people who seek therapy do so precisely because of their difficulties in getting along with others. It's not surprising, then, that it didn't take psychotherapists long to decide to treat people in groups. While both Sigmund Freud and his immediate follower, Carl Jung, believed strongly in the personal basis of psychopathology and did not explore group therapy, another early analyst, Alfred Adler, believed just as strongly in the role of social factors in causing emotional problems and in the use of social situations to cure them. He did, therefore, use the group format in child-guidance centers and with alcoholics (Bloch, 1979).

Today, practitioners from all the major schools of psychotherapy, as well as from the newer offshoots, do much of their work with groups of clients, as well as with individuals. Groups may be composed of people who have similar problems (such as drug abusers, overeaters, child beaters, or sex offenders), or they may consist of a mix of people with different problems.

What do people get from group therapy that they can't get from one-on-one treatment? They learn that they are not alone—that other people's problems are just as bad as their own, or worse. They get feedback about themselves from the other group members, as well as from the therapist. They play out in the group the problems in relating to other people that

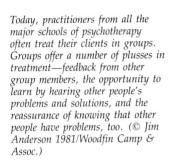

Today, practitioners from all the major schools of psychotherapy often treat their clients in groups. Groups offer a number of plusses in treatment—feedback from other group members, the opportunity to learn by hearing other people's problems and solutions, and the reassurance of knowing that other people have problems, too. (© Jim Anderson 1981/Woodfin Camp & Assoc.)

may have brought them into therapy in the first place. They learn from each other by seeing how other people work out their problems and by listening to advice and suggestions. They feel better about their own worth as they see that they can help others. They feel free to express their feelings in a safe environment.

What kinds of people do best in group therapy? In a discussion of long-term dynamic psychotherapy groups composed of people looking for help with a variety of different problems, and ultimately a basic personality change, Block (1979), not surprisingly, predicts success for the same clients who do best in other kinds of therapy—those who are motivated, relatively sophisticated in exploring and talking about their emotions, and convinced of the value of this kind of therapy. Poor candidates for group therapy include those who will get little from it (like the person with severe symptoms of schizophrenia who is too out of touch with reality to participate productively) and those who interfere with other people's ability to benefit (like the severe depressive, whose unreachability frustrates and dispirits the other group members).

Some problems that can be effectively tackled in a group are poor self-concept, inability to express or control emotions, anxiety, depression, ineffective coping with stress, and difficulties in getting along with or being intimate with other people (Bloch, 1979). Others, which respond very well to highly structured groups that focus on specific behavioral manifestations, are such behaviors as drinking or eating too much, mistreating children, and compulsive gambling.

Most groups are composed of between five and eight members, which provide enough people for the group experience to be effective and not so many that the individual gets lost. They usually meet once a week at a set time for an hour and a half to two hours. Some are *closed*, restricting membership to those who joined at the beginning, while others are *open*, permitting people to leave at different points and replacing them with new people.

FAMILY THERAPY   Family therapy is similar to group therapy in its focus on interaction among people, but it differs in several important ways. First, "The group does not have a history. It has no past and no future.

The family has both" (Foley, 1979, p. 464). Secondly, the family thera-pist's role is as a model or teacher, compared to the group therapist, who is more of a facilitator (Yalom, 1975). Perhaps most important, the goal of family therapy is to strengthen the family group itself, along with its individual members, whereas the therapy group's goal is to self-destruct when its individual members resolve their conflicts.

The basic premise of family therapy is that the *presenting problem*, the symptom that sends someone into therapy—a husband's drinking, a wife's depression, or a runaway child—is never the basic problem. In-stead, family therapists see these surface problems as signals that some-thing is radically wrong with the entire family (Napier, 1978). It is the family *system* that is not operating properly. This may be because of poor communication that prevents family members from knowing each other's feelings. It may be because a family believes in a "myth" that has been handed down from generation to generation ("Our family is unlucky" or "Our family likes to fight"). It may arise from a misguided conviction that everyone in a family has to think alike. Or it may be due to other reasons, such as alliances between some family members that exclude others (such as between one parent and one child) or inhibitions on the expression of feelings (Bentovim, 1979). Often a problem in the parents' marriage sur-faces in a child's rebelliousness, as she subconsciously reasons, "If I focus their attention on my troubles, they'll have to stay together to handle me."

In this kind of therapy, the entire family is the patient. By helping individuals to understand how their family works, counselors can often help them see what each one is doing to perpetuate disruptive patterns and how they can change these patterns. Family therapists, who may come from any of the major schools of psychotherapy, work in a number of different ways. They may see the entire family every time or alternate with separate sessions for one or more members. They may see a family for an hour a week, for one two-hour session every two to four weeks, or hew to some other schedule. They may be able to resolve a problem in four or five sessions—or they may stay with a family for a year or more. These variations depend on the therapist's orientation, the family's incli-nations, and the severity and kind of problem.

These, then, are the major kinds of psychotherapy. As we indicated, psychological problems are often treated in other ways, too—medically or socially. After we describe these latter two forms of therapy, we'll evalu-ate the comparative effectiveness of the various forms of treatment.

MEDICAL THERAPIES

We're all familiar with the bodily sensations tied to our emotional states— the butterflies zooming around in our stomach before an important exam or the tension headache that appears when we are worried. In Chapter 10 we saw how emotional characteristics can lead to such major illnesses as heart attacks. When the mind makes the body sick, the illnesses are called *psychosomatic*. While their cause is not *organic* (physical), but *functional* (emotional), they are real illnesses, with real physical manifestations. In such cases, physicians often recommend psychotherapy, along with medical care, in the treatment of physical symptoms that they believe to have an emotional basis. This is only one example of the close relationship between the body and the mind, a tie that has been recognized in varying degrees by physicians and philosophers through the ages.

Even before recorded history, people felt there are certain times when the body makes the mind sick. This belief has given rise to a range of therapies that aim to cure mental illness by treating the body.

The earliest kinds of such treatment took the form of surgery. Much later, electric shock therapy began to be used. Another kind of physical treatment for emotional distress—the administration of medicinal drugs—has become so common that it has amounted to a revolution in the care of the psychologically disturbed. We'll look briefly at surgery and shock treatment and then look more intensively at the way different kinds of drugs are used to treat different kinds of mental illness.

Psychosurgery

If you wander through the halls of a major museum of natural history, you are likely to see an exhibit of ancient human skulls with holes that have been drilled with a sharp instrument. Archeologists have determined that such holes were caused by the mental health experts of the day who practiced "trepanning" (also called "trephining"), a procedure that used a circular saw to cut out a portion of bone from the skull. The assumption is that this was done to treat mental illness or to relieve intractable pain.

In the more recent past another surgical technique, prefrontal lobotomy, came into common usage for a while. This operation, which involves cutting the nerve pathways in the two frontal lobes of the brain, was performed by the thousands during the 1940s and 1950s to relieve the symptoms of people with schizophrenic behavior disorders, obsessions, and severe pain. When all else failed, including shock therapy, a lobotomy was often prescribed.

Lobotomies were somewhat successful, providing at least temporary relief of symptoms in 30 to 60 percent of patients, letting some people leave institutions and come home to live. However, this irreversible operation had a much darker side. The patients' personalities often underwent severe change, leaving them apathetic shells of their former selves; some 5 percent developed convulsions; and more than 6 percent died (Rosen, 1982; Barahal, 1958). Because of these effects and because of the enormous successes in drug therapy in recent years, lobotomies are hardly ever performed any more.

Electroconvulsive (Shock) Therapy

Shock therapy, as described by the poet Sylvia Plath (see page 571) whose persistent bouts with depression led to her suicide at the age of 30, sounds like another frightening and inhuman relic from the past. It has been in use since the late 1930s and is still employed to treat some 100,000 Americans every year (Sobel, 1980).

Today the patient is first given a sedative and a muscle relaxant and is also strapped to a padded bed. The person administering the treatment attaches electrodes (devices that conduct electricity) to one or both sides of the patient's head and briefly passes a strong electric current through the brain. The patient usually becomes unconscious, goes rigid for a few seconds, has strong convulsions for a couple of minutes, stays unconscious for about half an hour, and is groggy and confused for hours.

Although its use is controversial, electroconvulsive (shock) therapy is effective in treating many cases of severe depression that fail to respond to drugs. (Parker Herring/ Time Magazine)

When she awakens, she'll remember neither the shock nor anything that happened just before it, but will probably regain her memory within two weeks.

A program of shock therapy, which may consist of just one experience or of repeated ones a couple of times a week for a period of up to several months, is often effective in alleviating the despair of the severely depressed and suicidal patient, but no one is sure about why it works. One theory is that depression is caused by an imbalance of chemicals in the brain and that the seizures affect these chemicals. A recent investigation (Costain, Gelder, Cowen, & Grahame-Smith, 1982) found that depressed patients given shock therapy showed brain changes ordinarily associated with the increased transmission of the brain chemical dopamine, supporting this theory. Another possibility is that the shock brings about temporary memory loss, thus breaking the patient's pattern of disturbing thoughts.

In any case, this form of therapy, too, has generally given way to drug treatment and is usually resorted to only when drug therapy would not be effective, as, for example, with elderly people who could not tolerate the side-effects of drugs. The treatment is quite controversial, with opponents charging that it is medical abuse forced on people who are psychologically unable to make an informed decision and who, as a result, suffer memory loss and psychological damage, and advocates maintaining that its safety has been demonstrated by controlled studies and that it often helps patients for whom no other treatment will work. Shock therapy is rarely effective with schizophrenic patients.

Drug Treatments

When Freud wrote about a powerful and vast unconscious that held the roots of our personality development and about the amazing results he achieved by taking neurotic patients into the depths of that storehouse of repressed memories, he started a revolution. Now, another monumental change has affected the way we look at and care for millions of people. Freud's was the revolution of the unconscious. Today, we are witnessing a revolution of the biochemical.

Today's revolutionaries are those psychiatrists and psychologists who explain psychological disturbance in terms of the balance of chemicals in the pathways of our brains and who treat it by administering drugs that travel through those pathways. Their influence has even spread to the general practitioner, who regularly dispenses psychoactive (mind-altering) drugs to some 17 million patients every year (Sobel, 1980).

Aside from lifting the spirits of the ordinary person at times of illness or other stress, this revolution has emptied out and closed down institutions that used to house the mentally ill. It has enabled people who were once a menace to themselves and to those around them to live freely in the community, hold jobs, and be among normal people, even though it has not cured their illnesses or magically made them normal. It has relieved the guilt of many parents, explaining their children's disturbances as the result of inborn chemical imbalances rather than emotionally scarring life experiences.

Because so many psychological disorders respond so well to psychoactive drugs, many researchers have become convinced that these disorders have biochemical causes. In some cases the successful drug treatment of a

"Don't worry," the nurse grinned down at me. "Their first time everybody's scared to death."

I tried to smile, but my skin had gone stiff, like parchment.

Doctor Gordon was fitting two metal plates on either side of my head. He buckled them into place with a strap that dented my forehead, and gave me a wire to bite.

I shut my eyes.

There was a brief silence, like an indrawn breath.

Then something bent down and took hold of me and shook me like the end of the world. Whee-ee-ee-ee-ee, it shrilled, through an air crackling with blue light, and with each flash a great jolt drubbed me till I thought my bones would break and the sap fly out of me like a split plant.

I wondered what terrible thing it was that I had done. (Plath, 1972, pp. 117–118)

condition has inspired research that has indeed shown a biological basis for the disorder. In other cases, the biochemical jury is still out.

What role do drugs play in the treatment of psychological disturbance? What can they do and not do? And when are they indicated?

WHO CAN BE HELPED BY DRUGS   The medications developed so far have been used most effectively with people suffering from the following conditions.

Schizophrenia   In the late1940s, physicians found that a certain antihistamine had a calming effect on patients undergoing surgery. Before long, scientists had developed a chemical relative of this drug that they administered to agitated schizophrenic patients. They then discovered that this new drug, *chlorpromazine* (trade name Thorazine), not only calmed these patients but also took away a number of the specific symptoms of their condition. Many patients who took it stopped hearing voices and hallucinating and were no longer oppressed by paranoid delusions. This drug and its chemical relatives in the family of the phenothiazines (which also includes *trifluoperazine*, marketed as Stelazine) have become known as *antipsychotic* drugs, as *neuroleptics* (because they produce neurological side effects), and as *major tranquilizers*. They are not addictive, and they do not put people to sleep.

For the great majority of schizophrenic patients, these drugs work dramatically, controlling their most disabling symptoms and enabling them to live outside an institution, in the community. They are not a cure-all, however. Some patients do not respond even to large doses, possibly because variation in metabolic rates apparently prevents adequate absorption of the drug into the system for some people (Shapiro, 1981). Even when the drugs do work, they do not cure the condition: When people with schizophrenic disorders stop taking their medicine, their old symptoms come right back within a couple of weeks. Furthermore, even when they are on the medication, many still need extensive social support and cannot lead a normal life (Wender & Klein, 1981b). The difference in the medicated and nonmedicated states of most such people is the difference between being able to walk alone on a public street, aware of the people and events in everyday life, and sitting on the floor of a bare hospital room, staring unseeingly at blank walls.

The antipsychotics are widely used today—too widely, according to critics, who maintain they are used mainly to make patients easy to manage. Critics point also to the drugs' troubling side-effects, which include blurred vision, trembling, constipation, and dryness of the mouth. The most worrisome one is tardive dyskinesia, a disorder that includes involuntary facial twitches and body contortions and affects a sizable number of those who have taken these drugs for a period of years. Some 40 to 50 percent of patients in state mental hospitals suffer from this disabling side-effect (Kolata, 1979).

When patients are taken off the drugs, the side-effects may or may not disappear—and the handicapping symptoms of schizophrenia reappear. This dilemma has caused a great deal of controversy in psychiatric and legal circles, with many hospitalized mental patients' currently taking to the courts to insist on their right to refuse antipsychotic drugs and many psychiatrists and hospital directors' maintaining that psychotic patients are unable to make sound decisions about their treatment (Appelbaum, 1982).

Depression   The discovery of chlorpromazine inspired the development of a major class of drugs used to treat depression, the tricyclics. They had been synthesized before the turn of the century but were not used until the late 1950s when chemists noted their chemical resemblance to chlorpromazine. Initial trials with them were successful in raising people's spirits, and they have become widely prescribed to treat clinical depression and certain other psychological disorders. The most common of the tricyclic compounds are Elavil, Tofranil, Sinequan, Vivactil, and Aventyl.

Another type of antidepressant in common use today is the monoamine oxidase (MAO) inhibitor (like Marplan, Nardil, and Parnate), also developed in the 1950s, when a new drug for tuberculosis "caused some elderly TB patients to dance in the corridors of their sanitariums" (Clark, 1979, p. 100).

There are limitations on the use of antidepressants. While they are very effective in treating the kind of despair that seems to well up from nowhere, helping some 70 percent of people with endogenous depression (Wender & Klein, 1981a), they do little, if anything, for the person depressed over an upsetting life event like the death of a family member or the loss of a job. Furthermore, even when they work well, they don't take effect for a week or longer. If a person is so desperately low in spirits that he is suicidal, it is dangerous to rely only on the antidepressants; immediate electric shock therapy may have to be given until the medicine has a chance to work.

Like all drugs, these also have side-effects. The tricyclics produce relatively minor ones like constipation, dryness of the mouth, and dizziness, but the MAO inhibitors can lead to dangerously high blood pressure if the patient eats certain foods such as chocolate or cheese which contain a certain amino acid.

Bipolar Disorder ("Manic-Depression")   At about the same time these other drugs were making their appearance in the late 1940s and early 1950s, the drug lithium carbonate was found to control the extravagant excesses of manic states. While it is a treatment rather than a cure, it often eliminates the manic symptoms entirely and has, therefore, been used increasingly over the past ten or fifteen years. Although lithium is not habit forming, it does have side-effects. It can affect the thyroid gland and the kidneys and can cause mild hand tremors and weight gain, as well as other slight effects. In excessive doses it can be poisonous, and since there is a fine line between therapeutic and toxic levels, anyone on lithium should have regular blood tests, as well as regular thyroid and kidney examinations (U.S. Department of Health and Human Services, 1981).

Another problem with lithium is in getting patients to take it. Since many manics don't like to give up the euphoria of their high states, some psychiatrists adjust the dosage of lithium to temper the mania without getting rid of it completely.

Anxiety and Neuroses In 1975, the antianxiety drug *diazepam* (Valium) was the most popular drug in America, with some 61.3 million prescriptions written for it during the year (Boffey, 1981). Since then, largely as the result of extensive publicity warning about its abuse and the danger of its being habit forming, Valium has dropped in popularity. In 1980, about 33.6 million prescriptions were written for it.

Valium—like its chemical cousins Miltown and Librium—is one of a class of drugs formally termed the *benzodiazepines* and informally (and somewhat misleadingly) referred to as "minor tranquilizers," to differentiate them from the phenothiazines, or "major tranquilizers." Despite the name, these two classes of drugs are very different. The two most important distinctions: The benzodiazepines do *not* alleviate psychotic symptoms, and they *do* have the potential for addiction. Their most common side-effects are drowsiness and unsteadiness from large dosages and a tendency to exaggerate the effect of alcohol when taken along with it. The benzodiazepines are effective in treating *general anxiety*, which a person feels in almost any kind of situation, as contrasted with a *specific anxiety* that shows up only in certain circumstances, like test taking or riding in an airplane.

Antidepressants and tranquilizers are sometimes prescribed together for specific goals. High rates of success have been reported in treating phobic patients with a combination of tricyclics and minor tranquilizers (Wender & Klein, 1981b).

HOW THE DRUGS WORK As we learned in Chapter 2, billions of nerve cells interconnect in the human brain. At the synapses where they form junctions, the nerve cells release chemicals called "neurotransmitters," which travel to other nerve cells and activate impulses that determine thought, mood, and movement. Once a neurotransmitter has activated a cell and a new impulse is initiated, the chemical is reabsorbed into the nerve cell that sent it out. According to the theory of chemical imbalance, problems arise when too much or too little of a particular neurotransmitter is released and when the receptors absorb it too quickly or too slowly. In other words, an excess or a deficiency of any particular neurotransmitter will cause deviations from the normal.

The neurotransmitter *dopamine* is the chemical that seems implicated in schizophrenia. Dopamine activates cells in parts of the brain that process thoughts and feelings, and when there is too much of it, it causes psychotic disorders of thought and mood. Antipsychotic drugs counter this effect by blocking the dopamine receptors so that the brain cells cannot absorb it.

Depression appears to be caused by a deficiency of other neurotransmitters, either *norepinephrine* or *serotonin*. The antidepressant drugs attack this problem in two ways: The tricyclics increase levels of one chemical or the other, and the MAO inhibitors block an enzyme that breaks down norepinephrine, allowing it to remain longer in the brain.

Lithium seems to act similarly to the antipsychotic drugs in reducing the sensitivity of dopamine receptors, while at the same time raising levels of serotonin, as the antidepressants do.

Institutionalization of the mentally disturbed has a long history, dating back to the seventeenth and eighteenth centuries. As recently as the 1950s, many institutions were nothing more than storehouses for the mentally ill. With the advent, during the early 1960s, of antipsychotic and antidepressant drugs, many patients have been able to leave the institutions, live in their own communities, and receive outpatient therapy. (Jerry Cooke/Photo Researchers, Inc.; M. E. Warren/Photo Researchers, Inc.)

EVALUATION OF DRUG THERAPY   Psychoactive drugs have taken millions of people from a half-life of misery to a richer life in the society of normal people. And yet these medications are still not a cure-all for all the psychological distresses humankind is heir to. As with any other drug, they don't always work. Even the ones with the highest success rates for a particular disorder are not effective with everyone suffering from that condition. And even when drugs *are* able to eliminate symptoms, the side-effects they leave in their wake sometimes seem as bad or worse than the original condition, and so their use has to be discontinued. (Later in this chapter we will compare drug therapy to the other therapies.) For people who cannot be helped by drugs, we need alternate forms of treatment—and we need continued research to find new ways to help.

ENVIRONMENTAL THERAPY

Sometimes the best course of treatment includes changing a person's environment. This may involve the most extreme kind of change—placement in a psychiatric hospital. Or it may constitute an alternative such as residence in a hostel, a small-group home, or a foster home. It may involve sending a person to a day-care center where she or he can remain all day long in a sheltered environment that provides an opportunity for therapy as well as for constructive activity. Such alternative care may offer training in daily living activities like personal grooming, using public transportation, budgeting, shopping, cooking, and doing laundry. It may also offer vocational training or work in a sheltered workshop.

Institutionalization of the mentally disturbed has a long history, stretching back to the seventeenth and eighteenth centuries. Its goal was humanitarian—to provide refuge, or "asylum" for the mentally ill. It was also protective of society: By locking up the disturbed, the normal were safeguarded. Eventually, in the nineteenth century, mental health professionals began to offer specialized treatment to the inmates of sanatoriums. By and large, however, attempts to cure institutionalized people have proved disappointing. People so disturbed that they needed to be

The following description could have been applied to hundreds of mental hospitals as recently as the 1950s:

The patients wandered aimlessly about, mumbling incoherently. Violent ones were wrapped in wet sheets with their arms pinned, or they wore "camisoles," the institutional euphemism for the straitjacket. Attendants, in frequent danger of assault, peered at their charges through screens. The floors lay bare, because rugs would have quickly been soiled with excrement.
(Clark, 1979, p. 98)

hospitalized were rarely able to benefit from inpatient treatment, and many people remained in mental hospitals from early adulthood until their deaths, as disturbed as the day they had entered. Fewer than 5 percent of those who were in an institution for more than two years ever left it (Paul, 1969).

Yet no one knew what else to do with the severely disturbed. So more and more hospitals were built, and more and more patients consigned to them. During the 1950s, more than half a million Americans were in the wards of mental hospitals, with their number increasing by nearly 10,000 per year (Clark, 1979). Hospitals were crammed with four times the number of patients they had originally been built to house and in many cases were nothing more than foul-smelling, dangerous storehouses for people who seemed barely human.

Then the antipsychotic and antidepressant drugs arrived on the scene and changed the whole picture. During the early 1960s millions of patients, now receiving medication, left the mental hospitals and went home to live in their own communities and to receive treatment as outpatients.

What happened in Ypsilanti, Michigan, is typical. The regional psychiatric hospital there was built in 1931, designed to house 900 patients. By the 1950s, it was straining to care for the 3400 packed within its walls. Then by 1979, the patient count was back down to 980 (Clark, 1979). Not only did this difference affect those patients who left the hospital; it had a great effect on those who remained, who were now able to receive more individual, humane attention in more pleasant surroundings.

Yet this story still has no happy ending for countless numbers of the mentally ill, many of whom live a revolving-door existence, going in and out of institutions until they issue the plaint that became the title of a recent book about a schizophrenic woman, *Is There No Place on Earth for Me?* (Sheehan, 1982). The typical destiny of the psychotic patient released from an institution is a life on the fringes of society. After struggling to get along either in a family thrown into turmoil by the disturbed person's presence or in a lonely furnished room, the patient shows up far too often at a hospital emergency room, once more to be readmitted to a psychiatric facility. About half of all released inpatients go back into the walls of an institution within a year of discharge (Bassuk & Gerson, 1978).

The promise of "community mental health," which was widely heralded in the 1960s to provide treatment and rehabilitation within the community setting has, by and large, not materialized. Those few excellent community-based programs that do exist can treat only a tiny minority of the patients who need them, and most released patients get little or no follow-up care or supervision and are left to flounder in relative isolation. The difficulty of their situation can be seen in the fact that so many of them keep going back to the hospital, even though there are clear indications that outpatient treatment is more effective and less costly.

In a review of ten studies comparing institutional and noninstitutional care of patients with serious mental illness, Kiesler (1982) concludes that patients who receive care outside an institution do better on psychiatric evaluations, job and school performance, maintenance of long-term relationships, and other measures of independent living. Furthermore, discharged hospitalized patients are more likely to return to mental hospitals than alternative-care patients are to ever be admitted at all. Hospitalization becomes "self-perpetuating."

While the number of patients in mental hospitals at any one time is two-thirds lower than it was twenty years ago, more people are admitted and readmitted for shorter stays. Mental hospitals in the United States receive about 1,800,000 admissions each year, and 70 percent of all national funds spent on mental health go to hospital care (Kiesler, 1982). One reason for this is that Medicaid has become the largest single mental health funding program in the country, and Medicaid pays primarily for institutional care rather than alternative types of care.

EVALUATION OF THE VARIOUS THERAPIES

We have discussed a large number of therapies available to treat psychological problems. To come to any conclusion about their effectiveness, we have to ask some critical questions. The rest of this chapter will attempt to answer the following queries:

1 Is therapy better than no therapy?
2 Is any one therapy "the best"?
3 Is a particular therapy best suited for a particular problem?
4 Is a combination of therapies better than a single therapy used alone?
5 Are there common denominators that cut across all therapies?

Is Therapy Better than No Therapy?

"Everyone has won and all must have prizes," the dodo bird announced as he judged the race in *Alice in Wonderland*. Luborsky, Singer, and Luborsky (1975) cited this "dodo bird verdict" to underscore their belief "that all the psychotherapies produce some benefits for some patients" (p. 995). This verdict is confirmed by a number of studies that have found that a high percentage of troubled people benefit by *any* kind of psychotherapy.

The consensus of contemporary researchers is far different from the early reports on the efficacy of psychotherapy, which now seem overly skeptical and negative. The most influential of these earlier critics of therapy was Hans J. Eysenck, (1952; 1965; 1969), who argued that about two-thirds of all neurotics improved over a two-year period whether they received therapy or not, that any effects of psychotherapy are small or nonexistent, and that "current psychotherapeutic procedures have not lived up to the hopes which greeted their emergence fifty years ago" (1965, p. 136). The only therapy Eysenck credited with positive results was behavior therapy. Since Eysenck came to his conclusion, there have been more and better-designed comparison studies. Luborsky and his colleagues (1975) point out that 80 percent of studies evaluating the benefits of psychotherapy have found mainly positive results even for minimal treatment, with about two-thirds of the comparisons of psychotherapy with control groups of untreated individuals showing significant differences.

Most of these studies deal only with short-term treatment, lasting from two to twelve months, and most rely on the therapist's judgment of the client's improvement. Since therapists like to feel that their efforts help people, they are apt to be biased in the direction of seeing improvement.

I am opposed to the advancement of psychoanalysis, to the advancement of Gestalt therapy, to the advancement of existential therapy, to the advancement of behavior therapy, or to the advancement of any delimited school of thought. I would like to see an advancement in psychological knowledge, an advancement in the understanding of human interaction, in the alleviation of suffering, and in the know-how of therapeutic intervention. (Lazarus, 1977, p. 553)

However, studies that have used more objective standards—such as the ratings of independent clinical judges or hospital discharge and readmission rates—show similar results to those based on therapists' judgments.

Is Any One Therapy "The Best"?

The fiercest contemporary controversies orbit around pro-drug versus anti-drug approaches and about the dynamic versus behavior therapies. Let's look at the evidence on these issues.

SHOULD CLIENTS USE THEIR MOUTHS TO TAKE DRUGS OR TO TALK?   The problem of the psychiatrist has been compared to that of the bartender in the controversy between pro-drug and anti-drug forces (Klerman, 1978). Should the psychiatrist mix a therapeutic "cocktail" blending, say, family therapy with a tranquilizer or group therapy with a neuroleptic? Or should she/he be a "prohibitionist" and avoid drugs altogether? Or be a dispenser of drugs alone, for "those who like their drinks straight"?

To answer these questions, it helps to review the arguments for each point of view. The drug controversy swirls around neurotic personality problems. The value of drugs in treating psychotic disorders such as schizophrenia, major depression, and mania is generally accepted.

The anti-drug people say that drug therapy makes patients too dependent on their doctors, that it increases their beliefs in magical treatment, and that it does not encourage them to struggle to gain insight into their personality problems. Social critics maintain that giving drugs to disturbed people labels their problems as biomedical, when, in fact, they may have arisen out of a discriminatory climate in society. Other critics question the drugs' effectiveness, maintaining that the improvement credited to them might be due to placebo* effects.

Even those people who feel there is a place for drug therapy raise questions. First of all, drugs don't always work. Even the ones with the highest success rates for a particular disorder are not effective with everyone suffering from that condition. And even when drugs *are* able to eliminate symptoms, the side-effects they leave in their wake sometimes seem as bad or worse than the original condition, and so their use has to be discontinued for that reason. Since their use is relatively recent on a large-scale basis, there is still a great deal of controversy about proper dosage, and we don't know much about their long-term effects. We still have to develop criteria for releasing hospitalized patients into the community, so that we will not have large numbers of people floundering about without a caring structure, simply because the drugs have helped them get rid of their obviously crazy symptoms. We have to ask ourselves how many people are getting drugs to alleviate the ordinary anxieties of everyday life, when they would be better advised to develop psychological reserves of strength to deal with adversity. We have to ask whether doctors prescribe pills because it's the fastest, easiest thing to do when some other treatment might be more useful.

The pro-drug professionals feel that medication is all the patient needs

---

*A placebo is a pill that substitutes sugar or something else for an active ingredient. Any effect such a "sugar pill" has on an individual is assumed to be psychological. Placebos are often given to control subjects in experiments so that any difference between an experimental and a control group will clearly be the result of the difference in the content of the medication and will not be affected by the fact that one group is getting medication and the other is not.

and that psychotherapy on top of drugs may interfere with the healing attributes of the drug regimen. They compare psychoactive drugs to those used in general medicine, like the insulin that diabetics take, and say nothing else is necessary. Many "biological psychiatrists" feel that psychotherapy will arouse patients and make them more tense by stirring up painful inner conflicts, thus undoing the valuable effects of the drugs.

Some people, whose conditions seem to have a biochemical basis respond dramatically to drug treatment. If they have not been severely handicapped emotionally by the consequences of their conditions, they can often walk away from their therapist's office clutching a prescription pad and requiring nothing more than a periodic checkup to be sure things are still going well.

For most people, however, drugs are most profitably used in conjunction with some kind of psychotherapy. No matter how effective the drugs are in getting rid of troubling symptoms, the individual still needs to develop some insight into his or her life or needs to learn behaviors that are more appropriate than those she or he had been practicing before therapy. The drugs may be the crucial catalyst enabling a person to participate actively in and derive benefit from psychotherapy, and the psychotherapy may be able to take a different focus because of the drugs' control of the individual's most troubling symptoms. We will look at the way drugs and therapy are combined in our answer to question 4.

WHICH IS BETTER: PSYCHOANALYTICALLY ORIENTED OR BEHAVIOR THERAPY? While neither one of these approaches has been shown to be of significant value in treating psychoses (either schizophrenia or severe depression), both kinds of therapy are commonly used in the treatment of a wide range of other disorders. In most studies comparing the two for the typical person who comes to therapy with a grab-bag of neurotic symptoms, very little difference emerges.

One explanation for this may lie in the findings from interviews of therapists from different schools. Behavior therapists, who emphasize the importance of persuading clients to practice new behaviors, said they often work with clients for "a year of corrective emotional experience" which can be "what the Freudians refer to as transference" (Russell, 1981, p. 20). And eclectic therapists, who emphasize the importance of helping a client achieve insight, give specific behavioral suggestions. In sum, these interviews confirm Gurman and Razin's (1977) conclusion that "the differences among therapists are more evident in how they think than in how they or their patients behave" (Russell, 1981, p. 17).

In some of these studies, behavior therapy does come out somewhat ahead of psychoanalytically oriented treatment. This superiority is not surprising since behavior therapy was born in the lab and endowed at birth with a propensity for scientific evaluation, whereas the dynamic, insight-oriented therapies lend themselves much less readily to objective measurement. Sloane and his colleagues (1975) found that behavior therapy is at least as effective as psychoanalytically oriented therapy, and maybe more so with neuroses and personality disorders.

They also found that psychoanalytically oriented therapy does better with "verbal, intelligent, well-educated young women of reasonably high

Over the past few years, behavior therapy has acquired "a bad press." Psychologist Arnold A. Lazarus protests:

One grows weary of explaining that behavior therapists do not deny consciousness, that they do not treat people like Pavlovian dogs, that they are not Machiavellian and coercive, that aversion therapy (except in the hands of a lunatic fringe) has always been a minor and relatively insignificant part of our armamentarium, and that we are not ignorant of the part played by mutual trust and other relationship factors among our treatment variables.
(1977, p. 553)

income, who are mildly neurotic, while behavior therapies are effective for a broader range of clients" (Sloane et al., 1975).

While behavior therapy has been successful in treating the whole range of neurotic problems, its superiority emerges most clearly in the treatment of certain specific, narrowly defined conditions, as seen in the discussion below of question 3.

Our answer, then, to question 2, is "sometimes." In some cases one particular therapy is best, and in many there is no clearly demonstrated superiority of one over another.

Is a Particular Therapy Best Suited for a Particular Problem?

The first report of the Commission on Psychiatric Therapies of the American Psychiatric Association stated that drug therapy is essential in the treatment of schizophrenia and that psychoanalytically oriented therapies "contribute little additional benefit to pharmacotherapy," though there is some value to various forms of behavior therapy and psychosocial rehabilitation (Pines, 1982). In major depressions, however, the commission recommends psychotherapy in addition to drugs. Drugs are also indicated in the treatment of other illnesses that appear to have a physiological basis, such as Tourette's syndrome, some forms of childhood hyperactivity, and some kinds of panic attacks.

One recent study found that people with schizophrenic disorders get more benefit from a combination of family therapy and neuroleptic drugs than from individual supportive therapy in conjunction with the drugs (Falloon et al., 1982). Therapists educated patients and their families about the nature, course, and treatment of schizophrenia, helped family members to identify tensions, and taught them how to improve their problem-solving skills. After nine months, only one patient in the family therapy group had relapsed, compared with eight who had been treated individually, and the family-treated patients spent less than one day in the hospital, on the average, compared with more than eight days for those in the other group.

Another treatment generally acknowledged as a specific "cure" for a specific problem is electroconvulsive, or shock, therapy, prescribed only for the severely depressed and suicidal and often quite effective. More specific recommendations about the best kind of treatment for depression may develop from a major study currently being conducted by the National Institute of Mental Health (NIMH) to compare three different treatments. Two are forms of psychotherapy: Beck's cognitive therapy and the interpersonal psychotherapy developed by Klerman, Weissman, and others. The third is a drug regimen consisting of a tricyclic antidepressant, compared to a placebo (Kolata, 1981; Pines, 1982).

One other major category of a specific type of therapy's being especially well adapted to a specific type of problem is the use of behavior therapy in the treatment of phobias, obsessions and compulsions, and certain kinds of sexual dysfunction.

So far, however, with most psychological disorders, the match between therapist and client seems much more important than the particular theory the therapist espouses. For more on this, see the discussion of question 5.

Is a Combination of Therapies Better than a Single Therapy Used Alone?

"In practice, most psychiatrists and even many nonmedical psychotherapists are active bartenders, mixing various 'cocktails' of drugs and psychotherapy" (Klerman, 1978, p. 221). The combination of these two kinds of therapy often operates as a "two-stage rocket" in the treatment of depression (p. 222). The first stage, the drug, attacks the prominent symptoms—anxiety, insomnia, tension, and so forth, getting the depressed person out of the "symptomatic orbit." The psychotherapy that constitutes the second stage helps the client become more competent in everyday life, adjust socially, and gain insight into his or her life situation. Drugs seem to make such a person more accessible to psychotherapy, and the combination seems superior to either treatment alone.

Luborsky and his associates (1975) also found plusses for combining treatments. When they compared drugs plus psychotherapy for a variety of psychological disorders with either drugs alone or psychotherapy alone, and when they compared medical care alone for psychosomatic illness to a combination of medical care plus psychotherapy, the combination won out almost all the time. They concluded, "A combination of treatments may represent more than an additive effect of two treatments—a 'getting more of one's money'" (p. 1004). We seem to have a synergistic effect here: The combination of two different treatments provides a therapy that is much more effective than just adding the benefits of one to the other. The combined force of the treatments has an energy all its own.

Are There Common Denominators that Cut across All Therapies?

What do all psychotherapies have in common? They all offer some kind of systematized explanation for a client's problems, with a set of principles she or he can use to guide future behavior, and they all offer a helping relationship with a professionally trained person. When they work, they raise clients' self-esteem, their sense of personal competence, and the confidence that they can make it in the world. "The chief problem of all patients who come to psychotherapy is demoralization, and the effectiveness of all psychotherapeutic schools lies in their ability to restore patients' morale" (Frank, 1974, p. 271).

In determining the success of treatment, the therapist is more important than the kind of therapy she or he practices. The therapist-client relationship is crucial. "You have to get along. It could be Sigmund Freud himself, but if he rubs you the wrong way, you should go to another therapist" (Cummings, quoted in Sobel, 1980, p. 104). Good therapists recognize the importance of the right fit between therapist and client.

Clients need to feel comfortable with their therapists' personality, orientation, and general approach. Sloane and his colleagues (1975) found that clients whose therapists like them, are comfortable with them, and find them interesting make better progress. The most successful clients of both psychotherapists and behavior therapists report finding their therapists warm, genuine, and empathetic.

Like anyone else, therapists continue to learn as they practice, and this learning pays off for their clients. By and large, experienced therapists from any school achieve better results with clients than do novices probably because they take more initiative, are more realistic, more patient, more interested in the client's history, more willing to wait for information, more prone to interpret material, more variable in the way they

Some therapists are effective hypnotists, others are not; some welcome emotional displays, others shy away from them; some work best with groups, others in the privacy of the dyad; some enjoy exploring psyches, others prefer to try to change behaviors. Ideally, a therapist should master as many rationales and procedures as possible and try to select those which are most appropriate for different patients. Most of us are capable of some flexibility, but very few can effectively handle all procedures.
(Frank, 1974, pp. 273–274)

BOX 16-2

CHOOSING THERAPY AND A THERAPIST

Faced with the bewildering array of therapies and therapists, how can people choose the best kind of therapy for their problems and the best person to administer it? There are no hard-and-fast answers, but the following dialogue may be helpful.

Q: How do I know if I need therapy?
A: Let's answer that question with other questions. Are you often unhappy? Do you have problems making and keeping close relationships? Do you have trouble doing schoolwork or holding a job? Do irrational fears get in the way of your daily life? Has there been a big change in your habits—sleeping too much or not enough, overeating or losing your appetite, losing interest in activities and people you used to enjoy? Do you think about suicide? Do you generally feel out of control of your life? If you have problems like these, it's time to speak to a therapist.
Q: How do I start?
A: With a thorough physical examination since some emotional problems are related to physical health. Your family doctor may be able to recommend a therapist. Someone you know who has had a good therapeutic experience can give you a name. You could go to your college's counseling/psychological service. Check the yellow pages to find a family service agency or a mental health

center. Or you could contact the closest school of medicine or major teaching hospital that has an outpatient psychiatric clinic. Such clinics often offer psychological testing, diagnostic screening by psychiatrists, and the ongoing services of psychologists and social workers.

If you go first to an interdisciplinary team, you'll find out whether your problems are physically caused, you'll have access to professionals qualified to prescribe medication, and you'll reap the benefits of several heads.
Q: How can I tell whether a particular therapist is right for me?
A: Only through a personal meeting. Besides checking out a therapist's basic professional qualifications, you'll know whether you feel comfortable with his or her personality, values and belief systems, and psychological orientation. Does she or he seem like a warm, intelligent person who would be able and interested in helping you? Is she or he willing to talk about the techniques she or he uses? Does she or he make sense to you?

If you get good vibrations from the first therapist you see, there's no need to shop around. If you feel at all uncomfortable, however, it's worthwhile setting up one-shot consultations with one or two others before you make up your mind. The therapist's attitude toward your interest in talking to

someone else may be the first barometer of his or her suitability. If you are not in need of emergency care, be prepared to spend at least as much time shopping for a therapist as you would for a new car. This decision may have lifelong ramifications, and it pays to invest time and money to make it as wisely as possible.
Q: How much will I have to spend?
A: As of this writing, costs for therapy vary from no fee on up to $100 per 45-minute session. Therapists in private practice charge more than those affiliated with centers or large institutions, and psychiatrists usually charge more than psychologists, who charge more than social workers. Many therapists charge on a sliding scale, based on what the client can afford, and many health insurance plans cover the costs.
Q: What should I do if I start with a therapist and then decide that she or he is not helping me?
A: First, ask yourself whether you're displeased because your therapy is raising difficult, painful issues that you don't want to deal with. Then express your dissatisfaction to your therapist and deal with it in your sessions. Finally, if you are convinced that your therapy is either ineffective or harmful, find another therapist (*not* one referred by your current therapist!).

behave during interviews, and more effectively expressive (Gurman & Razin, 1977; Russell, 1981).

Since the therapist-client fit is so vital to the success of therapy, how is someone seeking therapy to choose the right person? Luborsky (1979) has suggested that clients try several therapists and select one on the basis of their feelings. He has also proposed that, to make this process easier, therapists supply film strips or videotapes of themselves doing therapy. And Hogan (1979) recommends that therapists become aware of their own limitations, techniques, and values and that they share this awareness publicly, to make the selection of a therapist less like a blind date.

Therapy has made an enormous difference in the lives of untold numbers of people. It has opened their eyes to the possibilities around them. It has enabled them to be more loving, more productive, more content with themselves. It has allowed them to live in the company of their fellows in society rather than being forced into the isolation of institutionalization. In other instances, therapy has been a grave disappointment to those who sought and participated in it. The more we understand about what it can and cannot do, the better we will be able to unleash its power.

SUMMARY

1   About 3 percent of Americans, some 7 million people, are receiving *therapy*, or *treatment*, in a psychiatric facility, including private offices, outpatient clinics, community mental health centers, and hospitals. More people are hospitalized for mental disorders than for any other kind of ailment.

2   Recipients of therapy fall into several categories: *psychotics, neurotics, the psychologically shaken, the unruly, the discontent,* and *professional therapists.*

3   A *therapist* is someone who is specially trained to offer a definite kind of treatment. In our society a therapist is generally a *clinical psychologist, psychiatrist, social worker, psychoanalyst, psychiatric nurse,* or *counselor.*

4   There are many different approaches to therapy such as *psychotherapy, medical,* and *social.*

5   *Psychotherapy* refers to nonmedical forms of treatment. There are three major "schools" of psychotherapy: *dynamic, humanist,* and *behavioral.* Important current trends in psychotherapy include *cognitive, brief,* and *interpersonal* approaches. Many psychotherapists use elements from two or more approaches in their therapy, calling themselves "*eclectic.*"

6   The goal of *dynamic therapy* is to restructure personality by changing the way a person looks at and reacts to life. In this approach the patient is helped to develop insight into the vast and powerful psychological forces in his or her unconscious. *Psychoanalysis* is a type of dynamic therapy, developed by Freud, which uses techniques such as *free association* and *dream analysis* to determine the repressed instinctual drives and defenses in the unconscious which influence behavior. During psychoanalysis the patient gains insight into these forces.

7   Because classical psychoanalysis is so time-consuming and costly, many psychoanalytically oriented therapists have moved toward *psychoanalytically inspired psychotherapy,* which is more directive, less frequent, shorter, and goal directed.

8   The goal of *humanist psychotherapies* is to free personalities, to help clients grow. In *Carl Rogers' person-centered approach,* the therapist views the client as an individual in search of himself. The goal of therapy is *self-actualization.* The therapist provides the client with *unconditional positive regard* and *empathic understanding* so the client comes to accept his or her experiences as real and thus gets to know his or her *true* feelings and attitudes rather than those imposed by others.

9   The goal of *Gestalt therapy,* founded by *Fritz Perls,* is to make the client aware of the whole self. In Gestalt therapy the therapist actively seeks to make the client aware of contradictions in his or her actions. Gestalt therapists use a variety of techniques including *role-playing, games,* and *visual imagery.*

10   *Behavior therapy* is the use of experimentally established principles of learning to overcome habits that are not adaptive for the individual. The client is seen as someone who has learned inappropriate

behaviors, and the aim of therapy is to eliminate the undesirable behaviors and replace them with appropriate ones. Behavior therapists use a wide variety of techniques based on learning principles; these techniques include *systematic desensitization, aversive counterconditioning, modeling,* and *positive reinforcement (operant therapy)*.

11 *Cognitive therapies* such as *Ellis's rational-emotive therapy* and *Beck's cognitive therapy* consider *distortions in thinking* to be at the foundation of emotional problems. Cognitive therapists aim to show clients how such distortions contribute to their distress and to help clients substitute more correct appraisals and interpretations.

12 *Brief therapies* are time-limited therapeutic approaches, generally lasting for no more than fifteen or twenty sessions.

13 Today therapists from all the major schools sometimes do their work with *groups* rather than single individuals. In *family therapy* the entire family is the patient. The goal of family therapy is to strengthen the family group. By helping people understand how their family works, therapists can often help them see what each family member is doing to perpetuate disruptive patterns and how they can change these patterns.

14 *Medical therapies* include *psychosurgery, electroconvulsive (shock) therapy,* and *drug* treatments. The surgical technique prefrontal lobotomy was once quite common but is hardly ever used today. Electroconvulsive therapy, which is the application of electric current through the brain, is often effective with severely depressed, suicidal patients. Drug therapy is now extremely common. Disorders such as schizophrenia, depression, bipolar disorder, and anxiety disorders often respond successfully to drugs. The biochemical revolution has allowed numerous sufferers of mental disorders to live in the community. However, drug therapy is not always successful and frequently entails unwanted side-effects.

15 *Environmental or social therapy* includes *institutionalization*, or placement in a *hostel, small-group home*, or *foster home*. Individuals may spend time in *day-care centers* which provide a sheltered environment and the opportunity for therapy and constructive activity.

16 Although some early research questioned the value of psychotherapy, more recent research indicates that therapy *is* effective for many people. No one type of psychotherapy is generally *the* most effective although particular types of psychotherapy do seem especially well suited for particular problems. In many cases, however, the match between patient and therapist seems to be more important than the particular therapy used. Drug therapy is especially effective in treating disorders such as schizophrenia, depression, and mania; however, drugs are not equally effective for all patients. For most, drugs are most profitably used along with psychotherapy. Electroconvulsive therapy is particularly effective for major depressions. Behavior therapy is especially helpful in the treatment of phobias, obsessions, compulsions, and certain kinds of sexual dysfunction.

SUGGESTED READINGS

Goleman, D., & Speeth, K. R. (Eds.) (1982). *The essential psychotherapies.* New York: New American Library. A collection of essays by important psychotherapists including Freud, Adler, Jung, Ellis, Beck, Wolpe, and Rogers. The editors introduce each selection with a brief biography of the therapist.

Herr, J. J., & Weakland, J. H. (1979). *Counseling elders and their families.* New York: Springer. A practical guide to the problems of the elderly. Written primarily for health professionals, but other readers will also find this a useful aid in problem solving.

Napier, A., & Whitaker, C. A. (1978). *The family crucible.* New York: Harper and Row. A moving account of the process of family therapy. Focusing on the "Brice family," the authors demonstrate how the problem of the identified patient is a front for the serious malfunctioning of the entire family system.

Rogers, C. R. (1980). *A way of being.* Boston: Houghton Mifflin. A collection of essays written by the founder of person-centered psychotherapy. They provide insight into Rogers' personal experiences and attitudes.

Wender, P. H., & Klein, D. F. (1981). *Mind, mood, and medicine.* New York: Farrar, Straus, Giroux. Written for a lay audience by two psychiatrists. A comprehensive guide to the pharmacological advances which have revolutionized the treatment of mental disorders.

Peggy Bacon: *The Social Graces*, 1935. The Whitney Museum of American Art.

PART

7

SOCIAL PSYCHOLOGY

We human beings are social creatures. From the moment of birth we begin to be affected by those around us—our parents, our babysitters, our brothers and sisters, even other crying babies we don't know. This close tie with other human beings persists throughout life as we influence and are, in turn, influenced by others. The specific ways in which this influence flexes its muscle is often tempered by the situation in which we find ourselves. In the next two chapters we'll look at these influences in both group and intimate relationships.

In Chapter 17 "In a World with Other People: Social Influence," we look mostly at the group. We see how the influence of a group of strangers can make us doubt the evidence of our own senses, how someone we think of as an authority can influence us to harm a person who's done us no injury, and how easy it is to slip into socially accepted kinds of behavior even if they're not our usual way of acting. We'll also look at the "up" side, the factors that encourage us to reach out to help others. And finally, we'll look at the way we form our attitudes and how those attitudes can change, a phenomenon that's particularly relevant for modern society as we strive to overcome discrimination based on prejudices against certain ethnic and racial groups.

In Chapter 18, "Being with People Who Matter: Lovers and Friends," we focus on two important and very special types of relationships. We'll see what research tells us about why we like or love one person and not another, from such external factors as where people happen to live to their inner characteristics such as personal warmth. We'll also take a scientific look at that most unscientific emotion of love and see how it affects our close relationships with others, both in and out of marriage.

CHAPTER 17

IN A WORLD WITH OTHER PEOPLE: SOCIAL INFLUENCE

SPOTLIGHT ON

A study of the prison experience in which normal healthy college students randomly assigned to play either prisoner or guard rapidly assumed the behaviors "appropriate" for these roles.

How "groupthink"—an uncritical acceptance of an unwise course of action in order to maintain the unanimity of the group—can lead to disaster.

How many ordinary, decent people are, in some circumstances, ready to obey an authority who orders them to inflict pain on another person.

How our decision to help someone in distress is influenced by a number of situational factors.

How attitudes such as prejudice are formed and can be changed.

Today, four decades after the defeat of Nazi Germany in World War II, a steady succession of books, plays, TV shows, and movies about that era demonstrate the western world's continuing preoccupation with the mammoth riddle of the Holocaust: How could the citizens of a highly cultured, intellectual country have carried out a crusade of horror that resulted in the deaths of more than 12 million Jews, gypsies, political dissidents, and other "undesirables"? How could so many ordinary people who loved their families and behaved decently toward their neighbors have participated in or averted their eyes from millions of ghastly deaths?

The question underlying many of the recent fictional representations of the Holocaust, which focus on the Nazis rather than on their victims, is the terrifying one: "How would I have behaved? . . . What would I have done if I had lived in that place in that time?"

This same question has inspired a flood of psychological research on a wide range of issues that fall in the discipline of social psychology, the scientific study of how we feel, think, are affected by, and act toward other people. Much of psychology studies the individual alone—what she or he perceives, thinks, remembers, and feels—and only incidentally relates these processes to the influence of other people. Social psychology, however, emphasizes the fact that human beings are social creatures from birth till death and that it is impossible to understand us without understanding how we act and react to the other residents of this planet. Those others do not even have to be physically present: We learn social behavior and then make it part of our behavioral repertoire—so that even when you're alone at home, for example, you wear clothes and eat with knife and fork.

In view of the awesome questions raised by the unprecedented and previously unimaginable tragedy of the Holocaust, it's noteworthy that social psychology really came into its own only after World War II (Steiner, 1979).

In their research social psychologists use a wide variety of approaches and techniques. They conduct experiments in the laboratory and in the field, sometimes in such public places as subways, elevators, and restaurants. Some studies call for a certain amount of deception (which raises ethical issues, as we've indicated in Chapter 1), while other research is quite straightforward. While much research in social psychology explores such socially relevant topics as helping, obedience, and conformity, a considerable amount of attention is also devoted to more basic topics like attitude formation and change. A major concern of social psychologists is *group dynamics,* or the differences between the way people behave when they are alone and when they are with others.

We will now consider both new and classical research on various aspects of social impact. We'll see the importance of the social situation on conformity and obedience, while still remembering that personality characteristics interact with situational ones to determine what a given individual will do at any time. We'll look at one important kind of social behavior—altruism, or helping others. We'll see how attitudes are formed, how they can be changed, and how they relate to behaviors, and we'll look at one specific kind of attitude—prejudice—in detail. In this chapter we'll focus on the way people function in groups, and in the next chapter we'll talk about the influences and interdependencies of intimate relationships.

The tragedy of the Holocaust inspired a flood of research in the field of social psychology. This research has aimed to find answers to many questions, trying to find out, for example, what kinds of factors could have motivated so many people (like the Nazi soldiers shown at this rally in Nuremberg, who seemed to be decent, ordinary citizens) to carry out a crusade of horror that resulted in the often cruel and inhuman deaths of more than 12 million other decent, ordinary people, such as these concentration camp victims. (The Bettmann Archive, Inc.; Culver Pictures, Inc.)

PEOPLE IN GROUPS

According to psychologists, if you are interacting with one or more other people, you are in a group. What does interaction involve? That the members of the group be aware of each other, that they take one another into account, and that their relationship has some continuity, involving either the past or an anticipated future (McGrath & Kravitz, 1982). In other words, the people milling about you on a crowded city street would not constitute a group of which you are a member, unless some event were to happen that would make you stop and pay attention to each other. If, for example, you suddenly saw a man about to jump from a high building and you stopped with other passersby to watch, to help, or to dare him to jump, you would now be part of a group.

We belong to many different groups, from the basic one, the family, through children's clubs, school classes, and a variety of associations based on the common interests of their members. The most meaningful groups, those composed of friends and family, have long histories and the expectation of futures that stretch before them. Others—like the members of a seminar in psychology or the guests at a party—last for a short time and have no anticipated future. They are still groups because their members are interacting and interdependent at some time.

Norms and Roles

In the 1982 movie, *Best Friends*, Goldie Hawn and Burt Reynolds play a couple who marry after having lived together for three years. When they meet each other's parents for the first time, both mothers—his and hers—impress on Hawn her new responsibilities for pouring her husband's coffee and waiting on him at the table. "He knows how to do all of that himself—and he does it," she points out, only to receive the answer, "Yes, but *now* you're married—and that's a wife's job." Hawn's character was now supposed to behave according to the way both mothers interpreted the role of wife.

What is a role? It is a set of behavioral expectations for people of particular social positions. A role is made up of a group of norms, which are society's definitions of the way we should behave. Thus, norms in the United States dictate that men wear clothing that covers their pelvic area; a role dictates that a professional man wear a suit, shirt, and tie. Norms govern virtually every aspect of our behavior in society, with variations

People behave differently when they are alone than when they're with a group. When alone, they are more likely to answer a door, report a power failure, and help a fellow passenger pick up dropped pocket change. They tip more generously when alone, as well. After checking tips of 408 groups of 1159 customers at the Steak and Ale Restaurant in Columbus, Ohio, Freeman, Walker, Borden, and Latane (1975) found that lone diners tended to tip almost 19 percent of their bill, while groups of five or six left only 13 percent, probably because a larger group shares the responsibility for the tip. If you're planning to work your way through school by waiting on tables, you might want to pick up on Latane's suggestion to write separate checks, even for large parties. His findings indicate that "this might short-circuit diffusion of responsibility and result in larger tips" (p. 352). (Susie Fitzhugh/Stock, Boston)

depending on which particular society we live in. (Thus, Italian men commonly walk arm in arm, while American men ordinarily do not.) A particular position assumes the status of a *social role* when it accumulates a substantial number of norms. We have norms for the roles of parent and worker, as well as spouse. A worker, for example, is expected to be loyal, conscientious, hardworking, and so forth. But when a person travels by plane, the few behavioral expectations in the situation (buy the ticket, use the seat belt, etc.) don't justify according social role status to "airline passenger."

Norms have the capacity both for enhancing and restricting behavior. They oil the functioning of groups of people, so that once you learn your culture's norms, you know how to behave in many different situations. On the other hand, they can stifle independence since most people's natural tendencies seem to be to follow the norms, even when these are not the most effective or humane way to act. We will see in this chapter instances in which people obey orders because of previously learned norms and in which they conform to group decisions when they might think and act quite differently if they were alone. We also see that different people act differently in similar situations, showing the power of individual personality traits.

How much of our behavior is determined by the norms for the various roles we play? Philip G. Zimbardo and his colleagues at Stanford University established the powerful influence of a situation and society's definition of roles within that situation in an ingenious experiment (Zimbardo, Haney, Banks, & Jaffe, 1977). They recruited twenty-one emotionally stable, physically healthy, mature, and law-abiding college students to take part in a study on prison life. They randomly assigned eleven to act as prison guards for a two-week period and assigned the other ten to play the part of prisoners.

The "prisoners" were picked up in a surprise arrest, handcuffed, fingerprinted, deloused, given uniforms with ID numbers and stocking caps, and put in 6- by 9-foot windowless cells in the basement of a temporarily unused college building. The guards were issued khaki uniforms, reflector sunglasses (to prevent eye contact with prisoners), billy clubs, whistles, handcuffs, and keys. Rules that simulated the restrictiveness and depersonalization of prison life included requiring prisoners to obtain permission to write a letter, smoke a cigarette, or go to the toilet, and enforcing silence at many times during the day.

The researchers wanted to find out how these normal, healthy volunteers would react and whether their responses would give clues to the violence in real prison life. They found out so much that they had to

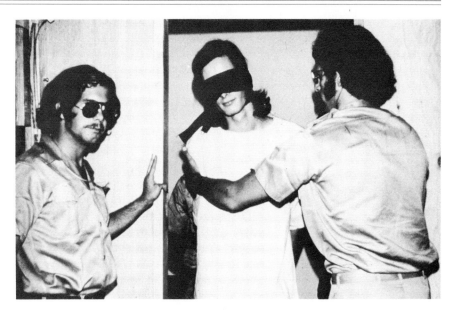

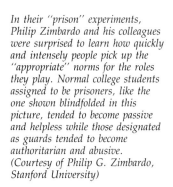

In their "prison" experiments, Philip Zimbardo and his colleagues were surprised to learn how quickly and intensely people pick up the "appropriate" norms for the roles they play. Normal college students assigned to be prisoners, like the one shown blindfolded in this picture, tended to become passive and helpless while those designated as guards tended to become authoritarian and abusive. (Courtesy of Philip G. Zimbardo, Stanford University)

release four prisoners within the first few days—and then to end the entire experiment early, after six days and nights.

The experiment had worked too well. These two groups of volunteers, at first indistinguishable in personality and health, developed traits related to their status as prisoner or guard. The four prisoners who were released early suffered from depression, anxiety, or, in one case, a psychosomatic rash over his entire body. One prisoner went on a hunger strike; some became "model" prisoners, obeying every command, no matter how arbitrary; others withdrew into themselves.

The guards all became authoritarian and abusive to varying degrees. Some were "good guys" who did little favors for the prisoners and were reluctant to punish them, and some were "tough but fair," just doing their job as they saw it. Over a third, however, acted hostile, arbitrary, and cruel, as they used their new power to degrade and humiliate prisoners. The guards' most typical way of acting toward the prisoners was to give commands and orders, threaten, and insult. The prisoners tended to become passive, increasingly doing and saying less and less that would call attention to themselves, behaving like the classic models of learned helplessness.

The researchers were surprised by "the relative ease with which sadistic behavior could be elicited from normal, non-sadistic people, and the extent of the emotional disturbance which emerged in young men selected precisely on the basis of their emotional stability" (p. 213). The kind of abnormal behavior that showed up during those six days seemed a direct product of the environment. Therefore, conclude Zimbardo and colleagues, "To change behavior we must discover the institutional supports which maintain the existing undesirable behavior and then design programs to alter these environments" (p. 214). Prisons need not be built of concrete and steel. They can exist in our minds as we play out our roles of either oppressor or victim in such "prisons of the mind" as racism, sexism, and ageism. This study helps us see how quickly people can pick up the "appropriate" norms for the roles they play.

Conformity

Before you read any farther, look carefully at the boxes in Figure 17-1. One of the lines in the square on the bottom is the same length as the single line in the square on the top. Which one?

You probably had no trouble choosing the matching line, which makes the findings from Solomon Asch's experiments (1955; 1956) all the more startling. College students were told they were participating in experiments on perception. Each subject sat at a table with a group of seven *confederates,* people posing as subjects who were actually working *with* the experimenter. All the "subjects" were then shown cards like the boxes in Figure 17-1 and posed the preceding problem with the confederates being called upon before the real subject. All participants gave their answers out loud in front of the entire group.

On some trials the confederates answered correctly, but on others every single confederate gave the wrong answer, contradicting what the subject saw before his eyes. In these trials, about one out of three of the real subjects *conformed,* that is, they went along with the majority, changing their opinions in response to the pressure they felt from the others in the group. Overall, about three out of four subjects gave the incorrect, conforming answer at least once. So while the majority of subjects did, in fact, trust their own judgment most of the time, a disturbingly large number of wrong answers were given.

Extreme differences showed up among individuals. Subjects who remained *independent* differed from each other, with some showing confidence in their own judgment, some acting withdrawn, and some tense and doubtful but determined to do as well as they could. The *yielding* subjects included some who were not aware how they had been influenced by the majority and some who still felt they were right but didn't want to seem different from the others. The largest subgroup of the yielders, however, came to doubt the evidence of their own senses.

Changing various conditions gave rise to a number of interesting findings. If only one other person agreed with the subject, he was likely to hold fast to his position, but if that person switched in midstream to the majority position, the subject was apt to shift, too. The size of the opposition was important, too. In different trials the size of the unanimous opposition varied from one to fifteen persons. A single dissenter had virtually no influence, two dissenters increased the pressure somewhat, and three produced the full effect. More than three dissenters did not increase the error rate further.

Despite the surprisingly high level of conformity that led so many people to mistrust the evidence before their eyes, however, *most* of the answers from subjects in Asch's experiments were, in fact, correct, even in the face of unanimously wrong answers offered by peers.

Conformity is not always bad. If no one's behavior conformed to group norms, we'd have a terrible time knowing what to expect, and we'd be faced constantly with thousands of decisions about everyday activities. We wouldn't be able to count on other drivers' stopping at a red light, on other passengers' making ways for us to get off a crowded bus, on other moviegoers' taking their proper turn in the ticket buying line. Much of the time, conforming behavior is simply convenient, both for ourselves and for others. The key is in knowing when it is appropriate and when it

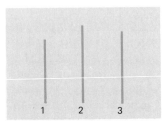

FIGURE 17-1 Asch's Line-Drawing Task *Subjects were shown the cards pictured and asked to choose the line in the picture on the bottom that was the same length as the line in the picture on the top. (From Asch, 1955)*

"Wait a minute, you guys—I've decided to make it unanimous after all."

Pressures to conform to the opinions held by other members of a group often make people disregard their own critical judgment, sometimes to the point where they even ignore the evidence of their own senses. (Drawing by Vietor; © 1978 The New Yorker Magazine, Inc.)

conflicts with more important norms and values. This is often difficult, even for people in high places.

GROUPTHINK, OR "HOW COULD WE HAVE BEEN SO STUPID?" John F. Kennedy asked this question after he and his close advisers had seen their decision to invade Cuba's Bay of Pigs turn into one of the United States' worst military and political fiascoes. The answer proposed by Irving L. Janis (1971) was groupthink, or an uncritical acceptance by members of a closely knit group of an unwise course of action.

The "two heads are better than one" approach gives us differing perspectives, which often result in a better solution than one person could come up with alone. Some closely knit groups, however, place a premium on maintaining unanimity. As the group becomes more concerned with complete agreement, critical thought often falls by the wayside. When groupthink takes over, the members of a cohesive group put loyalty to the group above all else. Individuals don't deliberately suppress any thoughts that would expose the folly of current or proposed plans. But they become so involved in wanting the group to continue being a "good group" that they unwittingly push to the back of their minds any nagging thoughts that would "spoil the cozy, 'we-feeling' atmosphere" (p. 218).

Groupthink makes people become overoptimistic, rationalize decisions instead of seriously reconsidering them, fail to consider ethical or moral consequences, hold onto stereotyped views of opponents that cloud realistic judgment, put pressure on any individual who casts doubt on the group's policy, self-censor critical thinking, believe falsely that everyone else fully agrees with policy, and try to protect the group from evidence that would question the wisdom of its policies (Janis, 1971).

President Kennedy learned a painful lesson from the Bay of Pigs and prevented groupthink in his handling of the Cuban missile crisis. He used some of the techniques recommended by Janis (1982), which include:

1 Alerting group members to the dangers of groupthink
2 Having the leader remain impartial
3 Instructing everyone to express their objections and doubts

4 Assigning one or more group members to play the role of devil's advocate by taking an opposing viewpoint
5 Occasionally subdividing the group into small groups that meet separately
6 Paying attention to all warning signals from a possible rival
7 Calling a "second-chance" meeting to reevaluate the preliminary decision
8 Inviting outside experts to come in to challenge the group's views
9 Encouraging group members to sound out group thought with trusted associates
10 Having several independent groups work on the same question at the same time

Obedience to Authority

Suppose that you have answered a newspaper ad calling for volunteers to take part in an experiment on memory and learning, directed by a professor at a prestigious university. You go into the psychology lab where you met a lab-coated experimenter and another volunteer, a pleasant-looking man in his fifties. After being chosen to be the "teacher" in this experiment on the effects of punishment on learning, you see the other volunteer, the "student," being strapped into a chair in the next room and attached to an electrode, and you hear the experimenter tell him that whenever he makes a mistake in learning a list of word pairs, he will receive an electric shock. The shocks will be painful, but they will not cause any permanent tissue damage.

Back in the main lab you are seated in front of a shock generator with thirty switches ranging from 15 to 450 volts, with labels ranging from "Slight Shock" to "Danger—Severe Shock." The experimenter tells you to give the learning test to the student and to give him a shock whenever he makes a mistake or fails to answer. You are to start at the lowest level and keep increasing the jolt with each error.

How far do you think you would go in following these instructions? Would you stop when the student began to show some discomfort—some grunting, say, at 75 volts? Or at 120 volts when he complained? At 150 when he demanded to be released? Or not until 285 volts, when the student was screaming in agony? What if, at any of these points, you turned to the experimenter for guidance and he told you to continue? Would you go all the way up to the maximum of 450 volts—even after you heard no more sounds from the next room?

If you react like a sample of college students, psychiatrists, and middle-class adults who were posed this same dilemma, you feel a sense of revulsion and are sure that you—and virtually all normal people, except for a lunatic fringe of 1 to 2 percent—would refuse to obey the experimenter at an early point (Milgram, 1974). Yet when this experiment was actually performed (with the cooperation of an actor who only pretended to be receiving shocks), the results were very different.

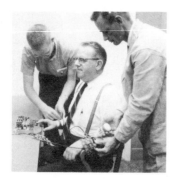

Stanley Milgram's famous experiments on obedience indicated that many ordinary people will hurt a complete stranger, even to the point of the threat of death, if they are ordered to do so by someone they consider an authority. If valid, this finding helps to explain many atrocities. (Copyright 1965 by Stanley Milgram. From the film Obedience, *distributed by the Pennsylvania State University, PCR.)*

Even those who disobeyed often showed great agitation, as we can see from this transcript of a defiant subject:

The man is banging. He wants to get out. . . . I'm sorry. If the man wants to get out I'd just as soon stop. . . . I don't want to administer any more [extremely excited]. . . . I will gladly refund the check, but I will not harm this man. . . . I'm sorry, I will not give him any more if he obviously wants to get out. There is no money in the world that will make me hurt another individual.
(Milgram, 1965, p. 67)

One 39-year-old social worker said, one year after his participation, "What appalled me was that I could possess this capacity for obedience and compliance to a central idea, i.e. the value of a memory experiment even after it became clear that continued adherence to this value was at the expense of violation of another value, i.e. don't hurt someone else who is helpless and not hurting you. I hope I can deal more effectively with any future conflicts of values I encounter" (Milgram, 1974, p. 54).

In 1963, Stanley Milgram conducted this experiment, which was not about learning and memory but about the extent of an ordinary person's willingness to obey an authority figure who orders him or her to hurt another person. Milgram and the rest of the psychological community were startled by the results. Of the forty men from a wide range of occupations who were the subjects in the first go-round, twenty-six—two out of three—obeyed commands fully and continued to give shocks to the highest voltage possible. Only fourteen broke off in response to the "student's" protests. Milgram (1974) pressed on with more experiments, introducing variations, until almost 1000 adults took part. The results were basically the same: A distressingly high proportion of subjects, many of whom disapproved of the "teaching tactics" of the experiment and were troubled by their own roles in it, obeyed orders and administered what they thought were painful shocks to an innocent person.

Subjects behaved differently under different conditions. Those in the same room as the victim were much more likely to defy orders (60 percent did), and those who actually had to place the victim's hand on the shock plate were even more likely to resist (70 percent defied orders). On the other hand, the closer the subject was to the experimenter, the more obedient: Obedience was three times greater when the experimenter was in the same room than when he gave orders by phone.

Even during the reign of terror that was Nazi Germany, some people found the strength to fight against officialdom. In these experiments, too, some people were able to resist authority. Which people? It's hard to identify those characteristics that made individuals stand their ground in the face of authority. The *situation* seemed to have more of an effect on whether a subject would obey or not than did any clearly identifiable personal characteristic.

There *was* one major difference between obedient and defiant subjects. The defiant ones saw themselves as principally responsible for the suffering of the learner, while the obedient ones felt less responsible than the experimenter. Furthermore, the obedient subjects attributed twice as much responsibility for the learner's suffering to the learner himself, offering arguments like "After all, he volunteered for the experiment, and he didn't learn very well in it" (Milgram, 1974).

There were no sex differences in obedience levels, although women experienced higher levels of conflict. Defiers tended to be better educated, in a "moral" profession (law, teaching, medicine) rather than a technical one, and to have had less military service and to have been officers rather than enlisted men (Milgram, 1974).

The frightening conclusion from Milgram's studies is the realization that many ordinary, decent people are, in some circumstances, ready to obey an authority who orders them to inflict pain on another person. If valid, this helps to explain many atrocities throughout history and leads us to examine the forces in society that exalt the value of obedience over the value of individual thought.

Milgram's work has been assailed on two major premises. First, critics maintain that the experiment itself was immoral since it deceived people into discovering and revealing a disturbing truth about themselves, causing them extreme stress for which they were not prepared and which may have caused long-term psychological harm (Baumrind, 1964). Milgram

(1974) has denied that his procedures caused lasting harm and has pointed to the fact that more than eight out of ten subjects said afterward that they were glad to have taken part, four out of five felt that more experiments like this should be carried out, and three out of four said they had learned something of personal importance.

Critics also claim that the findings have little relevance to the real world. The subjects trusted Yale University not to do anything cruel or immoral; as volunteers they may have been particularly prone to obey a scientific researcher; they were subjected to repeated proddings to continue if they showed any doubts; the lab situation was so different from what a person would encounter in, say, wartime that it's impossible to generalize from one to the other (Orne & Holland, 1968; Baumrind, 1964). Milgram (1974) has countered these arguments by setting up a similar experiment away from the university and by asking some hard questions, like the one in the margin.

WHY WE BEHAVE AS WE DO

So far in this chapter we have been talking about the ways our circumstances influence our actions: the way a situation is structured, the other people in it and what they do, our acceptance of cultural norms. In our discussion of personality in Chapter 14, we pointed out the important influence of the relatively consistent ways of dealing with people and situations that characterize us as individuals. One of the major questions in life—and one that psychologists are greatly concerned with—is "Why do people do what they do?" How do we draw our conclusions?

The conclusions we draw are important, first because we often base our behavior on them and secondly, because when we conclude that the situation carries the greater influence, we are motivated to change situations. If we conclude that jailers and prisoners both become brutalized by the prison experience, it makes sense for us to spend our efforts on coming up with alternatives to prison. If we conclude that people become brutal because of early influences upon personality but, once formed, do not react to situations in adulthood, we are not motivated to change their adult circumstances, other than to protect ourselves.

According to the attribution theory proposed by Fritz Heider (1958), we tend to attribute people's behavior to one of two basic causes—either something *internal* (like a personality trait or their own efforts) or to something *external* (like a social situation, someone else's actions, or luck). Attribution theory has been an important theoretical framework for social psychological research in recent years.

Much of the research we cite in this and the next chapter (where we discuss attribution theory in greater detail) point up the importance of the situation in determining behavior. We have seen how some people who by most accounts are perfectly nice, decent people—not monsters by any means—can be induced by the demands of a situation to inflict painful and possibly harmful shocks on strangers who never did them any harm. We have seen how intelligent people with normal vision can be influenced to deny the evidence of their own senses. We shall see how such factors as how much of a hurry a person is in can affect his willingness to stop and help an apparently sick person.

As a result of such experiments, some contemporary psychologists

Have Milgram's findings been attacked because they are so unpalatable, telling us something about ourselves that we don't want to know?

Is not the criticism based as much on the unanticipated findings as on the method? The findings were that some subjects performed in what appeared to be a shockingly immoral way. If, instead, every one of the subjects had broken off at "silent shock," or at the first sign of the learner's discomfort, the results would have been pleasant, and reassuring, and who would protest (Milgram, 1974, p. 194)?

Milgram's work shows to what lengths ordinary people will go in the name of obedience, it forces us to question our own commitment to values that transcend submission to authority, and it raises questions about society's ability to develop citizens who can learn to tell the difference between obedience for just and unjust causes.

have adopted a point of view that attributes almost all behavior to the impact of the situation, swinging the pendulum far in the other direction from the classical point of view that people acted according to their basic temperament and were relatively impervious to situational influences. A recent analysis of some of this research reminds us that when we talk about people, an "either-or" approach hardly ever provides the whole explanation. We human beings are far too complicated for that.

When Milgram's studies were analyzed according to characteristics of the situation—how many people were present, whether the experimenter was in or out of the room, and so forth—it turned out that *both* aspects of the situation and individual personality traits of the people in it affected behavior, a finding that confirms similar findings in a number of classic studies (Funder & Ozer, 1983).

Some of Milgram's subjects were horrified by the commands they received and flatly refused to administer electric shocks, and some "good Samaritans" in the bystander research studies (discussed below) stopped to help others even though that would make them late for their own appointments. Apparently, there were some aspects of these people's personalities that led them to transcend the situation. It is still, then, difficult to predict the way someone will behave, either from knowing that person's personality or from knowing the situation she or he is in. It's important for us to remember that what we do depends on the interaction between *who* we are and *where* we are. Even knowing that perfect prediction is not possible, it's still important to look for the roots of behavior, especially since certain kinds of behavior—such as aggression and altruism—have such a major impact on the way we function as a society and as individuals.

HELPING OTHER PEOPLE

Both helping and hurting other people are part of humankind's long history. What makes us behave one way or the other? Are the tendencies toward these behaviors built into us or drummed into us? What makes them surface when they do? In Chapter 9, "Motivation," we discussed some of the reasons for aggressive behavior. Now let's take a look at the underpinnings of altruism, which has been defined as "behavior carried out to benefit another, without anticipation of rewards from external sources" (Macaulay & Berkowitz, 1970, p. 3).

Altruism, or Prosocial Behavior

People help each other in many ways—giving money, giving blood, giving time. Most of this help is offered to family and friends, but a great deal is extended to strangers we will never meet. Most of us perform a wide variety of helping actions that entail some cost, self-sacrifice, or risk on our part. We take part in civil rights marches, participate in boycotts, put off our own goals to further another's well-being. These networks of assistance crisscross virtually everyone's life every day, and yet the great bulk of the helping, caring behavior we give and receive often goes unnoticed. Over the past generation, psychologists have been delving into the reasons underlying such altruistic behavior. First we'll look at a very specific kind of help—the kind rendered to a stranger in an emergency.

HELPING A STRANGER IN DISTRESS   The crowd at the New York City subway platform was aghast as they saw a 75-year-old blind man stumble and fall between the cars of a train about to pull out of the station. One man in the crowd—Reginald Andrews, a 29-year-old unemployed father on his way home after having filed still another job application—leaped onto the tracks, yelled out a plea to stop the train, and pulled the blind man to safety into a narrow crawl space under the edge of the platform. "I wasn't thinking about the danger, just that, hey, somebody needs help," Andrews said later about his feat in which he put his own life on the line to help a complete stranger (McFadden, 1982).

How different Mr. Andrews' action was from that of thirty-eight people who unwittingly spurred a long line of research studies designed to determine what makes some people take action to help a stranger, while others do nothing! Those thirty-eight people were also New Yorkers—residents of an apartment complex who watched from their windows in the middle of the night while a brutal attacker stabbed to death a young woman named Kitty Genovese. Despite her piercing screams and the obviousness of what was happening as the killer came back for three separate attacks, not one of these neighbors came to her aid, not even by picking up their phones to call the police, until she was already dead (Rosenthal, 1964). Why? Were these people monsters? Indifferent to her plight? Frightened for their own safety?

The answers that have emerged from dozens of experiments are complex, but they do shed some light on why one person will risk his life—while another will not give even a grain of help. Virtually all these studies have ruled out apathy as an answer. When people see that another person is in trouble, they are hardly ever indifferent. Even when they do not take any action that could help, they are often agitated and tense, concerned about the other person's health or safety, and in conflict about their own role. A number of factors help us explain why people do or do not stretch out a helping hand.

Recognition that an Emergency Exists   Before you take action, you first have to notice an event that is taking place and then you have to interpret it as an emergency (Latané & Darley, 1968). When a situation is clearly a serious emergency, like the blind man's fall under the subway train, impulsive, immediate rescue attempts like Reginald Andrews' are, in fact, more likely (Piliavin, Dovidio, Gaertner, & Clark, 1981).

If a situation is ambiguous, you'll look around at the people near you to see how they're interpreting it. If no one else seems to be doing anything, you may decide that you were overreacting and you won't do anything. This was brought out in a study in which smoke filled a room. When people were alone, they reported it; when they were with other people who did nothing, they ignored it, probably assuming that if there were a danger, somebody else would have done something (Latané & Darley, 1968). (How similar is this situation to those in Asch's conformity studies, in which people doubt their own judgment when the majority adopts a different point of view?)

Number of People on the Scene   Faulty interpretation was clearly not responsible for inaction on behalf of Kitty Genovese, but the sheer number of witnesses to her ordeal was, ironically, probably the major reason why *no* one helped her. Study after study has confirmed the fact that people who are alone are more likely to help someone in trouble (Latané & Nida, 1981). When other potential rescuers are around, barriers go up. The first barrier is the influence of other people in interpreting an event: If this is a crisis, why isn't someone else doing something about it?

The second is the ability of the observer to diffuse responsibility. It's the old "Let George do it" syndrome: "Why should I go out on a limb when there are all these other people around who can help?" Or the assumption that "if this really is important, surely someone else must have already done something, so I don't need to." Another major impediment is the average person's fear of looking foolish: "Suppose what looks like a crisis really isn't—and everyone will have seen me jump in with both feet—and then won't I look silly."

Who the Victim Is A man who collapses in a moving subway car is more likely to get help if he is carrying a cane than if he smells of liquor and is carrying a bottle wrapped in a brown paper bag (Piliavin, Rodin, & Piliavin, 1969). It's easier to understand why people would rather help a disabled person than a drunk than it is to understand the effects of other victim characteristics. For example, a man with a cane who collapses in a subway train is *less* likely to get help if he bleeds from the mouth (showing greater injury) than if he doesn't (Piliavin & Piliavin, 1972), and if he has a large red birthmark on his face than if he is unmarked (Piliavin, Piliavin, & Rodin, 1975). These findings seem to point to inaction as sometimes caused by fear or disgust toward the victim.

Pressures on the Bystander People in a hurry don't stop to help as often as people who don't feel the pressures of time or other obligations. This was brought out by a study in which divinity students practiced a speech in one building and then set out to record it in another building. Some students were told they were late for their taping appointments, some that they were on time, and some that they were early.

On the way each student passed a person lying in a doorway, his eyes closed and his head down, who coughed as the student went by. More than half the students who were early or on time stopped to help, while only one in ten of those who thought they were late did. The topic of the students' speeches? What else but the parable of "The Good Samaritan"? (Darley & Batson, 1973).

Predicting Who Will Help What happens when you see another person in serious trouble? You react on both feeling and thinking levels. You become emotionally aroused, a response that may have been bred into us as a means of preserving our species. Even day-old infants cry when they hear another baby cry (Simner, 1971; Sagi & Hoffman, 1976). Such a response probably occurs too early in life to have been learned. What we do learn, however, is the rationale for deciding what to do. In a crisis we ask ourselves what we stand to gain or lose by acting or by not acting. Will you feel too guilty if you do nothing? Will you be taking foolish risks by stepping in?

Jane A. Piliavin and her colleagues have provided a cost-benefit analysis of why we help. The overriding principle is that in deciding whether to help, we try to minimize our cost and maximize our rewards. According to this principle, you will help if you are so emotionally aroused that you respond impulsively, not even thinking of the costs to yourself, if your personal costs are low (you have time, you are not risking your life) or if the situation holds out other benefits to you (you find the victim attractive, you want to do something interesting, or you want to see yourself in the role of hero) (Piliavin, Dovidio, Gaertner, & Clark, 1981). Often people feel distressed when they don't help someone in need, but they still don't do it because the costs to themselves are too high.

WHY PEOPLE HELP OTHERS   What makes people go out of their way to help others, in a variety of situations, often putting themselves at a disadvantage? A number of explanations have been offered.

We Inherit the Tendency   Since some children show altruism from a very early age, while others do not, it's possible that some are born with more generous, sharing natures. Altruism may be in their genes. While altruism can, of course, hurt the individual who engages in it, it *is* beneficial to the species at large. The large amount of prosocial behavior in the animal kingdom suggests some hereditary, biologically adaptive reason for it.

Sociobiologists, scientists who study the biological basis of social behavior in various animals (including the human species), point to many altruistic activities among animals. Chimpanzees adopt orphaned chimps, small birds like robins and thrushes whistle to warn their fellows of the approach of a hawk (possibly drawing attention to themselves), and some honeybees commit suicide while defending their nests against intruders (Wilson, 1978). Many sociobiologists have concluded that there is some kind of genetic programming that makes us act altruistically. Most social psychologists, however, concentrate more on the contribution of learning and environmental factors in producing this kind of behavior.

We Learn to Do It   A great deal of research over the past twenty years has indicated that people learn to be sensitive to and to help other people. Altruistic children tend to have parents who help others, who expect their children to help others, and to let their children know in no uncertain terms how they should behave (Mussen & Eisenberg-Berg, 1977). In other words, among the norms such children learn are helping behaviors.

Marion R. Yarrow (1978) and her colleagues have studied the development of altruism in very young children and found that individual differences show up increasingly between $1\frac{1}{2}$ to 2 years of age, and the amount of helping behavior doesn't change by the age of 7, even though the form does. The first two or three years of life may be crucial for establishing these patterns.

The degree to which a child reaches out to help others seems to be related to how warm, responsive, and helpful parents are toward their children and to how intensely parents get the message across that children are not to hurt others. The mothers of the most altruistic children studied do not limit themselves to calmly pointing out, "Jimmy is crying because you hit him." Instead, they show strong emotion and conviction when they tell—and sometimes yell at—their children, "You do *not* hurt Jimmy!" or "Stop that!"

I maintain, despite the moment's evidence against the claim, that we are born and grow up with a fondness for each other, and that we have genes for that. We can be talked out of that fondness, for the genetic message is like a distant music and some of us are hard of hearing. Societies are noisy affairs, drowning out the sound of ourselves and our connection. Hard of hearing, we go to war. Stone deaf, we make thermonuclear missiles. Nonetheless, the music is there, waiting for more listeners. (Thomas, 1982, p. 59)

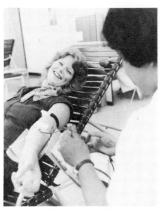

Donating blood has been compared to a daring sport like skydiving. At first people engaged in either activity are nervous and afraid, but the more often they do it, the more positive they feel about it, until they become "addicted" to the experience. (American Red Cross Photo; © Jose A. Fernandez 1979/ Woodfin Camp & Assoc.)

Helping Others Makes Us Feel Good   People like to feel virtuous. Since so many of us have been raised to think that charitable behavior is praise-worthy, we get an intrinsic reward in our own opinions of ourselves when we have helped somebody else. Helping behavior may be closely allied to two kinds of emotional states—happiness and sadness. When we're sad, helping others makes us feel better by making us feel as if we are better people (Baumann, Cialdini, & Kenrick, 1981). This would seem to bear out traditional advice to unhappy souls that they'll feel better if they don't brood about their own problems but do something nice for someone else instead.

We also seem to be more apt to help others when we're feeling happy, a conclusion reached by Baumann and his colleagues (1981) and confirmed by Rosenhan, Salovey, and Hargis (1981). In this study students who imagined they were being rewarded for hard work with a vacation in Hawaii were more likely to help a friend than those who imagined that their best friend was getting the holiday trip. When we feel fortunate, competent, and successful, our good feelings about ourselves often spur good actions toward others.

We Become "Addicted" to Altruism   Why do certain people give blood over and over again in a "community responsibility" blood collection system? In these systems donors don't get paid, nor do they or their families receive any reciprocal or insurance benefits if they should need blood themselves. Donors would appear to have nothing to gain from giving blood, while they do incur costs: They give up their time, feel weak for hours or days, and run risks of more serious effects. Yet some people become habitual blood donors.

Piliavin and her colleagues compare giving blood to parachute jumping: At first the participant feels all sorts of negative emotions revolving around fear and anxiety, but the more often she or he jumps (or gives blood), the more positive the feelings surrounding the activity—whether they're the exhilaration and sense of competence felt by the parachutist or the "warm glow" of having helped someone in need experienced by the blood donor (Piliavin, Callero, & Evans, 1982).

These authors explain both these shifts from negative to positive feelings by the *opponent-process theory* (H. Hoffman & Solomon, 1974; Solomon & Corbit, 1974). The initial negative-feeling state is opposed by a positive frame of reference; the opponent (positive) feelings are strengthened through use; and the initially aversive experience is eventually "transformed into a highly motivating, even addicting, experience" (Piliavin et al., 1982, p. 1204). So the more anxious we feel ahead of time, the better we'll feel later. For blood donors, the good feelings caused by doing good take over, and the third or fourth donation seems to be the "magic" point at which regular donors feel they get "hooked."

Encouraging Altruism

To survive in a perilous world populated by predatory animals and hostile tribes, early humans had to develop behavior patterns based on helping only those in their own small group and reacting with suspicion and aggression toward other groups. Today, however, as psychiatrist and behavioral biologist David A. Hamburg (1983) has pointed out, these attitudes are no longer adaptive. In a world in which strangers are often dependent on each other for the basics of life itself, we need to develop other ways of relating to those around us, both in and out of the family.

How, then, can we encourage altruism? One answer seems to lie in the way we teach children to learn how to solve their problems without resorting to violence, in the way we discourage them from aggressiveness early in life and reward them for other behaviors, and in the overall values we teach—helping rather than hurting, caring about other people rather than indifference, cooperation rather than competition, and equality between the sexes rather than male dominance and machismo. We could, for example, expose boys "to the same training that girls have traditionally received in our society and [encourage them] to develop similar kinds of socially positive, tender, cooperative, nurturant, and sensitive qualities, which are antithetical to aggressive behavior" (Eron, 1980, p. 244).

Another approach is biological. Recognizing that human beings do inhibit aggression in many situations, some researchers are trying to discover what brain chemicals are involved in the inhibitory process and whether similar substances can be developed to help people master antisocial aggression (Redmond, 1983). Still another approach emphasizes the importance of developing positive solutions for individual, family, community, and societal problems. The search is not easy, but in this nuclear age, it is essential.

ATTITUDES

You have an attitude toward practically everything and everyone in the world you've ever spent any time thinking about, and you have undoubtedly expressed opinions about many subjects. Your *opinion* is your attitude, put into words. An attitude is a way of responding to someone or something. It is something you have learned, and it is relatively permanent. Your attitude consists of three elements: *what you think* (the cognitive component); *how you feel* (the emotional component); and *how you tend to act* out your thoughts and emotions (the behavioral component). For example, you probably have an attitude about extramarital sex. Cognitively, you may think it's harmful to a marriage; emotionally, you may feel jealous at the idea of your spouse's having sex with anyone else; and behaviorally, you may remain monogamous.

One problem with studying attitude is that the three elements often contradict each other. For example, three separate national public opinion polls spanning the years from 1970 to 1977 showed that 75 to 87 percent of people in North America disapprove of married people's having sex with people they're not married to (National Opinion Research Center, 1977). At the same time, other surveys were finding that about half of all men and from a quarter to a half of all women were saying that they had *had* extramarital sex (Hunt, 1974). It seems, then, that the cognitive component of some people's attitudes about extramarital sex differs from their behavioral component.

Much research about attitudes has focused on the interrelationships among the different elements, how a change in one affects the others, and how we form and modify our opinions and our actions. Knowing the three different levels suggests ways to measure attitudes, using different scales for thoughts, feelings, and action. Furthermore, this approach has important implications for efforts to *change* attitudes. If we try to change only the cognitive element, for example, by trying to convince someone of the rationale behind civil rights laws, without taking into account the heavily charged emotions in interracial relationships, we won't get very far.

Measuring Attitudes

Most often social scientists measure attitudes the same way market researchers or ordinary people would, by asking people a number of questions about their beliefs, through interviews or questionnaires. Let's take a look at two of the most popular paper-and-pencil attitude scales, the Likert Scale and the Semantic Differential,

The Likert Scale (Likert, 1932) lists a number of statements or attitudes and asks the subject to respond on a continuum from "strongly agree" to "strongly disagree." A statement, or series of statements, are presented, such as, "The drinking age in my state should be raised to 21." The subject is then asked to indicate the extent to which she or he agrees or disagrees. Likert used a 5-point spread, from strongly agree, to agree, to undecided, to disagree, to strongly disagree. The subject gives the appropriate number or letter, and each response is given a point value, from 1 to 5 (or as many numbers as the scale includes—the range typically may go from 3 through 7). A person's attitude score is the sum of all his or her ratings.

The Semantic Differential (Osgood, Suci, & Tennenbaum, 1957) focuses on the meaning of a word or concept to an individual, asking the subject to rate the concept ("father," "nuclear power," "Democrat," etc.) in terms of a series of dimensions, such as fair-unfair *(evaluation of the item being assessed);* strong-weak *(perception of its power);* and hot-cold *(perception of its activity level).*

Relying on such self-reports poses problems. For one thing, the way a question is asked often affects the answer given. In a recent poll, 39 percent of Americans said that government spending for public welfare should be cut, while only 7 percent thought that "aid to the needy" should be cut (Marty, 1982). For another thing, people are not always honest with *themselves* on their true attitudes, let alone with researchers. So it's usually best to use several different methods to measure attitudes.

One ingenious method is the *bogus pipeline,* an important-looking machine that subjects believe can ferret out their real attitudes by measuring their physiological responses (Jones & Sigall, 1981). Researchers using the pipeline have elicited from college students statements that are more racially prejudiced and (from men) less favorable toward women's rights than they did with standard attitude scales (Sigall & Page, 1971; Faranda, Kaminski, & Giza, 1979).

How Do We Form Attitudes?

How did you develop your attitudes toward people of other ethnic groups? Toward the relative value of communism versus democracy? Toward the importance—or its lack—of a liberal arts education? Somehow, somewhere, you learned it. Here, too, as in every other psychological topic, different theories compete to explain the formation of attitudes.

LEARNING THEORIES   According to learning theory, we learn attitudes the same way we learn everything else. As we learn new information, we learn the feelings, the thoughts, and the actions associated with it. As we get rewarded *(reinforced),* the learning stays with us. Public relations, advertising, and sales personnel put this principle into effect every time they couple information about their product with a pleasant association—a satisfying meal or a picture that conjures up happy thoughts. These learning theories see people as reactors rather than initiators, as primarily passive beings whose learning "depends on the number and strength of the positive and negative elements previously learned" (Freedman et al., 1981).

COGNITIVE CONSISTENCY THEORIES   Suppose you are a network television executive who supports peace-oriented organizations and who believes strongly in the need for people to get along with each other. A major governmental report is published indicating that certain programs carried by your network foster aggressive attitudes that could lead to crime, or even war. These programs are the highest-rated, most profitable ones on the network; if you were to suggest dropping them, you are sure you would be fired the next day. What are you to do with these conflicts?

According to cognitive consistency theories, inconsistency between two sets of awareness makes people uncomfortable. So they change either their thinking or their actions to try to become consistent. In the example just given, you might achieve this by making one attitude (your desire to keep your good job) consistent with your other attitude (your belief in furthering goodwill among people). One way is to question the report by pointing out problems in the study design or maintaining that the findings do not justify the conclusions drawn. Another way is to make minor—and probably meaningless—program changes that won't jeopardize your job. Either way, you can continue to think of yourself as a person concerned with the common good—and you can keep your job.

Further consequences of making a difficult decision.

Cognitive Dissonance Theory: Sour Grapes and Sweet Lemons

We all know Aesop's tale about the fox who could not reach the grapes and decided he didn't want them because they were sour anyway. Then there's the story of the fruit-loving monkey who couldn't get anything besides lemons, so he decided they were the sweetest lemons he had ever tasted. According to cognitive dissonance theory, these opinions would have been even more strongly held if both fox and monkey had freely chosen their foods—if the grapes had been within reach but the fox didn't want to make the effort to get them or if the monkey had chosen the lemons instead of some other fruit. The natural tendency for human beings to enhance the value of whatever we have chosen and to play down what we haven't is part of the basis for this influential cognitive consistency theory proposed by Leon Festinger (1962).

Festinger maintains that whenever we hold two ideas, attitudes, or opinions that contradict each other, we are in a state of cognitive dissonance, or discord. This makes us psychologically uncomfortable. So we do something to reduce the discord. Dissonance is inevitable whenever we make a choice. Since few choices are perfect, whatever we choose has some negative aspects, and whatever we don't choose has some positives. If we think about these aspects, we'll experience an uncomfortable level of dissonance.

We'll wonder whether we made the right choice—whether some other college would have given us a better education, whether some other car would have held up longer, whether some other spouse would have been more satisfying to live with. So we try to reduce dissonance by telling ourselves that the alternative we chose really is the more desirable, and the one we didn't choose the less desirable (see Figure 17-2).

Other situations that can produce cognitive dissonance are those in which we do something contrary to our deeply held ideas about what's right and proper, when we hold a belief that appears to defy the rules of logic, when something happens that contradicts our past experience, or when we do something that doesn't fit our idea of who we are and what we stand for (Festinger, 1957).

A classic experiment demonstrating this effect was conducted by Festinger and Carlsmith (1959). They asked college students to work at a boring and tiring job for an hour and then asked them to tell the next subject about it, making the experience sound like fun. All the students were paid for their participation, but half received $1 and half $20. The first subjects were then interviewed to find out what they really thought of the experiment. Interestingly, those who received the large payment were more likely to say that the job was dull as dishwater, while the ones who got only $1 were more likely to give a favorable opinion of their dreary hour.

Why was this so? Because the subjects who earned $20 could easily tell themselves they lied to the other subjects because they had been paid a lot of money to do so, while the others couldn't come up with any good reason for misrepresenting the situation. To get rid of their uncomfortably dissonant feeling, they simply changed their minds and decided the job hadn't been so dull after all. They changed their attitudes to account for their behaviors.

According to the attributional analysis of attitude formation and change, people look at their behaviors and attribute how they feel to what they do. In this scene from Fiddler on the Roof, Golde *decides she* must *love Tevye because she has stayed with him for twenty-five difficult years. (From the United Artists' release* Fiddler on the Roof © *1971 Mirisch Productions, Inc. and Cartier Productions, Inc.)*

The practical lesson we can take from this is that if we want to change someone's attitude and future behavior, we'll do better to give modest rewards instead of large ones. If, for example, you want to encourage someone to lose weight, give him $2 for every pound he loses, not $50. Then he'll be more motivated to continue to eat less and won't be able to tell himself he did it only for the money. Like all influential theories, this one has stirred up a great deal of analysis—and its fair share of heated controversy.

Modifications of Dissonance Theory Dissonance theory can be modified in several ways. We can't ignore the fact that we're all different from one another: You may be able to tolerate dissonance better than I can and shrug it off without feeling you need to reduce it, or you may deal with it in a different way. Instead of downgrading the grapes, the fox could have boosted his self-esteem by upgrading something else in the situation—maybe the value of the exercise he got while trying to reach them. Furthermore, what is dissonant for me may be consonant for you.

Besides, sometimes dissonance-arousing information is useful. If we could not tolerate some of it, we would distort reality in many areas and never admit our mistakes. Admitting mistakes does create dissonance, but it is the only way we can profit from them and learn for the future. If, for example, I tell myself that the car I bought is the best one on the market, even though I am dissatisfied with its performance in many ways, I may be able to maintain a consonant view of myself as an intelligent purchaser—but I will not be able to change to a vehicle that will meet my needs better and I'll be trapped with an inferior product.

Bem's Attributional Analysis In the musical, *Fiddler on the Roof*, as Tevye the dairyman tells his wife, Golde, that their daughter has fallen in love, he asks her, "Golde, do you love me?" After some evasiveness, she sings, "Do I love him? For twenty-five years I've lived with him, fought with him, starved with him. Twenty-five years my bed is his. If that's not love, what is?" Tevye asks, "Then you love me?" and Golde replies, "I suppose I do" (Stein, Bock, & Harnick, 1964).

This exchange melodiously illustrates Bem's (1967; 1970) attributional analysis of attitude formation and change, also called self-perception theory. Bem disagrees with the principles in Festinger's cognitive dissonance theory, based on an internal process that first arouses dissonance and then reduces it. Bem says people form their attitudes much more simply. They look at their behavior and then attribute what they do to how they feel. If Golde didn't love Tevye, she thinks, why would she have stuck with him all through these difficult years? If you find yourself dressing with special care for what you had thought was going to be a casual evening, you realize, "This party and these people must mean more to me than I had thought." In other words, to figure out what our own attitudes are, we rely on the same external cues that we turn to when we try to decide what others think and feel.

This point was brought out in a famous experiment conducted by Stanley Schachter and Jerome Singer (1962), in which subjects were injected with a drug that made them sweat, made their hearts beat faster, and changed their breathing patterns, in the same way strong emotions do.

The subjects didn't know, however, that the injection caused these effects. Some subjects were placed in a room with a confederate (supposedly another subject) who acted very angry, others with one who acted very happy. Afterward, the subjects who had been with the angry person described themselves as angry and the ones who had been with the happy one said they themselves felt happy. These subjects were rating their own moods on the basis of both *internal cues* (what their bodies were telling them) and *external* ones (how the other person acted).

In two other conditions, subjects who were injected with a placebo that did *not* cause the physiological changes and subjects injected with the drug who *knew* what the effects of the drug would be both described themselves as relatively unemotional after the session with the confederate. The placebo subjects had no internal cues, and the informed ones had a ready explanation for them, so neither of them needed to draw on the external cues. Since two components seemed essential for subjects to label their emotions (the physiological arousal and the cognitive appraisal of that arousal), this is known as the *two-factor theory of emotion*. This research suggests that when our internal state is ambiguous, we tend to look for external cues to let us know what emotion we are feeling. We look beyond our behavior to elements in the environment that can explain that behavior.

This principle, too, has many practical applications. Bem (1970) maintains that it may make people accused of crime believe in their own guilt after they have been persuaded (but not forced) to make false confessions. After all, if a suspect said something in a situation where he was apparently free to say anything he wanted, what he said must be true. It also has implications for the value of participating in picket lines, sit-ins, and other protest demonstrations. If attitudes follow behavior, the more a person does on behalf of a particular cause—whether that be environmental preservation or union strength—the more strongly she or he will believe in that cause.

While this theory is intriguing, its findings have not been replicated by other researchers. Other reports indicate that subjects aroused by adrenaline usually report unpleasant emotions, no matter how positive the social context may be (Hogan & Schroeder, 1981).

How Are We Persuaded to Change Our Attitudes?

Everywhere you go, someone is trying to talk you into doing or believing something. Newspaper ads and radio and TV commercials urge you to buy products and vote for candidates. Religious leaders exhort you to act in a way befitting the dictates of their congregations. Special-interest groups urge you to fight for the right to bear arms or to restrict gun ownership; to keep the constitutional right to abortion or to overturn it; to support the Equal Rights Amendment or to defeat it. Teachers, friends, and relatives try to convince you of the wisdom and morality of some courses of action and the folly or evil of others.

What makes some of these persuasive communications more effective than others? The basic factors to consider are the source of the communication, its nature, and the characteristics of the audience. The following discussion is based on Elliot Aronson's (1980) clear analysis of these elements.

WHERE DOES THE MESSAGE COME FROM?   We're most likely to be influenced by people who are experts on the topic they're talking about, who have shown themselves to be trustworthy, who are arguing a point of view from which they personally have nothing to gain, who are not trying deliberately to win us over, and who are similar to us. For example, black junior high school students were more likely to have cleaner teeth after hearing a taped message on proper dental care from a black dentist rather than a white dentist (Dembroski, Lasater, & Ramirez, 1978). However, under the "sleeper effect," even though a highly credible source has more impact immediately after delivering a message, this greater believability dissipates after four weeks. This is probably because most people forget where they first heard a message (Kelman & Hovland, 1953).

In trivial matters the preceding considerations become very unimportant if we like, identify with, and find a person attractive. For example, a woman's beauty has a strong impact on audience opinion, even on topics irrelevant to her looks (Mills & Aronson, 1965). No wonder attractive young women look out on us from so many billboards, magazine ads, and TV screens!

HOW IS THE MESSAGE STATED?   Messages can appeal to our reasonableness or to our emotions; they can be one-sided or can present both sides to a question; they can differ in other ways. What makes one approach better in some situations but not in others? Sometimes it's the nature of the topic being discussed, sometimes it's the intelligence or self-esteem of the audience. Sometimes it's which message we heard first or last.

Appeals to our emotions seem more effective than appeals to our sense of logic. Many persuasive campaigns are based on *fear:* What will happen to the world if you don't vote for this candidate? What will happen to you if you combine drinking and driving? What will happen to your family if you don't buy life insurance? In general, messages that induce moderate levels of fear are most likely to change your attitude. If a message frightens you too much, you'll "tune out" to get rid of the discomfort, and if it doesn't scare you enough, it won't get your attention.

Fear arousal has induced students to stop smoking, to get chest x-rays, and to get tetanus shots (Leventhal, 1970). The most effective campaigns have combined the fear-arousing message with specific instructions about what to do; either element alone is less effective in changing behavior. The higher your opinion of yourself, the more likely you are to respond to a fear-arousing campaign, possibly because you have confidence in your ability to respond to the threat, possibly because you're not afraid of fear but are motivated by it, and possibly because the more you think of yourself, the better you want to take care of yourself.

Two-sided messages, those that include both sides of an argument and refute one viewpoint, are more effective with intelligent audiences who are at least aware of the opposing views and also with audiences that are already leaning in the opposite direction. So if someone is already leaning toward your position, don't confuse him or her by presenting arguments being offered by the other side, but if you feel you're on hostile territory, you'd do better to present the arguments they're already in agreement with and to show why they're wrong (Hovland, Lumsdain, & Sheffield, 1949).

WHO IS LISTENING TO THE MESSAGE?   What characteristics of an audience make it most receptive to a message? Poor self-esteem, for one, since people who don't think much of themselves are more easily influenced. A relaxed, well-fed state, for another. One reason so many politicians rely on an informal get-together in a private home to present their pitch is that people who have had something to eat and drink are more receptive (Janis, Kaye, & Kirschner, 1965; Dabbs & Janis, 1965). Another, of course, is that people are likely to be influenced by the fact that a friend or neighbor whom they like and respect is offering his or her home to help the candidate.

Furthermore, listeners need to feel in charge of their own opinions. If you forewarn them, ''I'm going to try to persuade you of the value of my point of view,'' they'll put their guard up and be less persuasible (Freedman & Sears, 1965). Experimenters who have used such phrases as ''You have no choice but to believe this'' are more likely to alienate listeners from their point of view than to persuade them (Worchel & Brehm, 1970). You may have found in your own experience that when parents try hard to change their adolescent and grown children's attitudes, the children often feel their freedom threatened and dig their heels in even more strongly. In this way, strenuous parental opposition can have the ''Romeo and Juliet effect,'' driving a young person into the arms of the sweetheart, the political involvement, or the way of life the parents are most against (Driscoll, Davis, & Lipetz, 1972).

Finally, an involved audience is more likely to change its attitude. Handing out blank stationery and asking members of an audience to write to their congressional representatives right then and there is likely to do two things—assure more mail than if you suggested they write when they get home and solidify the letter writers' own attitudes on the topic.

The importance of personal involvement was brought out by one study in which fourteen young women who smoked were asked to play the role of a person with lung cancer (Janis & Mann, 1965). They saw x-rays, talked with ''their doctor,'' pretended to await surgery, and so forth. Twelve control smokers heard tapes of role-playing sessions but didn't take part themselves. The role-players became more antismoking in their attitudes—more convinced that smoking is unhealthy and leads to lung cancer and more interested in giving up smoking. Eighteen months later, both groups were smoking less, with the role-players smoking less than the controls (Mann & Janis, 1968).

What Is the Relationship between Attitudes and Behavior?

A popular tale in the business community points up the difficulty of using people's expressed attitudes to predict what they'll do. Some years ago a major automobile manufacturer sponsored a survey to ask consumers what they wanted in a car. By an overwhelming majority, those polled said they wanted a simple car, with a minimum of fancy styling and a maximum in safety features. The manufacturer produced such a car, and it was a financial disaster. Hardly anyone bought it. So the manufacturer sponsored another poll. This time, researchers asked consumers, ''What does your neighbor like in a car?'' ''Oh, him,'' people would say: ''He likes something with a lot of chrome on it, that makes a quick getaway, that's capable of high speeds on the highway." The manufacturer made *this* car, and it made a fortune.

Research has shown, for example, that people's general attitude toward religion doesn't tell us whether they'll go to church next Sunday. That depends also on whether it's raining, whether they woke up with a hangover, whether they like the preacher, and whether there's something else they want to do. However, their religious attitudes do predict their overall religious conduct over time (Fishbein & Ajzen, 1974; Kahle & Berman, 1979).

There are, however, some instances when knowing what someone thinks can predict their actions two weeks, two months, and even two years later (Kahle, 1983; Kahle & Berman, 1979).

Prediction tends to be fairly accurate under the following conditions:

1 *When other influences on our behavior are minimized*—our concern about what others will think, for example.
2 *When the measured attitude corresponds closely to the situation being considered.* It's easier to predict a man's behavior toward a specific female coworker if we know how he feels about her than if we know only how he feels about the Equal Rights Amendment (Steiner, 1979).
3 *When we are conscious of our attitudes when we act,* either because we are reminded to focus on them (by being asked to think about them, as in an experiment by Snyder & Swann, 1976, or by looking in a mirror, as in experiments by Diener & Wallbom, 1976, and Carver & Scheier, 1981); because we acquired them in especially powerful ways—such as personal experience; or because we are "inner-directed" people who believe in judging each situation according to our principles rather than adjusting our principles and behavior to fit the situation (M. Snyder, 1982; Snyder & Campbell, 1982).

This point has been well demonstrated in psychological research, as well. A review of several dozen studies on attitudes and behaviors concluded that knowing what people *say* their attitudes are allow us to predict with less than 10 percent accuracy what they will actually *do* (Wicker, 1969). Why should this be? One major reason is that we often don't know what our attitudes about a specific topic are until we are forced to take action. (As a newspaper columnist said during a strike when the paper wasn't printed, "How do I know what I think if I don't write about it?") According to Bem's theory of self-perception, we often don't know what we think until we see how we act. A student may *think* she is opposed to cheating as a major moral principle, but if she is in a situation where she thinks that cheating on an exam will make a difference between passing or failing a crucial course and she thinks she won't get caught, she may well look over her neighbor's shoulder (Wicker, 1969).

Furthermore, in some cases our behavior seems to determine our attitudes. Schoolchildren who teach or enforce a moral code with other children end up following it better themselves (Parke, 1974); people induced to testify to something they're not really sure of end up believing it (Klaas, 1978); and soldiers who act brutally toward an enemy population end up hating and denigrating them.

The crucial issue in the relationship between attitudes and behavior is that both what we *do* and what we *say we believe* are subject to other

Predicting people's behavior is like predicting a baseball player's hitting. The outcome of any particular time at bat is nearly impossible to predict, because it is affected not only by what the batter brings to the plate, but also by what the pitcher throws and by unmeasurable chance factors. By averaging many times at bat we neutralize these complicating factors. Thus, knowing the players, we can predict their approximate batting *averages*. (Myers, 1983, p. 40)

influences. We have certain ideal standards of the kind of person we want to be, and the attitudes we express often conform to those standards, even though we don't always act the way we think we should. Also, we have a certain picture of ourselves that we want to present to the rest of the world, and we often say what we think other people want to hear—and end up believing it ourselves.

PREJUDICE

A black couple, both professionals, answer an ad for an apartment, only to be told, "Sorry, it's already rented," although a white couple who come afterward are shown the apartment. A woman seeking an entry-level job is asked by the personnel director, "Can you type?" and offered the job of secretary, while a man with the same education and experience is sent to the sales department. A 75-year-old man in excellent command of his faculties is not consulted about a decision on whether or not to perform surgery; instead, his physician discusses the man's medical condition with the man's middle-aged daughter. Prejudice exists against people of virtually every racial and ethnic group (*racism, antisemitism,* and so forth), the elderly *(ageism),* the female *(sexism),* the handicapped, the poor, people who pursue unpopular lifestyles.

Prejudice is a negative attitude held toward people solely because of their membership in some group without knowing them as individuals. Stereotypes are oversimplified beliefs about the characteristics of members of a group, with no allowance for individual differences. Whether stereotypes are positive or negative, they short-circuit logical thought and reasonable judgment, and they rob the individual of the right to be judged for him- or herself.

While prejudice is the attitude, encompassing both thoughts and feelings, discrimination is the behavior aimed at the person one is prejudiced toward.

How Do We Become Prejudiced?

The three major theories that explain prejudice focus on its development as a natural societal by-product of competition over scarce resources, as an attitude that we learn the same way we learn other attitudes, and as the manifestation of a certain kind of personality.

WE COMPETE—AND WE BECOME PREJUDICED AGAINST OUR COMPETITORS People of one ethnic or racial group often become violently prejudiced against the members of any group vying for the same jobs. This has shown up in the American Southwest, between Americans and Mexicans; in California, between whites and Chinese; in a small industrial town surrounded by farmland, between native Americans and German immigrants; in large cities around the country, between blacks and whites (Aronson, 1980).

WE ARE CAREFULLY TAUGHT When children hear the adults around them expressing prejudiced attitudes and see them showing prejudiced behavior, they acquire prejudice the same way they acquire any other societal norm. As we saw earlier, most people—children included—like to conform to society norms and like to be accepted by others. If the most important people in a child's world are prejudiced against certain groups, the child will be, too. Furthermore, it's hard even for the child of rela-

BOX 17-1

THE ROBBERS' CAVE EXPERIMENT: A STUDY IN THE CREATION OF PREJUDICE

To test the belief that one group's ability to achieve its ends only at the expense of another is a major cause of prejudice, Muzafer Sherif (1966) and his colleagues conducted the classic Robbers' Cave experiment. They assigned healthy, bright, well-adjusted 11- and 12-year-old boys to one of two groups—the Eagles and the Rattlers—at a summer camp. First, they posed various projects involving cooperation within each group, such as building a diving board, building a rope bridge, and cooking out in the woods.

Once each group had a strong, cohesive feeling, the next stage of the experiment pitted the Eagles and the Rattlers against each other in touch football, tug-of-war,

and other games that awarded prizes to the winning team. The boys in each team became hostile to the other team, scuffling, calling names, and burning the other team's banner. The researchers then escalated the conflicts, setting up situations designed to favor one group over the other. The less-favored group reacted—not against the camp directors setting the rules but against the boys in the preferred group.

Once the desired levels of hostility had been achieved, the researchers dropped the competitive activities and brought the two groups together as much as possible. By this time, however, so much ill will had grown up between the two groups that it

hung between them and even increased, even when the boys were all eating together or just sitting around watching movies.

The Robbers' Cave experiment had a happy ending. The researchers took the now mutually hostile Eagles and Rattlers and put them in situations where they had to cooperate to obtain a goal that was beneficial for all the boys. When they *had* to get together to repair the water-supply system and to rescue a disabled camp truck, they did. In the process the hostility between the groups evaporated. Eagles made friends with Rattlers, and both groups began to work and play together on their own.

tively unprejudiced parents to avoid the barrage of stereotypes that come from picture books, TV programs, and magazine ads.

Over the past several decades prejudice has become unfashionable, and more people have been expressing unprejudiced attitudes. In 1942 people were much more likely to openly disapprove of blacks and whites sitting together on buses, going to school together, or living in the same neighborhoods than they were in 1980 (Hyman & Sheatsley, 1956; National Opinion Research Center, 1980; Myers, 1983). This does not mean that prejudice itself has decreased as dramatically as people's public awareness of it. It still exists in less obvious forms. One issue that has brought this out is school busing. Since whites do not oppose busing students from one primarily white school to another but do oppose busing between largely white and largely minority-group school populations (McConahay, Hardee, & Batts, 1981), it seems clear that prejudice against the minority group exists.

THE PREJUDICE-PRONE PERSONALITY In an effort to determine whether certain individuals were more likely to develop prejudices, researchers devised the F Scale (F for fascism) to define what they called the authoritarian personality (Adorno, Frenkel-Brunswick, Levinson, & Sanford, 1950). Table 17-1 lists some of the questions from this scale. The authoritarian personality emerged as one that tends to think in stereotypes, is emotionally cold, identifies with power, and is intolerant of weakness in

TABLE 17-1   The F Scale

3	America is getting so far from the true American way of life that force may be necessary to restore it.
17	Familiarity breeds contempt.
20	One of the main values of progressive education is that it gives the child great freedom in expressing those natural impulses and desires so often frowned upon by conventional middle-class society.
23	He is, indeed, contemptible who does not feel an undying love, gratitude, and respect for his parents.
30	Reports of atrocities in Europe have been greatly exaggerated for propaganda purposes.
31	Homosexuality is a particularly rotten form of delinquency and ought to be severely punished.
32	It is essential for learning or effective work that our teachers or bosses outline in detail what is to be done and exactly how to go about it.
35	There are some activities so flagrantly un-American that, when responsible officials won't take the proper steps, the wide-awake citizen should take the law into his own hands.
39	Every person should have a deep faith in some supernatural force higher than himself to which he gives total allegiance and whose decisions he does not question.
50	Obedience and respect for authority are the most important virtues children should learn.
73	Nowadays when so many different kinds of people move around so much and mix together so freely, a person has to be especially careful to protect himself against infection and disease.
77	No sane, normal, decent person could ever think of hurting a close friend or relative.

Source: Adapted from Adorno et al., 1950.

himself as well as in others. Such a person is rigid and conventional, believes in the value of punishment, and willingly submits to higher authorities without much questioning.

Adorno and his colleagues traced these personality traits back to characteristic patterns of child rearing, finding that the parents of such individuals tend to discipline their children harshly, withdrawing love, and making their children feel insecure. The children feel dependent on, afraid of, and hostile toward their parents. Unable to express their anger toward their parents directly, they carry these negative feelings with them to adulthood, emerging as angry, fearful individuals who take out their aggression against groups they see as weaker than themselves.

While these findings do give us insight into prejudiced people, they don't provide a clear explanation. For one thing, while there is a correlation between child-rearing patterns, personality characteristics, and authoritarian thinking, we don't know what is cause and what is effect. For another, parents who raise their children in this authoritarian way tend to be prejudiced themselves, so their children may develop prejudices through identification and imitation, not necessarily through personality development.

How Can We Reduce Prejudice?

Looking at possible explanations for prejudice gives us clues for reducing it. Instead of competition, we can encourage cooperation. Instead of teaching prejudice, we can teach openmindedness. Instead of raising children who will be inclined to take out their own problems on others, we can raise children to accept responsibility for their own lives.

These workers turning a drill on a natural gas rig have learned that when they cooperate, they get the job done faster. In contemporary society, in which people depend on each other for many benefits, cooperation is often more adaptive than competition. (©John Blaustein 1983/Woodfin Camp & Assoc.)

ENCOURAGING COOPERATION   Aronson and his colleagues developed an approach called the jigsaw technique. In classrooms with children of different ethnic and racial backgrounds, teachers assigned different parts of a single project to different children, and the children learned that they could do their own assignments better and more easily if they consulted, taught, and listened to each other. They soon learned that encouraging other children had beneficial consequences for themselves, and they ended up liking school better, liking each other better, and liking themselves better (Aronson, Stephan, Sikes, Blaney, & Snapp, 1978; Aronson & Bridgeman, 1979; Geffner, 1978).

TEACHING OPENMINDEDNESS   We can change the kinds of messages we send throughout society. We can examine the mass media for evidence of prejudice against various groups, and we can send out new messages that show positive viewpoints. We can change the rules of society to uphold the rights of all people, as in the 1954 Supreme Court decision that outlawed school segregation and in many more recent laws and court decisions that have upheld the rights of racial and other minorities, of women, and of the elderly.

The importance of rules is borne out by the powerful influence of changed behavior. Enforcing equal access to housing, for example, requires people to live together on an equal-status basis, and we have known for years that white people who live in housing projects with black tenants develop more favorable attitudes toward black people than do white residents of segregated housing projects (Deutsch & Collins, 1951). This may support Daryl Bem's theory of attributional analysis: The white person may think, "If I live close to black people and we get along as neighbors, then I must like them."

RAISING INDEPENDENT, FAIR-MINDED CHILDREN   The implications for child rearing raised by the findings of Adorno and his colleagues (1950) on the authoritarian personality indicate that we can do a great deal to help our children become unprejudiced by raising them with respect and love, in ways that will help them think well of themselves.

In so many of the issues we have talked about in this chapter, self-esteem is, ultimately, the key to people's living well in groups. People who think highly of themselves are less apt to become slavish conformists, blind obeyers, cruel aggressors, and prejudiced discriminators. People who like themselves are more likely to like others—and less likely to feel the need to find someone to look down upon.

SUMMARY

1   *Social psychology* is the scientific study of how we feel, think, are affected by, and act toward other people. Social psychologists are concerned with the influence of the *group* on behavior. A group consists of two or more people who are interacting and interdependent at some time.

2   *Norms* are society's definitions of how we "should" behave. *Roles* are a set of behavioral expectations (or norms) for people of a particular social position. A particular position (such as parent) assumes the status of a *social role* when it accumulates a substantial number of norms. Norms have the capacity to restrict or enhance behavior.

3   Zimbardo's study of the prison experience demonstrated how rapidly presumably normal people assume "appropriate" norms for the roles they play. It shows the powerful influence of the situation on behavior.

4   *Conformity* refers to a change in opinion and/or behavior in response to the real or imagined pressure of others. Asch's classic study of conformity showed that individuals often conform to group opinions even when the group opinion is clearly wrong. Since not all people in Asch's experiments did conform, however, we see that the situation *and* the person affect behavior.

5   *Groupthink* refers to an uncritical acceptance by members of a close-knit group of an unwise course of action in order to preserve group unanimity.

6   Milgram's experiments on *obedience to authority* show that in some circumstances people will obey orders to inflict harm on another. A number of personal and situational factors influenced a person's decision to obey. Subjects were most likely to disobey if they were in the same room with the "victim" or actually had to place the "victim's" hand on the shock-plate. They were most likely to obey when in the same room as the experimenter. Participants who felt principally responsible for the victims suffering were least likely to obey.

7   *Altruism* is behavior carried out to benefit another, without anticipation of rewards from external sources. A number of factors contribute to whether we will help a person in distress. These include recognition that an emergency exists, the number of observers present, and other pressures on the bystander(s). According to Piliavin and her colleagues, we use cost-benefit analysis; in deciding whether to help, we try to minimize our costs and maximize our rewards.

8   Theoretical interpretations of why we help include the possibilities that we *inherit* the tendency, we *learn* to be altruistic, we help others because it *makes us feel good,* and we become *addicted* to altruism.

9   An *attitude* is a learned, relatively permanent way of responding to someone or something. Attitudes have three components: the *cognitive* (thoughts), the *emotional* (feelings), and the *behavioral* (actions). Attitudes are most frequently measured using *questionnaires* and *interviews*. Since subjects can readily distort answers during interviews and questionnaire items, social psychologists develop other techniques such as the *bogus pipeline* to overcome problems of distortion.

10   Social psychologists have showed considerable interest in attitude formation and attitude change. According to *learning theory,* we learn attitudes the same way we learn anything else, through conditioning. *Cognitive consistency* theories hold that incompatibility between our thoughts and our actions makes us uncomfortable and that we must try to reduce this discomfort. According to *Festinger's cognitive dissonance theory,* when there is an inconsistency between our attitudes and our behaviors, we are psychologically uncomfortable and are motivated to reduce the discomfort. In such a case our attitudes change to be more compatible with our behavior. According to *Bem's attributional analysis,* called *self-perception theory,* we infer our attitudes from our behaviors.

11   A number of factors determine the effectiveness of *persuasive communication* in changing attitudes. These include the source of the message, how the message is stated, and characteristics of the audience.

12   It is often difficult to predict a person's behavior by knowing his attitudes.

13   *Prejudice* is a negative attitude held toward people solely because of their membership in some group, without knowing them as individuals. *Stereotypes* are preconceived, oversimplified beliefs about the characteristics of members of a group. *Discrimination* is the behavior aimed at the person one is prejudiced toward.

14   Theories of prejudice include the contention that it is a natural societal by-product of competition over scarce resources, that it is an attitude we learn, and that it is a manifestation of a certain type of personality (the authoritarian personality). Ways to reduce prejudice include encouraging cooperation, teaching openmindedness, and raising independent, fair-minded children.

SUGGESTED READINGS

Aronson, E. (1984). *The social animal* (4th ed.). New York: W. H. Freeman. An award-winning introduction to many topics in social psychology including conformity, prejudice, and attraction. Written in an enjoyable style.

Janis, I. L. (1982). *Groupthink: Psychological studies of policy decisions and fiascoes* (2d ed.). Boston: Houghton Mifflin. Janis's most recent discussion of "groupthink"; contains an analysis of the Watergate cover-up.

Milgram, S. (1974). *Obedience to authority.* New York: Harper Colophon Books. Milgram's account of his famous experiments on obedience to authority; includes numerous transcripts of individuals' reactions in the experimental situation.

Myers, D. G. (1983). *Social psychology.* New York: McGraw-Hill. A textbook that is exceptionally well written and thorough. Contains discussions of all the major areas of social psychological research.

CHAPTER 18

BEING WITH PEOPLE WHO MATTER: LOVERS AND FRIENDS

SPOTLIGHT ON

The importance of beauty in attracting people to one another.

The powerful effect on attraction of living nearby and becoming familiar.

Our tendency to attribute another person's behavior more to his or her personality than to the situation (the reverse of the way we attribute our own behavior).

Factors that influence whether we are drawn into and stay in a relationship.

What makes us choose one person over another as a best friend, a lover, or a spouse? Social psychologists have studied the riddle of interpersonal attraction and have come up with some clues to the factors that draw us to others. (© 1979 Maureen Fennelli/Photo Researchers, Inc.)

People are basically social animals. In many of the chapters in this book we have seen how we affect other people and how they affect us. We influence and are influenced by both our parents, by our peers, our siblings, our teachers, our neighbors, our coworkers. We also interact with people we hardly know, through societal norms transmitted by the group, and sometimes these interactions can have life-and-death implications, as in the case of helping behavior or aggression between strangers.

In this chapter we will emphasize two specific types of ties with other people—friendships and love relationships between adults. The presence of friends and a special "significant other" in people's lives often predict the level of happiness in a person's life (Lowenthal & Haven, 1968). In recent years, a considerable amount of social psychology research has recognized the importance of such bonds and has tried to unravel the mysteries of how these relationships begin, develop, and either continue or dissolve.

During the mid-1970s, when the National Science Foundation awarded an $84,000 grant for research on love, Wisconsin Senator William Proxmire raged against this waste of taxpayers' money. He argued that falling in love is not a science but a mystery and that "200 million other Americans want to leave some things in life a mystery" (Harris, 1978, p. viii). Proxmire went on to urge: "So National Science Foundation—get out of the love racket. Leave that to Elizabeth Barrett Browning and Irving Berlin!"

Psychologists have not, however, left the study of love and friendship to the poets and the song writers. Instead, they have sponsored an increasingly wide range of studies to explore the reasons we are attracted to one person and not another and what happens during the course of friendships and love affairs.

BEING DRAWN TO OTHER PEOPLE: INTERPERSONAL ATTRACTION

While some studies of the way people select friends and spouses have gone on since the 1930s, as of 1958 Harry Harlow was able to write, "The little we know about love does not transcend simple observation, and the little we write about it has been written better by poets and novelists" (p. 673). This state of affairs has come about largely because of beliefs in the minds of the public—and among scientists themselves—that there is little about such complex relationships that can be scientifically explored.

Before going on, stop to think about your three closest friends. If you are in a loving relationship, think about that person, too. Why have you chosen these particular people to assume these special places in your life? What is it about them, of all the people you know? With an apology to Elizabeth Barrett Browning, let's ask ourselves, "Why do I like (or love) thee? Let me count the ways. . . ." Can you list the reasons you are attracted to each of these people?

Chances are that your "reasons" will focus on attributes of the other person (such as "sense of humor"). Yet social psychologists have found, and emphasize, that there are no attributes that absolutely predict attraction. It is how you interpret the other person's characteristics that determines whether you will be attracted to that person. In other words, attraction depends on the *interaction* between your own traits and the other person's traits, and the situation in which you get to know each other.

What do we mean when we talk about "interpersonal attraction"? In psychological terms, we are talking about a tendency to evaluate another person in a positive way. In other words, about an *attitude*. Evaluations of other people depend on many different factors. Let's take a look at how we study attraction, how we measure it, and how we discover the bases underlying it.

Studying Attraction

Over the years different research approaches have looked into different aspects of this complex social phenomenon. During the 1930s and 1940s, psychologists were exploring the factors leading us to choose our friends and our spouses and then trying to connect these factors to the success of marriage. At that time researchers emphasized the individual characteristics of the people involved. By the 1960s, emphasis shifted to study of the *processes* of attraction, an interest that continues to the present.

A number of recent theories (Bachman, 1981; Altman & Taylor, 1973; Levinger, 1974) describe the progression of relationships from a superficial level to the deep level of a close tie. As relationships deepen, the partners become more willing to disclose intimate facts and feelings, and they become more committed to each other. Although early studies focused on the easier-to-study early stages of relationship development, more recent research has shifted the emphasis to the later stages, including both maintenance or dissolution.

While some studies have taken place in naturalistic settings like housing developments (Festinger, Schachter, & Back, 1950) and dormitories (Newcomb, 1961), a large proportion of research has focused on ingenious laboratory-based studies. The subjects—as in so much psychological research—consist largely of white, middle-class college students. Since researchers interested in isolating a particular aspect of attraction have often set up situations that are more or less artificial, it is sometimes difficult to generalize their results to apply to real-life situations, a problem that must be considered for all lab-based experimental research. Recently, more social scientists have been merging the two approaches—using analytical procedures borrowed from the laboratory, along with survey procedures applied to the context of everyday life, making results more valid (Backman, 1981).

In this chapter we'll look at the ways we measure attraction, the factors that contribute to it (such as geographical closeness, physical appearance, and similarity of attitudes), and the theories that try to explain why we become attracted to one person and not to another. We'll look at friendship, love, marriage, and divorce.

Measuring Attraction

ASKING PEOPLE HOW THEY FEEL   One way psychologists assess the degree of attraction among people is to ask people to think about specific persons in their lives and then to think about them with regard to specific characteristics that they have and specific feelings that you have. These are called *self-report measures*. Another technique involves experimental manipulation of the other person's characteristics and/or your (the perceiver) situation before asking you to express your feelings. The researcher might vary such traits as the other person's physical attractiveness or how much the other person is said to like you, and then see how you feel about that person. Or the researcher may change the situation, possibly putting you in an anxiety-producing setting, and then ask about your attitude toward a person whom you meet in that setting.

The most widely used measure of attraction is the Interpersonal Judgment Scale developed by Donn Byrne (1971). On this scale you would rate someone on six different dimensions: intelligence, knowledge of current events, morality, adjustment, your feelings of like or dislike, and how

TABLE 18-1 The Interpersonal Judgment Scale: Measure of Attraction

Personal Feelings (Check One):

_____ I feel that I would probably like this person very much.

_____ I feel that I would probably like this person.

_____ I feel that I would probably like this person to a slight degree.

_____ I feel that I would probably neither particularly like not particularly dislike this person.

_____ I feel that I would probably dislike this person to a slight degree.

_____ I feel that I would probably dislike this person.

_____ I feel that I would probably dislike this person very much.

Working Together on an Experiment (Check One):

_____ I believe that I would very much dislike working with this person in an experiment.

_____ I believe that I would dislike working with this person in an experiment.

_____ I believe that I would dislike working with this person in an experiment to a slight degree.

_____ I believe that I would neither particularly dislike nor particularly enjoy working with this person in an experiment.

_____ I believe that I would enjoy working with this person in an experiment to a slight degree.

_____ I believe that I would enjoy working with this person in an experiment.

_____ I believe that I would very much enjoy working with this person in an experiment.

Source: Byrne, 1971.

much you would want to work with him or her. The two dimensions of this scale that are used to measure attraction are "liking" and "want to work with," which are reproduced in Table 18-1. On other scales designed to measure romantic attraction, you would be asked to indicate how much you would like to date the other person, how much you would like that person as a spouse, and how sexually and physically attractive he or she seems.

One widely used set of measures are the liking and love scales developed by Zick Rubin (1970). These are similar to the Likert scales (described in the previous chapter), which list a number of statements or attitudes and ask the subject to respond on a continuum from "strongly agree" to "strongly disagree." (For excerpts, see Table 18-2.)

The answers from these scales indicate that liking and loving are very different emotions. Love is not just liking to the nth degree; it is another feeling altogether. Why this conclusion? Because liking and loving scores are only moderately correlated. That is, if you like someone, there's not much basis for thinking you'll also love that person. While high scores on Rubin's dimensions of affection and respect go along with liking, love is associated with high scores on attachment, caring, and intimacy. Using still a different measure—the Love Scale developed by Alvin Pam and his colleagues (1975), which measures five different aspects of attraction (respect, altruism, physical attraction, attachment, and congeniality/trust)— Pam, Plutchik, and Conte conclude that friendship is marked by congeniality and respect, while love is highest on attachment and physical attraction.

LOOKING AT WHAT PEOPLE DO   Another way to measure attraction is by observing what people actually do, rather than how they say they feel.

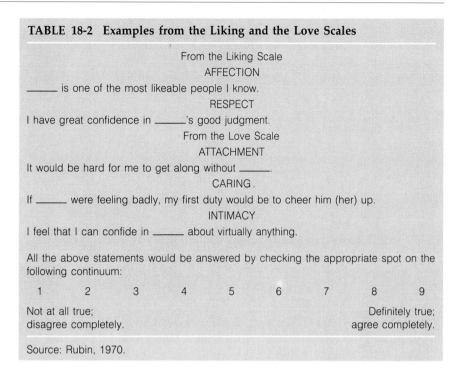

TABLE 18-2 Examples from the Liking and the Love Scales

From the Liking Scale

AFFECTION

_____ is one of the most likeable people I know.

RESPECT

I have great confidence in _____'s good judgment.

From the Love Scale

ATTACHMENT

It would be hard for me to get along without _____.

CARING

If _____ were feeling badly, my first duty would be to cheer him (her) up.

INTIMACY

I feel that I can confide in _____ about virtually anything.

All the above statements would be answered by checking the appropriate spot on the following continuum:

1	2	3	4	5	6	7	8	9

Not at all true;
disagree completely.

Definitely true;
agree completely.

Source: Rubin, 1970.

According to these so-called *unobtrusive measures*, psychologists look at people to see how much time they spend gazing into each other's eyes, how close they stand and whether they lean toward or away from each other, how much they touch, how willing they are to do favors for each other, whether their body postures are in *synchrony* (that is, whether they assume the same posture at the same time), whether they attempt to see each other again, and so forth (Rubin, 1970; Byrne & Griffitt, 1973; Perper, 1980).

Research has shown that all these behaviors are barometers of attraction. For example, people whose scores on the love scale indicate that they love each other a great deal spend more time gazing into each other's eyes than do those couples who love each other less, pointing to a likely validation of both measures (Rubin, 1970). By and large, however, very few studies have tried to find a relationship between the self-report scales and the behavioral measures of attraction, and more research is needed to explore the complexities involved (Triandis, 1977).

HOW WE MAKE DECISIONS ABOUT OTHER PEOPLE: PERSON PERCEPTION AND ATTRIBUTION THEORY

Whether we like or dislike someone depends very much on the way we perceive that person's attributes and motivations, and social psychologists have explored the ways by which we arrive at these perceptions. Say you are standing in line waiting for a bus and suddenly feel yourself being violently jostled. You will probably turn around to see who is pushing you—and to try to come up with some explanation for what is happening.

If you see that a man wearing dark glasses and carrying a white-tipped cane has bumped into you, you'll assume that the man is blind and you

As psychologists try to measure the degree to which two people are attracted to each other, they look to see whether the two assume the same posture at the same time. Often, when people feel close, their body postures are almost mirror images of each other. (Anestis Diakopoulos/Stock, Boston)

may help him to get where he wants to go. If the person who pushed you is wearing ragged clothes and reeks of alcohol, you'll assume he's drunk and may either ignore him or tell him to go away. If the jostler is a swaggering teenager who looks at you defiantly and curses you with a racial epithet, you may take a swing at him, call a law enforcement officer, walk away, or try to melt into the crowd. In each of these cases, the initial behavior was the same, but because of other clues, you attributed different reasons to the initial behavior—and you reacted very differently, depending on whatever your attributions were.

You formed inferences about each of these people based on what they did, what they themselves were like, and the context of their behavior (pushing a stranger in a public place). In your perception of these people, you didn't react passively. Even if you *did* nothing, your mental processes were active: You searched your memory, from a background of your own experience, to categorize what the clues to their behavior meant in your own frame of reference, and you gave a meaning to that behavior. The blind man couldn't help himself, the drunk man didn't care, and the tough kid acted out his aggressive feelings.

These examples were fairly clear-cut, but in most situations in life it is harder to decide why a person acts in a certain way. Yet we are continually examining the behavior of other people, trying to figure out their intentions and their emotional states, and trying to decide *why* they do what they do. The attributions we provide for other people's behavior are very important because they determine how we will feel and act toward those other people.

According to attribution theory (Heider, 1958), introduced in Chapter 17 in our discussion of Bem's self-perception theory, we tend to explain people's behavior either *dispositionally* (from some *internal* cause, like a

It is precisely common sense with which attribution theory is concerned. . . . However, it is our experience that the careful explication and systematization of what at first seems obvious eventually carries us into realms of discovery and insight. I believe social psychologists finally are realizing that their proper role is not to confound common sense, but rather to analyze, refine, and enlarge on it (Kelly, 1973, p. 108).

Psychological research sometimes does confirm common sense—what we knew all along—but sometimes it yields results directly opposed to common sense. Even when it confirms, it questions, it raises issues, and it offers new ways of looking at a wide range of topics dealing with the human mind.

basic personality trait) or *situationally* (through an *external* cause like a particular circumstance). This theory, then, is concerned with the way we make our judgments. If we feel, for example, that someone came up to us and shoved us for no good reason, then we're likely to be very angry. If we can come up with an explanation that seems logical (in other words, that would explain why we ourselves might do the same thing in such a situation), we will understand the behavior and not be angry.

When we are trying to answer the question, "Why did that person behave that way?" we rely on information about three attributes: *distinctiveness*, *consensus*, and *consistency* (Kelley, 1967).

Suppose you hear about Sue, who laughs at a particular comedian. Sue hardly ever laughs at comedians, but whenever she hears this one, she laughs at him. Almost everyone else who hears this particular comedian laughs at him, too. When a group of college students were asked whether they thought Sue's laughter was caused by an internal quality (her tendency to laugh at comedians) or an external circumstance (the effect of this particular comedian), 61 percent attributed the laughter to the situation, the effect of the comedian, while only 12 percent attributed it to something about Sue (McArthur, 1972). Sue's response was associated distinctively with this particular stimulus (the comedian), her response is similar to those of other persons (there is a consensus), and it is consistent over time. In other words, something about the situation brought about Sue's behavior.

On the other hand, when the students heard about Paul, who is enthralled by a painting, who has almost always been enthralled by the same painting (even though practically no one else who sees this painting is enthralled by it), and who is enthralled by almost every other painting, the subjects' reactions were quite different. Some 85 percent felt that the enthrallment arose from Paul himself, while practically none attributed it to the painting. Paul's reaction was consistent, but it was not distinctive and there was no consensus, indicating that the source of his enthrallment was internal. Paul's behavior is more appropriately attributed to something within himself (like his enthusiastic personality) rather than to something in the situation (such as the merit of a particular painting).

According to the fundamental attribution error (Ross, 1977), most of us tend to *overestimate dispositional* factors like personality traits and to *underestimate situational* ones like particular circumstances, in accounting for behavior. This error is most common when we try to explain the behavior of another person. When a professor heard that one of her students was dropping out of the Ph.D. program, for example, she immediately "blamed" his decision on his laziness and/or his inability to cope with the program's intellectual demands. After some reflection, she realized that situational factors also played an important part in his decision to leave. His father, who lived 1000 miles away had been quite ill, and the graduate student wanted to be close to him and be in a position to help his mother make decisions for his care. Furthermore, a government loan that the student had counted on to get him through the semester had not come through.

Research has supported this error in accounting for another's behavior. In one experiment students were presented with essays favoring a particular point of view. When the subjects knew that the writers of these papers were *told* to take this point of view, they made some allowance for this fact, but they still tended to assume that the writers really believed what they were saying (Jones & Harris, 1967).

Why do people tend to make assumptions about the personalities of other people without considering how the situation influences their behavior? A partial explanation is the fact that we *know* the influential factors in our own situation, while we don't know them for other people. We can easily point to various influences on our behavior, while we take the easiest path regarding other people and assume that they did something because that's the kind of people they are. Let's go back to our example of being pushed by a belligerent teenager: If we were to learn that someone who looked just like us had just moments before pushed him and had called out an ethnic slur while doing it, the boy's action would make more sense, and we wouldn't automatically assume that the pusher was showing pure, unmotivated aggression.

Another explanation is that we judge people by what actually happens because it requires more work to look for hidden reasons. Thus, if someone wrote an essay in favor of legalizing marijuana, it's easier to assume that that's his true opinion than having to remember that he was assigned to take that point of view.

The fundamental attribution error also serves the purpose of protecting our egos. We tend to attribute our *failures* to the situation ("I couldn't fix the car because it's a junk heap") and our *successes* to ourselves ("I must be a pretty good mechanic if I got rid of that rattle"). This can be seen in research that shows that the error doesn't seem to exist when it enhances our egos to attribute success to our own characteristics.

When the candidates in each of thirty-three political races in Wisconsin were asked why they thought they had won or lost, 75 percent of the winners attributed their victories to their own characteristics, emphasizing factors within their control (hard work, smart strategy, service to constituents), while the losers overwhelmingly (90 percent) blamed the results on outside factors beyond their control (party makeup of the district, national and state trends, lack of money) (Kingdon, 1967).

This way of thinking seems to be affected by cultural standards, as studies of shyness have indicated. In Japan, where 60 percent of the people consider themselves shy, children are expected to assume the full burdens of their failures, while they are expected to credit their successes to their parents, grandparents, teachers, or Buddha. In Israel, which has a low rate of shyness, individuals are encouraged to accept full credit for their successes and to blame their failures on such external factors as inadequate teaching or prejudice. Zimbardo and Radl (1982) maintain that the Japanese style discourages individuals from taking risks and fosters shyness, while the Israeli style encourages risk taking since the individual has little to lose.

The fundamental attribution error has important ramifications for intimate relationships. Any marriage counselor can recount tales of disputes in which partners explain their own behavior by referring to all sorts of mitigating circumstances, while they accuse their spouses of acting out of selfishness, inconsiderateness, thoughtlessness, repressed hostility, and other unfavorable personality traits. Also, since so many things that people do may stem from any of a number of different reasons, each person brings his or her own experience and way of thinking to bear on an incident and attributes thoughts and feelings to the other person that may never have entered his or her mind.

"Such a bias sows the seeds for interpersonal misunderstandings. . . . It is very likely that we assign to another's personality what we should be viewing as a complex interaction between person and situation" (Jones, 1977, p. 321). We don't make enough allowance for the roles people assume, for the external pressures they're subjected to, and for the differences in their experiences and ours—and so whenever other people do something we don't like or can't understand, the temptation arises to attribute their behavior to "a set of unwarranted personality characteristics" (p. 321). Once we've assigned this personality to them, we create self-fulfilling prophecies by giving off subtle cues that will induce people to act the way we expect them to.

WHAT ATTRACTS US TO OTHER PEOPLE?

The research on attraction is largely the study of first impressions among white middle-class college students in laboratory experiments. Even within these boundaries we have learned a number of principles that explain how we choose our friends and our lovers, and these principles are confirmed by a smaller body of field research that explores the development of relationships in the real world. Paramount among these principles is the interaction between another person's characteristics and our appraisal of those traits.

"The Nearness of You": Proximity

If you are a college student in the United States and I am a Sherpa tribesman living in a remote clearing in the Himalayas, it's highly unlikely that we will ever meet, let alone start a relationship. That seems fairly obvious. It's also unsurprising that there is a strong relationship between how close we live to someone and how friendly we become with that person. What *is* surprising, however, is the strength of that correlation. You can test it yourself by making your own friendship map. Plot out your neighbors, either in dorm, apartment building, or street. In all likelihood, you'll find that the closer you live to someone, the friendlier you are with that person, even though your proximity originally came about by chance.

The powerful impact of proximity was first brought out in a classic study of friendship patterns among married students living in a housing development named Westgate West (Festinger, Schachter, & Back, 1950). The development consisted of seventeen two-story buildings, with five apartments per floor. Residents could not choose which apartment they lived in: When a unit became vacant, the next person on the waiting list was assigned that apartment.

Again, it's not surprising that Westgate residents became friendlier with those in the same buildings than with those in other buildings. The surprising thing was the *extent* of architectural influence. The two major elements influencing friendships were the number of doors away two people lived and the direction a house faced. Next-door neighbors were most likely to be friends. After that, those two doors away were more likely to be friends than those separated by a relatively short hall. Those on the same floor were more friendly than those living on different floors.

The people who had the most friends were the ones whose apartments

The more we see of other people, the more likely we are to become friendly with them. According to some research, next-door neighbors are more likely to be friends than are people who live farther apart. (© Jim Anderson 1983/Woodfin Camp & Assoc.)

were near the mailboxes and near stairway entry and exits (where there was a lot of coming and going); those with the fewest friends lived in houses that faced outward toward the street. The people in these end houses, which had been assigned to them purely by chance, had less than half as many friends as did those whose houses faced inward on the courtyard.

Other research has shown that the closer their last names were alphabetically, the closer the friendships were among a group of police trainees whose seats and dorm rooms were assigned in alphabetical order. Trainees tended to choose friends whose names were, on the average, only 4.5 letters away from their own in the alphabet (Segal, 1974). Apparently, the more people see of each other, the better they're apt to like each other.

The practical conclusion to be drawn from all this is that if you want to be popular, you'll have a better chance of making friends if you go where the people are—get a room, an apartment, or a desk in a well-trafficked area and then go out of your way to see people often.

Why is there a relationship between geographical closeness and attraction? It isn't just availability and convenience. After all, people living two doors away are almost as available as next-door neighbors. Something else seems to be at work. It's possible that the more we see of someone, the more familiar that person becomes, and we become comfortable with familiar people. Familiarity breeds comfort because we can predict the behavior of people we know well: If I know how you will react, I can tailor my own reactions to do what will please you and avoid doing things that will make you angry.

Another possibility is that if I know I'll be seeing a lot of you, I'll be more highly motivated to see your good points and to do whatever I can to keep our interactions pleasant. This conclusion is suggested by a study that found that people who expected to spend time with another person had more positive feelings toward that person than they did toward another person whom they didn't expect to see again (Darley & Berscheid, 1967).

Then there is the mere-exposure effect (Zajonc, 1968; 1970) that suggests that we like something (someone) better after having been exposed to it (him or her) repeatedly. We often seem to like musical works, paintings, and other works of art simply because they are familiar. After we hear enough commercials, we are more favorably disposed toward that product. The same principle may hold for people.

Of course, proximity and familiarity don't always make us like someone. Even though proximity is related more often to attraction than to hostility, the great majority of violent assaults in this country are among relatives, neighbors, and others who know each other well (Steinmetz & Straus, 1974). Research has also shown that if we dislike someone the first time we meet him or her, then being close to that person will only increase this dislike (Schiffenbauer & Schiavo, 1976). So while proximity helps, it's not the only answer. What else draws us to someone?

"The Way You Look Tonight": Physical Appearance

Americans spend millions of dollars every year on clothing, makeup, hair care, weight loss, and other services and products to make us look better. On the basis of research, such expenditures are not so extravagant, after all. Study after study—most of them done since 1972—shows that physically attractive people are more sought after, more highly regarded, and generally treated better. This boost for beauty begins in early childhood, when attractive nursery school children are more likely to be chosen as friends and less likely to be blamed by teachers for misbehavior (Dion & Berscheid, 1974). It continues during the school years, when good-looking children are more popular (Lerner & Lerner, 1977; Kleck, Richardson, & Ronald, 1974); and it persists in adulthood, when better looking people are sought out, are treated better, and are thought to have better prospects for good sex lives, good marriages, good jobs, and general all-around happiness (Ecker & Weinstein, 1983; Walster, Aronson, Abrahams, & Rottmann, 1966; Snyder, Tanke, & Berscheid, 1977; Dion, Berscheid, & Walster, 1972).

How can we even study the effects of attractiveness when "beauty is in the eye of the beholder"? Originally, people thought that physical attractiveness could have no effect on a person's life because they believed that individuals differ so much on what is attractive. However, studies show a great deal of agreement among observers about people's physical attractiveness, and this discovery of agreement pointed to the impact that looks can have on a person's life (Berscheid, 1983).

In studying attractiveness, researchers generally ask an independent panel of judges to rate photographs or real people on their attractiveness, in the belief that if enough beholders agree, the person can be considered attractive. Then they set up their experiment involving subjects who were not involved in the ratings—and who don't even know that the effects of attractiveness are being studied—and correlate the results with the physical appearance of the target people.

One of the earliest studies on attraction sought to confirm the likelihood that we are drawn to those at about our own levels of social desirability, including physical attractiveness as one small part of this overall rating. In 1966, Elaine Walster and her colleagues sponsored a "computer-match" dance for University of Minnesota first-year students. The researchers obtained personality and aptitude test scores for the 752 first-

This boy's good looks probably help to explain the bevy of girls around him. Research shows that physically attractive people are more sought out, are treated better, and are thought to have a better chance for happiness. (David S. Strickler/The Picture Cube)

year students who had bought tickets, had them fill out questionnaires about themselves, and had them rated on attractiveness by four sophomores. Then they assigned them randomly to dates.

The first-year students evaluated their dates at intermission (two and a half hours into the dance) and then again four to six months later. The conclusions did not confirm the researchers' initial hypothesis that people of similar attractiveness levels will seek each other out. Nor did compatible personality and intelligence levels attract people to each other. To the contrary, the single most important determinant of how much the dates liked each other was how physically attractive they found each other. For both men and women, the more attractive their dates were, the more they wanted to and tried to date each other again (Walster, Aronson, Abrahams, & Rottmann, 1966). The often noted similarity in attractiveness levels between husbands and wives (Price & Vandenberg, 1979) must, therefore, have other causes. Maybe people drift toward their own level by trial and error. Studies indicate that people choose others of high social desirability when they expect those others to like them, but when they are afraid there is a strong chance of being rejected, they lower their sights to their same or lower levels of desirability (Berscheid, 1983).

The first-year students in this study may have been responding to something else about their dates that is correlated with good looks. That something may be the kind of personality an attractive person develops as a result of the self-confidence generated from a lifetime of favorable treatment.

The truth that we respond according to the way we are treated has been clearly brought out in another study in which male college students were shown photos of either a beautiful or an unattractive woman and told they would be having a 10-minute "get-acquainted" phone conversation with her. The men imagined the beautiful women to be friendly and socially skilled, with a good sense of humor, while the unattractive women were seen as lacking these qualities.

Observers who listened in on the phone conversations, which actually took place with an entirely different woman from those in the photos, found that the men acted according to their preconceived notions: The ones who *thought* they were talking to a beauty were friendlier, funnier, sexier, and more interesting. The significant finding with regard to the way our looks affect our personalities is that the women picked up these cues: The ones thought to be attractive acted friendlier, more animated, and more self-confident; the ones thought unattractive were more stand-offish and withdrawn (Snyder, Tanke, & Berscheid, 1977).

Recent studies have found more complexity in this matter of looks, possibly as a result of changing beliefs about sex roles. While sex-typed individuals of both sexes are more animated, enthusiastic, and interested in "phone-mates" they think are attractive, the freer college students are of sex-stereotyped thinking, the less likely they are to respond more positively over the phone to either men or women whom they think are attractive (Anderson & Bem, 1981). Men free from sex-stereotyped thinking don't differentiate at all between supposedly attractive and unattractive "phone-mates," and non-sex-typed women are actually *more* positive toward supposedly unattractive people, drawing them out in a way that lets them show more self-assurance and responsiveness than supposedly attractive people.

In another study, male and female college students rated as traditional, moderate, or liberal based on their attitudes toward women read either a well-written or a poorly written essay supposedly written by either an attractive or an unattractive woman, evaluated the essay, and rated the writer on her talent, likability, and competence (Holahan & Stephan, 1981). The women didn't seem to care what the writers looked like, focusing on their competence instead. The liberal women were less tolerant of incompetence: They were more critical of the poor essay and admired and liked the good writer better. The traditional women admired the good writer but felt the poor one was more likable and more likely to achieve personal fulfillment.

The men, however, were more influenced by looks. If the writer of the *poor* essay was supposed to be pretty, men tended to consider her more talented than if she was supposed to be plain. If the writer of the *good* essay was supposed to be pretty, however, men judged her as *less* talented. It looks as if many men still have trouble accepting the fact that a woman may be beautiful *and* brainy. Yet the liberal men liked the competent writer better if they thought she was attractive, while the traditional men liked the attractive woman better no matter which essay she wrote. We can see how complex the physical attractiveness effect is and how societal changes (in this case, changing sex-role attitudes) are reflected in research findings.

Why do looks matter so much? First, of course, there is the aesthetic advantage of looking at something (someone) you consider beautiful. Then, since we tend to assume that beautiful people have more desirable characteristics, we may believe that when we get a pretty package, we get more inside the package, too, than we would get from an unattractive person.

A third element is status by association: If most people attribute positive traits to attractive people, and if attractive people are more popular, with the ability to choose their friends and lovers freely, then whoever they do choose must be very special, too. So we enhance our own status by associating with the Beautiful People. And a fourth possibility is that beautiful people, by virtue of having been treated favorably over the years, may be more secure, more giving, more competent, and more satisfying to be with. Since the effects of looks on attraction go well beyond first impressions (Huston & Levinger, 1978), it's probable that there are many interlocking reasons for its power in bringing—and keeping—people together.

"That Certain Something": Other Personal Characteristics

There are, of course, many other personal characteristics that attract us to people. These characteristics do not exist in a vacuum but are filtered through our perceptions. It's not the trait in and of itself but the way we perceive it. So we may think that someone has a good sense of humor if she laughs at our jokes—and if we meet her in a situation that encourages laughter and high spirits. The factors we mentioned previously, proximity and physical attractiveness, are especially important attractants when we begin a relationship. Now we'll look at other factors that assume special importance as we decide whether to keep it up.

WARMTH To many people the quality of warmth embodies consideration of other people, informality, sociability, humanity, generosity, a sense of humor, and good nature. These are the specific traits that a group of students attributed to a guest lecturer when they had been told ahead of time that he was a warm person (Kelley, 1950). Some students in the same class, listening to the same lecturer, had been told he was a "rather cold" person. *All* the students were told that he was industrious, critical, practical, and determined. Not only did the students who expected the lecturer to be cold evaluate him less favorably after his 20-minute class but they also participated less in the discussion than did those who expected a warm person.

This classic experiment demonstrates the importance not only of personality characteristics themselves but also of the way our interpretation and expectations of other people's personalities affects the degree to which we'll like and feel comfortable with them, the way we'll act toward them, and, consequently, the way they're apt to feel and act toward us. We often create a self-fulfilling prophecy by giving off cues that make people act the way we expect them to.

COMPETENCE While people admire competence in others—and no evidence indicates that many people are attracted to those of mediocre abilities or talents, too much competence apparently makes other people feel insecure (Aronson, 1980). We like a competent person much better when she or he makes the kind of mistake that makes him or her seem less perfect and more human. This is known as the "pratfall effect." When competent people fall flat on their face as a result of their own errors, we tend to see them as more fallible, more human, and more likable. This was seen when President John F. Kennedy's popularity rose after his blunder in trying—and failing—to invade Cuba in the Bay of Pigs fiasco.

Aronson, Willerman, and Floyd (1966) demonstrated this point in experiments in which they played a series of four tape recordings to a group of subjects. The tapes consisted of interviews with either a person of mediocre ability or one so highly competent he was almost perfect (honor student, yearbook editor, track team member, and correct answerer of 92 percent of the difficult questions asked during the interview). One tape of each person (actually the same actor playing both parts) was without incident, while the other portrayed the interviewee clumsily spilling coffee all over his new suit. The subjects rated the superior person who committed the blunder as the most attractive of the four, the unblundering superior person next, the mediocre one third, and the mediocre coffee spiller least attractive.

Rivalry seems to play a part in the pratfall effect since follow-up studies showed that men preferred the competent blunderer while women preferred the competent nonblunderer. In addition, high-self-esteem men (who seemed to see the competent interviewee as a rival) preferred the competent blunderer, while low-self-esteem men (who felt out of the competent person's league and therefore did not have competitive feelings) preferred the competent nonblunderer (Deaux, 1972; Aronson, Helmreich, & LeFan, 1970).

"We Think Alike": Similarity

The thrill of getting to know another person is often the discovery that you both love the same books, hate the same politician, have similar goals in life, and do the same things in your leisure time. A great deal of research underscores this power of attitudinal similarity in bringing people together.

One way this is often done is through the "phantom other" procedure designed by Donn Byrne (1961; 1971). Assume you are a subject in such an experiment. After you had answered an opinion questionnaire, you would be presented with another person's answers to the same questions and you would be asked how you felt about this person. In fact, no such person exists. A researcher carefully filled out this second questionnaire to make it more or less similar to your own answers by an overlap of zero up to total agreement. Chances are that the closer the phantom's answers are to your own, the more you'll like that person (Byrne & Griffitt, 1973; Byrne, Clore, & Worchel, 1966; Byrne, London, & Reeves, 1968).

What about real life, though? Does the same principle hold? The evidence is that it does. One study differs from most experiments in the extended nature of the contact among the subjects and in the fact that they were not told how alike or different the others were (Griffitt & Veitch, 1974). Thirteen men who had not known each other lived together for ten days in a fallout shelter, after having expressed their attitudes on forty-four issues. At the end of the first, the fifth, and the ninth days of confinement, each man was asked to list the three people in the group he would *most* like to remain in the shelter and the three he would *least* like to stay. There was a clear-cut correlation: People wanted to keep the ones most like them and wanted to get rid of the ones least like them.

Other studies have found additional common grounds for close relationships. Both friends and spouses tend to be similar in race, age, socioeconomic status, religion, education, intelligence, values, and leisure activities (Murstein, 1982; Werner & Parmelee, 1979). Similarities in personality are also a basis of attraction (Byrne, 1969). Complementarity theory holds that opposite personalities attract—that, for example, a shy person is drawn to an outgoing one and a talker to a listener. This seems sensible but does not show up in actual studies, even though some friends, lovers, and spouses do seem to become more complementary as relationships develop (Berscheid & Walster, 1978; Nias, 1979; D. Fishbein & Thelen, 1981).

One limit to the attraction value of similarity brings to mind comedian Groucho Marx's famous avowal, "I wouldn't join any club that would have me for a member!" People who have a low opinion of themselves are not attracted to others who remind them of themselves. Leonard (1975) tested sixty-four college students on a measure of self-esteem; got information on their education, work history, and vital statistics; and asked their opinions about fourteen controversial topics. He then asked his subjects to rate several confederates, some of whom would give attitudinal and background information that would make them seem similar to the subject and some of whom would seem quite different. Only the high-self-esteem subjects were attracted to people who were like them; the reverse obtained for those who thought little of themselves.

Why do we like people like ourselves? Research has yielded a number of possible reasons for being attracted to similar people (Huston & Levinger, 1978). Being with someone who expresses similar attitudes and opinions is reinforcing because it validates our own experience: If she or he thinks the same way I do, you may think, I must be right myself. Since most of us like to be right, this provides a large reward. Also, since we tend to be convinced that our opinions are the correct ones, we will admire the judgment and right-thinking of those who share our outlook. We often assume that those who think like us will be favorably inclined toward us, which makes us favorably inclined toward them.

"If You Like Me, I Like You": Reciprocity

The natural tendency we have to be drawn toward those people who've shown their good taste and good judgment by liking us has been confirmed by research. If you were told that someone else liked you or gave you a favorable evaluation, you would be apt to like that person back (Backman & Secord, 1959; Kenny & Nasby, 1980; Berscheid & Walster, 1978). You might even have a standard with a fairly fine line to base your feelings on: If, for example, you heard that someone said seven complimentary things about you and one critical thing, you would like that person less than someone else who said all positive things (Berscheid, Walster, & Hatfield, 1969).

There are some exceptions to these findings. Sometimes we like people who compliment us, but sometimes we don't. People with high self-esteem respond favorably to compliments, probably because they believe in their truth, while flattery backfires with people who think little of themselves. They don't like to be complimented, probably because they don't believe the complimenters mean what they are saying and must, therefore, be acting falsely to manipulate them (Colman, 1980). Colman calls on *cognitive consistency theory* to explain these findings: We need to organize our thoughts, feelings, and behaviors in a consistent way, so we are more inclined to like those who share our attitudes.

Of 245 people interviewed in one study, 65 percent felt uneasy about being complimented, even when they viewed the compliments as sincere

In the second century B.C., the philosopher Hecato wrote: "I will show you a love potion without drug or herb or any witch's spell; if you wish to be loved, love" (Berscheid & Walster, 1978, p. 40).

We tend to be attracted to people who share our interests, values, and goals—and to people who like the same kinds of leisure-time activities. (David S. Strickler/The Picture Cube)

(Turner & Edgley, 1974). Why? Usually for one of these reasons: the felt obligation to return the compliment; the need to keep up a modest front and avoid seeming conceited by agreeing with the praise; suspicion of ulterior motives; fear that if someone compliments you now, she or he can criticize you later; resentment at being evaluated at all by someone else; or worry that it won't be possible to keep up whatever is being praised.

Who the complimenter is seems to make a difference in how you'll react. When higher-status complimenters (graduate students) praised undergraduates, they were better liked than when they made only neutral comments, while lower-status complimenters (high school dropouts) were less well liked when they praised the college students, especially when they praised them for qualities the students didn't feel they had (Colman, 1980). Colman explains these findings with *self-enhancement theory* (based on the personality theory of Carl Rogers), which would indicate that praise satisfies our needs to evaluate ourselves favorably. This study showed that we accept such praise only when it comes from someone we respect.

Virtually all theories of attraction have some sort of reward-punishment orientation. The problem in defining the nature of these rewards and punishments is that you and I are rewarded (and punished) by different things. So the course of any relationship depends on both people—what each one offers and how the other member takes to the offering. Thus social psychologists devote considerable effort to trying to find out what is rewarding to whom and under what circumstances.

WHY WE ARE DRAWN TO—AND STAY IN—RELATIONSHIPS

Psychologists are not, of course, just content to observe behavior; they want to explain it. How, for example, do we look at the large pool of possible marriage partners and zero in on one? (At least, one at a time.)

Robert F. Winch (1958) was the first social scientist to propose a theory of marital choice and try to provide solid support for it. He suggested the complementary-needs theory, which holds that people first screen the field of possible marriage partners on the basis of homogamy, a similarity of attributes, and then choose those individuals whose psychological characteristics meet our needs. So a man who needs to be nurtured will be attracted to a woman who needs to take care of someone, or a man who needs to be dominant will be attracted to a woman who needs to be told what to do. In other words, "birds of a feather" (with regard to social characteristics) "flock together," and then "opposites" (with regard to personalities) "attract." This theory has been very popular for some years because it seems to make such good sense. Since testing has not upheld it, however, it has fallen from favor and forced us to look for other explanations of marital choice.

Other researchers have developed theories to explain why people are attracted to each other as friends, as well as romantically. We'll take a look at a few of the most important.

We Get Rewarded: Reinforcement Theory

According to learning theory principles, we like to be with certain other people because we get something from the relationship. That something may include the fun we have doing things with them, the pleasure we get from looking at them, the satisfaction and self-validation of working toward common goals, the help they give us, or the boost in self-esteem that comes from feeling liked by them or admired by others because of them. Whatever it is, the relationship is reinforcing rather than punishing.

The principles of classical conditioning can explain the way reward theories of attraction work: Social contacts either make us feel good (reinforcing) or bad (punishing); whatever is associated with feeling good or bad can evoke that feeling in us; so we like people associated with our good feelings and don't like people associated with bad ones (Clore & Byrne, 1974).

In fact, sometimes people don't even have to do anything themselves to be reinforcing—they just have to be near us when we are feeling good for some other reason (Lott & Lott, 1974). Children who win at games like their teammates better than when they lose, and children who receive approval from their teachers like their classmates better than children whose teachers ignore or criticize them (Lott & Lott, 1960; 1968).

Adults like a stranger better when they meet him in a comfortable environment than in a hot, crowded room (Griffitt, 1970; Griffitt & Veitch, 1971). "It is through the relaxing evening before the fire, the excitement of a discussion, or the fun of a great party that the person who was always there will be liked even though he or she was not directly responsible for any of these pleasures" (Lott & Lott, 1974, p. 172). This carry-over effect provides one rationale for marriage counselors' common advice to couples in trouble that they make special efforts to plan good times together, so that they can each bathe in the halo of shared pleasures.

We Figure Out the Value of Our Rewards: Exchange Theory

Exchange theory, a more complex variant of basic reward theory, states that we consider the rewards and the costs in everything we do, even though we're not always consciously aware of what we're doing (Thibaut & Kelley, 1958; Homans, 1961). The rewards in a relationship can be the kind just described, while the costs can consist either of unpleasant aspects of the relationship or simply the fact that we have to give up something else, like another relationship or the freedom and solitude of the noncommitted.

We automatically deduct costs from rewards. If the reward is more than the cost, the relationship is profitable to us and we enter into it or stay in it. If the cost outweighs the reward, we have a loss situation, and we keep out or get out. To come up with our "bottom-line" assessment, we compare this relationship to its alternatives: What will we have if we don't have this? A man may be involved with a woman who insults him in public and gets him into debt. If he feels he'll be better off without her— either alone or with someone else—he'll get out. But he may decide that even though he doesn't like things as they are, he couldn't attract anyone who would treat him better, and he'd be too lonely with no woman at all in his life. So he stays with her.

The comparison level in a relationship refers to the minimum benefit a person expects from it; this determines his or her satisfaction. If you get more than the minimum, you'll be satisfied, but if you get less, you'll be dissatisfied (Thibaut & Kelly, 1959). The comparison level for alternatives refers to the attractiveness of other possible ties or to no relationship at all, compared with the present one. Commitment—the moral obligation to remain with someone or the dependence upon the other person—is rarely so total that a person never thinks, "Could I get more from an attachment to someone else? Or would I be better off even if I were alone? Do the problems in this relationship outweigh its benefits for me?" At this point you analyze your tie in terms of a comparison level. Even if you're dissatisfied with your present relationship, if you don't think you'd be better off with someone else or alone, you'll stay in the relationship. But if you think you'd be better off with an alternative, you won't.

Suppose you're in a less-than-perfect marriage. You may think about the alternatives. Can you support yourself financially? How will you feel about yourself if you leave? What will leaving your spouse do to your ties to children, in-laws, and friends? If the probable outcome of leaving doesn't look any worse than the unhappiness you're now suffering, you'll probably leave. If it seems worse, you'll stay.

Exchange theory rubs many people—including many psychologists— the wrong way. "It seems to make of human behavior a rather selfish, egocentric endeavor [with a motif of] 'What can you do for me?'" writes Murstein (1971, p. 17), objecting to the theory's businesslike assessment of one's emotional ledger. And yet, the theory *is* flexible enough to explain the behavior of an extremely generous, nurturant, giving person who considers the opportunity to take care of someone a reward. In such an individual's system of exchange, a relationship that someone else might consider a loss would be extremely profitable.

We Give and We Get: Equity Theory

Most of us are most comfortable in relationships in which we feel we're getting about what we deserve. We're uncomfortable both when we feel we are being shortchanged and when we feel we are shortchanging someone else, and in such situations we'll try to restore a fair and equitable balance. This is the basic premise of equity theory—that people will feel most comfortable in relationships in which there is an equitable (fair) distribution of rewards and costs and that they will strive to restore this state to relationships that they perceive as unbalanced. This theory has

According to equity theory, Great Britain's Lady Di and Prince Charles seem like a well-matched couple. Although he is in line for the throne, she can trace her lineage further back than he can. What other characteristics of both partners might affect the equitability of the alliance? (Wide World Photos)

Does equity affect the way we choose our friends and our lovers? Erving Goffman (1952) assumed it does when he wrote, "A proposal of marriage in our society tends to be a way in which a man sums up his social attributes and suggests to a woman that hers are not so much better as to preclude a merger or a partnership in these matters" (p. 456).

long been applied to relationships in business and to casual social relationships. Elaine Walster and her colleagues cite considerable evidence to apply it to relationships between friends, lovers/spouses, and parents and children (Walster, Walster, & Berscheid, 1978).

We can restore equity in two basic ways. We restore *actual equity* by changing what we are giving or what we are getting. A wife who feels she's being exploited may stop cooking dinner, have an extramarital affair, or withhold some of her earnings, putting them into a separate bank account. Or she may decide to restore *psychological equity* by convincing herself that the inequitable relationship is, in fact, fair. She can minimize her inputs ("After all, I'm not as good-looking, smart, or well educated as he is"); exaggerate her outcomes ("Even if I'm unappreciated, I get a chance to meet a lot of interesting people through his job"); exaggerate her husband's inputs ("He earns so much money that he can really give our family a good life"); or minimize her husband's outcomes ("He has to put up with a lot on his job that I don't have to on mine").

In casual relationships, the concept of equity is taken for granted. We do a neighbor a favor and expect that when we need one in return, we'll get help. After we go to a party, we feel we should invite the host to our own home or reciprocate some other way. If a classmate pays for coffee one day, we reach for the check next time. It's harder to calculate equity in intimate relationships because they are so multifaceted and involve more interactions. So while we don't measure or expect repayment for each service rendered, we do expect a certain fairness in the relationship—not only in the services we give and receive but in the "value" of the other person.

When Ellen Berscheid, Elaine Walster, and George Bohrnstedt (1973) analyzed 2000 questionnaires on mating and dating, they found that respondents who thought their partners were about as desirable as they were happier with their relationship than were those whose partners were much more or much less desirable than themselves. Furthermore, relationships in which partners thought they were fairly treated tended, on follow-up three and a half months later, to be more stable than those in which people thought they were either getting too much or too little (Walster & Walster, 1978).

When Burgess and Wallin (1953) looked at engaged couples, they found them fairly evenly matched on attractiveness, health, neuroticism, popularity, and parents' income, education, and marital happiness. Murstein (1967) gave the MMPI (Minnesota Multiphasic Personality Inventory) to engaged couples and followed them up six months later: The closer in mental health the two people were, the closer they had become in the interim.

When partners in an intimate relationship are not equally matched on one trait, they often balance that by an inequality in the other direction on some other characteristic. For example, in the Berscheid, Walster, and Bohrnstedt (1973) study just cited, people who considered their partners more attractive than themselves tended to be richer, more loving, and more kind and considerate than those whose partners were at the same or lower attractiveness levels.

A recent study examined married couples' perceptions of equity at four stages of the family life cycle—(1) when there is a child under 6; (2) when there are school-age children; (3) when the wife is over 45 and no children are in the home; and (4) when the wife is over 60 (Schafer & Keith, 1981). By and large, both husbands and wives felt that life got fairer with time, with the greatest increase in the equitability of the roles of cooking, home-making, and providing income occurring between stages 2 and 3, when children leave home. Interestingly, when couples did feel their marriages were unfair, they tended to feel the imbalance was in their favor, a perception that may have implications for the success of a marriage. People who feel they are getting the short end of the marital stick may be more likely to divorce so they wouldn't be in the later samples.

FRIENDSHIP

When we think of being attracted to another person, we tend to think of a romantic attraction. Yet attraction and attachment are important concepts in friendship, too. Friendships often endure longer than marriages, provide a great measure of emotional and practical support, and in immeasurable ways contribute to the quality of an individual's life.

What do people want from their friends? According to a survey of 216 people at four stages of life—high school seniors, newlyweds, parents whose youngest child was about to leave home, and people getting ready to retire—five specific dimensions of friendship are important (Weiss & Lowenthal, 1975). We look for *similarity* (in personality, values, or attitudes, with an emphasis on shared activities or experiences); *reciprocity* (helping, understanding, and accepting each other, with an emphasis on mutual trust and ability to share confidences); *compatibility* (enjoyment in being together); *structure* (geographic closeness, convenience, or long duration of acquaintance); and *role modeling* (admiration and respect for the friend's good qualities). Women emphasize the value of supportiveness, while men stress shared activities and interests.

Most of us have several different kinds of friends, to meet different needs (La Gaipa, 1977): We have social acquaintances (with whom we play tennis or study for an exam); good friends (whom we'll call up to go to a movie); close friends (whom we count on for help and support in times of need); and best friends (in whom we confide our deepest secrets). Friendships seem to develop first out of proximity, then out of similar background characteristics (such as age, sex, and race), then out of role relationships (coworkers, fellow students, fellow bowlers, etc.), and then out of similarities in values and attitudes (Huston & Levinger, 1978).

While we know, then, some of the factors that lead to making friends, there has been practically no research on keeping them—on what happens during a relationship, on what makes some friendships enduring and others fleeting, on what makes some people able to make and hold onto several friendships in a lifetime, while others drift along almost friendless. Friendship, then, offers a fertile field for social psychology research studies.

LOVE

Everyone is an expert on love. Out of common knowledge and personal experience, for example, we all know:

* women usually fall in love before men do and then keep carrying the torch after the men have called it quits;

- we don't fall in love and marry people we know too well, but instead become crazy about fascinating strangers we meet away from our normal life and work; and
- women need to be hard to get if they want to get a man.

These may be some of the "truths" that we all "know"—but psychological research conducted over the past twenty years has proved them all wrong (Walster & Walster, 1978). As an element in people's lives that is responsible for a major share of either happiness or unhappiness, love is finally coming in for its fair share of research and theorizing from social psychologists, as well as from poets, novelists, and popular song lyricists. Based on interviews, laboratory experiments, and other tools of research, we are learning facts about love, which may have a host of practical applications.

We have learned, for example, that contrary to the preceding mythical beliefs, men fall in love more quickly than women and cling more tenaciously to a dying affair; we do date, fall in love with, and marry the boy or girl next door or down the street in a startlingly high proportion; and men are most attracted to women who are easy for them to get but difficult for other men to get.

Kinds of Love

There seem to be two basic kinds of romantic love that engage our emotions—companionate and passionate. Companionate love, sometimes called *conjugal love,* is like a loving friendship between a man and a woman that includes affection, deep attachment, trust, respect, appreciation, loyalty, and close knowledge of each other (Driscoll, Davis, & Lipetz, 1972). Even though it may be intense enough to make a person sacrifice in time of need—sometimes to the point of giving his or her life—it is a sensible emotion that follows Byrne's (1971) "law of attraction," which attributes attraction to reinforcement.

Passionate love, on the other hand, is a "wildly emotional state, a confusion of feelings: tenderness and sexuality, elation and pain, anxiety and relief, altruism and jealousy" (Walster & Walster, 1978, p. 2). Psychologist Dorothy Tennov (1979) has coined a new word to describe passionate love—*limerence,* a state that some people experience over and over again, while others never do. According to Walster and Walster, this kind of love is time limited, rarely lasting more than from six to thirty months, even though it may surface from time to time in a basically companionate relationship.

Body and Soul: Physiological Correlates of Passionate Love

What happens when you see someone you love passionately? Your heart beats faster, your breath comes quicker, you get butterflies in your stomach, your hand trembles, your knees feel rubbery. You associate all these physical signs with the sight of your beloved and say, "I'm in love."

As Schacter's (1964) work showed, human beings often look to external reasons to explain ambiguous internal states. Walster and Walster (1978) suggest that people who experience the signs of physiological arousal in a potentially romantic situation may attribute such arousal to love. A number of experiments seem to confirm this.

When young men were frightened (by the threat of receiving severe electric shocks or by standing on a rickety bridge) and then introduced to

Psychological research has disproved many of the myths about love that have been commonly believed by poets, novelists, and the people who write the lyrics to popular songs. (©Jim Anderson 1980/Woodfin Camp & Assoc.)

an attractive young woman, they liked her more than did control subjects who had not experienced fear (Brehm, Gatz, Geothals, McCrimmon, & Ward, 1970; Dutton & Aron, 1974). Young men aroused physiologically by running in place or emotionally by hearing either a negative tape (describing a grisly murder) or a positive tape (comic routines) and then shown a videotape of an attractive or an unattractive young woman (actually the same person, made up and dressed differently) liked the attractive woman more and the unattractive woman less than did unaroused control subjects (White, Fishbein, & Rutstein, 1981). It seems, then, that passionate love can be awakened by all kinds of stimuli, including those that might ordinarily produce anxiety, guilt, hatred, jealousy, and confusion. Negative experiences may induce love by intensifying physiological arousal. And as long as physiological arousal takes place and as long as the individual attributes this agitated state to passion, she or he will experience passionate love (Walster, 1971).

The effect of negative experiences in inducing physiological arousal may help to explain the "Romeo and Juliet" effect—the fact that parental interference in a love relationship intensifies the feelings of passionate love between two people. When Driscoll, Davis, & Lipetz (1972) asked 140 dating, living-together, or married couples about the extent of their parents' disapproval of their relationships, they found that the more the parents interfered, the more passionately in love the couples were. Couples with interfering parents also, however, had lower levels of the attributes that usually go along with conjugal love—such as trust and uncritical acceptance. Apparently, if lovers don't resolve their problems with disapproving parents, the overall quality of their relationship with each other is likely to suffer.

When we talk about love and friendship and intimate relationships, we are talking about the kinds of attachments that often lead to marriage, with all its joys and complexities. Social psychologists have studied some aspects of marriage, including how we choose our mates and how marriage affects us in various ways. In recent years, with the increase in the divorce rate in the United States, research on the dissolution of relationships, both before and after marriage, has increased as well. Some of the findings from recent studies are presented in Box 18-1.

Interpersonal relationships—the source of our greatest joys and our deepest pain. While psychology is intrinsically the study of the individual, we have seen throughout this book how the individual affects and is affected by other people. The more we care about someone, the more we invest of ourselves in a relationship, the more deeply we are affected by our ties with others. The burgeoning interest among researchers in exploring the ways individuals get along with each other bodes well for the health of the individual psyche—as well as for society at large.

BOX 18-1

MARRIAGE AND DIVORCE

HOW WE CHOOSE SOMEONE TO MARRY

What would you want in a husband or wife? Chances are, you'd want someone you love who loves you, someone who would be your best friend, and someone with whom you could have a fulfilling sexual relationship. Today, in the United States, these attributes have largely replaced the bases for marriage that have been historically important—and that still are essential in many other societies around the world— such as financial or lineage considerations by the nuptial couple's parents and similarity in social background between bride and groom.

Similarity still is important, although not as much as it has been in times past. Most of us continue to pick spouses of the same race and religion, and of similar age, intelligence, education, and socioeconomic status, although with increasing rates of interracial and interreligious marriages, the number of exceptions to the rule of similarity is growing (Murstein, 1982).

Contemporary researchers tend to look at similarity as a screening device that "limit(s) the pool of marital eligibles rather than pushing the individual to marry anyone who has a similar cultural-social heritage" (p. 652). Most of us don't have a vast smorgasbord of potential marriage partners to select from; we tend to be exposed to those similar to ourselves, and we choose from them. So similarity works as a screening device devised by fate and circumstance. Once someone

gets through the screen, the theories of interpersonal attraction give insights into our ultimate choices.

HOW MARRIAGE AFFECTS US

While the scientific research on marriage lags behind general interest in the topic, we do know a little about how this almost universal state (entered into by nine out of ten Americans) affects us. For one thing, it seems to keep us healthy: Married people are physically and mentally healthier than single, separated, divorced, and widowed people (Bloom, Asher, & White, 1978). Another interpretation, of course, is that healthier people are more likely to marry or to stay married. Probably both explanations contribute to the positive correlation between health and marital status.

In some cases, marriage seems to advance personality development. Among a group of young men who had been delinquent and involved with drugs in high school, those who married young and became fathers before the age of 23 showed better adjustment and higher self-esteem than peers with the same background who had not married (Bachman, O'Malley, & Johnston, 1978). Again, of course, it's possible to explain this correlation by recognizing the possibility that those high school boys who continued to be maladjusted may have been less likely to marry. Still, this is a promising line of research "that marriage and parenthood may offer a positive socialization

experience into adult roles for previously maladjusted young adults" (Doherty & Jacobson, 1982).

BREAKING UP—BEFORE AND AFTER MARRIAGE
Before

"The best divorce is the one you get before you get married" seems to be as relevant today as it ever was. While the end of an intimate relationship is always painful, research bears out common experience that the end of a premarital affair is less traumatic than a divorce (Rubin, Peplau, & Hill, 1981; Hill, Rubin, & Peplau, 1976).

In a study of 103 break-ups among dating college students, part of a larger study of dating couples, a number of factors characterized affairs that ended. The young men and women who ended their relationships were more different from each other on such measures as age, educational aspirations, intelligence, and physical attractiveness than were the ones who stayed together. Furthermore, the couples who split were more apt to be unequally involved in the relationship; one was much more in love than the other. On Rubin's (1970; 1973) "love" and "liking" scales, the partners' love was a better predictor of their staying together than was their liking for each other. Whether the couples had had sexual intercourse or had lived together were, on the other hand, totally unrelated to whether they stayed together.

Couples often used external factors to help them separate, as shown by the fact that break-ups peaked at key turning points of the school year (May–June, September, and December–January), coinciding with changes in living arrangements, schedules, and questions regarding future plans ("Should we spend our vacation together?" "Should we get an apartment together?" "Should I accept a job out of town?").

The desire to break up is seldom mutual. One person usually initiates it—and that person is apt to feel freer, happier, and less depressed and lonely than is the other partner, who has to deal with his or her feelings of rejection, as well as the end of a relationship that she or he wanted to continue (Hill et al., 1976). Contrary to popular myth, women are more likely to end a relationship than men are—even when they are the more involved partner. Furthermore, they cope better with rejection when the man ends the affair. They may be more sensitive to their partner's feelings, better able to tell when he does not return their own depth of emotion, and thus more prepared either to accept or precipitate the break. Furthermore, women seem more in control of their feelings, possibly because of early socialization that emphasizes their power in the emotional domain (often at the expense of power in other aspects of life) (Rubin et al., 1981).

After

On the Holmes and Rahe Social Readjustment Scale of life stresses (1976), divorce is second only to the death of a spouse in the magnitude of stress. Aside from the emotional turmoil that precedes, accompanies, and follows it, it requires a change of residence for at least one partner, a changed financial situation for both, generally a series of legal skirmishes, and often the necessity to work out disagreements about the care of children. No wonder the year after the divorce (which is usually more than two years after the initial separation) is usually an emotional low point for both divorcing parents and their children (Hetherington, Cox, & Cox, 1977).

Despite today's high rate of divorce, the decision to separate is rarely made lightly. It is, however, made considerably more often than it used to be. Berscheid and Campbell (1981) point to some of the changing societal trends that have reduced the barriers to divorce: the fact that women are less financially dependent on their husbands today, that both sexes face fewer legal obstacles, less religious opposition, and less of a social stigma, and that current wisdom decrees that it's not always best to stay together "for the good of the children." But as these social psychologists point out, "Changes in societal conditions do not terminate relationships; people do"

(p. 210). The effect of these changed conditions, however, affect the comparison level for the person considering divorce. The alternatives to marriage are not so costly as they used to be, and so divorce is a viable option for more individuals.

In marital break-ups as in dating break-ups, it is often the woman who decides to sever the tie, often after months or years of contemplation (Kelly, 1982). And again, the partner who makes the decision to divorce is usually in better emotional shape than the other partner, largely because of the sense of control over his or her own life and the absence of the need to deal with rejection. Other factors that affect the way a person will react emotionally include the presence or absence of a network of supportive friends and family, the children's situation, the presence or absence of a lover who can serve as a "transitional person," and the degree of financial strain. While divorce is often a positive step that results in healthier psychological functioning, "the substantial minority of men and women who were overwhelmed and disorganized beyond their recuperative powers . . . remind us that divorce is not a panacea for all. Indeed there is evidence that divorce results in clear psychological gain for just one spouse in the marriage more often than both are benefited" (Kelly, 1982, p. 749).

SUMMARY

1 *Interpersonal attraction* is the tendency to evaluate another person in a positive way. It is an *attitude*. Attraction to another depends on interactions between your own traits, the other person's traits, and the situation in which you get to know each other.

2 Social psychologists interested in interpersonal attraction use a number of measures including naturalistic observation, self-report measures, and laboratory and field experiments.

3 *Person perception* refers to the way we form impressions or perceptions of others.

4   People try to give meaning to the behavior of others by attributing causes to their behavior. According to *attribution theory* we tend to explain people's behavior either *dispositionally* (as being based on some internal factor, like a basic personality trait) or *situationally* (as being the result of an external cause such as a particular circumstance). According to Kelley, three factors are important in attributing meaning to someone's behavior: *distinctiveness, consensus,* and *consistency* of the behavior.

5   The *fundamental attribution error* is the tendency to overestimate dispositional factors like personality traits and to underestimate situational ones (like a particular circumstance) in accounting for behavior. This error is particularly likely to operate when we are explaining the behavior of another. When we are explaining our own behavior, however, we tend to attribute it to situational factors. We are particularly likely to attribute our failures to the situation and our successes to ourselves.

6   Studies have shown that our attraction to another is related to a number of factors, like the following.

7   The *physical closeness* between two people affects their likelihood of becoming friends. A study by Festinger and his colleagues demonstrated that next-door neighbors in a student housing development were most likely to become friends.

8   From childhood on *physical attractiveness* is an important element in how we view others. Attractive people are thought to possess a wide array of desirable traits.

9   Other personal characteristics, such as *warmth* and *competence,* influence interpersonal attraction.

10 People, particularly those with high self-esteem, are attracted to others who hold similar opinions. We also tend to like people who like us.

11 There are a number of theories about why people stay in relationships. According to *reinforcement theory,* we stay in a relationship when we get something from it. *Exchange theory* holds that we consider the rewards and costs in the relationship as well as our alternatives in deciding whether to get into a relationship or stay in it. *Equity theory* maintains that we are most comfortable in relationships where there is a fair distribution of rewards and costs and that we will try to restore equity in relationships perceived as unbalanced.

12 People maintain a number of different types of *friendships* from social acquaintance to best friend. In choosing friends people look for *similarity, reciprocity, compatibility, structure,* and *role modeling.*

13 Psychologists have identified two basic types of love: *companionate* and *passionate.* Companionate love is like a loving friendship between two people that includes affection, deep attachment, trust, respect, appreciation, loyalty, and close knowledge of each other. Passionate love is a wildly emotional state which includes tenderness and sexuality, elation and pain, anxiety and relief, altruism and jealousy.

14 There appears to be a relationship between marriage and physical and psychological health as well as personality development. A number of factors influence breaking up, whether it occurs before or after marriage. Changing societal trends have reduced a number of barriers to divorce.

SUGGESTED READINGS

Berscheid, E., & Walster, E. (1978). *Interpersonal attraction* (2d ed.). Reading, Mass.: Addison-Wesley. A well-written and scholarly discussion about theories and measurement of interpersonal attraction by two leading researchers.

Kelley, H. H., et al. (1983). *Close relationships.* San Francisco: W. H. Freeman. Nine social psychologists discuss the impact of intimate relationships on human well-being. Information on therapy is included.

Walster, E., & Walster, G. W. (1978). *A new look at love.* Reading, Mass.: Addison-Wesley. A delightful discussion of passionate and companionate love with material on the dynamics of sexual attraction, how we choose a marriage partner, and the pain of passionate love. The book is liberally illustrated with cartoons and quizzes for the reader to answer.

Walster, E.; Walster, G. W.; & Berscheid, A. (1978). *Equity theory and research.* Boston: Allyn and Bacon. Presents an analysis of the application of equity theory to exploiter/victim, philanthropist/recipient, business, and intimate relationships.

APPENDIX

STATISTICS

BRANCHES OF STATISTICS

DESCRIPTIVE STATISTICS
Central Tendency
Variability
Normal Distributions
Skewed Distributions
Correlation

INFERENTIAL STATISTICS
Sampling Methods
Testing Research Hypotheses

SUMMARY

SUGGESTED READINGS

Would you describe yourself as above average in intelligence? Do you study less or more than other students? Is your sense of humor superior? Are you enduring an unusually stressful year? Are you likely to earn over $100,000 a year within the next decade?

The answers to all of these questions require statistics, a discipline that includes a variety of methods for collecting, organizing, analyzing and making inferences from numerical data. Statistics is a branch of mathematics that is used by psychologists as well as other social scientists to sort facts and draw conclusions. Psychology cannot use the precise measurements of pure sciences such as physics and chemistry. Height and weight can be measured accurately and precisely, but the measurement of memory, intelligence, humor, motivation and other broad personal attributes can only be estimated. Psychologists must rely heavily on statistics in developing tests of these attributes and in interpreting the results of research studies.

Although most mathematical calculations used in psychology are easily handled by computers, it is important to know how to accurately interpret the computer output. Therefore, the prime emphasis in this appendix will be on interpretation of statistics rather than on calculation.

BRANCHES OF STATISTICS

There are two branches of statistics: descriptive and inferential. Descriptive statistics provide a way to summarize data gathered from research. For example, you could determine the grade-point averages and study schedules of students in your psychology class and use descriptive statistics to summarize your findings. Inferential statistics use data from a sample to generalize and predict results in a larger population. You would need inferential statistics to predict the intelligence and study schedules of future psychology classes composed of students similar to those in your own class. Both descriptive statistics and inferential statistics are needed in psychological research.

DESCRIPTIVE STATISTICS

Suppose a researcher surveyed a psychology class with twenty-five students and asked each student to record the total number of hours he or she had studied psychology during a specified week. The researcher collected the information and recorded the data as shown in Table A-1. How can the researcher organize these data to make your interpretation easier? One way to organize the raw data in Table A-1 is to transform it to a tally, or frequency distribution. A frequency distribution lists each score or observation, statistically known as x (in our example the number of hours of psychology study), and indicates how frequently each score or observation x occurs (see Table A-2).

TABLE A-1 Raw Data

Student	Score x Hours of Psychology Study during Specified Week
John A.	6
Mike A.	3
Jane B.	4
Kara C.	9
Joann D.	10
Henry E.	20
Marshall G.	9
Jim I.	11
Tom J.	8
Bill J.	6
Tess L.	5
Dana M.	4
Leslie N.	6
Jack O.	0
Nancy O.	7
Ann P.	10
Sue Q.	6
Janice R.	7
Kenn S.	5
Louis S.	5
Willy T.	8
Lois T.	4
Carol V.	6
Tom W.	9
Bob Y.	7

TABLE A-2 Frequency Distribution

Hours of Psychology Study x	Frequency
0	1
1	0
2	0
3	1
4	3
5	3
6	5
7	3
8	2
9	3
10	2
11	1
12	0
13	0
14	0
15	0
16	0
17	0
18	0
19	0
20	1

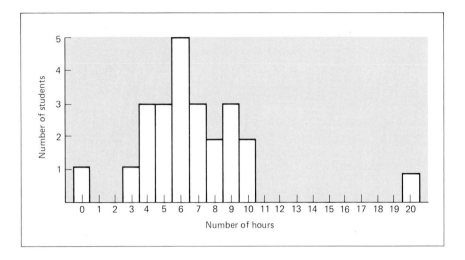

FIGURE A-1 Histogram

Another possibility is to create a visual outline of the data, a graph. One commonly used graph is the histogram, or bar graph. The *horizontal axis,* or *abscissa,* shows the score of each person, in our example the number of hours of psychology study. The *vertical axis,* or *ordinate,* represents the frequency of each score, in our example the number of students who studied a set number of hours. A glance at Figure A-1 reveals a histogram that is clearly more meaningful than Table A-1.

Often it is useful to compare the graphs of two or more sets of data. Constructing one histogram on top of another for this comparison would be confusing. One way to visually create this comparison is to construct another type of graph from the histogram. By connecting the midpoints of the tops of the bars of the histogram, you can construct a *frequency polygon,* as shown in Figure A-2. A polygon is a closed figure with many angles. The frequency at both ends of the distribution is zero, closing the figure and making a polygon. Frequency polygons can be constructed on top of each other for easy comparison of the two distributions. Figure A-3 uses frequency polygons to compare the amount of time twenty students

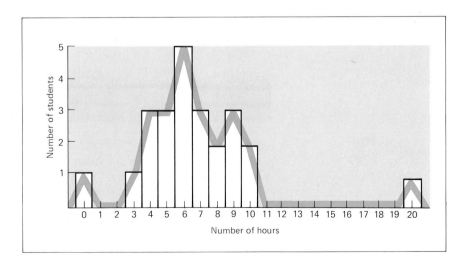

FIGURE A-2 Frequency Polygon

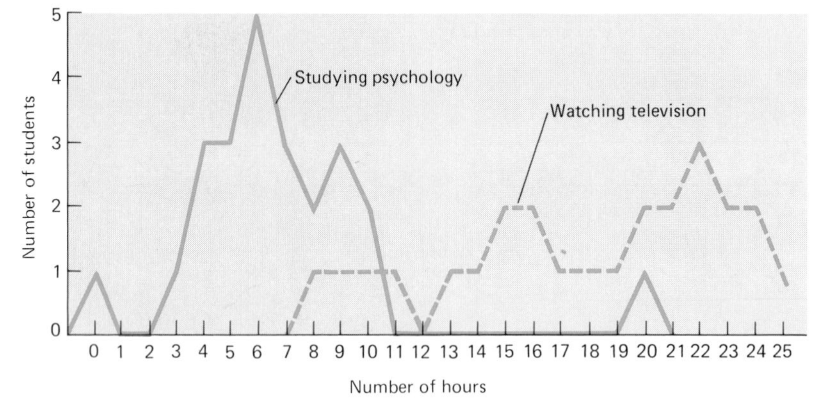

FIGURE A-3 Frequency Polygon Comparisons *This frequency polygon comparison demonstrates that students spend more time watching television than studying psychology.*

spent studying psychology with the number of hours they spent viewing television during the same week.

Central Tendency

The purpose of descriptive statistics is to organize, summarize, and simplify data. Frequency distributions and graphs provide organization but can be cumbersome and confusing. It is helpful to know the central tendency, or the most typical and representative score in a distribution. The three most common measures of central tendency are the mean, median, and mode.

MEAN   The mean, the arithmetic average of all scores, is the most frequently used measure of central tendency. The mean, often symbolized as $\overline{X}$, is calculated by adding all scores (x's) and dividing by the total number of scores, as shown in Table A-3. The Greek letter Σ (capital sigma) is used by statisticians to indicate summation or adding the sum of all scores. You are undoubtedly familiar with the mean in computing your college grade-point average. The mean is a useful measure of central tendency since it is an exact arithmetic measure. However, the mean can be affected by extreme scores. In our example, if the student who had studied psychology for 20 hours instead studied for 120 hours, the mean would increase from 7 hours to 11 hours. Thus the score of only one student would have a profound effect on the mean for the entire group.

MEDIAN   Just as a median strip divides a freeway in half, the median M as a statistic divides a distribution in half, so that one-half the scores are above the median and one-half are below. The median, or midpoint, is easiest to compute if there is an odd number of observations, as in the example in Table A-3. To calculate the median, observations or scores must be arranged in order from highest to lowest. If there is an odd number of scores, there will be only one middle score to represent the median. However, when there is an even number of observations, there will be two middle scores; the median will be found by averaging these two scores. For example, in the distribution:

1, 2, 3, 4, 5, 6

TABLE A-3   Calculation of the Mean, Median, and Mode

Mean $(\bar{X}) = \dfrac{\text{(Scores)}}{n\text{ (Total Number)}}$	Median (M) = Midpoint		Mode (M_o) = Most Frequent Score	
x (score)	x (in order)		x (in order)	
0	0		0	
3	3		3	
4	4		4	
9	4		4	
10	4		4	
20	5	12	5	
9	5	below	5	
11	5		5	
8	6		6	
6	6		6	
5	6		6	Mode
4	6		6	
6	6	Median	6	
0	7		7	
7	7		7	
10	7		7	
6	8		8	
7	8	12	8	
5	9	above	9	
5	9		9	
8	9		9	
4	10		10	
6	10		10	
9	11		11	
7	20		20	
$n = 25$ $\Sigma x = 175$	$M = 6$		$M_o = 6$	
$\bar{X}\ \dfrac{175}{25} = 7$				

the median is computed by averaging 3 and 4, and would be 3.5. The median is not affected by extreme scores. If the person who studied psychology for 20 hours during the week instead studied for 120 hours, the median would be unaffected.

MODE   The mode (M_o) of a distribution is the score that occurs most frequently. In our example in Table A-3, six hours was the most common score. Although it is easiest to compute, the mode is the least-used measure of central tendency. In some distributions, particularly small groups, scores occur only once and there is no mode. Likewise, in larger groups frequently there is more than one mode. The mode is more subject to fluctuation in sampling than either the median or mean. Generally, the mode is useful when only one or two scores occur extremely frequently.

Variability

After computing a measure of central tendency, a logical question is: How representative is this score? In other words, do the other scores spread out widely, or do they cluster around the mean and median? Consider the following sets of IQ scores:

IQ scores			
Set 1	99	100	101
Set 2	40	100	160

Although both sets share the same central tendency, there is an obvious difference in the spread of the scores, or variability.

THE RANGE   The simplest measure of variability is the range, the difference between the largest and smallest scores. The range for the distribution on Table A-2 would be $20-0 = 20$ hours. Although it is easy to compute, the range reflects only the difference between the highest and lowest values and does not include any other scores. One extremely high or low score could have a strong impact. Indeed, everyone could have the same score except two people and the range would reflect only the values of the two extremes.

THE VARIANCE   Another method to determine the variability of scores in a distribution is to compute the deviation of each score from the mean as shown in Table A-4, column 2. The deviation is computed by subtracting the value of the mean from each score. In the example in Table A-4, the mean value of 7 was subtracted. Values below the mean have negative deviations, while those above the mean have positive signs. The total shown at the bottom of column 2 is zero. As a matter of fact, the sum of the deviations from the mean in any distribution will always equal zero—not very helpful in estimating variability.

But these deviation computations do have further use. Statisticians have found that an interesting and widely used statistic can be derived by first squaring each deviation from the mean as in column 3 of Table A-4. The average of the squared deviations is then computed by totaling the figures in column 3 and dividing by the total number of cases, 25. This average of all the squared deviations from the mean score is called the variance and is symbolized by σ^2. In our example:

$$(x-\overline{X}) = 326; \quad n = 25; \quad \text{and} \quad = \frac{\Sigma\,(x-\overline{X})^2}{n} = 13.04$$

THE STANDARD DEVIATION   The preferred and most widely used measure of variability is the standard deviation. The standard deviation, symbolized by σ, is simply the square root of the variance.

$$\text{Standard deviation} = \sqrt{\text{variance}}$$
$$\sigma = \sqrt{\sigma^2}$$

In our example in Table A-4, the standard deviation is $\sqrt{13.04} = 3.6$. Like the variance, the standard deviation takes every score into account, rather than just the two extreme scores used in computing the range. The key advantage of the standard deviation over the variance is that the standard

TABLE A-4   Computation of the Variance and Standard Deviation

Column 1 Observation	Column 2 Deviation from Mean ($\overline{X}$) $(x-\overline{X})$	Column 3 Squared Deviation $(x-\overline{X})^2$
0	-7	49
3	-4	16
4	-3	9
4	-3	9
4	-3	9
5	-2	4
5	-2	4
5	-2	4
6	-1	1
6	-1	1
6	-1	1
6	-1	1
6	-1	1
7	0	0
7	0	0
7	0	0
8	1	1
8	1	1
9	2	4
9	2	4
9	2	4
10	3	9
10	3	9
11	4	16
20	13	169
$\Sigma = 175$	$\Sigma = 0$	$\Sigma = 326$
$\overline{X} = 7$		

Variance (average deviation squared):

$$\sigma^2 = \frac{\Sigma\,(x-\overline{X})^2}{n} = \frac{326}{25} = 13.04$$

Standard deviation:

$$\sigma = \sqrt{\sigma^2} = 13.04 = 3.6$$

deviation is expressed in terms of the original unit of measurement (in our example, number of hours), whereas the variance is expressed in squared units of measurement. Larger values of standard deviations indicate that scores are widely scattered from the mean. Smaller standard deviation values denote that most observations or scores are close to the mean. For example, suppose a researcher studied the level of job satisfaction of individuals in the accounting and public relations departments of a company. In both departments the average score was 70 percent satisfaction. However, the standard deviation in the accounting department was 1 while the standard deviation in the public relations department was 10. The researcher can conclude that there is considerably more variation in job satisfaction in the public relations department than in the accounting department. The standard deviation can be used for considerable additional statistical interpretation.

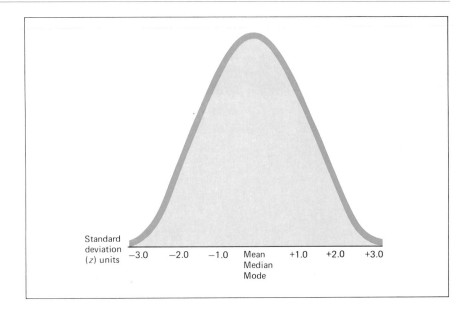

Standard deviation (z) units −3.0 −2.0 −1.0 Mean Median Mode +1.0 +2.0 +3.0

FIGURE A-4 The Normal Distribution

Normal Distributions

Fortunately, mathematicians and statisticians have more concrete descriptions of "normal" than do psychologists. The normal distribution, or normal curve, was suggested by a mathematician named Quetelet who noted that many measurements of people fall into an orderly pattern. For example, if you were to observe the heights of a crowd of women at an airport, you would probably note that most are average height; some are slightly taller or shorter; and very few of the women are extremely small or gigantic. If you were to continue with thousands of observations and plot the exact height values on a graph, your frequency polygon would probably resemble the smooth curve shown in Figure A-4.

The normal distribution is a symmetrical bell-shaped curve; the left half is the mirror reflection of the right half. In a normal distribution, the mean, median, and mode all fall in the same location, the exact center of the curve. Most of the scores are grouped around these measures of central tendency. Nearly all the scores in a normal distribution will appear within three standard deviation units on either side of the mean.

Consider the distribution of intelligence test scores. IQ tests have been developed to reflect a normal distribution of intelligence in the whole population. The mean IQ has been set at 100, and most intelligence tests have a standard deviation of 15 points. Since nearly all scores in a normal distribution are within ±3 standard deviation units, you can safely conclude that most people have IQs between 55 and 145.

The score of any individual on an IQ test can be translated into a standard score, or *z score*, by stating the number of standard deviations the score is from the mean. The mean of the distribution has a z score equal to zero since it has zero or no deviation from itself. Scores above the mean are positive z scores, and those below are negative z scores. A z score of +2 on an intelligence test would be 2 standard deviations above the mean, that is, 30 points above 100, or 130. Similarly, a z score of −1 on an IQ test would be 1 standard deviation below the mean or 100−15 = 85.

The standard score is always computed by subtracting the mean from the score and dividing by the standard deviation.

$$z = \frac{x - \overline{X}}{\sigma}$$

If you know the mean and standard deviation, you can determine a given individual's z score on any test. The z scores permit comparisons of scores on tests that have different means and standard deviations. Suppose you wanted to compare your score on a standardized test of perceptual speed with your IQ score of 120. You want to compare your relative standing on the two tests. Since the mean of the IQ test is 100 and the standard deviation is 15, you would compute your z score as follows:

$$z = \frac{120 - 100}{15} = \frac{20}{15} = \frac{4}{3} = 1.33$$

Your z score on the IQ test is 1.33. Assume your score on the test of perceptual speed was 85. The mean score on the test was 73, and the standard deviation was 12. Your z score on the test of perceptual speed would be computed:

$$z = \frac{85 - 73}{12} = \frac{12}{12} = 1.0$$

Thus, your score on the IQ test was relatively higher than your score on the test of perceptual speed. Psychologists often compare individual scores on different tests. For example, a psychologist might want to know whether an individual has a stronger aptitude for art or music or whether the person has more ability in language or math. By comparing the relative z scores, psychologists can answer many types of queries about test results.

As shown on Figure A-5, in a normal curve, more than two-thirds of the scores are within 1 standard deviation of the mean. Less than 5 per-

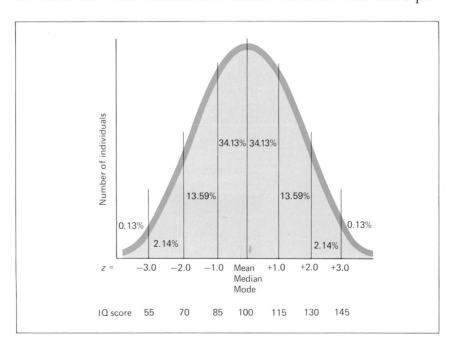

FIGURE A-5 Percentages in a Normal Curve *In a normal distribution more than two-thirds of the people will have IQs between 85 and 115. Only a fraction of a percent will have IQs below 55 and above 145.*

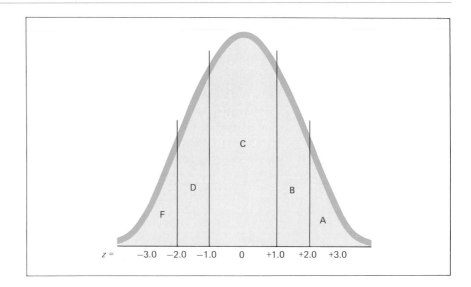

FIGURE A-6   A Distribution of Grades on a Normal Curve
One way to grade on a normal curve.

cent of the scores are more than 2 standard deviations away from the mean, and a mere fraction of a percent are beyond 3 standard deviations. If your IQ is 130, only slightly more than 2 percent of the population has scored above you.

College instructors sometimes transform raw scores on exams to z scores on a normal curve. The typical procedure is shown on Figure A-6. Of course, unless the class is extremely large, a perfect, normal distribution of grades is quite unlikely. Further, since college classes are often selective and have more abilities than the general population, a normal distribution is even less probable.

Skewed Distributions

Not all distributions of large populations are distributed normally. Often the mean, median, and mode fall at different places and the distribution is said to be skewed (not symmetric). For example, response time often forms a skewed distribution. When people are instructed to press a buzzer in response to a flashing light, most will respond very rapidly; only a few will lag behind (see Figure A-7). Since skewed distributions do not possess the same attributes as normal distributions, assumptions about the percentage distribution of standard scores are inappropriate. Thus it is more difficult to compare individual scores among skewed distributions.

Correlation

The focus thus far has been on describing distributions with only one variable. Correlation is the study of the relationship between the measurements of two variables. The purpose of correlations is to determine whether two sets of measurements have any association with each other. Assume, for example, you want to determine whether there is a relationship between high school grade-point average (GPA) and college GPA. To determine the relationship between these two variables, you might begin with a visual representation, a scatterplot. Figure A-8 presents a list of GPAs and a scatterplot. Each student is represented by 1 point on the scatterplot, with high school GPA located by the height along the vertical axis and college GPA indicated by the distance along the horizontal axis.

FIGURE A-7 Skewed
Distribution *In a normal
distribution the mean, median, and
mode are equal, but in a skewed
distribution the mean, median, and
mode have different values.*

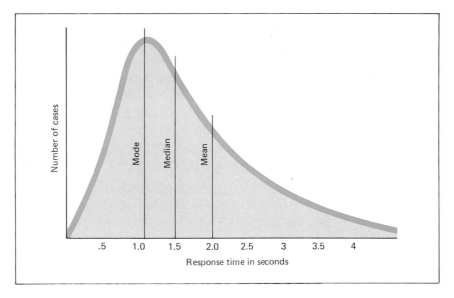

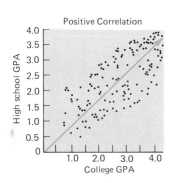

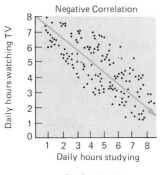

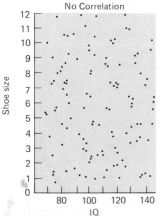

FIGURE A-9 Positive
Correlation
Negative Correlation
No Correlation

By glancing at the scatterplot, you can see that students with high GPAs in high school tend to have high GPAs in college (Ted, Tom, and Marcia). Similarly, those with low high school GPAs tend to earn low college GPAs (Bob and Susan). In other words, as high school GPA increases, college GPA tends to increase. There is then a *positive correlation* between the two variables because as one variable increases, the other tends to also increase.

When as the values of one variable increase, values on the other tend to decrease, correlation is said to be *negative*, or *inverse*. For example, as students spend more time watching television, they are likely to spend less time studying. As shown in Figure A-9, the plotted points on a scatterplot of positive correlation tend to slope upward, while the plotted

FIGURE A-8 Constructing a Scatterplot

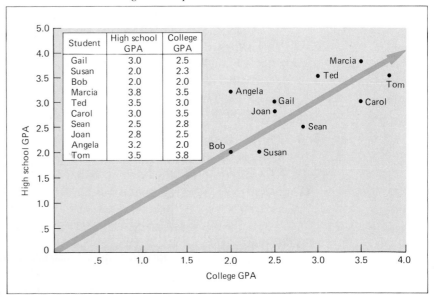

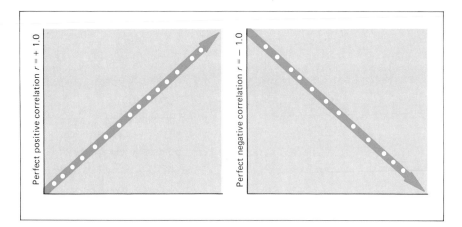

FIGURE A-10 Perfect Positive Correlation $r = +1.0$ Perfect Negative Correlation $r = -1.0$

points of negative correlation slope downward. When there is no correlation or relationship between two variables, points appear randomly and without a specific direction.

To determine the strength or extent of a relationship between two variables, you need to compute a correlation coefficient (r). A correlation coefficient (r) is a numerical value that indicates the strength and direction of the relationship between two variables. When there is no relationship between two variables, $r = 0$. Values of r range from -1.0 (perfect negative correlation) to $+1.0$ (perfect positive correlation). In perfect correlations, all values appear in an exact straight line on a scatterplot, as shown in Figure A-10.

However, most psychological variables have less than perfect correlation. The correlation coefficient is expressed as a decimal; the larger the numerical value of the decimal, the stronger the relationship. Usually r values of $\pm.80$ are considered very high. Note that strong correlations may be either positive or negative. The sign of the correlation coefficient merely indicates the direction of the relationship.

The actual computation of r is quite complex and, as promised, will not be included in this appendix. Most statistics software packages for microcomputers include the Pearson product moment coefficient of correlation, which will compute the value of r for any two variables.

Statisticians and psychologists stress that correlation does not imply causation. For example, suppose you found a perfect positive correlation between the number of librarians in X communities and the amount of alcohol consumed. Are the librarians alcoholics? Does reading books cause people to drink? Do alcoholics read more than others? Probably both of these variables are affected by another factor, the population of the community. The purpose of correlation is to determine the extent and direction of relationships rather than to identify causes.

INFERENTIAL STATISTICS

Often it would be either too expensive, too time-consuming, or totally impossible to measure an entire population. Inferential statistics allow researchers to predict and generalize from descriptive data they have collected and computed on just a small sample from the population. Whether standardizing an IQ test, assessing the popularity of a new product, or attempting to predict that an experiment can be replicated with the same results, psychologists must work with samples and rely on inferential statistics.

Sampling Methods

Several methods have been used to draw a sample from an entire population. You are undoubtedly familiar with the "man-on-the-street" technique. A reporter stands at a specific location and asks a sample of three or four passers-by for their opinions. This sampling technique is frequently seen on the evening news. There are two important defects to this sampling technique. First, the sample size is usually extremely small, consisting of only a few people. Second, the sample is usually biased, being limited to a specific location rather than representing many geographic areas. For example, attitudes toward physical fitness may be quite different if the interviewer stands at a cocktail lounge as opposed to a health center. The "man-on-the-street" technique is considered haphazard and is not an accepted sampling method for research.

A good sample should be representative of an entire population. As mentioned in Chapter 1, one appropriate sampling technique is the random sample. For a sample to be truly random, every member of the population must have the same chance of being selected for the sample. If you wish to use a random sample of 200 students from a college population of 2000, it is acceptable to select every tenth name from a roster of college students. It would not be appropriate to select only first-year students or only students whose last names begin with A and B.

A sample becomes even more representative of an entire population when it is stratified. In a stratified random sample, the sample must represent in proportion the various relevant elements of the population. For example, suppose you were requested to select a stratified sample for a nationwide survey on the study habits of college students. If 54 percent of the population of all college students is male, then 54 percent of your sample should be male. You would also want to have proportionate representation on other relevant variables such as college major, year of study, age, college size, grade average, geographic location, and job requirements. As you can imagine, the choice of categories or strata to be represented is critical to the accuracy of a stratified random sample. Even in the most rigorous stratified sampling, there is always some degree of uncertainty. However, as the size of the sample increases, the level of uncertainty decreases.

Testing Research Hypotheses

Since psychological experiments cannot be performed on entire populations, sampling and inferential statistics are critical for testing hypotheses and doing research. All psychological experiments must begin with a null hypothesis, a statement that an independent variable will not affect a dependent variable. The null hypothesis describes conditions as they currently are believed to exist. For example, a null hypothesis might state that consuming vitamin pills will not affect scores on an intelligence test, or increased ventilation will not affect pain tolerance, or attending ballets will not affect skiing skill. Until experimental evidence proves otherwise, we have no reason to believe that vitamin pills, ventilation, and viewing ballet will cause other specific changes in behavior.

The null hypothesis is a statement that the researcher attempts to disprove or reject and usually takes the following form:

> *If* . . . there is a change in the independent variable, *then* . . . this will not affect the dependent variable.

Suppose, for example, a psychologist wanted to determine whether financial motivation would affect scores on a psychology final examination. She intends to offer students $10 for scores over 80 percent. The null hypothesis would be stated:

> *If* students are offered a reward of $10 for grades over 80 percent on a final exam, *then* this will not affect their scores on the final exam.

The psychologist would then attempt to disprove the null hypothesis with some degree of certainty.

As mentioned in Chapter 1, the psychologist would need to assign students to two groups: an experimental group that is offered the $10 reward and a control group that is not offered any reward. Students must be randomly assigned to the two groups; stratification would enhance the equality of the two groups.

In addition to the random assignment of subjects, the experimenter would need to control many other variables that might intervene. The experimenter must be certain that both groups use the same text, hear the same lectures, participate equally in controlled discussions, and meet at approximately the same time of day. Conditions on the day of the final exam must be identical for both groups. The only difference in the treatment of the two groups should be the independent variable, the offer of a $10 reward.

Suppose the results of the final exam come in. The experimental group has an average score of 79, and the control group has an average score of 75. Is this difference meaningful or significant? Could this difference have occurred by chance? Would this difference hold for another group of students? To answer these questions, the experimenter must compare the means *and* standard deviations of the two groups. Consider the differences in the experimental and control groups illustrated in Figure A-11. Clearly the results with the smaller standard deviations show more noticeable differences.

How can you be sure the difference in the two groups did not occur just by chance? Can you say the difference is really *significant?* For results to be statistically significant, you must be certain that the obtained difference was not just due to chance variations. In psychological experiments, you can reject the null hypothesis if the odds are 5 percent or less that the difference could occur by chance. Or stated another way, you can reject the null hypothesis if a difference of that size would not occur by chance 95 times out of 100.

t TEST   Researchers use a *t* test to determine the significance of differences between experimental and control groups. The *t* test is a ratio of the means and standard deviations of the two groups. If there is a large difference in means and small variability, *t* will have increased value and be

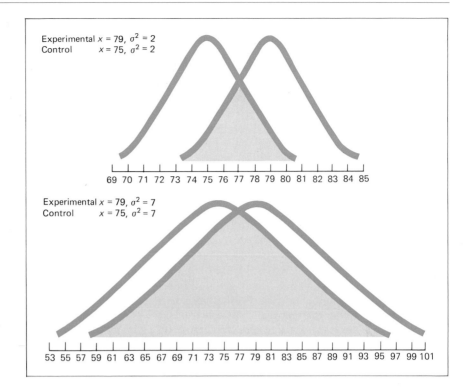

FIGURE A-11 Comparison of Experimental and Control Groups *Differences in means alone are not necessarily significant. In both illustrations the mean difference is the same. However, the illustration with less variability (a smaller value of σ) shows less overlap.*

significant. If there is a small difference in means and large variability, *t* will have less value and will not be significant.

ANALYSIS OF VARIANCE Suppose another researcher conducts a more complex experiment on motivation and psychology test scores. This psychologist is studying the affects of offering a $10 reward, a $25 reward, or a chance to win a microcomputer, upon scores on a final examination. The experimenter would need four groups: three separate reward groups and a control group. The *t* test is only useful for two groups. A more complex procedure, an *F test* or analysis of variance, is required. The *F* test is named after an English statistician, R. A. Fisher, and uses ratios similar to the *t* test. Like the *t* test, an analysis of variance yields statements of significant differences among the groups. Since most experiments reported in journals employ more than two groups, analysis of variance is among the most common statistics used by psychologists.

SUMMARY

1 There are two branches of statistics: *Descriptive statistics* summarize data, and *inferential statistics* make generalizations and predictions from data.

2 Descriptive statistics can be summarized in table form on a *frequency distribution* or graphed on *histograms* and *frequency polygons*.

3 *Central tendency* refers to the most typical or representative score in a distribution. The three measures of central tendency are the *mean, median,* and *mode*.

4 The *mean* of a distribution is the arithmetic average and is affected by extreme scores.

5 The *median* is the midpoint or the score that ranks in the center of a distribution.

6 The *mode* is the score that occurs most frequently in a distribution.

7 *Variability* refers to the spread or fluctuations within a distribution. The *range* is the simplest measure of variability and is computed by subtracting the lowest score from the highest score. The *standard deviation* is the best measure of variability since it takes every score into account and can be used for additional statistical interpretation.

8 A *normal distribution* is a symmetrical bell-shaped curve where the mean, median, and mode are equal. Almost all scores fall within ±3 standard deviation units of a normal curve.

9 Standard deviation units are called *z scores,* or *standard scores.* The z scores are used to compare scores on tests that have different means and standard deviations.

10 In a normal distribution, more than two-thirds of the scores are within one standard deviation of the mean.

11 When the mean, median, and mode fall in different places in a distribution, the distribution is labeled *skewed* rather than normal.

12 *Correlation* is the study of the relationship between two variables and can be represented graphically in a *scatterplot.* A *correlation coefficient* is a decimal value that indicates the strength and direction of the relationship. Correlation coefficient values vary from +1.0 (perfect positive correlation) to −1.0 (perfect negative correlation). Values close to zero indicate there is no relationship between the variables.

13 Although correlation can indicate the strength of relationships, it does not imply causation.

14 The two main techniques used in inferential statistics are *sampling* and *hypothesis testing.*

15 A good sample should be representative of an entire population. In a *random* sample, every member of the population should have an opportunity to be chosen. In a *stratified* sample, relevant elements in the populations are represented in appropriate proportions.

16 Psychological experiments begin with a *null hypothesis,* a statement of conditions as they currently exist. The purpose of the experiment is to reject or disprove the null hypothesis.

17 When differences occur between the experimental and control groups, researchers must use a statistical test to be certain the difference is significant and did not occur just by chance. If there are two groups in the experiment (one experimental group and one control group), a *t test* is used to measure the significance of the difference. If more than two groups are involved in the experiment, an *F ratio test,* or *analysis of variance,* must be used.

SUGGESTED READINGS

Huck, S. W.; Cormier, W. H.; & Bounds, W. G., Jr. (1974). *Reading statistics and research.* New York: Harper and Row. Focuses on the interpretation of statistics as used in research studies.

Huck, S. W., & Sandler, H. M. (1979). *Rival hypotheses: Alternative interpretations of data based conclusions.* New York: Harper and Row. Cleverly presents a number of well-known hypotheses of general interest and suggests alternative conclusions from possible data.

Kimble, G. (1978). *How to use (and misuse) statistics.* Englewood Cliffs, N.J.: Prentice Hall. Helps you to recognize how statistics can be used to intentionally distort data.

Young, R. K., & Veldman, D. J. (1981). *Statistics for the behavioral sciences.* (4th ed.). New York: Holt, Rinehart and Winston. Provides more extensive coverage of the topics in this Appendix along with specific applications of inferential statistics in the behavioral sciences.

GLOSSARY

ABC-X model of family stress A model proposed by Hill which holds that a family's outcome following a stressor event *X* depends on the stressor event *A*, the family's coping resources *B*, and the family's interpretation of the event *C*.

abnormal psychology The scientific study of the causes of emotional and behavioral disorders.

absolute threshold The smallest intensity of a stimulus that can be perceived.

accommodation The process by which the lens changes shape to focus near or far images onto the retina.

acetylcholine A neurotransmitter that has been implicated in Alzheimer's disease.

action potential The "firing" of a neuron, or sending a nerve impulse down its axon, from one end of the neuron to the other.

activation-synthesis model of dreaming Proposed by Hobson and McCarley, this model holds that dreams are the result of stimulation of the brain during sleep.

activity theory A theory that holds that successful aging depends on remaining as active as possible.

adaptation Decrease in response of sensory receptors with continued stimulation so that the individual ceases to be aware of the stimulus.

affective disorders Mental disturbances characterized by disorders of mood.

aggression Any behavior intended to hurt someone or something.

agoraphobia The most severe and most common *phobic disorder* generally expressed by the inability to go out of the house, be in large, unfamiliar places, drive, or travel by public conveyance.

algorithm A problem-solving strategy where every possible answer is exhausted until the correct solution is arrived at.

allele An alternate form of a gene. When alleles are identical, a person is homozygous for a trait; when alleles are dissimilar, the individual is heterozygous.

alternate state of consciousness Any qualitative change in consciousness from the normal waking state. Also called "altered state of consciousness."

altruism Behavior carried out to benefit another, without anticipation of rewards from external sources.

Alzheimer's disease An irreversible dementia characterized by memory loss, confusion, and other intellectual and personality deterioration.

amblyopia A visual disorder in which the brain does not receive visual messages from one eye.

amnesia A general term for a variety of memory disorders.

amniocentesis A prenatal medical procedure in which a sample of amniotic fluid is withdrawn and analyzed to determine the presence of certain birth defects.

amniotic sac The fluid-filled membrane encasing the fetus.

amphetamines Central nervous system stimulant drugs.

anaclitic depression A type of depression in which the individual emphasizes the need for gratification of dependency and nurturant needs.

anal stage According to Freudian theory, the psychosexual stage of toddlerhood (12 to 36 months) in which the child receives pleasure through anal stimulation; toilet training is the major situation in which gratification occurs.

analysis of variance A statistical test used to determine the significance of differences when there are more than two groups.

analytic introspection A technique developed by Wundt to analyze or break down the mind into its component elements.

androgens Male sex hormones.

androgynous A personality type integrating both typically "masculine" and typically "feminine" characteristics.

anima The feminine archetype in man.

animus The masculine archetype in woman.

anorexia nervosa An eating disorder, seen mostly in young women, in which an individual starves herself by not eating or by purging.

anterior chamber of eye The part of the eye located behind the cornea and in front of the lens, filled with aqueous humor.

anterograde amnesia A memory disorder in which new memories cannot be created.

antisocial disorder A personality disorder characterized by behaviors that violate the rights of others.

anxiety A state of apprehension, fearful uncertainty, or dread caused by some real or imagined anticipated threat.

anxiety disorders Mental disturbances affecting some 2–4% of the U.S. population. They include *phobic disorders, obsessive-compulsive disorders, posttraumatic stress disorders, panic disorders,* and *generalized anxiety disorders.*

applied social psychologist Social psychologist particularly concerned with solving practical problems related to people in groups.

approach-avoidance conflict The dilemma that occurs when a person is attracted to a desirable outcome or activity that also has associated with it an undesirable outcome or activity.

approach-approach conflict The need to choose between two or more desirable outcomes or activities.

aqueous humor A watery fluid that fills the anterior chamber of the eye and helps to "feed" the cornea.

archetype According to Jungian theory, the symbols or common themes that are found through the generations and in all parts of the world.

artificial insemination by a donor (AID) The placement of the sperm of an anonymous donor into a woman's uterus in order to enable her to conceive.

ascending reticular activation system The part of the reticular formation involved in awakening people.

associative learning A kind of learning in which an association is formed between two events. Two types of associative learning are *classical conditioning* and *operant conditioning.*

attachment An active, affectionate, reciprocal relationship between two individuals; their interaction reinforces and strengthens the bond.

attitude A learned, relatively permanent way of responding to someone or something. Has cognitive, emotional, and behavioral components.

attribution The process of drawing conclusions about ourselves and other people, based on behavior.

attribution theory A theory that offers an explanation for the way we make judgments about the causes of behavior.

auditory meatus The ear canal.

authoritarian personality A rigid, conventional, prejudice-prone person who thinks in stereotypes, is emotionally cold, identifies with power, and is intolerant of weakness.

autonomic arousal The heightened activity of a number of physiological responses such as heart rate and respiration. The increased action is controlled by the autonomic nervous system.

autonomic nervous system The part of the peripheral nervous system that controls involuntary functions. Consists of parasympathetic and sympathetic divisions.

autonomy versus shame and doubt According to Eriksonian theory, the second crisis of personality development. Between 18 months and 3 years, the child develops a sense of independence and self-assertion.

autosomal dominant inheritance A pattern of inheritance in which a specific gene is dominant; if it is inherited, it manifests itself in the individual.

autosomal recessive inheritance A pattern of inheritance in which a trait appears only if an individual inherits two genes for it, one from each parent. If the individual inherits only one gene for the trait, it will not appear in the individual but may be passed on to children.

autosomes Non-sex chromosomes.

aversive counterconditioning A behavior therapy technique based on classical conditioning in which an unpleasant situation is paired with the behavior a client wants to eliminate.

avoidance-avoidance conflict The need to choose between two or more undesirable outcomes or activities.

avoidant personality disorder A disturbance characterized by hypersensitivity to rejection or disapproval, preventing longed-for close ties.

axon A tail-like fiber extension of a neuron that carries nerve impulses to other neurons.

baby biography A journal recording a child's development.

basal ganglia Cell bodies in the cerebrum that control bodily movement.

basic-level categories Classifications of objects used in daily dealings.

basilar membrane A tissue inside the cochlea, in the inner ear, that moves at the same rate as the vibrations of the sound wave.

behavior therapy A psychotherapeutic approach that uses experimentally established learning principles to overcome maladaptive habits.

behavioral genetics The study of inherited aspects of behavior.

behavioral model An explanation of mental disorders that holds that abnormal ways of thinking and acting are learned, largely through the mechanisms of conditioning and modeling.

behaviorism A school of psychology that emphasizes the study of observable behaviors and events and the role of the environment in causing behavior.

benzodiazepines A class of anti-anxiety drugs, including Valium, Librium, and Miltown, also known as "minor tranquilizers."

beta-endorphin A morphinelike substance that occurs naturally in the body. It has been linked, among other things, to the conservation of energy, the attenuation of pain, and feelings of euphoria.

biofeedback A technique that gives people information about their internal processes (like blood pressure and heart rate) so they can learn to exert control over them.

bipolar disorder A mental disorder characterized by one or more *manic episodes* which generally alternate with episodes of *depression.*

birth trauma Birth-related brain injury caused by oxygen deprivation, mechanical injury, or disease at birth.

borderline personality disorder A disturbance characterized by instability in several areas, including mood, self-image, and relationships.

brain stem The part of the brain that contains the medulla, pons, and midbrain. The brain stem is responsible for many basic functions.

brief therapy A time-limited psychotherapy, generally lasting for no more than fifteen to twenty sessions, that tends to focus on one or two problem symptoms.

bulimia   An eating disorder in which an individual regularly eats huge quantities of food (binges) and then purges the body by laxatives or induced vomiting.

burnout   A syndrome of emotional exhaustion, depersonalization, and a reduction in personal accomplishments often experienced by people in the helping professions.

cardinal trait   According to Allport, a trait so dominant that it colors virtually every aspect of a person's behavior and attributes.

case history   A research method in which intensive information is collected about one or very few individuals.

cataract   The condition brought about when the lens in the eye loses its transparency, resulting in a progressive loss of vision.

catharsis   The reduction of an impulse, such as an aggressive impulse, as the result of draining off some of the energy associated with that impulse.

Cattell Infant Intelligence Scale   A standardized infant intelligence test measuring perception and motor abilities.

central nervous system   The brain and spinal cord.

central projection of the retina   Brain areas that receive visual information from the ganglion cells in the eyes.

central tendency   The most typical or representative score in a distribution.

central traits   According to Allport's theory, the characteristic tendencies used to describe an individual.

cephaocaudal principle   The principle that development proceeds in a head-to-toe direction. Upper parts of the body develop before lower parts do.

cerebellum   The part of the brain connected to the back of the brain stem, involved primarily in the coordination of motor activity.

cerebral cortex   The gray outer covering of the brain, involved in most higher-level functions, such as thinking, remembering, and problem solving.

cerebrum   The most highly developed part of the brain, which is multifunctional and contains the hypothalamus, thalamus, basal ganglia, limbic system, and cortex; the forebrain.

cesarean section   A surgical method of childbirth in which an incision is made in the mother's abdomen, from which the baby is lifted out.

chromatographic theory   The theory that various smells are perceived because different odors travel different distances inside the nasal cavity and the location where they land in the mucous lining of the nose determines the smell.

chromosomes   Tiny rod-shaped particles that carry genes, the transmitters of inheritance. In the normal human case, there are forty-six chromosomes.

chronionic villus biopsy   A new prenatal diagnostic technique in which a small sample of embryonic tissue is analyzed for certain birth defects.

chunking   A technique for expanding the capacity of short-term memory by grouping items together in the mind.

circadian rhythms   Biological rhythms that occur every twenty-five hours.

classical conditioning   A kind of learning in which a previously neutral stimulus (conditioned stimulus) acquires the power to illicit a response (conditioned response) after repeated pairing with an unconditioned stimulus that ordinarily elicits a particular response (unconditioned response).

climacteric   The medical term for menopause and the changes that occur at this time in a woman's life.

clinical method   A flexible method of interviewing in which additional questions are based on a respondent's earlier response.

clinical psychologists   Psychologists who diagnose and treat emotional and behavioral disorders.

clustering   A technique for organizing material to be remembered into categories.

cochlea   A coiled fluid-filled structure in the inner ear.

cognitive   Referring to thinking, abstracting, synthesizing, classifying, or any other mental operation that has to do with how we process information, make plans, or acquire knowledge.

cognitive-behavioral theory   The view that attaining the hypnotic state depends on a person's readiness to think along with and imagine themes suggested by the hypnotist rather than on any trance-induction techniques.

cognitive consistency   The theory that incompatibility between our thoughts and actions can cause discomfort, which we then try to reduce.

cognitive development   The process by which our thought processes change, affecting the ways we attain and use knowledge.

cognitive dissonance   The theory proposed by Leon Festinger, maintaining that any inconsistency between our attitudes and our behaviors motivates us to reduce this discomfort.

cognitive psychology   A psychological school concerned with the way the mind processes information.

cognitive therapy   A psychotherapeutic technique that helps clients overcome the distortions in thinking that contribute to emotional problems.

cohort   A group of people who grew up at about the same time.

collective unconscious   According to Jungian theory, that aspect of the mind which contains ancestral memories.

companionate love　A loving friendship between two people that includes affection, deep attachment, trust, respect, appreciation, loyalty, and close knowledge of each other; conjugal love.

comparison level　The minimum benefit a person requires from a relationship.

comparison level for alternatives　The attractiveness of other possible ties or of no relationship compared with an individual's present relationship.

complementarity theory　A theory of interpersonal relationships which holds that opposite personalities attract.

components of intelligence　According to Sternberg's information-processing approach, the steps in solving a problem.

compulsive personality disorder　A disorder characterized by perfectionism, insistence that others do things a certain way, workaholism, and restricted ability to express warmth and tenderness.

concepts　Categories of objects, events, or people.

concepts, ill-defined　Concepts in which features and rules that connect members of a category are not obvious.

concepts, well-defined　Concepts that can be specified by a set of clear, unambiguous features, connected by a rule.

conceptual blocks　Mental walls that prohibit correct perception and solution of problems.

concordant　Alike on a certain characteristic.

concrete operations stage　The third of Piaget's stages of cognitive development, roughly from 7 to 11 years, during which the child develops the ability to think logically but not abstractly.

concurrent validity　A measure of the relationship between test performance and some present criterion.

conditioned response　The classical conditioning term for a response that comes to be elicited by a conditioned stimulus which has been repeatedly paired with an unconditioned stimulus.

conditioned stimulus　The classical conditioning term for an initially neutral stimulus which, after repeated pairing with an unconditioned stimulus, comes to elicit a conditioned response.

conductive deafness　Hearing loss caused by a ruptured eardrum or a defect in the bones of the middle ear which blocks sound waves from reaching the cochlea.

cones　Receptors on the retina responsible for seeing color and small details.

conformity　A change in opinion and/or behavior in response to the real or imagined pressure of others.

consciousness　Our awareness of ourselves and the world around us.

conservation　A Piagetian term for the ability to recognize that two stimuli that were equal (in amount, weight, length, etc.) remain equal in the face of perceptual alteration, as long as nothing was added to or taken away from either stimulus.

content validity　The degree to which a test covers a representative sample of the material under consideration.

continuous reinforcement　A pattern of reinforcement by which the organism is reinforced every time it emits the desired response.

control group　Subjects who do not receive the treatment of interest in an experiment, who are then compared with the experimental group.

conversion disorder　A type of *somatoform disorder* in which a person may become paralyzed, lose the senses of smell or pain, suffer seizures, or experience false pregnancy.

coping　A response to stress designed to solve the stressful problem and manage stress-related emotional and physical responses.

cornea　The transparent protective tissue in front of the eye.

corpus collosum　A massive bundle of axons that enables the two hemispheres of the brain to communicate with each other.

correlation　A measure of the relationship (association) between variables.

correlational coefficient　The decimal value that indicates the strength and direction of a relationship, ranging from +1.0 (perfect positive correlation) to −1.0 (perfect negative correlation).

cortical arousal　Heightened activity of the cortex as measured by the electroencephalogram.

cost-benefit analysis　An explanation for altruistic behavior that maintains that we help other people when the reward to us is greater than the cost.

counseling psychologists　Psychologists who administer and interpret psychological tests, interview and observe clients, and help resolve their problems. Many work in schools.

creativity　The ability to see things in a new and unusual light and to come up with unusual solutions to problems.

crisis　A state of acute disequilibrium so severe that an individual or family can no longer function.

criterion-related validity　A measure of the relationship between test performance and some outcome (criterion).

criterion sampling　The development of a test based on what the test taker will be required to do in "real life."

cross-sectional method　A data collection technique that measures people of different ages on a single occasion to compare them with regard to one or more characteristics; gives information on age differences in development. Compare with *longitudinal method*.

crystallized intelligence The ability to use information that has been learned; this kind of intelligence is influenced by culture and education. Compare with fluid intelligence.

cue-dependent forgetting An inability to recall information because appropriate retrieval cues are lacking.

data Information collected through research.

defense mechanism According to Freudian theory, an unconscious way to combat anxiety through the distortion of reality. (See *displacement, sublimation, repression, regression, projection, reaction formation,* and *rationalization*.)

dementia Mental deterioration caused by organic brain disease; characteristic of about one in ten people over 65 years of age. Sometimes referred to as "senile dementia," or "senility."

dendrites Narrow, branching extensions of the cell body that receive incoming signals from neurons.

dependent personality disorder A disorder characterized by lack of self-confidence that leads to giving up responsibility for one's life.

depersonalization disorder A *dissociative disorder* in which a person temporarily loses or changes sense of his or her reality.

depression A psychological disturbance characterized by sadness and difficulties in eating, sleeping, and concentrating.

descriptive statistics A branch of statistics that provides a way to summarize data.

developmental psychologists Psychologists who describe, explain, predict, and modify changes in behavior throughout the life span.

developmental psychology The branch of psychology concerned with the ways physical, cognitive, and psychosocial characteristics change throughout the life span.

difference threshold The smallest noticeable difference in intensity between two stimuli.

discrimination Behavior aimed at member(s) of a group one is prejudiced against.

disengagement theory A theory that holds that successful aging is characterized by the normal, inevitable, mutual withdrawal of the elderly person and of society.

displacement A Freudian defense mechanism in which a person gratifies an urge indirectly, by substituting a safer or more available object, person, or activity.

dissociation A split in consciousness.

dissociative disorders Mental disturbances involving a sudden temporary alternation in either consciousness, identity, or motor behavior.

dizygotic twins (fraternal twins) Twins conceived by the union of two different ova and two different sperm.

DNA (deoxyribonucleic acid) A molecular material found in the chromosomes that carries the hereditary information that determines the makeup of all the cells in the body.

dopamine A neurotransmitter. Schizophrenia may result from too much dopamine, Parkinson's disease from too little.

double-blind technique A procedure in which both subject and experimenter do not know who is in the experimental group and who is in the control group.

Down's syndrome A disorder caused by an extra chromosome 21, which includes mental retardation and often heart defects and other physical abnormalities.

drug A chemical substance that produces physical, emotional, and/or behavioral changes in the user.

DSM-III The third edition of *The Diagnostic and Statistical Manual of Mental Disorders*, a guidebook to diagnosis, published by the American Psychiatric Association in 1980.

dynamic school of psychotherapy A therapeutic approach that emphasizes the need for insight into a troubled individual's thoughts, feelings, and past life as a way to bring about personality change.

dysthmic disorder Chronic mild depression.

echoic memory Auditory sensory memory.

ecological theory The theory that perceptual constancies occur because the relationships between different objects in a scene give information about their sizes.

educational psychologists Psychologists who do research on the learning process.

ego According to Freudian theory, the aspect of personality generally known as common sense; operates on the reality principle to mediate between the id and the superego.

egocentrism An inability to consider another person's point of view, which is characteristic of preoperational thought.

ego integrity versus despair According to Eriksonian theory, the eighth and final crisis of personality development, characterizing old age. A sense of acceptance of one's own life allowing one to accept death; the developmental alternative is despair, characterized by failure to accept one's life.

eidetiker A person, usually a child, with the ability to "see" an image after it is no longer in view.

Electra complex According to Freudian theory the female counterpart of the Oedipus complex in which the little girl in the phallic stage feels sexual attraction for her father and rivalry toward her mother.

electroconvulsive therapy (ECT) Shock therapy in which an electric current briefly passes through the brain; effective in treating severe depression.

electroencephalogram (EEG) An instrument that measures brain-wave activity.

electromyograph An instrument that measures muscle movements.

electronic fetal monitoring A procedure that uses a machine to check on the fetal heartbeat throughout labor and delivery.

electrooculograph An instrument that measures eye movements.

embryonic stage The second stage of pregnancy (2 to 8 weeks); characterized by rapid growth and development of major body systems and organs.

emotion A general term that refers to a person's subjective reaction to the environment. Emotions involve neural and hormonal responses. When activated, they elicit an adaptive reaction that is experienced by the individual as pleasant or unpleasant.

encoding The process of classifying information in memory.

endocrine system The network of glands that secrete hormones into the bloodstream.

endorphins Chemical substances produced by the brain that reduce or eliminate pain.

engineering psychologists Psychologists concerned with designing, evaluating, and adapting machines to meet human needs.

engram A memory trace.

enkaphalin The smallest endorphin, a powerful painkiller.

epinephrine One of the hormones secreted by the adrenal medulla, which plays an important role in autonomic arousal.

equity theory The theory that we are most comfortable in relationships in which there is a fair distribution of rewards and costs and that we will try to restore equity (balance) in relationships perceived as unbalanced.

erogenous zones Sexually sensitive areas of the body.

eros Life instincts in Freudian theory.

estrogen A female hormone.

ethologist A scientist who studies behavior in its natural environment.

exchange theory The theory that we consider the rewards and costs in a relationship, as well as our alternatives, in determining whether to enter a relationship or stay in it.

experiment A highly controlled, replicable (repeatable) procedure, in which the researcher assesses the effect of manipulating variables; provides cause-and-effect information.

experimental group Subjects who receive the treatment of interest in an experiment.

experimental psychologists Psychologists who study basic psychological processes in animals and humans.

experimenter bias Influence on experimental results caused by experimenter's expectations.

extinction The weakening and eventual disappearance of a learned (conditioned) response.

familial retardation Retardation that is generally less severe than organic retardation and probably involves an interaction between genetic and environmental factors.

family resemblance The degree to which members of a category share features in common.

family stress The concept that when stress affects one member of a family, other family members are also affected.

family therapy A group-therapy technique that aims to change maladaptive behaviors by changing family roles and communication patterns.

fetal alcohol syndrome A compound birth defect characterized by mental, motor, and growth retardation caused by maternal alcohol abuse during pregnancy.

fetal stage The final (third) stage of pregnancy (8 weeks to birth); characterized by rapid growth of organism.

fetoscopy Prenatal diagnostic technique which allows for direct visual examination of the fetus while still in utero.

fixed-interval schedule A pattern of reinforcement in which the organism is regularly rewarded according to a fixed time period.

fixed-ratio schedule A pattern of reinforcement in which the organism is reinforced after making a specified number of responses.

flashbulb memories Vivid recollections of what one was doing when one heard about a significant event.

fluid intelligence The ability to solve novel problems; this kind of intelligence is influenced by neurological development. Compare with crystallized intelligence.

formal operations stage According to Piaget, the final stage of cognition, characterized by the ability to think abstractly.

fovea A region of the retina specialized for detail vision.

free recall The reproduction of previously learned materials in any order.

frequency distribution A list of observations and how frequently each occurs.

frequency theory The theory that the rate with which the basilar membrane is stimulated determines what is heard.

frustration A psychological state that frequently occurs when goal-directed behavior has been blocked or thwarted.

functional fixedness Overreliance on traditional ways of solving problems which inhibit novel solutions.

functionalism A school of psychology represented by James and Dewey concerned with what the mind does rather than its elements or structure.

fundamental attribution error The tendency to overestimate the importance of personality traits and underestimate situational influences in explaining the behavior of other people.

g factor General intelligence that influences all-around performance. Compare with *s factor*.

ganglion cells Cells in the eyes that carry all visual information to the brain.

gene A tiny segment, carried on a chromosome, that transmits hereditary characteristics.

general adaptation syndrome (GAS) A three-phase reaction to stress, described by Selye, consisting of alarm, resistance, and exhaustion.

generalized anxiety disorder A mental disorder characterized by feelings of anxiety which cannot be ascribed to any particular event or situation.

generativity versus stagnation According to Eriksonian theory, the seventh crisis of personality development. At midlife the mature adult either expresses a concern with guiding the next generation or feels stagnation (personal impoverishment).

genetic counseling Analysis and communication of a couple's chances of producing a child with a birth defect.

genetics The study of inheritance.

genital stage The Freudian term for the psychosexual stage of mature adult sexuality, which begins during adolescence.

genotype An individual's actual genetic composition; may differ from the observable phenotype because of the possession of recessive genes.

germinal stage The first stage of pregnancy (fertilization to 2 weeks) characterized by rapid cell division and increasing complexity of the organism.

Gesell developmental schedules An intelligence test for children 4 weeks to 6 years old which assesses motor, adaptive, language, and social behavior.

Gestalt psychology The school of psychology that emphasizes the pattern formed by the elements in the mind rather than the individual elements themselves. These elements form a whole that is greater than the sum of its parts.

Gestalt psychotherapy A humanistic psychotherapeutic approach that aims to integrate the various aspects of the personality into a well-organized whole.

glaucoma An eye disease caused by an increase of pressure inside the eye.

glial cells Cells that support and protect neurons.

grammar The rules of sound, meaning, and syntax in a language.

groupthink An uncritical acceptance by members of a close-knit group of an unwise course of action in order to preserve group unanimity.

group therapy A therapeutic approach that sees clients in groups rather than individually.

habituation A simple type of learning in which an organism stops responding to something she or he has grown used to.

hallucination A sensation that seems to come from a stimulus in the environment but that actually arises within the individual (such as seeing illusions, hearing imaginary voices, feeling nonexistent bugs crawling on the skin, etc.); experienced in psychosis or from certain drugs.

hallucinogens Psychedelic drugs such as LSD and PCP that alter perception, thoughts, and emotions to produce hallucinations.

hemispheres The left and right halves of the brain.

heuristic A problem-solving strategy consisting of a rule of thumb that will lead to either a rapid solution or to no solution.

histogram A bar graph.

histrionic personality disorder A disorder characterized by very dramatic behavior.

homeostasis Equilibrium (balance) of vital functions maintained by coordinated adjustments of the autonomic nervous system.

homogamy A similarity of attributes.

hormones Internal secretions of the endocrine glands that are carried by the bloodstream. These hormones are important chemical integrators that affect how we act, think, and feel.

humanistic model An explanation of mental disorders that holds that they are the result of failure to achieve self-actualization.

humanistic psychology Considered the "third force" in psychology, humanistic psychology emphasizes healthy human behavior.

humanistic psychotherapy A therapeutic approach that aims to help clients grow by removing the constraints upon their self-fulfillment.

humanistic theory An approach to personality exemplified by the theories of Rogers and Maslow; sees people as striving for self-actualization.

hypnosis A state of heightened suggestibility or susceptibility to outside influence.

hypoglycemia A condition associated with low blood sugar levels.

hypothalamus A small, but important, area of the brain located just above the brain stem. It has been implicated in a number of motivated behaviors including hunger and eating, thirst and drinking, and sex. It has also been linked to a wide variety of emotional behaviors. It regulates endocrine activity and maintains body balance.

hypothesis A prediction about the results of research.

iconic memory Visual sensory memory.

id According to Freudian theory, the aspect of personality that is present at birth; operates on the pleasure principle and is characterized by the desire for immediate gratification.

identification The process of adopting the characteristic beliefs, attitudes, values, and behaviors of another person or group.

identity versus role confusion According to Eriksonian theory, the fifth crisis of personality development, in which an adolescent must determine his or her own sense of self (identity).

illusions False perceptions.

incus A tiny bone in the ear, known as the "anvil."

industrial and organizational psychologists Psychologists concerned with people, their work, and their workplaces.

industry versus inferiority According to Eriksonian theory, the fourth crisis of personality development, occurring during middle childhood. Children must learn the skills needed to succeed in their culture.

inferential statistics A branch of statistics that uses data from a sample to generalize and predict results in a larger population.

inferiority complex According to Adler, the basis for a person's drive to achieve, to complete oneself, and to overcome feelings of inadequacy.

insomnia Difficulty getting to sleep and/or staying asleep.

instinct An inborn, species-specific, relatively complex pattern of behavior that is biologically determined and usually important for species survival.

insulin A chemical secreted by the pancreas that is important for digesting such substances as blood glucose and carbohydrates.

intelligence A constantly active interaction between inherited ability and environmental experience, which results in an individual's being able to acquire, remember, and use knowledge; to understand both concrete and (eventually) abstract concepts; to understand relationships among objects, events, and ideas; and to apply and use all the preceding in a purposeful way to solve problems in everyday life.

intelligence quotient (IQ) The mathematical score computed by dividing an individual's mental age MA by his or her chronological age CA and then multiplying by 100: MA/CA × 100.

interneurons Intermediary neurons that send messages from one kind of neuron to another.

internal sense The sense that transmits information about the internal organs.

interpersonal attraction A tendency to evaluate another in a positive way.

interstimulus interval The classical conditioning term for the time interval between presentation of the neutral stimulus and the unconditioned stimulus.

intimacy versus isolation According to Eriksonian theory the sixth crisis of personality development, which occurs during young adulthood. Young adults want to make commitments to others; if they cannot, they may suffer from a sense of isolation and self-absorption.

in vitro fertilization The fertilization of an ovum outside the mother's body.

iris A pigmented set of muscles surrounding the pupil; the colored part of the eye.

karyotype A chart on which photographs of chromosomes are cut out and arranged. Demonstrates chromosomal abnormalities.

kinesthetic sense The sense that relates information about muscle tension.

Korsakoff's syndrome A neuropsychiatric disorder caused by prolonged, excessive alcohol use.

language A means of communicating, generally through spoken sounds, that express specific meanings and are arranged according to rules.

language acquisition device (LAD) An inborn ability to analyze language to exact grammatical rules.

lanugo Fuzzy prenatal hair.

latency stage According to Freudian theory, a period of relative sexual calm during middle childhood, which occurs after the Oedipus/Electra complex is resolved.

latent dream content The Freudian term for the symbolic, or hidden, meaning of a dream.

latent learning Learning that occurs but is not displayed until the organism is motivated to do so.

lateral hypothalamus The area of the hypothalamus that has been linked to the regulation of food intake. Electrical stimulation of this area will make animals start to eat while destruction of this area will make animals stop eating.

learned helplessness The conviction that one has no control over one's life and that one's actions make no difference.

learning A relatively permanent change in behavior, which reflects a gain of knowledge, understanding, or skill, achieved through experience which may include study, instruction, observation, or practice.

learning by observation Learning by observing and imitating the behavior of a model.

Leboyer method A childbirth technique designed to minimize the trauma of birth.

lens A round, elastic structure in

the eye that focuses light into a clear image.

levels of processing model of memory The memory model of Crick and Lockhart that holds that the ability to remember is dependent on how deeply we process information.

libido Sexual energy in Freudian theory.

life review As proposed by Butler, an examination of one's life as one nears death.

life structure According to Levinson, the basic pattern of a person's life, consisting of both internal and external aspects.

Likert scale An attitude measure in which a subject responds to a series of statements on a continuum from "strongly agree" to "strongly disagree."

limbic system The part of the cerebrum that mediates emotional responses and is involved in memory. Includes the septal area, hippocampus, amygdala, and parts of the thalamus.

linguistic relativity hypothesis Whorf's view that language affects perception and thought; the Worfian hypothesis.

linguistics The study of language.

lithium carbonate A drug used to treat bipolar disorder.

longitudinal method A data collection technique that measures the same individual or group more than once, giving information about age changes in development. Compare with cross-sectional method.

long-term memory A type of memory that seems to have unlimited capacity and may store information permanently.

male climacteric Hormonal/physical and related psychological changes in middle-aged men.

malleus A tiny bone in the ear known as the "hammer."

manic episode A manifestation in bipolar disorders, characterized by extreme elation, irrational behavior, and grandiose thinking.

manifest dream content The part of a dream we remember, as compared to the latent content.

mantra A specific word or thought used by someone practicing transcendental meditation.

maternal blood testing A prenatal diagnostic technique to determine blood alpha fetoprotein level, which is related to neural tube defects.

maturation The unfolding of biologically determined patterns of behavior.

mean Often called the "average," this is an arithmetic average, arrived at by adding up all the scores in a distribution and then dividing that total by the number of individual scores. This is the most frequently used measure of central tendency; compare with the other two measures of central tendency, the median and the mode.

mean length of utterance (MLU) The average length of utterances in morphemes.

median The midpoint of a distribution of scores, with the same numbers of scores above and below.

medical model An explanation of mental disorders that holds that they are the result of illness.

meditation An altered state of consciousness induced by a refocusing of attention.

memorist A person with an exceptional memory.

menarche The time of first menstruation.

menopause The cessation of menstruation which typically occurs between 48 and 52 years of age.

mental retardation Below-average general intellectual functioning, a deficiency in the level of adaptive behavior appropriate to current age, and the appearance of such retardation before age 18.

mere-exposure effect The tendency to like something or someone better after simply having repeated exposure.

metacomponents of intelligence According to Sternberg's information processing approach, the steps in deciding how to solve a problem.

method of loci A mnemonic in which items to be remembered are imagined to be placed along a familiar route.

Minnesota Multiphasic Personality Inventory (MMPI) An objective personality test.

mnemonic A device to aid memory.

mode The score that occurs most frequently in a distribution.

modeling therapy A behavior therapy technique through which the individual learns new behaviors by observing and imitating models.

monoamine oxidase (MAO) inhibitor A type of antidepressant drug.

monosynaptic reflex The simplest type of reflex; it occurs as a result of a direct connection between a sensory neuron and a motor neuron, with no intervening interneurons.

monozygotic twins (identical twins) Twins resulting from the division of a zygote after conception.

moral model An explanation of mental illness common during the Middle Ages that holds that mental illness is the result of sin and possession by the devil.

morpheme The smallest meaningful element of speech.

motivation A general term that refers to the study of the arousal, direction, and persistence of behavior. Contemporary researchers tend to focus on the question of what energizes or arouses behavior.

motor nerves Nerves that transmit information from the brain to the muscles and glands of the body.

multifactorial inheritance   Patterns of inheritance in which a trait is carried either by a combination of several genes or through the interaction of genes with environmental factors.

multiple approach-avoidance conflict   A conflict in which several options exist, containing positive and negative aspects.

multiple personality   A dissociative disorder in which one person has more than one distinct personality, each of which comes to prominence at different times.

myelin   A fatty tissue that covers some axons, allowing impulses to travel faster.

myelinization   The process that forms myelin on axons.

myopia   Nearsightedness.

narcissistic personality disorder   A disorder characterized by grandiose fantasies of unlimited success, craving for constant attention, feeling enraged, ashamed, or haughtily indifferent in response to criticism or failure, expectation of special favors, disregard of others' rights, lack of empathy.

narcolepsy   A disorder characterized by an uncontrollable urge to sleep.

narcotics   Central nervous system depressant drugs used to relieve pain and induce sleep.

narrative-chaining method   A mnemonic in which a story is made up containing the information to be remembered.

natural childbirth   An involvement by the parents in which the woman learns the physiology of reproduction, as well as techniques of breathing, relaxation, and physical fitness, to make childbirth more comfortable and thus reduce or eliminate the need for painkilling medication. This makes delivery safer for the baby and makes the father part of the experience since he is usually

present at and often assisting at the birth.

naturalistic observation   A research method in which subjects are studied in natural settings without experimental intervention.

nature-nurture controversy   The controversy over the relative influence of our inherited traits (nature) or our experience (nurture) on development.

negative reinforcer   An unpleasant stimulus which, when removed from a situation, increases the probability of the occurrence of a response.

neodissociation theory   A view that the hypnotized person is functioning on more than one level of awareness.

neonatal period   The first 2 weeks of life for full-term infants.

neurons   Nerve cells.

neuroses   Mental disorders arising from anxiety whose symptoms interfere with normal functioning but do not block it entirely. The term has been in use since its origination by Freud but has been dropped from *DSM-III*.

neurotransmitter   A chemical involved in transmitting messages between neurons.

neutral stimulus   A stimulus that does not automatically elicit a reflex response.

night blindness   The reduction of ability to see in dim light.

nightmares   Frightening dreams most likely to occur during childhood.

night terrors   A sleep disorder usually of childhood consisting of panic attacks which typically occur within an hour of falling asleep.

non-REM sleep   Non-rapid eye movement sleep. The sleeping person passes through four sleep stages, each with distinct EEG patterns, during non-REM sleep. Non-REM sleep is not typically associated with dreaming.

norepinephrine   A chemical involved in the transmission of

nerve impulses across neural synapses, which seems to affect mood. When norepinephrine levels as measured by blood plasma are high, people feel good; when levels are low, people are more apt to feel sad or depressed.

normal distribution   The distribution of scores in the orderly pattern of a symmetrical bell-shaped curve on which the mean, median, and mode are all equal.

norms   Society's definitions of how we "should" behave.

null hypothesis   A statement that an independent variable will *not* affect a dependent variable.

obedience   Compliance with the demands of an authority figure.

object permanence   The realization that an object or person continues to exist even if it can no longer be seen. According to Piaget, the most important cognitive acquisition of infancy.

obsessive-compulsive disorder   A disturbance characterized by obsessions (persistent, unwanted ideas, thoughts, or impulses) and/or compulsions (urges to repeat certain unwanted acts).

Oedipus complex   A phenomenon described by Freud in which the male child in the phallic stage feels sexual attraction for his mother and rivalry toward his father.

olfactory mucosa   A mucous membrane that contains the smell receptors.

operant   A response that operates on the environment to bring about an effect.

operant conditioning   A type of learning in which the consequences of a behavior (i.e., whether it is reinforced or punished) determine whether or not the behavior will be repeated.

operant therapy   A behavior therapy technique in which the therapist uses a system of rewards to change the client's behavior.

opponent-process theory of color vision A theory of color vision that proposes that opposite processes occur in three systems—blue-yellow, red-green, and achromatic; explains the phenomenon of afterimages.

optic disk A part of the eye with no photoreceptors; when an image is projected on this disk, it hits a blind spot.

oral stage According to Freudian theory the psychosexual stage of infancy (birth to 12–18 months) characterized by gratification in the oral region; feeding is the major situation in which this occurs.

organic retardation Generally severe mental retardation with a physical cause.

ovum (plural, ova) Egg; female sex cell.

panic disorder A disturbance characterized by attacks of terror that include physical symptoms such as dizziness, breathing difficulties, and sweating.

papillae Taste buds on the tongue.

parallel forms reliability The degree of similarity in scores between alternate or parallel forms of a test.

paranoid disorder A personality disorder characterized by suspiciousness.

parasympathetic system A division of the autonomic nervous system that restores the body by increasing its supply of stored energy. Compare with *sympathetic system.*

partial reinforcement A pattern of reinforcement where the desired response is rewarded only part of the time.

passionate love A wildly emotional state that includes tenderness and sexuality, elation and pain, anxiety and relief, altruism and jealousy.

passive-aggressive disorder A personality disorder characterized by indirect resistance to meeting demands through passively expressed aggression.

peg-word method A mnemonic in which items to be remembered are associated with ("pegged to") certain cues.

penis envy The Freudian concept that the female envies the penis and wants one of her own.

perception The way the brain organizes and interprets sensory information.

perceptual constancy The awareness that objects or events in the environment remain the same even though they may look different because of varying environmental conditions.

perceptual set The tendency to perceive what one expects.

peripheral nervous system The network of sensory and motor nerves that control muscles and glands.

person perception The way we form impressions or perceptions of others.

persona A Jungian archetype of the social mask one adopts.

personal unconscious According to Jungian theory that part of the mind which contains repressed or forgotten materials.

personality The constellation of relatively consistent ways of dealing with people and situations that makes each person unique.

personality disorders Mental disorders characterized by maladaptive behavior patterns that appear at an early age, become more engrained over time, and are not viewed as abnormal by the person exhibiting them.

person-centered psychotherapy A humanist psychotherapeutic approach (also called "client-centered therapy") developed by Carl Rogers, which aims to provide the climate for clients to draw upon their own resources to fulfill themselves.

person-situation controversy The conflict over whether "personality" is consistent over time and situations or whether behavior changes to meet the demands of different situations.

personality psychologists Psychologists who measure and describe individual differences in personality.

persuasive communication A communication designed to change attitudes.

phallic stage According to Freudian theory, the stage of psychosexual development in which the preschool child receives gratification in the genital area.

phenothiazines The class of antipsychotic drugs also known as "major tranquilizers."

phenotype Those characteristics of a person that can be seen or observed; may differ from genotype because of the presence of recessive genes.

phobic disorder A mental disorder characterized by a persistent, intense, and unrealistic fear of an object or situation.

phoneme The minimal sound unit of spoken language.

photons The smallest units of light that can be measured.

physical development Changes in the body such as height, weight, brain development, and motor skills.

physiological psychologists Psychologists who study the relationship between physiological processes and behavior.

pinna The outer ear.

pituitary gland An endocrine gland called the body's "master gland" that controls the activity of all the other glands.

place theory The theory that the ability to hear a certain sound depends on the particular spot on the basilar membrane that is stimulated.

placebo An inert substance or sugar pill often given to the control group in an experiment.

placenta The organ attached to the uterus that brings food and oxygen to the fetus and carries its body wastes away.

pleasure principle   In Freudian theory the operating principle for the id, which attempts to gratify needs immediately.

polysynaptic reflex   A reflex that involves many synapses in an unknown number of interneurons.

population   All the members of a group being studied.

positive reinforcer   A pleasant stimulus which, when added to a situation, increases the probability of the occurrence of a response.

posttest   Test given after an experimental treatment. Differences in performance between the experimental and control groups indicate the effectiveness of the experimental treatment.

posttraumatic stress disorder   A mental disorder, characterized by reexperiencing a traumatic event.

predictive validity   A measure of the relationship between test performance and some future criterion.

prefrontal lobotomy   A type of psychosurgery popular in the 1940s and 1950s, designed to overcome psychological problems; hardly ever performed today.

prejudice   A negative attitude held toward people solely because of their membership in a particular group.

premature baby   A baby born before the thirty-seventh week of gestation.

premenstrual syndrome (PMS)   A psychological and physical state experienced just before and during the early phases of menstrual period; characterized by feelings of physical discomfort and psychological tension.

prenatal psychology   The branch of psychology concerned with the effects of the prenatal environment on the unborn child.

preoperational stage   The second of Piaget's stages of cognitive development, occuring from about 2 to 7 years of age. Children develop a symbol system, but their ability to think logically is limited by their egocentrism.

prepared childbirth   Childbirth techniques developed by Lamaze, which teach a pregnant woman to substitute new relaxation responses for old responses of fear and pain during uterine contractions.

presbycusis   Hearing loss for high-frequency sounds.

presbyopia   Farsightedness

pretest   Test given before an experimental treatment, generally to both experimental and control groups.

primacy effects   The tendency to remember the items learned first in a list.

primary mental abilities   Thurstone's theory of intelligence which identified seven relatively distinct factors.

primary reinforcers   Objects or events that are biologically important, such as food or sex, and whose appearance increases the probability of a response.

proactive interference   A situation in which information learned first inhibits the ability to remember new information.

progesterone   A female sex hormone.

programmed theory of aging   The theory that bodies age because a pattern of aging is built into every organism. Compare with wear-and-tear theory.

projection   A Freudian defense mechanism characterized by attributing one's own unacceptable thoughts and motives to another.

projective tests   Personality tests which use relatively ambiguous material, the responses to which provide clues about the test taker's personality.

proprioception   The sense that provides information about movement of body parts and their position in space.

proximodistal principle   The principle that development proceeds in a near-to-far direction; parts of the body near the center develop before the extremities do.

psychoactive drugs   A drug that changes perception, mood, or thought processes.

psychoanalysis   A therapeutic approach originally developed by Freud that aims to eliminate anxiety by giving the patient insight into unconscious conflicts that affect behavior and emotions.

psychoanalytic model   An explanation of mental disorders that holds they are the result of a conflict between the id, ego, and superego.

psychoanalytic theory   The personality theory of Sigmund Freud which sees people in constant conflict between their biological urges and the need to tame them.

psychogenic amnesia   A *dissociative disorder* in which a person may forget events that occurred during a certain time period. It usually follows a traumatic event and may end suddenly.

psychogenic fugue   A dissociative disorder in which a person may forget his identity and assume a new one.

psychology   The scientific study of behavior and mental processes.

psychometric psychologists   Psychologists who develop psychological tests and methods to score them.

psychophysics   The study of the relationship between the physical aspects of stimuli and psychological perceptions of them.

psychosexual development   The essence of Freudian theory which claims that human personality develops through a sequence of stages whereby gratification (pleasure) shifts from one bodily zone to another (oral, anal, genital), accompanied by shifts in the agent of gratification (feeding, elimination, sexual activity).

psychosocial development   Changes in personality, emotional, and social development.

psychosocial development theory The theory of personality development across the life span described by Erikson which stresses cultural and societal influences on the ego.

psychosurgery Brain surgery performed to overcome psychological disorders.

psychotherapy Treatment of a person with a psychological problem by a person specially trained in procedures that may consist wholly of talk, may prescribe certain kinds of behaviors, or may involve the administration of psychoactive drugs.

puberty The physiological point at which an individual is sexually mature and able to reproduce.

pubescence The time of the life span just before puberty, characterized by rapid physiological growth, maturation of reproductive functioning, and the development of primary and secondary sex characteristics.

punishment An event that, when administered following a response, decreases the probability of the recurrence of that response.

pupil A small hole in the center of the iris, which allows light to enter the eye.

range The simplest measure of variability; the difference between the largest and smallest scores in a sample.

rational-emotive therapy (RET) A type of cognitive therapy that emphasizes irrational thought processes as the root of emotional problems.

reaction formation A Freudian defense mechanism characterized by the replacement of an anxiety-producing feeling by its opposite.

reality principle In Freudian theory, the operating principle for the ego, which attempts to find acceptable ways to gratify the id.

recall A measure of the retention of previously learned material in which the individual is asked to reproduce the material from memory. An essay test is an example. Compare with *recognition*.

recency effect The tendency to remember items learned last in a list.

receptive fields Specific areas of the retina to which given receptor cells respond.

receptor sites Specialized molecules on receiving neurons that bind with a transmitter substance (neurotransmitter).

recognition A measure of the retention of previously learned material in which the degree of retention is judged by the amount of time saved learning the material the second time, compared to the time taken to learn it the first time.

reflex An inborn, unlearned, involuntary reaction to stimulation.

regression A Freudian defense mechanism characterized by returning to the behaviors of earlier ages.

rehearsal The deliberate repetition of information to keep it in memory.

reinforcement An event (or consequence) following a behavior which increases the probability that the behavior will occur again.

relearning A measure of the retention of previously learned material in which the degree of retention is judged by the amount of time saved learning the material the second time, compared to the time taken to learn it the first time.

reliability The consistency of a test in measuring the performance of an individual or group.

REM sleep Rapid eye movement sleep; associated with dreaming; also called "active" or "paradoxical" sleep.

replicate Repeat an experiment using exactly the same methods and procedures as in the original.

repression A Freudian defense mechanism characterized by the unconscious blocking from consciousness of anxiety-producing urges or experiences.

research The systematic and objective collection of data.

research, applied Research performed to solve practical problems.

research, basic Research performed to advance human knowledge; "pure" research.

resting potential The potential energy stored within a neuron.

reticular activating system A system of nerve pathways and connections within the brain stem.

reticular formation The part of the brain stem involved with waking people up and putting them to sleep.

retina The most important part of the eye, this tissue lines the back of the eye and contains the light-sensitive rods and cones.

retrieval The process of recalling information from memory.

retroactive interference A situation in which information learned later inhibits the ability to remember previously learned information.

retrograde amnesia A memory disorder in which information learned before the onset of the amnesia cannot be recalled.

rods Receptors on the retina that are sensitive to black and white but not to color.

roles A set of behavioral expectations (or norms) for people of a particular social position.

role-playing theory The view that hypnosis is not a special state of consciousness but is a condition in which the hypnotized person acts as she or he thinks is the expected behavior.

Rorschach A projective personality test where an individual is asked to tell what he or she sees in a series of inkblots which are then scored on several dimensions.

S factor   Specific intelligence that influences performance on different tests. Compare with *g factor*.

sample   A subgroup of a target population.

sample, random   A sample in which every member of a population has an equal chance of being selected.

sample, stratified   A sample that demonstrates various characteristics in the same proportion as they are found in the population.

scatterplot   A visual representation of the relationship between two variables.

schedules of reinforcement   Patterns by which reinforcement is administered.

schizoid personality disorder   A disorder characterized by the inability to form relationships, coldness, aloofness, lack of humor, indifference to praise or criticism, and failure to show appropriate emotions.

schizophrenia   A *psychosis* characterized by at least one of the following: delusions, hallucinations, or thought disturbances.

schizotypal personality disorder   A disorder characterized by oddities of thought, perception, speech, and behavior not severe enough to be diagnosed as schizophrenic.

school psychologists   Psychologists who deal directly with school children and their parents and teachers to work on school-related problems.

sclera   The white, outer part of the eyeball that contains receptors for pressure, temperature, and pain.

secondary reinforcers   Stimuli that become reinforcing after becoming associated with primary reinforcers.

secondary traits   According to Allport, traits displayed occasionally which are not strong enough to be regarded as integral parts of a person's personality.

secular trend   A tendency toward the earlier attainment of adult height and sexual maturity today than in earlier generations.

sedatives   Central nervous system depressant drugs which are calming and induce sleep.

self-actualization   Self-fulfillment; the goal of humanistic psychotherapy.

self-perception theory   Bem's theory that people look at their behavior and then attribute how they feel to what they do.

semantic differential   An attitude measure by which a concept is measured on a series of dimensions.

semantics   The study of meaning in a language.

sensation   A feeling in response to information that comes in through the senses.

senescence   The period of the life span that ushers in old age and is accompanied by decrements in bodily functioning; begins at different ages for different people.

sense   A particular physiological pathway for responding to a specific kind of energy.

sensorimotor stage   The first of Piaget's stages of cognitive development characterizing the first two years of life, as infants learn about their world primarily through their senses and motor activities.

sensorineural hearing loss   Hearing loss due to damage to the hair cells of the cochlea or damage to the auditory nerve.

sensory memory   The type of memory that involves material that comes through the senses. This material disappears very rapidly unless it is transferred into short-term memory.

sensory nerves   Nerves that transmit information from the body to the brain.

serial position curve   The curve of remembering that demonstrates the tendency to remember items learned first and last in a series.

serial recall   The reproduction of previously learned material in the order in which it was originally presented.

sex chromosomes   The one pair of chromosomes that determines sex (XX in the normal female; XY in the normal male).

sex-linked inheritance   A pattern of inheritance in which characteristics are carried on an X chromosome. They are transmitted by the female and are generally expressed in the male.

sex-role stereotypes   Beliefs about characteristics that males and females *should* have.

shaping   The reinforcement of responses that come progressively closer to the desired behavior until the desired behavior is reached.

short-term memory   Working memory, with a limited capacity. Items remain in short-term memory for up to 20 seconds unless held there by rehearsal.

simple phobia   The most common kind of phobia in which a person has a persistent, irrational fear of some particular aspect of the environment, like snakes or heights.

single-blind technique   Technique where the experimenter who gives the posttest is unaware of which subjects are in the experimental group and which are in the control group.

skewed distribution   An asymmetrical distribution of scores in which the mean, median, and mode fall in different places.

sleep apnea   A sleep disorder characterized by periods of interrupted breathing.

small-for-date baby   A baby who is abnormally small for his or her gestational age.

social consequence model   An explanation of mental disorders that holds that many are more appropriately considered to be problems of living than medical illnesses.

social learning theory   A theory proposed by Bandura that behaviors are learned by observing and imitating models and are maintained through reinforcement.

social phobia   A fear in which the individual is terrified of being in a situation where he or she can be scrutinized by others.

social psychologists   Psychologists who study the way people affect and are influenced by others.

social psychology   The scientific study of how we feel, think, are affected by, and act toward other people.

somatic nervous system   Part of the peripheral nervous system that controls reflex and voluntary actions.

somatoform disorder   A mental disorder characterized by physical symptoms for which no physical basis can be found.

somatotypes   Body types.

sperm   The male sex cell.

split-half reliability   The degree of similarity in scores on half of a test's items compared to the other half.

spontaneous abortion   The expulsion of a fetus before it is sufficiently developed to live outside of the womb; miscarriage.

spontaneous recovery   The reappearance of an extinguished response with no additional conditioning trials.

standard deviation   The square root of the variance; the preferred and most widely used measure of variability.

standard score   The number of standard deviations a score is from the mean; z score.

standardization   In test construction, the development of procedures for giving and scoring a test. Test items are administered to a large group of subjects representative of the population for whom the test is intended in order to determine the distribution of test scores.

Stanford-Binet Intelligence Scale   An individual intelligence test with heavy verbal emphasis, used primarily with children.

stapes   A tiny bone in the ear known as the "stirrup."

state-dependent memory   The tendency to remember something when one is in the same mood as when the information was first learned.

statistics   A branch of mathematics that uses a variety of methods for collecting, organizing, analyzing, and making inferences from numerical data.

stereochemical theory   The theory that there are seven basic smells, that smell receptors have particular shapes, and that the molecular combinations of the various odor types fit into these shapes.

stereotypes   Preconceived, oversimplified beliefs about the characteristics of members of a group.

stimulants   Drugs which stimulate the central nervous system, producing increased energy, wakefulness, and mood elevation.

stimulus   A form of energy which can elicit a response.

stimulus generalization   The tendency to respond in the same way to a stimulus that is different from but similar to the one used in the conditioning trials.

storage and transfer model of memory   A memory model of Atkinson and Shiffrin which proposes that there are three types of memory: sensory, short term, and long term.

strabismus   An inborn defect of the eye muscles which keeps the two eyes from focusing together.

stranger anxiety   A normal, although not universal, wariness of strangers which usually appears between 8 and 12 months of age.

stress   According to Selye, the nonspecific response of the body to any demand made on it.

stress-inoculation training   A behavioral technique designed to prevent stress.

stressor   An event capable of producing stress although not necessarily doing so.

structuralism   Developed by

Wundt and Titchener, this psychological school emphasized the study of the elements of the mind.

structure of intellect   A model of intelligence proposed by Guilford. Intelligence is the result of the interaction of operations (the way we think), contents (what we think about), and products (the result of the application of a certain operation to a certain content, or our thinking a certain way about a certain issue).

sublimation   A Freudian defense mechanism characterized by rechanneling uncomfortable feelings (like sexual anxiety) into acceptable activities (like schoolwork).

superego   According to Freudian theory, the aspect of personality which represents the values that parents and other agents of society communicate to the child. Results from the resolution of the Oedipus/Electra complex.

superstitious behavior   Continuing to make a response that was accidentally reinforced or punished.

survey   A research method to gather information about large groups of people; includes questionnaires and interviews.

sympathetic system   A division of the autonomic nervous system that mobilizes the body's resources so it can expend energy. Compare with parasympathetic system.

synapses   Spaces between the axon of one neuron and the dentrites or cell body of a second, where neurons communicate with each other.

synaptic vesicles   Specialized organs on the axon terminal of the sending neuron that squirt neurotransmitters into the synapse.

syntax   The body of rules for structuring a language.

systematic desensitization   A behavior therapy technique based on classical conditioning, which gradually exposes clients to a hierarchy of anxiety-producing stimuli and teaches them to relax at each level until they have overcome their fear of the object or situation.

t test   A statistical test used to determine the significance of differences between two groups.

tardive dyskinesia   An antipsychotic drug side-effect that includes involuntary facial twitches and body contortions.

temperament   An individual's characteristic style of approaching people and situations.

teratogenic   Capable of causing birth defects.

terminal drop   A decrease in intellectual performance just before death.

test norms   In test construction, the determination of the distribution of scores. Standards of performance.

test-retest reliability   The degree of similarity in scores when a test is given to the same person or group more than once.

testosterone   The primary male hormone produced by the testes.

thalamus   The part of the cerebrum that acts as a relay center to the cortex, receiving sensory information that it sends to sensory areas of the cortex; it also sends motor information to the cortex.

thanatology   The study of death and dying.

thanatos   Death instincts in Freudian theory.

Thematic Apperception Test (TAT)   A projective personality test in which the individual makes up a story about the pictures on a series of cards; stories are scored for themes.

theory   An explanation about the cause of behavior; theories organize data and provide directions for research.

therapist   An individual specifically trained to offer a definite kind of treatment for psychological problems. May be a clinical psychologist, psychiatrist, psy-

choanalyst, social worker, psychiatric nurse, or counselor.

thinking   The use of symbols to stand for things, events, and ideas, which allows the manipulation of concepts and images.

tinnitus   A continuous ringing or hissing sound in the ears.

"tip-of-the-tongue" phenomenon   A retrieval problem in which an item cannot be remembered although there is some knowledge of it.

tracheostomy   A surgical opening of the windpipe used to treat some cases of sleep apnea.

trance-state theory   The view that the hypnotized state is a different state of consciousness from the normal one.

transcendental meditation (TM)   The best-known meditative technique in the West, developed by Maharishi Mahesh Yogi.

trichromatic theory of color vision (Young-Helmholtz theory)   A theory that holds that the visual system contains three color mechanisms and that combinations of the responses of these three mechanisms produce all colored light.

tricyclics   A major class of drugs; used to treat depression.

trimester   A three-month period, usually used to describe stages of pregnancy.

trust versus mistrust   According to Eriksonian theory the first crisis of personality development. From birth to 12–18 months the infant develops a sense of whether or not the world and the people in it can be trusted.

tympanic membrane   The eardrum; a tissue that moves back and forth as sound waves enter the ear.

Type A behavior pattern   An aggressive, impatient behavior pattern associated with coronary disease, compared to the more adaptive Type B pattern.

typicality   The degree to which a particular item is a good example of a concept.

unconditioned response   The classical conditioning term for the automatic response to an unconditioned stimulus.

unconditioned stimulus   The classical conditioning term for a stimulus which automatically elicits a response, without the organism's having to learn (be conditioned) to do so.

unconscious inference theory   The theory that perceptual constancies occur because of what is known from experience.

ultrasound   A method of scanning the uterus with high-frequency sound waves for detection of the fetal outline to determine whether pregnancy is progressing normally.

umbilical cord   The cord that attaches the embryo to the placenta.

unipolar disorder   Depression, without manic episodes.

validity   The degree to which a test measures what it is supposed to measure.

variability   The spread of the scores in a distribution.

variable, dependent   A factor which may (or may not) change as a result of the experimental manipulation of the independent variable.

variable, independent   A factor which is manipulated by the experimenter.

variable interval schedule   A pattern of reinforcement by which the time period that must pass before a response is reinforced varies; reinforcement may occur after 1 minute; next time after 2 minutes; next time after 3 minutes.

variable ratio schedule   A pattern of reinforcement by which the organism is reinforced after making a variable number of responses; reinforcement may occur after the first response; then not till the tenth; then after the fifth.

variance   A measure of variability

determined by computing the deviation of each score from the mean; the average of all the squared deviations from the mean score.

ventromedial hypothalamus An area of the hypothalamus that has been linked to the regulation of food intake. Electrical stimulation of this area will make an experimental animal stop eating, while destruction of this area will lead to overeating and eventually obesity.

vestibular labyrinth A complex arrangement of the canals in the inner ear that help maintain balance.

violence Destructive action against people or property.

visual capture The phenomenon by which visual information is more influential than information from the other senses.

vitreous humor The fluid that gives the eye its shape.

von Restorff effect The tendency to remember unusual items regardless of their position in a list.

wear-and-tear theory of aging The theory that bodies age because of continual usage. Compare with *programmed theory*.

Weber's law A law of psychophys-ics that states that the larger the stimulus, the larger any change in it has to be before it is perceived.

Wechsler scales Intelligence tests that include the Wechsler Adult Intelligence Scale (WAIS); Wechsler Intelligence Scale for Children (WISCR); and Wechsler Preschool and Primary Scale of Intelligence (WPPSI). These individual tests contain separate verbal and performance scales.

zygote The one-celled organism that results from the union of sperm and ovum.

BIBLIOGRAPHY

Abel, E. L. (1981). Behavioral teratology of alcohol. *Psychological
Bulletin,* **90**(3), 564–581.

Abroms, K. I., & Bennett, J. W.
(1981). Parental contributions to
trisomy 21: Review of recent cy-
tological and statistical findings.
In P. Mittler (Ed.), *Frontiers of
knowledge in mental retardation,*
vol. 2: *Biomedical aspects,* 149–157.

——— & ———. (1979). Paternal
contributions to Down's syndrome dispel maternal myths,
ERIC.

Adams, J. L. (1980). *Conceptual
blockbusting: A guide to better ideas*
(2d ed.). New York: Norton.

Adelson, J. (1979). Adolescence
and the generation gap. *Psychology Today,* **12**(9), 33–37.

Ader, R., & Cohen, N. (1982). Behaviorally conditioned immuno-
suppression and murine systemic lupus erythematosus.
Science, **215**, 1534–1536.

Adler, A. (1928). *Understanding
human nature.* London: Allen and
Unwin.

———. (1936). On the interpretation of dreams. *International Journal of Individual Psychology,* **1**, 3–
16.

Adorno, T.; Frenkel-Brunswik, E.;
Levinson, D.; & Sanford, R. N.
(1950). *The authoritarian personality.* New York: Harper.

Ainsworth, M. D. S. (1969). Object
relations, dependency, and attachment: A theoretical review of
the infant-mother relationship.
Child Development, **40**, 969–1025.

———. (1979). Infant-mother attachment. *American Psychologist,*
34(10), 932–937.

———; Blehar, M. C.; Waters, E.; &
Wall, S. (1978). *Patterns of a psychological study of the stranger situation.* Hillsdale, N.J.: Erlbaum.

ASJA Newsletter. (1982). Banning
sequel. American Society of Journalists and Authors, January,
p. 10.

Allport, G. W. (1937). *Personality: A
psychosocial interpretation.* New
York: Holt.

———. (1961). *Patterns and growth
in personality.* New York: Holt,
Rinehart, and Winston.

——— & Odbert, H. S. (1936).
Trait-names: A psycho-lexical
study. *Psychological Monographs,*
47, Whole No. 211.

——— & Postman, L. J., (1958).
The basic psychology of rumor.
In E. E. Maccoby, T. M. Newcomb, & E. L. Hartley (Eds.).
*Readings in social psychology (3d
ed.).* New York: Holt, Rinehart,
and Winston.

Altman, I., & Taylor, D. (1973). *Social penetration: The development of
interpersonal relations.* New York:
Holt, Rinehart, and Winston.

American Bar Association Journal.
(1978). Hypnotized man remembers too much, **64**, 187.

*American heritage dictionary of the
English language.* (1971). W. Morris (Ed.). Boston: Houghton Mifflin.

American Psychological Association. (1982). *Ethical principles in
the conduct of research with human
participants.* Washington, D.C.:
American Psychological Association.

Amoore, J. E. (1970). *Molecular basis
of odor.* Springfield, Ill.: Charles C
Thomas.

———; Johnston, J. W.; Rubin, M.
(1964). The stereochemical theory
of odor. *Scientific American,*
210(2), 42–49.

Anastasi, A. (1976). *Psychological
testing* (4th ed.). New York: Macmillan.

——— & Schaefer, C. E. (1971).
Note on concepts of creativity
and intelligence. *Journal of Creative Behavior,* **3**, 113–116.

Anders, T.; Caraskadon, M.; &
Dement, W. (1980). Sleep and
sleepiness in children and adolescents. In I. Litt (Ed.), *Adolescent medicine. Pediatric Clinics of
North America,* **27**(1), 29–44.

Anderson, J. R. (1980). *Cognitive
psychology and its implications.* San
Francisco: W. H. Freeman.

Appel, L.; Cooper, R.; McCarrell,
B.; Sims-Knight, J.; Yussen, S.; &
Flavell, J., (1972). The develop-
ment of the distinction between
perceiving and memorizing.
Child Development, **43**, 1365–1381.

Applebaum, P. S. (1982). Can mental patients say no to drugs? *The
New York Times Magazine,* March
21, pp. 46, 51–57.

Arend, R.; Gove, F.; & Sroufe, L. A.
(1979). Continuity of individual
adaptation from infancy to kin-
dergarten: A predictive study of
ego-resiliency and curiosity in
preschoolers. *Child Development,*
50, 950–959.

Ariès, P. (1962). *Centuries of childhood.* New York: Random House.

Aronson, E. (1980). *The social animal*
(3d ed.). San Francisco: W. H.
Freeman.

——— & Bridgeman, D. (1979). Jigsaw groups and the desegregated
classroom: In pursuit of common
goals. *Personality and Social Psychology Bulletin,* **5**, 438–446.

———; Helmreich, R.; & LeFran, J.
(1970). To err is humanizing—
sometimes: Effects of self-esteem, competence, and a pratfall
on interpersonal attraction. *Journal of Personality and Social Psychology,* **16**, 259–264.

———; Stephan, C.; Sikes, J.;
Blaney, N.; & Snapp, M. (1978).
The jigsaw classroom. Beverly
Hills, Calif.: Sage.

———; Willerman, B.; & Floyd, J.
(1966). The effect of a pratfall on
increasing interpersonal attractiveness. *Psychonomic Science,* **4**,
227–228.

Asch, S. E. (1955). Opinions and
social pressure. *Scientific American,* **193**(5), 31–35.

———. (1956). Studies of independence and conformity: A minority of one against a unanimous majority. *Psychological Monographs,* **9,** Whole No. 416.

Aserinsky, E., & Kleitman, N. (1953). Regularly occurring periods of eye motility and concomitant phenomena during sleep. *Science,* **118,** 273.

Ash, P.; Vennart, J.; & Carter, C. (1977). The incidence of hereditary disease in man. *Lancet* (April), 849–851.

Atkinson, J. W. (1957). Motivational determinant of risk-taking behavior. *Psychological Review,* **64,** 359–372.

Atkinson, R. C., & Shiffrin, R. M. (1968). Human memory: A proposed system and its control processes. In K. W. Spence and J. T. Spence (Eds.), *The psychology of learning and motivation: Advances in research and theory,* vol. 2. New York: Academic Press.

——— & ———. (1971). The control of short-term memory. *Scientific American,* **225,** 82–90.

Bachman, J. G.; O'Malley, P. M.; & Johnston, J. (1978). *Youth in transition,* vol. 6. Ann Arbor, Mich.: Institute for Social Research.

Bachrach, A. J.; Erwin, W. J.; & Mohn, J. P. (1965). The control of eating behavior in an anorexic by operant conditioning techniques. In L. Ullman and L. Krasner (Eds.), *Case studies in behavior modification.* New York: Holt, Rinehart and Winston.

Backman, C. W. (1981). Attraction in interpersonal relationships. In M. Rosenberg and R. H. Turner (Eds.), *Social psychology.* New York: Basic Books.

——— & Secord, P. F. (1959). The effect of perceived liking on interpersonal attraction. *Human Relations,* **12,** 379–384.

Baker, L., & Barcai, A. (1968). Personal interview with S. W. Olds, Philadelphia, Pa., December.

Balkwell, C. (1981). Transition to widowhood: A review of the literature. *Family Relations,* **30,** 117–127.

Ballinger, C. B. (1981). The menopause and its syndromes. In J. G. Howells (Ed.), *Modern perspectives in the psychiatry of middle age.* New York: Brunner/Mazel, pp. 279–303.

Baltes, P. B.; Reese, H. W.; & Lipsitt, L. P. (1980). Life-span developmental psychology. In M. R. Rosenzweig and L. W. Porter (Eds.), *Annual review of psychology,* vol. 31. Palo Alto, Calif.: Annual Reviews.

Bandura, A. (1964). The stormy decade: Fact or fiction? *Psychology in the Schools,* **1,** 224–231.

———. (1965). Vicarious processes: A case of no-trial learning. In L. Berkowitz (Ed.), *Advances in experimental social psychology,* vol. 2. New York: Academic Press.

———. (1968). A social learning interpretation of psychological dysfunctions. In P. London and D. Rosenhan (Eds.), *Foundations of abnormal psychology.* New York: Holt.

———. (1974). Behavior theory and the models of man. *American Psychologist,* **19,** 859–869.

———. (1970). Modelling therapy. In W. Sahakian (Ed.), *Psychopathology today: Experimentation, theory, and research.* Itasca, Ill.: Peacock, pp. 547–557.

———. (1971). *Social learning theory.* Englewood Cliffs, N.J.: Prentice-Hall.

——— & Huston, A. (1961). Identification as a process of incidental learning. *Journal of Abnormal and Social Psychology,* **63**(12), 311–318.

———; Ross, D.; & Ross, S. (1963). Imitation of film-mediated aggressive models. *Journal of Abnormal and Social Psychology,* **66**(1), 3–11.

———; Ross, D.; and Ross, S. (1961). Transmission of aggression through imitation of aggressive models. *Journal of Abnormal and Social Psychology,* **63,** 575–582.

——— & Walters, R. H. (1963). *Social learning and personality development.* New York: Holt.

Banks, M. S.; Aslin, R. N.; & Letson, R. D. (1975). Sensitive period for the development of human binocular vision. *Science,* **190,** 675–677.

Banta, D., & Thacker, S. (1979). Electronic fetal monitoring: Is it a benefit? *Birth and the Family Journal,* **6**(4), 237–249.

Barahal, H. S. (1958). 1,000 prefrontal lobotomies—A five `to ten-year follow-up study. *Psychiatric Quarterly,* **32,** 653–658.

Barber, T. X. (1970). *LSD, marihuana, yoga, and hypnosis.* Chicago: Aldine.

——— & Wilson, S. C. (1977). Hypnosis, suggestions, and altered states of consciousness: Experimental evaluation of the new cognitive behavioral theory and the traditional trance-state theory of hypnosis. In W. E. Edmonston, Jr. (Ed.), *Conceptual and investigative approaches to hypnosis and hypnotic phenomena.* New York: New York Academy of Sciences.

Bard, P. (1938). Studies in the cortical representation of somatic sensibility. *Harvey Lectures,* **33,** 143–169.

Barfield, R. E., & Morgan, J. N. (1974). *Early retirement: The decision and the experience and a second look.* Ann Arbor: Institute for Social Research.

——— & ———. (1978). Trends in satisfaction with retirement. *The Gerontologist,* **18**(1), 19–23.

Barlow, H. B., & Mollon, J. D. (1982). *The senses.* Cambridge, England: Cambridge University Press.

Barnes, A.; Colton, T.; Gunderson, J.; Noller, K.; Tilley, B.; Strama, T.; Townsend, D.; Hatab, P.; & O'Brien, P. (1980). Fertility and outcome of pregnancy in women exposed in utero to diethylstilbestrol. *New England Journal of Medicine,* **302**(11), 609–613.

Baron, R. A. (1977). *Human aggression.* New York: Plenum.

Barron, J. (1981). Ex-controllers facing hardships. *The New York Times,* December 5, p. 27.

Bartoshuk, L. M. (1974). Taste illusions: Some demonstrations. *Annals of the New York Academy of Sciences,* **237,** 279–285.

Baruch, G.; Barnett, R.; and Rivers, C. (1983). *Lifeprints.* New York: McGraw-Hill.

Bassuk, E. L., & Gerson, S. (1978). Deinstitutionalization and mental health services. *Scientific American,* **238**(2), 46–53.

Bateson, G.; Jackson, D. D.; Haley, J.; & Weakland, J. (1956). Double-bind hypothesis of schizophrenia. *Behavioral Science,* **1,** 251–264.

Baumann, D. J.; Cialdini, R. B.; & Kenrick, D. T. (1981). Altruism as hedonism: Helping and self-gratification as equivalent responses. *Journal of Personality and Social Psychology,* **40**(6), 1039–1046.

Baumrind, D. (1964). Some thoughts on ethics of research: After reading Milgram's "Behavioral study of obedience." *American Psychologist,* **19,** 421–423.

———. (1967). Child care practices anteceding three patterns of preschool behavior. *Genetic Psychology Monograph,* **75,** 43–88.

———. (1970). Socialization and instrumental competence in young children. *Young Children,* **26**(2).

——— & Black, A. (1967). Socialization practices associated with dimensions of competence in pre-school boys and girls. *Child Development,* **38,** 291–327.

Bayer, A. E. (1967). Birth order and attainment of the doctorate: A test of an economic hypothesis. *American Journal of Sociology,* **72,** 540–550.

Beard, R. J. (1975). The menopause. *British Journal of Hospital Medicine,* **12,** 631–637.

Beck, A. T., & Burns, D. (1978). Cognitive therapy of depressed suicidal outpatients. In J. O.

Cole, A. F. Schatzberg, and S. H. Frazier (Eds.), *Depression: biology, pschodynamics, and treatment.* New York: Plenum.

Behavioral Medicine. (1981). Special reports; Stress in the air—air traffic controllers: Casualities of stress? *Behavioral Medicine,* **8**(9), 30–35.

Behrman, R. E., & Vaughan, V. C. (1983). *Textbook of pediatrics* (4th ed.). Philadelphia: Saunders.

Bell, A. P., & Weinberg, M. S. (1978). *Homosexualities: A study of diversity among men and women.* New York: Simon and Schuster.

———; ———; & Hammersmith, S. K. (1981). *Sexual preference: Its development in men and women.* Bloomington: Indiana University Press.

Belmont, L., & Morolla, A. F. (1973). Birth order, family size, and intelligence. *Science,* **182,** 1096–1101.

Bem, D. J. (1967). Self-perception: An alternative interpretation of cognitive dissonance phenomena. *Psychological Review,* **74**(3), 183–200.

———. (1970). *Beliefs, attitudes and human affairs.* Belmont, Calif.: Brooks/Cole.

——— & Allen, A. (1974). On predicting some of the people some of the time: The search for cross-situational consistencies in behavior. *Psychological Review,* **81**(6), 506–520.

Bem, S. L. (1974). The measurement of psychological androgyny. *Journal of Consulting and Clinical Psychology,* **42**(2), 155–162.

———. (1976). Probing the promise of androgyny. In A. G. Kaplan and J. P. Bean (Eds.), *Beyond sex-role stereotypes: Readings toward a psychology of androgyny.* Boston: Little, Brown.

Bemis, K. M. (1978). Current approaches to the etiology and treatment of anorexia nervosa. *Psychological Bulletin,* **85,** 593–617.

Benderly, B. L. (1981). Flashbulb

memory. *Psychology Today,* **15**(6), 71–74.

Bennett, F. C.; Robinson, N. M.; and Sells, C. J. (1983). Growth and development of infants weighing less than 800 grams at birth. *Pediatrics,* **71**(3), 319–323.

Bennett, W., & Gurin, J. (1982). *The dieter's dilemma: Eating less and weighing more.* New York: Basic Books.

Benson, H. (1975). *The relaxation response.* New York: Morrow.

Bentovim, A. (1979). Family therapy when the child is the referred patient. In S. Bloch (Ed.), *An introduction to the psychotherapies.* Oxford, England: Oxford University Press.

Berger, R. M. (1982). *Gay and gray: The older homosexual male.* Urbana: University of Illinois Press.

Berlyne, D. E. (1971). *Aesthetics and psychobiology.* New York: Appleton-Century-Crofts.

Bernstein, A. C., & Cowen, P. (1977). Children's concepts of how people get babies. In E. M. Hetherington and R. D. Parke (Eds.), *Contemporary readings in child psychology.* New York: McGraw-Hill.

Berscheid, E. S. (1983). Personal communication to the authors, March 25.

——— & Campbell, B. (1981). The changing longevity of heterosexual close relationships. In M. J. Lerner, and S. C. Lerner (Eds.), *The justice motive in social behavior.* New York: Plenum.

——— & Walster, E. (1978). *Interpersonal attraction* (2d ed.). Reading, Mass.: Addison-Wesley.

———; ———; & Bohrnstedt, G. (1973). The happy American body, a survey report. *Psychology Today,* **7**(6), 119–131.

Bibring, E. (1954). Psychoanalysis and the dynamic psychotherapies. *Journal of the American Psychoanalytic Association,* **2,** 745–770.

Bing, E. (1963). Effects of child-rearing practices on development of different cognitive abilities. *Child Development,* **34,** 631–648.

Birns, B. (1976). The emergence and socialization of sex differences in the earliest years. *Merrill-Palmer Quarterly,* **22,** 229–254.

Blake, J. (1981). The only child in America: Prejudice vs. performance. *Population and Development Review,* **1,** 43–54.

Blakemore, C. (1977). *Mechanics of the mind.* Cambridge, England: Cambridge University Press.

Bloch, S. (1979). Group psychotherapy. In S. Bloch (Ed.), *An introduction to the psychotherapies.* Oxford, England: Oxford University Press.

Block, J. H. (1978). Another look at sex differentiation in the socialization behaviors of mothers and fathers. In F. Wenmark and J. Sherman (Eds.), *Psychology of women: future direction of research.* New York: Psychological Dimensions.

————. (1981). Some enduring and consequential structures of personality. In A. I. Rabin et al. (Eds.), *Further explorations of personality.* New York: Wiley.

Blodgett, H. C. (1929). The effect of the introduction of reward upon the maze performance of rats. *University of California Publication of Psychology,* **4**(8), 120.

Bloom, A. (1981). *The linquistic shaping of thought: A study in the impact on thinking in China and the West.* Hillsdale, N.J.: Erlbaum.

Bloom, B. L.; Asher, S. J.; & White, S. W. (1978). Marital disruption as a stressor: A review and analysis. *Psychological Bulletins,* **85,** 867–894.

Bluebond-Langner, M. (1977). Meanings of death to children. In H. Feifel (Ed.), *New meanings of death.* New York: McGraw-Hill.

Blum, J. E.; Fosshage, J. I.; & Jarvik, L. F. (1972). Intellectual changes and sex differences in octogenarians. A twenty-year longitudinal study of aging. *Developmental Psychology,* **7,** 178–187.

————; Jarvik, L. F.; & Clark, E. T. (1970). Rate of change on selective tests of intelligence. A twenty-year longitudinal study of aging. *Journal of Gerontology,* **25,** 171–176.

Blumstein, P. & Schwartz, P. (1983). *American couples: Money, work, sex.* New York: Morrow.

Boffey, P. M. (1981). Worldwide use of Valium draws new scrutiny. *The New York Times,* October 13, pp. C1–2.

————. (1981). Panel clears 2 accused of scientific fraud in alcoholism study. *The New York Times,* November 5, p. A12.

Boice, R. (1982). Increasing the writing productivity of 'blocked' academicians. *Behavioral Research and Therapy,* **20,** 197–207.

Bolles, R. C., & Fanselow, M. S. (1982). Endorphins and behavior. In M. R. Rosenzweig and L. W. Porter (Eds.), *Annual review of psychology.* Palo Alto, Calif.: Annual Reviews.

Bolton, R. (1973). Aggression and hypoglycemia among the Qolla: A study in psychobiological anthropology. *Ethnology,* **12,** 227–257.

Bootzin, M. (1975). *Behavior modification and therapy, an introduction.* Cambridge, Mass.: Winthrop.

Boss, P. G. (1985). Family stress: Perception and context. In M. Sussman and S. Steinmetz (Eds.), *Handbook of marriage and the family.* New York: Plenum.

————; McCubbin, H. J.; & Lester, G. (1979). The corporate executive wife's coping patterns in response to routine husband-father absence. *Family Process,* **18,** 79–86.

Boston Children's Medical Center. (1972). *Pregnancy, birth and the newborn baby.* Boston: Delacorte.

Bottoms, S. F.; Kuhnert, B. R.; Kuhnert, P. M.; & Reese, A. L. (1982). Maternal passive smoking and fetal serum thiocyanate levels. *American Journal of Obstetrics and Gynecology,* **144,** 787–791.

Botwinick, J.; West, R.; & Storandt, M. (1978). Predicting death from behavioral test performance. *Journal of Gerontology,* **33**(5), 755–762.

Bouchard, T. J. (1981). The study of mental ability using twin and adoption designs. *Twin research 3: Intelligence, personality and development.* New York: Liss, pp. 21–23.

————; Heston, L.; Eckert, E.; Keyes, M.; & Resnick, S. (1981). The Minnesota study of twins reared apart: Project description and sample results in the developmental domain. In *Twin research 3: Intelligence, personality and development.* New York: Liss.

Bouchard, T. J., & McGue, M. (1981). Familial studies of intelligence: A review. *Science,* **212**(29), 1055–1058.

Bourne, L. E. (1967). Learning and utilization of conceptual rules. In B. Kleinmuntz (Ed.) *Memory and the structure of concepts.* New York.

————. (1970). Knowing and using concepts. *Psychological Review,* **77,** 546–556.

————; Dominowski, R. L.; & Loftus, E. F. (1979). *Cognitive processes.* Englewood Cliffs, N.J.: Prentice-Hall.

Bousfield, W. A. (1953). The occurrence of clustering in the recall of randomly arranged associates. *Journal of General Psychology,* **49,** 229–240.

Bower, G. H. (1973). How to . . . uh . . . remember. *Psychology Today* (October), 63–70.

————. (1981). Mood and memory. *American Psychologist,* **36**(2), 129–148.

Bowers, K. (1973). Situationism in psychology: An analysis and a critique. *Psychological Review,* **80**(5), 307–336.

Brackbill, Y., & Broman, S. (1979). Obstetrical medication and development in the first year of life. Unpublished manuscript.

Brady, J. V. (1967). Emotion and

sensitivity of psychoendocrine systems. In D. C. Glass (Ed.), *Neurophysiology and emotion*. New York: Rockefeller University Press.

———. (1975). Towards a behavioral biology of emotion. In L. Levi (Ed.), *Emotions: Their parameters and measurement*. New York: Raven Press.

Bredehoft, D. (1981). Marital satisfaction: A comparison of childed, empty-nest, and childfree couples. Paper presented at the annual meeting of the National Council on Family Relations, Milwaukee, Wisconsin, October.

Bregman, E. O. (1934). An attempt to modify the emotional attitudes of infants by the conditioned response technique. *Journal of Genetic Psychology*, **45**, 169–198.

Brehm, J. W.; Gatz, M.; Goethals, G.; McCrimmon, J.; & Ward, L. (1970). Psychological arousal and interpersonal attraction.

Breland, K., & Breland, M. (1951). A field of applied animal psychology. *American Psychologist*, **6**, 202–204.

——— & ———. (1961). The misbehavior of organisms. *American Psychologist*, **16**, 681–684.

Brent, R. (1981). Ultrasonography in fetal diagnosis. *Pediatric Annals*, **10**(2), 49–60.

Brewster, A. B. (1982). Chronically ill hospitalized children's concepts of their illness. *Pediatrics*, **69**, 355–362.

Bridges, K. M. B. (1932). Emotional development in early infancy. *Child Development*, **3**, 324–341.

Briley, M. (1980). Burnout stress and the human energy crisis. *Dynamic Years* (July–August), 36–39.

Brim, O. G. & Kagan, J. (Eds.) (1980). *Constancy and change in human development*. Cambridge, Mass.: Harvard University Press.

Brittain, C. (1963). Adolescent choices and parent-peer cross-pressure. *American Sociological Review*, **28**, 385–391.

Brodbeck, A. J., & Irwin, O. C.

(1946). The speech behavior of infants without families. *Child Development*, **17**, 145–156.

Brody, E. B., & Brody, N. (1976). *Intelligence*. New York: Academic Press.

Brody, J. E. (1982). Noise poses a growing threat, affecting hearing and behavior. *The New York Times*, November 16, pp. C1, C5.

———. (1983). How drugs can cause decreased sexuality. *The New York Times*, September 28, pp. C1, C10.

Bromley, D. B. (1974). *The psychology of human aging* (2d ed.). Middlesex, England: Penguin.

Brooks, J., & Weintraub, M. (1976). A history of infant intelligence testing. In M. Lewis (Ed.), *Origins of intelligence*. New York: Plenum.

Brouilette, R. T.; Fernbach, S. K.; & Hunt, C. E. (1982). Obstructive sleep apnea in infants and children. *Journal of Pediatrics*, **100**(1), 31–40.

Brown, P., & Elliot, R. (1965). Control of aggression in a nursery school class. *Journal of Experimental Child Psychology*, **2**, 103–107.

Brown, R. (1973a). Development of the first language in the human species. *American Psychologist*, **28**(2), 97–106.

———. (1973b). *A first language: The early stages*. Cambridge, Mass.: Harvard University Press.

——— & Kulik, J. (1977). Flashbulb memories. *Cognition*, **5**, 73–99.

——— & Lenneberg, E. H. (1954). A study in language and cognition. *Journal of Abnormal Social Psychology*, **49**, 454–462.

——— & McNeill, D. (1966). The "tip of the tongue" phenomenon. *Journal of Verbal Learning and Verbal Behavior*, **5**, 325–337.

Bruner, J. S.; Goodnow, J. J.; Austin, G. A. (1956). *A study of thinking*. New York: Wiley.

Bukowski, C. (1972). *Mockingbird wish me luck*. Los Angeles: Black Sparrow Press.

Burgess, E. W., & Wallin, P. (1953).

Engagement and marriage. Philadelphia: Lippincott.

Burke, B. S.; Beal, V. A.; Kirkwood, S. B.; Stuart, H. (1943). Nutrition studies during pregnancy. *American Journal of Obstetrics and Gynecology*, **46**, 38–52.

Burstein, B.; Bank, L.; & Jarvik, L. F. (1980). Sex differences in cognitive functioning: Evidence, determinants, and implications. *Human Development*, **23**, 289–313.

Bush, T. L., Cowan, L. D., Barrett-Connor, E., Criqui, M. H., Karon, J. M., Wallace, R. B., Tyroler, H. A., & Rifkind, B. M. (1983). "Estrogen use and all-cause mortality: Preliminary results from the Lipid Research Clinics program follow-up study," *Journal of the American Medical Association*, vol. 249, no. 7, pp. 903–906.

Bustillo, M.; Buster, J. E.; Cohen, S. W.; Hamilton, F.; Thorneycroft, I. H.; Simon, J. A.; Rodi, I. A.; Boyers, S.; Marshall, J. R.; Louw, J. A.; Seed, R.; & Seed, R. (1984). Delivery of a healthy infant following nonsurgical ovum transfer. *Journal of the American Medical Association*, **251**(7), 889.

Butler, R. (1961). Re-awakening interests: Nursing homes. *Journal of American Nursing Home Association*, **10**, 8–19.

———. (1975). *Why survive? Being old in America*. New York: Harper and Row.

Butterfield, E., & Siperstein, G. (1972). Influence of contingent auditory stimulation upon non-nutritional suckle. In J. Bosma (Ed.), *Oral sensation and perception: The mouth of the infant*. Springfield, Ill.: Charles C Thomas.

Butters, N., & Cermak, L. S. (1980). *Alcoholic Korsakoff's syndrome*. New York: Academic Press.

Byrne, D. (1961). Interpersonal attraction and attitude similarity. *Journal of Abnormal and Social Psychology*, **62**, 713–715.

———. (1969). Attitudes and attraction. In L. Berkowitz (Ed.), *Advances in experimental social psychology.* New York: Academic Press, pp. 35–85.

———. (1971). *The attraction paradigm.* New York: Academic Press.

———; Clore, G. L.; & Worchel, P. (1966). The effect of economic similarity—dissimilarity on interpersonal attraction. *Journal of Personality and Social Psychology,* **4,** 220–224.

——— & Griffitt, W. (1973). Interpersonal attraction. In P. Mussen and M. R. Rosenzweig (Eds.), *Annual Review of Psychology,* vol. 24. Palo Alto, Calif.: Annual Reviews.

———; London, O.; & Reeves, K. (1968). The effects of physical attractiveness, sex, and attitude similarity on interpersonal attraction. *Journal of Personality,* **36,** 259–271.

Cain, W. S. (1981). Educating your nose. *Psychology Today* (July), 49–56.

Cannon, W. B. (1927). The James-Lange theory of emotions: A critical examination and an alternative theory. *American Journal of Psychology,* **39,** 106–124.

Cannon, W. B., & Washburn, A. L. (1912). An explanation of hunger. *American Journal of Physiology,* **29,** 441–454.

Carew, T. J.; Hawkins, R. D.; & Kandel, E. R. (1983). Differential classical conditioning of a defensive withdrawal reflex in *Aplysia californica. Science* (January 28), **219,** 397–400.

Carrera, M. A. (1983). Some reflections on adolescent sexuality. *SIECUS Report.* Published by Sex Information and Education Council of the U.S. New York, **11**(4), 1–2.

Carroll, M. (1982). Scores low, city ends civil service tests. *The New York Times,* December 8, pp. B1, B21.

Carstairs, G. M., & Kapur, R. L. (1976). *The great universe of Kota.* Berkeley, Ca.: University of California Press.

Cartwright, R. D. (1977). *A primer on sleep and dreaming.* Reading, Mass.: Addison-Wesley.

Carver, C. S., & Scheier, M. F. (1978). Self-focusing effects of dispositional self-consciousness, mirrorpresence, and audience presence. *Journal of Personality and Social Psychology,* **36,** 324–332.

Castillo, M., & Butterworth, G. (1981). Neonatal localization of a sound in visual space. *Perception,* **10,** 331–338.

Cattell, P. (1960). *The measurement of intelligence of infants and young children.* New York: Psychological Corp.

Cattell, R. B. (1965). *The scientific analysis of personality.* Baltimore: Penguin.

Cazden, C. B. (1971). Suggestions from studies of early language acquisition. In R. H. Anderson and H. G. Shane (Eds.), *As the twig is bent: Readings in early childhood education.* Boston: Houghton Mifflin.

Chase, M. H. (1981). The dreamer's paralysis. *Psychology Today,* **15**(11) 108.

Check, W. (1979). Antenatal diagnosis: What is "standard"? *Journal of the American Medical Association,* **241**(16), 1666ff.

Cherniak, N. S. (1981). Respiratory disrythmias during sleep. *New England Journal of Medicine,* **305**(6), 325–330.

Chesterfield, Lord. (1968). *Letters to his son.* In. B. Evans (Ed.), *Dictionary of quotations.* New York: Delacorte.

Chilman, C. S. (1982). Adolescent childbearing in the United States: Apparent causes and consequences. In T. M. Field, A. Huston, H. C. Quay, L. Troll, and G. E. Finley (Eds.), *Review of human development.* New York: Wiley.

Chomsky, C. (1969). *The acquisition of syntax in children from five to ten.* Cambridge, Mass.: MIT Press.

Chomsky, N. (1965). *Aspects of the theory of syntax.* Cambridge, Mass.: MIT Press.

———. (1968). *Language and mind.* New York: Harcourt, Brace, & World.

Cicirelli, V. G. (1980). Personal communication to S. W. Olds, November 14.

———. (1982). Sibling influence throughout the lifespan. In M. E. Lamb and B. Sutton-Smith (Eds.), *Sibling relationships: Their nature and significance across the lifespan.* Hillsdale, N.J.: Erlbaum.

Claridge, G. (1972). The schizophrenias as nervous types. *British Journal of Psychiatry,* **121,** 1–17.

Clark, M. (1979). Drugs and psychiatry: A new era. *Newsweek* (November 12), 98–104.

——— with Shapiro, D. (1980). Scanning the human mind. *Newsweek* (September 29), 63.

——— with Witherspoon, D. (1983). Reagan's hearing problem. *Newsweek* (September 19), 91.

Claudy, J. G.; Farrell, W. S.; & Dayton, C. W. (1979). *The consequences of being an only child: An analysis of project talent data.* Final Report (no. NO1-HD-82854). Center for Population Research, National Institutes of Health, December.

Clayton, V., & Overton, W. (1973). The role of formal operational thought in the aging process. Paper presented at the annual meeting of the Gerontological Society, Miami.

Clinical Pediatrics. (1979). NIH concensus development conference. *Clinical Pediatrics,* **18**(9), 535–538.

Clore, G. L., & Byrne, D. (1974). A reinforcement-affect model of attraction. In T. L. Huston (Ed.), *Foundations of interpersonal attraction.* New York: Academic Press, pp. 143–170.

Coe, W. C., & Ryken, K. (1979). Hypnosis and risks to human subjects. *American Psychologist,* **34**(3), 673–681.

——— & Sarbin, T. R. (1977). Hypnosis from the standpoint of a contextualist. In W. E. Edmonston, Jr. (Ed.), *Conceptual and investigative approaches to hypnosis and hypnotic phenomena*. New York: New York Academy of Sciences.

Cohen, D.; Schaie, K. W.; & Gribbin, K. (1977). The organization of spatial abilities in older men and women. *Journal of Gerontology*, **32**, 578–585.

Cohen, S. (1980). Aftereffects of stress on human performance and social behavior: A review of research and theory. *Psychological Bulletin*, **88**(1), 82–108.

Cohn, V. (1975). New method of delivering babies cuts down "torture of the innocent." *Capital Times*, November 5.

Colao, F., & Hosansky, T. (1982). *The key to having fun is being safe.* New York: The Safety and Fitness Exchange.

Cole, S. (1980). Send our children to work? *Psychology Today*, **14**(2), 44ff.

Colegrove, F. W. (1899). The day they heard about Lincoln. From F. W. Colegrove. Individual memories. *American Journal of Psychology*, 1899, **10**, 228–255. [Reprinted in A. Neisser (Ed.), *Memory observed*. San Francisco: W. H. Freeman. 1982.]

Coleman, J. (1980). Friendship and the peer group in adolescence. In J. Adelson (Ed.), *Handbook of adolescent development*. New York: Wiley.

Colen, B. D. (1982). Should the police use hypnosis? *This World, San Francisco Chronicle Magazine* (March 7), p. 22.

Colman, A. (1980). Flattery won't get you everywhere. *Psychology Today*, **13**(12), 80–82.

Condon, W., & Sander, L. (1974). Synchrony demonstrated between movements of the neonate and adult speech. *Child Development*, **45**, 456–462.

Condry, J. C. (1977). Enemies of exploration. Self-initiated versus other-initiated learning. *Journal of Personality and Social Psychology*, **35**, 459–477.

Conger, J. J. (1956). Reinforcement theory and the dynamics of alcoholism. *Quarterly Journal of Studies on Alcohol*, **17**, 296–305.

Conklin, E. S. (1933). *Principles of adolescent psychology*. New York: Holt.

Coons, S., & Guilleminault, C. (1982). Development of sleep-wake patterns and non-rapid eye movement sleep stages during the first six months of life in normal infants. *Pediatrics*, **69**(6), 793–798.

Cooper, C. L. (1981). *The stress check*. Englewood Cliffs, N.J.: Prentice-Hall.

Corby, J. C.; Roth, W. T.; Zarcone, V. P.; & Kopell, B. S. (1978). Psychophysiological correlates of the practice of tantric yoga meditation. *Archives of General Psychiatry*, **35**, 571–577.

Cornsweet, T. N. (1970). *Visual perception*. New York: Academic Press.

Costa, P. T. & McCrae, R. R. (1980). Still stable after all these years: Personality as a key to some issues in adulthood and old age. In P. B. Baltes and O. G. Brim (Eds.), *Life-span development and behavior*, vol. 3. New York: Academic Press.

Costain, D. W.; Cowen, P. J.; Gelder, M. G.; & Grahame-Smith, D. G. (1982). Electroconvulsive therapy and the brain: Evidence for increased dopamine-mediated responses. *Lancet* (August 21), 400–404.

Cowen, E. L. (1982). Help is where you find it: Four informal helping groups. *American Psychologist*, **37**(4), 385–395.

Coyle, J. T.; Price, D. L.; and DeLong, M. R. (1983). Alzheimer's disease: A disorder of cortical cholinergic innervation. *Science*, **219**, 1184–1190.

Craik, F. I. M., & Lockhart, R. S. (1972). Levels of processing: A framework for memory research. *Journal of Verbal Learning and Verbal Behavior*, **11**, 671–684.

——— & Tulving, E. (1975). Depth of processing and the retention of words in episodic memory. *Journal of Experimental Psychology* (General), **104**, 268–294.

Crandall, B. (1981). Alpha-fetoprotein: The diagnosis of neural-tube defects. *Pediatric Annals*, **10**(2), 38–48.

Cratty, B. (1979). *Perceptual and motor development in infants and children*. Englewood Cliffs, N.J.: Prentice-Hall.

Crawford, H. (1982). Cognitive processing during hypnosis: Much unfinished business. *Research Communications in Psychology, Psychiatry and Behavior*, **7**(2), 169–178.

Crick, F., & Mitchison, G. (1983). The function of dream sleep. *Nature*, **304**, 111–114.

———. (1982). Do dendritic spines twitch? *Trends in Neuroscience* (February), 44–46.

Crook, T., & Eliot, E. (1980). Parental death during childhood and adult depression: A critical review of the literature. *Psychological Bulletin*, **87**(2), 252–259.

Cross, D. T.; Barclay, A.; & Burger, G. K. (1978). Differential effects of ethnic membership, sex, and occupation on the California Personality Inventory. *Journal of Personality Assessment*, **42**, 597–603.

Crovitz, E. (1966). Reversing a learning deficit in the aged. *Journal of Gerontology*, **21**, 236–238.

Curtis, S. (1977). *Genre*. New York: Academic.

Custance, J. (1952). *Wisdom, madness, & folly*. New York: Farrar, Straus, and Cudahy.

Cytrynbaum, S.; Blum, L.; Patrick, R.; Stein, J.; Wadner, D.; & Wilk, C. (1980). Midlife development: A personality and social systems perspective. In L. Poon (Ed.), *Aging in the 1980's: Psychological issues*. Washington, D.C.: American Psychological Association.

Dabbs, J. M., & Janis, I. L. (1965). Why does eating while reading facilitate opinion change? An experimental inquiry. *Journal of Experimental Social Psychology*, **1**, 133–144.

Dalton, K. (1977). *The premenstrual syndrome and progesterone therapy*. London: Heinman.

Darley, J., & Bateson, C. D. (1973). From Jerusalem to Jericho: A study of situational and dispositional variables in helping behavior. *Journal of Personality and Social Psychology*, **27**, 100–108.

——— & Berscheid, E. (1967). Increased liking as a result of the anticipation of personal contact. *Human Relations*, **20**, 29–40.

Darwin, C. (1982). *The origin of species by means of natural selection*. 1859. London: New edition from the 6th edition with additions and corrections. New York: Appleton.

Deaux, K. (1972). To err is humanizing: But sex makes a difference. *Representative Research in Social Psychology*, **3**, 20–28.

DeCasper, A., & Fifer, W. (1980). Newborns prefer their mothers' voices. *Science*, **208**, 1174–1176.

Deci, E. L. (1975). *Intrinsic motivation*. New York: Plenum.

De Fries, J. C, & Plomin, R. (1978). Behavioral genetics. In M. R. Rosenzweig and L. W. Porter (Eds.), *Annual Review of Psychology*, vol. 29. Palo Alto, Calif.: Annual Reviews.

Dembroski, T. M.; Lasater, T. M.; & Ramirez, A. (1978). Communicator similarity, fear arousing communications, and compliance with health care recommendations. *Journal of Applied Social Psychology*, **8**, 254–269.

——— & MacDougall, J. M. (1978). Stress effects on affiliation preferences among subjects possessing the type A coronary-prone pattern. *Journal of Personality and Social Psychology*, **36**, 23–33.

Dement, W. (1960). The effect of dream deprivation. *Science*, 1705–1707.

——— & Baird, W. P. (1977). *Narcolepsy: Care and treatment*. Stanford, Calif.: American Narcolepsy Association.

Dennis, W. (1960). Causes of retardation among institutional children: Iran. *Journal of Genetic Psychology*, **96**, 47–59.

Deutsch, M., & Collins, M. E. (1951). *Interracial housing: A psychological evaluation of a social experiment*. Minneapolis: University of Minnesota Press.

deVilliers, D. A., & deVilliers, J. (1979). *Early language*. Cambridge, Mass.: Harvard University Press.

Diagnostic and statistical manual of mental disorders (DSM I). (1952). Washington, D.C.: American Psychiatric Association.

Diagnostic and statistical manual of mental disorders (DSM II). (1968). Washington, D.C.: American Psychiatric Association.

Diagnostic and statistical manual of mental disorders (DSM III). (1980). Washington, D.C.: American Psychiatric Association.

Dickey, W. (1981). I have had my vision. *The Key Reporter*, **67**(1), 1–4.

Dickson, W. P. (1979). Referential communication performance from age 4 to 8: Effects of referent type, context, and target position. *Developmental Psychology*, **15**(4), 470–471.

Diener, E., & Wallbom, M. (1980). Effects of self-awareness on antinormative behavior. *Journal of Research in Personality*, **39**, 449–459.

Dion, K. K., & Berscheid, E. (1974). Physical attractiveness and peer perception among children. *Sociometry*, **37**, 1–12.

———; ———; & Walster, E. (1972). What is beautiful is good. *Journal of Personality and Social Psychology*, **24**, 285–290.

Dittmann-Kohli, F., & Baltes, P. B. (In press). Toward a neofunctionalist conception of adult intellectual development: Wisdom as a prototypical case of intellectual growth. In C. Alexander and E. Langer (Eds.), *Beyond formal operations: Alternative endpoints to human development*.

Dodd, D. M.; Kinsman, R.; Klipp, R.; & Bourne, L. E., Jr. (1971). Effects of logic pretraining on conceptual rule learning. *Journal of Experimental Psychology*, **88**, 119–122.

Doering, C. H.; Kraemer, H. C.; Brodie, H. K. H.; & Hamburg, D. A. (1975). A cycle of plasma testosterone in the human male. *Journal of Clinical Endocrinology and Metabolism*, **40**, 492–500.

Doherty, W. J., & Jacobson, N. S. (1982). Marriage and the family. In B. B. Wolman (Ed.), *Handbook of developmental psychology*. Englewood Cliffs, N.J.: Prentice-Hall.

Dominick, J. R., & Greenberg, B. S. (1971). Attitudes towards violence: The interaction of television exposure, family attitudes, and social class. In G. A. Comstock and E. A. Rubinstein (Eds.), *Television and social behavior*, vol. 3: *Television and adolescent aggressiveness*. Washington, D.C.: Government Printing Office.

Donnerstein, E. (1980). Aggressive pornography and violence towards women. *Journal of Personality and Social Psychology*, **39**, 269–277.

——— & Malamuth, N. Pornography: Its consequences on the observer. In L. B. Schlesinger & E. Revitch (Eds.), *Sexual dynamics of antisocial behavior* (1983), Charles C Thomas.

Doob, A. N., & Climie, R. J. (1972). Delay of measurement and the effect of film violence. *Journal of Experimental Social Psychology*, **8**, 136–142.

Drachman, D. A., & Arbit, J. (1966). Memory and the hippocampal complex. *Archives of Neurology*, **15**, 52–61.

Dreyer, P. H. (1982). Sexuality during adolescence. In B. B. Wolman (Ed.), *Handbook of developmental psychology*. Englewood Cliffs, N.J.: Prentice-Hall.

Driscoll, R.; Davis, K. E.; & Lipetz, M. E. (1972). Parental interference and romantic love: The Romeo and Juliet effect. *Journal of Personality and Social Psychology,* **24**(1), 1–10.

Duncan, C. P. (1949). The retroactive effect of electroshock on learning. *Journal of Comparative and Physiological Psychology,* **42**, 32–44.

Dunker, K. (1945). On problem-solving. *Psychological Monographs,* **58**(5), Whole No. 270.

Dusek, D., & Girdano, D. A. (1980). *Drugs: A factual account.* Reading, Mass.: Addison-Wesley.

Dutton, D. G., & Aron, A. P. (1974). Some evidence for heightened sexual attraction under conditions of high anxiety. *Journal of Personality and Social Psychology,* **30**, 510–517.

Dyer, E. (1963). Parenthood as crisis: A re-study. *Marriage and Family Living,* **25**, 196–201.

Ebbinghaus, H. (1913). *Memory: A contribution to experimental psychology.* (1885). H. A. Roger and C. E. Bussenius (Trans.). New York: Teachers College.

Ecker, N., & Weinstein, S., (1983). The relationship between attributions of sexual competency, physical appearance and narcissism. Paper presented at conference of Eastern Region, Society for Scientific Study of Sex, April 16, Philadelphia.

Eckerman, C. O., & Stein, M. R. (1982). The toddler's emerging interactive skills. In K. H. Rubin and H. S. Ross (Eds.), *Peer relationships and social skills in childhood.* New York: Springer-Verlag.

Eckert, E. D.; Heston, L. L., & Bouchard, T. J. (1981). MZ twins reared apart: Preliminary findings of psychiatric disturbances and traits. In *Twin research 3: Intelligence, personality and development.* New York: Liss.

Ehrhardt, A. A., & Money, J. (1967). Progestin induced hermaphroditism: I. Q. and psychosocial identity. *Journal of Sexual Research,* **3**, 83–100.

Eimas, P.; Siqueland, E.; Juscrzyk, P.; & Vigorito, J. (1971). Speech perception in infants. *Science,* **171**, 303–306.

Eisenson, J.; Auer, J. J.; & Irwin, J. V. (1963). *The psychology of communication.* New York: Appleton-Century-Crofts.

Ekman, P.; Levenson, R. W.; & Friesen, W. V. (1983). Autonomic nervous system activity distinguishes among emotions. *Science,* **221**, 1208–1210.

Elliott, J. M. (1964). Measuring creative abilities in public relations and advertising work. In C. W. Taylor (Ed.), *Widening horizons in creativity.* New York: Wiley.

Ellis, A. (1958). Rational psychotherapy. *Journal of General Psychology,* **59**, 35–49.

———. (1974). *Humanistic psychotherapy.* New York: McGraw-Hill.

Emmerick, H. (1978). The influence of parents and peers on choices made by adolescents. *Journal of Youth and Adolescence,* **7**(2), 175–180.

Endler, N., & Edwards, J. (1982). Stress and personality. In L. Goldberger and S. Breznitz (Eds.), *Handbook of stress: Theoretical and clinical issues.* New York: Free Press.

Ericson, A.; Kallen, B.; & Westerholm, P. (1979). Cigarette smoking as an etiological factor in cleft lip and palate. *American Journal of Obstetrics and Gynecology,* **135**, 348–351.

Erikson, E. (1950, 1963). *Childhood and society.* New York: Norton.

———. (1965). Youth: Fidelity and diversity. In E. Erikson (Ed.), *The challenge of youth.* New York: Anchor.

———. (1968). *Identity: Youth and crisis.* New York: Norton.

Erlenmeyer-Kimling, L.; Cornblatt, B.; & Fleiss, J. (1979). High-risk research in schizophrenia. *Psychiatric Annals,* **9**(1), 79–102.

Eron, L. D. (1980). Prescription for reduction of aggression. *American Psychologist,* **35**(3), 244–252.

———; Huesmann, L. R.; Lefkowitz, M. M.; & Walder, L. Q. (1972). Does television violence cause aggression? *American Psychologist,* **27**, 253–263.

Estes, E. H. (1969). Health experience in the elderly. In E. Busse and E. Pfeiffer (Eds.), *Behavior and adaptation in later life.* Boston: Little, Brown.

Esquirol, J. E. D. (1838). *Des maladies mentales considerees sous les rapports medical, hygienique, et medico-legal.* (2 volumes) Paris: Bailliere.

Evans, F. J., & Orne, M. T. (1971). The disappearing hypnotist: The use of simulation subjects to evaluate how subjects perceive experimental procedures. *International Journal of Clinical and Experimental Hypnosis,* **19**, 277–296.

Eysenck, H. J. (1952). The effects of psychotherapy. *Journal of Consulting Psychiatry,* **16**, 319–324.

———. (1965). The effects of psychotherapy. *International Journal of Psychiatry,* **1**, 97–142.

———. (1967). *The biological basis of personality.* Springfield, Ill.: Charles C Thomas.

———. (1969). *The effects of psychotherapy.* New York: Science House.

——— & Kamin, L. (1981). *The intelligence controversy.* New York: Wiley.

——— & Prell, D. B. (1951). The inheritance of neuroticism: An experimental study. *Journal of Mental Science,* **97**, 441–446.

Fagan, J. F. (1982). Infant memory. In T. M. Field, A. Huston, H. C. Quay, L. Troll, and G. Finley (Eds.), *Review of human development.* New York: Wiley.

——— & McGrath, S. K. (1981). Infant recognition memory and

later intelligence. *Intelligence,* **5,** 121–130.

Falbo, T. (1977). The only child: A review. *Journal of Individual Psychology,* **33**(1), 47–61.

———. (1978). Reasons for having an only child. *Journal of population,* **1,** 181–184.

———. (1982). Only children in America. In M. E. Lamb and B. Sutton-Smith (Eds.), *Sibling relationships: Their nature and significance across the lifespan.* Hillsdale, N.J.: Erlbaum.

Falloon, I. R.; Boyd, J. R.; McGill, C. W.; Razini, J.; Moss, H. B.; & Gilderman, A. M. (1982). Family management in the prevention of exacerbations of schizophrenia. *New England Journal of Medicine.* **306**(24), 1437–1440.

Family Service Association. (1981). Family stress tops list of problems. *Highlights,* **7**(6), 1, 7–8.

Fantz, R. L. (1956). A method for studying early visual development. *Perceptual and Motor Skills,* **6,** 13–15.

———. (1963). Pattern vision in newborn infants. *Science,* **140,** 296–297.

———. (1964). Visual experience in infants: Decreased attention to familiar patterns relative to novel ones. *Science,* **146,** 668–670.

———. (1965). Visual perception from birth as shown by pattern selectivity. In H. E. Whipple (Ed.), *New issues in infant development, Annals of the New York Academy of Science,* **118,** 793–814.

———; Fagan, J.; & Miranda, S. B. (1975). Early visual selectivity. In L. Cohen and P. Salapatek (Eds.), *Infant perception: From sensation to cognition: basic visual processes,* vol. 1. New York: Academic.

——— & Nevis, S. (1967). Pattern preferences and perceptual-cognitive development in early infancy. *Merrill-Palmer Quarterly,* **13,** 77–108.

Faranda, J. A.; Kaminski, J. A.; & Gixa, B. K. (1979). An assessment of attitudes toward women with the bogus pipeline. Paper pre-

sented at the annual convention of the American Psychological Association, New York, N.Y.

Farber, S. (1981). Telltale behavior of twins. *Psychology Today,* **15**(1), 60ff.

Federal Bureau of Investigation. (1982). *Uniform crime reports for the United States.* Washington, D.C.: U.S. Department of Justice.

Fehr, L. A. (1976). J. Piaget and S. Claus: Psychological bedfellows. *Psychological Reports,* **39,** 740–742.

Fenton, G. W. (1975). Clinical disorders of sleep. *British Journal of Hospital Medicine* (August), 120–144.

Feron, J. (1982). Hypnosis is on trial at Stouffer hearing. *The New York Times,* February 5, pp. B1–2.

Festinger, L. (1957). *A theory of cognitive dissonance.* Stanford, Calif.: Stanford University Press.

———. (1962). Cognitive dissonance. *Scientific American* (January), 93–102.

——— & Carlsmith, J. M. (1959). Cognitive consequences of forced compliance. *Journal of Abnormal and Social Psychology,* **58,** 203–210.

———; Schachter, S.; & Back, K. (1950). *Social pressures in informal groups: A study of human factors in housing.* New York: Harper and Brothers.

Fishbein, D., & Thelen, M. H. (1981). Psychological factors in mate selection and marital satisfaction: A review. *Catalog of Selected Documents in Psychology,* **11,** 84.

Fishbein, M., & Ajzen. I. (1974). Attitudes toward objects as predictive of single and multiple behavioral criteria. *Psychological Review,* **81,** 59–74.

Fisher, S., & Greenberg, R. P. (1977). *Scientific creditability of Freud's theories and therapy.* New York: Basic Books.

Fiske, E. B. (1981). Youth outwits merit exam, raising 240,000 scores. *The New York Times,* March 17, pp. A1, C4.

Flavell, J.; Beach, D.; & Chomsky, J. (1966). Spontaneous verbal

rehearsal in a memory task as a function of age. *Child Development,* **37,** 238–200.

Fleming, A. (1980). New frontiers in conception. *The New York Times Magazine,* July 20, p. 144.

Foley, V. D. (1979). Family therapy. In R. J. Corsini and contributers, *Current psychotherapies* (2d ed.). Itasca, Ill.: Peacock, pp. 460–499.

Forman, G., & Siegel, I. (1979). *Cognitive development: A life-span view.* Belmont, Calif.: Wadsworth.

Foulkes, W. D. (1964). Theories of dream and recent studies of sleep formation consciousness. *Psychological Bulletin,* **62,** 236–247.

Fouts, R. S. (1974). Language: Origin, definitions, and chimpanzees. *Journal of Human Evolution,* **3,** 475–482.

Frank, J. (1974). Psychotherapy: The restoration of morale. *American Journal of Psychiatry,* **131**(31), 271–274.

———. (1979). What is psychotherapy? In S. Bloch (Ed.), *An introduction to the psychotherapies.* New York: Oxford University Press.

Franken, R. E. (1982). *Human motivation.* Monterey, Calif.: Brooks/Cole.

Frankenhauser, M. (1980). Psychoneuroendocrine approaches to the study of stressful person-environment interaction. In H. Selye (Ed.), *Selye's Guide to Stress Research,* vol. 1, New York: Van Nostrand Reinhold.

Freedman, D. (1983). *Margaret Mead and Samoa.* Cambridge, Mass.: Harvard University Press.

Freedman, J. L., & Sears, D. O. (1965). Warning distraction, and resistance to influence. *Journal of Personality and Social Psychology,* **1,** 262–266.

———; Sears, D. O.; & Carlsmith, J. M. (1981). *Social Psychology* (4th ed.). Englewood Cliffs, N.J.: Prentice-Hall.

Freeman, L. (1951). *Fight against fear.* New York: Crown.

——— & Strean, H. S. (1981). *Freud and women.* New York: Ungar.

Freeman, S.; Walker, M. R.;

Borden, R.; Latane, B. (1975). Diffusion of responsibility and restaurant tipping: Cheaper by the bunch. *Personality and Social Psychology Bulletin,* **1,** 584–587.

Freud, S. (1949). Three essays on the theory of sexuality (1905). In *Standard Edition,* vol. 7. London: Hogarth.

———. (1950). The ego and the id (1932). In J. Strachey (Ed.), *The standard edition of the complete psychological works.* London: Hogarth.

———. (1955). *The interpretation of dreams* (1900). New York: Basic Books.

Friedman, M., & Rosenman, R. H. (1974). *Type A behavior and your heart.* New York: Knopf.

Friedman, M. I. & Stricker, E. M. (1976). The physiological psychology of hunger: A physiological perspective. *Psychological Review,* **83,** 409–431.

Friedman, T. L. (1981). University head killed in Beirut; gunmen escape. *The New York Times,* January 19, p. A1, A8.

Fromkin, V.; Krashen, S.; Curtiss, S.; Rigler, D.; & Rigler, M. (1974). The development of language in Genie: Acquisition beyond the "critical period". *Brain and Language,* **1,** 81–107.

Frueh, T., & McGhee, P. (1975). Traditional sex role development and amount of time spent watching television. *Developmental Psychology,* **11**(1), 109.

Fuchs, F. (1980). Genetic amniocentesis. *Scientific American,* **242**(6), 47–53.

Funder, D. C., & Ozer, D. J. (1983). Behavior as a function of the situation. *Journal of Personality and Social Psychology,* **44**(1), 107–112.

Gaito, J. A. (1974). A biochemical approach to learning and memory: Fourteen years later. In G. Newton and A. H. Riesen (Eds.), *Advances in psychobiology,* vol. 2. New York: Wiley.

Gallagher, C. E. (1965). Opening

Remarks. Testimony before House Special Subcommittee on Invasion of Privacy of the Committee on Government Operations. *The American Psychologist,* **20,** 955–988.

Galton, F. (1979). *Hereditary genius: An inquiry into laws and consequences* (1869). New York: St. Martin's Press.

———. (1883). *Inquiries into human faculty and development.* London: Macmillan.

Garai, J. E., & Scheinfeld, A. (1968). Sex differences in mental and behavioral traits. *Genetic Psychology Monographs,* **77,** 169–299.

Garcia, J. (1981). The logic and limits of mental aptitude testing. *American Psychologist,* **36**(10), 1172–1180.

——— & Koelling, R. A. (1966). Relation of cue to consequence in avoidance learning. *Psychometric Science,* **4,** 123–214.

Geboy, M. J. (1981). Who is listening to the "experts"? The use of child care materials by parents. *Family Relations,* **30,** 205–210.

Geen, R. G., & Quanty, M. B. (1977). The catharsis of aggression; An evaluation of a hypothesis. In L. Berkowitz (Ed.), *Advances in experimental social psychology,* vol. 10. New York: Academic Press.

Geldard, F. A. (1972). *The human senses.* New York: Wiley.

Geschwind, N. (1972). Language and the brain. *Scientific American,* **226,** 186.

Gesell, A. (1929). Maturation and infant behavior patterns. *Psychological Review,* **36,** 307–319.

——— & Armatruda, C. (1941). *Developmental diagnosis.* New York: Paul B. Hoeber.

Getzels, J. W., & Jackson, P. W. (1963). The highly intelligent and the highly creative adolescent: A summary of some research findings. In C. W. Taylor and F. Barron (Eds.), *Scientific creativity: Its recognition and development.* New York: Wiley.

Gewirtz, H. B., & Gewirtz, J. L. (1968). Caretaking settings, background events, and behavior differences in four Israeli child-rearing environments: Some preliminary trends. In B. M. Foss (Ed.), *Determinants of infant behavior,* vol. 4. London: Methuen.

Gibson, J. J. (1950). *The perception of the visual world.* Boston: Houghton Mifflin.

Gil, D. G., (1971). Violence against children. *Journal of Marriage and the family,* **33**(4), 637–48.

Gilligan, C. (1977). In a different voice: Women's conception of self and of morality. *Harvard Educational Review,* **47**(4), 481–517.

———. (1982). *In a different voice.* Cambridge, Mass.: Harvard University Press.

Ginzburg, E., et al. (1951). *Occupational choice: An approach to a general theory.* New York: Columbia University Press.

Gittleson, N. (1979). Maturing of Woody Allen. *The New York Times Magazine,* April 22, p. 104.

Glanzer, M., & Cunitz, A. R. (1966). Two storage mechanisms in free recall. *Journal of Verbal Learning and Verbal Behavior,* **5,** 351–360.

Glass, A. L.; Holyoak, K. J.; & Santa, J. L. (1979). *Cognition.* San Francisco: W. H. Freeman.

Glass, D. (1977). *Behavior patterns, stress, and coronary disease.* Hillsdale, N.J.: Erlbaum.

——— & Carver, C. S. (1980). Environmental stress and the Type A response. In A. Baum and J. E. Singer (Eds.), *Advances in environmental psychology,* vol. 2: *Applications of personal control.* Hillsdale, N.J.: Erlbaum.

———; Neulinger, J.; & Brim, O. (1974). Birth order, verbal intelligence and educational aspirations. *Child Development,* **45**(3), 807–811.

——— & Singer, J. E. (1972). *Urban stress: Experiments on noise and social stressors.* New York: Academic Press.

Goertzel, V., & Goertzel, M. G.

(1962). *Cradles of eminence*. Boston: Little, Brown.

Goffman, E. (1952). On cooling the mark out: Some aspects of adaptation to failure. *Psychiatry*, **15**, 451–463.

Golden, N. L.; Sokol, R. J.; Kuhnert, B. R.; & Bottoms, S. (1982). Maternal alcohol use and infant development. *Pediatrics*, **70**, 931–934.

Goldfried, M. R.; Stricker, G.; & Weiner, I. R. (1971). *Rorschach handbook of clinical and research applications*. Englewood Cliffs, N.J.: Prentice-Hall.

Goldman, R.; Jaffa, M.; & Schachter, S. (1968). Yom Kippur, Air France, dormitory food and eating behavior of obese and normal persons. *Journal of Personality and Social Psychology*, **10**, 117–123.

Goldstein, E. B. (1980). *Sensation and perception*. Belmont, Calif.: Wadsworth.

Goleman, D. (1980). 1528 little geniuses and how they grew. *Psychology Today*, **13**(9), 28–53.

———. (1981). Deadlines for change. *Psychology Today*, **15**(8), 60–69.

———. (1982). Staying up. *Psychology Today*, **16**(3), 24–35.

———. (1984). The aging mind proves capable of lifelong growth. *The New York Times*, February 21, pp. C1, C5.

Goodenough, D. (1967). Some recent studies of dream recall. In H. Witkin and H. Lewis (Eds.), *Experimental studies of dreaming*. New York: Random House.

Goodner, C. J., & Russell, J. A. (1965). Pancreas. In T. C. Ruch and H. D. Patton (Eds.), *Physiology and biophysics*. Philadelphia: Saunders.

Gordon, E., & Terrell, M. (1981). The changed social context of testing. *American Psychologist*, **36**(10), 1167–1171.

Gottesman, I. I. (1962). Differential inheritance of the psychoneuroses. *Eugenics Quarterly*, **9**, 223–227.

———. (1963). Heritability of personality. A demonstration. *Psychology Monographs*. **77**(9), Whole No. 572.

———. (1979). Schizophrenia and genetics: Toward understanding uncertainty. *Psychiatric Annals*, **9**(1), 54–78.

——— & Shields, J. (1966). Schizophrenia in twins: 16 years consecutive admission to a psychiatric clinic. *British Journal of Psychiatry*, 72 **112**, 809–818.

Gould, R. (1972). The phases of adult life: A study in developmental psychology. *American Journal of Psychiatry*, **129**(5), 521–531.

———. (1978). *Transformations*. New York: Simon and Schuster.

Gould, S. J. (1981). *The mismeasure of man*. New York: Norton.

Great, H. T.; Wicks, J. W.; & Neal, A. G. (1980). *Differential consequences of having been an only child versus a sibling child*. Final Report (no. NIH-NO1-HD 92806), Center for Population Research.

Greenberg, M., & Morris, N. (1974). Engrossment: The newborn's impact upon the father. *American Journal of Orthopsychiatry*, **44**(4), 520–531.

Greenberg, S. B., & Peck, L. (1974). personal communication.

Greenberger, E.; Steinberg, L.; Vaux, A.; & McAuliffe, S. (1980). Adolescents who work: Effects of part-time employment on family and peer relations. *Journal of Youth and Adolescence*, **9**(3), 189–202.

——— & ———. (1985). *Work in teenage America*. Cambridge, Mass.: Harvard University Press.

Griffitt, W. B. (1970). Environmental effects on interpersonal affective behavior: Ambient effective temperature and attraction. *Journal of Personality and Social Psychology*, **15**, 240–244.

——— & Veitch, R. (1971). Hot and crowded: Influence of population density and temperature on interpersonal affective behavior.

Journal of Personality and Social Psychology, **17**, 92–98.

Grinspoon, L., & Bakalar, J. B. (1979). *Psychedelic drugs reconsidered*. New York: Basic Books.

Grotevant, H., & Durrett, M. (1980). Occupational knowledge and career development in adolescence. *Journal of Vocational Behavior*, **17**, 171–182.

Group for the Advancement of Psychiatry. (1973). *The joys and sorrows of parenthood*. New York: Scribner's.

Guilford, J. P. (1959). Three faces of intellect. *American Psychologist*, **14**, 469–479.

———. (1966). Intelligence; 1965 model. *American Psychologist*, **21**, 20–26.

———. (1967). *The nature of human intelligence*. New York: McGraw-Hill.

———. (1982). Cognitive psychology's ambiguities: Some suggested remedies. *Psychological Review*, **89**(1), 48–59.

Guilleminault, E.; Eldridge, F.; & Simmons, B. (1976). Sleep apnea in eight children. *Pediatrics*, **58**, 23–30.

Gummerman, K., & Gray, C. R. (1971). Recall of visually presented material: An unwonted case and a bibliography for eidetic imagery. *Psychonomic Monograph Supplements*, **4**(10).

Gurman, A. S., & Razin, M. (1977). *Effective psychotherapy: A handbook of research*. New York: Pergamon.

Gullotta, T., & Donohue, K. (1981). Corporate families: Implications for preventive intervention. *Social Casework*, **62**, 109–114.

Guttmacher Institute. (1981). *Teenage pregnancy: The problem that hasn't gone away*. New York: Alan Guttmacher Institute.

Gwirtsman, H. E., & Gerner, R. H. (1981). Neurochemical abnormalities in anorexia nervosa: Similarities to affective disorders. *Biological Psychiatry*, **16**, 991–995.

Gynther, M. D. (1972). White norms and black MMPIs: A prescription for discrimination? *Psychological Bulletin,* **5,** 386–403.

Haan, N., & Day, D. (1974). A longitudinal study of change and sameness in personality development: Adolescence to later adulthood. *International Journal of Aging and Human Development,* **5**(1), 11–39.

Haber, R. N. (1980). Eidetic images are not just imaginary. *Psychology Today,* **14**(6), 72–82.

Hall, C. S. (1966). *The meaning of dreams.* New York: McGraw-Hill.

——— & Lindzey, G. (1978). *Theories of personality* (3d ed.). New York: Wiley.

Hall, E. (1983). A conversation with Erik Erikson. *Psychology Today,* **17**(6), 22–30.

Hall, G. S. (1916). *Adolescence.* New York: Appleton.

Hall, J. A. (1978). Gender effects in decoding nonverbal cues. *Psychological Bulletin,* **85,** 845–857.

Hamburg, D. (1983). The evolutionary background of human behavior. Lecture given at the American Museum of Natural History, New York City, January 19.

Hamilton, S., & Crouter, A. (1980). Work and growth: A review of research on the impact of work experience on adolescent development. *Journal of Youth and Adolescence,* **9**(4), 323–338.

Hammond, C. B., Jelovsek, F. R., Lee, K. L., Creasman, W. T., & Parker, R. T. (1979). "Effects of long-term estrogen replacement therapy. II: Neoplasia," *American Journal of Obstetrics and Gynecology,* vol. 133, pp. 537–547.

Harlow, H. (1958). The nature of love. *American Psychologist,* **13,** 673–685.

——— & Harlow, M. K. (1962). The effect of rearing conditions on behavior. *Bulletin of the Menninger Clinic,* **26,** 213–224.

——— & Zimmerman, R. R. (1959). Affectional responses in the infant monkey. *Science,* **130,** 421–432.

Harmon, R.; Suwalsky, J.; & Klein, R. (1979). Infant's preferential response for mother versus unfamiliar adult. *Journal of the Academy of Child Psychiatry,* **18**(3), 437–449.

Harrell, R. F.; Woodyard, E.; & Gates, A. (1955). *The effect of mothers' diets on the intelligence of the offspring.* New York: Bureau of Publications, Teacher's College.

Harris, B. (1979). Whatever happened to little Albert? *American Psychologist,* **34**(2), 151–160.

Harris, J. E. (1978). External memory aids. In M. M. Gruneberg, P. E. Morris, and R. N. Sykes (Eds.), *Practical aspects of memory.* London: Academic Press. [Reprinted in U. Neisser (Ed.), *Memory observed.* San Francisco: W. H. Freeman, 1982.]

Harris, T. G. (1978). "Introduction" to Walster, E., & Walster, G. W., *A new look at love.* Reading, Mass.: Addison-Wesley, pp. x–xi.

Harrison, M. R.; Golbus, M. S.; Filly, R. A.; Nakayama, D. K.; & Delorimier, A. A. (1982). Fetal surgical treatment. *Pediatric Annals,* **11**(11), 896–903.

Hartmann, E. (1981). The strangest sleep disorder. *Psychology Today,* **15**(4), 14–18.

———; Baekeland, F.; & Zwilling, G. R. (1972). Psychological differences between long and short sleepers. *Archives of General Psychiatry,* **26,** 463–468.

——— & Brewer, V. (1976). When is more or less sleep required? A study of variable sleepers. *Comprehensive Psychiatry,* **17**(2), 275–284.

Hartshorne, H., & May, M. A. (1929). *Studies in the nature of character,* vol. 2: *Studies in service and self-control.* New York: Macmillan.

Hashim, S. A., & Van Itallie, T. B. (1965). Studies in normal and obese subjects with a monitored food dispensory device. *Annals of the New York Academy of Science* (vol. 131), 654–661.

Hassett, J., & the editors of *Psychology Today,* (1981). Is it right? An inquiry into everyday ethics. *Psychology Today,* **15**(6), 49–53.

Hawke, S., & Knox, D. (1978). The one-child family: A new lifestyle. *The Family Coordinator,* **27**(3), 215–219.

Hay, D. F.; Pedersen, J.; & Nash, A. (1982). Dyadic interaction in the first year of life. In K. H. Rubin and H. S. Ross (Eds.), *Peer relations and social skills in childhood.* New York: Springer-Verlag.

Hayden, A., & Haring, N. (1976). Early intervention for high risk infants and young children. Programs for Down's syndrome children. In T. D. Tjossem (Ed.), *Intervention strategies for high risk infants and young children.* Baltimore: University Park Press.

Hayes, C. (1951). *The ape in our house.* New York: Harper & Row.

Hayes, J. R. (1978). *Cognitive psychology: Thinking and creating.* Homewood, Ill.: Dorsey.

Hayflick, L. (1974). The strategy of senescence. *The Gerontologist,* **14**(1), 37–45.

Haynes, H.; White, B.; & Held, R. (1965). Visual accommodation in human infants. *Science,* **148,** 528–530.

Hearnshaw, L. S. (1979). *Cyril Burt: Psychologist.* Ithaca, N.Y.: Cornell University Press.

Hearst, E. (1979). One hundred years: Themes and perspectives. In E. Hearst (Ed.), *The first century of experimental psychology.* Hillsdale, N.J.: Erlbaum.

Hebb, D. O. (1955). Drive and the C.N.S. (central nervous system). *Psychological Review,* **62,** 243–254.

———. (1978). On watching myself get old. *Psychology Today,* **12**(6), 15–23.

Heider, F. (1958). *The psychology of interpersonal relations.* New York: Wiley.

Heider, E. R., & Olivier, D. C. (1972). The structure of the color space in naming and memory in two languages. *Cognitive Psychology*, **3**, 337–354.

Helmholtz, V. (1911). *Physiological optics*, vol. 2 (3d ed.). Rochester: Optical Society of America.

Helmreich, R. (1968). Birth order effects. *Naval Research Reviews*, **21.**

Henig, R. M. (1979). Ageism's angry critic. *Human Behavior*, **8**(1), 43–46.

Henker, F. O. (1981). Male climacteric. In J. G. Howells (Ed.), *Modern perspectives in the psychiatry of middle age.* New York: Brunner/Mazel.

Herbert, W. (1982). Schizophrenia: From adolescent insanity to dopamine disease. *Science News*, **121**(11), 173–175.

Herbst, A. L.; Ulfelder, H.; & Poskanzer, D. (1971). Adenocarcinoma of the vagina. *New England Journal of Medicine*, **284**(16), 878–881.

Hering, E. (1920). *Grundzuge der Lehr vs. Lichtsinn.* Berlin: Springer-Verlag.

Herr, J., & Weakland, J. (1979). Communication within family systems: Growing older within and with the double-bind. In P. K. Regan (Ed.), *Aging parents.* Los Angeles: University of Southern California Press.

Heston, L. L. (1966). Psychiatric disorders in foster-home-reared children of schizophrenic mothers. *British Journal of Psychiatry.* **112**, 819–825.

Hetherington, E. M. (1965). A developmental study of the effects of sex of the dominant parent on sex role preference, identification and imitation in children. *Journal of Personality and Social Psychology*, **2**, 188–194.

Hetherington, M.; Cox, M.; & Cox, R. (1975). Beyond father absence: Conceptualizing of effects of divorce. Paper presented at the biennial meeting of the Society for Research in Child Development, Denver.

Hier, D. B., & Crowley, W. F. (1982). Spatial ability in andro-

gen-deficient men. *New England Journal of Medicine*, **20**, 1202–1205.

Hilgard, E. R. (1977). The problem of divided consciousness: A neo-dissociation interpretation. In W. E. Edmonston, Jr. (Ed.), *Conceptual and investigative approaches to hypnosis and hypnotic phenomena.* New York: New York Academy of Sciences.

———. (1977). Hypnotic phenomena: The struggle for scientific acceptability. In I. Janis (Ed.), *Current trends in psychology.* Los Altos: William Kaufmann.

Hilgard, J. R. (1979). *Personality and hypnosis* (2d ed.). Chicago: University of Chicago Press.

Hill, C. T.; Rubin, Z.; & Peplau, L. A. (1976). Breakups before marriage: The end of 103 affairs. *Journal of Social Issues*, **32**(1), 147–168.

Hill, R. (1949). *Families under stress.* New York: Harper and Row.

Hingson R.; Albert, J. J.; Day, N.; Dooling, E.; Kayne, H.; Morelock, S.; Oppenheimer, E.; & Zuckerman, B. (1982). Effects of maternal drinking and marijuana use on fetal growth and development. *Pediatrics*, **70**(4), 539–546.

Hines, M. (1982). Prenatal gonadal hormones and sex differences in human behavior. *Psychological Bulletin*, **92**(1), 56–80.

Hobbs, D., & Cole, S. (1976). Transition to parenthood: A decade replication. *Journal of Marriage and the Family*, **38**(4), 723–731.

——— & Wimbish, J. (1977). Transition to parenthood by black couples. *Journal of Marriage and the Family*, **39**(4), 677–689.

Hobson, J. A., & McCarley, R. W. (1977). The brain as a dream state generator: An activation-synthesis hypothesis of the dream process. *The American Journal of Psychiatry*, **134**(12), 1335–1348.

Hochberg, J. E. (1964). *Perception.* Englewood Cliffs, N.J.: Prentice-Hall.

Hoffman, H. J., & Solomon, R. L. (1974). An opponent-process the-

ory of motivation III: Some affective dynamics in imprinting. *Learning and Motivation*, **5**, 149–164.

Hoffman, M. (1977). Sex differences in empathy and related behaviors. *Psychological Bulletin*, **84**, 712–722.

Hogan, R., & Schroeder, D., (1981). Seven biases in psychology. *Psychology Today*, **15**(7), 8–14.

Holahan, C. K., & Stephan, C. W. (1981). When beauty isn't talent: The influence of physical attractiveness, attitudes toward women, and competence on impression formation. *Sex Roles*, **7**(8), 867–876.

Holmes, L. (1978). How fathers can cause the Down's syndrome. *Human Nature*, **1**, 70–72.

Holmes, T. H., & Rahe, R. H. (1976). The social readjustment rating scale. *Journal of Psychosomatic Medicine*, **11**, 213.

Holroyd, K. A., & Lazarus, R. S. (1982). Stress, coping, and somatic adaptation. In L. Goldberger and S. Breznitz (Eds.), *Handbook of stress.* New York: Free Press.

Homans, G. C. (1961). *Social behavior: Its elementary forms.* New York: Harcourt.

Horel, J. A. (1978). The neuroanatomy of amnesia: A critique of the hippocampal memory hypothesis. *Brain*, **101**, 403–445.

Horn, J. L. (1968). Organization of abilities and the development of intelligence. *Psychological Review*, **75**, 242–259.

———. (1967). Intelligence—Why it grows, why it declines. *Transaction*, **5**(1), 23–31.

Horn, J. M.; Loehlin, J. C.; & Willerman, L. (1979). Intellectual resemblance among adoptive and biological relatives: The Texas Adoption Project. *Behavior Genetics*, **9**, 177–207.

Horner, M. S. (1969). Woman's will to fail. *Psychology Today*, **11**, 36–38, 62.

Horney, K. (1939). *New ways in psychoanalysis.* New York: Norton.

————. (1945). *Our inner conflicts.* New York: Norton.

Hoyer, W. F.; Hoyer, W. J.; Treat, N. J., & Baltes, P. B. (1978–1979). Training response speed in young and elderly women. *International Journal of Aging and Human Development, 9,* 247–253.

Hovland, C. I.; Lumsdaine, A. A.; & Sheffield, F. D. (1949). *Experiments on mass communication. Studies in social psychology in World War II,* vol. 3. Princeton, N.J.: Princeton University Press.

Hoyenga, K. B., & Hoyenga, K. T. (1979). *The question of sex differences.* Boston: Little, Brown.

Huesmann, L. R.; Eron, L. D.; Klein, R.; Brice, P.; & Fischer, (In press). Mitigating the imitation of aggressive behaviors by changing children's attitudes about media violence. *Journal of Personality and Social Psychology.*

Hull, C. (1952), *A behavior system.* New Haven, Conn.: Yale University Press.

Hull, C. L. (1943). *Principles of Behavior.* N.Y.: Appleton-Century-Crofts.

Hulse, S. H.; Egeth, H.; & Deese, J. (1980). *The psychology of learning.* New York: McGraw-Hill.

Hunt, D. (1970). *Parents and children in history: The psychology of family life in early modern France.* New York: Basic Books.

Hunt, E., & Love, T. (1982). The second mnemonist. A paper presented to the American Psychological Association in Honolulu, September, 1972. In U. Neisser (Ed.), *Memory observed.* San Francisco: W. H. Freeman.

Hunt, M. M. (1974). *Sexual behavior in the 1970's.* New York: Dell.

————. (1982). *The universe within: A new science explores the human mind.* New York: Simon and Schuster.

Hurvich, L. M. (1981). *Color vision.* Sunderland, Mass.: Sinauer Associates.

Huston, T. L., & Levinger, G. (1978). Interpersonal attraction and relationships. In P. Mussen

and M. Rosenzweig (Eds.), *Annual review of psychology.* Palo Alto, Calif.: Annual Reviews.

Hyden, H., & Lange, P. W. (1970). Brain cell protein synthesis specifically related to learning. *Proceedings of the National Academy of Sciences, 65,* 898–904.

Hyman, H. H., & Sheatsley, P. B. (1956). Attitudes toward desegregation. *Scientific American,* **195** (6), 35–39.

Ilfield, F. W. (1977). Sex differences in psychiatric symptomology. Paper presented at the annual meeting of the American Psychological Association, San Francisco, August.

————. (1978). Psychologic status of community residents along major demographic dimensions. *Archives of General Psychiatry,* **35,** 716–724.

Inouye, E. (1965). Similar and dissimilar manifestations of obsessive-compulsive neuroses in monozygotic twins. *American Journal of Psychology,* **121,** 1171–1175.

Isenberg, P., & Schatzberg, A. F. (1978). Psychoanalytic contribution to a theory of depression. In J. O. Cole, A. F. Schatzberg, and S. H. Frazier. (Eds.), *Depression: biology, psychodynamics, and treatment.* New York: Plenum.

Iverson, L. L. (1979). The chemistry of the brain. *Scientific American,* **242**(3), 134–147.

Izard, C. E. (1971). *The face of emotions.* New York: Appleton-Century-Crofts.

————. (1977). *Human emotions.* New York: Plenum.

————; Huebner, R. R.; Resser, D.; McGinnes, G. C.; & Dougherty, L. M. (1980). The young infant's ability to produce discrete emotional expressions. *Developmental Psychology,* **16**(2), 132–140.

Jacobsen, H. (1977). Current concepts in nutrition: Diet in pregnancy. *New England Journal of Medicine,* **297**(19), 1051–1053.

James, W. (1884). What is an emotion? *Mind,* **9,** 188–205.

————. (1890). *The principles of psychology.* New York: Holt.

Janis, I. L. (1971). Groupthink. *Psychology Today,* **5,** 43ff.

————. (1982). Counteracting the adverse effects of concurrence-seeking in policy planning groups: Theory and research perspectives. In I. H. Brandstatter, J. H. Davis, and G. Stocker-Kreichgauer (Eds.), *Group decision making.* New York: Academic Press.

————; Kaye, D.; & Kirschner, P. (1965). Facilitating effects of eating while reading on responsiveness to persuasive communication. *Journal of Personality and Social Psychology,* **1,** 181–186.

———— & Mann, L. (1965). Effectiveness of emotional role-playing in modifying smoking habits and attitudes. *Journal of Experimental Research in Personality,* **1,** 84–90.

Jarvik, L.; Kallman, F.; & Klaber, N. (1957). Changing intellectual functions in senescent twins. *Acta Genetica Statistica Medica,* **7,** 421–430.

Jensen, A. R. (1969). How much can we boost IQ and scholastic achievement? *Harvard Educational Review,* **39,** 1–123.

Johnson, J. (1983). Personal communication to authors.

Johnson, R. N. (1972). *Aggression in man and animals.* Philadelphia: Saunders.

Jones, E. (1977). How do people perceive the causes of behavior? In I. Janis (Ed.), *Current Trends in Psychology.* Los Altos, Calif.: William Kaufmann.

———— & Harris, V. A. (1967). The attribution of attitudes. *Journal of Experimental Social Psychology,* **3,** 2–24.

———— & Sigall, H. (1971). The bogus pipeline: A new paradigm for measuring affect and attitude. *Psychological Bulletin,* **76,** 349–364.

Jones, H. E. (1930). The retention of conditioned emotional reactions in infancy. *Journal of Genetic Psychology, 37,* 485–497.

Jones, K. L.; Smith, D. W.; Ulleland, C.; & Streissguth, A. P. (1973). Patterns of malformation in offspring of chronic alcoholic mothers. *Lancet,* 1(7815), 1267–1271.

Jones, M. C. (1924). A laboratory study of fear: The case of Peter. *Pedagogical Seminary, 31,* 308–315.

———. (1957). The late careers of boys who were early or late maturing. *Child Development,* 28, 113–128.

——— & Mussen, P. H. (1958). Self-conceptions, motivations, and interpersonal attitudes of early and late maturing girls. *Child Development, 29,* 491–501.

Jost, H., & Sontag, L. (1944). The genetic factor in autonomic nervous system function. *Psychosomatic Medicine, 6,* 308–310.

Jung, C. G. (1933). *Modern man in search of a soul.* New York: Harcourt, Brace, and World.

———. (1953). The stages of life. In H. Read, M. Fordham, and G. Adler (Eds.), *Collected works,* vol. 2. Princeton: Princeton University Press. (Originally published in 1931.)

Kacerguis, M., & Adams, G. (1980). Erikson stage resolution: The relationship between identity and intimacy. *Journal of Youth and Adolescence,* 9(2), 117–126.

Kagan, J. (1958). The concept of identification. *Psychological Review,* 65(5), 296–305.

———. (1971). *Personality development.* New York: Harcourt Brace Jovanovich.

———. (1982). Canalization of early psychological development. *Pediatrics,* 70(3), 474–483.

———. (1982). The ideas of spatial ability. *New England Journal of Medicine,* 306(20), 1225–1226.

Kahle, L. R. (1983). *Attitudes , attributes, and adaptation.* London: Pergamon.

——— & Berman, J. (1979). Atti-

tudes cause behaviors: A cross-lagged panel analysis. *Journal of Personality and Social Psychology.* 37, 315–321.

Kamin, L. J. (1974). *The science and politics of IQ.* Potomac, Md.: Erlbaum.

Kamiya, J. (1969). Operant control of the EEG alpha rhythm and some of its reported effects on consciousness. In C. Tart (Ed.), *Altered states of consciousness.* New York: Wiley.

Kandel, E. R. (1976). *The cellular basis of behavior.* San Francisco: W. H. Freeman.

Kanellakos, D. P. (1978). Transcendental consciousness: Expanded awareness as a means of preventing and eliminating the effects of stress. In C. D. Spielberger and I. G. Sarason (Eds.), *Stress and anxiety,* vol. 5. New York: Wiley.

Kaplan, H. S. (1979). *Disorders of sexual desire.* New York: Simon and Schuster.

Kaufman, L., & Rock, I. (1962). The moon illusion I, *Science,* 136, 953–961.

Keesey, R. E., & Powley, T. L. (1975). Hypothalamic regulation of body weight. *American Scientist,* 63, 558–565.

Kelley, H. H. (1950). The warm-cold variable in first impressions of persons. *Journal of Personality,* 18, 431–439.

———. (1973). The process of causal attribution. *American Psychologist,* 28, 107–128.

Kellogg, W. N., & Kellogg, L. A. (1933). *The ape and the child.* New York: McGraw-Hill.

Kelly, J. B. (1982). Divorce: The adult perspective. In B. Wolman (Ed.), *Handbook of developmental psychology.* Englewood Cliffs, N.J.: Prentice-Hall.

Kelman, H. C., & Hovland, C. (1953). "Reinstatement" of the communicator in delayed measurement of opinion change. *Journal of Abnormal and Social Psychology,* 48, 326–335.

Kenny, D. A., & Nasby, W. (1980).

Splitting the reciprocity correlation. *Journal of Personality and Social Psychology,* 38, 249–256.

Kermis, M.; Monge, R.; & Dusek, J. (1975). *Human sexuality in the hierarchy of adolescent interests.* Paper presented at the annual meeting of the Society for Research in Child Development, Denver.

Kerr, P. (1982). They help people looking for self-help. *The New York Times,* July 10, p. 46.

Kety, S. S.; Rosenthal, D.; Wender, P. H.; & Schulsinger, F. (1968). The types and prevalence of mental illness in the biological and adoptive families of adopted schizophrenics. In D. Rosenthal, and S. S. Kety (Eds.), *Transmission of schizophrenia.* London: Pergamon.

Kidwell, J. S. (1981). Number of siblings, sibling spacing, sex, and birth order: Their effects on perceived parent-adolescent relationships. *Journal of Marriage and the Family* (May), 315–332.

———. (1982). The neglected birth order: Middleborns. *Journal of Marriage and the Family,* 44 (1), 225–235.

Kiesler, C. A. (1982). Mental hospitals and alternative care: Noninstitutionalization as potential public policy for mental patients. *American Psycholgist,* 37(4), 349–360.

Kihlstrom, J. F., & Evans, F. J. (1979). *Functional disorders of memory.* Hillsdale, N.J.: Erlbaum.

——— & Harakiewicz, J. M. (1982). The earliest recollection: A new survey. *Journal of Personality,* 50(2), 134–148.

Kimmel, D. C. (1974). *Adulthood and aging.* New York: Wiley.

Kingdom, J. W. (1967). Politicians' belief about voters. *The American Science Review,* 61, 137–145.

Kinsey, A. C.; Pomeroy, W.; & Martin, C. E. (1948). *Sexual behavior in the human male.* Philadelphia: Saunders.

———; ———; ———; & Gebhard, P. H. (1953). *Sexual behavior*

in the human female. Philadelphia: Saunders.

Klaas, E. T. (1978). Psychological effects of immoral actions: The experimental evidence. *Psychological Bulletin*, **85**, 756–771.

Klatzky, R. L. (1980). *Human memory* (2d ed.). San Francisco: W. H. Freeman.

Klaus, M. H., & Kennell, J. H. (1976). *Maternal-infant bonding*. St. Louis: Mosby.

———— & ————. (1982). *Parent-infant bonding*. St. Louis: Mosby.

Kleck, R. E.; Richardson, S. A.; & Ronald, L. (1974). Physical appearance cues and interpersonal attraction in children. *Child Development*, **45**, 359–372.

Klein, R. F.; Bogdonoff, M. D.; Estes, E. H., Jr.; & Shaw, D. M. (1960). Analysis of the factors affecting the resting FAA level in normal man. *Circulation*, **20**, 772.

Kleinginna, P. R., Jr., & Kleinginna, A. M. (1981). A categorized list of emotion definitions, with suggestions for a consensual definition. *Motivation and Emotion*, **5**, 345–379.

Kleitman, N. (1960). Patterns of dreaming. *Scientific American*, **203**, 81–88.

Klerman, G. (1978). Combining drugs and psychotherapy in the treatment of depression. In J. O. Cole, A. F. Schatzberg, and S. H. Frazier (Eds.), *Depression: biology, psychodynamics, and treatment*. New York: Plenum.

Kobasa, S. C. (1982). The hardy personality: Toward a social psychology of stress and health. In J. Suls and G. Sanders (Eds.), *Social psychology of health and illness*. Hillsdale, N.J.: Erlbaum.

————. (1982). Committment and coping in stress resistance among lawyers. *Journal of Personality and Social Psychology*, **42**(4), 707–717.

Kohlberg, L. (1964). The development of moral character and moral ideology. In M. Hoffman and L. Hoffman (Eds.), *Review of child development research*, vol. 1.

New York: Russell Sage Foundation.

————. (1966). A cognitive-developmental analysis of children's sex-role concepts and attitudes. In E. E. Maccoby (Ed.), *The development of sex differences*, Stanford, Calif.: Stanford University Press.

————. (1968). The child as a moral philosopher. *Psychology Today*, **2**(4), 25–30.

———— & Gilligan, C. (1971). The adolescent as a philosopher: The discovery of the self in a postconventional world. *Daedalus* (fall), 1057–1086.

Kohler, W. (1927). *The mentality of apes*. New York: Harcourt, Brace and World.

Kolata, G. (1980). Prenatal diagnosis of neural tube defects. *Science*, **209**(12), 1216–1218.

————. (1981). Clues to the cause of senile dementia. *Science*, **211**(6), 1032–1033.

————. (1981). Clinical trial of psychotherapies is under way. *Science*, **212**, 432–433.

————. (1983). First trimester pregnancy diagnosis. *Science* (September 9), **22**, 1031–1032.

Kolb, B., & Whishaw, I. (1980). *Fundamentals of Neuropsychology*. San Francisco: W. H. Freeman.

Koulack, D. (1970). Repression and forgetting of dreams. In M. Bertini (Ed.), *Psicofisiologia del sonno e del sogno: Proceedings of an International Symposium*, Rome, 1967. Milan: Editrice vita e pensier.

———— & Goodenough, D. (1976). Dream recall and dream recall failure: An arousal-retrieval model. *Psychological Bulletin*, **83**, 975–984.

Kreugar, D. W. (In press). *Success phobia in women*. New York: Free Press.

Krueger, J. M.; Pappenheimer, J. R.; & Karnovsky, M. L. (1982). The composition of sleep-promoting factor isolated from humans. *The Journal of Biological Chemistry*, **257**(4), 1664–1669.

Kreutler, P. A. (1980). *Nutrition in*

perspective. Englewood Cliffs, N.J.: Prentice-Hall.

Kreutzer, M., & Charlesworth, W. R. (1973). Infant recognition of emotions. Paper presented at the biennial meeting of the Society for Research in Child Development, Philadelphia.

Kreuz, L. E., & Rose, R. M. (1972). Assessment of aggressive behavior and plasma testosterone in a young criminal population. *Psychosomatic Medicine*. **34**, 312–332.

Kübler-Ross, E. (1969). *On death and dying*. New York: Macmillan.

Labbe, R.; Firl, A.; Mufson, E. J.; & Stein, D. G. (1983). Fetal brain transplants: Reduction of cognitive deficits in rats with frontal cortex lesions. *Science*, **219**, 470–472.

La Gaipa, J. J. (1977). Testing a multidimensional approach to friendship. In S. W. Duck (Ed.), *Theory and practice in interpersonal attraction*. London: Academic, pp. 249–270.

Laing, R. D. (1964). Is schizophrenia a disease? *International Journal of Social Psychiatry*, **10**, 184–193.

————. (1967). *The politics of experience*. New York: Ballantine.

Lamb, M. (1979). Paternal influences and the father's role: A personal perspective. *American Psychologist*, **34**(10), 938–943.

————. (1982). The bonding phenomenon: Misinterpretations and their implications. *The Journal of Pediatrics*, **101**(4), 555–557.

————. (1982). Early contact and maternal-infant bonding: One decade later. *Pediatrics*, **70**(5), 763–768.

Lancet. (1982). Long-term outlook for children with sex chromosome abnormalities. *The Lancet* (July 3), 27.

Landesman-Dwyer, S., & Emanuel, I. (1979). Smoking during pregnancy. *Teratology*, **19**, 119–126.

Lange, C. (1922). *The emotions*. Baltimore: Williams and Wilkins. (Originally published 1885.)

Langer, E., & Rodin, J. (1976). The effects of choice and enhanced personal responsibility in an institutional setting. *Journal of Personality and Social Psychology*, **34**(2), 191–198.

Lashley, K. (1950). In search of the engram. *Symposia of the Society of Experimental Biology*, **4**, 454–482.

Lassen, N. A.; Ingevar, D. H., & Skinhoj, E. (1978). Brain function and blood flow. *Scientific American*, **239**, 62–71.

Latané, B., & Darley, J. M. (1968). Group inhibition of bystander intervention in emergencies. *Journal of Personality and Social Psychology*, **10**(3), 215–221.

―――― & Nida, S. (1981). Ten years of research on group size and helping. *Psychological Bulletin*, **89**(2), 308–324.

Lazarus, A. (1977). Has behavior therapy outlived its usefulness? *American Psychologist*, **32**(7), 550–554.

Lazarus, R. S. (1980). The stress and coping paradigm. In L. Bond and J. Rosen (Eds.), *Competence and coping during adulthood*. Hanover, N.H.: University Press of New England, pp. 28–74.

―――― & Launier, R. (1978). Stress-related transactions between person and environment. In L. A. Pervin and M. Lewis (Eds.), *Perspectives in interaction psychology*. New York: Plenum.

――――. (1981). Little hassles can be hazardous to health. *Psychology Today*, **15**(7), 58–62.

Leahey, T. H. (1980). *A history of psychology*. Englewood Cliffs, N.J.: Prentice-Hall.

Leboyer, F. (1975). *Birth without violence*. New York: Random House.

Lefcourt, H.; Miller, R.; Ware, E.; & Sherk, D. (1981). Locus of control as a modifier of the relationship between stressors and moods. *Journal of Personality and Social Psychology*, **41**(2), 357–369.

Leib, S.; Benfield, G.; & Guidubaldi, J. (1980). Effects of early intervention and stimula-tion on the preterm infant. *Pediatrics*, **66**, 83–90.

LeMasters, E. E. (1957). Parenthood as crisis. *Marriage and Family Living*, **19**, 352–355.

Lemon, B.; Bengston, V.; & Peterson, J. (1972). An exploration of the activity theory of aging: Activity types and life satisfaction among in-movers to a retirement community. *Journal of Gerontology*, **27**(4), 511–523.

Lenneberg, E. (1969). On explaining language. *Science*, **164**(3880), 635–643.

Leon, G. R.; Butcher, J. N.; Kleinman, M.; Goldberg, A.; & Almagor, M. (1981). Survivors of the holocaust and their children: Current status and adjustment. *Journal of Personality and Social Psychology*, **41**(3), 503–516.

Leonard, R. L. (1975). Self-concept and attraction for similar and dissimilar others. *Journal of Personality and Social Psychology*, **31**, 926–929.

Lerner, R., & Lerner, J. (1977). Effects of age, sex and physical attractiveness on child-peer relations, academic performance, and elementary school adjustment. *Developmental Psychology*, **13**(6), 585–590.

Lester, B. (1975). Cardiac habituation of the orienting response to an auditory signal in infants of varying nutritional status. *Developmental Psychology*, **11**(4), 432–442.

Lester, R., & Van Thiel, D. H. (1977). Gonadal function in chronic alcoholic men. *Advances in Experimental Medicine and Biology*, **85A**, 339–414.

Leventhal, H. (1970). Findings and theory in the study of fear communications. In L. Berkowitz and E. Walster (Eds.), *Advances in experimental social psychology*. New York: Academic Press.

Levine, M. W., & Shefner, J. (1981). *Fundamentals of sensation and perception*. Reading, Mass.: Addison Wesley.

Levinger, G. (1974). A three-level approach to attraction: Toward an understanding of pair relatedness. In T. L. Huston (Ed.), *Foundation of interpersonal attraction*. New York: Academic Press.

Levinson, D., with C. Darrow, E. Klein, M. Levinson, & B. McKee. (1978). *The seasons of a man's life*. New York: Knopf.

Levy, J.; Trevarthen, C.; & Sperry, R. (1972). Perception of bilateral chimeric figures following hemispheric disconnection. *Brain*, **95**, 61–78.

Lewin, K. (1938). *The conceptual representation and the measurement of psychological forces*. Durham, N.C.: Duke University Press.

――――. (1948). *Resolving social conflicts*. New York: Harper.

Lewis, C., & Lewis, M. (1977). The potential impact of sexual equality on health. *New England Journal of Medicine*, **297**(11), 863–869.

Lewis, E. J. (1972). Psychological determinants of family size: A study of white middle class couples ages 35–45 with zero, one or three children. Proceedings of the 80th Annual Convention of American Psychological Association, pp. 665–666.

Lickona, T. (Ed.) (1976). *Moral development and behavior*. New York: Holt, Rinehart and Winston.

Lidz, T., & Fleck, S. (1960). Schizophrenia, human integration, and the role of the family. In D. D. Jackson (Ed.), *The etiology of schizophrenia*. New York: Basic Books.

Lieberman, M., & Coplan, A. (1970). Distance from death as a variable in the study of aging. *Developmental Psychology*, **2**(1), 71–84.

Likert, R. (1932). A technique for the measurement of attitudes. *Archives of Psychology*, **40**.

Limber, J. (1977). Language in child and chimp? *American Psychologist*, **32**, 280–295.

Linn, S.; Schoenbaum, S. C.; Monson, R. R.; Rosner, B.; Stubblefield, P. G.; & Ryan, K. J.

(1982). No association between coffee consumption and adverse outcomes of pregnancy. *New England Journal of Medicine,* **306**(3), 141–145.

Lipsitt, L. (1980). Conditioning the rage to live. *Psychology Today,* **13**(9), 124.

———. (1982). Infant learning. In T. M. Field, A. Huston, H. C. Quay, L. Troll, and G. Finley (Eds.), *Review of human development.* New York: Wiley.

——— & Kaye, H. (1964). Conditioned sucking in the human newborn. *Psychonomic Science,* **1**, 20–30.

Livson, F. (1975). Sex differences in personality development in the middle adult years: A longitudinal study. Paper presented at the annual meeting of the Gerontological Society, Louisville, Kentucky.

Lloyd-Still, J.; Hurwitz, I.; Wolff, P. H.; & Schwachman, H. (1974). Intellectual development after severe malnutrition in infancy. *Pediatrics,* **54**, 306.

Locke, J. (1959). *An essay concerning human understanding,* vol. 1. New York: Dover. (Originally published 1690.)

Loehlin, J. C. (1979). Combining data from different groups in human behavior genetics. In Royce, J. R. (Ed.), *Theoretical advances in behavior genetics.* Leiden: Sijthoff & Hoordhoff.

Loftus, E. F. (1979). *Eyewitness testimony.* Cambridge, Mass.: Harvard University Press.

———. (1980). *Memory.* Reading, Mass.: Addison-Wesley.

——— & Loftus, G. R. (1980). On the permanence of stored information in the human brain. *American Psychologist.* **35**(5), 409–420.

———; Miller, D. G.; & Burns, H. J. (1978). Semantic integration of verbal information into a visual memory. *Journal of Experimental Psychology,* **4**, 19–31.

——— & Palmer, J. C. (1982). Re-construction of automobile destruction: An example of interaction between language and memory. *Journal of Verbal Learning and Verbal Behavior* (1974), **13**, 585–589. [Reprinted in U. Neisser (Ed.), *Memory observed.* San Francisco: W. H. Freeman.]

Looft, W. R. (1971). Toward a history of life-span developmental psychology. Unpublished manuscript, University of Wisconsin, Madison.

Loomis, A. L.; Harvey, E. N.; & Hobart, G. A. (1937). Cerebral states during sleep as studied by human potentials. *Journal of Experimental Psychology,* **21**, 127–144.

Lopata, H. (1973). Living through widowhood. *Psychology Today,* **7**(2), 87–98.

———. (1977). Widows and widowers. *The Humanist* (September/October), 25–28.

———. (1979). *Women as Widows.* New York: Elsevier.

Lott, A. J., & Lott, B. E. (1974). The role of reward in the formation of positive interpersonal attitudes. In T. L. Huston (Ed.), *Foundations of interpersonal attraction.* New York: Academic.

Lowenthal, M., & Haven, C. (1968). Interaction and adaptation: Intimacy as a critical variable. In B. Neugarten (Ed.), *Middle age and aging.* Chicago: University of Chicago Press.

Luborsky, L. (1979). *Predicting outcomes of psychotherapy.* New York: BMA Audio Cassettes (tape).

———; Singer, B.; & Luborsky, L. (1975). Comparative studies of psychotherapies. *Archives of General Psychiatry,* **32**, 995–1008.

Ludwig, A. M. (1969). Altered states of consciousness. *Archives of General Psychiatry* (1966), **15**, 225–234. [In C. Tart (Ed.), *Altered states of consciousness.* New York: Wiley.]

Luria, A. R. (1968). *The mind of a mnemonist.* Translated from the Russian by Lynn Solotaroff. New York: Basic Books.

Lutjen, P.; Trounson, A.; Leeton, J.; Findlay, J.; Wood, C.; & Renou, P. (1984). The establishment and maintenance of pregnancy using in vitro fertilization and embryo donation in a patient with primary ovarian failure. *Nature,* **307**, 174–175.

Lynn, D. (1974). *The father: His role in child development.* Monterey, Calif.: Brooks/Cole.

Lynn, R. (1966). *Attention, arousal and the orientation reaction.* Oxford, England: Pergamon.

———. (1982). IQ in Japan and the United States shows a growing disparity. *Nature,* **297**, 222–223.

Maccoby, E. E., & Jacklin, C. N. (1974). *The psychology of sex differences.* Stanford, Calif.: Stanford University Press.

Macfarlane, A. (1978). What a baby knows. *Human Nature,* **1**(2), 74–81.

Mackintosh, N. J. (1975). Blocking of conditioned suppression: Role of the first compound trial. *Journal of Experimental Psychology: Animal Behavior Processes,* **1** (4), 335–345.

MacLeod-Morgan, C. (1982). EEG lateralization in hypnosis: A preliminary report. *Australian Journal of Clinical and Experimental Hypnosis,* **10**, 99–102.

Malamuth, N. M., & Donnerstein, E. (1982). The effects of aggressive-pornographic mass media stimuli. *Advances in Experimental Social Psychology,* **15**, 103–135.

Mamay, P. D., & Simpson, P. L. (1981). Three female roles in television commercials. *Sex Roles,* **7**(12), 1223–1232.

Mann, L., & Janis, I. L. (1968). A follow-up study on the long-term effects of emotional role-playing. *Journal of Personality and Social Psychology,* **8**, 339–342.

Marcia, J. (1967). Ego identity status: Relationship to change in self-esteem, "general maladjustment," and authoritarianism.

Journal of Personality, **35**(1), 119–133.

Margules, D. L. (1979). Beta-endorphin and endoloxone: Hormones of the autonomic nervous system for the conservation and the expenditure of bodily resources and energy in the anticipation of famine or feast. *Neuroscience and Biochemical Reviews*, **3**, 155–162.

Margules, M. R.; Moisset, B.; Lewis, M. J.; Shibuya, H.; & Pert, C. (1978). Beta-endorphin is associated with overeating in genetically obese mice (ob/ob) and rats (fa/fa). *Science*, **202**, 988–991.

Marquis, D. P. (1931). Can conditioned responses be established in the newborn infant? *Journal of Genetic Psychology*, **39**(4), 479–492.

Martin, J. (1982). *Miss Manner's guide to excruciatingly correct behavior*. New York: Atheneum.

Marty, M. E. (1982). Watch your language. *Context* (April 15).

Maslach, C., & Jackson, S. E. (In press). Burnout in health professions: A social psychological analysis. In G. Sanders and J. Suls (Eds.), *Social psychology of health and illness*. Hillsdale, N.J.: Erlbaum.

Maslow, A. H. (1970). *Motivation and personality*. New York: Harper and Row.

———. (1973). Self-actualizing people: A study of psychological health. In R. J. Lowry (Ed.), *Dominance, self-esteem, self-actualization: Germinal papers of A. H. Maslow*. Belmont, Calif.: Wadsworth. (Originally published 1950.)

Mason, J. (1968). Organization of psychoendocrine mechanisms. *Psychosomatic Medicine*, **30**, 565–608.

Masson, J. M. (1983). *The Assault on Truth: Freud's Suppression of the Seduction Theory*. New York: Farrar, Straus & Giroux.

Masters, W. H., & Johnson, V. E. (1966). *Human sexual response*. Boston: Little, Brown.

Matas, L.; Arend, R. A.; & Sroufe, L. A. (1978). Continuity of adaptation in the second year: The relationship between quality of attachment and later competence. *Child Development*, **49**, 547–556.

Matthews, K., & Siegel, J. (1983). Type A behaviors by children, social comparison, and standards for self-evaluation. *Developmental Psychology*, **19**, 135–140.

May, R. (1969). *Love and will*. New York: Norton.

Mayer, R. E. (1983). *Thinking, problem-solving, and cognition*. San Francisco: W. H. Freeman.

McArthur, L. A. (1972). The how and what of why: Some determinants and consequences of causal attribution. *Journal of Personality and Social Psychology*, **22**, 171–193.

McCaskill, C. L., & Wellman, B. A. (1938). A study of common motor achievements at the preschool ages. *Child Development*, **9**, 141–150.

McClelland, D. C. (1965). Achievement and entrepreneurship: A longitudinal study. *Journal of Personality and Social Psychology*, **1**, 389–392.

———. (1973). Testing for competence rather than for "intelligence." *American Psychologist*, **28**(1), 1–14.

———; Atkinson, J. W.; Clark, R. A.; & Lowell, E. L. (1953). *The achievement motive*. New York: Appleton-Century-Crofts.

——— & Winter, D. G. (1969). *Motivating economic achievement*. New York: Free Press.

McConahay, J. B.; Hardee, B. B.; & Batts, V. (1981). Has racism declined in America? It depends upon who is asking and what is asked. *Journal of Conflict Resolution*, **25**(4), 563–579.

McConnell, J. V. (1962). Memory transfer through cannibalism in planarians. *Journal of Neuropsychiatry*, **3**, monograph supp. 1.

McFadden, R. D. (1982). Passenger saves blind man's life on IND tracks. *The New York Times*, December 22, p. B1.

McGrath, J. E., & Kravitz, D. A. (1982). Group research. In M. R. Rosenzweig and L. W. Porter (Eds.), *Annual review of psychology*. Palo Alto, Calif.: Annual Reviews.

McKinnon, D. W. (1968). Selecting students with creative potential. In P. Heist (Ed.), *The creative college student: An unmet challenge*. San Francisco: Jossey-Bass.

McLearn, G. E. (1969). Biological bases of social behavior with particular reference to violent behavior. In D. J. Mulvihill, M. M. Tumin, and L. A. Curtis (Eds.), *Crimes of Violence*, vol. 13. Staff report submitted to the National Commission on the Causes and Prevention of Violence. Washington, D.C.: Government Printing Office.

Mead, M. (1961). *Coming of age in Samoa*. New York: Morrow. (Originally published in 1928.)

———. (1935). *Sex and temperament in three primitive societies*. New York: Morrow.

——— & Newton, N. (1967). Fatherhood. In S. A. Richardson and A. F. Guttmacher (Eds.), *Childbearing—Its social and psychological aspects*. Baltimore: Williams and Wilkins, pp. 189–192.

Meichenbaum, D. A. (1974). Self-instructional strategy training: A cognitive prosthesis for the aged. *Human Development*, **17**, 273–280.

———. (1975). Self-instructional approach to stress management: A proposal for stress innoculation training. In C. D. Spielberger and I. G. Sarason (Eds.), *Stress and anxiety*, vol. 1. Washington, D.C.: Hemisphere.

——— & Butler, L. (1978). Toward a conceptual model for the treatment of test anxiety: Implications for research and treatment. In I. G. Sarason (Ed.), *Test anxiety: Theory, research, and applications*. Hillsdale, N.J.: Erlbaum.

——— & Novaco, R. (1978). Stress inoculation: A preventive approach. In C. D. Spielberger and

I. G. Sarason (Eds.), *Stress and anxiety,* vol. 5. New York: Wiley.

Metzger, B. E.; Ravnikar, V.; Vileisis, R. A.; & Freinkel, N. (1982). "Accelerated starvation" and the skipped breakfast in late normal pregnancy. *Lancet* (March 13), 588–592.

Milgram, S. (1963). Behavioral study of obedience. *Journal of Abnormal Psychology, 67,* 371–378.

———. (1965). Some conditions of obedience and disobedience to authority. *Human Relations,* **18,** 67–76.

———. (1974). *Obedience to authority.* New York: Harper.

Miller, B. C., & Sollie, D. L. (1980). Normal stress during the transition to parenthood. *Family Relations, 29,* 459–465.

Miller, E.; Cradock-Watson, J. E.; & Pollock, T. M. (1982). Consequences of confirmed maternal rubella at successive stages of pregnancy. *Lancet* (October 9), pp. 781–784.

Miller, G. A. (1956). The magical number seven, plus or minus two: Some limits on our capacity to process information. *Psychological Review, 63,* 81–97.

Miller, N. E. (1969). Learning of visceral and glandular responses. *Science, 163,* 434–445.

Mills, J., & Aronson, E. (1965). Opinion change as a function of communicator's attractiveness and desire to influence. *Journal of Personality and Social Psychology,* **1,** 173–177.

Mills, J. L.; Harlap, S.; & Harley, E. E. (1981). Should coitus in late pregnancy be discouraged? *Lancet,* **2,** 136.

Milner, B. (1966). Amnesia following operation on the temporal lobes. In C. Witty and O. Zangwill (Eds.), *Amnesia.* London: Butterworth.

———. (1970). Memory and the medial temporal regions of the brain. In K. H. Pribram and D. E. Broadbent (Eds.). *Biology of memory.* New York: Academic Press.

———. (1974). Hemispheric specialization: Scope and limits. The Neurosciences Third Study Program. Cambridge, Mass.: MIT Press.

Mischel, W. (1977). On the future of personality measurement. *American Psychologist, 32,* 246–254.

———. (1968). *Personality and assessment.* New York: Wiley.

———. (1973). Toward a cognitive social learning reconceptualization of personality. *Psychological Review, 80,* 252–283.

Mishkin, M.; Spiegler, B. O.; Saunders, R. C.; & Malamut, B. L. (1982). An animal model of global amnesia. In S. Corkin et al. (Eds.), *Alzheimer's disease: A report of progress.* New York: Raven Press.

Mitchell, D. E.; Freeman, R. D.; Millodot, M.; & Haegerstrom, C. (1973). Meridional amblyopia: Evidence for modification of the human visual system. *Vision Research, 13,* 535–558.

Molfese, D.; Molfese, V.; & Carrell, P. (1982). Early language development. In B. Wolman (Ed.), *Handbook of developmental psychology.* Englewood Cliffs, N.J.: Prentice-Hall.

Money, J., & Erhardt, A. A. (1972). *Man and woman, boy and girl.* Baltimore, Md.: Johns Hopkins University Press.

Monroe, L. (1967). Psychological and physiological differences between good and poor sleepers. *Journal of Abnormal Psychology,* **72,** 255–264.

Moore, T., & Ucko, C. (1957). Night waking in early infancy: Part I. **33,** 333–342.

Moore-Ede, M. C. (1982). Sleeping as the world turns. *Natural History* (October), **91**(10), 28–36.

Morgan, A. H. (1973). The heritability of hypnotic susceptibility in twins. *Journal of Abnormal and Social Psychology,* **82,** 55–61.

Morris, D. (1977). *Manwatching: A field guide to human behavior.* New York: Harry N. Abrams.

Morse, S. J. (1977). An introduction to dynamic psychotherapy. In S. J. Morse and R. J. Watson (Eds.), *Psychotherapies: A comparative casebook.* New York: Holt, Rinehart and Winston.

——— & Watson, R. J. (Eds.), (1977). *Psychotherapies: A comparative casebook.* New York: Holt, Rinehart and Winston.

Morris, C. D.; Bransford, J. D.; & Franks, J. J. (1977). Levels of processing versus transfer appropriate processing. *Journal of Verbal Learning and Verbal Behavior,* **16,** 519–533.

Moskowitz, B. A. (1978). The acquisition of language. *Scientific American,* **239**(5), 92–108.

Moss, H. A. (1967). Sex, age, and state as determinants of mother-infant interaction. *Merrill-Palmer Quarterly,* **13,** 19–36.

Mowrer, O. H. (1960). *Learning theory and the symbolic processes.* New York: Wiley.

Moyer, K. E. (1976). *The psychobiology of aggression.* New York: Harper and Row.

Murphy, D. P. (1929). The outcome of 625 pregnancies in women subjected to pelvic radium roentgen irradiation. *American Journal of Obstetrics and Gynecology,* **18,** 179–187.

Murray, H. A. (1938). *Explorations in personality.* New York: Oxford University Press.

Murstein, B. I. (1971). Critique of models of dyadic attraction. In B. I. Murstein (Ed.), *Theories of attraction and relationships.* New York: Springer.

———. (1982). Marital choice. In B. B. Wolman (Ed.), *Handbook of developmental psychology.* Englewood Cliffs, N.J.: Prentice-Hall.

Mussen, P. H., & Eisenberg-Berg, N. (1977). *Roots of caring, sharing, and helping: The development of prosocial behavior in children.* San Francisco: W. H. Freeman.

——— & Jones, M. C. (1957). Self-conceptions, motivation, and interpersonal attitudes of late and early maturing boys. *Child Development*, **28**, 243–256.

———— & Rutherford, E. (1963). Parent-child relations and parental personality in relation to young children's sex role preferences. *Child Development*, **34**, 589–607.

Muuss, R. E. (1970). Adolescent development and the secular trend. *Adolescence*, **5**, 267–284.

Myers, D. G. (1983). *Social psychology*. New York: McGraw-Hill.

Myers, N., & Perlmutter, M. (1978). Memory in the years from 2 to 5. In P. Ornstein (Ed.), *Memory development in children*. Hillsdale, N.J.: Erlbaum.

Naeye, R. (1979). Weight gain and the outcome of pregnancy. *American Journal of Obstetrics and Gynecology*, **135**(1), 3–9.

————. (1983). New data on the effects of coitus in pregnancy. Paper presented at seminar, Technological Approaches to Obstetrics: Benefits, Risks, Alternatives III, March 18, Moscone Convention Center, San Francisco.

Nagy, M. (1948). The child's theories concerning death. *Journal of Genetic Psychology*, **73**, 3–27.

Nagelman, D. B.; Hale, S. L.; & Ware, S. L. (1983). Prevalence of eating disorders in college women. Paper presented at the American Psychological Association, Anaheim.

Napier, A. (1978). *The family crucible*. New York: Harper and Row.

Nathan, P. E., & Harris, S. L. (1980). *Psychopathology and society* (2d ed.). New York: McGraw-Hill.

National Academy of Sciences. (1982). *Ability tests: Consequences and controversies*. Washington, D.C.: National Academy Press.

National Institute on Aging Task Force. (1980). Senility reconsidered: Treatment possibilities for mental impairment in the elderly. *Journal of the American Medical Association*, **244**(3), 259–263.

National Institutes of Health. (1981). *Cesarean childbirth. Consensus Development Conference Summary*. vol. 3, no. 6. Bethesda, Md.: U.S. Government Printing Office, 1981-0-341-132/3553.

National Opinion Research Center. (1977). *General social surveys code book for 1972–1977*. Chicago: University of Chicago Press.

————. (1980). *General social surveys, 1972–1980*. Storrs, Ct. Roper Public Opinion Research Center, University of Connecticut.

Neisser, U. (1982). Memory: What are the important questions? In U. Neisser (Ed.), *Memory observed*. San Francisco: W. H. Freeman.

Nelson, B. (1982). Why are earliest memories so fragmentary and elusive? *The New York Times*, December 7, pp. C1, C7.

Nelson, H.; Erkin, M.; Saigal, S.; Bennett, K.; Milner, R.; & Sackett, D. (1980). A randomized clinical trial of the Leboyer approach to childbirth. *New England Journal of Medicine*, **302**(12), 655–660.

Nelson, K. (1973). Structure and strategy in learning to talk. *Monographs of the Society for Research in Child Development*, **38**(Nos. 1–2).

————. (1979). The role of language in infant development. In M. Bornstein and W. Kessen (Eds.), *Psychological development from infancy*. Hillsdale, N.J.: Erlbaum.

————. (1981). Individual differences in language development: Implications for development and language. *Developmental Psychology*. **17**(2), 170–187.

Nelson, T. O. (1977). Repetition and depth of processing. *Journal of Verbal Learning and Verbal Behavior*, **16**, 151–172.

Neugarten, B., & Gutmann, D. L. (1958). Age-sex roles and personality in middle age: A thematic apperception study. *Psychological Monograph*, **72**(17). Whole No. 470.

Neugarten, B. (1968). Adult personality: Toward a psychology of the life cycle. In B. Neugarten (Ed.), *Middle age and aging*. Chicago: University of Chicago Press.

————. (1975). The rise of the young-old. *The New York Times*, January 18.

———— & Hagestad, G. (1976). Age and the life course. In H. Binstock and E. Shanas (Eds.), *Handbook of aging and the social sciences*. New York: Van Nostrand Reinhold.

————; Havighurst, R.; & Tobin, S. (1965). Personality and patterns of aging. In B. Neugarten (Ed.), *Middle age and aging*. Chicago: University of Chicago Press.

————; Moore, J. W.; & Lowe, J. C. (1965). Age norms, age constraints, and adult socialization. *American Journal of Sociology*, **70**, 710–717.

New York Times, The (1982). Sports people. August 11, p. B8.

————. (1983). Visual cues compensate for blindness in one eye, September 13, p. C2.

Newcomb, T. M. (1961). *The acquaintance process*. New York: Holt, Rinehart, and Winston.

Newman, H.; Freeman, F.; & Holzinger, K. (1937). *Twins: A study of heredity and environment*. Chicago: University of Chicago Press.

Newton, I. (1952). *Opticks*, 1730. Based on the 4th edition. London, 1730. New York: Dover Publications.

Nias, D. K. (1979). Marital choice: Matching or complementation? In M. Cook and G. Wilson (Eds.), *Love and attraction*. Oxford: Pergamon.

Nichol, S., & Heston, L. (1979). The future of genetic research in schizophrenia. *Psychiatric Annals*, **9**(1), 32–53.

Nickerson, R. S., & Adams, M. J. (1979). Long-term memory for a common object. *Cognitive Psychology*, **11**, 287–307.

Nisbett, R. E., (1968). Taste, deprivation and weight determinants of eating behavior. *Journal of Per-*

sonality and Social Psychology, **10**, 107–116.

Novaco, R. W. (1977). A stress inoculation approach to anger management in the training of law enforcement officers. *American Journal of Community Psychology*, **5**, 327–346.

O'Brien, C. P.; Stunkard, A. J.; & Ternes, J. W. (1982). Absence of naloxone sensitivity in obese humans. *Psychosomatic Medicine*, **44**, 215–218.

O'Connor, D. (1982). Personal communication to S. Olds, May 13, during meeting at sex therapy clinic, Department of Psychiatry, Roosevelt Hospital, New York City.

O'Connor, R. D. (1972). Relative efficacy of modeling, shaping, and the combined procedures for notification of social withdrawal. *Journal of Abnormal Psychology*, **79**(3), 327–334.

Oelsner, L. (1979). More couples adopting victims of genetic defects. *The New York Times*, March 8, pp. A1, B14.

Oetzel, R. (1966). Classified summary in sex differences. In Maccoby, E. E. (Ed.), *The development of sex differences*. Stanford, Calif.: Stanford University Press.

Offer, D. (1969). *The psychological world of the teenager: A study of normal adolescent boys*. New York: Basic Books.

——— & Offer, J. (1974). Normal adolescent males: The high school and college years. *Journal of the American College Health Association*, **22**, 209–215.

Olds, S. W. (1976). Shampoo, set and sympathy. *McCall's* (Oct.).

——— & Eiger, M. S. (1973). *The complete book of breastfeeding*. New York: Bantam.

Olton, D. S. (1979). Mazes, maps and memory. *American Psychologist*, **34**, 583–596.

Orlofsky, J.; Marcia, J.; & Lesser, I. (1973). Ego identity status and the intimacy vs. isolation crisis of young adulthood. *Journal of Per-*

sonality and Social Psychology, **27**(2), 211–219.

Orne, M. T. (1977). The construct of hypnosis: Implications of the definition for research and practice. In W. E. Edmonston, Jr. (Ed.), *Conceptual and investigative approaches to hypnosis and hypnotic phenomena*. New York: New York Academy of Sciences.

——— & Holland, C. C. (1968). On the ecological validity of laboratory deceptions. *International Journal of Psychiatry*, **6**(4), 282–293.

Orr, W. C.; Martin, R. J.; & Patterson, C. D. (1979). When to suspect sleep apnea—the Pickwickian syndrome. *Resident and Staff Physician* (May), 101–104.

Osgood, C. E.; Suci, G. J.; & Tennenbaum, P. H. (1957). *The measurement of meaning*. Urbana: University of Illinois Press.

Oskamp, S., & Mindick, B. (1981). Personality and attitudinal barriers to contraception. In D. Byrne and W. A. Fisher (Eds.), *Adolescents, sex, and contraception*. New York: McGraw-Hill.

———; ———; Berger, D.; & Motta, E. A. (1978). Longitudinal study of success versus failure in contraceptive planning. *Journal of Population*, **1**, 69–83.

Ostrove, N., (1978). Expectations for success on effort-determined tasks as a function of incentive and performance feedback. *Journal of Personality and Social Psychology*, **36**, 909–916.

Oswald, P. F., & Petzman, P. (1974). The cry of the human infant. *Scientific American*, **230**(3), 84–90.

Oursler, J. D. (1980). The role of extramarital involvement in personal adjustment, marital adjustment and counseling of middle class women. Unpublished doctoral dissertation, St. John's University, New York, N.Y.

Pagano, R. R.; Rose, R. M.; Stivers, R. M.; & Warrenburg, S. (1976). Sleep during transcendental meditation. *Science*, **191**, 308–309.

Paivio, A. (1975). Perceptual comparisons through the mind's eye. *Memory and Cognition*, **3**(6), 635–647.

Pam, A.; Plutchik, R.; & Conte, H. R. (1975). Love: A psychometric approach. *Psychological Reports*, **37**, 83–88.

Papalia, D. E. (1972). The status of several conservation abilities across the life-span. *Human Development*, **15**, 229–243.

——— & Bielby, D. D. (1974). Cognitive functioning in middle and old age adults: A review of research based on Piaget's theory. *Human Development*, **17**, 424–443.

Papalia, D., & Olds, S. W. (1982). *A Child's World: Infancy through Adolescence*. (3rd ed.). New York: McGraw-Hill.

——— & ———. (1981). *Human Development*. (2d ed.). New York: McGraw-Hill.

——— & Tennent, S. S. (1975). Vocational aspirations in preschoolers: A manifestation of early sex-role stereotyping. *Sex Roles*, **1**(2), 197–199.

Pape, K.; Buncic, R.; Ashby, S.; & Fitzhardinge, P. (1978). The status at 2 years of low-birth-weight infants born in 1974 with birth-weights of less than 2,001 gm. *Journal of Pediatrics*, **92**(2), 253–260.

Parke, R. D. (1974). Rules, roles, and resistance to deviation: Recent advances in punishment, discipline, and self-control. In A. Pick (Ed.), *Symposia of child psychology*, vol. 8. Minneapolis: University of Minnesota Press.

———. (1977). Some effects of punishment on children's behavior—revisited. In E. M. Hetherington and R. D. Parke (Eds.), *Contemporary readings in child psychology*. New York: McGraw-Hill.

———. (1978). Babies have fathers, too. Paper presented at seminar, Advances in Child Development Research, sponsored by American Psychological Association and Society for Research in Child

Development, New York Academy of Sciences, New York City, October 31.

Parkes, C. M.; Benjamin, B.; & Fitzgerald, R. (1969). Broken heart: A statistical study of increased mortality among widowers. *British Medical Journal*, **4**, 740–743.

Parkes, J. D. (1977). The sleepy patient. *Lancet* (May 7), 990–993.

Parmalee, A. H.; Wenner, W. H.; & Schulz, H. R. (1964). Infant sleep patterns: From birth to 16 weeks of age. *Journal of Pediatrics*, **65**, 576.

Paul, G. L. (1969). Chronic mental patients: Current status—future directions. *Psychological Bulletin*, **71**, 81–94.

Pavlov, I. P. (1927). *Conditioned Reflexes*. London: Oxford University Press.

Peel, E. A. (1967). *The psychological basis of education* (2d ed.). Edinburgh and London: Oliver and Boyd.

Pendery, M. L.; Maltzman, I. M.; & West, L. J. (1982). Controlled drinking by alcoholics? New findings and a reevaluation of a major affirmative study. *Science*, **217**, 169–175.

Penfield, W. (1969). Consciousness, memory, and man's conditioned reflexes. In K. H. Pribram (Ed.), *On the biology of learning*. New York: Harcourt Brace Jovanovich.

Perkins, D. V. (1982). The assessment of stress using life event scales. In L. Goldberger and S. Breznitz (Eds.), *Handbook of stress*. New York: Free Press.

Perkins, R. P. (1979). Sexual behavior and response in relation to complications of pregnancy. *American Journal of Obstetrics and Gynecology*, **134**, 498–505.

Perper, T. (1980). Flirtation behavior in public settings. Paper presented at the Society for Scientific Study of Sex, Eastern Regional Conference, Philadelphia, April 25–27.

Persky, H.; Lief, H. I.; Strauss, D.; Miller, W. R.; & O'Brien, C. P.,

(1978). Plasma testosterone level and sexual behavior of couples. *Archives of Sexual Behavior*, **7**(3), 157–173.

Peterson, I. (1983). Legal snarl developing around case of a baby born to surrogate mother. *The New York Times*, February 7, p. A10.

Peterson, L. R., & Peterson, M. J. (1959). Short-term retention of individual verbal items. *Journal of Experimental Psychology*, **58**, 193–198.

Petri, E. (1934). Untersuchungen zur erbedingtheit der menarche. *Z. Morph. Anth.*, **33**, 43–48.

Piaget, J. (1932). *The moral judgment of the child*. New York: Harcourt Brace.

———. (1951). *Plays, dreams, and initiation in childhood*. New York: Norton.

———. (1952). *The origins of intelligence in children*. New York: International Universities Press.

———. (1972). Intellectual evolution from adolescence to adulthood. *Human Development*, **15**, 1–12.

Pihl, R. O.; Zeichner, A.; Niaura, R.; Hagy, F.; & Zacchia, C. (1981). Attribution and alcohol-mediated aggression. *Journal of Abnormal Psychology*, **90**, 468–475.

Piliavin, J. A.; Callero, P. L.; & Evans, D. E. (1982). Addiction to altruism? Opponent-process theory and habitual blood donation. *Journal of Personality and Social Psychology*, **43**(6), 1200–1213.

———; Dovidio, J. F.; Gaertner, S. L.; & Clark, R. D. (1981). *Emergency intervention*. New York: Academic Press.

——— & Piliavin, I. M. (1972). Effects of blood on reactions to a victim. *Journal of Personality and Social Psychology*, **23**(3), 353–361.

Piliavin, I. M.; Piliavin, J. A.; & Rodin, J. (1975). Costs, diffusions, and the stigmatized victim. *Journal of Personality and Social Psychology*, **32**(3), 429–438.

———; Rodin, J.; & Piliavin, J. A.

(1969). Good samaritanism: An underground phenomenon? *Journal of Personality and Social Psychology*, **13**, 289–299.

Pines, M. (1982). Movement grows to create guidelines for mental therapy. *The New York Times*, May 4, p. C1.

———. (1981). The civilizing of Genie. *Psychology Today*, **15**(9), 28–34.

Pirenne, M. H. (1967). *Vision and the eye*. London: Science Paperbacks. (Originally published by Tinling, London, 1948.)

Plath, S. (1972). *The bell jar*. New York: Bantam.

Premack, A. J., & Premack, D. (1972). Teaching language to an ape. *Scientific American*, **277**, 92–99.

Prentice, A. M.; Whitehead, R. G.; Watkinson, M.; Lamb, W. H.; & Cole, T. J. (1983). Prenatal dietary supplementation of African women and birthweight. *Lancet* (March 5), 489–492.

Press, A. (1982). Judge to jury: Overruled. *Newsweek* (April 26), p. 59.

Price, R. A., & Vandenberg, S. G. (1979). Matching for physical attractiveness in married couples. *Personality and Social Psychology Bulletin*, **5**, 398–399.

Pugh, W. E., & Fernandez, F. L. (1953). Coitus in late pregnancy. *Obstetrics and Gynecology*, **2**, 636–642.

Purtilo, D., & Sullivan, J. (1979). Immunological bases for superior survival in females. *American Journal of Diseases of Children*, **133**, 1251–1253.

Rabkin, J. G., & Struening, E. L. (1976). Life events, stress, and illness. *Science*, **194**, 1013–1020.

———. (1980). Stressful life events and schizophrenia: A review of the research literature. *Psychological Bulletin*, **87**(2), 408–425.

Rachman, S. J., & Wilson, G. T. (1980). *The effects of psychological therapy* (2d ed.). Oxford, England: Pergamon.

Rayburn, W. F., & Wilson, E. A. (1980). Coital activity and premature delivery. *American Journal of Obstetrics and Gynecology*, **137**, 972–974.

Read, M. S.; Habicht, J. P.; Lechtig, A.; & Klein, R. E. (1973). Maternal malnutrition, birth weight, and child development. Paper presented before the International Symposium on Nutrition, Growth and Development. May 21–25, Valencia, Spain.

Redmond, D. E. (1983). Brain chemistry and human aggression, presentation in seminar, Recent Studies concerning Dominance, Aggression, and Violence, sponsored by the Harry Frank Guggenheim Foundation, Rockefeller University, New York City, January 18.

Reichard, S.; Livson, F.; & Peterson, P. (1962). *Aging and personality: A study of 87 older men*. New York: Wiley.

Reid, J. R.; Patterson, G. R.; & Loeber, R. (1982). The abused child: Victim, instigator, or innocent bystander? In D. J. Berstein (Ed.), *Response structure and organization*. Lincoln: University of Nebraska Press.

Reiff, R., & Scheerer, M. (1959). *Memory and hypnotic age regression: Developmental aspects of cognitive function explored through hypnosis*. New York: International Universities Press.

Relman, A. S. (1982). Marijuana and health. *New England Journal of Medicine*, **306**(10), 603–604.

Renfrew, B. (1984). Test-tube births prompt questions. *The Capital Times*, Monday, January 23, p. 7.

Rescorla, R. A., & Wagner, A. R. (1972). A theory of Pavlovian conditioning: Variations in the effectiveness of reinforcement and nonreinforcement. In A. Black and W. F. Prokasy, Jr. (Eds.), *Classical conditioning II*. New York: Appleton-Century-Crofts.

Rice, M. (1982). Child language: What children know and how. In T. M. Field, A. Huston, H. Quay, L. Troll, and G. Finley (Eds.), *Review of human development*. New York: Wiley.

Richter, C. P. (1957). On the phenomenon of sudden death in animals and man. *Psychosomatic Medicine*, **19**, 191–198.

Riegel, K. F., & Riegel, R. M. (1972). Development, drop, and death. *Developmental Psychology*, **6**(2), 306–319.

Rierdan, J., & Koff, E. (1980). Representation of the female body by early and late adolescent girls. *Journal of Youth and Adolescence*, **9**(4), 339–346.

Rips, L. P.; Shoben, E. J.; & Smith, E. E. (1973). Semantic distance and the verification of semantic relations. *Journal of Verbal Learning and Verbal Behavior*, **12**, 1–20.

Robb, D. M. (1951). *The Harper history of painting*. New York: Harpers.

Robbins, L. C. (1963). The accuracy of parental recall of aspects of child development and of child-rearing practices. *Journal of Abnormal and Social Psychology*, **66**, 261–270.

Roberts, C. L., & Lewis, R. A. (1981). The empty nest syndrome. In J. G. Howells (Ed.), *Modern perspectives in the psychiatry of middle age*. New York: Brunner/Mazel.

Robson, K. M.; Brant, H. A.; & Kumar, R. (1981). Maternal sexuality during first pregnancy and after childbirth. *British Journal of Obstetrics & Gynecology*, (September) **88**(9), 882–889.

Robson, K. S., & Moss, H. A. (1970). Patterns and determinants of maternal attachment. *Journal of Pediatrics*, **77**(6), 976–985.

Rock, I., & Kaufman, L., (1962). The moon illusion II, *Science*, **136**, 1023–1031.

Rodin, J. (1981). Current status of the internal-external hypothesis

for obesity. *American Psychologist*. **36**, 361–372.

———. (1983). Obesity: An update. Invited address, American Psychological Association, Anaheim, Ca.

——— & Langer, E. (1977). Long-term effects of a control-relevant intervention with the institutionalized aged. *Journal of Personality and Social Psychology*, **35**, 897–902.

———; Solomon, S. K.; & Metcalf, J. (1977). Role of control in mediating perceptions of density. *Journal of Personality and Social Psychology*, **91**, 586–597.

Roffwarg, H. P.; Herman, J. H.; Bowe-Anders, C.; & Tauber, E. S. (1976). The effects of sustained alterations of waking visual input on dream content. In A. M. Arkin, J. S. Antrobus, and S. J. Ellman (Eds.), *The mind in sleep: Psychology and psychophysiology*. Hillsdale, N.J.: Erlbaum.

Rogers, C. R. (1951). *Client-centered therapy*. Boston: Houghton Mifflin.

———. (1961). *On becoming a person*. Boston: Houghton Mifflin.

———. (1970). *Carl Rogers on encounter groups*. New York: Harper and Row.

———. (1980). *A way of being*. Boston: Houghton Mifflin.

Rohlen, T. P., quoted in Silk, L., (1982). Economic scene: A lesson from Japan, *The New York Times*, November 17, p. D2.

Rosch, E. H. (1975). Cognitive representations of semantic categories. *Journal of Experimental Psychology: General*, **104**, 192–233.

——— & Mervis, C. B. (1975). Family resemblances: Studies in the internal structure of categories. *Cognitive Psychology*, **7**, 573–605.

———; ———; Gray, W. D.; Johnson, D. M.; & Boyes-Braem, P. (1976). Basic objects in natural categories. *Cognitive Psychology*, **8**, 382–439.

Rosen, H. (1982). Lobotomy. In *Encyclopedia Americana*, vol. 17. Danbury, Conn.: Grolier, p. 635.

Rosenhan, D. L. (1973). On being sane in insane places. *Science*, **179**, 250–258.

———; Salovey, P., & Hargis, K. (1981). The joys of helping. Focus of attention mediates the impact of positive affect on altruism. *Journal of Personality and Social Psychology*, **40**(5), 899–905.

Rosenman, R. H., & Chesney, M. A. (1982). Stress, type A behavior, and coronary disease. In L. Goldberger and S. Breznitz (Eds.), *Handbook of stress*. New York: Free Press.

Rosenthal, A. M. (1964). *Thirty-eight Witnesses*. New York: McGraw-Hill.

Rosenzweig, M. R., & Leiman, A. L. (1982). *Physiological psychology*. New York: D.C. Heath.

Rosett, H. L., & Weiner, L. (1982). Prevention of fetal alcohol effects. *Pediatrics*, **69**(6), 813–816.

Ross, L. (1977). The intuitive psychologist and his shortcomings: Distortions in the attribution process. In L. Berkowitz (Ed.), *Advances in experimental social psychology*. New York: Academic Press.

Ross, H. G., & Milgram, J. I. (1982). Important variables in adult sibling relationships: A qualitative study, in M. E. Lamb and B. Sutton-Smith (Eds.), *Sibling relationships: Their nature and significance across the lifespan*. Hillsdale, N.J.: Erlbaum.

Rubenstein, C. (1982). Psychology's fruit flies. *Psychology Today*, **16**(7), 83–84.

———. (1983). Medical mnemonics. *Psychology Today*, **17**(1), 70.

Rubin, A. (1977). Birth injuries. *Hospital Medicine* (September), 114–130.

Rubin, L. B. (1979). *Women of a certain age: The midlife search for self*. New York: Harper and Row.

Rubin, Z. (1970). Measurement of romantic love. *Journal of Personality and Social Psychology*, **16**(2), 265–273.

———. (1981). Does personality really change after 20? *Psychology Today*, **15**(5), 18–27.

———; Peplau, L. A., & Hill, C. T. (1981). Loving and leaving: Sex differences in romantic attachments. *Sex Roles*, **7**(8), 821–835.

Rugh, R., & Shettles, L. B. (1971). *From conception to birth: The drama of life's beginning*. New York: Harper and Row.

Rumbaugh, D. M., & Gill, T. V. (1973). Reading and sentence completion by a chimpanzee. *Science*, **182**, 731–733.

Runck, B. (1980). *Biofeedback-Issues in treatment assessment*. Rockville, MD: National Institutes of Mental Health.

Russell, C. (1974). Transitions to parenthood: Problems and gratifications. *Journal of Marriage and the Family*, **36**(2), 294–302.

Russell, R. (1981). *Report on effective psychotherapy: Legislative testimony*. Presented at a public hearing on The Regulation of Mental Health Practitioners, conducted at the City University of New York, March 5, by Assemblyman Mark Alan Siegel of the New York State Assembly Committee on Higher Education.

Sabourin, M. (1982). Hypnosis and brain function: EEG correlates of state-trait differences. *Research Communications in Psychology, Psychiatry and Behavior*, **7**(2), 149–168.

Sagi, A., & Hoffman, M. (1976). Empathetic distress in newborns. *Developmental Psychology*, **12**(2), 175–176.

Sahakian, W. S. (1976). *Learning systems, models, and theories*. Chicago: Rand McNally College Publishing.

Salaman, E. (1970). *A collection of moments*. London: Longman.

Sameroff, A. (1971). Can conditioned responses be established in the newborn infant? *Developmental Psychology*, **5**, 1–12.

Samuel, W. (1981). *Personality:*

Searching for the sources of human behavior. New York: McGraw-Hill.

San Francisco Chronicle, This World Magazine. (1982). The latest in home dryers, March 7, p. 5.

Scarr, S., & Weinberg, R. (1976). IQ performance of black children adopted by white families. *American Psychologist*, **31**(10), 726–739.

Scarr-Salapatek, S., & Williams, M. (1973). The effect of early stimulation on low-birthweight infants. *Child Development*, **44**, 94–101.

Schacter, S. (1959). *The psychology of affiliation*. Stanford, Calif.: Stanford University Press.

———. (1971). *Emotion, obesity, and crime*. New York: Academic Press.

———. (1964). The interaction of cognitive and physiological determinants of emotional state. In L. Berkowitz (Ed.), *Advances in experimental social psychology*, vol. 1. New York: Academic Press.

———. (1982). Don't sell habit breakers short. *Psychology Today*, **16**(8), 27–34.

——— & Gross, L. P. (1968). Manipulated time and eating behavior. *Journal of Personality and Social Psychology*, **10**, 98–106

——— & Singer, J. (1962). Cognitive, social, and physiological determinants of emotional state. *Psychological Review*, **69**, 379–399.

Schaeffer, D. L. (1971). *Sex differences in personality*. Belmont, Calif.: Brooks/Cole.

Schafer, R. B., & Keith, P. M. (1981). Equity in marital roles across the family life cycle. *Journal of Marriage and the Family*, **43**(2), 359–367.

Schaie, K. W. & Gribbin, K. (1975). Adult development and aging. In M. Rosenzweig and L. Porter (Eds.), *Annual review of psychology*, vol. 26. Palo Alto, Calif.: Annual Reviews.

Schiffenbauer, A., & Schiavo, R. S. (1976). Physical distance and attraction: An intensification effect.

Journal of Experimental Psychology, **12,** 274–282.

Schildkraut, J. J., & Kety, S. S. (1967). Biogenic amines and emotion. *Science,* **156,** 21–30.

Schmeck, H. M., Jr. (1976). Trend in growth of children lags. *The New York Times,* June 10, p. 13.

Schreiber, F. R. (1975). *Sybil.* Chicago: Regenery.

Schultz, D. P. (1969). The human subject in psychological research. *Psychological Bulletin,* **72,** 214–228.

———. (1981). *A history of modern psychology.* New York: Academic Press.

Schulz, R. (1978). *The psychology of death, dying, and bereavement.* Reading, Mass.: Addison-Wesley.

Schwab, J. J.; Bell, R. A.; Warheit, G. J.; & Schwab, M. E. (1979). *Social order and mental health: The Florida Health Survey.* New York: Brunner/Mazel.

Scully, C. (1973). Down's syndrome. *British Journal of Hospital Medicine* (July), 89–98.

Sears, P. (1977). Life satisfaction of Terman's gifted women: 1927–72: Comparison with the gifted and with normative samples. Paper presented at 5th Annual Conference School of Education, University of Wisconsin, Madison.

——— & Barbee, A. (1978). Career and life satisfaction among Terman's gifted women. In *The gifted and the creative: A fifty-year perspective.* Baltimore: Johns Hopkins University Press.

Sears, R. R. (1977). Sources of life satisfaction of the Terman gifted men. *American Psychologist,* **32,** 119–128.

———; Maccoby, E. E.; & Levin, H. (1957). *Patterns of child rearing.* New York: Harper and Row.

Segal, J., & Yahraes, H., (1978). *A child's journey.* New York: McGraw-Hill.

Segal, M. W. (1974). Alphabet and attraction: An unobtrusive measure of the effect of propinquity in a field setting. *Journal of Personal-ity and Social Psychology,* **30**(5), 654–657.

Segerberg, O. (1982). *Living to be 100.* New York: Scribner's.

Seligman, M. (1975). *Helplessness: On depression, development and death.* San Francisco: W. H. Freeman.

Selltiz, C.; Jahoda, M.; Deutsch, M.; & Cook, S. W. (1959). *Research methods in social relations.* New York: Holt, Rinehart and Winston.

Selman, R. L., & Selman, A. P. (1979). Children's ideas about friendship: A new theory. *Psychology Today,* **13**(4), 71–80, 114.

Selye, H. (1939). A syndrome produced by diverse innocuous agents. *Nature,* **138,** 32.

———. (1956). *The stress of life.* New York: McGraw-Hill.

———. (1974). *Stress without distress.* Philadelphia: Lippincott.

———. (1980). The stress concept today. In I. L. Kutash, L. B. Schlesinger, and Associates (Eds.), *Handbook on stress and anxiety.* San Francisco: Jossey-Bass, pp. 127–143.

———. (1982). History and present status of the stress concept. In L. Goldberger and S. Breznitz (Eds.), *Handbook of Stress.* New York: The Free Press.

Sequin, E. (1907). Idiocy: Its treatment by the physiological method. New York: Bureau of Publications, Teachers College, Columbia University. (Reprinted from original edition, 1866.)

Shainess, N. (1961). A re-evaluation of some aspects of femininity through a study of menstruation: A preliminary report. *Comprehensive Psychiatry,* **2,** 20–26.

Shapiro, C. M.; Bortz, R.; Mitchell, D.; Bartel, P.; & Jooste, P. (1981). Slow-wave sleep: A recovery period after exercise. *Science,* **214,** 1253–1254.

Shapiro, S. (1981). *Contemporary theories of schizophrenia.* New York: McGraw-Hill.

Shatz, M., & Gelman, R. (1973). The development of communica-tion skills: Modifications in the speech of young children as a function of listener. *Monographs of the Society for Research in Child Development,* **38,** Whole No. 5.

Shaw, M. E. & Costanzo, P. R. (1982). *Theories of social psychology.* New York: McGraw-Hill.

Shaywitz, S.; Cohen, D.; & Shaywitz, B. (1980). Behavior and learning difficulties in children of normal intelligence born to alcoholic mothers. *Journal of Pediatrics,* **96**(6), 978–982.

Sheehan, S. (1982). *Is there no place on earth for me?* Boston: Houghton Mifflin.

Sheehy, G. (1976). *Passages.* New York: Dutton.

———. (1981). *Pathfinders.* New York: Morrow.

Sheldon, W. H. (1942). *The varieties of temperament: A psychology of constitutional differences.* New York: Harper.

Sheperd-Look, D. L. (1982). Sex differentiation and the development of sex roles. In B. B. Wolman (Ed.), *Handbook of developmental Psychology.* Englewood Cliffs, N.J.: Prentice-Hall.

Sherif, M. (1966). *In common predicament: Social psychology of intergroup conflict and cooperation.* Boston: Houghton Mifflin.

Sherman, M. (1927). The differentiation of emotional responses in infants. I. Judgments of emotional responses from motion picture views and from actual observations. *Journal of Comparative Psychology,* **7,** 265–284.

Sherrod, D. R. (1974). Crowding, perceived control, and behavioral aftereffects. *Journal of Applied Social Psychology,* **4,** 171–186.

Shields, J. (1962). *Monozygotic twins brought up apart and brought up together.* London: Oxford University Press.

Shiffrin, R. M., & Atkinson, R. C. (1969). Storage and retrieval processes in long-term memory. *Psychological Review,* **76,** 179–193.

Shipman, V. (1971). Disadvantaged

children and their first school experiences. Educational testing service, Head Start longitudinal study, Report PR-72-18, Princeton, N.J.

Shorter, M. A., & McDarby, D. (1979). *Chemical survival: A primer for western man* (2d ed.). Phoenix, Ariz.: Do It Now Foundation.

Shotland, R. L., & Straw, M. K. (1976). Bystander response to an assault: When a man attacks a woman. *Journal of Personality and Social Psychology.* **34,** 990–999.

Siegler, M., & Osmond, H. (1974). *Models of madness, models of medicine.* New York: Harper and Row.

Sigall, H., & Page, R. (1971). Current stereotypes: A little fading, a little faking. *Journal of Personality and Social Psychology,* **18,** 247–255.

Simner, M. L. (1971). Newborn's response to the cry of another infant. *Developmental Psychology,* **5**(1), 136–150.

Skeels, H. (1966). Adult status of children with contrasting early life experiences: A follow-up study. *Monographs of the Society for Research in Child Development,* **31**(3), Whole No. 105.

——— & Dye, H. B. (1939). A study of the effects of differential stimulation on mentally retarded children. *Program of the American Association of Mental Deficiency,* **44,** 114–136.

Skinner, B. F. (1938). *The Behavior of Organisms.* New York: Appleton-Century-Crofts.

———. (1951). How to teach animals. *Scientific American,* **185,** 26–29.

———. (1953). *Science and human behavior.* New York: Macmillan.

———. (1957). *Verbal behavior.* Englewood Cliffs, N.J.: Prentice-Hall.

———. (1982). Intellectual self-management in old age. Paper presented at the annual meeting of the American Psychological Association, Washington, D.C., August 23.

Skodak, M., & Skeels, H. (1949). A follow-up study of one hundred adopted children. *Journal of Genetic Psychology,* **75,** 85–125.

Slag, M. F.; Morley, J. E.; Elson, M. K.; Trence, D. L.; Nelson, C. J.; Nelson, A. E.; Kinlaw, W. B.; Bayer, H. S.; Nuttall, F. Q.; & Shafer, R. B. (1983). Impotence in medical clinic outpatients. *Journal of the American Medical Association* (April 1), **249**(13), 1736–1740.

Slater, E., with Shields, J. (1953). Psychotic and neurotic illnesses in twins. *Medical Research Council Special Report.* Series No. 278. London: HMSO.

Sloane, R. B.; Staples, F. R.; Cristol, A. H.; Yorkston, N.J.; & Whipple, K. (1975). *Psychotherapy.* Cambridge, Mass.: Harvard University Press.

Slobin, D. I. (1971). Universals of grammatical development in children. In W. Levelt & G. B. Flores d'Arcais (Eds.), *Advances in psycholinguistic research.* Amsterdam: New Holland.

Smith, C., & Forrest, A. D. (1975). The genetics of schizophrenia. In A. D. Forrest and J. Affieck (Eds.), *New perspectives in schizophrenia.* Edinburgh: Churchill Livingston.

Smith, D. (1982). Trends in counseling and psychotherapy. *American Psychologist,* **37**(3), 802–809.

——— & Wilson, A. (1973). *The child with Down's syndrome* (mongolism). Philadelphia: Saunders.

Snow, C. E. (1972). Mothers' speech to children learning language. *Child Development,* **43,** 549–565.

———. (1977). Mothers' speech research: From input to interaction. In C. D. Snow & C. A. Ferguson (Eds.), *Talking to children: Language input and acquisition.* Cambridge: Cambridge University Press.

———. (1961). Either-or. *Progressive* (February), p. 24.

———; Arlman-Rupp, A.; Hassing, Y.; Jobse, J.; Joosten, J.; &

Verster, J. (1976). Mothers' speech in three social classes. *Journal of Psycholinguistic Research,* **5,** 1–20.

Snyder, M. (1982). When believing means doing: Creating links between attitudes and behavior. In M. Zanna, E. Higgins, and C. Herman (Eds.), *Consistency in social behavior: The Ontario Symposium,* vol. 2. Hillsdale, N.J.: Erlbaum.

———; Campbell, B.; & Preston, E. (1982). Testing hypotheses about human nature: Assessing the accuracy of social stereotypes. *Social Cognition.*

——— & Swann, W. (1976). When actions reflect attitudes: the politics of impression management. *Journal of Personality and Social Psychology,* **34,** 1034–1042.

———; Tanke, E. D.; & Berscheid, E. (1977). Social perception and interpersonal behavior: On the self-fulfilling nature of social stereotypes. *Journal of Personality and Social Psychology,* **35,** 691–712.

Snyder, S. H. & Reivich, M. (1966). Regional location of lysergic acid diethylamide in monkey brain. *Nature,* **209,** 1093.

Sobel, D. (1980). Freud's fragmented legacy. *The New York Times Magazine,* October 26, pp. 28ff.

Sobell, M., & Sobell, L. (1975). The need for realism, relevance, and operational assumptions in the study of substance dependence. In H. D. Cappell and A. E. LeBlanc (Eds.), *Biological and behavioral approaches to drug dependence.* Toronto: Alcoholism and Drug Addiction Research Foundation of Canada.

Sobell, L.; Sobell, M.; & Ward, E. (1980). *Evaluating alcohol and drug abuse treatment effectiveness.* New York: Pergamon.

Sokolov, E. N. (1977). Brain functions: Neuronal mechanisms of learning and memory. *Annual Review of Psychology,* **20,** 85–112.

Soldo, B. J. (1980). *America's Elderly*

in the 1980's. Population Reference Bureau, **35**(4).

Solomon, R. L., & Corbit, J. D. (1974). An opponent-process theory of motivation I. Temporal dynamics of affect. *Psychological Review,* **81,** 119–145.

Sontag, S. (1975). The double standard of aging. In *No Longer Young: The Older Woman in America.* Ann Arbor: University of Michigan/Wayne State University, Institute of Gerontology. (Reprinted from *Saturday Review,* 1972.)

Sorensen, R. (1973). *The Sorensen report on adolescent sexuality in contemporary America.* New York: World.

Sostek, A. J., & Wyatt, R. J. (1981). The chemistry of crankiness. *Psychology Today,* **15**(10), 120.

Soule, B. (1974). Pregnant couples. Paper presented in a symposium on "Parents and infants: An interactive network." At the annual meeting of the American Psychological Association, New Orleans, August 29.

Spearman, C. (1904). General intelligence objectively determined and measured. *American Journal of Psychology,* **15,** 201–293.

Spelt, D. (1948). The conditioning of the human fetus in vitro. *Journal of Experimental Psychology,* 338–346.

Sperling, G. (1960). The information available in brief visual presentations. *Psychological Monographs,* **74,** 1–29.

Sperry, R. (1982). Some effects of disconnecting the cerebral hemispheres. *Science,* **217,** 1223–1226.

Spezzano, C. (1981). Prenatal psychology: Pregnant with questions. *Psychology Today,* **15**(5), 49–58.

Spielberger, C. (1979). *Understanding stress and anxiety.* New York: Harper and Row.

Spitzer, R. L. (1976). More on pseudo science in science and the case for psychiatric diagnosis: A critique of D. L. Rosenhan's "On

being sane in insane places" and "The contextual nature of psychiatric diagnosis." *Archives of General Psychiatry,* **33,** 459–470.

Squire, L. R., & Slater, P. C. (1978). Anterograde and retrograde memory impairment in chronic amnesia. *Neuropsychologia,* **16,** 313–322.

———; ———; & Chance, P. M. (1975). Retrograde amnesia: Temporal gradient in very long-term memory following electroconvulsive therapy. *Science,* **187,** 77–79.

Squire, S. (1983). *The slender balance.* New York: Putnam.

Srole, L., & Fischer, A. (1980). The Midtown Manhattan Longitudinal Study vs. "The Mental Paradise Lost" doctrine. *Archives of General Psychiatry,* **37,** 209–221.

———; Langner, T. S., & Michael, S. T. (1962). *Mental health in the metropolis,* revised and enlarged edition. New York: New York University Press.

Sroufe, L. A., & Wunsch, J. (1972). The development of laughter in the first year of life. *Child Development,* **43,** 1326–1344.

Stapp, J., & Fulcher, R. (1983). The employment of APA members: 1982. *American Psychologist,* **38**(12), 1298–1320.

Starr, B. D., & Weiner, M. B. (1981). *The Starr-Weiner report on sex & sexuality in the mature years.* New York: Stein & Day.

Steinberg, L. D. (1982). Jumping off the work experience bandwagon. *Journal of Youth and Adolescence,* **11**(3), 183–206.

Steiner, I. D. (1979). Social psychology. In E. Hearst (Ed.), *The first century of experimental psychology.* Hillsdale, N.J.: Erlbaum.

Stenchever, M. A.; Williamson, R. A.; Leonard, J.; Karp, L. E.; Ley, B.; Shy, K.; & Smith, D. (1981). Possible relationship between in utero diethylstilbestrol exposure and male fertility. *American Journal of Obstetrics and Gynecology,* **140**(2), 186–193.

Stephan, W. G.; Rosenfield, D.; &

Stephan, C. (1976). Egotism in males and females. *Journal of Personality and Social Psychology,* **34,** 1161–1167.

Stern, R. M., & Ray, W. J. (1977). *Biofeedback: Potential and limits.* Lincoln: University of Nebraska Press.

Sternberg, R. J. (1979). Stalking the IQ quark. *Psychology Today,* **13**(4), 27–41.

———. (1982). Who's intelligent? *Psychology Today,* **16**(4), 30–40.

———; Conway, B. E.; Ketron, J. L.; & Bernstein, M. (1981). Peoples' conceptions of intelligence. *Journal of Personality and Social Psychology,* **41**(1), 37–55.

——— & Davidson, J. (1982). The mind of the puzzler. *Psychology Today,* **16**(6), 37–44.

Sternberg, S. (1966). High-speed scanning in human memory. *Science,* **153,** 652–654.

———. (1967). Two operations in character-recognition: Some evidence from reaction-time measurements. *Perception and Psychophysics,* **2,** 45–53.

———. (1969). The discovery of processing stages. *Acta Psychologica,* **30,** 276–315.

Sternglanz, S., & Serbin, L. (1974). Sex role stereotyping in children's television programs. *Developmental Psychology,* **10,** 710–715.

Stewart, A., & Reynolds, E. (1974). Improved prognosis for infants of very low-birthweight. *Pediatrics,* **54**(6), 724–735.

Strasser, S., with Shapiro, D., (1984). A town on the edge of fear, *Newsweek* (January 23), **103,** (4), 27.

Streib, G. F., & Schneider, C. J. (1971). *Retirement in American society: Impact and process.* Ithaca: Cornell University Press.

Stroop, J. R. (1935). Studies of interference in serial verbal reactions, *Journal of Experimental Psychology,* **18,** 643–662.

Strupp, H. (1973). On the basic ingredients of psychotherapy. *Jour-*

nal of Consulting and Clinical Psychology, **41**, 1–8.

———. (1975). Psychoanalysis, "focal" psychotherapy, and the nature of the therapeutic inference. *Archives of General Psychiatry*, **32**, 127–135.

Stump, A. (1975). "That's him—the guy who hit me!" TV Guide (October 4–10), 32–35.

Suedfeld, P. (1975). The benefits of boredom: Sensory deprivation reconsidered. *American Scientist*, **63**, 60–69.

Sugarman, A., & Quinlan, D. (In press). Anorexia nervosa as a defense against anaclitic depression. *International Journal of Eating Disorders*.

Sulik, K.; Johnson, M. C.; & Webb, M. (1981). Fetal alcohol syndrome: embryogenesis in a mouse model. *Science*, **214**(2), 936–938.

Sundberg, N. D. (1977). *Assessment of persons*. Englewood Cliffs, N.J.: Prentice-Hall.

Suomi, S., & Harlow, H. (1972). Social rehabilitation of isolate-reared monkeys. *Developmental Psychology*, **6**(3), 487–496.

——— & ———. (1978). Early experience and social development in Rhesus monkeys. In M. Lamb (Ed.), *Social and personality development*. New York: Holt, Rinehart, and Winston.

Sutton-Smith, B. (1982). Birth order and sibling status effects. In M. E. Lamb and B. Sutton-Smith (Eds.), *Sibling relationships: Their nature and significance across the life-span*. Hillsdale, N.J.: Erlbaum.

Szasz, T. (1974). *The myth of mental illness*, (rev.). New York: Perennial Library, Harper and Row.

Talland, G. A. (1969). *The pathology of memory*. New York: Academic Press.

Tanner, J. M. (1968). Growing up. *Scientific American*, **218**, 21–27.

Tart, C. (Ed.). (1969). *Altered states of consciousness*. New York: Wiley.

———. (1975). Putting the pieces together: A conceptual framework for understanding discrete states of consciousness. In N. E. Zinberg (Ed.), *Alternative states of consciousness*. New York: Free Press.

Taub, H.; Goldstein, K.; & Caputo, D. (1977). Indices of neonatal prematurity as discriminators of development in middle childhood. *Child Development*, **48**(3), 797–805.

Taylor, C. W.; Smith, W. R.; & Ghiselin, B. (1963). The creative and other contributions of one sample of research scientists. In C. W. Taylor & F. Barron (Eds.), *Scientific creativity: Its recognition and development*. New York: Wiley.

Templeton, R. D., & Quigley, J. P. (1930). The action of insulin on the motility of the gastrointestinal tract. *American Journal of Physiology*, **91**, 467–474.

Tennov, D. (1979). *Love and limerence: The experience of being in love*. New York: Stein & Day.

Terman, L. M. (1921). In Symposium: Intelligence and its measurement. *Journal of Educational Psychology*, **12**, 127–133.

——— & Merrill, M. A. (1937). *Measuring intelligence: A guide to the administration of the new revised Stanford-Binet tests of intelligence*. Boston: Houghton Mifflin.

——— & Oden, M. H. (1959). *Genetic studies of genius, V. The gifted group at mid-life*. Stanford, Calif.: Stanford University Press.

Terrace, H. S. (1979). How Nim Chimsky changed my mind. *Psychology Today*, **13**(6), 65–76.

———; Petitto, L. A.; Sanders, R. J.; & Bever, T. G. (1979). *Science*, **206**(4421), 891–206.

Teuber, H.-L.; Milner, B.; & Vaughan, H. G., Jr. (1968). Persistent anterograde amnesia after stab wound of the basal brain. *Neuropsychologia*, **6**, 267–282.

Thibaut, J. W., & Kelley, H. H. (1959). *The social psychology of groups*. New York: Wiley.

Thomas, A.; Chess, C.; & Birch, H. G. (1968). *Temperament and behavior disorders in children*. New York: Brunner/Mazel.

——— & ———. (1977). *Temperament and development*. New York: Brunner/Mazel.

Thomas, L. (1982). On altruism. *Discover*, **3**(3), 58–60.

Thompson, J. K.; Jarvie, G. J.; Lahey, B. B.; & Cureton, K. J. (1982). Exercise and Obesity: Etiology, Physiology, and Intervention. *Psychological Bulletin*, **91**, 55–79.

Thompson, R. A., & Lamb, M. E. (1983). Security attachment and stranger sociability in infants. *Developmental Psychology*, **19**(2), 184–191.

Thompson, R. (1967). *Foundations of physiological psychology*. New York: Harper and Row.

Thorndike, E. L. (1911). *Animal intelligence*. New York: Macmillan.

Thurstone, L. L. (1938). *Primary mental abilities*. Chicago: University of Chicago Press.

Tolman, E. C. (1932). *Purposive behavior in animals and men*. New York: Century.

———. (1948). Cognitive maps in rats and men. *Psychological Review*, **55**, 189–208. (Reprinted in Gazzaniga, M. S., & Lovejoy, E. P. *Good reading in psychology*. Englewood Cliffs, N.J.: Prentice-Hall, 1971, pp. 224–243.)

Toman, W., & Toman, E. (1970). Sibling positions of a sample of distinguished persons. *Perceptual and Motor Skills*, **32**, 825–826.

Tomlinson, Keasey, C. (1972). Formal operations in females from eleven to fifty-six years of age. *Developmental Psychology*, **6**(2), 364.

Triandis, H. C. (1977). *Interpersonal behavior*. Monterey, Calif.: Brooks/Cole.

Tribich, D. (1982). Personal communication to S. W. Olds, New York, N.Y., January 14.

——— & Klein, M. (1981). On Freud's blindness. *Colloquium*, **4**, 52–59.

Troll, L. (1975). *Early and middle*

adulthood. Belmont, Calif.: Wadsworth.

Tryon, R. C. (1940). Genetic differences in maze learning in rats. *Yearbook of the National Society for Studies in Education,* **39,** 111–119.

Tulving, E. (1962). Subjective organization in free recall of "unrelated" words. *Psychological Review,* **69,** 344–354.

———. (1977). Cue-dependent forgetting. *American Scientist* (January–February 1974). (Reprinted in I. Janis (Ed.), *Current trends in psychology.* Los Altos, Calif.: William Kaufmann.)

Turnbull, C. (1972). *The mountain people.* New York: Simon and Schuster.

U.S. Department of Health and Human Services. (1980). Public Health Service, Alcohol, Drug Abuse, and Mental Health Administration. *Let's talk about drug abuse.* Rockville, Md.: National Institute on Drug Abuse.

———. (1980). *Project sleep: The national program on insomnia and sleep disorders.* Public Health Service, Rockville, Md.

———. (1980). *Smoking tobacco, and health.* DHHS Publication No. (PHS) 80-50150.

———. (1981a). *Pre-term babies.* Washington, D.C.: Government Printing Office.

———. (1981b). *ADAMHA data book.* DHHS Pub. No. (ADM) 81-662. Revised printing.

———. (1981c). *Information on lithium.* DHHS Pub. No. (ADM) 81-1078.

U.S. Department of Commerce & U.S. Department of Housing and Urban Development. (1981). *Part D, housing characteristics of recent movers for the United States and regions: 1978.* Series H-150-78D. Washington, D.C.: Government Printing Office.

U.S. Department of Health, Education, and Welfare. (1971). *The institutional guide to DHEW policy on protection of human subjects.* Washington, D.C., DHEW.

———. (1976). *Health, United States, 1975.* DHEW Pub. No. (HRA) 76-1232. Rockville, Md.: National Center for Health Statistics.

U.S. Public Health Service. (1982). *The health consequences of smoking: cancer.* Rockville, Md.

University of Texas Health Science Center at Dallas. (1980). Twins are double puzzles. *News* (July 8, 1980).

Upjohn Company. (1983). The menopausal woman: An enlightened view. *Writer's Guide to Menopause.* Kalamazoo, Mich.: Upjohn Company.

Vaillant, G., & McArthur, C. (1972). Natural history of male psychologic health. I. The adult life cycle from 18–50. *Seminars in Psychiatry,* **4**(4), 415–427.

Valentine, C. W. (1930). The innate bases of fear. *Journal of Genetic Psychology,* **37,** 485–497.

Vandell, D.; Wilson, K.; & Buchanan, N. (1980). Peer interaction in the first year of life: An examination of its structure, content, and sensitivity to toys. *Child Development,* **51,** 481–488.

Vandenberg, S. G. (1967). Hereditary factors in normal personality traits (as measured by inventories) (1965). In J. Wortes (Ed.), *Recent advances in biological psychiatry,* vol. 9. New York: Plenum, pp. 65–104.

Van Harreveld, A., & Fifkova, C. (1975). Swelling of dendritic spines in the fascia dentata after stimulation of the perforant fibers as a mechanism of post-tetanic potentiation. *Experimental Neurology,* **49,** 736–749.

Vaughan, V.; McKay, R.; & Behrman, R. (1979). *Nelson: Textbook of Pediatrics.* Philadelphia: Saunders.

Vener, A., & Stewart, C. (1974). Adolescent sexual behavior in middle America revisited: 1970–1973. *Journal of Marriage and the Family* (November), **36**(4), 728–735.

Verbrugge, L. (1979). Marital status and health. *Journal of Marriage and the Family,* **41,** 267–285.

Veroff, J.; Douvan, E.; & Kulka, R. (1981). *The inner American.* New York: Basic Books.

Victor, M.; Adams, R. D.; & Collins, G. H. (1971). *The Wernicke-Korsakoff syndrome.* Philadelphia: Davis.

Valins, S. (1966). Cognitive effects of false heart-rate feedback. *Journal of Personality and Social Psychology,* **4,** 400–408.

Wadden, T. A., & Anderton, C. H. (1982). The clinical use of hypnosis. *Psychological Bulletin,* **91**(2), 215–243.

Waid, W. M., & Orne, M. T. (1982). The physiological detection of deception. *American Scientist* (July-August), **70,** 402–409.

Wain, H. J. (1980). Pain control through use of hypnosis. *American Journal of Clinical Hypnosis,* **23**(1), 41–46.

Wagner, A. R., & Rescorla, R. A. (1972). Inhibition in Pavlovian conditioning: Application of a theory. In R. A. Boakes and M. S. Halliday (Eds.), *Inhibition and learning.* London: Academic Press.

Walk, R. D., & Gibson, E. (1961). A comparative and analytical study of visual depth perception. *Psychology Monographs,* **75** (15), 170.

Wallace, R. K., & Benson, H. (1972). The physiology of meditation. *Scientific American,* **226,** 85–90.

Walsh, B. J.; Katz, J. L.; Levin, J.; Kream, J.; Fukushima, D. K.; Hellman, L. D.; Weiner, H.; & Zumoff, B. (1978). Adrenal activity in anorexia nervosa. *Psychosomatic Medicine,* **40,** 499.

Walster, E. (1971). Passionate love. In B. Murstein (Ed.), *Theories of attraction and love.* New York: Springer.

———; Aronson, V.; Abrahams, D.; & Rottmann, L. (1966). Importance of physical attractiveness in dating behavior. *Journal of*

Personality and Social Psychology, **4**(5), 508–516.

———; Walster, C. W.; & Berscheid, E. (1978). *Equity theory and research.* Boston: Allyn and Bacon.

Wandersman, L. P. (1980). The adjustment of fathers to their first baby: The role of parenting groups and marital relationship. *Birth and the Family Journal,* **7**(3), 155–161.

Warrington, E. K., & Weiskrantz, L. (1970). Amnesic syndrome: Consolidation or retrieval? *Nature,* **228**, 628–630.

Waters, E.; Wippman, J.; & Sroufe, L. A. (1979). Attachment, positive affect, and competence in the peer group: Two studies in construct validation. *Child Development,* **50**(3), 821–829.

Watson, J. B. (1919). *Psychology from the Standpoint of a Behaviorist.* Philadelphia: Lippincott.

———. (1924). *Behaviorism.* New York: People's Institute.

——— & Rayner, R. (1920). Conditioned emotional reactions. *Journal of Experimental Psychology,* **3**(1), 1–14.

Watson, J. S. (1967). Memory and "contingency analysis" in infant learning. *Merrill-Palmer Quarterly of Behavior and Development,* **13**, 55–76.

Watson, J. S., & Ramey, C. T. (1972). Reactions to response-contingent stimulation in early infancy, *Merrill-Palmer Quarterly of Behavior and Development,* **18**, (3), 219–227.

Webb, W. B. (1971). Sleep behavior as a biorhythm. In P. Coloquhon (Ed.), *Biological rhythms and human performance.* London: Academic Press, pp. 149–177.

———. (1975). *Sleep: The gentle tyrant.* Englewood Cliffs, N.J.: Prentice-Hall.

Webb, W. (1979). Are short and long sleepers different? *Psychological Reports,* **44**, 259–264.

——— & Bonnet, M. H. (1979). Sleep and dreams. In M. E. Meyer (Ed.), *Foundations of con-*

temporary psychology. New York: Oxford University Press.

——— & Cartwright, R. D. (1978). Sleep and dreams. In M. Rosenzweig and L. Porter (Eds.), *Annual review of psychology,* vol. 29, pp. 223–252.

——— & Friel, J. (1971). Sleep stage and personality characteristics of "natural" long and short sleepers. *Science,* **171**, 587–588.

Webster, B. (1982). A pair of skilled hands to guide an artificial heart: Robert Koffler Jarvik. *The New York Times,* December 3, p. A24.

Wechsler, D. (1939). *The Measurement of Adult Intelligence.* Baltimore: Williams and Wilkins.

———. (1944). *The measurement of adult intelligence* (3d ed.). Baltimore: Williams and Wilkins.

———. (1955). *Wechsler adult intelligence scale manual.* New York: Psychological Corp.

———. (1958). *The measurement and appraisal of adult intelligence.* Baltimore: Williams and Wilkins.

———. (1974). *Manual: Wechsler intelligence scale for children* (rev.). New York: Psychological Corp.

Weitkamp, L. R.; Stancer, H. C.; Persad, E.; Flood, C.; & Guttormsen, S. (1981). Depressive disorders and HLA: A gene on chromosome 6 that can affect behavior. *New England Journal of Medicine,* **305**, 1301–1306.

Weitzman, L. J.; Eifler, D.; Hodaka, E.; & Ross, C. (1972). Sex role socialization in picture books for pre-school children. *American Journal of Sociology,* **77**, 1125–1150.

Wender, P. H., & Klein, D. F. (1981). The promise of biological psychiatry. *Psychology Today,* **15**(2), 25–41.

Werner, C., & Parmelee, P. (1979). Similarity of activity preferences among friends: Those who play together stay together. *Social Psychology Quarterly,* **42**, 62–66.

Werner, E.; Bierman, L.; French, F.; Simonian, K.; Connor, A.; Smith, R.; & Campbell, M. (1968). Reproductive and environmental

casualties. A report on the 10-year follow-up of the children of the Kauai pregnancy study. *Pediatrics,* **42**(1), 112–127.

Whisnant, L., & Zegons, L. (1975). A study of attitudes toward menarche in white middle class American adolescent girls. *American Journal of Psychiatry,* **132**(8), 809–814.

White, B. L. (1971). *Fundamental early environmental influences on the development of competence.* Paper presented at Third Western Symposium on Learning: Cognitive Learning. Western Washington State College, Bellingham, Washington, October 21–22.

White, G. L.; Fishbein, S.; & Rustein, J. (1981). Passionate love and the misattribution of arousal. *Journal of Personality and Social Psychology,* **41**(1), 56–62.

Whitehurst, G. J. (1982). Language development. In B. Wolman (Ed.), *Handbook of developmental psychology.* Englewood Cliffs, N.J.: Prentice-Hall.

Whorf, B. L. (1956). *Language, thought, and reality.* Cambridge: MIT Press.

Wickelgren, W. (1977). *Learning and memory.* Englewood Cliffs, N.J.: Prentice-Hall.

Wicker, A. W. (1969). Attitude versus actions: The relationship of verbal and overt behavioral responses to attitude objects. *Journal of Social Issues,* **25**, 41–78.

Will, J. A.; Self, P. A.; & Datan, N. (1976). Maternal behavior and perceived sex of infant. *American Journal of Orthopsychiatry,* **46** (1), 135–139.

Williams, D. R., & Williams, H. (1969). Auto-maintenance in the pigeon: Sustained pecking despite contingent nonreinforcement. *Journal of the Experimental Analysis of Behavior,* **12**, 511–520.

Williams, H. L.; Holloway, F. A.; & Griffiths, W. J. (1973). Physiological psychology: sleep. In M. Rosenzweig and L. Porter (Eds.), *Annual review of psychology,* vol.

24. Palo Alto, Calif.: Annual Reviews.

Wilson, E. O. (1978). *On human nature.* Cambridge, Mass.: Harvard University Press.

———. (1980). The ethical implication of human sociobiology. *Hastings Center Report* (December), 27–29.

Winch, R. F. (1958). *Mate selection.* New York: Harper and Row.

Wineburg, E. N. (1981). Should you incorporate biofeedback into your practice? *Behavioral Medicine* (August), **8**(8), 30–34.

Wingerson, L. (1982). Training the mind to heal. *Discover,* **3**(5), 80–85.

Winick, M. (1981). Food and the fetus. *Natural History* (January), **90**(1), 16–81.

———; Brasel, J., & Rosso, P. (1969). Head circumference and cellular growth of the brain in normal and marasmic children. *Journal of Pediatrics,* **74**, 774–778.

Winterbottom, M. R. (1958). The relation of need for achievement to learning experiences in independence mastery. In J. W. Atkinson (Ed.), *Motives in fantasy, action and society.* Princeton, N.J.: D. Van Nostrand, pp. 453–478.

Wittgenstein, J. (1953). *Philosophical investigations.* New York: Macmillan.

Wolff, P. H. (1969). The natural history of crying and other vocalizations in early infancy. In B. Foss (Ed.), *Determinants of infant behavior, IV.* London: Methuen.

Wolpe, J. (1978). Cognition and causation in human behavior and its therapy. *American Psychologist,* **33**(5), 437–446.

———. (1982a). Behavior therapy versus psychoanalysis. *American Psychologist,* **36**(2), 159–164.

———. (1982b). *The practice of behavior therapy* (3d ed.). New York: Pergamon.

Woodworth, R. S., & Schlosberg, H. (1954). *Experimental psychology.* New York: Holt.

Worchel, S., & Brehm, J. (1970). Effect of threats to attitudinal freedom as a function of agreement with the communicator. *Journal of Personality and Social Psychology,* **14**, 18–22.

Wyshak, G., & Frisch, R. (1982). Evidence for a secular trend in age of menarche. *New England Journal of Medicine,* **306**(17), 1033–1035.

Yalom, I. (1975). *The Theory and Practice of Group Psychotherapy* (2d ed.). New York: Basic Books.

Yarmey, A. D. (1973). I recognize your face but I can't remember your name: Further evidence on the tip-of-the-tongue phenomenon. *Memory and Cognition,* **1**(3), 287–290.

Yarrow, L. J.; Rubenstein, J. L.; & Pedersen, F. A. (1971). Dimensions of early stimulation: Differential effects of infant development. Paper presented at the biennial meeting of the Society for Research in Child Development.

Yarrow, M. R. (1978). *Altruism in children.* Paper presented at program, Advances in Child Development Research, New York Academy of Sciences, October 31.

Young, T. On the theory of light and colours. *Phil. Trans. R. Soc. Lond.,* **92**, 12–48.

Zajonc, R. B. (1968). Attitudinal effects of mere exposure. *Journal of Personality and Social Psychology,* **9**, Monograph Supplement No. 2, Part 2.

———. (1970). Brainwash: Familiarity breeds comfort. *Psychology Today* (February), 32–35, 60–62.

———. (1976). Family configuration and intelligence. *Science,* **197**(4236), 227–236.

——— & Bargh, J. (1980). Birth order, family size and decline in SAT scores. *American Psychologist,* **35**, 662–668.

Zaslow, F. (1984). Personal communication to the authors.

Zeigler, H. P. (1973). Trigeminal deafferentation and feeding in the pigeon: Sensorimotor and motivational effects. *Science,* **182**, 1155–1158.

———. (1975). The sensual feel of food. *Psychology Today* (August), 62–66.

——— & Karten, H. J. (1974). Central trigeminal structures and the lateral hypothalamic syndrome in the rat. *Science,* **186**, 636–638.

Zelazo, P., & Kearsley, R. (1981). *Cognitive assessment and intervention in developmentally delayed infants.* Final report to the Bureau of Education for the Handicapped, Grant No. G007603979, February.

Zelman, A.; Kabot, L.; Jacobsen, R.; & McConnell, J. V. (1963). Transfer of training through injection of "conditioned" RNA into untrained worms. *Worm Runners Digest,* **5**, 14–21.

Zelnik, M.; Kantner, J. F.; & Ford, K. (1981). *Sex and pregnancy in adolescence.* Beverly Hills, Calif.: Sage.

Zigler, E., & Seitz, V. (1982). Social policy and intelligence. In R. J. Sternberg (Ed.), *Handbook of human intelligence.* Cambridge: Cambridge University Press.

Zillmann, D., & Byant, J. (1982). Pornography, sexual callousness, and the trivialization of rape. *Journal of Communications,* **32**, 10–21.

Zimbardo, P.; Anderson, S.; & Kabat, L. (1981). Induced hearing deficit generates experimental paranoia. *Science,* **212**(26), 1529–1531.

———; Haney, C.; Banks, W. C.; & Jaffe, D. (1977). The psychology of imprisonment: Privation, power and pathology. In J. C. Brigham and L. S. Wrightsman (Eds.), *Contemporary Issues in Social Psychology.* Belmont, Calif.: Wadsworth.

——— & Radl, S. L. (1982). *The shy child.* New York: Doubleday/Dolphin.

Zimberg, S. (1982). Psychotherapy in the treatment of alcoholism. In E. M. Pattison and E. Kaufman (Eds.), *Encyclopedia handbook of alcoholism*. New York: Gardner Press.

Zimmerman, D. R. (1973). *RH: The intimate history of a disease and its conquest*. New York: Macmillan.

Zimmerman, W. (1970). Sleep mentation and auditory awakening thresholds. *Psychophysiology, 6,* 540–549.

Zuckerman, M. (1979). *Sensation seeking: Beyond the optimal level of arousal*. Hillsdale, N.J.: Erlbaum.

———; Buchsbaum, M. S.; & Murphy, D. L. (1980). Sensation-seeking and its biological correlates. *Psychological Bulletin, 88,* 187–214.

ACKNOWLEDGMENTS

TEXT, MARGINALIA, AND BOXES

Chapter 1

Hardy, T. L. *A History of Psychology: Main Currents in Psychological Thought.* ©1980 by Prentice-Hall, Inc. Used by permission.

Ruebhausen, O. M., & Brim, O. J., Jr. Privacy and behavioral research. *American Psychologist*, 1966, **21**, 423–444.

Chapter 2

Hunt, M. *The Universe Within.* Copyright ©1982 by Morton Hunt. Reprinted by permission of Simon & Schuster, Inc.

Geschwind, N. Language and the brain. Copyright ©1967 by Scientific American, Inc.

Chapter 4

Ludwig, A. M. Altered states of consciousness. *Archives of General Psychiatry*, 1966, **15**, 225–234. Copyright 1966, American Medical Association.

Moore-Ede, MC. C. Sleeping as the world turns. With permission from *Natural History*, **91** (10). Copyright the American Museum of Natural History, 1982.

Grinspoon, L., & Bakalar, J. B. *Psychedelic Drugs Reconsidered.* ©1979 by Lester Grinspoon and James B. Bakalar. Basic Books, Inc., Publishers.

Webb, W. B. *Sleep: The Gentle Tyrant.* ©1975 by Wilse B. Webb. Used by permission.

Chapter 5

Colao, F., & Hosansky, T. *The Key to Having Fun is Being Safe.* Safety and Fitness Exchange, New York, 1982. Used by permission. (Box 5-4)

Watson, J. B. *Behaviorism.* ©1928, 1954, W. W. Norton.

Bandura, A. *Social Learning Theory*, 12, 129. ©1977. Reprinted by permission of Prentice-Hall, Inc., Englewood Cliffs, N.J.

Chapter 6

Craik, F. I. M., & Tulving, E. Depth of processing and the retention of words in eposodic memory. *Journal of Experimental Psychology (General)*, 1975, **104,** 268–294. Copyright 1975 by the American Psychological Association. Adapted by permission of the authors.

Glass, A. L.; Holyoak, K. J.; & Santa, J. L. *Cognition.* ©1979 W. H. Freeman. *American Bar Association Journal*, 1978, **64**, 187. Used by permission.

Piaget, J. *Plays, Dreams, and Iniation in Childhood.* ©1951 W. W. Norton.

James, W. *The Principles of Psychology.* ©1980 Holt, Rinehart & Winston.

Colegrove, F. W. The day they heard about Lincoln. In individual memories. *American Journal of Psychology*, 1899, **10**, 255–288.

Martin, J. *Miss Manners' Guide to Excruciatingly Correct Behavior.* Text copyright ©1979, 1980, 1981, 1982 by United Feature Syndicate, Inc. Reprinted with the permission of Atheneum Publishers.

Lashley, K. In search of the engram. *Symposia of the Society of Experimental Biology*, 1950, **4**, 452–482.

Chapter 7

Adapted from American Psychiatric Association. *Diagnostic and Statistical Manual of Mental Disorders*, 3rd ed. ©1980 American Psychiatric Association; and Grossman, H. J. *Classification in Mental Retardation.* ©1983 American Association on Mental Deficiency. (Box 7-2)

Piaget, J. *The Origins of Intelligence in Children.* ©1952 International Universities Press. American Psychiatric Association. *Diagnostic and Statistical Manual of Mental Disorders*, 3rd ed. ©1980 American Psychiatric Association.

Chapter 8

Brown, R. Development of the first language in the human species. *American Psychologist*, 1973, **28**(2), 97–106.

Moskowitz, B. A. The acquisition of language. *Scientific American*, 1978, **239**(5), 92–108.

Cazden, C. B. Suggestions from studies of early language acquisition. *Childhood Education*, 1969, **46**(3), 127–131. Reprinted by permission of the author and the Association for Childhood Education International, Wheaton, MD. Copyright ©1969 by the Association.

Whitehurst, Grover J. Language development. In B. Wolman (ed.), *Handbook of Developmental Psychology*, 368–369. ©1982. Reprinted by permission of Prentice-Hall, Inc., Englewood Cliffs, N.J.

Brown, R. W., & Lenneberg, E. H. A study in language and cognition. *Journal of Abnormal Social Psychology*, 1954, **49**, 454–462.

Limber, J. Language in child and chimp? *American Psychologist*, 1977, 280–295.

Chapter 9

Horner, M. S. A woman's will to fail. *Psychology Today*, 1969, **62**, 36–38. Used by permission. (Box 9-2)

Suedfeld, P. The benefits of boredom: Sensory deprivation reconsidered. *American Scientist*, 1975, **63**, 60–69.

James, W. *The Principles of Psychology.* ©1890. Holt, Rinehart, & Winston.

James, W. What is an emotion? *Mind*, 1884, **9**, 188–205.

Chapter 10

Meichenbaum, D. In C. D. Spielberger & I. G. Sarason (Eds.), *Stress and Anxiety*, Vol. 1, 250–251. ©1983 Hemisphere Publishing Corporation. (Box 10-1)

Meichenbaum, D., & Novaco, R. Ibid., Vol. 5, 324–325. ©1983 Hemisphere Publishing Corporation. (Box 10-2)

Sheehy, G. *Pathfinders.* ©1981 William Morrow & Co.

Bukofsky, C. Shoelace. *Mockingbird Wish Me Luck.* ©1972 Black Sparrow Press.

Lazarus, R. W. The stress and coping paradigm. In L. Bond & J. Rosen (Eds.) *Competence and Coping During Adulthood.* ©1980 University Press of New England.

Chapter 11

Fleming, Anne Taylor. New frontiers in conception. *New York Times Magazine,*

7/20/80, 20. Copyright ©1980 by Anne Taylor Fleming. (Box 11-1)

Farber, S. Telltale behavior of twins. *Psychology Today*, 1981, **15**(1), 80. Used by permission of the American Psychological Association.

Chapter 12

Piaget, J. *The Origins of Intelligence in Children.* ©1952 International Universities Press.

McPhee, J. Department of Amplification. *The New Yorker*, 4/18/83. Used by permission.

Chapter 13

Peel, E. A. *The Psychological Basis of Education*, 2nd ed. ©1967 Oliver & Boyd Ltd. Used by permission of the author.

Hall, E. A conversation with Erik Erikson. *Psychology Today*, 1983, **17**(6), 27. Used by permission.

Baruch, G.; Barnett, R.; & Rivers, C. *Lifeprints.* ©1983 McGraw-Hill Book Company.

Chapter 14

Rogers, C. *A Way of Being.* ©1980 Houghton Mifflin Company.

Watson, J. B. *Behaviorism.* ©1928, 1954 W. W. Norton.

Chapter 15

Sheehan, S. *Is There No Place on Earth for Me?* Copyright ©1982 by Susan Sheehan. Reprinted by permission of Houghton Mifflin Company.

American Psychiatric Association. *Diagnostic and Statistical Manual of Mental Disorders*, 3rd ed. ©1980 American Psychiatric Association.

Nathan, P. E., & Harris, S. L. *Psychopathology and Society*, 2nd ed. ©1980 McGraw-Hill Book Company.

Townshend, P. You Didn't Hear It and Go to the Mirror Boy. *Tommy.* Copyright 1969 Fabulous Music Ltd. All rights in the United States, its territories and possessions, Canada, Mexico and the Philippines are controlled by Towser Tunes, Inc. All rights reserved. International copyright secured. Reproduced by kind permission of Peter Townshend, Fabulous Music Ltd., and Towser Tunes, Inc.

Illfeld, F. W. Sex differences in psychiatric symptomology. Paper given at Annual Meeting, American Psychiatric Association, 1977. Used by permission.

Carstairs, G. M., & Kapur, R. L. *The Great Universe of Kota.* ©1976 University of California Press.

Gottesman, I. R. Schizophrenia and genetics: Toward understanding uncertainty. *Psychiatric Annals*, 1979, **9**(1), 54–78.

Bateson, G.; Jackson, D. D.; Haley, J; & Weakland, J. Double-bind hypothesis of schizophrenia. *Behavioral Science*, 1956, **1**, 251–264. Used by permission.

Chapter 16

Freeman, L. *Fight Against Fears.* ©1951 Crown Publishers. Used by permission of the author.

The American Heritage Dictionary of the English Language. ©1982 Houghton Mifflin Company. Reprinted by permission.

Morse, S. J., & Watson, R. J. (Eds.). *Psychotherapies: A Creative Casebook.* ©1977 Holt, Rinehart & Winston.

Plath, S. *The Bell Jar.* Copyright ©1971 by Harper & Row, Publishers, Inc. ©1972 Faber & Faber Ltd. Reprinted by permission.

Clark, M. Drugs and psychiatry: A new era. Copyright 1979 by Newsweek, Inc. All rights reserved, reprinted by permission.

Lazarus, A. Has behavior therapy outlived its usefulness? *American Psychologist*, 1977, **32**(7), 550–554.

Frank, J. D. The restoration of morale. *The American Journal of Psychiatry*, 1974, **131**(3), 271–274. Copyright 1974, the American Psychiatric Association.

Chapter 17

Harnick, S., & Bock, J. Do you love me? *Fiddler on the Roof.* ©1964—Alley Music Corp. and Trio Music Co., Inc. All rights administered by Hudson Bay Music Corp. and Trio Music Co., Inc. Used by permission. All rights reserved.

Milgram, S. Some conditions of obedience and disobedience to authority. *Human Relations*, 1965, **18**, 67–76. Used by permission of the author.

Milgram. S. *Obedience to Authority: An Overview.* Copyright ©1974 by Stanley Milgram. Reprinted by permission of Harper & Row, Publishers, Inc.

Thomas, L. On altruism. ©1983 Discover Magazine, Time Inc.

Myers, D. G. *Social Psychology.* ©1983 McGraw-Hill Book Company.

Chapter 18

Kelly, J. B. Divorce: The adult perspective. In Wolman, B. B. (ed.), *Handbook of Developmental Psychology*, 749. ©1982. Reprinted by permission of Prentice-Hall, Inc., Englewood Cliffs, N.J. (Box 18-1)

Kelley, H. H. The process of causal attribution. *American Psychologist*, 1973, **28**, 107–128.

Berscheid, E. S., & Walster, E. *Interpersonal Attraction*, 2nd ed. ©1978 Addison-Wesley, Reading, Mass.

Goffman, E. On cooling the mark out: Some aspects of adaptation to failure. *Psychiatry*, 1952, **15**, 451–463.

TABLES AND ILLUSTRATIONS

Chapter 1

Figs. 1-1(*a*), 1-1(*b*): Stapp, J., & Fulcher, R. The employment of APA members: 1982. *American Psychologist*, 1983, **38**(12), 1298–1320. ©1983 by the American Psychological Association. Reprinted by permission of the publisher and author.

Chapter 2

Table 2-1: Crick, F. H. C. Thinking about the brain. Copyright ©1979 by Scientific American, Inc. All rights reserved. Adapted by permission.

Fig. 2-12: Hunt, M. *The Universe Within.* Copyright ©1982 by Morton Hunt. Reprinted by permission of Simon & Schuster, Inc.

Fig. 2-14: Rosenzweig, M. R., & Leiman, A. L. *Physiological Psychology.* Copyright ©1982 by D. C. Heath and Company. Reprinted by permission of the publisher.

Fig. 2-21: Jaynes, J. *The Origin of Consciousness in the Breakdown of the Bicameral Mind.* Copyright ©1976 by Julian Jaynes. Adapted by permission of Houghton Mifflin Company.

Figs. 2-22, 2-23: Rosenzweig, M. R., & Leiman, A. L. *Physiological Psychology.* Copyright ©1982 by D. C. Heath and Company. Reprinted by permission of the publisher.

Chapter 3

Table 3-2: Hurvitch, L. M. *Color Vision.* ©1981 Sinauer Associates.

Fig. 3-5(*b*); Mitchell, D. E.; Freeman, R. D.; Millodot, M.; & Haegerstrom, G. Meridional amblyopia: Evidence for modification of the human visual system. *Vision Research*, 1973, **13**(3),

535–558. Copyright 1973 Pergamon Press, Ltd. Reprinted by permission.

Fig. 3-6: Hubel, D. H. The visual cortex of the brain. Copyright ©1963 by Scientific American, Inc. All rights reserved.

Fig. 3-8(a): Levine, M. W., & Shefner, J. M. *Fundamentals of Sensation and Perception.* ©1981 Addison-Wesley, Reading, Mass. Reprinted by permission.

Fig. 3-9: Cornsweet, T. N. *Visual Perception.* ©1970 Academic Press.

Fig. 3-14: Reproduced by permission from the Dvorine Pseudo-Isochaomatic Plates. Copyright ©1944, 1953 by the Psychological Corporation. All rights reserved.

Fig. 3-16, 3-18: Levine, M. W., & Shefner, J. M. *Fundamentals of Sensation and Perception.* ©1981 Addison-Wesley, Reading, Mass. Reprinted by permission.

Fig. 3-19: Weinstein. In D. A. Kenshalo (ed.), *The Skin Senses.* By permission of Charles C Thomas, Publisher, Springfield, Ill.

Fig. 3-21: Murray, R. G., & Murray, A. The anatomy and ultrastructure of taste endings. In G. E. W. Wolstenholme & G. Knight (Eds.), *Taste and Smell in Vertebrates.* Ciba Found. Symp. 1970. Published by Churchill Livingstone Inc. Used by permission of the Ciba Foundation.

Fig. 3-22: Amoore, J. E.; Johnston, J. W. Jr.; & Rubin, M. The stereochemical theory of odor. Copyright ©1964 by Scientific American, Inc. All rights reserved.

Fig. 3-23: Geldard, F. A. *The Human Senses,* 2nd ed. ©1972 John Wiley & Sons.

Fig. 3-24: Julesz, B. *Foundations of Cyclopean Perception.* ©1971 Bell Telephone Laboratories, Inc. Used by permission of the author.

Fig. 3-32(b): Gregory, R. L. *Eye and Brain,* 2nd ed. ©1973 McGraw-Hill Book Company.

Fig. 3-34: Gibson, J. J. *The Perception of the Visual World.* Copyright ©1950, renewed 1977 by Houghton Mifflin Company. Used by permission.

Fig. 3-42: Deregowski, J. B. Pictorial perception and culture. Copyright ©1972 by Scientific American, Inc.

Chapter 4

Fig. 4-1: By permission of Dr. Wilse B. Webb.

Chapter 5

Fig. 5-3: Hulse, S. H.; Egeth, H.; & Deese, J. *Psychology of Learning,* 5th ed. ©1980 McGraw-Hill Book Company. Adapted by permission.

Fig. 5-4: Skinner, B. F. Teaching machines. Copyright ©1961 by Scientific American, Inc. All rights reserved.

Chapter 6

Table 6-2: Hulse, S. H.; Egeth, H.; & Deese, J. *The Psychology of Learning,* 5th ed. ©1980 McGraw-Hill Book Company.

Fig. 6-1: Atkinson, R. C., & Shiffrin, R. M. Human memory: A proposed system and its control processes. In K. W. Spence & J. T. Spence (Eds.), *The Psychology of Learning and Motivation: Advances in Research and Theory,* Vol. 2. ©1968 Academic Press, Inc.

Figs. 6-2, 6-3: Sperling, G. The information available in brief visual presentations. *Psychological Monographs,* 1960, **74** (Whole No. 498). Copyright 1960 by the American Psychological Association. Adapted by permission of the publisher and author.

Fig. 6-7: Loftus, E. *Memory.* ©1980 Addison-Wesley, Reading, Mass. Reprinted by permission.

Figs. 6-9, 6-10, 6-11: Nickerson, R. S., & Adams, M. J. Long term memory for a common object. *Cognitive Psychology,* 1979, **11,** 287–307. ©1979 Academic Press, Inc.

Fig. 6-12: Kandel, E. R. Small systems of neurons. Copyright ©1979 by Scientific American, Inc. All rights reserved.

Chapter 7

Fig. 7-1: Guilford, J. P. *Way Beyond the I.Q.* ©1977 Creative Education Foundation and Bearly Limited, Buffalo, N.Y. Used by permission.

Fig. 7-3: Anastasi, A. *Psychological Testing,* 5th ed. Copyright ©1982 by Anne Anastasi. Reprinted by permission of Macmillan Publishing Company.

Fig. 7-4: Reproduced by permission from the Gesell Developmental Schedules. Copyright ©1949 by Arnold Gesell and Associates. All rights reserved.

Fig. 7-6: *Preliminary Scholastic Aptitude Test.* Reprinted by permission of Educational Testing Service, copyright owner.

Chapter 8

Table 8-3: Lenneberg, E. On explaining language. *Science,* 1969, **164,** 636. Used by permission.

Fig. 8-2: Bruner, J. S.; Goodnow, J. J.; & Austin, G. A. *A Study of Thinking.* ©1956 Jerome S. Bruner. Adapted by permission.

Fig. 8-5: Bourne, L. E.; Dominowski, R. L.; & Loftus, E. F. *Cognitive Processes.* ©1979 Lyle E. Bourne. Adapted by permission.

Fig. 8-6: ©1982 Nina Wallace.

Fig. 8-8, 8-9: Adams, J. L. *Conceptual Blockbusting, A Guide to Better Ideas,* 2nd ed. Copyright ©1974, 1976, 1979 by James L. Adams. Used by permission of W. W. Norton & Company, Inc.

Chapter 9

Table 9-1: Zuckerman, M. The search for high sensation. *Psychology Today,* 1978, **11**(9), 38–46. Copyright ©1978 American Psychological Association.

Fig. 9-3: Schachter, S. *Emotion, Obesity and Crime.* ©1971 Academic Press, Inc.

Fig. 9-4: Berlyne, D. E. Novelty, complexity and hedonic value. *Perception and Psychophysics,* 1970, 284. ©1970 Psychonomic Society.

Fig. 9-9: In Waid, W. M., & Orne, M. T. The physiological detection of deception. *American Scientist,* **70,** 404. Adapted by permission.

Chapter 10

Table 10-1: Holmes, T. H., & Rahe, R. H. The social readjustment scale. *Journal of Psychosomatic Research* **11**: 213–218, 1967. Copyright 1967 Pergamon Press, Ltd. Adapted by permission.

Table 10-2: Papalia, D. E., & Olds, S. W. *A Child's World,* 3rd ed., ©1982 McGraw-Hill Book Company.

Fig. 10-1: Selye, H. *The Stress of Life.* ©1956 McGraw-Hill Book Company.

Fig. 10-2: Endler, N. S., & Edwards, J. Stress and personality. In L. Goldberger & S. Breznitz (Eds.), *Handbook of Stress.* Copyright ©1982 by The Free Press, a Division of Macmillan Publishing Co., Inc. Used by permission of Macmillan, Inc.

Chapter 11

Figs. 11-1, 11-2(a), 11-2(b), 11-3: Papalia, D. E., & Olds. S. W. *A Child's World,* 3rd ed. ©1982 McGraw-Hill Book Company.

Figs. 11-4: *New York Times,* 4/13/82. Copyright 1982 by The New York

INDEX

NAME INDEX

SUBJECT INDEX